Glory of the Empires
1880–1914

Glory of the Empires 1880–1914

The Illustrated History of the Military Uniforms and Traditions of Britain, France, Germany, Russia and the United States

Wendell Schollander

First published 2018

The History Press
The Mill, Brimscombe Port
Stroud, Gloucestershire, GL5 2QG
www.thehistorypress.co.uk

© Wendell Schollander, 2018

The right of Wendell Schollander to be identified as the Author
of this work has been asserted in accordance with the
Copyright, Designs and Patents Act 1988.

All rights reserved. No part of this book may be reprinted
or reproduced or utilised in any form or by any electronic,
mechanical or other means, now known or hereafter invented,
including photocopying and recording, or in any information
storage or retrieval system, without the permission in writing
from the Publishers.

Every effort has been made to contact the copyright owners of
the pictorial material herein. If anyone has been overlooked,
please accept my full apologies and contact the publisher to
correct the matter in a future reprint of the work.

British Library Cataloguing in Publication Data.
A catalogue record for this book is available from the British Library.

ISBN 978 0 7524 8634 5

Typesetting and origination by JCS Publishing Services Ltd
Printed and bound in India by Thomson Press India Ltd

To my wife, Jayn; we have stood together for two-thirds of our lives as we faced the good and the bad. The ways her help and sacrifice have aided me are legion. They range from taking on extra household work, in addition to her full-time job, to allowing me extra time to devote to my career and writing, to going on vacations built around military research, and include the endless hours she spent in typing and proofreading my manuscripts. I particularly want to thank her for her help with my hopeless spelling so that I, the most unlikely of authors, could commit my efforts to paper. All of this was done while living a life of style, endless grace, and genuine concern for others. It's no wonder that she with her gentle soul is loved by all, including me. I am the most fortunate of men.

CONTENTS

Acknowledgements xi
Preface xiii

Section I. Overview

Notes 4   Bibliography 4

Section II. British Empire

1 Country Background	5	e The Highland Regiments 150
2 The Army	7	f The Lowland Regiments and
3 Uniform Information	18	Highland Light Infantry 159
4 General Staff	94	9 West India Regiment 166
5 Guard Cavalry	96	10 West African Regiment 171
6 The Foot Guards Regiments	106	11 King's African Rifles 173
7 Line Cavalry	112	12 West African Frontier Force 176
a Dragoon Guards and Dragoons	112	13 The Malay State Guides 179
b Lancers	120	14 Egypt and the Sudan 180
c Hussars	127	15 The Hong Kong Regiment
8 Line Infantry	136	(1892–1902) 185
a Line Foot	136	16 The Chinese Regiment (1898–1906) 188
b Light Infantry	143	British Empire: Notes 190
c Fusiliers	143	British Empire: Bibliography 193
d Rifles	145	

Section III. India

1 Country Background	197	6 Infantry	315
2 The Army	204	7 Gurkhas	380
3 Uniform Information	228	India: Notes	387
4 General Staff	253	India: Bibliography	391
5 Cavalry	254		

Section IV. French Empire

1 Country Background	393	b Dragoons	415
2 The Army	395	c Light Cavalry	418
3 Uniform Information	401	i Hussars	422
4 General Staff	407	ii Chasseurs à Cheval	423
5 Cavalry	411	6 Infantry	424
a Cuirassiers	411	a Line Infantry	424

b Foreign Legion	429
c Chasseurs à Pied	431
d Chasseurs Alpins	432
e Alpine Infantry	435
7 North African Army	437
a Chasseurs d'Afrique	437
b Spahis	440
8 North African Infantry	446
a African Light Infantry	446
b Zouaves	447
c Tirailleurs Algériens and Marocains	452
d Foreign Legion	456

9 Colonial Infantry	457
a Line Colonial Infantry	457
b Senegalese Tirailleurs and Spahis	460
i Senegalese Tirailleurs	460
ii Senegalese Spahis	463
c Tonkinese and Annamite Tirailleurs	463
d Madagascan Tirailleurs	465
10 Sahara Tirailleurs and Spahis and the Compagnies Sahariennes	466
French Empire: Notes	469
French Empire: Bibliography	473

Section V. Russia

1 Country Background	475
2 The Army	477
3 Uniform Information	493
4 General Staff	518
5 Guard Cavalry	524
a Guard Cuirassier	524
b Guard Dragoons and Horse Grenadiers	534
c Guard Lancers	539
d Guard Hussars	544
e Guard Cossacks	552
f Emperor's Guard Escort	558
6 Guard Infantry	563
a Guard Infantry and Rifles	563
b Combined Guard Infantry	582
7 Line Cavalry	583
a Dragoons	583

b Lancers	600
c Hussars	606
8 Steppes (or Plains) Cossacks	615
9 Caucasus (or Mountain) Cossacks	621
10 The Native Horse Regiments	625
a The Crimean Cavalry	625
b The Dagestan Regiment and the Ossetian Demi-Regiment (Caucasus Native Horse)	626
d The Turkman Demi-Regiment	629
11 The Line Infantry and Grenadiers	633
12 Line Rifles	640
13 Cossack Infantry (Kuban Plastun Battalions)	643
Russian Empire: Notes	645
Russian Empire: Bibliography	647

Section VI. German Empire

1 Country Background	649
2 The Army	651
3 Uniform Information	660
4 General Staff	703
5 Prussian Guard Infantry	705
a Foot Guards	706
b Guard Fusilier Regiment	712
c Guard Grenadiers	712
d Guard Jäger and Rifles	714

6 Prussian Cavalry	715
a Prussian Cuirassiers	715
b Dragoons	733
c Lancers (Uhlans)	740
d Hussars	754
e Mounted Rifles (Jäger zu Pferde)	777
7 Bavarian Cavalry	780
a Bavarian Heavy Cavalry (Schwere Reiter)	780

	b Bavarian Lancers	782		g Bavarian Line Infantry	806
	c Bavarian Light Horse (Chevaulegers)	783	10	Jägers and Schützen (Rifles)	810
8	Saxon Cavalry	786	11	Overseas Troops	821
	a Saxon Heavy Cavalry (Schwere Reiter)	786		a German East Africa up to 1896	821
				b German South-West Africa	824
9	Line Infantry	792		c Cameroon	824
	a Prussian Line Grenadiers	793		d Togo	825
	b Prussian Line Infantry	795		e Tsingtao (Jiaozhou)	825
	c Hesse Line Infantry	797		f South Pacific Colonies	825
	d Saxon Line Infantry	800		g Common Uniforms of 1896	825
	e Baden Line Infantry	803	German Empire: Notes	838
	f Württemberg Line Infantry	805	German Empire: Bibliography	842

Section VII. American Empire

1	Country Background	845		c New Dress Uniforms	862
2	The Army	849		d Philippine Scouts	866
3	Uniform Information	854		e Porto Rico (Provisional) Regiment of Infantry	869
4	General Staff	857			
5	Cavalry and Infantry	859	American Empire: Notes	870
	a Cavalry	859	American Empire: Bibliography	872
	b Infantry	861			

Section VIII. Coda 875

Credits 877

Index 881

ACKNOWLEDGEMENTS

It is axiomatic that it takes many people to write a book. I have tried to list them below in no particular order. If I have omitted anyone, I apologise. My deep thanks to:

Bill Bowling, Mr. J.L. Powell, and W.L. Schollander, who, each in their different spheres, gave me a fresh start when I was at my nadir. All that has followed, including this work, is a result of their actions.

The late Bob Marrion, the kindly *éminence grise* of this project, as he was for so many others, generously sharing his vast knowledge and many original photographs. It is not given to many people to help make a forty-year dream come true; however, that is what he has done. Not only did he make this work possible, but I would like to flatter myself that we became friends.

Shaun Barrington breathed life into this project and nursed it along during his tenure as my editor.

Christine McMorris, who patiently shepherded the manuscript to completion.

Maria Salcedo, my main co-worker on this project, supplied a combination of initiative and attention to detail which kept us moving forwards. Without her, this work would have taken twice its five years to complete.

Jeff Millar, Kayleigh Heubel, and Marie-Louise Brunet provided yeoman help, going above and beyond.

David Reavis pulled together images for this work. His photographic skill is an integral part of this project.

Robin Smith, editor, confidante, advisor, factotum, and always a friend.

Natalia Tuchina, a true friend, for her wonderful help on matters Russian, and Vladimir Bakhirev for his help in St Petersburg.

Monte Campbell, whom I've known since we were teenagers going east to school full of inchoate dreams, some of which came true, provided help that showed the depth of her always-generous heart.

Ed Jacobson, my closest high school friend in Oregon, who is now living like a god in France, made research trips and provided moral support.

Mr and Mrs Stelletesky kindly allowed me access to the Motherland Museum on my schedule. They built one of the great collections of Nicholas II militaria in the Western world. It's too bad that it's been broken up.

The veterans of the czar's army and their sons were generous with their time and knowledge. As a bonus, most invited me into their homes. They include Tihon Kulikovsky, Alexis Wrangel, Gabriel Dolenga-Kovalevsky, Vladimir Littauer, V. Stelletesky, Alexis Uzfovich, Wladimir Zweguintzow, and Prince Nicholas Galitzine.

Alex Cheek and Brian Hawley, my good friends, provided crucial introductions. Without them, nothing would have happened.

Gordon Dine, a modest Englishmen of the old school, provided sage advice and the benefit of his extensive knowledge of the British army.

Peter Harrington at the Anne S.K. Brown Collection and my friend Jane Vogler (may she soon be in Bora Bora!) were always helpful and generous with their collections.

Ian Jones, Emma Lefley, Juliet McConnell and Richard Dabb of the National Army Museum, London, helped me locate the many photographs I needed.

Wes, my son, let me and my co-workers share his office to work on this book for years. Rene Wise, Pat Carrillo, and their fellow workers provided help and stoically bore our disruptions to their work.

Dr Anthony Clayton, a leading authority on the French army, not only answered questions but looked up information for me on trips to Sandhurst and worked with Monsieur Jose Maigre while he did research for me at St Cyr.

Henry Keown-Boyd, Captain Des Williams, Major Eddie Pickering, Major Gerald Davies, and Mary Presutti helped answer my questions and directed me.

Sally and Whitney Durand and Bob Rickert provided keys that led to finding Russian information and photographs.

Donna and Martin Thirlwell undertook research to help me.

The friendly staff at the Forsyth Public Library, too many to list, answered questions and found the many books that I needed. Librarians are the best of people.

David Linaker, Gordon Dine, and other members of the arm badge community generously helped me and allowed the use of items from their collections in this work.

Hermann Historica Auctions, Munich, kindly allowed the use of their photographs.

Cedric Demory, Jerome Discours, and Gary Schulze generously allowed the use of photographs in their collection.

Mark Conrad, a tireless researcher of Antebellum armies, has for years generously shared the fruits of his labour.

PREFACE

In 1914, the empires of Europe began the long, slow, and agonising process of blowing up their world. In the process, they discarded all the old certainties: the Divine Rights of Kings, the superiority of the wealthy and of nobles, the exalted status of white men, the certainty of religion, the belief in ever-improving technology, and the fascination with the military and uniforms.

Today, most of Europe has done away with monarchy, and in those countries that still have royalty, the royal families serve as mere fodder for the tabloids and gossip columns. The remaining nobles are seen as airheads, and the rich are viewed as crooks and often as downright evil. No serious person now claims a white person is superior to another race. Europe is a continent of empty churches, as many have rejected religion. Today, technology brings as many problems as blessings, and it seems to have unintended consequences that are worse than the problems it is trying to solve. European public opinion has turned away from the military: it tends to believe that fighting does not solve anything in the long run.

In the military sphere, today's attitude could not be more different from the pre-World War I viewpoint.

Military life was held in high regard by each of the great imperial powers of this study: Great Britain and its crown jewel India, France, Germany, Russia, and the United States. In many regiments of these countries, the money the government paid its officers was not sufficient to live on. These men needed subsidies from their families in order to serve. The prestige of being an army officer was so high that families were often happy to make this expenditure. In France, as an example, the extra money needed to support a family was often expected to come from the officers' wives. Regulations stated a minimum dowry that the wife of a French officer had to bring to the marriage. The interest on the dowry would make up the difference between the family's living expenses and the man's salary. The prestige of a French officer was high enough that many families were willing to put up money so that a daughter could be the wife of an army officer.

In India, the enlisted men were all volunteers. The lives of enlisted men in the pre-World War I Indian army were sufficiently high status that recruiting officers had to worry, not about getting enough volunteers, but rather about the wrong sort of man getting into the ranks. The British Indian army recruited only from certain ethnic classes. Other, less favoured classes would try to pass themselves off as members of the military classes to get a billet in the army. The recruiting manuals are full of sample questions that were asked in order to trip up and expose imposters who were trying to pose as members of one of the favoured classes.

The uniforms the soldiers wore added a great deal to the desirability of the military life, and to its expense. This was a time when men were proud to wear coats of pink or yellow and to have fur headdresses of possum, seal, or raccoon, decorated with egret, vulture, or ostrich feathers. Others flaunted metal helmets with statues of eagles or lions or short spikes on them. Uniforms were colourful and made one stand out as one set apart. In addition to the bright colours, uniforms often sported generous amounts of gold or silver braid, large badges, and plumes on the headdresses.

The uniform, in many cases, carried a record of some two hundred years of battles and incidents. The buttons on the tunic of the British Wiltshire Regiment, at one time, had a dent in them in memory of the regiment's courage in defending Carrickfergus Castle, Ireland in 1760. When they ran out of ammunition, the soldiers had used their uniform buttons as bullets. The Scots Greys Dragoons, a cavalry regiment, wear a bearskin grenadier headdress in memory of their 1706 defeat of the Regiment du Roi, a French grenadier regiment, at the Battle of Ramillies. The Greys rode off the field of battle wearing the Frenchmen's grenadier headdresses. The Gloucestershire Regiment had the unusual honour of wearing a regimental badge on both the front and the back of their helmets. They earned their back badge at the Battle of Alexandria in Egypt in 1801, fighting back-to-back when their rear rank was attacked by the French cavalry.[1]

In 1914 the Russian 81st Apsheronsk Regiment were awarded a red line along the top of their boots in memory of the Battle of Kunersdorf in 1759. At that battle, they are said to have stood up to their boot tops in blood. The 2nd Pskov Dragoons had a representation of a cuirassier's metal breastplate on their helmets. This represented the French cuirassiers' breastplate they were awarded in 1812. The officers of the 77th Tenga Infantry wore a regimental badge that recalled the actions of Arkhip Osipov and other members of the garrison of the Mikhailovskoe fortification in 1840.[2] Rather than let the fort be overrun and taken, Osipov, by agreement among the defenders, blew up the powder magazine, killing himself and most of the attackers. After that, until the czar fell, his name was kept on the regiment's roll, and at roll call the first man after him would answer, 'Died for the glory of the Russian arms in the Mikhailovskoe fortifications'.[3]

In the German army, historical or battle mementos were often carried on the helmet. The 1st and 2nd Battalions of Fusilier Regiment 34 carried a scroll on their helmet that referred to these units having their origin in the Royal Swedish Bodyguards. The helmet of the 4th Grenadiers carried a banner with 1626 on it, commemorating the year of the regiment's founding. It denoted its status as the oldest regiment in the Prussian army. Three Prussian units, Fusilier Regiment No. 73, Infantry Regiment No. 79, and Jäger Battalion No. 10, wore a Gibraltar armband on the right sleeve. This was in memory of the days when their predecessor units had been part of the army of Hanover, ruled by the British king. Those units had helped defend Gibraltar during the Great Siege of 1779 to 1783, and in 1784 King George III awarded a Gibraltar cuff band to men who had served at the siege. This award was revived in 1901 by Kaiser Wilhelm for the above three units.

The helmet of the German 2nd Cuirassier Regiment carried a banner with the inscription 'Hohenfriedberg, 4 Juni 1745'. This commemorated the outstanding work by the 2nd's predecessor regiment, the 5th Bayreuth Dragoons, at that battle. They destroyed 20 Austrian battalions, captured over 2,000 men, and took 66 regimental standards.[4]

The French army tended to adopt simple uniforms under the Third Republic, and did not have any unique reminders of past glories. Perhaps this was a reaction to the martial flamboyance of the First and Second Empires. However, the French had been the warrior race of Europe for a millennium, and as such, exercised a strong influence in other countries.

Military words such as *martinet*, *kepi*, *camouflage*, *campaign*, *triage*, and *bayonet* slipped into the English language. The style and cut of their uniforms were copied. For example, the French North African army formed Zouave regiments whose élan and dash impressed everyone who dealt with them. Their dress and style were widely adopted. In the American Civil War, many volunteer units marched out dressed as Zouaves – among them, to mention only two, were the Louisiana Tiger Zouaves and Ellsworth's First Fire (House) Zouaves (11th New York Infantry). The northern armies had over 55 Zouave units and the South a large but unknown number. The British dressed their West Indian troops and the Indian army in the Zouave style.

But the French troops did not forget their regiments' past heroic deeds. The 29th Infantry Regiment remembered they had been at Valmy in 1792 and had withstood the Prussian cannonade. By doing so they had kept alive the French Revolution and helped win one of the 15 decisive battles of the world. The 32nd Infantry Regiment had held the pass at Montenotte in 1796 against the Austrians – 1,500 men against an army. They held out all night, giving Napoleon time to come up and win his first victory for the French army of Italy.[5] The 8th Hussars took pride that they had achieved a feat unique in history: the capture of an enemy fleet by cavalry. This was done against a Dutch fleet at Texel in January 1795. Elements of the 8th had charged across the ice to capture the astonished sailors.[6]

In India, elements of the uniforms recall past military bravery and glory. The Sikh regiments wore a steel quoit on their turbans, a carry-over from the days of the independent Sikh army. A quoit is more or less a Frisbee with the centre removed, leaving a big steel ring. The outside edge is sharpened. In battle, the quoit can be taken off and thrown at the enemy.

The goal of this work is to describe the last of the dress uniforms of the old order. These uniforms are the last of the colourful dress worn by soldiers. By 1914, these bright uniforms were no longer worn in battle; weapons had become too deadly for that. However, the colourful uniforms were a common sight before August 1914, worn for parades, walking out in public, balls, and when attending court functions. The period covered is from about 1880 to 1914. The countries are Britain, India, France, Germany, Russia, and the United States.

I am only too aware that the British reading public, in this field, is probably the most knowledgeable in the world. A foolhardy author, who for one reason or another has errors in his work, will soon learn of the folly of his or her ways. That said, I will note in advance that, while every effort has been made to avoid errors, they are inevitable in a work so full of tables and lists. Computer programmers like to say that writing a complex computer program is like writing *War and Peace* without a single typo. What they do not tell us is that there are sub-routers to avoid problems, and often a program is self-correcting and will not run if it has an error. Writing this type of book is harder than writing a computer program. I know because I've written computer programs. I've never found a book of this type without typos. So, please bear in mind that typos come with the territory

With a subject matter as large as the uniforms of five countries – six if India is counted individually – certain uniform items must be left out through necessity. Therefore, the focus is narrowly on full dress uniforms and allied gala and palace dress in 1914 in most cases. Work dress, combat dress, and overcoats are not covered. Horse furniture and weapons, except for lances, are not covered. As much as I would have liked to, I have not generally addressed sabretaches or shabraques.

TERMINOLOGY

How to refer to the peoples of Sub-Saharan Africa and their descendants in the Diaspora has been a problem. This is a minefield of political correctness with swift attacks for use of the wrong term. Adding to the problem: there is not agreement within the community about what term is preferred. In Britain, the preferred term tends to be 'black'. In the United States, things are less clear cut; the preferred term tends to be 'African American', but other terms are also used.[7] Given that this work is published in Great Britain and has the possibility of being read in several countries, the term used herein is black. It seems to have the most general application.

The names used for African tribes and ethnic groups in this work are those used by the Europeans in the late nineteenth and early twentieth century. In about the middle third of the twentieth century, academically trained cultural anthropologists began using different names for a people and grouping them together in different ways. Some of the group names mentioned in this work, such as the Dinkas and the Masai, are still used. Others have been replaced by the new academic terms.

Locations in Africa are identified by the names used by the colonial powers and not the modern country and town names.

China, since the Communists came into power, has undergone a complete change in the spelling of place names. This has, for the most part, rendered earlier names unrecognisable. As a general practice, this work gives the old province and place names. In some cases, the new name is also noted if it does not interfere with the flow of the narrative.

The names of Indian provinces and cities are written as they were used under the British Raj. Since independence, and especially in the last ten to fifteen years, many of these have been given new names. For the most part, no effort has been made to update the old British terminology as this would be a Herculean task. Readers who wish to find out the new name in a specific case can fairly easily learn this using a internet resources such as Wikipedia or Google.

The Second Boer War (1899–1902) will often be referred to as the Boer War.

MONETARY VALUES

A present value for the cost of items purchased in the past is given in the book. For the pound, the Bank of England's inflation calculator (www.bankofengland. co.uk/education/Pages/resources/inflationtools/ calculator/flash/default.aspx) was used. For the dollar, the US Bureau of Labor Statistics' CPI inflation calculator (www.bls.gov/data/inflation_calculator. htm) was utilised. The dollar and pound original values were inflated to current values individually to avoid exchange rate problems. For values in dollars, marks, and francs an exchange rate into pounds found in Mitchell, *British Statistics* was used. This pound value was then inflated using Bank of England numbers. In spite of taking every care to compute present value, they were calculated over several years and should be viewed as approximate values.

For ease of use, notes and bibliographies appear at the end of the relevant empire section. In covering each of the empires, several government reports, books, and articles were cited. For convenient reference these citations are listed in a bibliography, with the abbreviated citations that are used in the endnotes.

PERSONAL NOTE

I first became interested in the armies of this period by playing with Britains™ toy soldiers, and I have conducted research for this work off and on for over forty years. The writing of this book had been, mostly, a joy. I hope you will find it enjoyable and informative.

PREFACE: NOTES

1. Carew, *Nicknames*, pp. 68–9.
2. Andolenko, *Badges*, p. 81.
3. Curtiss, *Russian/Nicholas I*, p. 159.
4. Johansson, *Pickelhauben*, p. 9.
5. Ogden, *Famous*, p. 73.
6. Ibid., p. 77.
7. See press release on the 2010 American census, Associated Press, 31 January 2012. It covers terms people used to classify themselves in place of the census term 'black', which once had been the preferred term. The answers were quite varied: African-American, Afro-American, African, Negro or a variation with Negro in it, mulatto, and brown, among others.

PREFACE: BIBLIOGRAPHY

Andolenko, *Badges* — Serge Andolenko, *Badges of Imperial Russia*, translated and enlarged by Robert Werlich (Washington, DC: Quaker Press, 1972).

Curtiss, *Russian/Nicholas I* — John Shelton Curtiss, *The Russian Army Under Nicholas I 1825–1855* (Durham, NC: Duke University Press, 1965).

Carew, *Nicknames* — Tim Carew, *How the Regiments Got Their Nicknames* (London: Leo Cooper, 1974).

Johansson, *Pickelhauben* — Eric J. Johansson, *Pickelhauben (Spiked Helmets) The Glittering Age: German Headdress from the Seventeenth to the Twentieth Century 1650–1918* (Independence, MO: HSM Publications, 1982).

Mitchell, *British Statistics* — B.R. Mitchell, *British Historical Statistics* (Cambridge: Cambridge University Press, 1988).

Ogden, *Famous* — H.A. Ogden (H.A. Hitchcock, collaborator), *Young People's Book of Famous Regiments* (New York: McBride Company, 1957).

§I

OVERVIEW

§I-1 COMPARING THE EMPIRES

Table I.1: Land Area of Major Empires Prior to World War I and Their Original Size

Land Area of Major Empire	Approximate Land Area of the Original State
1. British Empire (1914) 32,262,419 square kilometres 12,456,589.9 square miles	England (1065) 130,438 square kilometres 50,352 square miles
2. Russian Empire (end of nineteenth century)[a] 22,400,000 square kilometres 8,600,000 square miles	2. Moscow (1156) 0.012 to 0.016 square kilometres 0.005 to 0.006 square miles (3–4 acres)
3. French Empire (1914) 12,300,392.25 square kilometres 4,749,208 square miles	3. West Francia (843) 426,000 square kilometres 164,480 square miles
4. US Empire (1914) 10,333,374.5 square kilometres 3,989,738.2 square miles	4. Jamestown (1607) 0.083 square kilometres 0.032 square miles (20.63 acres)
5. German Empire (1914) 3,257,022 square kilometres 1,257,543.26 square miles	5. Brandenburg (1415–40) 29,525.86 square kilometres 11,400 square miles

Notes: [a] France was always considered the second largest empire, rather than Russia. Apparently because Russian land holdings were contiguous, it was considered a country rather than an empire.

Table I.2: Comparison of Ranks across Countries

Great Britain	India		France		Russia			Germany		United States
	Infantry	Cavalry	Infantry	Cavalry	Infantry	Cavalry	Cossacks	Infantry	Cavalry	
Brigadier	Below are ranks for Indians		General de Brigade	General de Brigade	Général-Maïor	Général-Maïor	Général-Maïor	General Major		Brigadier General
Colonel			Colonel	Colonel	Polkovnik	Polkovnik	Polkovnik	Oberst	Oberst	Colonel
Lieutenant Colonel			Lieutenant-Colonel	Lieutenant-Colonel	Pod-polkovnik[d]	Podpolkovnik[d]	Voïskovoï Starshina[d]	Oberst-Leutnant	Oberst-Leutnant	Lieutenant Colonel
Major			Chef de bataillon	Chef d'escadron				Major	Major	Major
Captain			Capitaine	Capitaine	Kapitan	Rotmistr	Esaoul	Hauptmann	Rittmeister	Captain
					Chtabs-Kapitan[c]	Chtabs-Rotmistr[c]	Podésaoul[c]			
Lieutenant	Subadar Major[a,b] Subadar[b]	Rissaldar Major[a,b] Rissaldar[b]	Lieutenant	Lieutenant	Poroutchik	Poroutchik	Sotnik	Oberleutnant	Oberleutnant	First Lieutenant
Second Lieutenant	Jemedar	Jemedar	Sous-Lieutenant	Sous-Lieutenant	Podporoutchik	Kornet	Khorounji	Leutnant	Leutnant	Second Lieutenant
			Adjutant Chef[c]	Adjutant Chef[c]	Podpraporchtchik[c]	Podpraporchtchik[c]	Podkhorounji[c]			
			Adjutant[c]	Adjutant[c]	Feldfébel[c]	Vakhmistr[c]	Feldfébel Vakhmistr[c]			
Regimental Sergeant Major			Soldat de 1ère Classe		Starchi Ounter-ofitzer	Starchi Ounter-ofitzer	Starchi Ouriadnik	Feldwebel	Wachtmeister	Master Sergeant
Company Sergeant Major; Platoon Sergeant Major; Colour Sergeant	Havildar Major	Kot Daffadar	Sergent-major	Marechal de logis chef					Vizefeldwebel (Vizewacht-meister)	Staff Sergeant
Sergeant	Havildar	Daffadar	Sergent	Marechal des logis	Mladchi Ounter-ofitzer	Mladchi Ounter-ofitzer	Mladchi Ouriadnik	Sergeant	Sergeant	Sergeant
Corporal	Naik	Lance Daffadar	Caporal	Brigadier	Iéfreïtor	Iéfreïtor	Prikazny	Unteroffizier	Unteroffizier	Corporal
Lance Corporal	Lance Naik	Acting Lance Daffadar						Obergefreiter	Gefreite	Private First Class
								Gefreiter		
Private	Sepoy	Sowar	Soldat	Cavalier	Riadovoï	Riadovoï	Riadovoï	[e]	[f]	Private

Notes: [a] These men are advisors to the British officers on matters concerning Indian troops, their customs, and morale.
[b] Indian soldiers could not give orders to European soldiers.
[c] No English equivalent.
[d] The regiments of the guard are commanded by major generals.
[e] A wide range of names are used depending on the state, type of branch, and even regiment. Examples are musketeer; grenadier, gardist (115th Regiment), Gemeiner (all Bavarians), Soldat (Saxon infantry), etc.[1]
[f] A wide range of names are used depending on the state, type of branch, and even regiment, e.g. hussar, Ulan Schwere Reiter, Gemeiner, etc.[2]

§I-2 CUFF TYPES

Throughout this work reference will be made to what type of cuffs the uniforms have. A standard terminology to describe cuffs has evolved, using a German outlook. Image I:1 shows six common cuff types: Brandenburg; Saxon; Swedish; French; lancer or Polish; and Gauntlet (found mostly on Scottish dress). References will be made to them throughout this work.

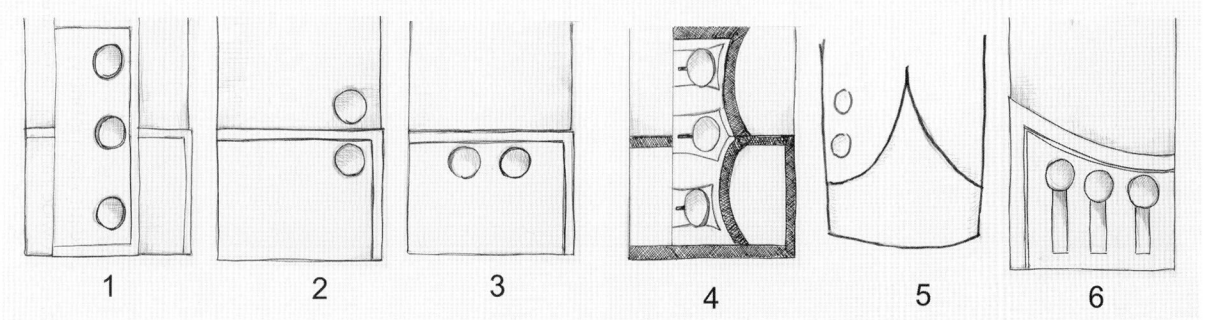

I:1 Cuff Types
1. Brandenburg; 2. Saxon; 3. Swedish; 4. French; 5: lancer or Polish. 6: gauntlet. See §I-2.

§I-3 PANTALOONS

The word pantaloons has different meanings in different countries. As used in the British section, it has the meaning given to it in the dress regulations: riding breeches. In the Indian section, the term is used to refer to baggy knickerbockers. In the French section, the term pantaloons refers to the very baggy trousers worn by North African troops. When the term pantaloons is used in the Russian section, it has yet another meaning: there, it means nether garments worn by guard and line infantry officers and Cossacks. These were baggy and typically tucked into boots just below the knee.

§I-4 ENLISTED MEN

At times I have used the American term 'enlisted men' rather than 'other ranks' because the term 'enlisted men' covers both NCOs and soldiers below that rank. 'Other ranks', on the other hand, leaves some ambiguity as to just what ranks are being covered.

§I-5 SECONDARY SOURCES

A sharp-eyed reader will observe the heavy use of secondary sources in preparing this work. When the author was in grad school, he took a course on research taught by a former CIA agent. That instructor said that during the Cold War, even in a tightly closed society like the USSR, 80 to 90 per cent of what one wanted to learn could be found in secondary sources, such as journals, magazines, and books. There was little need to try to read government files. I have followed this insight in preparing this work.

§I-6 COLOURS

On some issues, such as the colour of British enlisted men's coats, a careful distinction is made between red and scarlet. In other sources, the two terms are used interchangeably. In one book, both colours are used in a single paragraph.[3]

§I-7 HUNGARIAN KNOT

The text refers to the 'Hungarian knot'. British regulations and British books dealing with uniforms call this an Austrian knot, whereas Continental writers tend to use the term Hungarian knot. Austrian or Hungarian, the knot is exactly the same.

§I OVERVIEW: NOTES

1 See British Staff, *Handbook 1914*, pp. 301–2 for more examples.

2 Ibid.

3 Carman, *Uniforms Infantry*, p. 181, last ¶ on page.

§I OVERVIEW: BIBLIOGRAPHY

British Staff, *Handbook 1914* — British War Office, *Handbook of the German Army (Home and Colonial), 1912 (Amended to August 1914)*, 4th edition (London: Imperial War Museum, 2002).

Carman, *Uniforms Infantry* — W.Y. Carman, *Indian Army Uniforms Under the British from the 18th Century to 1947: Artillery, Engineers and Infantry* (London: Morgan-Grampian, 1969).

§II

BRITISH EMPIRE

§II-1 COUNTRY BACKGROUND

In the period before World War I, the British Empire appeared to be the most powerful in the world. It ruled one quarter of the world's land mass and about one quarter of the earth's population. Britain had painted the world map red as its holdings ran right round the globe, with hardly any signs of rebellion in the lands it ruled. Britain's navy was the most powerful in the world, and the traditional policy was to keep the fleet larger than the next two largest combined fleets. Britain's king-emperor or queen-empress and nobles were influential globally. The country's manufacturing base had for years led the world in innovation and production; it was known as the workshop of the world.

But, after 1890, things started to go wrong. Britain's rate of growth slowed. Between 1840 and 1870, industrial productions grew at an annual rate of just over 3 per cent; between 1875 and 1894 it grew at only 1.5 per cent, much less than its economic rivals.[1] In addition, Britain was the one country that practised free trade, so other nations sold into Britain's unprotected home markets while Britain was largely closed out of their markets.

In 1880, Great Britain had 22.9 per cent of the world's manufacturing output, but by 1913, this had fallen to 13.6 per cent. Britain's share of world trade in 1880 was 23.3 per cent; between 1911 and 1913, it was 14.1 per cent. The United Kingdom was now in third place in the industrial output race, behind the United States and Germany.[2] Britain in 1913 had 14 per cent of total world manufacturing production, while the United States had 36 per cent and Germany 16 per cent.[3]

The period also saw social change. The years from 1872 to 1896 are known as the Great Depression. During this period, increased production of industrial and agricultural products drove prices down and made for hard times. In the United States between 1865 and 1880, the grain-producing area more than doubled with the opening of the west to the plough.[4] This yielded a huge amount of additional grain for sale on the world market. There was more Russian grain on the market as well, the Russian government having worked out ways to extract more grain from its inefficient peasant farmers. This did not involve increases in productivity, but rather moving the date the farmers paid their taxes closer to the time of harvest. They thus had to sell more of their harvest to meet their tax obligations. This meant that the peasants had less to get them through the rest of the year, but all the government cared about was that it had more grain to sell on the world market to use to cover government debts. New land was also brought under the plough in Canada, Argentina, New Zealand, and Australia.[5] This, of course, added more grain for sale.

The flood of grain coming onto the market drove the price down. This in turn meant that the tenants of British landowners were unable to pay as much to the landlords. In the period 1875–85, land rents went down an average of 26 per cent in England, and in Ireland between 1881 and 1902 the fall was between 30 and 41 per cent, depending on the land's legal status.[6]

The British aristocracy was a small group. In 1880, there were 580 peers (nobles and baronets). Of these, 431 held seats in the House of Lords. The rank of noble was closely tied to land and wealth. It is said the leading politicians, Disraeli, Salisbury, and Lansdowne, all refused dukedoms on the grounds that they lacked the funds to support the rank.[7] There were another 4,500 large landowners known as the landed gentry. They had for generations lived off the income of their land as gentlemen should, and often spent their lives devoted to their hobbies or in political or military service to the state.

Younger sons of nobles and the landed gentry had no claim to the family estate. However, a younger son would often receive an allowance from his father while the father was alive, and perhaps after death, depending on the family's financial circumstances. The younger sons went into the law, the military, the Church, or the civil service. These were all high-status jobs where contacts could help build a career.

Prior to 1880, land ownership in England was among the most concentrated in Europe, and British landowners were the wealthiest in Europe. In 1873 in England there were 363 owners of 10,000 acres or more. One half of these were peers.

Before the 1880s peers and gentry held most of the government offices. This lock on power fell away as the franchise was broadened in the latter half of the nineteenth century. With new men coming into power, the way was open to attack the peers' and gentry's hold on the land. As one lord put it in 1881, 'The tendency of the extreme section of the Liberal Party is to buy the support of the masses by distributing among them the property of their own political opponents.'[8]

Thanks in part to these changes, landowners lost their grip on wealth in the United Kingdom. Between 1809 and 1879, some 88 per cent of British millionaires had been landowners, but this dropped to 33 per cent between the years 1880 and 1914. The wealth of the new men was made in finance, consumer goods, gold, diamonds, and newspapers. Their holdings were often much larger than those of the landowners, but smaller than the American fortunes being held by men such as Ford, Rockefeller, Mellon, Carnegie, Frick, and Huntington.

In 1894, death duties were introduced at a rate of 8 per cent on estates over £1 million, and increased to 15 per cent in 1909. Faced with fixed expenses and falling income, the landholders began to sell their assets. In the middle of the Great Depression, the return from land had fallen so low that there were no buyers. But, beginning in about 1905, the market picked up, and by late 1914 some 800,000 acres of English land had been sold for approximately £20 million. Landowners sometimes sold their London mansions and country houses, as well as business property such as collieries, rental property, market halls, and docks and harbours. In addition to real estate, land owners sold the contents of their London mansions and country houses. The buyers for all this property were mostly the newly rich Americans, whose wealth easily outshone that of the British.

§II-2 THE ARMY

§II-2-1   *British Cavalry Regiment Names and Dates Formed*
§II-2-2   *British Infantry Regiment Names and Dates Formed*
§II-2-3   *Distribution of British Army in 1914*
§II-2-4   *Special Uniform Items*

§II-2-1 BRITISH CAVALRY REGIMENT NAMES AND DATES FORMED

Regiment	Facings	Year Formed
1st Life Guards	Blue	1660
2nd Life Guards	Blue	1660
Royal Horse Guards (the Blues)	Scarlet	1661
1st (King's) Dragoon Guards	Blue	1685
2nd Dragoon Guards (Queen's Bays)	Buff	1685
3rd (Prince of Wales's) Dragoon Guards	Yellow	1685
4th (Royal Irish) Dragoon Guards	Blue	1685
5th (Princess Charlotte of Wales's) Dragoon Guards	Dark green	1685
6th Dragoon Guards (Carabiniers)	White	1685
7th (Princess Royal's) Dragoon Guards	Black	1688
1st (Royal) Dragoons	Blue	1661
2nd Dragoons (Royal Scots Greys)	Blue	1685
3rd (King's Own) Hussars		1685
4th (Queen's Own) Hussars		1685
5th (Royal Irish) Lancers	Scarlet	1689
6th (Inniskilling) Dragoons	Primrose yellow	1689

Regiment	Facings	Year Formed
7th (Queen's Own) Hussars		1689
8th (King's Royal Irish) Hussars		1693
9th (Queen's Royal) Lancers	Scarlet	1715
10th (Prince of Wales's Own Royal) Hussars		1715
11th (Prince Albert's Own) Hussars		1715
12th (Prince of Wales's Royal) Lancers	Scarlet	1715
13th Hussars		1715
14th (King's) Hussars		1715
15th (The King's) Hussars		1759
16th (The Queen's) Lancers	Blue	1759
17th (Duke of Cambridge's Own) Lancers	White	1759
18th (Queen Mary's Own) Hussars		1759
19th (Queen Alexandra's Own Royal) Hussars		1781
20th Hussars		1791
21st (Empress of India's) Lancers	French grey	1759

§II-2-2 BRITISH INFANTRY NAMES AND DATES FORMED

Regiment[a]	Facings	Year Formed[b]	Date Traditional Facing Colour Regained
Grenadier Guards	Blue	1661 (1656)	

Regiment[a]	Facings	Year Formed[b]	Date Traditional Facing Colour Regained
Coldstream Guards	Blue	1661 (1650)	

Regiment[a]	Facings	Year Formed[b]	Date Traditional Facing Colour Regained
Scots Guards	Blue	1685[c] (1660 in Scottish army)	
Irish Guards	Blue	1900	
The Royal Scots (Lothian Regiment) (1st Foot) Raised in 1633 in Scotland for service in France	Blue	1669 (1633)	
The Queen's (Royal West Surrey Regiment) (2nd Foot)	Blue	1661	
The Buffs (East Kent Regiment) (3rd Foot) Raised in 1572 in London for service in Holland	Buff	1665 (1571)	10/8/1890
The King's Own (Royal Lancaster Regiment) (4th Foot)	Blue	1680	
The Northumberland Fusiliers (5th Foot) Raised in 1674 as an Irish Regiment for service in Holland	Gosling green	1685 (1674)	15/7/1899
The Royal Warwickshire Regiment (6th Foot)	Blue	1685	
The Royal Fusiliers (City of London Regiment) (7th Foot)	Blue	1685	
The King's (Liverpool Regiment) (8th Foot)	Blue	1685	
The Norfolk Regiment (9th Foot)	Yellow	1685	24/03/1905
The Lincolnshire Regiment (10th Foot)	White	1685	
The Devonshire Regiment (11th Foot)	Lincoln green	1685	24/03/1905
The Suffolk Regiment (12th Foot)	Yellow	1685	22/9/1899
Prince Albert's (Somerset Light Infantry) (13th Foot)	Blue	1685	
The Prince of Wales's Own (West Yorkshire Regiment) (14th Foot)	Buff	1685	?/1/1900
The East Yorkshire Regiment (15th Foot)	White	1685	
The Bedfordshire Regiment (16th Foot)	White	1688	
The Leicestershire Regiment (17th Foot)	White	1688	
The Royal Irish Regiment (18th Foot) Raised in Ireland in 1684 but not placed in English service until 1688	Blue	1688 (1684)	
Alexandra, Princess of Wales's Own (Yorkshire Regiment) (19th Foot)	Grass green	1688	15/7/1899
The Lancashire Fusiliers (20th Foot)	White	1688	
The Royal Scots Fusiliers (21st Foot) Raised in 1678, but not placed in English service until 1688	Blue	1688 (1678)	
The Cheshire Regiment (22nd Foot)	Buff	1689	26/02/1904
The Royal Welsh Fusiliers (23rd Foot)	Blue	1689	
The South Wales Borderers (24th Foot)	Grass green	1689	24/03/1905
The King's Own Scottish Borderers (25th Foot)	Blue	1689	
The Cameronians (Scottish Rifles) (26th and 90th Foot) (1689 and 1794)	Blue	1689	

Regiment[a]	Facings	Year Formed[b]	Date Traditional Facing Colour Regained
The Royal Inniskilling Fusiliers (27th and 108th Foot) (1690 and 1854)	Blue	1690	
The Gloucestershire Regiment (28th and 61st Foot) (1694 and 1756)	White	1694	
The Worcestershire Regiment (29th and 36th Foot) (1694 and 1701)	White	1694	04/04/1920
The East Lancashire Regiment (30th and 59th Foot) (1694 and 1741)	White	1694	
The East Surrey Regiment (31st and 70th Foot) (1702 and 1756)	White	1702	
The Duke of Cornwall's Light Infantry (32nd and 46th Foot) (1702 and 1741)	White	1702	
The Duke of Wellington's (West Riding Regiment) (33rd and 76th Foot) (1702 and 1787)	Scarlet	1702	24/03/1905
The Border Regiment (34th and 55th Foot) (1702 and 1742)	Yellow	1702	19/03/1913
The Royal Sussex Regiment (35th and 107th Foot) (1702 and 1854) Regiment not placed in English establishment until 1702	Blue	1702 (1701)	
The Hampshire Regiment (37th and 67th Foot) (1702 and 1758)	Yellow	1702	26/02/1904
The South Staffordshire Regiment (38th and 80th Foot) (1702 and 1793)	White	1702	
The Dorsetshire Regiment (39th and 54th Foot) (1702 and 1755)	Grass green	1702	26/02/1904
The Prince of Wales's Volunteers (South Lancashire Regiment) (40th and 82nd Foot) (1717 and 1793)	White	1717	
The Welsh Regiment (41st and 69th Foot) (1719 and 1756)	White	1719	
The Black Watch (Royal Highlanders) (42nd and 73rd Foot) (1725 and 1758)	Blue	1725	
The Oxfordshire and Buckinghamshire Light Infantry (43rd and 52nd Foot) (1741 and 1755)	White	1741	
The Essex Regiment (44th and 56th Foot) (1741 and 1755)	White	1741	
The Sherwood Foresters (Nottinghamshire and Derbyshire Regiment) (45th and 95th Foot) (1741 and 1823)	Lincoln green	1741	19/02/1913
The Loyal North Lancashire Regiment (47th and 81st Foot) (1741 and 1793)	White	1741	
The Northamptonshire Regiment (48th and 58th Foot) (1741 and 1740)	White	1741	
Princess Charlotte of Wales's (Royal Berkshire Regiment) (49th and 66th Foot) (1744 and 1755)	Blue	1744	30/7/1885 (given Royal status)

Regiment[a]	Facings	Year Formed[b]	Date Traditional Facing Colour Regained
The Queen's Own (Royal West Kent Regiment) (50th and 97th Foot) (1755 and 1824)	Blue	1755	
The King's Own (Yorkshire Light Infantry) (51st and 105th Foot) (1755 and 1839)	Blue	1755	
The King's (Shropshire Light Infantry) (53rd and 85th Foot) (1755 and 1794)	Blue	1755	
The Duke of Cambridge's Own (Middlesex Regiment) (57th and 77th Foot) (1755 and 1787)	Lemon yellow	1755	09/04/1902
The King's Royal Rifle Corps (60th Foot) (1755)	Scarlet	1755	
The Duke of Edinburgh's (Wiltshire Regiment) (62nd and 99th Foot) (1756 and 1824) Raised as a second battalion to an existing regiment in 1756. Became a separate regiment in 1758	Buff	1756	24/03/1905
The Manchester Regiment (63rd and 96th Foot) (1756 and 1824) Raised as a second battalion to an existing regiment in 1756. Became a separate regiment in 1758	White	1756	

Regiment[a]	Facings	Year Formed[b]	Date Traditional Facing Colour Regained
The Princess of Wales (North Staffordshire Regiment) (64th and 98th Foot) (1756 and 1824) Raised as a second battalion to an existing regiment in 1756. Became a separate regiment in 1758	White	1756	
The York and Lancaster Regiment (65th and 84th Foot) (1756 and 1793) Raised as a second battalion to an existing regiment in 1756. Became a separate regiment in 1758	White	1756	
The Durham Light Infantry (68th and 106th Foot) (1756 and 1826) Raised as a second battalion to an existing regiment in 1756. Became a separate regiment in 1758	Dark green	1756	08/12/1902
The Highland Light Infantry (71st and 74th Foot) (1777 and 1787)	Buff	1777	17/11/1899
Seaforth Highlanders (Ross-Shire Buffs, The Duke of Albany's) (72nd and 78th Foot) (1778 and 1778)	Buff	1778	29/3/1899
The Gordon Highlanders (75th and 92nd Foot) (1778 and 1794)	Yellow	1778	
The Queen's Own Cameron Highlanders (79th Foot)	Blue	1793	

Regiment[a]	Facings	Year Formed[b]	Date Traditional Facing Colour Regained	Regiment[a]	Facings	Year Formed[b]	Date Traditional Facing Colour Regained
The Royal Irish Rifles (83rd and 86th Foot) (1793 and 1793)	Green	1793		The Prince of Wales's Leinster Regiment (Royal Canadians) (100th and 109th Foot) (1858 and 1854)	Blue	1858	
Princess Victoria's (Royal Irish Fusiliers) (87th and 89th Foot) (1793 and 1794)	Blue	1793		The Royal Munster Fusiliers (101st and 104th Foot) (1759 and 1839)	Blue	1759	
The Connaught Rangers (88th and 94th Foot) (1793 and 1823)	Green	1793		The Royal Dublin Fusiliers (102nd and 103rd Foot) (1746 and 1661)	Blue	1746	
Princess Louise's (Argyll and Sutherland Highlanders) (91st and 93rd Foot) (1794 and 1799)	Yellow	1794		The Rifle Brigade (The Prince Consort's Own)	Black	1800	

Notes: [a] Years in brackets in this column are the formation years of the two regiments that were joined to make these regiments.
[b] Years in brackets in this column are the dates the unit was first in existence before the regiments were officially formed on the English establishment.
[c] On English establishment

§II-2-3 DISTRIBUTION OF BRITISH INFANTRY IN 1914 (INCLUDES THE FOOT GUARDS)

British Regiments Infantry
Total number of battalions 157
52.9% at home
47.1% overseas

Locations of the 52.9% at home
71% England
24% Ireland
4% Scotland
1% Wales
Total 100%

Locations of the 47.1% overseas
64% India
4% Burma
18% Mediterranean, Egypt (Sudan) Aden (7% at Malta) (India lifeline)
7% Far East
7% South Africa (including 1 battalion in Mauritius)
1% Americas (Bermuda)
Total 101%

Distribution of British Battalions, 1914

Location	No. of Battalions	Percentage of Total Army
Home		
England	59	37.6%
Scotland	3	1.9%
Wales	1	0.6%
Ireland	20	12.6%
Total in home islands	83	52.9%
Overseas		
India	47	29.9%
Burma	3	1.9%
South Africa	4	2.5%
Gibraltar	2	1.3%
Malta	5	3.2%
Egypt	4	2.5%
Sudan	1	0.6%
Aden	1	0.6%
Malay	1	0.6%
Singapore	1	0.6%
Hong Kong	1	0.6%
Tientsin, China	2	1.3%
Mauritius Islands	1	0.6%
Bermuda	1	

Location	No. of Battalions	Percentage of Total Army
Total overseas	74	47.1%
Total	**157**	**100%**

The above figures are misleading. It is often pointed out that the battalions at home were hollow shells, holding only new enlistees and men about to be discharged, but the full extent of this statement is not realised until one looks at the composition of the battalions that went to France in August 1914: reservists formed 61.8 per cent of the personnel upon mobilisation.[9] This number would have been higher but for the fact the Expeditionary Force included six full-strength Guard battalions; they made up 8 per cent of the Old Contemptibles. It is no wonder people said that if you want to see the real British soldier you must go east of the Suez – the statement really should be 'east of Gibraltar', because of the large forces in the Mediterranean and Africa.

§II-2-4 SPECIAL UNIFORM ITEMS

The customs and mementos of British regiments can be broken down into eight different areas:

- uniforms
- badges
- animal mascots
- music
- practices outside the regimental mess
- mess silver
- souvenirs
- mess – mostly in how the table is set and how the loyal toast is performed.

In the interests of space, only the first area will be examined in detail, with the other areas only mentioned. T.J. Edwards's book *Military Customs* gives details on many of these items.[10] *Officer's Mess* by R.J. Dickinson provides a light-hearted and informative view on British mess practices.[11]

Additional Special Uniform Items

GLOUCESTERSHIRE REGIMENT: HELMET BADGE
At the Battle of Alexandria, Egypt, on 21 March 1801, the Gloucestershire's predecessor regiment, the 28th, was formed up in battle line when they were also attacked from the rear by the French cavalry. The back rank of the regiment was ordered to about face and fire on this new danger. Fighting back to back, they forced the enemy to retreat. In memory of this feat, the regiment wears a badge, a sphinx with a wreath on the back of their helmets. The back badge worn by officers between 1881 and 1914 was larger than that worn by enlisted men (see *§II-3 Appendix III*, Image II:31, row 4, last column, badges of the Gloucestershire Regiment, and Image II:118).[12]

The 2nd Battalion, old 61st Foot, which was the other battalion which went to form the Gloucestershire Regiment, had to fight back to back against the Sikhs at

Chillianwallah in 1849. They received no recognition for this feat.

GRENADIER GUARDS: BEARSKIN

As is well known, the Grenadier Guards were granted the honour of wearing a grenadier bearskin in 1815, after defeating Napoleon's Grenadiers at the Battle of Waterloo.

SCOTS GREYS: BEARSKIN

The Scots Greys, together with the 5th Royal Irish Lancers at the Battle Ramillies, captured most of the French Grenadier Regiment. Both regiments took the tall grenadier caps worn by the French and wore them for some years. This practice fell into disuse for the 5th Royal Irish Lancers, but the Scots Greys continued to do so, and these caps eventually became the bearskin worn by the regiment in the late nineteenth and twentieth centuries.

MINDEN REGIMENTS: ROSES

The Battle of Minden took place on 1 August 1759. The main action saw six British and two Hanover infantry regiments march into the centre of a numerically superior French army. The French could not believe that the infantry would march through artillery fire and defeat the three lines of French cavalry, which were said to number 10,000 men.[13] The British march took them past rose bushes, and the soldiers cut off roses and fastened them to their coats.

Five of the six British regiments who fought on that glorious day mark Minden Day (1 August) by wearing roses on their helmets. The table shows the regiments and the colours of their roses. Image II:1 shows a Minden regiment with roses attached to their helmets.

The Royal Welch Fusiliers did not wear roses on Minden Day.[14] Different reasons are given for this, ranging from the fact that their fusiliers' grenade cap badge had a small rose at its bottom, so they always were wearing a rose,[15] to the lordly 'We had more on our minds that day than picking flowers'.

Table II.2.4.1: Minden Regiments and Roses

Title of the Regiment in 1914	Number of Regiment in Battle of Minden	Rose Colour
Suffolk	12	Red and yellow[a]
Lancashire Fusiliers	20	Primrose yellow and burgundy red[b]
Welch Fusiliers	23	None[c]
King's Own Scottish Borderers	25	Red[d]
Royal Hampshire	37	Red[e]
Yorkshire Light Infantry	51	White[f]

Notes: [a] Conversation with Suffolk Regimental Museum, 18 November 2016.
[b] Conversation with Phil Mather, Fusilier Museum, Lancashire, 21 November 2016.
[c] Correspondence with Lt. Gen. Jonathon Riley, former Honorary Colonel of the Royal Welch Fusiliers, 21 November 2016.
[d] Conversation with Ian Martin of King's Own Scottish Borderers Regimental Museum, 21 November 2016. In 1921, red and white roses were authorised, but the regiment has always worn just red roses.
[e] Conversation with Royal Hampshire Regiment Museum, 21 November 2016.
[f] Correspondence with Malcolm Johnson, King's Own Yorkshire Light Infantry Museum, 25 November 2016.

ROYAL NORTHUMBERLAND FUSILIERS: PLUME

The Royal Northumberland Fusiliers wore a red and white plume on their fusilier's busby. This recalls the small battle at La Vigie on the island of St Lucia in the Windward Islands of the West Indies. There, on 18 December 1778, the old 5th Foot defeated twelve times their number of French-led forces. From the defeated French forces, they took the white feathers and wore them in their headdresses.[16]

How this changed to red over white is a somewhat complicated story. One prong of the story is how they came to be fusiliers wearing fusilier headdress. The 5th Foot at the Battle of Wilhelmstahl in 1762 was part of a force that captured some 3,000 French troops, mostly grenadiers. The men of the 5th took the French grenadier caps and began wearing them as war trophies. In fact, the regimental history states

II:1 The King's Own (Yorkshire) Light Infantry, 2nd Battalion on Minden Day (1 August) 1909 wearing white roses in their helmets.

that, from 1762 on, the regiment had always worn either grenadier or fusilier caps.[17] In this story, when the regiment were made fusiliers in 1836, it merely regularised the style of headdress the regiment had been wearing.[18]

There are some problems with this line of thought. A 2008 special study of British shakos showed that in 1835 the 5th wore shakos with red over white tuft balls while white tuft balls were standard for infantry.[19] At some point, a back story was developed that the soldiers of the 5th had dipped their feathers in the blood of the dead French. The same study shows a standard shako for the regiment in 1826 following the standard colours: in this case, white over red tufts or upright feather plumes for men and officers of the battalion company. Regular infantry companies did not seem to have tufts.[20] There was no exception shown for the 5th.

As noted above, in 1836, the 5th was made a fusilier regiment and thus entitled to wear a fusilier headdress, but the only change this involved was a flaming grenade to be worn on a plate on the front of a standard shako.[21] However, a provision was made for the 5th to wear red over white tuff balls rather than the normal infantry white balls. What had been implied in 1843 was specifically ordered in 1854: fusilier regiments were to no longer to wear bearskin caps.

When the regiment began wearing a fusilier busby, the colour combination was worn on a plume on the left side of the busby. This was almost unique; only one other fusilier regiment, the Royal Irish Fusiliers, had a plume until after the Boer War, when all the fusilier regiments were given coloured plumes. The Northumberland plume was still a little different, being shorter than the others, 11.43 cm (4½ inches) versus 16.51 cm (6½ inches).

Unconnected with Minden Day, the Royal Northumberland Fusiliers wore red and white roses on St George's Day, 23 April. St George killing a dragon is a regimental badge.[22]

Somerset Light Infantry: Sash

In the Somerset Light Infantry, the sashes were worn in an unusual way by sergeants. Before 1912, both sergeants and officers wore their sashes over their left shoulders, whereas sergeants would normally wear sashes over their right shoulders (while only officers would wear them over the left). It was said this custom was granted by the Duke of Cumberland after the Battle of Culloden in 1746, but the relevant documents have been lost.[23] The reason behind this custom is said to be that the officers took such high casualties in the battle that the sergeants had to act as officers. There is some doubt about this. A letter written immediately after the battle referred to the writer's joy that the regiment, then called Pulteney's Foot, suffered so few casualties, 'not twenty of our men were killed'.[24]

Regardless of what may or may not have happened, the wearing of the sash over the left shoulder by sergeants was authorised in 1865 in view of the length of time the custom had already existed. In 1912 all infantry officers began wearing their sashes around their waist. The officers of the Somerset Light Infantry then, quite against regulations, began tying their waist sash on the right instead of the more standard left. This was not approved until 1931.[25]

The regiment has another dress distinction, which, while not involving their dress uniform, might also be of interest. In 1707, the regiment, then known as Pierce's Foot, was serving in Spain. The commander of the British forces, the Earl of Peterborough, was short of dragoons, and hit upon the idea of mounting Pierce's Foot. In memory of this service, the officers wore a cavalry pattern mess vest.[26]

Staffordshire Regiment: Buff Cloth

The 38th Foot, later the 1st Battalion of the Staffordshire Regiment, was raised in 1702 and in 1707 sent to Antigua in the West Indies. This began a period of fifty-seven years' service in the West Indies. The 38th Foot was left with few supplies and reinforcements, while fevers tore huge holes in their ranks. Regimental lore says they were forgotten by the authorities in London and had to repair their tattered uniforms using brown holland cloth, which is the material used for bagging sugar.

It was customary when sending regiments to hot weather stations to leave them there for a long time. Overseas tours of twelve to fifteen years were often made. Medical opinion held that the highest losses from disease occurred when people first reached the tropical climate, and after that they built up a certain immunity. However fifty-seven years was way beyond any tour any other regiment ever performed.

Contrary to what is sometimes said, in the period 1880–1914 the South Staffordshires did not have an unofficial custom of wearing buff holland cloth behind the badges on their home and foreign service helmets in remembrance of this service.[27] In 1934 the regiment's long stay in the West Indies was recognised by the award of a dress distinction of buff cloth to be worn behind the cap and collar badges.[28] The regiment also began wearing a buff holland waistcoat with their mess kit.[29]

Black Lines on Lace and Shoulder Cords

Several regiments wear black lines in their lace and shoulder cords (see Image II:4(5)). Authorisation for some regiments to do this is found in a 1768 clothing warrant,[30] which clearly predates the normal reasons for these black lines: signs of mourning for or to commemorate the deaths of Sir John Moore at Corunna and James Wolfe at Quebec.

See §II-3-3 for the regiments that had these black lines and a discussion of their possible origins.

Wiltshire Regiment: Buttons

In 1760, a detachment of the 62nd Foot, later the 1st Battalion of the Wiltshire Regiment, defended Carrickfergus Castle against a raid by François Thurot, a well-known French privateer and terroriser of British shipping. When they ran out of ammunition, they fired their uniform buttons out of their muskets. For this, they won the right to have dents on their buttons in memory of their stand. However, according to the regimental museum, when uniform buttons became machine-made and mass produced it was no longer possible to strike a dent in them. Therefore this unique custom and honour fell by the wayside.

Royal Welsh Fusiliers: Back Flash

One of the best-known dress variations is the back flash of the Royal Welsh Fusiliers (as it was spelled in 1914.) When the army wore their hair powdered and tied in pigtails, it was customary to wear a shield of cloth on the collar to protect it from the grease and loose powder of the pigtail. Pigtails were abolished in July 1808, at which time the Welsh Fusiliers were stationed in Nova Scotia and continued to wear their pigtails, also called queues, and collar shields. Even when the regiment, at some point, ceased to wear pigtails, the officers continued to wear the pigtail/queue ribbons that served as collar shields on the back of their coat collars.

Finally, in 1834, they were ordered to stop this non-regulation practice. An appeal was made and the king approved of the use of the 'flash' as a peculiarity of the distinguished regiment. From 1834, the flash was worn by officers, warrant officers, and staff sergeants only. Then, in 1900, the right to wear it was extended to all ranks.[31] The flash consists of five swallow-tailed black silk ribbons 22.86 cm (9 inches) long for officers, 17.78 cm (7 inches) for soldiers, fastened to the back of the collar. See Image C20. They spread out from the collar in a fan shape.[32]

During World War I, the officers of the regiment wore the flash on the combat dress. This was objected to by the higher authorities on the grounds it would give the Germans information about the forces fighting them, and the regiment was ordered to remove their flashes. An appeal was made. In time, the king approved the regiment's wearing of their flashes in combat, saying he was sure the enemy would never see the backs of the Royal Welsh Fusiliers.

ROYAL FUSILIERS: SCABBARD AND STRIPE

The bandsmen of the 1st Battalion of the Royal Fusiliers wore brass scabbards for their swords. These were given to the 7th Foot in 1790 by the Duke of Kent, the father of Queen Victoria, when he was colonel of the regiment.[33]

Between World Wars I and II, the officers of the Royal Fusiliers wore a wider red stripe on their full dress trousers and breeches. The normal width was 0.64 cm (¼ inch), and they wore a 1.59 cm (⅝ inch) stripe.[34] This was done to show their old association, as fusiliers, with artillery. It is not clear if the wider stripe was worn prior to World War I. It is not provided for in the dress regulations of that period, but regimental customs often grew in spite of the regulations.

WORCESTERSHIRE REGIMENT: STAR

The 29th Foot, ancestor of the Worcestershire Regiment, wore a star on their pouches. When this first began is uncertain, but it is said to have been traced for certain back to the early part of the eighteenth century. Official approval was gained for

II:2 Royal Welsh Fusiliers Back Flash
The image also shows the trim pattern on the rear of the tunic.

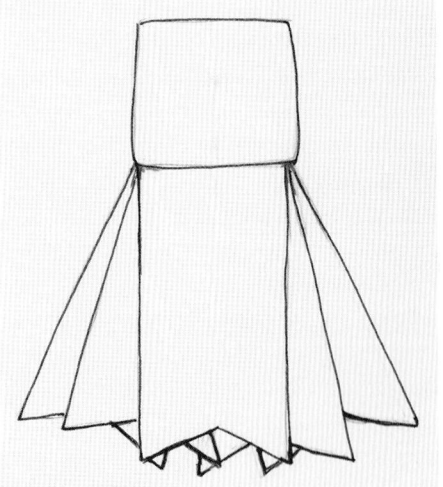

II:3 Royal Welsh Fusiliers Back Flash
Length: officers – 22.86 cm (9 inches); others – 17.78 cm (7 inches)

this practice in 1838. In 1877, the 29th Regiment was given permission to wear white ammunition pouches, like the foot guards, instead of black ones as used by the rest of the line infantry.

When the 19th and 36th merged in 1881 to form the Worcestershire Regiment, both battalions began to wear the star. The star badge consisted of a star of the Order of the Garter, similar to that worn by horse guards, only simpler. It had eight major rays and many lesser rays between them. On the star was a garter commemorating the order, along with its motto, *Honi soit qui mal y pense* – 'Shame upon him who thinks evil of it'. In the centre was a standing crowned lion.[35]

15th Hussars: Bourbon Flags

While not really a uniform distinction, mention should be made of a distinction granted to the 15th Light Dragoons, later the 15th Hussars. They, as a newly raised regiment in 1760, won an overwhelming victory at Emsdorff. In recognition of this, they were given the first battle honour granted by the British army and a special distinction for their horse furniture. The distinction was to show on cloth over the front wallets or on the shabraques. It was upside-down crossed Bourbon flags bearing fleur-de-lys. The depiction of the flags varied over the years, as did where they were shown. When the regiment underwent mechanisation, this special distinction was lost along with the horses.

Lace[36]

From 1880 to 1914 most regular cavalry regiments had one or more unique pattern of lace that went with the different types of dress. The line infantry had far fewer. Prior to 1850, the infantry had a large number of different lace patterns, but by 1900 these had dropped to just three for the tunic, one style each for Scottish, Irish, and another for English/Welsh regiments. These were the thistle, shamrock and rose style lace patterns respectively. The different lace patterns worn by the infantry are jointly called the infantry pattern. When used in text, it means one of these possible infantry lace patterns.

For line cavalry between 1880 and 1902, there were about seventy-five different patterns of lace that could be used on tunics, trousers, levee trousers, forage caps, mess jackets, shoulder belts, slings, etc.

In 1902, an effort was made to cut officers' costs by simplifying the lace situation. The number of lace patterns was cut to about sixty, and the different items of dress that called for lace was reduced to about four – tunic, shoulder, sling and girdle (lace waist belt).

Line rifles wore cord in place of lace. The Guards had their own individual bespoke lace and embroidery patterns.

The lace was woven from silver or gold thread in different widths and patterns. It could have coloured silk or cloth stripes on it.

§II-3 UNIFORM INFORMATION

§II-3-1	*Cavalry Brass Shoulder Titles*
§II-3-2	*Infantry Brass Shoulder Titles*
§II-3-3	*Black Lines in Lace and Shoulder Cords*
§II-3-4	*Shoulder Cords*
§II-3-5	*1900 and 1904 Uniform Composites*
§II-3-6	*British Badges, Errors and Changes*
§II-3 Appendix I	*Photographs of Cavalry Arm Badges*
§II-3 Appendix II	*1904 Dress Regulations: Descriptions of Officers' Buttons, Helmet Plates, Badges, and Belt Buckles*
§II-3 Appendix III	*1904 Dress Regulations: Photographs of Regimental Badges and of Standard Home Service Helmet Plate (With King's Crown)*
§II-3 Appendix IV	*1911 Dress Regulations: Descriptions of Officers' Buttons, Helmet Plates, and Badges*

§II-3-1 CAVALRY BRASS SHOULDER TITLES

Regiment	Title	Regiment	Title
1st Life Guards[a]	1 L.G.	7th Queen's Own Hussars	7 H.
2nd Life Guards[a]	2 L.G.	8th King's Royal Irish Hussars	8 H.
Royal Horse Guards[b]	R. H.G.	9th Queen's Royal Lancers	9 L.
1st King's Dragoon Guards	1 D.G.	10th Royal Hussars	10 H.
The Queen's Bays	2 D.G.	11th Hussars	11 H.
3rd Dragoon Guards	3 D.G.	12th Royal Lancers	12 L.
4th Royal Irish Dragoon Guards	4 D.G.	13th Hussars	13 H.
5th Dragoon Guards	5 D.G.	14th King's Hussars	14 H.
The Carabiniers (6th Dragoon Guards)	6 D.G.	15th The King's Hussars	15 H.
7th Dragoon Guards	7 D.G.	16th The Queen's Lancers	16 L.
1st The Royal Dragoons	1 R.D.	17th Lancers	17 L.
The Royal Scots Greys (2nd Dragoons)	2 D.	18th Royal Hussars	18 H.
3rd The King's Own Hussars	3 H.	19th Royal Hussars	19 H.
4th The Queen's Own Hussars	4 H.	20th Hussars	20 H.
5th Royal Irish Lancers	5 L.	21st Lancers	21 L.
The Inniskillings (6th Dragoons)	6 D.		

Notes: [a] Only one full stop shown in full title.
[b] Only one full stop shown in existing title.

§II-3-2 INFANTRY BRASS SHOULDER TITLES

Regiment	Title	Regiment	Title
Grenadier Guards	G.G. and grenade	Duke of Wellington's Regt	Duke of Wellington's
Coldstream Guards	C.G. and rose	Border Regt	Border
Scots Guards	S.G. and thistle	Royal Sussex Regt	Royal Sussex
Irish Guards	I.G. and star	Hampshire Regt	Hants
Royal Scots	Royal Scots	South Staffordshire Regt	S. Stafford
Queen's Royal Regt[a]	Queen's	Dorsetshire Regt	Dorset
The Buffs	Buffs	South Lancashire Regt	S. Lancashire
King's Own	King's Own	Welch Regt	Welch
Northumberland Fusiliers	N.F. and grenade	Black Watch	R.H.
Royal Warwickshire Regt	R. Warwickshire	Oxfordshire and Buckinghamshire Light Infantry	Oxf. & Bucks. with bugle
Royal Fusiliers	R.F. and grenade	Essex Regt	Essex
The King's	King's	Sherwood Foresters	Notts. And Derby.
Norfolk Regt	Norfolk	Loyal North Lancashire Regt	N. Lancashire
Lincolnshire Regt	Lincoln	Northamptonshire Regt	Northampton
Devonshire Regt	Devon	Royal Berkshire Regt	Royal Berks.
Suffolk Regt	Suffolk	Royal West Kent Regt	R.W. Kent
Somerset Light Infantry	Somerset and bugle	King's Own Yorkshire Light Infantry	Yorkshire and bugle
West Yorkshire Regt	W. York.	Middlesex Regt	Middlesex
East Yorkshire Regt	E. York	King's Royal Rifles	K.R.R.
Bedfordshire and Hertfordshire Regt	Bedford	Wiltshire Regt	Wilts.
Leicestershire Regt	Leicester	Manchester Regt	Manchester
Royal Irish Regt	Royal Irish	North Staffordshire Regt	N. Stafford
Green Howards	York	York and Lancaster Regt	Y. and L.
Lancashire Fusiliers	L.F. and grenade	Durham Light Infantry	Durham and bugle
Royal Scots Fusiliers	R.S.F. and grenade	Highland Light Infantry	H.L.I. and bugle
Cheshire Regt	Cheshire	Seaforth Highlanders	Seaforth
Royal Welch Fusiliers	R.W.F. and grenade	Gordon Highlanders	Gordon
South Wales Borderers	S.W.B.	Cameron Highlanders	Cameron
King's Own Scottish Borderers	K.O.S.B.	Royal Irish/Ulster Rifles	R.I.R.
Cameronians	S.R.	Royal Irish Fusiliers	R.I.F. and grenade
Royal Inniskilling Fusiliers	R. Inniskilling and grenade	Connaught Rangers	Conn. Rangers
Gloucestershire Regt	Gloster	Argyll and Sutherland Highlanders	A. and S.H.
Worcestershire Regt	Worcestershire	Leinster Regt	Leinster R.C.
East Lancashire Regt	E. Lancashire	Royal Munster Fusiliers	R.M.F. and grenade
East Surrey Regt	E. Surrey	Royal Dublin Fusiliers	R.D.F. and grenade
Duke of Cornwall's Light Infantry	Cornwall and bugle	Rifle Brigade	R.B.

Notes: [a] Apostrophe missing in new title.

§II-3-3 BLACK LINES IN LACE AND SHOULDER CORDS

Regiments with black lines in their lace and in the shoulder cords according to the 1911 Dress Regulations:

1. The Norfolk Regiment	To remember the part the regiment took in the burial of Sir John Moore in Spain in 1809.	
2. The East Yorkshire Regiment	To remember the death of James Wolfe at Quebec in 1759. The regiment had served under Wolfe.	
3. The Leicestershire Regiment	The black lines are in honour of James Wolfe. He did not serve in the regiment, but his father, Edward Wolfe, did serve in the old 17th Foot. The 17th Foot was in a brigade commanded by James Wolfe at the siege and capture of Louisburg, Nova Scotia in 1758. The regiment also lays out black crepe ribbons on its officers' table on guest nights and for regimental dinners. In addition, their band plays 'Wolfe's Dirge' at ceremonial parades.	
4. The Loyal North Lancashire Regiment	The 47th Foot played a major part in the capture of Quebec under James Wolfe and acquired the nickname 'Wolfe's Own'. They wore these black lines and black braid on mess waistcoats.[37]	
5. The Gordon Highlanders	To remember the part the regiment took in the burial of Sir John Moore in Spain in 1809.	
6. The Somersetshire Light Infantry	The reason for their black lines is unknown.[a]	
7. The York and Lancaster Regiment	The reason for their black lines is unknown, but it might be noted that one of its component, regiments, the 84th Foot, was massacred at Cawnpore, India.[38]	
8. The East Surrey Regiment	The reason for their black lines is unknown.[a]	
9. The Connaught Rangers	The reason for their black lines is unknown.[a]	

Notes: [a] An explanation for the black line in lace of the Somersetshire Light Infantry may lie in one of their predecessor regiments, the 13th Foot, affirming its loyalty to the Hanoverian monarchs. Black was the Hanoverian rulers' favoured colour, and it appeared often as black cockades and, sometimes, as facings on uniforms. It is said some regiments added black to their lace when the large black cockades were done away with in the change from tricorn hats to shakos.

Another explanation for the black line in lace is suggested by the history of the 41st Foot as reported in a military research journal.[39] The 41st became part of the Welsh Regiment, which did not have a black line in their lace c. 1900–14. The history is said to state that the 41st adopted black striped lace in 1787, before they had been in battle. The writer speculated that this was done because black lines improved the appearance of silver lace. When the silver lace was replaced by gold, there was no longer a need for the black line, and some regiments did away with them, although others may not have. This theory would account for, with perhaps one exception, the regiments with black lines in their lace.[40]

In the eighteenth and early nineteenth centuries, uniform details were not as closely regulated, and the regimental colonels had more freedom in setting uniform details.[41] This would explain why some regiments had black lines in their lace prior to the deaths of Moore and Wolfe.

It has even been suggested that regiments with black lace lines may have developed an *ex post facto* connection with Wolfe and Moore in Victorian times to explain the black lines in their lace, lines that had been originally placed there as a show of loyalty to the Hanoverians or for aesthetic reasons. They then had the lines officially approved on this new basis.

§II-3-4 SHOULDER CORDS

The British had different shoulder cords for different types of regiments. See Image II:4 to examine what these cords looked like. Eight service branches wore the different shoulder cords: household cavalry, dragoon guards and dragoons, hussars, lancers, infantry with black lines, rifles, infantry and other services, generals.

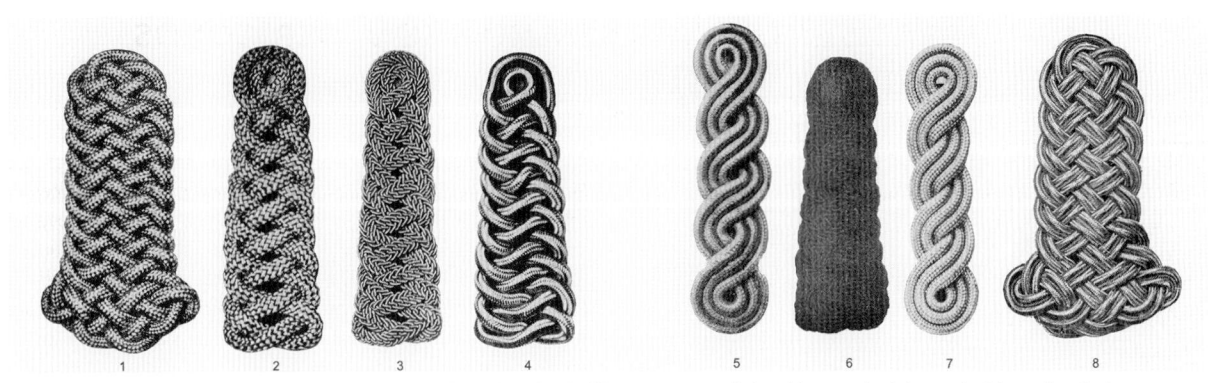

II:4 In the British army, the different branches of services had different types of shoulder cords. 1. household cavalry; 2. dragoon guards and dragoons; 3. hussars; 4. lancers; 5. infantry with black lines; 6. rifles; 7. infantry and other services; 8. generals

§II-3-5 1900 AND 1904 UNIFORM COMPOSITES

The period after the Boer War saw a simplification in design. The uniforms worn by the different branches in 1900 and then in 1904 are shown in Images II:5–24 to give a reference point as uniforms are discussed.

The uniforms shown are:

II:5: Household cavalry (1900 Regulations) – helmet, tunic, shoulder cords, epaulettes, cuff and rear skirt trim.

II:6: Household cavalry (1904 Regulations) – helmet, tunic, shoulder cords, epaulettes, cuff and rear skirt trim. Note how there have not been any changes from 1900.

II:7: Foot guards (1900 Regulations) – headdress, tunic, collars, shoulder straps, cuff and rear skirt trim. Note how trim varied by rank for the three foot guard regiments.

II:8: Foot guards (1904 Regulations) – headdress, tunic, collars, shoulder straps, cuff and rear skirt trim. Note how trim varied by rank for the four foot guard regiments.

II:9: Dragoon guards, dragoons, and 6th Dragoon Guards (1900 Regulations) – headdress, tunic, shoulder cords, and cuff and rear skirt trim. Note the braid pattern on the collar and cuffs and how complex the cuff trim was. They also varied by rank.

II:10: Dragoon guards, dragoons, and 6th Dragoon Guard (1904 Regulations) – headdress, tunic, shoulder cords, and cuff and rear skirt trim as of 1904. Note how the cuff trim has been greatly simplified.

II:11: Hussars (1900 Regulations) – headdress, tunic, shoulder cords, and cuff trim. Note how the collar and cuffs are very elaborate and vary by rank.

II:12: Hussars (1904 Regulations) – headdress, tunic, shoulder cords, cuff trim, and rear and back of skirt. Note how collar and cuffs have been simplified.

II:13: Lancers (1900 Regulations) – headdress, tunic (note braid pattern on collar and cuffs), shoulder cords, and cuff and rear skirt trim. When worn, the girdle olivet's position would be worn at the waist in line with the left arm, and not in front as shown.

II:14: Lancers (1904 Regulations) – headdress, tunic, shoulder cords, and cuff and rear skirt trim. Note how cuffs have been simplified.

II:15: Line infantry and fusiliers (1900 Regulations) – headdress, tunic, shoulder cords, and cuff trim. Note how rank is shown on collar and elaborate cuff braiding.

II:16: Line infantry and fusiliers (1904 Regulations) – headdress, tunic, shoulder cords, and cuff and rear skirt trim. Note how the cuff and collar trim has been simplified and how the helmet plate has changed. Notice also the reference to plumes, and how they were worn on all of the fusilier fur hats.

II:17: Colonial helmets (prior to 1904) – as the caption shows, the bottom helmet was worn in the African and Chinese Regiments. After 1904, this style would be known as the Wolseley helmet (Image II:18).

II:18: Colonial (Wolseley) helmet (1904 Regulations) – Egyptian pattern, and the styles of spikes worn on the helmets.

II:19: Rifles (1900 Regulations) – headdress, tunic, shoulder cords, and cuff trim. Note how elaborate the collar and cuff trim is.

II:20: Rifles (1904 Regulations) – headdress, tunic, shoulder cords, and cuff trim. Note how collar and cuffs have been simplified.

II:21: Highland Scots (1900 Regulations) – headdress, tunic, shoulder cords, cuff trim, and Inverness flap. The items that show rank are the gauntlet cuffs, slash cuffs, Inverness flaps, and the braiding on the shako.

II:22: Highland Scots (1904 Regulations) – headdress, tunic, shoulder cords, slash cuffs and Inverness flaps. Note how the collar, slash cuffs, and flaps no longer show rank, but the braid on the shako indicates rank.

II:23: Scottish Rifles (1900 Regulations) – headdress, tunic, shoulder straps, slash cuffs and Inverness flaps. Note how the collar, slash cuffs, and flaps show rank.

II:24: Scottish Rifles (1904 Regulations) – headdress, tunic, shoulder straps, slash cuffs and Inverness flaps. Note how the collar, slash cuffs, and flaps no longer show rank.

II:5 Household Cavalry (1900 Regulations)
1. Tunic.
2. Cuff.
3. Rear skirt.
4. Helmet.

§II-3 Uniform Information

II:6 Household Cavalry (1904 Regulations)
1. Tunic.
2. Cuff.
3. Rear skirt.
4. Helmet.

Note how there have not been any changes from 1900.

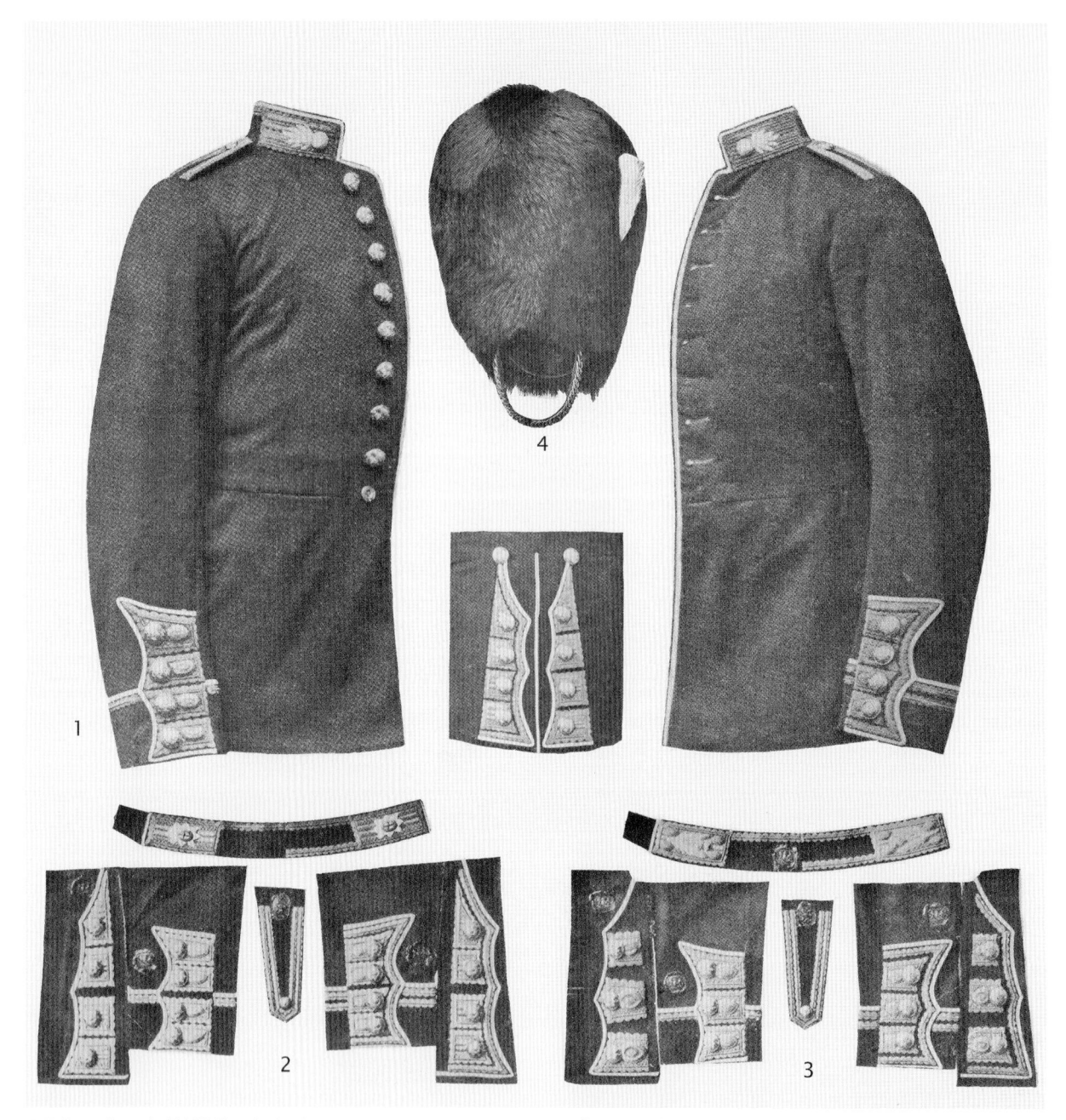

II:7 Foot Guards (1900 Regulations)
1. Grenadier Guard collar and cuffs with tunic buttons – junior officer;
    Centre – rear skirts: *left* – senior officers; *right* – junior officers;
    Right – tunic: senior officer collar and cuffs.
2. Coldstream Guards
    Top left – junior officer collar;
    Top right – senior officer collar;
    Bottom left – junior officer rear skirt and cuff;
    Bottom centre – shoulder strap;
    Bottom right – senior officer rear skirt and cuff.
3. Scots Guards
    Top left – junior officer collar;
    Top right – senior officer collar;
    Bottom left – junior officer rear skirt and cuff;
    Bottom centre – shoulder strap;
    Bottom right – senior officer rear skirt and cuff.
4. Bearskin Grenadier Guards headdress with plume. Note how trim varied by rank for the three foot guard regiments.

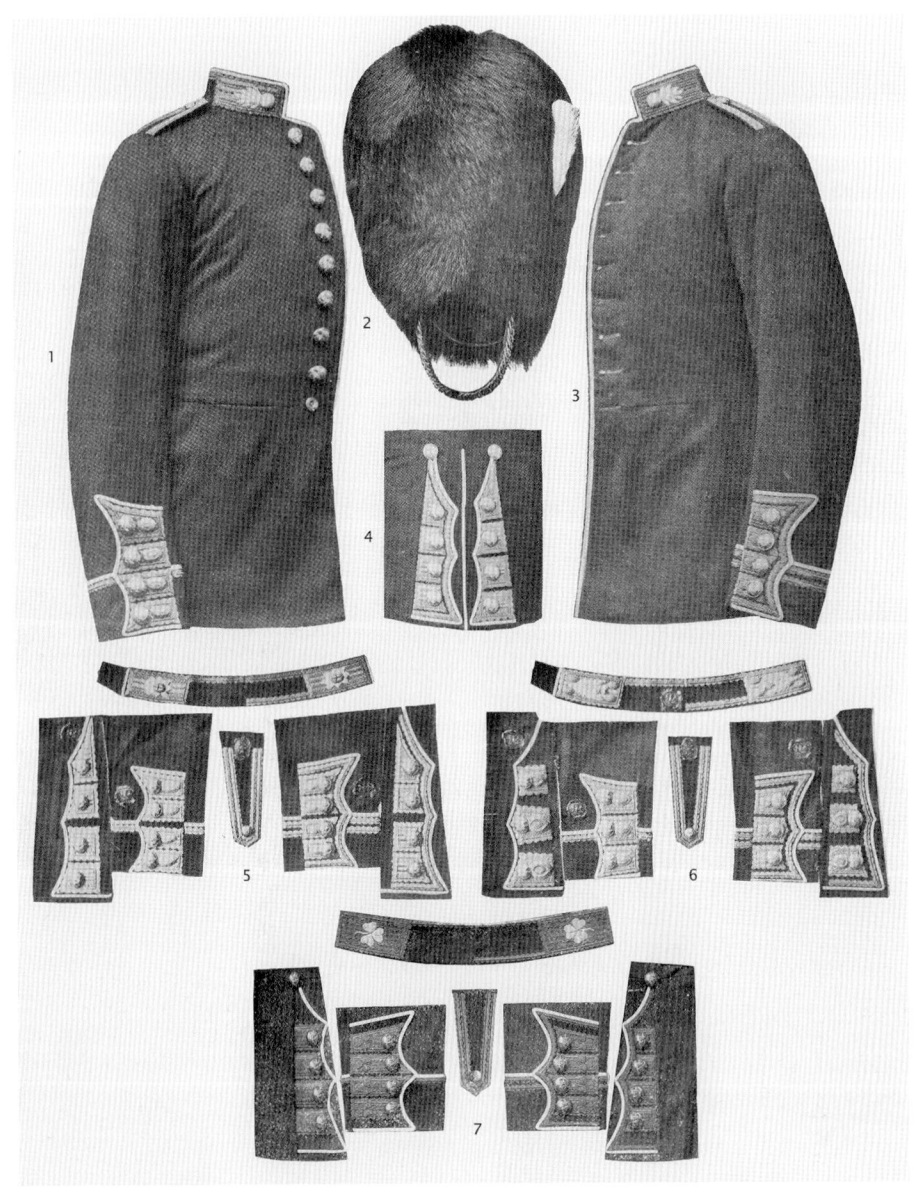

II:8 Foot Guards (1904 Regulations)
1. Tunic – collar and cuffs of junior officer of Grenadier Guards – with buttons.
2. Bearskin Grenadier Guards headdress with plume.
3. Tunic – collar and cuffs of senior officer of Grenadier Guards.
4. Tunic rear skirt: *left* – senior officer; *right* – junior officer.
5. Coldstream Guards
    Top left – junior officer collar;
    Top right – senior officer collar;
    Bottom left – junior officer rear skirt and cuff (note button pattern);
    Bottom centre – shoulder strap;
    Bottom right – senior officer rear skirt and cuff (note button and lace patterns).
6. Scots Guards
    Top left – junior officer collar;
    Top right – senior officer collar;
    Bottom left – junior officer rear skirt and cuff (note button pattern);
    Bottom centre – shoulder strap;
    Bottom right – senior officer rear skirt and cuff (note button and lace patterns).
7. Irish Guards
    Top left – junior officer collar;
    Top right – senior officer collar;
    Bottom left – junior officer rear skirt and cuff;
    Bottom centre – shoulder strap;
    Bottom right – senior officer rear skirt and cuff.
Note how trim varied by rank for the foot guard regiments.

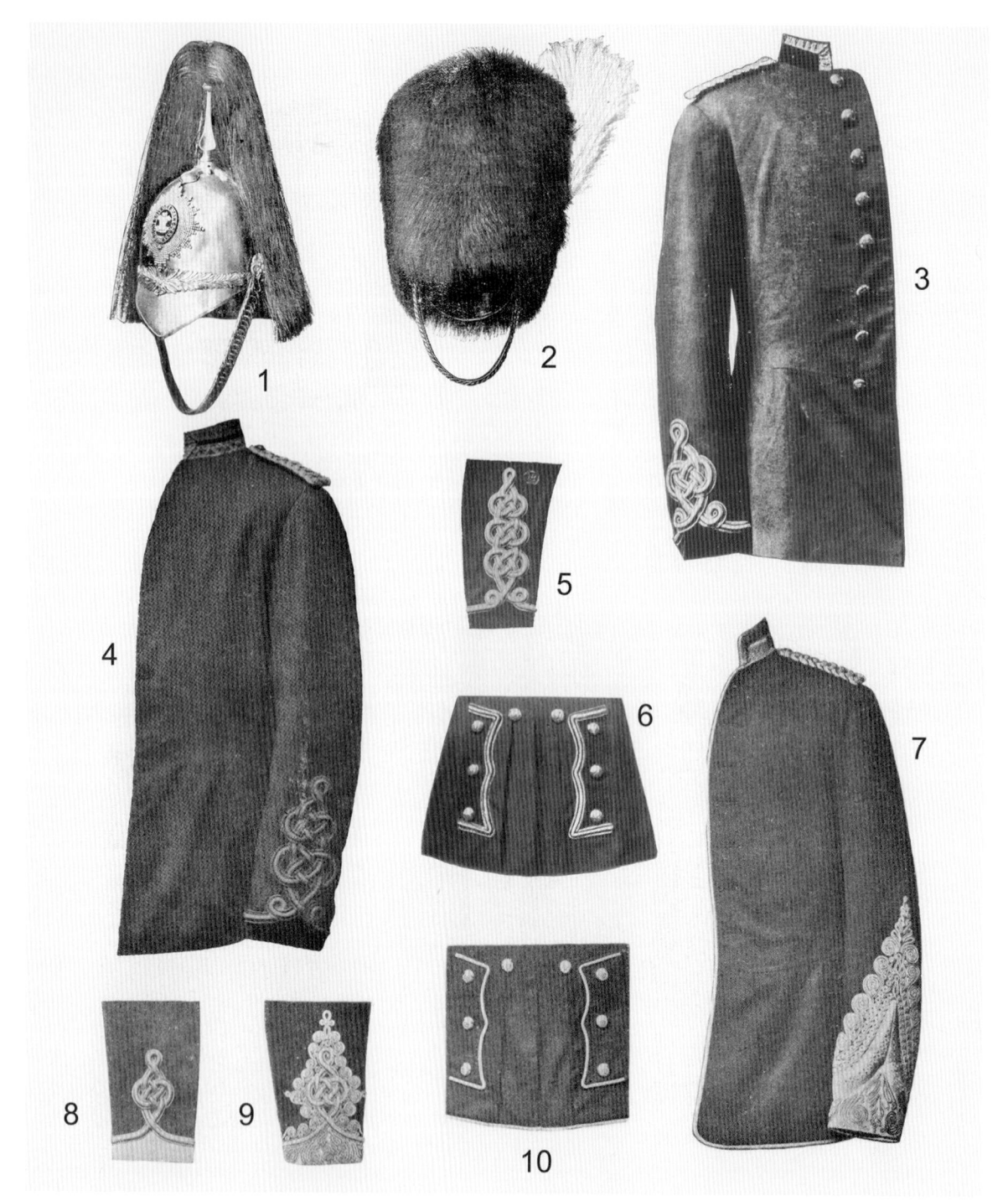

II:9 Dragoon Guards, Dragoons, and 6th Dragoon Guards (1900 Regulations)
1. Dragoon helmet.
2. Scots Greys (2nd Dragoons) bearskin headdress.
3. Tunic of lieutenant (note braid pattern on collar and cuffs).
4. Tunic – collar of field officer; cuffs of captain.
5. Cuff of field officer.
6. Tunic rear skirt.
7. 6th Dragoon Guards tunic of field officer (note braid pattern on collar and cuffs).
8. 6th Dragoon Guards tunic cuff of lieutenant.
9. 6th Dragoon Guards tunic cuff of captain.
10. 6th Dragoon Guards tunic rear skirt.

Note how complex the cuff trim was and how they varied by rank.

§II-3 Uniform Information 27

II:10 Dragoon Guards, Dragoons, and 6th Dragoon Guards (1904 Regulations)
1. Dragoon helmet.
2. 2nd Dragoons helmet.
3. Dragoon tunic.
4. 6th Dragoon Guards tunic.
5. Dragoon tunic rear skirt.
6. 6th Dragoon Guards tunic rear skirt.

Note how the cuff trim has been greatly simplified.

II:11 Hussars (1900 Regulations)
1. Tunic of captain (note braid pattern on collar and cuffs).
2. *Top* – tunic collar of field officer;
   Bottom – tunic collar of lieutenant.
3. Tunic cuff of lieutenant.
4. Tunic cuff of field officer.
5. Headdress (busby).

Note how the collar and cuffs are very elaborate and vary by rank.

§II-3 Uniform Information   29

II:12 Hussars (1904 Regulations)
1. Tunic.
2. Tunic, rear view.
3. Headdress (busby).
Note how collar and cuffs have been simplified.

II:13 Lancers (1900 Regulations)
1. Tunic of field officer (note braid pattern on collar and cuffs). When worn, girdle olivet's position would be worn at waist in line with left arm and not in front as shown.
2. Tunic cuff of officers below field rank.
3. Tunic rear skirt.
4. Headdress.

§II-3 Uniform Information   31

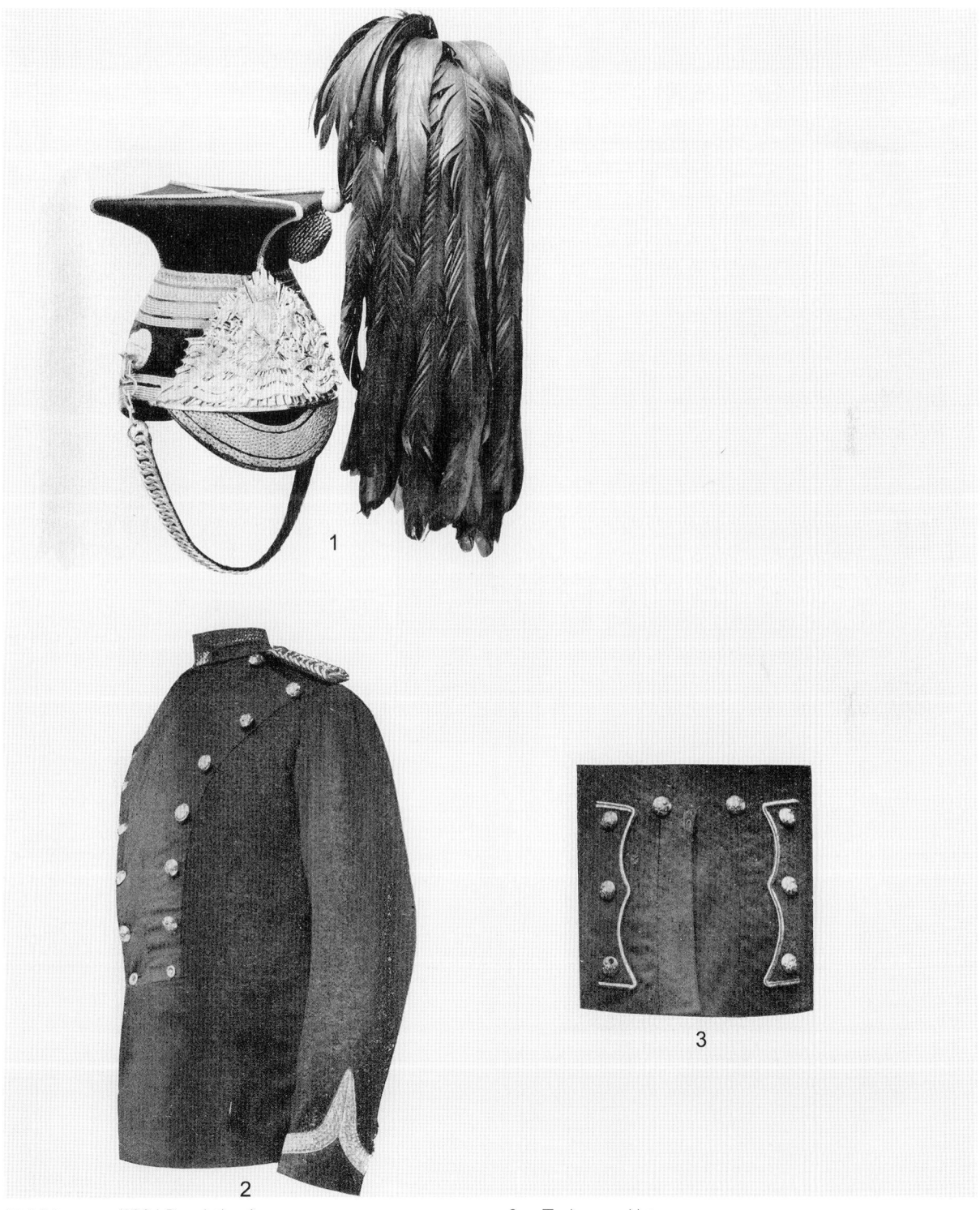

II:14 Lancers (1904 Regulations)
1. Headdress.
2. Tunic.
3. Tunic rear skirt.
Note how cuffs have been simplified.

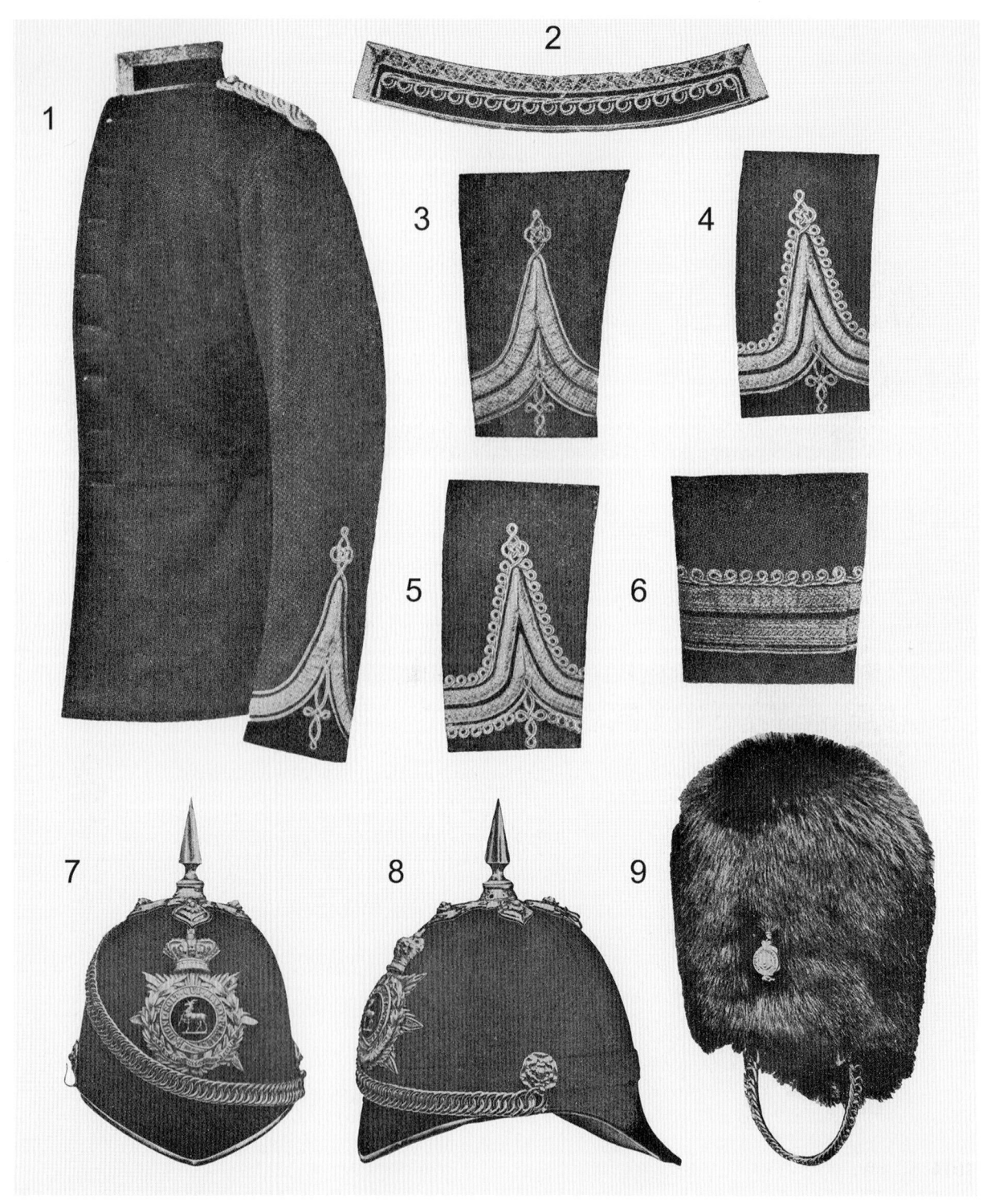

II:15 Line Infantry and Fusiliers (1900 Regulations)
1. Tunic with collar of captain and lieutenant; cuffs of lieutenant.
2. Tunic collar of field officer.
3. Tunic cuff of captain.
4. Tunic cuff of major.
5. Tunic cuff of colonel.
6. Rear view of tunic cuff of major.
7. Headdress – universal home pattern helmet.
8. Headdress – side view.
9. Headdress – fusiliers.
Note how rank is shown on collar and elaborate cuff braiding.

§II-3 Uniform Information   33

II:16 Line Infantry and Fusiliers (1904 Regulations)
1. Headdress – universal home pattern helmet.
2. Headdress – side view.
3. Headdress – fusiliers.
4. Tunic.
5. Tunic rear skirt.
6. Types of plumes for fusilier regiment headdresses.

Note how the cuff and collar trim has been simplified and how the helmet plate has changed. Notice also the reference to plumes, and how they were worn on all of the fusilier fur hats.

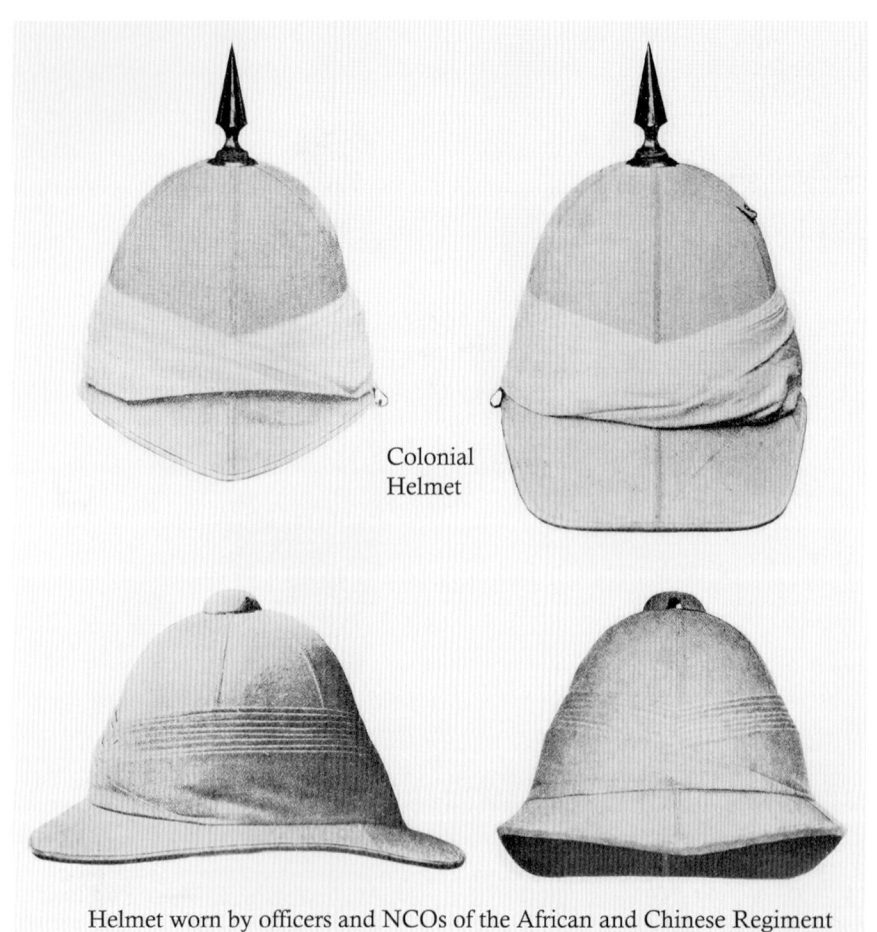

34 British Empire

Colonial
Helmet

Helmet worn by officers and NCOs of the African and Chinese Regiment

1

2

3

4

II:17 Colonial Helmets (Prior to 1904)
Top row – colonial helmets.
Bottom row – helmets worn in African and Chinese Regiments. After 1904, this style would be known as the Wolseley helmet (Image II:18).

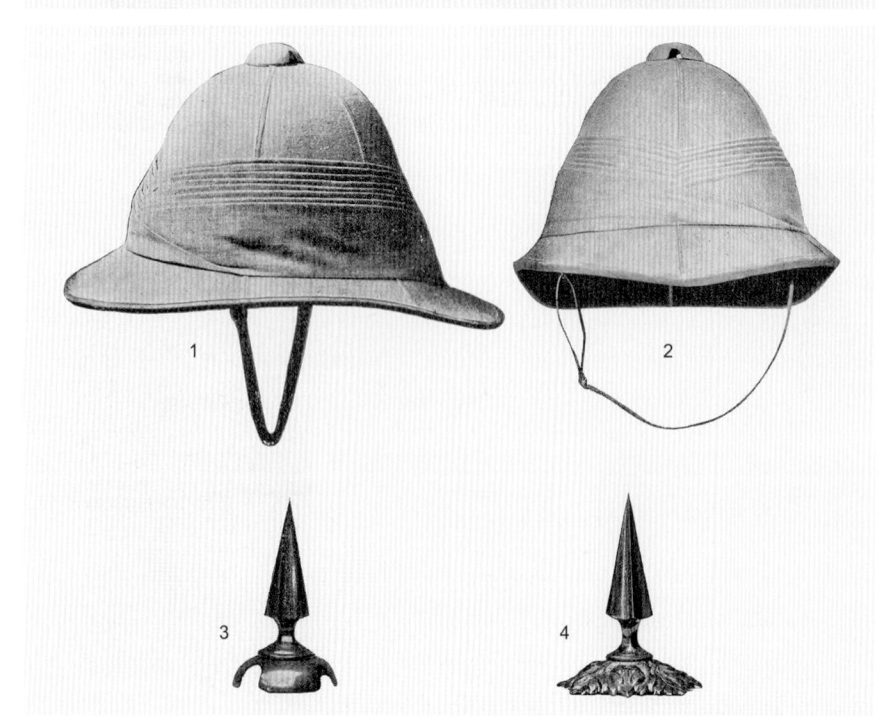

II:18 Colonial Wolseley Helmet (1904 Regulations) (Egyptian pattern)
1. Side view.
2. Front view.
3. Helmet furniture.
4. Helmet furniture – staff officer.

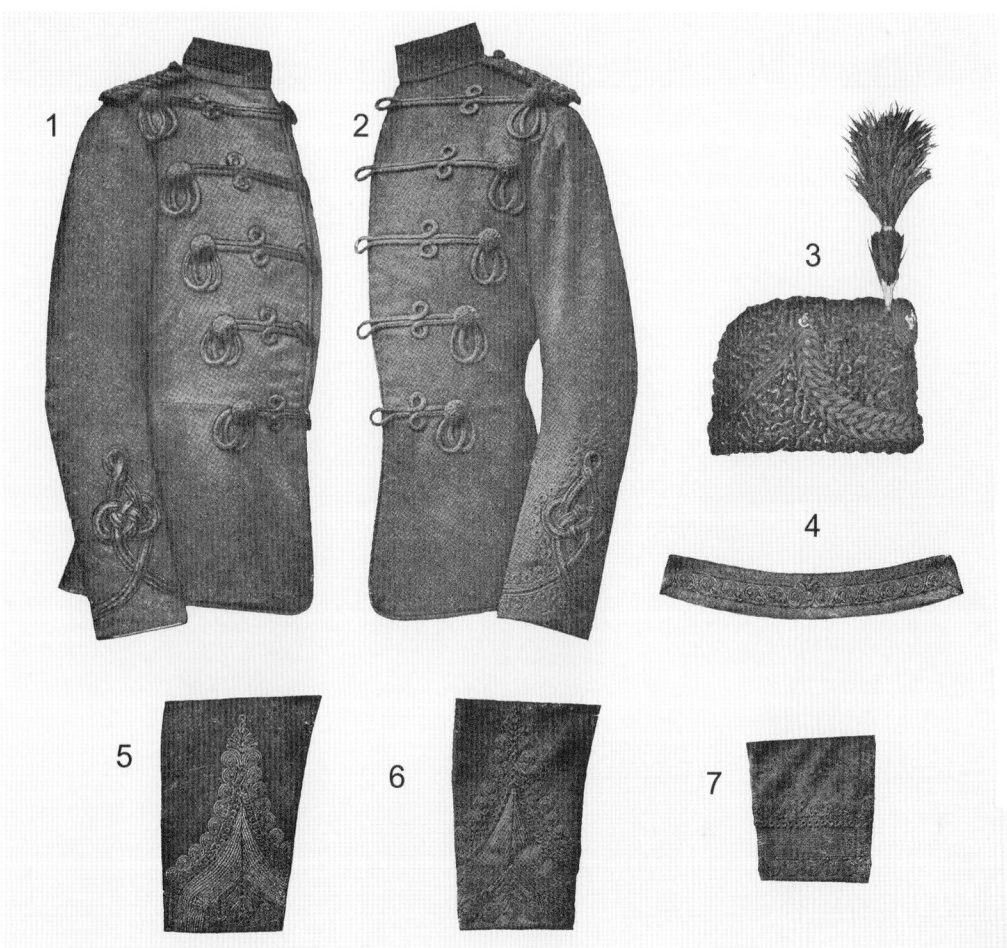

§II-3 Uniform Information   35

II:19 Rifles (1900 Regulations)
1. Tunic of lieutenant (note braid pattern on collar and cuffs).
2. Tunic of captain (note braid pattern on collar and cuffs).
3. Headdress.
4. Tunic collar of field officer.
5. Tunic cuff of field officer of the Royal Irish Rifles and the Rifle Brigade.
6. Tunic cuff of field officer of the King's Royal Rifle Corps.
7. Rear view of tunic cuff of field officer of the King's Royal Rifle Corps.
Note how elaborate the collar and cuff trim is.

II:20 Rifles (1904 Regulations)
1. Headdress.
2. Tunic, with shoulder cords and cuff trim.
Note how collar and cuffs have been simplified.

II:21 Highland Scots (1900 Regulations)
1. Tunic of major (note braid pattern on collar and cuffs).
2. Tunic of lieutenant (note braid pattern on collar and cuffs).
3. Tunic cuff of captain.
4. Tunic cuff of colonel.
5. Tunic cuff of lieutenant colonel.
6. Tunic back, Inverness flaps

left – officers below field rank;
right – field officer.
7. Highland Regiments headdress (bonnet).
8. Highland Light Infantry headdress (shako)
The items that show rank are the gauntlet cuffs, slash cuffs, Inverness flaps, and the braiding on the shako.

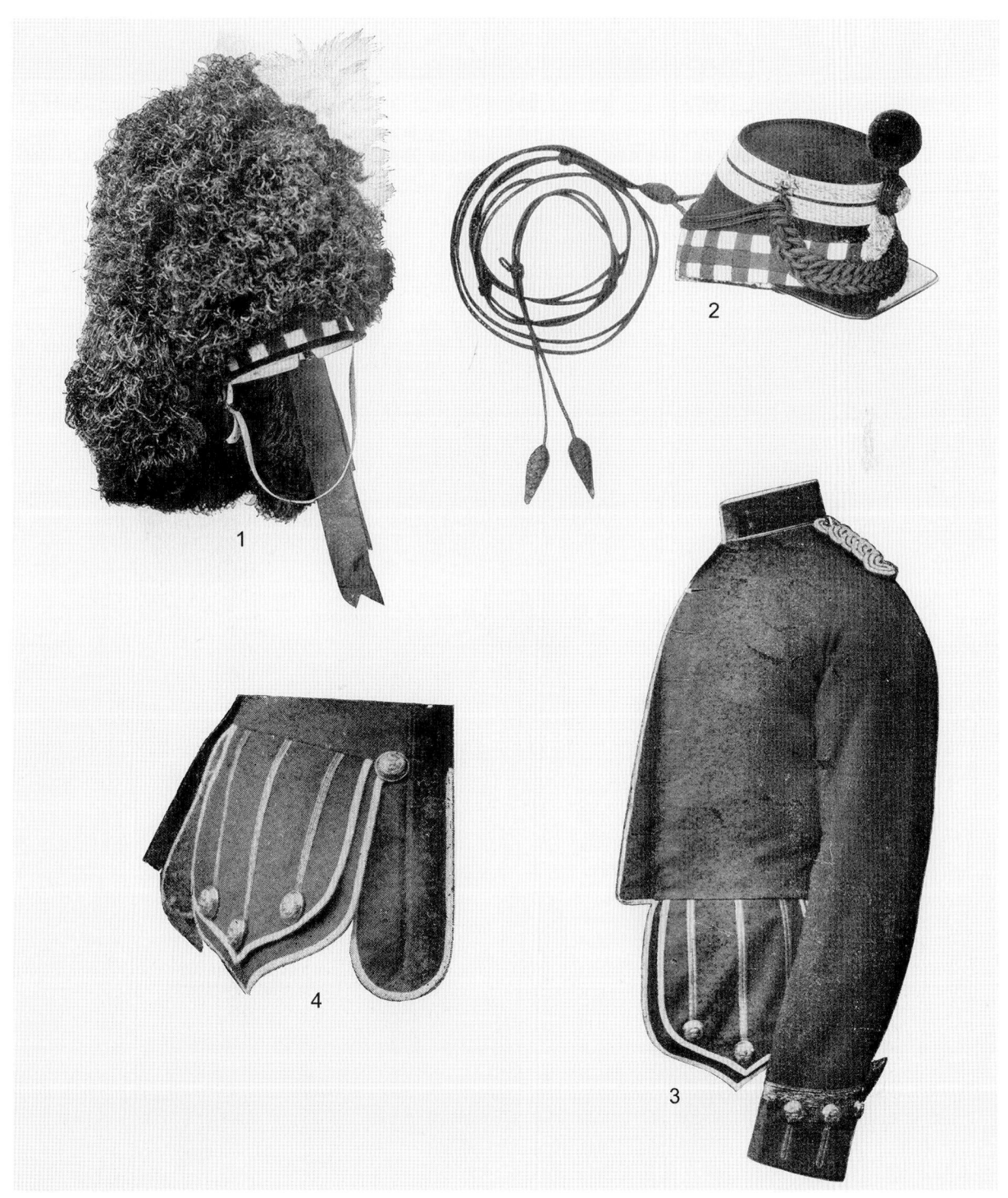

II:22 Highland Scots (1904 Regulations)
1. Highland Regiments headdress.
2. Highland Light Infantry headdress (1911 Regulations).
3. Highland Regiments tunic.
4. Tunic rear skirt.

Note how the collar, slash cuffs, and flaps no longer show rank, but the braid on the shako indicates rank.

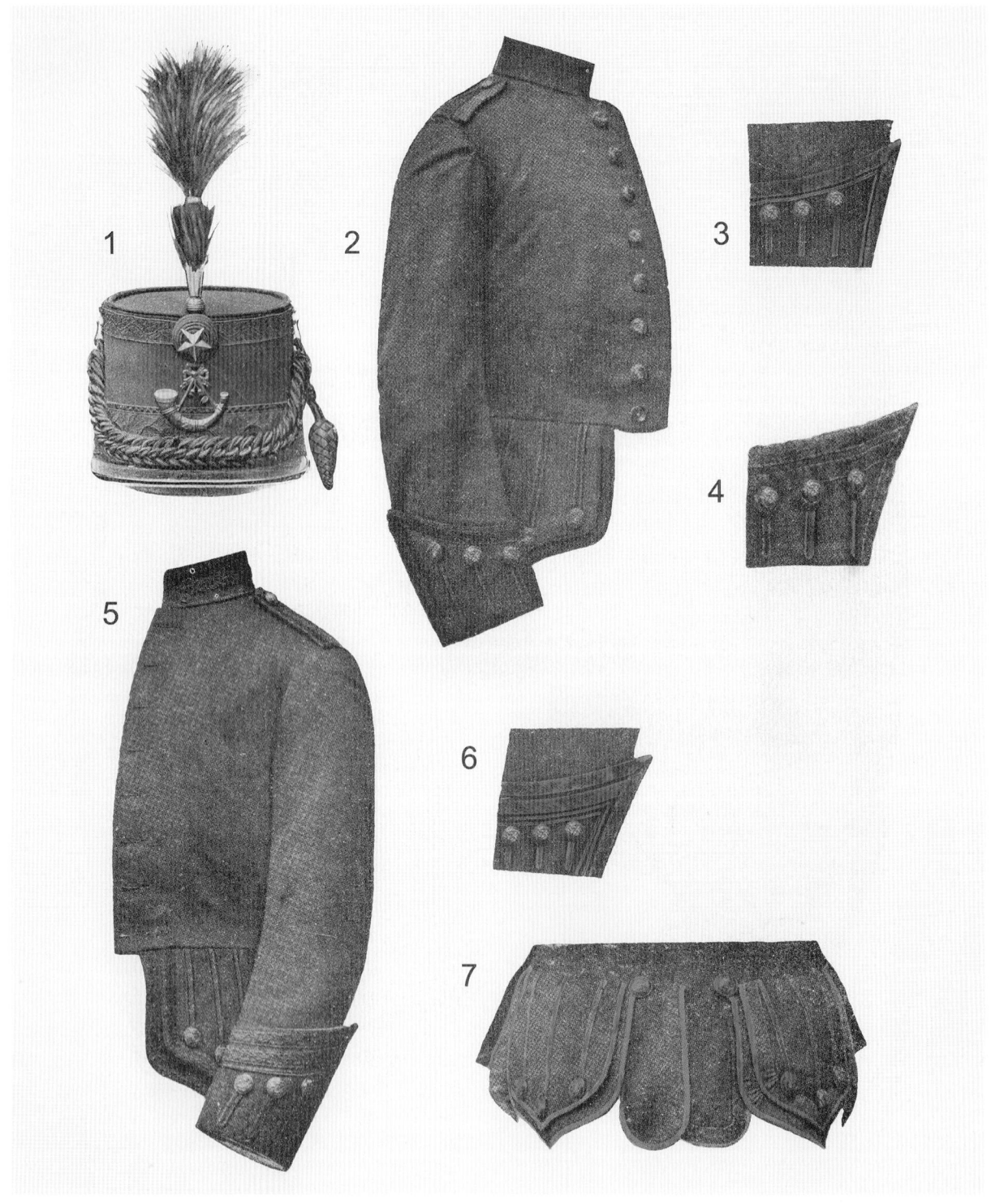

II:23 Scottish Rifles (1900 Regulations)
1. Headdress (shako).
2. Tunic of lieutenant (note braid pattern on collar and cuffs).
3. Tunic cuff of captain.
4. Tunic cuff of lieutenant colonel.
5. Tunic of lieutenant colonel (note braid pattern on collar and cuffs).
6. Tunic cuff of colonel.
7. Tunic Inverness flaps
   Left – officers below field rank;
   Right – field officers.
Note how the collar, slash cuffs, and flaps show rank.

II:24 Scottish Rifles (1904 Regulations)
1. Tunic.
2. Tunic Inverness flaps.

3. Headdress (shako).
Note how the collar, slash cuffs, and flaps no longer show rank.

§II-3-6 BRITISH BADGES, ERRORS, AND CHANGES

The British army wore badges on their headdress and collars, and for good measure, enlisted men in the foot guards, the dragoons, and the line infantry (including the rifles) wore abbreviated shoulder titles on their shoulder straps. See *§II-3-1 and 2* for shoulder strap titles. Also see the portion of *§II-6* dealing with uniforms of the guards for the devices worn by them.

The headdress and collar badges are extremely complicated subjects, and each has entire books devoted to them. For example, see Colin Churchill, *History of the British Army Infantry Collar Badges* and Arthur L. Kipling and Hugh L. King, *Head-Dress Badges of the British Army*.

These two subjects with their many details are beyond the scope of this work, but photographs of the 1904 badges, the last issued, and descriptions from the dress regulations for 1904 and 1911 as they summarise badges are included as *§II-3* Appendices II, III, and IV. To say these are complex subjects is an understatement. Even the military authorities can make errors. G. McWilliam pointed out that the photographs illustrating officers' badges in the 1900 Dress Regulations often showed other ranks' badges in lieu of officers' badges.[42] A study of the changes in badges pictured between 1900 and 1904 showed the following results:

Table II.3.6.1: Percent of Changes in Badges by Unit Type, 1900–4

Unit Type	Percent of Changes
Household Cavalry	0%
Foot Guards	25%[a]
Line Cavalry	19%[b]
Line Infantry	11%[c]

Notes: [a] One regiment of the four, the Grenadiers, had a change to their puggree badge.
[b] Four of the twenty-one regimental badges were changed.
[c] Eight of the seven regimental badges were changed.

Could this high percentage of changes be due to the need to correct the photos in 1904 to show officers' badges rather than other ranks' badges?

These changes can easily be spotted by looking at the two badges side by side. However, it should be noted that badges as a whole were undergoing constant changes. To give an idea of these changes, a study was made of the changes between the descriptions of infantry and cavalry badges in the 1904 and 1911 Dress Regulations. The results are given in the table below.

Table II.3.6.2: 1911 Regulation Changes from the 1904 Regulations

Regimental Branch	Number of Changes	% of Regiments with changes
Household Cavalry	0	0.00%
Foot Guards	0	0.00%
Line Cavalry		
Dragoons and Dragoon Guards	7[a]	6.80%
Hussars	9[b]	8.74%
Lancers	4[c]	3.88%
Line Infantry	23[d]	22.33%
Fusiliers	7[e]	6.80%
Highlanders	2	1.94%
Lowlanders	0	0.00%
Highland Light Infantry	1	0.97%
Scottish Rifles	1	0.97%
Rifles	3[f]	2.91%
Total	57	55.34%[g]

Source: Data based on *Dress Regulations, 1904* and *Dress Regulations, 1911*.

Notes: [a] Includes a spelling change for the 6th Dragoon Guards of the term 'Carabineers' (1904 spelling), which in the 1911 Regulations is spelled 'Carabiniers'. This change affected the title of the regiment as well as a scroll found on the garter.
[b] Includes two title changes, one making the description less specific, and one clarifying change with additions.
[c] Includes three making the descriptions less specific and one clarifying change.
[d] Includes six clarifying changes, one clarifying change with additions, one clarifying change with a title change, and one change with little meaning.
[e] Includes seven plume changes. One of the seven regiments also had additional changes. Another one of the seven regiments had a change with little meaning.
[f] Includes one clarifying change with additions.
[g] This is computed using the number of changes and the 103 regiments listed in the regulations. Thus, almost half of regiments saw their badges altered in just seven years.

§II-3 APPENDIX I: CAVALRY ARM BADGES

Image II:25 shows some good examples of some of these badges. NCOs could wear these over or near their chevrons. The image shows badges for: 1st Dragoon Guards; 2nd Dragoon Guards; 3rd Dragoon Guards; 4th Dragoon Guards; 7th Dragoon Guards; 1st Dragoons; 2nd Dragoons Scots Greys; 6th Dragoons; 11th Hussars; 18th Hussars; 14th Hussars; 15th Hussars; 19th Hussars; 9th Lancers; 17th Lancers; and 21st Lancers.

II:25 British Cavalry Arm Badges
NCOs could wear these over or near their chevrons.
1. 1st Dragoon Guards.
2. 2nd Dragoon Guards (shown out of scale to other badges. The original is larger).
3. 3rd Dragoon Guards.
4. 4th Dragoon Guards.
5. 7th Dragoon Guards.
6. 1st Dragoons.
7. 2nd Dragoons Scots Greys.
8. 6th Dragoons.
9. 11th Hussars.
10. 18th Hussars.
11. 14th Hussars.
12. 15th Hussars.
13. 19th Hussars.
14. 9th Lancers.
15. 17th Lancers.
16. 21st Lancers.

§II-3 APPENDIX II: 1904 DRESS REGULATIONS: DESCRIPTIONS OF OFFICERS' BUTTONS, HELMET PLATES, BADGES, AND BELT BUCKLES

Regiment.	On Buttons.	On Collar of Tunic, Mess Jacket, and Frock Coat.	On Full Dress Head-dress.	On Waist Belt.	On the Pouch.	On Puggaree and Cloth Forage Cap.
1st Life Guards.	The letters "L.G." reversed and intertwined, surmounted by a Crown. Between the letters and the Crown the number of the regiment.	...	Within a wreath of oak leaves and laurel, on a frosted gilt centre surmounted by a Crown, the Star of the Order of the Garter. Around the centre, the Collar of the Order, with the George upon the lower ends of the stems of the wreath. The colours of the Garter, cross, and field are carried out in enamel. The star in silver, the remainder gilt.	On frosted gilt rectangular plate, the star and collar of the Order or the Garter surmounted by a Crown. On either side of the collar the letters "L.G." reversed and intertwined. Below the letters a scroll upon a twig of laurel. The left scroll inscribed "Waterloo," the right, "Peninsula." On the undress belt a burnished plate is worn with a similar device, but with the motto and centre of the star in silver.	As for Waist plate, but larger.	The Star of the Order of the Garter, a Crown above in gilt metal.
2nd Life Guards.	Edge scalloped. The Imperial Crest between the letters "L.G." Below the Crown the figure 2.	...	As for 1st Life Guards, except that the field of the cross is in silver.	As for 1st Life Guards.	As for 1st Life Guards.	No badge on field cap. In gold and silver embroidery, the Royal Crest; below the crest, in gold embroidery, the letters "L.G." reversed and intertwined; within the letters the figure "2".
Royal Horse Guards.	The letters "R.H G." surmounted by a Crown.	...	As for 2nd Life Guards ...	On a dead gilt frosted rectangular plate, the Royal Arms.	The Royal Arms, on a scarlet cloth ground.	No badge.—On Field Cap the Star of the Order of the Garter.
1st (King's) Dragoon Guards.	The Star of the Order of the Garter surmounted by a Crown, within the Garter the letters "K.D.G."	The Austrian Eagle. In gold embroidery.	On the Garter star, in silver, the Garter with motto in gilt or gilding metal, pierced on a ground of blue enamel. Within the Garter on a ground of red enamel, the Royal Cypher in silver.	On a frosted gilt or gilding metal rectangular plate with burnished edges, in silver, the Royal Cypher and Crown. Within an oak-leaf wreath, a scroll on the bottom of the wreath inscribed *Diek et mon droit*.	In gilt or gilding metal, the Royal Cypher and Crown.	The Austrian Eagle in gilt metal. A scroll below inscribed "King's Dragoon Guards."
2nd Dragoon Guards (Queen's Bays)	Star of Order of the Garter surmounted by a Crown; within the Garter the word "Bays."	In gilt or gilding metal, within a laurel wreath, the word "Bays." Between the ends of the wreath, a Crown.	On the Garter star, the Garter, with motto pierced on a blue enamel ground; within the Garter the Royal Cypher in silver on a ground of red enamel.	As for 1st Dragoon Guards ...	As for 1st Dragoon Guards.	As for collar, but larger ...
3rd (Prince of Wales's) Dragoon Guards.	Within the Garter and motto the Prince of Wales's plume.	The Prince of Wales's plume. The Coronet in gilt or gilding metal, the plume and motto in silver.	On the Garter star, in silver, the Garter, with motto in gilt or gilding metal, pierced on a ground of blue enamel; within the Garter, in silver, the Prince of Wales's plume, on a scarlet enamel ground.	As for 1st Dragoon Guards ...	As for 1st Dragoon Guards. On the Cypher the Prince of Wales's plume in silver.	As for collar, with scroll below in gilt or gilding metal, inscribed "3rd Dragoon Guards."

	Buttons	Helmet Plates	Badges	Belt Buckles
4th (Royal Irish) Dragoon Guards.	The Star of the Order of St. Patrick, with "4th (Royal Irish) Dragoon Guards" round the star.	In silver, the Star of the Order of St. Patrick.	On the Garter star, in gilt or gilding metal, a circle inscribed *Quis separabit*, MDCCLXXXIII, on a blue enamelled ground. Within the circle, on a white ground, the Cross of St. Patrick. On the cross a shamrock-leaf in green enamel, with a red enamelled Crown on each petal.	As for 1st Dragoon Guards, but with shamrock instead of oak-leaf wreath.	As for 1st Dragoon Guards.	As for collar, with gilt or gilding metal scroll on the bottom of the star, inscribed "4th Royal Irish D. Guards."
5th (Princess Charlotte of Wales's) Dragoon Guards.	In gilt or gilding metal, a circle surmounted by a Crown. The circle inscribed *Vestigia nulla retrorsum*. Within the circle "5" D.G.	In gilt or gilding metal, a circle surmounted by a Crown. The circle inscribed *Vestigia nulla retrorsum*, on a frosted ground. On a burnished centre, in silver, the white horse with "V.," above and "D.G." below.	On the Garter star, in gilt or gilding metal, an elliptical ring, inscribed "P.C.W. Dragoon Guards." Within the ring "5" in silver.	...	As for 1st Dragoon Guards.	As for collar, but larger.
6th Dragoon Guards (Carabineers).	A circle inscribed "Carabineers," surmounted by a Crown. Within the circle "VI" D.G.	In gilt or gilding metal, upon crossed carbines the Garter and motto surmounted by a Crown. In silver, within the Garter, on a frosted ground, "VI"; below the garter a scroll inscribed "Carabineers."	On the Garter star, with motto in gilt or gilding metal, pierced on a ground of blue enamel. Within the Garter, on a ground of red enamel, the figure "6" in silver. The star has plain rays.	As for 1st Dragoon Guards	As for 1st Dragoon Guards.	As for collar, but larger.
7th (Princess Royal's) Dragoon Guards.	"P.R.D.G." surmounted by Princess Royal's Coronet.	In silver, the Earl of Ligonier's Crest—a lion issuing from a coronet, with a scroll below inscribed, *Quo fata vocant*.	On the Garter star, in silver, an elliptical ring, with "The Princess Royal's Dragoon Guards" in burnished gilt or gilding metal on a silver blue enamel ground. Within, on a ground of red enamel, the figure "7" in silver.	...	In gilt or gilding metal the letters "P.R.D.G." surmounted by the Princess Royal's Coronet.	As for collar, but larger, and the scroll inscribed "7 Dragoon Guards."
1st (Royal) Dragoons.	The Royal Crest. The Crown upon and the Lion within the Garter. A scroll below inscribed "Royal Dragoons."	In gold embroidery an eagle on a bar, below the bar "105" in silver. Upon the eagle a wreath in silver.	In gilt or gilding metal, the Garter star. On the star the Crest of England on a burnished silver ground within an elliptical ring in silver inscribed "The Royal Dragoons."	As for 1st Dragoon Guards	The Royal Cypher and Crown in gilt or gilding metal. On the Cypher, the Eagle in silver.	In gilt or gilding metal, the Royal Crest. A silver scroll below, inscribed "The Royal Dragoons."
2nd Dragoons (Royal Scots Greys).	Edge burnished and scalloped. An eagle above "Waterloo." Below "Waterloo," the letters "R.S.G." Mess dress button, plain gilt burnished, with eagle mounted thereon.	A grenade in silver embroidery.	A grenade in gilt or gilding metal. On the grenade the Royal Arms. In the centre below, St. Andrew and Cross, between sprays of rose, thistle, and shamrock; on a scroll beneath, the word "Waterloo."	On a seeded gilt rectangular plate with burnished edges, the Star and Collar of the Order of the Thistle; above the Star, a Crown. The Star and circle with motto in silver, the remainder of the device in gilt metal.	In gilt or gilding metal, an eagle above "Waterloo," with a gilt or gilding metal scroll below, inscribed "Royal Scots Greys."	In silver, an eagle above "Waterloo," with a gilt or gilding metal scroll below, inscribed "Royal Scots Greys."
3rd (King's Own) Hussars.	Full dome, gilt, burnished.	The white horse, in silver	...	...	In gilt or gilding metal, the Royal Cypher and Crown.	As for collar, with a scroll below, in gilt or gilding metal, inscribed "3rd King's Own Hussars."
4th (Queen's Own) Hussars.	Full dome, gilt, burnished.	In gilt or gilding metal, a circle inscribed "Queen's Own Hussars," with two	...	...	In gilt or gilding metal, the Royal Cypher and Crown.	As for collar, but larger.

II:26 1904 Dress Regulations, Descriptions
Officers' buttons, helmet plates, badges and belt buckles.

Regiment.	On Buttons.	On Collar of Tunic, Mess Jacket, and Frock Coat.	On Full Dress Head-dress.	On Waist Belt.	On the Pouch.	On the Puggaree and Cloth Forage Cap.
5th (Royal Irish) Lancers.	On crossed Lances a circle surmounted by a Crown, with a shamrock wreath below. On the circle, "Fifth Royal Irish." Within the circle the Harp.	The Harp and Crown in gilt or gilding metal.	On a gilt or gilding metal plate, universal pattern, in silver, the Royal Arms; below, the harp between sprays of shamrock. Across the bottom of the plate "Fifth Royal Irish Lancers." Above "Fifth," two scrolls inscribed "Blenheim," "Oudenarde." Above "Lancers," two scrolls inscribed "Ramillies," "Malplaquet."	...	In gilt or gilding metal, the Royal Cypher and Crown.	In gilt metal, on crossed lances, a circle inscribed *Quis separabit*. Within the circle, the figure "5." The "5" and the lower part of the pennons in silver.
6th (Inniskilling) Dragoons.	Scalloped edge. The Castle of Inniskilling, with "VI." below. For the mess waistcoat the design is in silver.	For tunic and frock coat, the Castle of Inniskilling, embroidered in silver. For mess jackets the same but smaller.	On a gilt or gilding metal beaded Garter star, an elliptical ring inscribed "Inniskilling Dragoons" in burnished letters on a frosted ground. Within the ring, in silver, the Castle over "VI" on a gilt or gilding metal ground.	...	In dead gilt or gilding metal, the Royal Cypher and Crown. On the Cypher the Castle in silver.	The Castle of Inniskilling in silver, with a scroll below in gilt or gilding metal, inscribed "Inniskilling."
7th (Queen's Own) Hussars.	Full dome, gilt, burnished.	In gilt or gilding metal, a circle inscribed "7th Queen's Own Hussars," surmounted by a Crown, within the circle, in silver, the letters "Q.O.," reversed and intertwined.	...	...	...	As for collar, but larger.
8th King's (Royal Irish) Hussars.	Full dome, gilt, burnished.	The Harp and Crown, the Harp in silver, the Crown in gilt or gilding metal.	...	...	In gold embroidery the Crest of England, and Harp and Crown, the Royal Cypher in silver embroidery. Round the Royal Cypher a wreath of shamrocks with eight scrolls in gold embroidery. The scrolls embroidered in silver, with the battles. A similar scroll below the Harp and Crown inscribed *Pristinæ virtutis memores*.	As for collar, with scroll in gilt or gilding metal below, inscribed "8th King's Royal Irish Hussars."
9th (Queen's Royal) Lancers.	On crossed lances, surmounted by a crown, the letters "A.R.," reversed and intertwined. Below the letters the figure 9.	In silver, the figure "9" on crossed lances, above the "9" a crown, below the "9" a scroll inscribed "Lancers."	In gilt or gilding metal the universal plate with the Royal Arms, on either side on sprays of laurel scrolls inscribed with the honours of the regiment. On a scroll below, "Royal Lancers." In silver, on the centre of the plate, "A.R.," reversed and intertwined.	...	In gilt or gilding metal "A.R.," reversed and intertwined, with a crown above.	As for collar, but larger.
10th (Prince of Wales's Own Royal) Hussars.	Full dome, gilt, burnished.	The Prince of Wales's Plume. The Plume and motto in silver. The coronet in gilt or gilding metal.	...	...	Within a laurel wreath, the Prince of Wales's Plume in silver, with the Royal Cypher and Crown underneath in gilt or gilding metal.	As for collar, with a gilt or gilding metal scroll below inscribed "10th Royal Hussars."

Regiment					
11th (Prince Albert's Own) Hussars.	Full dome, gilt, burnished. On frock coat,—special pattern.	On a ground of crimson cloth, in gold and silk embroidery, the Crest and Motto of the late Prince Consort. The motto on a blue velvet scroll.	...	Gilt or gilding metal flap and silver ornaments.	As for collar, but in gilt or gilding metal.
12th (Prince of Wales's Royal) Lancers.	Scalloped edge; "12" resting on crossed lances surmounted by a Crown.	Upon crossed lances in gilt metal the Prince of Wales's Plume. The Plume and motto in silver. The coronet in gilt metal. Above the plume the crown, below it the figure "XII." in gilt metal. The lower part of the pennons in silver.	In silver, the Royal Arms, with the Prince of Wales's Plume above, and the sphinx over Egypt below; the scroll inscribed *Dieu et mon droit* resting on two sprays of rose, thistle, and shamrock intertwined. Below, on three gilt or gilding metal scrolls, the battles; the outer ends of the scrolls finish in sprays of laurel.	The Royal Cypher, surmounted by a Crown.	As for collar, but larger ...
13th Hussars.	Full dome, gilt, burnished.	In gilt or gilding metal a circle, inscribed *Viret in æternum*, surmounted by a crown; around the circle a laurel wreath, with "Hussars" on a tablet on the lower bend; within the circle "XIII" in silver. A badge is not worn on tunic.	...	In gilt or gilding metal the Royal Cypher surmounted by a Crown.	On the puggaree, as for collar, but larger. On the forage cap the number "13," a scroll across it inscribed Hussars, above the scroll a crown, the whole in gilt metal.
14th (King's) Hussars.	Full dome, gilt, burnished.	The Eagle in black japanned metal with crown above. On Mess Jacket—the Eagle in black embroidery surmounted by a Prussian crown.	...	In gilt or gilding metal, the Royal Cypher and Crown reversed and intertwined. On the Cypher the Eagle in gilt.	The Eagle in black japanned metal with crown above.
15th (The King's) Hussars.	Full dome, gilt, burnished.	In gilt or gilding metal the Royal Crest, with a scroll below, in silver, inscribed "Merebimur."	...	...	In gilt or gilding metal, the Garter and Motto; below the Garter "XV K.H."; below the letters a scroll, inscribed "Merebimur," in silver, filled in blue enamel. Within the Garter, in silver, the Royal Crest.
16th (Queen's) Lancers.	A Crown with "Q. L." 16 below.	In silver, the figures "16" and a scroll below inscribed "Queen's Lancers" on a pair of crossed lances, between the pennons, a Crown; the lower part of the pennons in silver, the remainder of the lances and the Crown in gilt or gilding metal.	The universal plate in gilt or gilding metal. On the plate, in silver, the Royal Arms. On the lower part of the plate, scrolls inscribed with the honours of the regiment. In the centre of the plate at the bottom a scroll inscribed "16th Lancers."	In gilt metal, the Royal Cypher and Crown.	As for collar, but larger ...

II:26/cont. 1904 Dress Regulations, Descriptions/cont.

Regiment.	On Buttons.	On Collar of Tunic, Mess Jacket, and Frock Coat.	On Full Dress Head-dress.	On Waist Belt.	On the Pouch.	On the Puggaree and Cloth Forage Cap.
17th (Duke of Cambridge's Own) Lancers.	Full dome, gilt, burnished, with the death's head.	*On Tunic and Mess Jacket*:—No badge. *On Frock Coat*:—In silver, the death's head and scroll, inscribed "Or Glory."	In silver, the Royal Arms with the death's head and scroll, inscribed "Or Glory," and the letters "D.C.O." below. On the right a branch of laurel, and on the left a branch of oak; on the sprays are six scrolls inscribed with battles. A scroll at the bottom of the plate inscribed "Seventeenth Lancers."	...	The Royal Cypher and Crown in gilt or gilding metal.	As for collar, but larger ...
18th (Princess of Wales's) Hussars.	Full dome, gilt, burnished.	In gilt or gilding metal, within a laurel wreath, a circle inscribed *Pro regie pro legie, Pro patria conamur*, surmounted by a Crown. On the right side of the wreath a scroll inscribed "Waterloo," on the left side a scroll inscribed "Peninsula." Within the circle, in silver, "XVIII" H.	...	...	The Royal Cypher and Crown in gold embroidery, reversed and intertwined.	...
19th (Alexandra, Princess of Wales's Own) Hussars.	Full dome, gilt, burnished.	The Dagmar Cross, in silver...	...	...	The Royal Cypher and Crown in gilt or gilding metal.	In silver, the elephant, with a scroll below inscribed "19th (Alexandra P.W.O.) Hussars."
20th Hussars.	Full dome, gilt, burnished.	In gilt or gilding metal the letters "xHx," surmounted by a Crown.	...	...	The Royal Cypher and Crown in gilt or gilding metal.	As for collar, but larger ...
21st (Empress of India's) Lancers.	Scalloped edge. Between the numerals "XXI," a pair of upright lances. Between the pennons, a Crown.	As for forage cap but smaller	In silver, on crossed lances, the Royal Arms with a scroll below, inscribed "Khartoum." Below the scroll the Imperial Cypher, "V.R.I." On the right a spray of laurel with a scroll below, inscribed "21st (Empress of)," and on the left, palm leaves with a scroll below, inscribed "India's) Lancers."	...	The Imperial Cypher, "V.R.I." and Crown in gilt or gilding metal.	In gilt or gilding metal, a pair of crossed lances; between lances the Imperial Cypher, "V.R.I." and Crown; upon the staves, "XXI." "The lower part of the pennons in silver.

Grenadier Guards.	The Royal Cypher reversed and interlaced, surmounted by the Crown; a grenade beneath the Cypher in the centre.	*On Tunic*:—A grenade in silver embroidery, on a gold lace ground. *On the Mess Jacket and Frock*:—For service abroad, a grenade in gold embroidery. *On Frock Coat*:—No badge.	No badge ...	Not worn ...	On forage cap.—A grenade in gold embroidery. On the khaki helmet, In gilt metal, the Royal Cypher reversed and interlaced on a ground of red enamel within the Garter, surmounted by the Crown. The m.tto pierced on a ground of blue enamel.
Coldstream Guards.	The Star of the Order of the Garter.	*Tunic*:—In silver embroidery on a gold lace ground, the Star of the Order of the Garter, the Garter and motto in gold; the cross in scarlet silk. *Mess Jacket and Frock*:—A similar badge but not on a gold lace ground. *On the Frock Coat*:—No badge.	No badge ...	Not worn ...	In silver, the Star of the Order of the Garter. The Garter and motto in gilt metal, over blue enamel, the cross in red enamel. This badge is worn on the khaki helmet.
Scots Guards.	The Star of the Order of the Thistle, with Crown in place of the upper point of the Star.	*Tunic collar*:—The Thistle in silver embroidery, on a gold back ground. *Mess Jacket collar*:—The Star of the Order of the Thistle in silver embroidery. *Frock Coat*:—No badge ...	No badge ...	Not worn ...	In silver, the Star of the Order of the Thistle; the circle with motto, and the centre in gilt metal. On the khaki helmet—the Star of the Order of the Thistle.
Irish Guards.	The Harp and Crown ...	*On Tunic*:—A shamrock leaf in silver embroidery, on a gold ground. *On Mess Jacket*:—A star as for forage cap, embroidered in silver and colours. *On Frock Coat*:—No badge.	No badge ..	Not worn ...	The Star of the Order of St. Patrick in silver, the motto and circle in gilt metal on a blue enamel ground; within the circle the cross in red enamel, the Shamrock in green enamel and the crowns in gilt metal.

II:26/cont. 1904 Dress Regulations, Descriptions/cont.

Regiment.	On Buttons.	On Collar of Tunic, Mess Jacket, and Frock Coat.	On Helmet-Plates.	On the Puggaree, Cloth Forage Cap.	Special Badges.
The Royal Scots (Lothian Regiment).	The badge of the Order of the Thistle; below the badge, "The Royal Scots." On the mess dress button the title is omitted.	The Thistle, in gold embroidery, on a blue cloth ground on the tunic. On the mess jacket and frock coat, as for forage cap, but smaller.	Not worn	In silver, the Star of the Order of the Thistle; in gilt or gilding metal on the Star a raised circle inscribed *Nemo me impune lacessit*. Within the circle, on a ground of green enamel, the Thistle in gilt or gilding metal. Also worn on bonnet and glengarry.	On the waist-belt.—On a gilt or gilding metal rectangular plate, 2½ by 2¾ in., the badge in silver as for the glengarry and bonnet, but points of star more sharply defined. *On shoulder-belt.*—Badge as for bonnet, but larger—below on a scroll "The Royal Scots."
The Queen's (Royal West Surrey Regiment).	Within a circle, surmounted by the Crown, the Paschal Lamb, below the lamb "1661." On the circle, "The Royal West Surrey Regiment." Below the circle a scroll inscribed "The Queen's." For the mess dress, plain gold—the Lamb in silver,—mounted,—two sizes. For the cap, the Lamb on a plain dome.	The Paschal Lamb, in frosted gilt or gilding metal in pairs. In silver, a scroll below inscribed "The Queen's."	On a scarlet velvet ground, the Paschal Lamb in silver. On the universal scroll "The Royal West Surrey Regiment."	As for left collar badge, but 1½ inches in height.	... ...
The Buffs (East Kent Regiment).	A circle surmounted by the Crown. On the circle "The East Kent Regt. The Buffs"; within, the Dragon; below, on a scroll, *Veteri frondescit honore*. For the mess waistcoat, plain gilt. The Dragon over a scroll, inscribed "The Buffs," in silver,—mounted. For the cap, the same design die struck.	The Dragon, in silver	On a black velvet ground, the Dragon, in silver. On the universal scroll, "The East Kent Regiment." Above the Garter a scroll inscribed "The Buffs."	The Dragon, in silver. On a scroll beneath, "The Buffs."	... ...
The King's Own (Royal Lancaster Regiment).	The Lion of England with Crown above and Rose below. On circle "The King's Own Royal Lancaster Regt." For the mess dress, "K.O.R.L." in monogram, with the crown above.	The Lion, in silver	In silver, on a crimson velvet ground, the Lion of England. On the universal scroll, "Royal Lancaster Regt."	The Lion, in silver. Below the Lion, "The King's Own."	... ...
The Northumberland Fusiliers.	St. George and the Dragon within a circle inscribed *Quo fata vocant*. For the mess dress, the button is mounted. Ring with motto in gilt, dragon, &c., in silver.	A grenade in gold embroidery, with St. George and the Dragon in silver on the ball. Smaller pattern for mess jacket.	A grenade in gilt or gilding metal. On the ball, in silver, St. George and the Dragon within a circle, inscribed "Northumberland Fusiliers."	A grenade in gilt or gilding metal; on the ball, in silver, St. George and the Dragon within a circle, inscribed "Northumberland Fusiliers."	... ...
The Royal Warwickshire Regiment.	An antelope with collar and chain within a circle, inscribed "The Royal Warwickshire Regiment." The circle surmounted by the Crown. For the mess dress, the button is mounted, the Antelope in silver, within the Garter.	In frosted silver, the Antelope, with gilt or gilding metal collar and chain.	On a black velvet ground, the Antelope, in silver, with gilt or gilding metal collar and chain. On the universal scroll, "The Royal Warwickshire Regiment."	In silver, the Antelope, with gilt collar and chain. On a scroll below, "Royal Warwickshire."	... ...
The Royal Fusiliers (City of London Regiment).	The Garter, inscribed *Honi soit qui mal y pense*; on the Garter at the top, the Crown; within, the Rose. For the mess dress, "R.F." in monogram, surmounted by the crown,—mounted.	*On tunic and frock coat.*—A grenade, in silver embroidery, with the White Rose, in gilt metal, on the ball. *On mess jacket.*—A small grenade in gold embroidery with the white rose in silver metal on the ball.	In gilt or gilding metal, a grenade; on the ball, the Garter, surmounted by the Crown. The Garter pierced with the motto; the ground of blue enamel. Within the Garter, the Rose; below the Garter, in silver, the White Horse.	As for full dress head-dress, but smaller, the Rose in silver, and the White Horse omitted.	... ...

The King's (Liverpool Regiment).	A circle surmounted by the Crown within a laurel wreath; the circle inscribed "The Liverpool Regiment;" within the circle, the White Horse, with a scroll above inscribed *Nec aspera terrent*. Scroll on wreath at the bottom inscribed "The King's." For the mess dress, the button is mounted, design as for collar badge, a scroll above inscribed, "Nec aspera terrent."	In silver, the White Horse. A gilt or gilding metal scroll below, inscribed "The King's."	In silver, on a crimson velvet ground, the White Horse, with scroll above inscribed, in old English capitals, *Nec aspera terrent*. On the universal scroll, "The Liverpool Regiment."	In silver, the White Horse. A gilt or gilding metal scroll below, inscribed "The King's."
The Norfolk Regiment.	On the circle, "The Norfolk Regiment"; within the circle the figure of Britannia holding an olive branch in the right hand; the trident rests against the left shoulder. For the mess dress, the figure of Britannia mounted on a flat gilt button. For the cap, the same design, die struck.	The figure of Britannia, in gilt or gilding metal.	The figure of Britannia, in silver, on a black velvet ground. On the universal scroll, "The Norfolk Regiment."	In gilt or gilding metal, the figure of Britannia; a tablet below, inscribed "The Norfolk Regt."
The Lincolnshire Regiment.	Within a laurel wreath, a circle surmounted by the Crown. On the circle, "The Lincolnshire Regt."; within, the Sphinx over Egypt. For the mess dress, plain gilt; the Sphinx over Egypt in silver,—mounted. For the cap, the same design, die struck.	On a silver eight-pointed star, a circle in gilt or gilding metal, inscribed "Lincolnshire Regiment." Within the circle, on a ground of blue velvet, the Sphinx over Egypt, in silver.	In silver, on a black velvet ground, the Sphinx over Egypt. On the universal scroll, "The Lincolnshire Regt."	In gilt or gilding metal, on a silver eight-pointed star, a circle inscribed "Lincolnshire Regiment," the letters pierced. Within the circle, on a raised ground of blue velvet, the Sphinx over Egypt, in silver.
The Devonshire Regiment.	On an eight-pointed star a circle surmounted by the Crown. On the circle, "The Devonshire Regt.," within, the Castle of Exeter. For the mess dress, the design is in silver,—mounted.	In gilt or gilding metal, on a bright cut silver eight-pointed star, a circle surmounted by the Crown. On the circle, "The Devonshire Regiment"; within, in silver, the Castle of Exeter with scroll inscribed *Semper fidelis*, on a ground of blue velvet.	The Castle of Exeter, with scroll inscribed *Semper fidelis*, in silver, on a black velvet ground. On the universal scroll, "The Devonshire Regt."	As for collar, but larger.
The Suffolk Regiment.	Within a laurel wreath, the Castle and Key with scroll above, inscribed "Gibraltar," and above the scroll, the Crown. Below the Castle and Key, two scrolls, the upper inscribed *Montis Insignia Calpe*, the lower, "The Suffolk Regt." For the mess waistcoat the Castle and Key in silver,—mounted. For the cap, the same design, die struck.	The Castle and Key, in gold embroidery.	In silver, on a black velvet ground, the Castle and Key, with scroll above inscribed "Gibraltar," and scroll below inscribed *Montis Insignia Calpe*. On the universal scroll, "The Suffolk Regiment."	In silver, within a circle inscribed:— *Montis insignia calpe*, the Castle and Key, surmounted by a scroll inscribed "Gibraltar"; above the circle, the Crown; surrounding the circle, an oak-leaf wreath. Below the circle, upon the wreath, a scroll inscribed:—"The Suffolk Regiment."
The Prince Albert's (Somersetshire Light Infantry).	Within a laurel wreath, a circle surmounted by a mural crown. On the circle, "The Prince Albert's"; within, a bugle with strings. For the mess dress—the bugle surmounted by a mural crown, with a scroll above, inscribed "Jellalabad" —the whole in silver,—mounted on a flat gilt button. For the cap, the same design, die struck.	In gold and silver embroidery, on a ground of green cloth, a bugle with strings, surmounted by a mural crown embroidered "Jellalabad"; above the crown, in gold embroidery, a scroll inscribed "Jellalabad."	In silver, on a black velvet ground, a bugle with strings, surmounted by a mural crown with scroll above inscribed "Jellalabad"; the Sphinx over Egypt within the strings of the bugle. On the scroll, "Somersetshire Light Infantry."	In silver, a bugle; within the strings, the Cypher of H.R.H. the late Prince Consort. Above the bugle a mural crown surmounted by a scroll inscribed "Jellalabad."
The Prince of Wales's Own (West Yorkshire Regiment).	The Tiger, within a circle, inscribed at the top, "India," and at the bottom, "Waterloo." Outside the circle, "Prince of Wales's Own, West Yorkshire." For cap and mess waistcoat, the Tiger; for the latter mounted in silver.	The Prince of Wales's Plume, in gold and silver embroidery.	In silver, on a red velvet ground, the White Horse, with motto *Nec aspera terrent* on a scroll above. On the universal scroll, "The West Yorkshire Regiment."	In silver, the White Horse above a gilt or gilding metal scroll, inscribed "West Yorkshire."

Regiment.	On Buttons.	On Collar of Tunic, Mess Jacket, and Frock Coat.	On Helmet-Plates.	On the Puggaree, Cloth Forage Cap.	Special Badges.
The East Yorkshire Regiment.	A laurel wreath on an eight-pointed star. The White Rose within the wreath.	In gilt or gilding metal, an eight-pointed star; on the star a laurel wreath; within the wreath, on a ground of black enamel, the White Rose, in silver.	In gilt or gilding metal, on a ground of black enamel, a laurel wreath on an eight-pointed star. Within the wreath the White Rose, in silver. On the universal scroll, "The East Yorkshire Regiment."	In gilt or gilding metal, badges as for centre of helmet-plate; a scroll below, inscribed "East Yorkshire."	
The Bedfordshire Regiment.	On an eight-pointed star, a Maltese cross. On the cross, a circle inscribed "Bedfordshire." Within the circle, a Hart crossing a ford.	In dead gilt or gilding metal, a Hart crossing a ford; the water in silver. On a scroll below, "Bedfordshire."	In silver, on a black velvet ground, an eight-pointed star. On the star, in gilt or gilding metal, a Maltese cross. Within a gilt or gilding metal circle on the cross, in silver, a Hart crossing a ford, the Hart on blue enamel. On the universal scroll, "The Bedfordshire Regiment."	In silver, a Maltese cross on an eight-pointed star. On the cross, the Garter, with motto, within the Garter, on a raised ground of blue enamel, the Hart crossing a ford, in silver. A gilt scroll inscribed "Bedfordshire" below the Garter.	
The Leicestershire Regiment.	Within a laurel wreath, the Royal Tiger, with scroll above, inscribed "Hindoostan," and scroll below, inscribed "Leicestershire." For the mess dress, the Tiger in silver mounted on a flat gilt button.	The Royal Tiger, in silver, within a wreath in gilt or gilding metal.	On a black velvet ground, the Royal Tiger, in silver, with silver scroll above, inscribed "Hindoostan." On the universal scroll, "The Leicestershire Regiment."	In gilt or gilding metal, the Tiger. In silver, above the Tiger, a scroll inscribed "Hindoostan"; below the Tiger, another scroll, inscribed "Leicestershire."	
The Royal Irish Regiment.	Within a shamrock wreath, a circle inscribed Virtutis Namurcensis Praemium. Within the circle, the Harp; the circle surmounted by the Crown.	In silver, an Escutcheon of the arms of Nassau, with a silver scroll below, inscribed Virtutis Namurcensis Praemium.	In silver, on a scarlet ground, the Harp and Crown within a wreath of shamrock. On the universal scroll, "The Royal Irish Regiment."	In silver, the Harp and Crown, with a scroll below inscribed "The Royal Irish Regiment."	
Alexandra Princess of Wales's Own (Yorkshire Regiment).	The Cypher of H.R.H. the Princess of Wales combined with a cross, and surmounted by the Coronet of the Princess. On the cross the figures 1875. On scroll below, "Alexandra Princess of Wales's Own." For the mess dress, the Dagmar Cross is in silver, mounted. The scroll is omitted. For the cap, the same design, die struck.	In the cap and mess vest buttons the circle is omitted. The mess vest button mounted.	On a black velvet ground, the Cypher of H.R.H. the Princess of Wales combined with a cross, and surmounted by the Coronet of the Princess in silver metal. On the centre of the cross the figures 1875 and the word Alexandra. On a scroll in silver metal, "The Princess of Wales's Own Yorkshire Regiment."	In silver metal, the Cypher of H.R.H. the Princess of Wales combined with a cross, and surmounted by the Coronet of the Princess. On the centre of the cross the figures 1875, and the word "Alexandra." On a scroll below "The Princess of Wales's Own Yorkshire Regiment."	
The Lancashire Fusiliers.	Within a wreath of laurel, the Sphinx over Egypt, with the Crown above.	A grenade, in gold embroidery	A grenade in gilt or gilding metal; on the ball, in silver, the Sphinx over Egypt within a laurel wreath.	In gilt or gilding metal, a grenade. on the ball, the Sphinx over "Egypt" within a laurel wreath. Below the grenade, a scroll in silver, inscribed "The Lancashire Fusiliers."	
The Royal Scots Fusiliers.	The Thistle, surmounted by the Crown. For the cap and mess waistcoat, on a gilt-lined button, with burnished edge, the letters R.S.F. with the Crown above.	A grenade in silver embroidery; on the ball of the grenade, the Thistle, in silver metal. On the mess-jacket, gold embroidery, with thistle in silver.	A grenade in gilt or gilding metal; on the ball of the grenade, the Royal Arms.	On the Forage cap and Glengarry as for Fusilier cap, but smaller. On the puggaree, as for full dress head-dress.	On waist belt ... In silver, on a frosted gilt rectangular plate, a wreath of thistles; within the wreath, the figure of St. Andrew with cross. On the wreath, at the bottom, a silver scroll, inscribed "Royal Scots Fusiliers." On the shoulder belt.
The Cheshire Regiment.	On an eight-pointed star, a circle with acorn and oak-leaves in the centre. On the circle, "The Cheshire Regiment."	Acorn with oak-leaves. The leaves and cup in dead gilt or gilding metal; the acorn in burnished silver.	In silver, on a black velvet ground, an eight-pointed star. Within a gilt or gilding metal circle on the star, the Prince of Wales's Plume on a burnished silver ground. The plume in silver, the coronet in gilt or gilding metal. On the universal scroll, "The Cheshire Regiment."	In silver, an eight-pointed star, with a scroll below inscribed "Cheshire." On the star, in gilt or gilding metal, the acorn with oak-leaves.	Burnished gilt rectangular plate. In silver, a thistle, within a circle, inscribed Nemo me impune lacesset, surmounted by a crown. The Maltese cross in the lower band of the circle. Below the circle, a scroll inscribed "Royal Scots Fusiliers." Below the scroll, "1678" in gilt metal.

The Royal Welsh Fusiliers.	The Prince of Wales's Plume within the designation "The Royal Welsh Fusiliers." For the cap and mess waistcoat, a gilt-lined button with burnished edge, below the plume " R.W.F."	On tunic and frock coat. A grenade, in silver embroidery. On mess jacket. A grenade in gold embroidery with a Dragon in silver on the ball.	A grenade in gilt or gilding metal; the Prince of Wales's Plume, in silver on the ball.	A grenade in gilt or gilding metal; on the ball, in silver, a circle (frosted) inscribed "Royal Welsh Fusiliers." Within the circle, the Prince of Wales's plume, with gilt or gilding metal coronet.	...
The South Wales Borderers.	The Welsh Dragon within a wreath of laurel. For the mess dress, the dragon in silver,—mounted on a plain gilt button.	The Sphinx over Egypt in dead gilt or gilding metal.	In silver, within a wreath of immortelles, the sphinx over Egypt. On the lower bend of the wreath the letters "S.W.B." in burnished silver.	...
The King's Own Scottish Borderers.	The Royal Crest, within the designation "King's Own Scottish Borderers." For the mess dress, the Royal Crest over K.O.S.B. in silver,—mounted on a plain button.	On a dark blue cloth ground, the Castle of Edinburgh in silver embroidery. A flag in blue and crimson embroidery flies from each tower. The Castle rests on thistle leaves, etc., in gold embroidery. Beneath the gold embroidery a scroll, inscribed "The King's Own Scottish Borderers," on a ground of light blue silk.	In silver, a thistle wreath; within the wreath a circle pierced with the designation, "King's Own Scottish Borderers." Above the circle a scroll surmounted by the Royal Crest. The scroll pierced with the motto, *In veritate religionis confido*. Over the circle, the Cross of St. Andrew in burnished silver. On the cross, the Castle of Edinburgh. On the wreath at the bottom of the circle, a scroll with the motto in relief, *Nisi Dominus frustra*. Also worn on bonnet.	On the waist-belt. On a frosted gilt or gilding metal rectangular plate with bevelled edges burnished, the Cross of St. Andrew in burnished silver; on the cross, thistle wreath in silver; within the wreath and on the cross, the Castle of Edinburgh in silver. On the shoulder belt. On a burnished gilt rectangular plate the Cross of St. Andrew. On the Cross a ring inscribed "King's Own Scottish Borderers," within the ring and on the Cross the Caste of Edinburgh. Above the ring a scroll with the motto *In veritate religionis confido* surmounted by the Royal Crest. Below the ring a scroll with the motto *Nisi dominus frustra*. The Cross in burnished silver, remainder of the mount in frosted silver with burnished letters in relief.
The Cameronians (Scottish Rifles).	Within a thistle wreath, a bugle with strings; above the bugle the Crown.	No badge.	On the chaco, in bronze, a bugle and strings; above the bugle a mullet on a black corded boss.	On the waist-belt. In silver, on a frosted silver rectangular plate with burnished edges, a thistle wreath. Within the wreath, in burnished silver, a mullet surmounted by a Crown. On the bottom of the wreath, a bugle with strings. On the shoulder belt. In silver, a thistle wreath, surmounted by a Crown. Within the wreath, the mullet and bugle. On the lower bend of the wreath, a scroll inscribed "The Scottish Rifles." The ground of the plate frosted.
The Royal Inniskilling Fusiliers.	A castle with three turrets with St. George's colours flying, superscribed "Inniskilling." For the mess dress the castle is in silver,—mounted on a plain gilt button. For the cap, the same design, die struck.	A grenade in gold embroidery : the Castle, in silver, on the ball.	A grenade in gilt or gilding metal ; the Castle, in silver, on the ball.	As for full dress head-dress, but smaller. Below the Castle a scroll in silver, inscribed "Inniskilling."	...

II:26/cont. 1904 Dress Regulations, Descriptions/cont.

Regiment.	On Buttons.	On Collar of Tunic, Mess Jacket, and Frock Coat.	On Helmet-Plates.	On the Puggaree, Cloth Forage Cap.	Special Badges.
The Gloucestershire Regiment.	Within a laurel wreath of single leaves, inclining inwards, the Royal Crest above the monogram G.R. For the mess dress the wreath is omitted and the design is engraved.	In dead gilt or gilding metal, on two twigs of laurel, the Sphinx over Egypt. On collar of mess jacket the badge is in embroidery.	In silver, on a black velvet ground, the Sphinx over Egypt. On the universal scroll, "The Gloucestershire Regiment." Badge for back of helmet—In dead gilt or gilding metal, the Sphinx over Egypt within a laurel wreath.	In silver, within two twigs of laurel, the Sphinx over Egypt. On a scroll below, "Gloucestershire." Back badge as for helmet, but smaller.	...
The Worcestershire Regiment.	On an eight-pointed star, a circle surmounted by the Crown. The circle inscribed "The Worcestershire Regiment." Within the circle, a lion. Below the circle a scroll, inscribed "Firm." For the mess dress the design is engraved, the Crown omitted, and Garter substituted for circle.	On a silver eight-pointed star, in gilt or gilding metal, the Garter with motto, within the Garter, in silver, the Lion, pierced on a black velvet ground. Below the Garter, in gilt or gilding metal, a scroll inscribed "Firm."	On a black velvet ground, a silver eight-pointed star. On the star, in gilt or gilding metal, the Garter with motto. Within the Garter, the Lion, in silver on a black velvet ground. Below the Garter, a scroll in gilt or gilding metal, inscribed "Firm." On the universal scroll, "The Worcestershire Regiment."	As for centre of helmet-plate, but with enamel substituted for velvet. Below the star, a scroll in gilt or gilding metal, inscribed "Worcestershire."	...
The East Lancashire Regiment.	Within a circle inscribed "The East Lancashire Regiment," the Sphinx over Egypt; below the Sphinx, the Rose of Lancaster. For the mess dress, the sphinx and rose in silver, mounted.	The Rose of Lancaster, in red and gold embroidery.	In silver, on a black velvet ground, the Sphinx over Egypt. On the universal scroll, "The East Lancashire Regiment."	In silver, a laurel wreath surmounted by a Crown. Within the wreath the Sphinx over "Egypt"; on the lower part of the wreath a scroll inscribed "East Lancashire." Below "Egypt," and within the wreath, the Rose in gilt or gilding metal.	...
The East Surrey Regiment.	On a bright cut-silver star, the arms of Guildford, in silver, on a shield in frosted gilt or gilding metal, with burnished edges, surmounted by a gilt or gilding metal Crown. Within the circle, the arms of Guildford. For the mess waistcoat the design is mounted.		In silver, on a black velvet ground, an eight-pointed star; on the star, badge as for collar, but without the Crown. On the universal scroll, "The East Surrey Regt."	As for collar, but with a scroll in gilt or gilding metal, inscribed "East Surrey" below the star.	...
The Duke of Cornwall's Light Infantry	Within the designation "Duke of Cornwall's Light Infy.," a bugle with strings, surmounted by the Coronet of the Prince of Wales, and gateway as shown on His Royal Highness's Great Seal as Duke of Cornwall. For the mess dress, the design in silver, mounted.	In black enamel set in gilt or gilding metal, the badge of the County of Cornwall, surmounted by the Coronet, in gilt or gilding metal, of the Prince of Wales, as shown on His Royal Highness's Great Seal as Duke of Cornwall. On a scroll the motto One and All, pierced in gilt or gilding metal letters on a ground of blue velvet.	In gilt or gilding metal, on a ground of dark green velvet, a bugle with strings. On the strings of the bugle two red feathers set in gilt or gilding metal. On the stems of the feathers, in silver, a turreted archway. On the universal scroll, "The Duke of Cornwall's Lt. Infy."	In silver, a bugle with strings surmounted by the Coronet. Below the Coronet a scroll inscribed "Cornwall."	...
The Duke of Wellington's (West Riding Regiment).	Within the designation "Duke of Wellington's West Riding Regt." the Elephant with howdah in silver. For the mess vest the Elephant and howdah in silver,—mounted on a plain gilt ground. On mess jacket the small button is worn.	The Elephant in dead gilt or gilding metal, with howdah in silver. On the mess jacket, the Duke of Wellington's Crest, in gold embroidery. The flag, in silver, within a gold edging. The Cross scarlet.	In silver, on a black velvet ground, the Crest of the Duke of Wellington, with motto on a scroll below, Virtutis fortuna comes. On the universal scroll, "The West Riding Regiment."	In silver; badge as for helmet-plate. A gilt or gilding metal scroll below inscribed "The West Riding."	...
The Border Regiment.	The Dragon of China, with the word "China" above. In the 3rd and 4th Battalions the word "China" is omitted. For the mess dress, the design is as for the Collar badge, with the lions and scroll omitted, in silver, —mounted on a plain gilt ground. For the cap—the dragon.	In silver, a laurel wreath; on the wreath a Maltese cross with a Lion between each division. On the divisions of the cross, the battles of the Regiment. On the centre of the cross, a raised circle inscribed Wirroyo dels Molinos, "1811." Within the circle, on a ground of red enamel, the Dragon of China in silver and the word "China" on a silver ground. Below the wreath a scroll inscribed "The Border Regiment."	As for collar, but the Dragon and "China" in gold, and the upper part of the centre filled in with white enamel.	In silver, as for collar badge, on an eight-pointed diamond-cut star surmounted by a Crown.	...

The Royal Sussex Regiment.	Within a circle inscribed "The Royal Sussex Regt.," a Maltese cross on a feather; on centre of cross a wreath; within the wreath, St. George's Cross. For the mess dress the buttons are mounted. The circle and titles are omitted.	A Maltese cross, in gilt or gilding metal, on a feather in silver; on the cross a wreath in silver and green enamel; on the wreath the Garter and motto in blue enamel set with silver. Within the circle the Cross of St. George, in red enamel, set with silver; on a silver ground, on the mess jacket the feather in silver embroidery with the stem gilt. On the feather the star of the order of the Garter in gold embroidery. The centre of the star as above.	On a red velvet ground, badge as for collar. On the universal scroll, "The Royal Sussex Regiment."	In silver an eight-pointed star on a feather, the stem of the feather gilt. On the star the Garter and motto, on a ground of silver blue enamel. Within the Garter, the Cross of St. George, with the ground of silver red enamel. A scroll below inscribed "The Royal Sussex Regt."	... ...
The Hampshire Regiment.	Within a laurel wreath, the Royal Tiger; below the Tiger, the Hampshire Rose. For the mess dress the design is in silver,—mounted.	The Hampshire Rose, in gold and red and green embroidery.	On a black velvet ground, the Royal Tiger, in gilt or gilding metal, within a laurel wreath, in silver. On the universal scroll, "The Hampshire Regt."	In silver, an eight-pointed star, on the star the Garter and crown in gilt metal, within the Garter the rose. On the lower part of the star, a scroll inscribed "Hampshire."	... ...
The South Staffordshire Regiment.	The Staffordshire Knot with Crown above. For the mess dress waistcoat the design in silver, mounted on a flat gilt button.	The Staffordshire Knot, in gold embroidery.	In silver, on a black velvet ground, the Sphinx over Egypt. On the universal scroll, "The South Staffordshire Regiment."	In silver, the Staffordshire Knot, surmounted by a Crown, with a scroll below in gilt or gilding metal, inscribed "South Staffordshire."	... ...
The Dorsetshire Regiment.	The Castle and Key. Above the Castle, a scroll inscribed "Gibraltar," and one below, inscribed *Primus in Indis.* Above the top scroll, "The Dorsetshire Regiment"; below the bottom scroll, the Sphinx on a tablet inscribed "Marabout." For the forage cap the title and "Primus in Indis" are omitted. On the mess waistcoat, the Castle and Key in silver,—mounted.	The Sphinx in silver, on a gilt or gilding metal tablet. On the tablet "Marabout" in gilt or gilding metal letters on a ground of green enamel.	In silver, on a black velvet ground, the Castle and Key. A scroll above the Castle inscribed *Primus in Indis,* and one below, inscribed *Montis Insignia Calpe.* On the universal scroll, "The Dorsetshire Regiment."	In gilt or gilding metal, a laurel wreath, with a scroll inscribed "Dorsetshire," the wreath and scroll forming a circle. Within the circle, in silver—The Castle and Key. Above the Castle the Sphinx resting on a tablet inscribed "Marabout." Below the Castle, a scroll with the words *Primus in Indis.*	... ...
The Prince of Wales's Volunteers (South Lancashire Regiment).	Within a scroll inscribed "The Prince of Wales's Vols.," and a laurel branch issuing from either end, a circle surmounted by the Crown. On the circle, "The South Lancashire Regiment"; within, the Prince of Wales's Plume above the Sphinx over Egypt. For the mess dress the button is mounted. The plume in silver. The monogram P.W.V. n gilt metal below.	The Prince of Wales's Plume, in gold and silver embroidery, on a blue cloth ground; the scroll in blue silk, with the motto in silver embroidery.	In silver, on a black velvet ground, the Sphinx over Egypt. On the universal scroll, "South Lancashire Regiment."	In silver, the Sphinx over "Egypt"; above the Sphinx, the Prince of Wales's plume and motto, the coronet in gilt or gilding metal. In gilt or gilding metal on either side, a spray of laurel; between the top ends of the spray, a scroll inscribed "South Lancashire," between the bottom ends another scroll inscribed "Prince of Wales's Vols."	... ...
The Welsh Regiment.	Within a laurel wreath, a circle surmounted by the Crown. On the circle, "The Welsh Regiment"; within, the Prince of Wales's Plume. For the mess dress and forage cap the Prince of Wales's Plume, for the former it is in silver,—mounted.	The Welsh Dragon, in gilt or gilding metal.	In silver, on a black velvet ground, the Prince of Wales's Plume, with scroll below inscribed *Gwell angau na Chywilydd.* The coronet in gilt or gilding metal. On the universal scroll, "The Welsh Regiment."	The Prince of Wales's Plume as for centre of helmet-plate. In gilt or gilding metal, a scroll inscribed "The Welsh." For the puggaree badge the regimental motto is added.	... ...

II:26/cont. 1904 Dress Regulations, Descriptions/cont.

Regiment.	On Buttons.	On Collar of Tunic, Mess Jacket, and Frock Coat.	On Helmet-Plates.	On the Puggaree, Cloth Forage Cap.	Special Badges.
The Black Watch (Royal Highlanders).	Within the designation "The Royal Highlanders. Black Watch," the Star of the Order of the Thistle, indented. On the centre of the Star, a circle; within the circle, St. Andrew and Cross.	St. Andrew and Cross, in silver. On mess jacket, no badge.	In gilt metal, the Sphinx over "Egypt."	In silver, the Star of the Order of the Thistle; in gilt or gilding metal on the Star, a thistle wreath. Within the wreath, in gilt or gilding metal, an oval surmounted by the Crown. The oval inscribed, *Nemo me impune lacesset.* Within the oval, on a recessed seeded ground, St. Andrew and Cross, in silver. Below the wreath, the Sphinx, in gilt or gilding metal. In silver, a half scroll, to the left of the Crown, inscribed "The Royal"; another to the right inscribed "Highlanders." A half scroll to the left of the Sphinx, inscribed "Black"; another to the right, inscribed "Watch."	On the waist-belt. On a seeded gilt or gilding metal rectangular plate, with burnished edges, badge as for glengarry but smaller. On the shoulder belt. Badge as for glengarry, but larger, on a gilt seeded rectangular plate with raised burnished edges. Brooch ornament. In silver, on an engraved burnished plate, a thistle wreath. Within the wreath, on an open centre, St. Andrew and Cross.
The Oxfordshire Light Infantry.	Scalloped edge; within a laurel wreath a bugle with strings; below the bugle, "Oxfordshire." For the mess dress and cap an edgeless button as on collar.	Edgeless button; on the button, within a laurel wreath, a bugle with strings; above the bugle, the Crown; below the wreath "Oxfordshire." A loop of gold Russia cord 2½ inches long attached to the button connecting it with front edge of collar of tunic.	In silver, on a ground of black enamel, bugle with strings. On the universal scroll, "The Oxfordshire Lt. Infy."	In silver, a bugle and strings ...	... ...
The Essex Regiment.	Within an oak-leaf wreath, an eagle and the Castle and Key below. For mess dress, a gilt burnished button with the eagle in silver. For the cap, the county badge.	The County Badge. The shield in gilt or gilding metal; the blades of the seaxes in silver. On the mess jacket, an Eagle on a plain tablet in gilt or gilding metal.	An oak-leaf wreath is substituted for the universal wreath. In silver, on a black velvet ground, the Castle and Key, with the Sphinx over Egypt above, and a scroll below, inscribed *Montis Insignia Calpe.* On the universal scroll, "The Essex Regiment."	In silver, the Castle and Key within an oak-leaf wreath. The Sphinx over Egypt above the Castle, and scroll inscribed "The Essex Regt." on the wreath below the Castle.	... ...
The Sherwood Foresters (Nottinghamshire and Derbyshire Regiment).	A Maltese cross surmounted by the Crown; within an oak-leaf wreath on the cross, a Stag lodged. A half-scroll on the left division of the cross, inscribed "Sherwood"; another on the right division, inscribed "Foresters." On the lower division, a scroll inscribed "Notts and Derby." For the mess dress the button is mounted in gilt metal.	A Maltese cross surmounted by the Crown, in silver. Wreath and scrolls in gilt or gilding metal, as for buttons. Within the wreath, a Stag lodged, in silver, on a ground of silver blue enamel.	In the helmet-plate, the Garter, with motto, is omitted. Within the universal wreath, a Maltese cross, in silver. On the cross, in gilt or gilding metal, an oakleaf wreath; within the wreath, on a ground of silver blue enamel, a Stag lodged, in silver. In gilt or gilding metal, on the left division of the cross, the word "The"; on the right division, "Regt.," and on a scroll on the lower division, "Notts and Derby." A scroll of special pattern on the bottom of the universal wreath inscribed "Sherwood Foresters."	In silver, badge as for collar, but with scroll inscribed "Notts and Derby" in gilt or gilding metal below.	... ...
The Loyal North Lancashire Regiment.	Within a wreath the Arms of the City of Lincoln, surmounted by the Royal Crest, above the Crest the word "Tarifa," and inscribed "Loyal North Lancashire."	*On tunic and frock coat:*—In embroidery, the Arms of the City of Lincoln. The ground of the shield in silver, the Cross of St. George in red silk on the shield; the *fleur-de-lis* in gold on the cross. *On mess jacket:*—Centre of helmet-plate.	In silver, on a black velvet ground, the Royal Crest. Below the Crest, the Rose of Lancaster in silver gilt and red and green enamel. On the universal scroll, "Loyal North Lancashire Regiment."	In silver, the Royal Crest. In gilt or gilding metal, below the Crown, the Rose of Lancaster; below the Rose, a scroll inscribed "Loyal North Lancashire."	... ...

Regiment			
The Northamptonshire Regiment.	Within a scroll, inscribed "The Northamptonshire Regiment," the Castle and Key, with the Crown above. For the cap, the name is omitted. For the mess dress the button is mounted.	In gilt or gilding metal, within a laurel wreath, a gilt or gilding metal circle pierced "Northamptonshire"; the ground of silver blue enamel. In relief, within the circle, on a raised ground of silver George, in silver. Below the cross, and on the wreath, a horse shoe in silver. The circle surmounted by a Crown in gilt or gilding metal.	In silver, within a laurel wreath, the Castle and Key. Above the Castle a scroll inscribed "Gibraltar"; beneath a scroll inscribed "Talavera." On the lower bend of the wreath, in gilt or gilding metal, a scroll inscribed "Northamptonshire."	... ...
Princess Charlotte of Wales's (Royal Berkshire Regiment).	A circle inscribed "Pss Charlotte of Wales's"; within the circle, the Dragon of China; above, the Dragon, the Crown; below, "R. Berks." For the mess dress the Dragon and Crown are mounted on a plain gilt button. For the cap, the Dragon and Crown with "R. Berks." below.	The Dragon of China, in gold embroidery on a blue cloth ground.	In silver, on a scarlet cloth ground, a Stag under an oak. On the universal scroll, "Royal Berkshire Regiment."	In silver, the Dragon of China with a scroll below inscribed "Royal Berkshire."	... ...
The Queen's Own (Royal West Kent Regiment).	The Royal Crest	The Royal Crest, in gold embroidery.	In silver, on a black velvet ground, the White Horse of Kent on a scroll inscribed *Invicta*. Above the Horse, another scroll with motto *Quo fas et gloria ducunt*. On the universal scroll, "The Royal West Kent Regiment."	In silver, the White Horse of Kent on a scroll, inscribed *Invicta*. On another scroll below, "Royal West Kent."	... ...
The King's Own (Yorkshire Light Infantry).	A French horn surmounted by the Crown. In the centre of the horn the White Rose. For the mess waistcoat, the button is mounted, with monogram of regiment surmounted by the Crown.	A French horn, in gold embroidery; in the centre of the horn, on a raised ground of dark green cloth, the White Rose, in silver metal.	In silver, on a black enamel ground, a French horn with the White Rose in the centre. On the universal scroll, "The King's Own Yorkshire Light Infantry."	In gilt or gilding metal, a French horn; within the horn, the White Rose in silver.	... ...
The King's (Shropshire Light Infantry).	A circle surmounted by the Crown. On the circle, "Shropshire," with two twigs of laurel in the lower bend. Within the circle, the cypher K.L.I. For the mess dress the button is mounted.	A bugle with strings, in gold embroidery, on a ground of dark blue cloth.	In silver, on a ground of dark green enamel, a bugle with strings. In gilt or gilding metal, within the strings of the bugle, the cypher K.L.I. On the universal scroll, "King's Shropshire Lt. Infty."	In silver, the bugle and strings. Within the strings, the letters "K.S.L.I.," in gilt or gilding metal.	... ...
The Duke of Cambridge's Own (Middlesex Regiment).	Within a wreath of laurel, the Prince of Wales's Plume; on the bottom of the wreath, a scroll inscribed "Albuhera." For the mess dress the design is in silver,—mounted.	In silver, a laurel wreath; within the wreath, the Prince of Wales's Plume; below the Plume, the Coronet and Cypher of H.R.H. the Duke of Cambridge; on the lower bend of the wreath, "Albuhera."	In silver, on a black velvet ground, a laurel wreath; within the wreath, the Prince of Wales's Plume; below the Plume, the Coronet and Cypher of H.R.H. the Duke of Cambridge. On the bottom of the wreath a scroll inscribed "Albuhera." On the universal scroll "The Middlesex Regt."	In silver, as for collar, with scroll below inscribed "Middlesex Regiment."	... ...
The King's Royal Rifle Corps.	Within a laurel wreath, a bugle with strings; above the bugle, the Crown. No wreath on the shoulder strap and pocket buttons.	No badge	In bronze, a Maltese cross surmounted by a tablet, inscribed *Celer et Audax*. On the Cross a circle, inscribed "The King's Royal Rifle Corps"; within the circle, a bugle with strings. On each division of the cross, the battles of the Regiment. On the Boss a crown.	On the Forage Cap:—In silver, the bugle and strings on a scarlet cord boss. On the puggaree:—As for busby badge, but surmounted by a Crown, and with a scarlet cloth ground in the centre. The dimensions are:—From the top of the Crown to the bottom of the plate, back measurement, 4 inches; extreme width 2½ inches.	On the shoulder belt. As for Puggaree but in silver throughout.

II:26/cont. 1904 Dress Regulations, Descriptions/cont.

Regiment.	On Buttons.	On Collar of Tunic, Mess Jacket, and Frock Coat.	On Helmet-Plates.	On the Puggaree, Cloth Forage Cap.	Special Badges.
The Duke of Edinburgh's (Wiltshire Regiment).	The Cypher of H.R.H. the Duke of Edinburgh, with Coronet above, and "Wiltshire Regiment," below. For the mess dress the design is in silver,—mounted in two sizes; the title is omitted.	A Maltese cross in lined silver, with burnished edges. On the cross, a round convex plate, in burnished silver. On the plate, in gilt or gilding metal, the Coronet within the Cypher.	On a black velvet ground, the Maltese cross in lined gilt or gilding metal, with burnished edges. On the cross, a round convex burnished plate. On the plate, in silver, the Cypher surmounted by the Coronet. On the universal scroll, "The Wiltshire Regiment."	As for helmet plate, but with Cypher and Coronet in gilt or gilding metal; a scroll beneath inscribed "The Wiltshire Regiment"; above the cross the Coronet.	...
The Manchester Regiment.	The Garter, with motto, *Honi soit qui mal y pense*. Within the Garter, the Sphinx over Egypt with the Crown above. For the mess dress mounted in silver.	The Sphinx over Egypt in gold embroidery; the word "Egypt" embroidered in silver.	In silver, on a black velvet ground, the badge with motto of the City of Manchester. On the universal scroll, "The Manchester Regiment."	In silver, the badge and motto of the City of Manchester above a scroll in gilt or gilding metal inscribed "Manchester."	...
The Prince of Wales's (North Staffordshire Regiment.)	Within a scroll inscribed "Prince of Wales's" and a laurel branch issuing from either end, a circle inscribed "The North Staffordshire Regiment"; within the circle, the Staffordshire Knot; above the circle, the Prince of Wales's Plume. For the mess dress the button is mounted and the Knot and Plume are in silver.	The Staffordshire Knot in gold embroidery.	In silver, on a black velvet ground, the Prince of Wales's Plume. On the universal scroll, "The North Staffordshire Regiment."	The Staffordshire Knot surmounted by the Prince of Wales's plume, the Knot and Coronet in gilt or gilding metal; the plume and scroll in silver. Below the knot, in silver, a scroll inscribed "North Stafford."	...
The York and Lancaster Regiment.	A scroll inscribed "The York and Lancaster Regiment"; within the scroll, a laurel wreath; within the wreath the Royal Tiger; above the Tiger, a Coronet. On the wreath, at the bottom, the Union Rose. For the mess dress the tiger and rose are in silver,—mounted on a plain gilt button.	The Royal Tiger, in dead gilt or gilding metal, the rose above in gilt or gilding metal and silver.	In silver and gilt or gilding metal, on a black velvet ground, the Union Rose. On the universal scroll, "The York & Lancaster Regiment."	In gilt or gilding metal, the Tiger within a scroll inscribed "York and Lancaster" upon a laurel wreath. Between the ends of the wreath a coronet in silver; below the coronet, the Union Rose in gilt or gilding metal and silver.	...
The Durham Light Infantry.	Bugle, with the Crown on the strings. For the mess jacket "D.L.I." in cypher with the Crown above.	Bugle with strings, in gold embroidery on a dark green cloth ground.	In silver, on a dark green velvet ground, a bugle with strings. On the universal scroll, "The Durham Light infantry."	In silver, a bugle ornamented with laurel leaves. Upon the strings a crown. Within the strings "D.L.I."	...
The Highland Light Infantry.	Star of the Order of the Thistle. On the star, a horn: in the centre of the horn, the monogram H.L.I. Above the horn, the Crown; below the horn, a scroll, inscribed "Assaye"; under the scroll, the Elephant. For the mess dress a mounted button, the monogram H.L.I. with the crown above.	In silver, the Star of the Order of the Thistle. On the star a silver horn. In the centre of the horn, the monogram H.L.I. Above the horn, the Crown, in gilt or gilding metal. Above the horn, in gilt or gilding metal the Crown; below the horn, a scroll, in gilt or gilding metal, inscribed "Assaye"; under the scroll, in gilt or gilding metal, the Elephant. *On Mess Jacket.*— No badge.	As for collar badge, except that the cap of the Crown is of crimson enamel. The scroll is detached from the Elephant, and the badge is larger. A black boss is worn with gilt thistle mount.	As for chaco, but without boss	On the Waist Belt. On a seeded gilt or gilding metal rectangular plate, with badge as for chaco, mounted. On the Shoulder Belt. As for waist-plate, but larger.
Seaforth Highlanders (Ross-shire Buffs, the Duke of Albany's.	Raised edge, a stag's head, with the Cypher of H.R.H. the Duke of Albany above. A scroll below, inscribed "Seaforth Highlanders."	*On Tunic.*— Two badges in gilt metal— I. The Cypher of H.R.H. the late Duke of York with scroll inscribed "Caber Feidh." II. The Elephant. Both badges to be worn on each side of collar, the Cypher of the late Duke of York next the hooks and eyes. *On Mess Jacket.*— No badge.	As for glengarry but without the Coronet and Cypher.	In silver, a stag's head; above, the Coronet and Cypher of H.R.H. the Duke of Albany; below, a scroll inscribed "Cuidich'n Righ."	On the Waist Belt. Burnished gilt or gilding metal rectangular plate. Badge as for Highland head-dress, except that it is smaller, and that the motto on scroll is *Tulloch Ard.* On the Shoulder Belt. Plain gilt rectangular plate. In silver, the coronet, the Cypher of H.R.H. the late Duke of York, the Elephant, the stag's head, and scroll inscribed "Seaforth Highlanders."

The Gordon Highlanders.	The Cross of St. Andrew; on the cross a thistle wreath joined to a scroll let into the upper divisions of the cross, and inscribed "Gordon Highlanders." Within the scroll, on the upper divisions of the cross, the Sphinx over Egypt; within the wreath on the lower divisions of the cross, the Royal Tiger over India. Mounted button on Mess Vest.	The Royal Tiger, in gold embroidery *On Mess Jacket—* No badge.	In silver, the Crest of the Marquis of Huntly, within an ivy wreath. On the bottom of the wreath, *Bydland*.	As for Highland head-dress ...	Brooch Ornament. In silver, a thistle wreath intertwined with a scroll bearing the honours of the regiment. Within the wreath badges as for head-dress, without the scroll. On the Waist Belt. Burnished gilt or gilding metal rectangular plate. In silver, badge as on buttons, but larger. On the Shoulder Belt. On a burnished gilt rectangular plate in silver, the star of the Order of St. Andrew. On the top of the star the Sphinx over Egypt; on the lower part of the star the Tiger over India; on the centre the Crest of the Marquis of Huntly, above a spray of thistles; above the crest a scroll inscribed "Gordon Highlanders."
The Queen's Own Cameron Highlanders.	Within the designation "The Queen's Own Cameron Highlanders," the Thistle surmounted by the Crown. On Mess Vest a plain gilt button with St. Andrew and Cross in silver, mounted.	The Thistle surmounted by the Crown on a crimson velvet cushion, in silver embroidery, on a blue cloth ground. *On Mess Jacket—* No badge.	For Highland head dress and Puggaree. In silver, a thistle wreath; within the wreath the figure of St. Andrew with Cross, but with a scroll on the lower bend of the wreath inscribed "Cameron."	As for Highland head-dress ...	Brooch Ornament. In burnished silver, a plate with a scroll inscribed "Peninsula," "Egypt," on the right; "Waterloo," "India" on the left, and on the lower bend "Gordon Highlanders." On an open centre, badge as for Head-dresses. On the Waist Belt. Burnished gilt or gilding metal rectangular plate. In silver on the plate, a thistle wreath; within the wreath St. Andrew with Cross. On the Shoulder Belt. On a gilt seeded rectangular plate with raised burnished edges, the Cross of St. Andrew in cut bright silver with raised edges. On the Cross a gilt oval collar inscribed "Queen's Own Cameron Highlanders," surmounted by a Crown. Within the collar, on a burnished ground, the thistle and Crown in silver. Below the collar the Sphinx over Egypt in silver.

II:26/cont. 1904 Dress Regulations, Descriptions/cont.

Regiment.	On Buttons.	On Collar of Tunic, Mess Jacket and Frock Coat.	On Helmet-Plates; Ornaments for Bear or Racoon-skin Caps and Highland Head-dress.	On the Puggaree, Cloth Forage Cap or Glengarry.	Special Badges.
The Queen's Own Cameron Highlanders—	Scalloped edge: within a scroll and the shamrock leaves issuing from either end, the Harp and Crown. On scroll, "Royal Irish Rifles."	On Mess Jacket only, badge as on Forage Cap boss.			Brooch Ornament. In silver, a thistle wreath. Within the wreath the Sphinx over Egypt. Above the Sphinx a scroll inscribed "Peninsula," below a scroll inscribed "Waterloo."
The Royal Irish Rifles.			In bronze, the Harp and Crown; below the Harp, a scroll, inscribed *Quis separabit*, on a round boss, the Sphinx over Egypt; below the Sphinx, a bugle with strings.	On puggaree as for busby but without boss. On Forage Cap, a green cord boss with a Harp and Crown in silver across which is a scroll inscribed "Royal Irish Rifles."	On the Shoulder Belt. In silver, a shamrock wreath intertwined with a scroll, bearing the battles of the regiment; within the wreath the Harp and Crown; above the Harp a scroll inscribed *Quis separabit*; below the Harp, the Sphinx over Egypt; below the Sphinx a bugle with the strings. Over the strings of the bugle a scroll, inscribed "Royal Irish Rifles."
Princess Victoria's (Royal Irish Fusiliers).	Scalloped edge: an Eagle with a wreath of laurel; below the Eagle a small tablet inscribed with the figure 8. For the mess dress, plain edge with the eagle and tablet in silver—mounted.	A grenade in gold embroidery, with badge on ball as for buttons, but in silver. 2nd Badge—Coronet of H.R.H. the Princess Victoria in silver, worn next the hooks and eyes.	A grenade in gilt or gilding metal. In silver on the ball, the Eagle with a wreath of laurel. Below the Eagle a small tablet inscribed with the figure 8.	1st Badge:—The coronet of H.R.H. the Princess Victoria. 2nd Badge:—A gilt or gilding metal grenade with the Harp and Plume in silver on the ball.	... ...
The Connaught Rangers.	Scalloped edge. Within a wreath of shamrock, the Harp surmounted by a Crown; on the lower part of the wreath a scroll inscribed *Quis separabit*. For the mess waistcoat, the letters C.R. on a lined button with a raised edge.	*On Tunic and Frock Coat*—The Elephant, in silver. *On Mess Jacket collar*—The Harp and Crown in gold embroidery.	In silver, on a dark green velvet ground, the Harp, with scroll, inscribed *Quis separabit*. A sprig of laurel issues from either end of the scroll. On the universal scroll, "The Connaught Rangers."	In silver, the Harp and Crown; below the Harp a scroll inscribed "Connaught Rangers."	... ...
Princess Louise's (Argyll and Sutherland Highlanders).	A myrtle wreath interlaced with a wreath of butcher's broom. Within the myrtle wreath, a Boar's head on scroll inscribed, *Ne obliviscaris*; within the myrtle wreath, the Boar's head on scroll inscribed *Ne obliviscaris*. A Cat on scroll inscribed *Sans peur*. A label of three points above the Boar's head and the Cat. Above the wreaths, the Coronet of H.R.H. the Princess Louise.	*On Tunic*—In frosted silver, a myrtle wreath interlaced with a wreath of butcher's broom. In gilt or gilding metal, within the myrtle wreath, the Boar's head on scroll, inscribed *Ne obliviscaris*; within the wreath of butcher's broom, the Cat on scroll, inscribed *Sans peur*. A label of three points in silver above the Boar's head and the Cat. *On the Mess Jacket*—No badge.	In silver, a thistle wreath; within the wreath, a circle, inscribed "Argyll and Sutherland." Within the circle, the double Cypher of H.R.H. the Princess Louise. To the left of the Cypher, the Boar's head; to the right the Cat. Above the Cypher, and on the circle, the Coronet of the Princess.	As for Highland head dress ...	On the Waist Belt. Burnished gilt or gilding metal rectangular plate. Devices as for collar badge, but *all* in silver; above the wreaths, in frosted silver, a scroll surmounted by the Coronet of the Princess. The scroll inscribed "Princess Louise's"; below the wreath a silver scroll, inscribed "Argyll and Sutherland Highlanders." On the Shoulder Belt. As for waist-plate, but modified in shape, and with scrolls on the wreaths bearing the honours of the regiment. Brooch Ornament. Silver circular brooch with open centre. On the left, the boar's head and motto; on the right, the cat and motto. Above the opening, the Cypher and Coronet; below the opening a scroll inscribed "Argyll and Sutherland Highlanders."

The Prince of Wales's Leinster Regiment (Royal Canadians).	A Circle, inscribed "Prince of Wales's Leinster Regiment"; within the circle, the Prince of Wales's Plume. For the mess dress the plume in silver—mounted, on a plain gilt button.	The Prince of Wales's Plume, in silver; the Coronet in gilt or gilding metal.	In silver, on a black velvet ground, the Prince of Wales's Plume over two maple leaves. On a scroll, beneath the leaves, "Central India." On the universal scroll, "Prince of Wales's Leinster Regiment." The Coronet in gilt or gilding metal.	In silver, the Prince of Wales's Plume, the Coronet in gilt or gilding metal. Below the Coronet a scroll, in gilt or gilding metal, inscribed "The Leinster."	... ...
The Royal Munster Fusiliers.	Within the designation, "Royal Munster Fusiliers," a grenade, with the Royal Tiger on the ball. For the mess dress the Royal Tiger, in silver— mounted, on a plain gilt button.	A grenade in gold embroidery, with the Royal Tiger, in silver, on the ball.	A grenade, in gilt or gilding metal. On the ball a deep wreath of laurel intertwined with a scroll bearing the battles of the Regiment. Within the wreath, the Heraldic device for the Province of Munster, the Crowns in gilt or gilding metal, the shield in silver. On the bottom of the wreath, a scroll, in silver, inscribed "Royal Munster."	In gilt or gilding metal, a grenade. On the ball, in silver, the Tiger and scroll inscribed "Royal Munster."	... ...
The Royal Dublin Fusiliers.	Within the designation "Royal Dublin Fusiliers," a grenade; on the ball of the grenade, the Royal Tiger; below the Tiger, the Crown. For the mess waistcoat the elephant and the tiger on separate buttons in silver, mounted. For the cap, the same design, die struck.	A grenade in gold embroidery; in silver, on the ball, the Royal Tiger; below the Tiger, the Elephant.	A grenade in gilt or gilding metal: on the ball, in silver, the badge of the City of Dublin; below the shield—to the right, the Royal Tiger, on a silver tablet inscribed "Plassey," to the left, the Elephant, on a silver tablet inscribed "Mysore." Below the tablets a silver scroll inscribed *Spectamur agendo*. In silver on either side of the shield, a rich mounting of shamrock leaves.	In gilt or gilding metal, a grenade. On the ball, in silver, the Tiger; below the Tiger, the Elephant. Below the grenade, a scroll in silver inscribed "Royal Dublin Fusiliers."	... ...
The Rifle Brigade (The Prince Consort's Own).	Within a laurel wreath, and the designation Rifle Brigade, a bugle with strings; above the bugle, the Crown.	On mess jacket only, the bugle in silver.	On the busby, a bugle; on the boss, a Crown; small bugles at the side of the busby. The whole in bronze relieved.	In silver, a wreath of laurel intertwined with a scroll, bearing some of the battles of the Brigade. Within the wreath, a Maltese cross, with a Lion between each battles of the Brigade. On the centre of the cross, a circle inscribed "Rifle Brigade"; within the circle, a bugle with strings, surmounted by the Crown. Above the Cross, a Crown on a tablet, inscribed "Waterloo"; below the cross, a scroll, inscribed "Peninsula."	On the Shoulder Belt. As for puggaree, but 4 inches in height, and a scroll on the lower part of the wreath, inscribed "The Prince Consort's Own."
The West India Regiment.	A wreath of laurel and Carolina laurel leaves. Within the wreath, the cypher "W.I.R." surmounted by the Crown. For the mess dress, in silver, the letters "W.I.R." reversed and intertwined—mounted.	No badge	A wreath of laurel and palm leaves in gilt or gilding metal. Within the wreath, the Garter, with motto. Within the Garter, on a burnished ground, the cypher "W.I.R." The battles of the regiment on the larger rays of the star.	The wreath and garter as for the helmet-plate. The motto pierced on a silver blue enamel ground. Within the Garter, in silver, the cypher "W.I."	... ...
The Chinese Regiment.	The harbour of Wei-hai-wei with a junk in the foreground. On a circle round the design, "The Chinese Regiment."	In gilt metal the gate of Tientsin; above the archway the name of the town in Chinese characters, and below it in English characters on scrolls in silver. At the bottom of the badge, "1st Chinese Regiment" on a scroll in silver.	...	As for collar, but larger	... ...
West African Regiment.	Bronze, dome-shaped, with letters W.A.R. For mess dress, the button will be gilt with W.A.R. in silver, mounted.	...	...	In bronze, a leopard alighting. On a scroll below "WEST AFRICAN REGIMENT."	On shoulder straps "W.A.R."

II:26/cont. 1904 Dress Regulations, Descriptions/cont.

§II-3 APPENDIX III: 1904 DRESS REGULATIONS: PHOTOGRAPHS OF REGIMENTAL BADGES AND OF STANDARD HOME SERVICE HELMET PLATE (WITH KING'S CROWN)

II:27 1904 Dress Regulations, Photographs
Regimental badges and standard home service helmet plate (with King's Crown).

§II-3 Uniform Information 61

II:28 1904 Dress Regulations, Photographs
Regimental badges and standard home service helmet plate (with King's Crown).

II:29 1904 Dress Regulations, Photographs
Regimental badges and standard home service helmet plate (with King's Crown).

62 British Empire

FORAGE CAP BADGE.
GRENADIER GUARDS.

PUGGAREE BADGE (½ SIZE).
GRENADIER GUARDS.

PUGGAREE BADGE (½ SIZE).
COLDSTREAM GUARDS.

FORAGE CAP AND
PUGGAREE BADGE.
IRISH GUARDS.

FORAGE CAP BADGE.
COLDSTREAM GUARDS.

FORAGE CAP AND PUGGAREE BADGE.
SCOTS GUARDS.

THE ROYAL SCOTS
(LOTHIAN REGIMENT).

THE QUEEN'S
(ROYAL WEST SURREY REGIMENT).

THE BUFFS
(EAST KENT REGIMENT).

THE KING'S OWN
(ROYAL LANCASTER REGIMENT).

THE NORTHUMBERLAND
FUSILIERS.

THE ROYAL WARWICKSHIRE
REGIMENT.

THE ROYAL FUSILIERS
(CITY OF LONDON REGIMENT).

THE KING'S
(LIVERPOOL REGIMENT).

THE NORFOLK REGIMENT.

THE LINCOLNSHIRE REGIMENT.

THE DEVONSHIRE REGIMENT.

THE SUFFOLK REGIMENT.

II:30 1904 Dress Regulations, Photographs
Regimental badges and standard home service helmet plate (with King's Crown).

§II-3 Uniform Information

THE PRINCE ALBERT'S (SOMERSETSHIRE LIGHT INFANTRY).

(THE PRINCE OF WALES'S OWN). WEST YORKSHIRE REGIMENT.

THE EAST YORKSHIRE REGIMENT.

THE BEDFORDSHIRE REGIMENT.

THE LEICESTERSHIRE REGIMENT.

THE ROYAL IRISH REGIMENT.

ALEXANDRA, PRINCESS OF WALES'S OWN (YORKSHIRE REGIMENT).

THE LANCASHIRE FUSILIERS.

ROYAL SCOTS FUSILIERS.

THE KING'S OWN SCOTTISH BORDERERS.

THE CHESHIRE REGIMENT.

THE SOUTH WALES BORDERERS.

THE ROYAL WELSH FUSILIERS.

THE CAMERONIANS (SCOTTISH RIFLES).

THE ROYAL INNISKILLING FUSILIERS.

THE GLOUCESTERSHIRE REGIMENT. BACK BADGE.

THE WORCESTERSHIRE REGIMENT.

THE EAST LANCASHIRE REGIMENT.

THE EAST SURREY REGIMENT.

THE DUKE OF CORNWALL'S LIGHT INFANTRY.

II:31 1904 Dress Regulations, Photographs
Regimental badges and standard home service helmet plate (with King's Crown).

64　British Empire

THE DUKE OF WELLINGTON'S (WEST RIDING REGIMENT).

THE BORDER REGIMENT.

THE ROYAL SUSSEX REGIMENT.

THE HAMPSHIRE REGIMENT.

THE SOUTH STAFFORDSHIRE REGIMENT.

THE DORSETSHIRE REGIMENT.

THE PRINCE OF WALES'S VOLUNTEERS (SOUTH LANCASHIRE REGIMENT).

THE WELSH REGIMENT.

THE BLACK WATCH (ROYAL HIGHLANDERS).

THE OXFORDSHIRE LIGHT INFANTRY.

THE ESSEX REGIMENT.

THE SHERWOOD FORESTERS. NOTTINGHAMSHIRE & DERBYSHIRE REGIMENT.

THE LOYAL NORTH LANCASHIRE REGIMENT.

THE NORTHAMPTONSHIRE REGIMENT.

PRINCESS CHARLOTTE OF WALES'S. (ROYAL BERKSHIRE REGIMENT).

THE QUEEN'S OWN. (ROYAL WEST KENT REGIMENT).

FORAGE CAP AND PUGGAREE BADGE. THE KING'S OWN. (YORKSHIRE LIGHT INFANTRY).

THE DUKE OF CAMBRIDGE'S OWN. (MIDDLESEX REGIMENT).

THE KING'S. (SHROPSHIRE LIGHT INFANTRY).

THE KING'S ROYAL RIFLE CORPS.

FORAGE CAP BADGE.

II:32 1904 Dress Regulations, Photographs
Regimental badges and standard home service helmet plate (with King's Crown).

§II-3 Uniform Information   65

THE DUKE OF EDINBURGH'S (WILTSHIRE REGIMENT).

THE MANCHESTER REGIMENT.

THE PRINCE OF WALES'S (NORTH STAFFORDSHIRE REGIMENT).

THE YORK AND LANCASTER REGIMENT.

THE DURHAM LIGHT INFANTRY.

THE HIGHLAND LIGHT INFANTRY.

SEAFORTH HIGHLANDERS (ROSS-SHIRE BUFFS, THE DUKE OF ALBANY'S).

THE GORDON HIGHLANDERS. (RIGHT FRONT OF BADGE.)

THE QUEEN'S OWN CAMERON HIGHLANDERS.

FORAGE CAP BADGE.
PUGGAREE BADGE.
THE ROYAL IRISH RIFLES.

PRINCESS VICTORIA'S. (ROYAL IRISH FUSILIERS).

THE CONNAUGHT RANGERS.

PRINCESS LOUISE'S. (ARGYLL AND SUTHERLAND HIGHLANDERS).

THE PRINCE OF WALES'S LEINSTER REGIMENT. (ROYAL CANADIANS).

THE ROYAL MUNSTER FUSILIERS.

THE ROYAL DUBLIN FUSILIERS.

PUGGAREE BADGE. THE RIFLE BRIGADE. (THE PRINCE CONSORT'S OWN).

WEST INDIA REGIMENT.

II:33 1904 Dress Regulations, Photographs
Regimental badges and standard home service helmet plate (with King's Crown).

§II-3 APPENDIX IV: 1911 DRESS REGULATIONS: DESCRIPTIONS OF OFFICERS' BUTTONS, HELMET PLATES, AND BADGES

Regiment.	On Buttons.	On Full Dress Head-Dress.	On Waist Belt.	On the Pouch.
1st Life Guards.	The letters 'L.G.' reversed and intertwined, surmounted by a Crown. Between the letters and the Crown the number of the regiment.	Within a wreath of oak leaves and laurel, on a frosted gilt centre, surmounted by a Crown, the Star of the Order of the Garter. Around the centre, the Collar of the Order, with the "George" upon the lower ends of the stems of the wreath. The colours of the Garter, cross, and field are in enamel. The star in silver, the remainder gilt.	On a frosted gilt rectangular plate, the star and collar of the Order of the Garter surmounted by a Crown. On either side of the collar the letters "L.G." reversed and intertwined. Below the letters a scroll upon a twig of laurel. The left scroll inscribed "Waterloo," the right, "Peninsula." On the undress belt a burnished plate is worn with a similar device, but with the motto and centre of the star in silver.	As for Waist plate, but larger.
2nd Life Guards.	Edge scalloped. The Royal Crest between the letters "L.G." Below the Crown the figure 2.	As for 1st Life Guards, except that the field of the cross is in silver.	As for 1st Life Guards.	As for 1st Life Guards.
Royal Horse Guards.	The letters "R.H.G." surmounted by a Crown.	As for 2nd Life Guards.	On a dead gilt frosted rectangular plate, the Royal Arms.	The Royal Arms on a scarlet cloth ground.

II:34 1911 Dress Regulations, Descriptions Officers' buttons, helmet plates, and badges.

Regiment.	On Buttons.	On Collar of Tunic, Mess Jacket & Frock Coat.	On Full Dress Head-dress.	On Waist Plate.	On the Pouch.
(1st King's) Dragoon Guards.	The Star of the Order of the Garter surmounted by a Crown, within the Garter the letters "K.D.G."	The Austrian Eagle, in gold embroidery.	On the Garter star, in silver, the Garter with motto in gilt or gilding metal, pierced on a ground of blue enamel. Within the Garter on a ground of red enamel, the Royal Cypher in silver.	On a frosted gilt or gilding metal rectangular plate with burnished edges, in silver, within an oakleaf wreath, the Royal Cypher and Crown, a scroll on the bottom of the wreath inscribed *Dieu et mon droit*.	In gilt or gilding metal, the Royal Cypher and Crown.
2nd Dragoon Guards (Queen's Bays).	Star of Order of the Garter surmounted by a Crown; within the Garter the word "Bays."	In gilt or gilding metal, within a laurel wreath, the word "Bays." Between the ends of the wreath, a Crown.	On the Garter star, the Garter, with motto pierced, on a blue enamel ground; within the Garter the Royal Cypher in silver on a ground of red enamel.	As for 1st Dragoon Guards but larger.	As for forage cap with scroll bearing the motto "*Pro Rege et Patria*."
3rd (Prince of Wales's) Dragoon Guards.	Within the Garter and motto the Prince of Wales's plume.	The Prince of Wales's plume. The Coronet in gilt or gilding metal, the plume and motto in silver.	On the Garter star, in silver, the Garter, with motto in gilt or gilding metal, pierced on a ground of blue enamel; within the Garter, in silver, the Prince of Wales's plume, on a scarlet enamel ground.	As for 1st Dragoon Guards.	As for 1st Dragoon Guards. On the Cypher the Prince of Wales's plume in silver.
4th (Royal Irish) Dragoon Guards.	The Star of the Order of St. Patrick, with "4th (Royal Irish) Dragoon Guards" round the star.	In silver, the Star of the Order of St. Patrick.	On the Garter star, in gilt or gilding metal, a circle inscribed *Quis separabit* MDCCLXXXIII, on a blue enamelled ground. Within the circle, on a white ground, the Cross of St. Patrick in gold and red enamel. On the cross a shamrock-leaf in green enamel, with a red enamelled Crown on each petal.	As for 1st Dragoon Guards, but with shamrock instead of oak-leaf wreath. No scroll and motto.	As for 1st Dragoon Guards.
5th (Princess Charlotte of Wales's) Dragoon Guards.	Star of the Order of the Garter surmounted by a Crown. The circle inscribed "*Vestigia nulla retrorsum*." Within the circle, "5" D.G.	In gilt or gilding metal, a circle surmounted by a Crown. The circle inscribed "*Vestigia nulla retrorsum*," on a frosted ground. On a gilt burnished centre, in silver, the white horse with "V." above and "D.G." below.	On the Garter star, in gilt or gilding metal, an elliptical ring, inscribed "P.C.W. Dragoon Guards." Within the ring "5" in silver.	As for 1st Dragoon Guards, but larger.	As for 1st Dragoon Guards.

II:34/cont. 1911 Dress Regulations, Descriptions/cont.

Regiment.	On Buttons.	On Collar of Tunic, Mess Jacket & Frock Coat.	On Full Dress Head-dress.	On Waist Plate.	On the Pouch.
6th Dragoon Guards. (Carabiniers).	A circle inscribed "Carabiniers," surmounted by a Crown. Within the circle, "VI" D.G.	In gilt or gilding metal, upon crossed carbines, the Garter and motto surmounted by a Crown. In silver, within the Garter, on a frosted ground "VI" D.G. below the garter a scroll inscribed "Carabiniers."	On the garter star in silver, the Garter, with motto in gilt or gilding metal, pierced on a ground of blue enamel. Within the Garter, on a ground of red enamel, the figure "6" in silver. The star has plain rays.	As for 1st Dragoon Guards.	As for 1st Dragoon Guards.
7th (Princess Royal's) Dragoon Guards.	"P. R. D. G." in monogram, surmounted by the Princess Royal's Coronet.	In gold embroidery, the Earl of Ligonier's Crest — a lion issuing from a coronet, with a scroll below inscribed, "*Quo fata vocant.*"	On the Garter star, in silver, an elliptical ring, with "The Princess Royal's Dragoon Guards" in burnished gilt or gilding metal on a silver blue enamel ground. Within, on a ground of red enamel, the figure "7" in silver.	As for 1st Dragoon Guards, but larger.	In gilt or gilding metal the letters "P R. D. G." in monogram, surmounted by the Princess Royal's Coronet
1st (Royal) Dragoons.	The Royal Crest. The Crown upon, and the Lion within, the Garter. A scroll below inscribed "Royal Dragoons."	In gold embroidery an eagle on a bar, below the bar "105" in silver. Upon the eagle a wreath in silver.	In gilt or gilding metal, the Garter star. On the star, the Royal Crest in gilt on a burnished silver ground within an elliptical ring in silver inscribed "The Royal Dragoons."	As for 1st Dragoon Guards, but larger.	The Royal Cypher and Crown in gilt or gilding metal. On the Cypher, the Eagle, in silver.
2nd Dragoons (Royal Scots Greys).	Edge burnished and scalloped. An eagle above "Waterloo." Below "Waterloo," the letters "R.S.G." Mess dress button, plain gilt burnished, with eagle mounted thereon.	A grenade in silver embroidery	A grenade in gilt or gilding metal. On the grenade the Royal Arms. In the centre below, St. Andrew and Cross between sprays of rose, thistle and shamrock; on a scroll beneath, the word "Waterloo."	On a seeded gilt rectangular plate with burnished edges, the Star and Collar of the Order of the Thistle; above the Star, a Crown. The Star and circle with motto in silver, the remainder of the device in gilt metal.	In gilt or gilding metal, an eagle over "Waterloo."
6th (Inniskilling) Dragoons.	Scalloped edge The Castle of Inniskilling with "VI" below. For the mess waistcoat the design is in silver.	For tunic and frock coat, the Castle of Inniskilling embroidered in silver. For mess jackets the same but smaller.	On a gilt or gilding metal beaded Garter star, an elliptical ring inscribed "Inniskilling Dragoons" in burnished letters on a frosted ground. Within the ring, in silver, the Castle over "VI" on a gilt or gilding metal ground.	On a matted gilt or gilding metal plate with burnished edges in silver, an oak-leaf wreath with a scroll inscribed "Inniskilling Dragoons" on the lower bend. Within the wreath, the Castle over "VI."	In dead gilt or gilding metal, the Royal Cypher and Crown On the Cypher the Castle in silver, with scroll inscribed "Inniskilling."

Regiment.	On Buttons.	On Collar of Tunic, Mess Jacket, and Frock Coat.	On the Pouch.
3rd (King's Own) Hussars.	Full dome, gilt, burnished.	The white horse in silver.	In gilt or gilding metal, the Royal Cypher and Crown.
4th (Queen's Own) Hussars.	Full dome, gilt, burnished.	In gilt or gilding metal, a circle inscribed "Queen's Own Hussars," with two sprays of laurel below. Above the circle, a Crown. Within the circle, "IV," ornamented, in silver. Below the circle a silver scroll inscribed "Mente et Manu."	In gilt or gilding metal, the Royal Cypher and Crown.
7th (Queen's Own) Hussars.	Full dome, gilt, burnished.	In gilt or gilding metal, a circle inscribed "7th Queen's Own Hussars," surmounted by a Crown; within the circle, in silver, the letters "Q.O." reversed and intertwined.	The monogram "Q.O." surmounted by a crown. Special pattern edging, the whole in gold embroidery.
8th King's (Royal Irish) Hussars.	Full dome, gilt, burnished.	The Harp and Crown; the Harp in silver, the Crown in gilt or gilding metal.	In gold embroidery the Royal Crest and Harp and Crown, and the Royal Cypher in silver embroidery. Round the Royal Cypher a wreath of shamrocks with scrolls in gold embroidery. The scrolls embroidered in silver, with the honours as shown in the Army List. A similar scroll below the Harp and Crown inscribed "Pristinæ virtutis memores."
10th (Prince of Wales's Own Royal) Hussars.	Full dome, gilt, burnished.	The Prince of Wales's Plume. The Plume and motto in silver. The coronet in gilt or gilding metal.	Within a laurel wreath the Prince of Wales's Plume in silver, coronet in gilt, with the Royal Cypher and Crown underneath in gilt or gilding metal. Pouch belt ornaments of special pattern.
11th (Prince Albert's Own) Hussars.	Full dome, gilt, burnished. On frock coat—special pattern.	On a ground of crimson cloth, in gold and silk embroidery, the Crest and Motto of the late Prince Consort. The motto on a blue velvet scroll.	Gilt or gilding metal flap and silver ornaments. On pouch belt the sphinx over "Egypt" in silver.

II:34/cont. 1911 Dress Regulations, Descriptions/cont.

Regiment.	On Buttons.	On Collar of Tunic, Mess Jacket, and Frock Coat.	On the Pouch.
13th Hussars.	Full dome, gilt, burnished.	In gilt or gilding metal a circle, inscribed "*Viret in æternum*" surmounted by a crown; around the circle a laurel wreath, with "Hussars" on a tablet on the lower bend; within the circle "XIII" in silver. A badge is not worn on tunic.	In gilt or gilding metal the Royal Cypher surmounted by a Crown.
14th (King's) Hussars.	Full dome, gilt, burnished.	The Prussian Eagle in black and gold japanned metal with crown above. On Mess Jacket—the Eagle in black embroidery surmounted by a Prussian crown of blue silk and gold embroidery.	In gilt or gilding metal, the Royal Cypher and Crown reversed and intertwined. On the Cypher the Prussian Eagle in gilt.
15th (The King's) Hussars.	Full dome, gilt, burnished.	In gilt or gilding metal the Royal Crest, with a scroll below, in silver, inscribed "Merebimur."	Gold embroidery of special pattern, including battle honours.
18th (Queen Mary's Own) Hussars.	Full dome, gilt, burnished.	A ring resting on two sprays of laurel and surmounted by a crown. On the ring the title "Queen Mary's Own." Within the ring the numeral "XVIII" superimposed on the letter "H." The centre design *pierced* and the whole in silver.	Gold embroidery of special pattern, including battle honours.
19th (Queen Alexandra's Own Royal) Hussars.	Full dome, gilt, burnished.	In silver, the Dannebrog, interlaced with the letter "A," and surmounted by a coronet, on the arms of the cross the date "1885." For the mess jacket the badge is in gold embroidery.	The Royal Cypher and Crown in gilt or gilding metal; on pouch belt an elephant with "Assaye" above and "Niagara" below, on silver scrolls.
20th Hussars.	Full dome, gilt, burnished.	In gilt or gilding metal, the letters "xHx" surmounted by a Crown.	The Royal Cypher and Crown in gilt or gilding metal.

II:34/cont. 1911 Dress Regulations, Descriptions/cont.

Regiment.	On Buttons.	On Collar of Tunic, Mess Jacket and Frock Coat.	On Full Dress Head-dress.	On the Pouch.
5th (Royal Irish) Lancers.	On crossed Lances a circle surmounted by a Crown, with a shamrock wreath below. On the circle "Fifth Royal Irish." Within the circle, the harp.	The Harp and Crown in gilt or gilding metal.	On a gilt or gilding metal plate, universal pattern, in silver, the Royal Arms; below, the harp between sprays of shamrock. Across the bottom of the plate "Fifth Royal Irish Lancers." Silver scrolls inscribed with battle honours as per Army List.	In gilt or gilding metal, the Royal Cypher and Crown.
9th (Queen's Royal) Lancers.	On crossed Lances, surmounted by a crown, the letters "A.R.," reversed and interlaced. Below the letters the figure 9.	In silver, the figure "9" on crossed lances, above the "9" a crown, below the "9" a scroll inscribed "Lancers."	In gilt or gilding metal, the universal plate with the Royal Arms; on either side on sprays of laurel. scrolls inscribed with the honours of the regiment. On a scroll below, "Royal Lancers." In silver, on the centre of the plate, "A.R." reversed and interlaced.	In gilt or gilding metal "A.R." reversed and interlaced, with a crown above.
12th (Prince of Wales's Royal) Lancers.	Scalloped edge; "12" resting on crossed lances surmounted by a Crown.	Upon Crossed lances in gilt metal the Prince of Wales's Plume. The Plume and motto in silver. The coronet in gilt metal. Above the Plume the Crown, below it the figure "XII." in gilt metal. The lower part of the pennons in silver.	On a gilt or gilding metal plate in silver, the Royal Arms, with the Prince of Wales's Plume above, and the sphinx over Egypt below. Below, on gilt or gilding metal scrolls, the honours; the outer ends of the scrolls finish in sprays of laurel.	The Royal Cypher surmounted by a Crown in gilt or gilding metal.

II:34/cont. 1911 Dress Regulations, Descriptions/cont.

Regiment.	On Buttons.	On Collar of Tunic, Mess Jacket and Frock Coat.	On Full Dress Head-dress.	On the Pouch.
16th (The Queen's) Lancers.	A Crown with "Q.L." below. 16	In silver, the figures "16" and a scroll below inscribed "The Queen's Lancers." On a pair of crossed lances, between the pennons, a Crown; the lower part of the pennons in silver, the remainder of the lances and the Crown in gilt or gilding metal.	The universal plate in gilt or gilding metal. On the plate, in silver, the Royal Arms. On the lower part of the plate, silver scrolls inscribed with the honours of the regiment. In the centre of the plate at the bottom a silver scroll inscribed "Sixteenth Lancers."	In gilt metal the Cypher of Queen Charlotte, within the Garter.
17th (Duke of Cambridge's Own) Lancers.	Full dome, gilt, burnished, with the death's head.	*On Tunic and Mess Jacket:—* No badge. *On Frock Coat:—* In silver, the death's head and scroll, inscribed "Or Glory."	On a gilt or gilding metal plate, in silver, the Royal Arms with the death's head and scroll, inscribed "Or Glory." A second scroll below inscribed "Seventeenth Lancers." The letters D.C.O. On the right a branch of laurel, on the left a branch of oak; on the sprays, scrolls inscribed with the honours of the regiment.	The Royal Cypher and Crown in gilt or gilding metal.
21st (Empress of India's) Lancers.	Scalloped edge. Between the numerals "XXI," a pair of upright lances. Between the pennons a Crown.	In gilt or gilding metal, a pair of crossed lances; between the lances the Imperial Cypher of H.M. Queen Victoria, "V.R.I.," and Crown; upon the staves, "XXI." The lower part of the pennons in silver.	In silver, on crossed lances, the Royal Arms with a scroll below, inscribed "Khartoum." Below the scroll the Imperial Cypher of H.M. Queen Victoria, "V.R.I." On the right a spray of laurel with a scroll below, inscribed "21st (Empress of," and on the left, palm leaves with a scroll below, inscribed "India's) Lancers."	The Imperial Cypher of H.M. Queen Victoria, "V.R.I." and Crown in gilt or gilding metal.

II:34/cont. 1911 Dress Regulations, Descriptions/cont.

Regiment.	On Buttons.	On Collar of Tunic, Mess Jacket, and Frock Serge.
Grenadier Guards.	The Royal Cypher reversed and interlaced, surmounted by the Crown; a grenade beneath the Cypher in the centre.	*Tunic:*—A grenade in silver embroidery, on a gold lace ground. *Mess Jacket and Frock:*—A grenade in gold embroidery.
Coldstream Guards.	The Star of the Order of the Garter.	*Tunic:*—In silver embroidery on a gold lace ground, the Star of the Order of the Garter, the Garter and motto in gold; the cross in scarlet silk. *Mess Jacket and Frock:*—A similar badge, but not on a gold lace ground.
Scots Guards.	The Star of the Order of the Thistle, with Crown in place of the upper point of the Star.	*Tunic:*—The Thistle in silver embroidery on a gold ground. *Mess Jacket and Frock:*—The Star of the Order of the Thistle in silver embroidery.
Irish Guards.	The Harp and Crown	*Tunic:*—A shamrock leaf in silver embroidery on a gold ground. *Mess Jacket and Frock:*—A star as for forage cap, embroidered in silver and colours.

II:34/cont. 1911 Dress Regulations, Descriptions/cont.

Regiment.	On Buttons.	On Collar of Tunic, Mess Jacket, and Frock Coat.	On Helmet-Plates.
The Queen's (Royal West Surrey Regiment).	Within a circle surmounted by the Crown, the Paschal Lamb. Below the lamb "1661." On the circle "The Royal West Surrey Regiment." Below the circle a scroll inscribed "The Queen's." For the mess dress, plain gold—the Lamb in silver mounted.—two sizes. For the cap, the Lamb on a plain dome.	The Paschal Lamb, in frosted gilt or gilding metal, in pairs. In silver, a scroll below inscribed "The Queen's." For the mess jacket, the badge is in gold, silver and crimson embroidery, without a scroll.	On a scarlet velvet ground, the Paschal Lamb in silver. On the universal scroll "The Royal West Surrey Regiment." Above the Garter a silver scroll inscribed "The Queen's."
The Buffs (East Kent Regiment).	A circle surmounted by a Crown. On the circle "The East Kent Regiment. The Buffs;" within, the Dragon; below, on a scroll, "*Veteri frondescit honore.*" For the mess dress, plain gilt. The Dragon over a scroll inscribed, "The Buffs," in silver—mounted. For the cap, the same design, die-struck.	The Dragon in silver, in pairs.	On a black velvet ground, the Dragon, in silver. On the universal scroll, "The East Kent Regiment." Above the Garter a silver scroll inscribed "The Buffs."
The King's Own (Royal Lancaster Regiment).	The Lion of England with Crown above and Rose below. On circle "The King's Own Royal Lancaster Regiment." For the mess dress, "K.O.R.L." in monogram, with the crown above. For the cap, the Lion of England with Crown above and Rose below. Die-struck.	The Lion, in silver, in pairs.	In silver, on a crimson velvet ground, the Lion of England. On the universal scroll, "Royal Lancaster Regiment." Above the Garter, a silver scroll inscribed "The King's Own."
The Royal Warwickshire Regiment.	An antelope with collar and chain within a circle inscribed "The Royal Warwickshire Regiment." The circle surmounted by the Crown. For the mess dress, the button is mounted. The Antelope in silver, within the Garter. For the cap, gilt, same design as for mess dress but die-struck.	In frosted silver, the Antelope, with gilt or gilding metal collar and chain, in pairs.	On a black velvet ground, the Antelope, in silver, with gilt or gilding metal collar and chain. On the universal scroll, "The Royal Warwickshire Regiment."

II:34/cont. 1911 Dress Regulations, Descriptions/cont.

Regiment.	On Buttons.	On Collar of Tunic, Mess Jacket, and Frock Coat.	On Helmet-Plates.
The King's (Liverpool Regiment).	A circle surmounted by the Crown within a laurel wreath; the circle inscribed "The Liverpool Regiment"; within the circle, the White Horse, with a scroll above inscribed "*Nec aspera terrent.*" Scroll on wreath at the bottom inscribed "The King's." For the mess dress, the button is mounted, design as for collar badge, a scroll above inscribed, "*Nec aspera terrent,*" all gilt. For the cap, the button is gilt, die-struck; device the White Horse with scroll below inscribed "The King's."	In silver, the White Horse. A gilt or gilding metal scroll below, inscribed "The King's," in pairs.	In silver, on a crimson velvet ground, the White Horse, with scroll above inscribed in old English capitals, "*Nec aspera terrent.*" On the universal scroll, "The Liverpool Regiment." Above the Garter a silver scroll inscribed "The King's."
The Norfolk Regiment.	On the circle, "The Norfolk Regiment"; within the circle the figure of Britannia holding an olive branch in the right hand; the trident rests against the left shoulder. For the mess dress the figure of Britannia in silver, mounted on a flat gilt button. For the cap, the same design, die-struck, all in gilt.	The figure of Britannia, in gilt or gilding metal, in pairs.	The figure of Britannia, in silver, on a black velvet ground. On the universal scroll "The Norfolk Regiment."
The Lincolnshire Regiment.	Within a laurel wreath, a circle surmounted by the Crown. On the circle "The Lincolnshire Regt." within, the Sphinx over Egypt. For the mess dress, plain gilt; the Sphinx over Egypt in silver —mounted For the cap, the same design, die-struck.	On a silver diamond-cut eight-pointed star, a circle in gilt or gilding metal, inscribed "Lincolnshire Regiment." Within the circle, on a ground of blue velvet, the Sphinx over Egypt, in silver.	In silver, on a black velvet ground, the Sphinx over Egypt. On the universal scroll "The Lincolnshire Regt."

II:34/cont. 1911 Dress Regulations, Descriptions/cont.

Regiment.	On Buttons.	On Collar of Tunic, Mess Jacket, and Frock Coat.	On Helmet-Plates.
The Devonshire Regiment.	On an eight-pointed star a circle surmounted by the Crown. On the circle, "The Devonshire Regt."; within, the Castle of Exeter. For the mess dress, the design is in silver, mounted.	In gilt or gilding metal, on a diamond cut, silver eight pointed star, a circle surmounted by the Crown. On the circle, "The Devonshire Regiment"; within, in silver, the Castle of Exeter with scroll inscribed "*Semper fidelis*," on a ground of blue velvet.	The Castle of Exeter, with scroll inscribed "*Semper fidelis*," in silver, on a black velvet ground. On the universal scroll, "The Devonshire Regt."
The Suffolk Regiment.	Within a laurel wreath, the Castle and Key with scroll above, inscribed "Gibraltar," and above the scroll, the Crown. Below the Castle and Key, two scrolls, the upper inscribed "*Montis insignia Calpe*," the lower "The Suffolk Regt." For the mess dress the Castle in silver—mounted. For the cap, the same design, die-struck.	In gold embroidery the Castle and Key, within a laurel wreath, surmounted by a crown.	In silver, on a black velvet ground, the Castle and Key, with scroll above inscribed "Gibraltar," and scroll below inscribed "*Montis Insignia Calpe*." On the universal scroll, "The Suffolk Regiment."
The Prince Albert's (Somersetshire Light Infantry).	Within a laurel wreath a circle surmounted by a mural crown. On the circle, "The Prince Albert's"; within, a bugle with strings. For the mess dress—the bugle surmounted by a mural crown, with a scroll above inscribed "Jellalabad"—the whole in silver—mounted on a flat gilt button. For the cap, the same design, die-struck.	In gold and silver embroidery, on a ground of green cloth, a bugle with strings, surmounted by a mural crown embroidered in silver; above the crown in gold embroidery, a scroll inscribed, "Jellalabad."	In silver on a black velvet ground, a bugle with strings surmounted by a mural crown with scroll above inscribed "Jellalabad"; the Sphinx over Egypt within the strings of the bugle. On the scroll, "Somersetshire Light Infantry."
The Prince of Wales's Own (West Yorkshire Regiment).	The Tiger, within a circle, inscribed at the top, "India" and at the bottom, "Waterloo." Outside the circle "Prince of Wales's Own, West Yorkshire." For mess dress, the Tiger mounted in silver. For cap, the same design in gilt.	The Prince of Wales's Plume, in gold and silver embroidery.	In silver, on a scarlet velvet ground, the White Horse, with motto "*Nec aspera terrent*" on a scroll above. On the universal scroll, "The West Yorkshire Regiment."

II:34/cont. 1911 Dress Regulations, Descriptions/cont.

Regiment.	On Buttons.	On Collar of Tunic, Mess Jacket, and Frock Coat.	On Helmet-Plates.
The East Yorkshire Regiment.	A laurel wreath on an eight-pointed star. The White Rose within the wreath. For the mess dress, the button is mounted, the white rose in silver.	In gilt or gilding metal, an eight-pointed star; on the star a laurel wreath; within the wreath, on a ground of black enamel the White Rose, in silver.	In gilt or gilding metal, on a ground of black enamel, a laurel wreath on an eight-pointed star. Within the wreath the White Rose, in silver. On the universal scroll, "The East Yorkshire Regiment."
The Bedfordshire Regiment.	On an eight-pointed star, a Maltese cross. On the cross, a circle inscribed "Bedfordshire." Within the circle, a Hart crossing a ford. For the mess dress the button is mounted.	In dead gilt or gilding metal, a Hart crossing a ford; the water in silver. On a scroll below, "Bedfordshire."	In silver, on a black velvet ground, an eight-pointed star; on the star, in gilt or gilding metal, a Maltese cross. Within a gilt or gilding metal circle on the cross in silver, a Hart crossing a ford, the Hart on blue enamel. On the universal scroll, "The Bedfordshire Regiment."
The Leicestershire Regiment.	Within a laurel wreath the Royal Tiger, with scroll above, inscribed "Hindoostan," and scroll below, inscribed "Leicestershire." For the mess dress, the Tiger in silver mounted on a flat gilt button.	The Royal Tiger, in silver, within a wreath in gilt or gilding metal.	On a black velvet ground, the Royal Tiger, in silver, with silver scroll above inscribed "Hindoostan." On the universal scroll, "The Leicestershire Regiment."
The Royal Irish Regiment.	Within a shamrock wreath, a circle inscribed "*Virtutis namurcensis præmium.*" Within the circle, the Harp; the circle surmounted by the Crown. In the cap and mess dress buttons the circle is omitted. The mess dress button mounted, design in silver.	In silver, an Escutcheon of the arms of Nassau, with a silver scroll below, inscribed "*Virtutis namurcensis præmium.*"	In silver, on a scarlet ground, the Harp and Crown within a wreath of shamrock. On the universal scroll, "The Royal Irish Regiment."

II:34/cont. 1911 Dress Regulations, Descriptions/cont.

Regiment.	On Buttons.	On Collar of Tunic, Mess Jacket, and Frock Coat.	On Helmet-Plates.
Alexandra, Princess of Wales's Own (Yorkshire Regiment).	The Cypher of H.M. Queen Alexandra as Princess of Wales, combined with the Dannebrog, and surmounted by the Coronet of the Princess. On the cross the figures "1875." On scroll below, "The Princess of Wales's Own." For the mess dress, the Dannebrog, Cypher and Coronet are in silver — mounted. The scroll is omitted. For the cap, the same design, die-struck.	The Cypher of H.M. Queen Alexandra as Princess of Wales, combined with the Dannebrog. The Cypher and Coronet in gold embroidery on a crimson velvet cap; the cross in silver embroidery.	On a black velvet ground, the Cypher of H. M. Queen Alexandra as Princess of Wales, combined with the Dannebrog, and surmounted by the Coronet of the Princess, in silver metal. On the centre of the cross, the figures "1875" and the word "Alexandra." On a scroll in silver metal, "The Princess of Wales's Own Yorkshire Regiment." The White Rose in the centre of the scroll.
The Cheshire Regiment.	On an eight-pointed star, a circle with acorn and oak-leaves in the centre. On the circle, "The Cheshire Regiment."	Acorn with oak-leaves. The leaves and cup in dead gilt or gilding metal; the acorn in burnished silver.	In silver, on a black velvet ground, an eight-pointed star. Within a gilt or gilding metal circle on the star, the Prince of Wales's Plume on a burnished silver ground. The plume in silver, the coronet in gilt or gilding metal. On the universal scroll, "The Cheshire Regiment."
The South Wales Borderers.	The Welsh Dragon within a wreath of laurel. For the mess dress, the dragon, in silver, mounted on a flat gilt button.	The Sphinx over Egypt in dead gilt or gilding metal.	In silver, on a black velvet ground, the Welsh Dragon, within a laurel wreath. On the universal scroll "The South Wales Borderers."
The Gloucestershire Regiment.	Within a laurel wreath of single leaves, inclining inwards, the Royal Crest above the monogram G.R. For the mess dress the wreath is omitted and the design is engraved, on a flat gilt button. For the cap, the Royal Crest on a plain gilt button die-struck.	In dead gilt metal on two twigs of laurel, the Sphinx over Egypt. On collar of mess jacket the badge is in embroidery, but smaller.	In silver, on a black velvet ground, the Sphinx over Egypt. On the universal scroll, "The Gloucestershire Regiment." Badge for back of helmet—in dead gilt or gilding metal, the Sphinx over Egypt within a laurel wreath.

II:34/cont. 1911 Dress Regulations, Descriptions/cont.

Regiment.	On Buttons.	On Collar of Tunic, Mess Jacket, and Frock Coat.	On Helmet-Plates.
The Worcestershire Regiment.	On an eight-pointed star, a circle surmounted by the Crown. The circle inscribed "The Worcestershire Regiment." Within the circle, a lion. Below the circle a scroll, inscribed "*Firm.*" For the mess dress the design is engraved on a flat gilt button, the Crown omitted, and Garter substituted for circle.	On a silver eight-pointed elongated star, in gilt or gilding metal, the Garter with motto; within the Garter, in silver, the Lion pierced on a black velvet ground. Below the Garter, in gilt or gilding metal, a scroll inscribed "*Firm.*"	On a black velvet ground, a silver, eight-pointed elongated star. On the star, in gilt or gilding metal, the Garter with motto. Within the Garter, the Lion, in silver on a black velvet ground. Below the Garter, a scroll in gilt or gilding metal, inscribed "*Firm.*" On the universal scroll, "The Worcestershire Regiment."
The East Lancashire Regiment.	Within a circle inscribed "The East Lancashire Regiment," the Sphinx over Egypt; below the Sphinx, the Rose of Lancaster. For the mess dress the sphinx and rose in silver, mounted on a flat gilt button. For the cap, the same design on a plain gilt button, die-struck.	The Rose of Lancaster, in red velvet and gold embroidery.	In silver, on a black velvet ground, the Sphinx over Egypt. On the universal scroll, "The East Lancashire Regiment."
The East Surrey Regiment.	On an eight-pointed star, a circle surmounted by the Crown. The circle inscribed "East Surrey," with two twigs of laurel in the lower bend. Within the circle, the arms of Guildford. For the mess dress the design is mounted.	On a diamond cut silver star, the arms of Guildford in silver on a shield in frosted gilt or gilding metal, with burnished edges, surmounted by a gilt or gilding metal Crown.	In silver, on a black velvet ground, an eight-pointed diamond cut star; on the star, badge as for collar, but without the Crown. On the universal scroll "The East Surrey Regt."
The Duke of Cornwall's Light Infantry.	Within the designation "Duke of Cornwall's Light Infy.," a bugle with strings, surmounted by the Coronet of the Prince of Wales, and gateway as shown on His Royal Highness's Great Seal as Duke of Cornwall. For the mess dress, the design in silver mounted; the title is omitted. For the cap as for mess dress, but die-struck.	In black enamel set in gilt or gilding metal, the badge of the County of Cornwall, surmounted by the Coronet of the Prince of Wales, in gilt or gilding metal, as shown on His Royal Highness's Great Seal as Duke of Cornwall. On a scroll the motto "*One and All,*" pierced in gilt or gilding metal letters on a ground of blue velvet.	In gilt or gilding metal, on a ground of dark green velvet, a bugle with strings. On the strings of the bugle two red feathers set in gilt or gilding metal. On the stem of the feathers, in silver, a turreted archway. On the universal scroll "The Duke of Cornwall's Lt. Infy."

II:34/cont. 1911 Dress Regulations, Descriptions/cont.

Regiment.	On Buttons.	On Collar of Tunic, Mess Jacket, and Frock Coat.	On Helmet-Plates.
The Duke of Wellington's (West Riding Regiment).	Within the designation "The Duke of Wellington's West Riding Regt." the Elephant with howdah. For the mess vest the Elephant and howdah in silver—mounted on a flat gilt button. On mess jacket the small tunic button is worn. For the cap, the title is omitted.	The Elephant in dead gilt or gilding metal, with howdah in silver. On the mess jacket, the Duke of Wellington's Crest in gold embroidery. The flag in silver, within a gold edging. The Cross scarlet.	In silver, on a black velvet ground, the Crest of the Duke of Wellington, with motto on a scroll below, "*Virtutis fortuna comes.*" On the universal scroll, "The West Riding Regiment."
The Border Regiment.	The Dragon of China, with the word "China" above. For the mess dress the design is as for the collar badge, with the lions and scroll omitted, in silver—mounted on a gilt flat button. For the cap—the dragon.	In silver, a laurel wreath; on the wreath a Maltese cross with a Lion between each division. On the divisions of the cross, the honours of the Regiment. On the centre of the cross a raised circle inscribed "*Arroyo dos Molinos,*" "1811." Within the circle, on a ground of red enamel, the Dragon of China in silver and the word "China," on a silver ground. Below the wreath a scroll inscribed "The Border Regt."	As for collar, but the Dragon and "China" in gold, and the upper part of the centre filled in with white enamel.
The Royal Sussex Regiment.	Within a circle inscribed "The Royal Sussex Regt.," a Maltese cross on a feather; on centre of cross a wreath; within the wreath, St. George's Cross. For the mess dress the buttons are mounted. The circle and titles are omitted. For the cap, same design, but die-struck.	A Maltese cross, in gilt or gilding metal, on a feather in silver; on the cross a wreath in silver and green enamel; on the wreath the Garter and motto in blue enamel set with silver. Within the circle the Cross of St. George in red enamel set with silver, on a silver ground. On the mess jacket the feather in silver embroidery with the stem gilt. On the feather the star of the order of the Garter in gold embroidery. The centre of the star as in tunic badge.	On a scarlet velvet ground, badge as for collar. On the universal scroll, "The Royal Sussex Regiment."

II:34/cont. 1911 Dress Regulations, Descriptions/cont.

Regiment.	On Buttons.	On Collar of Tunic, Mess Jacket, and Frock Coat.	On Helmet-Plates.
The Hampshire Regiment.	Within a laurel wreath the Royal Tiger; below the Tiger, the Hampshire Rose. For the mess dress the design is in silver—mounted.	The Hampshire Rose, in gold and red and green embroidery.	On a black velvet ground, the Royal Tiger, in gilt or gilding metal, within a laurel wreath, in silver. On the universal scroll "The Hampshire Regt."
The South Staffordshire Regiment.	The Staffordshire Knot with Crown above. For the mess dress the design in silver, mounted on a flat gilt button.	The Staffordshire Knot, in gold embroidery.	In silver, on a black velvet ground, the Sphinx over Egypt. On the universal scroll, "The South Staffordshire Regiment."
The Dorsetshire Regiment.	The Castle and Key. Above the Castle, a scroll, inscribed "Gibraltar," and one below, inscribed "*Primus in Indis.*" Above the top scroll, "The Dorsetshire Regt."; below the bottom scroll, the Sphinx on a tablet inscribed "Marabout." For the cap, the title and "*Primus in Indis*" are omitted. For the mess dress, the Castle and Key in silver—mounted on a flat gilt button.	The Sphinx in silver, on a gilt or gilding metal tablet. On the tablet "Marabout" in gilt or gilding metal letters on a ground of green enamel.	In silver, on a black velvet ground, the Castle and Key. A scroll above the Castle inscribed "*Primus in Indis*," and one below, inscribed "*Montis insignia Calpe.*" On the universal scroll "The Dorsetshire Regiment."

II:34/cont. 1911 Dress Regulations, Descriptions/cont.

Regiment.	On Buttons.	On Collar of Tunic, Mess Jacket, and Frock Coat.	On Helmet-Plates.
The Prince of Wales's Volunteers (South Lancashire Regiment).	Within a scroll inscribed "The Prince of Wales's Vols.," and a laurel branch issuing from either end, a circle surmounted by the Crown. On the circle, "The South Lancashire Regiment"; within, the Prince of Wales's Plume above the Sphinx over "Egypt." For the mess dress the button is mounted. The plume in silver. The monogram P.W.V. in gilt metal below. For the cap, the same design die-struck.	The Prince of Wales's Plume, in gold and silver embroidery, on a blue cloth ground; the scroll in blue silk, with the motto in silver embroidery.	In silver, on a black velvet ground, the Sphinx over "Egypt." On the universal scroll, "South Lancashire Regiment."
The Welsh Regiment.	Within a laurel wreath, a circle surmounted by the Crown. On the circle, "The Welsh Regiment"; within, the Prince of Wales's Plume. For the mess dress and cap the Prince of Wales's Plume. For the former it is in silver-mounted.	In silver, the Prince of Wales's Plume with a scroll below bearing the motto "Gwell angau na chywilydd."	In silver, on a black velvet ground, the Prince of Wales's Plume, with scroll below inscribed "Gwell angau na chywilydd." The coronet in gilt or gilding metal. On the universal scroll, "The Welsh Regiment."
The Oxfordshire and Buckinghamshire Light Infantry.	Scalloped edge; within a laurel wreath a bugle with strings; below the bugle, "Oxfordshire and Buckinghamshire." For the mess dress and cap a plain edged button. On the button, within a laurel wreath, a bugle with strings; above the bugle, the Crown; below the wreath "Oxfordshire and Buckinghamshire."	Plain edged buttons, as on mess dress. A loop of gold Russia cord 2½-inches long attached to the button, connecting it with front edge of collar of tunic. On the frock coat the cord is dark blue. No badge on mess jacket.	In silver, on a ground of black enamel, a bugle with strings. On the universal scroll, "The Oxfordshire and Buckinghamshire Lt. Infy."
The Essex Regiment.	Within an oak-leaf wreath, an eagle and the Castle and Key below. For mess dress, a gilt burnished button with the eagle in silver. For the cap, the county badge instead of the eagle, with the Sphinx above.	The County Badge. The Shield in gilt or gilding metal; the blades of the seaxes in silver. On the mess jacket, an eagle on a plain tablet in gilt or gilding metal.	An oak-leaf wreath is substituted for the universal wreath. In silver on a black velvet ground, the Castle and Key, with the Sphinx over "Egypt" above, and a scroll below, inscribed "Montis insignia Calpe." On the universal scroll, "The Essex Regt."

II:34/cont. 1911 Dress Regulations, Descriptions/cont.

Regiment.	On Buttons.	On Collar of Tunic, Mess Jacket, and Frock Coat.	On Helmet-Plates.
The Sherwood Foresters (Nottinghamshire and Derbyshire Regiment).	A Maltese cross surmounted by the Crown: within an oak-leaf wreath on the cross a Stag lodged. A half-scroll on the left division of the cross, inscribed "Sherwood"; another on the right division, inscribed "Foresters." On the lower division a scroll inscribed "Notts and Derby." For the mess dress the button is mounted, in gilt metal.	A Maltese cross surmounted by the Crown, in silver. Wreath and scrolls in gilt or gilding metal, as for buttons. Within the wreath a stag lodged, in silver, on a ground of blue enamel.	In the helmet-plate, the Garter, with motto, is omitted. Within the universal wreath, a Maltese cross, in silver. On the cross, in gilt or gilding metal, an oakleaf wreath; within the wreath, on a ground of blue enamel, a stag lodged, in silver. In gilt or gilding metal, on the left division of the cross, the word "The"; on the right division, "Regt.," and on a scroll on the lower division "Notts and Derby." A scroll of special pattern on the bottom of the universal wreath inscribed "Sherwood Foresters."
The Loyal North Lancashire Regiment.	Within a wreath the Arms of the City of Lincoln, surmounted by the Royal Crest, above the Crest the word "Tarifa," and inscribed "Loyal North Lancashire."	*On tunic and frock coat:*—In embroidery, the Arms of the City of Lincoln. The ground of the shield in silver, the Cross of St. George in red silk on the shield; the *fleur-de-lis* in gold on the cross. *On mess jacket:*—Centre of helmet plate, in pairs	In silver, on a black velvet ground, the Royal Crest. Below the Crest, the Rose of Lancaster in silver gilt and red and green enamel. On the universal scroll. "Loyal North Lancashire Regiment."
The Northamptonshire Regiment.	Within a scroll, inscribed "The Northamptonshire Regiment," the Castle and Key, with the Crown above. For the cap, the scroll is omitted. For the mess dress the button is plain gilt with the Castle and Key mounted in silver.	In gilt or gilding metal within a laurel wreath, a gilt or gilding metal circle pierced "Northamptonshire"; the ground of blue enamel. In relief within the circle, on a raised ground of blue enamel, the Cross of St. George, in silver. Below the cross, and on the wreath, a horse shoe in silver. The circle surmounted by a Crown in gilt or gilding metal.	In silver, on a black velvet ground, the Castle and Key; on a scroll above, "Gibraltar," on a scroll below, "Talavera." On the universal scroll, "The Northamptonshire Regiment."

II:34/cont. 1911 Dress Regulations, Descriptions/cont.

Regiment.	On Buttons.	On Collar of Tunic, Mess Jacket, and Frock Coat.	On Helmet-Plates.
Princess Charlotte of Wales's (Royal Berkshire Regiment).	A circle inscribed "P⁸ Charlotte of Wales"; within the circle, the Dragon of China; above the Dragon, the Crown; below, "R. Berks." For the mess dress the Dragon and Crown are mounted on a plain gilt button. For the cap, the Dragon and Crown with "R. Berks" below.	The Dragon of China, in gold embroidery on a blue cloth ground.	In silver, on a scarlet cloth ground, a Stag under an oak. On the universal scroll, "Royal Berkshire Regiment."
The Queen's Own (Royal West Kent Regiment).	The Royal Crest. For the mess dress, the design is mounted in silver.	The Royal Crest, in gold embroidery.	In silver, on a black velvet ground, the White Horse of Kent above a scroll inscribed "*Invicta*." Above the Horse, another scroll with motto "*Quo fas et gloria ducunt.*" On the universal scroll, "The Royal West Kent Regiment."
The King's Own (Yorkshire Light Infantry).	A French horn surmounted by the Crown. In the centre of the horn the white rose in silver. For the mess waistcoat, the button is mounted, with monogram of regiment surmounted by the Crown. For the service dress the buttons are entirely of gilding metal, die-struck.	A French horn, in gold embroidery; in the centre of the horn, on a raised ground of dark green cloth, the White Rose in silver.	In silver, on a black enamel ground, a French horn with the White Rose in the centre. On the universal scroll, "The King's Own Yorkshire Light Infantry."
The King's (Shropshire Light Infantry).	A circle surmounted by the Crown. On the circle "Shropshire," with two twigs of laurel in the lower bend. Within the circle, the monogram "K.L.I." For the mess dress the button is mounted.	A bugle with strings, in gold embroidery, on a ground of dark blue cloth.	In silver, on a ground of dark green enamel a bugle with strings. In gilt or gilding metal, within the strings of the bugle, the cypher "K.L.I." On the universal scroll, "King's Shropshire Lt. Infty."

II:34/cont. 1911 Dress Regulations, Descriptions/cont.

Regiment.	On Buttons.	On Collar of Tunic, Mess Jacket, and Frock Coat.	On Helmet-Plates.
The Duke of Cambridge's Own (Middlesex Regiment).	Within a wreath of laurel, the Prince of Wales's Plume; on the bottom of the wreath a scroll inscribed "Albuhera." For the mess dress the design is in silver, mounted.	In silver, a laurel wreath; within the wreath, the Prince of Wales's Plume; below the Plume, the Coronet and Cypher of H.R.H. the *late* George, Duke of Cambridge; on the lower bend of the wreath, "Albuhera."	In silver, on a black velvet ground, a laurel wreath; within the wreath the Prince of Wales's Plume; below the Plume, the Coronet and Cypher of H.R.H. the *late* George, Duke of Cambridge. On the bottom of the wreath a scroll inscribed "Albuhera." On the universal scroll "The Middlesex Regt."
The Duke of Edinburgh's (Wiltshire Regiment).	The Cypher of H.R.H. the *late* Alfred, Duke of Edinburgh, with Coronet above, and "Wiltshire Regiment" below. For the mess dress the design is in silver—mounted in two sizes; the title is omitted. For the cap same as for mess dress, but gilt, die-struck.	A cross patee in lined silver, with burnished edges. On the cross, a circular convex plate, in burnished silver. On the plate, in gilt or gilding metal, the Coronet within the Cypher.	On a black velvet ground, a cross patee in lined gilt or gilding metal, with burnished edges. On the cross, a circular convex burnished plate. On the plate, in silver, the Cypher surmounted by the Coronet. On the universal scroll, "The Wiltshire Regiment."
The Manchester Regiment.	The Garter, with motto, "*Honi soit qui mal y pense.*" Within the Garter, the Sphinx over Egypt with the Crown above. For the mess dress the design is mounted in silver.	The Sphinx over Egypt in gold embroidery; the word "Egypt" embroidered in silver.	In silver, on a black velvet ground, the arms with motto of the City of Manchester. On the universal scroll, "The Manchester Regiment."

II:34/cont. 1911 Dress Regulations, Descriptions/cont.

Regiment.	On Buttons.	On Collar of Tunic, Mess Jacket, and Frock Coat.	On Helmet Plates.
The Prince of Wales's (North Staffordshire Regiment).	Within a scroll inscribed "Prince of Wales's" and a laurel branch issuing from either end, a circle inscribed "The North Staffordshire Regiment"; within the circle, the Staffordshire Knot; above the circle, the Prince of Wales's Plume. For the mess dress the button is mounted and the Knot and Plume are in silver.	The Staffordshire Knot surmounted by the Prince of Wales's Plume. The plume in silver, the remainder of the badge in gilt metal.	In silver, on a black velvet ground, the Prince of Wales's Plume. On the universal scroll, "The North Staffordshire Regiment."
The York and Lancaster Regiment.	A scroll inscribed "The York and Lancaster Regiment"; within the scroll, a laurel wreath; within the wreath the Royal Tiger; above the Tiger, a Coronet. On the wreath, at the bottom, the Union Rose. For the mess dress the tiger and rose in silver mounted on a plain gilt button. For the cap as for mess dress, gilt, die-struck.	The Royal Tiger, in dead gilt or gilding metal, the rose above in gilt or gilding metal and silver.	In silver and gilt or gilding metal, on a black velvet ground, the Union Rose. On the universal scroll, "The York & Lancaster Regiment."
The Durham Light Infantry.	Bugle, with the Crown on the strings. For the mess dress "D.L.I." in monogram with the Crown above.	Bugle with strings, in gold embroidery.	In silver, on a dark green velvet ground, a bugle with strings. On the universal scroll, "The Durham Light Infantry."
The Connaught Rangers.	Scalloped edge. Within a wreath of shamrock, the Harp surmounted by a Crown; on the lower part of the wreath a scroll inscribed "*Quis separabit.*" For the mess dress, the letters "C.R." on a lined button with a raised edge.	On tunic and frock coat— The Elephant, in silver. On mess jacket collar— The Harp and Crown in gold embroidery, strings in silver.	In silver, on a dark green velvet ground, the Harp, with scroll, inscribed "*Quis separabit.*" A sprig of laurel issues from either end of the scroll. On the universal scroll, "The Connaught Rangers."
The Prince of Wales's Leinster Regiment (Royal Canadians).	A Circle, inscribed "Prince of Wales's Leinster Regiment"; within the circle, the Prince of Wales's Plume. For the mess dress the plume in silver —mounted on a plain gilt button. For the cap, same as mess dress, but gilt, die-struck.	The Prince of Wales's Plume, in silver; the Coronet in gilt or gilding metal.	In silver, on a black velvet ground, the Prince of Wales's Plume over two maple leaves. The Coronet in gilt or gilding metal. On a scroll, beneath the leaves, "Central India." On the universal scroll, "Prince of Wales's Leinster Regiment."

II:34/cont. 1911 Dress Regulations, Descriptions/cont.

Regiment.	On Buttons.	On Collar of Tunic, Mess Jacket, and Frock Coat.	Ornaments for Bearskin or Racoon-skin Caps.
The Northumberland Fusiliers.	St. George and the Dragon within a circle inscribed "*Quo fata vocant.*" For the mess dress the button is mounted. Ring with motto in gilt, dragon, &c., in silver.	A grenade in gold embroidery, with St. George and the Dragon in silver on the ball. Smaller pattern for mess jacket.	A grenade in gilt or gilding metal. Mounted on the ball, a circle inscribed "*Quo fata vocant*"; within the circle, St. George and the Dragon.
The Royal Fusiliers (City of London Regiment).	The Garter, inscribed "*Honi soit qui mal y pense,*" on the Garter at the top, the Crown; within, the Rose. For the mess dress, "R.F." in monogram, surmounted by the crown—mounted.	*On tunic and frock coat.*—A grenade, in silver embroidery, with the White Rose, in gilt metal on the ball. *On mess jacket.*—A small grenade, in gold embroidery, with the white rose, in silver, on the ball.	In gilt or gilding metal, a grenade; mounted on the ball, the Garter, surmounted by the Crown. The Garter pierced with the motto; the ground of blue enamel. Within the Garter, the Rose; below the Garter, in silver, the White Horse.
The Lancashire Fusiliers.	Within a wreath of laurel, the Sphinx over "Egypt," with the Crown above. For the mess dress, the button is mounted.	A grenade, in gold embroidery. On the mess jacket the grenade is smaller.	A grenade in gilt or gilding metal; mounted on the ball, in silver, the Sphinx over "Egypt" within a laurel wreath.
The Royal Welsh Fusiliers.	Within a beaded circle the Prince of Wales's Plume surrounded by the designation "The Royal Welsh Fusiliers." For the cap and mess dress, a gilt-lined button with burnished edge, below the plume, "R.W.F."	*On tunic and frock coat.*—A grenade, in silver embroidery. *On mess jacket.*—A grenade in gold embroidery, with a Dragon in silver on the ball. A five-tailed flash of black silk ribbon is worn on the back of the collar of the tunic; the flash is worn with the tunic only.	A grenade in gilt or gilding metal; the Prince of Wales's Plume, mounted in silver on the ball.
The Royal Inniskilling Fusiliers.	A castle with three turrets with St. George's colours flying superscribed "Inniskilling." For the mess dress the castle is in silver—mounted on a plain gilt button. For the cap, the same design, die-struck.	A grenade in gold embroidery; the Castle, in silver, on the ball.	A grenade in gilt or gilding metal; the Castle mounted in silver, on the ball.
Princess Victoria's (Royal Irish Fusiliers).	Scalloped edge; an Eagle with a wreath of laurel; below the Eagle a small tablet inscribed with the figure "8." For the mess dress, plain edge with the eagle and tablet in silver—mounted. For the cap, as for mess dress, but die-struck.	1st Badge:—Coronet of H.R.H. the Princess Victoria in silver, worn nearer to the opening of the collar. 2nd Badge:—A grenade in gold embroidery, with badge on ball as for buttons, but in silver.	A grenade in gilt, or gilding metal. In silver on the ball, the Eagle with a wreath of laurel. Below the Eagle, a small tablet inscribed with the figure "8."

II:34/cont. 1911 Dress Regulations, Descriptions/cont.

Regiment.	On Buttons.	On Collar of Tunic, Mess Jacket, and Frock Coat.	Ornaments for Bearskin or Racoon-skin Caps.
The Royal Munster Fusiliers.	Within the designation, "Royal Munster Fusiliers," a grenade, with the Royal Tiger on the ball. For the mess dress, the Royal Tiger, in silver-mounted, on a plain gilt button. Same for cap, die-struck.	A grenade in gold embroidery, with the Royal Tiger, in silver, on the ball.	A grenade in gilt or gilding metal. Mounted on the ball a deep wreath of laurel intertwined with a scroll bearing the honours of the regiment. Within the wreath the Heraldic device for the Province of Munster, the Crowns in gilt or gilding metal, the shield in silver. On the bottom of the wreath, a scroll, in silver, inscribed "Royal Munster."
The Royal Dublin Fusiliers.	Within the designation "Royal Dublin Fusiliers," a grenade; on the ball of the grenade, the Crown. For the mess dress, the elephant and the tiger on separate buttons in silver, mounted. For the cap, the same design, die-struck.	A grenade in gold embroidery; mounted in silver, on the ball, the Royal Tiger; below the Tiger, the Elephant.	A grenade in gilt or gilding metal; mounted on the ball, in silver, the badge of the City of Dublin; below the shield—to the right, the Royal Tiger, on a silver tablet inscribed "Plassey," to the left, the Elephant, on a silver tablet inscribed "Mysore." Below the tablets a silver scroll inscribed "Spectamur agendo." In silver on either side of the shield, a rich mounting of shamrock leaves.

Regiment.	On Buttons.	On Collar of Doublet.	On Feather Bonnet.	On the F.S. Helmet and Glengarry Cap.	Special Badges.
The Black Watch (Royal Highlanders).	Within the designation "The Royal Highlanders, Black Watch," the Star of the Order of the Thistle, indented. On the centre of the Star, a circle; within the circle, St. Andrew and Cross.	St. Andrew and Cross, in silver.	In gilt metal the Sphinx over "Egypt."	In silver, diamond cut, the Star of the Order of the Thistle; in gilt or gilding metal on the Star, a thistle wreath. Within the wreath, in gilt or gilding metal, an oval surmounted by the Crown. The oval inscribed "Nemo me impune lacessit." Within the oval, on a recessed seeded ground, St. Andrew and Cross, in silver. Below the wreath, the Sphinx, in gilt or gilding metal. In silver, a half scroll, to the left of the Crown, inscribed "The Royal"; another to the right inscribed "Highlanders." A half scroll to the left of the Sphinx, inscribed "Black"; another to the right, inscribed "Watch."	**On the Waist Belt.** On a seeded gilt or gilding metal rectangular plate, with burnished edges, badge as for glengarry, but smaller. **On the Shoulder Belt.** Badge as for glengarry, but larger, on a gilt seeded rectangular plate with raised burnished edges. **Brooch Ornament.** In silver, on an engraved burnished plate, a thistle wreath. Within the wreath, on an open centre, St. Andrew and Cross.

Regiment.	On Buttons.	On Collar of Doublet.	On Feather Bonnet.	On the F.S. Helmet and Glengarry Cap.	Special Badges.
Seaforth Highlanders (Ross-shire Buffs, the Duke of Albany's).	Raised edge, a stag's head, with the Cypher of H.R.H. Leopold the *late* Duke of Albany above. A scroll below, inscribed "Seaforth Highlanders."	Two badges in gilt metal— I. The Cypher of H.R.H. Frederick the *late* Duke of York with scroll inscribed "*Caber Feidh.*" II. The Elephant. Both badges to be worn on each side of the collar, the Cypher next the hooks and eyes.	As for glengarry cap, but without the Coronet and Cypher.	In silver, a stag's head; above, the Coronet and Cypher of H. R. H. Leopold the *late* Duke of Albany; below a scroll inscribed "*Cuidich'n Righ.*"	On the Waist Belt. Burnished gilt or gilding metal rectangular plate. Badge as for feather bonnet except that it is smaller, and that the motto on scroll is "*Tulloch Ard.*" On the Shoulder Belt. Burnished gilt rectangular plate. In silver, the Coronet and Cypher of H.R.H. Frederick the *late* Duke of York, the Elephant, the stag's head, and scroll inscribed "Seaforth Highlanders." Brooch Ornament. In silver, a thistle wreath intertwined with a scroll bearing the honours of the regiment. Within the wreath badges as for glengarry cap without the scroll.
The Gordon Highlanders.	The Cross of St. Andrew; on the cross a thistle wreath joined to a scroll let into the upper divisions of the cross, and inscribed "Gordon Highlanders." Within the scroll, on the upper divisions of the cross, the Sphinx over Egypt; within the wreath on the lower divisions of the cross, the Royal Tiger over "India." Mounted buttons on mess vest.	The Royal Tiger, in gold embroidery.	In silver, the Crest of the Marquis of Huntly within an ivy wreath. On the bottom of the wreath, "*By-dand.*"	As for feather bonnet.	On the Waist Belt. Burnished gilt or gilding metal rectangular plate. In silver, badge as on buttons, but larger. On the Shoulder Belt. On a burnished gilt rectangular plate, in silver the star of the Order of the Thistle, diamond cut. On the top of the star the Sphinx over Egypt; on the lower part of the star the Tiger over India; on the centre, the Crest of the Marquis of Huntly, above a spray of thistles; above the crest a scroll inscribed "Gordon Highlanders," Brooch Ornament. In burnished silver, a plate with a scroll inscribed "Peninsula," "Egypt" on the right; "Waterloo," "India" on the left, and on the lower bend "Gordon Highlanders." On an open centre, badge as for headdresses.

II:34/cont. 1911 Dress Regulations, Descriptions/cont.

Regiment.	On Buttons.	On Collar of Doublet.	On Feather Bonnet.	On the F.S. Helmet and Glengarry Cap.	Special Badges.
The Gordon Highlanders.	The Cross of St. Andrew; on the cross a thistle wreath joined to a scroll let into the upper divisions of the cross, and inscribed "Gordon Highlanders." Within the scroll, on the upper divisions of the cross, the Sphinx over Egypt; within the wreath on the lower divisions of the cross, the Royal Tiger over "India." Mounted buttons on mess vest.	The Royal Tiger, in gold embroidery.	In silver, the Crest of the Marquis of Huntly within an ivy wreath. On the bottom of the wreath, "By-dand."	As for feather bonnet.	**On the Waist Belt.** Burnished gilt or gilding metal rectangular plate. In silver, badge as on buttons, but larger. **On the Shoulder Belt.** On a burnished gilt rectangular plate, in silver the star of the Order of the Thistle, diamond cut. On the top of the star the Sphinx over Egypt; on the lower part of the star the Tiger over India; on the centre, the Crest of the Marquis of Huntly, above a spray of thistles; above the crest a scroll inscribed "Gordon Highlanders." **Brooch Ornament.** In burnished silver, a plate with a scroll inscribed "Peninsula," "Egypt" on the right; "Waterloo," "India" on the left, and on the lower bend "Gordon Highlanders." On an open centre, badge as for headdresses.
The Queen's Own Cameron Highlanders.	Within the designation "The Queen's Own Cameron Highlanders," the Thistle surmounted by the Crown. On mess vest a plain gilt button with St. Andrew and Cross in silver, mounted.	The Thistle surmounted by the Crown in silver embroidery, on a blue cloth ground.	In silver, a thistle wreath; within the wreath, the figure of St. Andrew with Cross, with a scroll on the lower bend of the wreath inscribed "Cameron."	As for feather bonnet.	**On the Waist Belt.** Burnished gilt or gilding metal rectangular plate. In silver on the plate, a thistle wreath; within the wreath St. Andrew with Cross. **On the Shoulder Belt.** On a gilt seeded rectangular plate with raised burnished edges, the Cross of St. Andrew in cut bright silver with raised edges. On the Cross a gilt oval collar inscribed "The Queen's Own Cameron Highlanders," surmounted by a Crown. Within the collar, on a burnished ground, the thistle and Crown in silver. Below the collar the Sphinx over Egypt in silver. **Brooch Ornament.** In silver, a thistle wreath. Within the wreath the Sphinx over Egypt. Above the Sphinx a scroll inscribed "Peninsula," below a scroll inscribed "Waterloo."

II:34/cont. 1911 Dress Regulations, Descriptions/cont.

§II-3 Uniform Information

Regiment.	On Buttons.	On Collar of Doublet, Mess Jacket and Frock Coat.	On the Bonnet, F.S. Helmet, Forage Cap and Glengarry Cap.	Special Badges.
The Royal Scots (Lothian Regiment).	The Star of the Order of the Thistle; on the star the figure of St. Andrew and cross; below the star, "The Royal Scots." On the mess dress button the title is omitted, and the design is mounted in silver.	The Thistle, in gold embroidery, on a blue cloth ground on the tunic. On the mess jacket and frock coat, as for forage cap, but smaller.	In silver, the Star of the Order of the Thistle; in gilt or gilding metal on the Star a raised circle inscribed "*Nemo me impune lacessit.*" Within the circle, on a ground of green enamel, the Thistle in gilt or gilding metal.	**On the Waist-Belt.** On a gilt or gilding metal rectangular plate, 2⅝ by 2⅜ in., the badge in silver as for the bonnet, but points of star more sharply defined. **On the Shoulder Belt.** Badge as for bonnet, but larger—below on a scroll "The Royal Scots."
The Royal Scots Fusiliers.	The Thistle, surmounted by the Crown. For the cap and mess dress, on a gilt lined button, with burnished edge, the letters "R.S.F." with the Crown above.	A grenade in silver embroidery; on the ball of the grenade, the Thistle, in silver. On the mess-jacket, gold embroidery, with thistle in silver.	On the Fusilier cap, a grenade in gilt or gilding metal; on the ball of the grenade, the Royal Arms. The same on forage and glengarry cap, but smaller.	**On Waist Belt.** In silver, on a frosted gilt rectangular plate, a wreath of thistles; within the wreath, the figure of St. Andrew with cross. On the wreath, at the bottom, a silver scroll, inscribed "Royal Scots Fusiliers." **On the Shoulder Belt.** Burnished gilt rectangular plate. In silver, a thistle, within a circle, inscribed "*Nemo me impune lacessit*," surmounted by a crown. The Maltese cross in the lower bend of the circle. Below the circle, a scroll inscribed "Royal Scots Fusiliers." Below the scroll "1678" in gilt metal.
The King's Own Scottish Borderers.	The Royal Crest, within the designation "King's Own Scottish Borderers." For the mess dress, the Royal Crest over "K.O.S.B." in silver—mounted on a flat gilt button, in two sizes. For the cap, a gilt struck button, design as for mess dress.	On a dark blue cloth ground, the Castle of Edinburgh in silver embroidery. A flag in blue and crimson embroidery flies from each tower. The Castle rests on thistle leaves in gold embroidery. Beneath the gold embroidery a scroll inscribed "The King's Own Scottish Borderers," on a ground of light blue silk.	In silver, a thistle wreath; within the wreath a circle pierced with the designation, "King's Own Scottish Borderers." Above the circle a scroll surmounted by the Royal Crest. The scroll pierced with the motto, "*In veritate religionis confido.*" Over the circle, the Cross of St. Andrew in burnished silver. On the cross, the Castle of Edinburgh. On the wreath at the bottom of the circle, a scroll with the motto in relief, "*Nisi Dominus frustra.*"	**On the Waist Belt.** On a frosted gilt or gilding metal rectangular plate with bevelled edges burnished, the Cross of St. Andrew in burnished silver; on the cross, thistle wreath in silver; within the wreath and on the cross, the Castle of Edinburgh in silver. **On the Shoulder Belt.** On a burnished gilt rectangular plate the Cross of St. Andrew. On the Cross a ring inscribed "King's Own Scottish Borderers," within the ring and on the Cross the Castle of Edinburgh. Above the ring a scroll with the motto, "*In veritate religionis confido*" surmounted by the Royal Crest. Below the ring a scroll with the motto, "*Nisi Dominus frustra.*" The Cross in burnished silver, remainder of the mount in frosted silver with burnished letters in relief.

II:34/cont. 1911 Dress Regulations, Descriptions/cont.

Regiment.	On Buttons.	On Collar of Doublet.	On Chaco.	On the F.S. Helmet and Glengarry Cap.	Special Badges.
The Highland Light Infantry.	Star of the Order of the Thistle. On the star a horn; in the centre of the horn, the monogram "H.L.I." Above the horn the Crown, below the horn a scroll inscribed "Assaye"; under the scroll the Elephant. For the mess dress a mounted button, the monogram H.L.I. with the crown above.	In silver, the Star of the Order of the Thistle. On the star a silver horn. In the centre of the horn, the monogram "H.L.I." in gilt or gilding metal. Above the horn, in gilt or gilding metal, the Crown; below the horn a scroll, in gilt or gilding metal, inscribed "Assaye"; under the scroll, in gilt or gilding metal, the Elephant.	As for collar badge, except that the cap of the Crown is of crimson enamel, and the badge is larger. A black boss is worn with gilt thistle mount.	As for chaco, but without boss.	On the Waist Belt. On a frosted gilt or gilding metal rectangular plate badge as for chaco, mounted. On the Shoulder Belt. As for waist-plate but larger.

Regiment.	On Buttons.	On Chaco.	Special Badges.
The Cameronians (Scottish Rifles).	Within a thistle wreath, a bugle with strings; above the bugle the Crown.	In bronze, a bugle and strings; above the bugle a mullet on a black corded boss.	On the Waist Belt. In silver, on a frosted silver rectangular plate with burnished edges, a thistle wreath. Within the wreath, in burnished silver, a mullet surmounted by a Crown. On the bottom of the wreath, a bugle with strings. On the Shoulder Belt. In silver, a thistle wreath, surmounted by a Crown. Within the wreath, the mullet and bugle. On the lower bend of the wreath, a scroll inscribed "The Scottish Rifles." The ground of the plate frosted. Silver whistle and chain of special design. On the Pouch. A thistle in silver.

II:34/cont. 1911 Dress Regulations, Descriptions/cont.

Regiment.	On Buttons.	On Busby.	Special Badges.
The King's Royal Rifle Corps.	Within a laurel wreath, a bugle with strings; above the bugle, the Crown. No wreath on the shoulder strap and pocket buttons.	In black metal a Maltese cross surmounted by a tablet inscribed "*Celer et Audax*." On the Cross a circle, inscribed "The King's Royal Rifle Corps"; within the circle, a bugle with strings. On the divisions of the cross, the honours of the Regiment. On the Boss a Crown.	On the Shoulder Belt. In silver, a Maltese Cross surmounted by a tablet inscribed "Peninsula"; above the tablet a crown of special pattern. On the cross a circle inscribed "The King's Royal Rifle Corps"; within the circle a bugle with strings and the number "60." On the divisions of the cross battle honours as follows: "Roliça," "Vimiera," "Martinique," "Talavera," "Fuentes d'Onor," "Albuhera," "Ciudad Rodrigo," "Badajoz," "Nive," "Orthes," "Toulouse," "Salamanca," "Vittoria," "Pyrenees," "Nivelle." Whistle and chain of special pattern. On the Pouch. In silver, a bugle with strings.
The Royal Irish Rifles.	Scalloped edge; within a scroll with shamrock leaves issuing from either end, the Harp and Crown. On scroll, "Royal Irish Rifles."	In black metal the Harp and Crown; below the Harp a scroll, inscribed "*Quis separabit*." On a round boss, the Sphinx over Egypt; below the Sphinx, a bugle with strings.	Special Badges: On the Shoulder Belt. In silver, a shamrock wreath intertwined with a scroll, bearing the honours of the regiment; within the wreath the Harp; above the Harp a scroll inscribed "*Quis separabit*"; below the Harp the Sphinx over Egypt; below the Sphinx a bugle with strings. Over the strings of the bugle a scroll, inscribed "Royal Irish Rifles." The whole surmounted by a Crown. Whistle and chain of special pattern. On the Pouch. In silver, a bugle with strings surmounted by the Sphinx over "Egypt."
The Rifle Brigade (The Prince Consort's Own).	Within a laurel wreath, and the designation Rifle Brigade, a bugle with strings; above the bugle, the Crown.	In black metal a bugle; on the boss, a Crown.	On the Shoulder Belt. As for forage cap, but 4 inches in height, and a scroll on the lower part of the wreath, inscribed "The Prince Consort's Own." Whistle and chain of special pattern. On the Pouch. In silver, a bugle with strings.

II:34/cont. 1911 Dress Regulations, Descriptions/cont.

§II-4 GENERAL STAFF

Prior to 1897

Tunic

Prior to a simplification of staff uniforms in 1897,[43] staff officers wore a scarlet single-breasted tunic of hussar pattern with four rows of gold cord. The top was 20.32 cm (8 inches) long and the bottom was 10.16 cm (4 inches) long across the front.[44] On each side of the chest were four loops, close together: two above the individual row and two below. The bottom row consisted of only these loops. At the end of the row was a cap and two drooping loops of the same cord. In the middle of the chest was a gold olivet and loop to close the tunic.[45]

The gold cord came down the front and continued around the bottom of the tunic down to the rear vent. On the back seams was gold cording which formed a trefoil at the top, passed a netted button at waist level and, doubling, ended in a Hungarian knot.[46]

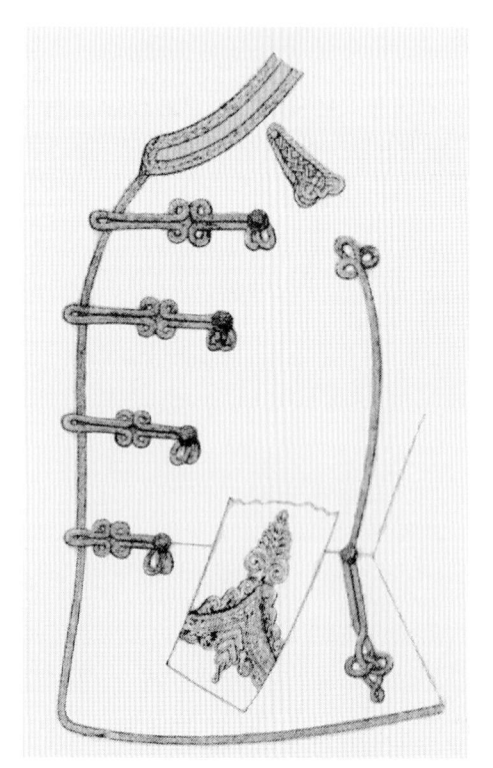

The tunic's collar and pointed cuffs were dark blue. Both carried a complex system of lace and gimp, which varied by rank and position held.[47] Because of their complexity, the subject cannot be covered here. However, an article in ***Tradition*** magazine provides good details.[48]

Gold shoulder cords completed the tunic. There was one type for generals and another, less elaborate, for officers below the rank of general.[49]

After 1897[50]

Cocked Hat

The staff uniforms became simpler after 1897. For generals, the cocked hat with 25.4 cm (10 inch) long white swan feathers, with red feathers under them, was retained. Staff officers, not on the cadre of a unit, with the rank of colonel or below kept the cocked hat with 20.32 cm (8 inch) long white swan feathers with red feathers under them.

II:35 General Staff Tunic as Worn Up to 1897
Notice the double loops on either side of the chest. The insert shows the cuff of an adjutant-general. Collar and cuff trim changed depending on the rank of the wearer.

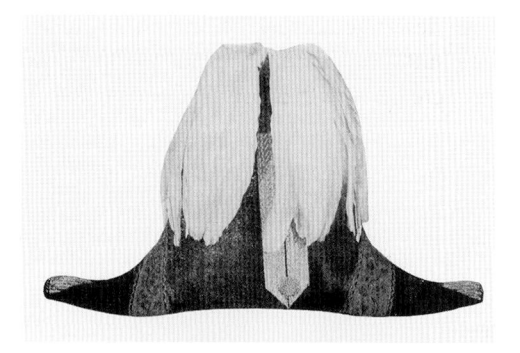

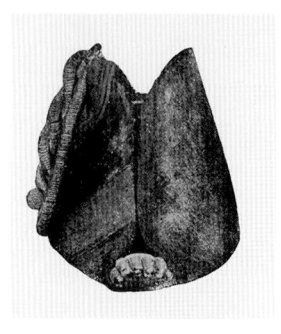

II:36 Cocked Hat
Side and front views. Worn by generals, staff officers, and some others.

Tunic

All staff officers wore a scarlet cloth single-breasted tunic with eight buttons down the front. The buttons of generals had one type of design, and colonels and below wore buttons with different designs.

The tunic had a standing collar and slash cuffs. Generals' collars had an oak-leaf design. The collars of those below general rank had trim on the top and bottom of their blue collar, depending on their rank. Colonels had gold staff pattern lace on the top and bottom of the collar. Officers below the rank of colonel had the lace only on the top of the collar.

The round blue cuffs were 7.62 cm (3 inches) deep. Two bands of lace 1.59 cm (⅝ inch) wide went around the top of the collar for colonels. The bands showed 0.32 cm (⅛ inch) of blue cloth between them. Staff officers below the rank of colonel had one lace band.

A scarlet three-pointed slash flap was on each arm. It lay over the cuff and sleeve, and looked similar to the flap on foot guard sleeves. The flap was 15.24 cm (6 inches) tall from the bottom of the cuff and 6.35 cm (2½ inches) wide at the points. The flap was edged along the inside edges with 1.59 cm (⅝ inch) wide lace.

The rear skirt of the tunic was decorated with the same slash design found on the sleeves. The rear slash had three buttons. The middle vent and each side of the slash were lined with lace 1.59 cm (⅝ inch) wide.

The lace was a gold staff pattern. The front collar, cuffs, flaps, and bands of lace on the skirts were edged with white cloth 0.48 cm (³⁄₁₆ inch) wide.

Trousers and Pantaloons

The trousers were blue with a 4.45 cm (1¾ inch) lace stripe down the outside seams.

The pantaloons (riding breeches) were blue with a 4.45 cm (1¾ inch) scarlet stripe down the outside seam.

Aiguillette

The staff-style aiguillette was the distinguishing mark of officers serving on the Headquarters' and General Staff. It was worn on the left shoulder by most staff officers, but officers of the Headquarters' Staff of the army wore it on the right shoulder.

Other

The regulations of 1911 carried forward the 1904 changes.

While not a part of full dress, the red gorget patch worn on the frock that became such a mark of staff officers was introduced in the 1900 Dress Regulations.[51]

§II-5 GUARD CAVALRY

Uniform

Helmet

In 1842, the Household Cavalry took into use a helmet in the Prussian style. Prince Albert, the Prince Consort to Queen Victoria, is said to have been the driving force behind the adoption of this style of helmet.[52] It is therefore known as the Albert Pattern helmet. It established the basic form of the helmets worn by the Household Cavalry regiments from 1842 to 1914 and by their successors today. This 1842 pattern was higher in the skull dome. The peak, or brim, edges on the front and back were heavily decorated with sprays of acanthus.[53]

The helmet took its final form in 1871. See helmet in Images II:5, II:6, and II:40. It consisted of a dome skull, front and rear peaks, a plume holder, and a plume.

For officers, the skull dome was of German silver. It consisted of two pieces soldered together. The front solder line is hidden by a helmet plate and the back by a band with a gilt scallop-shell pattern, which runs from the plume holder to the bottom of the rear brim. The front peak was in the shape of a point, the back peak was rounded. For officers only, both had gilt metal on their edges. There was no other decoration on the peaks.

In all the regiments of the Household Cavalry, there had been a tendency among some officers to wear the helmet in a way that caused the point of the front peak to come down almost to the tip of the wearer's nose. Queen Victoria complained about not being able to see the faces of her escort and it is said she caused a shorter peak to be introduced to make it easier to recognise the escort officers.[54] This way of wearing the helmet seems to have continued into modern times.

Royal Horse Guards (Blues) had a distinctive ear rosette.

The early helmet height was between 22.86 and 24.13 cm (9 and 9½ inches) from the crown of the skull to the tip of the front peak.[55] Later helmets were not as tall, about 17.8 and 19.05 cm (7 and 7½ inches).

Helmet Plate

In spite of confusing statements in the 1900, 1904, and 1911 Dress Regulations, the helmet plates for all regiments of the Household Cavalry were the same.

In the centre in the front was a silver eight-point star of the Order of the Garter. Resting on a gilt field on the silver star was a gilt garter of the Order, which rested on a blue enamel field with the motto of the order picked out so the blue enamel showed through. In the centre of the garter was a red enamel Cross of St George. This was set on a silver background.[56]

Around the silver field holding the star was the chain collar of the Order of the Garter. This in turn was surrounded by a wreath of oak and laurel leaves. The laurel leaves were on the wearer's right and the oak leaves on his left. This leaf trim had an offshoot which continued around to the ear rosettes on either side of the helmet (see below). Where the wreaths met in front, there was a small figure of St George on horseback killing a dragon, one of the symbols of England.

The whole was topped by a crown, which changed from the 'Queen's Crown' to the 'King's Crown' when Queen Victoria died.

David Rowe, in his *Head Dress of the British Heavy Cavalry*, notes there were two styles of Victorian crowns: one with a double arch on each side of the orb, which was mostly worn by Life Guards, and one with a single arch, worn mostly by the Royal Horse Guards. This is not an iron rule, and examples of each type are found in all Household Cavalry regiments.[57]

The parts of the centre of the officers' helmet plate came apart for cleaning. The star, the garter, the enamel red cross, and the blue border were all different pieces. This meant that when they are put back together on the helmet they stood well out from the skull if viewed from the side.

The chin chain was held to the helmet by large rosettes on either side of the helmet. The rosettes were in the shape of a flower and there were slight differences between the regiments. The Life Guards had a multi-petalled pattern. The Blues had a single rose with one inter-row of seven flat-pointed petals.[58]

The Chin Scales

The chin scales could be either 2.54 cm (1 inch) wide or a version which was 3.18 cm (1¼ inches) wide at the edges, and graduated down to 1.91 cm (¾ inch) at the centre of the chain.[59] The Life Guards wore their chin chains below their lower lip. The Horse Guards (Blues) wore them on the point of the chin.[60]

The Plume Holder

This consisted of a silver four-sided fluted stem above a gilt ball. The ball rested on a stem which in turn was mounted on a gilt eight-pointed star.[61] The plume holder and the plume were about 27.94 cm (11 inches) tall.

The Plume

The dress regulations for 1900, 1904, and 1911 state that the plumes are white horsehair for the two Life Guard Regiments and red horsehair for the Royal Horse Guards. This is another place where the regulations are not a complete guide.

In all three regiments the plume material went into the top of the plume stem and then up over a circular mould. The hair was then parted in the middle and was supposed to hang to a level even with the back of the helmet. However, often the plumes were worn shorter than this.

Officers of the Life Guards often wore plumes of shredded whalebone. It is thought the Blues began wearing yak hair plumes in about 1883.[62]

David Rowe believes that, prior to 1914, the officers of the Life Guards did not wear their plumes in the onion shape that is used today.[63]

Other Ranks' Helmets

The helmet of the other ranks was similar to that of the officers, but with cheaper and more mass-produced component materials. The helmet was of white metal. The plume holder was attached to the helmet skull. The ball shape on the holder was in white metal, and the star-shaped base was in gilding metal rather than the gilt of the officers' holder.

The oak and laurel wreath was in gilding metal. The eight-pointed garter star was of white metal; the rays were raised and not beaded. On the star was placed a

II:37 Trooper Life Guards, c. 1910

gilded metal garter with the motto and the cross of St George. There were of course no enamelled items.[64]

Other Ranks' Plume

The plume of the other ranks of both regiments of the Life Guards was white horsehair. As with the officers, the men in the Life Guards do not seem to have worn their plumes in an onion shape (see Image II:37). The men of the Blues wore red horsehair plumes.

Tunic

The tunic of the Life Guards was of scarlet cloth (see Image C11). The 1st Life Guards had a blue velvet collar and cuff, and edging of blue cloth. The 2nd Life Guards had the same blue velvet collar and cuffs, and theirs had stitched edges. The facings of the other ranks were cloth.

The collar had heavy gold embroidery consisting of a mixed laurel with an oak leaf and acorns pattern. It was 13.97 to 15.24 cm (5½ to 6 inches) long and

II:38 Trim Worn by Senior Officers of the Royal Horse Guards and Life Guards
A. (Left) Trim on rear skirt.
B. (Top right) Trim on collar. Note extra trim around the top of the collar denoting senior rank.
C. (Bottom right) Cuff trim. As a senior officer, the cuff also has an extra row of trim around the top.

5.08 cm (2 inches) wide – i.e. it went back to the midpoint of the shoulder.

The gauntlet-shaped cuff had a gold embroidery pattern similar to that on the collar. This was set in a slight 'V' pattern and had a specially designed button in the centre (see Images II:6 and II:38). The rear skirt had three sets of gold embroidery in the same pattern. The top edge of the cuff and collar of field officers had an extra line of embroidery 1.27 cm (½ inch) wide.

The Life Guards officers wore a Household Cavalry shoulder cord (see Image II:4(1)), which was also worn by senior NCO ranks in 1914.[65]

The collar of the 1st Life Guards was squared (Image II:40) and that of the 2nd Life Guards slightly rounded (Image II:41).[66] The rear skirts of officers had three blocks of slanted lace in the Life Guard pattern (Image II:6). The front edge of the tunic and the rear skirt was

II:40 Major, Life Guards, 1898
Note the heavy braiding on his aiguillette and the squared collar.

II:41 2nd Life Guards Regimental Quartermaster (wears cocked hat)
Note gap at slightly rounded collar, which denotes the 2nd Life Guards.

II:39 Household Cavalry Officer's Rear Skirt

§II-5 Guard Cavalry   99

II:42 Life Guard Officer, c. 1900
This shows a head to knee example of the Life Guard uniform.

II:43 Royal Horse Guards, Trooper, c. 1895
Note chevron trim on cuff and design on belt buckle. He has a long-service stripe.

edged in blue. The collars and gauntlet cuffs of the other ranks in the two Life Guards regiments were also blue. For the entire effect, see Image II:42.

The collars of other ranks had a hollow box that ran from near the front edge of each collar to the back, level with the shoulder strap of cords. First-class staff would wear extra gold lace that went all the way around the collar and a button at the end of the box of lace level with the shoulder cords (see below for shoulder cords) (Image II:43).

The buttons were of regimental pattern for both officers and men. The buttons on other ranks' tunics were brass.

The rear skirt of troopers and second-class staff had a three-point flap with three buttons. The top one was placed high enough to hold the belt in place. For first-class staff, a hollow three-sided box in gold lace was worn. The box had the shape of two chevrons of gold lace joined at the sides (Image II:44).

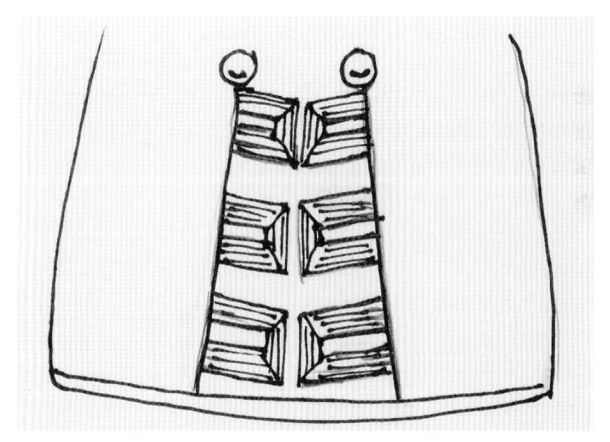

II:44 Rear Skirt Design of the First-Class Staff

The gauntlet cuffs for all other ranks had a hollow chevron of gold lace joined at the side. There was a button at the 'V' of the chevron (Image II:43).

The most noticeable thing about troopers was that they wore shoulder straps instead of should cords and did not wear aiguillettes. The blue shoulder straps were edged with gold lace on the two edges and the bottom.

The tunic of the Royal Horse Guards, often called the Blues or the Oxford Blues, was dark blue cloth with a scarlet collar and gauntlet-shaped cuffs (see Image C12). It had blue trim on the front edge and the rear skirt. This meant the colours of the Blues were the reverse of those of the Life Guards, but the lace of the Blues was in the regimental pattern. They carried heavy gold embroidery in the same location and shape as that of the Life Guards.

With very few other differences, the Blues' uniform was the same as the Life Guards'. This included the lace and embroidery. Field officers in the Blues also had an extra line of embroidery on their collars and cuffs. The rear skirt also had three sets of gold embroidery below the two buttons. Their officers and senior NCOs wore Household Cavalry shoulder cords.

Non-Officer Badges of Rank

Rank was not shown by chevrons. It was shown by aiguillettes worn on the left shoulder. These followed the same pattern in all three regiments.

First-Class Staff

First class staff wore gold shoulder cords of the Household Cavalry pattern and aiguillettes which had an extra cord near the needles (Images II:45 and II:46).[67]

II:45 Life Guards, Regimental Corporal Major (i.e. Sergeant Major) c. 1898
His army rank would be warrant officer. Note aiguillette with the extra coil denoting his high rank.

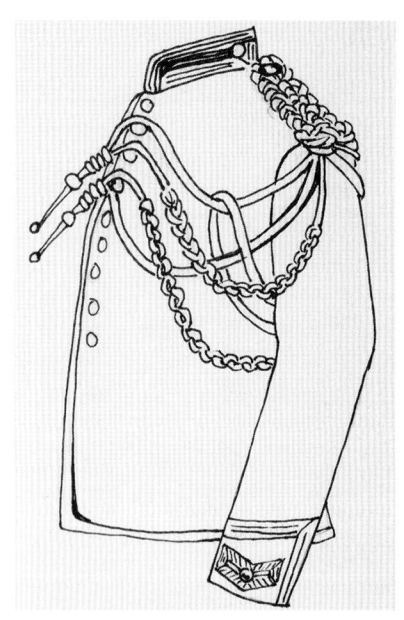

II:46 First-Class Staff Aiguillette
NCOs' aiguillettes were worn on the left shoulder. Notice extra coils near the needles.

The aiguillette went from the left shoulder cord and across the left breast to the top of the tunic. Shoulder cords rather than shoulder straps were worn as part of the aiguillette.

Second-Class Staff

Second-class staff also wore gold shoulder cords of the Household Cavalry pattern. These men wore a second-class aiguillette which is the same as the first-class, except it does not have the coils near the needles. It went from the left shoulder cord and across the left breast in the same way as the first-class aiguillette (Images II:47 and II:48).

Troopers

Troopers did not wear aiguillettes. This meant they wore shoulder straps. They had plain rear skirts (Images II:49 and II:50).

Field Officers

Field officers had, in addition to the normal gold trim on their collars and cuffs, an additional border of gold leaf embroidery 1.27 cm (½ inch) wide at the top of the collar and cuff.[68] They wore officers' aiguillettes,

§II-5 Guard Cavalry

II:47 Life Guards, Corporal of Horse Rank, c. 1895
His aiguillette is the same as worn by first-class staff, except it does not have extra coils near the needle. Note trim on collar, cuffs, and shoulder cords.

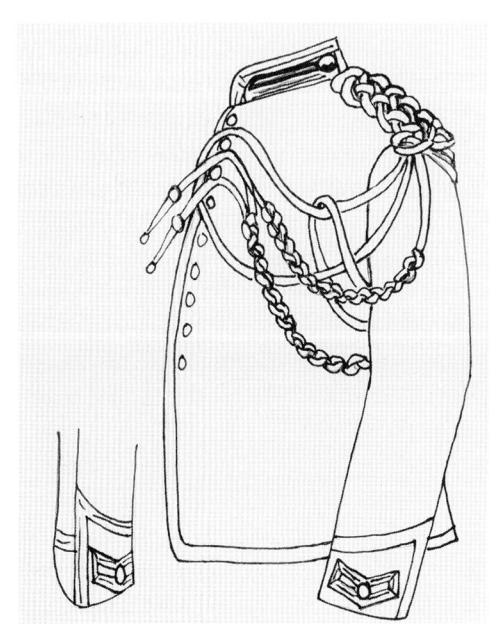

II:48 Second-Class Staff Aiguillette and Cuff
This does not have the extra cording near the needles.

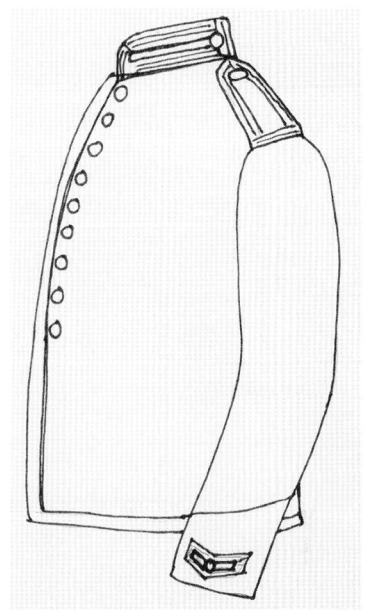

II:49 Trooper's Tunic
Troopers did not wear aiguillettes and therefore have shoulder straps in the facing colour with trim. They have shoulder straps with 1.27 cm (½ inch) gold trim on all sides.

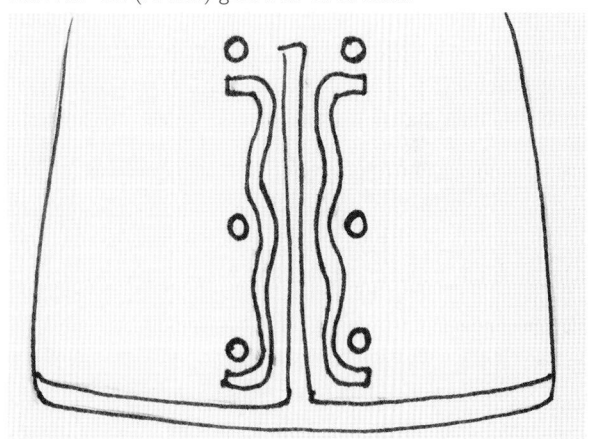

II:50 Rear Skirt of a Trooper

which were made of very heavy plated gold wire. Officers' aiguillettes were fastened from the right shoulder cord and worn across the right breast. Field officers' aiguillettes had an extra coil near the needle (Image II:42).

Junior Officers

This uniform was the same as that of field officers, except that the aiguillettes did not have the extra coil, and there was no extra trim on the top of the collar and cuffs.

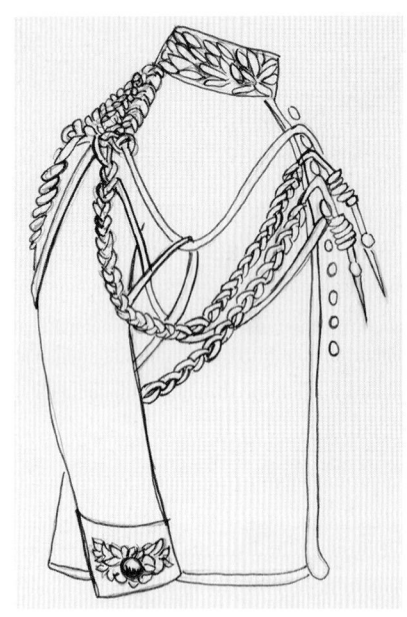

II:51 Household Cavalry Officer Aiguillette
Officers had a coil near the needle. Note embroidery on collar and cuff. Officer aiguillettes were worn on the right shoulder.

The aiguillette for officers and NCOs who wore them in the Life Guards was suspended from the shoulder cord and the collar when a tunic was worn. The Horse Guards' officers and applicable NCOs suspended their aiguillettes from the shoulder cords and the top button of the tunic. When cuirasses were worn, they attached to a clip on the front of the cuirass (Image II:40).[69]

Cartouche Belt

The cartouche or shoulder belt was in gold lace of the regimental pattern for the officers. In the centre of the belt was a flask cord. For officers, the cord was given as scarlet in the regulations for the 1st Life Guards, and the Blues in 1900, but the 1911 Regulations state their cords were crimson. The 2nd Life Guards wore blue. The Blues had a red stripe in the centre of the belt more or less under the cord.[70]

Other ranks wore a white leather shoulder belt. The other ranks of the 1st Life Guards wore a red flask cord, rather than the officers' crimson, and the 2nd Life Guards a blue cord; the Blues had a blue cord.

The cartouche pouch worn in the back of the belt was, for officers, of black patent leather. The device on it was in gilt. The other ranks' pouch was probably of black leather. At some point, the Life Guards officers and other ranks started putting a small piece of red cloth behind the device, but it is not clear when this happened. The device on the pouch of the 1st Life Guards was smaller than that worn by the 2nd Life Guards.[71]

See §II-3 *Appendix II* and *IV* for description of pouch lid and badges.

Trousers and Breeches

For mounted full levee dress, officers and men wore white buckskin pantaloons together with black leather jackboots and steel spurs (Image II:37).[72]

For dismounted full dress, officers and men wore dark blue overalls, ordinary type trousers only about 5.08 cm (2 inches) longer (Image II:47). The 1st Life Guards wore two scarlet stripes 3.81 cm (1½ inches) wide on their overalls. The 2nd Life Guards had two 3.18 cm (1¼ inches) wide scarlet stripes 1.27 cm (½ inch) apart. A scarlet welt was between the stripes.[73] These stripes were worn by the officers and other ranks of both regiments. The Blues had a single stripe 6.35 cm (2½ inches) wide on their blue trousers.

Black leather Wellington boots were worn with the overalls.

Cuirass

The cuirass was introduced at the coronation of King George IV.[74] The jackboots and white buckskins were adopted in 1812.[75] Both the front and back was of polished steel and had brass studs. For officers, the lining was blue Moroccan leather with blue velvet edges. The straps and buckles were of regimental pattern.

There was a noticeable difference between where the metal scale strap fastened on the front of the cuirass for other ranks and for officers. For other ranks, the two scale straps and their headpieces came close to touching in the centre of the cuirass (Images II:52 and II:53). For officers, the head that the metal scale strap went into was larger and further apart (see Image II:40) as well as varying in design from regiment to regiment.[76] In general the cuirasses of the officers were finer and fitted closer to the body than those of the other ranks (compare Image II:40 with Images II:52 and II:53).

Images II:54 and II:55 give an idea of how standard issue troopers' cuirasses fit on the side.

II:52 Life Guards Trooper, c. 1910, in Cuirass
Also notice the jackboots. The helmet plume does not have an onion shape.

II:54 1st Life Guards, c. 1910
Photo signed corporal. No NCO aiguillette, so he was not a corporal when photo taken. Note the jackboots.

II:53 Royal Horse Guards Trooper, c. 1910
The cuirass is essentially the same model as worn by the Life Guards.

II:55 Royal Horse Guards Trooper, c. 1910
Note how the cuirass comes together on the side and the jackboots.

The straps and buckles on the officers' cuirass were of regimental pattern.

In levee dress, the cuirass was not worn.

Gloves
White leather gauntlet gloves were worn in full dress.

Warrant Officers' Uniform
These uniforms were a mixture of officer and other rank elements.

Farriers
The farriers of the Life Guards had several uniform distinctions. Their tunics were blue instead of scarlet.

The plume for other ranks before 1914 were:

Table II.5.1: Farrier Plume Colour

Regiment	Plume Colour
1st Life Guards	Black
2nd Life Guards	Black
The Blues	Red

Farriers did not wear a cuirass. Rather than wear the white cartouche belt, they wore a ceremonial axe belt with a flask cord in the regimental colour. The axe belt had a frog at the back for carrying the axe on the march (Image II:56).[77]

For the Horse Guards, farriers now wear the following, and it is likely this was their dress in 1900–14: the cuffs are not scarlet, but are dark blue with scarlet cloth showing inside the gold chevron trim.[78] The same type of axe belt as worn by the Life Guards is worn by the Blues. This axe belt, however, has a red cord.

Miscellaneous

In 1903, an invoice showed the following costs for certain uniform items of an officer of the 2nd Life Guards:

Item	1903 Cost	Approximate current cost Pounds	Dollars
Helmet and plume	£12.00	£1,240	$1,450
Full dress tunic	£19.19	£1,980	$2,330
Aiguillette and case	£13.00	£1,340	$1,570
Cuirasses	£18.18	£1,870	$2,200
Sword	£6.00	£620	$730

Source: Rowe, Heavy Cavalry, p. 12.

In 1788, the 1st and 2nd Life Guards set a standard height for their men, not accepting any one under 1.8 m (5 feet 11 inches) nor over 1.85 m (6 feet 1 inch). This standard was followed down to World War II.[79]

Horses
Today, large black horses are an integral part of the Household Cavalry, but this was not always the rule.

II:56 Staff Corporal Farrier, 1st Life Guards
Note farrier's axe.

In the 1820s, officers' chargers were black, bay, brown, or chestnut, per Brigade Order 13 May 1814. One officer even had a grey horse.[80]

In the two Life Guard regiments, the horses' manes were combed to fall to the left (near) side of the horse, while those of the Royal Horse Guard fell to the right (off) side of the horse.[81]

The Blues were ordered to only ride black horses in 1813 by the Prince Regent. The Life Guards appear to have ridden only black horses from about 1830.[82]

§II-5 APPENDIX I: RANKS IN HOUSEHOLD CAVALRY

First-Class Staff

Regimental corporal major	First-class aiguillettes[83]	Troopers	No aiguillettes
Squadron corporal major	First-class aiguillettes	(Lance corporals added in 1922)	

Second-Class Staff

Farriers

Corporals of horse	Second-class aiguillettes	Farrier Corporal Major	First-class aiguillettes
Corporals	Second-class aiguillettes	Farrier Corporal of Horse	Second-class aiguillettes

§II-5 APPENDIX II: CROWN TYPES

Victorian Crown	Depressed arches
Tudor (Imperial) Crown	Raised arches
Elizabeth II Crown	St Edward's Crown (with slightly depressed arches)

§II-6 THE FOOT GUARDS REGIMENTS

Uniform

HEADDRESS

The headdress was a black bearskin 24.13 cm (9½ inches) tall for an officer who was 1.83 m (6 feet) tall. For taller officers, the height of the bearskin scaled up; for those shorter, it scaled down.

The black bearskin covered a cane frame built to form the required shape, slightly tapered down from front to back. It was often said that officers' bearskins were made from the skins of a female bear and the other ranks from that of a male bear, but it is difficult to identify a hard rule in this area.

The chin chain was worn under the lower lip, not under or on the chin. This custom set off a precedent that was unofficially followed by many regiments in the British and Indian armies. Chin straps were meant to be worn on the point of the chin, but some regiments, in violation of rules, elected to wear them under their lower lip.

The officers of the Grenadier Guards had a plume of white goat hair 15.24 cm (6 inches) long on the left side (Image II:57). The Coldstream Guards had scarlet feathers 15.24 cm (6 inches) long on the right side. The

II:58 Grenadier Guards Other Ranks and Drummers in the Corps of Drums
Notice the small size and square shape of their bearskins.

II:57 Grenadier Guards Field Officer
This photo offers an excellent view of the officer's 15.24 cm (6 inch) long white goat's hair plume, and the 5.08 cm (2 inch) scarlet stripe on his breeches.

Irish Guards wore St Patrick blue feathers that were 15.24 cm (6 inches) long on the right side. They were given a blue plume instead of a green one because the Royal Irish Fusiliers had already been given a green plume.[84] The Scots Guards did not wear a plume.

Enlisted guardsmen wore a smaller bearskin. It was less tapered and gave a less full, more squared, appearance. It was not as tall as an officer's bearskin and not as full (Images II:58 and II:60). Sergeants' and warrant officers' bearskins normally fell somewhere between those of the enlisted men and the officers. They were smaller than an officer's, but larger than a guardsman's (Image II:59 and II:60).

Image II:60 is a photograph of the King's Company, 1st Battalion, Grenadier Guards.[85] It shows the bearskins of officers, sergeants, and guardsmen. The variation in the size and shape of the bearskins worn by the different ranks can clearly be seen. Note how the sergeants on the right of the flag bearer in the first row wore two different shapes of bearskins. It also

II:59 Coldstream Guards Sergeants
The rear figure is the regimental sergeant major. Note design of rank chevrons on the right arm. The man in the centre with an axe is a pioneer sergeant. The gold crossed axes on his right arm can just be seen. One can also make out the silver rose of the Coldstreams above the axes. The man behind him on the left is a drill sergeant. His badge is a crimson flag with a device on it and crossed swords surmounted by a crown. The device on the flag would vary by regiment.

II:61 Senior Officer of the Grenadier Guards, Before 1902
This officer had a staff position, as shown by the aiguillettes on his left shoulder. Note how the grenadier badge stands out on the collar. His senior ranking is shown by the two lace stripes on his cuff. These would disappear in the uniform reforms of 1902. Also note the wide stripe on his trousers.

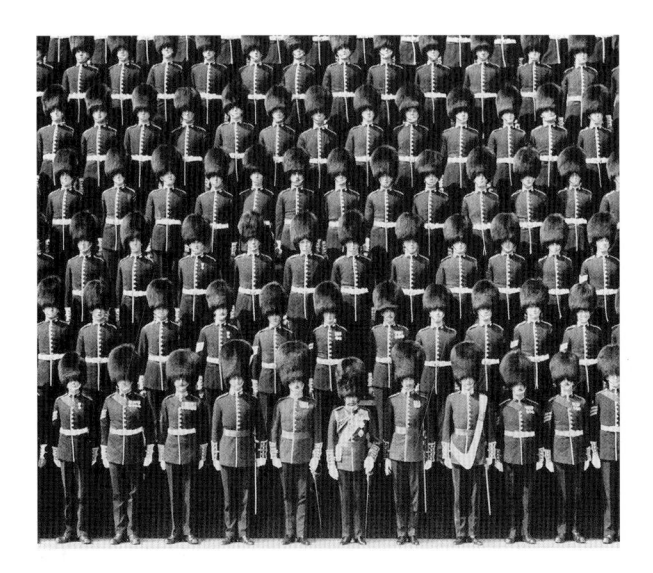

II:60 The King's Company, 1st Battalion, Grenadier Guards, 1926
George V is in the centre of the first row. Note the difference in the bearskins worn by NCOs, officers, and other ranks. Although the photo is taken after World War I, these uniforms and bearskins are the same as those worn prior to 1914.

II:62 Grenadier Guards' Inspection
This gives a good side view of the guardsmen's bearskins.

shows that the regimental plume was normally not visible from the front.

The guardsmen's plumes were of horsehair.[86] It was the same colour as that worn by the officers but other ranks' plumes were cut so as to not be seen from the front. Sergeants' and warrant officers' plumes were the cut feathers or other materials used by the officers.[87]

For the Grenadier Guards, the bearskin, and the uniform, was considered a battle honour, taken for defeating the French grenadiers at the Battle of Waterloo in 1815.[88]

Tunic

The tunic was of scarlet cloth with blue cloth collar and cuffs. The cuffs were 8.89 cm (3½ inches) deep with a blue 15.24 cm (6 inch) flap on each sleeve that had three points. The tunic, collar, and cuffs were edged with white trim 0.64 cm (¼ inch) wide. There were two buttons in the back to hold up the sash or belt. For the officers, the back of the tunic was cut in the middle and marked with white trim. The rear of the tunic was not split for non-officers, with only a white trim line on it.

The cuffs and collars had trim of the regimental pattern on the collar, and cuffs were varied by rank. This was quite complicated in 1900 and was somewhat simplified after 1902 (see §II-3-5, Image II:7 for examples of the rank lace). At a distance, the braid on an officer's cuff was noticeably different from the trim worn by sergeants and guardsmen. This can be seen in Image II:60, and then compare the cuffs of officers and sergeants in that photograph with the cuffs of guardsmen in Images II:63 and II:64.

The front edges of the collars of the other ranks were slightly rounded until 1905–6. After that, the collar edges had the square shape they still have today. Officers had square-edged collar openings both before and after 1905.

For other ranks, there were three quality levels of tunics: first-class, sergeant, and rank-and-file.[89] The first-class was worn by warrant officers. Confusingly, some ranks wore a mixture of first-class and sergeant quality tunics. The difference between the tunics had to do with the quality of the cloth, the fit, and the lack of braid worn. The rank-and-file tunic had white braid on the cuffs and skirt.

II:63 Grenadier Guard, c. 1914
He has the crossed flags of the signaller's proficiency badge. Note the badge on the collar and shoulder straps and horsehair plume on the bearskin.

II:64 Scots Guards Sergeant, c. 1904
For some unknown reason, he is wearing a cavalry sword belt. Note the badge on his collar. He is also wearing the unpopular and short-lived Brodrick cap.

The Grenadier Guards had nine buttons down the front, at equal distances, and officers had four bars of embroidery at equal distances on the skirts and cuff flaps (Images II:63, II:65, and II:67).

The Coldstream Guards had ten buttons in front, five sets of two. The lowest button was under the belt. Officers had four bars of embroidery, two by two, on the skirts and cuff flaps (Images II:66 and II:68).

The Scots Guards had nine buttons, three sets of three. The bottom button was flat so it could go under the waist belt plate.[90] The officers had three bars of embroidery at equal distances on the skirts and cuff flaps (Image II:64). This grouping of three has been traditional since 1775.[91]

The Irish Guards, after they were created in 1900, were to have, per the regulations, ten buttons in front – in theory, two sets of four and one set of two. However, the set of two were often not visible. Officers had four bars of embroidery on the skirts and flaps. On the cuffs, the buttons and embroidery were bunched together towards the middle, leaving a dark band at the top and bottom of the flap (Image II:69).

For officers, buttons on the cuffs, collar, and rear skirt were backed by lace of the regimental pattern. The cuffs, collars, and skirts were also trimmed with embroidery of the regimental pattern 1.27 cm (½ inch) wide. Officers above lieutenant had an extra row of embroidery on cuffs, collars, and skirts (see Images II:7 and II:67). For the original three guard regiments, the embroidery was affected by the changes of 1902 (*§II-3-5*, Image II:8). The Irish Guards, raised in 1900, did not have it on the cuffs and skirts of their officers.

Officers of the Grenadier Guards had a gold embroidered grenade at each end of the collar. The grenade was built up so it stood out from the collar (Image II:65). The Coldstream Guards had a gold embroidered star of the Order of the Garter (Image II:66). The Scots Guards had a silver embroidered thistle, and the Irish Guards a shamrock in silver embroidery.

Trousers and Breeches

The trousers, cut straight and allowing for fashion changes, were close to what we wear today. The colour was a very dark blue known as Oxford blue. Pantaloons were Oxford blue riding breeches, and they were cut loose in the thigh and tight at the knee. Prior to 1902

II:65 Elegant Senior Officer of the Grenadier Guards
Note how the grenadier badge stands out on the collar and the full dress sash worn only on state occasions.

II:66 Two Junior Officers of the Coldstream Guards
Note the very different look to their bearskins and the standard officer's crimson sash.

II:67 1st Regiment of Foot Guards-Grenadier Guards, Senior Officer

II:69 1st Irish Guards Regimental Sergeant Major, 1913
Note royal arms on the right arm as his badge of rank and four button pattern on his tunic front and cuffs. Also the badge on his collar.

trousers worn as levees, in drawing rooms and when in full dress had gold lace as specified for their regiment, 3.81 cm (1½ inches) wide down the side seam. On other occasions the side-seam stripe was 5.08 cm (2 inches) wide and scarlet. The pantaloons had 5.08 cm (2 inches) wide scarlet stripe. After 1902 both had a 5.08 cm (2 inch) scarlet stripe for officers. Other ranks had a scarlet welt along their side seams (Image II:62).

Field officers wore overalls rather than trousers.

Sash

There were two types of sashes. A sash worn on state occasions was crimson with gold stripes (Image II:65). It was 6.35 cm (2½ inches) wide. At other times a crimson silk sash of the same dimensions was worn (Image II:66).

II:68 Coldstream Foot Guards
Note regimental badge on collar.

Prior to 1904, the sash was worn over the left shoulder by officers and over the right by NCOs. The 1904 Dress Regulations call for the officers' sash to be worn around the waist with 17.78 cm (7 inch) tassels hanging down on the left side for an officer 1.83 m (6 feet) tall (Image II:62). The tassel length was to be adjusted up or down depending on the officer's height.

Shoulder Straps
Officers
Guard officers did not wear shoulder cords. They wore blue shoulder straps with, normally, two lines of gold trim marking the outside of the strap. A regimental button held the strap down near the collar.

Most officers wore badges of rank on their shoulder straps. However, in the guards, rank was shown by the number of rows of lace on the strap, as well as the stars and crowns. The Grenadier and Coldstream Guards used the garter star. The Scots Guards had a silver wire St Andrew's star with a gold thistle in the centre. The Irish Guards wore a silver wire St Patrick's star with a coloured silk shamrock in the centre.

The crown used during Victoria's reign was the so-called Queen's Crown. This was, in fact, the royal crown of England. It was very close in design to the St Edward's Crown which is used today by Queen Elizabeth II, and has been used in the reign of eight kings and two queens. When Edward VII became king, the crown changed to the Tudor Henry VII Crown. This was used as long as Great Britain held India, which was through the rule of four kings. This led to it being called the King's Crown.[92]

Other Ranks
The shoulder straps of the other ranks below the rank of officer were blue trimmed in white (Images II:63 and II:68). The devices they wore on their shoulder straps were distinctive. The Grenadier Guards had a crown over a garter bearing the motto of the Order of the Garter. Within the garter was a reversed cipher of the king or queen. The Coldstream Guards had a Tudor rose. The Scots and Irish Guards had St Andrew's and St Patrick's stars respectively.

Brass metal shoulder titles were worn on tunics from 1908 (see §II-3-2). In 1914 the Brigade of Guards began using embroidered shoulder titles.[93] These are still used today.

The shoulder straps of warrant officers were trimmed in gold lace, and they had two rows of gold lace below the white trim on the cuffs on each arm. In addition, the collar was trimmed top and bottom with gold lace.

Belts
Prior to 1904, officers wore a 'sword belt' over their tunic, which was made of gold lace 3.81 cm (1½ inches) wide. It had a buckle with a regimental badge on it. Once officers began wearing a sash around their waist, they did not wear a belt over their tunic. The sword belt was worn under the tunic and was of a workmanlike web design.

The belt for other ranks was white with a gilded metal clasp on which was written the regiment's title (Images II:63 and II:68).

§II-7 LINE CAVALRY

§II-7-a DRAGOON GUARDS AND DRAGOONS

Uniform
Table II.7.a.1: Dragoon Guards Dress Uniform

Regiment	Tunic Colour	Helmet	Plume Colour	Collar and Cuffs	Trouser and Pantaloon Stripe	Notes
1st	Scarlet	Gilt brass	Red	Blue	Yellow	A, B
2nd	Scarlet	Gilt brass	Black	Buff	White/buff	C
3rd	Scarlet	Gilt brass	Black over red	Yellow	Yellow	A, D
4th	Scarlet	Gilt brass	White	Blue	Yellow	A
5th	Scarlet	Gilt brass	White over red	Dark green	Yellow	A, B
6th	Blue	Gilt brass	White	White	Two white	
7th	Scarlet	Gilt brass	Black over white	Black	Yellow	A

Notes:
A: Collar and cuffs are velvet.
B: Rowe (*Lancers*, p. 101) states other ranks in these regiments wore crimped plumes, but there is no photographic evidence for this.
C: Mounted on bay coloured horses.
D: See Image C18 for an example of how the two plume colours lay.

Table II.7.a.2: Dragoons Dress Uniform in 1911–14

Regiment	Tunic	Helmet	Plume	Collar and Cuffs	Trouser and Pantaloon Trim	Notes
1st	Scarlet	White steel	Black	Blue	Yellow	
2nd	Scarlet			Blue	Yellow	A
6th	Scarlet	White steel	White	Primrose yellow	Yellow	B

Source: *Dress Regulations, 1911*, pp. 32–3, ¶ 337–60; MacLeod, *Glory*, pp. 16–17.
Notes:
A: Mounted on grey coloured horses.
B: The 1911 Dress Regulations call for primrose yellow stripes on trousers and pantaloons for the 6th Dragoon's officers.

Members of the band wore a different colour plume. Listed in the table are their plume colours, c. 1900.[94]

Regiment	Plume Colour
1st Dragoon Guards	White
2nd Dragoon Guards	White
3rd Dragoon Guards	White
4th Dragoon Guards	Black and white[a]
5th Dragoon Guards	Red
6th Dragoon Guards	Red
7th Dragoon Guards	Black
1st Dragoons	White
2nd Dragoons (Scots Greys)	Large scarlet feather plume[b]
6th Dragoons	White[c]

Notes: [a] Rowe states black and white, but many say white, based on photos.
[b] The plumes went from one side of the band's black bearskins to the other side across the top (MacLeod, *Glory*, p. 16 and see Rowe, *Lancers*, p. 132). The kettledrummer had a white bearskin with a red transverse plume, which during the pre-World War I period he often, but not always, wore on parades (Grant, *Scots Greys*, p. 40). There is a persistent myth that the white bearskin was given to Czar Nicholas II when he became Colonel-in-Chief of the regiment in 1894 (ibid., pp. 39–40). This story has been shown to be wrong many times as the white bearskin came into use in the 1880s (ibid., p. 40).
[c] Rowe (*Lancers*, p. 132) says red and white.

Helmet

The helmet was of gilt brass for officers and brass for the other ranks of the Dragoon Guards. Dragoons wore white metal. The helmets came down to a point that rested on the wearer's nose (Image II:10).

On top of the helmet there was a 10.16 cm (4 inch) stylised spike to which was fastened a horsehair plume. There were several different patterns of plume spikes used by officers of the different regiments. A rose-shaped piece of metal on top of the spike held the plume in place on the spike. Below the star was a metal laurel wreath, which circled the front half of the helmet. Officers had an oak leaf band running up the rear seam from the bottom to the spike.

Most of the Dragoon Guards' helmets carried a twelve-pointed star. Only the fourth regiment had an eight-pointed star. The star for all regiments except the 6th Dragoon Guards was diamond-cut. Officers' stars in the 6th Dragoon Guards were rayed like that worn by enlisted men. In the centre of the star was either the regiment's number or regimental badges. The 1st Regiment had, in addition, a scroll below the star.

For Dragoons, the helmets were basically the same pattern as those of the Dragoon Guards, but in white metal (instead of gilt) with gilt fittings. Both regiments of Dragoons that wore helmets, the 1st and the 6th, had twelve-pointed stars on them. In the centre of the stars were regimental devices.

The regulations state that the plume is to be horsehair. However, some officers paid extra to have their plumes made of shredded whalebone or yak hair. The plume rose 5.08 cm (2 inches) from the top of the spike and then fell to the back of the helmet. The plume was expected to fall to the bottom of the helmet at the back, but did not always do so, being sometimes short, other times long. Officers' plumes tended to be fuller and bushier than those of enlisted men.

Some regiments elected to have their plumes crimped – that is, to have waves put into the plumes. This was done in a similar way as waves are put into hair by a hairdresser or at home. The plume hair was dampened and put between wooden sticks or blocks that had an undulating pattern on the inside. This pattern was transferred to the hair as it dried. (Regiments also used wooden blocks to straighten the plume hair.) The decision to crimp the plume or not was made by the individual regiment and often not written down, so surviving photographs must be relied on for evidence, but these will not give a full picture. As noted elsewhere, it is believed that the 1st and 5th Dragoon Guards crimped their plumes before World War I (see Table II.7.a.1). Some regiments crimped their plumes after World War I. These were the 3rd Carabiniers Prince of Wales's Dragoon Guards (formed in 1922 by joining the 3rd Dragoon Guards (Prince of Wales) and Carabiniers (6th Dragoon Guards)) and the 5th Royal Inniskilling Dragoon Guards (formed in 1922 by joining the 5th Dragoon Guards and the Inniskillings (6th Dragoons)).[95] It is hard to detect a pattern in these sightings. The post-World War I use of crimping by the 5th Royal Inniskilling Dragoon Guards could be a carry-over of the use of crimping by the pre-war 5th Dragoon Guards, but the post-1918 use of crimping by the 5th Royal Inniskilling Dragoons has no known counterpart in the pre-war 5th Dragoons or the Inniskillings (6th Dragoons). It is equally possible that one of these regiments crimped their plumes without our knowing about it today, or that the composite regiment elected to begin crimping their plumes on some occasions.

The helmets of the other ranks were very similar in shape to those of officers, although the experienced eye could doubtless have spotted the difference. The helmet plate for all the other ranks of regiments was a twelve-pointed star. For other ranks, the star was rayed as opposed to the diamond-cut star worn by all officers except those in the 6th Dragoons. In the centre, on a black leather or black lacquered background, was the regimental number.

For both officers and men, the helmets had rosettes on each side over the ears where the chin chain joined the helmet.

The 2nd Scot Greys Dragoons wore a black bearskin rather than a metal helmet. For officers who were between 1.75 and 1.83 m (5 feet 9 inches and 6 feet) tall, the bearskin was 26.67 cm (10½ inches) tall (Image II:70). For shorter and taller officers, the height of the bearskin was scaled down or up. This was the tallest bearskin in the British army, being 2.54 cm (1 inch) higher for a man of the same height in the foot guards and 3.81 cm (1½ inches) higher than the bearskin fusilier officers could wear. On the left side of the bearskin, a 25.4 cm (10 inch) white hackle feather came out of the grenade-shaped holder (Image II:71). The officers' bearskin weighed 0.91 kg (2 lb). In 1896,

II:70 Czar Nicholas II, Colonel of the Scots Greys
Note the size of his bearskin and the pre-1902 cuff trim.

II:72 Badge on back of other ranks Scots Greys bearskin

these bearskins cost 15 guineas[96] (a guinea was worth around 21 shillings or £1.05), making the cost about £1,770 or $2,090 in current money.

The bearskin for enlisted men was less tall and of lesser quality. On the back it carried a white metal 'horse of Hanover', a horse running with all legs fully extended (Image II:72).

Tunic

For all regiments except the 6th Dragoon Guards, the tunic was scarlet with a standing collar and cuffs of the

II:71 Scots Greys
Dismounted review order with carbines, Main Gate Guard. This image gives a good view of the side of the other ranks' bearskin and the white hackle worn with the bearskin.

II:73 2nd Dragoon Guards, Captain, c. 1895
Note sword belt worn under tunic.

regiment's facing colour (see Tables II.7.a.1 and 2, and see Image C14). It had piping down the front of the tunic in the facing colour. The scarlet colour matched the colour worn by British infantry and recalled the dragoons' role as mounted infantry. The 6th Dragoon Guards wore a blue tunic with white cloth facings (see Image C13). There were eight buttons down the front and two sets of three at the waist behind. The tunic had a three-pointed flap on each rear skirt and was traced out on officers' tunics in double gold Russian braid (Image II:9(6)). Officers wore gold shoulder cords with a small button at the top.

Prior to 1902, officers' sleeves carried an elaborate system of Hungarian knots. The number of knots showed the wearer's rank. Lieutenants had one knot and captains two (Image II:73). Field officers had three knots, which extended almost to the bend of the elbow (Images II:74 and II:75). All officers had a preliminary loop on either side of the knot. After 1902, the knots were simplified. All officers wore the single Hungarian knot of a lieutenant and all regiments, except the 6th Dragoon Guards, had the extra loops on either side of the Hungarian knot (see §II-3-5, Image II:10). The 6th Dragoon Guards had come close to being converted to light cavalry in 1851, and their uniform had been changed to reflect their proposed new status. Because of this historical fact, the uniform of the 6th Dragoon Guards is unique among the dragoon guards. The most noticeable difference is that the tunic is blue rather than scarlet. This blue tunic was edged all around with gold cord. The top and bottom of the standing collar was also edged in gold cord. Prior to 1902, the officers' braid on the collar and cuffs was clearly different (§II-3-5, Images II:9 and II:10; also Images II:76 and II:77). In 1911–14, all dragoon guards and dragoon regiments, with two exceptions, had gold lace that was 1.91 cm (¾ inch) wide around their collar tops. The 1911 Regulations state that the 2nd Dragoon Guards and the 1st Dragoons had collar top lace that was 2.54 cm (1 inch) thick.

Field officers of the 6th Dragoon Guards had an inverted 'V' on the cuff with elaborate braiding and eyes above and below. The braiding extended to almost the bend of the elbow (Image II:76). Captains had a complex Hungarian knot with braid in the form of eyes above it. Below the line of the cord, where the facing colour would normally be shown, were more braids in a whirling pattern (Image II:77). Lieutenants

II:74 Field Officer of the 1st Dragoon Guards
The sleeve trim goes to the elbow. Note velvet cuffs.

II:75 Robert Baden-Powell
He is in 5th Dragoon Guards' field officer uniform, with the cuff trim going to the elbow. Note white over red plume on his helmet. His sword belt is worn under his tunic.

had a single complex Hungarian knot with the white facing colour showing below as if to make up for the complex cuffs (see §II-3-5, Image II:9(8)). The rear three-button flap was outlined by a single line of gold cord on either flap.

The 1900 and 1911 Regulations give the following information about collar and cuff facings: In the 1st, 3rd, 4th, 5th, and 7th Dragoon Guards, facings were velvet. In the 2nd and 6th Dragoon Guards, they were cloth. They were also cloth in the 1st, 2nd, and 6th Dragoons.[97]

The tunics of the other ranks were similar to those of the officers, but made of lesser quality cloth.

The other ranks' collar was of the regimental colour, as were the cuffs. The cuffs were trimmed with a Hungarian knot in roughly the same design as that worn by officers. All regiments except the 6th

II:76 Field Officer's Tunic of the 6th Dragoon Guards
The eyes surrounding the cuff trim are especially exuberant on this tunic and show you can never make any hard and fast rules about British uniforms. See §II-3-5, Image II:7 for the regulation cuff trim for 6th Dragoon Guard's field officers. Also note the pouch belt badge, chain, and pickers and shape of shoulder cords.

II:77 6th Dragoon Guards, Captains, c. 1880/90
Note the trim at their cuffs and the lace on their pouch belts and waist belts.

II:78 2nd Dragoon Guards, c. 1900
Note other ranks' cuff trim and S-clasp on belt.

§II-7 Line Cavalry 117

II:79 (left) 4th Dragoons Guards, Trumpeter, c. 1909
He used a bugle when mounted. Note other ranks' cuff trim and wide stripe on breeches. He is wearing a musician's aiguillette. Also note how the tip of the helmet rests on the bridge of the nose. The inside of the peak is lined with green skiver.

II:80 (below) Other Ranks' Tunic of 3rd Dragoon Guards
Note design on the rear skirts and cuffs and shape and colour of shoulder straps.

Dragoon Guards had the extra loops on either side of the Hungarian knot (Images II:78, II:79, and II:80). The shoulder straps were of regimental colour, and by 1909 the cloth shoulder strap was outlined in yellow. At first, a notation of the regiment's title was stitched into the shoulder straps. These embroidered titles were replaced in 1908 by brass titles worn 1.27 cm (½ inch) above the seam joining the shoulder strap to the sleeve.[98] The titles were a combination of the regiment's number and a 'D' or 'DG,' whichever was applicable[99] (see §II-3-1 and §II-3-2 for a list of the combinations).

The 6th Dragoon Guards did not wear a shoulder strap. Rather, they wore the yellow shoulder cords of the light cavalry.[100] The design on the tunic buttons for officers varied by regiment.

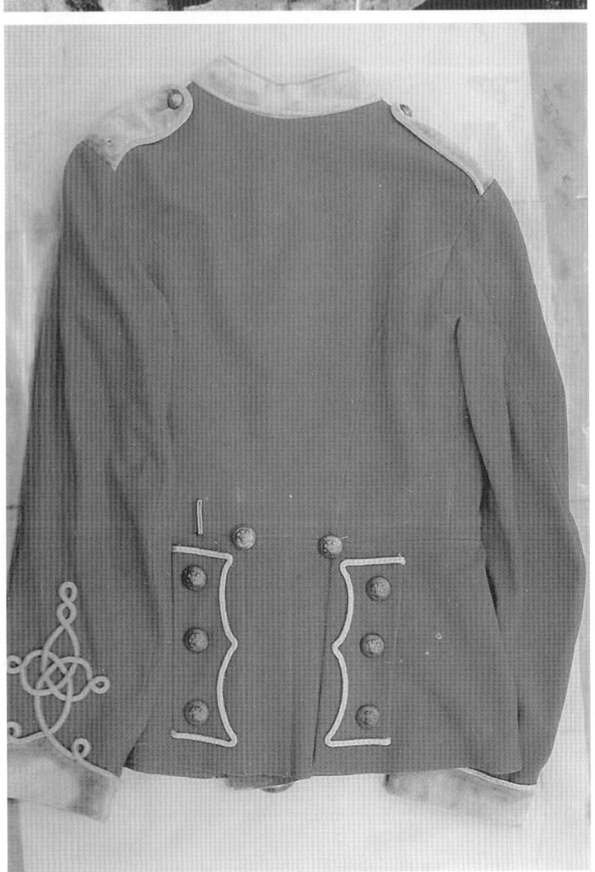

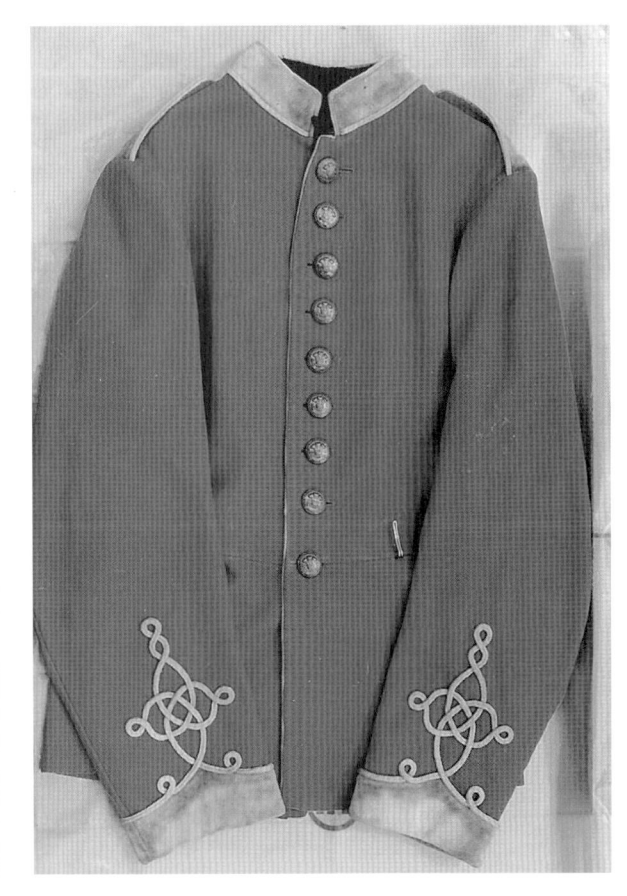

Pouch Belt

Officers wore a gold lace pouch belt over their left shoulder. The belt lace was of the regimental pattern. The 6th Dragoon Guards wore silver pickers and chains on their shoulder belts (Image II:76). This was a hold-over from their nearly being converted to light cavalry. The officers of the 6th Dragoons had a red stripe in the centre of their regimental lace that served as their pouch belt, both before and after 1900.[101] They were the only regiment among the dragoon guards and dragoons to have a stripe on their pouch belt (but see Image II:76). Prior to 1902, enlisted men wore a white leather pouch belt over their left shoulder. After 1902, this practice ended. The officers' pouch was black leather with a solid silver flap. The flap carried ornaments of the regimental pattern.

Waist Belt

For officers the waist belt was gold lace held in place by a gilt rectangular plate with a badge in the regimental pattern.

Other ranks wore a white leather belt closed with an S-shaped buckle.

Officers: Trousers and Pantaloons

Prior to the simplifying reforms of 1902, both the dragoon guards and dragoons wore a complex system of stripes on their blue trousers and pantaloons.

With two exceptions, stripes on the trousers of the dragoon guards and the dragoons consisted of gold lace of regimental pattern. The lace stripes were 4.45 cm (1¾ inches) wide and were centred on the side seam. The two exceptions were the 2nd and 6th Dragoon Guards, whose stripes were white cloth rather than lace. The 6th had another unique feature in that they had a double stripe on each leg. Each of the two stripes was 1.91 cm (¾ inch) wide, and they were set 0.32 cm (⅛ inch) apart. This reflected a light cavalry design as worn by British lancers and hussars.

The pantaloons had stripes made of cloth. They were the same width as the stripes on the trousers. The colour of the cloth stripe worn by officers of a given regiment was the same as that worn by the men of the regiment.

Around 1902, army dress was simplified for officers. The 1904 Regulations, repeated by the 1911 Regulations, provided, with two exceptions, that both trousers and pantaloons would have 4.45 cm (1¾ inches) yellow cloth stripes. The two exceptions were still the 2nd and 6th Dragoon Guards. Both of these regiments still had white cloth stripes. The 6th still had double stripes, but the fact that the space between the two stripes had a 'blue light' was added. The 1911 Regulations added that the stripe colour for the 6th Dragoons was primrose, a pale yellow.

Other Ranks: Pantaloons[102]

In full dress before the 1902 reforms, the other ranks of both the dragoon guards and the dragoons wore blue pantaloons (riding breeches) in full dress. With two exceptions, they had one yellow cloth stripe along the side seam of their pantaloon leg 1.91 cm (¾ inch) wide (see Image C18).[103] The exceptions were the 2nd Dragoon Guards, who had a wide white stripe, and the 6th Dragoon Guards. The 6th Dragoon Guards wore two cloth white stripes of the light cavalry pattern (see §II-7-b, Lancers and §II-7-c, Hussars, below). The dimensions of the stripes worn by other ranks were 4.45 cm (1¾ inches) in the 2nd Dragoons and two of 1.91 cm (¾ inch) in the 6th Dragoon Guards.

The colour of the blue pantaloons and the stripes was not changed in the 1902 reforms. However, it is likely the shade of yellow worn by the 6th Dragoons had changed to primrose yellow by 1911, as the 1911 Dress Regulations, which call for primrose, were probably recognising what had been done in the regiment for years.

Boots

In mounted full dress, the boot came to about 10.16 cm (4 inches) from the top of the knee. When not mounted, Wellington boots were worn for full dress and other orders of dress.

Sergeants' Arm Badges

One custom that separated the British army from all other armies was the wearing of special arm badges by sergeants and some other NCOs in the cavalry. Listed below are the badges worn by dragoon guards and dragoon NCOs in different cavalry regiments in 1914:

1st Dragoon Guards	Austrian double-headed eagle
2nd Dragoon Guards	The word 'Bays' within a laurel wreath, surmounted by a crown
3rd Dragoon Guards	Prince of Wales's plume
5th Dragoon Guards	None authorised, but, in practice wore running white horse of Hanover[104]
4th Dragoon Guards	Star of the Order of St Patrick
6th Dragoon Guards	None
7th Dragoon Guards	The Earl Ligonier's Crest in gilding metal in 1914
1st Dragoons	Royal crest (lion over a crown)
2nd Dragoons	French Napoleonic eagle
6th Dragoons	Castle of Inniskilling

The badges, with some exceptions noted below, were made of sterling silver. They were to be worn by sergeants of all grades above the rank of lance sergeant. The badges were not to be worn by warrant officers, but in several regiments warrant officers did wear them.

In the 2nd Dragoon Guards, the arm badge was authorised to be worn by corporals and lance sergeants in addition to sergeants. Rather than having a sterling silver badge, the 2nd Dragoon Guards had a white metal badge, and the 7th Dragoon Guards' badge was of gilded metal. For a sample of these badges, see *§II-3 Appendix I*.

Between 1890 and 1907, the front ranks of dragoon guards and dragoons were armed with lances.[105] The lances were the standard 2.74 m (9 feet) long. The men were eligible to earn crossed lances skill-at-arms badges, which would be worn on the lower left arm. The lance pennant was the standard red over white swallow-tailed pattern.

Table II.7.a.3: Battle Honours Held by Line Cavalry Regiments in 1914

1st Dragoon Guards	13	8th Hussars	9
2nd Dragoon Guards	4	9th Lancers	16
3rd Dragoon Guards	13	10th Hussars	10
4th Dragoon Guards	5	11th Hussars	11
5th Dragoon Guards	13	12th Lancers	8
6th Dragoon Guards	12	13th Hussars	12
7th Dragoon Guards	10	14th Hussars	15
1st Dragoons	12	15th Hussars	10
2nd Dragoons	13	16th Lancers	18
3rd Hussars	13	17th Lancers	7
4th Hussars	13	18th Hussars	4
5th Lancers	7	19th Hussars	10
6th Dragoons	7	20th Hussars	4
7th Hussars	9	21st Lancers	1

§II-7-b LANCERS

Uniform

Table II.7.b.1: Lancers Dress Uniforms in 1911–14

Regiment	Tunic	Plastron, Mortarboard Top, Cuffs, Collar (Facing Colour)	Double Trouser Stripes	Helmet Plume	Notes
5th	Blue	Scarlet	Yellow	Green	A
9th	Blue	Scarlet[a]	Yellow	Black and white	A, B
12th	Blue	Scarlet	Yellow	Scarlet	A
16th	Scarlet	Blue	Yellow	Black[b]	A, B
17th	Blue	White	White[c]	White	
21st	Blue	French grey	Yellow	White	A, B

Source: Dress Regulations, 1911, pp. 43–4; MacLeod, Glory, pp. 22–5.
Notes: [a] The 9th left the top in black patent leather and covered the sloped undersides of the mortarboard in blue cloth. Gold waist band was 2.54 cm (1 inch) high.
[b] The plume was red over white prior to 1883.
[c] For the 17th, the stripes were white for both officers and other ranks.

A Yellow trouser stripes for both officers and other ranks.
B: The 16th Lancers often put crimps or waves in their helmet plumes. This was adopted by the 9th and 21st Lancers. The 1st and 5th Dragoon Guards also crimped their plumes (Images II:81, II:83, and II:86) (Rowe, Lancers, p. 101).

HEADDRESS

The British lancer pattern cap had a compressed mid-section but was thicker in the middle than its continental cousins, much closer to the original Napoleonic model. For officers, it was made of black patent leather about 16.51 cm (6½ inches) high in front, 21.59 cm (8½ inches) in back, and the flat top (the mortarboard) was 17.78 cm (7 inches) square. The other ranks' cap was 22.54 cm (8⅞ inches) tall in front and 22.86 cm (9 inches) in the back. The sides were 17.78 cm (7 inches). The mortarboard was 16.83 cm (6⅝ inches) side to side and 24.77 cm (9¾ inches) diagonally.[106]

The cap of the 9th Lancers had many unique features. These will be best covered separately from the general discussion of lancer caps.

Officers' Lancer Caps

The following does not cover the 9th Lancers:

The lancer's cap was made of black patent leather. A band of lace 2.54 cm (1 inch) wide went around the waist. The lace was in the regimental pattern (see Image II:14(1)).[107] Three regiments had a colour

II:81 16th Lancers, Mounted Review Order, c. 1910/12
This regiment also crimped their plumes.

line in the centre of the lace (see Table II.7.b.2). Below the lace were two bands of gold braid. The upper one was 1.27 cm (½ inch) wide, and the lower was 0.64 cm (¼ inch) wide. There was 0.32 cm (⅛ inch) between the lower band of lace and the top band of braid and between the two bands of braid. Around the bottom of the lance cap were two bands of gold braid. The top band was 0.64 cm (¼ inch) wide and the bottom was 1.27 cm (½ inch) wide. There was 0.32 cm (⅛ inch) between them.

On the black patent leather peak (brim) was embroidered three stripes of gold purl. The widest stripe was the one in the centre.[108]

Table II.7.b.2: Central Colour Line on Lace

Regiment	Colour
5th	None
9th	Metal
12th	Blue
16th	Red
17th	Blue
21st	None

Source: Rowe, Lancers, pp. 73–5, 77, 78.

The lace was made with the coloured line as a part of the lace.

Except for the 9th Lancers, the top of the officers' lancer's caps were covered in cloth in the colours set out in Table II.7.b.1.[109]

Gold gimp and orris cord crossed the top of the mortarboard and went down the angles to the waist of the cap. Again the 9th Lancers were an exception.

9th Lancers' Officers' Caps

The caps of the 9th Lancers were different. In the 9th, the top was not covered by cloth and was left as plain black patent leather. The sides of the 9th's mortarboard were covered in a dark blue cloth. The edges of the top of the mortarboard were not trimmed, but the angles at the four corners had gold metal ornaments over the gilt metal strips. Down each angle of the mortarboard gilt metal strips ran from the top of the mortarboard to the waist of the cap.[110]

The front edge of the black patent leather peak had a simple gilt metal 0.64 cm (¼ inch) wide binding at its front edge.[111]

The waist of the cap did not have bands of lace. Rather, it had a gilt metal band 2.54 cm (1 inch) wide, which appeared to be a coil of rope. There was no braid around the bottom of the helmet.

Common Features

The top of the other ranks' lancer's cap was not covered in cloth, but instead black patent leather. The cloth-covered sides of the mortarboard were reinforced by having thin strips of cane inserted into pockets sewn into the cloth. This gave the sides a ribbed appearance.[112]

On the left front of the officers' cap, a gold bullion rosette with the royal cipher was embroidered in the centre on coloured velvet.

Table II.7.b.3: Colours of Velvet

Regiment	Colour
5th	Green
9th	See below[a]
12th	Blue
16th	Scarlet
17th	Blue[b]
21st	French Grey[c]

Notes: [a] In the 9th Lancers, in place of the gold bullion rosette, the cap had a gilt metal gimp boss, which appeared to be a coiled rope, each level reducing in size as it descended towards the centre. At the centre was a button with a regimental design on it (Rowe, Lancers, pp. 79, 71).
[b] Rowe, Lancers, p. 69.
[c] Rowe, Lancers, p. 80.

Officers wore swan feather plumes and, on occasion, horsehair or cock tail feather plumes. Rowe thought the cock tail feather plumes might have been worn at levees.[113] The plumes were normally 30.48 cm (12 inches) long, rising 11.43 cm (4½ inches) above the top of the cap.[114]

Other rank wore horsehair plumes in the same colours as the swan feathers shown in Table II.7.b.4. David Rowe collected information on what type of plume was worn, for how long and how it changed over the years.[115]

II:82 9th Lancers, Field Officer
Note the swan feather plume on his lancer cap and the pattern of his girdle. Also note cap lines worn twice around body of officer, four times in the other lancer regiments.

II:84 9th Lancers, Officer, c. 1896
Note the lance cap on the table and the unique design elements on the helmet worn only by the 9th Lancers.

II:83 9th Lancers, Dismounted Review Order, c. 1910/12
Note crimped black and white lance cap plume and the lancer's girdle.

II:85 17th Lancers, Colonel Sir Douglas Haig, 1912
He has double rank lace on his cuffs even though this is a 1912 photo. Note white swan feathers for his lance cap and the double cap lines which have been wrapped twice around his body.

Table II.7.b.4: Swan Feather Plume Colours in 1904

Regiment	Colour
5th	Green
9th	Black and white
12th	Scarlet
16th	Black[a]
17th	White
21st	White

Source: *Dress Regulations, 1904*, p. 22, ¶287.
Notes: [a] Prior to 1883 the plume was scarlet and white.

At the back of the cap, just below the left back edge of the mortarboard and in the middle of the regimental lace, was set a ring, the cap lines passed through this ring.

Other ranks wore horsehair plumes in the same colour as was worn by the officers in their regiment. The 9th Lancers crimped their plumes and lance pennants. The 16th and 21st Lancers also crimped their horsehair plumes.[116]

Two gold gimp and orris cap lines encircled the cap once at the waist, passed through the rear ring, and then dropped behind the wearer's body. From there, they looped up to pass around the officer's body once or twice, depending on the regiment (Image II:82), and then passed across his body to end on the left side of his chest[117] near the top left button of the tunic. The lines ended in a prominent accord shape. When not fastened to the helmet, the cap lines would be fastened around the neck and go twice around the body before looping across the front to be fastened on the left (Image II:85).

Warrant officers and senior NCOs wore caps that had elements of officers' quality.

Other Ranks

The other ranks had a yellow band at their cap's waist. On it, most regiments had a stripe. Table II.7.b.5 gives the colour of these stripes.

II:86 9th Lancers, Dismounted Review Order, c. 1910
Observe the crimped plume and the white pouch belt.

Table II.7.b.5: Other Ranks' Centre Stripe

Regiment	Colour
5th	Just yellow band
9th	Metal only
12th	Blue
16th	Red
17th	Blue
21st	Just yellow band

Source: Rowe, *Lancers*, p. 90.

In place of the officers' gold bullion rosettes, other ranks for all regiments except the 9th had a yellow wool cockade. In the centre of the yellow cockade was a coloured centre that varied by regiment as follows:

5th Lancers	Red
9th Lancers	A brass/gilding metal gimp boss
12th Lancers	Blue
16th Lancers	Red
17th Lancers	Blue
21st Lancers	French grey.[118]

The four edges of the mortarboard were covered by yellow worsted cord. This did not go over the top, as was the case on the officers' mortarboards. Senior NCOs, such as sergeants, had gold cord in lieu of the yellow cord. The 9th Lancers did not have cord. In its place gilding metal strips covered the angles, going down to the waist.[119]

The other ranks' peak was black japanned leather. Their plumes were horsehair. They were the same colour as the officers' plumes. The cap lines were made of yellow worsted cord. They were worn the same way as the officers' cords.[120]

The cap plate for British lancers was complex. It consisted of a rayed back plate upon which different designs for the different regiments were mounted. This was the royal coat of arms, battle honours, badges, and scroll bearing the regiment's name with, depending on regiment, sprays of laurel, oak, shamrock, or palm leaves. The lancer cap showed battle honours, so it had to be changed periodically. When Queen Victoria was succeeded by King Edward VII, the crown on the helmet plates was changed.

In addition to the royal arms and the battle honours, the plate could contain regiment badges and scrolls bearing the regiment's name.

For officers, the back plate was of gilt. The mounted devices were of gilt or silver. The other ranks' cap plate was of gilding metal and was die-struck, showing the same insignia as above.

Tunic

The double-breasted tunic was blue for all regiments except the 16th Lancers, who wore scarlet (compare Images C15 and C16). There were two rows of seven buttons in front that were 20.32 cm (8 inches) apart at the top and 10.16 cm (4 inches) apart at the bottom. The bottom two were flat to go under the girdle. The buttons for officers had a regimental design.

The coloured front was in the form of a plastron and was in the facing colour (see Table II.7.b.1.) This provided a distinct splash of colour to lancers who otherwise wore a rather dark uniform. The original function of the plastron was as a windcheater to give an extra bit of warmth to the wearer. The range of plumes and plastron colours made the lancers a colourful branch of service (Images II:87, II:88, and II:89).

II:87 17th (Duke of Cambridge's Own) Lancers, Dismounted Review Order
Notice the white plastron, which stands out against the blue of the tunic.

§II-7 Line Cavalry

The tunic had pointed cuffs of the regiment's facing colour. For officers the cuffs were trimmed in gold lace. The pattern of the lace roughly showed rank. The rank lace became less elaborate after the reforms of 1902. Prior to 1902, field officers had two V-shaped bands of trim above the cuff (Image II:82) and those below field grade only one (see §II-3-5, Image II:13, and Image II:84). After 1902, all carried one V-shaped band of trim (see §II-3-5, Image II:14, and Image II:89). Other ranks had a simple pointed cuff with two buttons off to the side. Field officers prior to 1902 also had two rows of gold lace on the collar and those below field rank one. After 1902, all had one row of lace.

The button colour was gilt. Each regiment had its own design on the button. In addition to this, each regiment, except the 17th Lancers, had a special badge they wore on their full dress collars. To describe each of these, much less show examples, would be to allow fine uniform details to swallow up this work.

Twisted lancer-style gold wire cords were on the shoulder for officers (see §II-3-4, Image II:4). These carried badges of rank on them. In most other regiments, the other ranks wore yellow cords on their shoulders. The lone exception was the 21st Lancers, who had an embroidered Imperial Crown and VRI cypher on a blue shoulder strap trimmed with French grey (French grey, a shade of light blue, was a colour much used by the East India Company).[121] Rank was also shown on the sleeves.

The back of the tunic had eight buttons: two at the waist and three on each side centre of the skirt. The three skirt buttons were trimmed with a gold cord for officers. The trim was the regiments' facing colour in the case of other ranks.

Lancer NCO Arm Badges

As noted elsewhere, one of the many unusual features of the British army was the wearing of regimental arm badges by cavalry NCOs. The designs for the lancer badges in 1914 were as follows:

5th Lancers	Harp and crown
9th Lancers	A.R. cypher reversed and interlaced and Crown
12th Lancers	Prince of Wales's plume
17th Lancers	Death's head, bones, and glory scroll motto
21st Lancers	Imperial VRI cypher and crown

II:88 9th Lancers Lieutenant, 1899
This photograph provides a view of the scarlet plastron. See cap lines going around body only twice, pouch belt, and lance cap with metal peak edging.

II:89 21st Lancers, Captain, Dismounted Review Order, Cairo, 1912
This provides a view of the 21st Lancers' French grey plastron.

The regulations state that the special NCO arm badges are to be worn above the chevron. Photographs show that, in fact, the badges were often worn on the chevrons by some regiments. In lancer regiments, the badge was worn by sergeants of all grades above the rank of lance sergeant, but in some regiments it was also worn by corporals. In this period, special arm badges were not worn officially by warrant officers, but this rule was, in some cases, not followed. For lancers, the special badges were made of sterling silver for all regiments.[122]

For a sample of these badges, see §II-3 Appendix I.

Pouch Belt
A pouch belt was worn over the left shoulder. The belt was gold lace of the regimental pattern for officers. On the pouch belt, there was a silk stripe of regimental facing colour for all regiments, except the 9th Lancers (see §II-2-1 for regimental facing colours). The 9th did not have a silk line in the lace. The 9th and the 17th Lancers did not wear collar badges, in spite of what the dress regulations may have stated. Up to 1902, the 21st Lancers wore a hussar-style pouch belt. Troopers wore a white pouch belt with a black leather pouch. It was withdrawn after 1902 and after that, other ranks did not wear a pouch belt. While worn, the pouch of the 17th Lancers was larger than the pouches worn in other regiments (Image II:90).

For officers, the pouch had different colours with a solid metal cover. Each regiment's pouch cover had a unique design on it.

Table II.7.b.6: Colours of Pouches Worn by Lancers

Regiment	Pouch Colour
5th	Scarlet
9th	Scarlet
12th	Scarlet
16th	Scarlet
17th	Blue
21st	Black

II:90 17th Lancers, c. 1898
Note the trim on the back skirts of the tunic. This photograph shows the extra large pouch worn by the 17th Lancers up to 1902 when pouches and pouch belts were done away with. The regiment's unique white stripes worn on trousers and breeches can just be seen in this photograph.

Girdle
Lancers wore around their waists a 6.35 cm (2 ½ inches) wide gold lace girdle. It had two narrow crimson silk stripes. For troopers, it was yellow worsted with two scarlet stripes.

Buttons
The buttons of each regiment had their own individual design.

Gauntlet Gloves
Gloves were white leather for officers and men.

Officers: Trousers and Riding Breeches (Pantaloons)
Up to 1902 in most regiments, the officers wore blue cloth trousers with two stripes of gold lace of regimental pattern. The lace was 1.91 cm (¾ inch) wide and set 0.64 cm (¼ inch) apart along each side

seam. The exception was the 17th Lancers, whose two stripes were white cloth. The pantaloons were also blue cloth with stripes that were the same colour as those worn by the men. When full dress was simplified around 1902, the regimental gold lace and different coloured stripes on the pantaloons were abolished. The 1904 and 1911 Dress Regulations state an officer's stripes were to be yellow for both the trousers and pantaloons. The stripes were required to be 1.91 cm (¾ inch) wide and 0.64 cm (¼ inch) apart.

Other Ranks: Pantaloons[123]

In full dress prior to the 1902 reforms, other ranks wore blue pantaloons (riding breeches). With one exception, all regiments had two yellow cloth stripes on their blue pantaloons. The exception was the 17th Lancers, whose two stripes were white. Citations giving the width of the stripes have not been found, but it is likely the width was the same as that of the officers (see above).

There were little or no changes to the other ranks' pantaloons in the 1902 reforms.

Boots

Mounted officers and men wore boots that came to within 10.16 cm (4 inches) of the knee. Dismounted officers wore a Wellington boot in review order and in the evening.

Lance and Pennant

Lancers carried a 2.74 m (9 foot) lance, which had a red over white pennant. The lance was made of ash until 1868; after that, it was made of bamboo from India.

§II-7-c HUSSARS

Table II.7.c.1: Hussar Dress Uniform in 1911–14

Regiment	Plume[a]	Bag	Collar	Stripe on Pouch Belt	Chain and Pricker	Pouch	Notes
3	White	Garter blue	Scarlet	Scarlet	Yes	Black leather silver flap	
4	Scarlet	Yellow		Scarlet	Yes	Black leather silver flap	
7	White	Scarlet		None	No	Scarlet cloth	A
8	White/red	Scarlet		None	No	Scarlet cloth	B
10	White/black	Scarlet		Chain on leather	Yes	Black patent leather	B, C, D
11	White/crimson	Crimson	V cut in front	None	Yes	Crimson leather gilt metal flap	B, E, F, G
13	White	Buff (white)	Buff (white)	Buff (white)	Yes	Black leather silver flap	H, I
14	White	Yellow		Gold	Yes	Black leather silver flap	J
15	Scarlet	Scarlet		Scarlet	No	Scarlet cloth	K
18	White/scarlet	Blue		None	Yes	Scarlet leather	B, L
19	White	White		White	Yes	Black leather silver flap	M
20	Yellow	Crimson		Crimson	Yes	Black leather silver flap	

Source: Dress Regulations, 1911, pp. 37–8; MacLeod, Glory, pp. 18–21.
Notes: [a] In 1901 officers' plumes, which had been osprey feathers, were replaced by a 38.1 cm (15 inch) high ostrich feather rising out of a base of vulture feathers. This change gave the officers a very different outline.

A: Officers' cap lines were worn shorter in the 7th than in other regiments. The cap lines were tied close to the tunic, just under collar, for both officers and men. The lines went under the top row of braid. Officers wore their white shirts so the shirt showed above the tunic collar.
B: The plume top colour is the ostrich feather (Hussar plumes for officers had been two parts since 1857).
C: The cap line goes under left arm rather than around the neck.
D: The top line of the chest frogging is worn under the shoulder's gold chain gimp. The pricker plate badge carried the Prince of Wales's feathers.
E: Officers' and other ranks' cap lines were worn plaited at times.
F: A pattern of small circles was worn around the button on the busby bag.
G: The pouch belt had a crown on it to hold the start of the pricker chain.
H: Battle honours are shown on the pouch belt. In 1914, these were: Albuhera, Vittoria, Orthes, Toulouse, Peninsula, Waterloo, Alma, Balaklava, Inkerman, Sevastopol, Relief of Ladysmith, and South Africa 1899–1902.
I: White double stripes on trousers and pantaloons. Regulations say buff, but really white.
J: Prussian eagle carried on the pouch plate where prickers go in. A cockade was not worn in the busby. In the 14th Hussars, both officers and other ranks, at times, wore plaited busby cap lines, although this was not authorised by the regulations. For the 14th and 15th Hussars, photographic evidence exists that they, at times, plaited their cap lines; the 14th seem to have done so more often than the 15th.
K: The cap line is not wrapped around the busby (MacLeod, *Glory*, p. 20; Bowling, *Hussars*, pp. 24 and 25, colour drawings nos. 32 and 41).
L: The pouch belt had a lion's head on it to hold the start of the pricker chain.
M: The pouch belt had the Assaya elephant, a battle honour given in 1803 to commemorate the Indian Battle of Assaya. They had the battle honours Assaya and Niagara above and below the elephant (*Dress Regulations, 1911*, p. 42, ¶ 432).

Uniform

HEADDRESS (BUSBY)

The officers' busby was constructed of black sable fur, 16.51 cm (6½ inches) high in front and 19.69 cm (7¾ inches) in the back (Image II:91). The top was slightly smaller than the base. A small gold cockade 5.08 cm (2 inches) tall and 3.81 cm (1½ inches) wide was at the top centre of the busby just under the plume, and was worn by all regiments except the 14th Hussars (Image II:92).

A cloth bag of regimental colour lay across the top of the busby and fell to the right side. The bag had a circular shape at the end (Image II:93). For colour, see Table II.7.c.1. The bag carried gold trim along the two edge seams and down the centre. It had a gold gimp button at the bottom. The 11th Hussars had extra decorations on their bags. There were small circles around the button on the busby bag (Image II:94).

The busby chain was a gilt corded chain. A line connecting the busby to the wearer's body was also part of the busby. Made of gold purl cord with slides and olive-shaped ends, the busby line encircled the busby three times, then around the body, and looped on the breast. The line of the 15th did not wrap around the busby, and in the 11th Hussars, the line was plaited as it crossed the chest (Images II:95 and II:96). Other regiments at times also plaited their busby lines (Image II:97).

The 10th Hussars wore their busby cords under their left arm rather than around their necks (Image II:98). The 7th Hussars wore short busby cords which ended close to the neck. The knot was worn under the top row of chest braid by officers, and the end acorns were close below the knot (Images II:99 and II:100).

The other ranks' busby followed the same pattern. However, their bag piping was yellow cord. Their busbies were made of black sealskin. The busby line was also a yellow cord.

TUNIC

The tunic consisted of dark blue cloth edged with gold gimp chain down the front and bottom for officers (see Image C17). It carried on the front six rows of gold gimp chain ending in two loops which dropped below the line of the braid. On either side the loops tilted inward. The rows of braid became progressively shorter as the decoration moved downwards from the upper chest to the waist (Image II:101).

The back of the tunic had two double lines of concave gold gimp chain edged with narrow gold braid. The top ended in a tri-fold and the bottom in a stylised inter-looped Hungarian knot (Image II:102).

The collar was blue, except for the 3rd Hussars, whose collar was scarlet, and the 13th, whose collar was buff (white). These exceptions were carried over from their service as light dragoons.

II:91 The German Crown Prince in the Uniform of the 11th Hussars
Note cockade at the top of the boots and an extra elaborate braid on his cuffs. He appears to be wearing field officer's decorated cuffs after c. 1900 changes.

II:93 15th Hussars, 1910 (although not wearing the 15th collar badge)
Even though this photo is dated 1910, he is still wearing a pouch belt that was officially done away with in 1902. Note the cap line is wrapped around the busby. Cap lines around the busby were worn by other ranks in the 15th, but officers did not wrap their cap lines around their busby.

II:92 Colonel Henry Blackbourne Hamilton of the 14th Hussars, c. 1887–91
Note lack of cockade at top of busby. He is wearing levee dress pantaloons and Hessian boots. Photo taken prior to 1902 as sabretache discontinued in November 1901.

II:94 11th (Prince Albert's Own) Hussars. Lieutenant Harold William Swithinbank c. 1883, Levee Dress
Swithinbank was also a sergeant in the 2nd Dragoons (Scots Greys) before becoming an officer in the 11th. Note the patent leather Hessian boots and bosses, crown on pouch belt, plaited busby cap lines across the right chest, and decoration around button on busby bag. Also note how the top chest braid is under the shoulder cord. The 11th Hussars were one of the regiments where the officers wore a Mameluk-type sword in levee dress. The sabretaches were not carried after 1901.

II:95 11th Hussars Trooper, c. 1905/6
Sword is pattern 1899. Note plaited cap lines.

II:97 13th Hussars
Note plaited cap line and battle honour scrolls.

II:96 11th Hussars Lieutenant, 1895
Note the plaited cap line.

II:98 10th Hussars Levee Dress
Note how top of chest braid ends under shoulder cords, 'chains' on pouch belt, and busby cap lines under left arm.

§II-7 Line Cavalry 131

II:99 Prince Arthur of Connaught in 7th Hussar Uniform
Note short busby cap line. Sash and decorations of the Royal Victorian Order.

II:101 Winston Churchill as a Young Officer in the 4th Hussars
Note the gimp chain on the tunic and cap line under the first row of frogging. This was a standard hussar uniform.

II:100 7th Hussars, Other Ranks
Note short busby cap line and attached inside rear of review order colonial helmet. Note swordsman and shooting qualification badges plus two good-conduct chevrons.

II:102 3rd Hussars
Note back of other ranks' tunic, the scout badge on the right arm of the mounted sergeant, and the arm badge above the chevrons.

The 1900 Regulations show field officers and captains with braided lace eyes on the collar. In the 1904 Regulations this was discontinued (see §II-3-5, Images II:11 and II:12). Officers wore plaited gold chain gimp shoulder cords that carried their badges of rank. The cord was held in place by a small button near the collar.

The cuff carried a Hungarian knot. Prior to 1902, the cuff, in general, showed the officer's rank. Field officers had an elaborate set of eye-shaped braids around the knot, reaching up the sleeve 27.94 cm (11 inches) from the bottom of the cuff. A captain had less elaborate eyes, reaching up 22.86 cm (9 inches) from the bottom of the cuff. Lieutenants had just the plain knot. After the 1902 reforms, all officers wore the plain knot of a lieutenant on their cuffs (see §II-3-5, Image II:12).

The officers' tunic was buttoned with toggle-shaped fasteners while other ranks had ball-shaped buttons.

POUCH BELTS AND POUCHES

In 1857, there were only five hussar regiments: the 7th, 8th, 10th, 11th, and 15th. These might be considered the old hussar regiments. This affected the pattern of pouch belts and pouches the regiments wore.

Other ranks wore a white leather pouch belt over their left shoulder until 1902 (Image II:93). After that, it was officially abandoned (Image II:103), but the belt seems to have been worn after that date by some troopers or regiments (Images II:93 and II:95).

The pouch belt for officers was also worn over the left shoulder. For officers, it consisted of gold lace on a leather belt for all regiments, except the 10th. The 10th had a plain black patent leather belt with chains on it (Image II:98). The other regiments' lace was of regimental pattern in the 1900 Dress Regulations. The 1904 Regulations no longer show different lace patterns for the different regiments.

The 13th had scrolls on their pouch belt that showed their battle honours (Images II:123 and II:104). See Table II.7.c.1 for a list of these honours in 1914. The 18th Hussars had a lion's head at the front top of the pouch belt, rather than the normal decoration, to hold the beginning of the pouch chains (Image II:105).

The belt was not wider than 5.08 cm (2 inches). It had regimental pattern buckle tips and slides. These were gilt for the 7th, 8th, 10th, 15th, and 18th Hussars. For the 4th, 11th, 13th, 14th, 19th, and 20th Hussars,

II:103 Probably 15th Hussars, Other Ranks, c. 1912
Cavalry collar badges were adopted in 1898, but were not always worn after that date. Note marksman badge and service chevron. Also note the cap line wraps around the busby. A distinguishing mark for officers of the 15th was not wrapping the cap line around the busby but enlisted men's busbies did have the cap line wrapped around their busbies. This exhibits the type of anomaly that so often appears among British regiments.

they were silver. The leather base was crimson for the 11th and 20th Hussars, buff for the 13th Hussars, and scarlet for all others.

The 7th, 8th, and 15th did not carry chains and prickers on their pouch belts and had the cloth pouches of the old hussar regiments. The pouch for the 3rd, 4th, and 13th Hussars had pouches of the old light dragoon pattern in that their pouches were black leather with silver flaps. The pouches for the 10th and 11th fall outside the above patterns and seem to be unique to each regiment (see Table II.7.c.1).

II:104 13th Hussars, Lieutenant Colonel
Note battle honour scrolls on the pouch belt.

II:105 18th Hussars, 1906
Note lion's head on pouch belt. This was unique to this regiment.

The 18th Hussars were one of the old hussar regiments. They were converted to hussars in 1807 and disbanded in 1821, but re-raised in 1858. Their pouch and pouch belt system was something of a hybrid. It was not cloth like the old hussar regiments as this was probably a bit impractical. It was leather and had the scarlet colour of a hussar regiment. The 19th and 20th were East India Company regiments that came into the British line as light dragoons in 1858 after the Indian Mutiny, and then converted to hussars (see Table II.7.c.1 above for their pouches).

OFFICERS: TROUSERS AND PANTALOONS

Trousers and pantaloons were the same shade of blue cloth as the tunic, except for the 11th Hussars who wore crimson. For levees, the 11th wore crimson and the 10th scarlet.

Prior to 1902, two 1.91 cm (¾ inch) gold lace stripes of regimental pattern, set 0.64 cm (¼ inch) apart, were along the outside seam of the trousers. The 13th Hussars wore white cloth in place of the lace. The pantaloons had two 1.91 cm (¾ inch) cloth stripes set 0.32 cm (⅛ inch) apart. The regulations state they were the same colour as those worn by the men (see below). After 1902, the stripes were of yellow cloth for both trousers and pantaloons, except for the 13th Hussars, who continued to wear white, or buff.

OTHER RANKS: PANTALOONS

Other ranks wore blue pantaloons (riding breeches) in full dress. With one exception, other ranks had two yellow cloth stripes on their pantaloons. The exception was the 13th Hussars, whose stripes were officially buff,[124] but in reality may have been white. Since the 1900 Dress Regulations, and presumably those before, provide that officers wear stripes of the colour worn by the other ranks, the officers would also wear yellow stripes on their pantaloons. A specific exemption was made for the 13th Hussars: there the other ranks of the regiment wore white stripes on the trousers.

The other ranks' stripes were 1.91 cm (¾ inch) wide and 0.32 cm (⅛ inch) apart, the same as the officers'. After 1902, the stripes on the other ranks' pantaloons were yellow, with the exception of the 13th. The width of the stripes and the width of the space between the stripes remained the same.

II:106 20th Hussars, Captain George C. Fitzgeorge, Review Order Uniform, c. 1875
The badge ranks are on the collar, and the hussar tunic does not have shoulder cords. After 1880, rank badges were moved to shoulder cords. The gold stripes on the riding breeches were discontinued after 1894.

Boots

Prior to 1902, two types of boots were worn by officers in full dress. The first was the universal riding boot. It came almost to the knee and was cut with a 'V' in front. Prior to 1902, hussar officers wore a gold gimp oval boss on the front of each boot just below each 'V' cut (Image II:92).

After 1902, a regular riding boot was worn. A 'V' cut in front was not specified in the 1911 dress regulations. It came to within 10.16 cm (4 inches) of the knee. The gold boss was still worn on the front of the boot (Image II:91). Other ranks wore the same type of riding boot as officers but without the boss (Image II:95).

A special boot, the Hessian boot, was also worn by officers in levee dress. The main feature of this boot was that it was scooped out in the back, where it reached only to mid-calf. Images II:94 and II:107 show two views of Hessian boots. The front was lower than the normal boot, being 3.81 cm (1½ inches) higher than the back of the boot. The top of each boot was trimmed with gold gimp chain, and it had an

II:107 4th Queen's Own Hussars, Major Cecil Wyburn Peters, c. 1891
He is in levee dress – note the Hessian boots. Levee pantaloons were to be worn skin-tight. As noted elsewhere, the sabretache was not part of the officers' uniform after 1901.

oval boss in front. These boots were normally patent leather and were cut so they crumpled near the ankle (Images II:94 and II:107).

Collar Badges

Hussar officers in some regiments, but not all, wore collar badges in full dress. The same was true for the other ranks. However, it is difficult to locate photos that show the man close enough to give a good view of his collar badge. Image II:108 clearly shows the Prussian eagle collar badge and its placement on the 14th Hussars, as worn just prior to 1914. Also see Images II:100 and II:95 for placement of the badges.

Arm Badges

As covered for other British cavalry types above, an unusual feature of the British cavalry was the wearing of regimental arm badges by cavalry NCOs. The designs for hussar arm badges in 1914 were as follows:

3rd Hussars	Wore a running white horse of Hanover[a]
4th Hussars	None
7th Hussars	None officially, but wore the letters 'QO' in interlocked monogram and crown above them[a]
8th Hussars	Crowned harp[a,b]
10th Hussars	Prince of Wales's plumes[a,b]
11th Hussars	Crest and motto of Prince Albert, the Prince Consort[b,c]
13th Hussars	None
14th Hussars	Prussian eagle[d,a]
15th Hussars	Royal crest, a lion over a crown
18th Hussars	'QMO' in interlocked monogram
19th Hussars	Elephant[a]
20th Hussars	None

Notes: [a] Worn by corporals.
[b] Worn on the chevrons as well as above them.
[c] Worn by warrant officers.
[d] In light of the bad feelings between Britain and Germany, led by Prussia, it may seem odd to have the Prussian eagle as a badge for a British regiment. However, this regiment's eagle goes back to 1798 when the Duchess of York was a Prussian.

The arm badges officially were to be worn above the chevron, but this rule was not always obeyed. For most regiments the badges were made of sterling silver. Among the hussars, exceptions were the 14th Hussars and the 18th Hussars. In the 14th Hussars, the badges of the corporals were made of oxidised German silver, while those of senior NCOs were made of sterling silver. The 18th Hussars had badges made from German silver.

Officially, the badge was to be worn by all sergeants above the rank of lance sergeant, except in the 14th Hussars. In the 14th, corporals were officially allowed

II:108 14th (King's) Hussars, Corporal
Note the Prussian eagle badge on his collar.

to wear the arm badge. However, as noted above, this rule was often not followed. Corporals were allowed to wear the arm badge, and in some regiments, the regimental sergeant major and/or the bandmaster elected not to wear the arm badge.

Likewise, officially, warrant officers were not allowed to wear these badges. But, in some regiments, their warrant officers went ahead and wore them. Some of these cases are noted above, but others may not have been preserved.[125]

§II-8 LINE INFANTRY

§II-8-a LINE FOOT

Uniform

HELMET

The line infantry regiments of this period wore the so-called home service pattern spiked helmet, which was introduced in May 1878 (Image II:109). The British spiked helmet took its inspiration from the Prussian pickelhaube, but it was taller and more delicate as it was made of cork rather than boiled leather. The cork body was covered by cloth – dark blue for most of the infantry, dark green for light infantry, and rifle green (close to black) for rifle regiments.

In 1890, three of the four rifle regiments gave up the spiked helmet, and then in 1892, the Cameronians (Scottish Rifles) gave up the helmet.

The helmet was 26.04 cm (10¼ inches) from the back to the centre of the crown and 20.32 cm (8 inches) from the front tip to the crown. At the top of the crown there was a metal piece in the shape of a stylised cross with a fluted spike rising from it. The height of the spike and cross base was 8.26 cm (3¼ inches). On the rear arm of the cross was a small hook where the chin chain could be hooked when not worn under the chin. On each side of the helmet there was a rose boss. The left boss anchored a metal chin chain. The boss on the right contained a hook where the chin chain could be hooked when worn under the chin.

The back had a 0.32 cm (⅛ inch) wide black patent leather trim. The front peak also had trim. For officers, it was 0.48 cm (³⁄₁₆ inch) wide gilded brass. For other ranks, it was leather. Officers, but not other ranks, also had a convex bar 0.64 cm (¼ inch) wide running down the centre of the back of their helmets. It ran from the bottom of the cross on the top of the helmet to the end of the back peak.

There were several differences between the helmets of officers and other ranks. For officers, the metal of the helmet was gilded; for the men it was brass. The officers' front peaks were pointed (Image II:110), while other ranks had rounded front peaks (Image

II:109 Soldier, the Sherwood Foresters (Nottingham and Derbyshire Regiment), c. 1903
Note shape of front of helmet. It is different from that worn by officers. He has the soldier's 'swagger stick', carried when walking out.

II:110 Officers, Hertfordshire Regiment
Note shape of front of helmet. It is different from that worn by most of the other ranks. This was a Territorial Force Regiment, not a regular unit.

II:109). In the back, officers' helmets were squared off while those of the rank and file wore rounded.

In general, the officers' helmets simply looked different as they were taller, narrower and showed that they cost more than the government-issued helmets the other ranks wore. While the rifle regiments still wore the helmet, they had bronze helmet items.

The standard-issue item for the front of the helmet was an eight-pointed garter star with a garter bearing the motto of the Order of the Garter (Image II:29). Around the garter was normally a laurel wreath. However, some regiments had other types of wreaths or devices. The Essex Regiment had an oak leaf wreath. The Sherwood Foresters omitted the garter and had a Maltese cross with an oak leaf wreath.[126] While the Royal Scots wore the helmet up to 1904, they omitted the garter and laurel wreath and wore the star of the Order of the Thistle. On the star was a silver circle with the motto of the Order of the Thistle, *Nemo me impune lacessit* ('No one provokes me with impunity').[127] Between 1878 and 1901, the plate was topped with a St Edward's Crown, also known as Queen's Crown. From 1901 on, an Imperial Crown was used, referred to as the King's Crown (compare the crowns on top of the helmet plates in Image II:109, King's Crown *c.* 1910, and Image II:111, Queen's Crown *c.* 1898). The size of the plate was 13.02 by 11.43 cm (5⅛ by 4½ inches).

The only regiment to show battle honours on the star was the West India Regiment, which had a special wreath of laurel and palm leaves.[128] Battle honours could be shown as part of the regiment's badge in the central space inside the garter.

Within the garter was an open space about 2.54 cm (1 inch) in diameter. This space was filled with regimental badges. For officers, the helmet badge was a three-piece item, and of two-piece construction for other ranks.

II:111 Connaught Rangers Officers, *c.* 1898
Sash over left shoulder.

The space inside the garter in a regiment's badge was often backed with velvet; black, scarlet, or dark green were common. Other badges used coloured enamelled backing – blue, black, red and white, or red and green. The backing was part of the badge's approval pattern, and any change had to be approved by the War Office.

The helmets were not cheap. In 1905, an infantry officer's helmet was listed as costing £2 9s 0d (£269 or $298 in current values).[129] The tin in which the helmet was kept cost another 8s to 13s 6d (£44–74 or $49–82 in current values).

The home service helmet was not universally popular. It was uncomfortable, expensive, and fragile. In 1897, a committee was set up to look into the question of headdress, and they suggested a shako be adopted for infantry in place of the helmet. This was rejected as not being suitable for active service. But in 1900 the helmet was replaced by a cloth cap for active service, thus opening the way for the shako to be considered again. Efforts were made in 1902 and 1906 to reintroduce shakos, but they were rejected on grounds of cost. In 1909 a shako model was approved by the secretary of state and King Edward VII.[130]

After this, the authorities periodically considered conducting trials of the shako prototype, but no action was ever taken and the helmet continued in use up to World War I.

Tunic

The tunic worn by the infantry had taken shape over a fifty-year period. The standard tunic was worn by the line infantry, the light infantry, and the fusiliers. For that reason, when the light infantry and the fusiliers are discussed in separate sections, only their headdress will be covered. They also wore the same trousers and belts as the line infantry.

In 1856, a shorter single-breasted patterned coat was introduced. In 1868, the tunic had pointed cuffs in regimental facing colours, edged with white piping. At this time, officers and senior NCOs wore scarlet while the other ranks still wore red.

In 1879, the cuff was again changed. The white centre edging was removed, and the outer piping was extended to form a trefoil knot above the cuff. In 1871, other ranks were also given a scarlet tunic. Now all line infantry soldiers, officers, and men were dressed

II:112 Lincolnshire Regiment, c. 1904/5
Note pointed cuffs, which were changed in 1902 from jampot cuffs.

in scarlet. However, there was a difference in quality between the tunics of the officers, the NCOs, and the rank and file.

In 1881, there was a further change to the rank-and-file tunic. It now had a low standing collar in the regiment's facing colour. With the exception of royal regiments, the War Office gave white facing colours to all English regiments, yellow to all Scottish regiments, and green to all Irish regiments.[131] Royal regiments had blue facing colours. Royal regiments are those with the title Royal, King's, or Queen's. The only non-royal regiment with blue facings was the Somerset Light Infantry.

The cuffs were changed to be rounded and in the facing colour: the so-called 'jam pot' cuffs. The shoulder straps were scarlet and had a rounded end. They carried white cloth abbreviated regimental titles.

At this time the basic format of the tunic was set. The tunic front had eight brass buttons showing for officer uniforms, with a flat button on the waist. Other ranks had seven brass buttons showing, and their tunics were of lesser quality. The tunic was piped down the left front and on the right front up to the waist in white. The shoulder straps had two buttons, and there were two at the waist in the back. All were brass. Two white piping lines ran down the back of the tunic skirt from the buttons to the bottom of the skirt.

Over the left cuff an enlisted man could wear long-service chevrons, point up. These were awarded for two, five, twelve, sixteen, eighteen, twenty-one, and twenty-six years of service.

In 1880, the method of showing rank for officers was changed. Prior to this, badges of rank had been shown on the collar. Now they would be worn on shoulder cords. The collar of the officers' tunic was made higher and squarer cut in front. English, Irish, and Scottish regimental officers wore different types of lace. The cuffs and collars of the officers had elaborate braiding showing their rank (see §II-3-5, Image II:15).

In 1902, following the Boer War, the tunic was again changed. A major concern in the government was that it was too expensive to be an officer, and this was keeping good men out of the army. Among other changes, this led to simpler rank braiding for officers on their tunics (see §II-3-5, Images II:15 and II:16).

In 1904, badges of rank were changed again, but were left on the shoulder cords. Rank was now shown as follows:

Colonels	A crown over two stars
Lieutenant colonels	A crown over a star
Majors	A crown
Captains	Three stars
Lieutenant	Two stars
Second lieutenant	One star

Prior to 1902, officers had worn their crimson silk sash over their left shoulder (Image II:111). After 1902, they changed to wearing it around the waist so they no longer needed their white leather belt with its gilded locket and round clasp fastening. A less showy belt was worn under the tunic to carry the sword. Sergeants and warrant officers continued to wear their sashes over their right shoulders (Image II:114), with one exception. That exception was the Somerset Light Infantry, who wore them over their left shoulder. This caused the officers to tie their sashes on the right side (see §II-2-4, Special Uniform Items, for a discussion of this regimental practice and its background).

II:113 Durham Light Infantry
Note long-service and good-conduct medal and chevrons. Note also bandsman's wings.

II:114 Colour Sergeant, Duke of Cornwall's Light Infantry, 1914
Note that in 1914, the shoulder strap was in the regiment's facing colour.

II:115 Middlesex Regiment
Note fleur-de-lys badge on right arm denoting a trained scout. Also note service stripes on the lower left sleeve. The combination of cuff facings and cuff strap shows the photo was taken after 1913.

During the Boer War, the army found that its city-bred soldiers did not know how to operate in the field. One officer, Robert Baden-Powell, had been training his men in outdoor skills, and after the war the army adopted scout training for selected men throughout the army. A fleur-de-lys badge worn on the left arm denoted a trained scout (Image II:115).

The collar carried a regimental badge on each side for both officers and other ranks. These badges were often different for officers and the rank and file. An exception was the Oxfordshire and Buckinghamshire Light Infantry, whose officers did not wear collar badges. Their collars had regimental buttons and cords on their collars.[132]

The back of the tunic was changed in 1902 to the 'Prussian' or slashed back (see Image C19). This had six buttons, three on either side of a central vent with all three in a vertical row. The central vent was trimmed in white. On either side of the vent were the three buttons, outlined by white piping.

In 1902, the shoulder strap remained scarlet, but was piped in white (Image II:109). Then in 1913, the shoulder straps were changed to be the regiment's facing colour.

Using the above changes as a reference, the date of a photograph or painting of an infantryman can be estimated. However, regiments often did more or less what they wanted, and uniform details could change yearly. This comes particularly into play when considering how collar and cuffs on tunics were trimmed.

A sealed pattern[133] from a 1912 infantry tunic, held in the Queen's Regimental Museum at Kingston-on-Thames in Surrey, shows the following: a dark blue collar (indicating it is a royal regiment) with white piping along the bottom edge where the collar joins the body of the tunic. The dark blue, pointed cuffs have a 0.64 cm (¼ inch) wide white tape edging. The pointed-ended parallel-sided shoulder straps are in the facing colour (dark blue), but have no piping at all.[134]

§II-8 Line Infantry

II:116 Royal Fusilier
Note that the collar and cuffs' white trim drawn on royal regiments cannot be trusted. The illustrators used a standard way to show this trim that often did not accurately reflect what was worn. Note also trim shape on rear skirts.

Since this was made up in 1912, could the authorities have been getting things ready for the 1913 changes? Perhaps, but the general rule was not always followed. A photo of the Royal Fusiliers c. 1913 shows them wearing white piping all around the collar.

One theory is that royal regiments, beginning in about 1912–13, had white piping around the lower edge of the collar. Earlier, beginning around 1902–6, piping around the top of the collar had been introduced.

During both periods, royal regiments with blue facing had white piping around the edge of the cuff piping. One non-royal regiment, the Somerset Light Infantry, had blue facings, and it seems to have used the piping scheme of the royal regiments. The regiments whose facing colour was not blue generally did not have piping around their collars or cuffs. However, the Duke of Wellington's Regiment, which had scarlet, was an exception. Their collar had white piping on the top, front and bottom. Their cuff was also set off by white piping.

The 1880 Cardwell reforms limiting facing colours to blue for royal (and one line) regiments, white for English, yellow for Scottish, and green for Irish regiments were not popular with the regiments. They tried to regain their old facing colours and by 1905–14 many were successful (see §II-2-2).

After 1907 the shoulder strap on full dress tunics had brass regiment titles.[135] For light infantry, they also had a hunting horn, and fusilier regiments had a flaming grenade in addition to their shortened title or initials.

A special tunic distinction was the back badge or flash of the Welsh Fusiliers. It consisted of five ribbons fanned out on the back of the tunic (Image II:3). The wearing of this item was allowed from 1834 on for officers, warrant officers, and staff sergeants. In 1900, it was extended to all ranks (Image C20, shown in colour). The flash was 22.86 cm (9 inches) long for officers and 17.78 cm (7 inches) for everyone else.[136]

Trousers
The trousers of officers and men were a dark blue known as Oxford blue. Up to 1902 officers' trousers had gold lace of infantry pattern 3.5 cm (1⅜ inch) wide with a crimson silk stripe 0.32 cm (⅛ inch) wide in the centre of the side seams. After 1902 officers' trousers and pantaloons had a scarlet stripe 0.64 cm (¼ inch) wide down the outside seam of each trouser leg. The rank and file and NCOs had a scarlet welt down each seam at the same location (Image II:116).

Sashes and Belts
Other ranks wore a white belt with a brass belt buckle (Image II:114). Prior to 1902, officers wore their sashes over their left shoulders (Image II:111). After that, they were worn around the waist with the tassels over the left hip (Image II:110). On state occasions a crimson and gold sash was worn, and at other times one of crimson silk net (Image II:117).

II:117 Officer wearing full dress sash over left shoulder

Footwear

Footwear for dismounted officers was black Wellington boots. Mounted officers wore boots that came to within 10.16 cm (4 inches) of the knee. Other ranks wore boots made to Derby shape.

Plumes, Special Badges, and Traditions

Most fusilier regiments did not have a plume on the cap between 1871 and 1900. However, the Northumberland Fusiliers were able to have a red over white hackle plume for a long period of time. See §II-2-4, Special Uniform Items, for a discussion on the background of the plume.

It is said that the Norfolk Regiment were given the figure of Britannia, symbolic of Britain, in 1707. At that time, they were part of an English army operating in Spain during the War of Spanish Succession. At the 1707 Battle of Alamanza they performed so well in covering the retreat of the allied army that they were considered worthy of bearing the country's symbol as their badge. Another theory is they were given the badge for bravery in the Battle of Rolica.[137] Others say they were wearing the badge at the Battle of Rolica.

The 35th (Royal) Sussex Regiment beat the French Rousillon Regiment outside Quebec and put their white plumes in their hats. White plumes were worn by the 35th until 1810, and later, a plume became part of their regimental badge.

The ever-sworded 29th, the Worcestershires in 1914 (29th and 36th Foot), were surprised while they were without arms in the Leeward Islands of the West Indies in 1746, and several were treacherously murdered. After that, they began a custom of carrying weapons everywhere, including to mess and church. In 1850, they changed to just the captain of the week and the orderly officer carrying weapons. The regiment are also known as vein-openers because of their actions in the Boston Massacre. In 1770 the 29th, pushed beyond endurance, fired into a mob, killing several people. The people of Boston and, indeed, all Americans made martyrs of the dead for propaganda purposes. This came to be known as the Boston Massacre. Two officers and eight soldiers were put on trial for murder in what was probably the longest trial in colonial history to that date. Two soldiers were found guilty of manslaughter and the rest were acquitted, in spite of the fact that every witness who testified at the trial perjured himself.[138]

The Cheshire Regiment wore oak leaves or, if they were not available – given the many different climates where the regiment served[139] – paper or cardstock oak leaves on their helmets (see Image C21). This was done in memory of the part their regiment is said to have played in protecting George II under an oak tree in the Battle of Dettingen after his horse ran away. They were worn only when the soldiers were in the presence of royalty or on Meeanee Day. The Battle of Meeanee was the key battle, fought in 1843, in the conquest of Sind (now in Pakistan). The Cheshire Regiment was the only British regiment at the battle.

The Somerset Light Infantry fought as dragoons in Spain 1706–13. For this they wore cavalry mess dress.

As noted above at §II-2-4, the Gloucestershire Regiment earned the right to wear a sphinx badge on the back of their headdress (Images II:118 and II:31, row 4, last column).

II:118 Gloucestershire Regiment
Note size of back badge.

§II-8-b LIGHT INFANTRY

The light infantry regiments were set apart by several things, such as having a French hunting horn or stringed bugle as part of their badges and, after 1878, having dark green cloth-covered helmets instead of the normal blue. They also had bugle bands in their battalions instead of fifes and drums.[140] In addition, they would march at 140 steps per minute with their rifle held at the trail, i.e. parallel to the ground.

Officers of the Oxfordshire and Buckinghamshire Light Infantry had a unique item on their collars. In about 1883, their standard collar badge was dispensed with. In its place the officers wore what seemed to be gorget buttons and cords. The button had a bugle, crown, and the name Oxfordshire, with Buckinghamshire, was added to the name in 1908. There was a line of gold Russian cord 6.35 cm (2½ inches) long attached to the button, which connected it to the front edge of the collar (see Insert 1). This regimental peculiarity came from the 52nd Regiment of Foot[141] when it was merged with the 43rd Foot in 1881.

Insert 1

§II-8-c FUSILIERS

Uniform

HEADDRESS

Fusiliers of other ranks wore a 22.86 cm (9 inch) tall cap made of raccoon skin or sealskin. Which regiment wore which type of skin is listed below. Officers wore bearskin or black raccoon skin caps; the choice seems to have been up to the officer, or perhaps the regiment.

The height of the officer's cap depended on the height of the officer. A 1.83 m (6 foot) tall fusilier officer would wear a 22.86 cm (9 inch) hat. By comparison, a 1.83 m (6 foot) tall guard officer's bearskin was 24.13 cm (9½ inches) high. The height of

II:119 Royal Fusiliers' Colours and Escort
Note the difference in size between the officers' and other ranks' fur cap.

II:120 Lancashire Fusiliers
Note the difference in size between the officers' and other ranks' fur cap. Images II:120 and II:121 show grenade partly covered by fur.

II:121 Officer, Inniskilling Fusiliers
It is unusual to see anything other than a flaming grenade on the front of a fusilier's fur cap.

the cap would vary up depending on the height of the officer.[142] There is reason to doubt these regulations were always followed. Actual measurements on an other ranks' fusilier fur cap shows a height of about 26.67 cm (10½ inches) in front and about 21.59 cm (8½ inches) in the back. They all had a slight depression in the centre.[143] Images II:119 and II:120 show that the officers' caps tower over the caps of the other ranks. Clearly, the officers' caps are taller than the 22.86 cm (9 inch) average. Some feel the cited height is actually the basic frame inside the pelt.

The fusilier cap for both officers and men were supposed to have a flaming grenade badge on the front, and the cap also carried a plume. This did not always happen, though (Image II:119), and at times it looked as if officers had put other badges on their caps (Image II:121). However, this undoubtedly was because the image of the grenade ball stood out and the grenade, at times, was wholly or partially covered by the fur.

As mentioned previously, the Northumberland Fusiliers' predecessors, the 5th Foot, defeated a French force on the West Indies island of St Lucia in 1778, despite being vastly outnumbered. For this they were given the right to wear a white feather in their headdress. In 1829, this was changed to a plume, having the top half red and the bottom half white. These colours came about because the 5th were said to have taken the French soldiers' white feathers and dipped them in their blood before putting them in their own hats (for the full story behind the plume, see §II-2-4, Special Uniform Items).

The plume on the Northumberland Fusiliers was a special distinction until the Boer War. Only the Irish Fusiliers also had a plume in 1900. Then plumes were granted to all fusilier regiments.

The details of the caps were as follows:

Fusilier Other Ranks' Headdress

Regiment	Other Ranks' Cap Skin[a]	Plume Location[b]	Plume Colour[c]	Plume Height[d]
Northumberland	Raccoon[e]	Left	Red over white	11.43 cm (4½")
Royal Fusiliers	Raccoon[e]	Right	White	16.51 cm (6½")
Lancashire	Raccoon[e]	Left	Primrose	16.51 cm (6½")
Royal Scots	Seal[f]	Right	White	16.51 cm (6½")
Royal Welsh	Raccoon[e]	Right	White	16.51 cm (6 ½")
Royal Inniskilling	Raccoon[e]	Left	Grey	16.51 cm (6½")
Royal Irish	Raccoon[e]	Left	Green	16.51 cm (6½")
Royal Munster	Raccoon[e]	Left	White over green	16.51 cm (6½")
Royal Dublin	Raccoon[e]	Left	Blue over green	16.51 cm (6½")

Notes: [a] Barthorp, *British Infantry*, p. 148. See generally, Bowling, *British Infantry*, p. 41. Others say other ranks' caps for all regiments were made of sealskin.
[b] Barthorp, *British Infantry*, p. 148.
[c] Bowling, *British Infantry*, p. 41; Bowling, *Scottish*, p. 54.
[d] *Dress Regulations, 1904*, p. 28.
[e] At different times, these regiments seem to have worn seal, then raccoon.
[f] Correspondence with Joyce Steele, development officer, and research team of the Royal Highland Fusiliers Museum, 24 November 2016.

Other than the cap and the grenades, the fusilier's uniform was exactly the same as that worn by the line infantry. See Image C20.

Tunic

The regulations called for tunics of officers in the fusiliers to have a flaming grenade badge on their collars. This rule was followed for the most part. Image II:122 shows an example of a fusilier officer's tunic. Other ranks' collars also had grenades. The Royal Irish Fusiliers wore a cornet with their grenades on each side of their collars.

§II-8-d RIFLES

Uniform

Headdress

Beginning in 1883, the four rifle regiments – the Cameronians (Scottish Rifles), the King's Royal Rifle Corps (KRRC), the Royal Irish Rifles, and the Rifle Brigade (Prince Consort's Own) – wore the home service helmet. The Cameronians had a thistle wreath that carried battle honours of the regiment. The KRRC had a Maltese cross with a scroll and crown over it. Between the arms of the cross, the battles of the corps were shown. The Irish Rifles had a shamrock wreath

II:122 Officer of the Royal Fusiliers
In this fine character study, note flaming grenade on collar and with rose mounted on ball of grenade.

II:124 Officer, King's Royal Rifle Corps (ex 60th Rifles)
Note badge on pouch belt and fur headdress. He has been awarded a Victoria Cross.

II:123 Rifle Busby
Front and side view. The busby with bugle badge is the Rifle Brigade's. Its plume is black.

that held the regiment's battles. There was not a star behind the wreath. The Rifle Brigade had a standard laurel wreath that carried the battles of the brigade. A Maltese cross was within the wreath. The helmets of the rifle regiments had bronze metal.[144]

In 1890, the helmet was discontinued for the KRRC, the Irish Rifles, and the Rifle Brigade. The helmet was discontinued from the Cameronians in 1892, and its replacement will be covered in the section on the dress of the Scottish regiments. In the other three rifle regiments, the home service helmet was replaced by a rifle busby.

Officers of the three non-Scottish rifle regiments wore a rifle busby of black Persian (astrakhan) lambskin. It had a bow shape, higher in the middle than at either end. The two sides joined at the ends. It had a central valley between the lambskin fur on either side, and it was 12.7 cm (about 5 inches) high at the ends and 15.24 cm (6 inches) in the middle (Image II:123). The top of the rifle busby was rifle green cloth.

The other ranks wore a black rifle busby made of sealskin and had the same cloth top.

The officers' rifle busby had a plume rising from a black oval boss located at the top front centre of the busby. For the KRRC, the plume was originally a black egret feather over scarlet vulture feathers. By 1904, this had changed to a 17.78 cm (7 inch) scarlet ostrich feather rising out of black vulture feathers.

The ostrich feather plume for the Royal Irish Rifles was the same height, but black, and the vulture feathers were dark green. The boss was dark green. The busby of the Rifle Brigade officers was the same as that worn by the KRRC except the ostrich feathers were black rather than scarlet.

Other ranks had a short horsehair plume in the same colour as the officers' plumes.

The front of the officers' rifle busby had a black silk, square, and plaited cord that went up to a small bronze bugle at the centre top of each side of the busby (Image II:124). There were two rows of square silk cord at the back, ending in a knot that held a bronze ring.

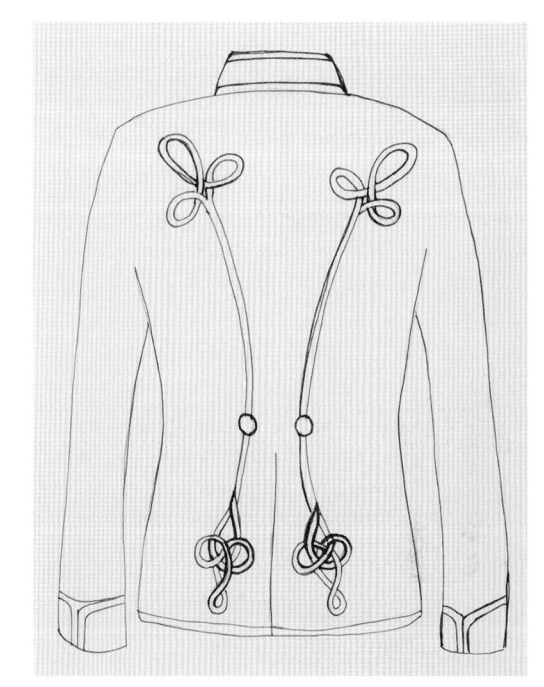

II:126 Back of Rifle Officer's Tunic

II:125 Officer, Rifle Brigade (ex 95th Rifles)
View of silver pouch belt badge is as seen on Image II:129.

A black cord that had been around the body held a bronze swivel that attached to the ring. The swivel was part of the body cap line. From this swivel silk cord lines came down the officer's back, passed around his neck, looped across his chest and fastened there. The cord line ended on the right side in acorns. The other ranks' busby was plainer. They had cords but did not have cap lines.

TUNIC

The tunic for the rifle regiments was dark green. This colour goes back to the founding 5th Battalion of the 60th (Royal Americans) Regiment, where it was thought to be suitable for their light infantry duties of skirmishing and sharp-shooting using a rifle. It was picked up when the 95th (Rifle Brigade) was formally created in 1801, and thereafter viewed as the proper colour for the riflemen.

The officers' tunic of the three rifle regiments had a black square cord trim that began at the top front of the tunic under the collar. From there, it went down the tunic's front and then around the bottom of the tunic to outline the bottom of the tunic on the sides and in the back (Image II:125). The front of these officers' tunics also had five olivets down the front and five rows and five loops of black square cord, in appearance much like that of hussars, who of course had six rows. This pattern of tunic is said to have derived from the Black Brunswick Hussars,[145] a group of German volunteers who came to England to fight against Napoleon and caused a great sensation (see Images II:19 and II:20 for the shape). The collar was of the regimental colour and edged by 1.27 cm (½ inch) wide black braid.

Prior to 1902, the officers' tunic had rows of braided eyes on the collar and cuff showing rank. The cuff design would differ according to regiment (see §II3-5, Image II:19). After 1902, these were done away with and a simple Hungarian-style knot was used on the cuff by all officers (see §II3-5, Image II:20). The collar was now edged with black braid with tracing lace below. The post-1902 Hungarian knot on the cuffs also had very thin tracing around it (Image II:125).

The collars of the Rifle Brigade were black, the King's Royal Rifle Corps were scarlet, and the Royal Irish Rifles were a dark green, one shade of green lighter than rifle green.[146] The cuffs were the same colour as the collar, and the Rifle Brigade had velvet collars and cuffs.

On the back of the tunic, there was the same cord, one on each side. It followed the seam of the tunic on either side of the back of the tunic. At the top, each ended in crows' feet, and at the bottom, each formed an Hungarian knot.

Other Ranks' Tunic

The tunic of the other ranks was much plainer. It was also dark green, but it did not have chest cords (see Image C23). However, it had trim in the regiment's facing colour down the front of the tunic, which was 0.64 cm (¼ inch) wide. The collar was in the regiment's facing colour, surrounded by black trim at the top, front, and bottom. The trim was 1.27 cm (½ inch) wide. The cuffs were the colour of the tunic, outlined by a simple V-shaped design with two trim lines (the men in Image C23 have full

II:127 Two Sergeants of the Rifle Brigade, *c.* 1890
Right figure is a colour sergeant. Note the S-shaped belt buckle worn by the man on the right and the cut of the bottom of the trousers.

II:128 Officer, King's Royal Rifle Corps (ex 60th Rifles Royal Americans)

§II-8 Line Infantry | 149

cuffs). The top trim line was in the regiment's facing colour, 0.32 cm (⅛ inch) wide. Just below it was a line of black trim 1.27 cm (½ inch) wide. The cuff was 15.24 cm (6 inches) tall at the top of the 'V' and 4.45 cm (1¾ inches) tall at the sides. The two rear skirts each had black buttons and a line of trim in the regiment's facing colour 0.64 cm (¼ inch) wide. The buttons were black.[147] Image II:127 shows two sergeants of the Rifle Brigade in this uniform.

The scarlet trim at the collar and cuffs and down the front gave the other ranks of the KRRC a splash of colour. On the other hand, the Rifle Brigade and

II:129 Officer, Rifle Brigade
Note badge on pouch belt.

II:130 Sergeant Bugler, Royal Irish Rifles, c. 1912
Note badge on pouch belt and headdress.

II:131 King's Royal Rifle Corps

the Irish Rifles, with their black and dark green trim, presented a sombre appearance.

Pouch Belt

Over the left shoulder the officers wore a black patent leather pouch belt which was 7.62 cm (3 inches) wide. A silver regimental badge was worn on the belt together with a whistle and chain (Images II:124, II:128, and II:129). High-ranking other ranks also wore a pouch belt with a badge (Image II:130). The pouch was also of black patent leather and carried a regimental badge on its lid.

Trousers

Officers' trousers were rifle green with 5.08 cm (2 inch) black mohair braid down the side of the seams. The other ranks also wore rifle green trousers in full dress. They did not have piping on their trousers.

Belts

Because of the hussar-type tunic, officers did not wear a belt. The waist belt for other ranks was black leather and was closed with an S-shaped buckle (Image II:127). Footwear was also black leather.

Image II:131 shows how the entire uniform looked.

Miscellaneous

The slings on riflemen's rifles were black rather than the line infantry's white. The sling was carried loose rather than tight as was done with non-rifle regiments.[148]

Rifle officers' spurs were straight rather than being swan-necked, and black leather gloves were worn.[149]

The Maltese cross badge of the King's Royal Rifle Corps was said, by the regiment's history, to date back to the forming of the rifle unit for the 60th Regiment in America under Hompesch. Hompesch was Bavarian, and it was suggested that the Maltese cross had come from a war medal given to Bavarian soldiers, or it might have come from a relative, Ferdinand de Hompesch, who was a knight of Malta.[150]

§II-8-e THE HIGHLAND REGIMENTS

Uniform

Headdress

One of the most impressive things about a Highland soldier was his bonnet, which, by 1880 to 1914, had grown to an imposing 27.94 cm (11 inches) tall for officers and was very full. An intimidating list of items was needed to make it: black ostrich feathers, wire, black cotton, velvet or cloth binding, silk ribbon cord, black thread, black buttons, strip leather for binding, 11.43 cm (4½ inches) deep pasteboard, a band of woven diced material, a chin strap with a buckle, and a vulture feather plume. The pasteboard, covered with the cloth in a diced version of the regimental pattern (see Table II.8.e.1), supported a wire frame about 25.4 cm (10 inches) high. Over the frame, flattened ostrich feathers were laid to about a 2.54 cm (1 inch) depth. Over the feathers were feathers made up into 'fox tails,' which hung down to the right. Each was about 76.2 cm (2 feet 6 inches) long, on strings, and fixed to the wire frame separately. The 'tails' were tied down to prevent them from blowing up and showing the wire frame. The number of tails varied by regiment (Table II.8.e.1). The bonnet of the other ranks was normally smaller than that of officers.

A little behind the right ear, there was a slit in the band. It had on it a black silk bow with 35.56 cm (14 inch) ends, which dropped onto the right shoulder. Just behind the left ear on the band was a cockade – black silk for officers, black leather for other ranks. A regimental badge was worn on the cockade. The vulture feather plume, red for the Black Watch, white for the other Highland regiments, was held by the cockade. The plume rose up the left side of the bonnet to a height of 3.81 cm (1½ inches) above the bonnet. The plume for the other ranks was also made of vulture feathers.

The diced border was partly covered, and when properly made up, only two rows of dicing showed below the feathers. The officers' bonnet, when complete, weighed about 0.68 kg (1½ lb).[151]

Table II.8.e.1: Highland Regiment Uniform Details

	Bonnet Tails	Bonnet Feather Plume[b]	Diced Border to Bonnet	Facing Colour on Doublet	Tartan[a]	Sporran Colour	Tails and Colour	Hose Tops	Gaiter Buttons	Notes
Black Watch (42nd & 73rd)	4	Red	Scarlet, blue, white	Blue	Government (C3)	White	5 Black	Black and red	White	A, B, C, D, E
Seaforth (72nd & 78th)	5	White	Scarlet, green, white	Buff	Mackenzie (C5)	White	2 Black	Red and white	White	A, C
Gordon (75th & 92nd)	5	White	Scarlet, green, white	Yellow	Gordon (C6)	White	2 Black	Red and black	Black	A, F, G, H, I
Cameron (79th)	5	White	Scarlet, blue, white	Blue	Cameron Erracht (C1)	Grey or black	2 White	Green and red	White	A, J, K
Argyll & Sutherland (91st & 93rd)	6	White	Scarlet, white	Yellow	Sutherland (C2)	Grey or black	6 Short white	Red and white	White	A, L, M, N, O

Notes: [a] For the design and colour of the tartan kilt, see the colour image indicated in brackets.
[b] The plumes for officers of all Highland regiments were made of vulture feathers (*Dress Regulations, 1911*, ¶677).

A: Sporran made of horsehair for other ranks.
B: V-shaped or square cut notch on gaiter at toe.
C: Officers wore five black horsehair tassels.
D: In levee dress officers wore five gold bullion tassels.
E: In levee and full dress, officers and sergeants wore two dark green silk bows. These were worn to the right of the sporran on the kilt apron (MacLeod, *Glory*, p. 50).
F: Officers wore five gold bullion tassels.
G: Officers' gaiters had ten buttons, and other ranks' had eight buttons. All other Highland regiments have eight buttons on their gaiters (MacLeod, *Glory*, p. 54).
H: Black gaiter buttons worn in memory of the death Sir John Moore in Spain.
I: Bandsmen had a red over white feather plume.
J: The officers' sporran was grey goat hair (*Dress Regulations, 1911*, p. 76).
K: Other ranks wore black horsehair sporrans (Bowling, *Scottish*, p. 28, Figure 14).
L: Sporran was made of dark badger hair (fur) for officers and sergeants (MacLeod, *Glory*, p. 54; Bowling, *Scottish*, pp. 25 and 26). Other ranks' sporrans were black horsehair and oval in shape (like those of the officers and sergeants).
M: Officers and senior NCOs had a badger's head at the top of the sporran.
N: The sporrans of the Argyll and Sutherlands were complex. The sporrans of other ranks were black horsehair with six short white horsehair tassels (MacLeod, *Glory*, p. 54). Senior NCOs and officers wore sporrans of dark grey badger hair with a badger head and six short white tassels on it. For officers and senior NCOs each white tassel had a thin red line at its top (Bowling, *Scottish*, p. 26). This distinctive sporran dates from 1829 (MacLeod, *Glory*, p. 54). For levee dress, a very different sporran was worn by the officers – a white horsehair sporran with five gold tassels (MacLeod, *Glory*, p. 54).
O: Their tartan was almost the same as that worn by the Black Watch. It is said to be the Government Tartan 2a, a slightly lighter shade than that of the Black Watch (Leishman, RHF Regimental Museum, correspondence, 12 September 2013; Bowling, *Scottish*, p. 26). It is sometimes known as Clan Sutherland tartan (Bowling, *Scottish*, p. 26). The Argylls, as a special distinction, wore an embroidered panel with green silk bows on the right side of the kilt apron (MacLeod, *Glory*, p. 54).

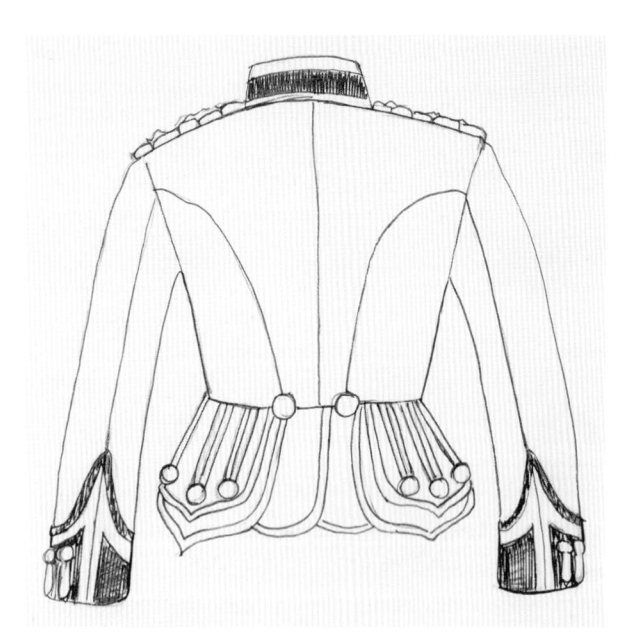

II:132 Back of Doublet, Inverness Skirt

II:133 Seaforth Highlanders
Note the double badges on the collar. Also the crossed flags and crown badge above the chevrons on the soldier on the left, denoting his rank as colour sergeant.

DOUBLET

The coat, called a doublet, consisted of a tunic with gauntlet cuffs and flapped 'Inverness' skirts. This item of 'Highland-style' dress seems to be a pure Victorian invention dating from the 1850s.[152] The gauntlet cuffs were cloth in the facing colour. The cloth was 8.89 cm (3½ inches) tall on the front of the sleeve (at the end of the cuff) and 15.24 cm (6 inches) tall on the back of the sleeve. The cuffs held three buttons along the top of the cuff. Officers had gold braid running from each button to just above the bottom of the cuff. Other ranks had white braid in the same location.

The Inverness skirt consisted of four flaps which hung from the belt line. Two were in the front, and two were in the rear. They had straight sides and then curved in to a point. A second flap was on top of the bottom flap, but it was 1.27 cm (½ inch) smaller. The bottom flaps were either 19.05 or 20.32 cm (7½ or 8 inches) long. The ones in front rested on the wearer's thighs, leaving enough space between them for the sporran. The ones in back were separated by two strips of cloth about 17.78 cm (7 inches) long that fell from the waist. These were straight on their sides and ended in a curve at the bottom (Image II:132). They had nothing on them except white or gold trim around the edge. In 1902, the trim on the cuffs and skirts was simplified (see §II-3-5, Images II:21 and II:22). Prior to that, the collar, cuff, and flap trim showed an officer's rank (Image II:134).

The top flaps had three buttons of the regimental pattern with loops running from the buttons, which were lined up across the bottom of the flap to the waist. The loops were gold braid for officers, and white trim for other ranks.

Each flap was outlined in white cloth as was the collar on the bottom. Officers carried gold lace on the collar, the cuffs, and the large flaps

SPORRAN

Another distinctive part of the highland dress was the sporran.[153] The 1911 Dress Regulations stated the sporrans were of regimental pattern. The top was not to exceed 15.24 cm (6 inches) and the breadth of the sporran leathers was not to exceed 21.59 cm (8½ inches). The length of the top and the leather together was not to exceed 27.94 cm (11 inches), except for the Argyll and Sutherland Highlanders,

II:134 Senior Officer of the Black Watch, Mounted Review Order
Note the plaid encircling the body, and the braid on his collar, on his cuffs, and on the back Inverness flap. See also the distinctive triple layer of braid on his Inverness flap.

who wore a badger head on their sporran; for them, it could be 33.02 cm (13 inches).

Unless stated otherwise, the material of the sporran and tails was horsehair. The body of the sporran was as follows:

Royal Highlanders (Black Watch): for officers and men, white horsehair, five short black horsehair tassels, a strap of white leather.

Seaforth Highlanders: white horsehair, six gold bullion tassels suspended by gold and crimson cords; other ranks had two long black tails, buff leather straps.

Gordon Highlanders: white horsehair, five gold bullion tassels hanging from looped gold cord, the heads of the tassels in teal and bright gold; other ranks had two long black tails, straps of white leather.

Cameron Highlanders: grey goat hair, six gold bullion tassels suspended by blue and gold twisted cords; other ranks had a black sporran with two long white tails, straps of black patent leather.

Argyll and Sutherland Highlanders: grey badger hair with a badger head on the top for officers and NCOs, six short white horsehair tassels below it; other ranks had a black sporran with six short white tails, black straps.

Over their right shoulder dismounted officers wore a white buff leather belt which was 6.35 cm (2½ inches) wide.

Kilt

A kilt was worn by all the Highland regiments. However, sometimes mounted officers in Highland regiments would wear pantaloons made up of cloth in the regiment's tartan pattern. They also wore trousers called trews. See Table II.8.e.1 for the different regiments' tartans.

The other Scottish regiments, the Highland Light Infantry, and the Scottish Lowland Regiments all wore trews. They will be considered at §II-8-f.

The plaid kilt was in the regimental pattern. For the name of the pattern, see Table II.8.e.1; for examples of the pattern, see below. In many cases, a regiment's tartan pattern was stated as being that of a Highland clan. There was, of course, a great deal of lore and mysticism around the clans and their tartans. However, it should be noted that there is a school of thought that the tie between the clans and their tartans is an invention that took place at the end of the eighteenth and beginning of the nineteenth centuries. For examples of this view point, see Hugh Trevor-Roper's 'The Invention of Tradition: The Highland Tradition of Scotland' and W.A. Thorburn's 'The Army and Scottish Dress'.[154]

The kilt was made of a hard textured cloth but was changed to a softer cloth after a parade in 1870 when Queen Victoria noticed that the back of soldiers' knees were bloody, caused by the cloth cutting into the back of their legs. A change to softer cloth took care of the problem.[155]

On the right side of the officers' and sergeants' kilts in the Black Watch were two dark green silk bows.[156] The Argylls, as a special distinction, wore an embroidered panel with green silk bows on the right side of the kilt apron.[157]

Shoulder Plaid

In Scottish regiments, officers continued to wear a sash over the left shoulder rather than around the waist. This was normally worn over the shoulder belt (see below). They would, in addition, wear a large piece of cloth across the front, over their left shoulder, and down the back on the left. The band and pipers also wore the plaid in the same way. Other ranks wore a 'shoulder plaid' hanging from the rear of the left shoulder. The cloth was woven in the regiment tartan colours.

In the Cameron Highlanders, officers did not wear a sash in levee dress; instead, they wore a portion of the shoulder plaid across the chest and under the right arm in its place.[158] The shoulder plaid was also worn by sergeants, who also wore the normal sash over their right shoulder.

The shoulder plaid was held in place by a large brooch worn at the left shoulder. The brooch was of the regimental pattern. The design of plaid brooches is beyond the scope of this work, but descriptions of regimental brooches can be found Grosart, 'Brooches'.[159]

Officers wore a wide white belt over their right shoulder to help hold up their Claymore broadswords. Each regiment's belt had its own style of shoulder belt plate, which was worn only by officers. In the Argyll Regiment, only the shoulder belt was worn over the sash.

Waist Belt

A waist belt of gold lace was worn by officers. The belt of the other ranks was of white leather. The buckle was of the regimental pattern.

The shoulder belt was worn under the waist belt by officers in Gordon Highlanders.

Garter Flashes

With their hose, the men wore red garter flashes, some of which differed regimentally:

Black Watch	Garter flash worn with one edge cutting the centre dice of the hose[160]
Seaforth	On the side garter flash single with two folds worn at side of leg[161]
Gordon	On the side garter flash double, the upper half being looped[162]
Cameron	On the side
Argyll and Sutherland	Garter flash worn with one edge cutting the centre dice of the hose[163]

See Table II.8.e.1 for the colour of the hose.

A dirk of the regimental pattern was worn on the right side. It was normally carried straight up in the Gordon rather than at the angle as in other regiments.[164]

A small knife known as a *sgian dubh* was carried in the hose top. Normally, this would be found in the right hose for a right-handed man. The knife was of the regimental pattern.

For examples of Highland dress, see:

Cameron Highlanders: Images II:135, II:136, II:137, and C1

Seaforth Highlanders: Images II:133, II:138, II:139, II:140, and C5

Gordon Highlanders: Images II:141, II:142, II:143, and C6

Black Watch: Images II:134, II:144, II:145, II:146, II:147, and C3

Argyll and Sutherland Highlanders: Images II:148, II:149, II:150, and C2

Levee Dress

This was almost the same as full dress, with only a few minor differences. The officers wore hose and a dancing pump-style of shoe with a large buckle in place of hose tops, gaiters, and plain shoes. As noted above, the Camerons wore a shoulder plate across their chest rather than a sash.[165] The Black Watch replaced their black horsehair tails on their sporrans with five tassels of gold bullion tassels. The Argylls (Argyll and Sutherland Highlanders) wore a special white hair sporran, the most notable features of which were five gold bullion tassels.

II:135 Other Ranks, Queen's Own Cameron Highlanders
He is wearing other ranks' plaid. This hangs from left shoulder only in front and back. It does not go around the body.

II:136 Officer, Cameron Highlanders, c. 1900
Note shoulder belt plate on white sword belt. Sword hung from shoulder belt.

II:137 Cameron Highlanders, Officer, c. 1890s
Note the six gold bullion tassels.

II:138 Seaforth Highlanders NCO, c. 1890s
Notice the star on his lower right sleeve awarded for distance judging and the crossed rifles on his lower left arm denoting best shot in company. After 1909, the crossed rifles were given for marksmanship.

II:139 Seaforth Highlanders Band Member, c. 1890s is a Drummer in the Pipes and Drums
Note the way he has spread his shoulder plaid completely across his chest and the regimental badge on his bonnet. There is drummer's lace on sleeves, collar, and shoulder wings.

II:140 Seaforth Highlanders Sergeant Drummer, c. 1900

II:141 Gordon Highlander Other Ranks, c. 1890s

II:142 Gordon Highlander Other Ranks, c. 1900
Note two long-service stripes on his left arm, although he still is a very low-ranking soldier.

II:143 Gordon Highlanders Officer in Levee Dress, c. 1890s
Note the five gold bullion tassels.

II:144 Black Watch Other Rank
Note sporran and tassels.

II:145 Captain, Black Watch, c. 1900
Note shoulder belt plate. Also note bullion tassels and part of the officers' crimson silk sash worn across the chest.

II:146 Black Watch Officer in Levee, Ball, and Court Dress, c. 1895
Note levee dress shoes and the scarlet officers' sash.

II:147 Grizzled Officer of the Black Watch
Note the other ranks' sporran and tassels. Note also his gaiters. The Black Watch had special shapes for their gaiters.

II:148 Other Ranks, Argyll and Sutherland Highlanders
The standing figure is a corporal. The seated man is a lance corporal. Note light horsehair tassels and regimental badge on the bonnet.

II:149 Regimental Sergeant Major, Princess Louise's (Argyll and Sutherland Highlanders), 1906
Note badger's head at the top of the sporran worn by officers and NCOs. Note also sergeant's sash and the part of shoulder plaid worn across chest.

II:150 Argyll and Sutherland Highlanders
Note the difference in sporran colours for NCOs (grey with badger head) and other ranks (black). Note also the close pressed pleats at the back of the kilt. The right figure is wearing a Highland regiment's undress white jacket.

§II-8-f THE LOWLAND REGIMENTS AND HIGHLAND LIGHT INFANTRY

Table II.8.f.1: Scottish Lowland Regiments and Highland Light Infantry

	Headdress	Plume	Diced Border	Facings	Tartan Trews[a]	Notes
Highland Light Infantry	Shako cap	Green	White, crimson, green[b]	Buff	MacKenzie (C4)	A
Royal Scots	Kilmarnock bonnet	Black cock feather	Scarlet, white, blue	Blue	Hunting Stewart (C9)	
Scottish Borderers (KOSB)	Kilmarnock bonnet	Black cock feather	Scarlet, white, blue	Blue	Leslie (C7)	
Royal Scots Fusiliers	Sealskin cap	White		Blue	Government (C8)[c]	B
Cameronians (Scottish Rifles)	Shako cap	Black		Dark green	Douglas (C10)	A, C

Notes: [a] For the design and colour of the tartan trews, see the colour image designated in the table for each regiment.
[b] Officers wore a darker green.
[c] Same as worn by the Black Watch, but with unofficial blue line added. This was added shortly after trews began to be worn.

See end note 180.

A: Black cap lines for officers.
B: Grenade badge on front of headdress.
C: Black lace for officers on the top and bottom of the shako.

THE HIGHLAND LIGHT INFANTRY

The Highland Light Infantry (HLI), as the name implies, is technically a Highland regiment. At first, a Highland regiment's wearing of trews was a fine distinction as they were associated with officers and the upper classes. However, when all the Lowland Scottish regiments were dressed in trews, the HLI's dress tended to call attention to the inconvenient fact that far too many of the HLI's men came not from the Highlands, but from Glasgow and the area around it. The HLI almost at once started a campaign to be put into kilts. They eventually achieved this goal, but it took them until 1947 to do so.

The HLI wore a Highland doublet with gauntlet cuffs and Inverness flaps. In 1881, their facing colour was the standard Scottish yellow. In 1899, the facing colour was changed back to buff.[166]

The case of the Highland Light Infantry gives an idea of how complicated the study of British regiments can be. In 1881, the 71st and 74th Regiments were joined to make the HLI. Each former regiment then formed a battalion of the new regiment: the 71st formed the 1st Battalion, and the 74th formed the 2nd Battalion. Until 1906, each battalion kept their old regiment's differences when it came to wearing different parts of the uniform.

Uniform

HEADDRESS: SHAKO

After 1882, the regiment wore a green cloth shako according to the dress regulations. It was actually dark blue for officers and other ranks by 1900.[167] For officers, it was 10.16 cm (4 inches) high in front and 16.51 cm (6½ inches) high in back. The crown was 15.24 cm (6 inches) long and 13.97 cm (5½ inches) across. Colonels had three rows of 1.59 cm (⅝ inch) gold lace, thistle pattern, round the top of the shako; lieutenant colonels had two, and majors one row. Dress regulations prior to 1911 called for two rows of lace for colonels and lieutenant colonels. This was a carry-over from the treatment of general infantry shako lace in 1869–78, prior to the use of the home service helmet.[168] The shako had a white, green (dark green for officers),[169] and crimson diced border around the bottom. At the top on the front was a dark green ball tuft.

II:151 Duke of Connaught in the Uniform of the Highland Light Infantry, c. 1912
Notice the three rows of rank braid on the top of his shako at the bottom right of the photo. Note how the crimson sash is partly covered by the plaid.

II:152 Young Officer of the Highland Light Infantry
Note how the pattern of his trews is cut so that a white line always appears at the centre front of the left. He is also wearing part of the shoulder plaid across his chest. As in Image II:151, the crimson sash is partly covered by the plaid. The plaid is encircling the body.

Black cord cap lines encircled the shako and were attached at the sides close to the top and then fell in loops in the front and back. The front loops were plaited and ended in two free-hanging acorns on the right (see §II-3-5).

For officers and senior NCOs, instead of the side acorns, cap lines of black silk cord hung down the back and then went around the person's neck. The cap lines were another example of regiments acting on their own when it comes to dress details. In 1880, the wearing of the cap lines around the neck by the 71st was questioned by the War Office. Their colonel answered they had been worn in that fashion since at least 1844 (in fact it had been since 1816). Upon receiving this answer, the department approved the custom.[170] The cords encircled the top doublet button and looped across the chest. Up to 1906, for the 1st Battalion, the lines joined a hook on the left breast (for an example of this, see Image II:160). For the 2nd, up to 1906, the line encircled a shoulder brooch and hung from the shoulder cord button.[171] After 1906, both battalions used the same system. The line hung from the shoulder cord, but did not go around the brooch.[172] The design of the brooch is beyond the scope of this work, but descriptions of regimental brooches can be found in Grosart, 'Brooches'.[173]

Other Ranks Shako[174]

The other ranks' shako was covered by dark blue cloth and had a chequered band of crimson, white, and green squares woven into it around the bottom. Black cord went around the shako. The cord was attached at the sides near the top of the shako and then looped down in front and back. The loop in the front was plaited. On the right-hand side of the shako, where

II:153 Other Ranks, Highland Light Infantry
Note white line down the front of their trews. They are wearing shoulder plaids and have part of it draped across their chests. Strictly speaking, one or both of them may not be entitled to wear this item of clothing.

the lines were attached, two free-hanging acorns fell from the shako. The regimental badge was in front, and above it was a black cord boss with a white metal thistle. A green, almost black, tuft ball on a 'Turk's head' support was above the boss.

Staff sergeants' shakos had a slightly finer pattern. Warrant officers wore a staff sergeant's shako and additional cap lines.[175]

A black ball and pouch belt were worn by the regiment (Image II:152).

Doublet and Trews

The HLI were considered to be a Highland regiment who wore trews, that is trousers with a tartan pattern.

From the waist up, except for the shako, the full dress of the HLI was just like that of the other Highland regiments. Below the waist, the fact that the regiment wore trews meant they did not wear hose, gaiters, or a *skean dhu*. For officers, the trews were cut tighter. For all ranks the trews were cut in such a way that a white stripe of the tartan always ran down the centre of the front of the leg (Images II:152 and II:153).[176] For the tartan pattern, see Image C4.

THE CLASSIC LOWLAND SCOTTISH REGIMENTS

For centuries, the regiments that had drawn their men from the Lowland areas of Scotland had been treated and dressed as any other line English infantry regiment. This changed in the 1881 reforms carried out under Hugh Childers. Under these changes, the Scottish element of the Lowland regiments was emphasised by dressing them in plaid trews. This did not make anyone very happy. It tied the Lowland regiments to the Highlanders, a group they had looked down on as uncouth. It took away the uniqueness of the plaid marker of the Highlanders. In addition, it made the HLI quite unhappy as it dressed regiments in the same trews that the HLI had felt marked their status as an elite regiment.

At first, all Lowland regiments wore the government pattern plaid, and this was known derisively as the MacChilders pattern. The regiments then began a quest to wear distinctive tartans in place of the government plaid. The King's Own Scottish Borderers, to commemorate the man who raised the regiment, David Leslie, the third Earl of Leven, received permission to wear a Leslie tartan in 1898.[177] The Cameronians (Scottish Rifles), to commemorate the man who raised them, the Earl of Angus, who was a Douglas, adopted the Douglas tartan in 1892.[178] The Royal Scots were granted the Hunting Stewart in 1901 in recognition of its royal status.[179] This doubtless was the product of effective lobbying. The Scots Fusiliers kept the government tartan, but the regiment added a bluish line to create their own unofficial tartan.[180]

ROYAL SCOTS AND KING'S OWN SCOTTISH BORDERERS

The classic Lowland Scottish regiments are the Royal Scots (the Lothian Regiments) and the King's Own Scottish Borderers (KOSB). There were two other Lowland regiments, the Royal Scots Fusiliers and the Cameronians (Scottish Rifles), both of which fell partly into other classifications.

The headdress for both the Royal Scots and the KOSB was a Kilmarnock bonnet with a black cock feather (Images II:155 and II:156). This was a stiffened version of the Balmoral bonnet, which dated back to the 1500s and was a cousin of the tam o' shanter. For both regiments, the bonnets were introduced in 1904. They replaced the home service helmet, which had

II:155 King's Own Scottish Borderers Other Ranks
Note shape of black cock feathers.

II:154 Royal Scots Officers
In this image, rank insignia shows the figure on the right is the adjutant. Within each infantry regiment, the commanding officer, second in command, and adjutant were mounted officers. Note the Kilmarnock bonnets with black cock feathers and diced border. The Hunting Stewart tartan is used for both trews and riding breeches; the cloth was cut so that the yellow or white lines always fell to the front.

II:156 King's Own Scottish Borderers Other Ranks and Sergeants in Dublin in 1914
A man on the second row had managed to acquire three long-service stripes and not risen much in rank. Note also the crossed flags on the right arms on some of the men in the front row, indicating colour sergeant status. Seated figure with plaid is a band sergeant.

been worn since 1878 with suitable changes to reflect changes to county organisation, the crowns, etc.

The bonnet was made of blue cloth, tilted to the left with a high diced band. The band consisted of a white background with a red horizontal line dividing the white area. The white field was divided by periodic vertical red lines. Where the red lines overlapped was a blue box. On the left side of the bonnet, above the border and at the base of the feathers, a large regimental badge was worn (Image II:156).

Doublet and trews were worn. See Table II.8.f.1, Images C7 and C9 for facing colours and tartan trews patterns. Colour Paintings of officers and an NCO and enlisted men are shown in Images II:154 and C22.

SCOTS FUSILIERS

The Scots Fusiliers, except for wearing a fusilier's busby, were dressed similarly to the other Lowland Scottish regiments (the fusilier's cap is discussed in §II-8-c). They wore a Highland doublet with gauntlet cuffs and Inverness flaps (Images II:157, II:158, and II:159). Their facings were blue to show their status as a royal regiment. Their trews were in the Government tartan pattern (Image C8).

II:157 Scots Fusiliers, c. 1900
Notice the fusilier headdress and grenade on his doublet. Other than that, he is all Scottish.

II:158 Royal Scots Fusilier
This man has a sergeant's sash.

II:159 Royal Scots Fusiliers Officer
Note his crimson silk sash and the wide belt to hold his sword coming across his right shoulder. His waist belt plate has a St Andrew's cross.

II:160 Cameronians Officers, c. 1890s
The cap lines go around the neck. Note also trim on cuff which shows rank and the badges on the shako. This regiment also had their trews cut in such a way that the white line of their Douglas tartan always came down the front of their leg.

CAMERONIANS (SCOTTISH RIFLES)

Shako

The Scottish Rifles wore a shako of dark rifle green cloth. For officers, it was 11.43 cm (4½ inches) high in the front and 19.685 cm (7¾ inches) high in the back. The crown was 15.24 cm (6 inches) long and 14.605 cm (5¾ inches) across. In front were a stringed bugle and a star. There was a band of black lace 4.445 cm (1¾ inches) wide around the bottom of the shako and another 1.59 cm (⅝ inch) wide around the top. The shako had a black horizontal peak and chin strap.[181]

The shako was decorated with a black silk square cord plaid in front, which began under the badge in front of the shako and went up to the hooks on either side of the shako near the top (Images II:23 and II:24). A double cord then went around to the lower rear of the shako and attached to a ring with a metal swivel. A double square black silk body line 1.93 m (6 feet 4 inches) long was attached to the ring swivel. The body line hung down in back, then went around the neck and was fastened on the chest.

A 17.78 cm (7 inch) high plume of black ostrich feathers was worn on the shako. The ostrich feathers rose out of black vulture feathers, which, in turn, rose out of a bronze socket with three upright flames.[182]

Doublet

The Scottish Rifles were a hybrid of Scottish and rifle elements. Their doublet was dark green. The cuffs, flaps, and front edge and bottom of the doublet were trimmed in black (Image II:161). As with other

II:161 Cameronian Scottish Rifles Officers
Note two-part plume on the shako and the pouch belt with chain and prickers. The field officers breeches are in the Douglas tartan.

regiments, the trim was more complex and showed officers' rank prior to 1902; after that date, the trim was simplified (see *§II-3-5*, Images II:23 and II:24). The buttons were black.

The officers wore a black patent leather shoulder belt 7.62 cm (3 inches) wide with a breast ornament of regimental pattern and a whistle and chain (Image II:161). On the back, they had a black patent leather pouch with a thistle in silver on it.[183]

TREWS
The regiment's trews were of the Douglas pattern (Image C10).

§II-9 WEST INDIA REGIMENT

Uniform

Regiment	Fez/Cap	Tassel[a]	Turban	Jacket	Jacket Trim	Shirt	Button Colour	Baggy Knickerbockers	Gaiters
1st	Red	White[b]	White	Scarlet	Yellow	White	Gold	Dark blue, yellow trim	White
2nd	Red	White[b]	White	Scarlet	Yellow	White	Gold	Dark blue, yellow trim	White

Notes: [a] The tassel was almost never worn, but the 1914 clothing regulations called for one fez and tassel to be issued to soldiers each year.

[b] The tassel was to be of the regiment's facing colour (Marrion, 'West India', 9/1987, p. 614).

By 1914, the force was one regiment of two battalions with white facings.

In 1858, the regiment was given a Zouave-type uniform. Legend says this was because Queen Victoria had seen the French Zouaves of the Guard in Paris and had been impressed by them. Maybe this is what happened. What is certainly true is that Zouave-type dress was being adopted in many countries as part of a Zouave fad following the French Zouaves' performance in the Crimean War.

II:162 West India Regiment Drum Corps, c. 1904
The black lines in the turban are actually yellow ribbons, which musicians wove through the turban cloth. Yellow during this period often showed as black in photographs.

II:163 West India Regiment Musicians
Note location of the stripe on their baggy knickerbockers and how the Zouave jacket fits when worn.

II:164 West India Regiment Officer and Men
Notice the shape of the men's gaiters and the size of the tassels on their headdress. The British officer's helmet dates this photograph to earlier than 1900.

II:165 Front of West India Jacket
Notice the shape of the zigzag braid on the front of the jacket and the trim around the collar, front, and bottom edges and armholes of this jacket.

II:166 Back of West India Jacket
This shows the shape of the trim on the back of the jacket.

As can be seen in Image II:162, the soldiers wore a close-fitting cap (red) surrounded by a turban of white cloth. The black lines in the turban of the man on the left are yellow ribbons (yellow appears black in many photos of this period). Band members would thread a yellow ribbon through the turban to show their membership of the band.

In full dress, a tassel was worn. Originally, in the 1860s, the colour of the tassel was to match the regiment's facing colour. It is not clear what colour the tassel was in the two battalions during the period 1900–14. The tassel was quite long, hanging down so far as to rest on the shoulders in some cases (see Images II:163 and II:164; note the different colours of the tassels).

The waistcoat jacket was red, and the trim was yellow. The trim outlined the front and bottom edges of the jacket. It also outlined the collar and sleeve openings (Image II:165). On the back there were stylised crows' feet at the top centre under the collar and at the bottom centre. The back seams on either side were covered in yellow braid, which ended in crows' feet near the arm opening (Image II:166). In the front, thin piping trim formed a zigzag pattern with a loop at the top of each extension (Image II:163).

II:167 The man on the left is a member of the West India band, as can be seen by the yellow ribbons that have been woven through the white cloth turban. The man on the right is probably a junior NCO infantryman, but it is possible he is a drummer of the bugle corps of his regiment. Note the gaiters the men are wearing.

The close-fitting long-sleeve shirt worn under the jacket was also trimmed in yellow at the cuffs and neck. The shirt had twenty small brass buttons down the front, which closed it (Image II:168; the top button is missing in this photograph). It is said by some that the yellow trim was limited to the 2nd Regiment, and the 1st Regiment had white trim, but this is difficult to verify, and other sources state yellow trim was worn by both regiments.

The regiment wore long baggy knickerbockers that were dark blue and had two yellow stripes, one on either side of the central side seam (Image II:169). A drawstring would pull the bottom of the knickerbockers together after they had been put on.

The men wore white gaiters (Images II:163 and II:164).

II:168 West India Shirt
The shirt is white, dress, with sleeves according to regulations. This shows the yellow trim at the sleeves, collar, and down the front of the shirt. In old photographs, this often shows as black. Note the many small buttons and the fact that a few of the top buttons are missing.

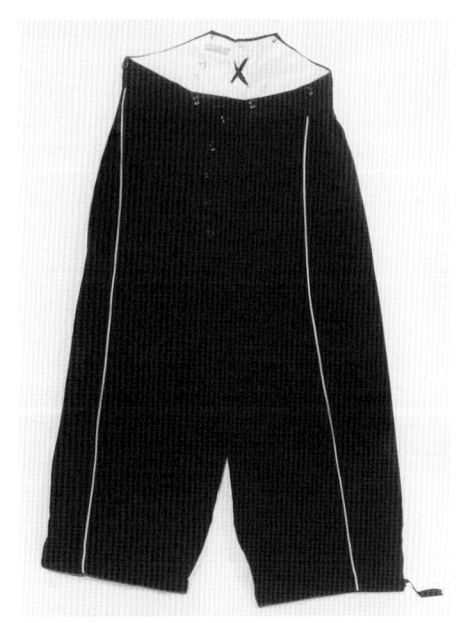

II:169 West India Baggy Knickerbockers
Note location of the stripe on the knickerbockers. There was a similar stripe in the same location on the other side of the central seam. The drawstring at the bottom of the knickerbockers is for pulling them tight.

II:170 West India Regiment Officer
The officer, being an officer in a regular line infantry regiment, wears the standard infantry tunic of a regiment with white facings. The only thing that sets him apart is his white colonial helmet, worn by the regiment in lieu of the home service helmet. Note the regimental badge worn on the front of the helmet.

NCOs

In the 1860s, the regiment had one British sergeant per company. In addition, the higher ranks of sergeant would be British; about half of all sergeants were British.[184] At first they wore a full Zouave-style full dress, but wore the regular British pattern uniform on other occasions.[185] About 1877, the NCOs began wearing a white colonial helmet of the type worn by officers in place of the turban and fez.[186]

Officers

The officers wore the uniforms of a regular British officer. However, serving in a tropical climate, there were some minor differences. About 1877, the officers stopped wearing a shako and began wearing a white helmet in full dress (Images II:164 and II:171).[187] The 1911 Dress Regulations say a white Wolseley helmet (*§II-3-5*, Image II:18 is the full dress headdress.

The tunic was the same tunic worn by British officers in other line regiments in full dress. The regiment had their own regimental buttons, as did all the other line infantry regiments.

Trousers and Breeches

The same trousers and breeches as were worn in Britain seem to have been worn in full dress. The 1904 Dress Regulations state that white trousers were to be worn 'on ordinary occasions'. The 1911 Dress Regulations repeat this.

II:171 West India Regiment Officer
A good character study. Since this regiment was a regular army regiment, his tunic and trim was exactly like British line infantry regiments. Note regimental badge on his white colonial helmet.

§II-10 WEST AFRICAN REGIMENT

Other Ranks' Uniform[188]

HEADDRESS
The men of the West African Regiment (WAR) wore a red fez. It had a black tassel that fell to the right to about even with the bottom of the fez. The tassel was fastened on the top.

SHIRT
The enlisted men wore a long-sleeve khaki blouse that was tucked into the cummerbund. It had four brass buttons down the front, but did not have any trim. The shoulder straps appear red in photographs, but it is hard to tell. The blouse had two patch pockets, one on each side of the chest (Image II:172).

CUMMERBUND AND BELT
The cummerbund was turkey red, and a belt was worn over it. The brown leather belt had an open brass buckle.

NETHERWEAR
The men wore khaki knickerbockers that did not have any trim on them. Shorts were issued in about 1909.[189]

PUTTEES
Puttees, when worn, were called drab, a colour slightly different from khaki, in the 1914 Dress Regulations. However, photographs of soldiers on full dress parades show them in dark-coloured puttees. One officer who served next to them stated they were either blue or black.[190] Whatever the colour, the men often went without puttees as they just added to the heat in an already hot, damp climate.

FOOTWEAR
The enlisted men did not generally wear boots.

NCOs' Uniform
In 1914–15, the regiment had fifteen British NCOs.[191] These NCOs basically wore the same dress as the

II:172 Band and Corps of Drums of the West African Regiment
In this regiment, the band did not have a special uniform, so this dress shows what the regiment wore: fez, khaki shirt, cummerbund, and knickerbockers. Note the men are all barefoot.

African enlisted men. They did seem to have the right to wear two officers' items: ties (at first black and, after 1913, drab), and khaki slacks.

Officers' Uniform

At first, the officers wore a khaki serge uniform for both full dress and levee dress.[192] Then, in 1911, the regulations called for the following:

Helmet
White Wolseley helmet with white puggree – a cloth in turban colours wrapped around the helmet (also spelled pagri, puggaree) – infantry pattern style.

Jacket
The jacket in full dress was to be a white frock coat with five small buttons down the front. The buttons were bronze and had 'WAR' (West African Regiment) on a frosted dome. The coat had a stand-up collar that was rounded where it met in front. The coat was to be long enough to clear the saddle when mounted. It had no trim and shoulder straps were white.

A bronze regimental badge was worn on the collar.

Trousers
The trousers of the officer's permanent unit were worn. The belt was the infantry web sword belt.

§II-11 KING'S AFRICAN RIFLES[193]

The King's African Rifles (KAR) were formed in 1902 with two battalions from the former Central African Regiment (CAR) in the Nyasaland area, now Malawi, one battalion from the East African Rifles (EAR) in Kenya, and two from the Uganda Rifles (UR).

Uniform

The clothing worn by the different contingents before the KAR was formed varied widely. The first British soldiers in the Central African area were Indians, and they wore an Indian uniform of turban, open-fronted jacket, white shirt, cummerbund, knickerbockers, and puttees. The colours were black for Africans, yellow for Arabs and other Asiatics, white for Europeans, and red for Britons. When the CAR was formed, this mutated into a black fez and tassel, khaki blouse and knickerbockers. The 2nd CAR when raised wore the same fez and tassels, but a blue blouse and knickerbockers; they also had blue puttees.[194] The UR, in theory, wore a blue tunic and breeches with a red fez, but the government had a great deal of trouble supplying these to the men, so they wore whatever they could get their hands on.[195] The EAR wore red fezzes, khaki blouses, knickerbockers, and puttees. This was their campaign and fatigue dress. They did not have a formal dress uniform.[196]

Other Ranks' Uniform 1901

When the KAR was formed the uniform in the table below was agreed upon by a committee that met in London in 1901.

KAR Other Ranks' Uniform

Battalion	Fez	Tassel	Blouse	Buttons	Shoulder Straps and Badge	Short Trousers[a]	Puttees
1st	Black	Black	Khaki	Brass	Khaki; brass KAR badge	Khaki	Blue
3rd	Red	Black	Khaki	Brass	Khaki; brass KAR badge	Khaki	Blue
4th	Red	Black	Khaki	Brass	Khaki; brass KAR badge	Khaki	Blue

Source: Moyse-Bartlett, The KAR, p. 691.
Notes: [a] Called shorts thereinafter. Originally, knickerbockers were called for in the regulations.

The fez was fairly tall and the tassel hung down to the right to below the bottom of the fez. The fez was worn square on the head (Image II:173).

The blouse was fairly long, coming down to the crotch. It had an opening in the front that went only part way down, which required the blouse to be put on over the head. The short front opening was closed with two brass buttons bearing a Tudor Crown in the centre and 'King's African Rifles' in an arc around the rim (Images II:173 and II:174). Some of the blouses had a stand-up collar (Image II:173) and some had no collar (Images II:174 and II:175). On the chest of the blouse were patch pockets, one on each side of the chest (Images II:173, II:174, and II:175). The shoulder straps were khaki (Images II:173 and II:174), and the blouse did not have any trim (Images II:173, II:174, and II:175).

Shorts were worn. These had no trim (Images II:173, II:174, and II:175). Blue puttees were normally worn, but not always (Image II:176).

While the authorities experimented with giving the men sandals, it seems not to have worked out, because the men normally went barefoot prior to World War I (Images II:173, II:174, II:175, and II:176).

Officers' Uniform 1901

The officers' khaki helmet was the colonial (Egyptian pattern at first) model with a khaki puggree (Image II:177). Officers could also wear the same fez and tassel as their men (Image II:178). After 1908, the regulations called for a cloth field service cap with a visor.

II:173 Yao Sergeant, 1st KAR, 1905
The 1st KAR wore black fezzes. The Yao ethnic group (tribe) were considered to be East Africa's finest soldiers.

II:174 Sudanese Corporal

II:175 Drummer Boy, KAR, Uganda

II:176 Atonga Company
1st KAR in 1902. They are not wearing puttees.

II:177 KAR Guard of Honour

Officers had a khaki jacket with patch pockets. They could wear either trousers or breeches of khaki. If they wore breeches, they would wear blue puttees, brown leather belts, and boots (Images II:177 and II:178).[197]

II:178 Richard Meinerzhagen. KAR Officer in 1903.

§II-12 WEST AFRICAN FRONTIER FORCE

Uniform

West African Frontier Force (WAFF) Dress Regulations
(Seems to be for 1903, Not Including Mounted Infantry)

Colony	Fez	Fez Tassel	Zouave Vest Colour	Vest Trim	Blouse Colour	Cummerbund	Shorts & Puttees
1st Northern Nigerian Battalion	Red	Red	Red	Yellow	Khaki	Red	Khaki
2nd Northern Nigerian Battalion	Red	Green	Red	Yellow	Khaki	Green	Khaki
Nigerian Artillery	Red	Royal Blue	Blue	Yellow	Khaki	Royal blue	Khaki
Southern Nigeria	Red	Red	Red	Yellow	Khaki	Long red; with fringed ends	Khaki
Gold Coast Infantry Battalion	Red	Old Gold	Red	Yellow	Khaki	Red	Khaki
Gold Coast Artillery	Red	Royal Blue	Blue	Yellow	Khaki	Royal blue	Khaki
Sierra Leone Battalion	Red	Blue	Red	Yellow	Khaki	Blue	Khaki
Lagos Battalion	Red	Red	Red	Yellow	Khaki	Red	Khaki
Gambia Company	Red	Brown	Red	Yellow	Khaki	Brown	Khaki

Source: Haywood, *W African FF*, p. 289.

However, Nevins[198] gives the following uniform for all units of the WAFF in 1914:

Type	Fez	Tassel	Zouave Vest	Vest Colour	Vest Trim	Blouse Colour	Cummerbund	Shirts & Puttees
Infantry	Red	Black	Red	Blue	Yellow	Khaki	Red	Khaki
Artillery	Red	Black	Blue	Red	Yellow	Khaki	Red	Khaki

Other Ranks

Images II:179 and II:180, which judging by the medals the men sport are probably taken after World War I, give a general idea of what the WAFF uniform looked like. It must be stressed that all the men in the photographs are sergeants and other high NCO ranks. The ordinary private did not have braid on the chest of his jacket.

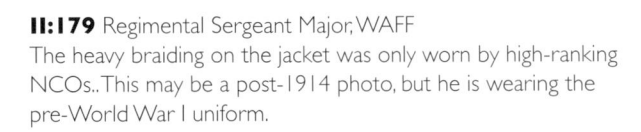

§II-12 West African Frontier Force 177

II:179 Regimental Sergeant Major, WAFF
The heavy braiding on the jacket was only worn by high-ranking NCOs.. This may be a post-1914 photo, but he is wearing the pre-World War I uniform.

II:180 NCOs, WAFF
This photo is post-1918, but they are wearing the pre-World War I uniform. World War I medals are being worn. Note the heavy braid on these NCOs' jackets, their puttees, and bare feet.

As to the colours of the uniforms, one can take one's pick of the schemes set out above.

Officers

In 1903, officers wore a Wolseley helmet with a puggree as shown in the table.[199]

Colony	Puggree	Flash on Helmet
1st North Nigeria	Khaki	Red
2nd North Nigeria	Khaki	Green
South Nigeria	Red	None
Gold Coast	Khaki	Old gold
Sierra Leone	Khaki	Blue
Lagos	Khaki and red	None
Gambia	Khaki and brown	None
Artillery	Khaki, topped with 0.64 cm (¼ inch) red and blue folds (red above blue)	None

They also wore a khaki jacket with red piping, khaki trousers (technically strapped overalls) or breeches, and black Wellington boots.

Mounted Infantry[200]

The mounted infantry up to 1907 wore khaki blouses and breeches. After 1907, they wore a kulla (long blouse), and a turban replaced the fez. In the early days, they went barelegged below the breeches. Later, they had puttees and boots.

§II-13 THE MALAY STATE GUIDES

To modern eyes, the Malay Peninsula prior to World War I was a somewhat confusing chequerboard of federate states, unfederated states, British-ruled areas, and states ruled by natives. Out of this rose the regiment Malay States Guides (MSG), an unusual hybrid of a regiment, commanded by British officers, manned by Indian soldiers, stationed in, and paid for, by three of the Malay states. Although not listed on the Indian army list, they were in effect an Indian army regiment.

Uniform[201]

The full dress of the enlisted men (Image II:181) was:

TURBAN
Green with silver trim.

TUNIC
An old-style Indian tunic with green facings and white trim. The stand-up collar, cuffs and shoulder straps were green. The tunic came down to about crotch level. The tunic was trimmed down the front and all the way around the bottom with white piping. The green cuffs were piped around the top in white, and this piping ended in crows' feet at the top of the piping. The green collar had white piping, as did the shoulder straps.

II:181 Malay State Guides
The Malay State Guides were a very obscure regiment, and this poor photograph is one of the few that shows them up close in their dress uniforms. Note the short tunic and the shape of the braid on their cuffs.

The tunics were closed down the front by buttons, but it is difficult to obtain a good count of how many. There seem to be five. The buttons were brass and had crossed *krises* in the centre (the *krise* is a Malay or Indonesian dagger with a wavy blade). The words 'Malay State Guides' were written around the rim. A tiger was at the top of the button. The regimental badge was a circular badge representing a wreath of ears of padi.

KNICKERBOCKERS
The knickerbockers were dark blue. Whether or not they had piping is unknown. In the few photographs showing the side, piping cannot be seen.

BELT
White, probably with a brass buckle.

GAITERS
White.

British and Native Officers' Uniform[202]

HEADDRESS
The British officers wore a white colonial helmet with spike, while the native officers wore turbans.

TUNIC
The commanding officer (who until 1912 was R.S. Frowd Walker) of the regiment wore a tunic very similar to that worn by field officers of the 6th Dragoon Guards in the British army prior to the changes of 1902 (see *§II-3-5*, Image II:9).[203] He had no connection with the 6th Dragoon Guards, having been an infantry ensign in the 28th Foot (Gloucestershires),[204] but since he raised and commanded the regiment for most of its life, doubtless he could design whatever uniform for himself he desired. Adding to his freedom was the fact that the regiment was not subject to direct British or Indian dress regulations. The other officers seem to have worn standard British infantry tunics in full dress.

TROUSERS AND BREECHES
The trousers and breeches worn in full dress were the same as those worn by the British army officers in full dress.

§II-14 EGYPT AND THE SUDAN

II:182 Senegalese Soldiers in the Egyptian Army
This group are in full dress. The Senegalese wore a Zouave-style uniform of light blue.

When problems arose in 1882 that threatened Britain's position in Egypt and its use of the Suez Canal, Britain sent a naval and land force to 'restore order'. The result was a *de facto* takeover of Egypt. The old Egyptian army was disbanded and a new one, largely under British command, was raised in 1883.

Uniform

The Egyptian and Sudanese other ranks wore different full dress uniforms.

Sudanese

The Sudanese wore a Zouave-type uniform (Image II:182).

Sudanese Full Dress

Fez	Turban	Jacket	Shirt	Cummerbund	Belt	Knickerbockers	Gaiters	Boots
Red	White	Light blue (really medium blue)	Light blue (really medium blue)	Red	Brown leather with 'S' buckle	Light blue (really medium blue), yellow trim	White	Black

Egyptian Winter Uniform

The winter uniform worn by the Egyptian other ranks was very different from that of the Sudanese soldiers and was one of the most attractive of the period.

Egyptian Winter Full Dress

Fez	Tassel	Tunic	Buttons	Collar, Trim, and Knickerbocker Stripes	Knickerbockers	Belt	Belt Buckle	Gaiters	Boots
Red	Black	Light blue (really medium blue) Trim: off white/cream	Brass	Off white/cream	Light blue (really medium blue)	Brown leather	Square brass with crescent and star on it	White	Black

Tunic

There were eight brass buttons down the front of the light blue (really medium blue) single-breasted tunic. The front of the tunic was piped in off white/cream. The cuff was the same colour as the tunic and outlined in an off-white/cream colour. The collar was all off white/cream (Image II:183).

The rear skirt had three buttons on each skirt, connected by off-white/cream trim in a scallop shape (Image II:184).

Knickerbockers

The knickerbockers were the same colour as the tunic and had a wide stripe in an off-white/cream colour (Image II:184).

Gaiters

White gaiters were worn.

Summer Uniform

There was also a summer full dress where the tunic and knickerbockers were white, and there was no trim or piping on either garment (Image II:184). Other than that, everything was the same as the winter full dress uniform.

II:183 An Egyptian Bugler of the Egyptian Army
He is wearing drummer's lace on sleeves, collars, and wings. He has bugler's wings and lace on his tunic. Other than that, his uniform is that of an Egyptian other ranks. Note in particular the collar badges and belt buckle. He has the British pattern drummer's sword.

British Empire

II:184 Egyptian Soldiers in Summer and Winter Uniforms
The man in the centre shows what the trim on the rear skirt looked like. This photo is especially useful in showing the width of the white/cream-coloured stripes on the knickerbockers.

II:185 Group of Egyptian Infantry Officers
They are wearing their double-breasted tunics. Note the rank lace on their sleeves. The men in the centre front of the photo are field officers and have three strands of cord looped across their chest to show their high rank.

II:186 Egyptian Kaimakan (Lieutenant Colonel)
His rank is shown by the lines on the braid on his sleeves, which entitles him to the three cords across his chest. Note the crescent and star on his collar.

Officers' Uniform

Egyptian infantry officers wore a double-breasted tunic of light blue (really medium blue) with eight buttons down each side. On their sleeves, they had gold braid that went up to near the elbow and came to a lance point at the top (Images II:185 and II:186). The number of threads and chevrons on the sleeve showed rank, as follows:

Sirdar	Seven threads
Ferik	Six threads
Lewa	Five threads
Miralai	Four threads with one around the bottom
Kaimakam	Four threads
Bimbashi	Three threads
Yuzbashi	Chevron with three threads, twist at the top
Mulazim Awal	Chevron with two threads, twist at the top
Mulazim Tani	Chevron with one thread, twist at the top

The different rank markers can be seen in Image II:185. In addition, field officers wore cords, normally three, usually gold, that hung from the end of each shoulder cord and across the chest (Images II:185 and II:186). Officers wore the same fez and tassel as the other ranks.

Officers' trousers were the same medium blue as the tunics and had two red stripes.

Cavalry Uniform

The cavalry wore a light blue (medium blue) tunic. Over this for full dress, they would button an off-white/cream plastron. The plastron had eight brass buttons on each side. They wore a red fez with a black tassel (Image II:187).

The breeches were also a medium blue with a wide off-white/cream stripe on them for troopers. Dark blue puttees were also worn (Image II:187). Officers had two stripes of gold lace on their breeches, each 1.91 cm (¾ inch) wide.

II:187 Egyptian Cavalry NCO
Note the white/cream plastron, collar, cuff trim, and riding breeches' stripes and dark, probably dark blue, puttees.

II:188 British Officer of the Egyptian Army
Note the frogging and loose braid on his tunic. Neck decoration is the Order of the Medjidie. He has the Distinguished Service Order.

British Officers

British officers were dressed differently from their brother Egyptian officers. The ruler of Egypt had made it a requirement that the British officers wore a fez in full dress, and the British, picking their battles, went along with this, and they wore a red fez with a black tassel.

However, they wore a black tunic that was very different from the Egyptians'. It had five rows of black braid across the chest. On either side of the chest, there was an elaborate knot and four strands of braid hung loose between them, falling across the chest (Image II:188). The sleeves had the gold lance pointed knot that showed rank (Image II:189). Since the lowest rank British officers held was bimbashi (major), they were all field officers, and they wore the three gold (normally) cords that hung across the chest (Images II:188 and II:189). Image II:189 shows how different Egyptian and British officers looked in full dress.

The trousers were dark blue with a gold lace stripe 4.45 cm (1¾ inches) wide.

For the summer months, the British officers had a white double-breasted tunic that was cut the same as the tunic worn by Egyptian officers (Image II:190). The white tunic had no trim. The fez, tassel, trousers, and gold cords across the chest were the same as was worn in winter full dress. This white tunic was also worn as levee dress.

II:189 Group of Egyptians and English Officer
Note the difference between the Egyptian officers' and the British officer's uniforms. Also note which officers are entitled to wear the three loose gold cords across their chests.

II:190 British Officer in Levee Dress

§II-15 THE HONG KONG REGIMENT (1892–1902)

Uniform[205]

HEADDRESS
In full dress, the sepoys wore a turban of indigo blue. The turban had gold bands to show rank. From period photographs, it also seems to have had yellow bands and stripes for lower-ranking soldiers. Indian officers in full dress wore the regimental badge on the centre of the turban. For the regiment's dress uniforms, see Image II:191.

KULLA
The kulla colour is not known. It is dark in photographs. One Indian officer in Image II:191 has a light-coloured kulla, which shows it has gold braid added to it.

LONG BLOUSE
All ranks of the Indians in the regiment wore a long scarlet blouse with yellow trim. It had a very low stand-up collar. This blouse did not have an opening which ran the length of the blouse and therefore had to be put on over the head. It had three buttons on the front. It also had two chest pockets, one on either side of the central rows of buttons.

For some ranks, both the central opening and the pockets were trimmed around the edges in either yellow or gold-coloured piping. The bottom of the central piping came to a point. Because of the vagaries of the light and film of the period, it is difficult to be sure what rank had what type of trim. Native officers had gold-coloured piping; privates had no piping; NCOs seem to have had yellow piping.

II:191 Hong Kong Regiment Officers and Other Ranks, c. 1895
Note the trim on the pockets of the kurta and how the trim on the chest opening ends in a point. Note also that the native officers (NOs) are wearing the regimental badge on their turbans and the fact that they have heavier gold-coloured trim on their turbans than the other ranks. The British officers are wearing the old-style tropical helmets, and their cuffs have the pre-1902 trim pattern, as do the NOs'. The cuff trim on the uniform of NOs is a little less elaborate than that worn by the British officers. Note the men's white gaiters.

II:192 Native Officer and Other Ranks of the Hong Kong Regiment, c. 1895
The other ranks are wearing a mix of full dress, No. 2 dress, and field dress. The native officer in the centre is facing left, which allows a good view of his shoulder strap and cuff trim. This can be compared with the NCO on the far right of the photograph. The image of the NO allows an excellent view of the gold trim, indicating high rank, on his turban. Compare the amount of gold trim on the turban of the NO and the NCO (far right) and the plain sepoy (far left). Note also the gold trim around the pockets and the chest opening of the NCO's kurta, which is absent on the kurta of the sepoy on the left. In full dress the men of the regiment wore white gaiters. For less than full dress the regiment wore dark, probably dark blue, puttees. The knickerbockers had piping on them.

For Indian officers the low stand-up collar had gold piping on the front, top, and bottom.

Shoulder Strap

The shoulder strap of enlisted men was yellow. It carried the regiment's title badge.

The shoulder straps of Indian officers had gold trim around the yellow shoulder strap. The trim was on the two edges and the top. The officers' shoulder strap also had their badges of rank and the regiment's title badge (Image II:192).

Cuffs

The cuffs were scarlet, the colour of the blouse. They were outlined by a yellow upside-down 'V' on each cuff. Unusually, at the top of each 'V', there was a small yellow trefoil (also called crows' feet) (Image II:192).

The cuffs of Indian officers carried a badge of rank. This was similar to the cuffs worn by British infantry officers prior to 1902 (see Image II:15(1) in §II-3-5). However, the braid on the cuff was thinner, and the cuff decoration as a whole was simpler (Image II:192).

Cummerbund

The cummerbund has been described as gold. This colour was probably worn by Indian officers. Enlisted men were more likely to wear a yellow cummerbund.

Knickerbockers

In full dress, all Indian ranks wore dark blue (Oxford blue) knickerbockers with red trim.

Belt

A brown belt was worn over the cummerbund in full dress. For enlisted men, it was closed with a full buckle. Indian officers had an S-shaped belt buckle.

Gaiters

For full dress, white gaiters were worn by all Indian ranks. For daily wear, blue puttees replaced the gaiters.

British Officers' Uniform

Headdress

The standard white tropical helmet of the period was worn (Image II:17). Around the helmet was a puggree. The regimental badge was worn on the front of the helmet pinned to the puggree. The full dress of an infantry officer in this regiment is shown in Image II:191.

Tunic

British officers wore the standard tunic worn by British officers serving with the Indian army during the period prior to 1902. It followed the rules set out for regiments wearing red or scarlet. The trim on the cuffs was the same as that worn in the British army during this period (Image II:191).

Trousers

The officers' trousers were dark blue (Oxford blue) with red piping.

Regimental Badges

Image II:193 shows two examples of Hong Kong Regiment badges, A and B. Badge A was the badge worn by British and Indian officers c. 1891–1900. The British wore it on the cloth wrapped around their helmet (the puggree). The Indians wore it on their turbans.

Badge B was the badge worn by British officers c. 1900–2. They wore it on their helmet puggree. Badge B consisted of a garter around a Chinese dragon facing left. The garter had the title of the regiment, 'The Hong Kong Regiment', on it. The garter was topped by a crown.

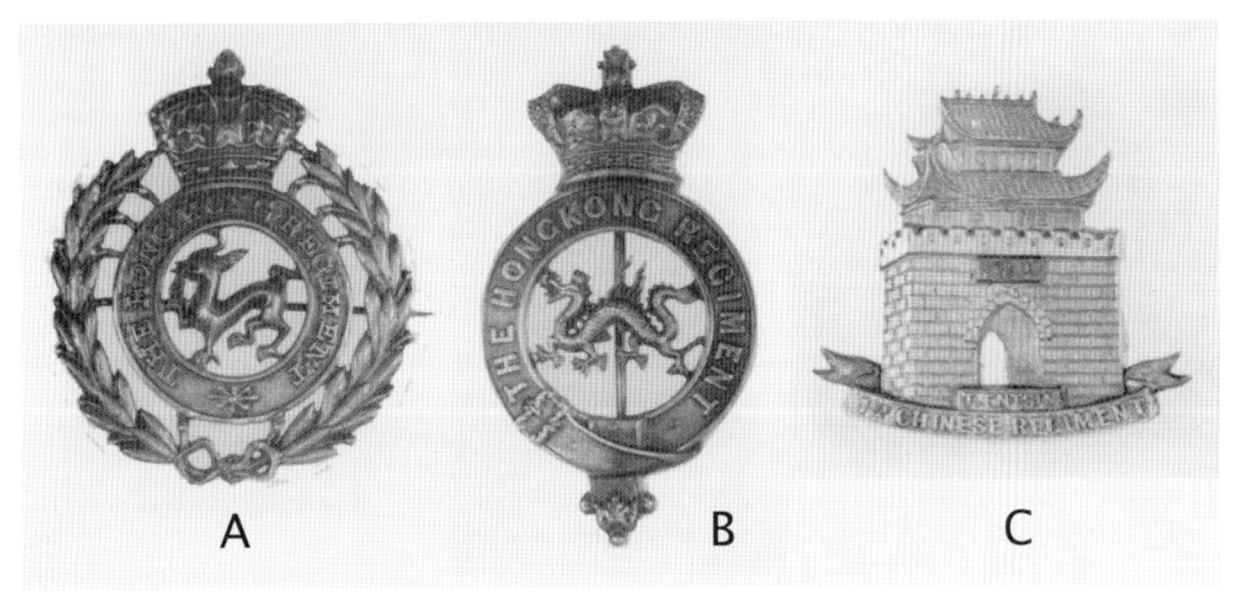

II:193 A. British officer's helmet badge and Indian officer's puggree badge, 1891–1900
B. British officer's helmet badge, c. 1900–2. Note the crown.
C. Cap badge of the 1st Chinese Regiment created after the Boxer Rebellion.

§II-16 THE CHINESE REGIMENT (1898–1906)

Original Uniform[206]

The first dress uniform for the Chinese Regiment (Image II:194) consisted of:

- A wide brimmed straw hat with a low crown similar to the hats worn in the Royal Navy. The brim was turned up in back.
- A white shirt with turn-down collar. The shirt was buttoned at the neck and wrists.
- Baggy dark blue trousers secured at the lower leg. On the lower leg, below the calf, the men wore a closing item that looked very much like the jambières worn by the French Zouaves (see §IV-8-b, Uniform – Gaiters and Jambières).
- A red cummerbund was worn around the waist over the shirt and trousers.
- The footwear consisted of white socks and Chinese shoes.

New Uniform

The original uniform was soon replaced by a totally different version (Image II:195). The following description was gleaned from an extract of a letter from an officer of the regiment published in *The Times* on 21 August 1899.

The headdress was a small, dark blue turban. The colour was often described as purple.[207] The blue smock (long blouse/frock-style shirt) was double-breasted with brass buttons. The letter in *The Times* said the smock had red shoulder straps, but photographs seem to show dark blue shoulder straps, the colour of the long frock (see Image II:195). However, many descriptions of the frock say it was grey. The frock fell to the knees and had a dark blue stand-up collar. Neither the collar nor the sleeves had trim. It had two

II:194 First Uniform of the Chinese Regiment Corporal Drummer
Drummers also carried bugles.

II:195 Chinese Regiment Uniform
His frock was very similar to a kurta, except it was double-breasted and had a high collar. Note the absence of trim.

rows of six buttons on its front; the bottom buttons were hidden by the cummerbund.

The regiment's buttons showed the harbour of Wei-hai-wei (also spelled Wei-hei-wei, Weihaiwei, etc.) with a junk under sail in the foreground. The regiment's buttons are not described in the 1900 Dress Regulations. There seem to have been three possible borders on the buttons; one of them has been described as a garter with the regiment's name on it, 'The Chinese Regiment'.[208] Photographs of officers' regimental buttons show two other versions.[209] One has a simple band around the edge of the button with the regiment's name on it. The other version has an irregular border that may be meant to show a coastline. At this late date, it is hard to divine the intent or the coastline. Whatever the border, the sailing junk motif makes the Chinese Regiment button one of the most attractive worn by the British army.

The trousers were dark blue.

The wide cummerbund was red and worn over the frock.

Dark blue puttees covered the lower legs from the ankles to over the calves.

The footwear was black boots.

The Chinese soldiers' pigtails were tucked up under their turbans.[210] That the men had pigtails indicates they were Chinese and not Manchu, the race that had conquered China and ruled it at this time. The Manchus had ordered all Chinese men to wear pigtails as a sign of submission. The belief that the regiment's soldiers were Manchus originates in the fact that the average height of the regiment's soldiers in 1900 was 1.73 m (5 feet 8 inches),[211] a far cry from the stereotypical small Chinese man. This height is comparable to the height the British soldiers of the period. In 1897, only 33.05 per cent of recruits were taller than 1.70 m (5 feet 7 inches) and 13.3 per cent were shorter than 1.63 m (5 feet 4 inches).

After the fighting against the Boxers around Tientsin, the regiment was granted the right to wear a badge depicting the ancient gate into Tientsin. Above the arch of the gate was a plaque which bore the name Tientsin in Chinese characters. Under the gate opening was another plaque with the English name 'Tientsin'. Below the badge was a scroll which bore the title '1st Chinese Regiment' (see Image II:193).[212] The badge was worn on the front of the turban and on the collars (Image II:195).

The British sergeants, based on their dress at the 1902 Coronation of Edward VII, wore the same uniform as the Chinese other ranks, except, in place of the turban, they wore a white tropical helmet. In 1902, this was the Wolseley-style helmet.[213]

Officers

The 1900 Dress Regulations simply state that for state occasions and levees, officers would wear the full dress of the regiment from which they had been seconded.[214] However, the 1900 Dress Regulations show a special helmet for officers and NCOs of the Chinese Regiment (Image II:17). The 1904 Dress Regulations add that, in hot weather, a Wolseley pattern helmet was to be worn.[215]

§II BRITISH EMPIRE: NOTES

1. Kennedy, *Rise/Fall*, p. 228.
2. Ibid.
3. Friedberg, *Titan*, p. 26.
4. Carsten, *Junkers*, p. 128.
5. Cannadine, *Aristocracy*, p. 91.
6. Ibid., pp. 92–3.
7. Ibid., p. 17.
8. Ibid., p. 62.
9. Watson, *Enduring/Great War*, p. 145.
10. Edwards, *Customs*, 4th ed.
11. Dickinson, *Mess*.
12. Grazebrook, 'Headdress/Gloucestershire', p. 97.
13. Brereton, *Queen's Own*, p. 50.
14. Beckett, *Traditions*, pp. 76–7.
15. Correspondence with Lt. Gen. Jonathon Riley, Royal Welch Fusiliers Museum, 22 November 2016.
16. Peacock, *Northumberland Fusiliers*, p. 35.
17. Ibid., p. 21.
18. Edwards, *Customs*, 4th ed., p. 116.
19. Fosten, *British Shako*, p. 35.
20. Ibid., p. 28.
21. Ibid., pp. 42–3.
22. Beckett, *Traditions*, p. 77. Correspondence with Lesley Frater, Fusilier Museum of Northumberland, 25 November 2016.
23. MacLeod, *Glory*, p. 44.
24. Edwards, *Customs*, 3rd ed., p. 103.
25. Ibid.
26. Edwards, *Customs*, 4th ed., p. 101.
27. Correspondence with Peter Duffen, research team Staffordshire Regiment, 24 November 2016.
28. Edwards, *Customs*, 4th ed., p. 101.
29. Ibid.
30. Ibid., p. 100.
31. Ibid., pp. 110–11.
32. Ibid., p. 111.
33. Ibid., p. 117.
34. Ibid., pp. 116–17.
35. Ibid., pp. 119–20.
36. Knight, 'British Laces'; *Dress Regulations 1900*, p. 118; *Dress Regulations 1904*, Index, p. iv.
37. Carew, *Nicknames*, p. 83.
38. Ibid., p. 95.
39. 'Black Line in Lace', p. 123.
40. Ibid.
41. I am grateful to Bruce Rogers, Somerset Military Museum Trust, for drawing my attention to this phenomenon.
42. McWilliam, 'Survey/Dress Regulations,' p. 72.
43. Nicholson, 'British Staff Uniforms, 1897', p. 7.
44. Ibid.
45. Ibid.
46. Ibid.
47. Ibid., pp. 7–8.
48. Ibid.
49. Ibid., p. 8, Figures 2 and 4.
50. *Dress Regulations, 1900*, ¶ 7, 37, 74–88, 106–43, Plate 13; *Dress Regulations, 1911*, ¶ 119–20, 122–3, 138–9.
51. *Dress Regulations, 1900*, ¶165.
52. MacLeod, *Glory*, p. 5.
53. Rowe, *Heavy Cavalry*, p. 16.
54. Ibid.
55. Ibid., pp. 16 and 38.
56. Ibid., p. 28.
57. Ibid.
58. Ibid., p. 31.
59. Ibid.
60. MacLeod, *Glory*, p. 6.
61. Rowe, *Heavy Cavalry*, p. 24.
62. Ibid., pp. 31 and 33.
63. Ibid., p. 38.
64. Ibid., pp. 37–8.
65. MacLeod, *Glory*, p. 10; Stadden, *Life Guards*, pp. 61–62.
66. Stadden, *Life Guards*, p. 65.
67. Manser, *Household Cavalry*, p. 56.
68. Ibid., p. 49.
69. Ibid., p. 56
70. Stadden, *Life Guards*, pp. 63 and 65.
71. For the red cloth, see Manswer, *Household Cavalry*, p. 56. For the size of the device, see Rowe, *Heavy Cavalry*, p. 15.
72. Manser, *Household Cavalry*, p. 69.
73. Stadden, *Life Guards*, p. 64.
74. MacLeod, *Glory*, p. 5.
75. Ibid.
76. Manser, *Household Cavalry*, p. 59.
77. MacLeod, *Glory*, p. 10.
78. Manser, *Household Cavalry*, pp. 29 and 53.
79. Hills, *Life Guards*, p. 41. After 1895, the requirement for cavalry were as follows:
    Household Cavalry: 1.80 m to 1.85 m (5'11" to 6'1")
    Heavy Cavalry: 1.73 m to 1.80 m (5'8" to 5'11")
    Medium Cavalry: 1.70 m to 1.75 m (5'7" to 5'9")
    Light Cavalry: 1.68 m to 1.73 m (5'6" to 5'8")
    (Rowe, *Heavy Cavalry*, p. 43, endnote 8A).
80. Stadden, *Life Guards*, p. 46.
81. Edwards, *Customs*, 4th ed., p. 183.
82. Manser, *Household Cavalry*, p. 76.
83. In general, see Manser, *Household Cavalry*, pp. 24–7.
84. MacLeod, *Glory*, p. 36.
85. This photograph was taken in 1926 but there had been few if any changes in the foot guards' bearskins since 1914. Victors seldom make changes to their uniforms.
86. MacLeod, *Glory*, p. 34.
87. Ibid., p. 36.
88. Ross, *Canadian*, pp. 111–12.
89. Bowling, *Foot Guards*, p. 31.
90. Ibid., p. 50.
91. Ibid., p. 45.
92. Tate, 'Crowns', pp. 65–6.
93. Westlake, *Shoulder Titles*, p. 1.
94. Rowe, *Heavy Cavalry*, pp. 103 and 132; Henshall, Royal Dragoon Guards Museum.
95. Rowe, *Heavy Cavalry*, pp. 104 and 106.
96. Ibid., p. 133.
97. These seem to date from the 1864 changes to the uniforms of dragoon guards and dragoons.
98. Westlake, *Shoulder Titles*, p. 1.
99. *Clothing Regulations*, p. 164.
100. Ibid.
101. See lace patterns for 6th Dragoons in *Dress Regulations, 1900* and *Dress Regulations, 1904*.

102 Dilley, *Modelling* 2/81, p. 119; Dilley, *Modelling* 10/79, p. 871; Hagger, *Modelling* 9/94, p. 30; Hagger, *Modelling* 11/94, p. 26; various Simkin prints.
103 *Dress Regulations, 1911*, p. 33.
104 Linaker, *Arm Badges*, p. 66.
105 Edwards, *Badges*, p. 45.
106 Rowe, *Lancers*, p. 89
107 Ibid., p. 76. See dress regulations for which lace pattern was worn by which regiment in a given year.
108 Ibid.
109 Ibid., p. 89.
110 Ibid., p. 68.
111 Ibid.
112 Ibid., p. 76.
113 Ibid., p. 79.
114 Ibid., p. 69.
115 Rowe, *Lancers*, pp. 252–3.
116 Rowe, *Lancers*, p. 101.
117 Ibid., p. 79.
118 Ibid., p. 89.
119 Ibid.
120 Ibid., p. 101.
121 *Clothing Regulations*, p. 164.
122 Ibid., p. 121. See Linaker, *Arm Badges*.
123 Various Simkin prints; Dilley, *Modelling* 11/78, p. 847; Hagger, *Modelling* 6/92, p. 28.
124 Bowling, *Hussars*, p. 25, illustration nos. 19–24, and pp. 24–5, illustration nos. 25–48; various Simkin prints.
125 For detailed coverage of this subject, see Linaker, *Arm Badges*. This is a detailed study of the type that can only be produced as a labour of love.
126 Wilkinson-Latham, *Helmet*, p. 17.
127 Ibid., p. 9.
128 Ibid., pp. 7 and 23.
129 Ibid., p. 7.
130 Fosten, *British Shako*, p. 59.
131 For Scotland, the exceptions overwhelmed the rule on yellow facings. The same thing happened with the Irish regiments. The only Scottish regiments with yellow facings were the Gordons and Argylls. The only Irish regiment with green facings was the Connaught Rangers.
132 Bowling, *British Infantry*, p. 41.
133 A sealed pattern uniform is one sent out by the central authorities to show regimental tailors how uniforms were to be made up
134 Fosten, *Modelling* 10/84, p. 740.
135 Westlake, *Shoulder Titles*, p. 1. Metal shoulder titles had been used on khaki tropical uniforms since 1881.
136 Captain Des Williams, assistant regimental secretary, Royal Welch Fusiliers.
137 Carew, *Nicknames*, p. 48.
138 Zobel, *Boston*.
139 Pickering, Cheshire Military Museum.
140 Dilley, *Modelling* 7/78, p. 541.
141 Churchill, *Collar Badges*, pp. 190–1.
142 *Dress Regulations, 1900*, p. 43; *Dress Regulations, 1904*, p. 28.
143 They had an average of 22.86 cm (9 inches) across the top and had an average circumference of 68.58 cm (27 inches) at the bottom and 71.12 cm (28 inches) at the top.
144 See Wilkinson-Latham, *Helmet*, pp. 13–21.
145 MacLeod, *Glory*, p. 56.
146 Charley, letter 8 March 1978.
147 MacLeod, *Glory*, p. 56.
148 Ibid.
149 Ibid.
150 Westlake, *Modelling* 4/92, p. 30.
151 Fosten, *Modelling* 5/84, p. 370.
152 McKay, *Highland Light*, p. 11.
153 The sporran descriptions are from *Dress Regulations, 1911*, p. 76.
154 Trevor-Roper, 'Invention', pp. 15–41; Thorburn, 'Scottish Dress', pp. 105–9.
155 Carman, *Simkin's Uniforms*, p. 149.
156 MacLeod, *Glory*, p. 50.
157 Ibid., p. 54.
158 Ibid., p. 50.
159 Grosart, 'Brooches', pp. 127–43.
160 MacLeod, *Glory*, p. 50.
161 Ibid., p. 52.
162 Ibid., p. 54.
163 Ibid.
164 Ibid., p. 54.
165 Ibid., p. 50.
166 McKay, *Highland Light*, pp. 51 and 53.
167 Ibid., p. 10.
168 Ibid., *Dress Regulations, 1911*, p. 82. See Fosten, *British Shako*, p. 54.
169 McKay, *Highland Light*, p. 10.
170 Ibid., pp. 10–11.
171 Ibid., p. 10.
172 Ibid., pp. 65 and 67.
173 Grosart, 'Brooches', pp. 127–43.
174 McKay, *Highland Light*, pp. 10–11.
175 Ibid., p. 10.
176 Ibid., p. 13.
177 KOSB regimental website.
178 Cameronians' regimental website. Source: *The Scottish Regiments* by Diana M. Henderson.
179 Gordon, Royal Scots Regimental Museum, 26 August 2013.
180 Leishman, RHF Regimental Museum, correspondence, 13 September 2013.
181 *Dress Regulations, 1911*, p. 86.
182 Ibid., p. 88.
183 Ibid., pp. 88–9.
184 Marrion, 'West India,' 6/1987, p. 395.
185 Marrion, 'West India,' 9/1987, p. 614.
186 Ibid., p. 617.
187 Ibid.
188 *Clothing Regulations*, p. 109.
189 Tylden, 'West African Regiment', p. 100.
190 Carman, *Journal Army Historical Research*, p. 101.
191 Tylden, 'West African Regiment', p. 99.
192 See *Dress Regulations, 1904*, p. 33
193 For an explanation of why these particular ethnic names and geographic terms are used in this section, see Preface – Terminology.
194 Moyse-Bartlett, *The KAR*, p. 689.
195 Ibid., pp. 689–90.
196 Ibid., p. 690.
197 Ibid, p. 691.
198 Nevins, *British Empire*, p. 274.
199 Haywood, *W African FF*, p. 289.
200 Ibid., p. 259.
201 Singh, *History MSG*, p. 16.
202 Ibid., pp. 16–17.

203 Wright, *Impressions Malaya*, p. 589.
204 Ibid.
205 Harfield, *Armies/China*, p. 188.
206 Marrion, 'Wei-Hei-Wei Regiment', p. 132; Harfield, *Armies/China*, pp. 283–4, 299.
207 Marrion, 'Wei-Hei-Wei Regiment', p. 132.
208 Harfield, *Armies/China*, p. 283.
209 Ibid., p. 301.
210 Marrion, 'Wei-Hei-Wei Regiment', p. 132.
211 Ibid.
212 Harfield, *Armies/China*, p. 283.
213 Marrion, 'Wei-Hei-Wei Regiment', p. 132.
214 *Dress Regulations, 1900*, ¶ 789.
215 *Dress Regulations, 1904*, ¶ 501, p. 34.

§II BRITISH EMPIRE: BIBLIOGRAPHY

Interviews and Correspondences

Charley, letter 8 March 1978	Colonel W.R.H. Charley, Regimental Association Secretary, Royal Irish Rangers, Belfast, letter dated 8 March 1978.
Gordon, Royal Scots Regimental Museum	Tom Gordon, Royal Scots Regimental Museum.
Henshall, Royal Dragoon Guards Museum	Alan Henshall, Royal Dragoon Guards Museum, York Army Museum.
Leishman, RHF Regimental Museum	A.B. 'Sandy' Leishman, Royal Highland Fusiliers Regimental Museum.
Pickering, Cheshire Military Museum	Major Eddie Pickering, Cheshire Military Museum.
Rogers, Somerset Military Museum Trust	Bruce Rogers, Trustee of the Somerset Military Museum Trust.

Government Reports

Clothing Regulations	War Office, *Clothing Regulations 1914, Part I: Regular Forces* (London: His Majesty's Stationery Office, 1914).
Dress Regulations, 1900	War Office, *1900 Dress Regulations* (London: Her Majesty's Stationery Office, 1900).
Dress Regulations, 1904	War Office, *1904 Dress Regulations* (London: His Majesty's Stationery Office, 1904).
Dress Regulations, 1911	War Office, *Dress Regulations for the Army 1911* (London: His Majesty's Stationery Office, 1911).

Books and Articles

1914 Hart's Annual Army List	Lieutenant General H.G. Hart, *Hart's Annual Army List: Militia List, and Imperial Yeomanry List, for 1914* (London: John Murray, 1914).
Barthorp, *British Infantry*	Michael Barthorp, *British Infantry Uniforms Since 1660* (Poole: Blandford Press, 1982).
Beckett, *Traditions*	Ian Beckett, *Discovering British Regimental Traditions* (Princes Risborough: Shire Publications, 1999).
'Black Line in Lace'	'W.Y.Q. Replies, 414, Black Line in Lace', *Journal of the Society for Army Historical Research*, vol. XIV (1935): p. 123.
Bond, *Staff College*	Brian Bond, *The Victorian Army and the Staff College, 1854–1914* (Fakenham: Eyre Methuen Ltd, 1972).
Bowling, *British Infantry*	A.H. Bowling, *British Infantry Regiments, 1660–1914* (London: Almark Publishing Co. Ltd, 1970).
Bowling, *Foot Guards*	A.H. Bowling, *The Foot Guards Regiments, 1880–1914* (London: Almark Publishing Co. Ltd, 1972).
Bowling, *Hussars*	A.H. Bowling, *British Hussar Regiments 1805–1914* (London: Almark Publishing Co. Ltd, 1972).
Bowling, *Scottish*	A.H. Bowling, *Scottish Regiments and Uniforms, 1660–1914* (London: Almark Publishing Co. Ltd, 1971).
Brereton, *Queen's Own*	J.M. Brereton, *The 7th Queen's Own Hussars* (London: Leo Cooper Ltd, 1975).
Cameronians' regimental website	'Uniform, Tartan & the Cap Badge', *The Cameronians (Scottish Rifles)*, http://www.cameronians.org/uniform-tartan-badge, accessed 26 August 2013.
Cannadine, *Aristocracy*	David Cannadine, *Decline and Fall of British Aristocracy* (New Haven, CT: Yale University Press, 1990).
Carew, *Nicknames*	Tim Carew, *How the Regiments Got Their Nicknames* (London: Leo Cooper Ltd, 1974).
Carman, *Journal Army Historical Research*	W.Y. Carman, 'Note 1408 (West African Regiment)', *Journal of the Society for Army Historical Research*, vol. XLII (42) (1964): pp. 100–2.

Carman, *Simkin's Uniforms*	W.Y. Carman, *Richard Simkin's Uniforms of the British Army: Infantry, Royal Artillery, Royal Engineers and Other Corps* (Exeter: Webb & Bower, 1985).
Carsten, *Junkers*	F.L. Carsten, *A History of Prussian Junkers* (England: Scolar Press, 1989).
Churchill, *Collar Badges*	Colin Churchill, *History of the British Army Infantry Collar Badges* (Uckfield: Naval & Military Press Ltd, 2002).
Dickinson, *Mess*	R.J. Dickinson, *Officers' Mess* (Tunbridge Wells: Midas Books, 1973).
Dilley, *Modelling* 7/78	Roy Dilley, 'The Somerset Light Infantry and the Dorset Regiment', *Military Modelling*, vol. 8, no. 7 (July 1978): pp. 541–2.
Dilley, *Modelling* 11/78	Roy Dilley, 'The 16th and 17th Lancers', *Military Modelling*, vol. 8, no. 11 (November 1978): pp. 846–7.
Dilley, *Modelling* 10/79	Roy Dilley, 'The Royal Scots Greys', *Military Modelling*, vol. 9, no. 10 (October 1979): pp. 870–1.
Dilley, *Modelling* 2/81	Roy Dilley, 'The 5th Dragoon Guards', *Military Modelling*, vol. 11, no. 2 (February 1981): pp. 119–20.
Edwards, *Badges*	Denis Edwards and David Langley, *British Army Proficiency Badges* (London: Wardley Publishing, 1984).
Edwards, *Customs*, 3rd ed.	Thomas J. Edwards, *Military Customs*, 3rd ed. (Aldershot: Gale and Polden Ltd, 1952).
Edwards, *Customs*, 4th ed.	Thomas J. Edwards, *Military Customs*, 4th ed. (Aldershot: Gale and Polden Ltd, 1954).
Fosten, *British Shako*	Bryan Fosten and Gary Gibbs, *The British Infantry Shako, 1800–1897* (London: Military Historical Society, 2008).
Fosten, *Modelling* 5/84	D.S.V. Fosten, 'The Cut of the Cloth', *Military Modelling*, vol. 14, no. 5 (May 1984): pp. 368–70.
Fosten, *Modelling* 10/84	Don and Bryan Fosten, 'The Cut of the Cloth', *Military Modelling*, vol. 14, no. 10 (October 1984): pp. 740–2.
Friedberg, *Titan*	Aaron L. Friedberg, *The Weary Titan: Britain and the Experience of Relative Decline, 1895–1905* (Princeton, NJ: Princeton University Press, 1988).
Grant, *Scots Greys*	Charles Grant, *Royal Scots Greys* (London: Osprey Publishing Ltd, 2005).
Grazebrook, 'Headdress/ Gloucestershire'	Lt. Col. R.M. Grazebrook, 'Headdress of the Gloucestershire Regiment, 1881–1914', *Bulletin of the Military Historical Society*, vol. 62, no. 246 (November 2011): pp. 97–101.
Grosart, 'Brooches'	Alan Grosart, 'Officers Plaid Brooches of the Highland Regiments Pre 1914', *Bulletin of the Military Historical Society*, vol. 62, no. 247 (February 2012): pp. 127–43.
Hagger, *Modelling* 6/92	Doug Hagger, '5th Royal Irish Lancers', *Military Modelling*, vol. 22, no. 6 (June 1992): pp. 28–31.
Hagger, *Modelling* 9/94	Doug Hagger and Bob Marrion, 'Forgotten Regiments: 7th (Princess Royal's) Dragoons Guards', *Military Modelling*, vol. 24, no. 9 (September 1994): pp. 30–5.
Hagger, *Modelling* 11/94	Doug Hagger and Bob Marrion, 'Forgotten Regiments: The 6th Dragoons Guards (Carabiniers)', *Military Modelling*, vol. 24, no. 11 (November 1994): pp. 26–33.
Harfield, *Armies/China*	Alan Harfield, *British and Indian Armies on the China Coast, 1785–1985* (Farnham: A and J Partnership, 1990).
Haywood, *W African FF*	A. Haywood and F.A.S. Clark, *The History of the Royal West African Frontier Force* (Aldershot: Gale & Polden Ltd, 1974).
Henderson, *Scottish Regiments*	Diana M. Henderson, *The Scottish Regiments* (London: Collins, 2001).
Hills, *Life Guards*	R.J.T. Hills, *The Life Guards* (London: Leo Cooper Ltd, 1971).
Kennedy, *Rise/Fall*	Paul Kennedy, *The Rise and Fall of the Great Powers* (New York: Random House Inc., 1987).
Kipling, *Kipling's Verse*	Rudyard Kipling, *Rudyard Kipling's Verse*, definitive edition (Garden City, NY: Doubleday and Co., Inc., 1940).
Kipling, *Head-Dress Badges*	Arthur L. Kipling and Hugh L. King, *Head-Dress Badges of the British Army, Volume 1: Up to the End of the Great War* (London: Frederick Muller, 1973).
Knight, 'British Laces'	David Knight, 'The Laces Worn By Officers of the British Army, 1820–1914', *Bulletin of the Military Historical Society*, vol. 67, no. 267 (February 2017): pp. 141–53.
KOSB regimental website	'Regimental Insignia', *The King's Own Scottish Borderer's Association and Museum*, http://www.kosb.co.uk/insignia.htm, 26 August 2013.
Lamothe, *Slaves/Sudanese*	Ronald Lamothe, *Slaves of Fortune: Sudanese Soldiers and the River War, 1896–1898* (Woodbridge: James Currey, 2011).

Linaker, *Arm Badges*	David Linaker and Gordon Dine (with assistance from Ron Harris and Walter Lambert), *Cavalry Warrant Officers and Non-Commissioned Officers' Arm Badges* (London: Military Historical Society, 1997).
MacLeod, *Glory*	Olaf MacLeod, *Their Glory Shall Not Be Blotted Out* (Oxford: Lutterworth Press, 1986).
Manser, *Household Cavalry*	Roy Manser, *The Household Cavalry Regiments* (London: Almark Publishing Co. Ltd, 1975).
Marrion, 'Wei-Hei-Wei Regiment'	Bob Marrion, 'The Wei-Hei-Wei Regiment', *Military Modelling*, vol. 11, no. 2 (February 1981): pp. 131–2.
Marrion, 'West India', 6/1987	Bob Marrion, 'The West India Regiment', *Military Modelling*, vol. 17, no. 6 (June 1987): pp. 392–5.
Marrion, 'West India', 9/1987	Bob Marrion, 'The West India Regiment', *Military Modelling*, vol. 17, no. 9 (September 1987): pp. 614–16.
McKay, *Highland Light*	James B. McKay and Douglas N. Anderson, *The Highland Light Infantry, The Uniforms of the Regiments, 1881 to 1914* (Glasgow: James B. McKay, 1977).
McWilliam, 'Survey/Dress Regulations'	G.F. McWilliam, 'A New Survey of Old Dress Regulations', *Bulletin of the Military Historical Society*, vol. 59, no. 234 (November 2008): pp. 66–72.
Mitchell, *British Statistics*	B.R. Mitchell, *British Historical Statistics* (Cambridge: Cambridge University Press, 1988).
Moyse-Bartlett, *The KAR*	H. Moyse-Bartlett, *The King's African Rifles: A Study in the Military History of East and Central Africa, 1890-1945* (Aldershot: Gale & Polden Ltd, 1956).
Nevins, *British Empire*	Edward M. Nevins, *Forces of the British Empire, 1914* (Arlington, VA: Vandamere Press, 1992).
Nicholson, 'British Staff Uniforms, 1897'	J.B.R. Nicholson, 'British Staff Uniforms, 1897', Parts I and II, *Tradition*, no. 39: pp. 7–10; no. 40: pp. 14–19.
Peacock, *Northumberland Fusiliers*	Basil Peacock, *The Royal Northumberland Fusiliers (The 5th Regiment of Foot)* (London: Leo Cooper Ltd, 1970).
Perry, 'Armies P1'	F.W. Perry, 'The Armies of the Commonwealth: Part One: The Regiments' (United Kingdom: n.p., typed manuscript held at the Imperial War Museum, 1977).
Ross, *Canadian*	David Ross and Renee Chartrand, *Canadian Militia Dress Regulations 1907* (Saint John, NJ: New Brunswick Museum, 1977).
Rowe, *Heavy Cavalry*	David J.J. Rowe, *Head Dress of the British Heavy Cavalry: Dragoon Guards, Household and Yeomanry Cavalry 1842–1934* (Atglen, PA: Schiffer Publishing Ltd, 1999).
Rowe, *Lancers*	David J.J. Rowe and William Y. Carman, *Head Dress of the British Lancers 1816 to the Present* (Atglen, PA: Schiffer Publishing Ltd, 2002).
Singh, *History MSG*	Inder Singh, *History of Malay State Guides (1873–1919)* (Revised by Singh Sidhu and Singh Dhaliwal) (Penang: privately printed, n.d.).
Stadden, *Life Guards*	Charles Stadden, *The Life Guards: Dress and Appointments 1660–1914* (New Malden: Almark Publishing Co. Ltd, 1971).
Tate, 'Crowns'	William T. Tate, 'Royal Crowns and Cyphers Heraldic Coronets', *Bulletin of the Military Historical Society*, vol. 23, no. 91 (February 1973): pp. 65–9.
Thorburn, 'Scottish Dress'	W.A. Thorburn, 'The Army and Scottish Dress', *Bulletin of the Military Historical Society*, vol. 26, no. 104 (May 1976): pp. 105–9.
Trevor-Roper, 'Invention'	Hugh Trevor-Roper, 'The Invention of Tradition: The Highland Tradition of Scotland', in Eric Hobsbawm and Terence Ranger (eds), *The Invention of Tradition*, (Cambridge: Cambridge University Press, 1983): pp. 15–41.
Tylden, 'West African Regiment'	G. Tylden, 'The West African Regiment, 1898 to 1928', *Journal of the Society for Army Historical Research*, vol. XLI (1963): pp. 98–100.
Watson, *Enduring/Great War*	Alexander Watson, *Enduring the Great War: Combat, Morale and Collapse in the German and British Armies, 1914–1918* (Cambridge: Cambridge University Press, 2008).
Westlake, *Modelling* 4/92	Ray Westlake, 'The King's Royal Rifle Corps', *Military Modelling*, vol. 22, no. 4 (April 1992): pp. 28–30.
Westlake, *Shoulder Titles*	Ray Westlake, *Collecting Metal Shoulder Titles*, 2nd ed. (London: Leo Cooper Ltd, 1996).
Wilkinson-Latham, *Helmet*	Robert Wilkinson-Latham and Christopher Wilkinson-Latham, *Home Service Helmet 1878–1914 with Regimental Plates* (London: Broadway Press, n.d.).
Wright, *Impressions Malaya*	Arnold Wright (ed.), *Twentieth Century Impressions of British Malaya: Its History, People, Commerce, Industries, and Resources* (London: Lloyd's Greater Britain Publishing Co. Ltd, 1908).
Zobel, *Boston*	Hiller B. Zobel, *The Boston Massacre* (New York: W.W. Norton and Co. Inc., 1970).

§III

INDIA

§III-1 COUNTRY BACKGROUND

The very word 'India' is something to conjure with. For centuries, it has summoned visions of the exotic and wealth, images which have built up in the West over millennia. The Ancient Greeks knew of India and its cotton; they thought little cotton-producing animals grew on plants. The Romans of Augustus Caesar's time complained of the outflow of wealth from Rome to India for spices and silk. The money raised from controlling just the penultimate leg of supply – from Alexandria to the Mediterranean ports – made Venice rich and powerful. And, of course, we all know both Columbus and Vasco de Gama were trying to reach India when they set sail. Their aim was to capture part of the wealth of the spice trade that, at that time, had been sending money into India for a thousand years.

Once the Europeans arrived, they found that India was very different from anything they had known: the landscape, customs, dress, and religion. This meant they had to adopt a host of new words to function in India. Some of these words flowed back into English and became so common that most people today do not realise they came from India. Some examples are: bandanna, bungalow, candy, juggernaut, shampoo, jungle, tom-tom, and swastika. Others, such as Brahmin, yoga, sari, and sati, are often used but their Indian background is recognised.

It is generally accepted that the Indians developed the Arabic numeral system and the concept of zero.[1] This was an intellectual breakthrough that has occurred only one other time, among the Mayans.

The Indians are also credited with one of the major developments in fighting technology, the stirrup. It is probably as important as gunpowder. Around 200 BC Indians were using a proto-stirrup of a rope with a loop for the big toe.[2] From this, it was only a short step to putting a wooden or metal platform under the foot. With the adoption of the stirrup, cavalry became dominant on the battlefield until the invention and development of gunpowder, when the balance began to tilt back to the infantry.

India has long been ranked as one of the world's most spiritual areas. Buddhism, a major world religion, was revealed to the world in upper India by the Buddha. The major religion in India is Hinduism, which dates back to India's very early days. It is also the home to Jainism, which is – with Hinduism – one of the world's oldest religions. Its origins are obscure: for Western writers, Jainism developed *c.* 599 BC with the teachings of Lord Mahavira; for Jains, he is simply one of a line of teachers.[3] Lord Mahavira is thought to have been born in the vicinity of Vaishali in the Ganges Basin and died in what is now the state of Bihar.[4] Sikhism is also centred in India.

The Europeans came to India seeking its spices and wealth. However, once in India, they learned that it was not as rich as they had dreamed. Certainly the ruling classes were very rich. It has been claimed that 'the flood of Bengal treasure' that flowed into Britain following the Battle of Plassey in 1757 helped create the capital base, along with West Indies' sugar profits, that led to the British Industrial Revolution.[5]

But, overall, India was not rich, and the peasants lived lives of grinding poverty. Although foreign money had been coming into the south of India for spices for centuries, it had flowed out from the north. This outward flow happened for several reasons. Two are of major importance. First is the issue of horses. Cavalry, during most of this period, was the queen of the battlefield. Unfortunately, horses do not breed well in India – Indian horses are small and of poor physique[6] – and will not breed at all in the south of India. This is why the British had to bring in Walers from Australia during the Raj. There are exceptions to every rule. With care, good cavalry horses can be bred in India. Several Indian cavalry regiments, for example the 12th (Probyn's) Horse, maintained their own stud farms in India.[7] In the pre-British era, the lack of good horses was overcome by importing them into India from the north. Given the constant state of war in India, there was a high demand for these animals, and a large amount of funds flowed north over the centuries to pay for them.

The second cause of the outflow money to the north was that India had been subject to constant invasions from the northwest that plundered the country and hauled away vast amounts of wealth. Perhaps the best-known example is the Peacock Throne of Persia, now Iran, which was taken from Delhi in an invasion in 1739.

Another point to consider is that India contains a vast number of people speaking different languages, with different religions, and leading different types of lives. Churchill once said words to the effect that the word 'India' no more reflects a unified country than does the word 'Equator'. Britain controlled more of India than any other ruler ever had in the past or has since. This vast expanse was ruled on behalf of the king-emperor or queen-empress by a large civil service which had, at its top, a force of about 1,000 British civil servants[8] chosen by stiff examinations in Britain. These men, with their helpers, were the day-to-day rulers and face of the British Raj in India.

India, in addition to being a source of fighting men for the British, also paid for the upkeep of the Indian soldiers, the costs connected with British soldiers stationed in India, and for certain campaigns in which the Indian army took part. When the East India Company controlled India, from the middle of the eighteenth century to the middle of the nineteenth, they maintained and paid for armies that consisted of European troops – both British and the East India Company (often called John Company) – and Indian troops.[9] They obtained the money to make these payments by selling Indian-grown opium to China in exchange for tea, and then selling the tea in Britain. Two products accounted for 70 to 90 per cent of the exports from Bombay in the period between 1820 and 1880: opium and raw cotton.[10]

When the British Crown took over the government of India after the Indian Rebellion or Mutiny of 1857, this new government, the British Raj, also took over the financial arrangements of the Company. These called for the costs connected with European soldiers in India to be paid for by the body that controlled India.[11]

In 1904, the military member of the Council of the Governor General estimated that military spending (which included money spent on military works and campaigns) took 46 per cent of the net revenues of the Indian government.[12] These costs were borne by the people of India, who, of course, had no say whatsoever in military affairs.

Table III.1.1 shows military spending for selected years from 1860–1 to 1898–9, when the rupee was valued at 10 Rs to £1. Care should be exercised in reading the figures, and many of the numbers that follow. The numbers in the table were produced by the Indian National Congress in 1931, who may have allowed an anti-British bias to influence their calculations. Further, the book the table is taken from seems to have a certain point of view, and there is a chance the numbers are wrong or have been cherry-picked. That said, the numbers shown in the table do show a general agreement with figures for military spending drawn up by a British Commission (the Welby Commission).[13] Even if no bias was used in compiling the numbers, the financial records of India for the period 1860–99 are very hard to work with, in part because of the falling value of the rupee and in part because of changes in classifications and methods of accounting.[14] Keeping all of this in mind, the numbers are quite interesting.

§III-1 Country Background

Table III.1.1: Military Spending, 1861–99

Year	Rupees	Pounds at 10 Rs to £1	Current Pounds	Current Dollars
1861–2	13,250,000 Rs	£1,325,000	£133,560,000	$158,001,900
1870–1	15,540,000 Rs	£1,554,000	£156,643,200	$185,309,300
1880–1	27,590,000 Rs	£2,759,000	£281,065,800	$332,501,700
1890–1	21,610,000 Rs	£2,161,000	£235,156,100	$278,190,400
1898–9	24,310,000 Rs	£2,431,000	£267,577,700	$316,545,100

Source: Sundaram, *India's Armies/Costs*, p. 47.

After 1900, military costs began to increase as the Indian army was reorganised and provided with more modern equipment. Table III.1.2 shows military spending from 1901 to 1914. The rupee was now valued at 15 Rs to £1 rather that the pre 1899 value of roughly 10 Rs to £1.[15] Note that different items are clearly included in military expenses in the post-1900 numbers from those considered in computing the pre-1900 numbers.

Table III.1.2: Military Spending, 1901–14

Year	Rupees	Pounds at 15 Rs to £1	Current Pounds	Current Dollars
1901–2	24,240,000 Rs	£1,616,000	£168,204,500	$198,986,500
1906–7	30,250,000 Rs	£2,016,700	£207,655,000	$245,652,600
1913–14	29,840,000 Rs	£1,989,300	£194,386,300	$229,955,700

Source: Sundaram, *India's Armies/Costs*, p. 61.

Table III.1.3 lists the significant campaigns and expeditions undertaken by British and Indian troops and how the costs were divided.

Table III.1.3: Campaigns and Expedition Costs, 1867–96

Year	Campaign or Expedition	Borne by India Ordinary	Borne by India Extra	Borne by Britain Ordinary	Borne by Britain Extra
1867	Ethiopia	All	None	None	All
1875	Perak (Malisa)	All	None	None	Colonial government all
1878	2nd Afghan	All	All but £5 million	None	£5 million
1882–92	Minor Northwest Frontier expeditions	Not computed			
1885	Sudan	All	None	None	All
1886	Burma	All	All	None	None
1896	Soukim Sudan	All	None	None	All

Source: Sundaram, *India's Armies/Costs*, p. 51.

There were several other costs borne by the people of India. For example: half the military charges for the garrison of Aden (£108,000 per year); half the costs of transporting British troops to and from India (India paid £130,000 per year); and payments for an Indian marine force or payments to the Royal Navy for ships in the Persian Gulf, the east coast of Africa and elsewhere. This last charge ranged between 436,000 and 798,000 Rs in the years 1875 to 1897. Then, beginning in 1892, India paid a set £300,000 to the Admiralty for Persian Gulf patrols. Later the charge was reduced to £100,000 a year.[16]

VICEROY COMMISSIONED OFFICER

The term 'viceroy commissioned officer' (VCO) is occasionally used herein in spite of the fact this term for Indian officers did not come into use until after World War I. It replaces the term 'native officer', as that term is considered slightly disparaging by some. At other times, native officer is used through inertia as this term was so common in the literature of the period 1880–1914.

INDIAN GLOSSARY[17]

Akalis, Akalees	Sikh regiments of strong religious believers	Bombay bowler	Service issue pith helmet (for BORs)
alkalak, alkaluk, alkhulak,	Long coat reaching to the knees with embroidered bib-shaped front, worn by horsemen, an example being the circular-fronted garments worn by the bodyguards. The length and decoration made it different from the kurta (qv)	BOR	British other ranks, i.e. NCOs and men
		Boy	Servant; call for servant (from *bhai* – younger brother)
		Bungalow	Country house (from *bungla* – country)
		Cantonment	Military area of station
		Carnatic	Southern part of Madras Presidency. Takes its name from an Indian kingdom of that name
Anglo-Indian	Originally British persons in India, but later specifically those of mixed blood (see Eurasian)	Chapatti, chapatty	Flat circular cake of unleavened bread, patted flat with the hand and baked on a griddle
Anna	One sixteenth of a rupee (qv)		
Babu, baboo	Semi-educated Indian who tries to act English. Originally, a word showing respect (lit. honorific for 'father'). Could mean 'sir' or 'your honour'. Often applied to clerks or other bureaucrats with an overtone of disparagement, but also derogatory, thus *babu* language, *babu*isms	Circar	Northern part of Madras Presidency
		Civil List	Warrant or Order of Precedence, also known as the Green, Red, or Blue Book
		Class regiment	Indian regiment drawn from one racial group, e.g. Gurkhas, Sikhs, as opposed to mixed regiments
		Coromandel Coast	The southeastern coast of India above the bottom tip of the subcontinent (Cape Comorin). It runs from Cape Comorin to about the midpoint of the east side of India.
Bahadur	A leader; distinguished man (often added to a name as a title)		
Banya	Moneylender, thus *banya ki raj* – rule of the moneylender		
Batta	Extra financial allowance	Crore	Ten million rupees or one hundred lakhs (qv)
Bazaar	Native market		
Bearer	House valet	Cummerbund, kamai band	Waistbelt (lit. 'loin-band'), a long cloth worn wrapped around the waist
Bhisti, bheesti, bheesty	Native water carrier, a job allocated to a low Hindu class. Gunga Din in Kipling's poem – 'You're a better man than I am, Gunga Din' – was a regimental *bhisti*		
		Dacoit, dacoo	Robber, thus *dacoity* – robbery
Blighty	England, Britain, home (from *billayat* – kingdom) thus also *billayat pani* – English water (soda water)		

Deccan	A large, flat plateau that lies behind the Western and Eastern Ghats. It covers most of southern India. On the north, it starts from the mountains of central India, the Satpura and Vindhya ranges. Originally, *deccan* meant south in Sanskrit
District	One of 250 units of administration in British India
Dome, Dhome	Untouchable sweeper
Durbar	Court; levee
Eurasian	Person of mixed descent, with derogatory overtones. The term Anglo-Indian was officially adopted in 1900 to replace it
Feringi	European (lit. foreigner)
Firman	Mogul emperor's edict
Furlough	Leave from the army (home or local)
Ghats	The mountain or hill ranges that lie inland from the coast along both sides of southern India (lit. steps)
Gymkhana	Sports ground; sports meeting
Hazur	Sir; honorific (lit. the presence)
Heaven-born	Honorific often used to denote the ICS (*qv*). This term came from the Hindu term for Brahmins, the highest of the four traditional class divisions of the Hindu religion
Hill station	Station above 5,000 feet to which state and central governments transferred in the hot weather
Hindustani, Hindostanee	Simple form of Urdu
Howdah, howder	Palanquin on elephant
ICS	Indian Civil Service
Kashmir shawl	Shawls originally woven or embroidered in the Indian state of Kashmir, but later in the Punjab (after 1556–1605) and the town of Paisley in Scotland (after 1803). Shawls from Kashmir were considered to be superior as only Kashmir weavers could obtain a goat fleece from Western Tibet, and, after 1800, from goat herds kept by nomadic Kirghiz tribes in Central Asia. A very few shawls were made of cashmere, which was made from fleece grown beneath a goat or wild Himalayan mountain sheep. The best grades of cashmere, *asli tus*, came only from wild animals. It was very soft, but extremely expensive to collect. In 1821, *asli tus* shawls were less than one-sixth of other shawl-wool imports. The shawls had designs on their entire surface or only on the ends. There was a wide range of designs produced, but a design known in the West as a cone or pine and in Kashmir as *buta*, which means flower, proved extremely popular. This design appeared on a large number of Kashmir shawls worn by Indian cavalry officers. (Image III:30) In the somewhat random sample of photographs that appear in this work and are clear enough to discern a pattern on the palloo (*qv*), fourteen have a pine design (Images III:8, III:10, III:12, III:14, III:15, III:39, III:40, III:42, III:46, III:48, III:49, III:51, III:54, and III:55) and five have stripes (Images III:37, III:47, III:50, III:52, and III:60). The manufacturers at Paisley printed the pine design on many different cotton items, including men's neckties. This explains why the Indian cavalry Kashmir shawl looks so similar to a Paisley pattern[18]
Khaki, khakee	From the Persian word for dust or earth. Khaki uniform was first worn by the Corps of Guides
Khalsa	The Sikh army
Khukri, khukuri,	Dog-legged shaped knife used by the Gurkhas. It comes in many different sizes. Contrary to popular myth, it does not act like a boomerang, and it can be drawn from its scabbard and returned without tasting blood — no need for the owner to nick his finger after cleaning it!
Konkan Coast	Coast running south from Bombay to the city of Goa
Kshatrias	Warrior caste among Hindus
Kulla, khulla, kullah	Pointed cap worn within the turban by some Muslims and Jats, the turban being worn around the cap. The British, when they wore a turban, also usually wore a kulla

Kurta	Long coat reaching to within three inches of the knees; a loose-fitting frock or blouse, as worn by Indian cavalry, sometimes slit at the sides, otherwise at the front or back
Lahk, lac, lack	A hundred thousand rupees
Lungi	Turban, term generally used in the cavalry; technically, a word used to describe the Indian headdress, tied looser than the turban, but often just used to mean turban. The words *pagri* and *safa* have the same meaning
Maharanee, maharani	Great queen
Mahout	Elephant driver
Malabar Coast	Coast that lies on the west side of southern India. It runs from the city of Goa south to the bottom tip of India (Cape Comorin)
Maranacha poshak	Literally 'clothes of the dead', long saffron-dyed gowns worn by Rajput men going out to fight to the death. This was the colour worn by Skinner's Regiment, the 1st Lancers, the 'Yellow Boys'
Mehtar	Sweeper or scavenger
Memsahib	European woman, by implication European lady, from 'madam-sahib'
Nawab	Mogul title for governor/nobleman
Padi, paddy	Rice field
Pag, pug	Cloth tied over the head beneath the turban. Worn by Sikhs, the colour was normally red or white
Palloo, paloo, palla	The falling end of a turban or cummerbund
Paltan	Battalion (corruption from the French *peloton*, meaning squad or platoon); hence, the infantry
Pandy	Colloquial name for sepoy mutineers, from Mangal Pandy, one of the first of them in 1857
Peon	Messenger, orderly
Pice, pie	Small copper coin worth one quarter of an anna or one sixty-fourth of a rupee
Piffers	Punjab Frontier Force
Pucka	Ripe, mature, cooked; often used of solid building materials such as local bricks and mortar, and by implications permanent or reliable. Also means 'true' or 'real' (see 'Pukka')
Puggree, puggaree, pugri, pagri	Word used for a turban, but generally used for cloth/scarf wrapped around the helmet
Pukka	Proper, thus *pukka* house – brick as against mud and thatch; *pukka* major – regimental major; *pukka* sahib – real gentleman; *pukka* road – tarred road (see 'Pucka')
Pultan, pultun	Indian for regiment (probably derived from the French *peloton* for platoon)
Punkah	Swinging fan hung from the ceiling; operated by a *punkah-wallah*
Purbiya, poohbeah, purabiya	The East. Term used by soldiers in the Punjab to refer to soldiers in the Bengal army, specifically Brahmins and Rajputs from Oudh and Bihar. These men formed the heart of the old Bengal army and were the men who mutinied in 1857. It had derogatory overtones
Puttees, putties	Cloth strips worn around the legs. Dark blue, black, green, and khaki puttees were worn by Indian cavalry and infantry. In the infantry, puttees were fastened at the ankle and wound up towards the knee. In the cavalry, puttees were the opposite, starting near the knee and wound down to the ankle
Quoit	Steel throwing ring with a very sharp outside edge. It was a hollow circle about 30.48 cm (1 foot) in diameter, and the steel portion was about 2.54 cm (1 inch) wide. It was worn on the turban, and a Sikh would spin it on his fingers and then throw it. It is said it could travel 91–183 metres (100–200 yards) or more and inflict quite serious wounds. Later, it became a decorative part of Sikh regimental dress
Raj	Kingdom or rule, used in the twentieth century chiefly to denote British rule in India from 1858 to 1947, hence rajah (ruler) and maharajah (great ruler)

Ranee	Queen
Ressala	Troop or squadron; hence, the cavalry
Rooty-gong	Long service medal (BOR, from *roti* – bread)
Rupee	Indian silver coin, valued at one-tenth of a pound sterling (gold) until about 1870. The fall in silver against gold thereafter led to a fall in the value of the rupee, at times to one-twentieth of a pound. In the 1890s it was stabilised at fifteen to the pound, a rate which continued until the end of the British period
Sardar	Distinguished leader
Sahib	Lord; master; a gentleman; sir; mister; European, also affixed rank, thus 'Collector sahib'
Sepoy	Indian soldier, a private
Silladar; sillidar	An Indian soldier, soldier of irregular cavalry, providing his own horse and equipment
Sircar	The government
Solar topee	Cork (see 'Topee') helmet
Suttee	The rite of widow-burning
Sweeper	Native of untouchable caste who cleans latrines
Syce	Horse groom
Topee	Cork helmet (*topi* – hat) (see 'Solar topee')
Touri	Small puff or wad of wool worn on the top centre of the other ranks' Gurkha Kilmarnock cap. Normally black in the pre-World War I period. Gurkha officers' caps did not have touris
Turban	A cloth headdress. The style of these became more tightly tied the closer the wearer was to 1914
Twice-born	Honorific, based on Hindu caste, often used to describe ICS
Urdu	Lingua franca of upper India (lit. language of the camp) see Hindustani
Waler	Horse imported from Australia (originally from New South Wales)
Wallah	Person employed or concerned with something, as in *dhobi-wallah* for laundryman. Developed to make words like *box-wallah*, initially a native itinerant peddler but then (somewhat derisively) a British businessman; and *competition-wallah* for member of the ICS appointed by competitive examination
Zouave jacket	Tunic with a panel of facing colour down the front

§III-2 THE ARMY

§III-2-1   The Indian Army: A Short History
§III-2-2   Indian Cavalry Regiments, Class Composition and Date Raised
§III-2-3   Indian Infantry Regiments, Class Composition and Date Raised
§III-2-4   Class Makeup of Indian Army in 1914
§III-2-5   Regimental Names
§III-2-6   Indian Military Rank
§III-2-7   Regimental Ratings after Inspections
§III-2-8   Expeditionary Forces
§III-2-9   Wartime Problems

§III-2-1 THE ARMY: A SHORT HISTORY

By 1914, the British had been in India for over three hundred years. They had started with a few small trading stations run by the East India Company, and ended with control of the subcontinent. They did not directly rule all portions of India: some Indian princes had sided consistently with Britain and were left with nominal control of their principalities. These native states accounted for approximately two-fifths of the area of India. They had their own military organisations and some undertook to supply the British with troops when the need arose.

The conquest of India had, in large part, been accomplished by the private armies of the East India Company. Valuable support had been provided by regular British regiments. The first of these, the 19th (the Dorsetshire Regiment), had come to India in 1754, and by 1914 one-third of the British army was stationed in India.

John Company (as the East India Company was known) had conducted its wars from three independent administrative areas, usually called presidencies, each of which maintained its own independent army. These were the presidencies of Bengal, Bombay, and Madras. In addition, a large number of local commands and corps were maintained to keep order in specific areas or to serve some special purpose. The most noteworthy were the Hyderabad Contingent and the Punjab Frontier Force.

The Bengal army, the strongest of the sepoy armies, mutinied in 1857 and the rebellion spread throughout the region. Although it is now known variously as the Indian Rebellion or India's First War of Independence – which perhaps better reflect the seriousness of the situation – I shall refer to it as the Indian Mutiny or the Sepoy Mutiny, which is how it was known at the time and for much of the twentieth century. The Mutiny ended Company rule in India, and the Crown assumed direct authority over the country. The British set up the Peale Commission to study the causes of the Mutiny. The Commission's conclusions shaped the British Indian army, for better or worse, for the rest of its existence.

The conclusions were:

1. There were too many British officers in the native regiments and thus too little chance for native advancement.

In the early days of Company rule, there had been few British available to command John Company's fighting forces, and natives had played an important part in recruiting and commanding the regiments. With the passage of time, the number of European officers in native regiments had grown steadily. This blocked advancement for ambitious Indians. It was thought that Indians thus blocked had played a key part in moving the regiments towards mutiny. To prevent this, the number of British officers, King's Commissioned Officers (KCOs), was reduced, and a class of Indian officers, Viceroy Commissioned Officers (VCOs), was created. At first, there were only seven British officers per regiment, but this had grown to fourteen by 1914. In 1914, KCOs held the senior regimental commands and command of companies. The VCOs were also officers and had power of command over native troops, although not over European troops. In fact, the actual authority held by the VCOs was greater than might appear from a table of organisation, as British officers were frequently absent or on leave. They were each entitled to two months of in-country leave every year and six months ex-India leave every four years, plus the odd week to ten days off to go to polo tournaments, races, horse shows, and skill-at-arms competitions.[19] In addition, officers were often seconded to other units. For example, in 1913, the 40th Pathans had one-half of the officers absent. Out of fourteen British officers, four were on leave outside India, and three were on duty outside the regiment. A typical 1914 British army company had six officers. An Indian company had one KCO in command, with the others VCOs.

This system meant the average enlisted man entering the Indian army had a far better chance of becoming an officer than his counterpart in the British army – indeed, a better chance than his counterpart in almost any army in the world, except for the French and, perhaps, the Russian armies. Although the system placed a limit on how high the Indians could rise, in practice this limit existed in all armies. In any army, for an enlisted man to become an officer, he first had to make his way through the non-commissioned officer ranks, and that took time. This meant that enlisted men were starting years behind officers commissioned directly from school. Since promotion through officer ranks in the earlier grades is largely a matter of time in grade, the older ex-ranker's chances of rising to high rank before retirement were quite limited.

2. Indian religious beliefs should be given more respect.

The spark point of the Indian Mutiny was the new greased cartridges issued to the men. The idea that the cartridges contained cow and pig grease, anathema to the Hindus and Muslims respectively, may have had a basis in fact. However, more importantly, it was believable. In the years prior to the Mutiny, the British had developed an open contempt for the religions of India. Many felt it was their duty to bring Christian salvation to the Indians and actively preached to the men in their command.

After the Mutiny great care was taken with the men's religious sensibilities. When a regiment recruited just one or two caste types, special kitchens made the food, and religious ceremonies were held in the regiment, with officers often taking part. They went to what many Indians thought were ridiculous extremes which at times made the usage of Indian troops awkward.

3. The different independent commands should remain separate, to minimise the chance of their combining against the government.

If the troops in Madras, Bombay, or the frontier areas had rebelled as well, it is doubtful the British could have put down the Mutiny. To lessen the chances of two or more commands breaking into mutiny at the same time, it was decided to hold each as separate as possible. The Frontier Force and the Bengal, Bombay, and Madras armies would remain as independent commands. Each would serve only in its own area and would, in theory, draw its recruits locally. In addition to these major groups, there were several smaller commands which also remained separate.

This system had an unforeseen side effect. The Mutiny and the raising of new regiments of the Bengal army had created a large number of promotional opportunities for officers. Conversely, the 1870s was a period of promotion stagnation for the Bombay and Madras armies, as they had seen little combat in the Mutiny. This, together with the fact that only the frontier and Bengal regiments were in a position to see active combat, meant that good ambitious young officers would try to move to these regiments. This led to a gradual lessening of the quality of officers in the Madras and Bombay armies. In addition, the regiments in these armies did not undergo the corrective effects of combat. As a result, Madras, and to a lesser extent Bombay, developed a reputation for being a backwater filled with poor soldiers officered by men of little ambition or ability.

4. Sufficient British troops should be maintained in each command to block incipient rebellions.

Because British troops might be needed to quell a mutiny in the early stages, the British made regular British army regiments an integral part of each command. At first a ratio of one British unit for two Indian units was attempted, but by 1914, this had become a ratio of approximately one to three. The

British regiments were known as the 'Army in India'. The regiments of the Army in India would spend several years in India and then move to another station, either back home or another overseas posting. Over time, the need to have British regiments on hand to quell mutinies was given less emphasis, and the common formula ran that the British units provided 'stiffening' for the Indian regiments. The common organisational format was to have one British battalion and three Indian regiments, each approximately equal to a British battalion, grouped into a brigade.

One of the Commission's conclusions that was never wholly followed and, ultimately, rejected was the recommendation that the native regiments be composed of different nationalities and castes, and, as a general rule, these should be mixed randomly throughout each regiment. In some ways, it might be the most important finding of the Peale Commission: the basis of recruitment in the Indian army and the relationship of service to religion. In the Bombay and Madras armies prior to 1857, little attention had been paid to a recruit's religion or race, and religious scruples were not allowed to interfere with operational necessities. This was understood by the men and accepted as part of the bargain when they enlisted.

In the old Bengal army a quite different tradition had developed. The Indian soldiers had been able to maintain their caste prerogatives. High-caste Hindus were often not required to do manual labour, and caste affected promotion. Bengal regiments often refused to serve overseas, either in Burma or eastern expeditions as this would be a violation of their caste beliefs. Mutinies or strikes often occurred when beliefs were threatened.

A logical conclusion stemming from the Mutiny was that the Bombay and Madras systems were preferable. This meant that while religious beliefs were to be respected, they should not dictate service or work in the way that had occurred in the Bengal army. In addition, an effort was to be made towards moving to a system of mixing all religions and castes within a regiment. This was called the 'plum-pudding' system as every element was mixed into one body.

It was not possible to implement the plum-pudding system in its entirety in the Bengal army. For one thing, two groups, the Sikhs and the Gurkhas, had supplied notable service in putting down the Mutiny, and there were many regiments made up entirely of these groups. Their vested interests in rank and promotional opportunities would have been harmed if outsiders were introduced into these regiments. Other regiments recruited from several religious groups but placed their men in homogeneous companies. In the end a compromise was reached for the Bengal army, and all of the systems were used. There were twenty mixed regiments on a plum-pudding basis, sixteen regiments with homogeneous companies, and seven regiments where all the men were of one religious or ethnic group.

The 1880s saw a shift in attitude. The 1885 Anglo-Russian crisis raised the possibility that the Indian army might be called upon to face Russian troops. Although it had been concluded by the English that the homogeneous regiment was the best fighting machine, it had not mattered that this was not the predominant format when there was no strong external threat. However, if the concern was fighting efficiency rather than preventing a mutiny or maintaining internal order, perhaps the plum-pudding system should be limited. These views were reinforced by the poor showing of the Madras regiments, who always had a plum-pudding system, in the Burma War of 1887–9. The views developing in the 1880s intersected with another trend, and together they had, by 1914, largely reversed the recommendations of the Peale Commission.

The other trend was the British acceptance of the tenets of the Indian caste system. Victorian Britain was organised on a rigid class system, so the idea of natural superiors and inferiors, each happy in his place, was an integral part of their world view. This is, of course, a caste system without the religious overtones. The Indian caste system also fitted neatly into simple racism. It was, at bottom, a stratification based on colour: as a general rule the higher the caste, the lighter the individual's skin colour. Thus, it was natural for the British to view themselves as a layer on top of the Indian caste system.

An outgrowth of the caste system was the 'martial race' theory. Its leading proponent was Lord Roberts, commander-in-chief of the Indian army from 1885 to 1893. The theory held that, because of caste history, certain groups or castes are natural fighters and others are not. It was recognised that certain events could affect the caste's natural propensity. The Muslim and Sikh religions were positive, while hot weather and peace were negatives. The more imposing physical stature of the men from the northern area of the country supported the theory as far as the military was concerned. It is natural to equate physical size with military prowess. For this reason the Bombay army had regularly poached recruits from this area, even though it was outside its assigned recruiting locale.

The effect of the merging of the political and military observations with the martial race theory was a dramatic reordering of the Indian army. The basis of recruiting in India shifted towards drawing the larger, light-skinned men from the colder northern climes. The British ended up recruiting two groups for their armies: Gurkhas and men from the Punjab. (Gurkhas are not tall or light skinned; they mostly belong to a different racial group from the bulk of the people who live in India. Their race used to be called Mongoloid, and is now known termed East Asian. They have been proven in battle time and again.) These two groups provided 57 per cent of the British Indian infantry. Two other northern groups, the Rajputs and the Pathans, provided another 12 per cent.

In addition to pulling more and more men from Punjab and Nepal, the British narrowed the caste basis they used for recruiting. As mentioned, Sikhism and Islam were seen as fighting religions and, as such, could in part overcome what might be seen as an individual's poor martial heredity. But, of course, if the Sikh or Muslim came from fighting stock, the prospect would be even better. Often a Muslim, whatever part of India he was recruited from, was the descendant of a foreign conqueror – usually of Afghan or Turkish origins. Hindus were in the main higher caste – Brahmins or warriors.

The main castes recruited for the army were: Pathans from the frontier area; Gurkhas and the closely related Garhwals from the northern part of the country; Jats and Dogras from the Punjab; Rajputs and Brahmins from Delhi and the northeast; Rajputs, Jats and Mers from central India; Marathas and Baluchs from the Bombay Presidency; Tamils, Christians, and Untouchables of the Madras Presidency; and Muslims from Madras and Bombay.

In addition to being of a certain racial background, the castes selected were typically well-to-do peasants – roughly equivalent to the English yeoman. Even within a caste, great care was taken to try and locate the perfect sub-caste or clan. The tendency was to use men home on leave to do the recruiting; it was natural that they would talk to friends and relatives of the same class, and these would be future recruits. In time, each regiment became its own narrow world, often different from other regiments who were supposed to recruit from the same class or classes.

The regiments were now reorganised. The plum-pudding basis was done away with. Regiments changed over to a class company basis or became homogeneous class regiments. A class regiment had a big advantage from a military point of view: since no Indian officer was allowed to command men of another class, having several different classes within a regiment presented organisational problems as casualties could not always be replaced by whoever was handy or next in command. The class company regiment did have the advantage of a *divide et impera* system within it. The Mutiny was still not forgotten. In 1914, three-quarters of the Indian regiments were still the class company type.

As already mentioned, when the British government assumed the rule of India after the Mutiny, it also took over the Company's armies. The different commands were left in place; it was felt that separate commands were less likely to join together in mutiny. This concept of different 'watertight compartments' held force up to the early 1900s. At that point, it was felt an invasion from Russia through Afghanistan was a greater danger than a mutiny or revolt by the Indian army or population. To maximise the potential response to the Russian threat, the old commands were done away with.

In 1903, the idea of separate water-tight presidential armies was officially laid to rest. All presidential and local units were placed under one central command. The change was reflected in a renumbering of the Indian regiments. The cavalry and infantry regiments were each numbered in one continuous sequence and references to presidential affiliations removed.[20] The Gurkha regiments were given their own numbering system outside the basic system – this was the main exception to the reordering in the centralised command structure.

The numbering of the Bengal army was not changed. It was assigned numbers 1 to 49 although not all numbers in this sequence were used in peacetime. The Frontier Force was given the numbers 51 to 59. The old Madras army took the numbers 61 to 94. The old Hyderabad Contingent had the numbers 94 to 99. The numbers 100 to 130 were allocated to the Bombay army. The Guides were left outside the numbering system.

Because of the racial recruiting policy, the Madras army was only a skeleton. The Madras component had been steadily reduced since 1889. The regiments retained the same numbers and names but the personnel were replaced by Punjab classes. So, while the Madras army showed thirty-four regiments, only eleven of these were composed of men of the Madras Presidency. Of that eleven, three were construction (pioneer) units and the other eight were garrisoned regiments – each with only 600 men. These eight regiments carried the denomination 'Carnatic', a component of the Madras Presidency – even the name Madras had fallen out of favour.

There were several gaps in the numbering system, caused by disbanding regiments or pulling out the Gurkha regiments for their own numbering system. Some of these were filled by former local contingents, such as the 42nd Deoli, 43rd Erinpura, and 44th Merwara Regiments. Other numbers remained empty.

The same system of renumbering was followed for the cavalry regiments. The Bengal cavalry was allotted numbers 1 to 19. Numbers 20, 29, and 30 went to the Hyderabad Contingent. The Frontier Force cavalry had numbers 21 to 25 with a gap at 24. Making one of the Hyderabad regiments number 20 allowed the Frontier Force regiment to keep the last digit of their old number. The Frontier Force was a storied organisation and well worth catering to.

The Madras cavalry regiments were assigned numbers 26 to 27. They lost all contact with their old numbers, as did the Hyderabad Contingent cavalry regiments. The southern regiments were out of favour, and someone had to lose to make the new system work.

The old Bombay cavalry received numbers 31 to 37. This allowed them to keep their original last digit. The Central India Horse, which had been a local corps, was given numbers 38 and 39.

The Corps of Guides, to denote their special status, were kept outside the numbering system and always listed at the end of the list. This was the same treatment given to the well-respected and prestigious Rifle Brigade in the British army.

As part of the 1903 changes, even the slight difference in uniforms between commands disappeared. However, special distinctions found on regimental uniforms lived on, for the most part. For infantry, the long blouse replaced the Zouave jacket. This was done at a deliberate pace, and it took several years to make the change. The changeover was taking place when A.C. Lovett was producing his illustrations for *The Armies of India*, and his paintings show some regiments still wearing Zouave tunics. The Lovett illustrations are the main source for Table III.6.3, Indian Infantry Other Ranks' Uniform. Thus, where Lovett showed a Zouave tunic for a regiment, that type of dress is listed in the table.

§III-2-2 INDIAN CAVALRY REGIMENTS, CLASS COMPOSITION AND DATE RAISED

Regiment	Facing Colour	Class Composition	Date Raised
1st Duke of York's Own Lancers (Skinner's Horse)[a]	Black velvet	4 squadrons of Hindustani Muslims	1803
2nd Lancers (Gardner's Horse)	Light blue	1 squadron of Sikhs, 1 of Rajputs, 1 of Jats, 1 of Hindustani Muslims	1809
3rd Skinner's Horse	Yellow	1 squadron of Sikhs, 1 of Jats, 1 of Rajputs, 1 of Rajput Muslims	1814
4th Cavalry	Blue	1 squadron of Rajput Muslims, 1 of Hindustani Muslims, 1 of Sikhs, 1 of Jats	1838
5th Cavalry	Blue	2 squadrons of Hindustani Muslims, 1 of Rajputs, 1 of Jats	1841
6th King Edward's Own Cavalry	Scarlet	1 squadron of Jat Sikhs, 1 of Sikhs other than Jat Sikhs, 1 of Jats, 1 of Hindustani Muslims	1842
7th Hariana Lancers	Blue	1 squadron of Jats, 1 of Sikhs, 1 of Dogras, 1 of Hindustani Muslims	1846

Regiment	Facing Colour	Class Composition	Date Raised
8th Cavalry	Scarlet	2 squadrons of Hindustani Muslims, 1 of Rajputs, 1 of Jats	1846
9th Hodson's Horse	White	1½ squadrons of Sikhs, ½ of Dogras, 1½ of Punjabi Muslims, ½ of Pathans	1857
10th Duke of Cambridge's Own Lancers (Hodson's Horse)	Scarlet	1½ squadrons of Sikhs, 1 of Dogras, 1 of Punjabi Muslims, ½ of Pathans	1857
11th King Edward's Own Lancers (Probyn's Horse)	Scarlet	2 squadrons of Sikhs, 1 of Dogras, ½ of Punjabi Muslims, ½ of Pathans	1857
12th Cavalry	Blue	2 squadrons of Sikhs, 1 of Dogras, 1 of Punjabi Muslims	1857
13th Duke of Connaught's Lancers (Watson's Horse)	Scarlet	2 squadrons of Punjabi Muslims, 1 of Sikhs, 1 of Dogras	1858
14th Murray's Jat Lancers	Scarlet	4 squadrons of Jats	1857
15th Lancers (Cureton's Multanis)	Scarlet	4 squadrons of Muslims (Multani Pathans and Muslims of the Derajat and Cis-Indus)	1857
16th Cavalry	Blue	2 squadrons of Sikhs, 1 of Dogras, 1 of Jats	1857
17th Cavalry	White	2 squadrons of Punjabi Muslims, 2 of Pathans	1857
18th King George's Own Lancers	White	3 squadrons of Punjabi Muslims, 1 of Sikhs	1858
19th Lancers (Fane's Horse)	French Grey	1½ squadrons of Sikhs, ½ of Dogras, 1 of Punjabi Muslims, 1 of Pathans	1860
20th Deccan Horse[b]	White	1 squadron of Sikhs, 1 of Jats, 2 of Dekhani Muslims	1826
21st Prince Albert Victor's Own Cavalry (Frontier Force) (Daly's Horse)	Scarlet	1½ squadrons of Sikhs, ½ of Dogras, 1 of Hindustani Muslims, 1 of Pathans	1849
22nd Sam Browne's Cavalry (Frontier Force)	Blue	1½ squadrons of Sikhs, ½ of Hindustani Hindus, 1 of Punjabi Muslims, ½ of Pathans, ½ of Hindustani Muslims	1849
23rd Cavalry (Frontier Force)	Scarlet	1½ squadrons of Sikhs, ½ of Dogras, 1 of Hindustani Muslims, ½ of Punjabi Muslims, ½ of Pathans	1849
25th Cavalry (Frontier Force)	Scarlet	1 squadron of Sikhs, 1 of Dogras, 1 of Punjabi Muslims, ½ of Hindustani Muslims, ½ of Pathans	1849
26th King George's Own Light Cavalry	Buff	1 squadron of Madras and Dekhani Muslims, 1 of Punjabi Muslims, 1 of Rajputana Rajputs, 1 of Jats	1787
27th Light Cavalry	Buff	1 squadron of Madras and Dekhani Muslims, 1 of Punjabi Muslims, 1 of Rathore Rajputs, 1 of Jats	unknown
28th Light Cavalry[c]	Buff	1 squadron of Madras and Dekhani Muslims, 1 of Punjabi Muslims, 1 of Rajputana Rajputs, 1 of Jats	1784
29th Lancers (Deccan Horse)[d]	White	2 squadrons of Jats, 1 of Sikhs, 1 of Dekhani Muslims	1826
30th Lancers (Gordon's Horse)	White	2 squadrons of Sikhs, 1 of Jats, 1 of Hindustani Muslims	1826
31st Duke of Connaught's Own Lancers	Scarlet	1 squadron of Dekhani Mahrattas, 1 of Jats, 1 of Sikhs, 1 of Pathans	1817
32nd Lancers	White	2 squadrons of Rajput Muslims, 1 of Rajputs, 1 of Sikhs other than Jat Sikhs	1817
33rd Queen Victoria's Own Light Cavalry	Scarlet	1 squadron of Jats, 1 of Sikhs, 1 of Kaimkhanis, 1 of Rajput Muslims	1820
34th Prince Albert Victor's Own Poona Horse	French grey	2 squadrons of Rathore Rajputs, 1 of Kaimkhanis, 1 of Punjabi Muslims	1817
35th Scinde Horse	White	2 squadrons of Derajat Muslims, 1 of Pathans, 1 of Sikhs	1839

Regiment	Facing Colour	Class Composition	Date Raised
36th Jacob's Horse	Primrose	2 squadrons of Derajat Muslims and Baluchs, 1 of Pathans, 1 of Sikhs	1846
37th Lancers (Baluch Horse)	Buff	2 squadrons of Derajat Muslims and Baluchs, 1 of Pathans, 1 of Sikhs	1885
38th King George's Own Central India Horse[e]	Maroon	2 squadrons of Sikhs, 1 of Pathans, 1 of Rajput Muslims	1858
39th King George's Own Central India Horse	Maroon	2 Squadrons of Sikhs, 1 of Punjabi Muslims, 1 of Muslim Rajputs	1858
Aden Troop[f]	Khaki		1867–8

Source: 1914 Army List, pp. 408–46; 1914 Hart's Annual Army List, pp. 678–91.

Notes: [a] Formed from a body of Perron's Horse (in Sindhia's service) who came over to the British after the Battle of Delhi.
[b] Formed from Captain Davis' and Captain Clark's risallahs of the Nizam's Reformed Horse.
[c] Formed from selected details of three regiments of native cavalry.
[d] Formed from Nawab Murtiza Yar Jung's Captains Hallis' and Smith's risallahs of the Nizam's Reformed Horse.
[e] Formed from the faithful remains of the cavalry of the Gwalior, Bhopal, and Malwah Contingents.
[f] Formed from volunteers from the 1st and 2nd Scinde Horse and the Poona Horse.

§III-2-3 INDIAN INFANTRY REGIMENTS, CLASS COMPOSITION AND DATE RAISED

Regiment	Facing Colour	Class Composition	Date Raised
1st Brahmins	White	8 companies of Brahmins	1776
2nd Queen Victoria's Own Rajput Light Infantry	Blue	8 companies of Rajputs	1798
3rd Brahmins	Black	8 companies of Brahmins	1798
4th Prince Albert Victor's Rajputs	Black	8 companies of Rajputs	1798
5th Light Infantry	Yellow	8 companies of Muslims of the Eastern Punjab and Hindustan	1803
6th Jat Light Infantry	White	8 of companies Jats	1803
7th Duke of Connaught's Own Rajputs	Yellow	8 of companies Rajputs	1804
8th Rajputs	Yellow	8 companies of Rajputs	1814
9th Bhopal Infantry[a]	Chocolate	2 companies of Sikhs, 2 of Rajputs, 2 of Brahmins, 2 of Muslims	1859
10th Jats	Yellow	8 companies of Jats	1823
11th Rajputs	Yellow	8 companies of Rajputs	1825
12th Pioneers (Kelat-i-Ghilzie Regiment)[b]	Black	4 companies of Jats, 4 of Lobana Sikhs	1838
13th Rajputs (Shekhawati Regiment)	Blue	8 companies of Rajputana Rajputs	1835
14th King George's Own Ferozepore Sikhs	Yellow	8 companies of Sikhs	1846
15th Ludhiana Sikhs	Emerald green	8 companies of Sikhs	1846

Regiment	Facing Colour	Class Composition	Date Raised
16th Rajputs (Lucknow Regiment)[c]	White	8 companies of Rajputs	1857
17th Infantry (Loyal Regiment)[d]	White	8 companies of Muslims of the Eastern Punjab and Hindustan	1858
18th Infantry	Black	8 companies of Muslims of the Eastern Punjab and Hindustan	1795
19th Punjabis[e]	Blue	4 companies of Sikhs, 2 of Punjabi Muslims, 2 of Pathans	1857
20th Duke of Cambridge's Own Infantry (Brownlow's Punjabis)[f]	Emerald green	4 companies of Pathans, 2 of Sikhs, 2 of Dogras	1857
21st Punjabis[g]	Scarlet	3 companies of Pathans, 1 of Punjabi Muslims, 3 of Sikhs, 1 of Dogras	1857
22nd Punjabis[h]	Blue	4 companies of Sikhs, 3 of Punjabi Muslims, 1 of Pathans	1857
23rd Sikh Pioneers	Chocolate	8 companies of Mazbi and Ramdasia Sikhs	1857
24th Punjabis	White	4 companies of Sikhs, 1 of Dogras, 2 of Afridis, 1 of Punjabi Muslims	1857
25th Punjabis	White	3 companies of Sikhs, 2 of Dogras, 2 of Punjabi Muslims, 1 of Pathans	1857
26th Punjabis	Scarlet	4 companies of Sikhs, 2 of Afridis, 2 of Punjabi Muslims	1857
27th Punjabis	Scarlet	3 companies of Sikhs, 1 of Dogras, 2 of Punjabi Muslims, 2 of Pathans	1857
28th Punjabis	Emerald green	3 companies of Sikhs, 1 of Dogras, 3 of Pathans, 1 of Punjabi Muslims	1857
29th Punjabis	Blue	4 companies of Sikhs, 2 of Dogras, 2 of Punjabi Muslims	1857
30th Punjabis	White	4 companies of Sikhs, 2 of Dogras, 2 of Punjabi Muslims	1857
31st Punjabis	White	4 companies of Sikhs, 2 of Dogras, 2 of Punjabi Muslims	1857
32nd Sikh Pioneers	Blue	8 companies of Mazbi and Ramdasia Sikhs	1857
33rd Punjabis	Emerald green	4 companies of Punjabi Muslims, 2 of Pathans, 2 of Sikhs	1857
34th Sikh Pioneers	Blue	8 companies Mazbi and Ramdasia Sikhs	1887
35th Sikhs	Yellow	8 companies of Sikhs	1887
36th Sikhs	Yellow	8 companies of Sikhs	1887
37th Dogras	Yellow	8 companies of Dogras	1887
38th Dogras	Yellow	8 companies of Dogras	1858
39th Garhwal Rifles	Black	16 companies of Garhwalis	1st Bn 1887; 2nd Bn 1901
40th Pathans	Emerald green	2 companies of Orakzais, 1 of Afridis, 1 of Yusufzais, 2 of Punjabi Muslims, 2 of Dogras	1858
41st Dogras	Yellow	8 companies of Dogras	1900
42nd Deoli Regiment	Scarlet	4 double companies of Rajputana Hindus and Muslims	1857
43rd Erinpura Regiment	Scarlet	4 double companies of Rajputana Hindus and Muslims	1860
44th Merwara Infantry	Gosling green	4 companies of Mers, 4 of Muslim Merats	1822
45th Rattray's Sikhs	White	8 companies of Sikhs	1856
46th Punjabis	Emerald green	4 companies of Punjabi Muslims, 1 of Afridis, 1 of Orakzais, 2 of Labana Sikhs	1900
47th Sikhs	Yellow	8 companies of Sikhs	1901
48th Pioneers	Black	4 companies of Jats, 4 of Labana Sikhs	1901

Regiment	Facing Colour	Class Composition	Date Raised
51st Sikhs (Frontier Force)	Yellow	4 companies of Sikhs, 1 of Dogras, 2 of Pathans, 1 of Punjabi Muslims	1846-47
52nd Sikhs (Frontier Force)	Scarlet	3 companies of Dogras, 2 of Sikhs, 2 of Punjabi Muslims, 1 of Pathans	1846-47
53rd Sikhs (Frontier Force)	Black	4 companies of Sikhs, 1 of Dogras, 2 of Khattaks, 1 of Punjabi Muslims	1846-47
54th Sikhs (Frontier Force)	Emerald green	4 companies of Sikhs, 1 of Dogras, 2 of Punjabi Muslims, 1 of Pathans	1846-47
55th Coke's Rifles (Frontier Force)	Scarlet (piping)	2 companies of Afridis, 1 of Yusufzais, 1 of Khattaks, 1 of Punjabi Muslims, 2 of Sikhs, 1 of Dogras	1849
56th Punjabi Rifles (Frontier Force)[j]	Black	2 companies of Sikhs, 2 of Dogras, 2 of Punjabi Muslims, 2 of Khattaks	1849
57th Wilde's Rifles (Frontier Force)[j]	Prussian blue	2 companies of Sikhs, 2 of Dogras, 2 of Punjabi Muslims, 2 of Pathans	1849
58th Vaughan's Rifles (Frontier Force)	Emerald green	3 companies of Sikhs, 1 of Dogras, 3 of Pathans, 1 of Punjabi Muslims	1849
59th Scinde Rifles (Frontier Force)	Scarlet	3 companies of Pathans, 1 of Punjabi Muslims, 2 of Sikhs, 2 of Dogras	1843
61st King George's Own Pioneers[k]	White	4 companies of Tamils, 2 of Madrasi Muslims, 2 of Paraiyans and Christians	December 1758
62nd Punjabis[l]	Emerald green	4 companies of Punjabi Muslims, 2 of Sikhs, 2 of Rajputs from Western Rajputana and the Eastern Punjab	1759
63rd Palamcottah Light Infantry[j]	Emerald green	4 companies of Madrasi Muslims, 2 of Tamils, 2 of Paraiyans and Christians	1759
64th Pioneers[l]	White	4 companies of Tamils, 2 of Madrasi Muslims, 2 of Paraiyans and Christians	1759
65th			Raised 1903; disbanded 1904
66th Punjabis	Emerald green	4 companies of Punjabi Muslims, 2 of Sikhs, 2 of Rajputs from Western Rajputana and the Eastern Punjab	1761
67th Punjabis	Emerald green	4 companies of Punjabi Muslims, 2 of Sikhs (other than Jats and Mazbis), 2 of Punjabi Hindus	1761
69th Punjabis	Emerald green	4 companies of Punjabi Muslims, 2 of Sikhs (other than Jats and Mazbis), 2 of Punjabi Hindus	1662–5
71st			Raised 1903; disbanded 1904
72nd Punjabis	White	4 companies of Sikhs, 2 of Punjabi Muslims, 2 of Pathans	1767
73rd Carnatic Infantry[m]	White	4 companies of Madrasi Muslims, 2 of Tamils, 2 of Paraiyans and Christians	1776
74th Punjabis[n]	Emerald green	4 companies of Punjabi Muslims, 2 of Sikhs (other than Jats and Mazbis), 2 of Punjabi Hindus	1776
75th Carnatic Infantry[o]	Yellow	4 companies of Madrasi Muslims, 2 of Tamils, 2 of Paraiyans and Christians	1776
76th Punjabis[p]	Emerald green	4 companies of Punjabi Muslims, 2 of Sikhs, 2 of Jats	1776

§III-2 The Army   213

Regiment	Facing Colour	Class Composition	Date Raised
77th			Raised 1903; disbanded 1907
78th			Raised 1903; disbanded 1907
79th Carnatic Infantry[q]	Yellow	4 companies of Madrasi Muslims, 2 of Tamils, 2 of Paraiyans and Christians	1777
80th Carnatic Infantry[r]	Emerald green	4 companies of Madrasi Muslims, 2 of Tamils, 2 of Paraiyans and Christians	1777
81st Pioneers[s]	White	4 companies of Tamils, 2 of Madrasi Muslims, 2 of Paraiyans and Christians	1786
82nd Punjabis	Emerald green	4 companies of Punjabi Muslims, 2 of Sikhs, 2 of Jats	1788
83rd Walajabad Light Infantry	Emerald green	4 companies of Madrasi Muslims, 2 of Tamils, 2 of Paraiyans and Christians	1794
84th Punjabis	Emerald green	4 companies of Punjabi Muslims, 2 of Sikhs, 2 of Rajputs from Western Rajputana and the Eastern Punjab	1794
86th Carnatic Infantry	Emerald green	4 companies of Madrasi Muslims, 2 of Tamils, 2 of Paraiyans and Christians	1794
87th Punjabis	Emerald green	4 companies of Punjabi Muslims, 2 of Sikhs, 2 of Jats	1798
88th Carnatic Infantry	Yellow	4 companies of Madrasi Muslims, 2 of Tamils, 2 of Paraiyans and Christians	1798
89th Punjabis	Blue	3 companies of Sikhs, 1 of Brahmins, 1 of Rajputs, 3 of Punjabi Muslims	1798
90th Punjabis[t]	Black	4 companies of Sikhs, 1 of Brahmins, 1 of Rajputs, 2 of Punjabi Muslims	1799
91st Punjabis (Light Infantry)	Cherry	3 companies of Punjabi Muslims, 1 of Hindustani Muslims, 2 of Sikhs, 2 of Dogras	1800
92nd Punjabis	White	4 companies of Sikhs, 4 of Punjabi Muslims	1800
93rd Burma Infantry	Yellow	4 companies of Sikhs, 4 of Punjabi Muslims	1800
94th Russell's Infantry	Dark green	3 companies of Rajputs, 2 of Jats, 3 of Dekhani Muslims	1813
95th Russell's Infantry	Dark green	3 companies of Rajputs, 3 of Hindustani Muslims, 2 of Ahirs of the Eastern Punjab	1813
96th Berar Infantry	Dark green	3 companies of Rajputs, 2 of Jats, 3 of Hindustani Muslims	1797
97th Deccan Infantry	Dark green	3 companies of Rajputs, 2 of Jats, 3 of Dekhani Muslims	1794
98th Infantry	Dark green	3 companies of Rajputs, 3 of Hindustani Muslims, 2 of Ahirs of the Eastern Punjab	1788
99th Deccan Infantry	Dark green	3 companies of Rajputs, 2 of Jats, 3 of Hindustani Muslims	1788
The 101st Grenadiers[u]	White	2 companies of Dekhani Mahrattas, 2 of Konkani Mahrattas, 2 of Rajputana Muslims, 2 of Punjabi Muslims	1779
102nd King Edward's Own Grenadiers	White	2 companies of Western Rajputana Jats, 2 of Bagri Jats and Jats from Eastern Rajputana, 2 of Rajputana Gujars, 2 of Punjabi Muslims	1796
103rd Mahratta Light Infantry	Black	4 companies of Dekhani Mahrattas, 2 of Konkani Mahrattas, 2 of Dekhani Muslims	1768

India

Regiment	Facing Colour	Class Composition	Date Raised
104th Wellesley's Rifles	Scarlet	4 companies of Rajputana Jats, 2 of Rajputana Rajputs, 2 of Punjabi Muslims	1775
105th Mahratta Light Infantry	Black	4 companies of Dekhani Mahrattas, 2 of Konkani Mahrattas, 2 of Dekhani Muslims	1788
106th Hazara Pioneers	Scarlet	8 companies of Hazaras	1904
107th Pioneers	White	2 companies of Pathans, 2 of Rajputana Muslims, 2 of Sikhs, 2 of Dekhani Mahrattas	1788
108th Infantry	White	2 companies of Dekhani Mahrattas, 2 of Konkani Mahrattas, 2 of Punjabi Muslims, 2 of Rajputana Muslims	1768
109th Infantry	Black	2 companies of Dekhani Mahrattas, 2 of Konkani Mahrattas, 2 of Rajputana Muslims, 2 of Punjabi Muslims	1788
110th Mahratta Light Infantry	Black	4 companies of Dekhani Mahrattas, 2 of Konkani Mahrattas, 2 of Dekhani Muslims	1797
112th Infantry	Yellow	2 companies of Western Rajputana Jats, 2 of Bagri Jats and Jats from Eastern Rajputana, 2 of Rajputana Gujars, 2 of Punjabi Muslims	1798
113th Infantry	Yellow	2 companies of Western Rajputana Jats, 2 of Bagri Jats and Jats from Eastern Rajputana, 2 of Rajputana Gujars, 2 of Punjabi Muslims	1800
114th Mahrattas	Yellow	4 Companies of Konkani Mahrattas, 2 of Dekhani Mahrattas, 2 of Dekhani Muslims	1800
116th Mahrattas	Yellow	4 companies of Konkani Mahrattas, 2 of Dekhani Mahrattas, 2 of Dekhani Muslims	1800
117th Mahrattas	Yellow	4 companies of Konkani Mahrattas, 2 of Dekhani Mahrattas, 2 of Dekhani Muslims	1800
119th Infantry (Mooltan Regiment)	Yellow	2 companies of Rajputana Gujars, 2 of Mers, 2 of Rajputana Rajputs, 2 of Hindustani Muslims	1817
120th Rajputana Infantry	Yellow	2 companies of Rajputana Gujars, 2 of Mers, 2 of Rajputana Rajputs, 2 of Hindustani Muslims	1817
121st Pioneers	White	2 companies of Dekhani Mahrattas, 2 of Rajputana Muslims, 2 of Western Rajputana Jats, 2 of Pathans	1777
122nd Rajputana Infantry	Emerald green	2 companies of Rajputana Gujars, 2 of Mers, 2 of Rajputana Rajputs, 2 of Hindustani Muslims	1818
123rd Outram's Rifles[v]	Scarlet	4 companies of Rajputana Jats, 2 of Rajputana Rajputs, 2 of Punjabi Muslims	1820
124th Duchess of Connaught's Own Baluchistan Infantry	Scarlet	2 companies of Hazaras, 2 of Punjabi Muslims, 1 of Khattaks, 1 of Mahsud Wazirs, 2 of Sikhs other than Jat Sikhs	1820
125th Napier's Rifles[w]	Scarlet	4 companies of Rajputana Jats, 2 of Rajputana Rajputs, 2 of Punjabi Muslims	1820
126th Baluchistan Infantry	Scarlet	2 companies of Hazaras, 1 of Khattaks, 1 of Wazirs, 2 of Baluchis and Brahuis, 2 of Sikhs other than Jat Sikhs	1825
127th Queen Mary's Own Baluch Light Infantry	Scarlet	2 companies of Punjabi Muslims, 3 of Mahsuds, 3 of other Pathans	1844
128th Pioneers	White	2 companies of Yusufzais, 2 of Rajputana Muslims, 2 of Sikhs, 2 of Dekhani Mahrattas	1846
129th Duke of Connaught's Own Baluchis	Scarlet	2 companies of Punjabi Muslims, 3 of Mahsuds, 3 of other Pathans	1846

Regiment	Facing Colour	Class Composition	Date Raised
130th King George's Own Baluchis (Jacob's Rifles)	Scarlet	2 companies of Punjabi Muslims, 3 of Mahsuds, 3 of other Pathans	1858
GURKHAS			
1st King George's Own Gurkha Rifles (Malaun Regiment)[x]	Scarlet	16 companies of Gurkhas[bb]	1815 (2nd Bn 1886)
2nd King George's Own Gurkha Rifles (Sirmoor Rifles)[y]	Scarlet	16 companies of Gurkhas[bb]	1815 (2nd Bn 1886)
3rd Queen Alexandra's Own Gurkha Rifles[z]	Black	16 companies of Gurkhas[bb]	1815 (2nd Bn 1891)
4th Gurkha Rifles	Black	16 companies of Gurkhas[bb]	1857 (2nd Bn 1886)
5th Gurkha Rifles (Frontier Force)	Black	16 companies of Gurkhas[bb]	1858 (2nd Bn 1886)
6th Gurkha Rifles	Black	16 companies of Gurkhas[cc]	1817 (2nd Bn 1904)
7th Gurkha Rifles	Black	16 companies of Gurkhas[cc]	1902 (2nd Bn 1907)
8th Gurkha Rifles[aa]	Black	16 companies of Gurkhas[cc]	1824 (2nd Bn 1835)
9th Gurkha Rifles	Black	16 companies of Gurkhas[dd]	1817 (2nd Bn 1904)
10th Gurkha Rifles	Black	16 companies of Gurkhas[ee]	June 1890 (2nd Bn 1908)
GUIDES			
Queen's Own Corps of Guides (Lumsden's) Cavalry	Red velvet (scarlet (cloth) for the ranks)	1 squadron of Sikhs, ½ squadron of Dogras and Punjabi Hindus, ½ squadron of Punjabi Muslims, 1 of Pathans	1846
Queen's Own Corps of Guides (Lumsden's) Infantry	Red velvet (scarlet (cloth) for the ranks)	2 companies of Sikhs, 1 of Dogras, 1 of Gurkhas, 2 of Pathans, 1 of Punjabi Muslims, 1 of mixed classes	1846

Source: 1914 Army List, pp. 469–585 and 448; *1914 Hart's Annual Army List*, pp. 696–741.

Notes: [a] Formed from the loyal remnants of the Bhopal, Gwalior, and Malwa Contingents.
[b] Raised as the 3rd Regiment of Infantry, Shah Shujah's Force for his use in Afghanistan.
[c] Formed from the remains of the 13th, 48th, and 71st Bengal Native Infantry.
[d] Formed from the remains of the 3rd, 36th, and 61st Bengal Native Infantry.
[e] Formed from four companies transferred from the 2nd and four from the 7th Punjab Police Battalion.
[f] Formed from eight companies transferred from the 4th and 5th Punjab Infantry.
[g] Formed from eight companies transferred from the 3rd and 6th Punjab Infantry.
[h] Formed from eight companies transferred from the 1st Sikhs Infantry and the 3rd Punjab Police Battalion.
[i] Formed from disbanded Sikh Darbar regiments.
[j] Formed from drafts from disbanded Sikh Darbar regiments.
[k] Formed from independent companies that had sporadically been in existence.
[l] Formed from independent companies already in existence.
[m] Formed from drafts from the 4th, 7th, and 11th Carnatic Battalions.
[n] Formed from drafts from the 5th, 9th, and 10th Carnatic Battalions.
[o] Formed from drafts from the 2nd, 6th, and 12th Carnatic Battalions.
[p] Formed from drafts from the 1st, 3rd, and 8th Carnatic Battalions.
[q] Formed from drafts from 1st, 3rd, 8th, and 16th Carnatic Battalions.
[r] Formed from drafts from the 2nd, 6th, 12th, and 15th Carnatic Battalions.
[s] Formed from the Ganjam Sebundy Corps and drafts from the 11th and 18th Madras Battalions.
[t] Formed principally from men who had belonged to Raymond's Brigade at Hyderabad.

[u] Formed from drafts from the 1st, 2nd, 3rd, 4th, 5th, and 6th Battalions of Bombay Sepoys and of two complete companies from the Marine battalions.
[v] Formed to a considerable extent from men who had served at the Battle of Kirkee in the disbanded Dapuri Battalion (Peishwa's service) under Major Ford, Madras army.
[w] Formed to a considerable extent from men who had served in the disbanded Dapuri Brigade (Peishwa's service), commanded by Major Ford.
[x] Formed chiefly from Gurkha soldiers of Amar Singh Thapa's army.
[y] Formed from Gurkha soldiers who took service with the British on the termination of the first phase of the Nepal War.
[z] Formed from Gurkha soldiers who took service with the British after the fall of Malaun and the conquest of Kumaon, supplemented by soldiers from the Gorakhpur Hill Regiment.
[aa] 2nd Bn formed from details already existing
[bb] Mostly Magar and Gurung classes from central Nepal. These are the beau ideal of what a Gurkha soldier should be (Vansittart, *Gurkhas*, p. 99).
[cc] Originally, mainly Limbus and Rais, by 1914, mostly Magars and Gurungs (Vansittart, *Gurkhas*, pp. 48 and 147).
[dd] The 9th was made up of Thakurs and Khas, high-class Gurkhas only (Vansittart, *Gurkhas*, pp. 65 and 70–2).
[ee] Mostly Rais and Limbus (Vansittart, *Gurkhas*, p. 101) from eastern Nepal. The British did not like men from western Nepal.

§III-2-4 CLASS MAKEUP OF INDIAN ARMY IN 1914

From Nepal   17% (Gurkhas)

From India
Approximately 41% of infantry came from the Punjab and border classes:

16.6%   Sikhs
13.9%   Punjabi Muslims
3.1%   Jats
3.9%   Pathans
3.7%   Dogras

§III-2-5 REGIMENTAL NAMES

The complicated history and class makeup of the Indian army is often reflected in the names and titles of the regiments.

The names of the Indian regiments typically had several elements. As well as the more common numbering and regimental type, there were other different elements that could be shown in a regiment's name: recruiting area; class makeup; where it was raised; battle honours; and an important figure in the past. Often a person's name and another element appeared together. The regiments also had a number that, in a general way, showed its seniority, but a significant point to remember is that the regimental numbers had first been assigned by block, according to presidencies, with local forces tucked in to fill up empty spaces.

As described above, the old Bengal army took numbers 1 to 48. Regimental numbers 51 to 59 were used by the Frontier Force infantry, rifles, etc. The Madras army was given a block of numbers that started with 61; however, the Madras regiments that still existed were among the oldest in the entire Indian army. Therefore, the 61st Regiment (formed 1758) would be older than the 15th Regiment (formed 1846), in spite of their numbers. The same holds true of the block of regiments beginning with 101. This is the Bombay army block, and the 101st dates back to 1779, far older than the 15th's 1846. It should also be noted that within each block of presidencies' numbers, the regiment's numbers did not always show seniority. Thus, for example, the 18th Infantry (1795) was far older than the 15th Sikhs (1846).

Number and Seniority

A regiment's number gave a rough idea of its seniority. However, it is a very loose guide, and understanding the code is important in its interpretation.

Type of Regiment

A reference to a specialised type of infantry – grenadiers, pioneers, or light infantry – often appeared. Except in the case of the pioneers, these names were of historical interest only and were typically a note of honour for past services. The pioneers were trained as construction troops as well as infantry.

Recruiting Area

Some examples of the regiments named after their recruitment area are those with Punjabis in them. Regiments showing their recruiting area were the Punjab regiments 19 to 31, 33 and 46 of the old Bengal army, and the regiments that changed over to Punjab personnel when the Madras army fell out of favour. Examples are the 62nd, 66th, 67th, etc. Punjabis. Another example of the recruiting area name being included in the regimental name is the term 'Carnatic'. The Madras army had lost support so much that the old term Carnatic for the area was revived and expanded. It was used for those regiments who still recruited the old classes from the Madras Presidency. In 1904, the 7th Lancers had 'Hariana' added to their title, for no apparent reason other than the fact that many of their troopers came from that district.[21] The Rajputana and Baluchistan regiments also indicated areas where recruiting took place. Others send false signals of where they were recruited or serve. The 93rd Burma, 96th Berar, and 99th Deccan Infantry were all full of men recruited entirely from the Punjab. Their names were merely historical carryovers.

Class Makeup

Many regiment names show the class makeup of the regiment. The 14th Lancers was an all Jat regiment. Other examples included the 1st and 3rd Brahmins; the 6th and 10th Jats; the 2nd, 4th, 11th, and 13th Rajputs; and the 37th and 38th Dogras. The 106th Hazara Pioneers was an all Hazara unit. The Hazaras lived in the Afghan highlands and were persecuted by the Afghans. A large number fled the country and settled in the British India frontier area. In 1904, the 106th Hazara Pioneers were raised from among the refugees and a core of Hazara soldiers serving in the 124th and 126th Baluchistan Infantry. Another class regiment was the 15th Lancers, or Cureton's Multanis. Multanis in the title, in addition to being obscure, is somewhat misleading. Multanis refers to Muslim Pathans who had moved to the Derajat district in Punjab, which is around the city of Multan (also known as Mooltan). Today, Multan is the third largest city in Pakistan; in the 1840s and 1850s, it was a strong fortification. The regiment, when first raised, consisted only of Punjabi Multanis,[22] but by 1914 it consisted of a mix of this class and other related Muslim tribes who lived in the area.

There were a large number of regiments with 'Sikh' in their title, and this can indicate an all Sikh makeup – for example, the 14th, 15th, 35th, 36th, 45th, and 47th Sikhs. But Sikh in the title does not always mean a regiment was made up entirely of Sikh personnel. The 51st, 52nd, 53rd, and 54th Sikhs of the Frontier Force, in spite of their name, were mixed-class regiments. They had Sikh in their title because they were recruited from men of the old Sikh army, which itself had men from many different Punjab classes in it. Another group of all Sikh regiments was the Sikh pioneer regiments. They were made up of men of the low-status sweeper caste. In the Sikh religion, in theory, there are no caste differences, but, in reality, everyone was aware of and to a certain extent followed caste rules as much as the rest of the Indian population. Examples of these regiments were the 23rd, 32nd, and 34th Sikh Pioneers.

Other regiments appeared to be class regiments, but were not. Examples were the 103rd, 110th, 114th, 116th, etc. Mahrattas. They all consisted of mostly Mahrattas, but each included two companies of Muslims.

The Baluch regiments were not made up of Baluchs. In fact, these regiments, the 127th, 129th and 130th, were very mixed and did not have any Baluchs in their makeup. The Baluchs are people who live in what is now the southwest part of Pakistan. These areas were once part of Persia, but some of the area's people have Mongol ancestry because in 1258–9 Hulagu Khan massed a Mongol army in Persia, said to be as large as 100,000 men, for an invasion of Egypt. The invasion never took place as the ruling Mongol khan died in 1259, and Hulagu was called home, with most of his army, to take part in the choosing of a new khan for the Mongol nation. A small army was left behind and were defeated by the Mamluks of Egypt in 1260, but while the Mongol army was there, some of them had integrated and married into the local population (see Image III:1 for the result).

III:1 Officer and Other Ranks of the 24th (Baluchistan) Regiment of Bombay Infantry (later 124th Baluchis)
Note the oriental appearance of some of the men.

Where the Regiment Was Raised

Distinguishing between where a regiment was raised and a battle honour can be extremely difficult. Examples of where a regiment was raised are the 14th Ferozepore and 15th Ludhiana Sikhs. They were raised in towns of those names taken over after the First Sikh War. Other examples are:

83rd Walajabad Infantry

This regiment took their name from the cantonment where they were stationed when they were made light infantry (LI). In their case, there does not seem to be a special action that led to their being named light infantry. The order went out that one regiment in each of the Madras army's four divisions would be made light infantry, and they were picked for their division.

9th Bhopal Infantry

This was the product of the loyal remnants of three local contingents raised by the British when the overwhelming majority of their fellow soldiers mutinied in 1857. The local contingents were the Bhopal Contingent raised in the Indian state of Bhopal in 1818 for British use;[23] and a large Gwalior Contingent (two cavalry regiments, seven infantry regiments, and five artillery batteries). This latter was raised in 1844 in the Indian state of Gwalior, but after the Indian ruler had been beaten he was forced to reduce his army.[24] While its officers were British and it was used for John Company purposes, the force was paid for by the Gwalior state. Also part of the 9th Bhopal Infantry was the Malwa Contingent, raised in 1840 as the Malwa Bhil Corps, a local force made up of Bhils. The Bhils were an aboriginal people who lived in the hills of Rajputana and Central India. They made their living largely through protection rackets in local villages and also charged merchants for safe conduct whenever they passed through their hills.[25] They were viewed by the British as being a group of lazy ruffians given to robbery. The Bhils were enlisted to local forces in different parts of India on the theory of 'set a thief to catch a thief.'

Shekhawati (or Skehawatee) Local Force

This was formed in 1839 to bring peace to the lawless Shekhawati district of Jaipur state, an area of about 10,880 square km (4,200 square miles). The force came to be known as the Shekhawati Brigade under Henry Forster. It consisted of a corps of cavalry, two regiments of infantry, and a six-gun artillery battery. In 1842 (some accounts say 1843), when it had established peace in the area, the brigade was disbanded, and one infantry regiment was transferred to the control of the Bengal army.[26] In the Bengal army, it was a local regiment and called the Shekhawati (or Shekhawatee) Regiment. In 1861, it was taken into the regular Bengal infantry, and for a few months was named the 14th Bengal Native Infantry. But, later in 1861, its number was changed, and it was named a Rajput regiment, taking the title it would carry, with minor modifications, until 1914, the 13th (Shekhawati) Rajput Infantry.[27]

The 34th Poona Horse were formed as an auxiliary cavalry in the city of that name in 1817. In about 1861, they became a regular cavalry regiment in the Bombay army with 'Poona' in their title. From that point on, until to the major changes of 1922, they always had Poona in their title.

Other regiments with local names are the three local corps: the 42nd, 43rd, and 44th Infantry Regiments. The 42nd Deoli Regiment took their name from the Deoli irregular force raised in 1857 as the Meena Battalion, from among the Meena class for service against the Indian Mutiny. The unit were stationed in the Deoli cantonment, located in Rajputana on the triple borders of Ajmer, Jaipur, and Mewar.[28] The Meenas are an aboriginal class found mostly in Rajputana. The British classified them as a criminal tribe, but because their so-called troublemaking showed a fighting spirit, and because they had rendered military service in the past, the British continued to recruit them.

The 43rd Erinpura Regiment were another local corps named after its cantonment. It was raised at Erinpura, Rajputana in 1860 as an irregular force. It consisted of cavalry as well as infantry.[29] The cantonment was given the name Erinpura in 1836 by a Captain Downing after the island of his birth.[30] The force was originally used under political control and detachments were sent out to help the police patrol disturbed areas and arrest dacoits. Later, its main mission was guard duty,[31] focusing on the railway station near Erinpura, an important British outpost in the otherwise Indian-controlled area of Rajputana. The station was also a key stopping point on the very important railway line between Bombay and Delhi. It was so important that the area around it was made British territory.

The 44th Merwara Infantry were a local battalion raised in 1822 in a village of that name in the state of Rajputana. By the late 1820s, their status seems to have changed to civil military police.[32] They were officially a civil unit in 1861, but returned to military status in 1871.[33] The battalion's composition was half Mers, an aboriginal tribe living in a range in central Rajputana, and half Muslim Merats.

The 1st Gurkha Rifles, the Malaun Regiment, and the 2nd Gurkha Rifles, the Simour Rifles, are yet more examples of regiments taking place names. The 1st Gurkhas were raised in 1815 from prisoners captured after the fall of the Gurkha Nepalese fortress of Malaun. In 1903, they took the fortress's name.[34] The 2nd Gurkhas were raised at Sirmoor near Dehra Dun in 1815.[35]

The 35th Scinde Horse is a regiment with a province name with several variations. Today, Sind is the southeast province of Pakistan and butts up against India in the east. In 1839, as the British under Napier were in the process of conquering the more-or-less-independent Mughal province of Sind, the 1st Scinde Irregular Horse was raised in 1839 in Hyderabad, Sind. It was not long after their raising that General Napier was reputed to have sent his famous message '*Peccavi*', Latin for 'I have sinned.' In the course of time, the regiment became the 5th Irregular Bombay Cavalry Regiment and the Scinde title was forgotten. Then, in 1903, the regiment was renamed the 35th Scinde Horse in honour of the province where it was raised.

Battle Honours

One example of battle honours in the regimental name is the 12th Pioneers, the 'Kelat-i-Ghilzie' Regiment. They were raised as part of a force for Shah Shujah (also spelled Shuja or Suja), whom the British restored to the throne of Afghanistan in the First Afghanistan War. His little army disappeared, but the force's 3rd Infantry Regiment performed so well at the siege of one town that they were brought into the Indian army establishment and given the town's name. The 16th Rajputs, the Lucknow Regiment, were formed from the parts of Bengal infantry regiments (13th, 48th, and 71st) that remained loyal and served with the small British garrison in the Siege of Lucknow, which gave the regiment their name. The 17th Infantry, the Loyal Regiment, gained their name the same way, changed from the 3rd, 36th, and 61st. The 119th Infantry was given the title the Mooltan Regiment in 1903 because of the outstanding part they played in the siege and capture in 1849 of the Sikh fortress at that town during the Second Sikh War. Today the town is known as Multan. The regiment were singled out for this notation from among twelve Indian regiments that took part in the siege.

§III-2-6 INDIAN MILITARY RANKS

Cavalry

Woordie Major	Adjutant
Rissaldar Major	Senior Indian officer
Rissaldar	Lieutenant
Jemedar	2nd Lieutenant
Kot Daffadar	Troop Sergeant Major
Daffadar	Sergeant
Lance Daffadar	Corporal
Acting Lance Daffadar	Lance Corporal
Sowar	Trooper

Infantry

Subadar Major	Senior Indian officer
Subadar	Lieutenant
Jemedar	2nd Lieutenant
Havildar Major	Sergeant Major
Havildar	Sergeant
Naik	Corporal
Lance Naik	Lance Corporal
Sepoy	Private

Source: Mollo, Army, p. 185.

§III-2-7 REGIMENTAL RATINGS AFTER INSPECTIONS

A wider understanding is provided through examining what the government authorities thought of the different regiments of the Indian army in the two years just before World War I. Even the mighty Gurkhas had feet of clay in some areas. When reading, bear in mind how class regiments are ranked and what the reviewers say about regiments from the Bombay area versus those from the Punjab and the frontier. Also note that, almost regardless of its problems, a regiment will be rated fit for combat.

Regimental Ratings for 1913 and 1914

Cavalry

Regiment	1913	1914	Fit for Service – 1914?
1st Lancers	A satisfactory report	On the whole satisfactory	Quite fit
2nd Lancers	A very satisfactory report	Very satisfactory	Fit
3rd Horse	On the whole, a satisfactory report	Satisfactory	Fit
4th Cavalry	A very satisfactory report	Very satisfactory	Fit
5th Cavalry	A very satisfactory report	Satisfactory, but field work evidently requires attention	Fit

§III-2 The Army

Regiment	1913	1914	Fit for Service – 1914?
6th Cavalry	A satisfactory report generally, except as regards the horses, for the condition of which, however, there were some extenuating circumstances	Unsatisfactory	Fit
7th Lancers	A fairly satisfactory report	Satisfactory	Fit
8th Cavalry	Quite a satisfactory report, showing much improvement	Satisfactory	Fit
9th Horse	A satisfactory report, showing improvement	On the whole, very satisfactory	Fit
10th Lancers	Quite a satisfactory report, showing great improvement	Very satisfactory	Fit
11th Lancers	A satisfactory report	On the whole, satisfactory	Fit
12th Cavalry	A very satisfactory report	Satisfactory	Fit
13th Lancers	A satisfactory report	On the whole, satisfactory	Fit
14th Lancers	A very satisfactory report	Very satisfactory	Fit
15th Lancers	A very satisfactory report	Rather a falling off, but on the whole satisfactory	Fit
16th Cavalry	A satisfactory report	Very satisfactory	Quite Fit
17th Cavalry	A very satisfactory report	On the whole, satisfactory	Fit
18th Lancers	A satisfactory report	Only a fairly satisfactory report	Fit
19th Lancers	A satisfactory report	Quite satisfactory	Fit
20th Horse	A satisfactory report	Satisfactory	
21st Cavalry	A very satisfactory report	Very satisfactory	Fit
22nd Cavalry	A very satisfactory report	A very satisfactory report	Fit
23rd Cavalry	A fairly satisfactory report	Very satisfactory	Fit
25th Cavalry	Quite a satisfactory report	Satisfactory	Fit
26th Light Cavalry	A satisfactory report	A fair report	Fit
27th Light Cavalry	A very satisfactory report	Very satisfactory	Fit
28th Light Cavalry	A very satisfactory report	Fairly satisfactory	Fit
29th Lancers	A very satisfactory report	Satisfactory	Fit
30th Lancers	A very satisfactory report	Very satisfactory	Fit
31st Lancers	A very satisfactory report	Very satisfactory	Fit
32nd Lancers	A very satisfactory report	Satisfactory	Fit
33rd Light Cavalry	A satisfactory report	Satisfactory	Quite fit
34th Horse	A very satisfactory report	Very satisfactory	Quite fit
35th Horse	A satisfactory report	On the whole, satisfactory	Fit
36th Horse	Satisfactory, under the circumstances	On the whole, satisfactory	Fit
37th Lancers	A very satisfactory report	Fairly satisfactory	Fit
38th Horse	Now a satisfactory report; improvement marked	Satisfactory	Fit
39th Horse	No comments – in Persia	Satisfactory, under the circumstances	Thoroughly fit
Corps of Guides (Cavalry)	A very satisfactory report	Very satisfactory	Fit

Infantry

Regiment	1913	1914	Fit for Service – 1914?
1st Brahmins	Satisfactory	Very satisfactory	Quite fit
2nd Rajputs	Satisfactory	Very satisfactory	Fit
3rd Brahmins	Satisfactory	Satisfactory	Fit
4th Rajputs	Not fit	Satisfactory	Fit
5th	Satisfactory, except for musketry	Satisfactory	Fit
6th Jats	Very satisfactory	Very satisfactory	Fit
7th Rajputs	Very satisfactory	Very satisfactory	Fit
8th Rajputs	Satisfactory	Satisfactory, except for arms and equipment	Fit
9th	Not satisfactory – 'Regiment must wake up'	'Very satisfactory improvement'	Fit
10th Jats	Very satisfactory	Satisfactory	Fit
11th Rajputs	Very satisfactory	Very satisfactory	Fit
12th	Very satisfactory	Very satisfactory	Fit
13th Rajputs	Very satisfactory	Satisfactory	Fit
14th Sikhs	Satisfactory	Satisfactory	Fit
15th Sikhs	Very satisfactory	Very satisfactory	Fit
16th	Satisfactory	Satisfactory	Fit
17th	Very satisfactory	Satisfactory	Fit
18th	Most unsatisfactory	Except for issues from 1913, satisfactory	No statement as to fitness
19th	With some exceptions, satisfactory	Quite satisfactory	Fit
20th	Very satisfactory	Very satisfactory	Fit
21st	Very satisfactory	Very satisfactory	Fit
22nd	Excellent	Excellent	Fit
23rd Mazbi Sikhs	Satisfactory	Satisfactory, except musketry	Fit
24th	Very satisfactory	Very satisfactory	Fit
25th	Satisfactory	Satisfactory	Fit
26th	Very satisfactory	Very satisfactory	Fit
27th	Satisfactory	Satisfactory, but needs smartening up	Fit
28th	Very satisfactory	Very satisfactory	Fit
29th	Very satisfactory	Very satisfactory	Fit
30th	Very satisfactory	Very satisfactory	Fit
31st	Very satisfactory	Very satisfactory	Fit
32nd Mazbi Sikhs	Satisfactory	Satisfactory	Fit
33rd	'In the circumstances, a satisfactory report'	Satisfactory	Fit
34th Mazbi Sikhs	Satisfactory	Satisfactory	Fit
35th Sikhs	Very satisfactory	Very satisfactory	Fit
36th Sikhs	Very satisfactory	Very satisfactory	Fit
37th Dogras	Satisfactory	Satisfactory	Fit

Regiment	1913	1914	Fit for Service – 1914?
38th Dogras	Very satisfactory	Very satisfactory	Fit
39th Garhwals (both battalions)	A fairly satisfactory report	On the whole, satisfactory	Fit, '1st Bt. not up to satisfactory'
40th	Very satisfactory	Very satisfactory	Fit
41st Dogras	Satisfactory	Satisfactory	Fit
42nd	Very satisfactory	Satisfactory	Localized Corps – no statement re fitness
43rd	Satisfactory	Satisfactory	Fit
44th	Satisfactory	Satisfactory	Fit
45th Sikhs	Satisfactory, as far as it goes	On the whole, very satisfactory	Fit
46th	On the whole, satisfactory	'Regiment is 14 years old and ought to be better'	Fit
47th Sikhs	Very satisfactory	Very satisfactory	Fit
48th	Satisfactory	Satisfactory	Fit
51st	Very satisfactory	Very satisfactory	Fit
52nd	Very satisfactory	Very satisfactory	Fit
53rd	Very satisfactory, except for musketry	Very satisfactory	Fit
54th	Very satisfactory	Satisfactory	Fit
55th	Satisfactory	On the whole, satisfactory	Fit
56th	Very satisfactory	Very satisfactory	Fit
57th	Very satisfactory	Satisfactory	Fit
58th	Very satisfactory	Very satisfactory	Fit
59th	Very satisfactory, except for recruits	Very satisfactory	Fit
61st	Very satisfactory	Satisfactory	Fit
62nd	Very satisfactory	Very satisfactory	Fit
63rd	Satisfactory	Very satisfactory	Fit
64th	Very satisfactory	Very satisfactory	Fit
66th	Very satisfactory	Satisfactory	Fit
67th	Satisfactory	Very satisfactory	Fit
69th	Very satisfactory	Very satisfactory	Fit
72nd	Very satisfactory	Satisfactory	Fit
73rd	Satisfactory, except for musketry	Quite satisfactory	Fit as far as they go
74th	Very satisfactory	Satisfactory	Fit
75th	Very satisfactory	Very satisfactory	Fit
76th	On the whole satisfactory	Very satisfactory	Fit
79th	Satisfactory	Fairly satisfactory	Fit as far as training
80th	Satisfactory	Satisfactory	Fit
81st	Very satisfactory	Very satisfactory	Fit
82nd	Quite a satisfactory report	Very satisfactory	Fit
83rd	Unfit for service, very unsatisfactory	Improvement is satisfactory	Fit
84th	Very unsatisfactory	Improvement is satisfactory	Fit
86th	Very satisfactory	Very satisfactory	Fit

Regiment	1913	1914	Fit for Service – 1914?
87th	Satisfactory	Satisfactory	Fit
88th	Very unsatisfactory	Some improvement, is satisfactory	Not fit
89th	Very satisfactory	Very satisfactory	Fit
90th	Satisfactory	Satisfactory	Fit
91st	Very satisfactory	Satisfactory	Fit
92nd	Very satisfactory	Not satisfactory	Fit
93rd	Very satisfactory	Satisfactory	Fit
94th	Very satisfactory	Satisfactory	Fit
95th	Satisfactory	Satisfactory, except for musketry	Fit
96th	Satisfactory	Very satisfactory	Fit
97th	Very satisfactory	Satisfactory	Fit
98th	Distinctly below average	Satisfactory	Fit
99th	Satisfactory	Satisfactory	Fit
101st	On the whole, satisfactory	Satisfactory, except for musketry	Fit
102nd	Very satisfactory	Satisfactory	Fit
103rd	Very satisfactory	Very satisfactory	Fit
104th	Very satisfactory	Very satisfactory	Fit
105th	Satisfactory	On the whole, satisfactory	Fit
106th	Satisfactory	Excellent	Fit
107th	Very satisfactory	Very satisfactory	Fit
108th	Satisfactory, on the whole	Satisfactory	Fit
109th	Very satisfactory	Satisfactory	Fit
110th	Very satisfactory	Very satisfactory	Fit
112th	Very satisfactory	Satisfactory	Fit
113th	Satisfactory	Satisfactory	Fit
114th	Satisfactory	Satisfactory, considering the conditions	Fit
116th	Very satisfactory	Very satisfactory	Fit
117th	Satisfactory, showing improvement	Fairly satisfactory	Fit
119th	Very satisfactory	Satisfactory	Fit
120th	On the whole, satisfactory	On the whole, satisfactory	Fit
121st (Pioneers)	Satisfactory	Indifferent	Fit in case of an emergency, below average
122nd	Unsatisfactory	Some improvement, more is needed	Fit
123rd	Very satisfactory	Very satisfactory	Fit
124th	Satisfactory	Satisfactory	Fit
125th	Satisfactory	Very satisfactory	Fit
126th	Very satisfactory	Satisfactory	Fit
127th	Very satisfactory	Satisfactory	Fit
128th	Satisfactory	Satisfactory	Fit

Regiment	1913	1914	Fit for Service – 1914?
129th	Quite satisfactory	Satisfactory except for some insubordination	Fit
130th	Very satisfactory	Very satisfactory	Fit
Guides Infantry	Very satisfactory	Very satisfactory	Fit
Corps of Guides (Infantry)	A very satisfactory report	Very satisfactory	Thoroughly fit for service

Gurkhas

Regiment and Battalion		1913	1914	Fit for Service- 1914?
1st	1st Bn	Quite satisfactory	Satisfactory, except for musketry	Fit
	2nd Bn	Very satisfactory	Satisfactory	Fit
2nd	1st Bn	Not good enough for this battalion	Satisfactory	Fit
	2nd Bn	Satisfactory	Satisfactory	Fit
3rd	1st Bn	Satisfactory on the whole	Only fairly satisfactory, work needed	Fit
	2nd Bn	Satisfactory in general	Satisfactory	Fit
4th	1st Bn	Excellent	Very satisfactory	Fit
	2nd Bn	Satisfactory	Generally, very satisfactory	Fit
5th	1st Bn	Satisfactory	Very satisfactory	Fit
	2nd Bn	Satisfactory, but needs work	Satisfactory	Fit
6th	1st Bn	Satisfactory	Very satisfactory on the whole	Fit
	2nd Bn	Satisfactory	Satisfactory, except for one incident	Fit, but with some questions
7th	1st Bn	Very satisfactory	Satisfactory	Fit
	2nd Bn	Very satisfactory	Very satisfactory	Fit
8th	1st Bn	Satisfactory, except for record keeping	Satisfactory	Fit
	2nd Bn	Satisfactory	Fairly satisfactory	Fit
9th	1st Bn	Very satisfactory	Satisfactory	Fit
	2nd Bn	Quite a satisfactory report	Satisfactory	Fit
10th	1st Bn	Satisfactory, except for account records	Satisfactory	Fit
	2nd Bn	Satisfactory	Satisfactory, on the whole	Fit

Source: L/MIL/7/17023, Blackfriars; supplemented by records at the British Library.

§III-2-8 EXPEDITIONARY FORCES

The Indian government agreed to allow most of the British troops to be sent to Europe, and also to supply Indian troops to trouble spots. The viceroy offered Indian troops for service in France. This was an act of some courage: with British and Indian troops gone, revolution or mutiny was a real possibility. If either happened, it would be the officers' families and the British civilians in India who would pay the price.

The Indian army supplied troops for several expeditionary forces. The Indian Expeditionary

Force (IEF)-A (the 3rd Lahore and the 7th Meerut divisions) left for France in September 1914. Shortly thereafter, troops were needed to invade East Africa (then Tanganyika), and IEF-B was sent, composed of two new formations, the 27th Bangalore and Imperial Service brigades. A second force, IEF-C, was organised and sent to East Africa to help hold off German attacks on British East Africa in Kenya. It was made up of one Indian army regiment and odds and ends of Imperial Service regiments from the Indian states. Because of organisational problems, IEF-C reached Africa before IEF-B.

India was then called upon to supply troops to protect the flow of oil from Persia. IEF-D sailed for the mouth of the Tigris on 16 October 1914. This force was the 16th Brigade of the 6th (Poona) Division. The rest of the division would soon follow.

Because of Turkey's threats against the Suez Canal, two additional forces were sent to Egypt, called IEF-E and IEF-F. IEF-E consisted of the 22nd Indian Brigade from the 8th Lucknow Division, which was sent to Egypt in November 1914. The IEF-F was made up of the 28th, 29th, and 30th Brigades, which were formed in November 1914 in Egypt. The 31st and 32nd Brigades, which were part of the force in Egypt, were formed in January 1915.[36] These divisions formed the 10th and 11th Indian Divisions respectively.[37]

§III-2-9 WARTIME PROBLEMS

The replacement of casualties and the expansion of troops necessary in a large bloody war, such as World War I, proved almost impossible for the Indian army as it was then organised. The underpinnings of the pre-war army had been a lessening in recruiting through narrow class intake and a close personal relationship between long-serving officers and men.

The first crisis faced was the problem of replacements. Earlier, the army had been organised, for the most part, on a system of linked regiments (or linked battalions). That is, several regiments, whose class makeup was similar, were to pool their resources when recruiting and were to be available for each other as a source of trained personnel. While the system was excellent for low-casualty frontier fighting, it had several drawbacks in a large war.

With heavy casualties, the regiments overseas would repeatedly draw men from the regiments at home, meaning a long trip for any replacements. This was done so often that the home regiments lost their ability to handle combat operations effectively. In this way, a good third of the army was reduced to serving as training battalions.

In the mixed-class regiments it was hard to replace Dogra for Dogra, Sikh for Sikh, etc., each in their own companies. Separate companies could not be combined – this would be mixing classes and placing men of one class under the command of a VCO of another class. The replacement of British officers also presented a grave problem. The replacement, merely to function, had to have a command of at least Urdu, and possibly another language as well. As the Indian divisions were made up of unrelated regiments, it was quite likely that the replacement officer with the necessary background would need to come all the way from India.

Moving an officer from a Sikh regiment to a Dogra regiment presented major problems. Then, upon arrival, the newcomer would need time to establish a personal relationship with his men. In addition, the number of officers with the basic linguistic skills and knowledge of India were limited. Some could be drawn from the civil community, but as a general proposition, officers were a limited resource. That shortage caused replacement problems, limited the expansion of the army, and was perceived as lowering the effectiveness of the Indian regiments. The British authorities felt that the native soldiers lacked initiative unless actively led by British officers who knew the men.

The narrow focusing of recruitment meant the war fell heavily on certain segments of the community, and most heavily on the Punjab area. Because the recruiting base was small, the authorities rapidly ran up against manpower limits. In 1914, recruiting was mostly through regimental officers, and some 28,000 men volunteered. In 1915–16, a further 222,000 men were recruited. But it was not enough to recruit men;

they had to be the right type or they were of little use. If enough men in the right class did not come forward, their regiments went undermanned, even though there might have been an excess of men of a different class.

The politics of race made it difficult for the British to expand the army. The narrowing of class recruiting had supplied peacetime efficiently, but gave the army a small population to draw on. It was not easy to turn to other classes to expand the army. First, one had the difficult problem of justifying war recruiting among classes that had not been deemed fit to serve in peacetime. Then the entire regiment must be trained from scratch as there was no cadre of experienced troops and NCOs to draw upon. This was partially overcome by sending out British NCOs to drill the men, but, to be added to the mix, the British NCOs first had to learn the men's language. Finding good NCOs who were also good linguists was not always easy. Finding British officers who could learn the language and who were willing to tie their future to a non-martial class was also difficult.

§III-3 UNIFORM INFORMATION

§III-3-1   *Lances and Forage Caps*
§III-3-2   *King's Indian Orderly Officers*
§III-3-3   *1900 Indian Cavalry Turban Colours*
§III-3-4   *1900 Indian Infantry Turban Colours*
§III-3-5   *Turban Shapes*

§III-3-1 LANCES AND FORAGE CAPS

In the 1901 Dress Regulations, there were only four cavalry regiments: the 3rd, 5th, 6th, and 12th. The others were lancers.[38] The British officers of the 17th Lancers continued to wear a cavalry uniform, and officers in the 4th, 7th, and 8th Lancers were allowed to wear out their cavalry uniforms, but lancer dress was to be gradually adopted.[39]

Uncertainty is common when dealing with the Indian army, and it is not clear which Indian army regiments actually carried lances. One possible clue is the officers' forage caps. Those for lancers had a coloured welt that ran across the top of the cap in a quartering pattern, like the top of a lancer's leather helmet. Some regiments that were not designated as lancers also had this lancer pattern, which seems to show they carried lances.

The regulations do not spell out what regiments had the quartering, and other evidence in the form of the actual caps from the period 1902–22 and the tailor's notes are incomplete. However, with these caveats in mind, an effort to list the regiments with lancer quartering was made by D.J. Knight and R.J. Smith.[40] Table III.3.1.1 shows the information presented in their article. Also shown are which regiments had lances in their regimental badges, *c.* 1911. The last column shows which regiments have been drawn carrying lances with lance pennants and the colours of the pennants. The tailor's notes also deal with the cap's colour, and some exceptions mentioned in these are included in the notes below the table

Table III.3.1.1: Lancer Quarterings, Regiment Badges, and Data from Period Images[a]

Regiment	Lancer Quartering	Lance(s) in Regimental Badge	Lance Pennant Colours (top/bottom)
1st Lancers	Yes	Yes	Red/white[n, o]
2nd Lancers	Yes (likely)	Yes	Red/white[o]
3rd Horse	Unknown (likely no)[b]	Yes	Blue/yellow[n, o]
4th Cavalry	Yes	Yes	Red/white[n, o]
5th Cavalry	Unknown (likely no)[b]	No	Red/white[n, p]
6th Cavalry	No[b]	No	Red/white[n, o, q]
7th Lancers	Unknown (likely yes)	Yes	Red/white[n, p]
8th Cavalry	Yes	Yes	Red/white[n, o]
9th Horse	Unknown (likely yes)[c]	Yes	Red/white[n, o]
10th Lancers	Unknown (likely yes)	Yes	Red/blue[n, o]
11th Lancers	Yes[h]	Yes	Blue/red[o, r]

§III-3 Uniform Information   229

Regiment	Lancer Quartering	Lance(s) in Regimental Badge	Lance Pennant Colours (top/bottom)
12th Cavalry	Unknown (likely no)[b]	No	Red/white[p, r]
13th Lancers	Unknown (likely yes)	Yes	Blue/white[o, s]
14th Lancers	Unknown (likely yes)	Yes	Red/white[n, o, q]
15th Lancers	No[d]	Yes	Red/white[n, p]
16th Cavalry	Yes[e]	Yes	Red/white[n, p]
17th Cavalry	No[d]	Yes	Red/white[n, p]
18th Lancers	Unknown (likely yes)[f]	Yes	Red/white[n, p]
19th Lancers	Yes	Yes	Blue/white[n, p]
20th Horse	Unknown (likely no)	No	Red/white[n, o]
21st Cavalry	Unknown (likely no)	No	None[n]
22nd Cavalry	No	No	None[n]
23rd Cavalry	Unknown (likely no)	No	None[n]
24th Cavalry	--[i]	--	--
25th Cavalry	No[j]	No	None[n]
26th Cavalry	Unknown (likely yes)[c]	Yes	Red/white[o]
27th Cavalry	Yes	Yes	Red/white[n, p]
28th Cavalry	Yes	Yes	Red/white[o]
29th Lancers	Yes	Yes	Red/white[n]
30th Lancers	Yes	Yes	Red/white[n]
31st Lancers	Unknown (likely yes)	Yes	Red/white[n]
32nd Lancers	Unknown (likely yes)	Yes	Red/white[n]
33rd Cavalry	Unknown (likely no)	No	None[n]
34th Horse	Unknown (likely no)	No	Red/white[o, q, t]
35th Horse	No	No	None[n]
36th Horse	No	No[m]	None[n]
37th Lancers	Yes[g, k]	Yes	Red/white[n]
38th and 39th Horse	No[l]	Yes	Red/white[n]
Corps of Guides Cavalry	Unknown (likely no)	Yes	Red/white[p, t]

Source: Knight, 'Forage Caps', pp. 30–6.
Notes: [a] The Governor General's Bodyguard and the other bodyguards are not covered by this table as they were no longer fighting units.
[b] Cavalry regiments listed in the 1901 Dress Regulations.
[c] Wore a lancer uniform.
[d] Per tailor's notes.
[e] Although they could have adopted a cap without lancer quarters, tailor's notes indicate lancer quarters present.
[f] Tailor's notes do not mention welts or lancer quartering, but Knight and Smith suggest this may have been an oversight as these details appear later.
[g] Caps have lancer quarters.
[h] Cap colours did not follow dress regulations. Regulations call for blue cap and scarlet trim. Caps seem to have been crimson with dark blue trim.
[i] There was no 24th Regiment.
[j] Tailor's notes record two all scarlet caps, even though the caps should have been green with scarlet trim.
[k] Two caps have been recorded. The first is blue with salmon buff trim. The second, which was likely worn by officers in khaki, is rifle green with drab trim.
[l] Cap colours did not follow dress regulations. Regulations call for drab cap with maroon trim. Caps seem to be maroon with drab welts.
[m] Their badge is a horseman carrying a lance.
[n] Bowling.
[o] *Tradition Magazine*, Special Indian Army issues.
[p] Nevins.
[q] Lovett.
[r] Bowling doesn't show this figure.
[s] Bowling and Nevins show red/blue.
[t] Bowling shows no lance.

§III-3-2 KING'S INDIAN ORDERLY OFFICERS

The British began a practice of having Indian officers come to London to serve as orderlies for the king. This was an honour for the officers and provides us with a good view of a cross-section of the uniforms of officers of the Indian army just prior to World War I.

After the war, the officers returned. They wore their old uniforms until 1922, when a reorganisation did away with old regiments and the old uniform. These images show the wide range of uniforms and turbans worn in the Indian Army.

For Images III:2–III:16, the captions show the regiments represented and the names of which officers are in the photographs, but the officers' names do not necessarily relate to the regiments listed across from them.

III:2 1903 King's Indian Orderly Officers

2nd Bengal Lancers	Risaldar Major Ali Muhammad Khan, Sardar Bahadur
2nd Punjab Cavalry	Risaldar Major Umdah Singh, Bahadur
2nd Lancers Hyderabad Contingent	Risaldar Ahmed Khan
45th (Rattray's) Sikh Infantry	Subadar Major Jiwand Singh, Bahadur
4th Madras Pioneers	Subadar Major Mir Abbas, Bahadur
3rd Bombay Light Infantry	Subadar Ram Chandra Ras Mohitay

III:3 1904 King's Indian Orderly Officers
2nd Lancers (Gardner's Horse)   Risaldar Kala Singh, Bahadur
31st Duke of Connaught's Own Lancers   Risaldar Tilok Singh, Sardar Bahadur
26th Punjabis   Subadar Major Magar Singh, Bahadur
76th Punjabis   Subadar Major Atar Singh, Bahadur

III:4 1905 King's Indian Orderly Officers
1st Bn 3rd Gurkhas
1st Bn 1st Gurkha Rifles (Malaun Regt)
1st Bn 2nd Prince of Wales's Own Gurkha Rifles (Sirmoor Rifles)
8th Gurkha Rifles
2nd Bn 10th Gurkha Rifles

Major A.P. Bateman-Champain
Subadar Major Karn Sing Gurung
Subadar Kirpa Ram Thapa, Sardar Bahadur
Subadar Nawal Sing Rana
Subadar Jas Lal Rai

§III-3 Uniform Information 233

III:5 1906 King's Indian Orderly Officers

Queen's Own Corps of Guides	Captain H. Campbell
9th Hodson's Horse	Risaldar Major Muhammed, Ali Beg
27th Light Cavalry	Risaldar Major Ali Jauha Khan
25th Mountain Battery	Subadar Dalel Khan
130th Baluchis	Subadar Major Alah Din

III:6 1907 King's Indian Orderly Officers
Hodson's Horse
13th Duke of Connaught's Lancers (Watson's Horse)
26th Prince of Wales Own Light Cavalry
13th Rajput (Shakhawati Regt)
41st Dogras

Major A.W. Pennington
Risaldar Major Parusottam Singh
Risaldar Thakin Mal Singh
Subadar Rohtan Singh
Subadar Gopala

III:7 1908 King's Indian Orderly Officers
Queen's Own Corps of Guides   Captain C.L. Norman
Queen's Own Corps of Guides   Subadar Major Safaras Khan
Prince of Wales Own Central India Horse   Risaldar Zahirulla Khan
17th Cavalry   Risaldar Major Mahammad Amir Khan
20th Duke of Cambridge's Own Punjabis Subadar Major Turabas Khan

III:8 1909 King's Indian Orderly Officers

13th Lancers	Major P. Holland-Pryor, DCO
3rd Skinner's Horse	Risaldar Major Hanway Singh
16th Cavalry	Risaldar Mangal Singh
6th Jat Light Infantry	Subadar Major Rekha Ram
32nd Sikh Pioneers	Subadar Major Prem Singh

III:9 1910 King's Indian Orderly Officers
8th Gurkha Rifles
2nd Bn 2nd King Edward's Own Gurkha Rifles (Sirmoor Rifles)
2nd Bn 3rd Queen Alexandra's Own Gurkha Rifles
2nd Bn 39th Garhwal Rifles
1st Bn 39th Garhwal Rifles

Major H. St. A. Wake
Subadar Major Santbir Gurung, Sardar Bahadur
Subadar Major Singbir Ghale, Bahadar
Subadar Bude Sing Negi
Subadar Baij Sing Rawat

III:10 1911 King's Indian Orderly Officers

5th Cavalry	Major L.C. Jones
51st Sikhs (Frontier Force)	Subadar Major Bahadur Ali Khan
26th King George's Own Light Cavalry	Risaldar Major Malik Sher Bahadur Khan
30th Lancers (Gordon's Horse)	Risaldar Major Abdul Karim Khan, Bahadur
32nd Mountain Battery	Subadar Muhammad Ismail

III:11 1912 King's Indian Orderly Officers
64th Pioneers
31st Duke of Connaught's Own Lancers
63rd Palamcottah Light Infantry
2nd Queen Victoria's Own Sappers and Miners
81st Pioneers

Major J.A. Bliss
Risaldar Lakshiman Rae Jadhu
Subadar Pandu Rao
Subadar Alexander, Sardar Bahadur
Subadar Somayya

III:12 1913 King's Indian Orderly Officers
23rd Cavalry Major C.H. Hawes
21st Prince Albert Victor's Own Cavalry (Frontier Force) (Daly's Horse) Risaldar Thakur Singh, Bahadur
Queen Victoria's Own Corps of Guides (Lumsden's) Risaldar Abnashi Ram
14th King George's Own Ferozepore Sikhs Subadar Major Bhagwan Singh, Sardar Bahadur
69th Punjabis Subadar Mul Raj

III:13 1914 King's Indian Orderly Officers

18th King George's Own Lancers	Major P.E. Ricketts
26th King George's Own Light Cavalry	Risaldar Zaman Khan
1st King George's Own Sappers and Miners No. 1 Company	Subadar Mihr Din, Bahadur
53rd Sikhs (Frontier Force)	Subadar Bostan Khan
63rd Palamcottah Light Infantry	Subadar Abdur Razzak

III:14 1920 King's Indian Orderly Officers
12th Cavalry   Risaldar Major Sukhdyal Singh
27th Light Cavalry   Risaldar Raswant Singh
4/39th Garhwal Rifles   Subadar Major Padan Singh Rewat
2/39th Garhwal Rifles   Subadar Tilk Sing Sauntiyal

III:15 1921 King's Indian Orderly Officers

52nd Sikhs (Frontier Force)	Major W.F.C. Gilchrist, CIE
92nd Punjabis	Subadar Muhammad Azim
10th Duke of Cambridge's Own Lancers	Risaldar Laurasib Khan
82nd Punjabis	Subadar Major Ghulam Muhiyuddin
19th Lancers	Risaldar Major Ghulam Husain

III:16 1922 King's Indian Orderly Officers

50th Kumaon Rifles	Major W.G. Strover
116th Mahrattas	Subadar Major Vishram Rao Chowan
64th Pioneers	Subadar Major Nanjappa
128th Pioneers	Hon. Lieutenant Krishna Bhosle
2nd Queen Victoria's Own Sappers and Miners	Hon. Lieutenant Joseph, Bahadur

§III-3-3 1900 INDIAN CAVALRY TURBAN COLOURS

1914 Regimental Number	1900 Regimental Titles and Numbers	Turban (Puggree) Colour(s)	Kulla Colour
Governor General's Bodyguard	Governor General's Bodyguard	Blue and gold lungi	Red and gold
Madras Bodyguard	Governor's Bodyguard of the Madras Army	Blue and gold	Scarlet
Bombay Bodyguard	Governor's Bodyguard of the Bombay Army	Red with yellow and blue ends	
1	1st (Duke of York's Own) Bengal Lancers	Black	
2	2nd Bengal Lancers	Dark and light blue	
3	3rd Bengal Cavalry	Blue	
4	4th Bengal Cavalry	Dark and light blue	
5	5th Bengal Cavalry	Dark blue	
6	6th (Prince of Wales's) Bengal Cavalry	Blue lungi	Scarlet
7	7th Bengal Cavalry	Blue lungi	Red
8	8th Bengal Cavalry	Dark and light blue	
9	9th Bengal Lancers	Blue	
10	10th (Duke of Cambridge's Own) Bengal Lancers	Blue lungi	
11	11th (Prince of Wales's Own) Bengal Lancers	Blue	
12	12th Bengal Cavalry	Blue lungi	
13	13th (Duke of Connaught's) Bengal Lancers	Blue and gold	
14	14th Bengal Lancers	Red	
15	15th (Cureton's Multani) Bengal Lancers	Blue lungi	
16	16th Bengal Cavalry	Blue	
17	17th Bengal Cavalry	Dark blue	White
18	18th Bengal Lancers	Blue	
19	19th Bengal Lancers	Blue	
20	1st Lancers of the Hyderabad Contingent	Dark blue and striped	
21	1st (Prince Albert Victor's Own) Punjab Cavalry	Blue	
22	2nd Punjab Cavalry	Blue and scarlet	
23	3rd Punjab Cavalry	Blue	
25	5th Punjab Cavalry	Scarlet	
26	1st Madras Lancers	Dark blue	Khaki
27	2nd Madras Lancers	Dark and light blue	White
28	3rd Madras Lancers	Dark blue and red	Grey
29	2nd Lancers of the Hyderabad Contingent	Blue regimental	
30	4th Lancers of the Hyderabad Contingent		
31	1st (Duke of Connaught's Own) Bombay Lancers	Dark blue, black, and yellow	
32	2nd Bombay Lancers	Dark and light blue and white	
33	3rd (Queen's Own) Bombay Light Cavalry	Dark blue, red, and white	
34	4th Bombay Cavalry	Green, red, blue, and yellow puggree and lungi	
35	5th Bombay Cavalry (Sindh Horse)	Blue, grey, and white with red kazlbash	

1914 Regimental Number	1900 Regimental Titles and Numbers	Turban (Puggree) Colour(s)	Kulla Colour
36	6th Bombay Cavalry (Jacob's Horse)	Dark blue and white	Red
37	7th Bombay Lancers (Belooch Horse)	Blue and gold	
38	1st Regiment of Central India Horse	Blue and white	
39	2nd Regiment of Central India Horse	Blue and white	
Aden Troop	Aden Troop	Khaki, black, and white	
Guides	Queen's Own Corps of Guides	Blue bronze	

Source: Table based on *Whitaker's List – 1900*, pp. 875–7, 886, 889, 894–5, 899, and 901.

§III-3-4 1900 INDIAN INFANTRY TURBAN COLOURS

1914 Regimental Number	1900 Regimental Titles and Numbers	Turban (Puggree) Colour(s)	Kulla Colour
1	1st Bengal Infantry	Khaki and red	
2	2nd (Queen's Own) Rajput Bengal Infantry	Dark blue	
3	3rd Bengal Infantry	Khaki and red	
4	4th (Prince Albert Victor's) Bengal Infantry	Red and black	
5	5th Bengal (Light) Infantry	Blue	
6	6th (Jat) Bengal (Light) Infantry	Dark blue	Red
7	7th (Duke of Connaught's Own Rajput) Bengal Infantry	Dark blue	
8	8th (Rajput) Bengal Infantry	Blue	
9	Bhopal Battalion		
10	10th (Jat) Bengal Infantry	Blue and yellow	
11	11th (Rajput) Bengal Infantry	(wore Kilmarnock cap with number 11 whenever possible)	
12	12th (Kelat-i-Ghilzie) Bengal Infantry	Red	
13	13th (Shekhawati) Rajput Bengal Infantry	Dark blue	
14	14th (Ferozepore) Sikhs	Red with steel quoit	
15	15th (Ludhiana) Sikhs	Red and yellow	
16	16th (Lucknow) Rajputs	Dark blue and red	
17	17th (Loyal Purbiyas)	Dark blue	
18	18th Bengal Infantry	Purple	
19	19th (Punjab) Bengal Infantry	Dark blue and khaki	
20	20th (Duke of Cambridge's Own Punjab) Bengal Infantry	Khaki and green	
21	21st (Punjab) Bengal Infantry	Khaki and red	
22	22nd (Punjab) Bengal Infantry		
23	23rd (Punjab) Bengal Infantry (Pioneers)	Chocolate	
24	24th (Punjab) Bengal Infantry	Dark blue and red	
25	25th (Punjab) Bengal Infantry	Dark blue and white	
26	26th (Punjab) Bengal Infantry	Khaki	

§III-3 Uniform Information   247

1914 Regimental Number	1900 Regimental Titles and Numbers	Turban (Puggree) Colour(s)	Kulla Colour
27	27th (Punjab) Bengal Infantry	Khaki and red	
28	28th (Punjab) Bengal Infantry	Khaki, Dark green, and red	
29	29th (Punjab) Bengal Infantry	Dark blue and yellow	
30	30th (Punjab) Bengal Infantry	Dark blue and white	
31	31st (Punjab) Bengal Infantry	Blue	
32	32nd (Punjab) Bengal Infantry (Pioneers)	Red	
33	33rd (Punjabi Muhammadan) Bengal Infantry	Dark blue and red	
34	34th (Punjab) Bengal Infantry (Pioneers)	Red	
35	35th (Sikh) Bengal Infantry	Red with yellow steel quoit	
36	36th (Sikh) Bengal Infantry	Red	
37	37th (Dogras) Bengal Infantry	Khaki and yellow	
38	38th (Dogras) Bengal Infantry	Blue	
39	39th (Garhwal Rifles) Bengal Infantry		
40	40th (Pathans) Bengal Infantry	Drab	Dark green
41[a]			
42	Deoli Irregular Force	Red and black	
43	Erinpura Irregular Force	Khaki and red	
44	Merwara Battalion	Khaki and red	
45	45th (Rattray's Sikhs) Bengal Infantry	Blue and white with steel quoit	
46[b]			
47[c]			
48[d]			
51	1st Sikh Infantry	Khaki with yellow fringe	
52	2nd (Hill Regiment) Sikh Infantry	Khaki with scarlet band	
53	3rd Sikh Infantry	Khaki with black and orange	
54	4th Sikh Infantry	Khaki with green border	
55	1st Punjab Infantry	Green	
56	2nd Punjab Infantry	Khaki with black	
57	4th Punjab Infantry	Khaki with blue	
58	5th Punjab Infantry	Khaki with green	
59	6th Punjab Infantry	Khaki with scarlet	
61	1st Madras Infantry (Pioneers)	Blue and red	
62	2nd Madras Infantry	Khaki and green	
63	3rd (Palamcottah) Madras (Light) Infantry	Khaki and green	Red
64	4th Madras Infantry (Pioneers)	Khaki, red, and white	Red
65	5th Madras Infantry	Khaki, yellow, and white	Red
66	6th Madras Infantry	Khaki and white	Khaki
67	7th Madras Infantry	Khaki and yellow	Khaki
68	8th Madras Infantry	Khaki and white	Red
69	9th Madras Infantry	Khaki, green, and yellow	Red
70	10th Madras Infantry (1st Burma-Gurkha Rifles)	Kilmarnock cap	

1914 Regimental Number	1900 Regimental Titles and Numbers	Turban (Puggree) Colour(s)	Kulla Colour
71	11th Madras Infantry	Khaki and green	
72	12th Madras Infantry (2nd Burma Battalion)	Khaki and white	
73	13th Madras Infantry	Khaki and white	
74	14th Madras Infantry	Khaki and white	
75	15th Madras Infantry	White and yellow	
76	16th Madras Infantry	Khaki, red, and white	
77	17th Madras Infantry[e]	Khaki and white	Red
78[f]			
79	19th Madras Infantry	Khaki and yellow	
80	20th Madras Infantry	Khaki and green	Khaki
81	21st Madras Infantry (Pioneers)	Khaki and white	Khaki
82	22nd Madras Infantry	Khaki and white	Black
83	23rd (or Walajabad) Madras (Light) Infantry	Khaki and green	
84	24th Madras Infantry	Khaki and green	Green
85	25th Madras Infantry	Khaki and dark green	
86	26th Madras Infantry	Khaki and green	
87	27th Madras Infantry	Dark blue, red, and yellow	Red
88	28th Madras Infantry	Khaki, red, and yellow	Red
89	29th (7th Burma Battalion) Madras Infantry	Khaki and blue	Red
90	30th (5th Burma Battalion) Madras Infantry	Khaki, black, and red	Red
91	31st (6th Burma Battalion) Madras (Light) Infantry	Khaki	
92	32nd (4th Burma Battalion) Madras Infantry	Dark blue, red, and white	Red
93	33rd (3rd Burma Battalion) Madras Infantry	Khaki and yellow	Khaki
94	1st Regiment of Infantry of the Hyderabad Contingent		
95	2nd Regiment of Infantry of the Hyderabad Contingent	Khaki	
96	3rd Regiment of Infantry of the Hyderabad Contingent	Khaki, edged green and orange	
97	4th Regiment of Infantry of the Hyderabad Contingent	Green	Red
98	5th Regiment of Infantry of the Hyderabad Contingent	Khaki and green	
99	6th Regiment of Infantry of the Hyderabad Contingent	Green and red	Green
101	1st Bombay Infantry (Grenadiers)	Khaki and white	Red
102	2nd (Prince of Wales's Own) Bombay Infantry (Grenadiers)	Khaki and red	Khaki
103	3rd Bombay (Light) Infantry	Khaki and red	Black
104	4th Bombay Infantry	Green	Scarlet
105	5th Bombay (Light) Infantry	Khaki and red	Black
106[g]			
107	7th Bombay Infantry	Khaki and red	Red

1914 Regimental Number	1900 Regimental Titles and Numbers	Turban (Puggree) Colour(s)	Kulla Colour
108	8th Bombay Infantry	Khaki and white	Red
109	9th Bombay Infantry	Khaki and white	Red
110	10th Bombay (Light) Infantry	Khaki and red	Black
112	12th Bombay Infantry	Khaki and red	White
113	13th Bombay Infantry	Khaki and red	Khaki
114	14th Bombay Infantry	Khaki and blue	Scarlet
116	16th Bombay Infantry	Khaki and blue	Scarlet
117	17th Bombay Infantry	Khaki and blue	Scarlet
119	19th Bombay Infantry	Khaki and yellow	Yellow
120	20th Bombay Infantry	Khaki	Yellow
121	21st Bombay Infantry (Marine Battalion)	Blue and striped[h]	Red
122	22nd Bombay Infantry	Khaki	Yellow
123	23rd Bombay Infantry	Green	Scarlet
124	24th (Baluchistan; Duchess of Connaught's Own) Bombay Infantry	Khaki and red	Red
125	25th Bombay Infantry	Green	Scarlet
126	26th (Baluchistan) Bombay Infantry	Khaki and red	Red
127	27th (1st Baluchistan Battalion) Bombay (Light) Infantry	Green	
128	28th Bombay Infantry (Pioneers)	Dark blue and white	
129	29th (Duke of Connaught's Own) Bombay Infantry (2nd Baluchistan Battalion)	Dark green	Red
130	30th Bombay Infantry (3rd Baluchistan Battalion)	Green	Red
Guides	Queen's Own Corps of Guides	Blue bronze	

Source: Table based on *Whitaker's List – 1900*, pp. 878–83, 886–8, 889–93, and 895–901.

Notes: [a] The 41st (Dogra) Bengal Infantry was raised in 1900. The uniform for this regiment is not listed in *Whitaker's List – 1900*.
[b] The 46th Bengal Infantry was raised in 1900. The uniform for this regiment is not listed in *Whitaker's List – 1900*.
[c] The 47th (Sikh) Bengal Infantry was raised in 1901.
[d] The 48th Bengal Infantry (Pioneers) was raised in 1901.
[e] Disbanded in 1907.
[f] Raised in 1903 and disbanded in 1907.
[g] Raised in 1904.
[h] Exactly as stated in *Whitaker's List – 1900*.

§III-3-5 TURBAN SHAPES

The turbans worn in the Indian army presented a wide range of shapes. Each ethnic group and sub-group had its own style. There were a very large number of such groups in the army, so it is impossible to show every turban shape. An idea of the wide range of turbans can be gained by looking at the images shown here. In addition, styles would change over the years, giving the turbans from one period a different shape from those of another era. People alive at the time could probably instantly identify a man's class by his turban, but for us today it is extremely difficult to do so.

Images III:17 to III:24 show the basic type of turbans worn by the main classes that made up the Indian army during the period 1900 to 1914. These photographs were made during World War I, and hence the turbans are tied somewhat tighter than they were in the 1900–14 period.

III:17 Punjab Muslim Turban

III:18 Sikh Turban

III:19 Jat Turbans

§III-3 Uniform Information 251

III:20 Rajput Turban

III:21 Another Style of Rajput Turban

III:22 Dogra Turban

III:23 Mahratta Turban

Image III:25 shows how the back of three of these turbans looked. (This image, by showing a soldier's back view, also shows how the smooth front of the infantry's long blouse was achieved.)

III:24 Dekhani Mahratta Turban

III:25 This composite shows how the smooth front on the long blouse was achieved. It also shows some common turbans. 1 and 2: Sikh; 3 and 4: Punjabi Muslim; 5 and 6: Afridi. All of the 26th Punjabis.

§III-4 GENERAL STAFF

Prior to a small number of Indian army officers going to the British Staff College in England, a practice which began in 1877, there were no Indian army officers trained in staff work.[41] Indian officers served next to officers from the British army on the staffs of Indian army formations, but the way for Indian army officers to gain this work was to catch the eye of a senior officer or to make personal contact, not through education. Subsequent employment depended on the impression made by the officer on the job.[42]

In 1877, in response to proposals to establish a staff college in India, the British Staff College at Camberley, England agreed to accept officers from the Indian army. Sources differ on the number taken. One says three a year. Another, who was a student in 1898, stated that three were taken one year and two in alternate years.[43] These men were selected by examination.

After 1886 the commander-in-chief could, in alternate years, nominate an Indian army officer for the school from a list of three. This officer did not need to take an exam to enrol in the staff college[44]

Few officers used this opportunity, however. A certificate was not essential for staff work in India, and the expense of going to Camberley was high.[45] Estimates of the cost range from £100 to £250 (£10,850 to £27,130 or $12,150 to $30,390 in current money) above pay per year.[46] This made staff college impossible for most Indian officers who were in the Indian army because they did not have a private income. In addition, if an officer did go to Camberley, his higher Indian army pay was cut back to the lower pay of the British army at the very time he was facing the higher cost of living in England.[47]

Having a staff college in India would alleviate the cost problems of going to England. There was, however, opposition, because of cost, control, and the risk of two schools of thought developing in the two colleges. Kitchener, who, as commander-in-chief of India, advocated for an Indian staff college, was able to use a combination of logic, his prestige, and contacts to overcome all objections.[48]

In 1905, a temporary Indian staff college opened. In 1906, the college moved to its permanent home at Quetta, and officially opened on 1 June 1907.[49] By 1914, the Indian Staff College had graduated 218 officers.[50]

Uniform

Even in the days when India did not have its own staff college, staff officers had dress distinctions.

HEADDRESS

A white overseas helmet (after *c.* 1901 the Wolseley style, see Image II:18). White swan feathers drooped down and outwards from the top of the helmet. Under the white feathers were red feathers, which reached to the bottom of the white swan feathers. The lengths of the white feathers were: 25.4 cm (10 inches) for general officers; 20.32 cm (8 inches) for colonels; and 15.24 cm (6 inches) for officers under the rank of colonel.[51]

TUNIC

In 1901, Indian staff officers wore the tunic provided for in the British War Office Dress Regulations.[52] The same tunic as British staff officers was also worn in the years prior to 1901. A description of these uniforms is given in §II-4 *British General Staff*.

NETHERWEAR

Pantaloons and trousers were of blue cloth with scarlet stripes 4.45 cm (1¾ inches) wide in 1913.[53] In 1897, they were 6.35 cm (2½ inches) wide.[54] In 1897, the stripes were gold in levee dress.[55]

AIGUILLETTE

One of the special marks of a staff officer was an aiguillette worn on the left side of the frock or, rarer, staff tunic.[56] Photographs show that officers wore the special staff tunic before it was abolished in 1897 and did not wear an aiguillette. After 1897, it became common to wear the aiguillette with the tunic.

The aiguillette consisted of a gold and red orris basket with the plait and the cord loop in front of the shoulder and behind it. The plaited cords end in plain cords with metal tips. The French call these metal tips pencil points, which gives an idea of their shape. The aiguillette is fixed to the tunic or frock coat under the left shoulder cords. The end is attached in front to the top of the tunic.[57]

§III-5 CAVALRY

The cavalry of all the presidencies, and then the frontier, played an active part in winning the battles that faced the East India Company. For the most part the cavalrymen served as regular cavalry. It was not until after the Mutiny that the silladar system took strong hold. As the silladar system came in, the men were more likely to wear turbans and native dress. For a long while the alkalak-style dress was favoured (see §*III-1* Indian Glossary and Image III:26). After that, the plainer kurta (see §*III-1* Indian Glossary) began to replace the alkalak in the 1890s.

The British officers wore tunics related to the tunics worn by cavalry in Great Britain. They made strong nods to lancer and dragoon-style tunics and to a lesser extent those of hussars. The lancer tunics had either full plastrons or turned-back lapels. It was the custom among British lancers who adopted a lancer tunic at the time of the Crimean War to turn back the tunic lapels to make a type of small plastron. The Indian cavalry lancer regiments adopted what was being done in England[58] (see Image III:27 and III:28 for an example of a turned-back lapel; Image III:34 shows a full plastron). Image III:29 shows a comparison of

III:26 Officers of the 15th Lancers, c. 1909
Note how the Indian officers are wearing alkalaks.

§III-5 Cavalry 255

III:27 Captain H.L. Dawson of the 9th Bengal Lancers (later Hodson's Horse), c. 1893
Note the partially turned-back lapel.

III:28 Lieutenant Frederick Atkinson of the 9th Hodson's Horse, c. 1907–8
Note the shape of the turned-back lapel on his lancer's tunic.

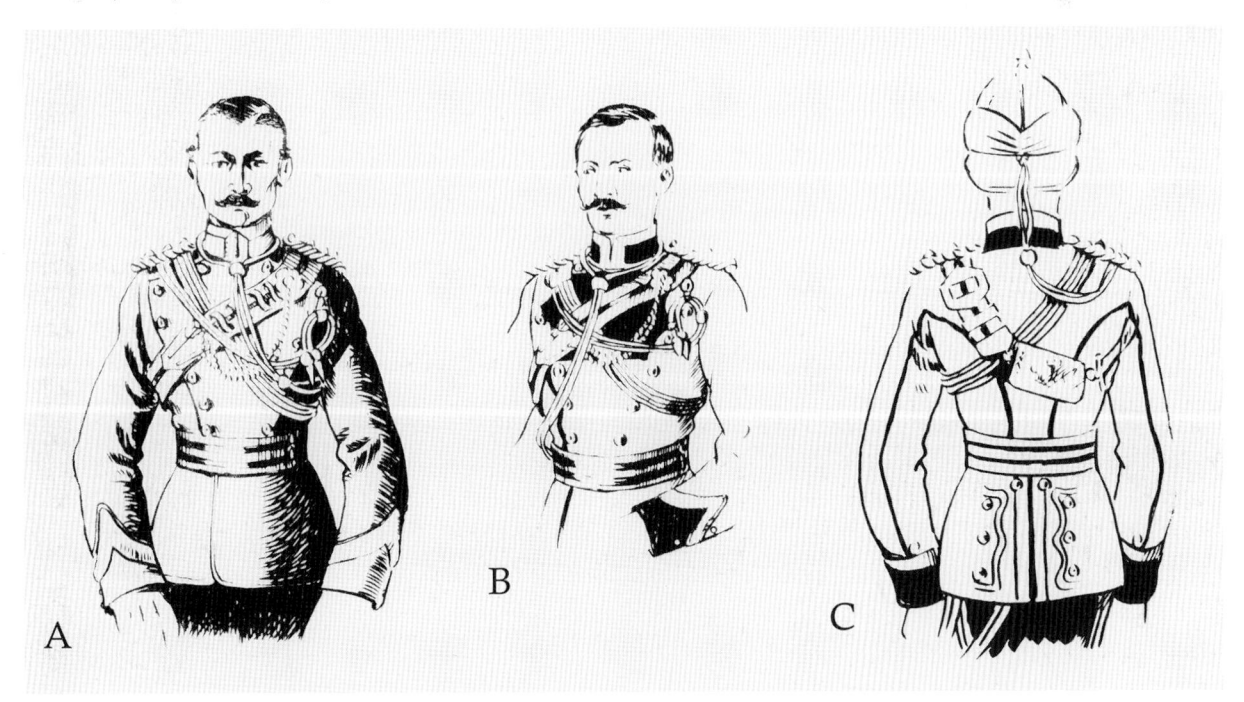

III:29 A. Lancer tunic without a plastron. The capline is worn around the body as the officer is not wearing a helmet.
B. Lancer tunic with a turned back lapel. Note how only a small area of the coloured front is shown.
C. Back of the lancer tunic showing trim pattern.

what would be a full plastron (A) and a turned-back lapel (B). It also shows the shape of the lancer's trim on the back of the tunic (C). The method of attaching the cap lines at the puggree, as shown in Image III:29(C), was common in the Indian cavalry. However, many cavalry regiments chose to attach the cap lines to the rear peak of the helmet. Many other regiments wore a tunic with loose cords across the front.

In the years closer to 1914, officers in many regiments began to adopt the kurta, turban, etc. for wear on parade with their men.[59] In 1907, King George V, impressed with the Indian-style uniforms he saw on his visit to India, expressed a wish for British officers in the Indian cavalry henceforth to wear Indian-style uniforms when they appeared before him.[60] A King's wish is an order. Image III:30 gives the names of the different parts of this uniform.

Then, in 1913, what had been a direction by the King-Emperor became part of the regulations. The 1913 Indian Dress Regulations call for British officers in all Indian cavalry regiments to wear kurtas in most full dress circumstances. For example, they were to be worn on parade with their men, when in the presence of the King-Emperor, at state balls, and at levees. Only five regiments were excepted from this general requirement: the 26th, 27th, and 28th (the old Madras regiments), the 23rd, and the Guides Cavalry (Frontier Force regiments).[61]

In contrast to the British officers who, prior to 1907, wore British-style uniforms in full dress, Indian officers wore Indian-style uniforms in all orders of dress. Many of the terms listed in Image III:30 would apply to them also.

Cavalry uniforms were subject to so many unwritten rules, exceptions, and just plain peculiarities that the best way to show the 1903–14 uniforms is to present tables backed by contemporary photographs and drawings.

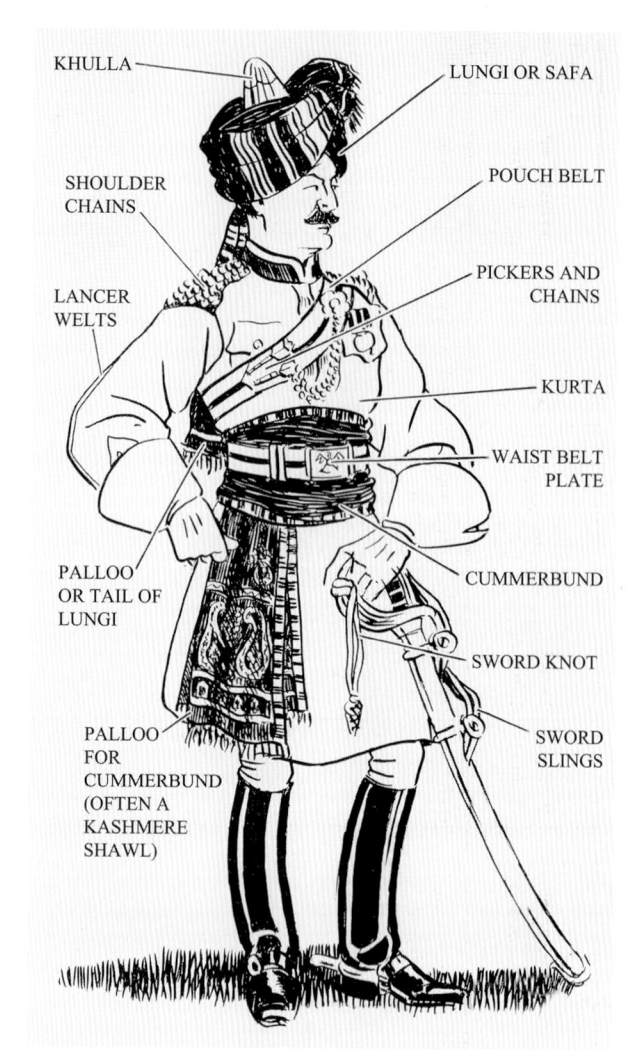

III:30 British Indian Officer in Kurta
This also shows terms used in India for component parts for items of dress used by Indian lancers.

Table III.5.1: Indian Cavalry British Officers' Standard Uniform (Kurta)

Regiment	Kurta	Kurta Trim (Facings)	Kurta Decorations	Lace	Shoulder Decorations	Button Colour	Lungi (Turban)	Kulla (Pointed Cap)	Cummerbund	Waist Belt or Girdle	Riding Breeches and Trousers
1st Lancers	Yellow	Black velvet	Front, chest, and cuffs – gold lace backed by red cloth; on each side of the central opening on the kurta, set at a 90-degree angle from the opening, were three elaborate gold loops on a black background	Gold	Chains on scarlet	Gilt	Black, gold, and light blue	Red with gold to show rank	Black with gold embroidered vertical stripes on the end	Gold girdle with one black stripe; Bowling says lace 6.35 cm (2½ inches) wide with two black stripes	White
2nd Lancers	Dark blue	Light blue	Collar edged with gold with a blue line around the inner edges; light blue cuffs with a Bengal knot; gold tracing braid forming eyes around the central panel is carried along the edges of the shoulder chains to form crow's feet at the point	Gold	Steel chains with gold foil tracing at the edges	Brass	Blue		Scarlet	Gold girdle with light blue line; Carman says gold girdle with two crimson stripes, lined with light blue morocco leather	White
3rd Horse	Dark blue	Yellow	Gold lace and embroidery down the front; cuffs also had lace and gold embroidery around their tops	Gold	Chains		Dark blue with gold, white, and light blue stripes	Blue with gold to show rank; the higher the rank the more gold; a lieutenant colonel in 1911 was all gold	Scarlet with light blue Kashmir ends	Gold	White

Regiment	Kurta	Kurta Trim (Facings)	Kurta Decorations	Lace	Shoulder Decorations	Button Colour	Lungi (Turban)	Kulla (Pointed Cap)	Cummerbund	Waist Belt or Girdle	Riding Breeches and Trousers
4th Cavalry	Not worn (see Table III-5-2)										
5th Cavalry	Red	Red (blue shown in dress regulations)	Gold lace curls around the collar and down the front; pockets edged with narrow gold gimp	Gold	Steel shoulder chains on dark blue cloth	Gilt	Very dark blue with gold, white, and blue stripes		Blue with gold, white, and blue vertical stripes	Gold with the zigzag light dragoon pattern lace	White; Carman says with scarlet cloth stripes 3.81 cm (1½ inches) wide
6th Cavalry	Dark blue	Red	Gold lace around the red standing collar and gold piping down the front; the cuff was red with gold lace and braid	Gold	Shoulder chains on red cloth[a]	Gold	Dark blue with yellow bar across the front and, on it, dark blue and white stripes	Red with gold to show rank	Red with Kashmir ends	Gold	White
7th Lancers	Red	Dark blue	Lace on top of the blue collar and down the front, finishing in a V shape; thin tracing on pocket flap	Gold	Shoulder chains on dark blue cloth[b]	Gold	Blue with gold stripes	Red with gold to show rank	Dark blue with gold, white, and blue stripes on the ends	Gold girdle in lancer fashion with two dark blue stripes	White
8th Cavalry	Dark blue	Red	Red stand-up collar trimmed around the top in gold braid; red piping outlined the front opening, the cuffs, and also went up the back seams; cuffs also trimmed in gold braid and lace	Gold	Shoulder chains with red backing	Gold	Blue with gold and white stripes	Red	Red Kashmir shawl	Gold with two red lines similar to lancer girdle	White

Regiment	Kurta	Kurta Trim (Facings)	Kurta Decorations	Lace	Shoulder Decorations	Button Colour	Lungi (Turban)	Kulla (Pointed Cap)	Cummerbund	Waist Belt or Girdle	Riding Breeches and Trousers
9th Horse	Dark blue	White	White collar edged with gold; trimmed gold down the front, extending from the collar to the waist	Gold	Shoulder chains with white backing	Gold	Dark blue with white and gold stripes; folds of turban show gold edge		Red Kashmir shawl	Gold with white central stripe and white edges	White
10th Lancers	Dark blue	Scarlet	Gold edging around the collar and front; scarlet collar and front panel had a tracing of eyes inside the collar lace and inside the edges of the front panel; lace also around cuffs	Gold	Metal shoulder chains; Bowling says shoulder straps of cloth embroidered with gold tracing	Gold	Blue with gold and white stripes		Scarlet Kashmir shawl	Gold with red line	White; velvet cord piping according to Carman
11th Lancers	Dark blue	Scarlet	Collar, shoulders, and front of the blouse along with the bottom edge and side slits were all embroidered; gold lace around cuff	Gold	Gold chain epaulette (with crescent) on kurta with Prince of Wales's plume badge (per Tradition No. 50); photos c. 1907 show embroidering under epaulettes coming down the shoulder and onto the upper arms.	Gold	Blue with white, yellow, and light blue stripes	Red with gold to show rank	Red Kashmir shawl, bars of red, yellow, and green	Gold girdle with red line; herringbone pattern and Prince of Wales's plumes on buckle	White

Regiment	Kurta	Kurta Trim (Facings)	Kurta Decorations	Lace	Shoulder Decorations	Button Colour	Lungi (Turban)	Kulla (Pointed Cap)	Cummerbund	Waist Belt or Girdle	Riding Breeches and Trousers
12th Cavalry	Dark blue	Dark blue	Collar had gold lace on the top and front edges with a line of gold tracing braid on the lower edge; tracing braid on front extending from collar to waist on either side of buttons.	Gold	Curb chain mounted on black leather; the regimental pattern shoulder chains extend over the point of the shoulder but do not fan out in the normal way; narrow shoulder pieces square at ends	Gold	Blue with gold rank marks		Red Kashmir work with unusual yellow, green, blue, white, and red fringe at the bottom	Plain gold, light dragoon lace	White
13th Lancers	Dark blue	Scarlet	Red trim on front extends from collar to waist on either side of buttons, begins around collar	Silver	Shoulder chains on red cloth	Silver	Gold with white and blue stripes	Silver and red	Red Kashmir design	Silver girdle with red line (Bowling shows single red stripe); Carman says silver girdle with two crimson stripes	White breeches, silver lace down the trouser seam
14th Lancers	Not worn (see Table III.5.2)										
15th Lancers	Dark blue	Dark blue	Lace around a small standing collar and down front opening; red piping on seams in lancer fashion	Gold	Steel shoulder chains	Gold	Blue and white with gold stripes and decoration	Red with gold to show rank	Red with Kashmir ends with grey embroidery	Gold	White

Regiment	Kurta	Kurta Trim (Facings)	Kurta Decorations	Lace	Shoulder Decorations	Button Colour	Lungi (Turban)	Kulla (Pointed Cap)	Cummerbund	Waist Belt or Girdle	Riding Breeches and Trousers
16th Cavalry	Dark blue; Bowling mentions a white kurta (possibly summer dress, but this is not mentioned)	Dark blue	Gold lace around collar's lower edge and down front, extending from collar to waist on either side of buttons; one pocket on the left breast also edged in gold; Bowling shows two pockets not edged gold; cuffs edged gold	Gold	Shoulder chains	Gold	Tied with stripes on right; navy blue with gold, white, and blue stripes	Red with gold to show rank	Red with Kashmir ends; embroidered green, blue, and yellow	Gold lace with centre blue stripe	White
17th Cavalry	Dark blue	White	Gold tracing around collar and three-button front opening	Gold	Shoulder chains	Gold	Dark blue with light blue and gold stripes	White; Bowling shows gold	Lighter blue than kurta, striped gold and blue like lungi	Light blue girdle with yellow and white horizontal stripes	White
18th Lancers	Red	Regulations say white; Carman and Bowling both say red	Gold lace around collar; then extends down centre from collar to waist; cuff trimmed in gold lace	Gold	Shoulder chains backed blue	Gold	Blue with gold and blue stripes; blue referred to as 'deep ultramarine shade'	Red with gold to show rank	Blue with embroidered Kashmir ends, which are very wide and short; blue referred to as 'deep ultramarine shade'	Red girdle	White
19th Lancers	Dark blue	Dark blue	Bowling states gold lace on centre opening	Silver	Steel shoulder chains, potentially silver cords instead of chains	Silver	Blue and grey with gold stripes	Red	Red and gold	Silver with two French grey stripes	White

Regiment	Kurta	Kurta Trim (Facings)	Kurta Decorations	Lace	Shoulder Decorations	Button Colour	Lungi (Turban)	Kulla (Pointed Cap)	Cummerbund	Waist Belt or Girdle	Riding Breeches and Trousers
20th Horse	Rifle green	White	1.91 cm (¾ inch) in hussar lace around collar, down the front, and around the cuffs	Gold, hussar pattern	Steel shoulder chains on white cloth	Gold	Blue and gold	Red with gold to show rank	Red with Kashmir embroidered ends	Gold with white line	White
21st Cavalry	Blue serge	Collar plain blue	Absolutely plain, per Bowling	Gold	Shoulder chains	Brass, per Bowling	Blue Peshawar type with blue, gold, and white bars with a single red 2.54 cm (1 inch) stripe near each end; blue, white, and gold stripes in between	Plain red	Scarlet with a tail of blue with gold and white bars with a few blue lines and a single red stripe near the end	Gold	White
22nd Cavalry	Red	Blue	Blue collar and pointed cuffs edged with gold lace; narrow gold lace down each side of chest opening	Gold			Dark blue with broad gold sections and red lines		Dark blue with broad gold sections and red lines		White
23rd Cavalry	Not worn (see Table III.5.2)										
25th Cavalry	Very dark green; Bowling says black	Red	Collar edged on the top and front with gold lace and eyes with buttons down the front to the waist; gold embroidery around cuffs	Gold	Shoulder chains on red cloth		Scarlet with gold and black bars, and down the back a tail of scarlet with gold and black bars reaching down to just above the gold waist belt	Red with gold to show rank	Scarlet with gold and black stripes	Gold with two red stripes	White breeches; rifle green trousers with red stripes were permitted on other occasions

Regiment	Kurta	Kurta Trim (Facings)	Kurta Decorations	Lace	Shoulder Decorations	Button Colour	Lungi (Turban)	Kulla (Pointed Cap)	Cummerbund	Waist Belt or Girdle	Riding Breeches and Trousers
26th Cavalry	Not worn (see Table III.5.2)										
27th Cavalry	Not worn (see Table III.5.2)										
28th Cavalry	Not worn (see Table III.5.2)										
29th Lancers	Dark green	White[c]	Two breast pockets (although Bowling shows no breast pockets); edged at the wrist with gold lace following the old style; gold around top of collar, also down front from collar to waist on either side of buttons	Gold	Shoulder chains	Gold	Dark green and gold		Red with blue, white, and red design and Kashmir ends	Gold and white girdle on green leather	White breeches; dark green trousers with double white stripe worn on other occasions
30th Lancers	Dark green serge	White	Edged at the wrist with gold lace following the old style; upper edge of collar edged in gold	Gold	Steel shoulder chains on white cloth	Gilt	Blue with gold ends and blue stripes; potentially green and gold as mentioned by Carman	Red; Bowling shows gold	Crimson shawl with blue Kashmir-work ends	Gold girdle with two white stripes	White breeches; dark green trousers with double white stripe worn on other occasions

Regiment	Kurta	Kurta Trim (Facings)	Kurta Decorations	Lace	Shoulder Decorations	Button Colour	Lungi (Turban)	Kulla (Pointed Cap)	Cummerbund	Waist Belt or Girdle	Riding Breeches and Trousers
31st Lancers	Dark blue	Scarlet	Back and sleeve seams piped in scarlet; edged at wrist in gold lace; top and bottom of collar also trimmed in gold lace; lancer cap lines worn	Gold	Steel shoulder chains on white cloth	Gold	Blue with white, light blue, and gold stripes	Red with gold to show rank	Red Kashmir design with blue fringe	Gold with red silk stripe	White moleskin breeches; blue trousers with scarlet stripes also permitted
32nd Lancers	Dark blue	White	Austrian knots braided according to rank on cuffs	Gold	Gilt shoulder chains	Gold	Blue	White (?)	Scarlet	Gold girdle with two crimson stripes	White moleskin breeches; blue trousers with scarlet stripes also permitted
33rd Cavalry	Dark blue	Scarlet	Scarlet collar laced with zigzag braid; pointed scarlet cuff outlined with gold braid	Narrow gold zigzag	Shoulder chains with leather backing	Gold	White, light blue, and dark blue with gold trim		Red cummerbund ends in Kashmir fashion and top edge around waist had a gold pattern	Gold	White
34th Horse	Dark blue	French grey	Collar edged all around with gold zigzag lace; cuffs edged in gold lace with a Hungarian knot at its top	Gold zigzag	Rectangular shoulder chains		Blue with gold and white stripes		Red with gold top edging and embroidery	Gold	White
35th Horse	Dark blue	White	Lace on collar, cuffs, and down the front, extending from collar to waist on either side of buttons	Gold	Shoulder chains on red cloth	Gold	Blue with white, gold, and red stripes	Red with gold to show rank	Red	Gold laced belt with red line	Likely white

Regiment	Kurta	Kurta Trim (Facings)	Kurta Decorations	Lace	Shoulder Decorations	Button Colour	Lungi (Turban)	Kulla (Pointed Cap)	Cummerbund	Waist Belt or Girdle	Riding Breeches and Trousers
36th Horse	Dark blue	Primrose yellow	Breast pockets; collar laced all around	Gold	Steel shoulder chains on blue cloth coming down the arms	Gold	Blue and white with gold bars	Red with gold to show rank	Red with gold decoration on top edge	Had red central stripes	White
37th Lancers	Khaki	Buff (salmon-pink shade)	Lace went around the collar and cuffs	Gold	Steel chains on dark blue cloth; Bowling shows chains on buff (salmon-pink shade) coming down the arms	Khaki	Blue, gold, and buff (salmon-pink shade)	Khaki; Bowling shows red with gold to show rank	Red with embroidered ends hanging on left; Bowling shows hanging from right	Sam Browne belt	Dark Bedford cord breeches
38th Horse	Drab	Maroon	Four patch pockets and a roll step collar;[d] gold tracing around the collar, down the front, and on the sleeves	Gold	Shoulder chains		Blue, white, and gold		Scarlet Kashmir	1913 Regulations state: maroon leather belt 4.45 cm (1¾ inches) wide topped with two stripes of gold light dragoon pattern lace 1.91 cm (¾ inch) wide with 0.64 cm (¼ inch) maroon velvet between them; oval buckle; Prince of Wales's plumes on the buckle.	Drab with double stripe of maroon with .64 cm (¼ inch) drab showing between

Regiment	Kurta	Kurta Trim (Facings)	Kurta Decorations	Lace	Shoulder Decorations	Button Colour	Lungi (Turban)	Kulla (Pointed Cap)	Cummerbund	Waist Belt or Girdle	Riding Breeches and Trousers
39th Horse	Drab	Maroon	Four patch pockets and a roll step collar;[e] gold tracing around the collar, down the front, and on the sleeves	Gold	Shoulder chains		Blue, white, and gold		Scarlet Kashmir	1913 Regulations state: maroon leather belt 4.45 cm (1¾ inches) wide topped with two stripes of gold light dragoon pattern lace 1.91 cm (¾ inch) wide with 0.64 cm (¼ inch) maroon velvet between them; oval buckle	Drab with double stripe of maroon with 0.64 cm (¼ inch) drab showing between
Aden Troop	Officers were seconded to this unit and wore the uniform of their permanent regiment										
Corps of Guides	did not wear; see Table III5-2										

Source: Compiled by Maria Salcedo and the author.

A note on sources and terms used in this table: *Tradition*, No. 50 is the primary source for Indian Cavalry Regiments 1, 2, 3, 4, 5, 8, 9, 10, 11, and 12. Carman, *Uniforms Cavalry* and Bowling, *Cavalry* were secondary sources for these regiments. *Tradition*, No. 73 is the primary source for Indian Cavalry Regiments 13, 16, 20, 21, 23, 25, 26, 28, 29, 30, 31, 32, and the Guides. Carman, *Uniforms Cavalry* and Bowling, *Cavalry* were also secondary sources for these regiments.

For Regiments 6, 7, 14, 15, 17, 18, 19, 22, 27, 33, 34, 35, 36, 37, 38, 39, and the Aden Troop, Carman, *Uniforms Cavalry* was the primary source with Bowling, *Cavalry* serving as a secondary reference. (There was not a 24th Regiment.)

The *Dress Regulations/India, 1901* and *Dress Regulations/India, 1913* were also viewed as a secondary source for several reasons. Often they merely stated 'wore regimental pattern'. In other places, they were maddeningly vague. Then, even when they were reasonably clear, the regiments – many with a background as irregular regiments – took a positive delight in finding loopholes in the regulations or just flouting them. A common saying was that the dress regulations were a reasonable basis for disagreement. An example of finding a loophole is observing that while the regulations stated a stripe or stripes on the pouch belt and girdles, they did not specify width. This left room for creative regimental officers, who were, after all, ordering and paying for the items, to make them quite wide if they thought that would look distinctive or smart. Then the fight with headquarters would begin.

Some of the regiments were classed as Horse and wore 'light dragoon lace' on their tunics (which are not covered here) and waist belts (which are covered). Light dragoon lace was a zigzag pattern lace where the lines of lace, as it zigged and zagged, formed small triangles (Carman, *Uniforms Cavalry*, p. 67). In general, see illustrations in MacMunn, *Armies*.

Notes: The 24th Regiment did not exist in 1914. Its predecessor, the 4th Punjab Cavalry, was disbanded in 1882.

[a] Document 6303/117, Blackfriars.
[b] Document 6303/117, Blackfriars.
[c] Bowling, *Cavalry*, p. 44.
[d] Carman, *Uniforms Cavalry*, p. 172.
[e] Carman, *Uniforms Cavalry*, p. 172.

Table III.5.2: Indian Cavalry British Officers Uniform (Tunics – i.e. regiments where kurta was not worn)

Regiment	Tunic	Tunic Trim (Facings)	Tunic Decorations	Lace	Shoulder Decorations	Button Colour	Waist Belt or Girdle	Riding Breeches and Trousers
4th Cavalry	Red	Blue	Gold lace around upper edge and sides of collar; lace also around pointed cuffs	Gold	Gold shoulder cords	Gold Bengal lancer pattern	Carman says (from a 1900 circular) gold girdle with two dark blue central stripes; Bowling says gold girdle with crimson stripes	Blue trousers with two red stripes; white breeches
14th Lancers	Blue	Scarlet	Turned-back lapel (Bowling says 'small plastron'); gold lancer lines were worn around the body and looped on the left side	Gold	Gold plaited shoulder cords	Gold	Gold girdle with two red stripes	Dark blue trousers with double gold lace stripes with a light of red between
23rd Cavalry	Dark blue	Scarlet	Hussar pattern tunic with scarlet collar and cuffs, edged all round, except collar, with gold cord; collar laced around the top with gold 1.91 cm (¾ inch) lace; Bengal cavalry knot of gold cord on each sleeve; five rows of hussar-style braid across the chest;[a] gold cord down the front edges and around the skirts	Gold	Gold gimp shoulder straps laid on red		5.08 cm (2 inch) wide gold laced belt with red silk stripe	Dark blue trousers with two scarlet stripes
26th Cavalry	French grey	Buff	Silver lace piped around and on sleeve and back seams with buff welts; wore full pale buff plastron; front of the tunic was trimmed in silver piping, only along the right side of where the plastron would be worn; this trim continued down to the bottom of the tunic and around its bottom; gold cap lines	Silver	Silver shoulder cords		Silver girdle with two French grey stripes	Sky blue trousers with two pale buff stripes

Regiment	Tunic	Tunic Trim (Facings)	Tunic Decorations	Lace	Shoulder Decorations	Button Colour	Waist Belt or Girdle	Riding Breeches and Trousers
27th Cavalry	French grey	Buff	Silver lace around the collar and cuffs; full pale buff plastron; front of the tunic trimmed in silver piping only along the right side of where the plastron would be worn; this trim continued down to the bottom of the tunic and around its bottom; gold cap lines	Silver	Silver shoulder cords	Silver	Gold with two red stripes	Dark blue trousers with two pale buff stripes
28th Cavalry	French grey	Light buff	Six rows of silver frogging; skirts lined drab; buff welts in the back and hind sleeve seams; silver trim around the collar, pointed cuffs, and down the front opening	Silver	Silver shoulder cords	Silver	Gold girdle with two crimson stripes; Bowling does not show a girdle	Dark blue breeches with cloth stripes
Corps of Guides	Khaki, some had a tendency towards pink	Red velvet	Edged all around, except collar, with drab lace cord; collar laced around the top with 1.91 cm (¾ inch) drab silk lace, and on the seam with one row of heavy Russia braid; five rows of hussar-style braid; Carman says cuff knot described as 'Austrian' appears on an actual tunic as the special Bengal pattern	Khaki silk lace	Shoulder chains	Silver	Not worn	Khaki with a double stripe of khaki lace 1.91 cm (¾ inch) wide with a welt of red velvet between the stripes

Source: Compiled by Maria Salcedo and the author. A note on sources and terms used in this table: *Tradition*, No. 50 is the primary source for Indian Cavalry Regiment 4. Carman, *Uniforms Cavalry* and Bowling, *Cavalry* were secondary sources for this regiment. *Tradition*, No. 73 is the primary source for Indian Cavalry Regiments 23, 26, 28, and the Guides. Carman, *Uniforms Cavalry* and Bowling, *Cavalry* were also secondary sources for these regiments.

For Regiments 14 and 27, Carman, *Uniforms Cavalry* was the primary source with Bowling, *Cavalry* serving as a secondary reference. (There was not a 24th Regiment.) *Dress Regulations/India, 1901* and *Dress Regulations/India, 1913* were also viewed as a secondary source for several reasons; see sources to Table III.5.1 for full explanation. In general, see illustrations in MacMunn, *Armies*.

Note: [a] The hussar-style braid consisted of two strands of flat cords. Each row of braid ended on the outside of the chest with two falling loops of cord. Halfway to the outside of the chest were two small loops in the braid, one above the line of the braid and one below it. At the end of each row was a large oval button with a netted cap. The tunic was fastened by a toggle and loop made out of the braid cord. On each of the two back seams there was the same cord braid. It formed crow's feet at the top, passed under a netted cap at the waist and on each skirt if doubled and formed a Hungarian knot.

Table III.5.3: Indian Cavalry Native Officers' Uniform

Regiment	Kurta	Kurta Trim (Facings)	Kurta Decorations	Lace	Shoulder Decorations	Button Colour	Lungi (Turban)	Kulla (Pointed Cap)	Cummerbund	Waist Belt or Girdle	Riding Breeches and Trousers
1st Lancers	Yellow	Black velvet	Front, chest, and cuffs – gold lace backed by red cloth and eyes; on each side of the chest three elaborate gold loops series on black which stand out at a 90-degree angle from the central line of lace	Gold	Chains on scarlet	Gilt	Black, gold, and light blue	Red with gold to show rank	Black with gold embroidered Kashmir ends	Gold girdle with black stripe; Carman says 6.35 cm (2½ inch) wide girdle with two black silk stripes, lined with black morocco leather	White
2nd Lancers	Dark blue	Light blue	Collar edged with gold with a blue line around the inner edges; gold tracing braid forming eyes around the central panel is carried along the edges of the shoulder chains to form 'crow's toes' at points; light blue cuffs with a Bengal knot	Gold	Steel chains with gold foil tracing on edges	Brass	Dark blue with grey stripes and gold threads		Scarlet	Gold with a light blue line; Carman says gold lancer lace girdle with two crimson stripes, lined with light blue morocco leather	White
3rd Horse	Dark blue	Yellow	Gold embroidery around the cuffs, down the front, and on collar edges	Gold	Shoulder chains	Gold	Blue with gold, white, and light blue stripes	Blue and gold	Red	Gold girdle	White

Regiment	Kurta	Kurta Trim (Facings)	Kurta Decorations	Lace	Shoulder Decorations	Button Colour	Lungi (Turban)	Kulla (Pointed Cap)	Cummerbund	Waist Belt or Girdle	Riding Breeches and Trousers
4th Cavalry	Red	Blue	Gold lace around collar, down front, extending from collar to waist, around two front pockets, and around cuffs	Gold	Shoulder chains	Bengal lancer pattern	Blue and gold	Red with gold to show rank	Blue with gold embroidery	Gold	White
5th Cavalry	Red	Red (blue shown in dress regulations)	Gold lace curls around the collar and down the front; gold lace also around cuff; pockets edged with gold; tracing of eyes around all the wide lace and around the patch pockets	Gold	Steel shoulder chains on blue cloth	Gold	Dark blue with gold, white, and blue stripes	Gold	Dark blue with gold, white, and blue (both light and dark) stripes	Gold	White with scarlet 2.81 cm (1½ inch) stripe
6th Cavalry	Dark blue	Scarlet	Gold lace and red piping on the cuffs, around the collar, and down each side of the front on either side of the buttons	Gold	Shoulder chains on red cloth[a]	Gold	Dark and light blue with gold stripes	Red with gold to show rank	Red with gold lower edge, gold embroidery, and red and dark blue fringe	Gold	White
7th Lancers	Scarlet	Blue	Gold lace around the bottom of the collar and continuing down the front, finishing in a V shape at the bottom; pocket flaps have narrow gold tracings around them	Gold	Steel shoulder chains on dark blue cloth[b]	Gold	Blue with gold stripes	Red with gold to show rank	Blue with gold and other (white) stripes on the ends	Gold	White

Regiment	Kurta	Kurta Trim (Facings)	Kurta Decorations	Lace	Shoulder Decorations	Button Colour	Lungi (Turban)	Kulla (Pointed Cap)	Cummerbund	Waist Belt or Girdle	Riding Breeches and Trousers
8th Cavalry	Dark blue	Scarlet	Two gold stripes down the front; gold lace around the top edges of the collar; the front extending down the front opening; gold lace on the pointed cuffs	Gold	Shoulder chains on red cloth	Gold	Dark blue with gold, light blue, and white stripes	Red with gold to show rank	Red Kashmir shawl with gold embroidery	Gold with two red lines and red edges	White
9th Horse	Dark blue	White	Gold lace on collar, down front (forming a panel down chest), and on the cuffs	Gold	Shoulder chains	Gold	Dark blue with white and gold stripes; folds of turban show gold edge		Red Kashmir shawl with white and gold embroidery and gold lace upper edge	Gold with white central stripe and white edges	White
10th Lancers	Dark blue	Scarlet	Gold braid around the top of the scarlet collar; tracing of cord eyes inside the braid; front scarlet panel had a tracing of eyes inside the edges of the front panel; cuffs were pointed, traced by elaborate tracing cord and topped by a series of cord	Gold	Shoulder chains not worn; red straps embroidered at the edges with small circles of gold lace; Carman says shoulder chains present	Gold	Dark blue with gold, light blue, and white stripes		Scarlet Kashmir with gold lace on upper edge; gold, red, and blue decoration; and red and blue fringe	Gold with red line	White velvet cord

Regiment	Kurta	Kurta Trim (Facings)	Kurta Decorations	Lace	Shoulder Decorations	Button Colour	Lungi (Turban)	Kulla (Pointed Cap)	Cummerbund	Waist Belt or Girdle	Riding Breeches and Trousers
11th Lancers	Dark blue	Scarlet	Gold lace around the cuffs and down the opening in the front; high collar, shoulders, and front of the blouse, along with the bottom edges and side slits, were embroidered with gold cord; gold cord embroidery at each of the four openings of the kurta (see Images III:31 and III:32)	Gold	Gold epaulettes with gold crescents worn over an embroidered representation of shoulder chains that came down far onto the upper arm (see Images III:31 and III:32)	Gold	Dark blue and light blue with gold stripes	Red with gold to show rank	Red Kashmir with gold lace on upper edge; red, white, and blue decoration; red and blue fringe	Gold with red line	White
12th Cavalry	Dark blue	Dark blue	Patch pockets; pointed cuffs outlined at the top with gold lace which joins at the back; collar had gold lace on the top and front edges with a line of tracing braid on the lower edge; tracing braid also carried on the front of the kurta in a line extending from the collar to the waist on either side of the buttons	Gold	Curb chain mounted on black leather; the narrow shoulder pieces were square at ends, the shoulder chains extended over the point of the shoulder but being square at the end, it did not fan out in the normal way	Gold	Gold and blue		Red Kashmir with unusual yellow, green, blue, white, and red fringe at the bottom	Plain gold, light dragoon lace	White

Regiment	Kurta	Kurta Trim (Facings)	Kurta Decorations	Lace	Shoulder Decorations	Button Colour	Lungi (Turban)	Kulla (Pointed Cap)	Cummerbund	Waist Belt or Girdle	Riding Breeches and Trousers
13th Lancers	Dark blue	Scarlet; Bowling shows white	Scarlet trim around lower edge of collar also found on the front, extending from collar to waist on either side of the buttons	Silver	Shoulder chains on scarlet cloth	Silver	Dark blue with gold and white stripes; lungi varies; Carman says stripes were shown in photos on both the right and left	Silver and scarlet; Bowling shows a gold kulla	Scarlet Kashmir design	Silver with scarlet line	White
14th Lancers	Dark blue	Scarlet	Gold lace on cuffs, around the collar, and on the edge of the skirt; broad gold lace around the front opening and an elaborate tracing, mainly in circles outside this; elaborate braid above the cuff that came up to near the elbow	Gold	False shoulder straps made of elaborate embroidered cloth which extended a bit further than normal down the arms	Gold	Red and gold; higher the rank, the more the gold; turban wound in two halves with the fringe appearing high up on the left side	Not worn	Red; upper and lower edges outlined in gold; gold embroidery; gold fringes	Gold with scarlet central stripe	White
15th Lancers	Dark blue	Scarlet; dark blue collar	Thick gold lace around top of the collar; another thin line of cord lace around the bottom; on the chest, the cord on the bottom of the collar extends from collar to waist on either side of buttons (ends in a V shape directly above cummerbund) (based on dress of British officers)	Gold	Steel shoulder chains	Gold	Blue and white with gold stripes	Red with gold to show rank	Red with special Kashmir ends; blue and white décor; white stripe on upper edge of cummerbund	Gold with red stripe	White

Regiment	Kurta	Kurta Trim (Facings)	Kurta Decorations	Lace	Shoulder Decorations	Button Colour	Lungi (Turban)	Kulla (Pointed Cap)	Cummerbund	Waist Belt or Girdle	Riding Breeches and Trousers
16th Cavalry	Dark blue	Dark blue	As of 1897, native officers had this trim: collar had gold lace outlined with tracing eyes; the front opening and cuffs were also outlined with braid and had tracing eyes outlining them	Gold	Shoulder chains		Navy blue with gold, white, and navy blue stripes; tied with stripes on right		Red	Gold lace with centre blue stripe	White
17th Cavalry	Blue	White	Gold lace around the collar and three-buttoned front opening; at least five sets of elaborate tracing cords came out at a 90-degree angle from the central lines of braid; this cord was on either side of the chest	Gold	Shoulder chains	Gold	Dark blue with light blue and gold stripes	White; Bowling shows gold trim to show rank	Blue (lighter blue than kurta stripes) and gold like lungi; Bowling shows white stripes also	Silver and gold girdle	White
18th Lancers	Scarlet	White	Gold lace on upper scarlet collar; lace extends from collar to waist on either side of chest opening; patch pockets on front of kurta; cuffs have elaborate fold braid that comes up to elbows	Gold	Shoulder chains on blue pieces	Gold	Light and dark blue with gold fringe (blue described as deep ultramarine shade) with gold stripes	Red with gold to show rank	Blue with Kashmir ends; blue described as a deep ultramarine shade; gold embroidery and fringe	Gold lancer girdle with red central stripe	White

Regiment	Kurta	Kurta Trim (Facings)	Kurta Decorations	Lace	Shoulder Decorations	Button Colour	Lungi (Turban)	Kulla (Pointed Cap)	Cummerbund	Waist Belt or Girdle	Riding Breeches and Trousers
19th Lancers	Dark blue	French grey	Silver lace appears on the seams of the collar and along right side of silver buttons down the front; Carman says gold lace on the centre opening	Silver	Silver cords instead of chains		Blue and grey with gold stripes; Bowling shows dark blue with gold, white, and light orange stripes	Red with gold to show rank	Red with gold embroidery	Silver with two French grey stripes	White
20th Horse	Green	White	1.91 cm (¾ inch) lace around the collar, down the front, and around the cuffs	Gold, hussar pattern	Steel shoulder chains on white cloth	Gold	Blue and gold		Red		White
21st Cavalry	Blue	Scarlet	Gold lace around upper portion of scarlet collar, continuing down front to the waist; gold lace also around scarlet pointed cuffs.	Gold	Shoulder chains		Blue with blue, gold, and white bars, a scarlet stripe near the fringe	Red with gold to show rank	Scarlet with embroidered ends similar to the Kashmir pattern	Gold	White
22nd Cavalry	Red	Blue	Blue collar and pointed cuffs edged with gold lace; narrow gold lace down each side of chest opening	Gold	Shoulder chains		Dark blue with broad gold sections and red lines		Dark blue with broad gold sections and red lines		White

Regiment	Kurta	Kurta Trim (Facings)	Kurta Decorations	Lace	Shoulder Decorations	Button Colour	Lungi (Turban)	Kulla (Pointed Cap)	Cummerbund	Waist Belt or Girdle	Riding Breeches and Trousers
23rd Cavalry	Blue	Scarlet	Edging of 1.91 cm (¾ inch) gold lace around top and bottom of scarlet collar and down the front all the way to the end of the kurta; kurta opened from top to bottom; narrow gold tracing also went around skirts; three quadruple rows of black cord hanging loosely across the breast with a black olivet at each end on top of black crow's feet; scarlet pointed cuffs with Hungarian knots come up to the elbow on each arm	Gold	Shoulder straps backed red		Light blue with gold and white stripes	Red with gold to show rank	Scarlet with gold embroidery	Gold lace with red silk stripe	White
25th Cavalry	Dark green; Bowling says black	Scarlet	Scarlet collar edged on top and front with broad gold lace; same lace down both sides of the front to the waist; gold cord forming eyes on bottom of collar lace and both sides of lace on front of the front trim; gold embroidery around scarlet cuffs	Gold	Shoulder chains on a red ground	Gold	Scarlet with gold and black bars, and down the back a tail of scarlet with gold and black bars; tail reaches down to just above the waist belt	Red with gold to show rank	Scarlet, with gold and black stripes	Gold	White

Regiment	Kurta	Kurta Trim (Facings)	Kurta Decorations	Lace	Shoulder Decorations	Button Colour	Lungi (Turban)	Kulla (Pointed Cap)	Cummerbund	Waist Belt or Girdle	Riding Breeches and Trousers
26th Cavalry	French grey	Buff	Silver lace around collar; on chest extending from collar to waist, and on pointed cuffs. Carman says a photo shows silver braid and eyes around chest pockets	Silver	Prince of Wales's plumes on shoulder chains	Silver	Dark and light blue with red bars	Khaki in 1900			Sky blue with two pale buff stripes
27th Cavalry	French grey	Facing colour buff (collar and cuff trim on native officers' kurtas was French grey)	Silver lace around collar; on chest extending from collar to waist on either side of the buttons, and on cuffs; a drawing in Carman seems to show a Bengal knot above a pointed cuff	Silver	Shoulder chains	Silver	French grey with gold and silver stripes	White	Dark blue (almost black) with gold embroidery	Silver with red central stripe	Blue with double silver stripes
28th Cavalry	French grey	Light buff	Silver lace around collar; on chest extending from collar to waist, and on cuffs	Silver	Shoulder chains	Silver	Dark blue	Red with silver embroidery to show rank		Gold girdle with two crimson stripes	Blue with double silver stripes
29th Lancers	Rifle green	White; rifle green collar	Gold lace around top of rifle green collar and on chest extending from collar to waist on either side of buttons; cuff edged at wrist in gold lace	Gold	Shoulder chains	Gold	Rifle green and gold		Red with blue, white, and red design and Kashmir ends	Gold and white girdle on green leather	White breeches; dark green trousers with double white stripes on other occasions

Regiment	Kurta	Kurta Trim (Facings)	Kurta Decorations	Lace	Shoulder Decorations	Button Colour	Lungi (Turban)	Kulla (Pointed Cap)	Cummerbund	Waist Belt or Girdle	Riding Breeches and Trousers
30th Lancers	Dark green	White	Gold lace on the upper edge of the white collar; white pointed cuffs edged at wrist with gold lace following the old style	Gold	Steel shoulder chains on white cloth	Gold	Blue with gold ends and blue stripes	Red with gold to show rank	Crimson shawl with blue Kashmir-work ends	Gold girdle with two white stripes	White breeches; dark green trousers with double white stripes on other occasions
31st Lancers	Dark blue	Scarlet	Back and sleeve seams piped in scarlet; lancer cap lines worn even though there was no helmet to attach them to	Gold	Steel shoulder chains	Gold	Blue with white, light blue, and gold stripes	Red with gold to show rank	Red Kashmir design with blue fringe	Gold girdle with red silk stripe	White moleskin breeches; blue trousers with scarlet stripes also permitted when not with troops
32nd Lancers	Dark blue	White	Same piping as 31st, but in white; lace on top and bottom of collar; gold tracing braid around cuff	Gold	Steel shoulder chains on leather straps	Brass	White, blue (both dark and light) with gold bars showing rank	Red with gold to show rank	Red	Gold girdle with two crimson stripes	White
33rd Cavalry	Dark blue	Scarlet	Narrow braid outlines pointed red cuffs and standing red collar; braid thickness tended to show rank	Gold	Shoulder chains fastened on leather straps	Gold	Red and blue		Red	Photo shows brown leather sword belt; may have also worn standard gold girdle	White
34th Horse	Dark blue	French grey	French grey collar laced on all three sides with gold lace; cuff outlined with gold braid	Gold zigzag	Shoulder chains on leather	Gold	Blue with gold and red stripes		Red with embroidered ends; top edged in gold	Gold	White

Regiment	Kurta	Kurta Trim (Facings)	Kurta Decorations	Lace	Shoulder Decorations	Button Colour	Lungi (Turban)	Kulla (Pointed Cap)	Cummerbund	Waist Belt or Girdle	Riding Breeches and Trousers
35th Horse	Dark blue	White	Gold lace on all three sides of collar; thin trim down front, extending from collar to waist on either side of buttons; pointed white cuffs have elaborate gold braid which reaches the elbow (see Image III:36)	Gold	Shoulder chains on red	Gold	Dark blue with white, gold, and red stripes	Red with gold to show rank	Red with dark blue embroidery	Gold with red central line	White
36th Horse	Dark blue	Primrose yellow	Gold lace on three edges of the standing primrose yellow collar; breast pockets	Gold	Shoulder chains, which come further than usual over the point of the shoulder and a bit down onto the upper arm on blue	Gold	Blue and white with gold bars	Red with gold to show rank	Red with gold edging on the top and decorations on hanging end	Gold with red central stripe	White
37th Lancers	Khaki	Buff (salmon-pink shade)	Gold lace around top and front of collar and cuffs	Gold	Carman says steel shoulder chains on dark blue cloth; Bowling shows shoulder chains on buff (salmon-pink shade)	Khaki	Blue and gold; Bowling shows blue, gold, and buff (salmon-pink shade)	Red with gold to show rank	Red with gold Kashmir-shaped embroidery	Sam Browne belt	Dark drab Bedford cord

Regiment	Kurta	Kurta Trim (Facings)	Kurta Decorations	Lace	Shoulder Decorations	Button Colour	Lungi (Turban)	Kulla (Pointed Cap)	Cummerbund	Waist Belt or Girdle	Riding Breeches and Trousers
38th Horse	Drab	Maroon	Pleats on chest; gold lace on all three sides of maroon collar and on chest from collar to waist on either side of buttons; cuffs maroon with elaborate gold braid, reaching to the elbows and eyelets below them, pointing into the maroon below	Gold	Shoulder chains	Gold	Blue and white with gold bars to show rank		Scarlet with Kashmir ends	Gold with scarlet central stripe	White
39th Horse	Drab	Maroon	Pleats on chest; gold lace on all three sides of maroon collar and on chest from collar to waist on either side of buttons; cuffs maroon with elaborate gold braid, reaching to the elbows and eyelets below them, pointing into the maroon below	Gold	Shoulder chains	Gold	Blue and white with gold bars to show rank		Scarlet with Kashmir ends	Gold with scarlet central stripe	White
Aden Troop	These men wore the uniform of the regiment from which they were seconded											

Regiment	Kurta	Kurta Trim (Facings)	Kurta Decorations	Lace	Shoulder Decorations	Button Colour	Lungi (Turban)	Kulla (Pointed Cap)	Cummerbund	Waist Belt or Girdle	Riding Breeches and Trousers
Corps of Guides	Khaki	Red	Turn-down red collar edged with drab silk cord and drab lace; pointed red cuffs ornamented with a Hungarian knot which came to the elbow and was traced all around with a row of eyes in silk tracing braid; chest had three rows of double silk loose drab braid edged with a row of eyes across the chest and with a silk olive at the end of each row	Khaki	Steel shoulder chains on red cloth		Dark blue with gold, white, and light blue stripes	Red	Red Kashmir shawl	Sam Browne belt	Khaki cord

Sources: Compiled by Maria Salcedo and the author. A note on sources and terms used in this table: *Tradition*, No. 50 is the primary source for Indian Cavalry Regiments 1, 2, 3, 4, 5, 8, 9, 10, 11, and 12. Carman, *Uniforms Cavalry* and Bowling, *Cavalry* were secondary sources for these regiments. *Tradition*, No. 73 is the primary source for Indian Cavalry Regiments 13, 16, 20, 21, 23, 25, 26, 28, 29, 30, 31, 32, and the Guides. Carman, *Uniforms Cavalry* and Bowling, *Cavalry* were also secondary sources for these regiments.

For Regiments 6, 7, 14, 15, 17, 18, 19, 22, 27, 33, 34, 35, 36, 37, 38, 39, and the Aden Troop, Carman, *Uniforms Cavalry* was the primary source with Bowling, *Cavalry* serving as a secondary reference. (There was not a 24th Regiment.)

Dress Regulations/India, 1901 and *Dress Regulations/India*, 1913 were also viewed as a secondary source for several reasons. see sources to Table III.5.1 for full explanation. In general.

Some of the regiments were classed as Horse and wore 'light dragoon lace' on their tunics (which are not covered here) and waist belts (which are covered). Light dragoon lace was a zigzag pattern lace where the lines of lace as it zigged and zagged formed small triangles (Carman, *Uniforms Cavalry*, p. 67). In general, see illustrations in MacMunn, *Armies*.

Notes: The 24th Regiment did not exist in 1914. Its predecessor, the 4th Punjab Cavalry, was disbanded in 1882.
[a] Document 6303/117, Blackfriars.
[b] Document 6303/117, Blackfriars.

III:31 British Officer, 11th King Edward's Own Lancers (Probyn's Horse), c. 1907
Note elaborate trim on kurta.

III:32 Officers of the 11th Lancers on the 50th Anniversary of Their Founding, 1907
The many different angles of their kurtas shown here give an excellent idea of what the trim and headdress looked like.

Table III.5.4: Indian Cavalry Other Ranks' Uniform

Regiment	Coat Type[a]	Coat Colour	Coat Facing Colour	Riding Breeches Colour	Riding Breeches Trim	Cummerbund Colour	Cummerbund Trim	Leggings Type[b]	Leggings Colour	Turban Pag or Kulla	Turban Pag or Kulla Colour	Turban Colour	Turban Fringe	Turban Stripes	Turban Special Trim Notes	Turban Hanging Where	Turban Hanging Trim	Turban Hanging Colour	Turban Hanging Fringe	Foot-wear
1	L	Yellow	Red	White	–	Black	–	P	Dark blue	Kulla	Red	Blue	–	White, blue, yellow	A	B†	Black, yellow	Black	Black	Black
2	L[d]	Blue	Light blue	White	–	Red	–	P	Black	Kulla	Red	Dark blue		Blue-grey						
3	L	Blue	Yellow, no trim	White	–	Red	–	P	Blue	Kulla	Red	Dark blue		White, light blue, dark blue		B†	Light blue, dark blue	Dark blue		Brown
4	L	Scarlet	Blue	White	–	Dark blue	–	P	Blue	Pag	White	Light blue, dark blue		Yellow, light blue, blue		–	–	–	Scarlet	Black
5	L	Scarlet	Blue	White	–	Dark blue	–	–	–	Kulla	Red	Grey blue		Yellow dark blue		B† R*	White Yellow	Blue		–
6	L	Blue	Scarlet	White	–	Scarlet	–	P	Dark blue	Kulla	Red	Dark blue	Dark blue white	Light blue-grey, white, dark blue		B† R*	Same as turban white	Same as turban red		Black
7	L[d]	Scarlet	Blue	White	–	Dark blue	Dark blue, light blue			Kulla	Red	Dark blue		Dark blue, light blue						
8	L	Blue	Scarlet	White	–	Red	–	P	Dark blue	Kulla	Red	Dark blue		Light blue-grey, dark blue, white	B	B†	Light blue-grey, dark blue, white	Dark blue	Scarlet	Black
9	L[d]	Blue	White	White		Scarlet		P	Dark blue											

Regiment	Coat Type[a]	Coat Colour	Coat Facing Colour	Riding Breeches Colour	Riding Breeches Trim	Cummerbund Colour	Cummerbund Trim	Leggings Type[b]	Leggings Colour	Turban Pag or Kulla	Turban Pag/Kulla Colour	Turban Colour	Turban Fringe	Turban Stripes	Special Trim Notes	Turban Hanging Where	Turban Hanging Trim	Turban Hanging Colour	Turban Hanging Fringe	Footwear
10	L	Blue	Scarlet	Khaki	–	Red				Pag, Kulla	White, Red	Blue		Light blue, blue		B†	Blue, light blue, white	Blue		
11	L	Blue	Scarlet	White	–	Scarlet	–			Pag, Kulla	Red	Grey-blue		Light blue, yellow		B†	Yellow	Light blue		
12	L[d]	Blue	Blue																	
13	L[d]	Blue	Scarlet	Drab	–	Red	–	P	Dark blue	Kulla	Red	Dark blue		White		B	White		Red	Black
14	L[d]	Blue	Scarlet, yellow trim	White		Red		P	Dark blue	–	–	Scarlet			C					
15	L[d]	Blue	Scarlet, no trim	White		Scarlet				Kulla	Red	Blue		Grey						
16	L[d]	Blue	Blue, no trim	White		Red		P	Dark blue	Pag	White	Dark blue				B†		Dark blue	–	Black
17	L	Blue	White	White		Light Blue		P	Dark blue	Kulla	White	Blue		White, light blue, blue		B†	White	Blue	Blue	
18	L[d]	Scarlet	White	White		Bright blue		P	Blue	Kulla	Red	Dark blue		Yellow, dark blue, white	D	B†	Yellow, dark blue, white	Dark blue	Blue	
19	L	Blue	French grey	White		Red		P	Dark blue	Kulla	Red	Dark blue		White, dark blue						Brown
20	L	Rifle green	White	White		Red		P	Rifle green	Kulla	White	Green		Grey, blue, white						Brown
21	L[d]	Blue	Scarlet	Drab		Scarlet		P	Dark blue	Kulla	Red	Blue		Light blue, blue						
22	L[d]	Scarlet	Blue	White		Dark blue		P	Dark blue	Pag	White	Dark Blue		Buff, dark blue						

Regiment	Type[a]	Coat Colour	Coat Facing Colour	Riding Breeches Colour	Riding Breeches Trim	Cummerbund Colour	Cummerbund Trim	Leggings Type[b]	Leggings Colour	Pag or Kulla	Pag or Kulla Colour	Turban Colour	Turban Fringe	Turban Stripes	Special Trim Notes	Turban Hanging Where	Turban Hanging Trim	Turban Hanging Colour	Turban Hanging Fringe	Footwear
23	L[d]	Blue	Scarlet	White		Dark blue		P	Dark blue	Kulla	Red	Dark blue		Dark blue, white, blue						
25	L[d]	Dark green	Scarlet	White		Red		P	Black	Kulla, Pag	Red, white	Red								
26	L	French grey	Buff, lace silver	Sky blue	W	Red		P	Black	Kulla	Red	Dark blue		Dark blue, red, yellow, white	E	B† R*	White	Blue	—	Brown
27	L[d]	French grey	Buff	Sky blue	White	Red		P	Black	Kulla	White	Dark blue		Dark blue, light blue, red		B†		Blue		
28	L[d]	French grey	Buff	Sky blue	White	Blue				Kulla	Red	Dark blue		Red, white						
29	L[d]	Rifle green	White	White		Red		P	Green			Green		Yellow, blue					—	Brown
30	L[d]	Rifle green	White	White		Red		P	Green	Pag	White	Green		Light blue, blue, white					White	Brown
31	L[d]	Blue	Scarlet	Buff		Red			Dark blue			Dark blue		Yellow, black		B†			—	
32	L	Blue	White	White		Red	—	P		Kulla	Red	Dark blue		Light blue, dark blue, white	F	B†	Light blue, white	Dark blue	—	
33	L	Blue	Scarlet	White		Red			Black	Kulla	Red	Dark blue		Red, blue, white	G	L†	—	Red	Scarlet	Black
34	L	Blue	French grey	White		Red		P	Blue	Kulla	Red	Dark blue		Yellow, red, blue		B†	Yellow, red, dark blue	Dark blue		Black

Regiment	Coat Type[a]	Coat Colour	Coat Facing Colour	Riding Breeches Colour	Riding Breeches Trim	Cummerbund Colour	Cummerbund Trim	Leggings Type[b]	Leggings Colour	Pag or Kulla	Pag or Kulla Colour	Turban Colour	Turban Fringe	Turban Stripes	Turban Special Trim Notes	Turban Hanging Where[c]	Turban Hanging Trim	Turban Hanging Colour	Turban Hanging Fringe	Footwear
35	L	Blue	White	White		Red		P	Blue	Kulla	Red	Blue		Grey, blue, yellow		R†	–	Red	Red	Brown
36	L	Blue	Primrose	White		Red		P	Blue	Kulla	Red	Blue		Yellow, white, blue		B†	Yellow, white, blue	Dark blue		Brown
37	L	Khaki serge	Buff			Red		P	Khaki	Kulla	Khaki	Khaki		Blue, white		B†	Blue, white	Khaki	Dark blue	Brown
38	L	Drab	Maroon	White	Red			P	Blue	Kulla	Red	Dark blue		Light blue, dark blue, white	Front pleats	B†	Blue, white	Light blue		Black
39	L[d]	Drab	Maroon												Front pleats					
Aden Troop		Khaki	Khaki																	
Guides	?	Khaki	Red	Khaki		Red		P	Blue	Kulla	Red	Blue	Blue	Light blue, blue	H	B†	Blue	Light blue	Red	Brown
Body guard	L[d]	Scarlet	Blue			Lancer's belt		Knee boots	Black						Red					

Sources: Sources consulted in constructing this table include: Lovett drawings, Whitaker's List – 1900, Carman, *Uniforms Cavalry*; Cassin-Scott, *Military Bands*; photos of King's Indian Orderlies; *Dress Regulations/India*, 1913; *Tradition*, No. 73; *Tradition*, No. 50; and *1914 Army List*. In case of conflict between Whitaker's List – 1900 and Lovett, we tended to take the colours shown in Lovett drawings.

Notes: Regiment 24 did not exist in 1914. Its predecessor, the 4th Punjab Cavalry, was disbanded in 1882.

[a] Coat type: L=long; Z=Zouave
[b] Leggings: P=puttees
[c] Palloo hanging, see Image III:30: *=from cummerbund; †=from turban; B=from back; R=right; L=left
[d] No source, but likely kurta.

Notes on *Special Trim*:
A: Solid black panel down front
B: Collar solid red
C: Solid collar, chest panel, and cuffs. All red, trimmed in yellow.
D: Solid dark blue chest panel and collar (Bowling, *Cavalry*, p. 42).
E: Solid red collar and chest panel
F: Solid white collar and cuffs
G: Full scarlet collar and cuffs
H: Full red cuffs, patch chest pockets trimmed yellow

CAVALRY UNIFORMS

Pre-Mutiny

As a general rule, the native troops of the East India Company in the presidencies were provided European-style uniforms.

The headdress was normally a shako, but in some years helmets or fur busbies were worn. British officers wore a jacket with braiding on the chest. Native ranks also wore a jacket. Both officers and native other ranks wore overalls.[62] There were some exceptions to the general rule of European dress. For example, as headdress, Madras native ranks wore a tall turban shaped like a large olive made of lacquered cloth which looked like leather. It swelled slightly outward at the top.[63]

Some commands used European dress for officers and men. The officers in the Hyderabad cavalry were dressed in European-style uniforms which closely followed those worn in the Madras command. However, they wore a Roman-style helmet up to the Mutiny, long after the Madras army had given it up. Native personnel, on the other hand, wore turbans and alkalaks.[64]

The Guides, raised in 1846, which had an infantry element, dressed the native soldiers in their native dress, turbans and alkalaks. They wore pyjama-like netherwear and boots. The same dress was worn by the sowars of the five Punjab cavalry regiments when they were raised in 1849. It is not clear what the British officers of the Guides wore during this period, but the British officers of the Punjab cavalry could wear either an alkalak or a European-style coat.[65] At least some of the officers' coats were hussar-style tunics with black hanging cords across the chest.[66] The European officers of the Punjab cavalry wore a dragoon-style plumed helmet.[67]

Colour Images

Prior to reviewing the uniform histories of each presidency it may be useful to see colour paintings of the Indian army as it existed just before World War I. The colour section has a selection of paintings by Major A.C. Lovett done c. 1905–12 as illustrations for *The Armies of India*. The list below indicates which regiments are shown in which painting.

Colour Image C26: Regiments 4, 5, 11, 16, 17, 23, and 26
C27: Regiments 1 and 3
C28: Regiments 6 and 8
C29: Regiment 14
C30: Regiment 19
C31: Regiments 27 and 28
C32: Regiments 20, 29, and 30
C33: Regiments 32, 33, and 34
C34: Regiment 38

It is interesting to compare a Lovett painting to a black and white photograph of the same subject. This allows us to see both the accuracy of the Lovett paintings and how colourful the Indian army uniforms were. For example, look at the officer in Image III:31 and the middle officer with a red cummerbund in colour Image C26.

Bengal Irregular Cavalry[68]

These regiments came and went with the Bengal establishment, but the tendency was for the number of them to grow over time. Both British officers and the men wore alkalaks and cummerbunds. For netherwear, they wore pyjamas. For officers, the three items came in a rainbow of colours. Alkalaks were yellow, green, red, blue, and scarlet. Pyjamas were red, yellow, and probably white. The cummerbunds were either blue or some shade of red. Headdress could be helmets, fezzes, turbans, or fur busbies.

There is less information on the other ranks, but contemporary watercolours show them in turbans and alkalaks.[69]

Post-Mutiny Cavalry

As has been noted elsewhere, under the East India Company, the military forces in India were divided into several different commands. These were: Bengal, Madras, Bombay, Punjab Frontier Force, and Hyderabad Contingent. After the Mutiny, Central Indian Horse regiments were added.

BENGAL

The Bengal cavalry organisation suffered the most upheaval because of the Mutiny. A common belief is that all the regular Bengal cavalry mutinied and all the irregular cavalry remained true to their salt. The ten regular regiments disappeared: seven because of mutiny and three upon being disarmed and disbanded.[70] But the irregulars also suffered a high level of mutinies and problems. Of the eighteen irregular regiments, Perry determined that only three stayed completely loyal. Among the others he found: part of the unit mutinied in six cases; three units mutinied; five were disarmed; and one was disbanded on the spot.[71]

Out of the wreckage eight irregular regiments formed the backbone of the new Bengal cavalry. The three regiments that had never mutinied were the 1st (Skinner's), 2nd (Gardner's) and the 6th, which was a descendant of the Oudh Irregular Horse. Two regiments where part of the unit had mutinied were taken into the post-Mutiny Bengal cavalry. One was the 4th Local Horse. This unit was once commanded by Robert Skinner, younger brother of James Skinner. Robert Skinner committed suicide because one of his wives might have been unfaithful.[72] The other unit was the 9th, raised in 1841, without much history. Surprisingly, three units that had been disarmed during the Mutiny were also made part of the new Bengal cavalry: the old 7th, 17th, and 18th.

Table III.5.5 shows which irregular unit became which regiment in the post-Mutiny Bengal army.

Table III.5.5: Bengal Cavalry Number and Title Changes, 1855–1914

Irregular Unit	Mutiny History	New Bengal Cavalry Number	1914 Name
1st Skinner's Horse	Loyal	1	1st Duke of York's Own Lancers (Skinner's Horse)
2nd Gardner's Horse	Loyal	2	2nd Lancers (Gardner's Horse)
4th Local Horse	Part mutinied	3	3rd Skinner's Horse
6th Irregular Cavalry	Loyal	4	4th Cavalry
7th Irregular Cavalry	Disarmed	5	5th Cavalry
8th Irregular Cavalry	Part mutinied	6	6th King Edward's Own Cavalry
17th Irregular Cavalry	Disarmed	7	7th Hariana Lancers
18th Irregular Cavalry	Disarmed	8	8th Cavalry

Source: Perry, 'Armies P1', pp. 116–18, 149; Indian Army List (July 1914), pp. 408–15; Carman, Uniforms Cavalry, pp. 49–73. Carman shows two 17th irregular cavalry regiments becoming the 7th Lancers and 8th Cavalry and no 18th Irregular. Perry shows the 18th Irregular becoming the 8th Cavalry, and that is what is shown here.

The 9th through the 18th were regiments that had been raised for service during the Mutiny and then retained to be part of the new Bengal army. They were the survivors among many wartime cavalry units raised.[73]

Uniforms 1861–1903

The 1863 Dress Regulations set out the dress of the eighteen post-Mutiny Bengal cavalry regiments. The eight pre-Mutiny irregular units were to wear alkalaks (see Table III.5.6 for their colours). The alkalak was worn by British and native officers, as well as the sowars of these eight regiments.[74]

The British officers of the old eight regiments in full dress wore alkalaks with a grey felt helmet and a plume.[75] The officers of the other ten regiments in 1863 wore cavalry tunics of regimental colour with collar and cuffs of the facing colour. The tunic had four rows of black cord that hung loosely. Overalls were blue except for regiments with green tunics. They wore green overalls.[76]

Table III.5.6: Uniforms of Eight Surviving Bengal Irregular Cavalry Regiments

Regiment	Colour of Alkalak or Tunic	Type	Facing Colour
1st Skinner's Horse	Yellow[a]	Alkalak	Red[b]
2nd Gardner's Horse	Emerald green[c]	Alkalak	None[c]
4th Local Horse	Scarlet[d]	Alkalak	Blue[d]
6th Irregular Cavalry	Scarlet[e]	Alkalak	Blue[e]
7th Irregular Cavalry	Scarlet[f]	Alkalak	Blue[f]
8th Irregular Cavalry	Blue[g]	Alkalak	Red[g]
17th Irregular Cavalry	Red[h]	Alkalak	Dark blue[h]
18th Irregular Cavalry	Blue[i]	Alkalak	Scarlet[i]

Notes: [a] Between 1878 and 1891 the colour of the tunic was a drab yellow or yellowish-khaki. Prior to and after these years, the yellow was a brighter shade (Rothero, *Skinner's Horse*, p. 12; Carman, *Uniforms Cavalry*, p. 54).
[b] Changed in 1879 to black (Mollo, *Army*, p. 113).
[c] Red facings were added in 1870. Garment and facing colours changed to blue and light blue in 1887 (Mollo, *Army*, p. 113).
[d] In 1881, colour was change to drab. Then, in 1891, the colour changed again to blue with yellow facings (Mollo, *Army*, p. 113).
[e] Mollo, *Army*, p. 113.
[f] Mollo, *Army*, p. 113.
[g] Mollo, *Army*, p. 113.
[h] This was carried over from pre-Mutiny days and lasted down to 1914 (Carman, *Uniforms Cavalry*, p. 72; Bowling, *Cavalry*, p. 22).
[i] This was carried over from pre-Mutiny days and lasted down to 1914 (Carman, *Uniforms Cavalry*, p. 72; Bowling, *Cavalry*, p. 22). But Bowling states the regiment's 1914 tunic was dark blue (Carman, *Uniforms Cavalry*, p. 22).

The 1874 Dress Regulations for Bengal cavalry set a general pattern for the dress of British officers in the Bengal cavalry that would be followed until 1913. For cold weather Review Order A (full dress when away from the troops), they would wear a tunic.[77]

The 1874 Dress Regulations provided the following for the five lancer regiments (the 10th, 11th, 13th, 14th, and 19th): a lancer jacket, crimson and gold girdle, white pantaloons, and Napoleon boots.[78] The other regiments wore a white cork helmet with gilt spike and a cavalry tunic.

The senior eight regiments had five gold or silver loops across the front of their tunics. Later photographs show the lancer tunics to be very similar to the lancer tunics worn in the British army (§II-*7-a Dragoon Guards and Dragoons*). The main difference was that some of the regiments didn't have full plastrons (see Table III.5.8) The other cavalry regiments had black cord loops. Pouch belts were of regimental lace, and the pouches were of cloth of the facing colour. All had white riding breeches and Napoleon boots.[79] The loops worn by the Bengal cavalry regiments tended to be plaited.[80]

When serving with the regiment on mounted duties, Review Order B, the British officer would wear a kurta (see §*III-1* Indian Glossary) of regimental colour and pattern and a regimental turban.[81] Image III:30 gives the names of the different parts of this order of dress.

The 1874 Bengal Dress Regulations state that the native officers of the first eight regiments would wear an alkalak, and the remainder a kurta. Both would be of regimental colour.[82] However, the wearing of alkalaks dropped away in the 1886 Dress Regulations.[83] It is interesting to observe that the 1874 Regulations specify a Kashmir shawl as an option, along with a gold embroidered shawl, for the cummerbund for British officers in Review Order B and for native officers in review dress.[84] In 1886, with the alkalak going out of style, the dress regulations called for these regiments to wear a 'coat' or loose frock, later known as a kurta.[85] The 1886 Regulations followed the 1874 systems of A and B dress. It states that the Bengal cavalry regiments where the British officers would wear a kurta, turban, and cummerbund were the 1st, 2nd, 5th, 6th, 7th, 8th, 12th, and 15th Bengal cavalry regiments. The British officers of the 9th, 10th, 11th, 13th, 18th, and 19th Bengal Lancers also wore the kurta, turban, and cummerbund of their men.[86] Table III.5.7 shows the colours of these items between 1860 and 1886 for Bengal cavalry regiments with higher numbers.

Table III.5.7: Bengal Cavalry Regiments Kurta, Turban, and Cummerbund Colours

Regiment	1860s and 1874 Kurta Colour	1860s and 1874 Kurta Trim	1860s and 1874 Turban Colour	1860s and 1874 Cummerbund	1886 Kurta Colour	1886 Kurta Trim	1886 Turban	1886 Cummerbund
9	Blue	Red	Red		Dark blue	White		
10	Blue	Scarlet	Scarlet	Red	Blue	Scarlet	Blue	Red
11	Blue	None?		Red	Blue	?	Blue and white	Red
12	Blue	Blue	Blue		Blue	Blue	Blue	Red?[a]
13	Blue?	Scarlet			Dark blue	Scarlet?		
14	Unknown	Unknown	Unknown	Unknown	Dark blue	Scarlet	Red?	
15	Rifle green	Scarlet			Blue	Scarlet?		
16[b]	Green[c]	Red			Blue	Blue		
17[d]	Blue	Red	Blue	Red Kashmir shawl	Blue	White		
18	Red	Blue			Scarlet or red, depending on rank	Blue		
19[e]	Blue	Light blue			Blue	Blue[f]		

Source: Carman, *Uniforms Cavalry*, p. 40, pp. 76–8, 82–4, 86, 88, 90, 92, 94, 96, 97, 99, 100, 102, and 103.

Notes: [a] Red cummerbund, c. 1900 (Carman, *Uniforms Cavalry*, p. 86).
[b] Raised during the Mutiny and became the 16th Cavalry. Dissolved in 1882 and reraised in 1885 (Carman, *Uniforms Cavalry*, pp. 94 and 96).
[c] It is not clear if the shade was pale or rifle green (Carman, *Uniforms Cavalry*, pp. 94).
[d] Raised during the Mutiny and became the 17th Cavalry. Dissolved in 1882 and reraised in 1885 (Carman, *Uniforms Cavalry*, pp. 97 and 99).
[e] Raised in 1860, after the Mutiny (Carman, *Uniforms Cavalry*, p. 102).
[f] Likely light blue, and maybe French grey (Bowling, *Indian Cavalry*, p. 42).

Over time, most of the Bengal regiments converted to become lancer regiments. Table III.5.8 gives the date of conversion and plastron type.

Table III.5.8: Bengal Cavalry Regiments: Plastron Worn and Date of Conversion to Lancer Status

Regiment	Plastron Type	Date Converted to Lancers
1	Full	1896
2	Lapel turned back	1890
3[a]		
4	Lapel turned back	1890
5[a]		
6[a]		
7	Lapel turned back	1900
8	Full	1900
9	Lapel turned back	1886
10	Full	1874
11	Full	1864
12[a]		
13	Full	1864
14	Full	1864
15	Full	1890
16	Lapel turned back	1900[b]
17	Lapel turned back	1900[c]
18	Full to 1901, then lapel turned back	1885
19	Lapel turned back	1864[d]

Sources: Mollo, *Army*, pp. 112 and 115; Carman, *Uniforms Cavalry*, pp. 55, 57, 72, 74, 76–7, 83, 88, 94, 96, 99, 100, and 103.
Notes: [a] Never converted to lancers.
[b] Carman says 1901.
[c] Carman states they became lancers in 1900, but uniform did not change at once.
[d] Carman says 1866.

Several regiments were lancers in spite of having 'Cavalry' or 'Horse' in their title, viz. the 4th, 8th, 9th, 16th, and 17th Regiments.

From the Mutiny to at least 1903, British officers wore British-style uniforms, as called for in the 1903 Regulations. An idea of what they looked like can be gained from looking at Images III:27, III:33, and III:34.

An Indian touch was added to these uniforms by having elaborate braid on the sleeves. This braid also appeared on the kurta. For examples of cuff braid, see Images III:35 and III:36.

III:33 Lieutenant Colonel J.C.F. Gordon, 6th Bengal Cavalry (Prince of Wales), c. 1896
Note the plaited braid across the front of the uniform worn by many Bengal cavalry regiments and the Bengal knot on his right sleeve.

After 1907 more and more regiments began to wear the kurtas and some of them tried out very elaborate designs. For examples, see Images III:37 to III:40.

The wearing of the kurtas caused the British officers to look more like the men they were commanding. This is true for both other ranks (see Images III:41 to III:44) and native officers (see Images III:26 and III:44 to III:51). To see Bengal cavalry in colour, see Images C26–C30.

§III-5 Cavalry

III:34 13th Bengal Lancers (later 13th Duke of Connaught's Lancers (Watson's Horse))
This photograph shows a full plastron. Note the pre-1902 double braid on cuffs showing rank.

III:36 A decoration that could be found on native officers' kurta sleeve bottoms. As the wearer achieved higher rank, additional loops would be added in the middle just above the top of the circular trim.

III:35 Bengal knot worn on the cuffs of tunics by British officers, as well as viceroy commissioned officers. As its name suggests, it was most commonly worn by Bengal regiments, but it was also worn by regiments of other presidencies. It was originally allowed to be worn by the first eight regiments of Bengal cavalry (Carman, *Uniforms Cavalry*, p. 91).

III:37 Lieutenant Campbell-Harris, 7th Hariana Lancers, Review Order, 1912

III:38 Lieutenant of the 9th Hodson's Horse, c. 1905

III:40 British Officer of the 16th Cavalry, c. 1900

III:39 12th Cavalry, Newly Joined Subaltern, Full Dress, c. 1914
Note how elaborate kurtas were becoming.

III:41 1st Lancers (Skinner's Horse) Other Ranks
The yellow kurta shows up dark in this photo.

III:42 6th Bengal Cavalry, Officers and Men, c. 1895

III:43 Other Ranks, 11th Bengal Lancers, c. 1895

III:44 Other Ranks and Officer of the 13th Lancers, c. 1895

India

§III-5 Cavalry 297

Opposite

III:45 (top, left) 11th King Edward's Own Lancers Risaldar Darrani (Afghan)
Note the chain and pricker on his pouch belt with the Prince of Wales's plumes on his badge.

III:46 (top, right) 12th Cavalry, Jemadar, Dogra

III:47 (bottom, left) Native Officer of 1st Duke of York's Own Lancers (Skinner's Horse) Note decoration on chest and cuffs. This was worn by both native and British officers. Also note the pouch belt decorations.

III:48 (bottom, right) 3rd Bengal Cavalry, Native Officer, 1897

III:49 Indian Officer, 13th Bengal Lancers, 1897 (later 13th Duke of Connaught's Lancers (Watson's Horse))
Note how the 1 and the 3 on the belt buckle were so close together that they formed a B.

III:50 British and Indian Officers of the 17th Cavalry, c. 1913
Note chest decorations on kurtas of both British and Indian officers.

III:51 Risaldar Major, 2nd Bombay Lancers (later 32nd Lancers), c. 1897

III:52 British Officers of 17th Cavalry, c. 1922
This photograph was taken just before the amalgamation of regiments that took place in 1922. It shows most of the different uniforms worn by an officer in the Indian cavalry. However, drill order and khaki service dress are not shown.

A negative effect of this for the British officers was buying the new kurtas, which added one more item to what was already a large and fairly expensive wardrobe. Image III:52 shows some of the many different orders of dress that British officers wore. The officers paid for their own uniforms.

MADRAS

In 1767, after raising troops that had a short existence, the Madras Presidency took under its command two thousand cavalrymen from the Nawab of Arcot.[87] These proved unreliable as they answered to the Nawab and themselves. Finally, in 1784, the Company took over four of the Nawab's regiments that they had been paying anyway. Most of these revolted, and only the 3rd entered Company service, becoming the 1st regiment. A second regiment was formed from the remains of the other regiments who were willing to serve the Company.[88] Until 1788, the regiments were numbered according to their commander's seniority, and thereafter retained that number.[89] The size of the Madras cavalry grew to eight regiments by the early 1800s, but the additional regiments – the 5th, 6th, 7th, and 8th – were disbanded in the Indian Mutiny era. The 8th was disbanded in 1857 and the other three in 1860.[90] The 4th was disbanded in 1891.[91]

In 1886, the 1st and 2nd Regiments became lancers. The 3rd followed in 1891. In the reorganisation of 1903, these regiments became respectively the 26th, 27th, and 28th Light Cavalry,[92] but they continued to wear their lancer uniforms.[93]

Uniform

Table III.5.9: Uniform and Trim of Madras Cavalry that Existed Past the Mutiny Era

Regiment	Coat	Facing	Date Raised
1	French grey	Pale yellow	1787
2	French grey	Orange	1784
3	French grey	Buff	1784
4	French grey	Deep yellow	1785

Source: Mollo, *Army*, p. 60.

On the path to 1914, there are several events that should be noted besides the normal minor regimental title changes, which will not be covered. Before it was disbanded in 1891,[94] the facings of the 4th changed to scarlet upon becoming the Prince of Wales's Own in 1876.[95] In 1886, the 1st and 2nd Regiments were converted to lancers and given new titles and dress. Then, in 1901, the 3rd was also converted to lancers and given a new title and dress.[96]

In the 1903 reorganisation, the Madras cavalry were given new numbers: the old 1st Madras Lancers became the 26th Light Cavalry, the 2nd Madras Lancers the 27th Light Cavalry, and the 3rd Madras Lancers the 28th Light Cavalry.[97]

The 1886 Regulations provide the following for the two new lancer regiments, the 1st and 2nd:

HEADDRESS
White helmet, probably foreign service-style, with a puggree of dark blue, French grey, and gold. Silver fittings.[98]

TUNIC
French grey lance tunic with full plastron in facing colour.[99] All three regiments originally had buff as their facing colour.[100] The collar and pointed cuffs were buff, as were welts on the sleeve and back seams. The buff piping went down the front of the tunic, around the lower skirt, and up the skirt divisions in the back. Lace was silver, as were the shoulder cords.[101] See Image C31 for pictures of a Madras officer of the 27th Light Cavalry and an other rank of the 26th Light Cavalry.

GIRDLE
The officers' lancer's girdle is shown in regulations between 1886 and 1901 as gold and crimson,[102] standard colours for the Indian cavalry. However, Carman states that they were, in reality, silver with two French grey stripes.[103]

OVERALLS AND RIDING BREECHES
The breeches were dark blue with double silver stripes.[104] However, Bowling states the blue worn by the Madras cavalry was a much lighter shade than that worn by the British cavalry.[105]

The 3rd Regiment of Madras light cavalry wore French grey hussar-style tunics until they were converted to lancers in 1891.[106] Their hussar tunic had six rows of frogging across the front. Each row ended in two dropped loops of frogging, one set on either end of each row (for more details on the frogging see §II-*7-c British Hussars*). The lace was silver. They wore a pouch belt with a red line on it.[107] Other than the tunic, all other items of dress, with the exceptions of the puggree colour design, its pouch belt and pouch, and the sabretache, were the same. Light cavalry carried sabretaches embroidered with a regimental design and battle honours. Lancers carried plain black ones, even in full dress.[108]

Apart from the post-1876 scarlet facings, and of course the puggree colours, pouch belt and pouch, and sabretache decorations, the 4th wore the same hussar-style uniform as the 3rd Madras Cavalry.[109] This was worn until the 4th were disbanded in 1891 and the 3rd became lancers.[110] After becoming lancers in 1891, the British officers of the 3rd Madras Light Cavalry wore a uniform that was similar to that of the other two lancer regiments. This is is outlined in the 1901 Dress Regulations.[111]

Native Officers

After 1861, the other ranks of the Madras cavalry gave up their European-style uniforms and, in Mollo's phrase, 'went irregular' in their dress, wearing turbans and alkalaks.[112] They wore alkalaks until about 1903, when they changed to kurtas.[113]

HEADDRESS
A turban of blue, French grey, and white was worn.[114] The native officers added gold stripes to indicate their rank.[115]

ALKALAK
A French grey alkalak was worn in full dress. It was trimmed with silver lace at the cuffs, neck, and the semi-circular design in the shape of a large bib was on the front of the garment. The braid on the front varied in quality, depending on the man's rank.

CUMMERBUND
The cummerbund followed the colours of the turban.[116]

PANTALOONS AND OVERALLS
The native officers wore sky blue pantaloons with two white cloth stripes.[117]

FOOTWEAR
Black cavalry boots were worn for mounted parades, ankle boots and puttees for dismounted duties.[118]

Rank and File
The rank and file of the Madras cavalry wore, basically, the same uniforms as the native officers. However, their alkalaks did not have silver braid,[119] nor, presumably, did they have gold stripes in their turban or cummerbund. In 1900, the kulla, the little cone worn under the turban, was listed as khaki for the 1st Madras Lancers, white for the 2nd, and grey for the 3rd. However, colour drawings often do not show these colours.[120] Officers' kullas would have gold added to them to show rank.

BOMBAY CAVALRY

PRE-MUTINY

The Bombay cavalry can trace its origins back to 1803 when a troop of cavalry was raised.[121] However, the first regiments did not come into being until 1817 when two regiments were raised using drafts from the Madras cavalry. Then, in 1820, a third regiment was formed with drafts from the two just formed regiments and the Poona Auxiliary Horse (see below).[122] These three regiments formed the Bombay regular cavalry corps until the Mutiny.

British Officers

HEADDRESS
Up until around 1824, the regiments wore a helmet. In 1824, a bell-top shako with silver lace and a white and red hackle was taken into use.[123] This may have been worn up to the Mutiny. Some officers in the 1850s seem to have begun wearing silver dragoon-style helmets with plumes. At least one had a white horsehair plume.[124] Carman makes reference to other helmets, one for the 2nd Regiment and one for the 3rd, which had black and scarlet horsehair plumes respectively.[125] The jury is definitely out on the colour of the plumes.

JACKET
The single-breasted jacket was French grey with white collars and cuffs. Regulations called for it to have five rows of buttons, three to a row, with braid behind the buttons.[126] However, an actual officer's uniform had silver braid across the front that was so thick it hid the cloth because it had extra braid between the five rows of buttons and their braid.[127]

The back seams of their jacket had braid along its seams.

The collar was white, laced all around the edges with 2.54 cm (1 inch) wide silver lace and narrow Russia braid.[128] Pointed cuffs were 7.62 cm (3 inches) deep at the point. They were ornamented with silver lace and Russia braid, which outlined the cuff.[129]

Trousers

The trousers in different orders of dress were either sky blue cloth or white linen. Both had two stripes down the outside seam. The stripes were of silver lace 1.91 cm (¾ inch) wide, leaving a light between them.[130]

Lancers

In 1842, the 1st Cavalry was converted to lancers,[131] which affected their uniforms. As lancers, they wore the following:

Headdress

The 1st Lancers wore the lancer helmet of the period, one with a thick waist. It was black with a red top.[132] The regulations called for a black horsehair plume, but dark cock's feathers seem to have been worn instead.[133] The regulations state the plume was to be 39.37 cm (15½ inches) long.[134]

Jacket

The 'cavalry grey' double-breasted jacket had two rows of nine buttons spaced at equal distance from each other down the front.[135] The two rows were fairly close to each other in the centre of the tunic.[136] Cavalry grey is not defined, but Mollo states, 'portraits show a dark blue-grey colour' for lancer jackets.[137]

Indigenous Troops[138]

The dress uniforms of the native officers and other ranks were generally the same as those worn in the Bengal command. There were differences in the shako and the chest braid.

The Bombay shako was adopted in about 1814 and did not change until the Mutiny. It was taller than the Bengal shako for much of this period. The red Bombay coatee had seven sets of white braids on the chest.

Bombay Irregular Cavalry

In the pre-Mutiny period, the Bombay command had two regiments of irregular cavalry: the Poona Horse and the Scinde Horse. The Poona Horse were descendants of men who had come from the Peishwa's troops.[139] In the 1850s, the British officers wore a dragoon helmet and a double-breasted coatee.[140] The coatee was dark with red facings.[141] Other ranks wore a red turban with a dark green alkalak with red facings and gold lace. They had a red cummerbund.[142]

The Scinde Horse was descended from a Kutch Levy, a group of men from the Scinde Horse sent out to keep the peace on the Kutch–Sind border. In 1839, men of the Kutch Levy were sent to Sind and became the Scinde Irregular Horse.[143]

The British officers of the Scinde Horse wore a silver dragoon helmet with a black plume. They wore a dark green hussar-style jacket with heavy cording on the front and a hussar-style sash with silver slides. Their overalls were dark green with two stripes of silver lace.[144]

Other ranks wore a red turban and a (dark?) green alkalak with red facings and silver lace. The cummerbund was red. They seem to have worn green pyjamas.[145] As can be seen, except for the lace colour, the uniform looks back to the parent unit, the Poona Horse. A 2nd Scinde Horse was raised in 1846.[146] Carman wrote that it dressed the same as the 1st.[147]

Following the Mutiny, the Poona Irregular Horse were put on a more regular establishment in 1861, but were not made the 4th Bombay Cavalry until 1885.[148] The same thing happened to the 1st and 2nd Scinde Irregulars in 1861, which were made the 5th and the 6th Bombay Cavalry in 1885.[149]

There were other irregular units raised before the Mutiny that did not survive – for example, the 1st and 2nd South Mahratta Horse (1850 and 1858) and the Gujarat Horse (1839).[150]

POST-MUTINY

Following the Mutiny, British officers seem to have worn the uniform prescribed by the 1850 Regulations for cavalry, wearing it between 1860 and the 1880s.

Headdress

The regulations of 1850 called for a fur cap for British officers in full dress, but, instead, the officers may have continued to wear the pre-Mutiny dragoon-style helmet. Over time, it was replaced with the foreign service helmet.[151]

In 1884, new dress regulations were issued. By this time, two of the three old Bombay regiments were lancers, the 1st in 1880 and the 2nd in 1883.[152] All three regiments wore a white helmet, presumably an overseas helmet, with a regimental puggree.[153]

Lancers

Tunic

The British officers (BOs) of the 1st Lancers, when not with the men, wore a dark green lancer tunic with a scarlet plastron and scarlet piping.[154] The 2nd Lancers' BO tunic was likely also dark green. Its plastron and piping were white (see Table III.5.10).

The collar and pointed cuffs were scarlet with gold trim lace for the 1st.[155] The facings were white for the 2nd.[156]

Pouch Belt

For both regiments, the pouch belt consisted of gold zigzag lace. On it was an unusual feature, a chain and whistle. They were worn on the pouch belts of all Bombay cavalry regiments. The pouch had a silver top.[157]

Girdle

The girdle for the 1st Regiment was gold with two crimson silk stripes.[158] The same girdle was probably worn by the 2nd Lancers. The basis for this supposition is that the 1901 Dress Regulations state that the uniform of the 2nd Lancers, except for the facings, is the same as that of the 1st.[159]

Overalls

The 1st Lancers wore dark green overalls with a gold stripe on either side of the outside leg seam.[160] Again, this was likely true for the 2nd Bombay Lancers.

Lancers British Officers

When in full dress with their men, British officers wore a dark green kurta. The collar and cuffs were scarlet for the 1st Lancers and probably white for the 2nd. In both regiments, the cummerbund was red, and they wore drab cord breeches. In 1903, the kurta colour became dark blue, and the kurta became full dress for all occasions. The breeches were changed to white moleskin. In addition, British officers could wear blue trousers or breeches with scarlet stripes.[161]

Lancers Viceroy Commissioned Officers

The VCOs wore a green kurta up to 1903. After 1903, it was dark blue. The kurta had collar, cuff, and kurta piping in the regimental colour, red for the 1st and white for the 2nd. The turban colour would vary by regiment. The VCOs had gold stripes added to show their rank.

Their breeches were white, and in the 1880s and 1890s, they wore knee boots.

III:53 British Officer of the 3rd Bombay Cavalry (later the 33rd Light Cavalry), c. 1897
He is wearing a dragoon-style tunic. Note the whistle carried on his pouch belt. This was standard in all Bombay cavalry regiments.

3rd Bombay Cavalry Regiment

The conversion of the 1st and 2nd regiments to lancers left the 3rd to soldier on as a regular cavalry regiment.

HEADDRESS

The British officers of the 3rd Cavalry Regiment wore a white overseas helmet with a regimental puggree.

TUNIC

British officers wore a dragoon-style tunic with eight buttons down the front (see §II-7-a, British Dragoons).[162] The tunic was dark green up to 1903, and thereafter, dark blue (see Image III:53).[163]

Table III.5.10 shows the plastron colours for all the cavalry/lancer regiments.

4th, 5th, and 6th Bombay Cavalry

The Poona Horse and the 1st and 2nd Scinde Regiments were tied more closely to the Bombay cavalry establishment after the Mutiny. All were known for a short period in 1861 as silladar cavalry, but reverted back to their previous name in the same year. The three were placed in the Bombay cavalry line in 1885 as the 4th, 5th, and 6th Bombay Cavalry respectively.[164]

Table III.5.10: Cavalry Plastrons and Date of Conversion to Lancers

Regiment	Name	Plastron Type	Date Became Lancers	Plastron Colour
1	Lancers	Full[a]	1880	Scarlet
2	Lancers	Full[b]	1883	White
3	Light Cavalry			
4	Horse			
5	Horse			
6	Horse			
7	Lancers	Full[c]	1890	Buff (pink)[d]

Source: Bowling, *Cavalry*, pp. 56–64.
Notes: [a] Bowling, *Cavalry*, p. 56, drawing, last figure, front row.
[b] Bowling, *Cavalry*, p. 59, drawing, figure no. 4.
[c] Bowling, *Cavalry*, p. 64, p. 32, figure no. 106.
[d] The official facing colour was buff, but in fact it was salmon pink.

Between the early 1880s and 1901, the 3rd, 4th, 5th, and 6th Bombay Cavalry all wore similar uniforms.[165] The facing colour, turban colour, and cummerbund colour details would have been the main differences. The 3rd has already been covered. The other three regiments wore the colours set out in Table III.5.11.

Table III.5.11: Bombay Cavalry Tunic and Kurta Colours, and Facing Colours

Regiment	British Officers — Tunic Colour	British Officers — Type	British Officers — Facing Colour	VCOs and Other Ranks — Kurta Colour	VCOs and Other Ranks — Facing Colour	Cummerbund	Breeches
34th (Poona Horse)	Dark green	Dragoon	French grey	(Dark) green	Light French grey	Red	Yellow
35th (1st Scinde)	(Dark) green	Hussar (1870)	Likely white	Dark green	White		
36th (2nd Scinde)	Likely dark green		Primrose	Dark green	Primrose	Red	White

Source: Carman, *Uniforms Cavalry*, pp. 160, 163 (nos. 150 and 151), and 166.

See Image III:54 for a photograph of an other rank of the 1st Bombay Lancers and Image III:55 for a photograph of an officer of the 34th Poona Horse in his kurta.

For a painting of Bombay other ranks of the 32nd, 33rd, and 34th Regiments in full dress, see Image C33.

III:54 Indian Officer, 1st Bombay Lancers (later 31st Lancers), c. 1897
In 1897, this kurta was dark green. It changed to dark blue in 1903.

III:55 Frank Alexander de Pass of the 34th Poona Horse
This officer earned a Victoria Cross in France in 1914.

7th Bombay Cavalry

The 7th Bombay Cavalry were the last Bombay cavalry regiment raised. They were raised in 1885 in Scinde. In 1886, they were given the subtitle Baluch Horse, and in 1890 became lancers.[166]

At first, the regiment wore dark green, the same as the other regiments. Soon after they became lancers in 1890, khaki with buff (salmon pink) facings replaced the green uniforms.[167] The pouch belt was brown leather and, unusually, had a silver curb chain on its edges.[168] As a Bombay regiment, it had the expected chain and whistle.[169] The breeches were khaki,[170] and the cummerbund was red.[171]

III:56 Officer in Review Order and Trumpeter in Drill Order of the 7th Bombay Lancers (Baluch Horse) (later 37th Lancers (Baluch Horse))

CAVALRY OF FRONTIER FORCE AND GUIDES

After conquering the Sikhs and annexing the Punjab, the British faced two problems. The first was raids by tribesmen from across the border. The other was potential problems from the unemployed men who had been in the now disbanded Sikh army. Soldiers from the regular Bengal army did not like to serve on the frontier, so they were of limited help in guarding against raids.[172]

To solve these problems, the British raised four regiments of Sikh infantry for service on the frontier in 1846/7.[173] In December 1846 they also raised a the Corps of Guides, consisting of both cavalry and infantry.[174] Neither of these forces was sufficient, and in 1849, five Punjab cavalry and five Punjab infantry regiments were raised.[175] These were combined together with the guides to form the Punjab Irregular Frontier Force,[176] known as the 'Piffers'. The Piffers viewed themselves as the Indian army's *corps d'élite*,[177] although the Gurkhas were certain to disagree.

The Punjab Frontier Force regiments, from their formation, were under the command of the civil authorities, first the lieutenant governor of the Punjab, and, above him, the Foreign Department of the Government of India.[178] This civilian control lasted until 1886, when the Piffers were 'brought directly under the commander-in-chief, India, as part of the Bengal army'.[179]

THE GUIDES

Pre-Mutiny

From the first, H.B. Lumsden, the lieutenant who commanded the first Guides, had his men dress in a loose turban and body garments. Then, in 1849, he had their clothes dyed in river mud. This earned the men the title 'Mudlarks.'[180]

Post-Mutiny British Officers

HEADDRESS
A drawing by R. Simkin shows British officers wearing a white helmet with a blue and gold puggree.[181]

TUNIC
The dress regulations of 1886 describe a drab tunic of hussar pattern with five rows of drab silk cord hanging loosely across the front of the tunic. The full dress tunic had red velvet facings, and the lace was drab silk.

III:57 Guide's Special Dress Kurta, c. 1900
Drawing shows uniform worn after the Guides were equipped as a lancer regiment in 1896. Lancer pickers and chains are worn on the pouch belt. Note the chest design of three double rows of trim worn by king's viceroy officers and NCOs. These trim rows were the same on both sides of the center column. The trim was made of drab braid. The same braid appears on the cuffs. The collar and the pointed cuffs are red.

POUCH AND POUCH BELT
According to the dress regulations of 1886 these were of brown leather. The pouch had a silver lid.

PANTALOONS AND OVERALLS
The dress regulations of 1886 call for breeches of drab cord, worn with high boots. The dress overalls had two drab lace stripes with a welt of red between them. In 1896, it was ordered that the Guides be equipped as lancers. The most obvious effect this had on their dress was on the pickers and chains on the pouch belt.[182]

Post-Mutiny Viceroy Commissioned Officers

HEADDRESS
A blue and gold turban was worn. If the officer's religion called for a kulla, it was red.

KURTA
The drab kurta of the Guides VCOs was unusual. On the front of the kurta were three sets of drab braid. The braid on the front of the kurta consisted of two columns of braid, one on each side of the front centre line of the kurta. From a column, the braid came out, made a loop, and extended towards the front edge of the chest (see Image III:57). These sets of braid were repeated three times. The top one extended to the edge of the shoulder cords. The next one from the top was shorter in length, and the bottom one, which was just above the cummerbund, was the shortest of the three.

The braid designs were on both sides of the kurta, making six of them in all.

The kurta had a turn-down red collar and pointed cuffs. Both had drab braid around them.

CUMMERBUND
The cummerbund was red.

III:58 Officer and Other Ranks of the Guides (Cavalry), c. 1895
The three figures on the right are the other ranks.

Post-Mutiny NCOs and Other Ranks
The NCOs wore a dress uniform that was very similar to that of the VCOs. The main difference was that their turn-down collar was scarlet cloth, and they seem to have worn khaki puttees.[183]

Other ranks wore a collarless khaki kurta and pouch belt and pickers.[184]

PUNJAB CAVALRY

Five cavalry regiments were raised in the Punjab by the British in 1849.

Pre-Mutiny Uniforms[185]
Prior to the Mutiny, the Punjab regiments wore the following uniforms:

British officers wore a dragoon-style helmet with a plume. They wore either an alkalak or a European-style coat.[186]

The uniform of enlisted men is described in Table III.5.12.

Table III.5.12: Punjab Cavaly Enlisted Men, Pre-Mutiny

Regiment	Alkalak Colour	Facing Colour	Lace Colour
1	Dark blue	Buff	Silver
2	Scarlet	Black	Silver
3	Dark blue	—	Silver
4	Scarlet	Scarlet	Gold
5	Scarlet	Scarlet	Gold

Post-Mutiny British Officers[187]

The following uniforms were worn by British officers when not parading with their men (Review Order A): Up to 1903, this was considered full dress.

Table III.5.13: British Officers' Uniforms

Regiment	Uniform Style	Uniform Colour	Collar and Cuff Colour	Hanging Cord Colour[a]	Loose or Plaited	1914 Regimental Number
1	Hussar	Dark blue	Red	5 black	Loose	21
2	Hussar	Red	Blue	5 gold	Loose	22
3	Hussar	Blue	Scarlet	5 black	Loose	23
4	Disbanded in 1882[b]					
5	Single-breasted	Dark green	Scarlet	6 gold	Plaited	25

Note: [a] The colour of the hanging chest cords is based on Carman, *Uniforms Cavalry*. Mollo states British officers wore cavalry tunics with five loops down the front, black before 1874, gold after, but the 2nd and 4th adopted gold before (Mollo, *Army*, p. 117).
[b] Bowling, *Cavalry*, p. 50.

When in full dress with the men, Review Order B, BOs wore a helmet, a kurta the colour of their tunics, a red cummerbund, and white breeches.[188] After 1903, Review Order B became full dress, and a turban replaced the helmet. Image III:59 shows British officers of the 25th Cavalry in European dress, and Image III:60 shows the officers of this regiment after they changed to kurtas.

III:59 Group of British Officers of the 25th Cavalry, c. 1908
Note the loose cording across the chest and the braiding coming down the sleeves. Loose-hanging cords were unusual in the Frontier Force; usually they wore their cords plaited. Note how only the senior officer has a Bengal knot on his sleeves.

III:60 Officers of the 25th Cavalry, c. 1911
The regiment had now changed over to kurtas in conformity with the rest of the Indian cavalry.

Post-Mutiny Viceroy Commissioned Officers[189]

The VCOs wore a turban of regimental pattern. Until the early 1880s, the VCOs wore alkalaks, probably in the regimental colour: 1st – dark blue; 2nd – red; 3rd – blue; and 5th – dark green. The VCOs of the 2nd continued to wear alkalaks until around 1900.[190] When the alkalak fell out of favour, they changed to kurtas of regimental colour and gold lace. The VCOs of the 1st Punjab had the distinction of wearing three black cords hanging loosely across the chest of their kurta.[191] The VCOs of the 5th had twisted gold cord on the shoulders of their kurtas.[192] This was a most unusual distinction.

All regiments had gold lace, red cummerbunds, and white breeches.[193]

HYDERABAD CONTINGENT CAVALRY

The regiments that became the Hyderabad Contingent Cavalry can trace their origins back to three local regiments of the nizam of Hyderabad. These were reorganised in 1816 under the command of viceroy commissioned officers with British advisors. In 1825, British officers took command of the regiments. In 1826, a 4th regiment was raised, and an existing regiment, numbered the 5th, was brought under British control.[194] However, the 5th was disbanded in 1853.[195] In 1854, the title of the regiments was changed from Nizam's Cavalry to the 1st through 4th Cavalry, Hyderabad Contingent.

By and large, the Hyderabad regiments remained loyal during the Mutiny. Only elements of the 1st gave reason for doubt; part of it was disarmed in 1857.[196]

All four regiments continued after the Mutiny, earning one battle honour.[197] The honour was awarded to the 3rd Cavalry for service in Burma in 1885–7, but they were disbanded shortly thereafter.[198] The lack of honours was to be expected, because the contingent was considered a local corps.

In 1890, all four regiments became lancers.[199] In 1903, the contingent ceased being a local corps and became a part of the wider Indian army. As part of this change, the 3rd Regiment was disbanded and the other regiments given new numbers as follows: the 1st became the 20th, the 2nd the 29th, and the 4th the 30th.[200] Also in 1903, the 1st was converted from lancers to horse, becoming the 20th Deccan Horse.[201] There were no further noteworthy changes to the regiments between 1903 and 1914.[202]

Pre-Mutiny Uniforms, 1824–57[203]

In general, the uniforms worn by the Hyderabad Contingent followed those worn by the Madras army, except their jackets and alkalaks were dark green.

British officers of the five regiments wore hussar jackets with heavy frogging as worn by Napoleon's hussars and early British hussars.[204] Native officers wore a turban and alkalak with gold lace to show rank. Other ranks wore a plain alkalak and a turban.

Post-Mutiny British Officers

Headdress

Cork helmets with a brass spike. Wrapped around the helmet was a cloth of regimental pattern, usually the same design as the cummerbund.

Tunic

Until 1890, the regiments wore a rifle green single-breasted tunic with six rows of frogging on the front made of gold chain braid. Each row ended in a cap and drops. The tunic was fastened closed with olivets. The gold chain braid also went down the front of the tunic, around the bottom edges to the back, where it outlined the rear skirts. The back seams were traced by double gold chain. At the top of the back it ended in an elongated crow's foot, and at the bottom it terminated in a trefoil knot.[205]

The collar and cuffs were the same colour as the tunic. The collar was trimmed on top with gold lace.[206] If the uniform carefully followed the British hussar pattern, the cuffs would have a Hungarian knot on it, with its complexity depending on the wearer's rank.[207] The shoulder straps were of the hussar pattern. It was made of plaited gold chain gimp.[208]

Pantaloons and Overalls

British officers wore either white Melton riding breeches or rifle green overalls with a double gold stripe. The stripes were 1.91 cm (¾ inch) wide.[209]

Post-Mutiny Viceroy Commissioned Officers

Headdress

Blue turbans.[210]

Long Blouses (Kurtas)

Viceroy commissioned officers wore a kurta of rifle green with gold lace.[211]

Netherwear

Brown pyjamas.[212]

British Officers After 1890

In 1890, all four regiments were converted to lancers, and British officers adopted lancer tunics.[213]

The headdress and nether garments did not change except for style changes in the helmet.

Lancer Tunic

The adoption of the lancer-style tunic was the main uniform change made in 1890. The new double-breasted lancer tunic was rifle green with a white plastron.[214]

The Hyderabad regiments wore their plastrons and lapels in different ways as shown in Table III.5.14 (Image III:29(A and B)).

The double-breasted rifle green tunic had two rows of seven buttons down the front. These began just below the shoulder cords and ended at the waist under the lancer's girdle. The buttons tapered down from 20.32 cm (8 inches) apart at the top to 10.16 cm (4 inches) at the bottom. In addition to the buttons, the tunic had white piping down the front, around the skirts, and marking the split in the skirt at the back. The rear skirts had two slashes. Each had three buttons. The seam on the back of the tunic was marked with piping (Image III:29(C)).[215]

Table III.5.14: Hyderabad Plastrons

Regiment	Full Plastron	Lapel Turned Back
1 (20th)	Ceased being lancers in 1903[a]	
2 (29th)	Yes	
3[b]		
4 (30th)		Yes

Source: Carman, *Uniforms Cavalry*, pp. 113–14; Bowling, *Cavalry*, p. 45; Mollo, *Army*, p. 118, plate 108.
Notes: [a] Whether they wore a plastron or lapel turned back during the thirteen years of being lancers is unknown.
[b] Disbanded 1903. Whether they wore a plastron or lapel turned back during the thirteen years of being lancers is unknown.

Collar

The standing square collar was white. For field officers, it had gold lace at the front, top, and bottom. For officers below field rank, the gold lace was only at the front and top.[216] See Image II:13(1) for an example of the collar.

Cuffs

The white cuffs were pointed. Field officers had two rows of 2.54 cm (1 inch) gold lace above the cuff. Captains and ranks below had one row. All had two small buttons on the cuff.[217] See Image I.1(5) (Polish cuff).

Lancer Girdle

The girdle was 6.35 cm (2½ inches) wide and made of gold lace. It had two white stripes on it.[218]

Lancer Pouch Belt and Pouch

In 1890, the four regiments adopted a pouch belt of gold 'train' lace with a white silk central stripe.[219] The belt had chains and prickers that were fixed to a crown-shaped fastening. The pouch had a silver top with the letters 'HCL' and was said to have crossed lances behind the letters. However, Carman included a drawing of a pouch made in 1892 that did not have lances.[220] A crown was above the letters and, if they appeared, the lances.[221]

Pantaloons and Overalls

On duty with the men, white leather pantaloons were worn. On other occasions, cloth pantaloons of rifle green with double gold lace stripes could be worn. Officers also could wear cloth rifle green overalls.[222]

1903 and After

In 1903, the Hyderabad Contingent ceased being a local force and became part of the Indian army. The regiments were given new numbers. The British officers of the new 29th and 30th (old 2nd and 4th Hyderabad Lancers) continued to wear lancer's tunics until 1913.[223]

Under the 1913 Dress Regulations, the British officers of both the 29th and 30th began to wear a dark green kurta in full dress. The lancer tunic was now optional.[224]

In addition, as noted above, the 1st Lancers stopped being lancers and became the 20th Deccan Horse. As such, they no longer wore lancer dress. However, perhaps seeing the future, they do not seem to have adopted a tunic. Rather, they began wearing a kurta when they would have worn a tunic.[225]

The 20th Deccan Horse Post-1903 Uniform

Headdress

British officers wore a white Wolseley helmet with a spike – referred to as a hog spear – and regimental puggree. Viceroy commissioned officers wore a turban.

Kurta

A green cloth kurta with a white collar was worn. There was 1.91 cm (¾ inch) wide hussar lace around the collar, down the front, and around the cuffs. There were chains on the shoulders.[226]

Pouch Belt and Pouch

Their pouch belt was now gold hussar lace with a white stripe and silver devices. The pouch was dark green leather. It had a gilt flap which had silver devices on it.[227]

Viceroy Commissioned Officers[228]

In 1886, viceroy commissioned officers wore rifle green kurtas. Rank was shown by gold lace at the collar and cuffs. The lace was 2.54 cm (1 inch) wide for rissaldars and 1.91 cm (¾ inch) wide for jemedars. They had a blue turban and brown pyjamas, but white breeches were also worn.

In the early 1890s, the kurta seems to have been blue, but the 1901 Dress Regulations call for rifle green again.

The 1901 Regulations called for steel shoulder chains with silver rank badges on them. The same regulations also describe the cummerbund as a red shawl with different regimental designs on it. It stated that the breeches of the 1st, 2nd, and 3rd were khaki and the 4th yellow. Then, confusingly, the pantaloons were mentioned as being of a white material.

Other Ranks

The enlisted men wore basically the same uniform as the viceroy commissioned officers. The main difference was that the enlisted men did not have rank lace.

Dress Uniform

The Hyderabad Contingent cavalry officers followed the same general pattern as the Bengal cavalry officers when it came to their dress uniforms. The 1886 Dress Regulations state that European officers would wear a tunic with six loops of gold chain lace across the breast.[229] For undress, a kurta could be worn. A Kashmir cummerbund and a turban were worn on mounted parades.[230] The cummerbund clearly signals that a kurta was being worn on mounted parades.

The native officers wore a kurta.[231] The skirts of the kurtas were to reach within 7.62 cm (3 inches) of the knee. This was standard for all Indian army kurtas.

In 1890, the four Hyderabad cavalry regiments became lancers, and as the British officers began wearing a lancer's tunic,[232] the native officers continued to wear kurtas.[233]

Other ranks wore a kurta, cummerbund, turban, and, where appropriate, a kulla (see Image III:61 and also Image C32).

THE CENTRAL INDIA HORSE

The Central India Horse (CIH) at first consisted of three regiments, the amalgamation of several regiments that had been raised to put down and control unrest in central India.[234] The 3rd CIH was disbanded in 1861, leaving two regiments for the post-Mutiny period.[235] There is disagreement about exactly which units were used to form the 1st and 2nd CIH.[236]

The new regiments were a local corps, although they could be pulled away for other duties. They were under the command of the Government of India,[237] like the Piffers had been in their early days. The CIH remained under civilian control until 1914.

To stress that they were an elite corps, the CIH discharged all their low-caste men as soon as possible after the Mutiny.[238] So much for loyalty and gratitude to the type of men who had helped the British in their crisis.

UNIFORMS

After 1870, the two regiments of the CIH wore practically the same uniform. The descriptions below apply to both regiments. Differences will be specifically noted.

At first, though, the uniforms were very different. The 1st Regiment based their organisation and drab uniform on the Corps of Guides.[239] The 2nd and 3rd Regiments wore red turbans and green alkalaks. Their commander, William Beatson, had once served with the Nizam of Hyderabad's Cavalry and may have brought their colour scheme with him for his new regiments.[240]

III:61 2nd Hyderabad Lancers (later 29th Lancers), Other Ranks

Early on, perhaps as soon as 1868, the CIH regiments were dressed in drab.[241] This is confirmed by the 1886 Dress Regulations.

British Officers

The 1886 Dress Regulations specify the uniform listed below.

HEADDRESS
The British officers were to wear a drab-coloured helmet, probably the pre-1902 colonial helmet (Image II:17, top row). It had a small puggree of blue and gold.[242]

TUNIC
The drab single-breasted full dress tunic was braided with gold cord.[243] The chest had five drop loops with single eyes in the centre, and olivets. There were gold Hungarian knots for all ranks. The two buttons on each cuff and the one button on each shoulder were gilt half-balls.[244] The tunic was edged all around with gold cord. Gold cord also traced out the back seams. There was a crow's foot at the top of each corded seam. The cord continued down to the tunic's rear skirt, where the cords doubled and ended in a Hungarian knot 1.91 cm (¾ inch) from the bottom of the skirt.[245]

Collar and Cuffs
The collar was maroon velvet. It had gold light dragoon lace around the top and was edged with gold cord.[246]

The cuffs also consisted of maroon velvet braided with gold cord.[247]

Shoulder Straps
The shoulder straps were of the hussar pattern and made of plaited gold gimp chain. They were lined with drab.[248]

Pouch Belt and Pouch
The pouch belt consisted of gold light dragoon lace with a 0.64 cm (¼ inch) light of velvet maroon in the middle of the lace. The pouch was a binocular case of maroon velvet with a gilt 'CIH' monogram and crown on the flap.[249]

Breeches and Boots
The breeches were white doeskin, and Napoleon-style boots were worn.[250]

1901 Dress Regulations and After
The 1901 Regulations follow the same pattern as above, with a few points that should be noted. The pouch belt did not have chains and pickers. There was a 0.64 cm (¼ inch) velvet maroon light between the two gold stripes on the officers' drab overalls. The 1st Regiment wore Napoleon boots with their doeskin breeches, and the 2nd wore black knee boots.[251]

In 1903, along with most of the army, the Central Indian Horse received new numbers. The 1st became the 38th and the 2nd the new 39th. British officers continued to wear their European-style uniforms.[252]

However, in the years after 1901, the kurta grew in popularity. By the 1913 Regulations, European uniforms were optional. The 1913 Regulations say a kurta of regimental pattern would be worn by British officers.

Viceroy Commissioned Officers (VCOs)
The 1886 regulations called for the following for VCOs.

Headdress
A turban of blue and white, with perhaps yellow to show rank, was worn.[253]

Kurta
In cool weather full dress, a khaki kurta was worn. It had gilt buttons, gold tracings down the front, and braided sleeves.[254]

Cummerbund
The Kashmir cummerbund was scarlet.[255]

Netherwear and Boots
The netherwear of VCOs were yellow pyjamas.[256] They wore the same boots as the British officers.[257]

1901 Dress Regulations
The 1901 Dress Regulations for VCOs called for more of the same for their uniforms. VCOs could now wear shoulder chains like British officers. The pyjamas were now white.[258]

Other Ranks
Other ranks wore a drab kurta, drab turban, and netherwear. See Image C34.

§III-6 INFANTRY

The British, via the East India Company, conquered and ultimately held India because its locally raised infantry, the sepoys, proved able to beat any foe put against them. These opponents ranged from French-trained infantry to native cavalry and native infantry, the Sikhs. The one enemy they could not defeat was the British themselves, as shown by the fighting in the Mutiny.

The soldiers who won India for the British were hired by the East India Company. The military forces of the East India Company, for historical reasons, were divided into several presidencies' commands: Bengal, Madras, Bombay, the Punjab Frontier Force, and the Hyderabad Contingent. While each was dressed in generally the same manner, they often had differences in their uniforms. When the Crown replaced the Company as the ruler of India, it left in place the different army commands.

This concept of different presidencies' commands held force up until the early 1900s. At that point, it was felt that an invasion from Russia through Afghanistan was a larger danger than a mutiny or revolt by the Indian army or population. To maximise the ability to respond to the Russians, the old commands were done away with.

PRE-MUTINY UNIFORMS

BENGAL INFANTRY

Prior to the Mutiny, the uniform followed the style of that worn by British soldiers. They wore a shako whose shape changed over the years. A Kilmarnock cap, introduced in 1847, was worn in undress. A red, fairly tight single-breasted coatee was worn, with five sets of double braid on the front. White cross belts were worn on the chest.[259] The trousers were normally dark blue with a red stripe for full dress. In hot weather, white trousers were allowed.[260]

Bengal Gurkhas

In 1829, Gurkha other ranks were ordered to wear a special uniform. Their headdress was a peaked (brimmed) shako (the shako worn by the infantry of the Bengal line did not have a peak). The dark green jacket had five decorations on the chest. Loops formed part of the decorations. These units wore black cross belts on the chest. The trousers were (dark?) green.[261]

MADRAS INFANTRY[262]

In general, the uniforms of the native other ranks of the Madras force followed those of the Bengal other ranks. They also wore a fairly tight red coatee with braiding behind the coat buttons that stretched most of the way across the chest. They seem to have had five rows of white braid across their chest. They, like the Bengal troops, also wore white cross belts. Loose trousers of dark blue or white, depending on the season, were worn.

The main difference between the uniforms of the Bengal and the Madras commands was the type of headdress they wore. Instead of a shako, the Madras native enlisted men wore a cylinder that was about as tall as a shako. The cylinder swelled slightly outward at the top. It was made by covering a stiff bamboo frame with dark blue or black cloth. The cloth was then lacquered and polished to look like leather. On the top of this cloth imitation shako was a grooved knob. Traditionally, the groove was to act as a musket rest.

BOMBAY INFANTRY[263]

The dress uniforms of the native other ranks were generally the same as that worn in the Bengal command. There were differences in the shako and the chest braid.

The Bombay shako was adopted in about 1814, and didn't change until the Mutiny. The Bombay shako was taller than the Bengal shako for much of this period. The red Bombay coatee had seven sets of white braids on the chest.

INDIAN INFANTRY UNIFORMS AFTER THE MUTINY

Infantry uniforms, while more alike than those of the cavalry, still had great variety. Therefore, the best way to give a picture of the uniforms is to present tables backed by contemporary photographs. The tables are heavily based on the regulations, which everyone knows are unreliable, but one must start somewhere and the regulations for infantry are a better guide than those for cavalry.

Table III.6.1: Indian Infantry, British Officers' Uniforms, c. 1913

Regiment	Tunic Colour[a]	Facing Colour	Lace Colour	Tunic Decoration	Collar and Cuff Colour[a]	Shoulder Cord Colour	Pantaloon and Trouser Colour[a]	Pouch Belt	Pouch	Notes
1	Scarlet	White	Gold[b]	None	White t: gold[c,d]	Gold backed scarlet[e]	Blue t: scarlet[f]			A
2	Scarlet	Blue	Gold[b]	None	Blue t: gold[c,d]	Gold backed scarlet[e]	Blue t: scarlet[f]			A
3	Scarlet	Black	Gold[b]	None	Black t: gold[c,d]	Gold backed scarlet[e]	Blue t: scarlet[f]			A
4	Scarlet	Black	Gold[b]	None	Black t: gold[c,d]	Gold backed scarlet[e]	Blue t: scarlet[f]			A
5	Scarlet	Yellow	Gold[b]	None	Yellow t: gold[c,d]	Gold backed scarlet[e]	Blue t: scarlet[f]			A
6	Scarlet	White	Gold[b]	None	White t: gold[c,d]	Gold backed scarlet[e]	Blue t: scarlet[f]			A
7	Scarlet	Yellow	Gold[b]	None	Yellow t: gold[c,d]	Gold backed scarlet[e]	Blue t: scarlet[f]			A
8	Scarlet	Yellow	Gold[b]	None	Yellow t: gold[c,d]	Gold backed scarlet[e]	Blue t: scarlet[f]			A
9	Drab	Chocolate	Drab mohair	Five rows of hussar-style braid[g]	Chocolate t: drab[h]	Drab, Hussar-style[i]	Drab t: one stripe drab mohair lace[j]	Brown leather[k,o]	Brown leather[w,x]	
10	Scarlet	Yellow	Gold[b]	None	Yellow t: gold[c,d]	Gold backed scarlet[e]	Blue t: scarlet[f]			A
11	Scarlet	Yellow	Gold[b]	None	Yellow t: gold[c,d]	Gold backed scarlet[e]	Blue t: scarlet[f]			A
12	Scarlet	Black	Gold[b]	None	Black t: gold[c,d]	Gold backed scarlet[e]	Blue t: scarlet[f]			A
13	Scarlet	Blue	Gold[b]	None	Blue t: gold[c,d]	Gold backed scarlet[e]	Blue t: scarlet[f]			A
14	Scarlet	Yellow	Gold[b]	None	Yellow t: gold[c,d]	Gold backed scarlet[e]	Blue t: scarlet[f]			A
15	Scarlet	Emerald green	Gold[b]	None	Emerald green t: gold[c,d]	Gold backed scarlet[e]	Blue t: scarlet[f]			A
16	Scarlet	White	Gold[b]	None	White t: gold[c,d]	Gold backed scarlet[e]	Blue t: scarlet[f]			A

Regiment	Tunic Colour[a]	Facing Colour	Lace Colour	Tunic Decoration	Collar and Cuff Colour[a]	Shoulder Cord Colour	Pantaloon and Trouser Colour[a]	Pouch Belt	Pouch	Notes
17	Scarlet	White	Gold[b]	None	White t: gold[c,d]	Gold backed scarlet[e]	Blue t: scarlet[f]			A
18	Scarlet	Black	Gold[b]	None	Black t: gold[c,d]	Gold backed scarlet[e]	Blue t: scarlet[f]			A
19	Scarlet	Dark blue	Gold[b]	None	Dark blue t: gold[c,d]	Gold backed scarlet[e]	Blue t: scarlet[f]			A
20	Drab	Emerald green	Drab mohair	Five rows of Hussar-style braid[g]	Emerald green t: drab[h]	Drab, Hussar-style[i]	Drab t: one stripe drab mohair lace[j]	Brown leather[k,o]	Brown leather[w,x]	
21	Drab	Scarlet	Drab mohair	Five rows of Hussar-style braid[g]	Scarlet t: drab[h]	Drab, Hussar-style[i]	Drab t: one stripe drab mohair lace[j]	Brown leather[k,o]	Brown leather[w,x]	
22	Scarlet	Blue	Gold[b]	None	Blue t: gold[c,d]	Gold backed scarlet[e]	Blue t: scarlet[f]			A
23	Drab	Chocolate	Drab mohair	Five rows of Hussar-style braid[g]	Chocolate t: drab[h]	Drab, Hussar-style[i]	Drab t: one stripe drab mohair lace[j]	Brown leather[k,o]	Brown leather[w,x]	
24	Scarlet	White	Gold[b]	None	White t: gold[c,d]	Gold backed scarlet[e]	Blue t: scarlet[f]			A
25	Scarlet	White	Gold[b]	None	White t: gold[c,d]	Gold backed scarlet[e]	Blue t: scarlet[f]			A
26	Drab	Scarlet	Drab mohair	Five rows of Hussar-style braid[g]	Scarlet t: drab[h]	Drab, Hussar-style[i]	Drab t: one stripe drab mohair lace[j]	Brown leather[k,o]	Brown leather[w,x]	
27	Drab	Scarlet	Drab mohair	Five rows of hussar-style braid[g]	Scarlet t: drab[h]	Drab, Hussar-style[i]	Drab t: one stripe drab mohair lace[j]	Brown leather[k,o]	Brown leather[w,x]	
28	Scarlet	Emerald green	Gold[b]	None	Emerald green t: gold[c,d]	Gold backed scarlet[e]	Blue t: scarlet[f]			A
29	Scarlet	Blue	Gold[b]	None	Blue t: gold[c,d]	Gold backed scarlet[e]	Blue t: scarlet[f]			A
30	Scarlet	White	Gold[b]	None	White t: gold[c,d]	Gold backed scarlet[e]	Blue t: scarlet[f]			A
31	Scarlet	White	Gold[b]	None	White t: gold[c,d]	Gold backed scarlet[e]	Blue t: scarlet[f]			A

Regiment	Tunic Colour[a]	Facing Colour	Lace Colour	Tunic Decoration	Collar and Cuff Colour[a]	Shoulder Cord Colour	Pantaloon and Trouser Colour[a]	Pouch Belt	Pouch	Notes
32	Scarlet	Dark blue	Gold[b]	None	Dark blue t: gold[c,d]	Gold backed scarlet[e]	Blue t: scarlet[f]			A
33	Drab	Green	Drab mohair	Five rows of hussar-style braid[g]	Green t: drab[h]	Drab, hussar-style[i]	Drab t: one stripe drab mohair lace[j]	Brown leather[k,o]	Brown leather[w,x]	
34	Scarlet	Dark blue	Gold[b]	None	Dark blue t: gold[c,d]	Gold backed scarlet[e]	Blue t: scarlet[f]			A
35	Scarlet	Yellow	Gold[b]	None	Yellow t: gold[c,d]	Gold backed scarlet[e]	Blue t: scarlet[f]			A
36	Scarlet	Yellow	Gold[b]	None	Yellow t: gold[c,d]	Gold backed scarlet[e]	Blue t: scarlet[f]			A
37	Scarlet	Yellow	Gold[b]	None	Yellow t: gold[c,d]	Gold backed scarlet[e]	Blue t: scarlet[f]			A
38	Scarlet	Yellow	Gold[b]	None	Yellow t: gold[c,d]	Gold backed scarlet[e]	Blue t: scarlet[f]			A
39	Rifle green t: black	Black	Black mohair	Five rows of Hussar-style braid[g]	Black t: black[h,p]	Black, hussar-style[i]	Rifle green t: black[l]	Black enamelled seal leather[n,o]	Black enamelled seal leather; a binocular case	
40	Drab	Emerald green	Drab mohair	Five rows of hussar-style braid[g]	Emerald green t: drab[h]	Drab, hussar-style[i]	Drab t: one stripe drab mohair lace[j]	Brown leather[k,o]	Brown leather[w,x]	
41	Scarlet	Yellow	Gold[b]	None	Yellow t: gold[c,d]	Gold backed scarlet[e]	Blue t: scarlet[f]			A
42	Rifle green t: black	Scarlet	Black mohair	Five rows of hussar-style braid[g]	Scarlet t: black velvet[h,p,q]	Black, hussar-style[i]	Scarlet	Brown leather[l,n]	Brown leather[w,x]	B
43	Rifle green t: black	Scarlet	Black mohair	Five rows of hussar-style braid[g]	Scarlet t: black velvet[h,p,q]	Black, hussar-style[i]	Rifle green t: two stripes black mohair braid, scarlet ground with a light between stripes[t]	Brown leather[m,n,s]	Brown leather with gilt chain edging[w,x]	B
44	Scarlet	Gosling green	Gold[b]	None	Gosling green t: gold[c,d]	Gold backed scarlet[e]	Blue t: scarlet[f]			A
45	Scarlet	White	Gold[b]	None	White t: gold[c,d]	Gold backed scarlet[e]	Blue t: scarlet[f]			A

Regiment	Tunic Colour[a]	Facing Colour	Lace Colour	Tunic Decoration	Collar and Cuff Colour[a]	Shoulder Cord Colour	Pantaloon and Trouser Colour[a]	Pouch Belt	Pouch	Notes
46	Drab	Emerald green	Drab mohair	Five rows of hussar-style braid[g]	Emerald green t: drab[h]	Drab, Hussar- style[i]	Drab t: one stripe drab mohair lace[i]	Brown patent leather[k,o]	Brown leather[w,x]	
47	Scarlet	Yellow	Gold[b]	None	Yellow t: gold[c,d]	Gold backed scarlet[e]	Blue t: scarlet[f]			A
48	Scarlet	Black	Gold[b]	None	Black t: gold[c,d]	Gold backed scarlet[e]	Blue t: scarlet[f]			A
51	Drab t: drab	Yellow	Drab	Five rows of hussar-style braid[g]	Yellow t: drab[h]	Drab, hussar-style[i]	Drab t: two stripes drab mohair lace with facing colour piped between[r]	Brown leather[k,o]	Black leather[w,x]	
52	Drab t: drab	Scarlet	Drab	Five rows of hussar-style braid[g]	Scarlet t: drab[h]	Drab, hussar-style[i]	Drab t: two stripes drab mohair lace with facing colour piped between[r]	Brown leather[k,o]	Black leather[w,x]	
53	Drab t: drab	Black	Drab	Five rows of hussar-style braid[g]	Black t: drab	Drab, hussar-style[i]	Drab t: two stripes drab mohair lace with facing colour piped between[r]	Brown leather[k,o]	Black leather[w,x]	
54	Drab t: drab	Emerald green	Drab	Five rows of hussar-style braid[g]	Emerald green t: drab[h]	Drab, hussar-style[i]	Drab t: two stripes drab mohair lace with facing colour piped between[r]	Brown leather[k,o]	Black leather[w,x]	
55	Dark green t: black	Scarlet	Black mohair	Five rows of hussar-style braid[g]	Scarlet t: black[h,p,q]	Black, hussar-style[i]	Rifle green t: two stripes black mohair braid, scarlet ground with a light between stripes[t]	Black patent leather[k,o]	Black leather[w,x]	B
56	Drab t: drab	Black	Drab	Five rows of hussar-style braid[g]	Black t: drab[h]	Drab, hussar-style[i]	Drab t: two stripes drab mohair lace with facing colour piped between[r]	Black patent leather[k,o]	Black leather[w,x]	
57	Drab t: drab	Blue	Drab	Five rows of hussar-style braid[g]	Blue t: drab[h]	Drab, hussar-style[i]	Drab t: two (lancer pattern) stripes drab mohair lace with facing colour piped between[r]	Brown leather[k,o]	Black leather[w,x]	
58	Drab t: drab	Emerald green	Drab	Five rows of hussar-style braid[g]	Emerald green t: drab[h]	Drab, Hussar-style[i]	Drab t: two stripes drab mohair lace with facing colour piped between[r]	Brown leather[k,o]	Black leather[w,x]	

Regiment	Tunic Colour[a]	Facing Colour	Lace Colour	Tunic Decoration	Collar and Cuff Colour[a]	Shoulder Cord Colour	Pantaloon and Trouser Colour[a]	Pouch Belt	Pouch	Notes
59	Drab t: drab	Scarlet	Drab	Five rows of hussar-style braid[g]	Scarlet t: drab[h]	Drab, Hussar-style[i]	Drab t: two stripes drab mohair lace with facing colour piped between[r]	Black patent leather[k,o]	Black leather[w,x]	
61	Scarlet	White	Gold[b]	None	White t: gold[c,d]	Gold backed scarlet[e]	Blue t: scarlet[f]			A
62	Scarlet	Green	Gold[b]	None	Green t: gold[c,d]	Gold backed scarlet[e]	Blue t: scarlet[f]			A
63	Scarlet	Emerald green	Gold[b]	None	Emerald green t: gold[c,d]	Gold backed scarlet[e]	Blue t: scarlet[f]			A
64	Scarlet	White	Gold[b]	None	White t: gold[c,d]	Gold backed scarlet[e]	Blue t: scarlet[f]			A
66	Scarlet	Green	Gold[b]	None	Green t: gold[c,d]	Gold backed scarlet[e]	Blue t: scarlet[f]			A
67	Scarlet	Emerald green	Gold[b]	None	Emerald green t: gold[c,d]	Gold backed scarlet[e]	Blue t: scarlet[f]			
69	Scarlet	Emerald green	Gold[b]	None	Emerald green t: gold[c,d]	Gold backed scarlet[e]	Blue t: scarlet[f]			A
72	Drab	White	Drab mohair	Five rows of hussar-style braid[g]	White t: drab[h]	Drab, hussar-style[i]	Drab t: one stripe drab mohair lace[j]	Brown leather[k,o]	Brown leather[w,x]	
73	Scarlet	White	Gold[b]	None	White t: gold[c,d]	Gold backed scarlet[e]	Blue t: scarlet[f]			A
74	Scarlet	Emerald green	Gold[b]	None	Emerald green t: gold[c,d]	Gold backed scarlet[e]	Blue t: scarlet[f]			A
75	Scarlet	Yellow	Gold[b]	None	Yellow t: gold[c,d]	Gold backed scarlet[e]	Blue t: scarlet[f]			A
76	Scarlet	Emerald green	Gold[b]	None	Emerald green t: gold[c,d]	Gold backed scarlet[e]	Blue t: scarlet[f]			A
79	Scarlet	Yellow	Gold[b]	None	Yellow t: gold[c,d]	Gold backed scarlet[e]	Blue t: scarlet[f]			A
80	Scarlet	Emerald green	Gold[b]	None	Emerald green t: gold[c,d]	Gold backed scarlet[e]	Blue t: scarlet[f]			A
81	Scarlet	White	Gold[b]	None	White t: gold[c,d]	Gold backed scarlet[e]	Blue t: scarlet[f]			A

Regiment	Tunic Colour[a]	Facing Colour	Lace Colour	Tunic Decoration	Collar and Cuff Colour[a]	Shoulder Cord Colour	Pantaloon and Trouser Colour[a]	Pouch Belt	Pouch	Notes
82	Scarlet	Emerald green	Gold[b]	None	Emerald green t: gold[c,d]	Gold backed scarlet[e]	Blue t: scarlet[f]			A
83	Scarlet	Emerald green	Gold[b]	None	Emerald green t: gold[c,d]	Gold backed scarlet[e]	Blue t: scarlet[f]			A
84	Scarlet	Emerald green	Gold[b]	None	Emerald green t: gold[c,d]	Gold backed scarlet[e]	Blue t: scarlet[f]			A
86	Scarlet	Emerald green	Gold[b]	None	Emerald green t: gold[c,d]	Gold backed scarlet[e]	Blue t: scarlet[f]			A
87	Scarlet	Emerald green	Gold[b]	None	Emerald green t: gold[c,d]	Gold backed scarlet[e]	Blue t: scarlet[f]			A
88	Scarlet	Yellow	Gold[b]	None	Yellow t: gold[c,d]	Gold backed scarlet[e]	Blue t: scarlet[f]			A
89	Drab	Blue	Drab mohair	Five rows of hussar-style braid[g]	Blue t: drab[h]	Drab, hussar-style[i]	Drab t: one stripe drab mohair lace[j]	Brown leather[k,o]	Brown leather[w,x]	
90	Drab	Black	Drab mohair	Five rows of hussar-style braid[g]	Black t: drab[h]	Drab, hussar-style[i]	Drab t: one stripe drab mohair lace[j]	Brown leather[k,o]	Brown leather[w,x]	
91	Drab	Cherry	Drab mohair	Five rows of hussar-style braid[g]	Cherry t: drab[h]	Drab, hussar-style[i]	Drab t: one stripe drab mohair lace[j]	Brown leather[k,o]	Brown leather[w,x]	
92	Drab	White	Drab mohair	Five rows of hussar-style braid[g]	White t: drab[h]	Drab, hussar-style[i]	Drab t: one stripe drab mohair lace[j]	Brown leather[k,o]	Brown leather[w,x]	
93	Drab	Yellow	Drab mohair	Five rows of hussar-style braid[g]	Yellow t: drab[h]	Drab, hussar-style[i]	Drab t: one stripe drab mohair lace[j]	Brown leather[k,o]	Brown leather[w,x]	
94	Scarlet	Dark green	Gold[b]	None	Dark green t: gold[c,d]	Gold backed scarlet[e]	Blue t: scarlet[f]			A
95	Scarlet	Dark green	Gold[b]	None	Dark green t: gold[c,d]	Gold backed scarlet[e]	Blue t: scarlet[f]			A
96	Scarlet	Dark green	Gold[b]	None	Dark green t: gold[c,d]	Gold backed scarlet[e]	Blue t: scarlet[f]			A
97	Scarlet	Dark green	Gold[b]	None	Dark green t: gold[c,d]	Gold backed scarlet[e]	Blue t: scarlet[f]			A

Regiment	Tunic Colour[a]	Facing Colour	Lace Colour	Tunic Decoration	Collar and Cuff Colour[a]	Shoulder Cord Colour	Pantaloon and Trouser Colour[a]	Pouch Belt	Pouch	Notes
98	Scarlet	Dark green	Gold[b]	None	Dark green t: gold[c,d]	Gold backed scarlet[e]	Blue t: scarlet[f]			A
99	Scarlet	Dark green	Gold[b]	None	Dark green t: gold[c,d]	Gold backed scarlet[e]	Blue t: scarlet[f]			A
101	Scarlet	White	Gold[b]	None	White t: gold[c,d]	Gold backed scarlet[e]	Blue t: scarlet[f]			A
102	Scarlet	White	Gold[b]	None	White t: gold[c,d]	Gold backed scarlet[e]	Blue t: scarlet[f]			A
103	Scarlet	Black	Gold[b]	None	Black t: gold[c,d]	Gold backed scarlet[e]	Blue t: scarlet[f]			A
104	Rifle green t: black	Scarlet	Black	Five rows of hussar-style braid[g]	Scarlet t: black velvet[h,p]	Black, hussar-style[i]	Rifle green t: black[j]	Black leather[k,o]	Black leather[w,x]	B
105	Scarlet	Black	Gold[b]	None	Black t: gold[c,d]	Gold backed scarlet[e]	Blue t: scarlet[f]			A,C
106	Drab	Red	Drab mohair	Five rows of hussar-style braid[g]	Red t: drab[h]	Drab, hussar-style[i]	Drab t: one stripe drab mohair lace[l]	Brown leather[k,o]	Brown leather[w,x]	
107	Scarlet	White	Gold[b]	None	White t: gold[c,d]	Gold backed scarlet[e]	Blue t: scarlet[f]	Brown leather[w,x,y]	Binocular case of brown leather[u,w,x]	D
108	Scarlet	White	Gold[b]	None	White t: gold[c,d]	Gold backed scarlet[e]	Blue t: scarlet[f]			A
109	Scarlet	Black	Gold[b]	None	Black t: gold[c,d]	Gold backed scarlet[e]	Blue t: scarlet[f]			A
110	Scarlet	Black	Gold[b]	None	Black t: gold[c,d]	Gold backed scarlet[e]	Blue t: scarlet[f]			A
112	Scarlet	Yellow	Gold[b]	None	Yellow t: gold[c,d]	Gold backed scarlet[e]	Blue t: scarlet[f]			A
113	Scarlet	Yellow	Gold[b]	None	Yellow t: gold[c,d]	Gold backed scarlet[e]	Blue t: scarlet[f]			A
114	Scarlet	Yellow	Gold[b]	None	Yellow t: gold[c,d]	Gold backed scarlet[e]	Blue t: scarlet[f]			A
116	Scarlet	Yellow	Gold[b]	None	Yellow t: gold[c,d]	Gold backed scarlet[e]	Blue t: scarlet[f]			A

Regiment	Tunic Colour[a]	Facing Colour	Lace Colour	Tunic Decoration	Collar and Cuff Colour[a]	Shoulder Cord Colour	Pantaloon and Trouser Colour[a]	Pouch Belt	Pouch	Notes
117	Scarlet	Yellow	Gold[b]	None	Yellow t: gold[c,d]	Gold backed scarlet[e]	Blue t: scarlet[f]			A
119	Scarlet	Yellow	Gold[b]	None	Yellow t: gold[c,d]	Gold backed scarlet[e]	Blue t: scarlet[f]			A
120	Scarlet	Yellow	Gold[b]	None	Yellow t: gold[c,d]	Gold backed scarlet[e]	Blue t: scarlet[f]			A
121	Scarlet	White	Gold[b]	None	White t: gold[c,d]	Gold backed scarlet[e]	Blue t: scarlet[f]			A
122	Scarlet	Emerald green	Gold[b]	None	Emerald green t: gold[c,d]	Gold backed scarlet[e]	Blue t: scarlet[f]			A
123	Rifle green t: black	Scarlet	Black mohair	Five rows of hussar-style braid[g]	Scarlet t: black velvet[h,p]	Black, hussar-style[i]	Rifle green t: black[j]	Black leather[k,o]	Black leather[w,x]	B
124	Drab	Scarlet	Gold[b]	None	Scarlet collar t: scarlet	Gold cord lined drab	Red	Brown leather[k,v]	Brown leather[w,x]	
125	Rifle green t: black	Scarlet	Black mohair	Five rows of jussar-style braid[g]	Scarlet t: black velvet[h,p]	Black, hussar-style[i]	Rifle green t: black[j]	Black leather[k,o]	Black leather[w,x]	B
126	Drab	Scarlet	Gold[b]	None	Scarlet collar t: scarlet	Gold cord lined drab	Red	Brown leather[k,v]	Brown leather[w,x]	
127	Rifle green t: black	Scarlet	Black mohair	Five rows of Hussar-style braid[g]	Scarlet t: black velvet[h,p]	Black, hussar-style[i]	Red	Brown leather[k,o,cc]	Brown leather[w,x]	B
128	Scarlet	White	Gold[b]	None	White t: gold[c,d]	Gold backed scarlet[e]	Blue t: scarlet[f]	Brown leather[w,x,y]	Binocular case of brown leather[u,w,x]	C,D
129	Rifle green t: black	Scarlet	Black mohair	Five rows of hussar-style braid[g]	Scarlet t: black velvet[h,p]	Black, hussar-style[i]	Red	Brown leather[k,o,cc]	Brown leather[w,x]	B
130	Rifle green t: black	Scarlet	Black mohair	Five rows of hussar-style braid[g]	Scarlet t: black velvet[h,p]	Black, hussar-style[i]	Red	Brown leather[k,o,cc]	Brown leather[w,x]	B
Guides	Khaki	Red velvet	Drab silk lace		Red	Khaki	Khaki	Brown leather[z,aa]	Brown leather[x,bb]	

Source: Compiled by Maria Salcedo and the author: *Dress Regulations/India, 1913* is the primary source for this table.

Notes: Regiments 49, 50, 60, 65, 68, 70, 71, 77, 78, 85, 100, 111, 115, and 118 did not exist in 1913. Regiments 65, 71, 77, and 78 were raised in 1903 and disbanded in 1904.

a t: = trim.
b 1.27 cm (½ inch) vellum pattern.
c 1.27 cm (½ inch) lace along the top of collar and gold Russia cord at the bottom.
d 1.27 cm (½ inch) lace around top of the pointed cuffs; lace extends to 19.05 cm (7½ inches) with a tracing of gold Russia braid 0.48 cm (3/16 inch) above and below the lace, which forms a Hungarian knot at the top extending from 24.13 cm (9½ inches) from the bottom of the cuff.
e Shoulder cord of the type used in the British army.
f 0.64 cm (¼ inch) down side seams.
g The hussar-style braid consisted of two strands of flat cords. Each row of braid ended on the outside of the chest with two falling loops of cord. Halfway to the outside of the chest were two small loops in the braid, one above the line of the braid and one below it. At the end of each row was a large oval button with a netted cap. The tunic was fastened by a toggle and loop made out of the braid cord. On each of the two back seams there was the same cord braid. It formed crow's feet at the top, passed under a netted cap at the waist and on each skirt if doubled, and formed a Hungarian knot.
h Cuff topped by Hungarian knot, with a tracing of braid around it, extending 17.78 cm (7 inches) from the bottom of the cuff.
i See §II-3.
j 5.08 cm (2 inches) wide down the side seams.
k 7.62 cm (3 inches) wide.
l Bronze regimental device, whistle, and chain.
m Edging, whistle, and chain in gilt.
n 7.30 cm (2⅞ inches) wide.
o With silver regimental plate, whistle, and chain.
p Collar edged with 1.27 cm (½ inch) black braid with tracing of braid below.
q Black tracing of braid on collar seam.
r Stripes 2.54 cm (1 inch) wide; piping between edging 0.32 cm (3/16 inch) wide.
s Gilt buckles, tip and slides.
t 2.22 cm (⅞ inch) wide braid.
u Binocular case dimensions: 12.7 by 5.08 cm (5 by 2 inches); top 8.89 by 3.18 cm (3½ by 1¼ inches); bottom 10.16 cm (4 inches) deep with brown leather cover.
v Gilt regimental plate, whistle and chain.
w Regimental pattern.
x Badges.
y 1.9cm (¾ inch) gilt chain on the edge.
z Edges with silver.
aa Chain, bucklet, tip and slide of regimental pattern with chain and pickers.
bb Silver flap cover.
cc Brown, black when not parading with troops.

A: Crimson sash.
B: Rounded collar.
C: The facings were velvet for officers (Carman, *Uniforms Infantry*, p. 178).
D: Brown leather belt and slings edged with 0.95 cm (6/16 inch) gold stitching.

Table III.6.2: Indian Infantry, Native Officers' Uniforms, c. 1913

Regiment	T or B[a]	T or B Colour[b]	Facing Colour	Lace Colour	Collar & Cuff Colour[b]	Shoulder Strap Colour[b]	Turban[c]	Sash	Knicker-bockers[b]	Pouch Belt	Pouch	Leggings[d]	Notes
1	T	Scarlet p: white[e]	White	Gold	White t: gold[f,g]	White t: gold[h]	Khaki with red fringe and stripes plus a badge	Crimson	Blue p: scarlet[i,j]			Gaiters; white	
2	B	Scarlet p: blue[k,j]	Blue	Gold	Blue t: gold[g,m]	Blue t: gold[h]	Dark blue with red fringe and a badge	None	Blue p: scarlet[i,j]			Puttees; dark blue; gaiters; white	A
3	T	Scarlet p: black[e]	Black	Gold	Black t: gold[f,g]	Black t: gold[h]	Khaki with red fringe	Crimson	Blue p: scarlet[i,j]			Gaiters; white	
4	T	Scarlet p: black[e]	Black	Gold	Black t: gold[f,g]	Black t: gold[h]	Dark blue with red and black stripes plus a badge	Crimson	Blue p: scarlet[i,j]				
5	T	Scarlet p: yellow[e]	Yellow	Gold	Yellow t: gold[f,g]	Yellow t: gold[h]	Dark blue with yellow stripes	Crimson	Blue p: scarlet[i,j]			Puttees; dark blue	
6	T	Scarlet p: white[e]	White	Gold	White t: gold[f,g]	White t: gold[h]	Dark blue with yellow fringe plus a badge	Crimson	Blue p: scarlet[i,j]			Puttees; dark	
7	T	Scarlet p: yellow[e]	Yellow	Gold	Yellow t: gold[f,g]	Yellow t: gold[h]	Dark blue with red fringe and a badge	Crimson	Blue p: scarlet[i,j]			Gaiters; white	
8	T	Scarlet p: yellow[e]	Yellow	Gold	Yellow t: gold[f,g]	Yellow t: gold[h]	Dark blue with Prussian blue and white stripes and a badge	Crimson	Blue p: scarlet[i,j]			Puttees; dark blue; gaiters; white	
9	T	Drab p: chocolate[e]	Chocolate	Khaki silk	Chocolate t: khaki[n,o]	Choc-olate t: khaki[p]	Blue Peshawan	Crimson	Drab[i]	Brown leather[q]	Brown leather[r,s,s]	?	
10	B	Scarlet t: yellow[k,j]	Yellow	Gold	Yellow t: gold[g,m]	Yellow t: gold[h]	Blue with yellow fringe	None	Blue p: scarlet[i,j]			?	B

Regiment	T or B[a]	T or B Colour[b]	Facing Colour	Lace Colour	Collar & Cuff Colour[b]	Shoulder Strap Colour[b]	Turban[c]	Sash	Knicker-bockers[b]	Pouch Belt	Pouch	Leggings[d]	Notes
11	T	Scarlet p: yellow[e]	Yellow	Gold	Yellow t: gold[f,g]	Yellow t: gold[h]	Kilmarnock cap with number 11	Crimson	Blue p: scarlet[i,j]			Gaiters: white	
12	T	Scarlet p: black[e]	Black	Gold	Black t: gold[f,g]	Black t: gold[h]	Red with light and dark blue and white stripes	Crimson	Blue p: scarlet[i,j]			Puttees: dark blue	
13	T	Scarlet p: blue[e]	Blue	Gold	Blue t: gold[f,g]	Blue t: gold[h]	Blue with red fringe	Crimson	Blue p: scarlet[i,j]			Gaiters: white	
14	T	Scarlet p: yellow[e]	Yellow	Gold	Yellow t: gold[f,g]	Yellow t: gold[h]	Blue with a quoit and badge	Crimson	Blue p: scarlet[i,j]			Gaiters: white	
15	T	Scarlet p: emerald green[e]	Emerald green	Gold	Emerald green t: gold[f,g]	Emerald green t: gold[h]	Red with yellow stripes and a badge worn only by native officers. A quoit was worn by other ranks	Crimson	Blue p: scarlet[i,j]			Gaiters: white	
16	T	Scarlet p: white[e]	White	Gold	White t: gold[f,g]	White t: gold[h]	Dark blue with a badge	Crimson	Blue p: scarlet[i,j]			Puttees: blue; gaiters: white	
17	T	Scarlet p: white[e]	White	Gold	White t: gold[f,g]	White t: gold[h]	Dark blue with a badge	Crimson	Blue p: scarlet[i,j]			Puttees: dark blue	
18	T	Scarlet p: white[e]	Black	Gold	Black t: gold[f,g]	Black t: gold[h]	Purple with gold fringe and a badge	Crimson	Blue p: scarlet[i,j]			Puttees: drab	
19	T	Scarlet p: dark blue[e]	Dark blue	Gold	Dark blue t: gold[f,g]	Dark blue t: gold[h]	Khaki with gold and dark blue fringe and stripes	Crimson	Blue p: scarlet[i,j]			Gaiters: white	

Regiment	T or B[a]	T or B Colour[b]	Facing Colour	Lace Colour	Collar & Cuff Colour[b]	Shoulder Strap Colour[b]	Turban[c]	Sash	Knicker-bockers[b]	Pouch Belt	Pouch	Leggings[d]	Notes
20	T	Drab p: emerald green[e]	Emerald green	Khaki silk	Emerald green t: khaki[n,o]	Emerald green t: khaki[p]	Khaki with green fringe		Drab p: none	Brown leather[q,ss]	Brown leather[r,ss]	Puttees: khaki	
21	T	Drab p: scarlet[e]	Scarlet	Khaki silk	Scarlet t: khaki[n,o]	Scarlet t: khaki[p]	Khaki with red fringe		Drab p: none	Brown leather[q,ss]	Brown leather[r,ss]	Puttees: khaki	
22	T	Scarlet p: blue[e]	Blue	Gold	Blue t: gold[f,g]	Blue t: gold[h]	Blue with red, white, and blue stripes	Crimson	Blue p: scarlet[i,j]			Puttees: blue	
23	B	Drab p: chocolate[k,l]	Chocolate	Khaki silk	Chocolate t: khaki[n,o]	Chocolate t: khaki[p]	Khaki		Drab[i]	Brown leather[q]	Brown leather[r,ss]	Puttees and gaiters: khaki[s]	C
24	T	Scarlet p: white[e]	White	Gold	White t: gold[f,g]	White t: gold[h]	Dark blue and red	Crimson	Blue p: scarlet[i,j]			Puttees: dark blue	
25	T	Scarlet p: white[e]	White	Gold	White t: gold[f,g]	White t: gold[h]	Dark blue with yellow, white, and dark blue stripes	Crimson	Blue p: scarlet[i,j]			Puttees: dark blue	
26	T	Drab p: scarlet[e]	Scarlet	Khaki silk	Scarlet t: khaki[n,o]	Scarlet t: khaki[p]	Khaki with khaki fringe		Drab[i]	Brown leather[q]	Brown leather[r,ss]	Puttees: khaki	
27	T	Drab p: scarlet[e]	Scarlet	Khaki silk	Scarlet t: khaki[n,o]	Scarlet t: khaki[p]	Khaki with red and white fringe		Drab[i]	Brown leather[q]	Brown leather[r,ss]	Puttees: khaki	
28	T	Scarlet p: emerald green[e]	Emerald green	Gold	Emerald green t: gold[f,g]	Emerald green t: gold[h]	Khaki with white and green fringe plus a badge		Blue p: scarlet[i,j]			Puttees: dark blue	
29	T	Scarlet p: blue[e]	Blue	Gold	Blue t: gold[f,g]	Blue t: gold[h]	Dark blue with yellow fringe	Crimson	Blue p: scarlet[i,j]			Puttees: dark blue	
30	T	Scarlet p: white[e]	White	Gold	White t: gold[f,g]	White t: gold[h]	Dark blue with white fringe and a badge	Crimson	Blue p: scarlet[i,j]			Puttees: dark blue	

Regiment	T or B[a]	T or B Colour[b]	Facing Colour	Lace Colour	Collar & Cuff Colour[b]	Shoulder Strap Colour[b]	Turban[c]	Sash	Knicker-bockers[b]	Pouch Belt	Pouch	Leggings[d]	Notes
31	T	Scarlet p: white[e]	White	Gold	White t: gold[f,g]	White t: gold[h]	Dark blue with dark and light blue stripes and a badge	Crimson	Blue p: scarlet[i,j]			Gaiters: white	
32	T	Scarlet p: dark blue[e]	Dark blue	Gold	Dark blue t: gold[f,g]	Dark blue t: gold[h]	Red with blue and yellow fringe and a quoit plus a badge	Crimson	Blue p: scarlet[i,j]			Puttees: dark blue	
33	T	Drab p: green[e]	Green	Khaki silk	Green t: khaki[n,o]	Green t: khaki[p]	Yellow with khaki fringe		Drab[j]	Brown leather[q]	Brown leather[r,x,ss]	Puttees: khaki	
34	T	Scarlet p: dark blue[e]	Dark blue	Gold	Dark blue t: gold[f,g]	Dark blue t: gold[h]	Red with a quoit and a badge	Crimson	Blue p: scarlet[i,j]			Puttees: dark blue	
35	T	Scarlet p: yellow[e]	Yellow	Gold	Yellow t: gold[f,g]	Yellow t: gold[h]	Red with yellow fringe and a quoit	Crimson	Blue p: scarlet[i,j]			Puttees and gaiters: white	
36	T	Scarlet p: yellow[e]	Yellow	Gold	Yellow t: gold[f,g]	Yellow t: gold[h]	Red with a quoit	Crimson	Blue p: scarlet[i,j]				
37	T	Scarlet p: yellow[e]	Yellow	Gold	Yellow t: gold[f,g]	Yellow t: gold[h]	Khaki with yellow fringe	Crimson	Blue p: scarlet[i,j]			Puttees: khaki	
38	T	Scarlet p: yellow[e]	Yellow	Gold	Yellow t: gold[f,g]	Yellow t: gold[h]	Dark blue with yellow, blue, and white stripes on the left	Crimson	Blue p: scarlet[i,j]			Puttees: dark blue; gaiters: white	
39	T	Dark green p: black[t]	Black	Black silk	Black t: black[u,v]	Dark green, plain	Rifle green Kilmarnock cap		Rifle green trousers	Black enamelled seal leather[w]	Black enamelled seal leather with a binocular case[x]	Puttees: black	
40	T	Drab p: emerald green[e]	Emerald green	Khaki silk	Emerald green t: khaki[n,o]	Emerald green t: khaki[p]	Khaki with khaki fringe		Drab[j]	Brown leather[q]	Brown leather[r,x,ss]	Gaiters: drab	

Regiment	T or B[a]	T or B Colour[b]	Facing Colour	Lace Colour	Collar & Cuff Colour[b]	Shoulder Strap Colour[b]	Turban[c]	Sash	Knicker-bockers[b]	Pouch Belt	Pouch	Leggings[d]	Notes
41	T	Scarlet p: yellow[e]	Yellow	Gold	Yellow t: gold[f,g]	Yellow t: gold[h]		Crimson	Blue p: scarlet[i,j]			Puttees: khaki	
42	T	Dark green p: scarlet[y]	Scarlet	Black silk	Scarlet t: black[z,aa]	Scarlet t: black[bb]	Khaki with red fringe on the front and red band edged black	Crimson	Scarlet	Brown leather[cc]	Brown leather[x]	Gaiters: white	
43	T	Dark green p: scarlet[y]	Scarlet	Black silk	Scarlet t: black[z,aa]	Scarlet t: black[bb]	Yellow with red fringe on the front and red stripes		Green	Brown leather[dd]	Brown leather[x,ee]	Gaiters: white reinforced brown	
44	T	Scarlet p: gosling green[e]	Gosling green	Gold	Gosling green t: gold[f,g]	Gosling green t: gold[h]	Light blue with blue fringe on the front and blue and yellow stripes	Crimson	Blue p: scarlet[i,j]			Gaiters: white/ brown	
45	T	Scarlet p: white[e]	White	Gold	White t: gold[f,g]	White t: gold[h]	Blue with white stripes and a quoit plus a badge	Crimson	Blue p: scarlet[i,j]			Gaiters: white	
46	T	Drab p: emerald green[e]	Emerald green	Khaki silk	Emerald green t: khaki[n,o]	Emerald green t: khaki[p]	Khaki with green fringe on the left		Drab[l]	Brown leather[q]	Brown leather[x,x]	Puttees: khaki	
47	T	Scarlet p: yellow[e]	Yellow	Gold	Yellow t: gold[f,g]	Yellow t: gold[h]	Red and Yellow, with dark blue stripes and a quoit	Crimson	Blue p: scarlet[i,j]			Puttees: dark blue	
48	B	Scarlet t: black[k,l]	Black	Gold	Black t: gold[g,m]	Black t: gold[h]	Black with pale orange stripes and a badge	None	Blue p: scarlet[i,j]			Puttees: dark blue	D
51	T	Drab p: yellow[e]	Yellow	Khaki silk	Yellow t: khaki[n,o]	Yellow t: khaki[p]	Khaki with yellow fringe		Drab[l]	Regimental pattern[x]	Regimental pattern[r]	Puttees: khaki	

Regiment	T or B[a]	T or B Colour[b]	Facing Colour	Lace Colour	Collar & Cuff Colour[b]	Shoulder Strap Colour[b]	Turban[c]	Sash	Knicker-bockers[b]	Pouch Belt	Pouch	Leggings[d]	Notes
52	T	Drab p: scarlet[e]	Scarlet	Khaki silk	Scarlet t: khaki[n,o]	Scarlet t: khaki[p]	Khaki with red fringe		Khaki drill	Regimental pattern[x]	Regimental pattern[r]	Puttees: black	
53	T	Drab p: black[e]	Black	Khaki silk	Black t: khaki[n,o]	Black t: khaki[p]	Khaki with black and orange fringe on the left		Khaki drill	Regimental pattern[x]	Regimental pattern[r]	Puttees: black	
54	T	Drab p: emerald green[e]	Emerald green	Khaki silk	Emerald green t: khaki[n,o]	Emerald green t: khaki[p]	Khaki with green fringe		Khaki drill	Regimental pattern[x]	Regimental pattern[r]	Puttees: khaki	
55	T	Dark green p: scarlet[y]	Scarlet	Black mohair	Dark green p: scarlet[f,gg]	Dark green: scarlet[hh]	Green with green fringe		Green	Black leather[ii,uu]	Black leather[x]	Puttees: green	
56	T	Drab p: black[e]	Black	Khaki silk	Black t: khaki[n,o]	Black t: khaki[p]	Khaki with black fringe		Khaki drill	Regimental pattern[x]	Regimental pattern[r]	Puttees: black	
57	T	Drab p: blue[e]	Blue	Khaki silk	Blue t: khaki[n,o]	Blue t: khaki[p]	Khaki with Prussian blue fringe on the left		Khaki drill	Regimental pattern[x]	Regimental pattern[r]	Puttees: khaki	
58	T	Drab p: emerald green[e]	Emerald green	Khaki silk	Emerald green t: khaki[n,o]	Emerald green t: khaki[p]	Khaki with dark green fringe		Khaki drill	Regimental pattern[x]	Regimental pattern[r]		
59	T	Drab p: scarlet[e]	Scarlet	Khaki silk	Scarlet t: khaki[n,o]	Scarlet t: khaki[p]	Khaki with red fringe		Khaki drill	Regimental pattern[x]	Regimental pattern[r]	Puttees: khaki	
61	T	Scarlet t: white[e]	White	Gold	White t: gold[f,g]	White t: gold[h]	Blue and red plus a badge	Crimson	Blue p: scarlet[i,j]			Gaiters: khaki	
62	T	Scarlet t: green[e]	Green	Gold	Green t: gold[f,g]	Green t: gold[h]	Khaki with green fringe and stripes	Crimson	Blue p: scarlet[i,j]				
63	T	Scarlet t: emerald green[e]	Emerald green	Gold	Emerald green t: gold[f,g]	Emerald green t: gold[h]	Khaki with emerald green fringe on the left and a badge	Crimson	Blue p: scarlet[i,j]			Puttees: khaki; gaiters: white	

Regiment	T or B[a]	T or B Colour[b]	Facing Colour	Lace Colour	Collar & Cuff Colour[b]	Shoulder Strap Colour[b]	Turban[c]	Sash	Knicker-bockers[b]	Pouch Belt	Pouch	Leggings[d]	Notes
64	T	Scarlet t: white[e]	White	Gold	White t: gold[f,g]	White t: gold[h]	Khaki with red (on the left) and white fringe and a badge	Crimson	Blue p: scarlet[i,j]			Gaiters: white	
66	B	Scarlet t: green[k,l]	Green	Gold	Green t: gold[g,m]	Green t: gold[h]	Khaki with green fringe	None	Blue p: scarlet[i,j]				E
67	T	Scarlet t: emerald green[e]	Emerald green	Gold	Emerald green t: gold[f,g]	Emerald green t: gold[h]	Dark blue with green fringe and a quoit badge	Crimson	Blue p: scarlet[i,j]				
69	T	Scarlet t: emerald green[e]	Emerald green	Gold	Emerald green t: gold[f,g]	Emerald green t: gold[h]	Khaki with green and yellow fringe and a quoit badge	Crimson	Blue p: scarlet[i,j]				
72	T	Drab p: white[e]	White	Khaki silk	White t: khaki[n,o]	White t: khaki[p]	Khaki with white fringe plus a badge		Drab[j]	Brown leather[r]	Brown leather[r,ss]	Puttees: khaki	
73	T	Scarlet t: white[e]	White	Gold	White t: gold[f,g]	White t: gold[h]	Khaki with white fringe on the right	Crimson	Blue p: scarlet[i,j]			Puttees: khaki	
74	T	Scarlet t: emerald green[e]	Emerald green	Gold	Emerald green t: gold[f,g]	Emerald green t: gold[h]	Khaki and dark blue with red fringe and a badge	Crimson	Blue p: scarlet[i,j]			Puttees: dark blue	
75	T	Scarlet t: yellow[e]	Yellow	Gold	Yellow t: gold[f,g]	Yellow t: gold[h]	Khaki with yellow (on the left) and white fringe	Crimson	Blue p: scarlet[i,j]			Puttees: khaki	
76	T	Scarlet t: emerald green[e]	Emerald green	Gold	Emerald green t: gold[f,g]	Emerald green t: gold[h]	Khaki with yellow fringe	Crimson	Blue p: scarlet[i,j]				

Regiment	T or B[a]	T or B Colour[b]	Facing Colour	Lace Colour	Collar & Cuff Colour[b]	Shoulder Strap Colour[b]	Turban[c]	Sash	Knicker-bockers[b]	Pouch Belt	Pouch	Leggings[d]	Notes
79	T	Scarlet t: yellow[e]	Yellow	Gold	Yellow t: gold[f,g]	Yellow t: gold[h]	Khaki, plus a badge	Crimson	Blue p: scarlet[i,j]				
80	T	Scarlet t: emerald green[e]	Emerald green	Gold	Emerald green t: gold[f,g]	Emerald green t: gold[h]	Green with khaki fringe and green, red, and white stripes and a badge	Crimson	Blue p: scarlet[i,j]			Puttees: dark blue	
81	T	Scarlet t: white[e]	White	Gold	White t: gold[f,g]	White t: gold[h]	Khaki with white fringe plus a badge	Crimson	Blue p: scarlet[i,j]			Gaiters: white	
82	T	Scarlet t: emerald green[e]	Emerald green	Gold	Emerald green t: gold[f,g]	Emerald green t: gold[h]	Khaki with green fringe	Crimson	Blue p: scarlet[i,j]				
83	T	Scarlet t: emerald green[e]	Emerald green	Gold	Emerald green t: gold[f,g]	Emerald green t: gold[h]	Khaki with emerald green fringe on the front and a badge	Crimson	Blue p: scarlet[i,j]			Puttees: khaki	
84	T	Scarlet t: emerald green[e]	Emerald green	Gold	Emerald green t: gold[f,g]	Emerald green t: gold[h]	Khaki with green fringe	Crimson	Blue p: scarlet[i,j]			Gaiters: white	
86	T	Scarlet t: emerald green[e]	Emerald green	Gold	Emerald green t: gold[f,g]	Emerald green t: gold[h]	Green with white fringe plus a badge	Crimson	Blue p: scarlet[i,j]			Puttees: green	
87	T	Scarlet t: emerald green[e]	Emerald green	Gold	Emerald green t: gold[f,g]	Emerald green t: gold[h]	Dark blue with yellow and red fringe	Crimson	Blue p: scarlet[i,j]			Puttees: green	
88	T	Scarlet t: yellow[e]	Yellow	Gold	Yellow t: gold[f,g]	Yellow t: gold[h]	Khaki with yellow and red fringe	Crimson	Blue p: scarlet[i,j]				
89	T	Drab p: blue[e]	Blue	Khaki silk	Blue t: khaki[n,o]	Blue t: khaki[p]	Khaki with blue fringe		Drab[i]	Brown leather[r]	Brown leather[r,x,ss]		

Regiment	T or B[a]	T or B Colour[b]	Facing Colour	Lace Colour	Collar & Cuff Colour[b]	Shoulder Strap Colour[b]	Turban[c]	Sash	Knicker-bockers[b]	Pouch Belt	Pouch	Leggings[d]	Notes
90	T	Drab p: black[e]	Black	Khaki silk	Black t: khaki[n,o]	Black t: khaki[p]	Khaki, plus a badge		Drab[j]	Brown leather[q]	Brown leather[r,x,ss]		
91	T	Drab p: cherry[e]	Cherry	Khaki silk	Cherry t: khaki[n,o]	Cherry t: khaki[p]	Khaki with black and red fringe and stripes plus a badge		Drab[j]	Brown leather[q]	Brown leather[r,x,ss]	Puttees: light grey brown	
92	T	Drab p: white[e]	White	Khaki silk	White t: khaki[n,o]	White t: khaki[p]	Dark blue with red and white fringe		Drab[j]	Brown leather[q]	Brown leather[r,x,ss]		
93	T	Drab p: yellow[e]	Yellow	Khaki silk	Yellow t: khaki[n,o]	Yellow t: khaki[p]	Khaki with yellow fringe		Drab[j]	Brown leather[q]	Brown leather[r,x,ss]	Puttees: khaki	
94	T	Scarlet t: dark green[e]	Dark green	Gold	Dark green t: gold[f,g]	Dark green t: gold[h]	Green with green fringe on the front	Crimson	Blue p: scarlet[i,j]			Puttees: green	
95	B	Scarlet t: dark green[k,l]	Dark green	Gold	Dark green t: gold[g,m]	Dark green t: gold[h]	Green with green fringe on the front	None	Blue p: scarlet[i,j]			Puttees: green	F
96	T	Scarlet t: dark green[e]	Dark green	Gold	Dark green t: gold[f,g]	Dark green t: gold[h]	Green with green fringe on the front	Crimson	Blue p: scarlet[i,j]			Brown leather wraparound	
97	B	Scarlet t: dark green[k,l]	Dark green	Gold	Dark green t: gold[g,m]	Dark green t: gold[h]	Green with red fringe plus a badge	None	Blue p: scarlet[i,j]			Puttees and gaiters: white	F
98	T	Scarlet t: dark green[e]	Dark green	Gold	Dark green t: gold[f,g]	Dark green t: gold[h]	Green with green fringe on the front	Crimson	Blue p: scarlet[i,j]			Puttees: green	
99	B	Scarlet t: dark green[k,l]	Dark green	Gold	Dark green t: gold[g,m]	Dark green t: gold[h]	Green with red fringe	None	Blue p: scarlet[i,j]				F
101	T	Scarlet t: white[e]	White	Gold	White t: gold[f,g]	White t: gold[h]	Khaki with white fringe and a badge	Crimson	Blue p: scarlet[i,j]			Gaiters: white	

Regiment	T or B[a]	T or B Colour[b]	Facing Colour	Lace Colour	Collar & Cuff Colour[b]	Shoulder Strap Colour[b]	Turban[c]	Sash	Knicker-bockers[b]	Pouch Belt	Pouch	Leggings[d]	Notes
102	T	Scarlet t: white[e]	White	Gold	White t: gold[f,g]	White t: gold[h]	Khaki with red fringe on the front plus a badge	Crimson	Blue p: scarlet[i,j]			Gaiters: white	
103	T	Scarlet t: black[e]	Black	Gold	Black t: gold[f,g]	Black t: gold[h]	Khaki with yellow and red fringe	Crimson	Blue p: scarlet[i,j]			Puttees: khaki	
104	T	Dark green p: scarlet[y]	Scarlet	Black silk	Scarlet t: black[z,aa]	Scarlet t: black[bb]	Dark green with bugle-horn badge		Green	Black leather[uu]	Black leather[x]	Puttees: green[jj]	
105	T	Scarlet t: black[e]	Black	Gold	Black t: gold[f,g]	Black t: gold[h]	Khaki with red fringe and stripes	Crimson	Blue p: scarlet[i,j]				G
106	T	Drab p: red[e]	Red	Khaki silk	Red t: khaki[n,o]	Red t: khaki[p]	Khaki with khaki fringe and yellow and red stripes		Drab, peg tops style	Brown leather[q]	Brown leather[rr,ss]	Puttees: khaki	
107	T	Scarlet t: white[e]	White	Gold	White t: gold[f,g]	White t: gold[h]	Khaki with red fringe plus a badge	In place of sash, brown leather belt and slings	Blue p: scarlet[i,j]	Brown leather[kk]	Binocular case of brown leather[ll,r]	Gaiters: white	
108	T	Scarlet t: white[e]	White	Gold	White t: gold[f,g]	White t: gold[h]	Khaki with white fringe and a badge	Crimson	Blue p: scarlet[i,j]				
109	B	Scarlet t: black[k,l]	Black	Gold	Black t: gold[g,m]	Black t: gold[h]	Blue/black with white fringe black	None	Blue p: scarlet[i,j] Black knee-pad on right knicker-bocker leg			Gaiters: black	D

Regiment	T or B[a]	T or B Colour[b]	Facing Colour	Lace Colour	Collar & Cuff Colour[b]	Shoulder Strap Colour[b]	Turban[c]	Sash	Knicker-bockers[b]	Pouch Belt	Pouch	Leggings[d]	Notes
110	T	Scarlet t: black[e]	Black	Gold	Black t: gold[f,g]	Black t: gold[h]	Khaki with black fringe and red stripes plus a badge	Crimson	Blue p: scarlet[i,j]			Gaiters: white/brown	
112	T	Scarlet t: yellow[e]	Yellow	Gold	Yellow t: gold[f,g]	Yellow t: gold[h]	Yellow with yellow fringe and white and yellow stripes	Crimson	Blue p: scarlet[i,j]			Puttees: blue	
113	T	Scarlet t: yellow[e]	Yellow	Gold	Yellow t: gold[f,g]	Yellow t: gold[h]	Khaki with red fringe, blue and brown stripes, and a badge	Crimson	Blue p: scarlet[i,j]			Puttees: blue	
114	T	Scarlet t: yellow[e]	Yellow	Gold	Yellow t: gold[f,g]	Yellow t: gold[h]	Khaki with blue fringe	Crimson	Blue p: scarlet[i,j]			Puttees: blue	
116	T	Scarlet t: yellow[e]	Yellow	Gold	Yellow t: gold[f,g]	Yellow t: gold[h]	Khaki with blue fringe	Crimson	Blue p: scarlet[i,j]				
117	T	Scarlet t: yellow[e]	Yellow	Gold	Yellow t: gold[f,g]	Yellow t: gold[h]	Khaki with blue stripes	Crimson	Blue p: scarlet[i,j]				
119	T	Scarlet t: yellow[e]	Yellow	Gold	Yellow t: gold[f,g]	Yellow t: gold[h]	Yellow with yellow fringe and red and grey stripes	Crimson	Blue p: scarlet[i,j]			Puttees: blue	
120	T	Scarlet t: yellow[e]	Yellow	Gold	Yellow t: gold[f,g]	Yellow t: gold[h]	Khaki	Crimson	Blue p: scarlet[i,j]				
121	T	Scarlet t: white[e]	White	Gold	White t: gold[f,g]	White t: gold[h]		Crimson	Blue p: scarlet[i,j]				
122	T	Scarlet t: emerald green[e]	Emerald green	Gold	Emerald green t: gold[f,g]	Emerald green t: gold[h]	Khaki	Crimson	Blue p: scarlet[i,j]			Gaiters: white/brown	
123	T	Dark green p: scarlet[y]	Scarlet	Black silk	Scarlet t: black[z, aa]	Scarlet t: black[bb]	Dark green		Green	Black leather[tt,uu]	Black leather[x]	Puttees: green[jj]	

Regiment	T or B[a]	T or B Colour[b]	Facing Colour	Lace Colour	Collar & Cuff Colour[b]	Shoulder Strap Colour[b]	Turban[c]	Sash	Knicker-bockers[b]	Pouch Belt	Pouch	Leggings[d]	Notes
124	T	Drab p: scarlet[e]	Scarlet	Khaki silk	Scarlet t: khaki[n,o]	Scarlet t: khaki[p]	Khaki with red fringe		Red, peg tops style	Brown leather[mm]	Brown leather[rr,ss]	Gaiters: white[nn]	
125	T	Dark green p: scarlet[y]	Scarlet	Black silk	Scarlet t: black[z,aa]	Scarlet t: black[bb]	Rifle green with a badge		Green	Black leather[ii,uu]	Black leather[x]	Gaiters: white/black[jj]	
126	T	Drab p: scarlet[e]	Scarlet	Khaki silk	Scarlet t: khaki[n,o]	Scarlet t: khaki[p]	Khaki with white fringe and red stripes		Red, peg tops style	Brown leather[mm]	Brown leather[rr,ss]	Gaiters: white[nn]	
127	T	Green p: scarlet[y]	Scarlet	Black silk	Scarlet t: black[z,aa]	Scarlet t: black[bb]	Green		Red p: none peg tops style	Brown leather[ii,uu,vv]	Brown leather[x]	Gaiters: white[nn]	
128	T	Scarlet t: white[e]	White	Gold	White t: gold[f,g]	White t: gold[h]	Dark blue with white fringe and a badge	In place of sash, brown leather belt and slings	Blue p: scarlet[i,j]	Brown leather[kk]	Binocular case of brown leather[ll,r]	Puttees: blue	
129	T	Green t: black[oo]	Scarlet	Black silk	Scarlet t: black[pp,qq]	Green t: black[rr]	Dark green p: red and black		Red p: none peg tops style	Brown leather[ii,uu,vv]	Brown leather[x]	Gaiters: white[nn]	
130	T	Green p: scarlet[y]	Scarlet	Black silk	Scarlet t: black[z,aa]	Scarlet t: black[bb]	Dark green with green fringe		Red p: none peg tops style	Brown leather[ii,uu,vv]	Brown leather[x]	Gaiters: white[nn]	
Guides	T	Khaki	Red	Khaki	Red	Red	Red	Red	Khaki	Brown leather[ss]	Brown leather[r]	Puttees: khaki	

Source: Compiled by Maria Salcedo and the author. *Dress Regulations/India, 1913* is the primary source for this table. The *1914 Army List* was consulted for uniform and facing colours.
Notes: Regiments 49, 50, 60, 65, 68, 70, 71, 77, 78, 85, 100, 111, 115, and 118 did not exist in 1913. Regiments 65, 71, 77, and 78 were raised in 1903 and disbanded in 1904.

[a] T = tunic; B = long blouse.
[b] t = trim; p = piping.
[c] This was a regimental pattern item. It would have been the same as the other ranks, probably with the addition of gold stripes to denote rank. For badge descriptions, see Table III.6.4. The badge worn by native officers of the 15th is not listed in this table but evidence of it being worn by only native officers can be seen in Image III:79 (a painting c. 1905 by Lovett from *Armies of India*). This painting shows only the other ranks of the 15th wearing a quoit in full dress.
[d] This would have been the same as the other ranks.
[e] Piping of facing colour 0.64 cm (¼ inch) wide down left front and from bottom button to the bottom of tunic on the right front, also right centre of back skirt.
[f] Collar 3.81 cm (1½ inches) in depth with 1.27 cm (½ inch) gold lace around the ends and along the top.
[g] Cuffs pointed 16.51 cm (6½ inches) deep in front and 5.72 cm (2¼ inches) at the sides and back, 1.27 cm (½ inch) gold lace all around showing 0.32 cm (⅛ inch) of facing cloth.
[h] 1.27 cm (½ inch) gold lace all around except at base.
[i] Knickerbockers cut loose with the spare material being fitted into a waist band 5.72 cm (2¼ inches) wide to give plenty of room over the hips. Bottoms are made loose and provided with a drawstring for fastening below the knee, the string being covered as the knickerbockers are cut long enough to fall over about 10.16 cm (4 inches).
[j] Piping of scarlet down side seam 0.64 cm (¼ inch) wide.
[k] Length 101.6 cm (40 inches) to fit a man 1.75 m to 1.78 m (5 feet 9 inches to 5 feet 10 inches) varying 3.81 cm (1½ inches) for every 5.08 cm (2 inches) in height.
[l] Opening in front 41.91 cm (16½ inches) in length made up 6.35 cm (2½ inches) wide, edged on both sides with 0.64 cm (¼ inch) of facing cloth. Opening at side seam at bottom 15.24 cm (6 inches) in length.
[m] 3.81 cm (1½ inches) in depth with 0.85 cm (⅓ inch) gold lace around the ends and along the top of the collar.
[n] Collar 3.81 cm (1½ inches) in depth with 1.27 cm (½ inch) khaki silk lace around the ends and along the top.
[o] Cuffs pointed 16.51 cm (6½ inches) deep in front and 5.72 cm (2¼ inches) at the sides and back, 1.27 cm (½ inch) khaki silk lace all around, showing 0.32 cm (⅛ inch) of facing cloth.
[p] 1.27 cm (½ inch) khaki silk lace all around except at base.
[q] 7.62 cm (3 inches) wide with silver regimental plate, whistle and chain.
[r] Regimental device on lid of pouch.
[s] One-piece puttees and gaiters.
[t] Piping of facing colour 0.64 cm (¼ inch) wide down left front, skirt, pleats, and centre of back, and from bottom button to the bottom of tunic on the right front.
[u] Collar 3.81 cm (1½ inches) in depth with 1.27 cm (½ inch) black silk lace all around.
[v] Cuffs pointed 13.97 cm (5½ inches) deep in front and 1.27 cm (½ inch) black silk lace all around.
[w] 7.3 cm (2⅞ inches) wide.
[x] With badge(s).
[y] Piping of facing colour 0.64 cm (¼ inch) wide down left, front and from bottom button to the bottom of tunic on the right front, also down centre of back of skirt.
[z] Collar 3.81 cm (1½ inches) in depth with 1.27 cm (½ inch) black silk lace all around the ends and along the top.
[aa] Cuffs pointed 16.51 cm (6½ inches) deep in front and 5.72 cm (2¼ inches) at the sides and back, 1.27 cm (½ inch) khaki silk lace all around showing 0.32 cm (⅛ inch) of facing cloth.
[bb] 1.27 cm (½ inch) black silk lace all around, showing 0.32 cm (⅛ inches) of facing colour.
[cc] With regimental device, whistle, and chain in bronze.
[dd] With gilt buckles, tip, and slide; edging, whistle, and chain in gilt.
[ee] With gilt chain edging.
[ff] Collar 3.81 cm (1½ inches) in depth, piped with facing colour around the end and along the top, 1.27 cm (½ inch) black silk lace around the collar below the piping.
[gg] Cuffs 13.97 cm (5½ inches) deep in front, piped with facing cloth and rounded off at hind of arm seam, with piping carried down each side of the seam, finishing off 1.91 cm (¾ inch) from the bottom.
[hh] Piped all round, except at base,
[ii] 7.62 cm (3 inches) wide.
[jj] Black canvas leggings with buckles and studs, according to 1913 Regulations.
[kk] 1.71 cm (¾ inch) gilt chain on the edges and regimental badges.
[ll] 12.7 by 5.08 cm (5 by 2 inches); top 8.89 by 3.18 cm (3½ by 1¼ inches); bottom 10.16 cm (4 inches) deep with brown leather cover.
[mm] Gilt regimental plate, whistle, and chain.
[nn] White canvas leggings with cord loops.
[oo] Tunic edged all around with 0.64 cm (¼ inch) black braid.
[pp] Collar edged with 1.27 cm (½ inch) black braid with a tracing of plain braid below.
[qq] Cuff topped by Hungarian knot, with a tracing of braid around it, extending 17.78 cm (7 inches) from the bottom of the cuff.
[rr] Edged with 0.64 cm (¼ inch) black braid.
[ss] Regimental pattern.
[tt] Edging, whistle and chain in gilt.
[uu] Silver regimental plate, whistle and chain.
[vv] Black when not parading with the troops.

A: Blue cummerbund.
B: Yellow cummerbund.
C: Chocolate or khaki cummerbund.
D: Black cummerbund.
E: Green cummerbund.
F: Dark green cummerbund.
G: The facings were velvet for officers (Carman, *Uniforms Infantry*, p. 178).

Table III.6.3: Indian Infantry – Other Ranks Uniform, c. 1913

Regiment	Coat Type[a]	Coat Colour	Coat Facing Colour	Knicker-bockers Colour	Knicker-bockers Trim[b]	Cummerbund Colour	Cummerbund Trim	Leggings Type[c]	Leggings Colour	Turban Pag or Kulla	Turban Pag or Kulla Colour	Turban Colour	Turban Fringe[d]	Turban Special	Turban Stripes	Hanging Where[e]	Hanging Colour	Hanging Trim	Shoes
1	L	Scarlet	White	Blue	R	White	Red	G	White	–	–	Khaki	Red	Badge	Red				Brown
2	L	Scarlet	Blue	Blue	R	Dark blue	–	P, G	Dark blue White	–	–	Dark blue	Red	Badge	–	LA	White	Blue	Black
3	L	Scarlet	Black	Blue	R	Black[f]		G	White	–	–	Khaki	Red	–	–				Brown
4		Scarlet	Black	Blue	R	Black[f]				–	–	Dark blue		Badge	Red, black				
5	L	Scarlet	Yellow	Blue	R	Belt only		P	Dark blue	–	–	Dark blue		–	Yellow				Brown
6	L	Scarlet	White	Blue	R	Yellow	Black	P	Dark blue	Kulla	Yellow	Dark blue	Yellow	Badge	–				Brown
7	L	Scarlet	Yellow	Blue	R	Yellow[f]		G	White			Dark blue	Red	Badge	–				Black
8	L	Scarlet	Yellow	Blue	R	Yellow	Black	P, G	Dark blue White			Dark blue	–	Badge	Prussian blue, white				Black
9	Z	Drab	Chocolate	Drab	R	–			?			Blue	Peshawan lungi						
10	L	Scarlet	Yellow	Blue	R	Yellow[f]			?			Blue	Yellow						
11	L	Scarlet	Yellow	Blue	R	Yellow[f]		G	White	Kilmarnock cap until c. 1912 or so, with number 11 on it.									Black
12	L	Scarlet	Black	Blue	R	Black	–	P	Dark blue	Kulla	Red	Red	–	–	Light blue, white/dark blue	LA	Light Blue	White, dark blue	Brown
13	L	Scarlet	Blue	Blue	R	Blue	–	G	White	–	–	Blue	Red	–	–				Black
14	L	Scarlet	Yellow	Blue	R	Yellow[f]	–	G	White	Pag	Red	Blue	–	Quoit badge	–				
15	Z	Scarlet	Emerald green	Blue	R	–		G	White	Pag	Red	Red	–	Quoit,	Yellow				Brown
16	T	Scarlet	White	Blue	R	White[f]		P, G	Blue White	Kulla	Dark blue	Dark blue	–	Badge	–				Black

Regiment	Coat Type[a]	Coat Colour	Coat Facing Colour	Knicker-bockers Colour	Knicker-bockers Trim[b]	Cummerbund Colour	Cummerbund Trim	Leggings Type[c]	Leggings Colour	Pag or Kulla	Pag or Kulla Colour	Turban Colour	Turban Fringe[d]	Turban Special	Turban Stripes	Hanging Where[e]	Hanging Colour	Hanging Trim	Shoes
17	N	Scarlet	White	Blue	R	—		P	Dark blue	—	—	Dark blue		Badge					
18	N	Scarlet	Black	Blue	R	—		P	Drab			Purple	Gold	Badge	Gold stripes for native officers				
19	L	Scarlet	Blue	Blue	R	Blue[f]		G	White	Kulla	Red	Khaki	Gold, dark blue	—	Gold, dark blue				Brown
20	L	Drab	Emerald green	Drab		Emerald green		P	Khaki	Kulla	Dark green	Khaki	Green	—	—				
21	L	Drab	Scarlet	Drab		Belt only		P	Khaki	Kulla	Red	Khaki	Red	—	—				Brown
22	L	Scarlet	Blue	Blue	R	Blue	Red	P	Blue	Kulla	Red	Blue	—	—	Blue, red/white				Black
23	L[g]	Drab	Chocolate	Drab		Chocolate		P & G[h]	Khaki	Pag	White	Khaki	—	—	—				Black
24	L	Scarlet	White	Blue	R	White[f]		P	Dark blue	Pag	Red	Dark blue/red	—	—	—				Brown
25	L	Scarlet	White	Blue	R	White[f]		P	Dark blue	Pag	Red	Dark blue	—	—	Yellow, dark blue/white				Brown
26	L	Drab	Scarlet	Drab	—	Belt only		P	Khaki	Kulla	Khaki	Khaki	Khaki	—	—				
27	T	Drab	Front/cuff 1st scarlet	Drab	R	Belt only		P	Khaki	Pag	Red	Khaki	Red, white	—	—	—	—	—	Brown
28	L	Scarlet	Emerald free[n]	Blue	R	Emerald green[f]		P	Dark blue	Pag	Red	Khaki	White, green, red	Badge	—				Black
29	L	Scarlet	Blue	Blue	R	Blue[f]		P	Dark blue	Kulla	Red	Dark blue	Yellow	—	Yellow				Brown

Regiment	Coat Type[a]	Coat Colour	Coat Facing Colour	Knickerbockers Colour	Knickerbockers Trim[b]	Cummerbund Colour	Cummerbund Trim	Leggings Type[c]	Leggings Colour	Pag or Kulla	Pag or Kulla Colour	Turban Colour	Turban Fringe[d]	Turban Special	Turban Stripes	Hanging Where[e]	Hanging Colour	Hanging Trim	Shoes
30	L	Scarlet	White	Blue	R	Belt only		P	Dark blue	Kulla	Red	Dark blue	White	Badge					Black
31	Z	Scarlet	White	Blue	R			G	White	Pag	Red	Dark Blue		Badge	Yellow, dark blue, light blue				Brown
32	Z	Scarlet	Blue	Blue	R			P	Dark blue	Pag	White	Red	Blue Yellow	Quoit, badge	–	–	–	–	
33	L	Drab	Emerald Green	Drab	–	Green	–	P	Khaki	Kulla	Green	Yellow	Khaki	–	–	L	Green		Brown
34	Z	Scarlet	Blue	Blue	R			P	Dark Blue	Pag	White	Red	–	Quoit, badge	–	–	–	–	Brown
35	L[g]	Scarlet	Yellow	Blue	R	Yellow	–	P G	White	Pag	Yellow	Red	Yellow	Quoit					Brown
36	L	Scarlet	Yellow	Blue	R	Yellow[f]						Red	Yellow	Quoit					Brown
37	L	Scarlet	Yellow	Blue	R	Yellow[f]		P	Khaki	–	–	Khaki							Brown
38	Z	Scarlet	Yellow	Blue	R			P G	Dark blue White	Pag	Red	Blue			Yellow, blue, white[i]	–	–	–	
39	T	Dark green	Black	Dark green	–	Belt only		P	Black	Kilmarnock cap – black						–	–		Brown
40	L	Drab	Emerald green	Drab	–	Green	–	G	Drab	Kulla	Dark green	Khaki	Khaki	–	–	B	Khaki		
41	L	Scarlet	Yellow	Blue	R	Yellow[f]		P	Khaki										Brown
42	T	Dark green	Full cuff scarlet	Scarlet	–	Belt only		G	White	–	–	Khaki	Red (F)	–	Red band edged in black	–	–	–	
43	T	Dark green	Full cuff scarlet	Red	–	Belt only		G	White, reinforced brown	–	–	Yellow	Red (F)	–	Red	–	–	–	Brown

Regiment	Coat Type[a]	Coat Colour	Coat Facing Colour	Knickerbockers Colour	Knickerbockers Trim[b]	Cummerbund Colour	Cummerbund Trim	Leggings Type[c]	Leggings Colour	Pag or Kulla	Pag or Kulla Colour	Turban Colour	Turban Fringe[d]	Turban Special	Turban Stripes	Hanging Where[e]	Hanging Colour	Hanging Trim	Shoes
44		Scarlet	Full cuff gosling green	Blue	R	Belt only		G	White/brown	–	–	Light blue	Blue (F)	–	Blue yellow				Brown
45	L	Scarlet	White	Blue	R	White	–	G	White	Pag	Red	Blue		Quoit, badge	White				Brown
46	L	Drab	Emerald green	Drab	–	Belt only		P	Khaki	Kulla	Khaki	Khaki	Green (L)	–	–				
47	T	Scarlet	Yellow	Blue	R	Belt only		P	Dark blue	–	–	Red? Yellow		Quoit	Dark blue				Brown
48	L	Scarlet	Black	Blue	R	Black	–	P	Dark blue	–	–	Black		Badge	Pale orange	RA	Black, pale orange, buff		
51	T	Drab	Full cuff yellow	Drab	–	Belt only		P	Khaki	Kulla	Red	Khaki	Yellow						Brown
52	T	Drab	Scarlet	Drab		Belt only		P	Black	Kulla	Khaki	Khaki	Red						
53	T	Drab	Black	Drab		Belt only		P	Black	Kulla	Black	Khaki	Black, orange (L)						Slippers
54	T	Drab	Emerald green	Drab		Belt Only		P	Khaki	Pag	Red	Khaki	Green						Brown
55	T	Dark green	Scarlet[k]	Dark Green		Belt only		P	Green	–	–	Green	Green						Brown
56	T	Drab	Black	Drab		Belt only		P	Black	Kulla	Pale yellow	Khaki	Black						Brown
57	T	Drab	Full cuff, Prussian blue	Drab	–	Belt only		P	Khaki	Kulla	Khaki	Khaki	Prussian blue (L)						Black
58	T	Drab	Emerald green	Drab		Belt only						Khaki	Dark green?						

Regiment	Coat Type[a]	Coat Colour	Coat Facing Colour	Knickerbockers Colour	Knickerbockers Trim[b]	Cummerbund Colour	Cummerbund Trim	Leggings Type[c]	Leggings Colour	Pag or Kulla	Pag or Kulla Colour	Turban Colour	Turban Fringe[d]	Turban Special	Turban Stripes	Hanging Where[e]	Hanging Colour	Hanging Trim	Shoes
59	T	Drab	Full cuff, scarlet	Drab		Belt only		P	Khaki	Kulla	Red	Khaki	Red	—	—				Black
61	Z	Scarlet	White	Blue		—		G	Khaki			Blue Red		Badge					Brown
62		Scarlet	Emerald green	Blue		Emerald green[f]				Kulla	Green	Khaki	Green	Badge	Green				Brown
63	Z	Scarlet	Emerald green	Blue	R	—		G P	White Khaki	Kulla	Red	Khaki	Emerald green (L)	Badge	—	BT	Khaki		Brown
64	Z	Red	White	Blue		—		G	White	Kulla	Red	Khaki	Red, white (F)	Badge					Brown
65		Scarlet	Yellow			Yellow[f]													
66	L	Scarlet	Emerald green	Blue		Emerald green[f]				Kulla	Khaki	Khaki	Green						Brown
67	L	Scarlet	Emerald green	Blue		Emerald green[f]				Pag	Khaki	Dark Blue	Green	Quoit					Brown
69	L	Scarlet	Green	Blue		Green[f]				Pag	Dark blue	Khaki	Green, yellow	Quoit					
71		Dark green	Scarlet			Scarlet[f]						Khaki							
72	L	Drab serge	White	Khaki		Khaki	—	P	Khaki	Kulla	Red	Khaki	White	Badge					Brown
73	L	Scarlet	White	Blue	R	White[f]		P	Khaki	Kulla	Khaki	Khaki	White (R)						Brown
74	L	Scarlet	Emerald green	Blue		Green	—	P	Dark blue	Pag	Red	Khaki, dark blue	Red	Badge					Brown
75	Z	Scarlet	Yellow	Blue	R	—		P	Khaki			Khaki	Yellow, white (F)		—				Black
76		Scarlet	Emerald green	Blue	R	Emerald green[f]				Kulla	Burnt orange	Khaki	Yellow						Brown
77		Scarlet	Green			Green[f]						Red fez							

Regiment	Coat Type[a]	Coat Colour	Coat Facing Colour	Knickerbockers Colour	Knickerbockers Trim[b]	Cummerbund Colour	Cummerbund Trim	Leggings Type[c]	Leggings Colour	Pag or Kulla	Pag or Kulla Colour	Turban Colour	Turban Fringe[d]	Turban Special	Turban Stripes	Hanging Where[e]	Hanging Colour	Hanging Trim	Shoes
78		Scarlet	Green			Green[f]						Red fez							
79		Scarlet	Yellow			Yellow[f]						Khaki		Badge					
80	N	Scarlet	Emerald green	Blue	R	–		P	Dark blue	Kulla	Khaki	Green	Khaki	Badge	Green, red/white				Brown
81		Scarlet	White	Blue	R	White[f]		G	White	Kulla	Khaki	Khaki	White	Badge					
82		Scarlet	Emerald green	Blue	R	Emerald green[f]				Kulla	Red	Khaki	Green						
83	N	Scarlet	Emerald green	Blue	R	–		P	Khaki			Khaki	Emerald green (F)	Badge	–	BT	Khaki		Black
84	L	Scarlet	Emerald green	Blue	R	Green		G	White	Kulla	Green	Khaki	Green			RA	Green	Red, white	Brown
86	N	Scarlet	Emerald green	Blue	R	–		P	Green	Kulla	Khaki	Green	White	Badge		BT	Green	–	Brown
87	L	Scarlet	Emerald green	Blue	R	Green	–	P	Green			Dark blue	Yellow, red			LA	Green	Green, red/white	Brown
88		Scarlet	Yellow	Blue	R	Yellow[f]				Kulla	Red	Khaki	Yellow, red	Badge					
89		Drab serge	Blue	Drab	–	Blue[f]				Kulla	Khaki	Khaki	Blue						
90		Drab serge	Black	Drab	–	Black[f]				Kulla	Red	Khaki		Badge					
91	T	Drab	Cherry	Khaki	–	Cherry[f]		P	Light grey/khaki,	Kulla	Red	Khaki	Black, red	Badge	Black, red				Brown
92		Drab serge	White	Drab	–	White[f]				Kulla	White	Dark blue	Red, white						
93	T	Drab serge	Yellow	Drab	–	Yellow[f]		P	Khaki	Kulla	Khaki	Khaki	Yellow		–				Brown
94	L	Scarlet	Dark green	Blue	R	Green	–	P	Green			Green	Green (F)	–	–	RA	Green		Brown

Regiment	Coat Type[a]	Coat Colour	Coat Facing Colour	Knickerbockers Colour	Knickerbockers Trim[b]	Cummerbund Colour	Cummerbund Trim	Leggings Type[c]	Leggings Colour	Pag or Kulla	Pag or Kulla Colour	Turban Colour	Turban Fringe[d]	Turban Special	Turban Stripes	Hanging Where[e]	Hanging Colour	Hanging Trim	Shoes
95	L	Scarlet	Dark green	Blue	R	Green	–	P	Green	Kulla	Yellow	Green	Green (F)	–	–	RA	Green	Yellow	Brown
96	L	Scarlet	Dark green	Blue	R	Green	–	o	Brown			Green	Green (F)		Yellow	RA	Green	Yellow	Brown
97	L	Scarlet	Dark green	Blue	R	Green	–	G P	White	Kulla	Red	Green	Red	Badge	–	LA	Green	Red, White	Brown
98	L	Scarlet	Dark green	Blue	R	Green	–	P	Green	Kulla	Yellow	Green	Green (F)	–	–	LA	Green	–	Brown
99	L	Scarlet	Dark green	Blue	R	Dark green[f]				Kulla	Green	Green	Red						
101	L	Scarlet	White	Blue	R	White	Red	G	White	Kulla	Red	Khaki	White	Badge	–	RA	White	Red	Black
102	L	Scarlet	White	Blue	R	White	–	G	White	Kulla	Khaki	Khaki	Red (F)	Badge	–				Brown
103	L	Scarlet	Black	Blue	R	Black[f]	–	P	Khaki	Kulla	Black	Khaki	Yellow, red	–	–				Brown
104	L	Dark green	Scarlet	Rifle green	–	Scarlet[f]	?	P	Green	Kulla	Scarlet	Dark green	–	Badge	–				Black
105	T	Scarlet	Black	Blue	R	Black[f]	?			Kulla	Black	Khaki	Red		Red				
106	T	Drab	Scarlet	Drab		Scarlet[f]		P	Khaki	Kulla	Khaki	Khaki	Khaki		Yellow Red				Brown
107	Z	Scarlet	White	Blue	R	–		G	White			Khaki	Red						Brown
108	T	Scarlet	White	Blue	R	White[f]				Kulla	Red	Khaki	White	Badge	–				Brown
109[m]	L	Scarlet	Black	Blue, black knee pad on right knickerbockers leg	R	Black	White	G	Black	Kulla	Red	Blue/black	White	Black right kneepad patch	–	RA	Black	White	

Regiment	Coat Type[a]	Coat Colour	Coat Facing Colour	Knickerbockers Colour	Knickerbockers Trim[b]	Cummerbund Colour	Cummerbund Trim	Leggings Type[c]	Leggings Colour	Pag or Kulla	Pag or Kulla Colour	Turban Colour	Turban Fringe[d]	Turban Special	Turban Stripes	Hanging Where[e]	Hanging Colour	Hanging Trim	Shoes
110	L	Scarlet	Black	Blue	R	Black	White	G	White/Brown	Kulla	Black	Khaki	Black	Badge	Red	–	–		Black
112	T	Scarlet	Yellow	Blue	R	Yellow[f]		P	Blue	Kulla	White	Yellow	Yellow	–	White, yellow, red				Brown
113	L	Scarlet	Yellow	Blue	R	Yellow	–	P	Blue	Kulla	Khaki	Khaki	Red	–	Blue, brown				Brown
114	L	Scarlet	Yellow	Blue	R	Yellow	Blue	P	Blue	Kulla	Khaki	Khaki	Blue		–				Brown
116	L[n]	Scarlet	Yellow	Blue	R	Yellow[f]				Kulla	Scarlet	Khaki	Blue	–	–				Brown
117	L[n]	Scarlet	Yellow	Blue	R	Yellow[f]		P	Blue	Kulla	Scarlet	Khaki		–	Blue				
119	L	Scarlet	Yellow	Blue	R	Yellow[f]				Kulla	Yellow	Yellow	Yellow	–	Red, grey				Brown
120	L[n]	Scarlet	Yellow			Yellow[f]				Kulla	Yellow	Khaki							
121	L[n]	Scarlet	White			White[f]				–	–		–						
122	L	Scarlet	Emerald green	Blue	R	Black	Yellow/red	G	White/brown	Kulla	Scarlet	Khaki	–	–	–	RA	Very dark green	Red, white	Brown
123	L	Dark green	Scarlet	Rifle green	–	Red	Dark green	P	Green	Kulla	Scarlet	Dark green				–	–	–	Brown
124	L	Drab	Scarlet	Scarlet	–	Red	White, blue	G	White	Kulla	Red	Khaki	Red						Black
125	L	Rifle green	Scarlet	Rifle green	–	Red	–	G	White/black	Kulla	Red	Rifle green	–	Badge		–			
126	L[n]	Drab	Scarlet	Scarlet		Red		G	White	Kulla	Red	Khaki	White		Red				Brown
127	T	Green	Scarlet	Scarlet		Red	–	G	White	Kulla	Red	Green							Brown
128	L	Scarlet	White	Blue	R	White	–	P	Blue	Kulla	Dark blue	Dark blue	White	Badge	–				
129	T	Green	Scarlet	Red		Belt only		G	White	Kulla	Red	Dark green			Piped, red/black				

Regiment	Coat Type[a]	Coat Colour	Coat Facing Colour	Knicker-bockers Colour	Knicker-bockers Trim[b]	Cummerbund Colour	Cummerbund Trim	Leggings Type[c]	Leggings Colour	Turban Pag or Kulla	Turban Pag or Kulla Colour	Turban Colour	Turban Fringe[d]	Turban Special Stripes	Hanging Where[e]	Hanging Colour	Hanging Trim	Shoes
130	L	Green	Scarlet	Red		Scarlet[f]		G	White	Kulla	Red	Dark green	Green					Black
Guides	L	Khaki	Red	Khaki		Red		P	Khaki	Kulla	Red	Khaki			RA	Red		Brown

Sources: Sources consulted in constructing this table include: Lovett drawings, *Whitaker's List – 1900*; Carman, *Uniforms Infantry*; Cassin-Scott, *Military Bands*; photos of King's Indian Orderlies; *Dress Regulations/India, 1913*; and *1914 Army List*. In case of conflict between *Whitaker's List – 1900* and Lovett, we tended to take the colours shown in Lovett's drawings.

Notes: Regiments 49, 50, 60, 65, 68, 70, 71, 77, 78, 85, 100, 111, 115, and 118 did not exist in 1913. Regiments 65, 71, 77, and 78 were raised in 1903 and disbanded in 1904.

[a] L = long blouse; Z = Zouave-style; T = tunic.
[b] R = red trim.
[c] G = gaiters; P = puttees.
[d] Turban fringe usually fell to the right. (F) = trim fringe to the front; (L) = fringe fell to the left.
[e] F = front; L = left, R = right; B = back; A = from cummerbund; T = from turban.
[f] The 1913 Dress Regulations for India state in several places the cummerbunds for wear with the blouse are to be the colour of the regimental facings (*Dress Regulations/India, 1913*, pp. 48 and 55, ¶ 173 and 193).
[g] Native officers wore a long blouse.
[h] One-piece puttee and gaiters.
[i] Left.
[j] Special cuff with a valley where point would be, so there were two points on either side of the valley (Carman, *Infantry*, p. 127).
[k] Officer's tunic had shoulder straps of green-piped with red.
[l] The 1st Bombay Grenadiers (later the 101st Infantry) wore grenades on their collars (Mollo, *Army*, p. 135). However, Carman state these were worn in all khaki dress (Carman, *Uniforms Infantry*, p. 177).
[m] The regiment traditionally wore a black patch on their right trouser leg (Carman, *Uniforms Infantry*, p. 178).
[n] Assumed.
[o] Leather wraparound.

Table III.6.4: Indian Infantry, Unofficial Turban Badges

These turban badges were worn by only infantry regiments.

1st Brahmins	In brass two carp (crest of Oudh) upon a tablet bearing '1776', the date this regiment was raised
2nd Rajput LI	Brass bugle with numeral between the strings
4th Rajputs	Brass *khanjar* (dagger)
6th Jat LI	Brass bugle with numeral below
7th Rajputs	Brass cypher of Duke of Connaught with Roman number and title
8th Rajputs	Brass circle bearing title, surrounded by laurels, and surmounted by crown[a] with numeral in centre
14th Sikhs	The Prince of Wales's plumes, adopted at the time it was made a Prince of Wales regiment
15th Sikhs	Gaylor, in *Sons/Company*, states black steel quoit worn in khaki only. MacMunn, in *Armies*, shows only other ranks wearing quoits in full dress (see Image III:79). The regiment had a very distinctive red and yellow turban. The colours showed on all sides of the turban (see Image C24)
16th Rajputs	Brass gateway of Lucknow surmounted by numeral, and scroll 'Defence of Lucknow'
17th Infantry	Large crescent
18th Infantry	Crescent and five-pointed star
28th Punjabis	White metal crescent and quoit below a crown[a]
30th Punjabis	Brass Roman numerals within a laurel wreath, surmounted by a crown[a]
31st Punjabis	White metal circle bearing title, surmounted by crown;[a] within circle a star of eight points, numeral in centre
32nd Sikh Pioneers	White metal quoit bearing Roman numeral and title, surmounted by a crown[a] and crossed axes. Below quoit the motto 'Aut viam inveniam aut faciam'
34th Sikh Pioneers	Upon a brass Star of India, a white metal crowned garter, bearing the title and containing the number. Below, crossed axes
45th Sikhs	White metal quoit with *kirpan* (Sikh dagger) above
48th Pioneers	Brass crossed axes upon a white metal six-pointed star
61st Pioneers	Brass and white metal
	(i) Crowned[a] circle bearing title. 'LXI' inside (brass)
	(ii) Prince of Wales's plumes over oval, 'LXI' inside title scroll 'Prince of Wales' Own'
	(iii) Prince of Wales's plumes over circle, 'LXI' inside, title scroll 'King George's Own'
	(iv) Prince of Wales's plumes over garter, 'GRI' within, numeral and title scroll below
63rd Palamcottah LI	Brass French horn with number in the curl and crown[a] above
64th Pioneers	Numeral over crossed axes in brass
72nd Punjabis	White metal peacock and title
74th Punjabis	Brass Chinese dragon
79th Carnatic Infantry	Brass circle bearing the title and containing the numbers, surrounded by laurels and surmounted by a crown[a]
80th Infantry	Brass numerals within a laurel wreath
81st Pioneers	Brass circle bearing the title and containing the number, surmounted by a crown[a] and surrounded by laurels
83rd Walajabad LI	Brass bugle with number between the strings
86th Carnatic Infantry	Brass circle bearing the title and containing the number, upon a crowned[a] eight-pointed star
88th Carnatic Infantry	Solid brass circle, containing the title and number, surmounted by a crown[a] and surrounded by laurels
90th Punjabis	White metal Burmese *chinthe* (lion-like creature) with number and title below

91st Punjabis	White metal crossed *dahs* (Burmese sword or knife)
97th Infantry	Numeral within crowned[a] circle, title scroll and *nagpur*
101st Grenadiers	Brass grenade with white metal horse on grenade ball
102nd Grenadiers	Brass grenade with white metal Prince of Wales's plumes on flame and sphinx on ball
104th Rifles	A black crowned[a] bugle with numeral between the strings
107th Pioneers	Brass garter bearing the number and title, within the garter, crossed axes
108th Infantry	Numeral on brass rising sun; title scroll below (brass)
110th Mahratta LI	Brass bugle with strings
125th Rifles	A black crowned[a] bugle with numeral between the strings
128th Pioneers	Brass garter bearing the number and title. Within the garter, crossed axes, and a crown[a] above

Source: Gaylor, *Sons/Company*, pp. 326–7
Note: [a] Crown would be Queen's or King's Crown, depending on who was ruling.

Colour Images

As was the case with cavalry, prior to reviewing the uniform histories of each presidency it may be useful to see colour paintings of infantry in the Indian army as it existed just before the Great War. The colour section has a selection of paintings by Major A.C. Lovett done *c.* 1905–12. The list below shows which regiments are shown in which painting.

Colour Image C24: Infantry Regiment 15
C25: Infantry Regiment 42
C35: Infantry Regiments 5 and 6
C36: Infantry Regiment 35
C37: Infantry Regiment 33
C38: Infantry Regiment 39
C39: Infantry Regiment 45
C40: Infantry Regiments 101 and 102
C41: Infantry Regiment 127
C42: Gurkha Regiment 6

It is interesting to compare a Lovett painting to a black and white photograph of the same regiment. This allows us to test the accuracy the Lovett painting – for example, compare Image III:91 with colour Image C39.

BENGAL INFANTRY AFTER THE MUTINY

Proposals had been made to modify the uniforms before the Mutiny, but events overtook those efforts. In 1863, the uniforms underwent an extensive change.[264]

British Officers

The red or scarlet full dress uniforms of British officers (BOs) in regiments followed the uniforms of British line officers' uniforms. The collar and cuffs were in the facing colour. Their dark blue trousers had narrow red stripes. If the BO was in a regiment dressed in drab or dark green, his uniform followed those of British rifle regiments.[265] Image III:62 shows an officer in a scarlet uniform.

Their collar and cuffs were in their facing colour, and BOs dressed in dark green or drab had black or drab lace loops down the front, and green or drab overalls with drab piping.[266] Image III:63 shows an officer in a drab uniform, and Images III:64 and III:65 show details of the front and back of a drab tunic. Green tunics had the same pattern of braid on the front and back of the tunic.

Turbans were approved for use in 1860, but some regiments wore the Kilmarnock cap into the 1890s.[267]

III:62 (far left) Second Lieutenant Claude Auchinleck, 62nd Punjab Regiment, c. 1904
This is the standard uniform for a British officer of a regiment dressed in scarlet. It is just like the British line uniform except for trim details and the helmet. The collar badge of an elephant in silver followed by a golden dragon wearing a crown can just be made out. The very busy helmet badge of quoit, elephant, scroll, and dragon is hard to distinguish.

III:63 (left) 20th Punjab Officer in his Drab Uniform
This photo shows the stripe on the breeches particularly well.

III:64 Front of a Full Dress Tunic of the 9th Bhopal Infantry, c. 1910

III:65 Back of a Full Dress Tunic of the 9th Bhopal Infantry, c. 1910

Viceroy Commissioned Officer and Other Ranks

Headdress

Immediately after the Mutiny, the enlisted men continued to wear a round cap. This cap was not as high as the pre-Mutiny headdress and was more like a Kilmarnock cap. (See Image III:66 for an example of a Kilmarnock cap). In 1860, the government approved the wearing of turbans, the colour to be set regimentally.[268] By 1900, almost all the regiments had adopted turbans (see §*III-3-4* for their colours). The exceptions were the 11th Rajputs (Image III:67), the Gurkha regiments, and the 39th Garhwal Rifles, who dressed in the Gurkha style (Image III:68), and all were listed as wearing Kilmarnock caps in 1914.[269]

III:66 Subadar Major Parsu Khattri, Sardar Bahadur of the 5th Royal Gurkhas
Note the badge on the pouch belt and the fine collection of medals this man has accrued.

III:67 11th Bengal Infantry in old-style headdress (Kilmarnock cap) and Zouave jacket, c. 1900
The regiment was very fond of these caps and jackets and continued wearing them long after other regiments began wearing turbans and long blouses.

III:68 39th Garhwal Rifles
This ethnic group had once served in the Gurkha army, and so their uniform was like that worn by the Gurkhas. Based on his impressive medals, this photograph may have been taken after World War I.

III:69 Native Officer of the 1st Brahmins
Note the badge on his turban in this fine character study.

III:70 Native Officer and a Sepoy of the 7th Bengal Infantry (later the 7th Rajputs), c. 1895
The two figures on the right are in full dress. Note the officer is wearing gaiters, and the sepoy is wearing puttees.

§III-6 Infantry

III:71 Officers and Men in Review Order of the 13th Bengal Infantry (later 13th Rajputs)
Notice the difference between the officer's turban on the far right and the other turbans belonging to other ranks.

III:72 Note turban badge. This photo was likely taken after the Great War.

III:73 Subadar Major, 34th Sikh Pioneers after 1902
Note turban badge.

354   India

III:74 Indian Native Officers, 36th Sikhs, c. 1890s
Note the quoit. This regiment is wearing a regulation badge on their turbans. It was one of sixteen Indian regiments that had regulation badges for their VCOs' turbans. These regiments were the 8th, 16th, 32nd, 34th, 36th, 48th, 63rd, 72nd, 73rd, 74th, 81st, 83rd, 88th, 91st, 97th, and 102nd. A description of these badges is found under the regiment's name in Appendix I, Dress Regulations, India 1913. Note also the shape of the Sikh turbans.

III:75 45th Bengal Infantry (later 45th Rattray's Sikhs), c. 1895
Note the regimental unofficial badge on their turban shows up clearly in this photograph. Note the difference between the turbans of the officer holding flags and the turbans of the other ranks in the colour party.

§III-6 Infantry 355

III:76 12th (Kelat-i-Ghilzie) Regiment of Bengal Infantry (later 12th Pioneers (Kelat-i-Ghilzie Regiment)) in Review Order, c. 1895
Notice the Zouave-style jacket with a square-cut bottom to central panel.

III:77 17th Bengal Infantry
Note the more sedate crescent moon unofficial badges compared to those found in Image III:86.

III:78 Pathan Native Officer, 19th Punjab Infantry, c. 1896
Note the square-cut bottom to the central panel to the Zouave-style tunic.

Zouave Jacket

In 1863, the Zouave jacket was taken into use for native ranks.[270] The Indian army Zouave jacket was a tunic with a panel of the facing colour down the front. The panel was trimmed in white.[271] See Images III:69 to III:75 for examples of a Zouave front worn by officers. Images III:76 to III:79 show the Zouave front being worn by other ranks. In Bengal, initially, the panel was cut away so it was curved at its bottom. But, by the 1890s, in the Bengal army the curve was removed and the panel was square at the bottom.[272]

However, not all Bengal native officers wore Zouave tunics; particularly after the Zouave tunics fell out of favour in the late 1890s. For examples of non-Zouave tunics among officers, see Images III:80 to III:85. For non-Zouave tunics and long blouses among other ranks, see Images III:86 to III:92.

The Bengal army for historical reasons recruited from certain groups that were not considered military classes. The uniforms of the regiments raised from among these groups were often different – sometimes markedly, sometimes subtlely – from those worn in the general Bengal army. For an example of an officer wearing a unique uniform, see Image III:93. For examples of other ranks wearing unique uniforms, see Images III:94 to III:98.

III:79 Colour Party of the 15th Sikhs in Zouave Jackets
Note their 'humbug' red and yellow pattern turbans and the regimental badges on the officers' turbans. Also note the quoits on the other ranks' turbans (see Table III.6.4 and Image C24).

III:80 (left) An Other Ranks and Officer of the 1st Bengal Infantry (later 1st Brahmins), c. 1895

III:81 (opposite, top left) Native Officer of the 19th Punjab Infantry, c. 1912 The Zouave jacket has been replaced by a tunic. The sash around the shoulder has been replaced by the waist sash and white gaiters have replaced the puttees. Adding white puttees was common as it was a way to add colour in place of the vanished central coloured panel of the Zouave jacket.

§III-6 Infantry   357

III:82 Officer and Sergeant of the 30th Infantry, c. 1895
Note neither of these men is wearing a Zouave jacket.

III:83 32nd Punjab Infantry (Pioneers) (later 32nd Sikh Pioneers)
The man on the left is a native officer in review order.

III:84 45th Rattray's Sikhs
The turban badge shows up very clearly here. This native officer is wearing the new-style tunic. This regiment gave up Zouave tunics in 1903 and began wearing gaiters the same year.

III:85 Fine Study of a 1st Brahmins Officer

III:86 17th Infantry (Loyal Regiment) Pipe Band
Note the large crescent moon badge on their turban. As behooves a pipe band, they are wearing special Scots doublets with Inverness skirts. Several Indian army regiments had bagpipe units.

§III-6 Infantry 359

III:87 33rd Punjab Infantry (later 33rd Punjabis), c. 1895
All three men are in review order. Note they are all wearing tunics and not Zouave jackets.

III:88 38th Bengal Infantry (later 38th Dogras), c. 1895
The two men on the left are a sergeant and a native officer. Note the difference between the sergeant's and the officer's turbans.

III:89 40th Pathans, c. 1907
Note the many different styles of turbans. Officially there are five different classes supplying soldiers to this regiment. Examples of those classes with their distinctive turbans shown in the photograph are as follows:
Jammu Dogras (4), Orakzai (3), Akora Khattak (2), Afridi (3), and Yusufzai (3) Pathans, and Punjabis from the Salt Range (2) and Murree Hills (2).

III:90 40th Pathan NCO
Note the long blouse, kulla, turban, and puttees, which show up well in this photo. The colour of the 40th's uniform is drab, and this uniform seems a little dark for that. However, often the drab worn in India was a dark shade, and the film stock of the period could produce odd effects.

III:91 (above) Band of the 45th Infantry
Note the quoit with dagger badge on turbans.

III:92 (left) Other Rank of the 22nd Punjabis
The long blouse comes to just above the knees.

III:93 (below) Malwa Bhil Corps, c. 1895
This photograph was taken before the regiment began to wear the Kilmarnock cap. It clearly shows the belt with the S buckle and the tunic with five buttons. The full trousers are shown. The regulations call them Zouave trousers, but it is clear that they are nowhere close to being true Zouave trousers. The tunic cuff has an indentation where most tunic cuffs would have pointed cuffs. This can be clearly seen in the original photograph.

III:94 18th Infantry
They are wearing the new style long blouses. Note the star and crescent on their turbans.

III:95 Other Rank Native Officer and Sergeant of the Deoli Irregular Force (later 42nd Deoli Regiment) in Review Order

Note the tunic with four buttons and white gaiters. Also note that the officer is distinguished by piping around the collar, down the front of the tunic, and around the bottom. During the 1890s, native officers in India wore their sash over their left shoulder, and NCOs, such as this havildar, wore a sash over their right shoulder. The Deoli Force consisted of both infantry and cavalry. However, the cavalry drew on classes other than the Mina (Meena). In this photo, the cavalryman is a Sikh. The Deoli Infantry drew men from the high-status Mina clans.

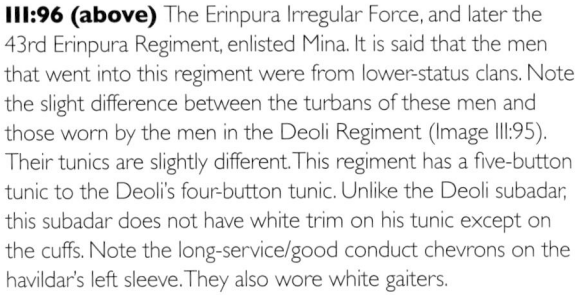

III:96 (above) The Erinpura Irregular Force, and later the 43rd Erinpura Regiment, enlisted Mina. It is said that the men that went into this regiment were from lower-status clans. Note the slight difference between the turbans of these men and those worn by the men in the Deoli Regiment (Image III:95). Their tunics are slightly different. This regiment has a five-button tunic to the Deoli's four-button tunic. Unlike the Deoli subadar, this subadar does not have white trim on his tunic except on the cuffs. Note the long-service/good conduct chevrons on the havildar's left sleeve. They also wore white gaiters.

III:97 (top right) Native Officer and Sergeant of the Merwara Battalion (later 44th Merwara Infantry) in Review Order, c. 1895
Notice how the tunic is cut with a pronounced V in front. The tunic cuff has an indentation where most tunic cuffs would have pointed cuffs.

III:98 (right) Meywa Bhil Corps and Their Distinctive Tunic, c. 1895
The tunic has only four buttons and is cut away at the bottom. These features are clearly shown in the photograph. There was no collar on the tunic, but there was trim along the neck opening. The pointed cuffs were scarlet. The regulations state that the rifle green trousers were to be peg-topped, but this image shows them loose. All ranks wore leather gaiters as per regulations. The regulations stated that native officers had a black leather pouch and pouch belt without ornamentations. However, this photograph clearly shows a plate, chains, and whistle on the native officer's pouch belt. Note how the officer's Kilmarnock cap does not have a badge while that of the enlisted men does.

Netherwear

In 1869, dark blue baggy knickerbocker trousers for review order were introduced. These had red piping down the side seams. Normally, in review order, these were worn with white gaiters.[273] However, photos exist showing troops wearing dark puttees in review order.

MADRAS INFANTRY AFTER THE MUTINY

Up to the 1890s, when the Burma battalions were created, all Madras infantry regiments wore scarlet.[274]

Until 1883 the Madras infantry wore a single-breasted tunic. The collar, cuffs, and shoulder straps seem to have been in the facing colour.[275] In 1883, a Zouave jacket was adopted.[276] It was very similar to the Bengal Zouave tunic with a central panel of the facing colour. The bottom of the panel was cut away to form a V shape (Image III:100),[277] and in 1897, the skirt of the Zouave jacket was lengthened by 3.81 cm (1½ inches).[278] The central panel was piped in white cloth and had gold lace 1.91 cm (¾ inch) wide around the neck and down the front to the waist seam. The cuffs were the slash style, and there were eight buttons down the front.[279]

By 1913, the Madras VCOs were wearing a tunic. In the 66th Madras, the officers and men wore scarlet long blouses in full dress, which were 101.6 cm

III:99 Sepoy of the 61st Pioneers
Note the Madras-style Zouave tunic with the V at the bottom of the central panel. Several of the Madras army regiments wore Zouave tunics right up to 1914.

III:100 Native Officer Mukhlis Ali Khan of the 14th Madras Infantry, c. 1896
Note his Madras-style Zouave tunic and the style of turban he is wearing. This regiment later had its personnel drawn from men from the Punjab.

(40 inches) long for men 1.75 metres (5 feet 9 inches) or taller.[280] The 3.81 cm (1½ inch) tall collar, as well as shoulder straps and cuffs, was in the regiment's facing colour,[281] emerald green. A few other regiments, the 2nd, 10th, 48th, 95th, 97th, 99th, and 109th, also wore a blouse rather than a tunic.[282]

British Officers

HEADDRESS

In 1870, a cork helmet covered with a white cloth was adopted for Madras British officers. This, together with a regimental puggree,[283] became standard headdress. The shape of the helmet would change over the years (see Images II:17 and II:18 for two of the shapes).

TROUSERS AND PANTALOONS

These were the same as worn by the British infantry, and the 1885 Dress Regulations state they had a 0.64 cm (¼ inch) scarlet welt down the side seams.[284]

Viceroy Commissioned Officers

Viceroy commissioned officers wore the same uniform as the Bengal infantry with only minor exceptions.[285]

BURMA REGIMENTS

One unusual feature of the Madras army was the so-called Burma units. These were formed in 1886–7 after Upper Burma was annexed. The area suffered from lawlessness and military police battalions were raised in India from Sikhs and Gurkhas. By 1890–1, they had the area under control, but rather than disband the military police battalions, the authorities decided to add them to the Madras army. In one case, a police battalion adopted the regimental number of a disbanded regiment, but in most cases an existing regiment had its personnel from southern classes replaced by the Punjabi men of the military police or Gurkhas. Table III.6.5 shows the process.

The Burma Battalion numbers were carried as part of the Madras regimental title (noted in brackets) from the early 1890s to the reorganisation of 1903.[286] At that time, the 93rd took the title Burma Infantry, and references to Burma were removed from the other Madras regiments' titles.[287]

The Burma infantry wore drab in full dress.[288] This has been described as a practical uniform,[289] but it should be viewed as more of a fashion statement. Drab, however useful it was in the Northwest Frontier, offered no more camouflage than a red coat in green jungles and rice paddies in Burma.

See Table III.2.3 for the Burma units' facing colours, and Table III.3.4 for their turban colours.

Table III.6.5: Military Police into Madras Regiments and a Gurkha Regiment

Military Police Unit	Madras Regiment	1903–14 Title
1	10[a]	10 Gurkha Rifles
2	12	72 Punjabis
3	33	93 Punjabis
4	32	92 Punjabis
5	30	90 Punjabis
6	31	91 Punjabis
7	29	89 Punjabis

Sources: Perry, 'Armies PI', pp. 134–6, 142; Carman, *Uniforms Infantry*, pp. 158–9

Note: [a] The original regiment was disbanded in 1885 according to Carman, *Uniforms Infantry*, p. 159; Perry, 'Armies PI', p. 134, says 1890.

HYDERABAD CONTINGENT AFTER THE MUTINY

The Hyderabad Contingent traces its origins back to a favourite device used by the East India Company to raise troops. The Company would recruit soldiers, who would be stationed in or near the territory of a native state, and that state would pay for them. When the Mutiny came in 1857, most of these contingents mutinied. The Hyderabad Contingent was an exception, and it and the state of Hyderabad stayed loyal to the British.

After the Mutiny, when the Crown took over the Company's armies, the Hyderabad Contingent was treated as a local force.

Officers' Dress

The 1886 Regulations state that the dress uniform of British officers in the contingent is the same as that for British infantry officers.[290] The uniform of VCOs was the same as that supplied for VCOs by the Madras army.[291]

The 1900 Regulations provide for a scarlet uniform with dark green facings. The British officers were to wear the same uniform as the Bengal infantry officers who dressed in scarlet. The native officers were to wear the same uniform as Madras native officers who dressed in scarlet.[292]

After 1903, the Hyderabad regiments were no longer treated as a local force. They took the numbers 94 to 99 in the new continuous listing of Indian regiments. Because they were now in the Indian army proper, they were covered in the 1913 Dress Regulations with regiments dressed in scarlet with little further comment.

Native officers of the 95th, 97th, and 99th Regiments wore a scarlet long blouse in full dress. The native officers in the other three regiments wore scarlet tunics.[293]

Other Ranks

Whitaker's List of 1900 states that all six regiments wore a red uniform with dark green facings.[294] This was presumably a long blouse for other ranks; a painting by Lovett in *The Armies of India* shows other ranks men from five Hyderabad regiments c.1905. Their turbans, trim, and cummerbunds were all dark green. Three had dark green puttees, one a leather sheath, and one a combination of white gaiters-puttees in place of the dark green puttees. The knickerbockers were Oxford blue with a red stripe on the outside side of each leg.

The 1900 *Whitaker's List* gives the colours of the turbans at that point in time.

Regiment	Turban (Puggree) Colour	Kulla
1	Not listed	
2	Khaki	—
3	Khaki edged with green and orange	—
4	Green	Red
5	Khaki and green	—
6	Green and red	Green

Source: Whitaker's List – 1900, pp. 899–900.

BOMBAY INFANTRY AFTER THE MUTINY

Throughout the period between the Mutiny and 1914, the Bombay infantry wore a single-breasted tunic; they never dressed in a Zouave tunic.[295]

The Bombay regiments can be divided into three types: line, rifle, and Baluch.[296]

LINE REGIMENTS

British Officers

The uniforms of BOs in the Bombay army during the period after the Mutiny closely followed the dress of the British army and other presidencies.[297] By the 1900s, British officers of regiments dressed in scarlet wore a single-breasted eight button tunic. Officers of regiments dressed in drab or green wore coats with five rows of frogging on the chest and braid on the back (see Images III:64, III:65, and III:101). Officers dressed in drab and green wore pouch belts.

Viceroy Commissioned Officers

The native officers' dress closely followed the uniforms of the Bombay army's BOs. The main differences were the VCOs wore a turban[298] and were much more likely to wear knickerbockers than BOs (Images III:102, III:103, and III:104).

Other Ranks

By 1861, the other ranks wore a tunic which followed the undress tunic of the British infantry. In 1880, a new tunic was issued, which was basically the same except it had a coloured collar and shoulder straps of the facing colour, but was without coloured trim on the cuffs.[299] This left the tunic sleeves plain.[300] The single-breasted tunic had five buttons down the front (Images III:105, III:106, and III:107).

III:101 Lieutenant Colonel A.P. Elphinstone of the 106th Hazara Pioneers in Full Dress
This is a standard tunic for British officers wearing drab uniforms. Note the pouch belt badge and chain and whistle. A whistle was standard for Bombay regiments.

III:102 Native Officers of the 101st (Bombay) Grenadiers
They are wearing the standard tunic of officers from regiments dressed in scarlet. It is a slightly simplified version of the tunic worn by British officers of these regiments. Note also the type of turbans these officers are wearing.

368 India

III:103 Ram Sarup Subadar of the 107th Pioneers in Scarlet Full Dress
Note his pouch belt, unusual for a regiment wearing scarlet. Also note that there is no officer's sash, which is also unusual for a regiment wearing scarlet.

III:104 107th Pioneers Officer
Note the non-regulation garter badge bearing regimental number and crossed axes on his turban (see Table III.6.4).

III:105 The 28th Bombay Infantry (Pioneers) (later 128th Pioneers)
The two men on the right are an officer and sergeant. Notice the type of tunic worn in the Bombay army. Also note the type of turbans worn by the men of this regiment. This regiment also had a pouch belt of brown leather and a brown leather belt. These took the place of sashes.

NETHERWEAR

VCOs and other ranks wore dark blue knickerbockers with red piping along the outside seams.

GAITERS

The gaiters worn by Bombay regiments were distinctive as they had a piece of leather behind the buttons and at the ankles to provide strengthening. For line regiments, the leather was left its natural colour so they were easy to spot (Images III:106 and III:107).

RIFLE REGIMENTS

The first of the rifle units in the Bombay army was the old 4th Bombay Infantry. They were made rifles in May 1841 and claim to be the first Indian regiment so honoured.[301] Two other regiments followed, the 23rd and the 25th in 1890 and 1888 respectively.[302]

III:106 Sepoy of the 105th Infantry
Note the Bombay-style gaiters with the leather reinforcements. Also note the style of turban. This man has put in long years of service and does not seem to have received any promotions.

III:107 20th Bombay Infantry (later 120th Rajputana Rifles)
The two men on the left are in full dress. Notice the Bombay-style gaiters with the leather reinforcement.

British Officers

Headdress
The BOs wore a tropical helmet covered with white cloth.[303]

Tunic
The tunic was rifle green with scarlet facings for all three regiments,[304] and the trim was scarlet. It had a black velvet collar in 1913,[305] and in 1901 it had a collar the colour of the regimental facings (scarlet).[306] It is likely this distinction predated 1901.

In 1901, on both sides of the chest opening were five cords.[307] These follow the pattern of the British rifle tunic's chest cords (see §II-3-5, Image II:19 for a photograph and §II-8-d for a description of the cording).

Trousers
The 1901 Dress Regulations state that three rifle regiments wore the uniform of officers of the Bengal infantry – dressed in green with certain exceptions.[308] The British officers dressed in green wore rifle green overalls and pantaloons with a 5.08 cm (2 inch) black braid down the side seams.[309] The trousers in 1913 were almost certainly rifle green because the 1901 Dress Regulations call for rifle green trousers and pantaloons with 5.08 cm (2 inch) black braid down each side seam.[310]

Viceroy Commissioned Officers

Headdress
The VCOs of the three rifle regiments wore green turbans.[311] The kulla was scarlet or red for all three regiments.[312]

Tunic
The VCOs' tunic c. 1909 was green with a red collar and cuffs. The piping down the front was also red.[313] The 1901 Dress Regulations call for a rifle green tunic with scarlet collar.[314]

Trousers
VCOs of the 125th wore dark green trousers c. 1905.[315] The 1901 Regulations state that VCOs of all three regiments were to wear rifle green knickerbockers without piping.[316]

Gaiters
The 4th Bombay Rifles wore black gaiters c. 1891, but later green puttees replaced them.[317] The 1901 Dress Regulations stated black gaiters for all three regiments.[318] The 125th (formerly the 25th) wore white gaiters c. 1905.[319]

Rifle Other Ranks

Turban
The other ranks of all three regiments wore a green turban with a red or scarlet kulla, if a kulla was called for.[320]

Blouse
The other ranks of two of the three rifle regiments, the 23rd and 25th (after 1903 the 123rd and 125th), wore a long dark green blouse.[321] It is probable that the 4th (104th) also had a green blouse.

The green blouse had red shoulder straps, red trim on the cuffs, and, around 1905 at least, red trim down the front.[322]

Cummerbund
The basic cummerbund was red. The 23rd had in addition what seem to have been dark green stripes.[323]

Trousers
The pipe band of the 25th Bombay Infantry (later 125th) wore sepoy dress, and their trousers were dark green.[324] From this, it can be concluded that other ranks in the three rifle regiments all wore dark green trousers.

Gaiters
A Lovett watercolour, c. 1905 shows a pipe band of the 125th in sepoy's dress. They wore white gaiters.[325] The 4th wore black gaiters in 1891 and later black puttees.[326]

BALUCH REGIMENTS

The first Baluch regiment, the 27th Bombay, traces its origins to an experimental 'Baluch battalion' raised in 1844 after the conquest of Scinde. In 1861, this unit became the 27th Bombay Infantry. A second Baluch unit was raised in 1846 and became the 29th Bombay Infantry in 1861.[327] In 1858, two Baluch rifle regiments were formed as silladar infantry. In 1861, the second rifle regiment was disbanded and the first became the 30th Bombay Infantry.[328]

The 24th and 26th Bombay became Baluchistan regiments in 1891 and 1896 respectively. They both wore drab coats with red facings and trousers.[329]

This meant that by the mid-1890s there were five Baluch regiments: the 24th, 26th, 27th, 29th, and 30th. All wore the distinctive red trousers, the mark of Baluch troops, and most – the 27th, 29th, and 30th – wore dark green coats and turbans. The reason for the use of these colours may lie in the fact that red and dark green were the state colours of Khairpur and were a popular colour combination in Scinde.[330]

The 24th and 26th, when they became Baluch troops, were given drab coats and turbans (khaki turbans for the 26th) to go with their red trousers.[331]

The 27th, 29th, and 30th Bombay Infantry

After 1903, these were the 127th, 129th, and 130th Infantry respectively. These were the regiments that wore green turbans and coats and red trousers (Image C41).

British Officers of the 27th, 29th, and 30th Infantry

HEADDRESS

BOs wore a white colonial helmet (Images II:17 and II:18 show the different styles, which changed over the years). The 27th had a red puggree, the 29th a

III:108 26th (Baluchistan) Regiment of Bombay Infantry
The men on either end are in review order dress. Note the difference in tunics between the sergeant on left and the officer on the right.

green puggree with the top fold being scarlet, and the 30th a dark green puggree with a green fringe and a red kulla.[332]

Tunic

The tunic worn by the British officers was similar to the British rifle regiments' tunic, and the 27th Bombay (127th) and 30th Bombay (130th) were said to be the same as the British 60th Regiment (KRRC). This meant these tunics were rifle or dark green with scarlet facings[333] and had black braid across the chest and along the back seams. (See §II-3-5, Image II:19 for an image of the braid and §II-8-d for a description of the braid.)

In the 29th (129th), the collar and cuffs were scarlet.[334] This was likely true of the 27th and 30th also.

Trousers and Overalls

Trousers were plain red in the 29th (129th).[335] Mollo says BOs of the 27th, 29th, and 30th Bombay Baluch Infantry wore red overalls.[336]

Viceroy Commissioned Officers of the 27th, 29th and 30th Infantry

Headdress

The 29th (129th), in 1882, had a plain green turban with a red kulla.[337] Image III:5 shows a King's Orderly Officer VCO of the 130th Baluchis in 1906. His turban seems to be striped dark green and gold.[338] A green turban was, generally speaking, a distinguishing mark of a Baluch regiment dressed in green. However, a Lovett drawing of c. 1905 shows a blue turban (Image C41).

Tunic

The tunic of VCOs of these three regiments was green, often dark green, with red collars, cuffs, and piping on the seams.[339] The tunic had black rifle-style braid.[340]

Knickerbockers and Trousers

Red netherwear were a distinguishing mark of the Baluch units. They were worn by all three regiments.

Gaiters

White gaiters were worn with the red knickerbockers and trousers (Image C41).[341] White gaiters were worn by the VCOs of the 29th when they were in Egypt in 1882.[342] Another painting of 1886 shows the same thing.[343] The other two regiments, the 27th and 30th, also wore white gaiters.[344]

Other Ranks of the 27th, 29th, and 30th Infantry

Headdress

In the 27th Bombay Regiment, 'the sepoys had green pugris with two upstanding ends over the red kullah'.[345] The other two regiments, the 29th and 30th, wore dark green turbans.[346] *Whitaker's List* for 1901 shows the 27th as having a green puggree, the 29th as having a dark green puggree with red kulla, and the 30th as having a green puggree with red kulla.[347]

Tunic

All three regiments, the 27th, 29th, and 30th, wore a dark green tunic with a red collar and cuffs and red piping on the seams.[348]

Knickerbockers

All three regiments wore red knickerbockers.[349]

Gaiters

White gaiters were worn in full dress by all three regiments.[350]

Drab Baluch Regiments

After 1903, the drab Baluch regiments were the 124th and 126th Bombay Infantry. The 24th Bombay Infantry became a Baluch regiment (124th) in 1891, and the 26th became one (126th) in 1896.[351]

British Officers of the Drab Baluch Regiments

HEADDRESS
The 1901 Dress Regulations state that BOs wore a cork helmet covered in white cloth. The helmet was then covered in drab cloth.[352] This would have been the colonial helmet shown in Image II:17.

TUNICS
The 1901 Dress Regulations state the tunic is drab. It was cut the same as that worn by Bengal infantry dressed in scarlet. It had scarlet edging on the collar, down the front, on the plaits behind, and on the skirts and shoulder straps.[353]

The 1913 Dress Regulations say that BOs of these two regiments will wear drab tunics in a pattern like those worn by the regiments dressed in scarlet. The only difference is that the two Baluch regiments had pleats on the tunic skirts' behind.[354] The 1901 Regulations do not mention pleats; however, Carman states that pleats were on the chest for the 26th, but is silent as to the 24th.[355]

OVERALLS AND PANTALOONS
The 1901 Dress Regulations state that overalls and pantaloons should consist of plain red cloth.[356]

Viceroy Commissioned Officers of the Drab Baluch Regiments

TURBAN
The 1901 Dress Regulations state the VCOs' turban was khaki with gold ends. The kulla, if worn, was scarlet, embroidered with gold.[357]

TUNIC
The tunic was the same as that worn by Bengal regiments dressed in drab (see above).[358] See Images III:64 and III:65 for an idea of the shape of the braid on a drab tunic.

NETHERWEAR
The 1901 Dress Regulations state that the VCOs' netherwear was scarlet pyjamas without trim.[359] By 1913, their netherwear was described as red knickerbockers.[360]

GAITERS
The 1901 Dress Regulations called for white gaiters to be worn in full dress.[361]

Other Ranks of the Drab Baluch Regiments

TURBAN
The 1900 *Whitaker's List* describes the 24th and 26th as having a khaki and red turban with red kulla.[362]

BLOUSE (KURTA)
When the long blouse was introduced for war by other ranks, the 24th wore one that was light drab with red piping.[363] It is very likely the 26th (126th) also wore a drab blouse with red facings and piping.

CUMMERBUND
The 24th wore a cummerbund that had no ends. It was red with stripes edged green.[364]

TROUSERS
Red trousers, the mark of a Baluch unit, were worn by both regiments.[365]

GAITERS
In full dress, the 26th's red trousers were tucked into white gaiters.[366] White gaiters are also likely for the 24th.

PUNJAB INFANTRY AFTER THE MUTINY

The Punjab Infantry was raised in 1849. A sixth regiment, the old Scinde Camel Corps of the Bombay army, was added in 1853. The four Sikh regiments joined in 1851.[367] A Gurkha battalion, the Hazara Gurkha Battalion, was formed in 1858 (later the 5th Gurkhas) and served with the Frontier Force. The Guides, while they held themselves somewhat apart, were added to the Frontier Force in 1851.[368]

There is little information on uniforms before 1860. The 1st Punjab Infantry (after 1903 the 55th Coke's Rifles) wore dark blue tunics with red piping and dark blue trousers with a yellow stripe. The 4th Punjab Infantry (PI) was dressed in a drab uniform. After 1853, the 5th Punjab Infantry wore a drab tunic with green facings. Before that, they had a red tunic.[369]

1ST REGIMENT

British Officers

The British officers of the 1st PI in the early 1860s wore blue uniforms. The 1865 Regulations describe red facings on a dark green uniform. The uniform was piped red. The green trousers and pantaloons had two 1.91 cm (¾ inch) stripes of black mohair braid on a scarlet ground with a light in between.

The 1901 Regulations follow this pattern, but the width of the two braids on each leg had changed to 2.22 cm (⅞ inch) wide. The 1913 Dress Regulations are the same.[370]

Native Officers

In the 1890s, the native officers' turban 'was dark green and blue with yellow (or gold) stripes', according to Carman.[371] It had a green fringe. Their dark green eight-button tunic was piped red down the front and around the top of the cuffs. They wore loose dark green pyjamas and probably dark green puttees. The shoulder straps were dark green piped red.

The 1913 Dress Regulations provide similar details for the tunic. They state Indian officers were to wear knickerbockers.[372]

Other Ranks

The other ranks wore dark green tunics with red piping that were similar to those of the native officers. Dark green knickerbockers can be assumed.

OTHER PUNJAB REGIMENTS

The other Punjab regiments, the 2nd, 3rd, 4th, 5th, and 6th, all dressed in drab.

British Officers

In 1865, BOs wore a drab single-breasted tunic with five rows of drab silk square cord. The collar and cuffs were the colour of the regimental facings. The trousers were a dark drab cloth with a double stripe of drab silk lancer pattern braid 1.91 cm (¾ inch) wide.[373]

In the 1866 and 1891 Dress Regulations, the description of the BOs' tunic is basically the same. They note the pouch belt of the 2nd and 6th Punjab Infantry was black leather, and the others had brown.[374] The 1913 Regulations also call for five rows of frogging on the front of the single-breasted tunic with braid on the back seams and skirt (see Images III:64 and III:65). The trousers and pantaloons were drab with a 5.08 cm (2 inch) black braid down the outside seams.

Indian Officers

The Indian officers dressed in drab according to the 1886 and 1891 Dress Regulations wore a drab single-breasted tunic. The collar, shoulder straps, cuffs, and piping were in the regimental facing colour (see table below). The pointed cuffs were 12.7 cm (5 inches) deep.[375]

The 1913 Dress Regulations called for a single-breasted drab tunic edged with cord. On the front were five sets of drab frogging (see Image III:64), and the seams on the back of the tunic were traced with a cord (see Image III:65). The collar and cuffs were in the facing colour.[376]

The trousers and pantaloons were of drab cloth with two stripes, each 2.54 cm (1 inch) wide, of drab mohair down the side seams of each leg. There was piping in the colour of the facings 1.27 cm (½ inch) wide between each side seam. The 57th (old 4th) Regiment had stripes of lancer pattern.

The 56th and 59th Rifles had pouch belts of black patent leather; the pouch belts of the other regiments were brown leather. All pouch belts were 7.62 cm (3 inches) wide with a silver plate, whistle and chain. The pouch was of black leather of regimental pattern with regimental number in silver on the flap.[377]

Original Regiment Number[a]	Original Coat Colour	Original Facing Colour	1903 Regiment Number
1	Green	Green[b]	55
2	Drab	Black	56
3	Drab	Green[c]	Disbanded 1882
4	Drab	French grey[d]	57
5	Drab	Green	58
6	Red	Green[e]	59

Notes: [a] Mollo, Army, p. 130.
[b] Red piping in 1870.
[c] Green piping in 1870.
[d] Khaki coat and Prussian blue facings in 1870; drab coat in 1898.
[e] Drab coat and red facings in 1870.

SIKH REGIMENTS BEFORE THE MUTINY

As they came into contact with the tribes of the Northwest Frontier and made peace with the Sikhs, the British faced two problems: raids from across the frontier and a large number of ex-soldiers from the disbanded Sikh army, who might cause problems now that they had no way to make a living. Both of these problems were solved by hiring veterans of the Sikh wars. These men went into the British Sikh infantry of the Frontier Force and guarded the frontier.

The new regiments, raised in 1846/7, were titled Sikh infantry because their personnel came from the old Sikh army. The regiments, like the Sikh army itself, were never wholly Sikh.[378]

Headdress

The headdress went through a dizzying array of changes. The original intent was for the Sikh regiments to wear turbans. But the regiments were hardly formed when, in 1847, the headdress was changed to a type of Kilmarnock cap. Then, in 1853, it was changed to a drab cap. Finally, in 1857, the headdress was changed to a drab turban with yellow.[379]

Tunic

When formed, the 1st, 3rd, and 4th Sikh regiments were to wear red coats with yellow facings. The 2nd Regiment was assigned a green coat with black facings. According to Carman, trousers were 'as in the line'.[380]

No sooner was this set than the uniforms were changed to drab. A request to change the uniform colour to drab or green was approved in 1852, and clothing was made up in a drab colour.[381] In 1859, drab tunics and pantaloons were issued.[382]

SIKH REGIMENTS AFTER THE MUTINY

All four Sikh regiments wore khaki or drab uniforms after the Mutiny, including the 2nd Sikhs, who exchanged their green uniforms for khaki ones in 1861 (by 1865, the uniform colour was described as drab).[383]

Table III.6.6: Sikh Regiment Facing Colours and Turban Colours, *c.* 1886

Regiment Number	Facing Colour	Turban Colour	Turban Stripe	Post-1903 Number
1	Yellow	Khaki	Yellow – several	51
2	Scarlet	Khaki	Red[a]	52
3	Black	Khaki	Black; orange fringe	53
4	Emerald green[b]	Khaki	Green	54

Source: Carman, *Uniforms Infantry*, pp. 221–4.
Notes: [a] NCOs also had a red fringe.
[b] Was dark green up to 1884.

British Officers

HEADDRESS
BOs in the Sikh regiments of the Frontier Force wore the overseas helmet used during their time of service (Image II:17). BOs of the 2nd Sikhs had a red square silk flash worn on the left side of their overseas helmet. This was worn up to 1921.[384]

III:109 Lieutenant Colonel of 52nd Sikhs in Review Order, c. 1907
This was standard dress for regiments wearing drab uniforms.

TUNIC
BOs wore a drab tunic with five rows of hussar-type braid and olivets on the chest (Image III:64). The tunic's back had two lines of braid, with netted caps, on the seams (Images III:64, III:109, and III:110).[385]

Viceroy Commissioned Officers

HEADDRESS
After the Mutiny, the facings of the 2nd Sikhs changed from black to red. The VCOs' turban was khaki with a khaki fringe and a red stripe.[386] In the 3rd Sikhs, the turban for VCOs was khaki with a 7.62 to 10.16 cm (3 to 4 inch) stripe above an orange fringe.[387] In the early 1860s, the VCOs of the 4th Sikhs wore a khaki turban with a dark green fringe at each end.[388]

TUNIC
All four regiments wore tunics of either khaki or drab,[389] the two shades blending into each other. Their facing colours are shown in Table III.6.6. The 3rd Sikhs' tunic, *c.* 1900, had black collars edged with drab braid, black shoulder straps, pointed black cuffs, and black piping down the front of the tunic.[390]

III:110 British Officer of the 58th Vaughan's Rifles (Frontier Force) (this was the regiment's title after 1903)
The uniform is khaki, and the collar is emerald green. The crown on the brown leather pouch belt device seems to be a Queen's Crown, which would probably date this photo to before Queen Victoria's death in 1901. However, it was not uncommon for officers to continue to wear uniform items, such as helmet plates, with Queen's Crowns after Victoria died. That may have happened here with the pouch belt badge.

In the 1860s, the 4th Sikhs' VCOs wore a summer uniform of a khaki blouse without a collar, but with dark green cuffs. The 1886 Regulations call for the summer uniform to be khaki coats for all.[391]

The 1913 Dress Regulations call for VCOs to wear a drab tunic with piping of facing cloth down the front and around to the rear vent. The collar, pointed cuffs, and shoulder straps were in the facing colour.[392] Thus, in most regiments dressed in drab, the native officers did not have the elaborate braiding on the front of their tunics as worn by British officers (see Image III:111).

III:111 British and Native Officer of the 53rd Sikhs (Frontier Force) in Full Dress Uniforms
Notice the difference between the tunics worn by British and native officers. Also notice the different types of turbans worn by the native officers. Two scarlet-clad officers have slipped into this photo. The one on the far left is a British line officer, as shown by the Staffordshire knot on his collar.

III:112 Naik of the 57th Wilde's Rifles and an Officer of the 53rd Sikhs
Notice how the cuff of the tunic of the naik is filled in with the facing colour.

Netherwear

In the 1860s, the 4th Sikhs wore very full khaki pyjamas formed into knickerbockers.[393] Other than vague mentions of khaki or drab uniforms, which imply wear of that colour, Carman is silent on netherwear.[394] The 1913 Regulations state that khaki knickerbockers were to be worn.[395]

Other Ranks

With few exceptions, other ranks in the Sikh infantry wore the same uniform as the regiments' VCOs. One exception was that NCOs of the 2nd Sikhs had a red fringe on their khaki turbans in 1864.[396] Image III:112 shows how two regiments of the Frontier Force, one of them a Sikh regiment, looked just prior to World War I.

III:113 Corps of Guides (Infantry)
The officer in the middle is in review order dress.

GUIDES INFANTRY AFTER THE MUTINY

Little is known about the pre-Mutiny uniforms of the Guides infantry. This means their uniform must be assumed to be generally the same as the cavalry element of the Guides. In 1849, their uniforms were dyed a sort of khaki, and dress regulations in 1855 give red piping for their uniform.[397] The description below is of the post-Mutiny uniform.

British Officer

In 1877, a watercolour by Simkin shows BOs wearing drab jackets with red collars and pointed cuffs.[398]

Viceroy Commissioned Officers

VCOs in 1890 wore basically the same uniform as the BOs. They also wore a khaki turban and a red kulla.[399] During this period, infantry VCOs did not wear a cummerbund – they were only worn by cavalry.[400]

Other Ranks

In 1877, Simkin shows sepoys in a plain drab uniform. In 1901, he shows the sepoys' drab tunic as having a red collar, cuffs, shoulder straps, and piping. The trousers and puttees were khaki.[401] Lovett, c. 1907, shows the sepoy in a long blouse with three buttons down the front, with red piping on either side of the buttons. The outline of a pointed cuff was traced in red. A red cummerbund was worn.[402]

A photograph of c. 1895 (Image III:113) shows a native officer in a tunic with a coloured collar and cuffs. The colour was probably red as this was the regiment's facing colour. The tunic was drab, and the knickerbockers and puttees were a lighter shade of khaki. The turban was also khaki.

§III-7 GURKHAS

The Gurkhas were recruited in Nepal, an independent kingdom located between the northeastern border of India by Tibet.[403] The East India Company went to war with Nepal in 1814 and fighting lasted until early 1816. While fighting was going on in 1815, the British were able to raise four battalions of Gurkhas to serve under them.[404] These were the 1st and 2nd Nasiri Battalions, the Sirmoor Battalion, and the Kumaon Battalion.[405] The 1st Gurkha Rifles (the Malaun Regiment) and the 2nd Gurkha Rifles (the Simour Rifles) were descendants of units raised during the war and took place names. The 1st Gurkhas were raised in 1815 from prisoners captured after the fall of the Gurkha Nepalese fortress of Malaun. They, in time (1903), took the fortress's name.[406] The 2nd Gurkhas were raised at Sirmoor near Dehra Dun in 1815.[407] In 1914, the four original battalions had morphed into the 1st, 2nd, and 3rd Gurkha Rifles.

By the time of the Mutiny, these units had been joined by the three Gurkha local battalions.[408]

PRE-MUTINY UNIFORM

British Officers

HEADDRESS
Regulations issued in 1829 stated that British officers were to wear a black bell-top shako with black lace and a black tuft.[409]

JACKET
The jacket was a dark green rifle pattern with a black collar and cuffs. There were three columns of black buttons down the front, and it had black braid. The pouch belt and pouch were black leather.[410]

Other Ranks

HEADDRESS
The first headdress worn by sepoys was a small, low, black cap with a black cloth wrapped around it.[411] By the 1830s, the other ranks also wore a bell-topped shako with a peak (brim). (The Bengal line infantry's shakos did not have a peak.[412]) In 1847, a form of Kilmarnock cap was adopted. It was generally dark blue with a band of dark green. However, the Sirmoor Battalion adopted a chequered (diced) red and green band.[413]

JACKET
The dark green single-breasted jacket had five buttons down the front. Each button had a bastion style loop going out from it.[414] In 1850, the Nasiri Battalion was taken into the Bengal line as the 66th Bengal Native Infantry[415] and, therefore, they wore red cutaways.

NETHERWEAR
While separate Gurkha units wore green,[416] the 66th wore the Bengal line's dark blue knickerbockers with red piping.[417]

POST-MUTINY UNIFORM

British Officers

HEADDRESS
The early post-Mutiny headdress for British officers (BOs) was a Kilmarnock cap.[418]

The 1886 Dress Regulations provide for a helmet covered with rifle green cloth.[419] This dark headdress was still being worn in 1911. It is said the King-Emperor in 1911 disapproved of the dark helmets, and they were soon changed to white.[420] Cap lines for

III:114 Colonel E. Mollo of the 5th Royal Gurkhas
Note his pouch belt and his collection of metals. Note also the difference between this British officer's tunic and the tunic of the Gurkha officer, c. 1900.

III:115 Officer of the 2nd Gurkhas
This character study clearly shows the size of the diced border on the Kilmarnock cap. Also note the ram's head on the pouch belt, a form of battle remembrance given very early in the regiment's history.

the helmet were approved in 1911.[421] The cap lines were worn by mounted officers and were fastened at the back of the helmet.[422]

Tunic

BOs wore a rifle green tunic with regimental facings, black braid, and five rows of cord with loops across the front. The 1901 dress regulations state that the collar and cuffs of BOs in all Gurkha regiments, except the 1st and 2nd, were black velvet.[423] The 1st and 2nd Gurkhas had scarlet cloth on their collars and cuffs.[424] The back was trimmed with black braid.[425] Images III:64 and III:65 show the shape of this braid. See Table III.7.1 for facing colours.

BOs and some native officers of the 2nd Gurkhas wore a pouch belt with a ram's head. This unusual chain finial commemorates an 1824 attack on a bandits' fort where a tree was cut down and used as a battering ram.[426] The Gurkhas were outnumbered three to one, but they still captured the fort.[427]

Table III.7.1: Gurkha and 39th Garhwal British Officers' Tunics, c. 1913

Regiment	Tunic Colour[a]	Facing Colour	Lace Colour	Tunic Decoration	Collar and Cuff Colour[a]	Shoulder Cord Colour	Pantaloon and Trouser Colour[a]	Pouch Belt	Pouch
1st Gurkha	Rifle green t: black[b]	Scarlet	Black	Five rows of hussar-style braid[c]	Scarlet t: black velvet[d,e,f]	Black chain gimp	Rifle green t: black[g]	Black patent leather[h,i,r]	Black leather with a binocular case[i]
2nd Gurkha	See note[j]	Scarlet		See notes[j,m]				Black patent leather[i,k,n,p,q]	Black patent leather[i]
3rd Gurkha	Rifle green t: black[b]	Black	Black	Five rows of hussar-style braid[c]	Black t: black[d,e,f]	Black chain gimp	Rifle green t: black[g]	Black enamelled seal leather[h,i,r]	Black enamelled seal leather[i]
4th Gurkha	Rifle green t: black[b]	Black	Black	Five rows of hussar-style braid[c]	Black t: black[d,e,f]	Black chain gimp	Rifle green t: black[g]	Black patent leather[h,i,r]	Black patent leather[i]
5th Gurkha	Rifle green t: black[b]	Black	Black	Five rows of hussar-style braid[c]	Black t: black[e,f,o]	Black chain gimp	Rifle green t: black[g]	Black patent leather[i,q,r]	Black leather with a binocular case[i]
6th Gurkha	Rifle green t: black[b]	Black	Black	Five rows of hussar-style braid[c]	Black t: black[d,e,f]	Black chain gimp	Rifle green t: black[g]	Black patent leather[h,i,r]	Black patent leather[i]
7th Gurkha	Rifle green t: black[b]	Black	Black	Five rows of hussar-style braid[c]	Black t: black[d,e,f]	Black chain gimp	Rifle green t: black[g]	Black enamelled seal leather[h,i,r]	Black enamelled seal leather[i]
8th Gurkha	Rifle green t: black[b]	Black	Black	Five rows of hussar-style braid[c]	Black t: black[d,e,f]	Black chain gimp	Rifle green t: black[g]	Black patent leather[h,i,r]	Black patent leather[i]
9th Gurkha	Rifle green t: black[b]	Black	Black	Five rows of hussar-style braid[c]	Black t: black[d,e,f]	Black chain gimp	Rifle green t: black[g]	Black enamelled seal leather[h,i,r]	Black enamelled seal leather[i]
10th Gurkha	Rifle green t: black[b]	Black	Black	Five rows of hussar-style braid[c]	Black t: black[d,e,f]	Black chain gimp	Rifle green t: black[g]	Black patent leather[h,i,r]	Black patent leather[i]
39th Garhwal	Rifle green t: black[b]	Black	Black	Five rows of hussar-style braid[c]	Black t: black[e,f,o]	Black chain gimp	Rifle green t: black[g]	Black enamelled seal leather[h,i,r]	Black leather with a binocular case[i]

Sources: Compiled by Maria Salcedo and the author. *Dress Regulations/India, 1913* is the primary source for this table.
Notes: [a] t = trim.
[b] Tunic trimmed all around, except the collar, with black square cord.
[c] The hussar-style braid consisted of two strands of flat cords. Each row of braid ended on the outside of the chest with two falling loops of cord. Halfway to the outside of the chest were two small loops in the braid, one above the line of the braid and one below it. At the end of each row was a large oval button with a netted cap. The tunic was fastened by a toggle and loop made out of the braid cord. On each of the two back seams there was the same cord braid. It formed crow's feet at the top, passed under a netted cap at the waist, and on each skirt if doubled, and formed a Hungarian knot.
[d] Collar edged with 1.27 cm (½ inch) black braid with a tracing of plain braid below.
[e] Cuff topped by Hungarian knot, with a tracing of braid around it, extending 17.78 cm (7 inches) from the bottom of the cuff.
[f] Badges of rank in bronze.
[g] 5.08 cm (2 inches) down side seams.
[h] 7.3 cm (2⅞ inches) wide.
[i] With badge(s).
[j] Wore the same pattern as the King Royal Rifle Corps
[k] Ram's head on their pouch belt in memory of making a battering ram from a tree in 1824 at Koonja

[l] Collar edged with 2.54 cm (1 inch) black braid and after 1902 with a tracing of braid below. Prior to 1902 the collar had eye braid whose nature depended on the officer's rank.
[m] After 1902 cuff topped by Hungarian knot, with a tracing braid around it, extending 21.59 cm (8½ inches) from the bottom of the cuff. Prior to 1902, depending on the officer's rank, the braid could be more elaborate and could extend higher from the bottom of the cuff. See the 1900 British Army Dress Regulations.

[n] Bronze plate with regimental badge.
[o] Collar edged with 1.27 cm (½ inch) black braid with no tracing of braid below the edging of 1.27 cm (½ inch) braid
[p] Bronze whistle and chain attached to ram's head (confirmed by Gavin Edgerley-Harris, director, Gurkha Museum, 14 June 2017).
[q] 7.62 cm (3 inches) wide.
[r] Silver regimental plate, whistle and chain.

Netherwear

The BOs' trousers, overalls, and pantaloons were rifle green with 5.08 cm (2 inch) black braid down the side seams.[428]

Native Officers

Headdress

Photographs c. 1870 show native officers wearing a Kilmarnock cap with a netted button like those of BOs.[429]

Tunic

In 1863, the dark green Zouave jacket was introduced in the Bengal army for wear by native ranks.[430] The change applied to the Gurkhas, where native officers wore a rifle green Zouave jacket trimmed with 1.27 cm (½ inch) black lace around the collar[431] and down either side of the front panel. Normally the front panel was of the unit's facing colour.[432] However, the Gurkhas' Zouave jacket had a dark green panel.[433]

The Zouave jacket was worn until the 1890s, when it was replaced by a plain single-breasted tunic[434] with eight buttons down the front.[435]

The 1891 Dress Regulations call for a slashed cuff with three buttons on each cuff[436] of the type worn on the Zouave jacket. The three-button slashed cuff is shown in Images III:67, III:79, and III:99. The slashed cuff was edged in the regiment's facing colour, scarlet for the 1st,[437] red or scarlet (depending on the source) for the 2nd Gurkhas,[438] and black for all other Gurkha regiments.

In the late 1890s, the slashed cuffs gave way to pointed cuffs[439] for all regiments (Images III:9 and III:118), except the 1st and 2nd, who kept the slashed cuffs piped in scarlet.[440]

Table III.7.2: Gurkha and 39th Garhwal Native Officers' Tunics, c. 1913

Regiment	Tunic Colour[a]	Facing Colour	Lace Colour	Collar & Cuff Colour[a]	Shoulder Strap Colour	Trouser colour[a]	Pouch Belt	Pouch	Notes
1st Gurkha	Dark green patrol jacket t: black[b,c]	Scarlet	Black mohair	Scarlet t: black[d,e]	Black chain gimp	Rifle green t: none	Black patent leather[f,g,p]	Black patent leather[g]	A,E
2nd Gurkha	Dark green t: black[c,h]	Scarlet	Black mohair	Scarlet t: black[i,j]	Black chain gimp	Rifle green, almost black t: black[k]	Black patent leather[n,q,r]	Black patent leather[c]	B,C,D,E
3rd Gurkha	Dark green p: black[m]	Black	Black	Black t: black[n,o]	Dark green, rifle pattern[s]	Rifle green t: none	Black enamelled seal leather[f,g,p]	Black enamelled seal leather[g]	E
4th Gurkha	Dark green p: black[m]	Black	Black	Black t: black[n,o]	Dark green, rifle pattern[s]	Rifle green t: none	Black patent leather[f,g,p]	Black patent leather[g]	E

Regiment	Tunic Colour[a]	Facing Colour	Lace Colour	Collar & Cuff Colour[a]	Shoulder Strap Colour	Trouser colour[a]	Pouch Belt	Pouch	Notes
5th Gurkha	Dark green p: black[m]	Black	Black	Black t: black[n,o]	Dark green, rifle pattern[s]	Rifle green t: none	Black patent leather[g,p,q]	Black patent leather with a binocular case[g]	E
6th Gurkha	Dark green p: black[m]	Black	Black	Black t: black[n,o]	Dark green, rifle pattern[s]	Rifle green t: none	Black patent leather[f,g,p]	Black patent leather[g]	E
7th Gurkha	Dark green p: black[m]	Black	Black	Black t: black[n,o]	Dark green, rifle pattern[s]	Rifle green t: none	Black enamelled seal leather[f,g,p]	Black enamelled seal leather[g]	E
8th Gurkha	Dark green p: black[m]	Black	Black	Black t: black[n,o]	Dark green, rifle pattern[s]	Rifle green t: none	Black patent leather[f,g,p]	Black patent leather[g]	E
9th Gurkha	Dark green p: black[m]	Black	Black	Black t: black[n,o]	Dark green, rifle pattern[s]	Rifle green t: none	Black enamelled seal leather[f,g,p]	Black enamelled seal leather[g]	E
10th Gurkha	Dark green p: black[m]	Black	Black	Black t: black[n,o]	Dark green, rifle pattern[s]	Rifle green t: none	Black patent leather[f,g,p]	Black patent leather[g]	E
39th Garhwal	Dark green p: black[m]	Black	Black	Black t: black[n,o]	Dark green, rifle pattern[s]	Rifle green t: none	Black patent leather[g,p,q]	Black patent leather with a binocular case[g]	E

Sources: Compiled by Maria Salcedo and the author. *Dress Regulations/India, 1913* is the primary source for this table. The *1914 Army List* was consulted for uniform and facing colours.

Notes: [a] t = trim; p = piping.

[b] 71.12 cm (28 inches) long from the bottom of the collar behind, for an officer 1.75 m (5 feet 9 inches) in height, with a proportionate variation for any difference in height. 2.54 cm (1 inch) black mohair braid traced inside with Russia braid down the front, at the bottom of the skirts, and on the slits. Back seams were also trimmed with 2.54 cm (1 inch) black mohair braid, but with Russia braid trimmed on both sides of mohair braid.

[c] Five rows of hussar-style braid. The hussar style braid consisted of two strands of flat cords. Each row of braid ended on the outside of the chest with two falling loops of cord. Halfway to the outside of the chest were two small loops in the braid, one above the line of the braid and one below it. At the end of each row was a large oval button with a netted cap. The tunic was fastened by a toggle and loop made out of the braid cord. On each of the two back seams there was the same cord braid. It formed crow's feet at the top, passed under a netted cap at the waist and on each skirt, if doubled, and formed a Hungarian knot.

[d] Collar edged all around with a 1.91 cm (¾ inch) mohair braid, traced inside with Russia braid, forming an eye at each end.

[e] Cuff edged with 2.54 cm (1 inch) black mohair, traced with Russia braid.

[f] 7.3 cm (2⅞ inches) wide.

[g] With badge(s).

[h] Tunic trimmed all around, except the collar, with black square cord.

[i] Collar edged with 2.54 cm (1 inch) black braid with a tracing of braid below.

[j] Cuff topped by Hungarian knot, with a tracing braid around it, extending 21.59 cm (8½ inches) from the bottom of the cuff.

[k] 5.08 cm (2 inches) down side seams.

[l] 7.3 cm (2⅞ inches) wide with bronze plate.

[m] Tunic piped in facing colour 0.64 cm (¼ inch) wide down left front, skirt, pleats, and centre of back, and from bottom button to the bottom of the tunic on the right front.

[n] Collar 3.81 cm (1½ inches) in depth made of facing cloth with 1.27 cm (½ inch) black silk lace all round.

[o] Pointed cuffs of facing cloth pointed 13.97 cm (5½ inches) deep in front, 1.27 cm (½ inch) black silk lace all round. The lace carried down each side of seam, finishing off inside cuff.

[p] Silver regimental plate, whistle and chain.

[q] 7.62 cm (3 inches) wide.

[r] Bronze ram's head, whistle and chain.

[s] See British Empire Image II:4(6) for the shape of these cords.

A: Patrol jacket is the same model as that worn by the King's Royal Rifle Corps.

B: Wore the same model tunic, collar, and cuffs as the King's Royal Rifle Corps.

C: Pillbox cap (Kilmarnock) has red and dark green/black dicing around its lower edges.

D: Ram's head worn on pouch belt.

E: Regimental badge often, but not always, worn on the front of the dark green Kilmarnock (see photographs and illustrations in Marrion, *Gurkhas*).

NETHERWEAR

Native officers wore dark green pyjamas and trousers without piping for most regiments.[441] The exception was the 1st Gurkhas, who had scarlet piping listed in the 1901 Dress Regulations. By the 1913 Regulations, this distinction was no longer listed.[442]

PUTTEES AND GAITERS

Photographs *c.* 1896 show native officers of the 1st Gurkhas wearing high black gaiters.[443] It is said that gaiters were the normal Gurkha dress in the 1880s.[444] After that, black puttees were the norm.

QUEEN'S TRUNCHEON[445]

The 2nd Gurkhas, as recognition for their tremendous bravery at the Seige of Delhi, were granted a third colour. When they became a rifle regiment in 1858, they no longer carried colours and consequently lost their third colour. Queen Victoria had a truncheon made to replace the third honorary colour and had the truncheon presented to the regiment in 1863. The truncheon stands approximately 1.83 metres (6 feet) tall and can be broken down into five pieces so it can be taken apart and carried by five different soldiers. The truncheon is treated with the same honour as the Queen's colours of a regiment that carries colours and an extra officer is carried on the regimental establishment to carry it. For pictures of the truncheon, see Images III:116 and III:117.

III:116 Queen's Viceroy Officer with Queen's Truncheon, c. 1860
The truncheon was given to the regiment by Queen Victoria in 1863. It is just under 1.83 m (6 feet) high.

III:117 2nd Gurkha's Truncheon
This close-up shows the detail of its top.

Other Ranks

Table III.7.3: Gurkha Other Ranks

Regiment	Tunic Colour	Facing Colour	Lace Colour	Collar & Cuff Colour[a]	Shoulder Strap Colour	Trouser colour	Notes
1st Gurkha	Dark/rifle green	Scarlet	Black	Collar: scarlet cuff t: scarlet	Dark/rifle green	Dark/rifle green	C
2nd Gurkha	Dark/rifle green	Scarlet	Black	Collar: scarlet cuff t: scarlet	Dark/rifle green	Dark/rifle green	A,C
3rd Gurkha	Dark/rifle green	Black	Black	Black	Dark/rifle green	Dark/rifle green	C
4th Gurkha	Dark/rifle green	Black	Black	Black	Dark/rifle green	Dark/rifle green	C
5th Gurkha	Dark/rifle green	Black	Black	Black	Dark/rifle green	Dark/rifle green	C
6th Gurkha	Dark/rifle green	Black	Black	Black	Dark/rifle green	Dark/rifle green	B,C
7th Gurkha	Dark/rifle green	Black	Black	Black	Dark/rifle green	Dark/rifle green	C
8th Gurkha	Dark/rifle green	Black	Black	Black	Dark/rifle green	Dark/rifle green	C
9th Gurkha	Dark/rifle green	Black	Black	Black	Dark/rifle green	Dark/rifle green	C
10th Gurkha	Dark/rifle green	Black	Black	Black	Dark/rifle green	Dark/rifle green	C

Sources: Sources consulted in constructing this table include: *1914 Army List*, Carman, *Uniforms Infantry*, and Marrion, *Gurkhas*.
Notes: [a] t = trim
A: Band on Kilmarnock cap diced (checkered) red and black.
B: Red touri worn on top of the Kilmarnock cap of the other ranks.
C: See photographs and illustrations in Marrion, *Gurkhas*.

The Gurkha other ranks closely tracked the uniforms of the Gurkha VCOs. There was little except badges of rank and accessories, swords, etc. to mark the two classes as different.

The other ranks of the 6th Gurkhas wore a red touri on their Kilmarnock cap (Image C42). This was not worn by VCOs. For a general overview of other ranks' uniforms, see Table III.7.3 and Image III:118.

III:118 Troops of the 5th Royal Gurkhas (Frontier Force) Order of Merit Men in 1899 Note how they wear their chin strap under their lip.

§III INDIA: NOTES

1. 'Numeration Systems', *World Book*, N–O, vol. 14, p. 453; 'Zero', *World Book*, W–X–Y–Z, vol. 21, pp. 495–96.
2. White, *Medieval Technology*, p. 14.
3. Dundas, *Jains*, p. 17. Lord Mahavira, while it is hard to be sure, is believed to be a contemporary of the Buddha (563 BC?–483 BC?). 'Buddha,' *World Book*, B, vol. 2, p. 555.
4. Dundas, *Jains*, p. 22.
5. Bose, 'Foreign Capital', p. 492.
6. Heathcote, *Garrison*, p. 66.
7. Sumner, *Army, 1914–1947*, p. 51.
8. Gilmour, *Ruling Caste*, p. xiii.
9. See Sundaram, *India's Armies/Costs*, p. 18, for a count and location of European and Indian troops which the Company had under arms in 1857 at the start of the Mutiny.
10. Fukazawa, 'Cotton', p. 227.
11. Ibid., p. 43.
12. Ibid., p. 6.
13. Compare numbers on p. 45 to those on p. 47 in Sundaram, *India's Armies/Costs*.
14. Vakil, *Financial India*, pp. 85–91.
15. Vakil, *Financial India*, p. 96; Joshi, 'Currency', pp. 385–6.
16. Sundaram, *India's Armies/Costs*, pp. 54 and 48–9.
17. Sources used in creating this glossary include the following: Yule, *Hobson-Jobson*; Bowling, *Cavalry*, p. 71; Mollo, *Army*, p. 185; Allen, *Plain Tales*, pp. 273–87; Holmes, *Sahib*, pp. 507–11; Heathcote, *Garrison*, p. 203.
18. Irwin, *Kashmir Shawl*, pp. 5, 9, 11–12, and 20.
19. Ismay, *Memoirs*, pp. 16–17.
20. Mollo, *Army*, p. 139.
21. Gaylor, *Sons/Company*, p. 98.
22. Gaylor says there were Baluch tribesmen of the Derajat District in the regiment when it was first formed. Ibid., p. 103.
23. Bakshi, *Madya Pradesh*, p. 449.
24. Roberts, *Forty-One Years*, p. 154, footnote ‡.
25. Bonarjee, *Fighting Races*, pp. 142–4.
26. Das, *Rajputana Rifles*, p. 2.
27. Perry, 'Armies P1', pp. 129 and 167; 'Shekhawati', *Imperial Gazetteer*, vol. 22, pp. 268–70.
28. 'Deoli', *Imperial Gazetteer*, vol. 11, pp. 246–7; 'Ajmer-Merwara', *Imperial Gazetteer*, vol. 5, pp. 137, 165.
29. Carman, *Uniforms Infantry*, p. 124.
30. 'Erinpura', *Imperial Gazetteer*, vol. 12, p. 27.
31. Ibid.
32. Carman, *Uniforms Infantry*, p. 191.
33. Ibid., p. 127.
34. Marrion, *Gurkhas*, p. 8.
35. Farwell, *Gurkhas*, p. 33.
36. Perry, *Order Battle 5B*, pp. 115–20.
37. Ibid., pp. 115–22.
38. Carman, *Uniforms Cavalry*, p. 47.
39. Ibid.
40. Knight, 'Forage Caps', pp. 29–39.
41. Bond, *Staff College*, p. 199.
42. Heathcote, *Garrison*, p. 139.
43. Bond, *Staff College*, p. 199; Barrow, *Fire of Life*, p. 41.
44. Bond, *Staff College*, pp. 138–9; Barrow, *Fire of Life*, p. 41.
45. Ibid., pp. 199–200.
46. Ibid., pp. 161, 200.
47. Heathcote, *Garrison*, pp. 139–40.
48. Bond, *Staff College*, pp. 200–4.
49. Ibid., pp. 204–5.
50. Ibid., p. 208.
51. *Dress Regulations/India, 1913*, p. 6, ¶29; *Dress Regulations/India, 1901*, pp. 12–13.
52. *Dress Regulations/India, 1901*, p. 35.
53. Ibid., p. 25, ¶81.
54. Nicholson, 'British Staff Uniforms, 1897', p. 19.
55. Ibid.
56. *Dress Regulations/India, 1901*, pp. 38–40; *Dress Regulations/India, 1913*, p. 24, ¶76.
57. *Dress Regulations/India, 1913*, p. 24, ¶76; *Dress Regulations, 1904*, p. 14, ¶157.
58. *Tradition*, No. 50, p. 11.
59. Ibid., p. 9.
60. Information on the wishes of King George V came from text drafted by the staff of the (British) National Army Museum in connection with the 18th Lancers. See 2015 NAM webpage.
61. *Dress Regulations/India, 1913*, ¶104, p. 32.
62. Mollo, *Army*, pp. 52, 55, 58–62; Carman, *Uniforms Cavalry*, pp. 29–31.
63. Mollo, *Army*, p. 78; Carman, *Uniforms Cavalry*, pp. 138–39, drawing no. 123, and p. 10, drawing nos. 8, 9, and 10.
64. Carman, *Uniforms Cavalry*, pp. 108–9.
65. Mollo, *Army*, pp. 56–7.
66. Carman, *Uniforms Cavalry*, p. 125.
67. Mollo, *Army*, p. 56.
68. Ibid., pp. 55–6.
69. Ibid., pp. 56–7, plates 40 and 41.
70. Perry, 'Armies P1', p. 149.
71. Ibid.
72. Holman, *Sikander Sahib*, p. 195. Robert and James's mother was a Rajput. They grew up heavily influenced by Rajput mores. Neither saw any problem with having several wives, i.e. a harem.
73. Perry, 'Armies P1', pp. 117–18. Perry lists several other wartime cavalry units that were short-lived. Ibid., p. 118.
74. Mollo, *Army*, pp. 114–15.
75. Ibid., p. 114.
76. Ibid.
77. Carman, *Uniforms Cavalry*, pp. 38–9.
78. Mollo, *Army*, p. 115.
79. Ibid.
80. See photos and drawings, Harris, *Bengal Cavalry*.
81. Carman, *Uniforms Cavalry*, p. 40.
82. Ibid., pp. 44–5.
83. Ibid., p. 47.
84. Ibid., pp. 40 and 44–5.
85. Ibid., p. 52.
86. Ibid., p. 47.

87 Carman, *Uniforms Cavalry*, p. 128.
88 Ibid.
89 Ibid.
90 Perry, 'Armies P1', p. 119.
91 Carman, *Uniforms Cavalry*, p. 128.
92 Ibid., p. 129.
93 Ibid., p. 145.
94 Perry, 'Armies P1', p. 119.
95 Carman, *Uniforms Cavalry*, p. 145.
96 Ibid.
97 Bowling, *Cavalry*, pp. 52 and 54.
98 Ibid., p. 52; Carman, *Uniforms Cavalry*, p. 145.
99 Mollo, *Army*, p. 118.
100 Bowling, *Cavalry*, pp. 52–4.
101 Carman, *Uniforms Cavalry*, p. 145.
102 Ibid.
103 Ibid.
104 Ibid.
105 Bowling, *Cavalry*, p. 52.
106 Ibid., p. 54.
107 Ibid., p. 28, drawing 79.
108 Carman, *Uniforms Cavalry*, p. 145.
109 Bowling, *Cavalry*, p. 55.
110 Carman, *Uniforms Cavalry*, p. 145.
111 Ibid.
112 Mollo, *Army*, p. 118.
113 Carman, *Uniforms Cavalry*, p. 148.
114 Mollo, *Army*, p. 118.
115 Carman, *Uniforms Cavalry*, p. 148.
116 Ibid.
117 Ibid.; Mollo, *Army*, p. 118.
118 Carman, *Uniforms Cavalry*, p. 148; Mollo, *Army*, p. 118.
119 Carman, *Uniforms Cavalry*, p. 148.
120 Ibid.
121 Ibid., p. 149.
122 Ibid.
123 Mollo, *Army*, p. 61.
124 Ibid.; Carman, *Uniforms Cavalry*, p. 156.
125 Carman, *Uniforms Cavalry*, p. 156.
126 Ibid., p. 155.
127 Ibid., p. 156.
128 Ibid., p. 155.
129 Ibid.
130 Ibid.
131 Mollo, *Army*, p. 62.
132 Ibid.
133 Carman, *Uniforms Cavalry*, pp. 151 and 153.
134 Ibid., p. 153.
135 Ibid.
136 Ibid., p. 152, drawing no. 143; Mollo, *Army*, p. 72, plate 50.
137 Mollo, *Army*, p. 62.
138 Ibid., p. 78.
139 Carman, *Uniforms Cavalry*, p. 159.
140 Mollo, *Army*, p. 62.
141 Carman, *Uniforms Cavalry*, p. 160.
142 Mollo, *Army*, p. 62.
143 Carman, *Uniforms Cavalry*, p. 162.
144 Ibid.
145 Mollo, *Army*, p. 62.
146 Bowling, *Cavalry*, p. 63.
147 Carman, *Uniforms Cavalry*, p. 164.
148 Bowling, *Cavalry*, p. 61.
149 Ibid., p. 63.
150 Perry, 'Armies P1', p. 120.
151 Carman, *Uniforms Cavalry*, pp. 155–6.
152 Bowling, *Cavalry*, pp. 56, 58.
153 Carman, *Uniforms Cavalry*, p. 158.
154 Ibid.
155 Ibid.
156 Ibid.
157 Ibid.
158 Ibid.
159 Ibid.
160 Ibid.
161 Ibid.
162 Bowling, *Cavalry*, p. 55 photograph.
163 Ibid., p. 60.
164 Bowling, *Cavalry*, pp. 61 and 63.
165 Carman, *Uniforms Cavalry*, p. 166.
166 Carman, *Uniforms Cavalry*, p. 166; Bowling, *Cavalry*, p. 64.
167 Bowling, *Cavalry*, p. 64.
168 Ibid.
169 Ibid.
170 Carman, *Uniforms Cavalry*, p. 166.
171 Mollo, *Army*, p. 121.
172 Heathcote, *Garrison*, p. 27.
173 Carman, *Uniforms Infantry*, p. 220.
174 Ibid., p. 115.
175 Perry, 'Armies P1', pp. 119 and 133.
176 Heathcote, *Garrison*, p. 27.
177 Ibid., p. 29.
178 Ibid., p. 27.
179 Ibid., p. 29.
180 Carman, *Uniforms Cavalry*, p. 115.
181 Ibid., p. 116.
182 Ibid.
183 Ibid.
184 Ibid.
185 Mollo, *Army*, pp. 56–7.
186 Ibid.
187 Carman, *Uniforms Cavalry*, pp. 118–19, 122, 123, 125; Mollo, *Army*, p. 117.
188 Mollo, *Army*, p. 117.
189 Carman, *Uniforms Cavalry*, pp. 118–19, 122, 123, 125; Mollo, *Army*, p. 117.
190 Mollo, *Army*, p. 117.
191 Ibid.
192 Carman, *Uniforms Cavalry*, p. 127. See *Dress Regulations/India, 1913*, ¶144.
193 Mollo, *Army*, p. 117.
194 Carman, *Uniforms Cavalry*, p. 106.
195 Mollo, *Army*, p. 60.
196 Perry, 'Armies P1', p. 150.
197 See *1914 Army List*, pp. 427, 435–6.
198 Mollo, *Army*, p. 122.
199 Carman, *Uniforms Cavalry*, p. 111.
200 Ibid., p. 113.
201 Ibid.
202 Bowling, *Cavalry*, pp. 43–5.
203 Mollo, *Army*, pp. 60–1.
204 Bowling, *Hussars*, pp. 36–7.
205 Carman, *Uniforms Cavalry*, p. 110.
206 Bowling, *Cavalry*, see e.g. plate 86 on p. 29.
207 Bowling, *Hussars*, pp. 28–9, 47, and 50.
208 Carman, *Uniforms Cavalry*, p. 110.
209 Mollo, *Army*, p. 122; Carman, *Uniforms Cavalry*, p. 110.
210 Carman, *Uniforms Cavalry*, p. 111.
211 Mollo, *Army*, p. 122; Carman, *Uniforms Cavalry*, p. 111.
212 Mollo, *Army*, p. 122; Carman, *Uniforms Cavalry*, p. 111.
213 Mollo, *Army*, p. 122.
214 Carman, *Uniforms Cavalry*, pp. 111–12.

215 Carman, *Uniforms Cavalry*, p. 112.
216 Ibid.; Mollo, *Army*, p. 118, plate 108.
217 Carman, *Uniforms Cavalry*, p. 112.
218 Ibid.
219 Ibid., p. 111.
220 Ibid., p. 110, drawing 99.
221 Ibid., p. 111.
222 Ibid., p. 112.
223 Ibid., p. 113.
224 Ibid., pp. 113–14.
225 Ibid., p. 113.
226 Ibid.
227 Ibid.
228 Ibid., pp. 111–12.
229 Ibid., pp. 109–10.
230 Ibid., p. 111.
231 Ibid.
232 Ibid.
233 Ibid., pp. 111–12.
234 Perry, 'Armies P1', p. 121. Perry lists the different regiments.
235 Ibid.
236 See ibid. and Mollo, *Army*, p. 122.
237 Mollo, *Army*, p. 122.
238 Heathcote, *Garrison*, p. 88.
239 Mollo, *Army*, p. 122, but see Carman, *Uniforms Cavalry*, p. 169. Carman seems to imply that the case for khaki is not certain.
240 Carman, *Uniforms Cavalry*, p. 169.
241 Ibid.
242 Ibid., p. 170.
243 Ibid.
244 Ibid.
245 Ibid., p. 169.
246 Ibid., pp. 169–70.
247 Ibid., p. 169.
248 Ibid., p. 170.
249 Ibid.
250 Ibid.
251 Ibid.
252 Ibid.
253 Ibid.
254 Ibid.
255 Ibid.
256 Ibid.
257 Ibid.
258 Ibid., p. 172.
259 Mollo, *Army*, p. 66; MacMunn, *Armies*, p. 106.
260 Mollo, *Army*, pp. 62, 66–7.
261 Ibid., p. 73.
262 Ibid., p. 78.
263 Ibid.
264 Carman, *Uniforms Infantry*, p. 108.
265 Mollo, *Army*, p. 127.
266 Ibid.
267 Ibid., p. 128.
268 Ibid.
269 Ibid. Text mistakenly identifies the 38th instead of the 39th.
270 Mollo, *Army*, p. 127.
271 Ibid.
272 Ibid.
273 Ibid.
274 Ibid., p. 133.
275 Carman, *Uniforms Infantry*, p. 154.
276 Ibid.
277 Ibid.
278 Ibid.
279 Ibid.
280 Ibid.
281 Ibid., pp. 154–5.
282 *Dress Regulations/India, 1913*, p. 48.
283 Carman, *Uniforms Infantry*, p. 157.
284 Ibid., p. 156.
285 Ibid., p. 158.
286 Carman, *Uniforms Infantry*, p. 159.
287 Ibid.
288 Ibid.
289 Ibid.
290 Ibid., p. 197.
291 Ibid.
292 Ibid., pp. 197–8.
293 *Dress Regulations/India, 1913*, p. 48, ¶173.
294 Carman, *Uniforms Infantry*, p. 197.
295 Mollo, *Army*, p. 135.
296 Ibid.
297 Ibid.
298 Ibid.
299 Ibid.
300 Ibid.
301 Carman, *Uniforms Infantry*, p. 177.
302 Ibid., pp. 180–1.
303 Ibid.
304 Ibid., pp. 177, 180–1.
305 *Dress Regulations/India, 1913*, p. 49, ¶174.
306 *Dress Regulations/India, 1901*, pp. 149–50.
307 Ibid., pp. 149–50.
308 Ibid., p. 150.
309 Ibid., p. 131.
310 Ibid., pp. 149–50, 131.
311 Carman, *Uniforms Infantry*, pp. 177, 180–1.
312 Ibid.
313 Ibid., p. 177.
314 *Dress Regulations/India, 1901*, p. 152.
315 Carman, *Uniforms Infantry*, p. 181.
316 *Dress Regulations/India, 1901*, p. 152.
317 Carman, *Uniforms Infantry*, p. 177.
318 *Dress Regulations/India, 1901*, p. 152.
319 Carman, *Uniforms Infantry*, p. 181.
320 Ibid., pp. 180–1, 177.
321 Ibid., p. 181.
322 Ibid.
323 Ibid.
324 Ibid.
325 Ibid.
326 Ibid., p. 177.
327 Ibid., pp. 182–3.
328 Ibid., p. 183.
329 Ibid., p. 181.
330 Ibid., p. 182.
331 Ibid., p. 181.
332 Ibid., pp. 182–3.
333 Ibid., pp. 183–4.
334 Ibid., p. 183.
335 Ibid.
336 Mollo, *Army*, p. 137.
337 Carman, *Uniforms Infantry*, p. 183.
338 Ibid., p. 184.
339 Mollo, *Army*, p. 137.
340 Carman, *Uniforms Infantry*, pp. 183–4.
341 Ibid., p. 183.
342 Ibid.
343 Ibid.
344 Mollo, *Army*, p. 137.
345 Carman, *Uniforms Infantry*, p. 183.
346 Ibid.
347 *Whitaker's List – 1900*, p. 898.
348 Carman, *Uniforms Infantry*, p. 183.
349 Ibid.
350 Ibid.
351 Ibid., p. 181.
352 *Dress Regulations/India, 1901*, p. 153.

353 Ibid.
354 *Dress Regulations/India, 1913*, p. 53, ¶187.
355 *Dress Regulations/India, 1901*, p. 153; Carman, *Uniforms Infantry*, p. 181.
356 *Dress Regulations/India, 1901*, p. 153.
357 Ibid., p. 156.
358 Ibid.
359 Ibid.
360 *Dress Regulations/India, 1913*, p. 55, ¶199.
361 *Dress Regulations/India, 1901*, p. 156.
362 *Whitaker's List – 1900*, pp. 897–8.
363 Carman, *Uniforms Infantry*, p. 181.
364 Ibid.
365 Ibid.
366 Ibid.
367 Ibid., p. 213; Mollo, *Army*, p. 72.
368 Carman, *Uniforms Infantry*, p. 213.
369 Mollo, *Army*, p. 73.
370 Carman, *Uniforms Infantry*, p. 214.
371 Ibid.
372 *Dress Regulations/India, 1913*, p. 51, ¶178.
373 Carman, *Uniforms Infantry*, p. 215.
374 Ibid., p. 217.
375 Ibid.
376 *Dress Regulations/India, 1913*, p. 54, ¶189.
377 Ibid.
378 Gaylor, *Sons/Company*, p. 171.
379 Carman, *Uniforms Infantry*, p. 221.
380 Ibid., p. 220.
381 Ibid., p. 221.
382 Ibid.
383 Ibid., pp. 221–3.
384 Carman, *Uniforms Infantry*, p. 222.
385 Ibid., pp. 222–3.
386 Ibid., p. 222.
387 Ibid., p. 223.
388 Ibid., p. 224.
389 Ibid., pp. 222–4.
390 Ibid., p. 223.
391 Ibid.
392 *Dress Regulations/India. 1913*, p. 55, ¶192.
393 Carman, *Uniforms Infantry*, p. 223.
394 Ibid., pp. 222–3.
395 *Dress Regulations/India, 1913*, p. 55, ¶192.
396 Carman, *Uniforms Infantry*, p. 222.
397 Ibid., p. 213.
398 Ibid.
399 Ibid.
400 Ibid.
401 Ibid., pp. 213–14.
402 Ibid., p. 214.
403 Nicholson, *Gurkha Rifles*, p. 3.
404 Ibid., p. 6.
405 Ibid.
406 Marrion, *Gurkhas*, p. 8.
407 Farwell, *Gurkhas*, p. 33.
408 Marrion, *Gurkhas*, pp. 20–1, 25, and 31.
409 Mollo, *Army*, p. 72.
410 Ibid., pp. 72–3.
411 Nicholson, *Gurkha Rifles*, p. 5.
412 Mollo, *Army*, p. 73, plate 57, p. 77.
413 Ibid., p. 73.
414 Ibid., pp. 72–3, plate 57, p. 77.
415 Ibid., p. 73.
416 Ibid.
417 Ibid., p. 128.
418 Carman, *Uniforms Infantry*, pp. 200, 203, 206, and 209.
419 Ibid., p. 200.
420 Ibid., pp. 203, 205, 201 (1912).
421 Ibid., p. 201.
422 Ibid., p. 205.
423 *Dress Regulations/ India, 1901*, p. 130.
424 Ibid.
425 Carman, *Uniforms Infantry*, p. 200.
426 Farwell, *Gurkhas*, p. 36.
427 Ibid.
428 Carman, *Uniforms Infantry*, pp. 200 and 201.
429 Ibid., p. 207.
430 Mollo, *Army*, p. 128.
431 Carman, *Uniforms Infantry*, p. 200.
432 Mollo, *Army*, pp. 185 and 128.
433 Ibid., p. 129.
434 Ibid.
435 Ibid., p. 207.
436 Carman, *Uniforms Infantry*, pp. 200–1.
437 Ibid., p. 200.
438 Ibid., p. 202; Nicholson, *Gurkha Rifles*, p. 32.
439 Carman, *Uniforms Infantry*, p. 201.
440 Nicholson, *Gurkha Rifles*, p. 32.
441 Carman, *Uniforms Infantry*, pp. 201 and 207.
442 Ibid., p. 201.
443 Ibid.
444 Ibid., p. 204.
445 Marrion, *Gurkhas*, pp. 11–12.

§III INDIA: BIBLIOGRAPHY

Books, Articles, and Website

1914 Army List	Great Britain, *The Quarterly Indian Army List July 1914* (Calcutta: Superintendent Government Printing, 1914).
1914 Hart's Annual Army List	Lieutenant General H.G. Hart, *Hart's Annual Army List: Militia List, and Imperial Yeomanry List, for 1914* (London: John Murray, 1914).
2015 NAM webpage	Description for NAM Accession Number 1953-05-55 (tunic and body lines of 18th Lancers, National Army Museum, www.nam.ac.uk/inventory/objects/results.php?shortDescription=king+george+v+preferred+kurta, accessed 23 March 2017.
Allen, *Plain Tales*	Charles Allen, *Plain Tales From the Raj* (London: Futura Publications Limited, 1978).
Bakshi, *Madya Pradesh*	S.R. Bakshi and O.P. Ralhan, *Madya Pradesh Through the Ages*, vol. 4 (Social Revolution Towards Swaraj) (New Delhi: Sarup & Sons, 2007).
Barrow, *Fire of Life*	George Barrow, *The Fire of Life* (London: Hutchinson & Co. Ltd, 1942).
Bonarjee, *Fighting Races*	Pitt D. Bonarjee, *A Handbook of the Fighting Races of India* (India: Asian Publication Services, 1975).
Bond, *Staff College*	Brian Bond, *The Victorian Army and the Staff College, 1854–1914* (Fakenham: Eyre Methuen Ltd, 1972).
Bose, 'Foreign Capital'	Arun Bose, 'Foreign Capital', in V.B. Singh (ed.), *Economic History of India, 1857–1956* (Bombay: Allied Publishers Private Limited, 1983): pp. 485–527.
Bowling, *Cavalry*	A.H. Bowling, *Indian Cavalry Regiments, 1880–1914* (London: Almark Publishing Co. Ltd, 1971).
Bowling, *Hussars*	A.H. Bowling, *British Hussar Regiments 1805–1914* (London: Almark Publishing Co. Ltd, 1972).
Carman, *Uniforms Cavalry*	W.Y. Carman, *Indian Army Uniforms Under the British from the 18th Century to 1947: Cavalry* (London: Leonard Hill, 1961).
Carman, *Uniforms Infantry*	W.Y. Carman, *Indian Army Uniforms Under the British from the 18th Century to 1947: Artillery, Engineers and Infantry* (London: Morgan-Grampian, 1969).
Cassin-Scott, *Military Bands*	Jack Cassin-Scott and John Fabb, *Military Bands and Their Uniforms* (Poole: Blandford Press, 1978).
Das, *Rajputana Rifles*	Chand Das, *The Rajputana Rifles: A Brief History* (New Delhi: Reliance Publishing House, 1995).
Dasgupta, 'Jute'	Ajit Dasgupta, 'Jute Textile Industry', in V.B. Singh (ed.), *Economic History of India, 1857–1956* (Bombay: Allied Publishers Private Limited, 1983): pp. 260–80.
Document 6303/117, Blackfriars	Document 6303/117, India Office Library and Records at Blackfriars. This document has since disappeared, and the reference number does not work at the British Library.
Dress Regulations, 1904	War Office, *1904 Dress Regulations* (London: His Majesty's Stationery Office, 1904).
Dress Regulations/India, 1901	India, Army Department, *Army Regulations, India, 1901, Volume 1, Dress* (Calcutta: Superintendent Government Printing, 1901) (NAM Accession No. 8913).
Dress Regulations/India, 1913	India, Army Department, *Army Regulations, India, 1913, Volume 7, Dress* (Uckfield: Naval & Military Press, 2001) (reprint of Calcutta: Superintendent Government Printing, 1913).
Dundas, *Jains*	Paul Dundas, *The Jains* (London: Routledge, 1992).
Farwell, *Gurkhas*	Byron Farwell, *The Gurkhas* (New York: W.W. Norton & Co., 1984).
Fukazawa, 'Cotton'	H. Fukazawa, 'Cotton Mill Industry', in V.B. Singh (ed.), *Economic History of India, 1857–1956* (Bombay: Allied Publishers Private Limited, 1983): pp. 223–59.
Gaylor, *Sons/Company*	John Gaylor, *Sons of John Company* (Tunbridge Wells: Spellmount, 1992).
Gilmour, *Ruling Caste*	David Gilmour, *The Ruling Caste: Imperial Lives in the Victorian Raj* (New York: Farrar, Straus, and Giroux, 2001).
Harris, *Bengal Cavalry*	R.G. Harris, *Bengal Cavalry Regiments, 1857–1914* (Men-at-Arms Series, ed. Martin Windrow), (London: Osprey, 1979).
Heathcote, *Garrison*	T.A. Heathcote, *The Indian Army: The Garrison of British Imperial India, 1822–1922* (London: David & Charles, 1974).

Holman, *Sikander Sahib*	Dennis Holman, *Sikander Sahib: The Life of Colonel James Skinner, 1778–1841* (London: Heinemann, 1961).
Holmes, *Sahib*	Richard Holmes, *Sahib: The British Soldier in India, 1750–1914* (Hammersmith: HarperCollins, 2005).
Imperial Gazetteer	*The Imperial Gazetteer of India* (Oxford: Clarendon Press, 1908).
Indian Army List	*The Quarterly Indian Army List* (Calcutta: Superintendent Government Printing, India, Yearly).
Irwin, *Kashmir Shawl*	John Irwin, *The Kashmir Shawl* (London: His Majesty's Stationery Office, 1973).
Ismay, *Memoirs*	Lionel Ismay, Baron Hastings, *The Memoirs of General Lord Ismay* (New York: Viking Press, 1960).
Joshi, 'Currency'	M.D. Joshi, 'Currency', in V.B. Singh (ed.), *Economic History of India, 1857–1956* (Bombay: Allied Publishers Private Limited, 1983): pp. 375–413.
Knight, 'Forage Caps'	D.J. Knight and R.J. Smith, 'Staff Pattern Peaked Forage Caps of the Indian Cavalry, 1902–1922', *Bulletin of the Military Historical Society*, vol. 63, no. 249 (August 2012): pp. 29–39.
L/MIL/7/17023, Blackfriars	L/MIL/7/17023 Confidential Reports on Regiments, etc. –1914. India Office. Library and Records, Blackfriars, now in the British Library.
MacMunn, *Armies*	Major G.F. MacMunn, DSO, *The Armies of India* (London: Adam and Charles Black, 1911).
Marrion, *Gurkhas*	R.J. Marrion and D. Fosten, *The Tradition Book of the Gurkhas* (London: Belmont Maitland, 1974?).
Mollo, *Army*	Boris Mollo, *The Indian Army* (Poole: Blandford Press, 1981).
Nicholson, 'British Staff Uniforms, 1897'	J.B.R. Nicholson, 'British Staff Uniforms, 1897', Parts I and II, *Tradition*, no. 39: pp. 7–10; no. 40: pp. 14–19.
Nicholson, *Gurkha Rifles*	J.B.R. Nicholson, *The Gurkha Rifles* (Men-at-Arms Series, ed. Martin Windrow), (London: Osprey, 1974).
Perry, 'Armies P1'	F.W. Perry, 'The Armies of the Commonwealth: Part One: The Regiments' (United Kingdom: n.p., typed manuscript held at the Imperial War Museum, 1977).
Perry, *Order Battle 5B*	F.W. Perry, *Order of Battle of Divisions Part 5B, Indian Army Divisions* (Newport: Ray Westlake Military Books, 1993).
Roberts, *Forty-One Years*	Field Marshal Lord Roberts of Kandahar, *Forty-One Years in India*, 2 vols in 1 (New York: Longmans, Greens, & Co., also London: Richard Bentley and Sons, 1898).
Rothero, *Skinner's Horse*	Christopher Rothero, *Skinner's Horse* (London: Almark Publications, 1979).
Sumner, *Army, 1914–1947*	Ian Sumner, *The Indian Army, 1914–1947* (Oxford: Osprey, 2001).
Sundaram, *India's Armies/Costs*	Lanka Sundaram, *India's Armies and Their Costs: A Century of Unequal Imposts for an Army of Occupation and a Mercenary Army* (Bombay: Avanti Prakashan, 1946).
Tradition, No. 50	Lieutenant Colonel Frank Wilson, *Tradition*, ed. Lt. Col. J.B.R. Nicholson, No. 50 (Special Cavalry Edition No. 1) (n.d.).
Tradition, No. 73	*Tradition*, ed. Lt. Col. J.B.R. Nicholson, No. 73 (Special Cavalry Edition No. 2) (n.d.).
Vakil, *Financial India*	Chandulal Vakil, *Financial Developments in Modern India, 1860–1924* (Bombay: D.B. Taraporevala Sons & Co., 1935).
Vansittart, *Gurkhas*	Eden Vansittart, *Gurkhas: Handbook for the Indian Army* (Calcutta: Office of the Superintendent, Government Printing, 1906; reprinted New Delhi: Asian Educational Services, 1991).
Whitaker's List – 1900	*Whitaker's Naval and Military Directory and Indian Army List, 1900* (London: J. Whitaker & Sons, 1900).
White, *Medieval Technology*	Lynn White, Jr., *Medieval Technology & Social Change* (Oxford: Oxford University Press, 1964).
World Book	*The World Book Encyclopedia* (USA: World Book, 1983).
Yule, *Hobson-Jobson*	Henry Yule, A.C. Burnell, and William Crooke, *Hobson-Jobson; A Glossary of Colloquial Anglo-Indian Words and Phrases*, 2nd ed. (Delhi: Munshiram Manoharlal, 1968).

§IV

FRENCH EMPIRE

§IV-1 COUNTRY BACKGROUND

It has been fashionable in some quarters to denigrate the French fighting ability. This is a relatively recent phenomenon, growing mostly out of the French army's experience in World War II. Perhaps their experience in the colonial wars of the 1950s also influenced this view. The French were the first, in modern times, to launch an all-out effort to battle widespread guerilla movements in an attempt to hold on to colonies. The task is now viewed as nearly impossible but, at the time, it was seen as another example of the French's lack of toughness.

This view is ironic, given that, for most of European history, the French were seen as the great warrior race of Europe. In fact, in 1940, during the Phoney War, American magazines writing about the European situation automatically described the French army as the finest in Europe.

If we go back to the birth of the nation, the Franks under Charlemagne (r. 768–814) conquered a large portion of Western Europe. Two hundred years later, the First Crusade (1095–9) was largely a French effort.[1] In many ways this was the most successful crusade because it captured Jerusalem. The heavy French contingent explains why the king of Jerusalem had a French name and why the Arab name for European became Frank.[2]

At about the same time, the Normans, who technically owed allegiance to the French Crown but more or less acted independently, were exploding out of Normandy. That they conquered England in 1066 is well known, but what are less well known are their conquests in southern Europe. In the 1040s, Normans began conquering parts of southern Italy. Calabria was largely won by them by 1059. In 1061, they began the process of retaking Sicily from the Saracens and completed that conquest in 1091.[3] The Normans went on to take parts of North Africa and carried out attacks into Byzantine Greece.

Charlemagne's death in 814, along with his sons' and grandsons' manoeuvring, had left one of his grandsons the core of what would become modern France. It included some of the best land in Europe.

Modern France, after taking in portions of the Alps, still has one of the highest percentages of arable land in Europe, indeed in the world: 33.5 per cent. The percentage for the United Kingdom is 25 per cent. The modern numbers for other countries are Russia, 7.4 per cent; United States, 17.8 per cent; Germany, 34.3 per cent; and Spain, 25.1 per cent.[4] This resource was particularly important during a period when there was no or little industry. The ability to grow crops directly translated into how many people the nation could support, and thus how many fighting men and knights it could field.

The history of France is one of battles and campaigns. Around 1150, Eleanor of Aquitaine married the very masculine Henry Plantagenet, Duke of Anjou, after her unhappy marriage to Louis VII of France. That first marriage was annulled: Louis thought her a strumpet; she called him a monk. Eleanor helped Henry gain the throne of England, and this opened the door for the Hundred Years War.

About 1200, the French conquered Normandy. The extensive English holdings in France fell back to their Aquitaine core. In 1494, Charles VIII of France invaded Italy and is said to have conquered Italy with a piece of chalk in his hand. That is to say his artillery was so powerful he only needed to write out the plan of attack with a piece of chalk for the resisting city's fate to be sealed. By 1495, Charles had taken Naples. But then, a combination of long supply lines and an outbreak of syphilis – freshly brought from the New World by the Spanish, according to most sources – caused his army to fall apart.

Following that, France was engaged in a merry-go-round of wars for the next century. It did manage, by and large, to stay out of the Thirty Years War that devastated Germany, although there was a revolt in France by Huguenots during that period.

At the Battle of Rocroi in 1643, French troops destroyed the Spanish tercios, and France became the great military power in Europe just as Louis XIV came to the throne. France's population now dwarfed most other European countries'. The French population was 20 million strong; the others on the whole much smaller: England and Spain had 5 million each; Italy had 6 million and Holland had 2 million. The Holy Roman Empire had 21 million people, but it was divided into over 400 different states, impoverished and jealous of each other.[5] France took a position of cultural and military leadership that would last until 1940, with a brief interruption in 1870.

The Third Republic brought a period of political instability. There were forty-nine prime ministers between 1871 and 1914, counting two that served twice. There were forty-seven ministers of war during that period; this was the death of long-term planning. The Dreyfus Affair of 1894–1906 and its aftermath of left-wing anti-military politicians in power only made things worse.

Note on Units of Measurement

By this period, the metric system was well established in France, and sources give measurements in millimetres and centimetres. These do not convert into simple fractions of inches, so I quote the imperial measurement as decimal numbers.

§IV-2 THE ARMY

§IV-2-1   Cavalry Regiments and Dates Formed
§IV-2-2   Infantry Regiments and Dates Formed
§IV-2-3   Regimental Histories

§IV-2-1 FRENCH CAVALRY REGIMENTS AND DATES FORMED

Cuirassiers

Regiment	Date Formed
1st Cuirassiers	1631
2nd Cuirassiers	1635
3rd Cuirassiers	1645
4th Cuirassiers	1643
5th Cuirassiers	1653
6th Cuirassiers	1635
7th Cuirassiers	1659
8th Cuirassiers	1638
9th Cuirassiers	1666
10th Cuirassiers	1643
11th Cuirassiers	1652
12th Cuirassiers	1668

Dragoons

Regiment	Date Formed
1st Dragoons	1656
2nd Dragoons	1635
3rd Dragoons	1649
4th Dragoons	1667
5th Dragoons	1656
6th–7th Dragoons	1673
8th Dragoons	1674
9th Dragoons	1673
10th–11th Dragoons	1674
12th Dragoons	1675
13th Dragoons	1676
14th Dragoons	1672
15th Dragoons	1688
16th Dragoons	1718
17th Dragoons	1743
18th Dragoons	1744
19th–20th Dragoons	1793
21st Dragoons	1796
22nd Dragoons	1630
23rd Dragoons	1670
24th Dragoons	1671
25th Dragoons	1665
26th Dragoons	1673
27th Dragoons	1674
28th Dragoons	1792
29th–30th Dragoons	1803
31st Dragoons	1893
32nd Dragoons	1913

Chasseurs à Cheval

Regiment	Date Formed
1st Chasseurs à Cheval	1651
2nd Chasseurs à Cheval	1673
3rd–5th Chasseurs à Cheval	1675
6th Chasseurs à Cheval	1676
7th Chasseurs à Cheval	1745
8th–9th Chasseurs à Cheval	1749
10th Chasseurs à Cheval	1758
11th Chasseurs à Cheval	1762
12th Chasseurs à Cheval	1769
13th–16th Chasseurs à Cheval	1793
17th Chasseurs à Cheval	1792
18th–21st Chasseurs à Cheval	1793

Hussars

Regiment	Date Formed
1st Hussars	1720
2nd Hussars	1734
3rd Hussars	1764
4th–5th Hussars	1783
6th–7th Hussarss	1792
8th–11th Hussars	1793
12th Hussars	1794
13th Hussars	1795
14th Hussars	1813

Chasseurs d'Afrique

Regiment	Date Formed
1st–2nd Chasseurs d'Afrique	1831
3rd Chasseurs d'Afrique	1832
4th Chasseurs d'Afrique	1839
5th–6th Chasseurs d'Afrique	1887

Spahis

Regiment	Date Formed
1st–3rd Spahis	1831
4th Spahis (Tunisian)	1882
5th Spahis (Algerian)	1914

Other

Regiment	Date Formed
Moroccan Spahis Régiment de Marche	1912

§IV-2-2 FRENCH INFANTRY REGIMENTS AND DATE FORMED

Infantry

Regiment	Date Formed
1st Infantry	1480
2nd Infantry	1776
3rd Infantry	1507
4th Infantry	1776
5th Infantry	1521
6th Infantry	1776
7th Infantry	1521
8th Infantry	1776
9th Infantry	1562
10th Infantry	1776
11th Infantry	1621
12th Infantry	1776
13th Infantry	1597
14th Infantry	1776
15th Infantry	1576
16th Infantry	1776
17th Infantry	1597
18th Infantry	1776
19th Infantry	1597
20th Infantry	1776
21st Infantry	1589
22nd Infantry	1776
23rd Infantry	1644
24th Infantry	1775
25th Infantry	1585
26th Infantry	1775
27th Infantry	1616
28th Infantry	1775
29th Infantry	1617
30th Infantry	1775
31st Infantry	1610
32nd Infantry	1775
33rd Infantry	1625
34th Infantry	1775
35th Infantry	1604
36th Infantry	1775
37th Infantry	1587
38th–39th Infantry	1629
40th Infantry	1598
41st Infantry	1634
42nd Infantry	1635
43rd Infantry	1638
44th Infantry	1642
45th Infantry	1643
46th–47th Infantry	1644
48th Infantry	1610
49th Infantry	1647
50th–51st Infantry	1651
52nd Infantry	1654
53rd Infantry	1656
54th Infantry	1657
55th Infantry	1644
56th Infantry	1635
57th Infantry	1627
58th Infantry	1667
59th Infantry	1668
60th–61st Infantry	1669
62nd Infantry	1667
63rd–67th Infantry	1672
68th–69th Infantry	1673
70th–75th Infantry	1674
76th–77th Infantry	1671
78th–84th Infantry	1684
85th–89th Infantry	1690

90th Infantry	1691	158th Infantry	1887
91st Infantry	1692	159th Infantry	1794
92nd Infantry	1661	160th Infantry	1887
93rd Infantry	1706	161st–164th Infantry	1794
94th Infantry	1709	165th Infantry	1793
95th Infantry	1734	166th–167th	1794
96th Infantry	1745	168th Infantry	1913
97th Infantry	1752	169th–173rd Infantry	1794
98th–99th Infantry	1757		
100th Infantry	1758	***Chasseur Battalions***	
101st Infantry	1787	**Battalion**	**Date Formed**
102nd Infantry	1560	1st Chasseurs à Pied	1838
103rd–104th Infantry	1791	2nd–5th Chasseurs à Pied	1840
105th Infantry	1575	6th–7th Chasseurs à Pied (Alpins)	1840
106th Infantry	1766	8th–10th Chasseurs à Pied	1840
107th Infantry	1772	11th–14th Chasseurs à Pied (Alpins)	1854
108th Infantry	1766	15th–20th Chasseurs à Pied	1854
109th Infantry	1772	21st Chasseurs à Pied	1855
110th Infantry	1773	22nd Chasseurs à Pied (Alpins)	1855
111th Infantry	1793	23rd Chasseurs à Pied (Alpins)	1870
112th Infantry	1794	24th Chasseurs à Pied (Alpins)	1854
113th–114th Infantry	1795	25th–26th Chasseurs à Pied	1871
115th Infantry	1808	27th–28th Chasseurs à Pied (Alpins)	1871
116th–118th Infantry	1794	29th Chasseurs à Pied	1871
119th–120th Infantry	1808	30th Chasseurs à Pied (Alpins)	1871
121st – 122nd Infantry	1794	31st Chasseurs à Pied	1913
123rd Infantry	1793		
124th–125th Infantry	1795	***Zouaves***	
126th Infantry	1793	**Regiment**	**Date Formed**
127th–128th Infantry	1794	1st Zouaves	1830
129th Infantry	1793	2nd–3rd Zouaves	1852
130th Infantry	1795	4th Zouaves	1855
131st–132nd Infantry	1794		
133rd Infantry	1811	***Tirailleurs***	
134th Infantry	1795	**Regiment**	**Date Formed**
135th–137th Infantry	1813	1st–3rd Tirailleurs (Algerian)	1842
138th–141st Infantry	1794	4th Tirailleurs (Tunisian)	1884
142nd–143rd Infantry	1795	5th–9th Tirailleurs (Algerian)	1913
144th Infantry	1794		
145th–146th Infantry	1795	***Foreign Legion***	
147th–148th Infantry	1793	**Regiment**	**Date Formed**
149th–150th Infantry	1794	1st–2nd Foreign Legion	1831
151st Infantry	1813		
152nd Infantry	1794	***African Light Infantry Battalions***	
153rd Infantry	1813	**Battalion**	**Date Formed**
154th Infantry	1794	1st–3rd African Light Infantry	1832
155th–156th Infantry	1813	4th–5th African Light Infantry	1889
157th Infantry	1795		

Moroccan Auxiliary Tirailleur Battalions

Battalion	Date Formed
1st–5th Moroccan Auxiliary Tirailleurs	1912

A sixth battalion was being formed in July of 1914.[6]

Colonial Troops

Regiment	Date Formed
1st–22nd Colonial	1822
3rd Colonial	1838
4th Colonial	1854
5th–8th Colonial	1890
9th Colonial	1886
10th Colonial	1888
11th Colonial	1869
16th Colonial	1900
21st–22nd Colonial	1899
23rd–24th Colonial	1902

The 12th–15th and 17th–20th Colonial Regiments were disbanded in the early 1900s.

Senegalese Units

Regiment	Date Formed
1st Senegalese Tirailleurs	1857
2nd Senegalese Tirailleurs	1892
3rd Senegalese Tirailleurs	1900
4th Senegalese Tirailleurs	1904

Battalion	Date Formed
1st Senegalese Battalion in Mauritania	
2nd Senegalese Battalion in Timbuktu	
3rd Senegalese Battalion in Zinder	
1st–2nd Senegalese Battalion in Algeria	1910

Vietnamese Units

Regiment	Date Formed
1st–2nd Tonkinese Tirailleurs	1884
3rd Tonkinese Tirailleurs	1885
4th Tonkinese Tirailleurs	1897
1st Annamite Tirailleurs	1879

Madagascar Units

Regiment	Date Formed
1st Malgaches Tirailleurs	1885
2nd Malgaches Tirailleurs	1886
3rd Malgaches Tirailleurs	1903
Battalion of Senegalese in Madagascar	1911?

Other Tirailleurs Units

Regiment of Native Tirailleurs in Gabon	1912
Regiment of Senegalese in l'Oubangui – Chad (now part of the Central African Republic)	1900

Senegalese in Morocco

1st–4th Regiment of Senegalese Tirailleurs in Morocco	1913

(These regiments did not exist as separate regiments. They were mixed with colonial infantry in six *régiments de marche,* temporary regiments formed to perform a particular task or fight in a particular campaign. *Régiments de marche* typically contain troops from several different units; in this case there was a ratio of two Senegalese battalions and one colonial battalion per mixed *régiment de marche.*)

§IV-2-3 REGIMENTAL HISTORIES[7]

INFANTRY

The formation dates in *§IV-2-2* should be viewed with scepticism. French regiments do not have an unbroken chronology leading back to an original ancestor, as found in the British and American armies. Instead, French regiments were disbanded and recreated as the French rulers changed back and forth among kings, republics, and an emperor between 1785 and 1825.

Before the French Revolution of 1789, the royal army had been reorganised so that the infantry regiments each had two battalions,[8] except for the Regiment du Roi, the King's Bodyguard (later the 28th), which had four.[9] In 1793, many of the Bourbon royal regiments were separated, and one of their battalions joined with two battalions of volunteers.[10] It was hoped that the regulars would stiffen the enthusiastic but unstable mass of volunteers. These new formations were called demi-brigades and given numbers.

During the amalgamation of 1793, the 1st Amalgamation, some account of the seniority of the royal regiments was taken. Thus, the 1st Royal Regiment became the core of the 1st and 2nd Demi-brigades. The 2nd Royal Regiment became the core of the 3rd and 4th, and so on.[11] The first battalion became part of a demi-brigade with an odd number, and the second battalion became part of a demi-brigade with an even number.[12]

The forming of demi-brigades was an ongoing process and took place between the major amalgamations. For example, in 1794, two regiments, the 13th and 99th, formed the 25th, 26th, 177th, and 178th Demi-brigades. Later that year, the second battalions of the 40th and the 82nd Infantry were amalgamated into the 80th and 152nd Demi-brigades. The first battalions were left in place until the second amalgamation.[13]

The second amalgamation, which took place in 1795, created additional demi-brigades out of volunteers and many of the line regiments that had not been broken up earlier, primarily in 1793. The new demi-brigades were allocated numbers on a more or less random basis.[14] See Smith, *Napoleon's Regiments*,[15] for dates and reasons for the two main amalgamations.

The process of amalgamating the regular and volunteer battalions sounds neat and logical. But, in application, it was anything but smooth. The Ministry of War was in disorder. Sometimes it was in the hands of people who cared more about ideology than record keeping, supplying the troops, and payrolls. New units were being formed while earlier ones were being amalgamated or disbanded. The confusion was so serious that War Ministry researchers in 1894 concluded that the confused record 'escapes analysis'.[16] This period is the weak link in tracing the lineage of royal regiments through demi-brigades to Napoleonic regiments.

These numbers carried over to the Napoleonic period (*c.* 1804–14) as the numbers for Napoleon's regiments. When Louis XVIII was placed on the throne in 1814, he kept most of Napoleon's regiments, the bulk of which went over to Napoleon when he returned from Elba. Faced with this mass disloyalty, in 1815 Louis XVIII disbanded the entire army. In its place, he raised a new army consisting of one legion per department. The ninety-four resulting legions were named after their departments.[17]

In 1820, the army changed back to numbering its foot units. Sixty line infantry regiments, numbered 1 to 60, and twenty light infantry regiments, numbered 76 to 95, were created. Regimental numbers were assigned by numbering the legions according to the alphabetical order of their departmental names.[18] These numbers, at least for the first sixty regiments, and those between 76 and 95, would be kept until 1914. In 1823, when France sent an army to restore the king of Spain to his throne, four additional regiments were created: the 61st, 62nd, 63rd, and 64th. This started the expansion of the army that would take place between the 1820s and 1914.

Detaille, a historian of the French army, states that 1820 is the 'true birth of today's [1882] regiments'.[19] When an earlier date for regiment formation is given, authors have just assumed that the number given to the royal Bourbon regiments in 1791[20] is connected to the regimental number of 1820 or later, and so give the new regiment the history of the royal regiment.

The dates shown in §IV-2-2 are from *Recueil D'Historiques de l'Infanterie Française* by General Serge Andolenko. *Napoleon's Regiments* by Digby Smith gives a history of regimental title changes, but unfortunately the two sources, in many places, do not agree.[21]

CAVALRY

In spite of the early formation dates for many French cavalry regiments shown in §IV-2-1, the cavalry, like the infantry, does not have an unbroken lineage back to these dates. They suffered disbandment and changes in function.

The cavalry regiments came through the early days of the French Revolution almost completely unscathed. In 1792, two German-speaking regiments, the 15th (Royal Allemand) Cavalry and the 4th (Saxe) Hussars, emigrated, or deserted – choose your word –

to the enemy.[22] Their numbers were dropped from the regimental lists, and all regiments of their type below them moved up one number.[23]

The cavalry regiments were given numbers in 1791.[24] But, as Detaille shows, the numbers often did not reflect a regiment's seniority.[25] Between 1791 and 1802, additional cavalry regiments were formed from odds and ends of volunteer units.[26] Then, in 1803, nine new dragoon regiments, the 22nd to 30th, were created by changing six regiments in the cavalry group (regiments classed as 'cavalry' under the Bourbons would become cuirassiers under Napoleon) and three hussar regiments into dragoons.[27]

During the Second Restoration, in 1815, the government disbanded all the cavalry regiments that had not been disbanded in 1814.[28]

When the cavalry arm was recreated, the number of cavalry regiments was drastically reduced from that maintained by Napoleon. Decrees in 1815 fixed the number of line cavalry regiments at forty-seven. There were, in addition to eight guard cavalry regiments,[29] one regiment of carabiniers; six of cuirassiers; ten of dragoons; twenty-four of chasseurs à cheval; and six of hussars.[30]

It had been planned that the new regiments would be given numbers, but this did not happen. Instead, the heavy cavalry, carabiniers, and cuirassiers were given the names of princes. The other regiments were given the names of government departments. When it came to assigning numbers to the regiments, heavy cavalry was assigned numbers by the rank of their prince or leader. The other regiments were assigned numbers using the alphabetical order of the their departments' names.[31]

When the regiments that were reformed in 1815–16, there seems to have been an attempt to destroy regimental traditions by sending men from one old regiment to a different new one. For example, the men of the old 5th Dragoons were sent to the 3rd Dragoons, and the old 11th Chasseurs à Cheval became the new 23rd Chasseurs à Cheval, and then the 11th Dragoons in 1825.[32]

This type of thing also happened later. Consider the changes made in 1825: four regiments of dragoons, the 7th through 10th, were converted into four regiments of cuirassiers, the 7th through 10th. At the same time six regiments of chasseurs, the 19th through 24th, became the 7th through 12th Dragoons.[33] It would have been simpler to leave the dragoons in place and only move the chasseurs. That this was not done was either because of Gallic logic or it is possible that it was been done to break the bonds of regimental loyalty.

As was the case with the infantry, cavalry founding dates need to be taken with a grain of salt. Consider the 11th Cuirassiers, which were created in 1871 as successors to the Carabiniers of the Guard, which, in turn, were successors to a regiment of carabiniers formed in 1693.[34] Then, for no apparent reason other than that they have the same number and name, the history of the Napoleonic 11th Cuirassiers was assigned to the regiment.[35]

Trying to follow cavalry lineage, given the many disbandments and the cases where a lineage is assumed based on having the same number, presents many traps for the unwary. The dates given in §IV-2-1 are from Andolenko, *Historiques Cavalerie*. Smith's *Napoleon's Regiments* often gives different dates and lineages.

§IV-3 UNIFORM INFORMATION

§IV-3-1   *The Old Pre-1900 Uniforms*
§IV-3-2   *Lances and Pennants*
§IV-3-3   *Coat, Kepi and Epaulette Colours*
§IV-3-4   *Officer Rank Markings*

§IV-3-1 THE OLD PRE-1900 UNIFORMS

Image IV:1, a photograph taken during the Universal Exposition of 1900, is instructive: it shows the different branches of the French army of the period and their tremendous range of uniforms. It also shows many men wearing uniforms with braid on their chest. This was to be replaced in short order by the model 1900 single-breasted tunic, although it took time for the stocks of the old uniforms to be used up.

§IV-3-2 LANCES AND PENNANTS

The fact that some regiments of the French cavalry carried lances is not well known. They had originally carried bamboo lances and in 1903, the steel lance was introduced to replace the bamboo. The steel lance was about 3 m (9 feet 10 inches) long[36] and used up to and during early World War I. The bamboo lance of the period was 2.9 m (9 feet 6 inches) long. A steel lance was carried by the 2nd, 3rd, 4th, 8th, 11th, and 12th Hussars[37] and the steel lance was also issued to the 13th, 14th, 15th, 17th, and 18th Regiments of Chasseurs.[38]

All dragoons were armed with lances. They were bamboo for Regiments 10, 15, 19, 20, 24, and 25, and steel for the other regiments.

The lances had lance pennants of crimson over white.

IV:1 Paris Universal Exhibition, showing all the different uniforms worn in the French army, marines, and navy as of 1900. Note the Brandenburg braid on the front of some of the uniforms. Shortly after this photo, this style of uniform was replaced.

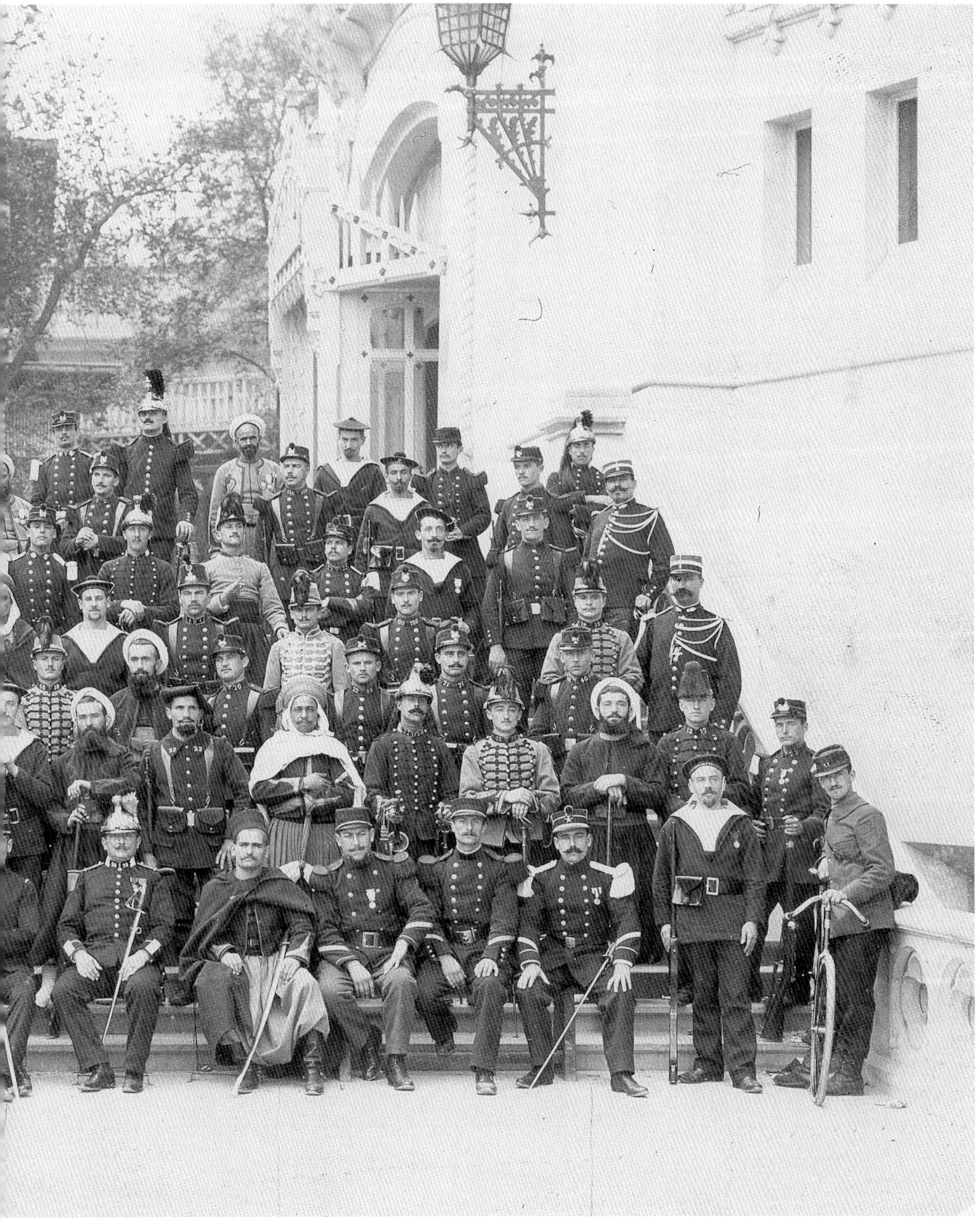

§IV-3-3 COAT, KEPI AND EPAULETTE COLOURS

To make the information more manageable, the table showing this information has been split into two.

French Uniforms, Other Ranks: Kepi and Epaulette Colours, Part I

	Coat	Epaulette and Trefoils		Collar		Button	Kepi and Shako	
		Base	Fringe	Collar	Shield	Button	Base	Top
Line infantry	Dark blue[a]	Crimson	Crimson	Crimson	Dark blue [b,c]	Gold	Dark blue[b,c]	Crimson[d,e]
Foreign Legion (FL)	Dark blue[a]	Crimson	Green	Crimson	Crimson[f,g]	Gold	Dark blue[b] or f,h	Crimson[d,e]
Alpine Infantry (IA)	Dark blue[a]	Crimson	Crimson	Crimson	Dark blue[b,c]	Gold	Dark blue beret[f,g]	
Chasseurs à Pied	Dark blue[j]	Green	Green	Dark blue	Dark blue[j,k]	Silver	Dark blue[j,k]	Dark blue[i,l]
Chasseurs Alpins	Short dark blue jacket	None[m]		Large, fold down[j]		Silver	Dark blue beret[n,o]	
Cuirassiers	Dark blue[p]	Crimson	Crimson	Crimson	Dark blue[b,k]	Silver	Helmet	
Chasseurs à cheval	Light (mid) blue[p]	White	Trefoils	Crimson	Crimson[k,q]	Silver	Light (mid) blue[n or b,r]	Crimson[s,l]
Hussars	Light (mid) blue[p]	White	Trefoils	Sky blue	Sky blue[b,k]	Silver	Light (mid) blue[t, or b,r]	Crimson[s,l]
Dragoons	Dark blue[p]	White	Trefoils	White	Dark blue[b,k]	Silver	Helmet	
African Light Infantry	Dark blue[p]	Crimson	Green	Dark Blue	Dark blue[j,k]	Silver	Dark blue[j,k]	Crimson[i,l]
Chasseurs d'Afrique	Light (mid) blue	White	Trefoils	Yellow	Sky blue[j,u]	Silver	Light (mid) blue[b,k]	Crimson[i,l]

Notes: The table shows the dress of other ranks unless otherwise noted
[a] Crimson trim.
[b] Crimson number.
[c] Officers' number was gold.
[d] Dark blue trim.
[e] Officers had gold trim.
[f] Grenade (the grenades of the FL and IA were of different shapes).
[g] Officers' grenade was in gold.
[h] Officers' grenade or number in gold.
[i] Yellow trim.
[j] Yellow number.
[k] Officers' number was silver.
[l] Officers' number was sky blue.
[m] Other ranks did not wear tunic.
[n] French hunting horn.
[o] Officers' horn was silver.
[p] No trim except for a cuff flap the same colour of the collar.
[q] Sky blue number.
[r] Shako or kepi.
[s] Sky blue trim.
[t] Hussar knot.
[u] Officers had yellow shield with silver number.

French Uniforms, Kepi and Epaulette Colours, Part II

	Coat	Epaulette		Collar		Button	Kepis and Shako	
		Base	Fringe	Collar	Shield	Button	Base	Top
Zouaves								
Other ranks	Short dark blue vest/jacket & closed waistcoat	None		None		n/a	Crimson chechia[a] & white turban	
Officers	Dark blue[b]	None		Dark blue	Dark Blue[c]	Gold	Dark blue[c]	Crimson[d]

§IV-3 Uniform Information

	Coat	Epaulette		Collar		Button	Kepis and Shako	
		Base	Fringe	Collar	Shield		Base	Top
Tirailleurs								
Other ranks	Short light blue vest/jacket, & closed waistcoat	None		None		n/a	Crimson chechia[a] & white turban	
Officers	Very light blue[d]	None		Yellow	Very light blue[c or e]	Gold	very light blue[c or e]	Crimson[d]
Moroccans								
Other ranks	Khaki shirt	None		None		n/a	Crimson chechia[a]	
Officers	Light blue[d]	None		Yellow	Light blue[f]	Gold	Very light blue[f]	Crimson[d]
Spahis								
Other ranks	Crimson jacket/waistcoat & crimson waistcoat (vest)	None		None		n/a	Dark blue guenhour & white haik[g]	
Officers	Crimson[d]	Gold	Gold	Crimson	Crimson[c or e]	Gold	Light blue[c or e]	Crimson[d]
Colonial infantry								
Other ranks	Dark blue	Yellow	Yellow	Dark blue	Dark blue[h]	Gold	Dark blue[h]	Dark blue[i]
Officers	Dark blue/black	Gold	Gold	Coat colour	Coat colour[c or j]	Gold	Dark blue/black	Dark blue[i]
Senegalese								
Other ranks	Short dark blue jacket[k]	None[l]		None[m]		Gold	Crimson chechia[a]	
Officers	Dark blue/black	Gold	Gold	Coat colour	Coat colour[c or j]	Gold	Dark blue/black	Dark blue[i]
Indo Chinese								
Other ranks	Short dark blue jacket[n]	None[l]		None		None	Coolie-style hat	
Officers	Dark blue/black	Gold	Gold	Coat colour	Coat colour[c or j]	Gold	Dark blue/black	Dark blue[i]
Malgaches								
Other ranks	Short dark blue jacket[k]	None		None[o]		Gold	Crimson chechia[a]	
Officers	Dark blue/black	Gold	Gold	Coat colour	Coat colour[c or j]	Gold	Dark blue/black	Dark blue[i]

Notes: [a] A chechia is a larger, softer version of a fez.
[b] Officers only; other ranks did not wear tunic.
[c] Gold number.
[d] Gold trim.
[e] Crescent moon and number.
[f] Gold crescent moon and star.
[g] See §IV-7-b.
[h] Crimson number or crimson anchor.
[i] Crimson trim.
[j] Gold anchor.
[k] New jackets were introduced in 1914, but not worn until 1915 or later (Mirouze, *French Army*, p. 245).
[l] Other ranks did not wear tunic.
[m] Crimson letters 'TS' on either side of jacket on a level just below first button.
[n] Unique jacket style.
[o] Crimson letters 'MS' on either side of jacket on a level just below the first button.

§IV-3-4 OFFICER RANK MARKINGS

Rank	Kepi – Vertical Braid	Kepi – Quatrefoil on Top of Kepi	Tunic – Horizontal Rings	Tunic – Cuff Rings	Tunic – Epaulettes
Colonel	3; Button colour	3; Button colour	5; Button colour	5; Button colour	2; Large fringe. Button colour
Lt. Colonel	3; Button colour	3; Button colour	5; Bottom, 3rd & 5th button colour, 2nd and 4th opposite colour	5; Bottom, 3rd & 5th button colour, 2nd and 4th opposite colour	2; Large fringe. Top surfaces opposite colour, crescents and fringes button colour
Chef de Battalion (Major)	3; Button colour	3; Button colour	4; Button colour	4; Button colour	Large fringe button colour on left; no fringe on right
Commandant Major 1871–83	3; Button colour	3; Button colour	4; Button colour	4; Top opposite button colour over 3 that are button colour	Large fringe button colour on left; no fringe on right
Commandant Major 1883–1914	3; Button colour	3; Button colour	4; Button colour	4; Top opposite button colour over 3 that are button colour	Large fringe button colour on right; no fringe on left
Captain	2; Button colour	2; Button colour	3; Button colour	3; Button colour	2; Fine. Button colour
Captain Adjutant Major[a]	2; Button colour	2; Button colour	3; Button colour	3; Bottom and top opposite colour. Centre ring button colour	2; Fine. Button colour with scarlet stripe down centre of top surfaces
Captain de Tir[a]	2; Button colour	2; Button colour	2; Button colour	3; Top opposite colour. Centre and bottom rings button colour	2; Fine. Button colour; top surface opposite to button colour; crescents and fringes are button colour
Lieutenant	1; Button colour	1; Button colour	2; Button colour	2; Button colour	Fine fringe on left; no fringe on right; button colour
Sous-Lieutenant	1; Button colour	1; Button colour	2; Button colour	1; Button colour	Fine fringe on right; no fringe on left; button colour
Adjutant Chef, after 1913	1; Button colour with scarlet band	1; Button colour with scarlet band	1; Button colour with scarlet band	1; Button colour with scarlet band	Fine fringe on right; no fringe on left; button colour, but scarlet stripe down centre of top surface
Adjutant	1; Button colour with scarlet band	1; Button colour with scarlet band	1; Opposite colour with scarlet band	1; Opposite colour with scarlet band	Fine fringe on right; no fringe on left; opposite colour

Source: Robert, Uniformes, vol. 4, pp. 6–7; Windrow, Foreign Legion, pp. 70–1; Sumner, French Army, p. 17.
Note: [a] Rank done away with in 1890.

§IV-4 GENERAL STAFF

The Revolutionary Wars ended the French staff system in the traditional sense. Army purges removed Ancien Régime staff officers, and the young generals being promoted on merit learned how to function without them.[39] A staff college was established in 1818, but its training proved defective, and its graduates were isolated from army life.[40]

An effort at reform was made after Prussia defeated Austria in 1859, but there was too little time and the forces of inertia were too strong. Poor staff work contributed to the French defeat in the Franco-Prussian War in 1870.[41]

Following this loss, the leaders of the new Third Republic became convinced that a central system for planning and executing military operations was needed. It would be something like the Prussian General Staff.[42] The system, set up in 1874, created a much weaker staff than that found in Prussia. The general staff was made the General Staff of the Minister of War, and its head was appointed by the minister.[43] In setting it up, the government, remembering past power grabs and coups, carefully limited the power of the General Staff of the Minister of War.[44]

The years that followed showed a number of flaws with the new system. First was government instability. The government fell often, thirty-two times between 1871 and 1900.[45] When a government fell, it was customary for the minister of war to resign, although sometimes he was held over. The thirty-two governments during this period had twenty-six ministers of war. The average tenure was under one year, and only ten held the post for a year or longer.[46] Thus, the ministers had little experience in office and little time to make reforms. When he came into office, almost every new minister brought with him a new chief of staff who was junior to him.[47]

Second, quality generals avoided the post of minister of war because of the office's unappealing half-military, half-political demands overlaid with an unsettling sense of intrigue.[48] Therefore, the post went to less eminent and more junior generals. This left them without moral authority over the older, more senior generals who ostensibly reported to them. In addition, the ministers always had, in the back of their minds, the knowledge that they would return to the army junior to the many men they now commanded.[49] That the ministers were aware of their humble status is shown by a letter written in the late 1880s by General Ferron, an ex-minister of war and Assistant Chief of Staff, asking for help in securing a command. The letter-writer did not seek a prestigious command, such as the upcoming vacancy in the Sixth Army Corps. Rather, his request was that he be given the command of the corps of whoever was named head of the Sixth.[50]

Third, the mediocre ministers of war made sure they chose mediocre chiefs of staff so as to not be overshadowed by them.[51]

In 1890, the problems of the general staff were addressed by creating a General Staff of the Army. This office was still under the authority of the minister of war, but the officeholder had more influence on the army in peacetime than any general before him. In wartime the holder of the office would become the chief of staff to the general commanding the main group of armies fighting Germany on the eastern front.[52] This commander was known as the Generalissimo.[53]

A strengthened high command, the Conseil Superieur de la Guerre (CSG), was reorganised. It had the power to direct war operations. The general staff directed training and made the war's operational plans. The rub was that, officially, the two bodies did not consult with each other. The only time they had contact was at the moment of mobilisation.[54] In reality, the two bodies usually found ways to talk to each other in peacetime.[55]

As part of the leftists' backlash following the Dreyfus Affair, the radicals were able to place General Louis André as minister of war. He took several steps that damaged the morale and functioning of the army.[56] One of them was directed against the general staff. He began handpicking officers in the general staff to place officers with republican views and also cut the functional powers of CSG.[57]

Then, at the last minute, during the Moroccan Crisis of 1911, more power was given to the chief of the general staff. The most important change was to unite the offices of Generalissimo and the chief of the general staff. Thanks to this move, one person had control of training, drawing up war plans, and of fighting using those plans. This one person had more power than the chief of the Prussian General Staff,[58] and more than any French general since Napoleon, and Napoleon had also been head of state.[59]

This was the staff organisation that France took into World War I.

Staff Uniforms

Headdress

As of 1872, in full dress, officers of the general staff wore a cocked hat (Image II:36) made of black felt bordered by black silk lace. It had gold braid and a gold button.[60] It had a plume of drooping cock feathers coloured red, white, and blue (red on top).[61] Image II:36 shows a British cocked hat, but the shape was the same. The main difference was that the plume of a French hat all fell to the right side.[62]

In 1884, the cavalry full dress headdress shako and helmet was said to have the following plumes:

White	General staff and the Staff of the Minister of War
White and red	Staffs of army corps (white on top)
Red	Staffs of division
Blue	Staffs of brigades[63]

In 1886, the kepi became the full dress headdress for foot troops. The plume colours remained the same, except for the staff of the chasseurs à pied (CaP) – they wore a drooping green black plume like other CaPs.

Generally speaking, where an officer served could be identified by the colour of his plume and armband design.

Table IV.4.1: Staff Plume Colours, 1914

Office	Years	Plume Colour
President of the Republic	1872–84	No details nor text
	1884–87	Regulatory white plume (actually tricolour)
	1887–1914	Tricolour (blue on top)
Minister of war – special general staff	1872–80	White and red (of the General Staff of the Army)
	1880–1914	Entirely white
Corps of General Staff	1872–1880[a]	Tricolour (red on top)
Staff of the army/armies	1872–1914	White and red (white on top)
General staffs of body of army	1872–87	White and red (white on top)
	1887–1914	Tricolour (white on top)
General staff of division	1872–1914	Entirely scarlet
General staffs of brigades	1872–1914	Fully dark sky blue
General staffs of regiments	1872–1914	Tricolour (red on top)
Staff in colonies, East Africa		Entirely red
Staff in colonies, Equatorial Africa		Entirely blue
Staff in colonies, Indochina		Tricolour (blue on top)

Source: Robert, *Uniformes*, vol. 4, p. 22.
Note: [a] Corps of General Staff disbanded in 1880.

Tunic

Staff officers wore the standard blue French infantry officers' tunic of the period 1880–1914. The buttons were gold.[64] The cuffs were the same as other infantry officers' cuffs, and a system of rings showed rank. The collar was all blue. For officers who were certified members of the staff, the collar had a stylised winged lightning bolt, the insignia of the general staff (Image

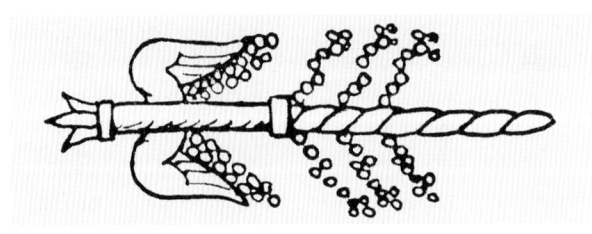

IV:2 Insignia of French General Staff Officers
Generally known as a winged lightning bolt, it is also referred to as a thunderbolt.

IV:2).⁶⁵ For officers seconded to the staff, the lightning bolt, when worn after 1900, was either gold or silver to match the button colour of the officer's mother branch.⁶⁶ Up to 1900, officers serving on the staff who had not gone through staff training and therefore were not certified staff officers, wore a grenade on their collars (Image IV:3). In 1900, their insignia changed to the lightning bolt.⁶⁷

Full dress epaulettes for staff officers were the same as those worn by army infantry officers (Table IV.6.a.2).⁶⁸ Clerks and staff secretaries were enlisted men and not officers in the general staff.⁶⁹ They wore staff epaulettes with white fields and fringe.⁷⁰

After 1886, silk armbands were a part of the staff officers' dress uniform.⁷¹ They showed that an officer was a staff officer and where he was assigned. They were worn on the left sleeve above the elbow. The armband was bordered on both sides by a narrow gold braid, regardless of the uniform's button colour.⁷² The designs of the bands are shown in Table IV.4.2.

Table IV.4.2: General Staff Armband Colours and Insignia, 1914

Officer	Years	Colour and Detail
Military staff of the president	1886	White
	1887–1914	Tricolour (blue at the top). Gold lightning bolts on white area
General staff of minister of war		Completely white (golden lightning bolts at the centre)
General staff of the army and the armies		White and red (red on bottom). Golden lightning bolts riding on the white and red
General staff of the army corps		Tricolour (blue on top). Golden lightning bolts on blue and white
General staff division of infantry		Entirely red. Gold grenade at the centre, number of the division below in figures
General staff division of cavalry		Entirely red. Eight-pointed star at the centre, number of the division below in Roman numerals
General staff of brigade of infantry		Entirely dark sky blue. Gold grenade at the centre, number of the brigade below in figures
General staff brigade of cavalry of corps		Entirely dark sky blue. Eight-pointed star at the centre, number of brigade in figures
General staff brigade of divisional cavalry		The same armband as above. Number in Roman numerals
General staff artillery of corps		Entirely dark sky blue. Two gold guns crossed at the centre, beneath number of the army corps
General staff of army engineering		Entirely red. At the centre (embroidered in gold) the attributes of engineers: cuirass and pot on head
General staff of governor of a stronghold		Entirely red with gold lightning bolts at the centre
General staff of the governor of colony (including Algeria)		Red – white – red, without lightning bolts
Staff in West Africa		Entirely red with lightning bolts
Staff in Equatorial Africa		Entirely blue with lightning bolts
Staff in Indochina		Tricolour (blue on top)

Source: Robert, *Uniformes*, vol. 4, pp. 23–4.

Staff officers who had gone through staff college and were full members of the staff wore gold aiguillettes on their right shoulder.[73] Officers who had successfully completed the two-year staff college course and who were serving as interns on the general staff wore a lanyard.[74] The officers seconded to the staff, and therefore without formal staff training, wore the uniforms of their original branch with some staff distinctions, grenade, or lightning bolt added. Their aiguillettes were in their uniform's button colour and were worn on the right shoulder.[75]

Officers seconded to the general staff from cuirassiers and dragoons wore the appropriate helmet and epaulettes. But, from 1892 on, cuirassier officers did not wear a cuirass.[76]

Officers of foot units wore the same trousers as those worn in the army (§IV-6-a). Mounted officers wore riding breeches.[77] The trousers and breeches of staff assigned to the president and the ministers of war and the navy had two braids of gold or silver, depending on the button colour, that ran along either side of the garment's side seams. The space between the braid was the colour of the piping on the officer's trousers or breeches or his parent branch. For officers assigned to the staff, in general the space between the gold or silver braid was the colour of the officer's branch.[78] The braid was 20 mm (0.79 inches) wide with 4 mm (0.16 inches) between them.[79]

IV:3 Captain of Dragoons
The grenade on his collar shows he is on detached duty away from the regiment, probably with the staff.

IV:4 Close-Up of Cuirassier's Crest and Marmouset

§IV-5 CAVALRY

In 1914, the French cavalry was divided into two branches: heavy and light cavalry. This was almost entirely for historical reasons since, by 1914, all cavalry regiments had the same functions. They all scouted ahead, acted as a screen for the army, and, as necessary, skirmished.

§IV-5-a CUIRASSIERS

Uniform

HELMET

Under the old Bourbon kings, heavy cavalry wore a cocked hat. In 1802, the 8th Cuirassiers – formally the Cuirassiers du Roi[80] – were given helmets of the type already worn by dragoons, but of steel rather than brass, and with a black skin turban rather than the dragoons' brown sealskin turban.[81]

Then, between 1802 and 1804, the other heavy cavalry regiments received their steel helmets with red plumes. The fully developed cuirassier helmet consisted of five parts: (1) the helmet body; (2) a metal crest; (3) a horsehair plume that came out of the back of the metal crest; (4) a small holder and short brush that rose out of the front top of the metal crest, called a marmouset; and (5) a large plume that rose out of the left side of the helmet (Image C46).

The horsehair brush and holder was added to helmets in the 1820s.[82] The short brush on the front of the metal crest was red (see Image C46). It was made of horsehair and about 45 mm (1.77 inches) high, and came out of a 25 mm (0.98 inch) holder stamped with a waterleaf decoration (Image IV:4).[83] The plume on the side of the helmet was also red. At first plumes were worn in all orders of dress, but it was soon found that they came off easily in the field. This caused their use to be limited to parades.[84]

The metal of the helmet was, at various times, copper or steel. After 1871, it was steel. When the cuirassiers were first formed, the helmet was wrapped in a black skin placed just above the helmet's peak (or brim). This wrapping was normally called a turban. Thereafter, some sets of regulations provided for a turban, some did not. The regulations in force just prior to World War I did not. Instead, the helmet (model 1872–4) had a thin sheet of decorated brass attached to the front. In its centre was a flaming grenade, and, on each side, laurel branches.

The metal crest had, at its front end, a Medusa's head. The sides of the crest had palmettes separated by water lilies.[85] The model 1858 (M1858) helmet had a 29.5 cm (11.61 inch) plume on the left side of the helmet, and the size of the plume was carried over to the new, smaller helmet adopted in 1872. At the base of the plume, other ranks wore small balls of wool cording, called olives, whose colour showed the squadron. These were:

1st Squadron	Dark blue
2nd Squadron	Crimson
3rd Squadron	Dark green
4th Squadron	Sky blue
5th Squadron	Daffodil yellow
6th Squadron	Orange
Service platoon	Scarlet on top, royal blue on the bottom
General staff	Tricolour with red on top and blue on the bottom.

Officers wore silver wire cord as their olive (Image C46).[86]

The plume was scarlet cocks' feathers for other ranks. It was tricolour for the regiment's staff, red on top (Image IV:5). The officers' plume was scarlet vulture feathers or tricolour if they were on the general staff.[87]

In lieu of the standard scarlet plume that rose out of a small holder on the left side of the helmet, certain officers wore other types of plumes. The colonel commanding a regiment wore white egret feathers (Image IV:6); brigadier generals wore sky blue egret feathers; and major generals wore scarlet egret feathers. Divisions and brigade staff officers had

IV:5 Cuirassier Staff Officer
Note the tricolour plume in his helmet (red on top).

IV:6 Colonel of Cuirassiers
Note the white egret feathers. His cuirass has been nickelled to produce a high shine.

tricolour plumes, red on top. They also wore a silver thunderbolt on the front of their helmets.[88]

A 75 cm (29.53 inch) black horsehair 'mane' (scarlet for trumpeters and musicians) came off the M1858 helmet.[89] On this model, the mane was attached to the back of the crest. However, on the M1872, the mane was attached in two rows to the top of the lower crest, starting just behind the marmouset plate. It appears the length of the mane did not change.

A brigadier general also had two small stars on the front of the helmet band each side of the grenade with sky blue egret plumes,[90] and major generals had three stars with the third star on the grenade, with scarlet egret plumes.[91]

Tunic

The heavy cavalry of the royal army normally wore short blue coats. This uniform was carried over to the Republic's army and beyond. In the early 1860s, the short blue jacket was replaced by a long blue tunic whose skirts were buttoned back to show a red lining.[92]

After the Franco-Prussian War, the blue tunic underwent several modifications.[93] These produced the blue tunic worn prior to World War I.

In 1914, enlisted men wore a dark blue M1900 tunic with nine buttons down the front. The collar was crimson with a dark blue patch on each side of the collar where it closed. On the patch, the regimental number was shown in crimson. The collar was trimmed in dark blue. The cuff had a crimson vertical bar but no other trim. The crimson bar held three buttons. The tunic skirt did not have any trim but had three buttons on each side of the centre line. The cuirassiers' buttons were yellow and had a flaming grenade on them. The cuirassiers' epaulette consisted of a crimson shoulder board and fringe (Image IV:7).

IV:7 Cuirassier Other Rank
Note how his extra long epaulettes stick out beyond the cuirass and how the other rank's cuirass differs from the officer's cuirass in Image IV:6. The black horsehair 'mane' has been thrown over his shoulder and so gives us an idea of how long it is. Note the large crossed axes badge on his upper left arm, denoting a cavalry pioneer.

Cuirassier officers wore a tunic of the same basic cut as that of the enlisted men (see Image C47). Theirs was a darker colour, a dark blue/black. Prior to 1911, the officers' tunics had seven gold buttons down the front. After 1911, this was changed to nine buttons. Badges of rank in gold stripes were worn on the officers' sleeves. The number worn on the crimson patch on the collar was also gold (see §IV-3-4 for the number worn by each rank).

The officer's rank was also shown by the epaulettes.

Cuirass

The thing that made a cuirassier was his cuirass, the armour he wore on his chest and back. The first cuirasses were issued to modern French cavalry in 1802. By 1803–4, all heavy cavalry had been changed to cuirass armour.[94] The French cuirassiers who wore their

IV:8 Group of Mounted Cuirassiers, 1913
They wear a covering over their helmet to avoid giving off tell-tale glare.

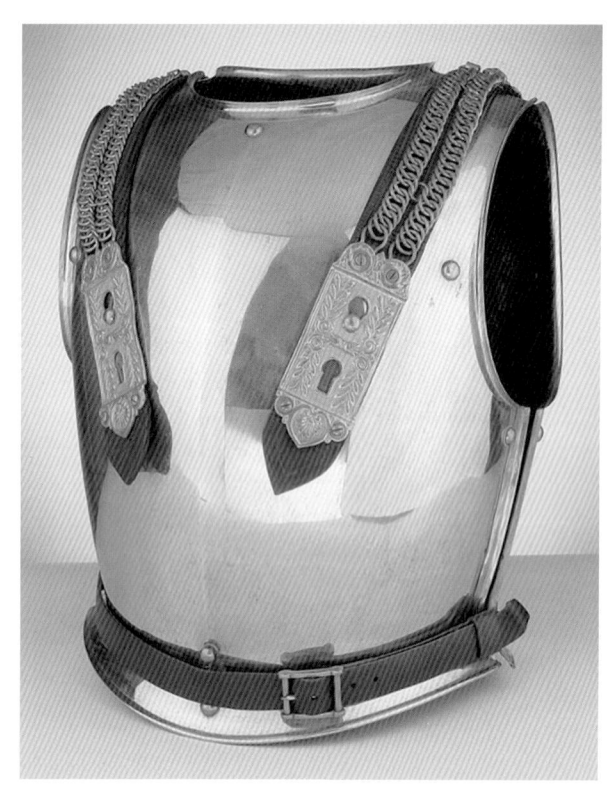

IV:9 Front of an Officer's Cuirass

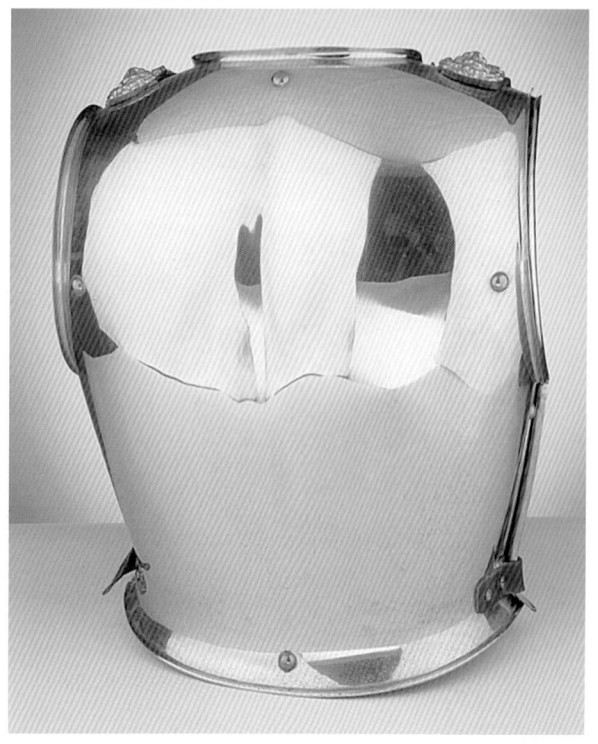

IV:10 Back of an Officer's Cuirass
The lion at the top of the strap can just barely be seen.

cuirasses into the field in 1914 were the last European army – and maybe the last major army in the world – to wear metal armour into battle (Image IV:8.[95])

The cuirass, which consisted of front and back chromed steel plates, weighed, on average, 7 kg (15.43 lb) (Images IV:9 and IV:10).[96] The basic design was set in 1855, and it was later slightly modified in the right shoulder area to allow for the firing of a carbine.

The two plates were held together by leather straps that went over each shoulder and a thin black leather belt at the waist. Each leather shoulder strap had two strands of linked chain on it. The shoulder straps ended in a metal plate, known as the buttonhole, with two openings and ending in a curved point. The openings were used to fasten the two plates together by hooking the key holes over the raised nuts in the chest area of the front breastplate.

The cuirass of an officer was of high quality and had several differences from those of the other ranks. The chain of the shoulder strap for officers was thicker. The leather of the shoulder strap and waist belt were of patent leather. The plate of the buttonhole, instead of being plain like the enlisted men, was decorated with an oak leaf design (compare Image IV:7 to Image IV:9). The officers' armour sheets have a shape that is more tailored to the wearer's body than the standard-issue plates. Most officers had their plates nickel-plated to make upkeep easier, even though this was against the rules for most regiments.[97]

The armour plates would tarnish easily, and this required a great deal of polishing. The 6th Regiment is said to have been exempt from this requirement and just let their plates go. At the other extreme, the enlisted men of the 1st and 2nd Cuirassiers, after 1902, were allowed to nickel-plate their armour.[98] They also nickel-plated their helmets after 1902. The 1st and 2nd were garrisoned in Paris and formed an unofficial guard unit for the Republic. They were the troops, who, because of their picturesque appearance, more often than not escorted visiting foreign dignitaries or French high officials on ceremonial occasions.

WAISTCOAT/VEST

To ease the weight of the cuirass, and to prevent its edge cutting into the person wearing it, a padded waistcoat (to use the British term – or vest in America) was worn. The standard issue item was buff with crimson built-up areas around the armholes and neck opening which showed outside the cuirass, serving as a crimson trim. These protected the wearer from the cuirass shifting. Officers wore a waistcoat/vest which was similar to that of the other ranks. Many officers had theirs made for them and were silk or satin.[99]

Riding Breeches

By the 1880–1914 period, the cuirassiers had long worn crimson breeches. The M1905 breeches were cut very loose above the knee, but were tight from the knee down. In 1909, the area between the legs was re-enforced with extra crimson cloth.[100] The quality of the cloth improved as the wearer's rank increased. Other ranks had narrow dark blue piping; officers had a wide band of dark blue/black (Image IV:11).

Gauntlet Gloves

White gauntlet gloves were issued to the 1st and 2nd Cuirassiers in 1912[101] because they were, for the most part, stationed in Paris. For this reason, as noted above, they often took part in ceremonial duties involving high dignitaries. The white gauntlet gloves, which only these two regiments wore, dressed them up just a little bit more.

IV:11 Crimson Other Rank's Breeches
Note the added cloth reinforcements between the legs added in 1909 and the thin dark blue piping.

§IV-5-b DRAGOONS

Dragoons were one of the oldest types of soldiers in the French army. In 1914, they were classed as heavy cavalry, but their duties were the same as those of the light cavalry.

Uniform

Headdress

Brass helmets had been worn by the Saxe Cavalry in 1745, and a version of this was issued to dragoons in 1763. This helmet was adopted by the cuirassiers.

By 1810, the helmets had a metal crest with a long horsehair tail, a plume rising out of the left side of the helmet, and tufts rising out of the top front of the metal crest.[102]

After the Napoleonic Wars, the dragoons, for a time, wore a helmet with a curving Greek-style crest, and then went back to the old helmet with the metal crest and long horsehair plume. In the 1820s, a horsehair brush, much like the marmouset and brush of the cuirassiers, was added to the top of the metal crest to go with the large plume on the left of the helmet. In 1854, the helmet took more of a First Empire look, but the metal crest, brush, side plume, and long tail remained.[103]

After the Franco-Prussian War, a new helmet was adopted. The helmet worn by the dragoons was basically identical to that worn by the cuirassiers. The only difference was that the cuirassiers' marmouset and brush were not worn by dragoons. This left a hole in the metal crest; a metal plug was placed in the hole

IV:12 Dragoon's Helmet
This is exactly like a cuirassier's helmet, except it does not have a marmouset. The hole where the marmouset would set would be plugged up. This helmet is fresh from combat. The horsehair 'mane' is still tied up to keep it from blowing into the wearer's eyes.

on the metal crest where the marmouset would have been inserted (Image IV:12).

Other than this, the helmets were the same: steel with a red plume on left, a black flowing horsehair plume, and the same metal crest. Even the brass front piece attached to the front of the helmet had the same flaming grenade (Image IV:12).

TUNIC

The traditional colour for dragoons' coats had been green. Their collars and cuffs would often show their regimental colour, or the colour of the group of regiments to which they were assigned.[104] In 1867, the traditional green jacket was replaced by a single-breasted blue tunic.[105] This would mark dragoons from that point on.

By 1914, dragoons wore a blue tunic with a white standing collar. The collar had dark blue piping and a dark blue shield on either side of the closure in front. The shield of other ranks had the regiment's number in crimson. There was an upright cuff patch of white which had three buttons (Images C50 and IV:13). The other ranks' tunic had nine white dome buttons without a device on them down the front (Image IV:14). The rear skirt of the tunic did not have piping, but had three white buttons on each side of the centre line.

IV:13 Group of Dragoons
Note colour of collar and the collar shield. Notations of rank are on the lower left sleeve.

On their shoulders the enlisted men wore a white shoulder piece that ended in the trefoil of the light cavalry (Image IV:15).

The tunic worn by officers was almost the same as that of the other ranks. It was a darker colour – dark blue/black. This meant the collar patch was of this colour. The regiment's number on the patch was silver. The regulation height for the collars was 6 cm (2.36 inches), but fashionable officers liked to wear higher collars (Image IV:16).

The tunic buttons for officers in the dragoons were also plain half-domes. The colour was silver. There was one exception: in 1913, the 13th Cuirassiers were converted into the 32nd Dragoons; the new dragoons kept their old flaming grenade on their buttons in memory of their former status.

Image IV:3 shows a dragoon on detached duty, for which there is no specific uniform badge. As such,

IV:14 Dragoon Other Ranks
This gives a clear view of the buttons down the tunic.

IV:15 Shoulder-Piece on Other Ranks' Tunic
One can see why it is often referred to as a cat's paw.

he is wearing grenades on his collar. An example of detached duty would be working as a staff officer without being certified as such by the staff college.

Riding Breeches

The dragoons followed the rest of the French army in wearing crimson riding breeches. They wore the same breeches as the cuirassiers.

Lance

All the dragoon regiments were armed with a lance (see *§IV-3-2*). Bamboo lances were carried by the 10th, 15th, 19th, 20th, 24th, and 25th Dragoons. The other regiments of the thirty-two-strong dragoon army carried steel lances after 1903.[106]

IV:16 Officer of Dragoons
Note how epaulettes show rank. There is fringe only on the left epaulette, denoting rank of lieutenant. The two rings on the sleeves also show his rank.

The bamboo lance had an overall length of 2.9 m (9 feet 6 inches). The other regiments' steel lances were about 3 m (9 feet 10 inches) long. The French lance pennant was crimson over white, roughly the same colours as the British lance pennants.[107]

§IV-5-c LIGHT CAVALRY

Hussars and chasseurs à cheval were classified as light cavalry. After the Franco-Prussian War, the French authorities tended to treat all units of light cavalry the same when it came to the assignment of men, uniforms, and armaments.

As light cavalry, the smaller men in each draft were assigned to the hussars and chasseurs. The men in these forces were to be between 1.59 and 1.68 m (5 feet 2.5 inches and 5 feet 6 inches) tall and could not weigh more than 65 kg (145 lb).[108]

Uniform

HEADDRESS: SHAKOS, KEPIS, AND HELMETS

A shako was adopted for the light cavalry, hussars, and chasseurs in 1874. This was said to be the brainchild of General du Barail, the minister of war at the time.[109] The body for both types of regiments was mid-blue. NCOs had a lighter shade of blue for the body of their shakos. The cloth was supported by a cardboard frame. On the front there was a white branch badge, a Hungarian knot for hussars (Image C48) and a French hunting horn for chasseurs (Image C49). A metal cockade of white iron was embossed with the tricolour (red, white, and blue, red to the outside) and worn above the branch badge. The peak (brim) was patent leather bordered with brass.[110]

Hussars' shakos had an upper border in the form of a stripe of white braid 28 mm (1.1 inches) wide (Image C48). Chasseurs' shakos had an upper border in the same width made of black wool – yes, wool (Images C49 and IV:17).

At first, the shakos were fairly large and sloped inward, making them slightly narrower on top than at their base. In later years, closer to 1914, the shakos became shorter and rounder.[111] The top was flat, and there was a bottom band of about the same height as the top band (Image IV:17).

IV:17 Side View of Light Cavalry Shako (Chasseurs à Cheval) The upper border is made of black wool. At the front top, it has a pompom, which was worn between the 1880s and 1910. Note how the chinstrap chain hooked up in the back of the shako.

Between the 1880s and 1910, the shako carried pompoms in different colours, marking the different squadrons. These were: 1st, dark blue; 2nd, crimson; 3rd, dark green; 4th, sky blue; depot squadron and general staff, tricolour with red on the top. The pompom was 35 mm (1.38 inches) in diameter and slightly flattened on the top and the bottom. After 1910, in full dress, both hussars and chasseurs wore plumes of cock feathers on the front of their shakos (Images IV:18, IV:19, and IV:20). The feathers were a black-green shade.[112] In 1913, other ranks' shakos cost 9.40 francs, which was equal to about 7 shillings 4.3 pence or $1.93 (about £36 or $46 in current funds).[113]

The officers' shako from the first was lower and had a different shape. The cloth of the body was a lighter blue and, as might be expected, the shako's materials were of a better quality. The braid at the top of the shako and the Hungarian knot were a silver colour, the light cavalry's button colour.

IV:18 Chasseurs à Cheval Marechal des Logis (Sergeant) with Plume on Shako
Note chinstrap chain on side of shako.

IV:20 Hussar Other Rank with Plume on Shako
Note the nine buttons down front of tunic, and the collar shield and the cuff trim are all the same colour as the tunic. Also note the white cat's paw shoulder-piece.

IV:19 Chasseur à Cheval Officer with Cock's Feathers on Shako
These replaced the pompoms. Note stripes on breeches.

For less than full dress, chasseurs and the hussars wore a kepi. For other ranks of both hussars and chasseurs, the upper body and top were crimson with mid-blue piping. The lower band was a mid-blue. Officers had an upper body and top of a brighter crimson with a silver trim according to rank (§IV-3-3). The trim was in a type of braid known as soutache. Their lower band was a light blue. The rank markings followed the French standard pattern, and silver was the predominant colour.

Up to about 1900, the bottom band of an officer's shako or kepi had a branch badge (see Images C48 and C49). After that, a silver regimental number was worn by most regiments. However, photos show the branch badge being worn on shakos and kepis up to 1914.

Much ink has been wasted on the M1910 helmet, which was, in fact, issued to very few regiments by 1914. These few helmets were basically the same helmets worn by dragoons.[114] The most noticeable

IV:21 Hussar Officer's Helmet
This was essentially the same as the dragoon's helmet, with minor differences. Note the star on the front.

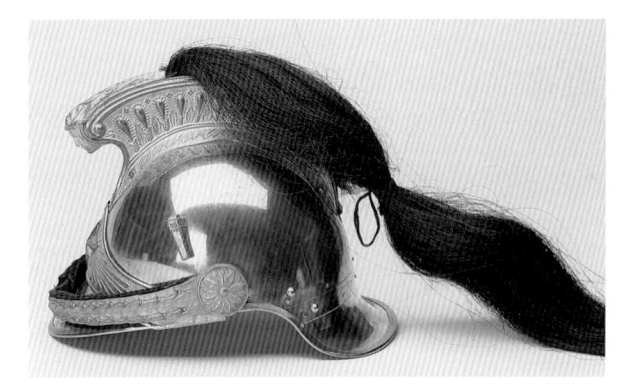

IV:22 Side View of Hussar's Helmet

difference was the front plate. For hussars, it held a five-pointed star in the centre of it rather than the dragoons' flaming grenade (Image IV:21). Image IV:22 shows a side view of the helmet.

The experiment of helmets for light cavalry also reached the chasseurs. Their helmet was just like that of the hussars except the front piece had a French hunting horn rather than the star of the hussars. Although a widespread adoption was planned, it seems that they were only officially issued to the 8th Hussars and the 5th Chasseurs by August 1914.[115] However, other regiments received the M1910 helmet, either soon after the Great War began or before it started, as there are existing samples from other regiments of these helmets with bullet holes in them.

The helmets cost 22.65 francs, which was equal to 18 shillings or $4.40 (£88 or $104 in current money).

DOLMANS AND TUNICS

Following the Franco-Prussian War, a dolman was worn by the French light cavalry. The light cavalry dolman was the same for the chasseurs and the hussars, though some say the chasseur dolman was a slightly darker blue than that of the hussars. In reality, the only difference was the trim colours.

The dolman had nine rows of braid down the front. Each row had three buttons and two sets of loops

IV:23 Dolman
This style of dolman was worn by both hussars and chasseurs à cheval. However, the colour of the braid was different. The hussars had white braid and the chasseurs à cheval wore black. Some felt the colour of the hussar dolman was a slightly lighter blue than that of the chasseurs. This style of braid was known as Brandenburg braid, and the tin half-ball buttons were at the end of each double row of white square braid. Some of the buttons on this example have come loose. Note the stylised crow's feet at the top and bottom of each set of braid. Also note the bugler's multicoloured braid in the shape of a chevron worn above the simple white cuff braid on the sleeves. The bugler's braid can just be seen on the collar. The dolmans with Brandenburg braid were worn in full dress until just after 1900. See Image IV:1, taken in 1900. The back of the dolmans had braid tracing the seam above the waistline and divided into three branches at the waist, each ending in a crow's foot on the skirt of the dolman. The braid on the back, like that on the front, was white for the hussars and black for the chasseurs à cheval.

between them. There was also a loop at the end, just below the end of each row of braid, connecting one row to another. This style of braid was known in the French army as 'Brandenburg' (Image IV:23).[116] Both cuffs had braid that did a simple one loop turn. The back also had braid in the form of hussar braid. For chasseurs, the braid was black; for hussars, it was white. Image IV:1 shows uniforms of all arms of the French military in 1900 and has several men in dolmans with Brandenburg braid.

For hussars, the low collar was the same colour as the dolman, and its regiment number was crimson. For chasseurs, the low-standing collar and its shield were crimson. It carried a regimental number in the same colour as the dolman. The collars were trimmed on the top and the bottom, in black for the chasseurs and in white for hussars.

The dolman was worn officially up to about 1900, when it was replaced by a single-breasted mid-blue tunic. However, examples of the dolman with its Brandenburg braiding could be seen long after 1900 as the French were thrifty and their military great believers in continuing to use items that had not worn out.

The M1900 tunic that replaced the dolman was the same for both chasseurs and hussars except for identifying details. It was a mid-blue colour, officially called light blue. It was closed with nine white-coloured half-dome buttons down the front. The buttons did not have a design or device on them.

The shoulder-piece was the white wool shoulder cords that end in a trefoil. This end device has been described as looking like a cat's paw (Image IV:15). The shoulder-piece itself was made of eight square-cut, thick pieces of white wool.

The light cavalry badges of rank were worn as an inverted V on both arms.

For hussars, the collar, the shield, and the cuff bar were all light blue, the colour of the tunic. The shield on the collar carried the regimental number in crimson (Image IV:20). The cuff bar had three buttons on it. Chasseurs had a crimson collar, shield, and cuff bar. The regimental number worn on the shield was light blue, the colour of the coat. Their cuff bar had three buttons on it (Image IV:18).

The tunic of officers was of a finer cloth and a lighter shade than that worn by other ranks (Images IV:24 and IV:25). Sometimes it was such a light blue as to be almost white. (The French also had white summer tunics, and the light blue winter tunics should not be confused with them). The regimental numbers were made of silver embroidery. Regulations limited officers' collars to 60 mm (2.36 inches), but the younger officers often wore them higher since French and German officers thought it fashionable to wear their collars as high as they could get away with.

The officers' tunic had seven half-dome buttons down the front until 1911. After that, it had nine. The buttons were silver-plated and were plain. Rank stripes were worn on the cuffs. Since the light cavalry's button colour was silver, the major colour in the stripes was silver (§IV-3-3).

IV:24 Hussar Officer
Officers preferred to wear a very light shade of light blue.

For hussar officers, the collar, collar shield, and cuff bar were all light blue, the colour of the tunic. For chasseurs, the collar, collar shield, and cuff bar were all crimson. The regiment's number was shown in silver on the collar shield.

In full dress, light cavalry officers wore epaulettes. In accord with their button colour, silver predominated in the epaulettes.

Trousers and Riding Breeches

There were two types of nether garments worn by officers and men of the light cavalry: trousers and riding breeches. The trousers were worn for dismounted dress and the breeches for mounted duties. These were worn by officers and men of both hussars and chasseurs à cheval.

Both the trousers and breeches were crimson. After 1900, the breeches had leather reinforcements between the legs.

Other ranks had narrow light blue trim on the outside seam of their trousers and breeches.

Officers had a wide light blue band. In the middle of this band were two narrow crimson stripes with a sky blue band showing between them. From a distance, the crimson stripes gave the appearance of being one crimson band. See Image IV:46 in §IV-7-a, Chasseurs d'Afrique, for an example of these stripes; the Chasseurs d'Afrique were considered light cavalry and had many of the same uniform items as the metropolitan light cavalry.

IV:25 Chasseur à Cheval Officer in a Very Light Blue Tunic

§IV-5-c-i HUSSARS

Hussars in the French army go back to the 1700s. During that period, the army had four hussar regiments composed mostly of Hungarians and Germans.[117] By the time of the Revolution, the number of hussar regiments had grown to six. The old hussars were taken over by the new Republic and given numbers up to six. By 1793, the regiments had increased to fourteen, but the numbers thereafter varied.

After Waterloo (1815), the new royal army had six regiments of hussars. In 1841, three additional hussar regiments were added to the army list;[118] the 9th Hussars were disbanded in 1856.

Following the Franco-Prussian War, additional hussar regiments were created by converting guard guide and line lance regiments (in 1871) and forming new hussar regiments (in 1873, two; 1891, one; and 1893, one). This brought the number of regiments to fourteen in 1914.[119]

Uniform

TUNIC

After the Napoleonic Wars, the reformed hussars followed the old traditions of continental hussars by wearing dolmans of different colours. Their pelisses were the same colour as the dolmans. The 1st wore sky blue, the 2nd brownish maroon, the 3rd light grey, the 4th red, the 5th dark blue, and the 6th green. All but the 4th wore red trousers and a red shako. The lone exception, the 4th, wore a black shako and sky blue trousers.[120]

This same colour scheme was followed up to the end of Napoleon III's rule in 1870, when the two new regiments were given their own colours. For example, the 8th had a white pelisse and a sky blue dolman, which was a slight variation from the standard colour programme.[121]

After 1870–1, the hussars followed the dress of the light cavalry (see §IV-5-c, above).

§IV-5-c-ii CHASSEURS À CHEVAL

Traditionally, there were six regiments of chasseurs à cheval in the army of the Ancien Régime. Six more were added in 1788. After that, more were added so the total stood at twenty-six in 1801 and thirty-one in 1811.[122] They were the workhorses of the Empire's army.

When the Bourbons came back in 1815, they created a line arm of twenty-four chasseurs à cheval. In 1831, a reorganisation changed a great deal, and the number of chasseur regiments was reduced to fourteen. One of the main reasons for the reduction was that five of them had been converted into lancers.[123]

Under Napoleon III, there were twelve line chasseurs à cheval regiments. In 1871, after the Franco-Prussian War, this number grew to fourteen as the Chasseurs à Cheval de la Guard Imperial were converted to the 13th Chasseurs, and the 7th Lancer Regiment to the 14th Chasseurs. Then in 1873, six new chasseur regiments, the 15th to 20th Chasseurs à Cheval, were formed. In 1888, the chasseurs à cheval reached their pre-World War I total of twenty-one regiments by the addition of the 21st Chasseurs.[124]

Uniform

HEADDRESS

In the early days of the Revolution, most of the chasseurs à cheval wore a Tarleton helmet. Some regiments wore a tapered felt cap. In general, confusion reigned. During the Empire, the chasseurs wore a shako.[125]

After Napoleon, in the 1830s, the chasseurs wore a very tall shako and had a hanging black plume in the front. Then, around 1845, the shakos were replaced by hussar fur caps. The fur was replaced in 1848 by the infantry sloping shako, which in turn was replaced in 1853 by a sloping hussar cap made with curled lamb's wool dyed black. The cap carried a green and red plume and was worn up to 1870.[126]

After the Franco-Prussian War, the light cavalry shako, M1874, was introduced by chasseurs à cheval and hussars. The two differed only in outward details. The subsequent developments are covered in the light cavalry section, §IV-5-c.

TUNIC

The chasseurs wore a dizzying array of different types of coats. In 1792, they wore a dolman with heavy braiding on the front. This was replaced about 1805 by a plain green jacket. In 1822, they were back to the green hussar-style dolmans with frogging on the front. Then, in 1831, it was back to a green single-breasted jacket with red epaulettes. This, in turn, was replaced in 1853 by a green hussar dolman with eighteen black loops on the chest.[127]

After the war with Prussia, the chasseurs wore standard light cavalry dress. See §IV-5-c, Light Cavalry, for details.

§IV-6 INFANTRY

After the splendour of the First and Second Empires, the uniforms of the Third Republic were downright plain. The Armée d'Afrique, which retained oriental touches, provided most of the colourful uniforms that were to be found in the French army during the period 1880–1914.

§IV-6-a LINE INFANTRY

Uniforms

Kepi

The kepi began life as an unofficial item to wear in the field in place of the heavier full headdress. The French soldiers in North Africa sought something to wear in place of the heavy leather shako. A lighter version of the leather shako was made by the soldiers out of cloth. During the early period, 1832–3, they were still tall and on a cardboard frame.

By the time of fighting in Italy and Crimea, c. 1854–9, the cloth hat had become shorter and assumed a shape closer to what we think of when we hear the term kepi. The word was originally a slang term and did not become official until 1874. Prior to that, it was officially referred to as a *bonnet de police à visière*.[128]

IV:26 Officer's Kepi
The four bands on the kepi and three lines on the quatrefoil on the top of the kepi denote a colonel. This kepi was owned by Pétain when he was a colonel of the 33rd Infantry Regiment. Charles de Gaulle was a junior officer under Pétain in the 33rd.

The kepi was made part of official dress wear after the Franco-Prussian War. The first version was somewhat higher than the final form adopted in 1884. The model 1884 kepi usually consisted of two parts. At the bottom there was a band of one colour, and above it, a top, sometimes called a turban, normally of another colour. The colours of the bands and tops were different for each branch of service (see *§IV-3-3*). The band for infantry was dark blue, and the top was red (Image C43). The officers wore a band of a darker shade of blue, more of a dark blue/black. The shade of red worn by French troops on their kepis, riding breeches, and trousers is known as madder or *garance*, a French name for a specific shade of red. Others called it crimson, a term we shall adopt.

Other ranks had blue trim on the kepi, while the officers' trim was in gold soutache.

Table IV.6.a.1: Officers' Kepi Rank Markings

Rank	Verticals & Quatrefoil on Top of Kepi	Horizontal rings
Colonel	Three	Five gold
Lt. Colonel	Three	Gold/silver/gold/silver/gold
Major	Three	Four gold
Captain	Two	Three gold
Lieutenant	One	Two gold
Sous-Lieutenant	One	One gold
Adjutant Chef	One, gold and red	One, gold and red after 1913
Adjutant	One, gold and red	One silver

Source: Windrow, *Foreign Legion*, p. 71.

IV:27 Kepi with Quatrefoil Showing Rank of Adjutant Chef

IV:28 Kepi with Top Showing a Rank Equivalent to General de Brigade

In the infantry, other ranks carried a red regimental number on the band, while an officer's number was in gold.

An officer's rank was noted by a system of braid on the top and the side of the kepi, as noted in Table IV.6.a.1 (and see Image IV:26).

The bottom rank ring was always butted down against the edge of the blue/black band, with subsequent higher rings at 1 mm (0.04 inch) intervals, with the crimson of the crown showing between them (Image IV:26). The verticals normally showed in the spaces between the horizontal rings. The quatrefoils were on the top of the kepi (Images IV:27 and IV:28).

Beginning in 1886, on the front of the kepi, there was the insignia of the branch, a flaming grenade, in the case of infantry, a tricolour cockade of painted metal and a single wool pompom (Image IV:29) whose colour would vary as follows:

1st Battalion	Dark blue
2nd Battalion	Scarlet red
3rd Battalion	Yellow
4th Battalion	Dark green
Depot company and regimental staff	Tricolour (red on top)

IV:29 Line Infantryman in Full Dress, after 1910

Junior officers wore a gold pompom. The pompom for adjutants was a mix of silver and scarlet cording. Superior officers had a straight tricolour (red on top) plume of vulture feathers that came out of a small olive-shaped ball.

The regiment's colonel, as a special mark of rank, wore an upright plume of white egret feathers (Image IV:30).[129]

The pompom, cockade, and grenade were done away with for full dress in 1910. Other ranks in the line infantry after that date wore nothing on their kepis except their regimental number in red (Image C43).

Junior officers after 1910 wore a drooping plume of red cock's feathers. The feathers came out of an olive-shaped ball of gold cording. The adjutant's ball was silver.

IV:30 Colonel Brunck, Commander of the 10th Infantry of the Line
Note the egret feathers in his plume, the mark of a colonel.

For superior officers, the drooping plume was tricolour, red at the top. The colonel continued to wear a white egret plume. The regiment's drum major often, although unofficially, wore an upright tricolour plume on an adjutant's kepi.[130]

From the 1850s, officers and adjutants had a false gold lace chinstrap on their kepis. This was worn in a permanent up position on the front of the kepi, above the peak. A second black leather chinstrap that could be used to keep the kepi on the head when needed was worn inside the cap. In 1874, sergeant majors and sergeants gained the right to wear the folded false chinstrap.[131]

The kepi was an ideal dress head covering for a France that was trying to recover from the destruction of the Franco-Prussian War – which had been fought on their territory – and the crushing monetary payments to the Germans that followed the war. The kepi was cheap, distinctive, and easy to produce. While it did not give any protection to the wearer in the field, it was no worse than most other headwear in this regard. Its only real drawback is that in the rain, water tended to puddle in the slightly sunken crown.

It is often claimed that both Russia and the United States adopted a kepi-style headdress. To a certain extent this is true. It should be remembered that France, prior to the Franco-Prussian War and especially after the Crimean War, was the leading military power in Europe, and its army was the most fashionable. French military dress was often copied by other countries.

In the 1860s and 1870s, the French army, or at least stylish officers, wore a low kepi that sloped forward from the back.[132] In 1862, a low kepi-style hat called a *shapka* was adopted for full dress in the Russian army. It was worn until the late 1870s to early 1880s.[133] Its shape was very close to the shape of kepi worn by officers in France in the 1860s and 1870s. It was smaller on top than on the bottom, so the sides sloped in. The shapka was worn with gold braid to show rank and a hair plume on the front, rather like that of a German Jäger. (See Jäger Helmets at §VI-10.)

The American version also looked very much like the French low kepi. In the American Civil War, the soldiers of the North and the South did not like the regulation headdress, the so-called Hardee or Jeff Davis hat.[134] Other ranks and some officers developed the habit of wearing their forage cap whenever possible. The forage cap, which was introduced in 1858, was said to be a faithful copy of the kepi.[135] This would have been the tall kepi of the late 1850s. It was without stiffening, and so, when worn, it tended to collapse on itself, and the crown would bend forward, which made it look like a true kepi. The dress regulations for the Southern Confederate armies state that the forage cap for officers is to be a cap similar to that known as a French kepi.[136] The forage cap never became an item of full dress, but it did live on after the Civil War in a somewhat smarter form. It was worn until the 1890s.[137]

In the French army, the kepi could be privately purchased by officers and NCOs. They took advantage of the privilege to slightly change their kepis from the standard to reflect their tastes and the styles of the day. Thus, from 1880 to 1900, a 'Saumur' style was worn by officers. From the 1900s to 1914, officers wore kepis in the shapes and cuts known as 'polo' and 'half-polo', depending on the period when it was made.

LINE INFANTRY TUNIC

The Ancien Régime of the Bourbons dressed their French line infantry in white coats. The Swiss, Irish, and German infantries wore coloured coats.[138]

The uniform of the National Guard under the Bourbons had been blue. In the early days of the Revolution, the old regulars in white and the new blue-clad troops served side by side. Of course, the regulars looked down on the novices. They called themselves the 'soldiers of porcelain', because they had been through the fire. The French army term '*bleu*' for a recruit or novice comes from this period. As used by the white-coated regulars, it was not a term of endearment.

In 1793, blue became the standard uniform colour for French line infantry and has remained that ever since, except for a very short experiment with white coats by Napoleon I and a five-year period (1815–19) right after the Bourbon restoration ('They learned nothing and forgot nothing', as the politician and diplomat Talleyrand is said to have declared).

Prior to the Franco-Prussian War, French infantry had worn double-breasted tunics with yellow trim. After the war, this was changed to a single-breasted tunic with red trim. Just before to the war, in 1868,

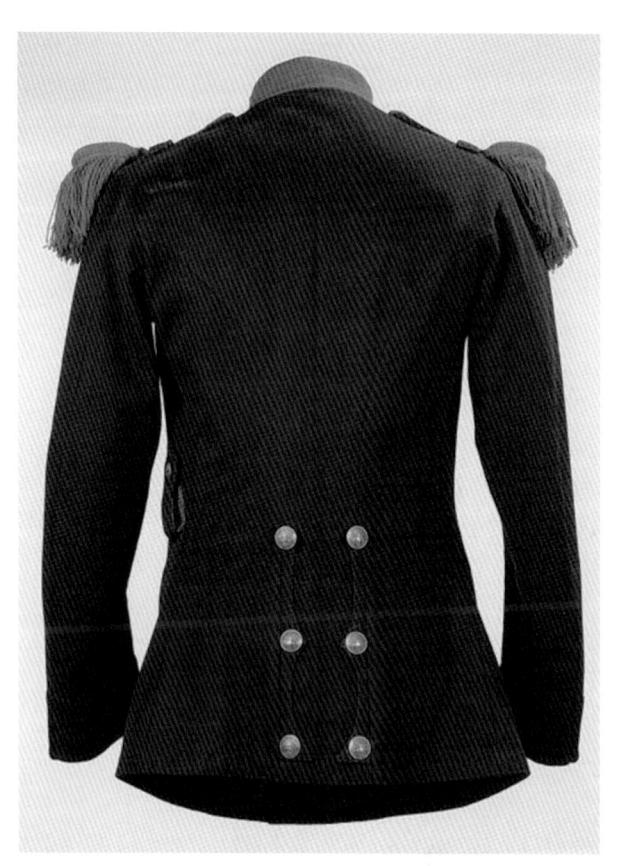

IV:31 Back of Other Rank's Tunic, c. 1914

the army did away with elite flank companies, which allowed the red epaulettes of the grenadiers to be taken into wear by all the infantry.

By the 1880s, infantry other ranks in full dress wore a dark blue single-breasted tunic with crimson trim and seven brass buttons down the front. The trim consisted of a crimson stand-up collar and a bar on each cuff. On either side of the front curved collar opening was a dark blue shield with a crimson regimental number on it.

In addition to the seven buttons down the front, each tunic had three buttons on the red bar on each cuff (Images IV:29 and C44). In the back, there were two false pockets with scalloped flaps, one on each tail, each with three buttons. There was no coloured trim (Image IV:31). For a better view of the stitching on the rear skirts, see Image C58.

The button colour was yellow, and each carried a flaming grenade device.

The tunics of the officers followed the same general pattern. Their tunics, however, were a darker blue, almost black. The 1872 tunic had seven gilt buttons

Table IV.6.a.2 Officer's Army Rank as Shown on the Cuffs and Epaulettes

Rank	Cuff Rings	Epaulettes
Colonel	Five gold	Two gold, short thick fringes
Lt. Colonel	Gold/silver/gold/silver/gold	As colonel, but top surfaces silver, crescents and fringes gold
Chef de Battalion	Four gold	Gold, fringed, on left; fringeless on right
Commandant Major, 1871–83	One silver over three gold	As chef de battalion
Commandant Major, 1893	One silver over three gold	Gold, fringed, on right; fringeless on left
Captain	Three gold	Two gold, long thin fringes
Captain Adjutant Major[a]	Silver/gold/silver	As captain, but red stripe down centre of top surfaces
Captain de Tir[a]	Silver/gold/gold	As captain, but top surfaces silver, crescents and fringes gold
Lieutenant	Two gold	Gold, fringed, on left; fringeless on right
Sous-Lieutenant	One gold	Gold, fringed, on right; fringeless on left
Adjutant Chef[b]	One gold, with red central light	As sous-lieutenant, in gold, with red stripe down centre of top surfaces
Adjutant	One silver, with red central light	As sous-lieutenant, but silver, with red stripe down centre of top surfaces

Source: Windrow, Foreign Legion, p. 70.
Notes: [a] Rank abolished in 1890.
[b] Rank introduced in 1913.

down the front. In 1911, this was changed to nine. The crimson bar on each cuff had three buttons. On the back, there were two false pockets with scalloped flaps. The pockets were decorated with three buttons on each side, similar to that of the other ranks. These buttons were gold-coloured and also carried a flaming grenade.

The number on the officers' dark blue/black collar patch was gold. Rank for officers was shown through a system of kepi markings, cuff rings, and the fringes on epaulettes (Tables IV.6.a.1 and 2).

NCOs' rank was shown by a system of stripes on the lower sleeve, as well as marks on the kepi and epaulettes. Long service and re-enlisted status was also shown on the sleeve.

Rank was shown by a diagonal strip of cloth worn on both forearms. These sloped from the inside up towards the outside (Image IV:29). The number and colours for infantry were as follows: first-class soldiers had one crimson stripe; corporals had two crimson stripes; sergeants had one gold stripe and sergeant majors had two gold stripes.[139] For junior NCOs, the cloth was crimson; for senior NCOs, it was gold.

Prior to 1887, re-enlisted soldiers wore chevrons on the upper left arm, one chevron for each five years served. Other ranks wore red, and NCOs wore gold. After 1887,[140] the chevrons were replaced by a crimson line for troopers and a line of mixed crimson and gold line for NCOs. These were worn just above the cuff.

TROUSERS

During our period, the French wore the famous red trousers. The shade of red introduced in 1829, as noted above, has been called madder, *garance*, and crimson. The colour came from the madder root, and had been used since the time of the pharaohs. It is said to be the basis for the red found in early English uniforms. In 1827, French chemists Pierre-Jean Robiquet and Jean-Jacques Colin began producing *garancine*.[141] It is believed that the army adopted the red trousers to support the French madder industry.

These red trousers became something of a symbol of France. Former War Minister Eugene Etienne in 1912 said, '*Le pantalon rouge c'est la France!*' ('The red trousers are France!').[142] He made the statement in opposition to the plan to eliminate red trousers in combat dress in favour of a more drab colour, as was being done by all the other major powers. His opposition is not as irrational as it seems to us today;

many defenders of the army saw this action as yet another of the left's many efforts to hamstring the army and reduce the dignity and authority of the officer corps.[143]

Other ranks' trousers did not have a stripe. Officers had a dark blue/black stripe on their trousers. Field officers, being mounted, wore riding breeches with a wide 45 mm (1.77 inch) stripe of the same colour on them.[144]

Spats
In 1881, the white spatterdash gaiter was ordered out of use in campaigns. However, a smaller relative, spats, werre retained for parades and other full dress events.[145] Spats were widely worn in the 1880s and 1890s, but less so after that. However, as late as 1913, the regulations provided that a regiment could have its men wear spats in full dress if they wished to do so.

§IV-6-b FOREIGN LEGION

The French Foreign Legion, or Regiments Etranger, was considered part of the North African army, but it will be considered here, because it does not occur to most people – including the author for many years – that the Legion, which is manned overwhelmingly by Europeans and has served around the world, is not part of the metropolitan army. In addition, its uniform, with a few minor differences, is essentially identical to that of the line infantry during the period 1880 to 1914.

Uniform

Kepi
The regulation kepi worn by the Legion was the same as that worn by line infantry, and the rank stripes worn by officers were the same. Prior to 1870, the line infantry had yellow trim, and the Legion had crimson trim; thus, the trim on the Legion's kepi was crimson. Up to the Franco-Prussian War, the distinguishing mark for the Legion was a five-pointed star. This was worn on the blue band at the front of the kepi.

Around 1872, the star was changed to a crimson seven-flamed grenade.[146] The white kepi cover was not worn in regulation full dress. In fact, the first time the white cover, now so tied into the Legion myth, was officially recognised as a full dress item was at the Bastille Day Parade in 1939.[147]

The white cover would normally start its life as a khaki cover. The desert sun, sweat, heat, and washing would fade it to white. The white kepi cover became the mark of long-serving veterans. Younger soldiers, wanting to look like old hands, would help the process along by repeated unnecessary washings and would even bleach their covers.[148]

Tunic
The Legion wore the tunic of the line infantry. In theory, the two dress uniforms were to be exactly the same, with the exception of the regimental markings. But, in practice, Africa was a long way away from the army bureaucrats in Paris, and the Legion was at the bottom of the pecking order when it came to receiving supplies and equipment. This led to a certain variance from the spit-and-polish dress norm. This showed up mostly in combat and daily dress, but it could be found, at times, in full dress.

The tunic was dark blue. In 1867, regulations, which formed the basis for future developments in other rank tunics, provided for a double-breasted tunic of dark blue. It had a standing collar of crimson piped down the front, round the top of the straight patchless cuff, and on the rear skirt. The rear skirt was cut in a design known as the '*soubise*' pattern,[149] but in fact it was the standard line infantry skirt pattern of no piping and three buttons on each skirt. An order of 1871 removed all piping.[150] When the Legion was broken out into two regiments in 1884, the individual's regimental number was shown on the collar in dark blue (Image IV:32).

In 1899, the other ranks received a new tunic. It was single-breasted with seven buttons down the front, a crimson standing collar, and collar patches. The regimental number on the patch was still dark blue. There was an upright crimson cuff bar which had three buttons. As infantry, the button colour

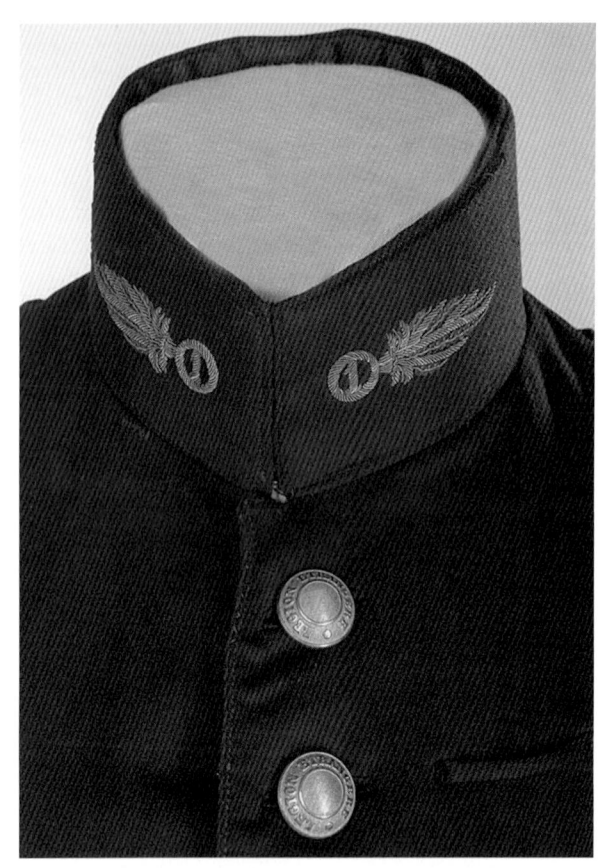

IV:32 French Foreign Legion Officer's Tunic Collar
Note flaming grenade badge on the collar with the regimental number inside the body of the grenade. Also note the 'Legion Etranger' on the tunic buttons.

IV:33 French Foreign Legion Officer's Tunic
Note that the collar and cuff plate are the same colour as the tunic.

was gold. The rear still had the *soubise* cut on the rear skirts.[151] There was no piping, but re-enlistment and rank stripes were worn. The buttons had 'Legion Etranger' in capital letters in an arc around the outside of the button.

Between 1883 and 1893, along with the rest of the army, Legion officers wore a dolman. This jacket, with its seven Brandenburg braids across the front, was a sartorial dead end, and thus beyond the scope of this work.

In 1893, officers and warrant officers were given a dark blue/black tunic. It, like the line officer's tunic, had seven buttons down the front.[152] In 1910, the number of buttons was changed to nine. The buttons had the same 'Legion Etranger' working around the outside as on the other ranks' buttons.

There was no piping, and officers in the Legion had collars and cuffs of dark blue/black, rather than the crimson of the line infantry.[153] Rank was shown by the same system used in the line infantry.

Trousers

The trousers were crimson with the same stripes as worn by line infantry.

Spatterdash Gaiters

The Legion followed the same general rules as the line infantry in only wearing spats for parades after 1881, but in reality they tended to use them on campaigns and parades for longer than the metropolitan troops.

Sash

A uniform item that is closely identified with the Legion is the blue sash or cummerbund. This was officially recognised in 1882. It was worn with several orders of dress, but officially never with the tunic.[154] Therefore, it was not part of the Legion's full dress uniform.

§IV-6-c CHASSEURS À PIED

The armed forces of France had a long history of tirailleurs, chasseurs, voltigeurs, and light infantry. A regimental organisation was restored to the French army after a system of departmental legions from 1815 to 1820 was done away with. The revised army had twenty light infantry regiments.

In 1838, a separate unit, the Tirailleurs de Vincennes, was raised. In 1842, this force was increased to a force of ten battalions and given the name Chasseurs d'Orléans. They served alongside the army's twenty-five regiments of light infantry. The Revolution of 1848 ended the rule of King Louis Philippe and the House of Orléans; so the Orléans titles in regimental and battalion names were removed. These battalions became known as chasseurs à pied and are the ancestors of the chasseurs à pied of 1914.[155] They wore basically the same uniforms as the line infantry. The only difference was in the colours, trim, and badges.

Uniform

Kepi

The size and shape of the kepi was the same as that of the line infantry. Both the top and band were dark blue cloth. For other ranks, the battalion number on the front of the kepi and trim was yellow, often described as daffodil yellow. By tradition, the chasseurs did not use the word yellow. The term for their trim was *jonquille*, a colour approximating yellow.[156]

The officer's kepi was similar to that of the line infantry officer's. It would change slightly as the style of the officer's kepi changed in the line infantry – for example, from a Saumur cut to a half-polo style (see discussion at §IV-6-a). The top was in dark blue/black cloth. The cap band was in black velvet, a peculiarity that is said to go back to the founding of the corps.[157]

The officer's rank braid followed the standard pattern set out above. The braid and number were in silver since that is the chasseurs' button colour.

Between 1886 and 1910, officers and men wore a silver French hunting horn, the badge of the chasseurs, on the front of their kepis. After 1910, they wore their battalion number.

Tunic

The tunic of the chasseurs à pied was identical to that of the line infantry except for button and trim colour. The chasseurs had a French hunting horn on their silver (tin) buttons (Image IV:34). The officers' tunics had silver rank stripes, epaulettes, and a fringe on the epaulettes (Image C45).

Trousers

Chasseurs' trousers for other ranks were a lighter shade of blue than the blue used for the tunic; it was often described as tending toward blue with a grey tint and the difference in colour was quite noticeable when the two were worn next to each other. Other ranks' trousers had daffodil yellow piping. Those of the officers were of a dark blue/black colour, and the trim followed the same pattern as those of the infantry, except it was in daffodil yellow.

IV:34 Other Ranks, Chasseur à Pied
On his sleeve, he has an unusual combination of badges showing he is a musician and a marksman.

§IV-6-d CHASSEURS ALPINS[158]

The chasseurs Alpins have an interesting story behind their formation. The origins of the story are in North Africa, in Tunisia. After some jockeying within the Great Powers, France obtained clearance at the Congress of Berlin to take over Tunisia. It did so in 1881, and Tunisia became a French protectorate.

This upset Italy, which viewed the area as lying within its sphere of influence. The two are just across the Mediterranean from each other, and many Italians lived in Tunisia. The bad feelings would taint French–Italian relations for a generation. In response, Italy, in 1882, allied itself with Germany and Austria-Hungary in the Triple Alliance. Since 1872, Italy had had soldiers, the Alpini, specially trained to fight in mountains. A hostile Italy with mountain troops created a potential problem for which France had no answer.

When the Triple Alliance was renewed, France responded in 1888 by converting twelve battalions of chasseurs à pied into chasseurs Alpins, trained for mountain warfare.[159] This conversion was fairly easy to do because the chasseurs already served as covering troops along the borders of France, so the men in these converted battalions came, by and large, from mountainous areas.

The new mountain troops were given a special practical dress to help them operate in the mountains. This specialised dress was worn by the other ranks in both full dress and in the field.

Uniform

BERET

The most distinctive item of wear adopted by the Alpins was their headdress, the beret. It was called a 'Basque beret', but seems to have been commonly worn in the mountainous regions along the Italian border where the men for the chasseurs Alpins were largely recruited. However, the Alpins also drew men from the Pyrenees, bordering Spain. The beret was dark blue like the chasseurs' kepi. Other ranks carried a French hunting horn device in daffodil yellow cloth. The beret worn prior to 1914 was rather large; one sample had a diameter of 34.5 cm (13.58 inches).[160] It is said that the classic test to check if the beret is the correct size is to see if the man who is to wear it can fit both his feet in it when the tie strings are drawn up. The hunting horn symbol of NCOs was embroidered silver, bordered by a daffodil yellow trim.[161] The hunting horn is normally worn on the right side of the beret, but photos of it on the left exist (Image IV:35).

The beret was known as a 'tarte'. In drawings, the convention is to show that it tilted to the left (Image IV:36), but photographs show it tilted to both the right, left, and front (Image IV:37). Some companies, or perhaps whole battalions, bent it so it presented a point to the front (Image IV:38).

Officers in full dress did not wear a beret. They wore the standard chasseurs' kepi.

JUMPER

A new item of wear was the dark blue loose jumper worn by the Alpins. It is cut to allow freer movement than a standard tunic. For that reason, it does not look quite as smart. It is closed down the front with seven silver buttons with the standard chasseur French hunting horn device on it. These were the only buttons on the jumper (Images IV:35 and IV:36).

The jumper had a simple fold-over cuff with no trim. The rear was without trim. At the end of each shoulder, just above where the sleeve meets it, there was a roll of cloth. This was there to help packs and rifle straps stay on the shoulder.

The jumper had a large fold-over collar, which could be turned up for protection in case of bad weather. The end of each collar came to a rounded point. At the point was placed the battalion's number in daffodil yellow (Image IV:35).

Rank was shown on the sleeves by pointed stripes in daffodil yellow or silver. First-class soldiers had one yellow stripe, corporals had two. Sergeants had one silver stripe and sergeant majors had two silver stripes. The stripes were diagonal, sloping from the inside of both forearms towards the outside. Alpins wore the standard specialised insignias in daffodil yellow on the right arm of their jumpers (Image IV:35).

In full dress, officers did not wear a jumper. They wore a standard chasseurs à pied tunic instead.

IV:35 Studio Photo of a Man in the 12th Chasseur Alpins
The way he wears his beret was fairly popular before World War I.

IV:36 Postcard Showing Chasseurs Alpins in the Field
The field uniform and the dress uniform were almost exactly the same.

IV:37 Group of 13th Chasseurs Alpins
Note the different ways the men are wearing their berets. Note the large chasseur pioneer badge of crossed axe and shovel on the right arm of a man on the front row and the telegrapher's badge of star with a lightning bolt coming out of it on the left upper arm of the man standing next to him.

IV:38 Group of Men in the 14th Chasseurs Alpins
This entire group has elected to wear their berets bent so that they come to a point in the front.

IV:39 Officer of the 30th Chasseur Alpins, in 1905
Note the more tailored uniforms and the variety of ways they wear their berets.

Trousers

Other ranks and officers wore standard-issue blue-grey trousers with daffodil yellow trim. In the summer, white trousers were often worn (Images IV:35, IV:36, and IV:37).

Puttees

Other ranks wore dark blue wool puttees over their trousers, up to mid-calf. The puttees were worn in all orders of dress. In 1910, they were 26 cm (10.23 inches) long and 12 cm (4.72 inches) wide.[162] The Senegalese Tirailleurs had long worn leggings that looked like puttees, but they had an entirely different shape, that of a triangle.[163]

Footwear

The mountain troops wore the 'Neapolitan shoe'. This had an enlarged sole and no heel. It would be made waterproof with animal fats.

Alpenstock

The mountain troops also carried an 'alpenstock'. This was basically a sturdy, round-handled cane with a steel top that was pointed. The alpenstock was very useful in walking in areas where there was ice. I have personally known people who went on hikes in mountainous environments where the trail had ice, and they just could not move forward. Women and children with alpenstocks zipped by them with no problem. The height and size of an alpenstock was a matter of individual preference.

Blue Devils

Today, the term Blue Devils is often applied to the chasseurs Alpins, because of their dark blue berets and jumpers. It is thought by many that this term was first applied to the chasseurs Alpins because of the battle to hold and then retake the mountain outcrop of Hartmannswillerkopf (commonly abbreviated to HWK, also referred to as Hartmannsweilerkopf and Vieil Armand), a key point in the German defence, in the Vosges. The battle began around Christmas 1914 and continuing, with varying levels of intensity, into early 1916. During this time, positions on the summit changed hands several times.[164]

Newspapers covered these events and the French Chasseur Battalion were referred to as Blue Devils because the ferocity of fighting. Soon the Blue Devils and HWK were famous.[165] An American sportswriter saw a newspaper story about the fighting at HWK and the 28 BCA Blue Devils, and used the nickname when writing about a local sports team. The name stuck, and today, the Duke University Blue Devils are one of the best-known sports teams in the United States.

§IV-6-e ALPINE INFANTRY[166]

The chasseurs Alpins served in the XIV and XV Army Corps. In addition, certain line infantry regiments in these army corps were trained and dressed for mountain service. They were referred to as Alpine infantry and dressed very similarly to chasseurs Alpins.

There were primarily four line infantry regiments in the Alpine infantry. First, the 157th, 158th, and 159th were included. Then, in 1889, the 1st Battalion of the 97th Infantry Regiment was added. Finally, in 1913, the other two battalions of the 97th were added. These four regiments, the 97th, 157th, 158th, and 159th were considered Alpine infantry.

The duty of the 157th, 158th, and 159th Regiments was to man fortresses – sometimes no more than fortified buildings – along the high mountains of the Italian border during the winter. As such, they were part of the border's static defence.

The chasseurs Alpins only operated during the summer and were part of a mobile defence in the same high mountains. The 97th Regiment was part of this mobile defence. In 1913, the 158th was sent to serve in the Vosges mountains as part of the new XXI Army Corps.

Other regiments in the XIV Army Corps, namely the 96th, 99th, and 140th, were given Alpine equipment and training but were not considered Alpine infantry or given their dress. The other regiments in these corps were trained in a general way to operate in the mountains, and given some equipment to do so.

IV:40 Soldier of the 159th Alpine Infantry
His uniform is a standard line infantry uniform with Alpine touches. Notice the edelweiss flower on the beret, indicating this photo was probably made before 1896.

IV:41 Soldier of the 97th Infantry
He is wearing a French army uniform and chasseur Alpin puttees, cummerbund, and beret. The flaming grenade badge of the Alpine infantry can just be seen on the right side of his beret.

Uniform

The Alpine infantry wore the normal uniform of a line infantry regiment. Just a few touches set them apart as Alpine troops: the beret; the cummerbund; the puttees; and the alpenstock. The line infantry were dressed in blue tunics with red collars and cuffs with blue trim. Their trousers were crimson. The Alpine infantry wore this same uniform with four differences.

They wore a dark blue beret. Up to 1896, the beret had an edelweiss flower device and the regiment's number. Both were in crimson. After 1896, they wore a grenade with seven flames. Photographs show these devices being worn on both the left and right side of the beret, but on the right side is far more common.

Their blue wool cummerbund was the type worn by Turcos. It was 4.2 m (13.78 feet) long and 40 cm (15.75 inches) wide.[167]

The Alpine Infantry wore the crimson trousers of the line infantry. Over them, they wore the same puttees issued to the chasseurs Alpins.

Since the Alpine Infantry also operated in the mountains, they also carried the same steel-tipped alpenstock carried by their brothers, the chasseurs Alpins (Image IV:40).

IV:42 97th Infantry, an Alpine infantry regiment, in Parade Dress
In parades, Alpine infantry often did not wear Alpine items.

In full dress, officers of the four Alpine infantry regiments wore regular uniforms and did not wear berets, cummerbunds, or puttees (Image IV:42).

§IV-7 NORTH AFRICAN ARMY

Several of the great European powers maintained separate troops with uniforms that were very different from those worn by their main army regulars. These separate troops were from areas that were, or at one time had been, outside the country's heartland, and they wore colourful and exotic uniforms. These units showed the scope of their country's power and added a touch of barbaric colour to military displays. For Britain, it was the Scots and the Indians. For the Russians, it was the Cossacks. For France, it was the army of North Africa, the Armée d'Afrique.

The Armée d'Afrique consisted of one French cavalry regiment, the Chasseurs d'Afrique; and three European infantry units, the Zouaves, the African Light Infantry, and the French Foreign Legion. It also had several units made up of indigenous peoples commanded by native and French officers. These were the Spahis, the Tirailleurs, the Marocains, and Compagnies Sahariennes.

These troops were treated as an integral part of the French army, and in time of war formed the French XIX Corps. When WWI began, North African troops were at once sent to France to take part in the Great War.[168]

§IV-7-a CHASSEURS D'AFRIQUE

The Chasseurs d'Afrique, often shortened to Chass d'Af, were created in 1831 from a grab bag of different troops: former Zouaves, chasseurs à cheval, line cavalry, and members of the Foreign Legion. Some forty troopers for each squadron were recruited from the local population. Natives with light-coloured skin were normally selected.[169] A second unit of Chass d'Af followed in April 1832, and a third in 1833.

It did not take long for the Chass d'Af to become a desirable arm. There was never a shortage of volunteers, and it was even said that metropolitan officers would volunteer to serve as other ranks. In addition, up and coming officers tried to serve as officers in the regiment.[170] The regiments offered a special combination of cavalry duty, dash, and combat opportunities. There may also have been volunteers from non-Frenchmen. The novel *Under Two Flags* by Ouida is about an Englishman who elects to serve in the Chasseurs d'Afrique.

The four regiments of the Chass d'Af went to the Crimea. There, at Balaclava, the 1st and 4th Regiments charged the Russian artillery battery that was firing into the survivors of the British Light Brigade, forcing the artillery's withdrawal.[171]

The Chass d'Af served in Mexico during France's Mexican adventure of 1861–7. The 1st Chass d'Af were awarded the Legion d'Honneur for their action there; they were the first cavalry regiment to be awarded this honour.[172]

In the Franco-Prussian War, all four regiments went to France and served with the armies. They all were captured at Sedan and Metz. Prior to that, they had taken part in many charges against the German armies. It is claimed that during one charge by the 3rd Regiment across the front of the 81st Infantry Regiment of the Prussian army,[173] the regiment's officers, out of admiration for the bravery of the Chass d'Af, ordered their men to cease firing into the horsemen and saluted their foe with their swords.[174] The 81st was made up of men from Hesse-Cassel, which was a Hessian state that had been absorbed, along with Hanover, by Prussia at the end of the Austro-Prussian War.[175]

Uniform

HEADDRESS

In the early days, the Chasseurs d'Afrique wore a Polish lancer helmet, the *czapska*. By the Second Empire, 1852–70, a shako with red body and sky blue band was worn in full dress. The shako carried a pompom in different colours for each squadron.[176] The pompom colours followed the normal colour

IV:43 Group of Chasseurs d'Afrique
Note French hunting horn high on the shako of the man on the far right of the photograph. This was peculiarity of the chasseurs d'Afrique. A man in the front row has the crossed axes of a cavalry pioneer on both sleeves.

pattern, with an addition for a 6th squadron: 1st, dark blue; 2nd, crimson; 3rd, dark green; 4th, sky blue; 5th, daffodil yellow; and 6th, orange. The staff had a tricolour pompom, crimson, white, and blue, crimson end uppermost.[177]

A shako was still worn, model 1873, after the Franco-Prussian War. It had a crimson body and top with a sky blue (really mid-blue) band. The trim was light blue. The front had the same French hunting horn worn by chasseurs à cheval. The other ranks often wore the horn above the lower band on the shako, almost at the top of the shako, rather than on the band, as was done in most cavalry regiments (see man on the far right in Image IV:43).[178] The chass d'Af also had a painted metal cockade of red, white, and blue on the front of the shako. In 1901, the shako trim was changed from light blue to daffodil yellow.[179] The Chass d'Af often unofficially referred to the shako as a 'Taconnet' after the original manufacturer.[180]

They also wore a chechia, which is a larger, softer version of a fez. The chechia, M1858, was 28 cm

IV:44 Crimson Chechia Worn by Other Ranks in the Chasseurs d'Afrique

(11.02 inches) tall in worsted or felted crimson wool. It was provided with a black sheepskin internal sweatband after March 1903. The chechia was worn rather than the kepi for all Chass d'Af up to the rank of warrant officer.[181] The chechia inevitably had three dark stripes around its bottom (Image IV:44) and tassels in squadron colours. The colour system was the same as that set out above for pompoms.[182] The tassels were at the end of a very short 30 mm (1.18 inch) cord, which came out of the middle of the top of the chechia. The cord's short length meant the tassels normally just peeked over the edge of the top of the chechia.

For NCOs, the top of the tassel had narrow silver braid (6 mm or 0.24 inches). The chechia occasionally carried a badge of the regimental number inside a crescent moon. This same badge could also, at times, be seen on Chass d'Af shakos in place of the hunting horn.[183]

Often, and probably the great majority of the times the other ranks wore them on parade, the shakos were covered with a cloth cover (Image IV:45 shows it on the table). Up to 1910, the cover was white, and then it was khaki linen. The white covers, together with the colourful uniforms, white cloaks, and the white/grey horses they normally rode, gave the chass d'Af a very dashing appearance.[184]

IV:45 Other Ranks of the Chasseurs d'Afrique
Note shako on table covered with white cloth, which was worn in most orders of dress.

Tunic

In 1872, like the other light cavalry regiments, the chass d'Af were dressed in a dolman. It had nine rows of black Brandenburg braid and nine rows of three silver-coloured buttons.

In 1900, the dolman was replaced by a M1900 jacket with nine silver-coloured buttons. The jacket stopped at the waistline and was called *ras de cul*, which means bare-arsed. It had a daffodil yellow collar and a shield on either side of the central neck opening. The shield was mid-blue, like the jacket (Image IV:46) and the regiment number was shown on on it in daffodil yellow. There was no trim bar on the cuffs, but as was common in North Africa, the rear of the sleeve was slit. The slit was outlined wherever the wearer's jacket had braid indicating re-enlistment or a rank above plain trooper.

At the shoulder the *ras de cul* carried the white wool light cavalry shoulder strap of cords that ended in a trefoil. It had an upside-down yellow V at each cuff.

The jacket was almost always worn with a crimson cummerbund, 5.6 m (18 feet, 4.47 inches) long and 42 cm (16.54 inches) wide that had the end turned back to show three sets of daffodil yellow stripes. The stripes were in a two, three, two pattern.[185]

Warrant officers were allowed to wear the tunic, whose button count changed from seven to nine in 1911. The warrant officer's tunic colour was purported to be sky blue, but it was more of a mid-blue, as was the case for the chasseurs à cheval. They also wore the white wool shoulder strap that ended in a trefoil.

Officers and adjutants wore a very light-coloured sky blue tunic. The tunic had a stand-up daffodil yellow collar with a daffodil yellow shield. This meant the collar was all yellow. The regiment's number was shown in silver on the collar shield. The buttons were half-dome without a device on them and silver in colour.

IV:46 Other Rank of Chasseurs d'Afrique
The collar shield is the same colour as the tunic. Note the cat's paw shoulder-piece and the light blue piping on the crimson riding breeches.

Officers had a daffodil yellow upright bar on each cuff. Each cuff had three plain domed buttons. The officer's rank was shown by lines of silver braid, as was the case for all light cavalry regiments.

In full dress, silver epaulettes were worn. The fringe, or lack of it, showed the officer's rank (see §IV-3-3).[186] The epaulettes were seldom seen as officers typically wore the white wool shoulder strap that ended in a trefoil.

Riding Breeches and Trousers

The Chass d'Af wore the standard light cavalry riding breeches of crimson with light blue trim. These breeches were exactly like those worn by the French continental light cavalry. Other ranks had piping in light blue. Officers had a wide light blue stripe with two narrow stripes of crimson in the middle of the light blue stripe (Image C52). In walking-out dress, the Chass d'Af could wear crimson trousers. Many of the overseas officers adopted a 'peg-leg' cut for their trousers – a very loose cut from the waist down to the ankles and then very tight at the ankles. For an example of this style being worn, see Image IV:68 in §IV-8-c. This style was known as '*flottard*'.

The Chass d'Af rode, for the most part, North African Barbary horses, also known as Barbs, and preferred light-coloured animals. (As every racing fan knows, one of the three founding stallions of English thoroughbred racing stock is thought to have been a Barb.)[187]

§IV-7-b SPAHIS

The Spahis have their origins in irregular local cavalry formed to help the French early in their invasion of Algeria. Officially, in 1831, there were three units of spahi irregulars, one each for Algiers, Oran, and Bone.[188] They each became regular troops in 1836, and all were joined together in one command in 1840. Finally, in 1845, each group was made a Spahi regiment. The 1st was in the Algiers Province, the 2nd in Oran, and the 3rd in Constantine.[189]

From the beginning, Colonel Marey-Monge, father of the Spahis, had wanted the Spahis to be from noble families and required that recruits supply their own horses.[190] They had not been able to maintain quite that standard, but, in general, the regiments were made up of sons of respected Arab notables, helped no doubt by the fact that after 1871, horses were supplied to the troops.[191]

In 1882, shortly after the 1881 conquest of Tunisia, mixed companies of spahis were formed for service in Tunisia. In 1886, these were joined into a 4th Regiment of Spahis.[192] The 4th Spahis were Tunisian while the other three regiments were Algerian. On 15 May 1914, a 5th Regiment of Spahis was authorised, but it was not formed before the war began.[193]

The different spahi regiments took an active part in the battles of conquest in Algeria, usually as small detachments. In some cases, whole regiments took part in large battles. Both the 1st and 2nd Spahis were present and did well at the Battle of Isly in 1844.[194] Under the Second Empire, the only service outside North Africa was one troop sent to China in 1860 and another to Syria. After the regular French armies surrendered in 1870, all three regiments were sent to France to try to help salvage the situation. They, along with the ad hoc units raised, failed. About this time, the 5th Squadron of the 3rd Spahis mutinied and murdered many of their French officers. This helped set off a wider general uprising, which involved some 800,000 people and took several months to put down.[195]

Between 1871 and 1914, all three regiments served in Indochina, and the 3rd took part in the occupation of Tunisia. Later, detachments of all four regiments served in Morocco. Sub-units also went to Dahomey, Senegal, and Madagascar.

The dress of the Spahis was, from the beginning, eye-catching, if somewhat impractical. It changed very little down to 1914.

Uniform

HEADDRESS

The Spahis wore a headdress called a *guenhour*. This consisted of a felt base headscarf called a *haik* (also spelled *haick*) of white and blue calico, which covered the head and normally went from the top of the head to under the chin (Image IV:47). The haik was around 5 m (16 feet 4.84 inches) long, 1.5 m (4 feet 11.06 inches) wide.[196] The extra tails were worn wrapped around the body under the wearer's clothes.

The use of the haik was officially stopped in 1906.[197] The Spahis thereafter wore a cheche in place of the haik as part of the guenhour. A cheche is a piece of cloth that goes over the head and can be wrapped under the chin. It is not as large as the haik (Image IV:48). This change highlighted a long-term movement which had been taking place, towards the use of the cheche, versus the chechia, which is a fez-like hat.

The haik had alternating bands of white cloth, 70 mm (2.76 inches) wide, and then a band with six sets of 5 mm (0.2 inch) blue lines separated by 8 mm (0.31 inch) white spaces.[198]

As the cheche came into use, the use of stripes on the headscarf stopped. The white cheche still covered

IV:47 Group of Spahis
Note several men (possibly Frenchmen) are wearing just cloth wrappings on their head. All the Algerians have their under cloak is folded up. Note that several men have tied up the bottom of the burnous with a cloth that hangs over the shoulder.

IV:48 Group of French Officers and Native and French NCOs
Note smaller chechia cloth headdress over the head.

the head and could still go under the chin, but there was just not as much excess cloth.

The haik or cheche was held together by cords made of camel hair. The camel hair cords of the guenhour were looped together in such a way that could make the guenhour rather tall. The height of the headdress would vary by regiment and served to distinguish one regiment from another.

1st Spahis	Very high
2nd Spahis	A little lower
3rd Spahis	Lower still
4th Spahis	Very low[199]

The very high guenhour of the 1st Spahis is what is normally shown in photographs of spahis, thereby giving the impression that this was the normal way the spahi headdress was worn. This style of headdress may have shown up so often because the 1st Spahis who wore it were from Algiers Province, and thus easier to reach and photograph than other spahis.

The whole headdress was normally worn tilted towards the back of the head.

In photographs, the guenhour cords appear to be dark, perhaps dark blue (Images IV:47 and IV:48).

After 1901, in addition to the cords of the guenhour, extra camel hair cords in different colours were worn.[200] The colours show the squadron as follows: dark blue for the 1st, dark pink for the 2nd, green for the 3rd, light blue for the 4th, and yellow for the 5th. These coloured cords were normally worn on top of the camel hair cords of the guenhour and were about 2.7 m (8 feet 10.3 inches) long, each ending in a silk tassel. Since the cord was folded in half before being put on, this meant there were four tassels. In theory, the tassels were to rest on the right shoulder of the wearer, but in practice, they could fall anywhere the person pleased. These tassels do not seem to have been worn by Frenchmen in the first three regiments of Spahis but do seem to have been worn by the French in the 4th Regiment in Tunisia. The other ranks of all regiments were subject to wearing the tassels, but there is little photographic evidence. They may be an item that was only worn in full dress.[201]

Spahis could wear a crimson chechia, which could have a dark blue/black tassel. In practice, it was worn mostly by French personnel (Image IV:48). The chechia could also be worn in walking-out dress. Sometimes, the cheche was worn around the chechia as a rough form of turban.[202]

French officers would often wear a kepi. It had a light blue bottom band, and the upper band and top were crimson. The normal hat rings showed rank, as did the horizontal bands and braid on the top of the kepi (Image IV:49).

On the bottom band, the kepi showed the regiment. This could be the number alone or a crescent moon with the regiment's number inside the moon (Image IV:49).

IV:49 Kepi of a Spahi Officer
Note the regimental number within a crescent moon. This crescent motif was used in the spahi, Turkos, and Moroccan regiments.

JACKET

A sky blue waistcoat was worn. This waistcoat's cut is identical to that worn by the Zouaves. It had black braid down the front and around the collar. It also had additional arabesque-shaped tracings around this braid and in the open spaces on the front and back of the waistcoat.

The jacket was crimson. It had black braid across the front of it. At the end, on either side, it made a loop called a *tombeau* (or tombo), which contained different colours to mark the regiments (see below). This front braid ended with trim in the shape of an ear of wheat rather than the three-ring clover shape found on the jacket of Zouaves and tirailleurs (Image C59). The sleeves had sky blue pointed cuffs. On the back of each cuff was a slash opening, like that worn by Zouave officers, with the same type of small gold buttons. The bottom and front of each side of the waistcoat/jacket was trimmed in black braid. The same braid was also placed at the bottom of each cuff and in a line across the jacket about two-thirds of the way down from the top.

The back of the waistcoat/jacket had two small notches on both sides at the bottom. These notches were outlined in the black braid. The black bands

IV:50 Back of Sergeant's Jacket
This shows how elaborate NCOs' extra braid could be.

could be trimmed in small circles and other intricate designs made of black braid.

The open spaces on the front and back of the waistcoat/jacket were often decorated with thin braid in arabesque shapes. These appeared on the jacket of both other ranks and officers. A higher rank yielded more ornate decorations.

As noted above, the jacket had tombeaus in regimental colours. After 1885, these were crimson for the 1st regiment, white for the 2nd, daffodil yellow for the 3rd, and sky blue for the 4th.[203]

French officers, up to 1900, wore a dolman. From about 1900, the Spahis, together with the rest of the cavalry, changed over to the tunic. The Spahi officers' tunic was one of the most striking in the French army (Image C60). It was crimson, and its stand-up collar, collar shield, and upright cuff trim were all crimson. The collar had the regimental number in gold, as were the officer rank stripes on the sleeves. The gold buttons down the front, at first seven, then after 1911, nine, were plain domes, like the three on each cuff. This bright, all crimson tunic with its gold buttons could not help but be noticeable.

French officers had two forms of full dress, with and without the burnous (see below). When the tunic was worn without a burnous, epaulettes were worn. These followed the standard pattern of fringe and colour for showing rank. When a burnous was worn over the tunic, epaulettes were not worn.[204]

Native officers could wear either the tunic or the waistcoat and waistcoat/jacket (native dress), as they elected. The tunic followed the general French army rules. The native dress sported ever-more elaborate trim as the man's rank grew higher. However, there do not seem to have been any rules governing the shape or amount of the trim.

Cummerbund

The Spahis' cummerbund seems to be scarlet wool, but it must be noted that several sources say crimson.[205] The cummerbund could be worn in full dress and walking-out dress. The cummerbund, when worn in walking-out dress, had stripes on it.

Pantaloons

The first regulations in 1841 listed royal blue pantaloons for Spahis. However, in 1842, a lieutenant of the Spahis took it upon himself to wear sky blue pantaloons. Everyone found this colour so pleasing that the darker blue pantaloons quickly disappeared.[206]

The other ranks wore pantaloons that were close to the shape of the very baggy pantaloons worn by the Zouaves. However, they differed from those of the Zouaves since, at the bottom, they were divided into two legs, which made riding a horse easier.

The officers' walking-out, number two pantaloons were cut to be very loose. It is said their cut was different from those of the Zouaves. The Zouaves' were cut in a flottard style, and the Spahis' were cut *à la houzarda*.[207] To the untrained eye, they look remarkably similar, and only the cognoscenti could see the difference. Most writers on Spahis are content to state that the Spahis wore their pantaloons in the flottard style.

When on mounted duty with their men, the officers wore the standard light cavalry riding breeches. For full dress, officers wore crimson trousers or riding breeches, depending on whether they had mounted or dismounted duties, with light cavalry stripes, just like those of the French light cavalry in the metropolitan army (§IV-5-c).

Boots

French personnel in the Spahis generally wore normal-style riding boots. Native officers, and occasionally French officers, wore a local heelless boot called a *themaggs* or *khoffes* (both will be referred to as themaggs below). Many of the themaggs had the leather worked to show arabesque designs.

The sources are silent on what type of footwear the other ranks wore, and photographs do not show enough detail to make a judgement.

Burnous

One element that made the Spahis' uniform so impressive was the two-layer burnous, one crimson and one white. These were worn in full dress and cold weather, but not in the summer, in combat or in service dress.[208]

IV:51 Spahi
This photograph dates from 1863, but little changed between then and 1914. It shows a spahi fully rigged out.

The Spahi burnous consisted of two large capes with hoods. A white one was worn next to the body, and it formed a lining for the crimson burnous, with a hood that laid over it. In cold weather, the burnous was worn closed in front, and this allowed a panel that went down from the collar of the burnous to be seen. This panel showed the squadron colours as follows: the 1st Squadron, dark blue; the 2nd Squadron, dark pink; the 3rd Squadron, green; the 4th Squadron, light blue; and the 5th Squadron, yellow.

Normally, the burnous, when worn, was worn folded back so that the white under burnous showed clearly from the front (Image IV:47). From the back, the crimson burnous would still show clearly.

The burnous was very long, reaching almost to the ground, and in some cases, depending on the lie of the land, would touch the ground. This could be quite cumbersome. To resolve this problem, the Spahis would tie the ends of the burnous to a cloth that hung down from their body in front. The hanging cloth was short enough that when the burnous ends were tied to it, the ends were raised up off the ground (Images IV:47 and IV:51).

MOROCCAN SPAHIS

The Moroccan Spahis, by 1914, consisted of eleven squadrons and had a strength of about 2,200 men.[209] The dress of the Moroccan Spahis other ranks was different from the regular spahis in some ways. The following differences are noteworthy.

The cheche was sand-coloured. The turban was also sand-coloured, and it took different shapes depending on what tribe the man came from. It was made from a long band of cloth.

The waistcoat/jacket was crimson and did not have braid or tombeaus.

The cummerbund was crimson.

The burnous had a front panel of crimson.

The French officers' kepi was all sky blue. This is said to be because the original troops came from the Moroccan army.[210] The kepi normally had a badge on the front that was a crescent with a star in the middle of it.

The pantaloons of the Moroccans were normally sand-coloured.

§IV-8 NORTH AFRICAN INFANTRY

§IV-8-a AFRICAN LIGHT INFANTRY

The light infantry was formed in 1832 to meet the French manpower needs in Algeria as the French regular army was being withdrawn. By 1833, there were three battalions.[211]

By 1914, there were five battalions d'infanterie legère d'Afrique. The name of these units was often shortened to Bat d'Af, or they were called 'Les Joyeux' ('the Joyful Ones') because of their constant complaining and grumbling.

Writers often confuse the African light infantry with disciplinary companies of the army. The African light infantry was a permanent assignment. A man was sent to a disciplinary company for a set period of time for an infraction of rules while in the army. Men who went to the African light infantry had been sentenced to prison in France for at least six months prior to going into the army. It was understood that petty criminals would be the type of men sent to the African light infantry. The classic example would be a pimp.

The men in the battalions were subject to harsh discipline and rough living conditions. When not fighting, they would be kept busy on construction projects, a life very much like that of the Foreign Legion.

Their pre-1914 uniform has been said to be modelled on that of the Foreign Legion, leading to great similarities between the uniforms of the Joyeux and the legion.[212]

Uniform

Kepi

The kepi had a dark blue band and a crimson top. The other ranks had daffodil yellow trim. The battalion number was in daffodil yellow at the front of the kepi on the dark blue band. NCOs had their piping in soutache braid, and their number was in silver.

Officers also had their piping in soutache-type braid with the battalion number in silver at the front of the kepi. They wore the standard rank markings with silver as the predominant colour.

Tunic

The African light infantry wore the standard infantry tunic with minor differences involving the collar, cuff, and the buttons. As is the norm, the tunic for other ranks was dark blue. It had seven silver buttons. The buttons had hunting horns. The design of this horn was the same as that worn by the chasseurs à pied. It also had three buttons at each cuff and three buttons, six in total, at each side of the rear skirt. The stand-up collar was the same colour as the tunic. The collar shield was also the colour of the tunic. This meant the other ranks wore a solid dark blue tunic. The shield for other ranks had the battalion number in daffodil yellow (Images IV:52 and C51).

The other ranks' epaulettes in 1914 were the same as those of the Foreign Legion. The shoulder board

IV:52 Corporal of African Light Infantry
They wore the same uniform as the Foreign Legion, except for trim details. The Bat d'Af were not disciplinary units but rather held men who had been in jail or prison for short periods of time prior to entering the army.

was crimson, and the fringe was green (Image C51). NCOs had silver edging on the crescent at the top of the fringe.

The officers' tunic was the same except it was a dark blue/black colour, and the battalion number on the shield was silver.

The collar and the cuff bar was the same colour as the tunic. The officers also had three buttons on each cuff and three on each side of the rear skirt.

Officers' epaulettes were silver and followed the normal fringe pattern for regiments whose button colour was silver.

SHORT TUNIC
The Joyeux often wore a short tunic, called a *ras de cul* (see §IV-7-a) which came to the waist (see Image C51). It was worn with the cummerbund covering the waist. Apart from its length, it was exactly like the standard tunic.

TROUSERS
The African light infantry wore the standard crimson infantry trousers.

§IV-8-b ZOUAVES

The well-known Zouaves were raised in 1830 from the Berber Zouagha tribe and a few others among the Kabyle-speaking population of Algeria. The tribe lived in the Djurjurah area of the Atlas mountains, some 100 km (62 miles) east of Algiers, and had served as mercenary troops for the dey and the ruling Turks.[213]

Left without work when the dey was overthrown by the French, the tribe was more than willing to work with the French. In turn, the arrangement allowed the French to establish ties with the indigenous population.[214]

Uniform

HEADDRESS
The other ranks wore a crimson chechia, which is a larger, softer version of a fez (Image IV:53). The chechia was about 25 cm (9.84 inches) high, and in full dress had a tassel of dark blue at the end of a short, dark blue cord. NCOs had a 6 mm (0.24 inch) gold band at the top of the tassel.[215]

Around the chechia, a turban was worn. There is disagreement on the colour of turban. Some say the colour of the turban varied by the area the unit was stationed in, with those in the Algiers area wearing red turbans, those in the Oran area white, and so on.[216] Others state it changed over time from red to green and then to white.[217] Whatever colour of turban was worn in the past, all agree that by 1880–1914 the turban was white (Image IV:55).

It is said that there was a custom among the Zouaves to wear their chechias in different ways, depending on the regiment. The 1st Regiment wore theirs tilted to the right, sometimes down to the ear (Image IV:54 and IV:56); the 2nd to the left, again occasionally almost to the ear; and the 3rd tilted to the back of the head (Image IV:54). It may be that these extreme tilts showed up in studio photos more than in the real world, where such a tilt would be hard to keep on the head. Image IV:57 shows the 4th with their chechias on the right side of their heads.

WAISTCOAT AND JACKET
Under their other items the Zouaves wore a long-sleeve undyed cotton shirt with no collar. If one could see it, the shirt appeared to be white. However, in practice, the shirt was almost always completely covered up.

Over the shirt, Zouaves wore a fairly tight tubular waistcoat that buttoned on the right side and at the shoulder. The waistcoat extended down to the belt level. It was dark blue with crimson trim around the collar and down the front (Image IV:58). NCOs were allowed to wear extra crimson trimming on their waistcoats (Image IV:59)[218].

Over the tubular waistcoat, Zoauves wore a dark blue open jacket called a *shama*. The shama had crimson trim around the collar, down the front and bottom edge of the jacket, and on the cuffs (Image C53). In the front of the cuff, there was a small upside-down V, and in the back a slash opening lined with

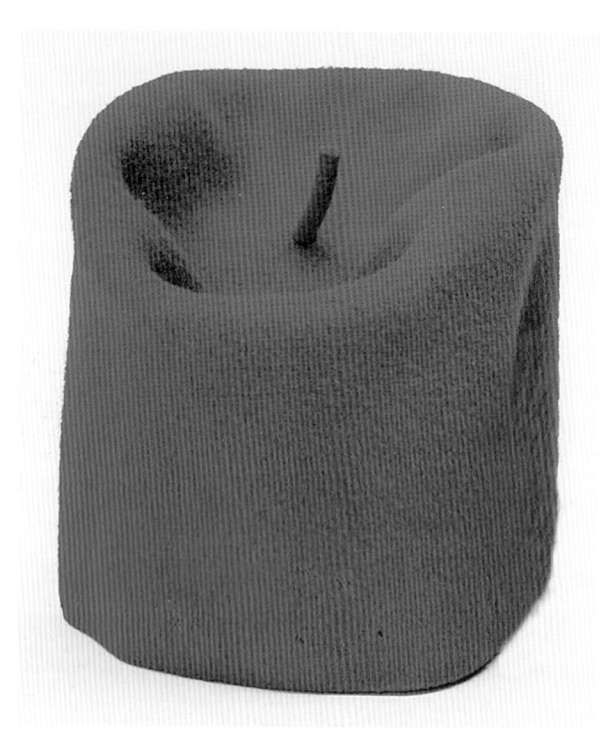

IV:53 Chechia Worn by Zouaves and Algerian Tirailleurs

IV:55 Zouave NCO
Note rank braids on his forearms and marksman badge on his upper left sleeve. He has his chechia tilted well to the back of his head.

IV:54 Zouave NCO
Zouaves loved to put their chechia on the side of their heads. Note how large the tassels are.

IV:56 Zouave First-Class Soldier
Note how he has been able to put arabesque-style lines on his waistcoat and jacket.

IV:57 Sergeant and Sergeant Majors of the 4th Regiment of Zouaves
They have their chechias on the right side of their heads. The officer with the kepi is a sous-lieutenant. Note the braid on the side of the men's pantaloons (saroual).

IV:58 Zouave Waistcoat
This is the basic soldier's model without any ornamentation.

IV:59 Zouave Waistcoat with Arabesque Trim
There was not an established pattern for the trim.

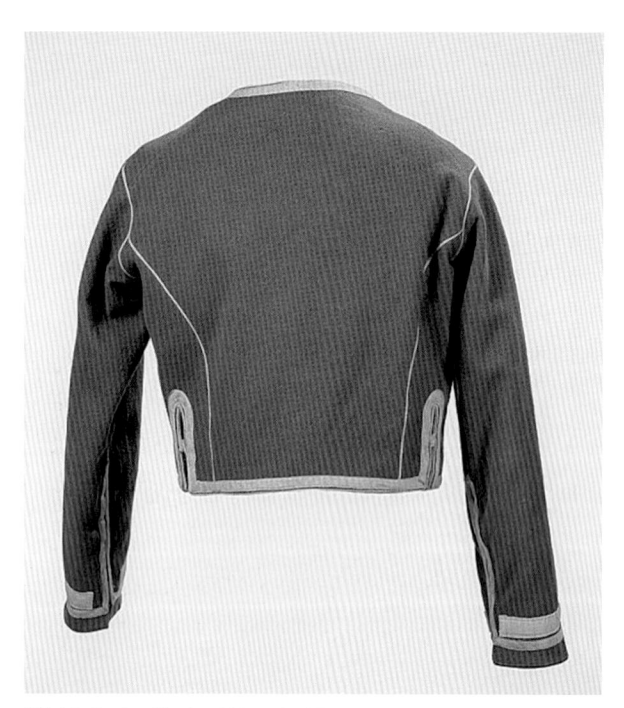

IV:60 Back of Jacket Worn by Zouaves and Tirailleurs
Note the slit on the inside of the sleeves.

IV:61 Jacket Back of a Zouave Sergeant Major
Note the heavy arabesque trim on the back and around the jacket's braid. Also notice the slit on the back side of the sleeve and the sixteen small, gold-coloured buttons.

crimson. The opening was framed by sixteen small, gold-coloured buttons (see Image C55 and IV:61). The back and armhole had a crimson welt along the seam and two lines of braid that came down from the armhole. There was a small notch on either side of the back of the shama, which the braid along the bottom edge outlined (Image IV:60).

The front panels on the left and right side of the jacket had crimson trim. It drew a line across the front of the jacket, creating a false pocket or tombeau, and curled up to form a trefoil (Image C54).

Inside the tombeau was a different colour, depending on the regiment: red for the 1st, white for the 2nd, yellow for the 3rd, and dark blue, the same colour as the jacket, for the 4th (Image C54 shows all four colours).

NCOs wore a more elaborate braid on the chest panels of their waistcoat and shama. The NCO braid did not end in the trefoil of the other ranks, but rather a single head of different designs. The line of braid on the front panel also had small loops of crimson braid coming off it, making it more elaborate. The centre of each front panel and the centre back of the shama had elaborate crimson arabesque patterns, which added greatly to the richness of the garment (Images C53 and IV:61). Just how elaborate it was depended to a certain extent upon the NCO and his budget. Some men completely covered the front panels and had braid on their upper sleeves and cuffs.

The cuffs of the garment were traced with gold lines to mark an NCO's rank. The gold line was in an upside V shape to follow the shape of the crimson cuff trim. Re-enlisted men had a thin red or gold line, depending on their rank, along the bottom of the cuff.

The tubular waistcoat for NCOs also had extra crimson arabesque-patterned lines. These went out from the centre line of crimson braid at about mid-chest level.

Tunic

Officers wore a dark blue/black tunic with a stand-up collar and collar shield of the same colour. The tunic was closed in front by seven gold buttons up to 1911, and thereafter by nine. The plain dome buttons were gold-coloured.

The rear of the tunic had a false pocket with scaled flaps and three gold-coloured buttons on each side of the centre line.

The cuffs were marked by gold Hungarian knot-type braid that ended in points at or above the elbow, depending on the wearer's rank. The number of lines in the braid depended on the officer's rank, and followed the line system for rank set out in §IV-3-4. The Zouaves were the first to adopt this type of dress, but it soon became the norm for North African officers.[219] Officers of the Turcos (see below) wore the same knots on their tunics; see Images IV:68 and C57 for examples of these sleeve rank stylised Hungarian knots.

The back of the cuffs, like that of the other ranks, had a slit. The slit on an officer's tunic was 25 cm (9.84 inches) long and lined by scarlet silk. The slit was worn open, but it had eighteen small gold-coloured buttons and corresponding loops that could close the slit (Image C55).[220] The total effect of the large lance-point knot and the cuff slit trimmed with scarlet silk and gold buttons was a very rich and elaborate uniform.

Because Zouave officers wore the knot on their sleeves, they did not wear epaulettes.

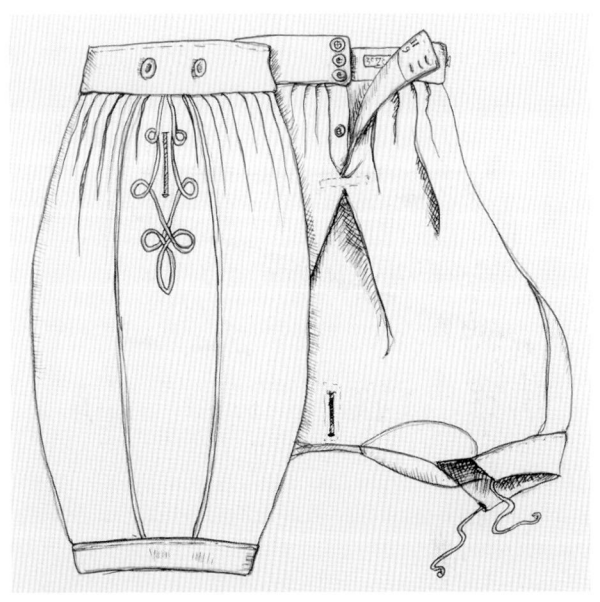

IV:62 Zouave and Turko Pantaloons
Note the stripes on the side and the braid between the stripes. Also note how the bottoms of the pantaloons were tightened to the leg. A slit was at the bottom of the pantaloons.

Cummerbund

The Zouaves wore a light blue cummerbund over the waistcoat and under the shama. It was 4.2 m (19 feet 9.36 inches) long and 40 cm (15.75 inches) wide.

Pantaloons and Trousers

Zouave other ranks wore very full crimson baggy pantaloons, called *saroual*. Each leg had a dark blue design on the side, stopping just above the bend of the knee. The design was in the form of a lance-head trefoil (Image IV:62). There were also two dark blue trim lines on either side of the lance-head that went from the waist to the bottom of the saroual. The pantaloons were mostly one piece and, until the very bottom, did not separate for the left and right legs. They had a slit at the bottom.

In the summer, the crimson saroual was often replaced by a white cotton saroual, which made more of a division for the legs and was, in general, cooler. The white summer saroual did not have any trim.

Officers wore crimson trousers with their tunics. For full dress, the trousers tended to follow those worn by the line infantry. Those trousers had a black band 50 mm (1.97 inches) wide on each leg.

For walking-out dress, Zouave officers, in common with other North African and colonial officers, preferred to wear their trousers in the flottard style. In this style, the leg had pleats at the waist and was cut very loose down to the ankles. The bottom of the trousers was gathered together tightly, peg-leg style. The total effect is reminiscent of the trousers of the zoot suiters of the 1940s (see Image IV:68 for an example of the flottard cut in trousers).

Gaiters and Jambières

Below the short pantaloons, the Zouaves wore gaiters or a combination of gaiters and jambières, depending on the year. The jambières were yellow-orange-coloured leather stockings that were buttoned around soldiers' legs. North African soldiers often wore them in combination with gaiters or spats from the time of Napoleon III and up to around 1900. After that, only white or dark gaiters were worn (Image IV:57). White was the more formal of the two (Image IV:56).

IV-8-c TIRAILLEURS ALGÉRIENS AND MAROCAINS

The Tirailleurs Algériens, better known as 'Turcos', had their beginnings in 1842, when the North African men in the Zouave units were removed in order to make the Zouaves more French. The removed men were formed into existing companies of Kouloughlis, Kabyles, and Arabs to form three battalions, formally known as Tirailleurs Indigenes d'Algerie.

Kouloughlis were the offspring of Turks and local Moorish women.[221] It is likely that the Kouloughlis' origins are the reason these troops were given the nickname Turcos. The Indian equivalent was the Moplahs (also spelled Moplas or Mopillas), who were a mix of Arabs and Indians.[222] The British, of course, created the Anglo-Indians from their relations with the local Indian women. The Kabyles were the Berber group that included the Zouagha tribe, who supplied the first men for the Zouaves. Over time, all three companies became more and more Berber.

In 1855, a second battalion was added to each existing battalion. In 1856, the units were named the 1st, 2nd, and 3rd Regiments de Tirailleurs Algériens.[223]

In 1884, following the 1881 French takeover of Tunisia, a 4th regiment of Turcos was added. Under their local dey (ruling official), Tunisia had a draft, and the French took this over for the 4th after making some minor changes. The 4th Regiment was known officially as the 4th Regiment de Tirailleurs Algériens up to 1914, in spite of being composed of Tunisians and stationed in Tunisia. Perhaps they did this to maintain the idea that the French were not in Tunisia permanently.

The number of regiments in Algeria remained at three from 1856 to 1914 because the colon (colonial) community, like colonial communities everywhere, was worried about the effect of arming the native people and training them to use modern weapons.[224] This was not an irrational fear. There had been revolts and uprisings in 1871, 1876, and 1879. Another rebellion, among the Batna, took place in 1916. To get around colon concerns about creating additional regiments, the French authorities instead merely enlarged the number of battalions in each regiment as the populations grew. In 1907, the 1st had eight battalions, the 2nd nine, the 3rd eight, and the 4th twelve.[225] In 1913, they used these extra battalions to form additional regiments, the 5th through the 9th.[226]

The Turco regiments raised in Algeria, whether volunteers or draftees, were largely drawn from the Kabyle and other Berbers in the mountain areas of Algeria. The French tried to follow a policy of *divide et impera* in North Africa by siding with the Berbers and freezing out the Arabs. Ultimately, this policy did not work because the Berbers were more drawn to the Arab culture, which shared the same religion, rather than the French.

Since the tirailleurs had their origins in the Zouaves, it is only natural that their uniform should closely resemble that of the Zouaves.

Uniform

Headdress
Like the Zouaves, the Turcos also wore a crimson chechia with tassels, which had a narrow gold band on the tassel heads for NCOs. The difference was that tirailleurs wore light blue tassels. Under the chechia, they wore a white cotton skullcap, which just showed as a narrow white edge around the bottom of the chechia. It is said that all Turco regiments wore their chechias tilted toward the back of their heads,[227] but photographs do not support this claim (Image IV:63).

The Turcos' chechia also had a turban wrapped around it in full dress, which followed the same colour changes over time as those of the Zouaves. By 1880–1914, it was white (Image IV:64).

Jacket
The Turcos also wore a whitish long-sleeve shirt. In addition, they wore the side- and top-buttoned waistcoat and the open jacket called a shama (Image IV:65). The waistcoat and the shama were identical to those worn in the Zouaves, except they were sky (light) blue with daffodil yellow trim. At first, the shama and waistcoat were green, and the pantaloons (saroual) were blue. After the expansion of 1855, all of these clothing items were changed to light blue with daffodil yellow trim.[228] See Image C56.

The tombos were the same colours as used for the Zouave regiments: red for the 1st, white for the

§IV-8 North African Infantry

IV:63 Soldier of the 2nd Regiment of Algerian Tirailleurs
Note to his right a chechia with white turban wrapped around it. Note also trim on pantaloons.

IV:64 Sergeant of 3rd Tirailleurs
He has his chechia and turban on his head.

2nd, and yellow for the 3rd (Image C56). When a 4th regiment was created, it was given a dark blue tombo. Additional regiments were created in 1913. The 1st budded off the 5th and 9th Zouaves, who received red tombos. The 2nd budded off the 6th, who received white tombos. The 3rd budded off the 7th, who received yellow tombos. The 4th created the 8th Turcos, who received dark blue tombos. Other than the tombos, the dress uniforms of the new regiments were exactly the same as the first four regiments. With the duplication of tombos, this could make for confusion. After the Great War was over, the confusion was addressed by placing a regiment's number on the shama.

NCOs had their daffodil yellow trim end in a wheat head rather than the trefoil of the other ranks (compare Image IV:65 with Image IV:66), and could add an additional arabesque trim as was done in the Zouaves. In addition, the Tirailleurs had roughly a 50-50 mix of French and natives in the NCO and lieutenant ranks. The ranks of captain and above were all French.[229]

IV:65 Tirailleur Without Headdress
In this fine character study, note how his hair has been shaved back to fit under his chechia.

Native officers would tend to have the trim of their shamas in black braid. They also had gold pointed Hungarian knots on their sleeves. They could elect to have extra trim on the shama.

Cummerbund

Tirailleurs wore the same 4.2 meter (13 feet 9.36 inches) by 40 cm (15.75 inches) wide cummerbund as the Zouaves, except for the Turcos, it was crimson.

Pantaloons

The Tirailleurs also wore the same very full pantaloons (saroual) as the Zouaves, except the Turcos' were light blue with daffodil yellow trim for the other ranks. This trim followed the same design as that worn by the Zouaves. NCOs and native officers could have extra braiding to their sarouals. The braid of native officers was more complex and in black. In the summer, white sarouals without trim would be worn.

French Officers

French officers wore European uniforms. Their kepi had a light sky blue band with a crimson top. They wore the standard rank bands in gold. The regiment would be noted on the kepi band by either a gold number or a gold number inside a gold crescent moon (Image IV:67). For an example of a number and moon, see Image IV:49 in §IV-7-b.

Their light blue tunics had a daffodil yellow collar adorned with a light blue shield. On the shield was the regiment's number in gold. Turcos wore the same shaped lance-head Hungarian-knot rank stripes as the Zouaves on their sleeves (see Image C57). The back of the sleeves was slashed and had small buttons just like the Zouaves' (see Image C58). In theory, the lining of the slash was daffodil yellow rather than the crimson of the Zouaves but, as Image C58 shows, some linings were crimson. Because of the large gold rank knots on their sleeves, the officers did not wear epaulettes.

The officers' trousers were crimson, and had a 50 mm (1.97 inch) wide stripe of sky (light) blue on them (Image IV:68). In number two dress, French Turco officers were also inclined to wear their trousers in the flottard style (Image IV:68).

IV:66 NCO of Tirailleurs
Note the exaggerated rank braid on his forearms and the wheat head ending in place of the trefoil on his chest braid. This man also added an arabesque tracing and trim to his jacket.

IV:67 Tirailleur French Officer
Note that yellow on uniforms during this period would often show up as a dark colour. This photograph gives a good view of the rank braid used on the sleeves in North African regiments.

Native officers seem to have been free to elect to wear either native or French dress. If they wore French tunics, they would replace the kepi with a crimson chechia and perhaps oriental pantaloons that resembled loose-cut knickerbockers.

TIRAILLEURS MAROCAINS

The Marocains came into being at the turn of the twentieth century, when the French needed local help from men who knew the terrain and local politics as they fought to control Morocco. The force grew rapidly from an initial four companies in 1912 to five battalions in 1914.[230]

These five battalions were sent to France when war broke out in 1914. Their first job was to fight in the defence of Paris, where they performed well and started to build the outstanding reputation the Marocains gained during the war. By the end of September 1914, the original 5,000 men had been reduced to 800.[231] In December 1914, the battalions became the 1st Régiment de Marche de Tirailleurs Marocains and fought the balance of the war on the Western Front. They did well there, earning honours, just one step below the most honoured Zouave and Algerian regiments.[232]

Prior to 1914, the other ranks came mostly from the coastal and lowland areas of Morocco. This made them Arab in the eyes of the French. Later, as their mountain homelands were conquered, more Berbers were enlisted.[233]

HEADDRESS
A crimson chechia was worn, probably with a light blue tassel. Since the Moroccans were always in combat, they typically had a khaki covering on their chechia and did not wear a tassel.

COAT/SHIRT
A long-sleeve khaki coat/shirt with a low collar was worn by the Marocains. It had eight buttons and was buttoned to the neck. There were no decorations on the sleeves and no buttons on the cuffs. The shoulders had simple cloth epaulettes. The cloth was held down by one button on each shoulder.

CUMMERBUND
The Moroccans wore a standard crimson cummerbund, which was 4.2 m (13 feet 9.36 inches) long and 40 cm (15.75 inches) wide.

KNICKERBOCKERS
For their netherwear, the Moroccans wore a type of loose-cut knickerbockers. The colour of this garment was khaki.

IV:68 The yellow collar shows up in black because of photographic limitations during this period. The trousers are in the flottard style. The trim on the crimson trousers is sky blue.

Gaiters/Puttees

The Moroccans do not seem to have worn gaiters. Rather, they wore puttees, which were probably made from the same triangle-shaped dark blue cloth that was used by the Senegalese tirailleurs.[234]

Officers

Since the tirailleurs Marocains were such a recent creation, the officers had not had time to develop their own unique uniform by 1914. Therefore, their uniform was, except for small details, like that of officers of the Algerian tirailleurs. The kepi was crimson with a sky blue band and gold trim. The band had a crescent moon with a star inside it, all in gold. The tunic was sky or light blue with a daffodil yellow collar. The collar shield was the same colour as the tunic and had a gold battalion number in it. The bar on each cuff was daffodil yellow. The front of the tunic was closed with seven gold buttons up to 1911. After 1911, there were nine gold buttons. Each cuff had three gold buttons on the daffodil yellow trim and three on each skirt in the rear of the tunic. The buttons did not carry any device.

The trousers were likely crimson with a sky blue stripe 50 mm (1.97 inches) wide, which is what officers of the tirailleurs Algériens wore. However, others state that the trouser stripe was divided by two narrow crimson stripes, which made it appear as if there were two sky blue stripes on the trousers.

§IV-8-d FOREIGN LEGION

(see *§IV-6-b* above)

§IV-9 COLONIAL INFANTRY

§IV-9-a COLONIAL LINE INFANTRY

The origins of what would become the colonial infantry lie in troops raised in 1621. These units guarded naval bases in France and trading stations overseas. They had an on-and-off existence until 1822, when permanent marine companies were formed. In 1831, two regiments of infanterie de Marine, the 1st and 2nd, were created out of independent companies. They were charged to garrison overseas colonies and could use local native recruits to do so.[235] In 1838, a 3rd regiment was formed. From 1829 to 1849, these regiments supplied men for duty in the Caribbean, Senegal, and India (Pondicherry). They also were involved with the landings in Algiers, and in operations in Madagascar, Gabon, Morocco, New Caledonia, Greece, and Tahiti.[236] Under Napoleon III, who sent six companies to Senegal, a 4th regiment was added in 1854.

Under the Third Republic, all four regiments contributed to a battalion de marche for the 1883–5 Tonkin Campaign in Indochina.[237] Then, in 1890, the 5th through 12th Regiments were raised. The 5th to 7th were holding regiments; the 9th to 11th served in Indochina. These regiments were created by reorganising existing companies and converting régiments de marche already in country: the 9th in Tonkin, the 10th in Annam, and the 11th in Cochinchina.[238] The 12th was in New Caledonia. A 13th regiment was raised in 1895 for service in Madagascar. In 1899, the 14th was created for West Africa, and another regiment, the 15th, was created for Madagascar. In 1900, the 16th through 18th were formed for service in Senegal and China. Two garrison regiments to serve in France, the 21st and 22nd, were also raised in 1900. Then, in 1902, a further two regiments were raised, the 23rd and 24th, for service in France. These marked the high point of the colonial list in terms of number of regiments.[239]

Soon after they were raised, some of the newly created regiments were disbanded. The 12th, 13th, 14th, and 15th regiments were disbanded in 1903, 1908, 1903, and 1903 respectively. The 17th was disbanded in 1908. The 18th was disbanded in 1902. There never was a 19th or 20th regiment. Thus, in 1914, the Colonial Army List read as set out in Table IV.9.a.1.

Table IV.9.a.1 Colonial Army List, 1914

Regiment	Year Raised	Where Stationed
1	1831	Cherbourg
2	1831	Brest
3	1838	Rocheford
4	1854	Toulon
5	1890	Lyon
6	1890	Lyon
7	1890	Bordeaux
8	1890	Toulon
9	1890	Tonkin
10	1890	Annam
11	1890	Saigon
16	1900	North China
21	1899	Paris
22	1899	Hyeres
23	1902	Paris
24	1902	Perpignan[a]

Source: Conrad, 1914 Army, pp. 57–8. Years raised are from Andolenko, Historiques Infanterie, pp. 344–59.
Note: [a] In the Marseille area

Prior to 1900, infantry that operated overseas, the infanterie de marine, was under the control of the navy. In 1900 control was transferred to the colonial department, and it became infanterie coloniale. Early on the infantry's nickname was *marsouins*, or porpoises. The colonial artillery were called sea snails (*bigors*).[240]

Uniform

HEADDRESS

In 1872, the other ranks continued to wear a shako with a pompom showing the colour of the regiment. The pompom did not show the company number. The colours were: 1st Regiment, turquoise blue; 2nd Regiment, scarlet; 3rd Regiment, daffodil yellow; and 4th Regiment, green.

In 1886, the kepi became the headdress for first-class dress. For officers, it had an anchor in gilded brass and a tricolour cockade of silk. Field officers had a tricolour plume, and the colonel had a white egret feather plume. Subordinate officers had a pompom of twists of gold, and adjutants had strands of silver mixed in with the gold.[241]

Both the troupes de marine and, after 1900, the troupes coloniales wore kepis that had dark blue tops and dark blue bands (Image IV:69). For officers, these items were a dark blue/black colour. The other ranks had crimson piping.

Officers had gold piping and a gold anchor or number (Image IV:69).[242]

There is confusion about the wearing of numbers versus anchors on the front of the band of the kepi and when it was worn. The device on the front of the band of the other ranks' kepi was crimson and was either a regimental number or a fouled anchor. The book *The French Army*, which was made extensive use of Musée de l'Armée material, stated that, after 1909, regiments stationed in France wore their regimental number on their kepi and uniform, and those overseas wore the fouled anchor.[243] However, period photographs do not entirely support this theory.

On the other hand, Claude Robert in his *Les Uniformes de l'Armée Française* gives the following

IV:69 Captain of the 1st Colonial Marine Regiment
The large anchor on his kepi indicates that this is probably an early photograph.

IV:70 16th Colonial Infantry in China, c. 1910
The tricolour plume of the field officer in the left front of the image is clear. Less clear is the white egret plume of the colonel in the right front.

sequence for the use of numbers and anchors: In 1890, the number of the regiment replaced the anchor.[244] NCOs after 1901 wore either a number or an anchor.[245] In 1904, the number was replaced by a fouled anchor in daffodil yellow, and gold for officers and adjutants.[246] After 1904, the regimental number was not to be worn except in the event of mobilisation.[247] In summary, the regimental number was worn on the band from 1890 to 1904; the anchor was worn from 1904 to 1914.

In 1910, junior officers and adjutants began wearing a plume of blue-grey cock's feathers. Field officers wore a tricolour plume. The regimental colonel continued to wear the white egret feather plume (Image IV:70).[248]

Photographs show officers wearing two different styles of anchor on their kepis. Type A is a large non-fouled anchor (Image IV:69), taller than the band. Type B (Image IV:71) is smaller; it is fouled and rests completely within the band. There is ambiguity present in the photographs showing the different anchors and the style of the kepis, Type A seems to be an early version, and Type B seems to have come into use around 1900 or a bit earlier, but the dates are not at all clear. Compare Images IV:69 and IV:71.

Coat

Other ranks wore a dark blue jacket with a stand-up collar (Image IV:72). The tunic for other ranks was abolished in 1886, so all they had to wear was the jacket. It had two rows of tombac (brass alloy) buttons, which continued the corps gold button theme. The buttons had a fouled anchor design on them.

There were no buttons on the cuffs or the rear of the jacket.

The stand-up collar and the cuffs were the same colour as the jacket. The collar shield area had a cloth patch, which was also the same colour as the jacket. Sewn on to the patch was either a crimson fouled anchor or number, as set out above under kepis. The patch was then sewn onto the collar. This allowed the fouled anchor and number to be switched as a man moved between stations in France and overseas. In France, in 1909, the regimental number replaced the anchor on the collar of the other ranks' and officers' tunic for wear while in France.[249]

On the jacket in full dress, the men wore daffodil yellow epaulettes. The stripe(s) showing rank worn on the lower sleeves were crimson or gold and

IV:71 Officer of the 4th Colonial Infantry
The small anchor on his kepi indicates this photo was taken shortly before World War I.

IV:72 Infanterie Coloniale Other Rank
Note the double-breasted tunic and the open-faced belt buckle, both marks of colonial infantry.

followed the same pattern as those for line infantry. The narrow stripe of a re-enlisted man worn just above the cuff on both arms was crimson.

A white uniform was often worn because of the heat in overseas stations and sometimes in southern French ones. It was single-breasted and all white except for a shield on the collar bearing the regiment's number or anchor (Image IV:73).

Officers wore a dark blue/black single-breasted tunic with a standing collar. The naval tunic, adopted in 1893, was closed with eight gold-coloured buttons down the front. Later, the number of buttons increased to nine (Image IV:71). Each cuff had three buttons where an upright bar would have been, and the rear skirt had two sets of three buttons. The rear skirts were without coloured trim. The collar and cuffs were the same colour as the body of the coat, as was the area that would have been the shield on the collar.

An officer's rank was shown by rings on the cuff. The system for these rings followed that of the metropolitan army (see §IV-3-4).

Officers wore standard gold epaulettes on their tunics. The system of colour and fringe followed that used by the metropolitan line infantry.

IV:73 Soldier of the 9th Colonial Infantry in Tropical Walking-Out Dress

Belts and Buckles

The other ranks of the marsouins wore a wide black belt very similar to that of the line infantry. However, the marsouins' other ranks, after 1870, wore a distinctive belt with a wide hollow buckle, very different from the solid buckle worn by other French soldiers (Image IV:72).

Trousers

The shape of the trousers was the same as worn by metropolitan infantry, and their colour was bluish-grey. Re-enlisted NCOs wore a dark iron-grey coloured trousers, the same shade as worn by the chasseurs à pied. The other ranks' trousers carried crimson piping along the side seams of both legs.

Officers' trousers were quite different from those worn in the metropolitan line infantry. First, the colour was not the same: officers and adjutants wore trousers of a special shade of blue, which is slightly different from the dark iron-grey worn by re-enlisted NCOs. Second, rather than having the wide trouser stripe of the line infantry officer, the colonial and then the marine officers had crimson piping, like the other ranks.

§IV-9-b SENEGALESE TIRAILLEURS AND SPAHIS

§IV-9-b-i SENEGALESE TIRAILLEURS

In 1914, France had the world's second largest empire.[250] Much of it was in Africa, and a great deal of the conquest was achieved by the Senegalese tirailleurs under the command of French marine and army officers.

Local native men, as early as 1765, had been organised to provide military services by the French trading companies along the coast of Senegal, but these men were only needed sporadically. It was not until 1857 that the Senegalese tirailleurs were organised as a standing military force. This was achieved through the efforts of Louis Faidherbe, who, after two tours of duty in North Africa, had become governor of Senegal.[251] The strength of the Senegalese grew from four companies in 1857, to a two-battalion regiment, the 1st Régiment de Tirailleurs Sénégalais, in 1884.

Ahead of the French colony lay the Sahel, an area that, on average, is some 700 km (435 miles) wide, south of the Sahara Desert and north of the equatorial forests of Central Africa. The Sahel is huge – by some accounts it extends all the way from the Atlantic to the Red Sea. It is a flat, dry area of arid grass and shrubs. The people who lived there were constantly at war with each other.

Serious French expansion into the Sahel began under the ministry of Jules Ferry, a leftist politician in power in 1880–1 and 1883–5, who said, 'For the time being, forget *revanche* [revenge against Germany for 1870] and concentrate on the expansion of the empire.'[252] The first column of conquest went out in 1881; it consisted of 400 men. This was typical of what followed in the next twenty years, although larger columns, up to 2,000 men at times, would be used later. The French generally used columns of a small number of men, made up of mostly Senegalese tirailleurs, against large numbers of enemy soldiers.

During these wars of conquest, the French officers developed a deep respect for the courage of some of their foes. 'Not one fled; all died at their stations,' wrote Lieutenant Felix-Anthelm Orsat, and 'If instead of having the Tukulors as enemies, we could have had them with us, Africa would not have been long to take.'[253] Orsat was killed in 1891 at the age of twenty-three. His letters to his brother about life and fighting in the Sahel were published after his death.[254] 'The men ... died superbly,' claimed Charles-Emmanuel Mangin (1866–1925). As a young man Mangin had fought in the Sahel, in 1910 publishing *La force noir*, advocating extensive French use of black soldiers from the Sahel. In World War I he was a successful general.

Uniform

HEADDRESS

The Senegalese tirailleurs wore a crimson chechia with a light blue tassel. They tended to wear them tilted well towards the back of their heads (Images IV:74 and IV:76).

IV:74 Senegalese Tirailleurs
These men are not in full dress. They only have a belt, but they do give a good idea of what a Senegalese uniform looked like. Note how they wear their chechias towards the back of their heads.

Jacket

They wore a dark blue collarless long-sleeve jacket (M1898). The jacket closed in front using four gold-coloured half-dome tombac buttons. There was daffodil yellow trim at the neckline and cuffs. The cuff trim was in the shape of an upside down V. The capital letters 'TS' in scarlet cloth were worn below the yellow trim on either side of the central line of buttons (Image IV:75).

A new style of jacket for the Senegalese was approved in June 1914. However, it was not issued until early 1915 and falls under wartime dress. It was dark blue with a fold-over collar, trimmed in daffodil yellow and with a fouled anchor in the same colour. In the front, it had two rows of five tombac buttons. The cuffs had the same trim as the M1898 jacket.[255]

Cummerbund

A crimson cummerbund was worn, the same as the one worn by the Armée d'Afrique.

Breeches

Dark blue knickers with daffodil yellow trim were worn.

Leggings

In photographs, these appear to be puttees, but the Senegalese wore special leggings of triangle-shaped cloth, which was wrapped around the calf area.[256] Traditionally, these had been dark blue for field and full dress. When khaki dress was introduced, they were coloured khaki to match the rest of the field dress. In addition, photographs of troops in ceremonial events show them wearing white leggings rather than the dark blue (compare Image IV:76 with Image IV:74).

Footwear

The Senegalese in full dress wore either standard French army boots or tan leather sandals with a big strap.[257] This seems to have been decided regimentally, with sandals being worn more often in the Sahel and seldom, if ever, in Europe and North Africa.

IV:75 Senegalese Tirailleur Jacket M1898
The trim is yellow, the 'TS' is scarlet, and the jacket is dark blue.

IV:76 1st Senegalese in 1913
Note the sandals and white leggings.

§IV-9-b-ii SENEGALESE SPAHIS[258]

The first squadron of Senegalese spahis was created in 1885, and in 1893, a second squadron was formed. When in 1900 the marine forces passed control of the Senegalese to the colonial army, in theory, the Senegalese Spahis were disbanded. However, they seem to have continued in existence, as in 1914 there were two squadrons shown on the army list – one at Saint Louis in Western Africa and one in Morocco.[259]

Uniform in 1900

HEADDRESS
These troopers could wear either a red cloth chechia with a blue tassel or a colonial helmet covered in white cloth. The helmet had a crescent and star insignia on the front.

TUNIC
The tunic was all bright red. It had nine copper buttons down the front. The standing collar was all red, as were the cuffs.

RANK BADGES
Rank badges were yellow.

CUMMERBUND
The bright red cummerbund was worn over the tunic in full dress.

BURNOUS
When a burnous was worn, it consisted of two capes, a bright red cloth cape over a white cotton cape.

PANTALOONS
The baggy sky blue pantaloons did not have any braiding or piping.

§IV-9-c TONKINESE AND ANNAMITE TIRAILLEURS

France's entry into Indochina began with French missionaries and the navy, seeking ports for its ships. An expedition to avenge murdered missionaries followed in 1858, and France gained control of part of south Vietnam. Between 1874 and 1884, it gained protectorates in north (Tonkin) and central (Annam) Vietnam. Southern Vietnam (Cochinchina) became a colony. The French had already occupied Cambodia and established a protectorate in 1863. The late 1880s and early 1890s saw them moving into and taking over Laos. All of these areas formed French Indochina.[260]

This takeover was not achieved without long, hard fighting by marine regiments, the Legion troops, troops from the Armée d'Afrique, and help from metropolitan regiments. Disease took more lives than enemy action. To help hold the area, local regiments were raised. In 1914, these were the 1st to 4th Tonkin Regiments and the Annamite Regiment.

Thus, the French mostly relied on men from the northern and central parts of Vietnam and did not use men from Cambodia or the southern part of Vietnam. This reflects the areas where the fighting against the French was the most intense and prolonged.

Uniform

HEADDRESS
The headdress, called the *salacco*, was made of strips of bamboo or rice straw. It was topped by a small brass plate and either an olive- or ball-shaped piece on top of the plate. The hat was held on by a strip of scarlet cloth that tied behind the head under a bun of hair. Sometimes these strips of cloth hung down to about midway on the soldier's back.

IV:77 Indochinese Soldiers
Photo probably taken during World War I. Note the coolie-style hat worn by the troops from Annam and Cochinchina and the flat hat worn by some men (Tonkinese style). Both of these hats were called salaccos.

The salacco came in two shapes. The Annamite model, worn by troops from Annam and Cochinchina, took a coolie-style shape. It came to a point, and the sides fell sharply away to form a deep cone (Image IV:77). The other style was the Tonkinese model, worn by troops from the north of Indochina. It had a smaller diameter and was almost flat. It was topped by a small ball (Images IV:77 and IV:78). It would not be surprising if some pre-World War I salaccos were varnished.

It should be noted that after World War I, the regulation salacco was made of varnished bamboo and had a conical shape.

Blouse

The tirailleurs wore a blouse, called a *keo*, with a low collar. It was closed in front with five copper buttons. The top, bottom, and front of the low collar had scarlet trim. A line of scarlet trim ran down the front and bottom of the keo (Image IV:78). There was no trim on the cuffs, but they did have badges of rank in an upside down V shape, and bugler's braid in the same shape, if called for.

On the front of the keo, at each of the five visible buttons, a line of scarlet extended from the centre line, maybe by 6.35 cm (2.5 inches), to each side.

Belt

A black belt with the open marine buckle was worn.

Loin Cloth

Under the keo and belt, a scarlet loin cloth was worn under the keo. It hung out in the front at different lengths, although it never came down past mid-thigh. It was a solid piece of cloth and did not have fringe (Images IV:77 and IV:78).

Trousers and Knickerbockers

The tirailleurs, in earlier days, wore dark blue pyjama-style trousers (Image IV:78). After about 1895 or so, knickerbockers became more common (Image IV:77), although the pyjama-style seems to have still been worn. It may be that men wore pyjama-type trousers because of the heat, or that different provinces followed different styles. Neither style had trim on them.

IV:78 Tonkinese Tirailleurs, c. 1885
Note flat salacco held on by a ribbon (usually red) that is tied behind the head. Note also the front red loin cloth that has different lengths. Because of the heat, the pyjama-style trousers are worn loose.

IV:79 This 1905 photograph appears to be of a Compagnies Saharienne trooper. Two elements of his dress support this conclusion. First are the ammunition belts crossed on his chest. Second are the trousers and shoes that show below the white duster. Sahariennes were to supply their own clothing, and this man is wearing rough-and-ready trousers and well-worn shoes or boots, as opposed to the elegant white pantaloons and Arab boots worn by the Sahara spahis.

LEGGINGS
If knickerbockers were worn, a type of leggings would be needed. These probably would be the French triangle-style leggings, not the Indian army-style puttees.

The colour in full dress could be dark blue, white, or even scarlet.

FOOTWEAR
The footwear would be either sandals or boots.

§IV-9-d MADAGASCAN TIRAILLEURS

In addition to the far better-known Senegalese tirailleurs, France maintained a force of Madagascan tirailleurs. This force in 1914 stood at three regiments, the 1st to 3rd Régiment de Tirailleurs Malgaches. Each regiment had three battalions.[261] The regiments were all stationed in Madagascar, keeping the peace.

Uniform
There has been almost no coverage of the uniforms of the Madagascan tirailleurs. From the little that has been written, it appears they dressed exactly like the Senegalese tirailleurs. The only thing to mark them as different was the letters 'TM' on both sides of the jacket, in place of the 'TS' worn by the Senegalese.[262]

§IV-10 SAHARA TIRAILLEURS AND SPAHIS AND THE COMPAGNIES SAHARIENNES

Almost unknown among the last thrusts of French colonial conquest, the French movement into the Sahara owes its impetus to the French national humiliation at Fashoda. There is so much attention paid to the Dreyfus Affair that people often forget that other important events were occurring in France during those years. One was France's desire not to suffer another humiliation at the hands of the British. The best way to avoid this was to be able to apply significant pressure on Britain in the event of crisis.[263] This was not easy to do, given Britain's command of the sea. Nigeria was picked as the target; it involved only a short sea passage close to French home waters, followed by troop movements over land. Plans for a trans-Sahara railway, a generation old, were brought out and adjusted.[264] Building the railway would be very costly, but national honour was at stake.

The plans were altered for a change of route to Nigeria, which placed a group of oases, the Tuat, in the path of the railroad.[265] A scientific mission was sent with a small military escort, ostensibly to study mineral conditions in the Tuat. The inhabitants of the Tuat were not fooled; they told the French they were not welcome, and when the mission would not leave, they attempted to eject the French by force. While the escort was small, it had modern weapons, and it easily defeated a party of townspeople and captured the first village in the Tuat.[266]

One thing followed another in the old colonial minuet, and eventually the French had, by 1900, conquered all of the oases complex.[267]

This was not the end of the story. As the French garrisons were reduced, a series of revolts broke out.[268] To garrison the oases with French soldiers was expensive. In addition, they required more supplies from the north, which meant more supply columns that were subject to attack, and, therefore, needed to be guarded. To solve this problem, the French first tried to garrison the southern oases with native troops from Algeria, but these men hated this duty so much they would refuse to re-enlist.[269]

The French then formed new units – the Sahara spahis and Sahara tirailleurs – both formed in 1894.[270] The Sahara tirailleurs, in theory, drew on two sources for its soldiers: the Haratin, a mixed-race group of Berber and negro heritage who did agricultural work in the oases on a sharecrop basis, and black ex-slaves who, as slaves, had kept the oases water system working.[271] When the French arrived, as a rule, they declared all slaves to be free; the slaves then stopped working – with disastrous effects on the agricultural system. The sharecroppers, the Haratin, also stopped working.[272]

It was from the ex-slaves and the Haratin that the French elected to recruit men for two companies of the Sahara tirailleurs.[273] In drawing on these two classes – the lowest two classes in the local social system – the French seemed to have had a divide-and-rule strategy in mind. They felt the low-class men would be happy to ally themselves with the French against their former overlords.[274] NCOs were to be volunteers from the Algerian tirailleurs and the officers a mix of Algerian tirailleurs and French.[275]

For mobility, the Sahara spahis were formed in 1894, a camel company of Chaamba Arabs.[276] The Chaambas were a nomadic people who lived in the north-central Sahara and moved their herds of camels and sheep from one pocket of vegetation to another.[277]

The new units turned out to be less than elite troops. The ex-slaves and sharecroppers lacked the physical and mental robustness to make good soldiers.[278] The poor quality of their NCOs and officers did not help. The Algerians sent the worst of their men to be junior officers and NCOs in the Sahara tirailleurs. These new arrivals did not know their men and had no interest in their jobs. French NCOs came from supply depots or desk jobs and were too young or unable to stand the hot climate.[279]

Porch states that many of the tirailleurs were not local men, but men from Algeria – soldiers and native men. Both made poor soldiers.[280] The Sahara spahis were next to useless in stopping raids against the supply convoys. As a general rule, the better class of the population never volunteered for military service. One 1887 report stated that for the period reported on, the Sahara spahis had not killed a dissident or recaptured a stolen camel. The unit suffered from many of the same problems as the Sahara tirailleurs and just were not as good as the men they were trying to fight.[281]

COMPAGNIES SAHARIENNES

The Sahara tirailleurs and spahis were good enough to serve as garrison troops, hold the towns, and perform escort duty with the supply convoys. They could not be used successfully to conquer the Sahara: a new type of unit was needed. This unit was the Compagnies Sahariennes, the Sahariennes, formed in 1902. Initially, they recruited from several nomad peoples, including the Chaamba and the Tuareg.[282] Later, the unit was almost all Chaamba. Volunteers brought their own food, clothing, and camels. The government supplied the rifles, and, apparently later the white dusters worn over the men's clothing.

Enlistment was for four months.[283] This relatively short term was very important; service with the French was looked down upon. Some enlisted after committing crimes and, in general, the recruits were the sweepings of the oases. In response to being scorned by the population, the men of the Sahariennes grew very sensitive about their honour and any infringements of it.[284] At the same time, discipline was hard and firm. It was not as brutal as that found in the Foreign Legion, but it could be quite coercive.[285] This type of discipline could not help but impinge on the recipient's honour, and the four-month enlistment allowed a soldier a way out of what could be an uncomfortable situation. On the other side, the French sometimes enlisted men who were not good soldiers. Therefore, the four-month enlistment allowed both the officers and the men a face-saving way to end the relationship.[286]

To command the three companies raised, Affaires Indigènes military officers were used. These officers generally had a cavalry or spahi background, but some came from the different tirailleur regiments.[287] In this way, they were much like the Guides of India, who were also under civil control in their early years and had a reputation as crack troops.

Porch ventures the opinion that the Sahariennes became one of the most exotic units in the French colonial army, an army known for exotic and colourful regiments. They became sufficiently well-known before World War I to attract British and other tourists to what was, essentially, the end of the world.[288] The three companies – there would be more later – succeeded in creating a presence that would linger long after they were gone.

The purpose of the Sahariennes was to conquer and hold that portion of the Sahara occupied by the Tuareg, a Berber people who controlled much of the deep Sahara.[289] The Tuareg obtained and kept this control without firearms, which they scorned as 'the arms of treachery'. Instead, they used broadswords, spears, and shields.[290]

In 1902, before the Sahariennes were fully organised, a patrol set out for Tuareg territory. The 130 men had five experienced soldiers among them; the bulk of the rest were Chaamba, acting as a *goum* (a goum is much like an armed posse, put together from whichever men were on hand).[291] Part of the patrol – seventy men – were attacked at Tit. Outnumbered by more than three to one by the attacking Tuareg, who, for once, were armed with modern rifles, the patrol held on until another part of the patrol came back and put the attackers under crossfire.

The victory at Tit took the heart of the Tuareg, and after that the French could send patrols into the Sahara almost without challenge. The Battle of Tit demonstrates a larger point. The Sahariennes did not conquer the Tuareg – that was done by goumiers and Sahara spahis.[292] The Sahariennes did keep control of the area once it was conquered.[293]

The French began to work with the different groups of the Tuareg to reconcile them to French rule. In this work they were aided by the death, in 1900, of the chief of the Ahaggar Tuareg, one of France's main foes.[294]

After several years' work, the French were able to make peace with different Tuareg groups living of the Tuareg heartland.[295] Then, in 1905, the man they had picked for paramount chief of the Ahaggar Tuareg became chief, made formal peace with the French, and was given a salary.[296] With this action, the Sahara could be considered conquered, and all that remained to do was send out patrols to make sure peace was maintained.

The conquest of the Sahara brought an area twice as large as France under French control.[297] But, economically, it was a hollow victory. In 1910, it produced 300,000 francs (current value £1,240,200, $1,505,000) in taxes and cost 3 million francs (current value £12,401,800, $15,049,600) a year to operate and man.[298]

Sahara Tirailleurs Uniform[299]

HEADDRESS
This was a cheche, possibly white, held in place by a camel cord.

BLOUSE AND PANTALOONS
These were of white cloth. The blouse had a blue chest ornament with a yellow cross on it.

CUMMERBUND
This was of red wool.

BURNOUS
This was perhaps the most distinctive uniform item for this unit. It, like all burnouses, consisted of two capes. The over cape was brown and the under one white.

STRAW HAT
Soldiers of this unit were often shown wearing a multicoloured sombrero-like straw hat. Presumably, this was to protect them from the pounding desert sun. It should be pointed out that the wearing of straw hats was not limited to Sahara tirailleurs. Drawings also exist showing Algerian tirailleurs with them.

BELT
The wide belt was light brown in colour with a copper belt plate.

BOOTS
These were also light brown.

Sahara Spahis Uniform[300]

BLOUSE AND NETHERWEAR
These were of white cloth. The blouse had a sky blue cloth chest plate with yellow cloth on it.

CUMMERBUND
This was bright red wool.

BURNOUS
The burnous can be considered the most distinctive uniform item worn by these soldiers. It consisted of two capes, a black one worn over a white one.

HAT
The Sahara Spahis could wear a sombrero-like hat woven of various coloured palm leaves.

BELT
It was in red leather.

BOOTS
The Arabic boots were red leather.

FRENCH OFFICERS
These men were seconded from the Algerian spahis and, with one alteration, wore their Algerian spahi uniform in full dress while serving with the Sahara spahis. That exception involved the kepi. While seconded, the officers wore a kepi that was entirely sky blue, with gold trim and a gold star over a crescent insignia. French sub-officers wore the same uniform.

Compagnies Sahariennes Uniform
The men who served in the Compagnies Sahariennes supplied their own clothing, and there was not a standard uniform for them. The closest the unit came to distinguishing uniform items was red belts crossed on their chests[301] and white dusters.[302] Image IV:79, c. 1905 shows a Compagnies Saharienne in a white duster. Apparently dusters, while more common after 1918, were also used before World War I.

§IV FRENCH EMPIRE: NOTES

1. Durant, *Age-Faith*, p. 589.
2. Ibid.
3. Neveux, *Normans*, pp. 208–9.
4. *World in Figures*, pp. 148, 234, 204, 236, 150, and 218.
5. Durant, *Age-Louis*, p. 3.
6. Conrad, *1914 Army*, p. 64.
7. The main sources used in this section are: Smith, *Napoleon's Regiments*; Detaille, *L'Armée Française*; Andolenko, *Historiques Infanterie*; and Andolenko, *Historiques Cavalerie*. All are works of extensive scholarship. They cover somewhat different subjects, and, unfortunately, their dates and details of regimental history do not always agree.
8. Detaille, *L'Armée Française*, p. 24; Elting, *Swords/Throne*, p. 14.
9. Elting, *Swords/Throne*, p. 14.
10. Smith, *Napoleon's Regiments*, p. 19.
11. Ibid., p. 14.
12. Detaille, *L'Armée Française*, p. 30.
13. Scott, *Yorktown/Valmy*, pp. 177–8.
14. Smith, *Napoleon's Regiments*, p. 14.
15. Ibid., pp. 19–21.
16. Elting, *Swords/Throne*, p. 34.
17. Detaille, *L'Armée Française*, pp. 45–6.
18. Ibid., p. 49.
19. Ibid.
20. Smith, *Napoleon's Regiments*, p. 19.
21. Andolenko, *Historiques Infanterie* was used for the formation date and lineage because it covered more of each regiment's history.
22. Scott, *Response/Revolution*, pp. 114–5 and 182.
23. Ibid., p. 115, footnotes 1 and 3.
24. Detaille, *L'Armée Française*, p. 87.
25. Ibid.
26. Ibid., table.
27. Ibid., table and pp. 99–100.
28. For one example of an 1814 disbanding, see the 13th Chasseurs à Cheval in Smith, *Napoleon's Regiments*, p. 273, and for disbanding dates in general, see Smith, *Napoleon's Regiments*, pp. 229–91.
29. Detaille, *L'Armée Française*, p. 127.
30. Ibid.
31. Ibid.
32. Smith, *Napoleon's Regiments*, pp. 242 and 270–1. See generally Smith, *Napoleon's Regiments*, pp. 240–91.
33. Detaille, *L'Armée Française*, p. 133.
34. Andolenko, *Historiques Cavalerie*, p. 38.
35. Ibid.
36. Mirouze, *French Army*, pp. 317–18.
37. Ibid., p. 330.
38. Ibid., p. 352.
39. Bond, *Staff College*, pp. 41–2.
40. Ibid., pp. 42–3.
41. Ibid., pp. 41 and 43.
42. Ralston, *Army/Republic*, p. 143.
43. Ibid., pp. 143, 155–6.
44. Ibid., pp. 143, 145.
45. Ibid., pp. 29 and 150.
46. Ibid., p. 150.
47. Ibid., p. 156.
48. Ibid., p. 152.
49. Ibid., pp. 154–5.
50. Ibid., p. 154.
51. Ibid., p. 156.
52. Ibid., p. 184.
53. Ibid.
54. Ibid., pp. 190–1.
55. Ibid., p. 191.
56. Ibid., p. 264–72, 281–8.
57. Ibid., pp. 289–95.
58. Ibid., p. 338.
59. Ibid., p. 337.
60. Robert, *Uniformes*, vol. 4, p. 11.
61. Ibid.
62. Ibid., drawing following p. 11.
63. Ibid., p. 16.
64. Mirouze, *French Army*, p. 503.
65. Robert, *Uniformes*, vol. 4, p. 14. This insignia was also called a thunderbolt.
66. Ibid.
67. Ibid.
68. Ibid., p. 11.
69. Mirouze, *French Army*, pp. 502–3 (by implication).
70. Ibid.
71. Robert, *Uniformes*, vol. 4, p. 17.
72. Ibid.
73. Ibid., p. 11.
74. Ibid., p. 12.
75. Ibid., p. 14.
76. Ibid., p. 17.
77. Ibid., p. 15.
78. Ibid., p. 12.
79. Ibid., p. 16.
80. Thorburn, *French Army*, p. 66.
81. Ibid., p. 46.
82. Ibid., p. 78.
83. Delperier, *Cuirassiers*, p. 32.
84. Thorburn, *French Army*, p. 73.
85. Mirouze, *French Army*, p. 256.
86. Delperier, *Cuirassiers*, pp. 4, 6 and 18.
87. Ibid., pp. 4, 6, 17, and 18.
88. Mirouze, *French Army*, p. 254.
89. Delperier, *Cuirassiers*, p. 4.
90. Ibid., p. 18; Mirouze, *French Army*, p. 254.
91. Mirouze, *French Army*, p. 254.
92. Thorburn, *French Army*, p. 84.
93. Delperier, *Cuirassiers*, pp. 33–5. See also, Mirouze, *French Army*, pp. 264–5.
94. Thorburn, *French Army*, p. 73.
95. During World War I, experiments with armour were tried for infantry, mainly snipers and lookouts, to stop rifle bullets. They were unsuccessful. To be even close to useful, it had to be too heavy.
96. Mirouze, *French Army*, p. 289. Another writer states that in 1900, the cuirass weighed between 5.9 kg and 7.26 kg (13 and 16 lb). Jerram, *Armies of the World*, p. 120.
97. Mirouze, *French Army*, p. 291.
98. Ibid., p. 289.
99. Ibid., pp. 268–71.
100. Ibid., pp. 276–7.
101. Delperier, *Cuirassiers*, p. 53.
102. Thorburn, *French Army*, p. 71.
103. Ibid., p. 82.
104. Ibid., pp. 78, 82.
105. Ibid., p. 82.

106 Mirouze, *French Army*, p. 296.
107 Ibid., pp. 316–18.
108 Delperier, 'Cavalerie', p. 8.
109 Ibid., p. 13.
110 Mirouze, *French Army*, pp. 336–7.
111 Ibid., p. 356.
112 Delperier, 'Cavalerie', p. 13.
113 Ibid., p. 15.
114 The light cavalry helmet was said to be slightly smaller, and the metal tail sheet had two rivets rather than three. Ibid.
115 Ibid.; Mirouze, *French Army*, p. 332.
116 Robert, *Uniformes*, vol. 2, p. 39.
117 Kannik, *Military Uniforms*, p. 169, no. 107.
118 Thorburn, *French Army*, pp. 66–8.
119 Andolenko, *Historiques Cavalerie*, pp. 112–17.
120 Thorburn, *French Army*, p. 74.
121 Ibid., p. 83.
122 Ibid., p. 66.
123 Ibid., p. 67.
124 Andolenko, *Historiques Cavalerie*, pp. 91–100.
125 Thorburn, *French Army*, pp. 68–9.
126 Ibid., pp. 76 and 81.
127 Ibid., pp. 69, 76, and 81.
128 Windrow, *Foreign Legion*, p. 28.
129 Robert, *Uniformes*, vol. 1, p. 23.
130 Ibid., pp. 25 and 27.
131 Windrow, *Foreign Legion*, p. 71.
132 Examples of these kepis can be seen at (1) Delperier, *Cuirassiers*, p. 19 (M1868), p. 43 (M1873); (2) Martin, *Military Uniforms*, p. 129.
133 Mollo, *Uniforms*, p. 136 and drawings 101 to 103.
134 Lord, *Uniforms/Civil War*, p. 43. The Hardee or Jeff Davis hat was a 15.24 cm (6 inch) tall felt hat with a brim. The brim would be turned up on the left side. Jefferson Davis, later president of the breakaway Confederate States of America during the American Civil War, was secretary of war for the United States during the years 1853–7. During this period, the hat was designed, and it was introduced in 1858. The man who designed the hat was William Hardee (1815–73). He was an army officer, instructor at the US Military School Academy at West Point, and author of the drill manual used by both sides during the Civil War. He is said to have written the manual and designed the hat in about 1855. When the American Civil War began, because he was from the state of Georgia, he joined the South. He rose to the rank of lieutenant general.
135 Ibid., p. 29.
136 Ibid., p. 104.
137 This is implied by the fact that the 1889 Dress Regulations provided for a slightly modified kepi-style forage cap. Steffen, *Horse Soldiers*, vol. 3, p. 27.
138 Swiss and Irish, in red; Germans, in cornflower blue.
139 Sumner, *French Army*, p. 17.
140 There is dispute about the date and what was done. Windrow, *Foreign Legion*, p. 73.
141 en.wikipedia.org/wiki/Rose_madder.
142 Tuchman, *Guns of August*, p. 38.
143 Brogan, *France/Republic*, p. 447, footnote 3.
144 Mirouze, *French Army*, p. 91.
145 Windrow, *Foreign Legion*, p. 72.
146 Ibid., p. 69.
147 Ibid., p. 108.
148 Ibid., p. 75.
149 Ibid., p. 53.
150 Ibid., p. 69.
151 Ibid., p. 75.
152 Ibid., p. 73.
153 Ibid.
154 Ibid., p. 72.
155 Thorburn, *French Army*, pp. 48–9.
156 Mirouze, *French Army*, p. 160. They would also avoid the use of the word red. That was for the infantry. Instead the words *bleu cerise*, cherry blue, were used. Sumner, *French Army*, p. 35.
157 Mirouze, *French Army*, p. 166.
158 In general, see Delperier, 'Chasseurs Alpins', pp. 14–20.
159 Melegari, *Greatest Regiments*, p. 106.
160 Mirouze, *French Army*, p. 177.
161 Ibid.
162 Ibid., p. 179.
163 Ibid., p. 247.
164 Greenhalgh, *French/World War*, pp. 75, 77.
165 Ibid., p. 75.
166 Material for this write-up came from www.alpins.fr, which is maintained by Cedric Demory, and from Louis Delperier, 'Des Régiments d'Infanterie Alpine'; see also Delperier, 'L'Infanterie Alpine'.
167 Cedric Demory, 2 April 2012; Mirouze, *French Army*, p. 216.
168 General Staff, *Handbook/French*, p. 106; Clayton, *France*, pp. 94–7. The units sent to France in 1914 were formed into régiments de marche, and in August 1914 formed French Infantry Divisions 37 and 38. *Armées Françaises*, 10-2, pp. 298–9, 306–7.
169 Clayton, *France*, p. 216.
170 Ibid., p. 217.
171 Ibid.
172 Vauvillier, *Chass Afrique*, p. 10.
173 In 1914, Infantry Regiment Count Friedrich I of Hesse-Cassel (1st Electorate of Hesse). However, Howard, *War*, states on p. 216, footnote 2, that the 81st was not at the battle, and it might have been the 2nd Electorate of Hesse Infantry Regiment 82 or the Infantry Regiment von Wittich (3rd Electorate of Hesse) 83.
174 Clayton, *France*, p. 218.
175 Hesse-Cassel is the state that used to supply Britain with a great many of its mercenary soldiers. Whole regiments were hired from the ruler of the state. See §VI-9-c for more details.
176 Thorburn, *French Army*, p. 79.
177 Vauvillier, *Chass Afrique*, p. 23.
178 Sumner, *French Army*, p. 44. See Vauvillier, *Chass Afrique*, p. 27 photo.
179 Vauvillier, *Chass Afrique*, pp. 22–3.
180 Sumner, *French Army*, p. 44.

181 Vauvillier, *Chass Afrique*, p. 23.
182 Ibid.; Mirouze, *French Army*, p. 380.
183 See, for example, the photo in Vauvillier, *Chass Afrique*, p. 27.
184 Ibid., p. 22; Thorburn, *French Army*, p. 79.
185 Vauvillier, *Chass Afrique*, pp. 22 and 23.
186 Delperier, 'Cavalerie', pp. 28 and 30.
187 Reddick, *Horses*, p. 60; Whyte, *British Turf*, vol. I, p. 64. Whyte notes that some believe that the Godolphin Barb was really an Arabian.
188 Andolenko, *Historiques Cavalerie*, pp. 138–40.
189 Clayton, *France*, p. 272.
190 Porch, *Conquest/Morocco*, pp. 71–2.
191 Clayton, *France*, pp. 272–3.
192 Conrad, *1914 Army*, p. 33.
193 Ibid.
194 The Battle of Isly was fought near the Algerian–Moroccan border in 1844 between the French Armée d'Afrique and an army under the command of the emir of Morocco. The numbers involved were large for colonial fighting: about 8,000 on the side of the French, and maybe as many as 45,000 on the Algerian side. The battle is said to have been fought in a temperature of 60 degrees Celsius (140 degrees Fahrenheit). It was a victory for the French. See Perrett, *Battle Book*, p. 143.
195 Clayton, *France*, pp. 66 and 273.
196 Noulens, *Spahis*, p. 37.
197 Ibid., p. 52.
198 Ibid., p. 37.
199 Robert, *Uniformes/Afrique*, p. 45.
200 Mirouze, *French Army*, p. 393.
201 Noulens, *Spahis*, p. 43.
202 Ibid., p. 53.
203 Robert, *Uniformes/Afrique*, p. 45. The tombeau colours used prior to 1885 were set in 1858. See Noulens, *Spahis*, p. 37.
204 Noulens, *Spahis*, p. 52.
205 Ibid., p. 51.
206 Ibid., p. 35.
207 Ibid., p. 52.
208 Mirouze, *French Army*, p. 399.
209 Ibid., p. 390.
210 Girard, *Cavaliers/Soleil*, pp. 42–3.
211 Clayton, *France*, p. 211.
212 Ibid., p. 213.
213 Martel, 'Zouaves', p. 33.
214 Clayton, *France*, p. 199.
215 Mirouze, *French Army*, pp. 188–9.
216 Clayton, *France*, p. 200.
217 Norman, 'War', p. 6; Martel, 'Zouaves', p. 54.
218 Mirouze, *French Army*, pp. 193–4.
219 Clayton, *France*, p. 200.
220 Mirouze, *French Army*, p. 196.
221 Fisher, *Book/World*, p. 631.
222 Bonarjee, *Fighting Races*, p. 163.
223 Clayton, *France*, p. 245.
224 It is noteworthy that before 1914 the Armée d'Afrique and the Senegalese, like the Indian army, did not have anything heavier than pack artillery.
225 Clayton, *France*, pp. 246–7.
226 Andolenko, *Historiques Infanterie*, pp. 267–71.
227 Norman, 'War', p. 7.
228 Clayton, *France*, p. 245.
229 Ibid.
230 Clayton, *France*, p. 262; four of the battalions had four companies, and one had two. A 6th battalion was being raised in July 1914. Conrad, *1914 Army*, p. 64.
231 Clayton, *France*, p. 263.
232 They earned a Croix de Guerre with five palms and one silver star. A few other Armée d'Afrique regiments won the Legion d'Honneur for their flags. Conrad, *1914 Army*, p. 64.
233 Clayton, *France*, p. 262.
234 Mirouze, *French Army*, p. 247.
235 Clayton, *France*, p. 311.
236 Ibid., p. 312.
237 Ibid.
238 Andolenko, *Historiques Infanterie*, pp. 325–54. It should be noted that the 9th, in spite of being created in 1890 in Indochina, managed to have battle honours for Alma, 1854, and Timbuktu 1890, in North Africa, on their flag. This is said to be because of their ties to the 2nd Marine Infantry's Régiment de Marche. Ibid., p. 352.
239 Clayton, *France*, pp. 312–13; Andolenko, *Historique Infanterie*, pp. 344–59.
240 Clayton, *France*, p. 310.
241 Robert, *Uniformes*, vol. 1, p. 54.
242 Mirouze, *French Army*, p. 232.
243 Ibid., pp. 233–7.
244 Robert, *Uniformes*, vol. 1, p. 55.
245 Ibid., p. 56.
246 Ibid.
247 Ibid.
248 Ibid.
249 Ibid.
250 Russia, which was larger, was considered a country, not an empire.
251 Balesi, *Adversaries*, pp. 2–6.
252 Ibid., p. 8.
253 Ibid., p. 13.
254 Ibid., p. 11.
255 Mirouze, *French Army*, p. 245.
256 Ibid., p. 247.
257 Robert, *Uniformes*, vol. 1, drawing of Senegalese in full dress after p. 59.
258 Funcken, *La Guerre 1914*, p. 35. Robert, *Uniformes/Afrique*, pp. 21, 48–50, plate after p. 48.
259 Conrad, *1914 Army*, pp. 61, 64.
260 'Indochina', *World Book*, I, vol. 10, p. 169.
261 Conrad, *1914 Army*, pp. 59–60.
262 Sumner, *French Army*, p. 45.
263 Porch, *Conquest/Sahara*, p. 211.
264 Ibid., p. 213.
265 Ibid., p. 212.
266 Ibid., p. 215.
267 Ibid., pp. 221–2.
268 Ibid., pp. 222–5.
269 Ibid., p. 244.
270 Clayton, *France*, p. 282.
271 Porch, *Conquest/Sahara*, pp. 57–8, 238.
272 Ibid., p. 238, but see p. 61.
273 Ibid., p. 282; Robert, *Uniformes/Afrique*, p. 21.
274 Porch, *Conquest/Sahara*, pp. 210, 244.
275 Ibid., p. 245.
276 Clayton, *France*, p. 282.
277 Porch, *Conquest/Sahara*, p. 7.
278 Clayton, *France*, p. 76.

279 Porch, *Conquest/Sahara*, p. 245.
280 Ibid., pp. 245–6.
281 Ibid., p. 246.
282 Ibid., p. 7.
283 Clayton, *France*, p. 282.
284 Porch, *Conquest/Sahara*, pp. 254–5.
285 Ibid., p. 255.
286 Ibid., p. 274.
287 Clayton, *France*, p. 282.
288 Porch, *Conquest/Sahara*, p. 253.
289 Ibid., p. 7.
290 Ibid., p. 65.
291 Ibid., p. 242.
292 Ibid., p. 256.
293 Ibid., p. 265–70.
294 Ibid., p. 258.
295 Ibid., pp. 271–2.
296 Ibid., pp. 260, 272.
297 Ibid., p. xi.
298 Ibid., p. 8.
299 Robert, *Uniformes/Afrique*, p. 21, plate after p. 18.
300 Ibid., plate after p. 48, p. 49.
301 Porch, *Conquest/Sahara*, p. 253.
302 See photographs in Verchin, *Burnous/Vent*.

§IV FRENCH EMPIRE: BIBLIOGRAPHY

Books, Articles, and Websites

alpins.fr	www.alpins.fr, maintained by Cedric Demory, accessed 24 June 2014.
Andolenko, *Historiques Cavalerie*	General Andolenko, *Recueil d'Historiques de l'Armée Blindée et de la Cavalerie* (Paris: Eurimprim, 1968).
Andolenko, *Historiques Infanterie*	General Andolenko, *Recueil d'Historiques de l'Infanterie Française* (Paris: Eurimprim, 1968).
Armées Françaises, 10-2	Porch Pompe, Etats-Major des l'Armées, Service Historique, *les Armées Françaises dans la Grande Guerre*, Part X, vol. 2, Ordre de Bataille des Divisions (Paris: Imprimerie Nationale, 1924).
Balesi, *Adversaries*	Charles John Balesi, *From Adversaries to Comrades-in-Arms: West Africans and the French Military, 1885–1918* (Waltham, MA: Crossroads Press, 1979).
Bonarjee, *Fighting Races*	Pitt D. Bonarjee, *A Handbook of the Fighting Races of India* (India: Asian Publication Services, 1975).
Bond, *Staff College*	Brian Bond, *The Victorian Army and the Staff College, 1854–1914* (Fakenham: Eyre Methuen Ltd, 1972).
Brogan, *France/Republic*	D.W. Brogan, *France Under the Republic: The Development of Modern France (1870–1939)* (New York: Harper & Brothers Publishers, 1940).
Clayton, *France*	Anthony Clayton, *France, Soldiers and Africa* (London: Brassey's Defence Publishers, 1988).
Conrad, *1914 Army*	Mark Conrad, *French Army Order of Battle, 1914* (privately printed, n.d.), a reprinting of the 1914 French Army List with annotations.
Delperier, 'Cavalerie'	Louis Delperier, 'La Cavalerie Legère 1900–1914', *Uniformes*, no. 72 (1983), pp. 8–28.
Delperier, 'Chasseurs Alpins'	Louis Delperier, 'Les Chasseurs Alpins 1890–1914', Uniformes, no. 73 (1983), pp. 14–20.
Delperier, *Cuirassiers*	Louis Delperier, et al., *Les Cuirassiers 1845–1918* (Paris: Argout Editions, 1981).
Delperier, 'L'Infanterie Alpine'	Louis Deperier, 'L'Infanterie Alpine 1896–1917', loose magazine article in author's collection; magazine uncertain, likely *Uniformes* (1983), pp. 13–18.
Delperier, 'Des Régiments d'Infanterie Alpine'	Louis Delperier, 'Des Régiments d'Infanterie Alpine', www.alpins.fr/infanterie_alpine.html, accessed 24 June 2014.
Detaille, *L'Armée Française*	Edouard Detaille, *L'Armée Française: An Illustrated History of the French Army, 1790–1885* (New York: Waxtel & Hasenauer, 1992).
Durant, *Age-Faith*	Will Durant, *The Age of Faith* (New York: Simon and Schuster, 1950).
Durant, *Age-Louis*	Will Durant, *The Age of Louis XIV* (New York: Simon and Schuster, 1963).
Elting, *Swords/Throne*	John R. Elting, *Swords Around a Throne: Napoleon's Grande Armée* (New York: Free Press, 1988).
en.wikipedia.org/wiki/The_Egyptian_Gazette	Wikipedia, 'The Egyptian Gazette', http://en.wikipedia.org/wiki/The_Egyptian_Gazette, accessed 26 March 2014.
en.wikipedia.org/wiki/Rose_madder	Wikipedia, 'Rose Madder,' http://en.wikipedia.org/wiki/Rose_madder, accessed 27 March 2017.
Fisher, *Book/World*	Richard Fisher, *Book of the World* (New York: J.H. Colton, 1849).
Funcken, *La Guerre 1914*	Liliane Funcken and Fred Funcken, *L'uniforme et les armes de soldats de la guerre, 1914–1918, vol. I, Infanterie, etc* (Tournai: Casterman, 1970).
General Staff, *Handbook/French*	British War Office, *Handbook of the French Army, 1914* (reprinted) (Nashville, TN: Battery Press, Inc., 1995).
Girard, *Cavaliers/Soleil*	Claude Girard, *Les Cavaliers du Soleil* (Ottignies: Editions Quorum, 1995).
Greenhalgh, *French/World War*	Elizabeth Greenhalgh, *The French Army and the First World War* (Cambridge: Cambridge University Press, 2014).
Head, *Napoleonic Lancer*	Michael Head, *French Napoleonic Lancer Regiments* (London: Almark Publishing, 1971).
Howard, *War*	Michael Howard, *The Franco-Prussian War: The German Invasion of France, 1870–1871* (New York: Macmillan, 1962).
Jerram, *Armies of the World*	Charles S. Jerram, *The Armies of the World* (London: Lawrence & Bullen, 1899).

Kannik, *Military Uniforms*	Preben Kannik, *Military Uniforms of the World in Color*, ed. William Carman (New York: Macmillan, 1968).
Lord, *Uniforms/Civil War*	Francis A. Lord and Arthur Wise, *Uniforms of the Civil War* (New York: A.S. Barnes and Co., 1970).
Martel, 'Zouaves'	Col. J.L. Martel, 'Les Zouaves', *Campaigns*, vol. 2, no. 8 (Jan/Feb 1977): pp. 32–5 and 54.
Martin, *Military Uniforms*	Paul Martin, *European Military Uniforms: A Short History* (London: Spring Books, 1967).
Melegari, *Greatest Regiments*	Vezio Melegari, *The World's Greatest Regiments*, trans. Ronald Strom (Milan: P.G. Putnam's Sons, 1968, 1969).
Mirouze, *French Army*	Laurent Mirouze and Stéphane Dekerle, *The French Army in the First World War*, vol. 1, *To Battle 1914* (Vienna: Verlag Militaria, 2007).
Mollo, *Uniforms*	Boris Mollo, *Uniforms of the Imperial Russian Army* (Poole: Blandford Press, 1979).
Neveux, *Normans*	François Neveux, in collaboration with Claire Ruelle, *A Brief History of the Normans: The Conquest that Changed the Face of Europe*, trans. Howard Curtis (London: Constable and Robinson, 2008).
Norman, 'War'	C.A. Norman, 'The French Army in Franco-Prussian War, 1870–71, Part II', *Tradition*, no. 64 (n.d.), pp. 6–12.
Noulens, *Spahis*	Raymond Noulens, *Les Spahis Cavaleries de l'Armée d'Afrique* (Paris: Musée de l'Armée, 1997).
Perrett, *Battle Book*	Bryan Perrett, *The Battle Book: Crucial Conflicts in History from 1469 B.C. to the Present* (London: Arms and Armour Press, 1992).
Porch, *Conquest/Morocco*	Douglas Porch, *The Conquest of Morocco* (New York: Alfred A. Knopf, 1982).
Porch, *Conquest/Sahara*	Douglas Porch, *The Conquest of the Sahara* (New York: Fromm International, 1986).
Ralston, *Army/Republic*	David Ralston, *The Army of the Republic* (Cambridge, MA: MIT Press, 1967).
Reddick, *Horses*	Kate Reddick, *Horses* (New York: Bantam Books, 1976).
Robert, *Uniformes*	Andre Galot and Claude Robert, *Les Uniformes de l'Armée Française ... (de 1872 à 1914)* (Paris: Societé des Collection de Figurines Historiques, 1967).
Robert, *Uniformes/Afrique*	Andre Galot and Claude Robert, *Les Uniformes de l'Armée Française ... Armée d'Afrique* (Floirac: Association pour l'Etude de l'Histoire Militaire, privately published, n.d.).
Scott, *Response/Revolution*	Samuel Scott, *The Response of the Royal Army to the French Revolution* (Oxford: Clarendon Press, 1978).
Scott, *Yorktown/Valmy*	Samuel Scott, *From Yorktown to Valmy* (Niwot, CO: University Press of Colorado, 1998).
Smith, *Napoleon's Regiments*	Digby Smith, *Napoleon's Regiments: Battle Histories of the Regiments of the French Army, 1792–1815* (London: Greenhill Books, 2000).
Steffen, *Horse Soldiers*	Randy Steffen, *The Horse Soldier, 1776–1943* (Norman, OK: University of Oklahoma Press, 1978).
Sumner, *French Army*	Ian Sumner, *The French Army 1914–18* (London: Osprey, 1995)
Thorburn, *French Army*	W.A. Thorburn, *French Army Regiments and Uniforms: From the Revolution to 1870* (London: Arms and Armour Press, 1969).
Tuchman, *Guns of August*	Barbara W. Tuchman, *The Guns of August* (New York: Bonanza Books, 1982).
Vauvillier, *Chass Afrique*	François Vauvillier, *Les Chasseurs d'Afrique* (Paris: Histoire & Collections, 1999).
Verchin, *Burnous/Vent*	Jean Verchin, *Burnous au Vent, et Saber au Clair* (Bobigny: Sogico, 1983).
Whyte, *British Turf*, vol. I	James Whyte, *History of the British Turf, from the Earliest Period to the Present Day*, vol. 1 (London: Henry Colburn, 1840).
Windrow, *Foreign Legion*	Martin Windrow, *Uniforms of the French Foreign Legion 1831–1981* (Poole: Blandford Books, 1981).
Windrow, *Foreign Legionnaire*	Martin Windrow, *French Foreign Legionnaire, 1890–1914* (Oxford: Osprey, 2011).
World Book	*The World Book Encyclopedia* (USA: World Book, 1983).
World in Figures	*Pocket World in Figures*, 2013 edn (London: Profile Books in association with *The Economist*, 2013).

§V

RUSSIAN EMPIRE

§V-1 COUNTRY BACKGROUND

By 1914 Russia had grown from an insignificant fort and trading post to the second largest empire on earth. It first started gathering power through collecting taxes for the Mongols and then spent centuries absorbing the smaller states around it.

The government style was autocratic. Examples abound where the orders or even perceived orders of the czar were followed blindly and without thinking. The proper functioning of Czarist Russia was hampered by incompetence, mismanagement, theft, and drunkenness.

Political and social unrest were constants in the pre-World War I period, as they were in all the Great Powers. The poor conditions endured by Russian factory labourers appeared very much like those in the other Great Powers during this period. Although strikes proved very common in Russia up to World War I, the individuals who participated in them – as in the other powers – were the skilled and relatively well-paid workers.[1]

The Revolution of 1905 is now considered a harbinger of the Revolution of 1917, but before 1914, the situation was viewed differently. The 1911 *Encyclopedia Britannica* compared the 1905 Revolution to the 1789 French Revolution and concluded that Russia would not have a general revolution that would overthrow the government because of the reforms made and because Russia did not have a middle class.[2]

The Revolution of 1905 ultimately resulted in the creation of the Duma. Although 75 per cent of the population were peasants, the Duma was aligned in viewpoint with the czar and his government. It relieved revolutionary pressure without changing things.

The Russian economy prior to 1914 grew at a stellar pace. The Russian economy started to take off during the 1890s, growing by some 8 per cent per year on average during the decade. The railway network grew by 40 per cent between 1881 and 1894, albeit from a small base, and doubled again between 1895 and 1905.[3]

Then, around 1890, Russia, together with most of Europe, experienced depression. This lasted through the Russo-Japanese War of 1904–5 and until the first Duma was seated in 1906. After that, the country grew at a rate of 6 per cent per year until 1914.[4] Much of this growth was driven by foreign investment, which grew nine-fold between 1880 and 1900.[5] Even at this increased rate, Russia's productive strength paled in comparison to that of Germany. For example, between 1900 and 1913, Russia's steel production grew by 218 per cent while Germany's expanded by 279 per cent.[6]

Defence spending accounted for 25 to 33 per cent of the total Russian budget for the years 1907 to 1913. The 6 per cent per year overall increase in the military budget was double the rate of increase of the other Great Powers.[7]

In summary, Russia was growing fast and building up its army and navy after the losses of the Russo-Japanese War. Germany may have been growing faster economically in some areas, but Russia's growth was very impressive. Had it not been for the dislocations and hardships of World War I, there is a good chance that Russia would not have suffered a general revolution and the bloodbaths that followed.

REGIMENTAL NAMES

It might be appropriate, at this point, to mention the logic behind the Russian regimental names and certain other terms used in preparing this work. In translating Russian regimental names, I have generally followed the system used in the book *Badges of Imperial Russia* as translated by Robert Werlich. The only times I have not done so is with guard regiments, whose names under other systems are too well-known to vary.

NOTE ON UNITS OF MEASUREMENT

By this period, the metric system was well established in France, and sources give measurements in millimetres and centimetres. These do not convert into simple fractions of inches, so I quote the imperial measurement as decimal numbers.

§V-2 THE ARMY

§V-2-1   *Russian Regiment Names in 1914 and Dates Formed*
§V-2-2   *Russian Regiments with Distinction Banners*
§V-2-3   *Physical Characteristics*
§V-2-4   *Marching*

§V-2-1 RUSSIAN REGIMENT NAMES IN 1914 AND DATES FORMED[8]

Imperial Guard Regiments

Imperial Guard Infantry Regiments

Regiment	Date Formed
Preobrazhensky Regiment of the Imperial Guard	1683
Semenovsky Regiment of the Imperial Guard	1683
Izmailovsky Regiment of the Imperial Guard	1730
Yegersky Regiment of the Imperial Guard	1796
Moscow Regiment of the Imperial Guard	1811
Grenadier Regiment of the Imperial Guard	1756
Paul Regiment of the Imperial Guard	1790
Finland Regiment of the Imperial Guard	1806
Lithuanian Regiment of the Imperial Guard	1811
Kexholm Regiment of His Imperial Majesty, Emperor of Austria and King of Hungary Imperial Guard	1710
St Petersburg Regiment of the King of Prussia, Frederick-William III Imperial Guard	1790
Volynsky Regiment of the Imperial Guard	1817
His Imperial Majesty's Combined Guard Infantry Regiment	1881

Imperial Guard Rifle Regiments

Regiment	Date Formed
1st His Majesty's Imperial Guard Rifle Regiment	1856
2nd Tsarskoe-Selo Imperial Guard Rifle Regiment	1856
3rd His Majesty's Rifle Regiment of the Imperial Guard	1799
4th Imperial Guard Rifle Regiment of the Imperial Family	1854

Imperial Guard Cavalry Regiments

Regiment	Date Formed
Chevalier Guard Regiment of Empress Maria Feodorovna	1799
Cheval (Horse) Guards Regiment of the Imperial Guard	1721
Imperial Guard Cuirassiers Regiment of His Majesty	1702
Imperial Guard Cuirassiers Regiment of the Empress Maria Feodorovna	1704
Imperial Guard Cossack Regiment of His Majesty	1775
Imperial Guard Cossack Ataman Regiment of the Czarevich	1775
Combined Cossack Regiment of the Imperial Guard	1798 (Sotnia of Ural), 1906 (Combined Regiment)
Horse Grenadier Regiment of the Imperial Guard	1809, claimed 1651
Imperial Guard Lancer Regiment of Her Majesty	claimed 1651
Dragoon Regiment of the Imperial Guard	1814
Imperial Guard Hussar Regiment of His Majesty	1775
Imperial Guard Lancer Regiment of His Majesty	claimed 1651
Grodno Hussar Regiment of the Imperial Guard	1824
His Imperial Majesty's Personal Escort Convoy	1811

Infantry

Infantry Grenadiers

Regiment	Date Formed
1st Ekaterinoslav Imperial Grenadier Regiment of Emperor Alexander II	1756
2nd Rostov Grenadier Regiment of Grand Duke Michael Alexandrovich	1700
3rd Pernov Regiment of King Frederick William IV of Prussia	1710
4th Nesvizh Grenadier Regiment of Field Marshal Prince Barclay de Tolly	1797
5th Kiev Grenadier Regiment of the Czarevich	1700
6th Tavrida Grenadier Regiment	1756
7th Samoguitia Grenadier Regiment of Adjutant General Count Totleben	1797
8th Moscow Grenadiers of the Grand Duke of Mecklenburg Frederick II	1790
9th Siberian Grenadier Regiment of Grand Duke Nicholas Nicolaevich	1700
10th Little Russia Grenadier Regiment of Field Marshal Count Rumyantsev-Zadunaisky	1756
11th Phanagoria Grenadier Regiment of Generalissimo Prince Suvorov	1790
12th Astrakhan Regiment of Emperor Alexander III	1700
13th Erivan Imperial Grenadier Regiment of Czar Michael Fedorovich	1642
14th Georgian Grenadier Regiment of the Czarevich	1700
15th Tiflis Grenadier Regiment	1726
16th Mingrelia Regiment of Grand Duke Dimitri Constantinovich	1763

Regular Infantry Regiments

Regiment	Date Formed
1st Neva Infantry Regiment of His Highness the King of Greece	1706
2nd Sofia Infantry Regiment of Emperor Alexander III	1811
3rd Narva Infantry Regiment of Field Marshal Prince Michael Golitsyn	1703
4th Koporia Infantry Regiment of His Majesty the King of Saxony	1803
5th Kaluga Infantry Regiment	1805
6th Libau Infantry Regiment of Prince Frederick Leopold of Prussia	1806
7th Revel Infantry Regiment of General Tuchkov	1769
8th Estland (Estonia) Infantry Regiment	1711
9th Ingria Infantry Regiment of Emperor Peter I	1703
10th New Ingria Infantry Regiment	1790
11th Pskov Infantry Regiment of Field Marshal Prince Kutuzov Smolensky	1700
12th Velikie-Luki Infantry Regiment	1711
13th Belozersk Infantry Regiment of Field Marshal Prince Wolkonsky	1708
14th Olonets Infantry Regiment of Peter I, King of Serbia	1798
15th Schlusselburg Infantry Regiment of Field Marshal Prince Anikita Repnin	1700
16th Ladoga Infantry Regiment	1708
17th Archangelgorod Infantry Regiment of Grand Duke Vladimir Alexandrovich	1700
18th Vologda Infantry Regiment of the King of Rumania	1803
19th Kostroma Infantry Regiment	1700
20th Galich Infantry Regiment	1811
21st Murmom Infantry Regiment	1708
22nd Nizhi-Novgorod Infantry Regiment	1700
23rd Nizovsky Infantry Regiment of Field Marshal Count Saltykov	1726
24th Simbirsk Infantry Regiment of General Neverovsky	1811
25th Smolensk Infantry Regiment of General Rayevsky	1700
26th Mogilev Infantry Regiment	1805
27th Vitebsk Infantry Regiment	1703
28th Polotsk Infantry Regiment	1769
29th Chernigov Infantry Regiment of Field Marshal Count Dibich-Zabalkansky	1700
30th Poltava Infantry Regiment	1798
31st Alexeiev Infantry Regiment	1731
32nd Kremenchug Infantry Regiment	1806
33rd Velets Infantry Regiment	1763
34th Sevsk Infantry Regiment of General Count Kamensky	1763
35th Bryansk Infantry Regiment of Adjutant General Prince Gorchakov	1809
36th Orel Infantry Regiment of Field Marshal the Duke of Warsaw, Count Paskevich-Erivansky	1711

Regiment	Year
37th Yekaterinburg Infantry Regiment	1796
38th Tobolsk Infantry Regiment of General Count Miloradovich	1703
39th Tomsk Infantry Regiment	1796
40th Kolyvan Infantry Regiment	1798
41st Selenga Infantry Regiment	1796
42nd Yakutsk Infantry Regiment	1806
43rd Okhotsk Infantry Regiment	1806
44th Kamchatka Infantry Regiment	1806
45th Azov Infantry Regiment of Grand Duke Boris Vladimirovich	1700
46th Dnieper Infantry Regiment	1769
47th Ukrainian Infantry Regiment	1798
48th Odessa Infantry Regiment of Emperor Alexander I	1811
49th Brest Infantry Regiment of Grand Duke Michael Michaelovich	1806
50th Belostok Infantry Regiment	1807
51st Lithuanian Infantry Regiment of the Czarevich	1809
52nd Vilna Infantry Regiment of Grand Duke Cyril Vladimirovich	1811
53rd Volynsky Infantry Regiment of Grand Duke Nicholas Nikolaevich	1803
54th Minsk Infantry Regiment of His Majesty the King of Bulgaria	1806
55th Podolsk Infantry Regiment	1798
56th Zhitomir Infantry Regiment of Grand Duke Nicholas Nikolaevich	1811
57th Modlinsky Infantry Regiment	1831
58th Praga Infantry Regiment	1831
59th Lublin Infantry Regiment	1831
60th Zamosc Infantry Regiment	1831
61st Vladimir Infantry Regiment	1700
62nd Suzdal Infantry Regiment of Generalissimo Prince Suvorob	1700
63rd Uglich Regiment of Field Marshal Apraksin	1708
64th Kazan Infantry Regiment	1700
65th Moscow Infantry Regiment of His Majesty	1700
66th Butyrki Infantry Regiment of General Dokhturov	1796
67th Tarutino Infantry Regiment of the Grand Duke of Oldenburg	1796
68th Borodino Infantry Regiment of Emperor Alexander III	1796
69th Ryazan Infantry Regiment of Field Marshal Prince Golitsyn	1703
70th Ryazhsk Infantry Regiment	1763
71st Belev Infantry Regiment	1763
72nd Tula Infantry Regiment	1769
73rd Crimean Infantry Regiment	1856
74th Stavropol Infantry Regiment	1845
75th Sevastopol Infantry Regiment	1856
76th Kuban Infantry Regiment	1845
77th Tenga Infantry Regiment	1700
78th Navaga Infantry Regiment of General Kotlyarevsky	1777
79th Kura Infantry Regiment of Field Marshal Prince Vorontsov, now of Grand Duke Paul Alexandrovich	1802
80th Kabarda Infantry Regiment of Field Marshal Prince Baryatinsky	1726
81st Apsheron Infantry Regiment of Catherine II, now of Grand Duke George Mikhaylovich	1700
82nd Dagestan Infantry Regiment	1845
83rd Samur Infantry Regiment	1845
84th Shirvan Infantry Regiment	1724
85th Vyborg Infantry Regiment of His Majesty William II, Emperor of Germany, and King of Prussia	1700
86th Wilmanstrand Infantry Regiment	1806
87th Nyslot Infantry Regiment	1863
88th Petrovsky Infantry Regiment	1863
89th White Sea Infantry Regiment of the Czarevich	1803
90th Onega Infantry Regiment	1803
91st Dvinsk Infantry Regiment	1805
92nd Pechora Infantry Regiment	1803
93rd Irkutsk Infantry Regiment of Grand Duke Michael Alexandrovich	1797
94th Yenisei Infantry Regiment	1813
95th Krasnoyarsk Infantry Regiment	1797
96th Omsk Infantry Regiment	1797
97th Laflyand Infantry Regiment of Field Marshal Count Sheremetev	1700
98th Yuriev Infantry Regiment	1763
99th Ivangorod Infantry Regiment	1805
100th Ostrov Infantry Regiment	1806
101st Perm Infantry Regiment	1797
102nd Vyatka Infantry Regiment	1803
103rd Petrozavodsk Infantry Regiment	1803

Regiment	Year
104th Ustyug Infantry Regiment of General Prince Bagration	1797
105th Orenburg Infantry Regiment	1811
106th Ufa Infantry Regiment	1811
107th Troitsk Infantry Regiment	1797
108th Saratov Infantry Regiment	1797
109th Volga Infantry Regiment	1797
110th Kama Infantry Regiment of Adjutant General Count Toll	1813
111th Don Infantry Regiment	1797
112th Ural Infantry Regiment	1797
113th Staraya-Russa Infantry Regiment	1796
114th Novy-Torzhok Infantry Regiment	1763
115th Vyazma Infantry Regiment of General Nesvetaev	1798
116th Maloyaroslavets Infantry Regiment	1797
117th Yaroslavl Infantry Regiment	1763
118th Shuja Infantry Regiment	1711
119th Kilomna Infantry Regiment	1797
120th Serpukhov Infantry Regiment	1813
121st Penza Infantry Regiment of Field Marshal Count Milyutin	1813
122nd Tambov Infantry Regiment	1797
123rd Kozlov Infantry Regiment	1797
124th Voronezh Infantry Regiment	1775
125th Kursk Infantry Regiment	1806
126th Rylsk Infantry Regiment	1807
127th Putivl Infantry Regiment	1809
128th Starooskolsky Infantry Regiment	1831
129th Bessarabian Infantry Regiment of Grand Duke Michael Alexandrovich	1806
130th Kherson Infantry Regiment of Grand Duke Andrew Vladimirovich	1811
131st Tiraspol Infantry Regiment	1700
132nd Bendery Infantry Regiment	1811
133rd Simferopol Infantry Regiment	1831
134th Feodosia Infantry Regiment	1831
135th Kerch-Yenikale Infantry Regiment	1798
136th Taganrog Infantry Regiment	1831
137th Nezhin Infantry Regiment of Grand Duchess Maria Pavolvna	1796
138th Bolkhov Infantry Regiment	1703
139th Morshansk Infantry Regiment	1700
140th Zaraysk Infantry Regiment	1798
141st Mozhaysk Infantry Regiment	1796
142nd Zvenigorod Infantry Regiment	1806
143rd Dorogobuzh Infantry Regiment	1806
144th Kashira Infantry Regiment	1806
145th Novocherkassk Infantry Regiment of Emperor Alexander III	1796
146th Tsaritsyn Infantry Regiment	1769
147th Samara Infantry Regiment	1798
148th Caspian Infantry Regiment of Grand Duchess Anastasia Nikolaevna	1811
149th Black Sea Infantry Regiment	1863
150th Taman Infantry Regiment	1863
151st Pyatigorsk Infantry Regiment	1863
152nd Vladikavkaz Infantry Regiment	1863
153rd Baku Infantry Regiment	1863
154th Derbent Infantry Regiment	1863
155th Kuba Infantry Regiment	1863
156th Elizabetpol Infantry Regiment	1863
157th Imeretinsky Infantry Regiment	1863
158th Kutais Infantry Regiment	1863
159th Guriya Infantry Regiment	1863
160th Abkhaz Infantry Regiment	1863
161st Alexandropol Infantry Regiment	1874
162nd Akhaltsykhe Infantry Regiment	1874
163rd Lenkoran-Nasheburg Infantry Regiment	1874
164th Zakataly Infantry Regiment	1874
165th Lutsk Infantry Regiment	1811
166th Rovno Infantry Regiment	1877
167th Ostrog Infantry Regiment	1877
168th Mirgorod Infantry Regiment	1877
169th Novi-Troki Infantry Regiment	1811
170th Molodechno Infantry Regiment	1877
171st Kobrin Infantry Regiment	1811
172nd Lida Infantry Regiment	1811
173rd Kamenets Infantry Regiment	1811
174th Romny Infantry Regiment	1811
175th Baturin Infantry Regiment	1877
176th Perevolochna Infantry Regiment	1877
177th Izborsky Infantry Regiment	1877
178th Venden Infantry Regiment	1877
179th Ust-Dvinsk Infantry Regiment	1811
180th Vindau Infantry Regiment	1811
181st Ostrolenka Infantry Regiment	1720
182nd Grokhov Infantry Regiment	1811
183rd Pultusk Infantry Regiment	1811
184th Warsaw Infantry Regiment	1811
185th Bashkadyklar Infantry Regiment	1811
186th Aslanduz Infantry Regiment	1763
187th Avaria Infantry Regiment	1805
188th Kars Infantry Regiment	1796
189th Izmail Infantry Regiment	1811

Regiment	Date
190th Ochakov Infantry Regiment	1804
191st Larga-Kagul Infantry Regiment	1811
192nd Rymnik Infantry Regiment	1811
193rd Sviyaga Infantry Regiment	1711
194th Troitske-Sergujevsky Infantry Regiment	1796
195th Oravais Infantry Regiment	1811
196th Insar Infantry Regiment	1811
197th Lessnaya Infantry Regiment	1803
198th Alexander Nevsky Infantry Regiment	1720
199th Kronshtadt Infantry Regiment	1806
200th Kronshlot Infantry Regiment	1803
201st Poti Infantry Regiment	1889
202nd Gori Infantry Regiment	1887
203rd Sukhum Infantry Regiment	1805
204th Ardagan Mikhaylov Infantry Regiment	1806
205th Shemakha Infantry Regiment	1889
206th Salyany Infantry Regiment of the Czarevich	1805
207th Novoboayazet Infantry Regiment	1887
208th Lori Infantry Regiment	1887

European Rifles

Regiment	Date Formed
1st–12th Rifle Regiments – formed 1835, 1834, 1826, 1839, 1834, 1835, 1809, 1808, 1839, 1826, 1841, and 1854, sequentially	
13th Rifle Regiment of General-Field Marshal Grand Duke Nicholas Nikolaevich	1843
14th Rifle Regiment of General-Field Marshal Gurko	1856
15th Rifle Regiment of His Majesty King Nicholas I of Montenegro	1856
16th Rifle Regiment of Emperor Alexander II	1845
17th–20th Rifle Regiments – formed 1856, 1841, 1864, and 1864, sequentially	

Caucasus Rifles

Regiment	Date Formed
1st Caucasus Rifle Regiment of Grand Duke Michael Nikolaevich	1837
2nd–4th Caucasus Rifle Regiments: all formed	1856
5th Caucasus Rifle Regiment of Grand Duke George Mikhailovich	1831
6th–8th Caucasus Rifle Regiments – formed 1888, 1851, and 1888, sequentially	

Siberian Rifles

Regiment	Date Formed
1st Siberian Rifle Regiment of His Majesty	1883
2nd–10th Siberian Rifle Regiments – formed 1823, 1720, 1889, 1849, 1889, 1883, 1883, 1880, and 1849, sequentially	
11th Siberian Rifle Regiment of Grand Duchess Maria Feodorovna	1898
12th Siberian Rifle Regiment of the Czarevich	1898
13th–20th Siberian Rifle Regiments – formed 1890, 1886, 1892, 1854, 1720, 1880, 1882, and 1893, sequentially	
21st Siberian Rifle Regiment of Grand Duchess Alexandra Feodorovna	1865
22nd–24th Siberian Rifle Regiments – formed 1882, 1890, and 1900, sequentially	
25th Siberian Rifle Regiment of Lieutenant General Kondratenko	1900
26th–44th Rifle Regiments – formed 1903, 1903, 1903, 1771, 1899, 1903, 1903, 1903, 1903, 1903, 1886, 1896, 1900, 1900, 1865, 1711, 1711, and 1711, sequentially	

Finnish Rifles

1st–12th Finland Rifle Regiments – formed 1811, 1877, 1855, 1877, 1811, 1877, 1855, 1877, 1811, 1845, 1811 and 1806, sequentially

Turkestan Rifles

1st–22nd Turkestan Rifle Regiments – formed 1855, 1771, 1709, 1869, 1873, 1771, 1711, 1771, 1711, 1882, 1771, 1701, 1720, 1869, 1885, 1893, 1830, 1801, 1893, 1798, 1771, and 1809, sequentially

Cavalry

Dragoon Regiments

Regiment	Date Formed
1st Moscow Life Dragoon Regiment of Emperor Peter the Great	1700
2nd Pskov Life Dragoon Regiment of Empress Maria Feodorovna	1668
3rd New Russia Dragoon Regiment of Grand Duchess Helen Vladimirovna	1803
4th New Russia-Ekaterinoslav Regiment of Field Marshal Prince Potemkin	1708
5th Kargopol Dragoon Regiment	1707

Regiment	Date Formed
6th Glukhov Dragoon Regiment of Empress Catherine II	1668
7th Kinburn Dragoon Regiment	1798
8th Astrakhan Dragoon Regiment of Field Marshal Grand Duke Nicholas Nikolaevich	1811
9th Kazan Dragoon Regiment of Grand Duchess Maria Nikolaevna	1701
10th Novgorod Dragoon Regiment of the King of Württemberg	1701
11th Riga Dragoon Regiment	1709
12th Starodub Dragoon Regiment	1782
13th Military (St George) Order Dragoon Regiment of Field Marshal Count Minikh	1709
14th Little Russian Dragoon Regiment of the Crown Prince of Germany, and Prussia	1785
15th Pereyaslav Dragoon Regiment of Emperor Alexander III	1798
16th Tver Dragoon Regiment of the Czarevich	1798
17th Nizhni-Novgorod Dragoon Regiment of His Majesty	1701
18th Seversk Dragoon Regiment	1701
19th Archangelgorod Dragoon Regiment	1895
20th Finland Dragoon Regiment	1901
Premorsky Dragoon Regiment	1869

Lancer Regiments

Regiment	Date Formed
1st St Petersburg Lancer Regiment of Field Marshal Prince Menshikov	1705
2nd Kurland Lancer Regiment of Emperor Alexander II	1803
3rd Smolensk Lancer Regiment of Emperor Alexander III	1708
4th Kharkov Lancer Regiment	1651
5th Lithuanian Lancer Regiment of King Victor Emmanuel III of Italy	1803
6th Volynsky Lancer Regiment	1807
7th Olviopol Lancer Regiment of Alfonso XIII, King of Spain	1812
8th Voznesensk Lancer Regiment of Grand Duchess Tatiana Nikolaevna	1812
9th Bug Lancer Regiment	1803
10th Odessa Lancer Regiment of the Grand Duke of Nassau and Luxemburg	1812
11th Chuguev Lancer Regiment of Empress Maria Feodorovna	1749
12th Belgorod Lancer Regiment of the Emperor of Austria and King of Hungary Franz-Joseph I	1701
13th Vladimir Lancer Regiment	1701
14th Yamburg Lancer Regiment of Grand Duchess Maria Alexandrovna	1806
15th Tatar Lancer Regiment	1891
16th New Archangel Lancer Regiment	1897
17th New Mirgorod Lancer Regiment	1897

Hussar Regiments

Regiment	Date Formed
1st Sumy Hussar Regiment of General Seslavin	1651
2nd Pavlograd Hussar Regiment of Emperor Alexander III	1764
3rd Elizabetgrad Hussar Regiment of Grand Duchess Olga Nikolaevna	1764
4th Mariupol Hussar Regiment of Empress Elizabeth Petrovna	1748
5th Alexandria Hussar Regiment of Her Imperial Majesty Alexandra Feodorovna	1776
6th Klyastitsi Hussar Regiment of Grand Duke Ernst-Ludwig of Hesse	1806
7th White Russian Hussar Regiment of Emperor Alexander I	1803
8th Lubny Hussar Regiment	1807
9th Kiev Hussar Regiment	1668
10th Ingermanland Hussar Regiment of the Grand Duke of Saxony-Weimar	1704
11th Izyum Hussar Regiment of Prince Henry of Prussia	1651
12th Akhtyrka Hussar Regiment of Grand Duchess Olga Alexandrovna	1651
13th Narva Hussar Regiment of the Emperor of Germany and King of Prussia William II	1705
14th Mitau Hussar Regiment	1805
15th Ukrainian Hussars of Grand Duke Nicholas Nikolaevich	1891
16th Irkutsk Hussars of Grand Duke Nicholas Nikolaevich	1895
17th Chernigov Hussars of Grand Duke Nicholas Nikolaevich	1668
18th Hezhin Hussar Regiment	1783

Other Mounted Troops

Regiment	Date Formed
Crimean (Tartar) Horse Regiment	1784
Dagestan Regiment	1851

Turkman Demi-Regiment 1890
Ossetian Demi-Regiment 1890

Don Cossack Host
All formed 1570
1st Don Cossack Regiment of Generalissimo Prince Suvorov
2nd Don Cossack Regiment of General Sysoev
3rd Don Cossack Regiment of Yermak Timofeev
4th Don Cossack Regiment of Graf Platov
5th Don Cossack Regiment of Host Ataman Vlasov
6th Don Cossack Regiment of General Krasnoshehekov
7th Don Cossack Regiment of General Denisov
8th Don Cossack Regiment of General Ilovaiskii XII
9th Don Cossack Regiment of General-Adjuntant Graf Orlov-Denisov
10th Don Cossack Regiment of General Lukovikin
11th Don Cossack Regiment of General of Cavalry Graf Denisov
12th Don Cossack Regiment of General Field Marshall Prince Potemkin of Taurica
13th Don Cossack Regiment of General Field Marshall Prince Kutuzov of Smolensk
14th Don Cossack Regiment of Host Ataman Yefremov
15th Don Cossack Regiment General Krasnov I
16th Don Cossack Regiment of General Grekov VIII
17th Don Cossack Regiment of General Baklanov
1st–6th Separate Don Cossack Sotnias

Caucasian Cossack Host
Viceroy of the Caucasus's Escort Sotnia

Kuban Cossack Host
Kuban Cossack Half-Regiment 1830
1st Yekaterinodar Regiment of Koshevoi Ataman Chepega 1788
1st Kuban Regiment 1788
1st Uman Regiment of Brigadier Golovatov 1788
1st Black Sea Regiment unknown
1st Poltava Regiment of Koshevoi Ataman Sidor Belyi 1788
1st Zaporozhian Regiment of Empress Catherine the Great 1788
1st Laba Regiment of General Zass 1842
1st Caucasian Regiment of Viceroy of Catherine, General Field Marshall Prince Potemkin 1788
1st Line Regiment of General Velyaminov 1858
1st Taman Regiment of General Bezkrovnyi 1788
1st Khoper Regiment of Grand Duchess Anastasia Mikhailovna 1696

Kuban Plastun Brigade
Formation dates of battalions unknown
1st Plastun Battalion of General Feldzeugmeister Grand Duke Michael Nikolaevich
2nd–6th Plastun Battalions

Terek Cossack Host
1st Kizlyar-Grebenskii Regiment of General Yermolov 1732
1st Mountain-Mozdok Regiment of General Krukovskii 1732
1st Volga Regiment 1732[9]
1st Sunsha-Vladikavkaz Regiment of General Sleptsov 1832

Astrakhan Cossack Host
Formed 1750
1st Astrakhan Cossack Regiment

Orenburg Cossack Host
Formed 1574
1st Orenburg Cossack Regiment
2nd Orenburg Cossack Regiment of Voevod Nagyi
3rd Orenburg Cossack Regiment of Ataman Mogutov
4th Orenburg Cossack Regiment
5th Orenburg Cossack Regiment of Ataman Ugletskii
6th Orenburg Cossack Regiment
Separate Orenburg Cossack Demi-Regiment
1st–2nd Separate Orenburg Cossack Sotnias

Ural Cossack Host
Formed 1591
1st–3rd Ural Cossack Regiments
Temir Detachment of the Ural Cossack Host
Uil Detachment of the Ural Cossack Host

Siberian Cossack Host
Formed 1582
1st Siberian Cossack Regiment of Yermak Timofeev
2nd–3rd Siberian Cossack Regiments

Semirechye (Seven Rivers) Cossack Host
Officially formed 1582, but budded off from the Siberian Cossacks in 1867[10]
1st Semirechye Cossack Regiment of General Kolpakovskii

Trans-Baikal Cossack Host
Officially formed 1655 but assembled from fragmented troops of the Irkutsk government and along the border in 1851[11]
1st Verkhneudinsk Cossack Regiment
1st Chita Cossack Regiment
1st Nerchinsk Cossack Regiment

Amur Cossack Host
Officially formed 1655, but budded off from Trans-Baikal Cossacks in 1879[12]
Amur Cossack Regiment of General Adjutant Graf Muravev of the Amur

Ussuri Cossack Host
Formed 1655
Ussuri Cossack Troops

Other Cossacks
Irkutsk Cossack Sotnia
Krasnoyarsk Cossack Sotnia

§V-2-2 RUSSIAN REGIMENTS WITH DISTINCTION BANNERS[13]

For examples of distinction banners, see Images V:1 and V:2.[14]

In the following tables, 'S' indicates that the unit received a 'simple' decorative banner, bearing only the words За Отличие (For Distinction). Generally, the simple 'For Distinction' award was given prior to c. 1830. After that, the banners began to describe the battle. If the banner describes a battle or action before c. 1830, and especially if it describes an action during the Napoleonic Wars, it is very likely it was awarded long after the event. 'C' indicates that the banner was of this more complex type, often including details about the exact dates, years, or battles for which the award had been given. The number following 'C' gives the number of different awards the banner shows.

Finally, the superscript number or numbers are made up of two parts: the first figure, either a number or a letter, indicates the decade in which the award was earned. The second number indicates the specific award years, as indicated in the accompanying table. For example, C1[73] would mean a complex banner with a description on the banner. The superscript 7 means it was awarded in the 1870s, and the superscript 3 point more specifically to 1877. A banner designated as C2[32, B5] is a complex banner, with two descriptions covering actions in 1831 and 1904–5.

Regiments, battalions, or companies receiving multiple awards, therefore, will likely have multiple superscript numbers separated by commas. Note that awards were not always given to entire regiments, but could be different from battalion to battalion or company to company. In some regiments, all of the battalions received different awards, while in other regiments only a single battalion or company earned a distinction banner.

Sometimes different battalions or other subunits within a regiment will appear to have the same award but are listed separately, such as the 195th Infantry. In such cases, the different battalions received awards in the same time period, but the wording on the two banners is different.

Generally speaking, the regiments were divided into four battalions of four companies each. Thus, the 1st battalion comprised companies 1–4, the 2nd battalion comprised companies 5–8, and so on. Exceptions to this rule are noted where applicable. The various Cossack hosts were made up of six sotnias, or groups of one hundred, rather than traditional battalions. Each sotnia was then divided into two 'fifties', or halves, in place of companies. Abbreviations for groupings of men are as follows: Bn = Battalion; Co = Company; Sqd = Squadron; Sot = Sotnia (100).

The information below covers only infantry and cavalry. As can be seen, it is quite complex. The subject of distinction banners is even more complex if one considers that the banners were given to all combat branches. The authors of *La Garde Imperiale Russe, 1896–1914* note that Zweguintzow in his book *Russian Army 1914* lists over 200 banners, with different wording for each, that had been awarded by the start of World War I.[15]

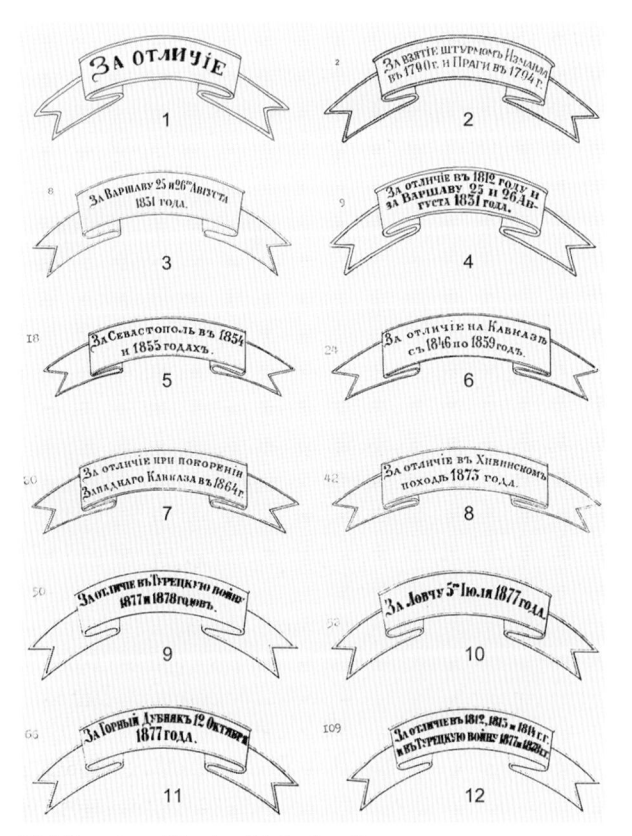

§V-2 The Army   485

V:1 Samples of Russian Distinction Banners
See §V-2-2, Distinction Banners, for the regiments that carried these banners on their headdress.

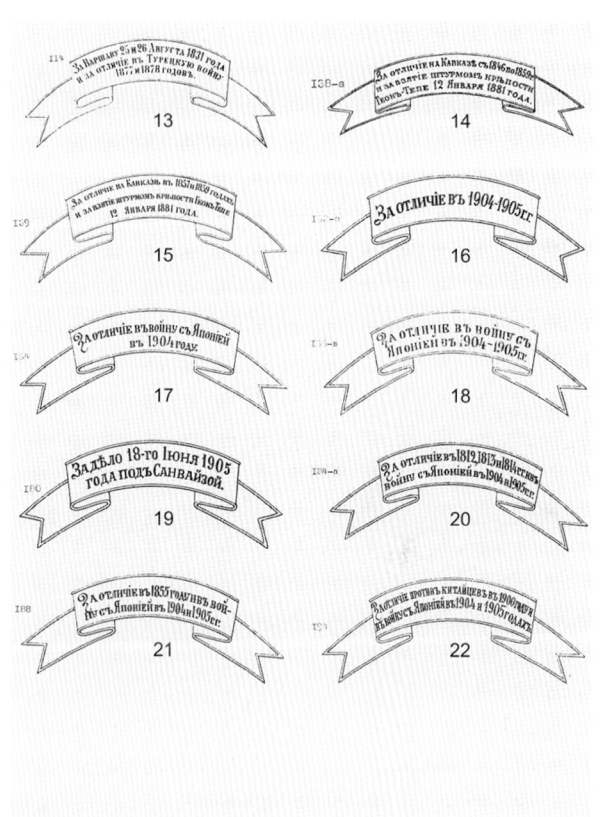

V:2 Samples of Russian Distinction Banners
See §V-2-2, Distinction Banners, for the regiments that carried these banners on their headdress.

SUPERSCRIPT AWARD YEAR ABBREVIATIONS

1700s (A)
1790 = 1
1794 = 2

1810s (1)
1811 = 1
1812 = 2
1812 & 1813 = 3
1812, 1813 & 1814 = 4
1812–14 = 5
1813 = 6
1813 & 1814 = 7
1814 = 8

1820s (2)
1826 = 1
1826 and 1827 = 2

1828 = 3
1828 & 1829 = 4
1828–9 = 5

1830s (3)
1830 = 1
1831 = 2
1833 = 3

1840s (4)
1846–1849 = 1

1850s (5)
1852 = 1
1853 = 2
1853, 1854 & 1855 = 3
1854 = 4

1854 & 1855 = 5
1855 = 6
1857 = 7
1857, 1858 & 1859 = 8
1857–9 = 9

1860s (6)
1860 = 1
1862 = 2
1864 = 3
1866 = 4
1868 = 5

1870s (7)
1873 = 1
1875 = 2
1877 = 3

1877 & 1878 = 4
1877–8 = 5
1878 = 6

1880s (8)
1881 = 1

1900s (B)
1900 = 1
1900-1901 = 2
1904 = 3
1904 & 1905 = 4
1904–5 = 5
1905 = 6

Imperial Guard Regiments

Imperial Guard Infantry Regiments
Preobrazhensky: C1[73]
Semenovsky: C1[73]
Izmailovsky: C1[73]
Yegersky: C1[73]
Moscow: 1st, 2nd, 3rd Bn: C1[73]
    4th Bn: C1[73]
Grenadier: C1[73]
Paul: C1[73]
Finland: C1[76]
Lithuanian: C1[76]
Kexholm: S
St Petersburg: S
Volynsky: C1[73]
Combined Infantry: –

Imperial Guard Rifle Regiments
1 Guard Rifle: C1[76]
2 Guard Rifle: C1[73]
3 Guard Rifle: –
4 Guard Rifle: –

Imperial Guard Cavalry Regiments
Chevalier: –
Horse Guards: –
Cuir. (his): –
Cuir. (hers): –
Cossacks (his): 1st Sot: C1[75]
    2nd Sot: C1[73]
    3rd, 4th Sot: C1[75]
Ataman Cossacks: C1[32]
Comb. Coss.: –
Horse Gren: C1[73]
Lanc. (hers): C1[73]
Lanc. (his): C1[74]
Dragoons: –
Hus. (his): C1[73]
Grodno Hussars: –
Convoy: 1st, 2nd Sot: C1[74]
    3rd, 4th Sot: C1[73]

Infantry

Infantry Grenadiers
1Gren: S
2Gren: S
3Gren: S
4Gren: C2[12, 32]
5Gren: S
6Gren: S
7Gren: 3rd Bn: C1[73]
8Gren: S
9Gren: S
10Gren: S
11Gren: C2[A1, A2]
12Gren: S
13Gren: S
14Gren: S
15Gren: S
16Gren: S

Regular Infantry Regiments
1: C1[74]
2: C1[74]
3: S
4: C1[74]
5: S
6: C1[32]
7: C1[32]
8: –
9: C2[32, B5]
10: C2[32, B5]
11: S
12: C1[32]
13: C1[32]
14: C1[32]
15: S
16: S
17: S
18: –
19: S
20: S
21: S
22: S
23: C1[32]
24: S
25: –
26: S
27: S
28: C1[55]
29: S
30: –
31: –
32: –
33: C1[32]
34: 7th Co: C2[14, 56]
    All others: C1[14]
35: S
36: C1[B3]
37: –
38: S
39: S
40: S
41: S
42: S
43: S
44: S
45: S
46: C1[73]
47: C1[73]
48: S
49: –
50: –
51: C1[55]
52: 1st, 2nd Bn: C1[55]
    3rd, 4th Bn: C1[53]
53: C1[55]
54: C1[55]
55: –
56: C1[73]
57: C1[B6]
58: C1[B6]
59: C1[B6]
60: C1[54]
61: C1[73]
62: C1[73]
63: C1[73]
64: C1[73]
65: –
66: –
67: C1[55]
68: C1[55]
69: S
70: 1st Bn: C1[54]
    2nd Bn: C1[55]
    3rd Bn: C1[58]
    4th Bn: C2[55, 58]
71: C1[54]
72: C1[54]
73: 1st, 2nd Bn: C1[63]
    9th, 10th Co: C2[63, 81]
    11th, 12th Co: C1[63]
    4th Bn: C1[63]

§V-2 The Army   487

74: C1[63]
75: C1[63]
76: C1[63]
77: C1[58]
78: C1[58]
79: S
80: 1st, 2nd Bn: S[31]
   3rd, 4th Bn: S[18]
81: 1st Co: C2[57, 71]
   2nd, 3rd, 4th Co: C1[57]
   5th, 6th, 7th Co: C2[57, 73]
   8th Co: C1[57]
   3rd Bn: C2[57, 81]
   13th, 14th, 15th Co: C2[57, 81]
   16th Co: C3[57, 71, 81]
82: 1st Bn: C2[41, 81]
   4th Bn: C1[41]
83: 1st Bn: C1[59]
   5th, 6th, 7th Co: C1[59]
   8th Co: C2[59, 71]
   3rd Bn: C2[59, 81]
   4th Bn: C1[59]
84: 1st Bn: C2[21, 81]
   2nd Bn: S
   3rd Bn: C2[21, 81]
   4th Bn: S
85: –
86: C1[B5]
87: 7th Co: C1[B4]
   All others: C1[B5]
88: C1[B5]
89: –
90: –
91: C1[32]
92: S
93: C2[32, 74]
94: C2[32, 74]
95: C2[24, 74]
96: C1[74]
97: C1[32]
98: S
99: S
100: S
101: –
102: C1[32]
103: S
104: C1[32]
105: C1[32]

106: –
107: S
108: S
109: S
110: S
111: C1[32]
112: S
113: S
114: S
115: S
116: –
117: C1[74]
118: C1[74]
119: C1[74]
120: C1[74]
121: C1[32]
122: C1[14]
123: C2[14, B4]
124: C1[B5]
125: 1st Bn: C1[55]
   2nd Bn: C1[74]
   3rd Bn: C1[55]
   4th Bn: C1[55]
126: C1[55]
127: C2[55, 74]
128: C1[74]
129: C1[74]
130: C1[74]
131: 1st, 2nd Bn: C1[55]
   3rd Bn: C1[55]
   4th Bn: C1[55]
132: –
133: –
134: –
135: –
136: –
137: 1st Bn: C2[74, B4]
   2nd, 3rd, 4th Bn: C1[B4]
138: S
139: 1st, 2nd Bn: C2[24, B5]
   3rd, 4th Bn: C2[74, B5]
140: S
141: S
142: S
143: S
144: S
145: S
146: C1[B6]

147: C1[B6]
148: 1st, 2nd Bn: C2[14, B4]
   3rd Bn: C2[14, B3]
   4th Bn: C2[14, B4]
149: 1st Co: C1[63]
   2nd Bn: C1[74]
   4th Bn: C1[74]
150: 1st, 2nd, 3rd Bn: C1[73]
   13th Co: C2[63, 73]
   14th, 15th, 16th Co: C1[73]
151: 1st Bn: C3[22, 25, 75]
   2nd, 3rd Bn: C1[74]
   13th Co: C2[63, 74]
   14th, 15th, 16th Co: C3[62, 63, 74]
152: 1st Bn: C3[22, 25, 75]
   2nd Bn: C2[22, 74]
   3rd Bn: C1[74]
   4th Bn: C2[63, 74]
153: 1st Bn: S
154: 13th Co: C1[63]
155: 4th Bn: C1[65]
156: –
157: C1[74]
158: C1[74]
159: 1st Bn: C1[74]
   2nd, 3rd, 4th Bn: C1[74]
160: 1st Bn: C1[74]
   2nd, 3rd, 4th Bn: C1[74]
161: S
162: C1[63]
163: 1st, 2nd Bn: C1[58]
   3rd, 4th Bn: S
164: 1st Bn: C1[57]
   2nd Bn: C1[41]
   3rd Bn: C1[59]
   4th Bn: S
165: –
166: –
167: –
168: –
169: –
170: –
171: –
172: –
173: –
174: –
175: –
176: –

177: –
178: –
179: –
180: –
181: –
182: –
183: –
184: 3rd Bn: C1[B4]
185: 1st Co: C1[63]
   3rd Bn: C1[B4]
   4th Bn: C1[B4]
186: 1st Bn: C1[65]
   2nd Bn: C1[B4]
   9th Co: C1[65]
   4th Bn: C1[B4]
187: 3rd Co: C1[73]
188: 1st, 2nd Co: C1[63]
   3rd Co: C2[63, 73]
   4th Co: C1[63]
189: 2nd Bn: C1[B4]
   4th Bn: C1[B4]
190: 4th Bn: C1[B4]
191: 2nd Bn: C1[B4]
   4th Bn: C1[B4]
192: 2nd Bn: C1[B4]
193: –
194: –
195: 1st, 2nd Bn: C1[B4]
   4th Bn: C1[B4]
196: 1st, 2nd Bn: C1[B4]
197: –
198: –
199: –
200: –
201: –
202: –
203: 1st–5th Co: C1[74]
204: 1st–5th Co: C2[24, 73]
205: –
206: –
207: –
208: –

European Rifles
1ER: C1[B4]
2ER: C1[B4]
3ER: C1[B4]
4ER: 1st Bn: C2[56, B4]
   2nd Bn: C2[56, B6]
5ER: –
6ER: –
7ER: C1[B4]
8ER: C1[B4]
9ER: C1[54]
10ER: –
11ER: C1[73]
12ER: –
13ER: C1[54]
14ER: C1[B1]
15ER: 7th, 8th Co: C1[B1]
16ER: C1[55]
17ER: C1[B6]
18ER: C1[B6]
19ER: –
20ER: C1[B6]

Caucasus Rifles
1CR: 1st Bn: C1[63]
2CR: 1st Bn: C1[63]
3CR: 1st Bn: C1[65]
4CR: 1st Bn: C1[63]
   5th Co: C1[63]
5CR: 5th Co: C1[63]
6CR: 5th Co: C1[63]
7CR: –
8CR: 5th Co: C1[63]

Siberian Rifles
1SR: C1[B1]
2SR: –
3SR: C1[B1]
4SR: C1[B2]
5SR: C1[B1]
6SR: C2[B1, B4]
7SR: C1[B1]
8SR: –
9SR: C1[B3]
   Machine guns: C1[B6]
10SR: C1[B4]
11SR: C1[B1]
   Machine guns: C1[B4]
12SR: C1[B3]
13SR: 1st, 2nd Co: C1[B1]
   4th Co: C1[B1]
   6th, 7th Co: C1[B1]
14SR: 1st Bn: C1[B1]
15SR: 1st Bn: C1[B1]
   5th Co: C1[B1]
16SR: 1st Bn: C1[B1]
17SR: 1st Bn: C1[B1]
18SR: 1st Bn: C1[B1]
19SR: –
20SR: 1st, 2nd Co: C1[B1]
   4th Co: C1[B1]
21SR: 1st Bn: C1[B1]
22SR: 1st Bn: C1[B1]
23SR: –
24SR: –
25SR: C1[B3]
26SR: C1[B3]
27SR: C1[B3]
28SR: C1[B3]
29SR: –
30SR: –
31SR: –
32SR: –
33SR: C1[B1]
34SR: –
35SR: –
36SR: –
37SR: 1st, 2nd Bn: C1[B1]
   9th Co: C1[B1]
38SR: 1st, 2nd Bn: C1[B6]
39SR: 1st, 2nd Bn: C1[B6]
40SR: 1st, 2nd Bn: C1[B6]
41SR: –
42SR: –
43SR: –
44SR: –

Finnish Rifles
1–12FR: –

Turkestan Rifles
1TR: 1st Bn: C1[64]
   6th Co: C1[71]
   8th Co: C1[71]
2TR: Units formed from the 1st and 2nd Co of the 2nd Bn and the 1st and 3rd Co of the 8th Bn: C1[71]
3TR: 1st Co: C1[65]
   7th, 8th Co: C1[71]
4TR: –
5TR: –

§V-2 The Army   489

6TR: 1st, 2nd Co: C1[61]
    5th, 6th Co: C1[65]
    7th Co: C2[65, 81]
    8th Co: C1[65]
7TR: –
8TR: 1st Bn: C2[52, 63]
9TR: 1st, 2nd Co: C1[81]
10TR: –
11TR: 1st Bn: C1[65]
12TR: –
13TR: 4th Co: C1[63]
14TR: 1st Bn: C1[81]
15TR: –
16TR: –
17TR: 4th Co: C1[63]
18TR: –
19TR: 5th Co: C1[81]
20TR: –
21TR: 3rd Co: C1[61]
22TR: –

Cavalry
Dragoon Regiments
1Drag: –
2Drag: –
3Drag: S
4Drag: S
5Drag: S
6Drag: S
7Drag: –
8Drag: –
9Drag: –
10Drag: –
11Drag: C1[74]
12Drag: C1[74]
13Drag: –
14Drag: S
15Drag: C1[63]
16Drag: C1[63]
17Drag: S
18Drag: S
19Drag: –
20Drag: –
Premorsky Drag: 1st Sqn: C2[B1, B4]
    2nd Sqn: C1[B4]
    3rd, 4th Sqn: C2[B1, B4]
    5th Sqn: C1[B4]
    6th Sqn: C2[B1, B4]

Lancer Regiments
1Lanc: S
2Lanc: S
3Lanc: S
4Lanc: S
5Lanc: –
6Lanc: –
7Lanc: S
8Lanc: S
9Lanc: S
10Lanc: S
11Lanc: –
12Lanc: C1[75]
13Lanc: C1[74]
14Lanc: –
15Lanc: –
16Lanc: –
17Lanc: –

Hussar Regiments
1Hus: S
2Hus: S
3Hus: S
4Hus: C1[16]
5Hus: C1[16]
6Hus: S
7Hus: C1[16]
8Hus: S
9Hus: S
10Hus: –
11Hus: S
12Hus: C1[16]
13Hus: C1[74]
14Hus: –
15Hus: –
16Hus: –
17Hus: 1st Sqn: C1[B5]
    2nd, 3rd Sqn: C1[B6]
    4th, 5th Sqn: C1[B5]
    6th Sqn: C1[B6]
18Hus: S

Other Mounted Troops
Crimean Horse Regt: –
Dagestan Regt: 3rd, 4th Sot: C1[71]
Turkman Demi-Regt: –
Ossetian Demi-Regt: –

Don Cossack Host
1DCoss: –
2DCoss: –
3DCoss: –
4DCoss: –
5DCoss: –
6DCoss: –
7DCoss: –
8DCoss: C1[74]
9DCoss: C1[74]
10DCoss: –
11DCoss: C1[74]
12DCoss: C1[74]
13DCoss: C1[74]
14DCoss: –
15DCoss: –
16DCoss: –
17DCoss: C1[74]

Separate Don Cossack Sotnias
1–6DCossSot: –

Kuban Cossack Host
KubanCoss Half-Regt: –
1Yekaterinodar: C2[63, B6]
1Kuban: 1st Sot: C2[54, 74]
    All others: C1[74]
1Uman: 1st ½ 1st Sot: C2[54, 74]
    2nd ½ 1st Sot: C2[63, B4]
    2nd Sot: C3[64, 73, B4]
    3rd, 4th Sot: C2[64, B4]
    5th Sot: C3[64, 73, B4]
    6th Sot: C2[64, B4]
1Black Sea: –
1Poltava: C2[64, 81]
1Zaporozhian: C1[64]
1Laba: 5th, 6th Sot: C1[81]
1Caucasian: 1st ½ 1st Sot: C1[54]
    2nd ½ 1st Sot: C1[64]
    2nd–6th Sot: C1[64]
1Line: –
1Taman: C1[64]
1Khoper: 1st ½ 1st Sot: C1[54]
    2nd ½ 1st Sot: C1[56]

Kuban Plastun Brigade
1Bn: C1[64]

2Bn: 1st Sot: C2[64, 73]
    All others: C1[64]
3Bn: –
4Bn: –
5Bn: –
6Bn: –

Terek Cossack Host
1Kizlyar-Grebenskii: 1st ½ 1st Sot: C2[54, 73]
    2nd ½ 1st Sot: C2[56, 73]
    2nd, 3rd Sot: C1[73]
1Mountain-Mozdok: 1st ½ 1st Sot: C1[54]
    2nd ½ 1st Sot: C1[56]
1Volga: 1st Sot: C2[56, 74]
    2nd, 3rd, 4th Sot: C1[74]
1Sunsha: 1st ½ 1st Sot: C2[54, 73]
    2nd ½ 1st Sot: C2[56, 73]
    2nd Sot: C1[74]
    3rd Sot: C2[74, B6]
    4th Sot: C1[74]

Astrakhan Cossack Host
1Astrakhan: –

Orenburg Cossack Host
1OCoss: 1st Sot: C2[71, B4]
    All others: C1[B4]
2OCoss: 1st, 2nd, 3rd Sot: C1[81]
3OCoss: –
4OCoss: 1st Sot: C1[81]
5OCoss: –
6OCoss: 2nd, 3rd Sot: C1[71]
Orenburg Demi-Regt: –
1–2Separate Orenburg Cos Sot: –

Ural Cossack Host
1UCoss: 1st Sot: C1[74]
2UCoss: 1st Sot: C1[71]
    3rd Sot: C1[71]
    4th Sot: C1[63]
3UCoss: 1st Sot: C1[81]

Siberian Cossack Host
1SCoss: 1st, 2nd Sot: C1[72]

2SCoss: –
3SCoss: –

Semirechye (Seven Rivers) Cossack Host
1Semirechye Coss: 1st Sot: C1[71]

Trans-Baikal Cossack Host
1Verkhneudinsk: 4th, 5th Sot: C1[81]
1Chita: C1[B4]
1Nerchinsk: C1[B4]

Amur Cossack Host
Amur Coss Regt: C1[B4]

Ussuri Cossack Host
Ussuri Coss Regt: C1[B4]

Other Cossack Hosts
None awarded

§V-2-3 PHYSICAL CHARACTERISTICS

HORSE COLOURS

The Russian Imperial Army, by tradition, reserved certain colours of horses for different regiments of cavalry. The army, with some exceptions, mounted odd-numbered hussar regiments on black or dark brown horses and the regiments with an even number on greys, although the 15th Ukrainian, the 12th Akhtyrka, the 16th Irkutsk, and the 17th Chernigov Hussars were exceptions. The 15th Ukrainian Hussars rode mouse grey horses, and the 12th Akhtyrka Hussars had cream-coloured mounts – three squadrons rode palominos,[17] the preferred colour, and three rode duns with black manes and tails. The 16th Irkutsk Hussars rode bays, and the 17th Chernigov Hussars did not have a prescribed colour for the regiment, but each squadron had its own preferred colour. The 1st Squadron rode chestnuts, the 2nd blacks with white markings, the 3rd and 4th bays, the 5th chestnuts or dark browns, and the 6th blacks or greys.

Many regiments also made an effort to mount their squadrons on horses with similar markings. For those regiments mounted on greys, this would be done by having one squadron on dark greys, another squadron on speckled greys, and yet another squadron on light greys. Regiments riding black animals with different marking were placed in different squadrons. For example, in the 1st Sumy Hussars, the 1st Squadron rode pure blacks, the 2nd blacks with white forehead blazes, the 3rd and 4th dark browns, the 5th blacks with white leg marking, and the 6th blacks with white face and leg markings. This system ran counter to everyone's natural desire to have the best mount in spite of the rules. The Sumy Hussars achieved a happy compromise by using the practical system of allowing exceptions to their rules on markings, but requiring the correct markings be painted on the horses for parades.

Table V.2.3.1: Guard Cavalry Horse Colours

Regiment	Horse Colour
Emperor's Escort	Bay
Chevalier Guards	Bay
Horse Guards	Black
Emperor's Cuirassiers	Dark brown
Empress's Cuirassiers	Chestnut
Emperor's Cossacks	Bay
Ataman Cossacks	Chestnut
Combined Cossack Regiment:	
1st Sotnia	Bay
2nd Sotnia	Grey
3rd Sotnia	Bay
4th Sotnia	1 bay platoon; 1 grey platoon
Horse Grenadiers	Black
Guard Dragoons	Bay
Empress's Lancers	Chestnut
Emperor's Lancers	Bay
Emperor's Hussars	Grey
Grodno Hussars	Dark Brown
Guard Squadron of Gendarmes	Grey
Reserve Cavalry of the Guard	All colours

Table V.2.3.2: Physical Characteristics of Guard Infantry and Rifles

Regiment	Physical Characteristics
Preobrazhensky	Tall, blond. 3rd and 5th Companies: beards
Semenovsky	Tall, chestnut/light brown hair. No beards
Izmailovsky	Brunette. 1st Company: beards
Yegersky (Chasseurs)	Small, slender, all colours hair
Moscow	Red hair, beards
Grenadiers	Brunette. 1st Company: beards
Paul	Pug-nosed. 1st Company: tall; 5th Company: blond with beards; 9th Company: brown hair
Finland	Small and slender, with all colours of hair.
Lithuanian	Tall, and blond. No beards.
Kexholm	Tall, with chestnut/light brown hair. No beards
St. Petersburg	Brunette
Volynsky	Small, slender, all colours of hair
1st Rifles	Blond
2nd Rifles	Brunette
3rd Rifles	No specific physical characteristics
4th Rifles	Short-nosed, thick eyebrows growing together

Table V.2.3.3: Physical Characteristics of Guard Cavalry

Regiment	Physical Characteristics
Chevalier Guards	Tall and blond, blue or grey eyes, no beards
Horse Guards	Tall and brunette, small moustaches. 4th Squadron: beards
Emperor's Cuirassiers	Tall, red hair, long noses
Empress's Cuirassiers	Tall, brunette, dark skin
Emperor's Cossacks	Brunette or chestnut/light brown hair, beards
Ataman Cossacks	Blond, beards
Combined Cossack Regiment	All hair colours, beards
Horse Grenadiers	Brunette, moustaches but no beards
Guard Dragoons	Chestnut/light brown hair, no beards
Empress's Lancers	Blond or red hair, long-noses, no eyebrows, short moustaches
Emperor's Lancers	Dark chestnut or brunette hair, small moustaches
Emperor's Hussars	Of a nice size, chestnut/light brown hair. 1st Squadron: blond beards
Grodno Hussars	Brunette, goatees

The line lancers were all supposed to be mounted on bays, but in reality the 14th Lancers rode black horses, while the 16th and 17th Lancers were mounted on chestnuts. The cuirassier dragoons were assigned light chestnut, while all the other line dragoons were to ride dark chestnuts. In practice, the 'light' and 'dark' distinction was dropped, and most of the dragoon regiments simply rode chestnuts. However, the 15th, 17th, and 18th Caucasus Dragoons rode black, bay, and dark brown mounts respectively, and the Premorsky Dragoons had horses varying by squadron: chestnut for the 1st and 3rd, black for the 2nd, bay for the 4th, grey for the 5th, and dark brown for the 6th. The Crimean (Tartar) Horse Regiment were mounted on blacks, bays, or chestnuts depending on the squadron. Line Cossacks were mounted on horses of all colours.[18]

Because such large numbers of horses were needed for the line regiments, the correct colour could not always be obtained in sufficient quantity, so the horses which were the right colour were used for the squadrons on the edges of formation, and horses deviating from the appropriate colour were kept in the centre of the formation, where they were less likely to be seen.

Guard cavalry regiments were assigned specfic colours for their horses as well, but because the number of horses needed for the guard was smaller there were not always the same obstacles to following the colour regulations. Guard horse colours are indicated in Table V.2.3.1.

SOLDIERS' CHARACTERISTICS

The other ranks, less so the officers, of the Russian Imperial Guard were also classified and assigned to a particular regiment according to their physical characteristics, a practice which was often deeply rooted in tradition, which would be deemed highly inappropriate in modern society. At the time, however, the practice of physical classification was seen as a way of giving each regiment a more uniform appearance. Tables V.2.3.2 and V.2.3.3 show the 'ideal' characteristics which were assigned for each regiment's men.

§V-2-4 PAINTING WITH THE TOE

The marching step used by the czar's armies is hard to describe. The often-used low goose step characterization does not quite capture it.

When learning to march, recruits were told to think in terms of 'painting with the toe'. Drawing V:3 is labelled 'Painting with the Toe' and dates from the 1820s or 1830s.

V:3 Painting with the Toe
This style of marching used by the Russian army was a variation on the goose step used by the German army. Russian recruits were told to obtain the light march steps by visualising painting with their toes. See *§V-2-3*.

§V-3 UNIFORM INFORMATION

§V-3-1   Standard Uniform Items
§V-3-2   The Army Uniform
§V-3-3   Collar and Cuff Lace
§V-3-4   Guard Uniforms Before 1908
§V-3-5   Infantry and Cavalry Monograms
§V-3-6   Shenk Plates
§V-3-7   Pouch Belt Badges
§V-3-8   Regimental Badges
§V-3-9   Service Chevrons
§V-3-10 Gorgets
§V-3-11 Guard Other Rank Rifle Straps
§V-3-12 Complete Uniform Changes of 1881–2 and 1907–8

§V-3-1 STANDARD UNIFORM ITEMS[19]

Some articles of clothing, accessories, and equipment were common uniform items, found in several branches of the Russian army. To avoid repetition of the description of these items, a description of several of these items follows. Specific information as to the colour of an item, ranks entitled to wear an item, decorative details, etc. for an individual branch of service or regiment can be found with the more detailed descriptions of these individual uniforms in later sections.

Uniform Colours

While regulations cite dark green as the colour of other ranks' tunics, headdress, and netherwear, in reality these garments were black, for economic reasons. This applied to almost all other ranks in the Russian army, including infantry, grenadiers, rifles, dragoons, artillery, engineers, and auxiliary troops, among others.[20] The uniforms of officers are also often cited as being dark green[21] (see Image C61). However, in fact, they were a mid-green shade, often referred to as 'czar's green', a very distinctive almost iridescent shade. This does not show well in photographs, but is easy to spot when looking at a tunic.

Cockades

Cockades were worn as decoration on many uniforms, and were most often found on the headdress. The cockades were made of embossed metal, painted in the colours of the Imperial Family, black and orange, and were generally oval in shape. The shape, size and design varied slightly according to rank.

Regular soldiers and corporals wore the basic cockade, which was slightly convex and oval, measuring 3.89 cm (1.53 inches) on its vertical diameter and 2.78 cm (1.09 inches) on its horizontal. The centre of the cockade was painted black. There were three additional rings of colour painted around the centre, alternating orange and black. Around the edge of the outermost ring of orange, a wide band of the unpainted shining white metal of the cockade was visible, creating a border.

For NCOs, the dimensions of the cockade were the same, but instead of having a rounded convex shape, it was flat with only the bevelled white metal border giving it depth. The embossing of the white metal border was supposed to look like large grains of barley.

Officers and chief adjutants had larger cockades which were 4.17 cm (1.64 inches) on the vertical diameter and 3.06 cm (1.20 inches) on the horizontal. The bands of colour which were orange for other ranks were gold for officers. The white metal border was again bevelled so the flat centre of the cockade stood out, and embossed with a series of rays pointing outwards.

The white outer band was the widest of five concentric ovals. Troopers had a plain white band, and under-officers had a flat white band with highlights. Warrant officers and regimental officers had a scalloped outer band. The cockade was somewhat larger for the latter group. The centre of the cockade consisted of three narrow bands and a black oval centre. The middle three bands were in an orange–black–orange pattern.

There were a few exceptions to the above descriptions. The 4th Guard Rifles had regular cockades, but had the gilt Cross of the Mass Conscription mounted on them. The Guard Cuirassiers, Line Dragoons, Guard Horse Grenadiers and Guard Paul Regiment all had large round – not oval – cockades on the right side of the headdress under the attachment of the chinstrap. These cockades were the same colours as the oval cockades.

Litzen

Many regiments had a special type of trim called *litzen* at the collar, cuffs, or both. The most common type of litzen was the 'chapter' or 'chapel' – the names are used interchangeably. The chapter shape was rectangular with ends that flared out slightly. A coloured stripe ran lengthwise along the centre of the rectangle. The stripe was called a *spiegel* (both *litzen* and *spiegel* are German terms) or a central light. Normally the spiegel was the colour of the collar or cuff under it, but there were exceptions. For example, the guard's Lithuanian Regiment had a red spiegel when its collar was yellow.

Epaulettes

Many officers' full dress uniforms and even some other ranks' full dress uniforms included epaulettes. The epaulettes passed under special epaulette straps that were part of the shoulder of the tunic, and then attached to either shoulder with an epaulette button. Epaulette buttons bore the same design as the tunic buttons, but were smaller in size, located at the end of the shoulder board closest to the collar. There were several different models of epaulette that could be worn with a particular uniform. Descriptions of the four models pertinent to this work follow.

Guard Infantry Model

These officer's epaulettes were made entirely of either gold or silver metallic cloth. The outer rounded portion of the epaulette was bordered with four successive crescents of twisted cording in different thicknesses. The fringe hanging from the epaulette crescents varied by rank: generals had a thick fringe, field officers had a fine fringe, and subalterns did not have a fringe. The colour of the lining and piping of the officer's epaulettes varied by regiment, but was typically the same colour as the shoulder straps worn by the troops of the regiment. If the regiment bore the monogram of its *chef*, the monogram was mounted in silver or gold inside the crescent.

Line Infantry Model

This was an officer's epaulette. The base of the epaulette was made of cloth that varied in colour by regiment, but was the same colour as the shoulder straps worn by the troops of that regiment. The shoulder board was trimmed with metallic braid in the colour of the button, and the crescent was bordered with decorative twists and fringe. The lining and piping were the same colour as the shoulder straps worn by the troops. If the regiment bore the monogram of its *chef*, the monogram was mounted in silver or gold inside the crescent.

Cavalry Model

These officer's epaulettes were made of gold or silver metal. The rectangular shoulder board was made of eleven rows of metal scales joined to the rounded metal epaulette crescent. The crescent was bordered with decorative twists and fringe. The lining and piping of the epaulettes varied in colour by regiment and were the colour of the shoulder straps that were worn by the troops of that regiment. If the regiment bore the monogram of its honorary *chef*, the monogram was created by repoussé work on the smooth metal inside the epaulette crescent (repoussé – literally 'beaten out' in French – is a raised area in metal created by hammering from the reverse side). The resulting monogram was either left the same metal colour as the rest of the epaulette or plated with the contrasting metal colour.

Trooper Model

There were relatively few regiments where the other ranks were permitted to wear epaulettes in full dress. They were the Guard Horse Grenadiers, Guard Dragoons, Guard and Line Lancers, and Guard Cossacks. Officers of these units wore one of the models of officer epaulettes described above to preserve the distinction of rank, so the other ranks wore the special trooper model which was made entirely of metal, either gold or silver colour, depending on the regiment's button colour. The shoulder board was made of metal scales joined to a rounded metal crescent. Unlike the officer models, the crescent was plain, without decorative twists or fringe, with the exception of the Guard Horse Grenadiers, whose trooper model epaulettes had a red fringe. If the regiment bore the monogram of its *chef*, the monogram was in repoussé work for cavalry model epaulettes.

Shoulder Straps

If uniforms did not include epaulettes, the full dress uniforms of the other ranks or the regular and walking-out uniforms of both officers and other ranks often included shoulder straps. The shoulder straps were made of cloth, 6.67 cm (2.63 inches) wide. They varied in length according to the length of the trooper's shoulder, but were a maximum of 17.78 cm (7 inches) long. They varied in colour by regiment. Shoulder straps of some units included coloured piping as well. The shoulder straps started with a straight edge at the end of the shoulder and ended in a point near the collar, where it buttoned on to the tunic. The strap point extended 1.39 cm (0.33 inch) beyond the straight sides of the strap. For adjutants, however, the tip of the point was cut off so the strap came to a blunt end near the collar.

Shoulder straps could have a variety of markings, including the monogram of the regiment's *chef* where applicable, the regimental number, the army subdivision emblem, etc. The colour of the marking varied depending on the colour of the shoulder strap. Markings were generally painted in yellow on straps that were red, raspberry, blue, green, or black. They were painted in red on white, yellow, and orange straps. However, there were some exceptions to this rule, and some monograms were white; for example, the monogram worn by the 2nd Dragoons was white on a pink shoulder strap. The shoulder strap marking was placed 2.22 cm (0.88 inch) from the outer edge of the strap. Uppercase letters and numbers were 3.33 cm (1.31 inches) high, and lowercase letters were 1.67 cm (0.66 inch) high. If the monogram was made up of two rows of text, the second row was 1.67 cm (0.66 inch) high and was placed 0.56 cm (0.22 inch) below the upper row. Other markings, such as a crown or the emblem of an army subdivision, were placed 0.28 cm (0.11 inch) above the monogram.

Trooper shoulder straps had braids immediately below the shoulder strap button, laid horizontally across the strap to denote rank. The basic rank braids were 1.11 cm (0.44 inch) wide, and were orange for the guard and white for the line. Corporals had one of these braids, sergeants had two, and chief sergeants had three. Adjutants had a 2.78 cm (1.09 inch) wide braid that was either gold or silver according to the button colour. Chief adjutants had gold or silver square-weave braid that ran lengthwise down the centre of the shoulder strap instead of widthwise below the button.

Officers' shoulder straps were worn only with standard or walking-out dress, not full dress. They were the same size and shape as adjutant shoulder straps, with the cut-off point near the collar. Officers' shoulder straps had different types and arrangements of braid depending on rank. Subalterns had two stripes of square-weave braid separated by a 0.28 cm (0.11 inch) spacing band. Field officers had one stripe of square-weave braid with a stripe of 'superior officer' style – combined square and zigzag design – braid on either side. The three stripes were again separated by 0.28 cm (0.11 inch) spacing bands. Generals had a single stripe of 6.67 cm (2.63 inch) wide general's (zigzag) braid that ran the length of the shoulder strap.

Uniform Buttons[22]

With a few exceptions, all regiments and battalions of line infantry and cavalry had, since 1904, worn buttons that had a double-headed eagle (the imperial eagle) on them. The cavalry exception was the 2nd Dragoons. Between 1881 and 1904, button design was not an issue for line regiments of infantry and cavalry since, under Alexander III's uniform reforms, they wore uniforms that did not have buttons. Instead, the coats were fastened closed with internal hooks. Plastuns and mounted Cossacks did not wear buttons. Their uniforms were also closed by internal hooks. See Images V:57 (other ranks of the Guard Cossacks), V:59 (officers of the Guard Combined Cossack Regiment), V:123 (line Cossack), and V:133 (plastuns).

The line grenadiers all wore buttons with a grenade on them, with one exception: the 13th Grenadiers. Both the 2nd Dragoons and the 13th Grenadiers had a crown on their buttons. Prior to 1907, all line units that had the emperor or empress as regimental chief had a crown on the button. Only the 2nd and the 13th kept this design after 1907. It used to be said that the 2nd Dragoons 'forgot' to change their button design.[23] An exception may have been made for the 13th because it was the oldest regiment in the Russian army.

Guard infantry and cavalry units had worn double-headed eagles on their button from 1829.[24]

Cuff Buttons

The bottom cuff button of officers was, by tradition, undone on officers' Russian tunics and similar coats. This dates back to the early years of Czar Alexander I's reign when coat sleeves were cut too tight to allow freedom of movement.[25]

Pouch Belt

The uniforms of some units included a pouch belt in full dress. The pouch belt was covered with different styles of gold or silver braid, depending on button colour, for different units, and was 4.45 cm (1.75 inches) wide. The Chevalier Guards, Ataman Guard Cossacks, Emperor's Guard Hussars, and Crimean Cavalry Regiment each had a unique braid on their pouch belt (see individual units for descriptions). The Grodno Guard Hussar Regiment and regiments of line hussars had 'hussar-style' (zigzag) braid on the pouch belt. For all other units assigned a pouch belt, the covering was made of standard square-weave 'belt-style' braid.

The pouch belt was worn over the left shoulder, where it typically passed under the epaulette or shoulder strap. When the pouch belt was worn with a cuirass, the pouch belt passed over the epaulette or shoulder strap, but under the right cuirass strap.

The pouch belt buckled in different locations, depending on what type of pouch it was worn with. In the standard *lyadunka* pouch, it buckled at the back; if the *patrontach* style, the pouch belt buckled at the chest.

Pouch

There were two styles of pouch that could be worn on the pouch belt (described above) in full dress. The standard pouch worn by most of the units had a silver-coloured cover flap and was called a *lyadunka*. The other model, or *patrontach*, had a black leather cover flap with a metallic border in the colour of the button. It was worn only by the Crimean cavalry and the line Cossacks.

The cover flap of the pouch had a central metallic ornament. It was typically a St Andrew guard star (sometimes known simply as a guard star) or a double-headed eagle, but could also be a St George's star or a monogram in special cases noted in individual regiments. The pouch was worn low on the right-hand side of the back. When a cuirass was worn, the pouch was worn on the right side.

Regimental and School Badges

Russian officers wore badges showing their regiment, what military school they had attended, and any advanced military academies they attended. There were several other reasons an officer could obtain a badge, such as attending an officers' training school, some type of jubilee or anniversary taking place, being part of the czar's escort or suite, etc.

Regimental badges were usually created on a regiment's 100th anniversary, but in some cases they marked the regiment's bicentennial or even its 250th anniversary. Having a regimental badge would show the antiquity of the regiment. But, since a large number of regiments were created during the Napoleonic Wars, many were entitled to badges by 1914 – so many that several of the really old guard regiments, such as the Chevalier Guards, the Horse Guards, the Hussars of the Emperor, and the Lancers of the Empress, did not adopt regimental badges.[26]

The badge of a regiment was worn on the left side of the chest. Also on the left side was the badge of the officer's cadet schools and military colleges. On the right side of the chest, the officer would wear badges of the Czar's Suite and the academies and any upper-level schools he had attended.[27] It is believed the badge denoting the Cossack Host was also worn on the left side.

The regimental badges were typically designed by an officer of the regiment, often the colonel or his deputy, and then approved by the czar. They varied a great deal. Some were very artistic and others quite pedestrian. Some were very colourful, having gold, silver, and colour enamelling. Others were plain. They were privately made by different jewellers over the years so they could vary in size and even in design. Image V:15 in §V-3-8 shows a group of modern reproductions of regimental badges to give an idea of what they looked like. The skull regimental badge for the 5th Hussars is shown in the Russian Hussar section, §V-7-c at V:122.

Officer's Sash

Officers wore a single model of sash. It was worn in both full and standard dress, but not with service or walking-out dress. The sash was 5 cm (1.97 inches) wide and was made of woven fabric that was silver with three rows of mixed black and orange silk stitching. It fastened at the front, above the bottom tunic button, by means of a buckle covered in the same silver fabric.

Riding Breeches, Pantaloons, Trousers, and Charivari

Both officers and other ranks of most cavalry regiments wore riding breeches in full dress. The colour of the breeches varied by unit or regiment. Breeches sometimes had coloured stripes or piping along the outside seams of the legs. Infantry officers in full dress wore a type of short pantaloons. These were baggy and typically tucked into boots just below the knee.

Officers often had full-length trousers in addition to the breeches. Trousers could be worn in walking-out dress.

Several regiments, most notably those of the guard, had an additional type of breeches called *charivari* – from the Russian *šarawary*, or 'flowing trousers' – that were worn in full dress instead of the regular breeches.

These were full-length trousers, but of a looser cut. They varied in colour according to regiment or unit and usually had coloured stripes or piping along the outside seams of the legs.

Cossacks wore what is probably best described as Cossack charivari. These were loose trousers that tucked into the boots. They differed from infantry pantaloons in the looseness of their cut. Like other nether garments, they could have bands in various colours on them.

Bands on Riding Breeches, Pantaloons, etc.

While the styles and colours of the bands on riding breeches, pantaloons, etc. varied from unit to unit, there were at least two specific styles delineated by regulation.

The first was the simple or 'Cossack' style, a single 4.45 cm (1.75 inch) band of colour that ran down the outside leg seam. As might be expected, these were commonly worn on Cossack charivari.

The second was the double or 'general's' style. The outside leg seam was highlighted with 0.28 cm (0.11 inch) coloured piping. On either side of the piping, placed at a spacing of 0.56 cm (0.22 inch), was a band of general's (zigzag) braid in the same colour as the piping.

Footwear

The most common form of footwear was the basic black leather boot that came to the knee, which was worn by all officers and troops except those of the hussars (§V-5-d and §V-7-c), the 4th Guard Rifles (§V-6-a), and the 81st Apsheron Line Infantry. The 81st Apsheron Line Infantry had the basic black boots, but with a flap of red wool 7.78 cm (3.06 inches) wide at the top, in remembrance of the Battle of Kunersdorf, fought in 1759, where the regiment was said to have stood up to its boot tops in blood.

Several regiments also had jackboots, worn for court dress or palace duty, made of stiff black leather lined with white chamois leather, extending above the knee 17.78 cm (7 inches). The toes of the boots were cut straight across.

Officers also had black leather ankle boots, worn only when were wearing long trousers, not breeches.

Spurs

Silver metal or white metal spurs were standard ware in the Imperial Russian Army.[28]

Gloves

In full dress, standard, short white chamois gloves were typically worn. Chamois is a species of mountain goat native to Eurasia. But in time the word acquired a wider meaning: a type of smooth leather typically made of goat, sheep or deerskin.

Several regiments also had white chamois gloves in the gauntlet style, meaning they flared out above the wrist and extended about halfway up the forearm.

For uniforms other than full dress, standard gloves of brown leather could be worn. There were also white and brown cotton gloves for summer and white and brown woollen gloves for winter.

Side Arms

Full dress uniforms usually included side arms such as swords, sabres, etc. Detailed descriptions of these weapons are outside the scope of this work. However, it should be noted that the Russian army was unique in that its full dress uniforms included black leather holsters and Nagant revolvers in 1914.[29] The pistol cord worn in full dress was white silk, mixed with black and orange thread, for all regiments regardless of button colour.

The dress sword, the *shashka*, worn by most of the Russian army was carried with the cutting edge to the back. The scabbard was wood and covered with black leather, the metal parts gilt brass. Other ranks carried basically the same sword and scabbard, but the scabbard of other ranks was fitted to carry a bayonet.

Many cavalry officers, when in full dress but not parading with their men, were allowed to substitute a sabre for the shashka. This option was normally exercised as the sabre was considered smarter than the pedestrian shashka. The scabbard worn with the sabre was steel.

The dress sword knot for officers was a cone covered with thick silver wire. Below the knot, the wire was allowed to hang loose in thick tassels. The knot was decorated with two thin strips of orange and black striped silk placed to divide the silver knot into three equal parts. The tassel was solid rather than having loose cords. There was also an officer's 'dress sword knot'. This consisted of a silver lace strap edged on both sides with black and orange strips. The knot was gathered silver strips covered with silver thread and decorated with applied sequin ornaments.[30] The sword knot of other ranks was brown leather and the cords consisted of brown leather strips.

Decorations

Decorations were worn on the coat in full dress. Because of the plastron, these were often worn in the centre of the chest. In addition, officers wore badges of their regiments if one existed.

Cavalry Lance Pennants

In considering the uniforms of Russian cavalry, another item should be noted: the lance pennant. Most Russian cavalry regiments had a pennant that was unique to it. This was accomplished by having four patterns of pennants. There was one pattern for the hussars, one for the lancers, and two patterns for line dragoons – one for the standard dragoons, one for the cuirassier dragoons. The four pennant patterns are shown in Line Drawings V:4 through V:7. Each regiment was assigned special colours for its pennant, usually colours which matched different parts of the regiment's uniform. The colours of each regiment's pennant are shown in Tables V.3.1.a–d. The pennants were made of muslin cloth and were attached to the top of the lances.

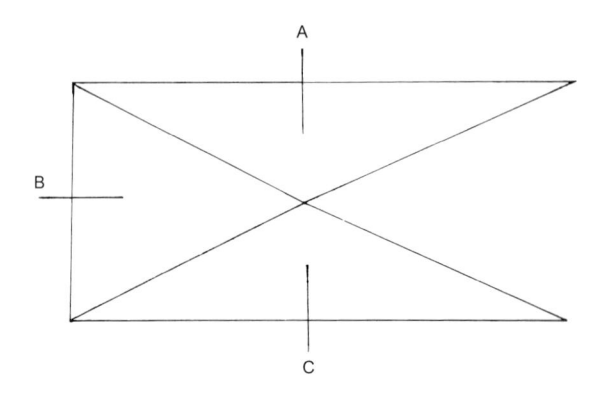

V:4 Cuirassier Lance Pennant

§V-3 Uniform Information

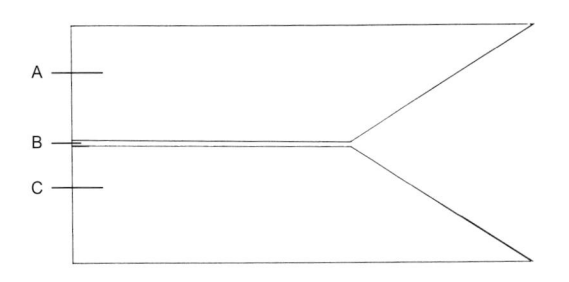

Table V.3.1.a: Cuirassier Lance Pennant Colours

Regiment Name	Triangle A	Triangle B	Triangle C
Chevalier Guards	Red	White	Red
Horse Guards	Yellow	White	Dark Blue
Emperor's Cuirassiers	Light blue	White	Yellow
Empress's Cuirassiers	Light blue	Yellow	Light blue
2nd Pskov Life Dragoons	Pink	White	Pink
4th New Russia-Ekaterinoslav Dragoons	Orange	White	Orange
6th Glukhov Dragoons	Light blue	White	Light blue
8th Astrakhan Dragoons	Yellow	White	Yellow
9th Kazan Dragoons	Red	Yellow	Red
10th Novgorod Dragoons	Raspberry	Yellow	Raspberry
12th Starodub Dragoons	Light blue	Yellow	White
13th Military (St George) Order Dragoons	Black	Orange	Black
14th Little Russian Dragoons	Light green	Yellow	Light green

Table V.3.1.b: Dragoon Lance Pennant Colours

Regiment Name	Square A	Triangles and Stripe B
Guard Dragoons	Red	White
1st Moscow Life Dragoons	White	Red
3rd New Russia Dragoons	White	Raspberry
5th Kargopol Dragoons	White	White
7th Kinburn Dragoons	White	Yellow
11th Riga Dragoons	Light Blue	White
15th Pereyaslav Dragoons	Raspberry	White
16th Tver Dragoons	White	Raspberry
17th Nizhni-Novgorod Dragoons	Raspberry	White
18th Seversk Dragoons	White	Raspberry
19th Archangelgorod Dragoons	White	Red
20th Finland Dragoons	Yellow	White
Premorsky Dragoons	Dark Green	Yellow
Crimean Cavalry	Black	Red

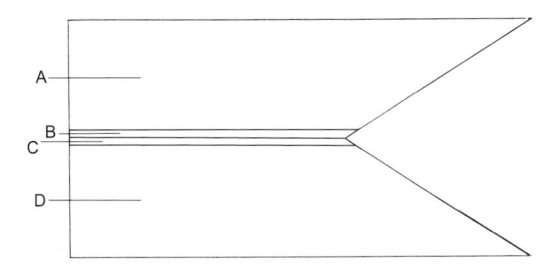

V:6 Lancer Lance Pennant

V:5 Dragoon Lance Pennant

V:7 Hussar Lance Pennant

Table V.3.1.c: Lancer Lance Pennant Colours

Regiment Name	Stripes A and C	Stripes B and D
Empress's Lancers	White	Red
Emperor's Lancers	Yellow	Red
Horse Grenadiers	Red	White
1st St Petersburg Lancers	Red	White
2nd Kurland Lancers	Light blue	White
3rd Smolensk Lancers	White	Dark blue
4th Kharkov Lancers	Yellow	White
5th Lithuanian Lancers	Red	White
6th Volynsky Lancers	Light blue	White
7th Olviopol Lancers	White	Dark blue
8th Voznesensk Lancers	Yellow	White
9th Bug Lancers	Red	White
10th Odessa Lancers	Light blue	White
11th Chuguev Lancers	White	Dark blue
12th Belgorod Lancers	Yellow	White
13th Vladimir Lancers	Yellow	White
14th Yamburg Lancers	Yellow	White
15th Tatar Lancers	Raspberry	White
16th New Archangel Lancers	White	Dark blue
17th New Mirgorod Lancers	Raspberry	White

Lance Poles

The lance poles, to which lance pennants could be attached, were carried by the first rank of all the guard and line cavalry and by the first and second ranks of the Cossacks, except the Emperor's Escort, the Kuban Cossacks, and the Terek Cossacks, who did not carry lances. Adjutants and chief adjutants did not carry lances. In full dress, all except the Cossacks had the lance pennant attached to the top of the lance by means of three hooks. In the guard, some units even bore the lance pennant in ordinary dress on certain occasions.

From 1910, the standard lance was made of steel and painted khaki. Previously, lances had been made of wood. Several regiments retained the old wooden lances, though, which were slightly shorter and painted in the regimental colour. They used these more decorative lances instead of the new steel lances during times of peace in both full and ordinary dress. The regiments which retained these wooden lances, along with the colours of the lances, can be seen in Table V.3.1.e.

One other exception to the 1910 standard-issue lance is that carried by the Guard Lancers of the Empress. In recognition of their service at the Battle of Adrianople during the Russo-Turkish War of 1877–8, this regiment was given special bamboo lances.

Table V.3.1.d: Hussar Lance Pennant Colours

Regiment Name	Stripe A	Stripe B	Stripe C
Emperor's Hussars	Red	Yellow	Yellow
Grodno Hussars	Raspberry	White	Dark green
1st Sumy Hussars	Red	Yellow	Light blue
2nd Pavlograd Hussars	Turquoise	Yellow	Dark green
3rd Elizabetgrad Hussars	White	Yellow	Light blue
4th Mariupol Hussars	Yellow	Yellow	Dark blue
5th Alexandria Hussars	Red	White	Black
6th Klyastitsi Hussars	Light blue	White	Dark blue
7th White Russian Hussars	White	White	Light blue
8th Lubny Hussars	Yellow	White	Dark blue
9th Kiev Hussars	Red	Yellow	Dark green
10th Ingermanland Hussars	Light blue	Yellow	Light blue
11th Izyum Hussars	Red	Yellow	Red
12th Akhtyrka Hussars	Yellow	Yellow	Brown
13th Narva Hussars	Yellow	White	Light blue
14th Mitau Hussars	Yellow	White	Dark green
15th Ukrainian Hussars	Light blue	White	Pink-orange
16th Irkutsk Hussars	Raspberry	Yellow	Dark green
17th Chernigov Hussars	White	Yellow	Dark green
18th Hezhin Hussars	Light blue	White	Dark green

Table V.3.1.e: Wooden Lance Pole Colours

Regiment Name	Lance Pole Colour
Guard Cuirassier Regiments[a, c]	
Chevalier Guards	Red
Horse Guards	Dark blue
Emperor's Cuirassiers	Yellow
Empress's Cuirassiers[a]	Light blue
Guard Cossack Regiments[b, c]	
Emperor's Cossacks	Red
Ataman Cossacks	Sky blue

Regiment Name	Lance Pole Colour
Combined Regiment:[b, c]	
1st Ural Sotnia	Raspberry
2nd Orenburg Sotnia	Sky blue
3rd Mixed Sotnia:	
½ Siberian Sotnia	Red
Semirechya Platoon	Raspberry
Atrakhan Platoon	Orange
4th Mixed Pri-Amur Sotnia:	
½ Trans-Baikal Sotnia	Orange
Amur Platoon	Orange
Ussuri Platoon	Orange

Notes: [a] Undated letter (c. 1975) from Kovalevsky.
[b] The colour of the lance pole matches the colour of the shoulder straps for guard Cossack regiments, sotnias, and platoons.
[c] Zweguintzow, *Uniformes Russe*, p. 66.

§V-3-2 THE ARMY UNIFORM

Embroidery and Litzen of the Guard Infantry[a]

Regiment	Officers – Embroidery[b]			Other Ranks – Litzen[c]		
	Collar	Cuffs	Colour	Collar	Cuffs	Colour
Preobrazhensky	2	3	Gold	2	3	Yellow-orange[d]
Semenovsky	2	3	Gold	2	3	Yellow-orange[d]
Izmailovsky	2	3	Gold	2	3	Yellow-orange[d]
Yegersky	2	3	Gold	2	3	Yellow-orange[d]
Moscow	2	3	Gold	2	3	Yellow-orange[d]
Grenadiers	2	3	Gold	2	3	Yellow-orange[d]
Paul	2	3	Gold	2	3	Yellow-orange[d]
Finland	2	3	Gold	2	3	Yellow-orange[d]
Lithuanian	2	3	Silver	2	3	Yellow-orange[e]
Kexholm	2	3	Silver	2	3	Yellow-orange[d]
St Petersburg	2	3	Silver	2	3	Yellow-orange[d]
Volynsky	2	3	Silver	2	3	Yellow-orange[d]
1st Rifles	2	3	Gold	2	3	Yellow-orange[d]
2nd Rifles	2	3	Silver	2	3	Yellow-orange[d]
3rd Rifles	2	3	Silver	2	3	Yellow-orange[d]
4th Rifles	None	2 Vertical	Gold	None	2 Vertical	Orange wool[f]

Notes: [a] Litzen and embroidery are used as decoration on the collar and go around the buttonholes on the cuffs.
[b] Officers' embroidery is unique for nearly all of the guard regiments, with the following exceptions: the Preobrazhensky and Lithuanian regiments have the same embroidery, and the Finland and Volynsky regiments have the same embroidery. The numbers show the number of times an embroidered design appears on a collar or cuff.
[c] The numbers show the number of times litzen appears on a collar or cuff.
[d] Red thread along the sides. Central thread in the colour of the collar or cuff to which it is sewn.
[e] Although their collar is yellow, the Lithuanian regiment's litzen has a red central thread.
[f] With black central thread.

Collar and Cuff Litzen of the Line Infantry: Regiments with Exceptions[a]

Regiment	Officers Collar	Officers Cuffs	Officers Colour	Troops Collar	Troops Cuffs	Troops Colour
2nd Sofia[b]	2	2	Gold	2	---	White[c]
9th Ingria[b]	2	2	Gold	2	---	White
17th Archangelgorod	2*	2*	Gold	---	---	---
34th Sevsk	2*	2*	Gold	2	2	St George's[d]
48th Odessa[b]	2	2	Gold	2	---	White
65th Moscow	2	2	Gold	2	2	White
68th Borodino[b]	2	2	Gold	2	---	White
80th Kabarda[e]	2*	2*	Gold	2	2	White
81st Apsheron[b]	2	2	Gold	2	---	White
84th Shirvan[e]	2*	2*	Gold	2	2	White
145th Novocherkassk[b]	2	2	Gold	2	---	White
16th Rifles[b]	2	2	Gold	2	---	White
1st Siberian Rifles[e]	2	2	Gold	2	2	White
11th Siberian Rifles[e]	2	2	Gold	2	2	White
21st Siberian Rifles[e]	2	2	Gold	2	2	White
1st Caucasus Rifles	2*	2*	Gold	2	2	St George's[d]

Notes: [a] The normal line infantry regiment uniform was: Officers – 2 regular litzen at the collar and on each cuff in gold. Troops – No litzen.
[b] Denotes regiments whose honorary chief is a dead emperor or empress: litzen at collar only for other ranks.
[c] With a central thread in the colour of the collar for each regiment bearing this distinction.
[d] Orange and black.
[e] Denotes regiments whose honorary chief is a reigning emperor or empress or the dowager empress: litzen at collar and cuffs.
* Distinction-type litzen.

Collar and Cuff Litzen of the Guard Cavalry

Regiment	Officers Collar	Officers Cuffs	Officers Colour	Troops Collar	Troops Cuffs	Troops Colour
Emperor's Cuirassiers[a]	1	2	Silver	1	2[b]	Yellow-orange[c]
Empress's Cuirassiers	1	2	Gold	1	2[b]	Yellow-orange[c]
Chevalier Guards	1	2	Silver	1	2[b]	Yellow-orange[c]
Horse Guards	1	2	Gold	1	2[b]	Yellow-orange[c]
Guard Dragoons	2	1	Silver	2	1	Yellow-orange[d]
Horse Grenadiers	2	1	Gold	2	1	Yellow-orange[d]
Emperor's Lancers	2	1	Silver	2	1	Yellow-orange[d]
Empress's Lancers	2	1	Gold	2	1	Yellow-orange[d]
Emperor's Cossacks[e]	2[d]	1	Silver	2	1	Yellow-orange[c]
Ataman Cossacks	2	1	Silver	2	1	Yellow-orange[c]
Combined Cossack Regiment	2	1	Silver	2	1	Yellow-orange[c,f]

Notes: ᵃ In this regiment only, the litzen at the collar contains a button for both officers and troops, in addition to the buttons at the cuffs.
ᵇ Only the bottom part of the button and/or litzen is visible because of the trim.
ᶜ With a central thread the colour of the cloth underneath.
ᵈ With red central thread.
ᵉ Starting in 1914, the Emperor's Cossacks have embroidery instead of litzen.
ᶠ In the Combined Cossack Regiment only, when the distinction mark is orange, the central thread of the litzen is red.

Collar and Cuff Litzen of the Line Dragoons

Regiment	Officersᵃ Collar	Officersᵃ Cuffs	Officersᵃ Colour	Troops Collar	Troops Cuffs	Troops Colour
1st Moscow	1	1	Gold	1	---	White
2nd Pskov	1	2	Silver	1	2	Whiteᵇ
3rd New Russia	1	1	Gold	---	---	---
4th New Russia-Ekaterinoslav	1*	2*	Silver	---	---	---
5th Kargopol	1	1	Gold	---	---	---
6th Glukhov	1	2	Silver	1	---	Whiteᵇ
7th Kinburn	1	1	Silver	---	---	---
8th Astrakhan	2	2	Silver	---	---	---
9th Kazan	1	2	Gold	---	---	---
10th Novgorod	1	2	Gold	---	---	---
11th Riga	1	1	Gold	---	---	---
12th Starodub	1	2	Gold	---	---	---
13th Military Order of St Georgeᶜ	1	2	Gold	---	---	---
14th Little Russian	1	2	Gold	---	---	---
15th Pereyaslav	1	1	Silver	1	1	White
16th Tver	1*	1*	Gold	---	---	---
17th Nizhni-Novgorod	2*	1*	Gold	2	1	St George's
18th Seversk	2*	1*	Silver	2	1	St George's
19th Archangelgorod	1	1	Silver	---	---	---
20th Finland	1	1	Silver	---	---	---
Premorsky	1	1	Gold	---	---	---

Notes: ᵃ In dragoon regiments classified as dragoons, the normal officer's uniform has a single standard litzen at the collar and cuffs. In dragoon regiments formerly classified as cuirassiers, the normal officer's uniform has a single standard litzen at the collar and two at the cuffs.
ᵇ At the collar: with a central thread the colour of the shoulder tab. At the cuffs: with a central thread the colour of the cuffs.
ᶜ With grenade-shaped decorations. Troops also have grenade-shaped decorations at the collar, although they do not have litzen. Cuffs have plain buttons for both officers and troops, but only officers have litzen at the cuffs.
* Distinction-type litzen.

Collar and Cuff Litzen of the Line Lancers

Regiment	Officers Collar[a]	Officers Cuffs[a]	Colour	Troops Collar	Troops Cuffs	Colour
1st St Petersburg	1*	1*	Gold	---	---	---
2nd Kurland	1	1	Gold	1[b]	---	White
3rd Smolensk	1	1	Gold	1[b]	---	White
4th Kharkov	1	1	Gold	---	---	---
5th Lithuanian	1	1	Silver	---	---	---
6th Volynsky	1	1	Silver	---	---	---
7th Olviopol	1	1	Silver	---	---	---
8th Voznesensk	1	1	Silver	---	---	---
9th Bug	1*	1*	Gold	---	---	---
10th Odessa	1	1	Gold	---	---	---
11th Chuguev	1	1	Gold	1[b]	1[c]	White
12th Belgorod	1	1	Gold	---	---	---
13th Vladimir	2	1	Silver	---	---	---
14th Yamburg	2	1	Silver	---	---	---
15th Tatar	1	1	Silver	---	---	---
16th New Archangel	1	1	Silver	---	---	---
17th New Mirgorod	1	1	Gold	---	---	---

Notes: [a] A single standard litzen was a normal part of an officer's uniform.
[b] With central thread the colour of the cloth underneath.
[c] With central thread the colour of the cuff.
* Distinction-type litzen.

Collar and Cuff Litzen of the Line Infantry Grenadiers

Regiment	Officers Collar	Officers Cuffs	Colour	Troops Collar	Troops Cuffs	Colour
1st Ekaterinoslav	2	3	Gold	2	3	White
2nd Rostov	2	3	Gold	---	---	---
3rd Pernov	2	3	Gold	---	---	---
4th Nesvizh	2	3	Gold	---	---	---
5th Kiev	2	3	Gold	---	---	---
6th Tavrida	2	3	Gold	---	---	---
7th Samoguitia	2	3	Gold	---	---	---
8th Moscow	2	3	Gold	---	---	---
9th Siberian	2	3	Gold	---	---	---
10th Little Russia	2	3	Gold	---	---	---
11th Phanagoria	2	3	Gold	---	---	---
12th Astrakhan	2	3	Gold	2	3	White
13th Erivan	2*	3*	Silver	2	3	St George's
15th Tiflis	2*	3*	Silver	2	3	St George's
16th Mingrelia	2*	3*	Silver	2	3	St George's

Notes: * Distinction-type litzen.

Litzen of the Cossacks of the Steppes

Officers			Troops		
Collar	Cuffs	Colour	Collar	Cuffs	Colour
1	1	Silver	1	1	White[a]

Notes: [a] With central thread the colour of the collar piping.

§V-3-3 COLLAR AND CUFF LACE

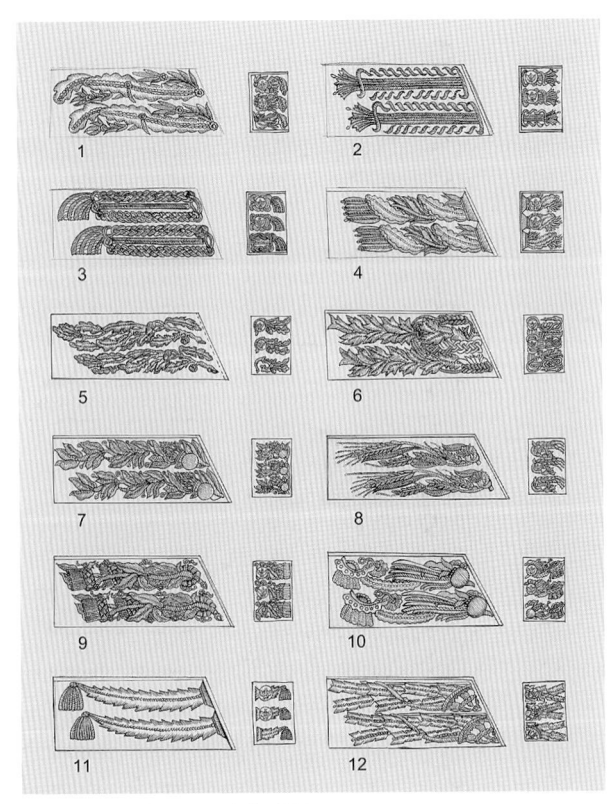

V:8 Russian Collar and Cuff Trim
1. Preobrazhensky Regiment of the Imperial Guard and Lithuanian Regiment of the Imperial Guard.
2. Semenovsky Regiment of the Imperial Guard.
3. Izmailovsky Regiment of the Imperial Guard.
4. Yegersky Regiment of the Imperial Guard.
5. Moscow Regiment of the Imperial Guard.
6. Grenadier Regiment of the Imperial Guard.
7. Paul Regiment of the Imperial Guard.
8. Finland Regiment of the Imperial Guard and Volynsky Regiment of the Imperial Guard.
9. Kexholm Regiment of His Imperial Majesty, Emperor of Austria and King of Hungary Imperial Guard.
10. St Petersburg Regiment of the King of Prussia, Frederick-William III Imperial Guard.
11. 1st His Majesty's Imperial Guard Rifle Regiment.
12. 2nd Tsarskoe-Selo Imperial Guard Rifle Regiment.

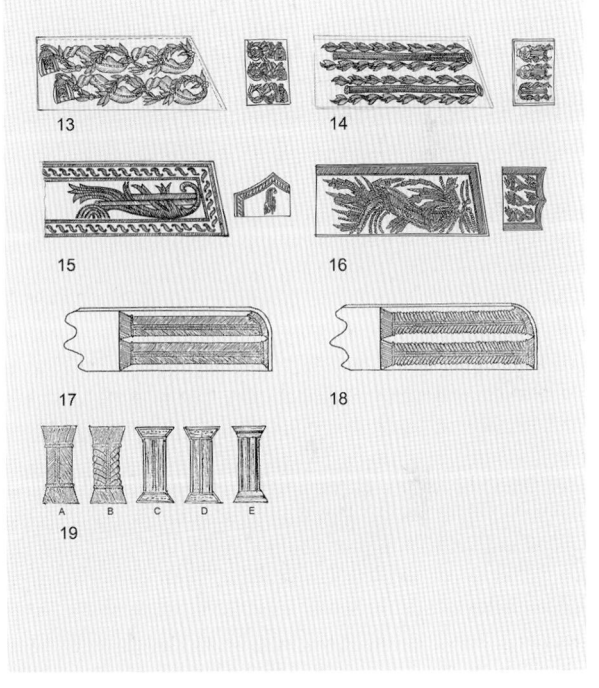

V:9 Russian Collar and Cuff Trim
13. 3rd His Majesty's Rifle Regiment of the Imperial Guard.
14. Russian Guard Artillery and Engineers.
15. Imperial Guard Cossack Regiment of His Majesty.
16. General Staff.
17. Standard collar litzen (some regiments had only one litzen). Litzen were gold or silver, depending on button colour.
18. Distinction litzen. It is ribbed (corduroyed), which is the mark of a distinction litzen.
19a. Officer's standard cuff button litzen.
19b. Officer's distinction cuff button litzen. Note the ribbing.
19c. Guard other rank's standard cuff button litzen. Guard other rank litzen is red-orange with red thread along the length of the sides of litzen. In the guards, the centre line of the litzen is the colour of the collar or cuff behind it. The exception to this rule is the Lithuanian Regiment of the Imperial Guard where the litzen sat on a yellow collar, but had a red 'central light' line.
19d. Line other rank's standard cuff button litzen.
19e. Other rank's St George's cuff button litzen. This litzen had three black columns and two orange columns.

Image V:8 shows the collar and cuff lace for the Guard Infantry regiments and the 1st and 2nd Guard Rifles regiments. Image V:9 shows the collar and cuff lace for: the 3rd and 4th Guard Rifles; the Guard Artillery and Engineers; the General Staff and different types of collar and cuff litzen.

There were complicated rules about where and when litzen were worn when the regiment's chief was the czar, the czar's wife, his mother, or a member of the Imperial Family. These are beyond the scope of this work.[31]

The lower cuff button of the uniform was not buttoned (see §V-3-1).

Certain patterns of lace or embroidery were used by more than one regiment when a second regiment was budded off from an older regiment (see Images V:8(1) and V:9(8)).

§V-3-4 GUARD UNIFORMS BEFORE 1908

Image V:10 of a graduating class of the Corps de Pages before 1908 provides a clear view the uniforms worn by the exclusive guards regiments during most of the reign of the last czar.

The men shown are from the following regiments (with the number from each in brackets):

Imperial Guard Lancer Regiment of Her Majesty (6)
Cuirassiers (5)
Cheval (Horse) Guards Regiment of the Imperial Guard (4)
Imperial Guard Cuirassiers Regiment of the Empress Maria Feodorovna (1)

V:10 Corps de Pages Graduating Class before 1908
The photograph shows guard uniforms worn during most of the reign of Nicholas II from his coronation up to 1908. Only men connected with the Russian guards were allowed to wear the white papakha. See §V-3-4, Guard Uniforms Before 1908.

Grodno Hussar Regiment of the Imperial Guard (4)

44th Nizhni-Novgorod Line Dragoons (later the 17th Nizhni-Novgorod Dragoon Regiment of His Majesty)(4)

Dragoon Regiment of the Imperial Guard (3)

Horse Grenadier Regiment of the Imperial Guard (2)

3rd Plastun Battalion, Kuban Cossacks had ties to the Preobrazhensky Guard Regiment. They are the men in the white papakha (hat) (2)

Semenovsky Regiment of the Imperial Guard (1)

4th Imperial Guard Rifle Regiment of the Imperial Family (1)

Line Dragoons (2)
    Finland Dragoons (later the 20th Finland Dragoon Regiment) (1)
    Sumy Dragoons (later the 1st Sumy Hussar Regiment) (1)

Horse Artillery (2)

Artillery (2)

§V-3-5 INFANTRY AND CAVALRY MONOGRAMS

Images V:11 and V:12 show the infantry and cavalry monograms and also lists the names of the rulers, nobles and cities whose monograms are shown in Images V:11 and V:12. The number of each monogram is associated with the person or city to which the monogram applies.

This list shows which regiment wore a given monogram. The first number relates back to the numbers of the monograms. For example, the number 2 shows that the monogram 'A' is for Czarevich Alexander. The entry after the number then lists the number of regiments (eight) that carried this monogram. Further down the list is the number 15, which relates to monogram 15, a 'K', which was Grand Duke Konstantin's monogram. It was carried by one regiment: the 15th Tiflis Grenadier Regiment.

1: 4th Nesvizh Grenadier Regiment of Field Marshal Prince Barclay de Tolly, 13th Erivan Imperial Grenadier Regiment of Czar Michael Fedorovich, 65th Moscow Infantry Regiment of His Majesty, 1st Company of 80th Kabarda Infantry Regiment of Field Marshal Prince Baryatinsky, 84th Shirvan Infantry Regiment, 1st Siberian Rifle Regiment of His Majesty, 17th Nizhni-Novgorod Dragoon Regiment of His Majesty, and many other regiments.

2: 5th Kiev Grenadier Regiment of the Czarevich, 14th Georgian Grenadier Regiment of the Czarevich, 51st Lithuanian Infantry Regiment of the Czarevich, 89th White Sea Infantry Regiment of the Czarevich, 206th Salyany Infantry Regiment of the Czarevich, 12th Siberian Rifle Regiment of the Czarevich, 16th Tver Dragoon Regiment of the Czarevich, 2nd Don Cossack Regiment of General Sysoev, and 1st Orenburg Cossack Regiment.

3: 48th Odessa Infantry Regiment of Emperor Alexander I, and 7th White Russian Hussar Regiment of Emperor Alexander I.

4: 1st Ekaterinoslav Imperial Grenadier Regiment of Emperor Alexander II, and 2nd Kurland Lancer Regiment of Emperor Alexander II.

5: 12th Astrakhan Regiment of Emperor Alexander III, 2nd Sofia Infantry Regiment of Emperor Alexander III, 68th Borodino Infantry Regiment of Emperor Alexander III, 145th Novocherkassk Infantry Regiment of Emperor Alexander III, 15th Pereyaslav Dragoon Regiment of Emperor Alexander III, 3rd Smolensk Lancer Regiment of Emperor Alexander III, and 2nd Pavlograd Hussar Regiment of Emperor Alexander III.

6: 16th Rifle Regiment of Emperor Alexander II.

7: Crimean (Tartar) Horse Regiment, 21st Siberian Rifle Regiment of Grand Duchess Alexandra Feodorovna, and 17th Chernigov Hussars of Grand Duke Nicholas Nikolaevich.

8: 11th Siberian Rifle Regiment of Grand Duchess Maria Feodorovna, 2nd Pskov Life Dragoon Regiment of Empress Maria Feodorovna, and 11th Chuguev Lancer Regiment of Empress Maria Feodorovna.

9: 13th Erivan Imperial Grenadier Regiment of Czar Michael Fedorovich.

V:11 Russian Infantry and Cavalry Monograms
1. Czar Nicolas II.
2. Czarevich Alexander Nikolaevich.
3. Alexander I.
4. Alexander II.
5. Alexander III.
6. Alexander III.
7. Empress Alexandra Feodorovna.
8. Empress Maria Feodorovna.
9. Czar Mikhail Feodorvich.
10. Peter the Great.
11. Peter the Great and Alexander III.
12. Katherine the Great.
13. Grand Duke Dmitri Konstantinovich.
14. Alphonse XIII of Spain.
15. Grand Duke Konstantin.
16. King of Rumania.
17. Emperor Franz Joseph of Austria.
18. Prince Frederick Leopold of Prussia.
19. Grand Duke Luke Ludwig Victor of Austria.
20. King Victor Emmanuel III of Italy.
21. Grand Duke Dmitri Pavlovich.
22. Grand Duke Mikhail Alexandrovich.
23. Grand Duke Mikhail Nikolaevich.
24. City of Malo-Russiski.
See below for which regiments wore these monograms.

V:12 Russian Infantry and Cavalry Monograms
25. Grand Duke Nikolai Nikolaevich.
26. City of Samogitski.
27. King Christian IX of Denmark.
28. Duke of Oldenburg.
29. Duke Frederich of Mecklenburg.
30. King Frederick Wilhelm IV of Prussia.
31. Emperor Wilhelm II of Germany.
32. Emperor Wilhelm I of Germany.
33. King of Württemberg.
34. Peter I of Serbia.
35. Nicolas I of Montenegro.
36. Emperor Ferdinand of Bulgaria.
37. King of Greece.
See below for which regiments wore these monograms.

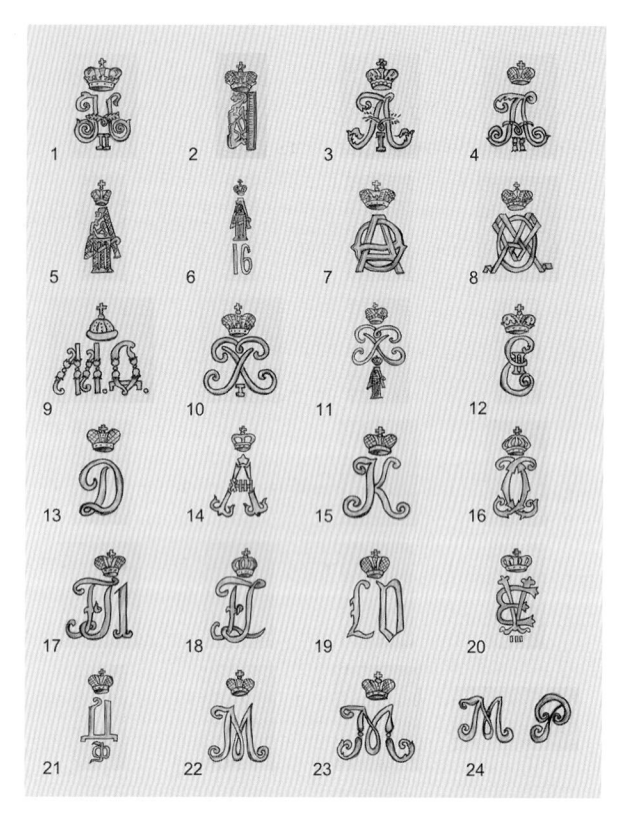

10: 9th Ingria Infantry Regiment of Emperor Peter I.
11: 1st Moscow Life Dragoon Regiment of Emperor Peter the Great.
12: 81st Apsheron Infantry Regiment of Catherine II, now of Grand Duke George Mikhaylovich, 6th Glukhov Dragoon Regiment of Empress Catherine II, and 1st Zaporozhian Regiment of Empress Catherine the Great.
13: 16th Mingrelia Regiment of Grand Duke Dimitri Constantinovich.
14: 7th Olviopol Lancer Regiment of Alfonso XIII, King of Spain.
15: 15th Tiflis Grenadier Regiment.
16: 18th Vologda Infantry Regiment of the King of Rumania.
17: 12th Belgorod Lancer Regiment of the Emperor of Austria and King of Hungary Franz-Joseph I.

18: 6th Libau Infantry Regiment of Prince Frederick Leopold of Prussia.
19: 39th Tomsk Infantry Regiment.
20: 5th Lithuanian Lancer Regiment of King Victor Emmanuel III of Italy.
21: 11th Phanagoria Grenadier Regiment of Generalissimo Prince Suvorov.
22: 2nd Rostov Grenadier Regiment of Grand Duke Michael Alexandrovich.
23: 6th Tavrida Grenadier Regiment, 1st Caucasian Regiment of Viceroy of Catherine, General Field Marshall Prince Potemkin, 1st Kuban Regiment, and 1st Plastun Battalion of General Feldzeugmeister Grand Duke Michael Nikolaevich.
24: 10th Little Russia Grenadier Regiment of Field Marshal Count Rumyantsev-Zadunaisky.
25: 9th Siberian Grenadier Regiment of Grand Duke Nicholas Nicolaevich, 13th Rifle Regiment of General-Field Marshal Grand Duke Nicholas Nikolaevich, and 8th Astrakhan Dragoon Regiment of Field Marshal Grand Duke Nicholas Nikolaevich.
26: 7th Samoguitia Grenadier Regiment of Adjutant General Count Totleben.
27: 18th Seversk Dragoon Regiment.
28: 67th Tarutino Infantry Regiment of the Grand Duke of Oldenburg.
29: 8th Moscow Grenadiers of the Grand Duke of Mecklenburg Frederick II.
30: 3rd Pernov Regiment of King Frederick William IV of Prussia.
31: 85th Vyborg Infantry Regiment of His Majesty William II, Emperor of Germany and King of Prussia and 13th Narva Hussar Regiment of William II, Emperor of Germany and King of Prussia.
32: 5th Kaluga Infantry Regiment.
33: 10th Novgorod Dragoon Regiment of the King of Württemberg.
34: 14th Olonets Infantry Regiment of Peter I, King of Serbia.
35: 15th Rifle Regiment of His Majesty King Nicholas I of Montenegro.
36: 54th Minsk Infantry Regiment of His Majesty the King of Bulgaria.
37: 1st Neva Infantry Regiment of His Highness the King of Greece.

§V-3-6 SHENK PLATES

In response to the 1908 changes in the Russian uniforms, booklets showing details of the new uniforms were published. Without a doubt the best was that created by V.K. Shenk in 1910. These are shown in Images C64 through C74:

C64a: Dragoon uniforms 1881–1910 (pre-1910 name followed by post-1910 name). The colours shown here for the 9th, 17th, 18th, and 21st Dragoons do not agree with the colours listed at Table V.7.a.1.1 in the text. This schematic was made by Moritz Ruhl in 1890. The text in the table is from a book by a Russian researcher *c.* 1980.

Row A:
1. 7th New Russia Dragoons (3rd New Russia Dragoons)
2. 8th Smolensk Dragoons (3rd Smolensk Lancers)
3. 9th Elizabetgrad Dragoons (3rd Elizabetgrad Hussars)
4. 10th Ekaterinoslav Dragoons (4th New Russia-Ekaterinoslav Dragoons)
5. 11th Kharkov Dragoons (4th Kharkov Lancers)
6. 12th Mariupol Dragoons (4th Mariupol Hussars)

Row B:
1. 13th Kargopal Dragoons (5th Kargopol Dragoons)
2. 14th Lithuanian Dragoons (5th Lithuanian Lancers)
3. 15th Alexandria Dragoons (5th Alexandria Hussars)
4. 16th Glukhov Dragoons (6th Glukhov Dragoons)
5. 17th Volynsky Dragoons (6th Volynsky Lancers)

6. 18th Klyastitsi Dragoons (6th Klyastitsi Hussars)

Row C:
1. 19th Kinburn Dragoons (7th Kinburn Dragoons)
2. 20th Olviopol Dragoons (7th Olviopol Lancers)
3. 21st White Russian Dragoons (7th White Russian Hussars)
4. 22nd Astrakhan Dragoons (8th Astrakhan Dragoons)
5. 23rd Voznesensk Dragoons (8th Voznesensk Lancers)
6. 24th Lubny Dragoons (8th Lubny Hussars)

C64b: Plates of the Russian Imperial Army Uniforms by V.K. Shenk (1910)

Row 1:
1. Preobrazhensky Regiment of the Imperial Guard
2. Semenovsky Regiment of the Imperial Guard
3. Izmailovsky Regiment of the Imperial Guard
4. Yegersky Regiment of the Imperial Guard

Row 2:
1. Moscow Regiment of the Imperial Guard
2. Grenadier Regiment of the Imperial Guard
3. Paul Regiment of the Imperial Guard
4. Finland Regiment of the Imperial Guard

C65
Row 3:
1. Lithuanian Regiment of the Imperial Guard
2. Kexholm Regiment of the His Imperial Majesty Emperor of Austria and King of Hungary Imperial Guard
3. St. Petersburg Regiment of the King of Prussia, Frederick-William III Imperial Guard
4. Volynsky Regiment of the Imperial Guard

Row 4:
1. Guard Rifle Regiment
2. 1st His Majesty's Imperial Guard Rifle Regiment
3. 2nd Tsarskoe-Selo Imperial Guard Rifle Regiment
4. 4th Imperial Guard Rifle Regiment of the Imperial Family

Row 5:
1. Chevalier Guard Regiment of Empress Maria Feodorovna
2. Cheval (Horse) Guards Regiment of the Imperial Guard
3. Imperial Guard Cuirassiers Regiment of His Majesty
4. Imperial Guard Cuirassiers Regiment of the Empress Maria Feodorovna

Row 6:
1. Undress uniform of Chevalier Guard Regiment of Empress Maria Feodorovna
2. Undress uniform of Cheval (Horse) Guards Regiment of the Imperial Guard
3. Undress uniform of Imperial Guard Cuirassiers Regiment of His Majesty
4. Undress uniform of Imperial Guard Cuirassiers Regiment of the Empress Maria Feodorovna

C66
Row 7:
1. Gala dress of Chevalier Guard and Horse Guards
2. Full dress of His Majesty's Personal Cossack Escort
3. Walking-out dress of His Majesty's Personal Cossack Escort
4. Don Cossack Guard artillery battery

Row 8:
1. Full dress of His Majesty's Cossacks
2. Walking-out dress of His Majesty's Cossacks
3. Full dress of Ataman Guard Cossacks
4. Walking-out dress of Ataman Guard Cossacks

Row 9:
1. Dragoon Regiment of the Imperial Guard
2. Horse Grenadier Regiment of the Imperial Guard
3. Imperial Guard Lancer Regiment of Her Majesty
4. Imperial Guard Lancer Regiment of His Majesty

Row 10:
1. Imperial Guard Hussar Regiment of His Majesty
2. Grodno Hussar Regiment of the Imperial Guard
3. Cavalry Reserve Regiment
4. Gendarmes Squadron

C67
Row 11:
Sotnias of the Combined Cossack Regiment of the Imperial Guard
1. 1st Ural Sotnia
2. 2nd Orenburg Sotnia
3. 3rd Mixed Sotnia (Siberian Sotnia)
4. 3rd Mixed Sotnia (Semerechya Platoon)

Row 12:
Sotnias of the Combined Cossask Regiment of the Imperial Guard
1. 3rd Mixed Sotnia, (Astrakhan Platoon)
2. 4th Trans-Amur Sotnia (Transbaikal Sotnia)
3. 4th Trans-Amur Sotnia (Amur Platoon)
4. 4th Trans-Amur Sotnia (Ussuri Platoon)

Row 13:
1. Example of full dress and walking-out dress of the Combined Cossack Regiment of the Imperial Guard
2. Palace Grenadiers
3. Palace Grenadiers, undress uniform
4. a- Example of gorget
   b- Side view of the 4th Fusilier Battalion mitre of the Paul Regiment
   c- Examples of guard star, cockades, and 4th Imperial Guard Rifle Regiment cross worn over cockades
   d- Example of monograms

Row 14:
1. Infantry summer uniform
2. Cavalry summer uniform
3. Equipage of the Guard winter uniform
4. Equipage of the Guard summer uniform

C68
Row 15:
1. 1st Ekaterinoslav Imperial Grenadier Regiment of Emperor Alexander II
2. 2nd Rostov Grenadier Regiment of Grand Duke Michael Alexandrovich
3. 3rd Pernov Grenadier Regiment of King Frederick William IV of Prussia
4. 4th Nesvizh Grenadier Regiment of Field Marshal Prince Barclay de Tolly

Row 16:
1. 5th Kiev Grenadier Regiment of the Czarevich
2. 6th Tavrida Grenadier Regiment
3. 7th Samoguitia Grenadier Regiment of Adjutant General Count Totleben
4. 8th Moscow Grenadiers of the Grand Duke of Mecklenburg Frederick II

Row 17:
1. 9th Siberian Grenadier Regiment of Grand Duke Nicholas Nicolaevich
2. 10th Little Russia Grenadier Regiment of Field Marshal Count Rumyantsev-Zadunaisky
3. 11th Phanagoria Grenadier Regiment of Generalissimo Prince Suvorov
4. 12th Astrakhan Grenadier Regiment of Emperor Alexander III

Row 18:
1. 13th Erivan Imperial Grenadier Regiment of Czar Michael Fedorovich
2. 14th Georgian Grenadier Regiment of the Czarevich
3. 15th Tiflis Grenadier Regiment
4. 16th Mingrelia Grenadier Regiment of Grand Duke Dimitri Constantinovich

C69
Row 19:
1. 113th Staraya-Russa Infantry Regiment
2. 114th Novy-Torzhok Infantry Regiment
3. 115th Vyazma Infantry Regiment of General Nesvetaev
4. 116th Maloyaroslavets Infantry Regiment

Row 20:
1. 1st Neva Infantry Regiment of His Highness the King of Greece
2. 2nd Sofia Infantry Regiment of Emperor Alexander III
3. 9th Ingria Infantry Regiment of Emperor Peter I
4. 34th Sevsk Infantry Regiment of General Count Kamensky

Row 21:
1. 65th Moscow Infantry Regiment of His Majesty
2. 68th Borodino Infantry Regiment of Emperor Alexander III

3. 80th Kabarda Infantry Regiment of Field-Marshal Prince Baryatinsky
4. 17th Archangelgorod Infantry Regiment of Grand Duke Vladimir Alexandrovich

Row 22:
1. 84th Shirvan Infantry Regiment
2. 145th Novocherkassk Infantry Regiment of Emperor Alexander III
3. 146th Tsaritsyn Infantry Regiment
4. a- Examples of belt buckles and tunic buttons
   b–d- Examples of monograms

C70
Row 23:
1. 16th Rifle Regiment of Emperor Alexander II
2. 1st Siberian Rifle Regiment of His Majesty
3. 11th Siberian Rifle Regiment of Grand Duchess Maria Feodorovna
4. 21st Siberian Rifle Regiment of Grand Duchess Alexandra Feodorovna

Row 24:
1. 4th Rifle Regiment
2. 6th Eastern Siberian Rifle and a reserve regiment
3. Summer or combat uniform
4. a- Distinction braid on collar, tunic button, and belt buckle
   b–d- Examples of monograms

Row 25:
1. 1st Moscow Life Dragoon Regiment of Emperor Peter the Great
2. 3rd New Russia Dragoon Regiment of Grand Duchess Helen Vladimirovna
3. 5th Kargopol Dragoon Regiment
4. 7th Kinburn Dragoon Regiment

Row 26:
1. 11th Riga Dragoon Regiment
2. 15th Pereyaslav Dragoon Regiment of Emperor Alexander III
3. 19th Archangelgorod Dragoon Regiment
4. 20th Finland Dragoon Regiment

C71
Row 27:
1. 16th Tver Dragoon Regiment of the Czarevich

2. 17th Nizhni-Novgorod Dragoon Regiment of His Majesty
3. 18th Seversk Dragoon Regiment
4. Premorsky Dragoon Regiment

Row 28:
1. 2nd Pskov Life Dragoon Regiment of Empress Maria Feodorovna
2. 4th New Russia-Ekaterinoslav Regiment of Field Marshal Prince Potemkin
3. 6th Glukhov Dragoon Regiment of Empress Catherine II
4. 8th Astrakhan Dragoon Regiment of Field Marshal Grand Duke Nicholas Nikolaevich

Row 29:
1. 9th Kazan Dragoon Regiment of Grand Duchess Maria Nikolaevna
2. 10th Novgorod Dragoon Regiment of the King of Württemberg
3. 12th Starodub Dragoon Regiment
4. 14th Little Russian Dragoon Regiment of the Crown Prince of Germany and Prussia

Row 30:
1. 13th Military (St George) Order Dragoon Regiment of Field Marshal Count Minikh
2. 1st–8th Reserve uniform
3. Crimean (Tartar) Horse Regiment
4. Cavalry summer and combat dress

C72
Row 31:
1. 1st St Petersburg Lancer Regiment of Field Marshal Prince Menshikov
2. 2nd Kurland Lancer Regiment of Emperor Alexander II
3. 3rd Smolensk Lancer Regiment of Emperor Alexander III
4. 4th Kharkov Lancer Regiment

Row 32:
1. 5th Lithuanian Lancer Regiment of King Victor Emmanuel III of Italy
2. 6th Volynsky Lancer Regiment
3. 7th Olviopol Lancer Regiment of Alfonso XIII, King of Spain

4. 8th Voznesensk Lancer Regiment of Grand Duchess Tatiana Nikolaevna

Row 33:
1. 9th Bug Lancer Regiment
2. 10th Odessa Lancer Regiment of the Grand Duke of Nassau and Luxemburg
3. 11th Chuguev Lancer Regiment of Empress Maria Feodorovna
4. 12th Belgorod Lancer Regiment of the Emperor of Austria and King of Hungary Franz-Joseph I

Row 34:
1. 13th Vladimir Lancer Regiment
2. 14th Yamburg Lancer Regiment of Grand Duchess Maria Alexandrovna
3. 15th Tatar Lancer Regiment
4. 16th New Archangel Lancer Regiment

C73
Row 35:
1. 17th New Mirgorod Lancer Regiment
2. Dagestan Regiment
3. Ossetian Demi-Regiment
4. Turkman Demi-Regiment

Row 36:
1. 1st Sumy Hussar Regiment of General Seslavin
2. 2nd Pavlograd Hussar Regiment of Emperor Alexander II
3. 3rd Elizabetgrad Hussar Regiment of Grand Duchess Olga Nikolaevna
4. 4th Mariupol Hussar Regiment of Empress Elizabeth Petrovna

Row 37:
1. 5th Alexandria Hussar Regiment of Her Imperial Majesty Alexandra Feodorovna
2. 6th Klyastitsi Hussar of Grand Duke Ernst-Ludwig of Hesse
3. 7th White Russian Hussar Regiment of Emperor Alexander I
4. 8th Lubny Hussar Regiment

Row 38:
1. 9th Kiev Hussar Regiment
2. 10th Ingrermanland Hussar Regiment of the Grand Duke of Saxony-Weimar
3. 11th Izyum Hussar Regiment of Prince Henry of Prussia
4. 12th Akhtyrka Hussar Regiment of Grand Duchess Olga Alexandrovna

C74
Row 39:
1. 13th Narva Hussar Regiment of the Emperor of Germany and King of Prussia William II
2. 14th Mitau Hussar Regiment
3. 15th Ukrainian Hussars of Grand Duke Nicholas Nikolaevich
4. 16th Irkutsk Hussars of Grand Duke Nicholas Nikolaevich

Row 40:
5. 17th Chernigov Hussars of Grand Duke Nicholas Nikolaevich
6. 18th Hezhin Hussar Regiment
7. Cavalry school uniform
8. General's gala uniform

§V-3-7 POUCH BELT BADGES

Some regiments wore decorations on their pouch belts. They are shown in Images V:13 and V:14:

V:13: The monogram 'HII' (Cyrillic for Nicholas II), worn by the Imperial Guard Hussar Regiment of His Majesty, Imperial Guard Cossack Regiment of His Majesty, Imperial Guard Cossack Ataman Regiment of the Czarevich, and some units of the Combined Cossack Regiment of the Imperial Guard.

V:14: A helmet and trophies, worn by the Imperial Guard Hussar Regiment of His Majesty and Imperial Guard Cossack Ataman Regiment of the Czarevich.

V:13 Pouch Badge
The badge worn on the lower front of the pouch belt of Hussars of His Majesty, Cossacks of His Majesty, Ataman Guard Cossacks, and some units of the Combined Guard Cossacks.

V:14 Pouch Badge
The badge worn on the upper end of the pouch belt of the Hussars of His Majesty and the Ataman Guard Cossacks.

V:15 Modern Examples of Regimental Badges Worn on Tunics
1. Semenovsky Regiment of the Imperial Guard.
2. Moscow Regiment of the Imperial Guard.
3. Finland Regiment of the Imperial Guard.
4. 108th Saratov Infantry Regiment.
5. 180th Vindau Infantry Regiment.
6. Ural Cossack Host.

§V-3-8 REGIMENTAL BADGES

Image V:15 shows the regimental badges of: the Semenovsky Regiment of the Imperial Guard; the Moscow Regiment of the Imperial Guard; the Finland Regiment of the Imperial Guard; the 108th Saratov Infantry Regiment; the 180th Vindau Infantry Regiment; and the Ural Cossack Host.

§V-3-9 SERVICE CHEVRONS

Prior to 1825, service for the other ranks was for life. In 1825, it was reduced to twenty-five years for the line and twenty-two for the guards.[32] In 1834, the term of service was reduced to fifteen years in the active army for soldiers with good service records. These men then went into the reserves for five years.[33] With these long-term soldiers, obtaining NCOs with experience was not a problem.

Following the Crimean War, the army saw a need for a better system of reserves. In the Miliutin military reforms of 1874, the draft system was changed. The duty to serve in the army ranks was extended from just the lower classes to all subjects of the czar. The length of service was reduced to six years, and many exemptions were made. This allowed for the creation of a larger military reserve that could be called up in time of war.[34]

But, once short-term service was introduced, almost all the drafted soldiers elected to return to civilian life. This choked off the supply of experienced men who might become NCOs. To induce men to re-enlist when their first service term expired, the authorities tried several things: increases in pay, preferences in employment once they left the army, limited pensions, and service chevrons for their uniforms.[35]

An NCO during his first five-year period as a re-enlisted man wore a silver chevron. If he re-enlisted for a second five-year period, he would be given a gold chevron,[36] the third a silver medal. If there was a fourth five-year re-enlistment, the soldier was awarded a gold and silver medal worn around the neck. The chevrons were worn on the upper left arm, and the medal on the chest.[37]

In 1882, the British intelligence service stated that a silver chevron was awarded to re-enlisted soldiers. Gold chevrons were awarded to men who re-enlisted after their first five-year re-enlistment period. All chevrons were worn on the left upper arm (Image V:38 shows an example).[38]

Men who had served longer than six years wore a chevron of yellow braid, and sub-ensigns and sub-cornets[39] wore an extra-wide gold chevron also on their upper left arm.[40]

In the early part of the twentieth century, service chevrons were described as follows: the first chevron was awarded after ten years' service, thereafter another chevron was awarded for each subsequent five years of service. Nothing was said about the colour of the chevrons.[41]

Service chevrons seem to have continued to be worn up to 1914, and were probably in the regiment's button colour.[42]

§V-3-10 GORGETS

Gorgets were not a normal part of Russian uniforms. However, the officers of many guard and line infantry units wore gorgets as an old honour or a battle distinction.

Image V:16 shows gorgets worn by Russian guard infantry, line infantry, grenadier, and rifle regiments: gorget for senior officers of the Preobrazhensky and Semenovsky Imperial Guard Regiments; gorget for subalterns of the Preobrazhensky and Semenovsky Imperial Guard Regiments; gorget for the Izmailovsky Imperial Guard Regiment officers; gorget for the Moscow, Finland, Lithuanian and Volynsky Imperial

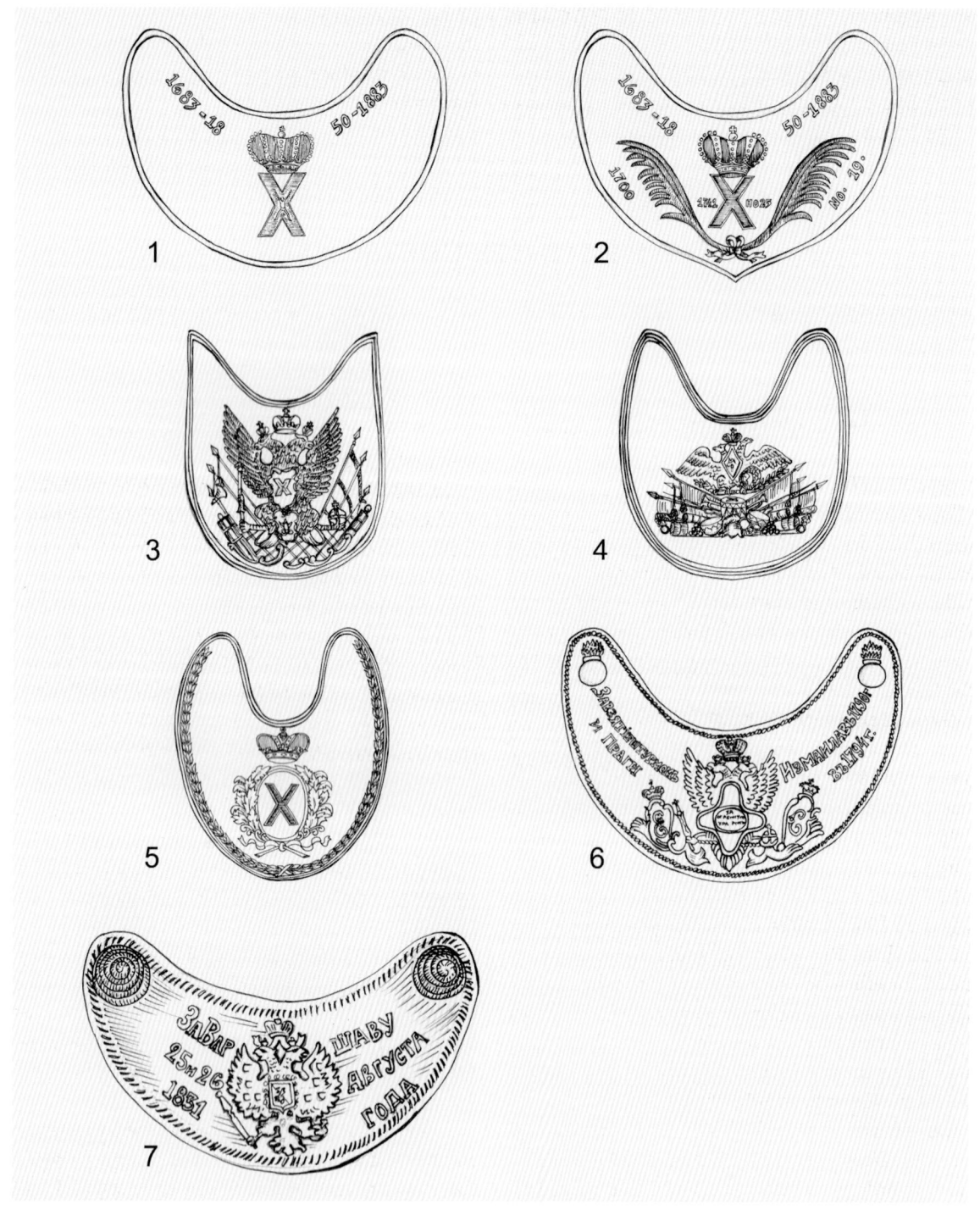

V:16 Gorgets
Worn by Russian guard infantry, line infantry, grenadier, and rifle regiments. For details of what is on these gorgets, see §V-6-a.
1. Gorget for senior officers of the Preobrazhensky and Semenovsky Regiments.
2. Gorget for subalterns of the Preobrazhensky and Semenovsky Regiments.
3. Gorget for the Izmailovsky Regiment officers.
4. Gorget for the Moscow, Finland, Lithuanian and Volynsky Regiment officers.
5. Gorget for the St Petersburg Regiment officers.
6. Gorget for the 11th Phanagoria Grenadier Regiment.
7. Gorget for officers of all other line infantry, grenadier, and rifle regiments.

Guard Regiment officers; gorget for the St Petersburg Imperial Guard Regiment officers; gorget for the 11th Phanagoria Grenadier Regiment; gorget for officers of all other line infantry, grenadier, and rifle regiments. For line infantry, grenadier and rifle regiments the gorget was where honour distinctions are listed, so the wording on the gorget changed from regiment to regiment. (See §V-2-2 for a list of units with distinction wording.)

§V-3-11 GUARD OTHER RANK RIFLE STRAPS

In full dress the rifle straps of guard regiments were red. The line regiments' straps were brown.

§V-3-12 UNIFORM CHANGES OF 1881–2, 1907–8, AND 1913

The period 1880–1914 saw two complete changes in the design of the uniforms worn by the Russian line soldiers. The first was in 1881–2, the other 1907–8. There is confusion about when these changes occurred as different authorities state different dates. Below is a clarification of why the Shenk illustrations shown at Images C64 to C74 at times do not match descriptions in the text.

When Alexander III came to the throne, an early reform was to change the uniforms of the line regiments in 1881 or 1882. The uncertainty of the date is that the order for the change was given in November of 1881,[43] but most of the changes to the uniforms occured in 1882.[44]

The same thing happened with the uniform changes of 1907–8 after the Russo-Japanese War of 1904–5 and the Revolution of 1905. The authorities decided for efficiency reasons to replace the service uniforms worn by the line regiments and to boost morale by bringing back the old colourful full dress uniforms for these soldiers.

First, in November 1907, khaki service dress was introduced, which would also be the summer full dress.[45] In December 1907, a new double-breasted tunic was ordered for the guard and line infantry,[46] but this could not be issued until 1908. In April 1908, new full dress was introduced for the line cavalry regiments.[47] More changes were made to the new line infantry and cavalry uniforms, particularly to the cavalry headdress, right up to the start of World War I.

During 1911–12 thoughts turned to transforming the summer khaki dress uniform into a winter full dress uniform by adding a plastron, collar and cuffs of regimental colour and pattern. These were black with red trim for the general staff, yellow for the grenadiers, and raspberry for the rifles. The first regiment in a line infantry division had a red plastron, the second had a light-blue one, the third white, and the fourth dark green (black for other ranks) with red trim. The 1st Neva and 2nd Sofia Infantry Regiments had white trim on their plastrons. (Zweguintzow, *Uniformes Russe*, p. 114.) The dress of the guard and cavalry were not affected. A new papakha with a double-headed eagle and any distinction awards would also be worn (Mollo, *Uniforms*, p. 48; Zweguintzow shows papakhas with cockades rather than eagles in *Uniformes Russe*, plate A19).

These changes were formally introduced as part of the Romanoff house's tercentenary celebrations in 1913. The changes were so late that the army bureaucracy was not able to make the conversions to the uniforms before World War I began, so they are largely unknown.

The change by trying to convert one dress item into another with the addition of the plastron produced some odd results. When added to an officer's khaki jacket, the plastron did not quite cover the bottom outside corners of the breast pockets. Some officers went to the expense of having a special full dress jacket made, which showed this flaw (see Mollo, *Military Fashion*, p. 223). Maybe it is just as well these uniforms weren't widely adopted.

§V-4 GENERAL STAFF

Available to both line and guard officers, the general staff provided an opportunity to achieve a brilliant military career. Like the German general staff, it was difficult to gain a place in the Russian general staff. In 1895, 3.33 per cent of those who took the first test were chosen for the general staff. In 1907, with fewer applying, 16 per cent were chosen.[48]

A young officer had to pass successfully through five levels of tests and filters in order to earn this right. Officers had only three chances to take the tests to enter the academy. After that, they could never try again.[49]

Entry into the general staff tended to be easier for some. Guard officers, for example, received a better education and had better access to resources, such as crammers[50] and lectures, as they were for the most part stationed in the city where the academy entrance tests were administered. Thus, they were statistically more likely to be appointed to the general staff.

Upon being accepted as a general staff (hereafter GS) officer, a man might be assigned to one of three areas: the Central GS, the GS serving with the guard and in the St Petersburg Military District (St PMD), or the GS serving with line formations, or other GS duties.

As might be expected, general staff officers had several uniform elements to set them apart. The uniform could have variations depending on whether an officer served in the Central GS or with a battle formation. These in turn would be different for officers serving with guard units versus those serving with line units.

§V-4-a CENTRAL GENERAL STAFF[51]

UNIFORM

Headdress
Central GS officers wore a general staff model kiver, which was 13.34 cm (5.25 inches) tall in the front and 12.22 cm (4.81 inches) tall in the back. The black patent leather top was flat, in contrast to the slight scoop on the regular guard kiver. On the front of the kiver was a silver double-headed eagle.

The top had red piping. Below the piping was a thin silver band whose thickness showed rank. The same rules as those used by the guard infantry were followed (see *§V-6-a*). On the centre front above the eagle was an officer's style cockade.

The body of the kiver was covered with cloth of czar's green. Around the kiver's base was a black velvet band with red piping. The front, back, and both sides had a smooth silver cord looping down from four silver buttons. The buttons had an imperial double-headed eagle on them. Below these cords were woven cords hanging down on all four sides of the kiver. The smooth cords and the woven cord in front of the kiver partially covered the eagle on the front. The way the two sets of cord hung down and how the front badge was partially covered by the two front cords is shown in Image V:17. The officer's kiver had a patent leather peak (visor) with a metallic silver border.

Officer in full dress wore a tall white horsehair line infantry model plume (Image V:17). For daily wear they had a shorter white horsehair plume or a silver pompom.[52]

Tunic
The tunic, collar, cuff elements, epaulette fringe, aiguillette, and breeches discussed below can all be seen in Image V:17.

The double-breasted tunic was czar's green and had two rows of six silver buttons down the front. The tunic top where it folded over was cut straight because GS officers and men did not wear plastrons. The buttons had the double-headed eagle on them. The top and front edges of the tunic were piped in red.

of silver trim.[53] The body of the collar contained GS embroidery. See Image V:9(16) for the design in 1914.

Cuffs

The GS tunic had Brandenburg cuffs piped in red (see §V-6-a for size). Both the horizontal and vertical parts of the cuffs were black velvet. Slightly above the red trim on the horizontal part of each cuff was a thin silver band. The vertical bar of black velvet was almost completely covered by sets of silver GS-style embroidery (Image V:9(16)). On top of the top two sets of embroidery there was a silver button with an imperial eagle. Since it was the custom in the Russian army not to button the bottom button, the bottom embroidery did not have a button on it. However, a silver button with an imperial eagle was sewn on the cuff off to the side (Image V:17).

Epaulettes

Central GS officers wore silver epaulettes of the guard infantry model. The hanging fringe was silver, and its thickness indicated rank. It had red piping around the edges, and its lining was red. See §V-3-1 for details on epaulettes.

Aiguillette

A silver aiguillette was worn on the right shoulder.

Breeches

The breeches were blue with red piping. Generals serving on the GS wore the same blue breeches with two wide stripes.

Footwear

In full dress, Central GS members wore black boots.

V:17 Uniform of a Member of an Elite within an Elite, a General Staff Officer Serving with the Guards
His tunic has many of the attributes of a Central General Staff officer's uniform: silver buttons, silver fringe on his epaulettes, cuffs of black velvet with silver trim on it, and silver aiguillettes. He also has a St Andrew's star, guard star, on a double-headed eagle on his kiver.
However, the embroidery on his collar does not match the general staff embroidery of Image V:9(16). For a discussion of this mystery and fuller coverage of the general staff uniform, see §V-4-b, the Mystery of Collar Embroidery.

Each rear skirt of the tunic had a simple straight two-button trim that made a 90-degree turn. There was a silver button with imperial eagle at each end. The edge of each skirt between the buttons was piped red.

Collar

The collar was cut at a sharp angle like those of the guard. It was made of black velvet with red piping on the front and top edges. These edges also had bands

§V-4-b OFFICERS WITH GUARD AND ST PETERSBURG MILITARY DISTRICT UNITS

UNIFORM

GS officers serving with guard units or the St PMD wore a uniform that was a blend of the GS uniform and the uniform worn by the parent guard unit. Officers working with a guard infantry division wore, with a few exceptions, the uniform of the 4th regiment of the division. Officers assigned to the Guard Rifle Brigade wore the uniform of the 1st Regiment of the brigade because the 4th Regiment had a unique history and therefore wore a special uniform (see §V-6-a).

With some exceptions, they wore the same uniform as those serving in the Central GS. For that reason, only exceptions to this dress will be set out below.

Headdress

The officers serving with the guard units wore the GS kiver with the same dimensions, silver double-headed eagle, and cords set out above. In addition, they had a guard silver star of St Andrew on top of the breast of the eagle. This marked them as an elite within an elite. This meant the cords hanging down in front of the GS kiver partially covered both the eagle and guard star on the front of the kiver (Image V:17).

They also had different colour bottom cloth bands and trim on their kivers (see Table V.4.2).

Tunic

The double-breasted tunic was the same colour and cut in the same way as the Central GS tunic. The button colours and trim colours were different, depending on whether a GS officer served in the St PMD or a guard unit. Then, if he served in a guard unit, his button colour and trim would be different, depending on where he served (see Table V.4.2).

Table V.4.2: Uniform Trim of GS Officers Serving with Guard Units and in the St Petersburg Military District, c. 1914

Unit	Button Colour	Kiver Bottom Band	Piping on Top of Kiver	Tunic Collar and Trim	Cuffs[a]	Cuff Tabs[b]	Overall Trim	Breeches' Trim
General Staff and St PMD[c]	Silver	Red Trim: none	Red	Red Trim: none	Red No trim	Red Trim: none	Red	Red
Guard Corps	Gold	Czar's green Trim: red	Red	Czar's green Trim: red	Czar's green Trim: red	Red Trim: none	Red	Red
1st Guard Division	Gold	Czar's green Trim: red	Red	Czar's green Trim: red	Czar's green Trim: red	Red Trim: white	Red	Red
2nd Guard Division	Gold	Czar's green Trim: red	Red	Czar's green Trim: red	Czar's green Trim: red	Red Trim: none	Red	Red
3rd Guard Division	Silver	Czar's green Trim: yellow	Yellow	Czar's green Trim: yellow	Czar's rreen Trim: yellow	Yellow Trim: none	Yellow	Yellow
Guard Rifle Brigade	Gold	Czar's green Trim: raspberry	Raspberry	Czar's green Trim: raspberry	Czar's green Trim: raspberry	Raspberry Trim: none	Raspberry	Raspberry

Notes: [a] Brandenburg cuffs were worn.
[b] Cuff tabs refer to the vertical portion of the Brandenburg cuff.
[c] Officers serving in these units wore a combined monogram made up of a gold monogram of Nicholas II and a silver monogram of Alexander I.

Collar and Cuff

The collar was probably cut the same way as those of the Central GS. The cuffs were also the Brandenburg style, but the colour of the cuffs could vary from the Central GS black (see Table V.4.2 for the colours of collars, cuffs, cuff tabs, and their trim).

This leads to another mystery about the officer in Image V:17. Why does he have a double-headed eagle and a guard star on his kiver, while the rest of his uniform – excepting the collar – seem to be that of an officer serving on the Central GS? With the guard star, one would expect the tunic collar and cuffs to show one of the colours from Table V.4.2.[54]

BREECHES

The breeches were also blue, but in some units the seam piping was not red (Table V.4.2).

Table V.4.2 shows the uniform details referred to above. Also see the table, note c, for the special monogram worn by officers and other ranks serving in the St PMD and the Guard GS.

THE MYSTERY OF COLLAR EMBROIDERY

The collar embroidery shown in line drawing V:9(16) does not quite match the collar embroidery worn by the man in Image V:17. There are a number of possibilities:

1. The line drawing is inaccurate. The drawing was based on a drawing in Zweguintzow's *Uniformes Russe*. It is very unlikely that W. Zweguintzow was wrong.
2. The collar embroidery differed by rank. This is unlikely because Zweguintzow does not mention this in *Uniformes Russe*, and he is normally careful to include this type of information.
3. The GS officers had different embroidery depending on where they were assigned. Again, this is unlikely as *Uniformes Russe* does not mention it.
4. The embroidery worn by GS personnel varied over the years. *Uniformes Russe* describes uniforms in 1914, so would not deal with collar embroidery in earlier years. In a small sample of photographs of GS officers, different years show different collar embroidery for the different years.[55]

Until a specific explanation of why the embroidery is different appears, this last is probably the best theory.

GENERAL STAFF OTHER RANKS

The Russian GS had other ranks assigned to it to assist the GS officers and perform clerical duties. In this the Russian GS was different from the Prussian/German GS, which did not have any enlisted men assigned to it.

GUARD GS OTHER RANKS

The other ranks did not wear a kiver, even in full dress. In its place, they wore a cap without a peak (visor), but with a cap band whose colour varied by parent unit.[56]

They wore a double-breasted tunic without a plastron.[57]

Their belts were black if they worked with the GS of a guard unit or the St PMD.[58]

Other than these differences the other ranks serving with the GS generally wore what the GS officers wore. However, some different uniform items were worn, caps and shoulder straps for example, because they were enlisted men. The colours of these are covered in Table V.4.3.

Table V.4.3: Uniform Trim of Other Ranks Serving with the GS among Guard Units and in the St Petersburg Military District, c. 1914

Unit	Cap Headband	Piping on Top of Cap	Shoulder Strap
GS and St PMD[a]	Red Trim: none	Red	Red Trim: none
Guard Corps	Black[b] Trim: red	Red	Red Trim: none
1st Guard Division	Black[b] Trim: red	Red	Red Trim: black[b]

Unit	Cap Headband	Piping on Top of Cap	Shoulder Strap
2nd Guard Division	Black[b] Trim: red	Red	Red Trim: black[b]
3rd Guard Division	Black[b] Trim: yellow	Yellow	Red Trim: black[b]
Guard Rifle Brigade	Black[b] Trim: raspberry	Raspberry	Raspberry Trim: black[b]

Notes: [a] Other ranks serving in these units wore a combined monogram made up of a gold monogram of Nicholas II and a silver monogram of Alexander I.

[b] For other ranks, this was the same colour as their tunic or blouse.

§V-4-c LINE GENERAL STAFF

GS officers do not appear to have had anything to mark their status as GS men. This is the implication from the coverage in Zweguintzow's *Uniformes Russe*,[59] where no distinctions were listed for GS officers – not even aiguillettes or GS collar embroidery – but it was noted that some other ranks working for GS officers wore trousers and shoes instead of breeches and boots.[60]

OTHER RANKS

GS other ranks wore the general uniform of the line troops they served, with only a few trim details marking them as serving with the GS. Their cap and uniform trim was, with one exception, the same as the trim worn by GS officers serving with line units (Table V.4.4). The exception was that the other ranks did not have trim on their breeches or trousers.

For example, their cap bands were the colour of their tunics, with red trim for those serving with staff officers working with grenadiers and line units, raspberry trim for rifles. The same pattern was followed for the tunic collars.

Most other ranks wore black boots with their breeches tucked into them. But, as was noted above, some were allowed to wear long trousers with shoes.

The real distinguishing mark was in the numbers and letters showing the corps worn on the shoulder strap. The number and initials were red for grenadiers and yellow for all GS other ranks serving with line infantry and rifle units (Table V.4.4).

Table V.4.4: Caps, Collars, Cuffs, Buttons, Trim, and Initials of GS Officers Serving with Line Formations

Unit	Button Colour	Cap Headband	Cap Trim	Tunic Collar and Trim	Cuff Trim Colour	Rear Trim	Other Trim	Trim of Breeches and Trousers	Initials and Colour
Grenadier Corps	Gold	Czar's green or black[a] Trim: red	Red	Czar's green or black[a] Trim: red	Red	Red	Red	Red	Г К Red
1st Grenadier Division	Gold	Czar's green or black[a] Trim: red	Red	Czar's green or black[a] Trim: red	Red	Red	Red	Red	Number Г Red
2nd Grenadier Division	Gold	Czar's green or black[a] Trim: red	Red	Czar's green or black[a] Trim: red	Red	Red	Red	Red	Number Г Red
3rd Grenadier Division	Gold	Czar's green or black[a] Trim: red	Red	Czar's green or black[a] Trim: red	Red	Red	Red	Red	Number Г Red
Caucasus Grenadier Division	Silver	Czar's green or black[a] Trim: red	Red	Czar's green or black[a] Trim: red	Red	Red	Red	Red	К$_В$ Г Red
Infantry Army Corps	Gold	Czar's green or black[a] Trim: red	Red	Czar's green or black[a] Trim: red	Red	Red	Red	Red	Number АК Yellow[b]
Infantry Division	Gold	Czar's green or black[a] Trim: red	Red	Czar's green or black[a] Trim: red	Red	Red	Red	Red	Number Yellow
Rifle Brigade or Division	Gold	Czar's green or black[a] Trim: raspberry	Raspberry	Czar's green or black[a] Trim: raspberry	Raspberry	Raspberry	Raspberry	Raspberry	Number Yellow

Notes: [a] The same colour as the tunic: officers – czar's green, other ranks – black.   [b] Or number and К$_В$ К for the Caucasus Corps, number and С$_Б$ К for the Siberian Corps, or Т К for the Turkistan Corps.

§V-5 GUARD CAVALRY

§V-5-a GUARD CUIRASSIERS[61]

The cuirassier, or heavy cavalry, branch of the guard cavalry consisted of four regiments: the Chevalier Guard Regiment; the Cheval (Horse) Guards Regiment; the Imperial Guard Cuirassiers Regiment of His Majesty; and the Imperial Guard Cuirassiers Regiment of the Empress Maria Feodorovna. While every guardsman considered his regiment the best, most felt these four regiments had the highest prestige in the old Imperial Army.

CHEVALIER GUARD REGIMENT[62]

A tradition in this regiment allows it to trace its founding back to 1712. A body of troops, called the 'Kavalergardia', consisting of sixty men with high rank, was created by Peter the Great especially for the purpose of taking part in the coronation of Catherine, his second wife. Following the coronation, the Kavalergardia was disbanded. In the years that followed, this type of unit would be formed several times for special ceremonial occasions and then disbanded.

On 11 January 1799, Czar Paul I formed a unit of one hundred men, all nobles, to act as the escort of the Grand Master of the Order of the Knights of Malta. The Grand Master just happened to be Czar Paul. One year later, on 11 January 1800, with Paul still on the throne, the escort was converted to a regiment named the Regiment of Cavalier Guards. Several name changes regarding *chefs* followed until 1894, when it was given the name it would carry into World War I.

The regiment was one of the most prestigious in the old Imperial Army. Both the czar and the czarevich had been listed on its officers' rolls at the time of their birth.

CHEVAL GUARDS[63]

The Cheval (Horse) Guards was formed in March of 1721 as a dragoon regiment by pulling together units from other dragoon regiments and elements from the Life Guard squadron. In April 1722, the czar ordered that the regiment should be composed entirely of nobles and provide officers for other dragoon regiments. In 1725, it had the name 'Life Regiment'. Following that, in 1730, it was incorporated into the guard and given the name 'Regiment of the Cheval Guards'. Its name was changed in 1800, but in 1801 it changed back to Garde à Cheval, a name it kept until 1914.

CUIRASSIERS OF THE EMPEROR[64]

This regiment was derived from one of the older regiments in the Russian army, the Dragoon Regiment of Prince Volkonsk, and it took the dragoons' formation date of 21 June 1702 as its own. The dragoon regiment went through several name changes. In 1733, it became a cuirassier regiment and in 1761, it was given the name 'Life Cuirassiers of His Imperial Majesty'. Shortly thereafter, in 1761, Czarevich Paul became *chef* of the regiment, and the regiment was given the name 'Cuirassiers of the Czarevich'. Then, in 1796, when Paul became czar, the name changed to Cuirassiers of the Emperor, which was its final name.

CUIRASSIERS OF THE EMPRESS[65]

This regiment was another that could trace its origins back to an early date. Its founding is said to go back to the Dragoons of the Portés, which was formed in 1704 by a close companion of Peter the Great. In 1733 or 1744 (sources differ) it became a cuirassier regiment. After this, there was a period of title changes until 1855, when it was given the name 'Cuirassiers of the Empress'. In 1856, it became a guard regiment, and in 1884 it was named a member of the Old Guards. In 1894, it was given the title it would carry until 1914: Cuirassiers of Her Majesty the Empress Maria Feodorovna. She was the mother of Nicholas II and the widow of Alexander III.

UNIFORM

Table V.5.a.1: Guard Cuirassiers

Regiment	Button Colour	Facing Colour	Collar and Cuff Colour	Collar Shield Colour	Collar Trim	Cuff Trim	Officer Epaulettes[a]	Troopers Shoulder Strap[b]	Stripe on Koller Braid	Supra-vest	Notes
Chevalier Guards	Silver	Red	Red	None	Red	Red	Silver	Red	Red	Red[c]	A, C, D, E
Horse Guards	Gold	Red	Red	None	Red	Red	Gold[d]	Red[d]	Dark blue	Red[c]	B, C, D, F
Emperor's Cuirassiers	Silver	Yellow	Yellow	Light blue	Light blue	Yellow	Silver[e]	Yellow[e]	Light blue	None	A, C, D
Empress's Cuirassiers	Gold	Light blue	Light blue	None	Light blue	Light blue	Gold	Light blue	Light blue	None	B, C, D

Notes: [a] Epaulettes were made of gold or silver cloth, rather than metal.
[b] Trim on shoulder straps was white.
[c] Supravest of regimental pattern worn for certain palace duties.
[d] Gold monogram H II for Nicholas II in the 1st Squadron only.
[e] Silver monogram H II for Nicholas II in the 1st Squadron only.
A: Silver eagle on the helmet in full dress.
B: Gold eagle on the helmet in full dress.
C: Guard star (of St Andrew) on the helmet.
D: A single litzen on the collar and double litzen on the cuffs were standard for all ranks. Litzen were in the chapter shape in all cases.
E: St Andrew's star on supravest.
F: Double-headed eagle on supravest.

Headdress

The helmet worn in full dress was made of a brass shell that included a visor in the front and a curved neck-cover in the back. The metal borders on the visor and neck-cover, along with all of the metal studs, were silver. On the front of the helmet was a silver St Andrew guard star with an enamelled centre (Images V:18 and V:19). A metal double-headed eagle was affixed to the top of the helmet in full dress, although on some occasions a metal grenade decoration was used instead. The eagle and its support piece were in the regiment's button colour, gold for the Horse Guards and the Empress's Cuirassiers, silver for the Chevalier Guards and the Emperor's Cuirassiers (Images V:20 and V:21). Positioned above the visor was a decorative chinstrap, made of overlapping scales, also of the button colour. On the right side of the helmet beneath the point where the chinstrap attached was a large round black, orange, and silver cockade. The curved neck-cover at the back of the helmet was lined with coloured fabric for officers and black leather for the other ranks. The coloured fabric for officers of the Chevalier Guards and Horse Guards was red, while for the Emperor's Cuirassiers and Empress's Cuirassiers it was yellow and light blue, respectively. The shape of the front visor and rear neck-cover gave the Russian helmet a very different look from that of the Prussian cuirassiers of 1900–14.

V:18 Russian Guard Star

V:19 Centre of the Russian Guard Star

V:21 Officer's Helmet of the Chevalier Guards
A side view of the helmet with double-headed eagle on it. Note how the rear lobster tail is not as deep as the Prussian model.

V:20 Officer's Helmet of the Chevalier Guards with Double-Headed Eagle

V:22 Guard Cuirassier Officer's Koller

§V-5 Guard Cavalry

WHITE KOLLER

In full dress, all officers and troops of the four guard cuirassier regiments wore a special type of white tunic known by the German word *koller*. As was common for this garment, it was single-breasted, and fastened by means of hooks instead of buttons (Image V:22).

It had straight-cut false pockets on the rear skirts trimmed with piping the colour of the collar (Table V.5.a.1, and see Image V:23). There were two buttons, one at the top edge of the false pocket at waist level and the other on the bottom (Image V:23). The lining of the koller was also white.

Other ranks had piping in the colour of the collar and cuffs (Table V.5.a.1) which outlined the seam where the sleeve joined the body of the tunic. Officers did not have this piping.

V:24 Subaltern of One of the Guard Cuirassier Regiments
Note the corduroy design on his pouch belt and also his school and regimental badges on the left side of his koller.

COLLAR

The collar was rounded, with braid which differed by rank (see below) running along the outer edges of the collar and continuing down the front edges of the tunic. There was supposed to be one litzen on each side of the collar for all four regiments, but only the Emperor's Cuirassiers were to have a button in it (Images V:22 and V:24). The Emperor's Cuirassier Regiment was also the only one of the four which had a rectangular collar shield, so the litzen and button were on the shield rather than directly on the collar. The light blue shield extended from the front of the collar around on both sides and ended lining up with the back edge of the shoulder straps.

SWEDISH CUFFS

The cuffs, which varied in colour by regiment (Table V.5.a.1), were Swedish style and trimmed with the same braid as the collar. On the outside of the braid the cuffs also had piping. Each cuff had two vertical litzen, both containing a button, but they are not found on all kollers (Image V:22). See Table V.5.a.1 for details on cuffs.

V:23 Subalterns of His Majesty's Cuirassiers
Note the helmet of the man on the left has a column with a flame on top. This was worn in less than full dress. Also note the holster and pistol cords. The man on the right is wearing breeches. Note the shape of the piping on his rear skirt.

Officers' Braid and Litzen

Officers had special 'cuirassier-style' braid, distinguishable by its alternating horizontal stripes of flat weave and raised welts which ran the entire length of the trim (Image V:25). This type of braid trimmed the collar, the front edges of the tunic, and the cuffs. The braid was either gold or silver, according to the button colour, with two stripes of colour running through it (see Table V.5.a.1 for colour).

Officers' litzen were gold or silver according to the button colour. There was one litzen on either side of the collar and two on each cuff. The cuff litzen was entirely visible for officers, unlike that of the troops.

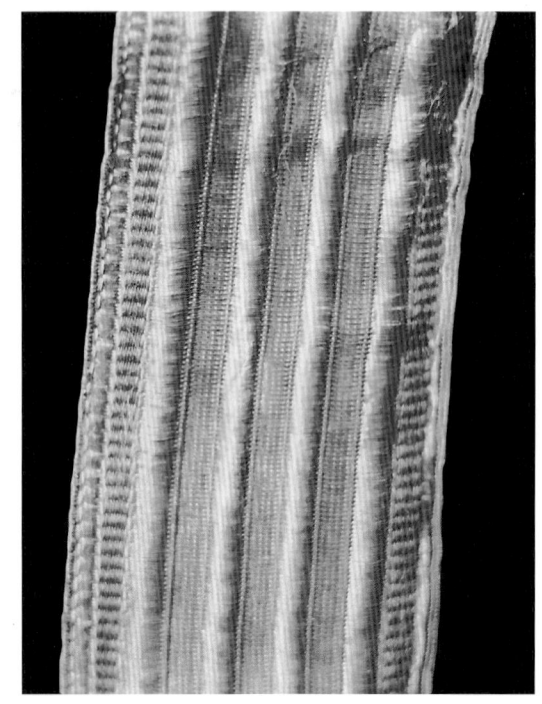

V:25 Close-Up of Cuirassier Corduroy Style Braid

Other Ranks' Braid and Litzen

Other ranks had braid which was made of three coloured stripes. The central stripe varied by regiment and matched the stripes in the officers' cuirassier braid. The two outer stripes were orange for all four regiments. This braid trimmed all the same parts of the tunic listed above for officers. See the section on Prussian Cuirassiers, §VI-6-a, for a view of similar trimming for other ranks.

Other ranks' litzen were orange. Collar litzen included a thread in the colour of the fabric that the litzen was sewn to – collar shield colour for the Emperor's Cuirassiers, collar colour for other regiments. Cuff litzen and the buttons in the cuff litzen were only partially visible. The upper part of the litzen and buttons were covered by the striped braid which decorated the cuff, described above.

Gala Dress Red Koller

Generals and officers of the Chevalier Guards and the Horse Guards had a red koller in addition to the white full dress koller (Images C62 (bottom left man) and Image V:26) The red koller was only worn in gala dress. It was the same cut and style as the white full dress koller, but made with red cloth. The collar and its piping, cuffs and their piping, coloured stripes in the cuirassier-style braid, and pocket piping were all light blue for the Chevalier Guards and dark blue for the Horse Guards. The braid, litzen, and epaulette straps were all in the button colour, silver for the Chevalier Guards and gold for the Horse Guards.

V:26 Subaltern in the Red Koller Worn by the Chevalier Guards and the Horse Guards for Gala Occasions

BRITISH EMPIRE

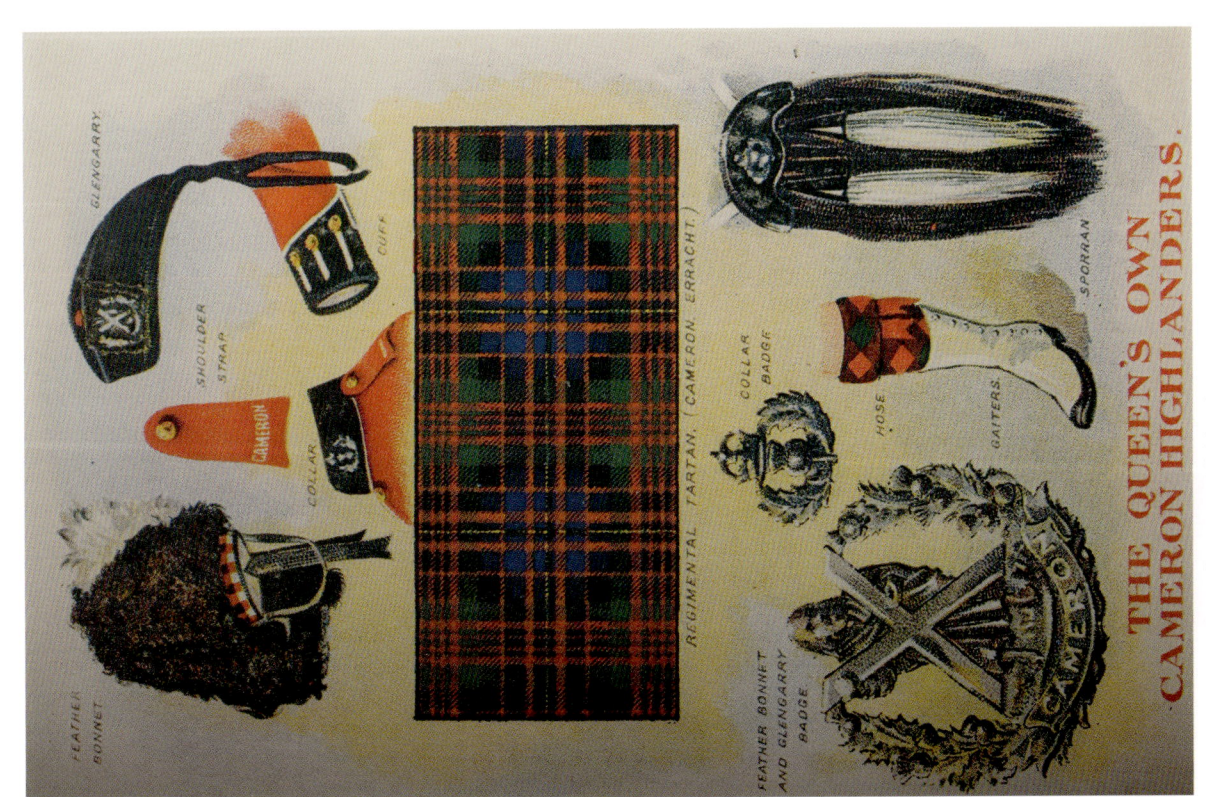

C1 The Queen's Own Cameron Highlanders

C2 Princess Louise's Argyll and Sutherland Highlanders

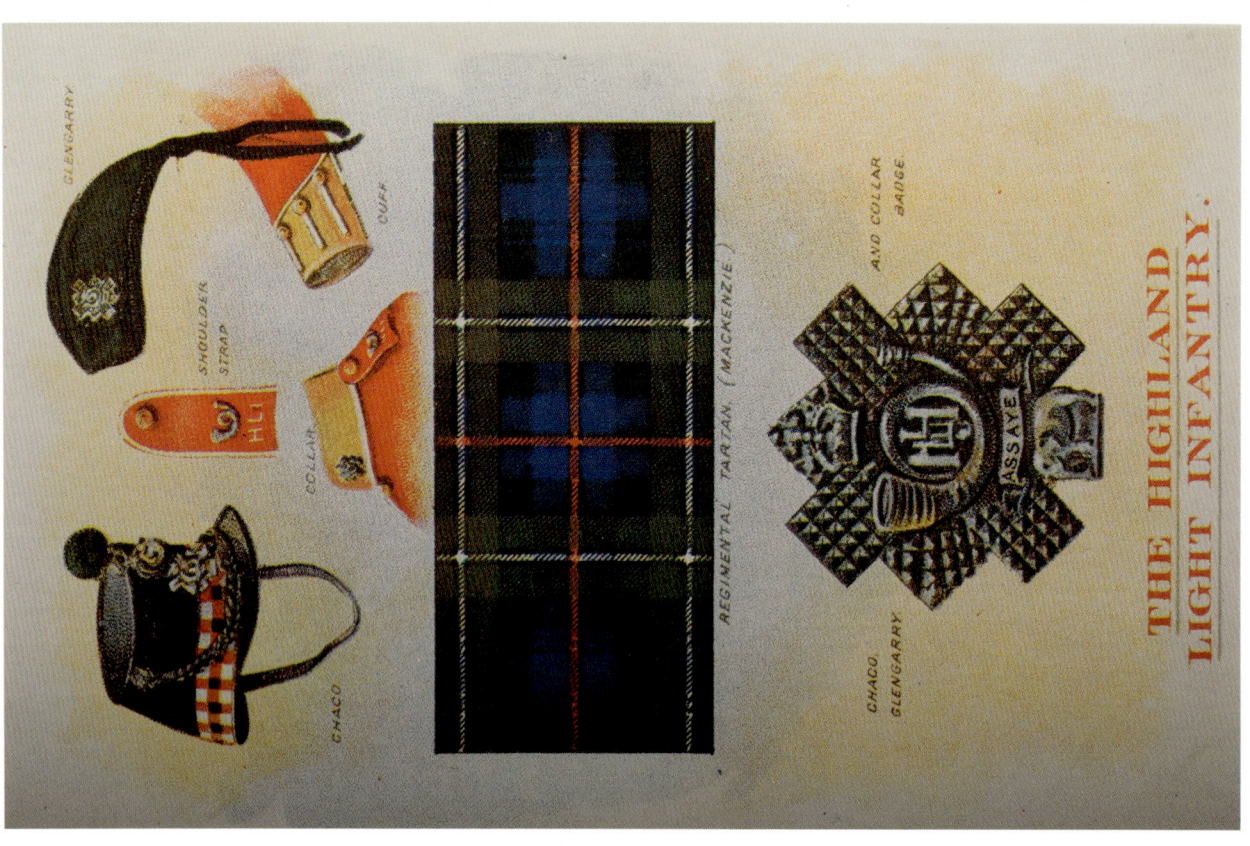

C4 The Highland Light Infantry

C3 The Black Watch (Royal Highlanders)

C6 The Gordon Highlanders

C5 Seaforth Highlanders (Ross-Shire Buffs)

C8 The Royal Scots Fusiliers

C7 The King's Own Scottish Borderers

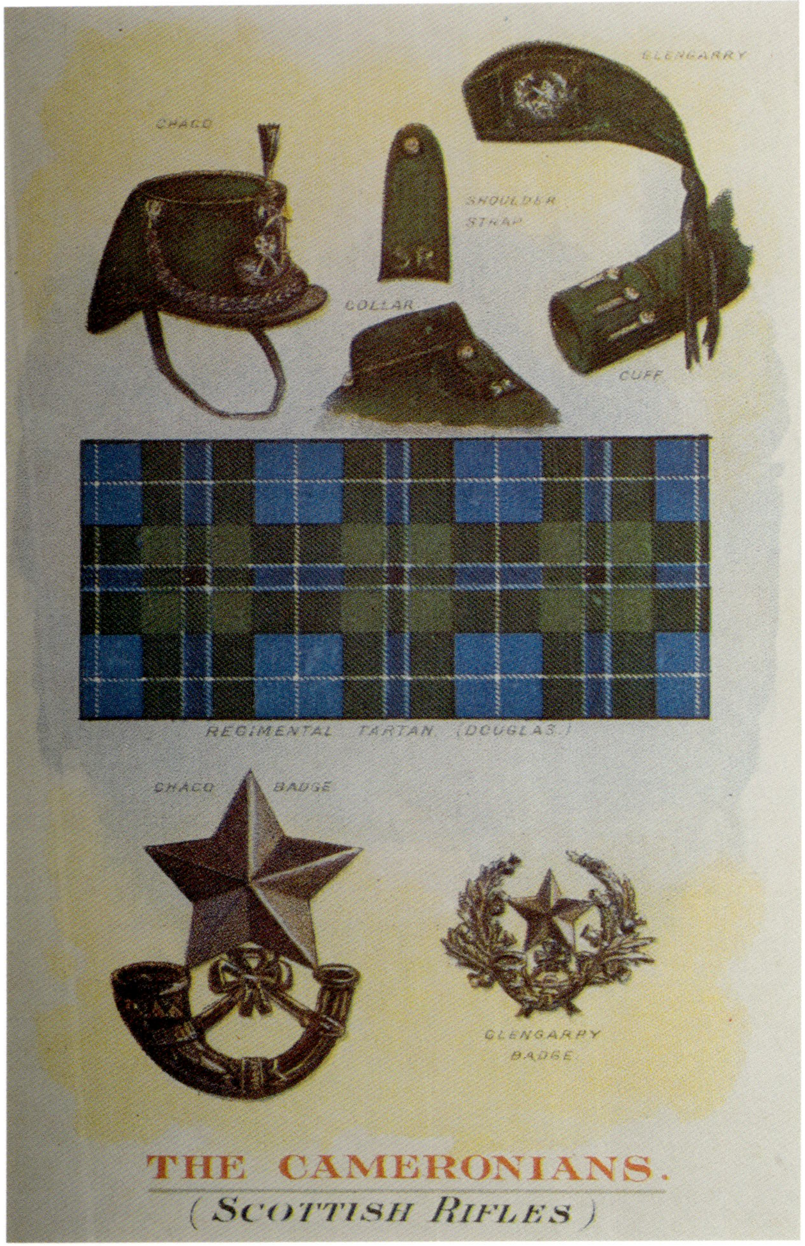

C10 The Cameronians (Scottish Rifles)

C9 The Royal Scots (Lothian Regiment)

C11 1st Life Guards Lieutenant (Mounted Review Order)

C12 Royal Horse Guards (The Blues) Lieutenant (Mounted Review Order)

C13 6th Dragoon Guards (Carabiniers) Lieutenant (Mounted Review Order)

C14 6th (Inniskilling) Dragoons Lieutenant (Mounted Review Order)

C15 5th (Royal Irish) Lancers Lieutenant (Mounted Review Order)

C16 16th (The Queen's) Lancers Captain (Mounted Review Order)

C17 19th (Princess of Wale's Own) Hussars Lieutenant (Mounted Review Order)

C18 3rd Dragoon Guards (Prince of Wales's)

C19 The Manchester Regiment

C21 The Cheshire Regiment
They are wearing paper oak leaves, which were only worn in the presence of royalty and on the anniversary of the Battle of Meeanee. This recalls their claim to have protected George II at the Battle of Dettingen in 1743.

C20 Royal Welsh Fusiliers
Left figure, 1st Class Scouts badge; right figure, Regimental Sergeant Major. Note the 'flash' ribbons worn on the back of the tunic. They are 17.78 cm (7 in) long for other ranks and (22.96 cm (9 in) long for officers in 1914.

C22 NCO and other ranks, Royal Scots

C23 The Rifle Brigade

INDIAN EMPIRE

C24 Indian army officers
The two officers on the left are in Zouave uniform of the 15th Sikhs'. Note 'humbug' pattern turbans. The man on the right is in a post-1903 infantry officer's uniform.

C25 42nd Deoli Regiment
Lt. Col. C.E.N. Priestley
Photo hand coloured by his wife.

C26 Left to right: 5th Cavalry; 23rd Cavalry (Frontier Force); 17th Cavalry; 26th King George's Own Light Cavalry; 11th King Edward's Own Lancers (Probyn's Horse); 4th Cavalry, (Daffadar, Jat Sikh); 16th Cavalry, (Jemedar, Jat).

C27 From left: 1st Duke of York's Own Lancers (Skinner's Horse), Hindustani Muslim; 3rd Skinner's Horse, Rajput Muslim.

C28 From left: 6th King Edward's Own Cavalry; 8th Cavalry

C29 14th Murray's Jat Lancers, Rissaldar Major

C30 19th Lancers (Fane's Horse), Punjabi Muslim

C31 From left: 27th Light Cavalry, British Officer; 28th King George's Own Light Cavalry, Daffadar, Madrasi Muslim of the Carnatic

C32 The Former 'Hyderabad Contingent' Cavalry
From left: 30th Lancers (Gordon's Horse), Lance Daffadar, Jat; 20th Deccan Horse, Sikh; 29th Lancers (Deccan Horse), Rissaldar, Dekhani Muslim.

C33 From left: 33rd Queen's Own Light Cavalry, Daffadar, Kaimkhani; 34th Prince Albert Victor's Own Poona Horse, Ratore Rajput; 32nd Lancers, Lance Daffadar

C34 38th King George's Own Central India Horse, Lance Daffadar, Gakkar, Punjabi Muslim

C35 From left: 5th Light Infantry; 6th Jat Light Infantry

C36 35th Sikhs

C37 33rd Punjabis

C38 39th Garhwal Rifles

C39 45th Rattray's Sikhs 'The Drums', Jat Sikhs

C40 101st and 102nd Grenadiers

C42 6th Gurkhas
Note red touri on the Kilmarnock hat top.

C41 127th Queen Mary's Own Baluch Light Infantry

FRENCH EMPIRE

C43 NCO's kepi

C44 French infantry other ranks tunic

C45 Chasseur à Pied, lieutenant officer's tunic

C46 Cuirassier officer's helmet

C47 Cuirassier officer's tunic

C48 Hussar other ranks shako

C49 Chasseur à Cheval adjudant's shako

C50 Dragoon other rank's tunic

C51 'Half-assed tunic'
Note sergeant's chevron of rank at the bottom of each sleeve.

C52 Chasseur d'Afrique officer's trousers

C53 Zouave sergeant major jacket

C54 The four different tombeau colours
Left to right: red for the 1st, white for the 2nd, yellow for the 3rd, and dark blue for the 4th.

C55 Zouave sergeant major jacket sleeve opening

C56 Algerian Tirailleur other ranks jacket

C57 Algerian Tirailleur officer's tunic (front)

C58 Algerian Tirailleur officer's tunic (back)

C59 Spahi sergeant's jacket

C60 Spahi officer's tunic

RUSSIAN EMPIRE

C61 Paul Regiment

C62 Above: 4th Guard Rifles
Below left: Horse Guards gala dress
Below right: Kexholm Regiment

C63 Above: Crimean (Tartar) Horse Regiment
Right: Turkman Horse Demi-Regiment

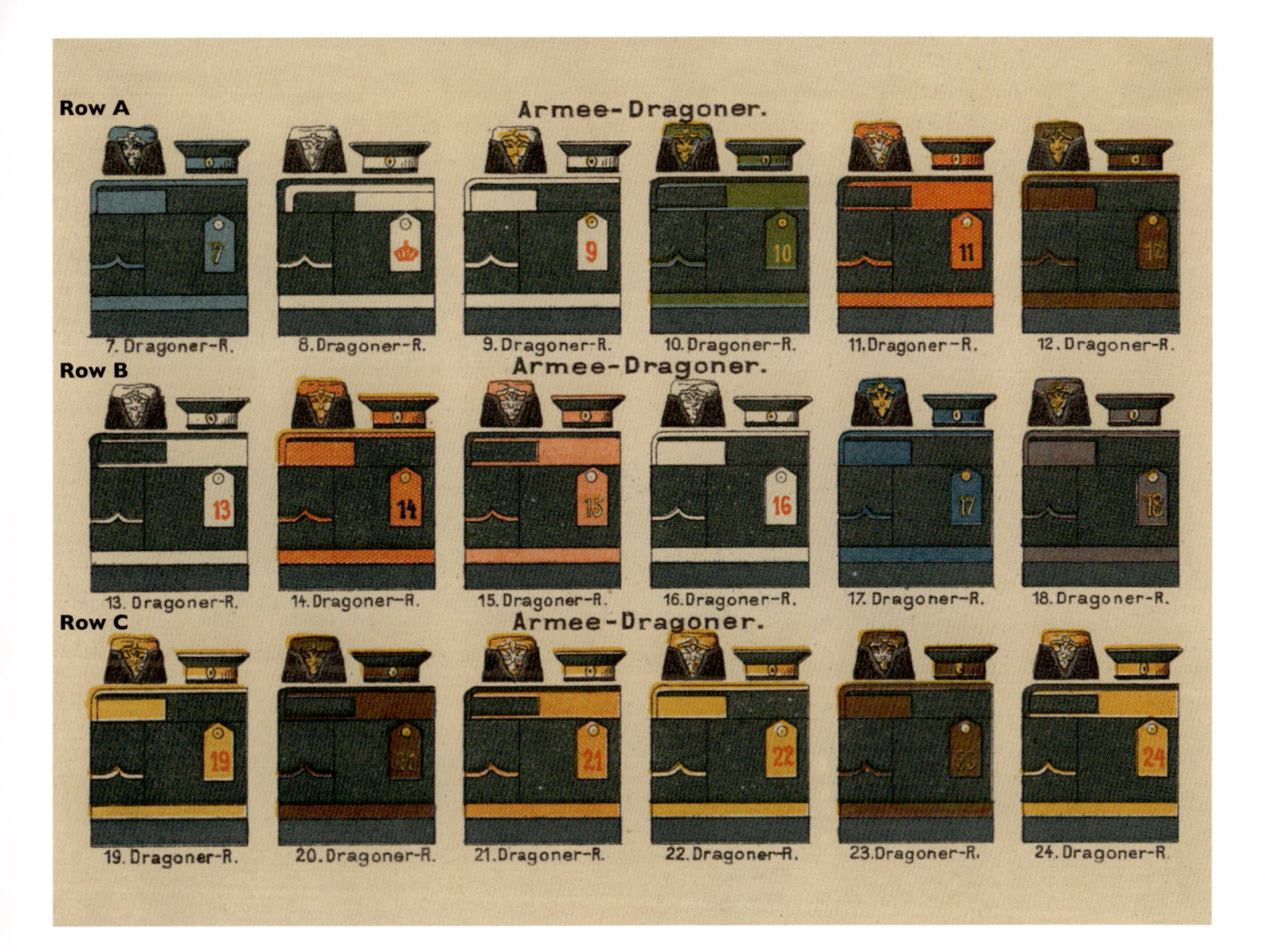

C64a

Dragoon uniforms 1881–1910 (pre-1910 name followed by post-1910 name). The colours shown here for the 9th, 17th, 18th, and 21st Dragoons do not agree with the colours listed at Table V.7.a.1.1 in the text. This schematic was made by Moritz Ruhl in 1890. The text in the table is from a book by a Russian researcher c. 1980.

Row A: (left to right)
1. 7th New Russia Dragoons (3rd New Russia Dragoons)
2. 8th Smolensk Dragoons (3rd Smolensk Lancers)
3. 9th Elizabetgrad Dragoons (3rd Elizabetgrad Hussars)
4. 10th Ekaterinoslav Dragoons (4th New Russia-Ekaterinoslav Dragoons)
5. 11th Kharkov Dragoons (4th Kharkov Lancers)
6. 12th Mariupol Dragoons (4th Mariupol Hussars)

Row B: (left to right)
1. 13th Kargopal Dragoons (5th Kargopol Dragoons)
2. 14th Lithuanian Dragoons (5th Lithuanian Lancers)
3. 15th Alexandria Dragoons (5th Alexandria Hussars)
4. 16th Glukhov Dragoons (6th Glukhov Dragoons)
5. 17th Volynsky Dragoons (6th Volynsky Lancers)
6. 18th Klyastitsi Dragoons (6th Klyastitsi Hussars)

Row C: (left to right)
1. 19th Kinburn Dragoons (7th Kinburn Dragoons)
2. 20th Olviopol Dragoons (7th Olviopol Lancers)
3. 21st White Russian Dragoons (7th White Russian Hussars)
4. 22nd Astrakhan Dragoons (8th Astrakhan Dragoons)
5. 23rd Voznesensk Dragoons (8th Voznesensk Lancers)
6. 24th Lubny Dragoons (8th Lubny Hussars)

C64b Plates of the Russian Imperial Army Uniforms by V.K. Shenk (1910)

Row 1: (left to right)
1. Preobrazhensky Regiment of the Imperial Guard
2. Semenovsky Regiment of the Imperial Guard
3. Izmailovsky Regiment of the Imperial Guard
4. Yegersky Regiment of the Imperial Guard

Row 2: (left to right)
1. Moscow Regiment of the Imperial Guard
2. Grenadier Regiment of the Imperial Guard
3. Paul Regiment of the Imperial Guard
4. Finland Regiment of the Imperial Guard

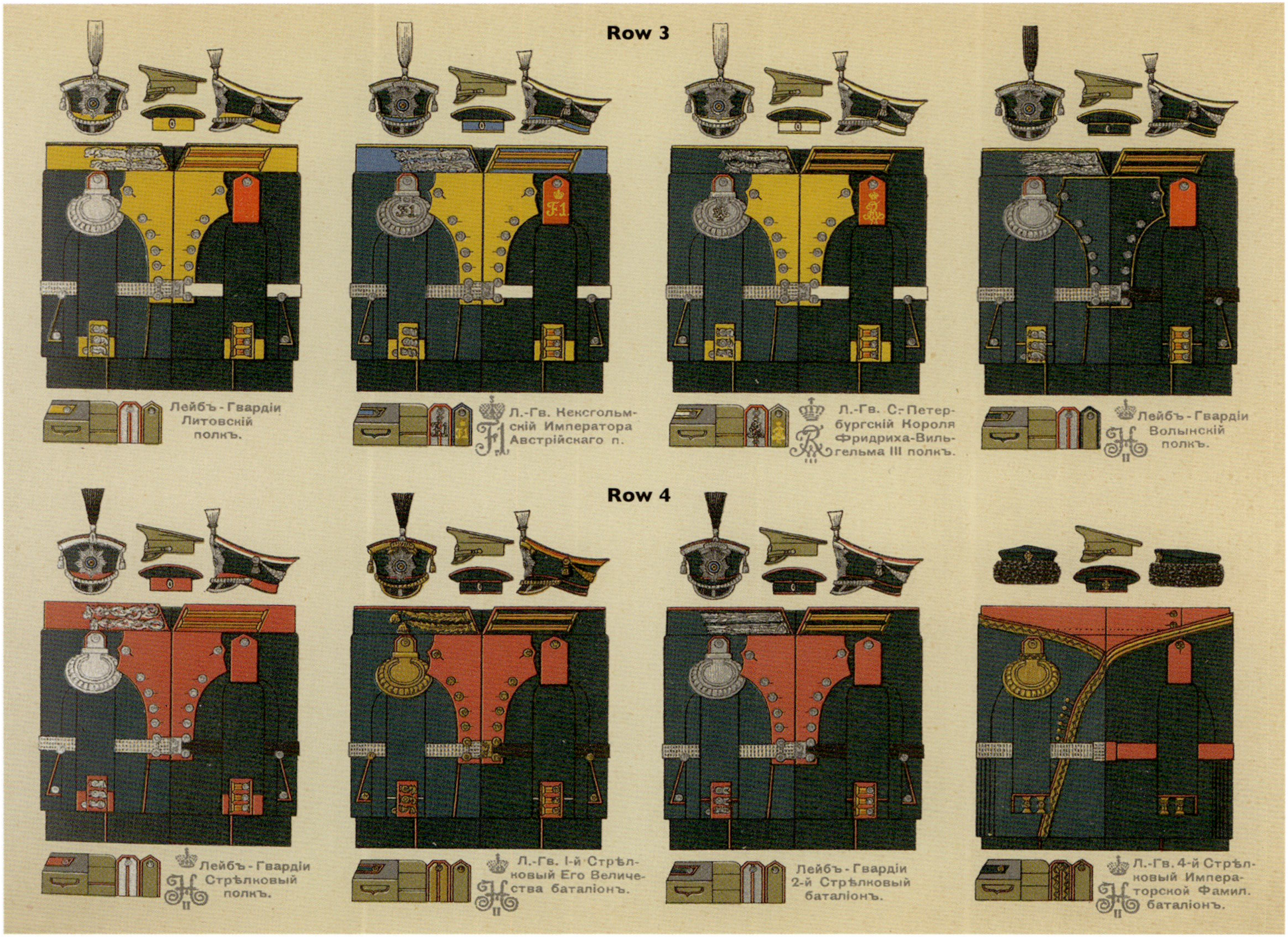

C65a Plates of the Russian Imperial Army Uniforms by V.K. Shenk (1910)

Row 3: (left to right)
1. Lithuanian Regiment of the Imperial Guard
2. Kexholm Regiment of His Imperial Majesty, Emperor of Austria and King of Hungary Imperial Guard
3. St Petersburg Regiment of the King of Prussia, Frederick-William III Imperial Guard
4. Volynsky Regiment of the Imperial Guard

Row 4: (left to right)
1. Guard Rifle Regiment
2. 1st His Majesty's Imperial Guard Rifle Regiment
3. 2nd Tsarskoe-Selo Imperial Guard Rifle Regiment
4. 4th Imperial Guard Rifle Regiment of the Imperial Family

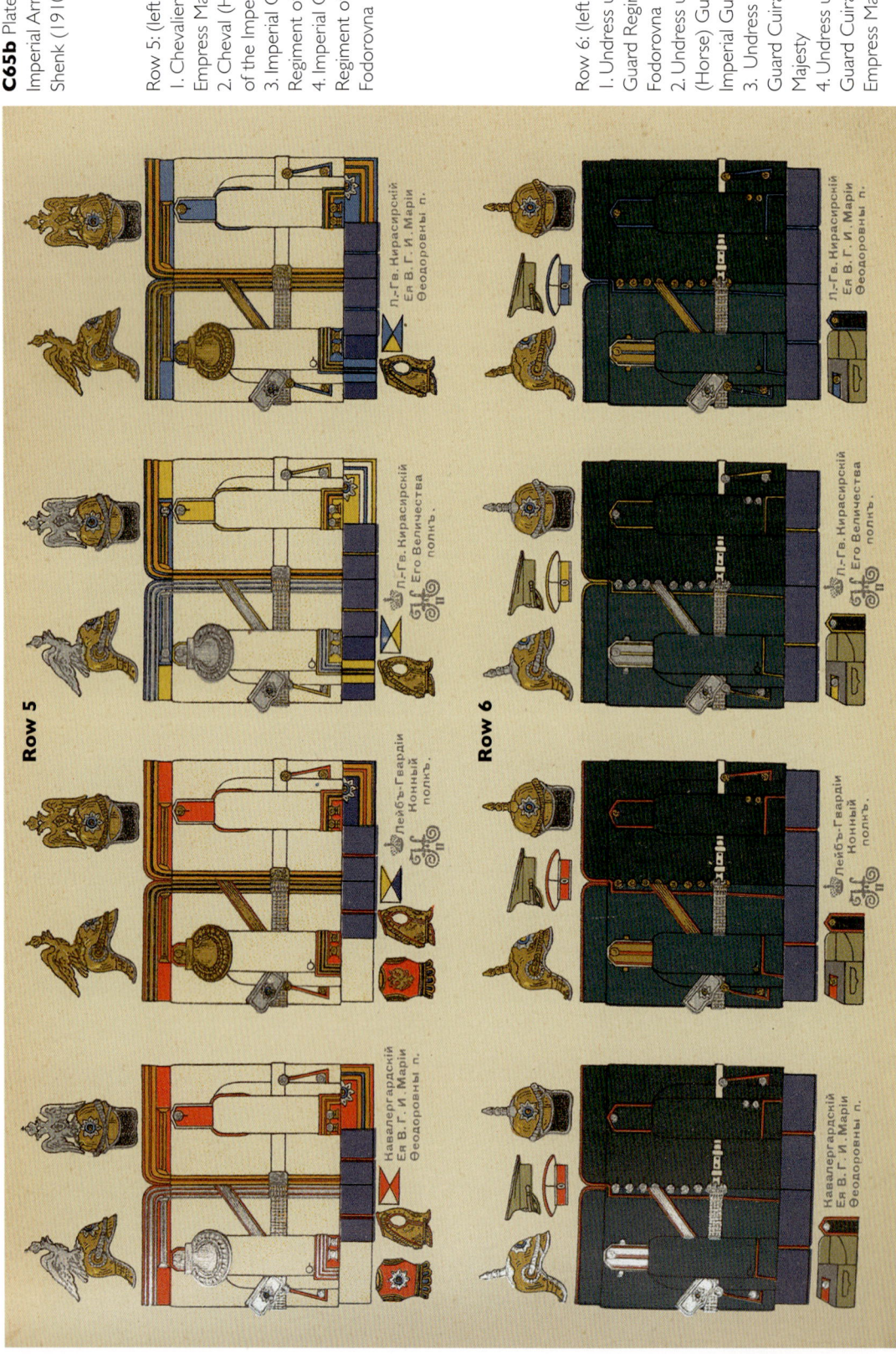

C65b Plates of the Russian Imperial Army Uniforms by V.K. Shenk (1910)

Row 5: (left to right)
1. Chevalier Guard Regiment of Empress Maria Fodorovna
2. Cheval (Horse) Guards Regiment of the Imperial Guard
3. Imperial Guard Cuirassiers Regiment of His Majesty
4. Imperial Guard Cuirassiers Regiment of the Empress Maria Fodorovna

Row 6: (left to right)
1. Undress uniform of Chevalier Guard Regiment of Empress Maria Fodorovna
2. Undress uniform of Cheval (Horse) Guards Regiment of the Imperial Guard
3. Undress uniform of Imperial Guard Cuirassiers Regiment of His Majesty
4. Undress uniform of Imperial Guard Cuirassiers Regiment of the Empress Maria Fodorovna

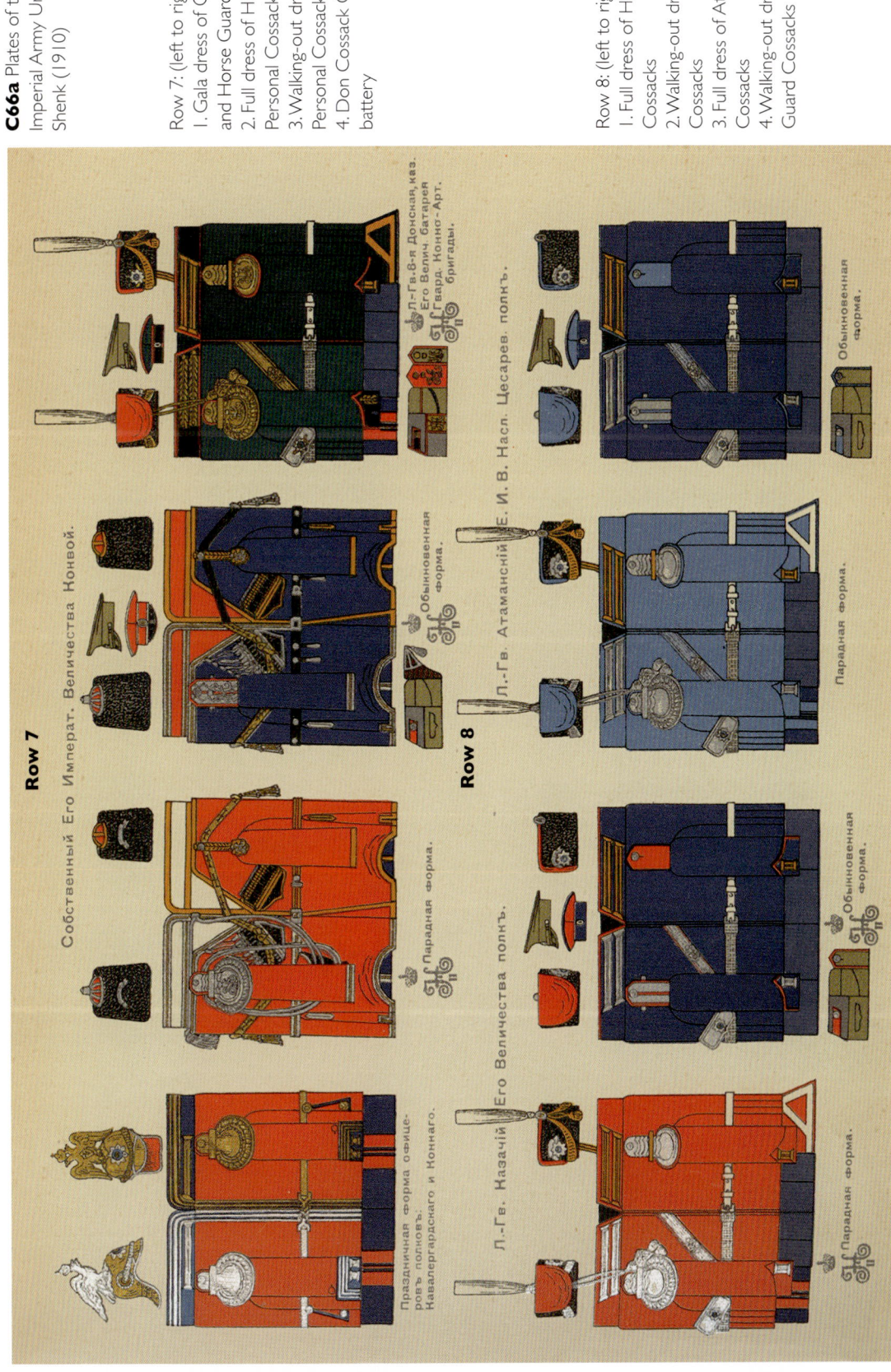

C66a Plates of the Russian Imperial Army Uniforms by V.K. Shenk (1910)

Row 7: (left to right)
1. Gala dress of Chevalier Guard and Horse Guards
2. Full dress of His Majesty's Personal Cossack Escort
3. Walking-out dress of His Majesty's Personal Cossack Escort
4. Don Cossack Guard artillery battery

Row 8: (left to right)
1. Full dress of His Majesty's Cossacks
2. Walking-out dress of His Majesty's Cossacks
3. Full dress of Ataman Guard Cossacks
4. Walking-out dress of Ataman Guard Cossacks

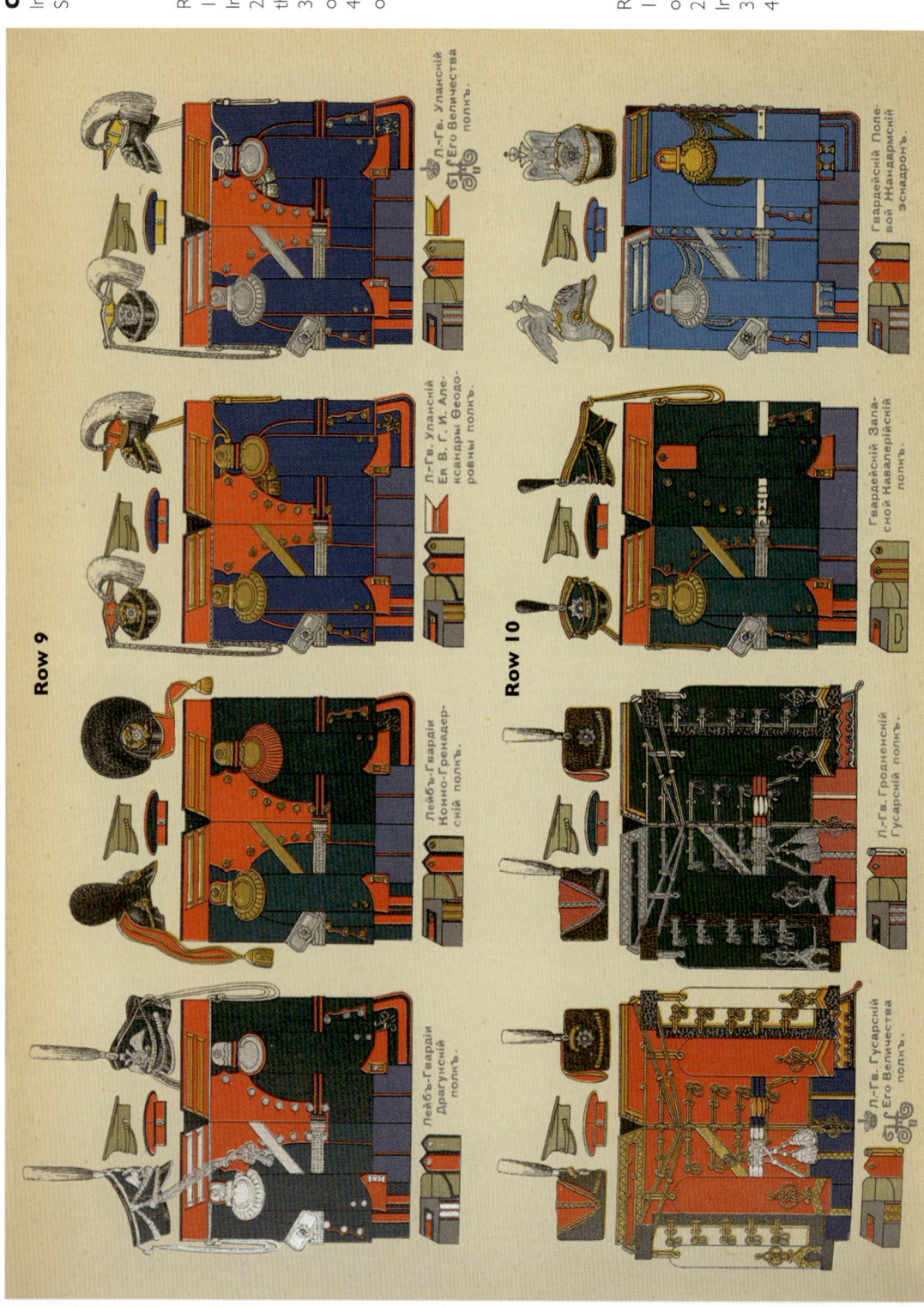

C66b Plates of the Russian Imperial Army Uniforms by V.K. Shenk (1910)

Row 9: (left to right)
1. Dragoon Regiment of the Imperial Guard
2. Horse Grenadier Regiment of the Imperial Guard
3. Imperial Guard Lancer Regiment of Her Majesty
4. Imperial Guard Lancer Regiment of His Majesty

Row 10: (left to right)
1. Imperial Guard Hussar Regiment of His Majesty
2. Grodno Hussar Regiment of the Imperial Guard
3. Cavalry Reserve Regiment
4. Gendarmes Squadron

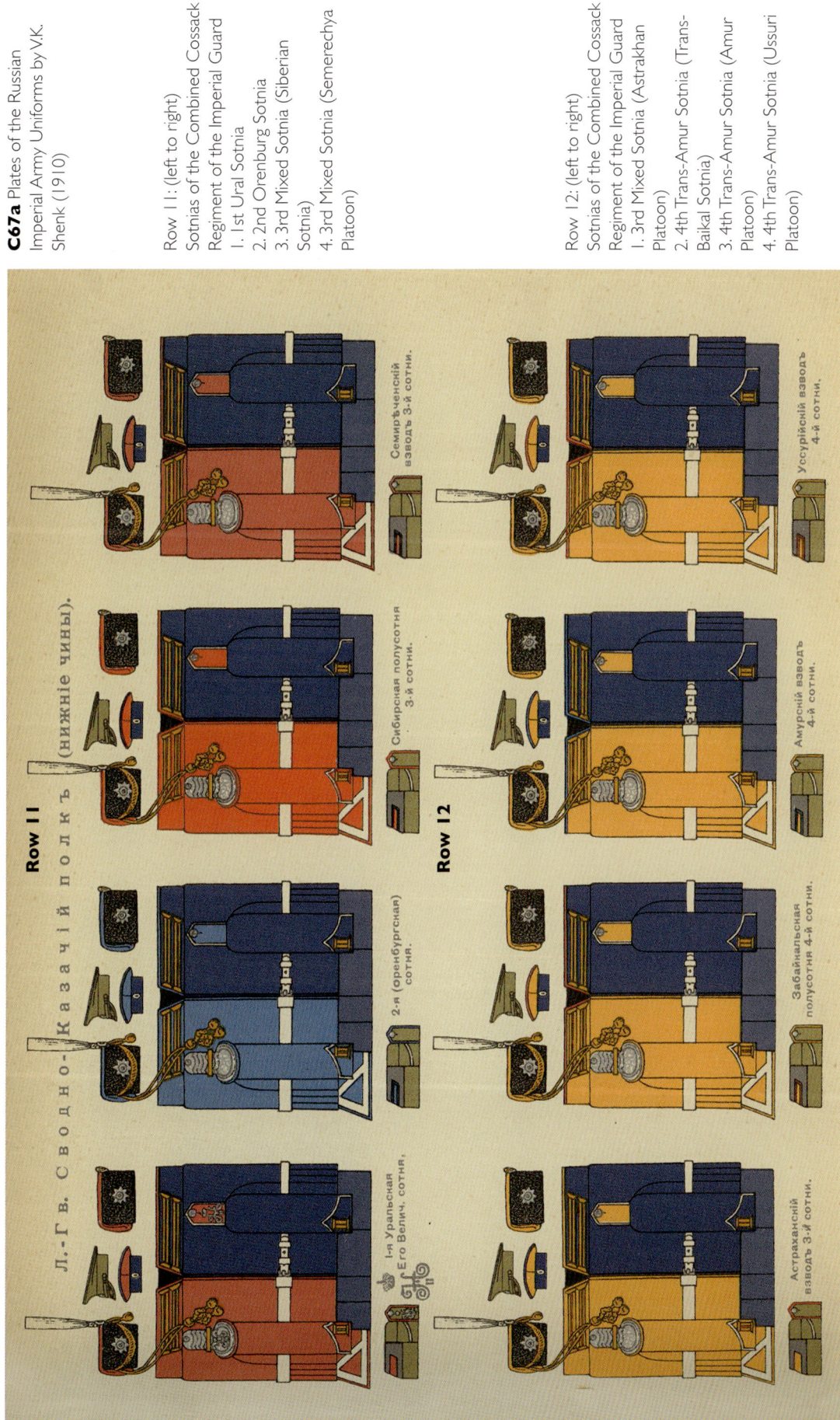

C67a Plates of the Russian Imperial Army Uniforms by V.K. Shenk (1910)

Row 11: (left to right) Sotnias of the Combined Cossack Regiment of the Imperial Guard
1. 1st Ural Sotnia
2. 2nd Orenburg Sotnia
3. 3rd Mixed Sotnia (Siberian Sotnia)
4. 3rd Mixed Sotnia (Semerechya Platoon)

Row 12: (left to right) Sotnias of the Combined Cossack Regiment of the Imperial Guard
1. 3rd Mixed Sotnia (Astrakhan Platoon)
2. 4th Trans-Amur Sotnia (Trans-Baikal Sotnia)
3. 4th Trans-Amur Sotnia (Amur Platoon)
4. 4th Trans-Amur Sotnia (Ussuri Platoon)

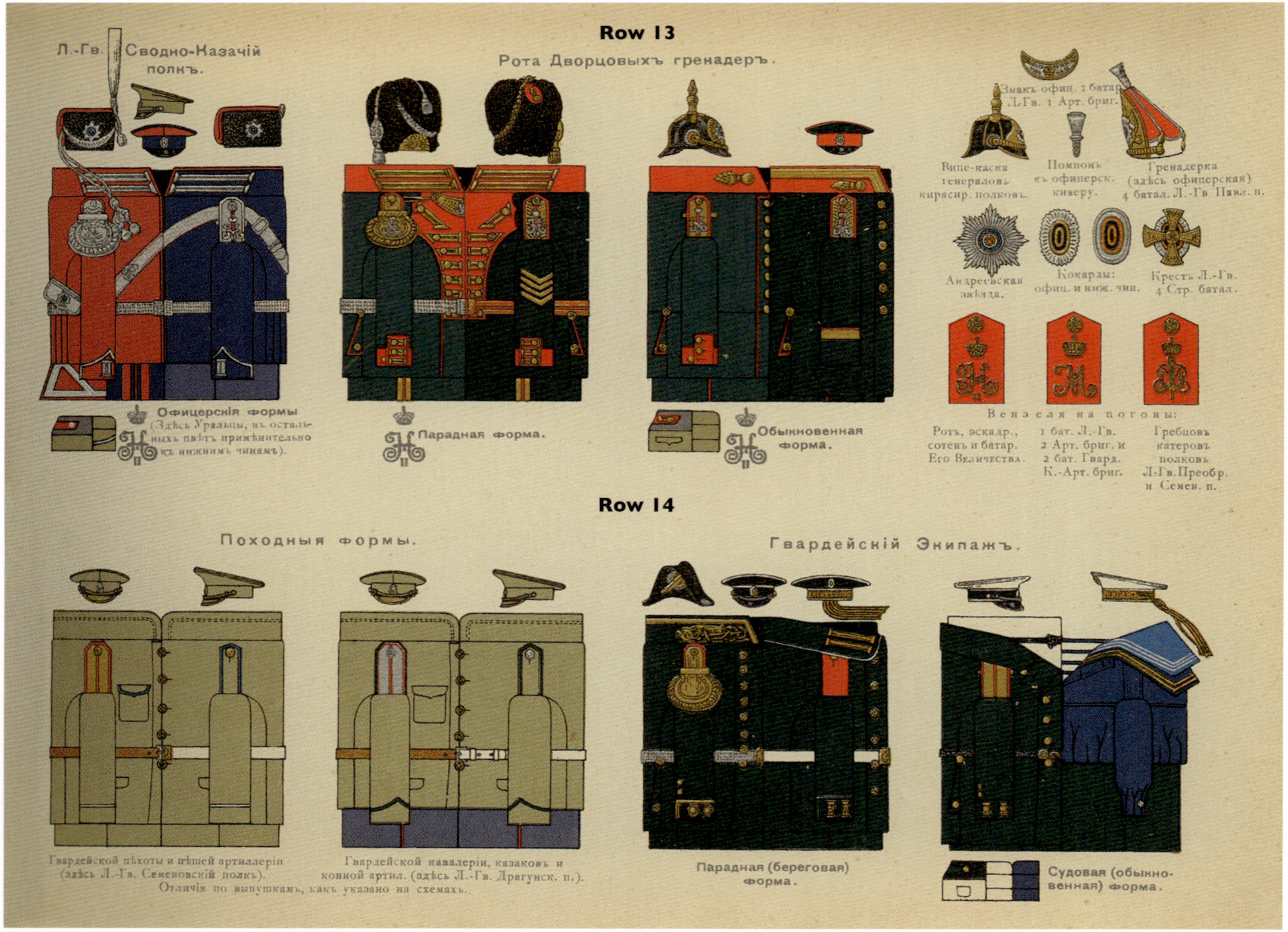

C67b Plates of the Russian Imperial Army Uniforms by V.K. Shenk (1910)

Row 13: (left to right)
1. Example of full dress and walking-out dress of the Combined Cossack Regiment of the Imperial Guard
2. Palace Grenadiers
3. Palace Grenadiers, undress uniform
4: (from top)
a. Example of gorget
b. Side view of the 4th Fusilier Battalion mitre of the Paul Regiment
c. Examples of guard star, cockades, and 4th Guard Rifle Regiment cross worn over cockades
d. Examples of monograms

Row 14: (left to right)
1. Infantry summer uniform
2. Cavalry summer uniform
3. Equipage of the Guard winter uniform
4. Equipage of the Guard summer uniform

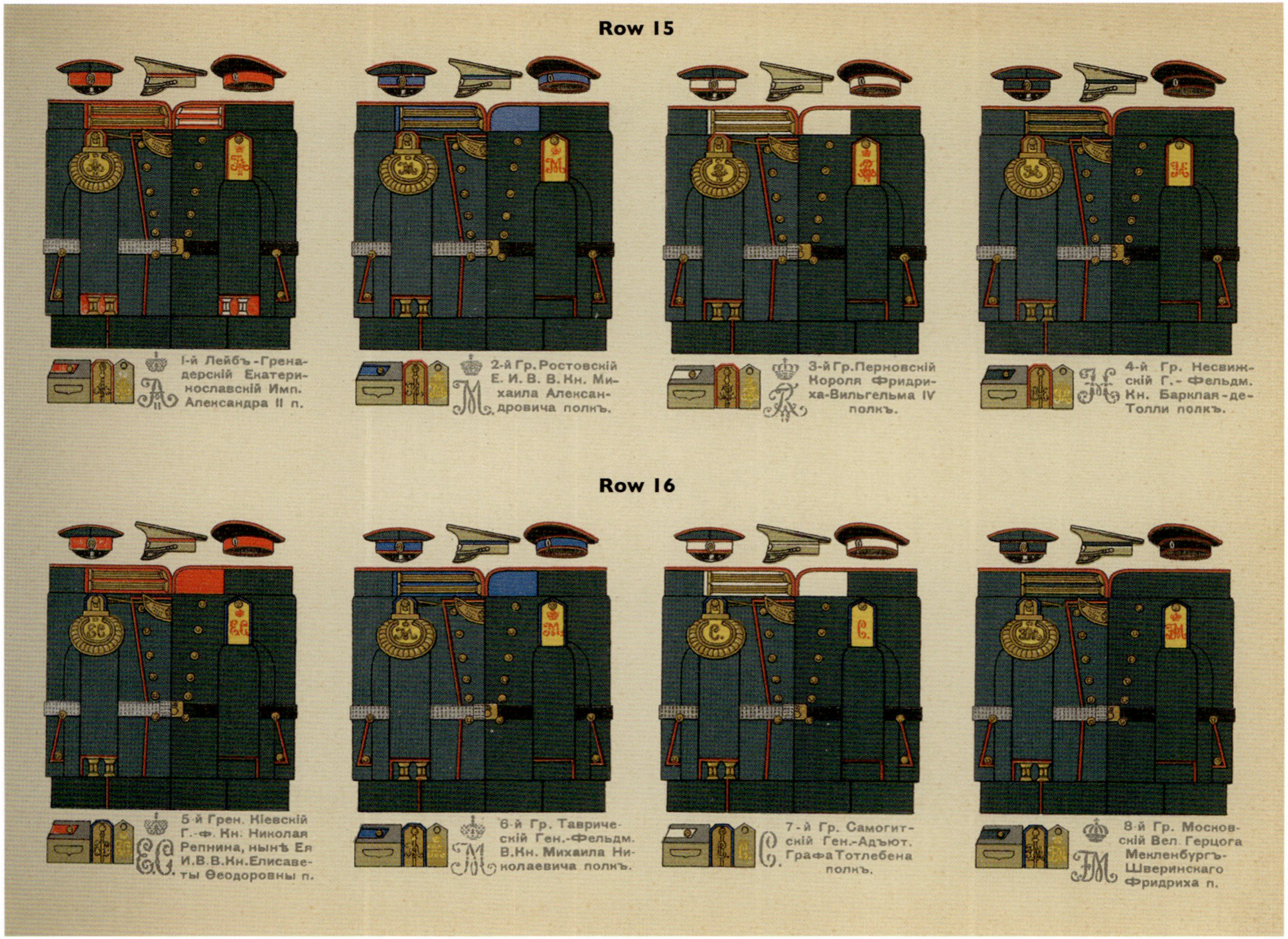

C68a Plates of the Russian Imperial Army Uniforms by V.K. Shenk (1910)

Row 15: (left to right)

1. 1st Ekaterinoslav Imperial Grenadier Regiment of Emperor Alexander II

2. 2nd Rostov Grenadier Regiment of Grand Duke Michael Alexandrovich

3. 3rd Pernov Grenadier Regiment of King Frederick William IV of Prussia

4. 4th Nesvizh Grenadier Regiment of Field Marshal Prince Barclay de Tolly

Row 16: (left to right)

1. 5th Kiev Grenadier Regiment of the Czarevich

2. 6th Tavrida Grenadier Regiment

3. 7th Samoguitia Grenadier Regiment of Adjutant General Count Totleben

4. 8th Moscow Grenadiers of the Grand Duke of Mecklenburg Frederick II

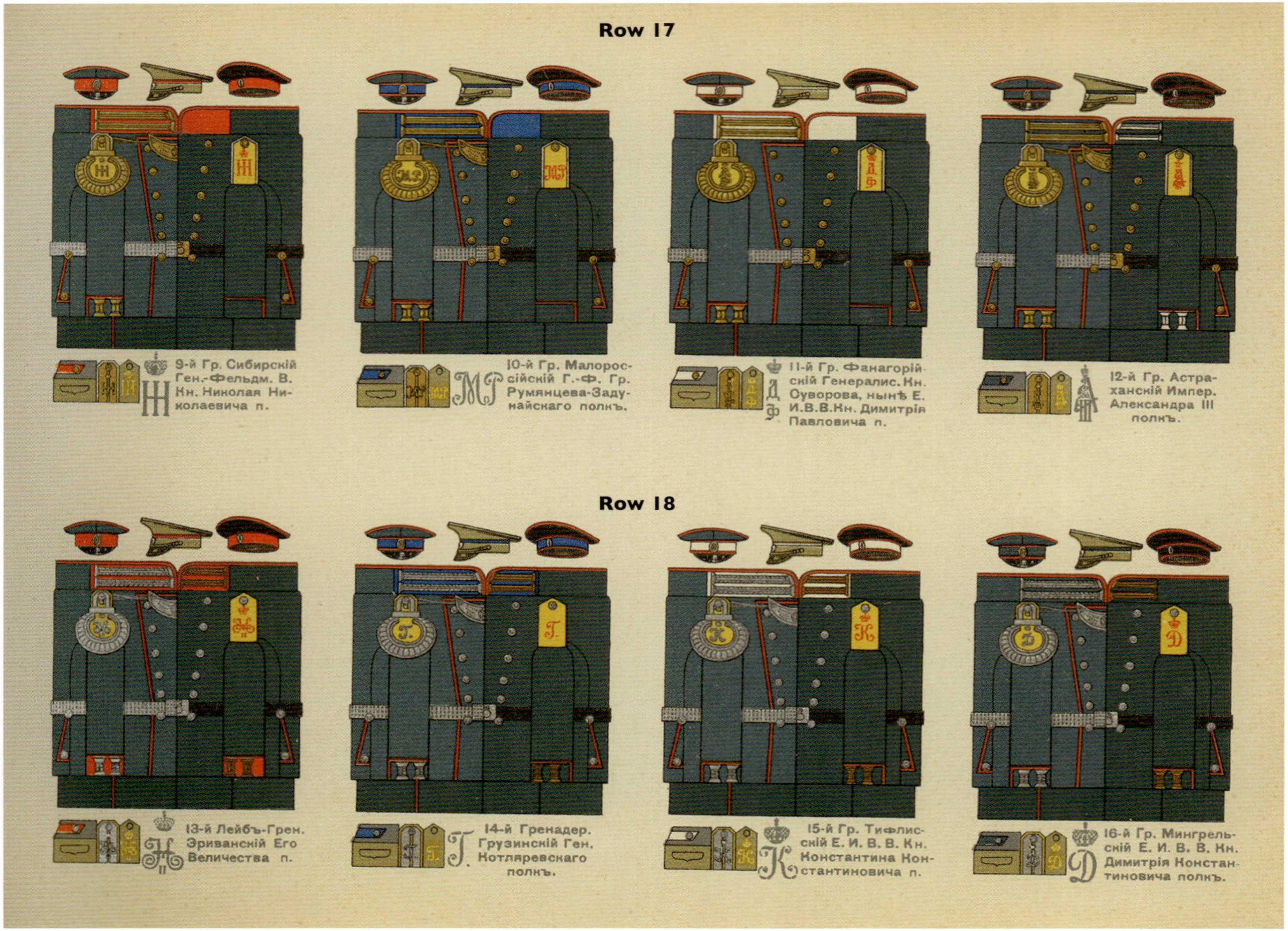

C68b Plates of the Russian Imperial Army Uniforms by V.K. Shenk (1910)

Row 17: (left to right)
1. 9th Siberian Grenadier Regiment of Grand Duke Nicholas Nicolaevich
2. 10th Little Russia Grenadier Regiment of Field Marshal Count Rumyantsev-Zadunaisky
3. 11th Phanagoria Grenadier Regiment of Generalissimo Prince Suvorov
4. 12th Astrakhan Grenadier Regiment of Emperor Alexander III

Row 18: (left to right)
1. 13th Erivan Imperial Grenadier Regiment of Czar Michael Fodorovich
2. 14th Georgian Grenadier Regiment of the Czarevich
3. 15th Tiflis Grenadier Regiment
4. 16th Mingrelia Grenadier Regiment of Grand Duke Dimitri Constantinovich

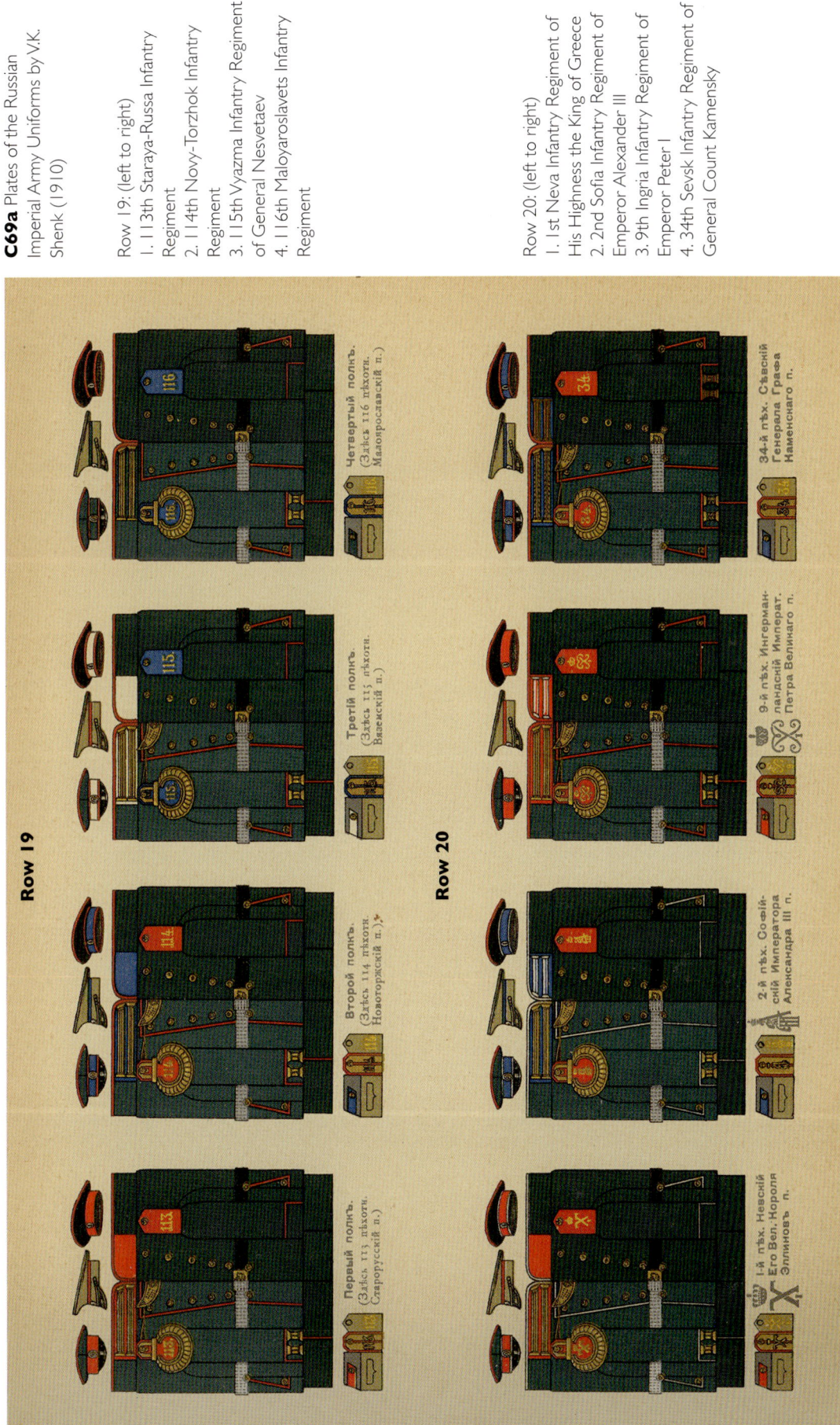

C69a Plates of the Russian Imperial Army Uniforms by V.K. Shenk (1910)

Row 19: (left to right)
1. 113th Staraya-Russa Infantry Regiment
2. 114th Novy-Torzhok Infantry Regiment
3. 115th Vyazma Infantry Regiment of General Nesvetaev
4. 116th Maloyaroslavets Infantry Regiment

Row 20: (left to right)
1. 1st Neva Infantry Regiment of His Highness the King of Greece
2. 2nd Sofia Infantry Regiment of Emperor Alexander III
3. 9th Ingria Infantry Regiment of Emperor Peter I
4. 34th Sevsk Infantry Regiment of General Count Kamensky

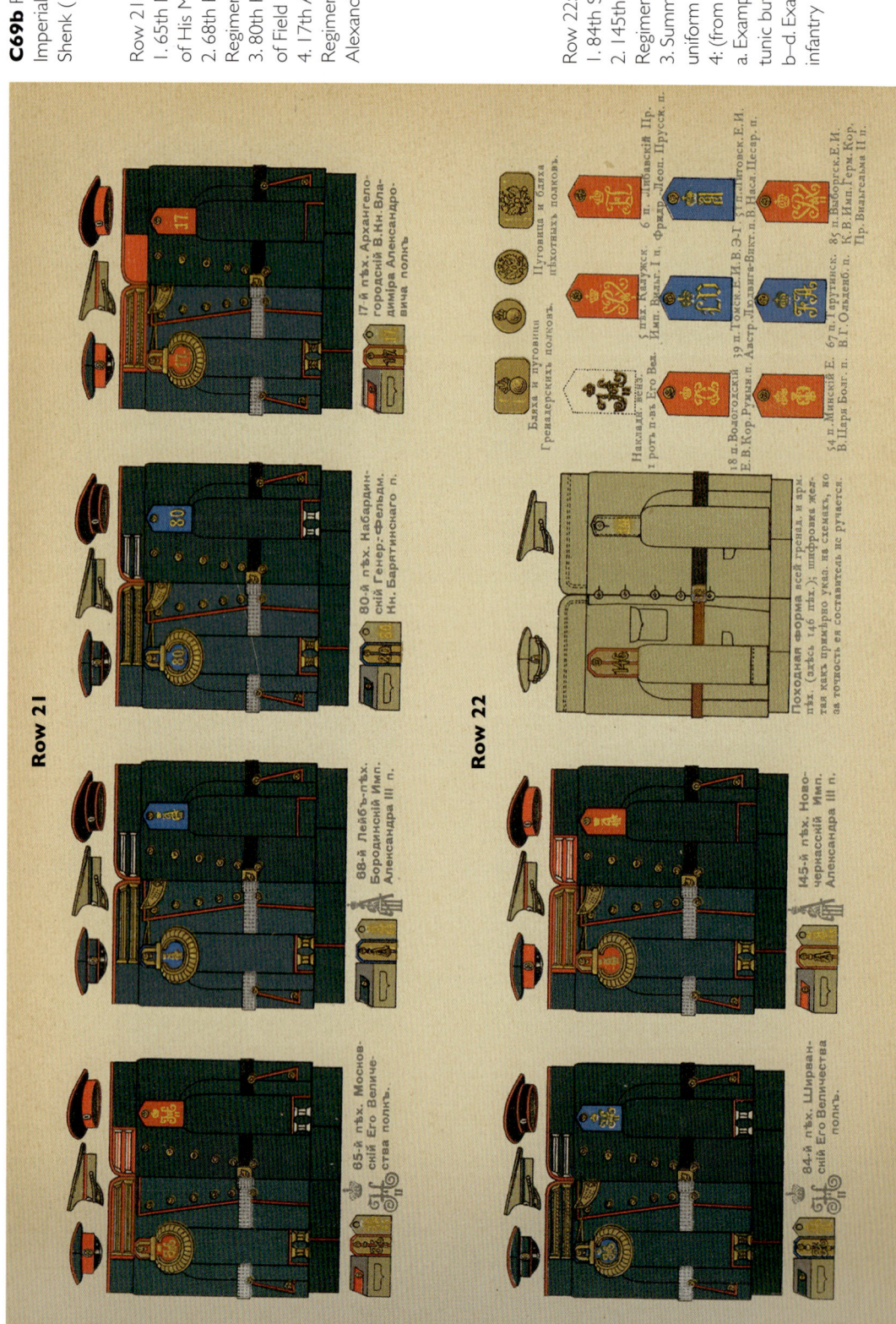

C69b Plates of the Russian Imperial Army Uniforms by V.K. Shenk (1910)

Row 21: (left to right)
1. 65th Moscow Infantry Regiment of His Majesty
2. 68th Borodino Infantry Regiment of Emperor Alexander III
3. 80th Kabarda Infantry Regiment of Field Marshal Prince Baryatinsky
4. 17th Archangelgorod Infantry Regiment of Grand Duke Vladimir Alexandrovich

Row 22: (left to right)
1. 84th Shirvan Infantry Regiment
2. 145th Novocherkassk Infantry Regiment of Emperor Alexander III
3. Summer dress and combat uniform (infantry)
4: (from top)
a. Examples of belt buckles and tunic buttons
b–d. Examples of monograms for infantry

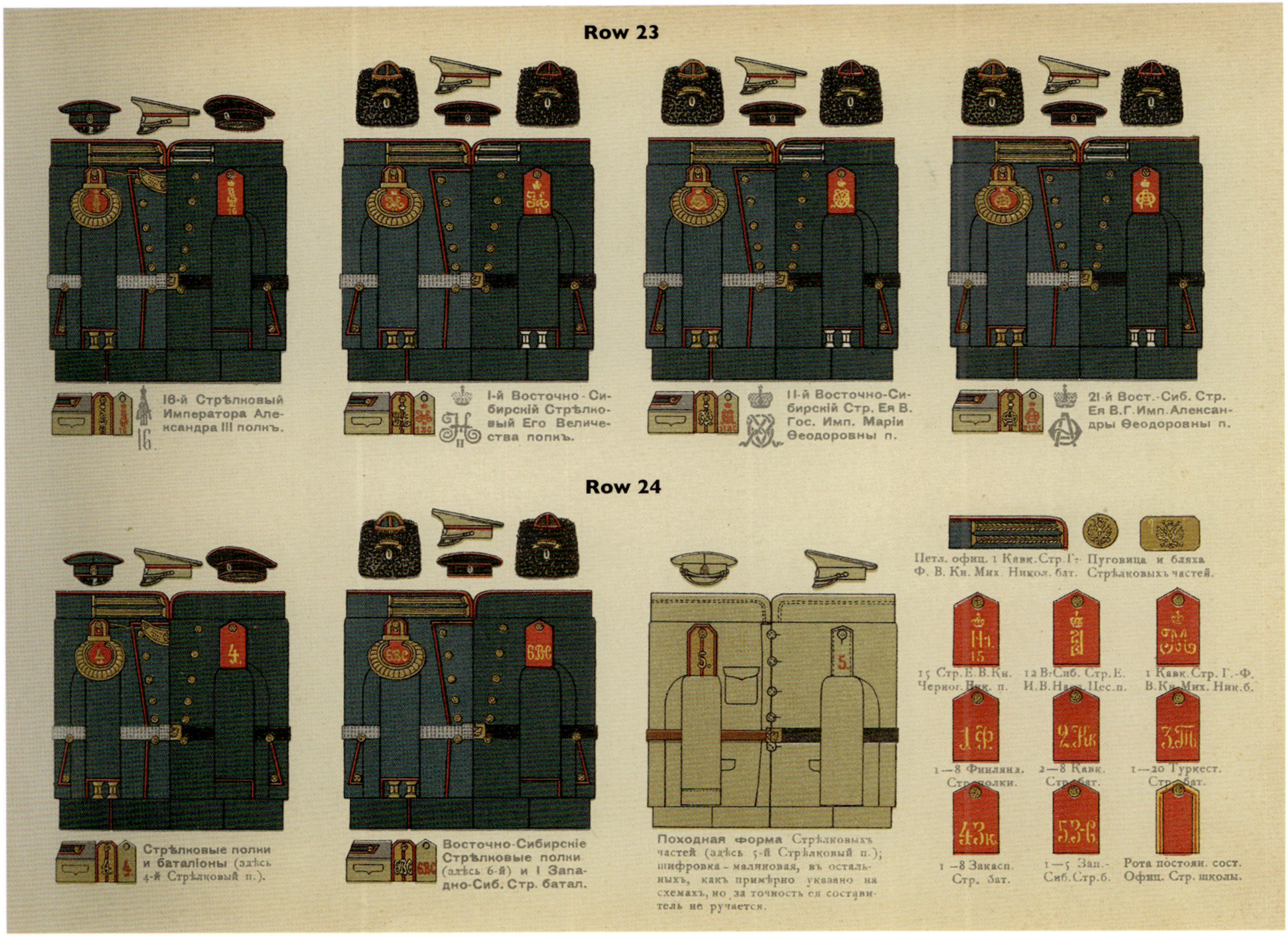

C70a Plates of the Russian Imperial Army Uniforms by V.K. Shenk (1910)

Row 23: (left to right)
1. 16th Rifle Regiment of Emperor Alexander II
2. 1st Siberian Rifle Regiment of His Majesty
3. 11th Siberian Rifle Regiment of Grand Duchess Maria Feodorovna
4. 21st Siberian Rifle Regiment of Grand Duchess Alexandra Feodorovna

Row 24: (left to right)
1. 4th Rifle Regiment
2. 6th Eastern Siberian Rifle and a reserve regiment
3. Summer or combat uniform
4: (from top)
a. Distinction braid on collar; tunic button, and belt buckle
b–d. Examples of monograms and shoulder strap markings for rifles

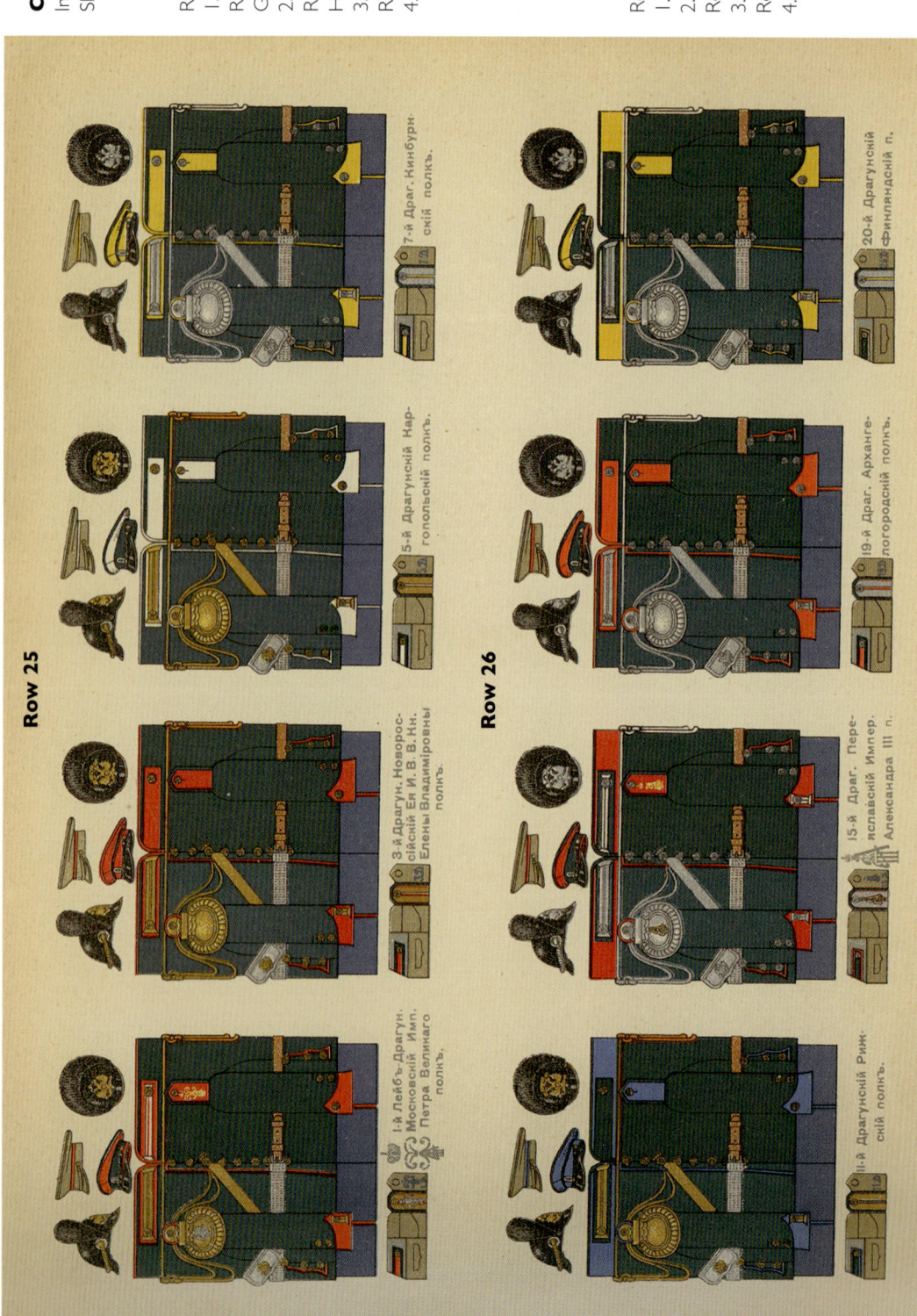

C70b Plates of the Russian Imperial Army Uniforms by V.K. Shenk (1910)

Row 25: (left to right)
1. 1st Moscow Life Dragoon Regiment of Emperor Peter the Great
2. 3rd New Russia Dragoon Regiment of Grand Duchess Helen Vladimirovna
3. 5th Kargopol Dragoon Regiment
4. 7th Kinburn Dragoon Regiment

Row 26: (left to right)
1. 11th Riga Dragoon Regiment
2. 15th Pereyaslav Dragoon Regiment of Emperor Alexander III
3. 19th Archangelogorod Dragoon Regiment
4. 20th Finland Dragoon Regiment

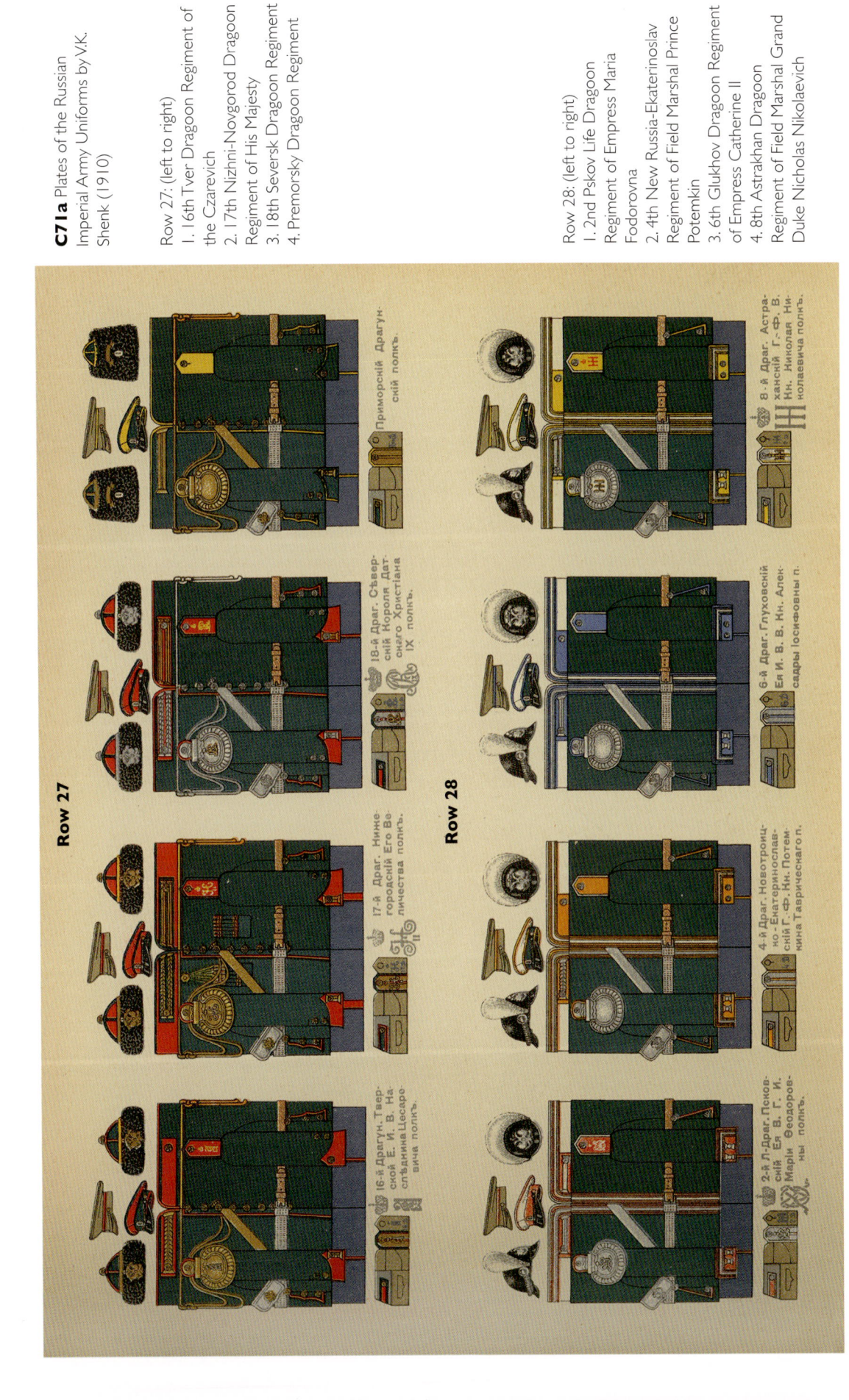

C71a Plates of the Russian Imperial Army Uniforms by V.K. Shenk (1910)

Row 27: (left to right)
1. 16th Tver Dragoon Regiment of the Czarevich
2. 17th Nizhni-Novgorod Dragoon Regiment of His Majesty
3. 18th Seversk Dragoon Regiment
4. Premorsky Dragoon Regiment

Row 28: (left to right)
1. 2nd Pskov Life Dragoon Regiment of Empress Maria Fodorovna
2. 4th New Russia-Ekaterinoslav Regiment of Field Marshal Prince Potemkin
3. 6th Glukhov Dragoon Regiment of Empress Catherine II
4. 8th Astrakhan Dragoon Regiment of Field Marshal Grand Duke Nicholas Nikolaevich

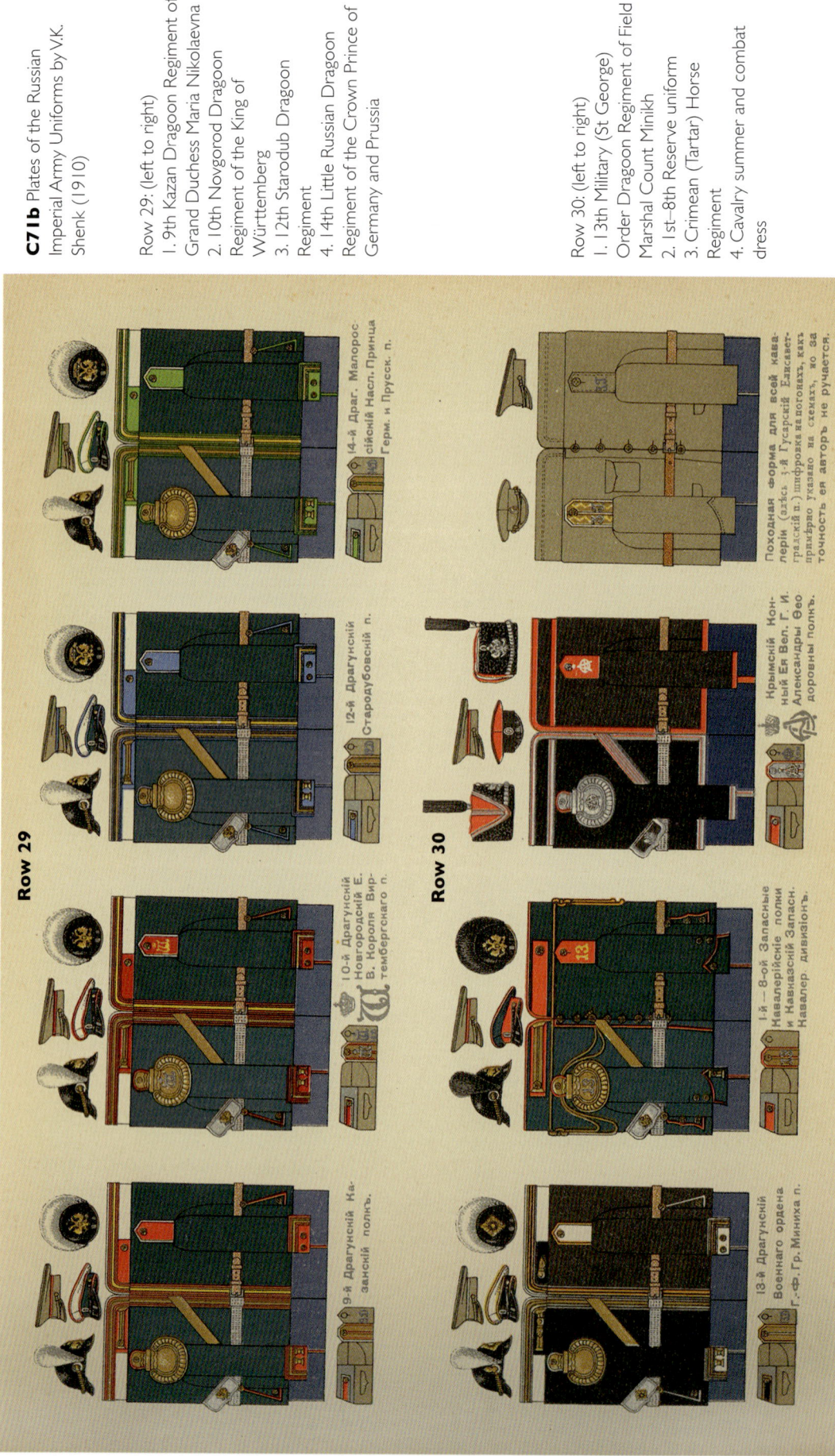

C71b Plates of the Russian Imperial Army Uniforms by V.K. Shenk (1910)

Row 29: (left to right)
1. 9th Kazan Dragoon Regiment of Grand Duchess Maria Nikolaevna
2. 10th Novgorod Dragoon Regiment of the King of Württemberg
3. 12th Starodub Dragoon Regiment
4. 14th Little Russian Dragoon Regiment of the Crown Prince of Germany and Prussia

Row 30: (left to right)
1. 13th Military (St George) Order Dragoon Regiment of Field Marshal Count Minikh
2. 1st–8th Reserve uniform
3. Crimean (Tartar) Horse Regiment
4. Cavalry summer and combat dress

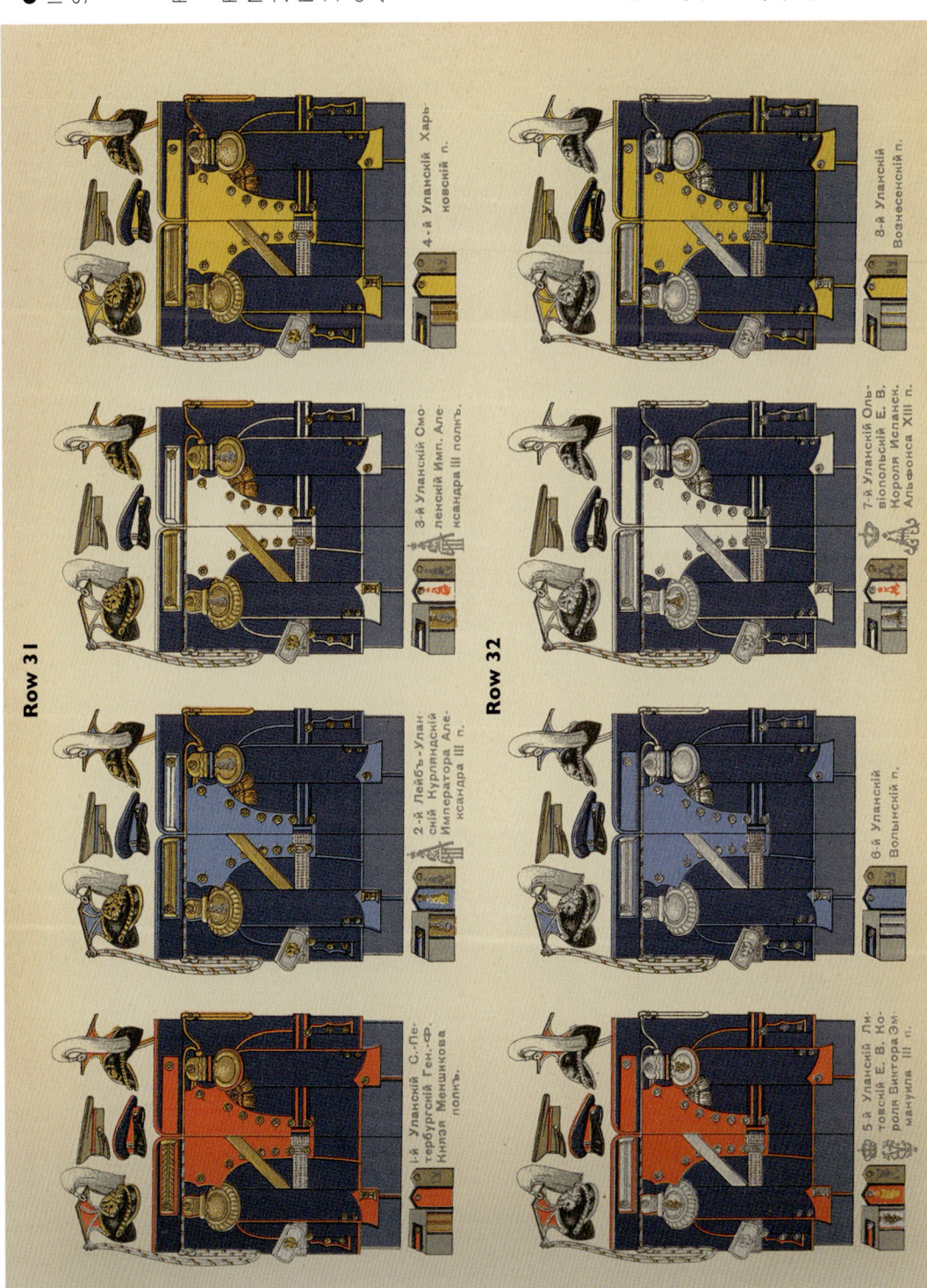

C72a Plates of the Russian Imperial Army Uniforms by V.K. Shenk (1910)

Row 31: (left to right)
1. 1st St Petersburg Lancer Regiment of Field Marshal Prince Menshikov
2. 2nd Kurland Lancer Regiment of Emperor Alexander II
3. 3rd Smolensk Lancer Regiment of Emperor Alexander III
4. 4th Kharkov Lancer Regiment

Row 32: (left to right)
1. 5th Lithuanian Lancer Regiment of King Victor Emmanuel III of Italy
2. 6th Volynsky Lancer Regiment
3. 7th Olviopol Lancer Regiment of Alfonso XIII, King of Spain
4. 8th Voznesensk Lancer Regiment of Grand Duchess Tatiana Nikolaevna

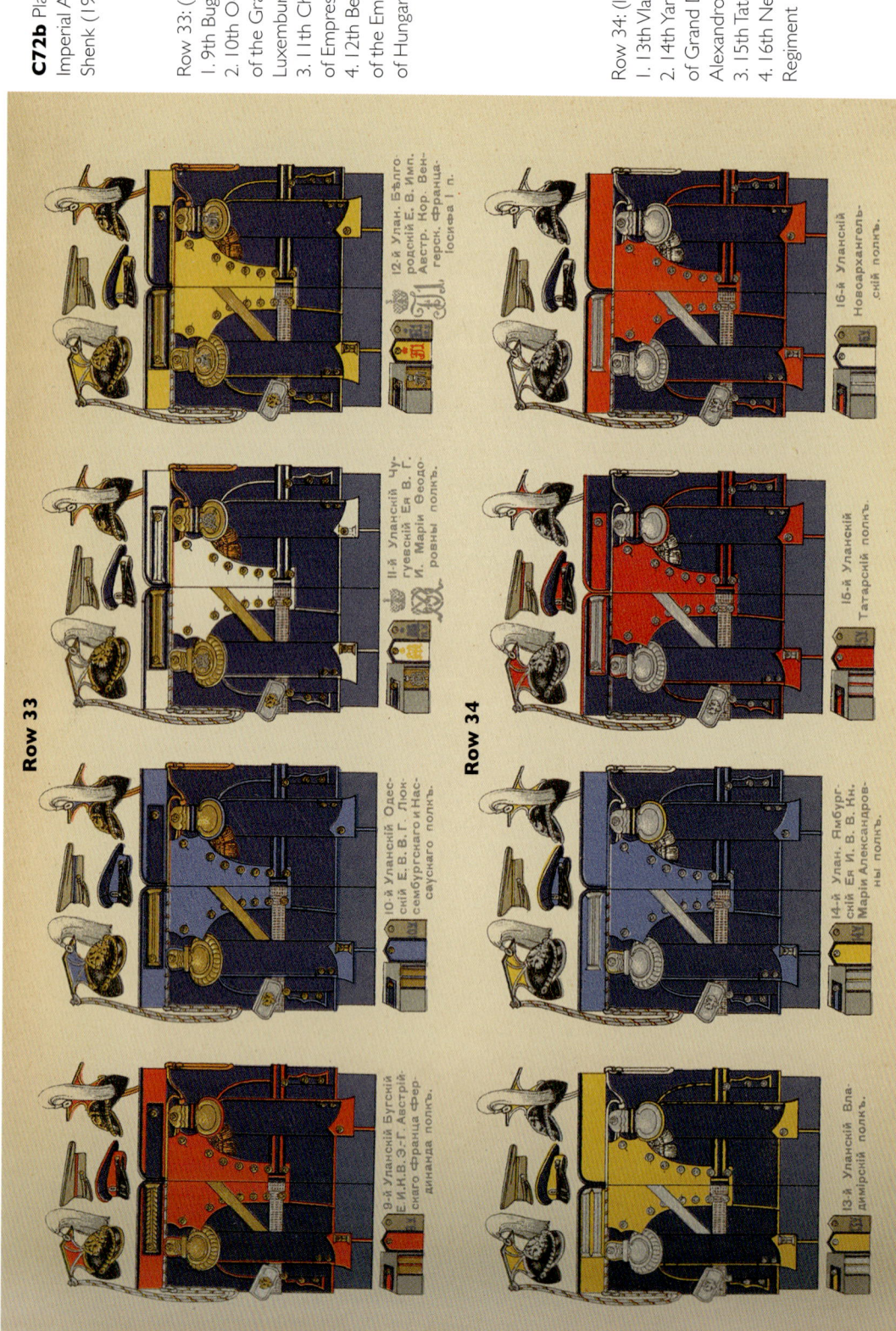

C72b Plates of the Russian Imperial Army Uniforms by V.K. Shenk (1910)

Row 33: (left to right)
1. 9th Bug Lancer Regiment
2. 10th Odessa Lancer Regiment of the Grand Duke of Nassau and Luxemburg
3. 11th Chuguev Lancer Regiment of Empress Maria Feodorovna
4. 12th Belgorod Lancer Regiment of the Emperor of Austria and King of Hungary Franz-Joseph I

Row 34: (left to right)
1. 13th Vladimir Lancer Regiment
2. 14th Yamburg Lancer Regiment of Grand Duchess Maria Alexandrovna
3. 15th Tatar Lancer Regiment
4. 16th New Archangel Lancer Regiment

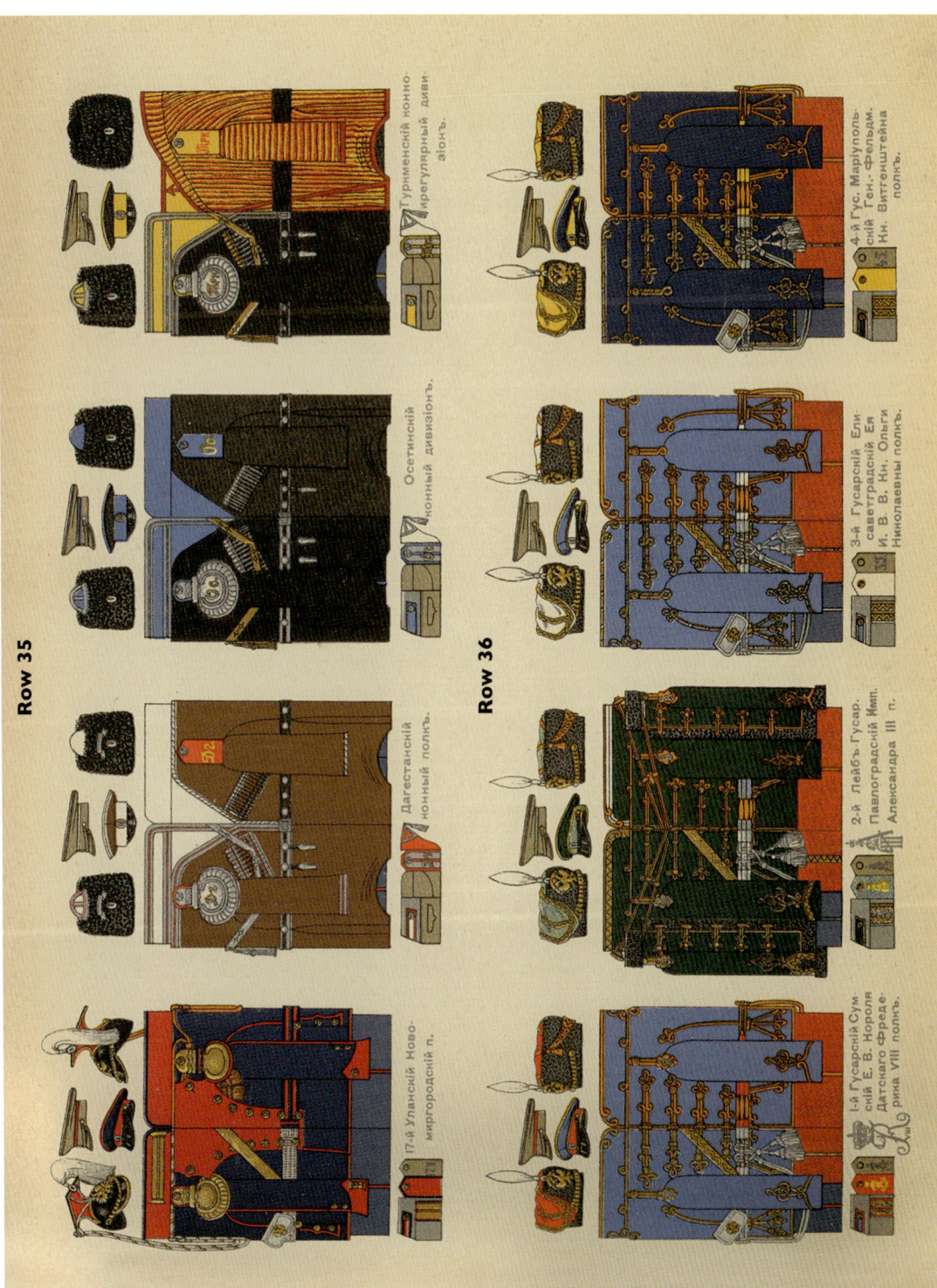

C73a Plates of the Russian Imperial Army Uniforms by V.K. Shenk (1910)

Row 35: (left to right)
1. 17th New Mirgorod Lancer Regiment
2. Dagestan Regiment
3. Ossetian Demi-Regiment
4. Turkman Demi-Regiment

Row 36: (left to right)
1. 1st Sumy Hussar Regiment of General Seslavin
2. 2nd Pavlograd Hussar Regiment of Emperor Alexander III
3. 3rd Elizabetgrad Hussar Regiment of Grand Duchess Olga Nikolaevna
4. 4th Mariupol Hussar Regiment of Empress Elizabeth Petrovna

Row 35

Row 36

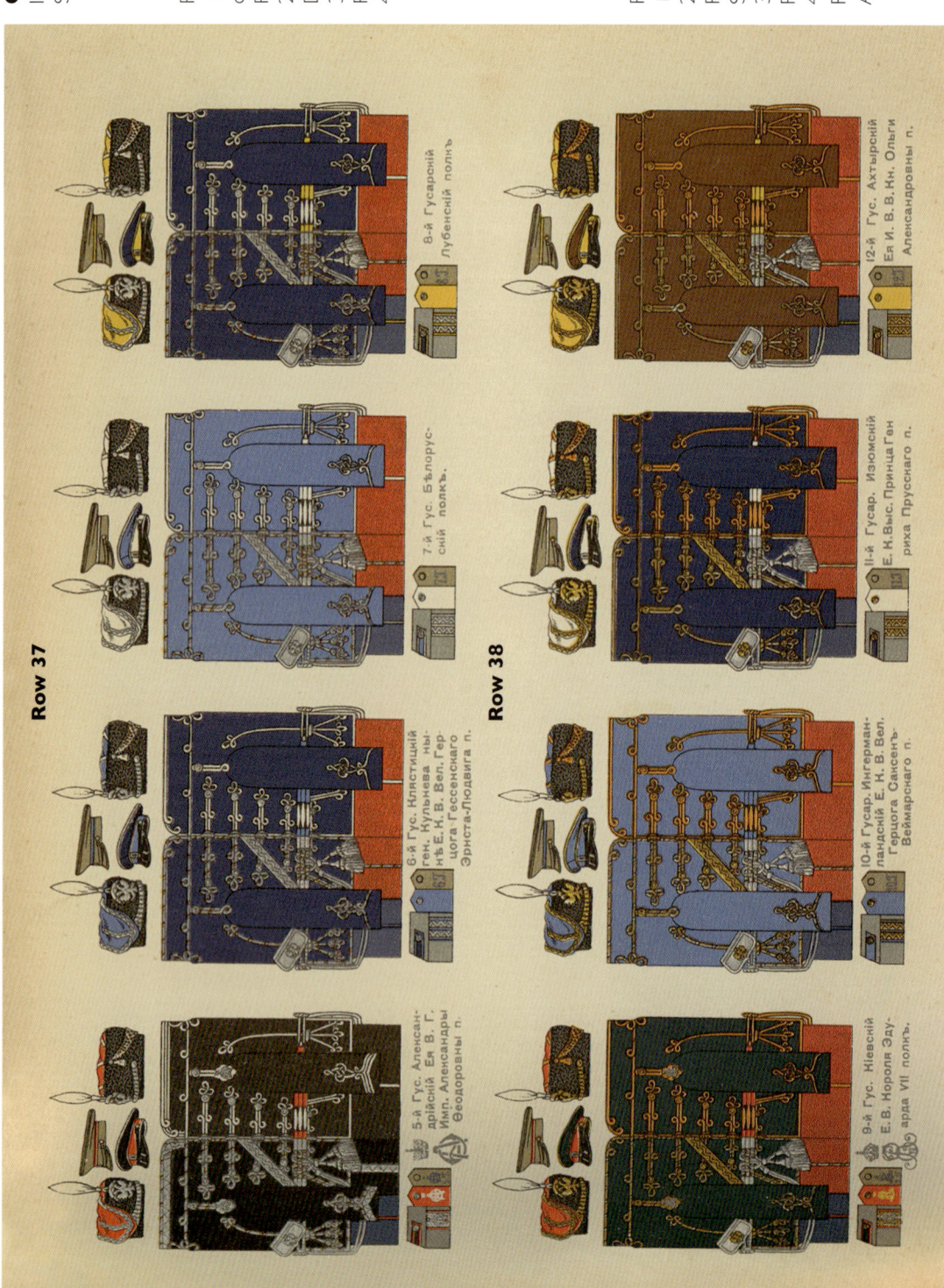

C73b Plates of the Russian Imperial Army Uniforms by V.K. Shenk (1910)

Row 37: (left to right)
1. 5th Alexandria Hussar Regiment of Her Imperial Majesty Alexandra Feodorovna
2. 6th Klyastitsi Hussar of Grand Duke Ernst-Ludwig of Hesse
3. 7th White Russian Hussar Regiment of Emperor Alexander I
4. 8th Lubny Hussar Regiment

Row 38: (left to right)
1. 9th Kiev Hussar Regiment
2. 10th Ingermanland Hussar Regiment of the Grand Duke of Saxony-Weimar
3. 11th Izyum Hussar Regiment of Prince Henry of Prussia
4. 12th Akhtyrka Hussar Regiment of Grand Duchess Olga Alexandrovna

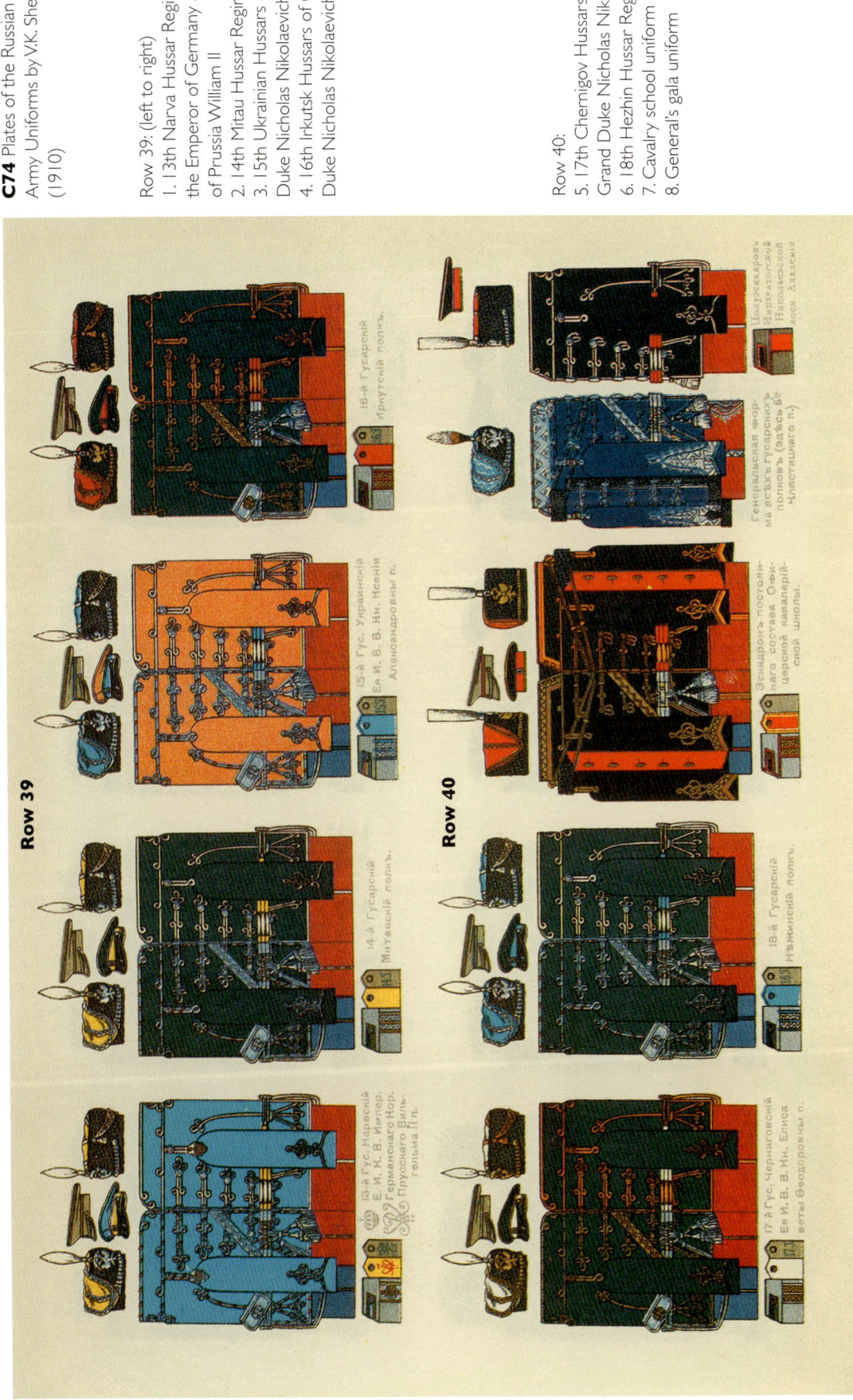

C74 Plates of the Russian Imperial Army Uniforms by V.K. Shenk (1910)

Row 39: (left to right)
1. 13th Narva Hussar Regiment of the Emperor of Germany and King of Prussia William II
2. 14th Mitau Hussar Regiment
3. 15th Ukrainian Hussars of Grand Duke Nicholas Nikolaevich
4. 16th Irkutsk Hussars of Grand Duke Nicholas Nikolaevich

Row 40:
5. 17th Chernigov Hussars of Grand Duke Nicholas Nikolaevich
6. 18th Hezhin Hussar Regiment
7. Cavalry school uniform
8. General's gala uniform

GERMAN EMPIRE

C77 Guard Cuirassiers gala tunic

C76 Gardes du Corps gala tunic

C75 See §V.13-17, Lance Pennant Colours

C80 1st Guard Dragoons

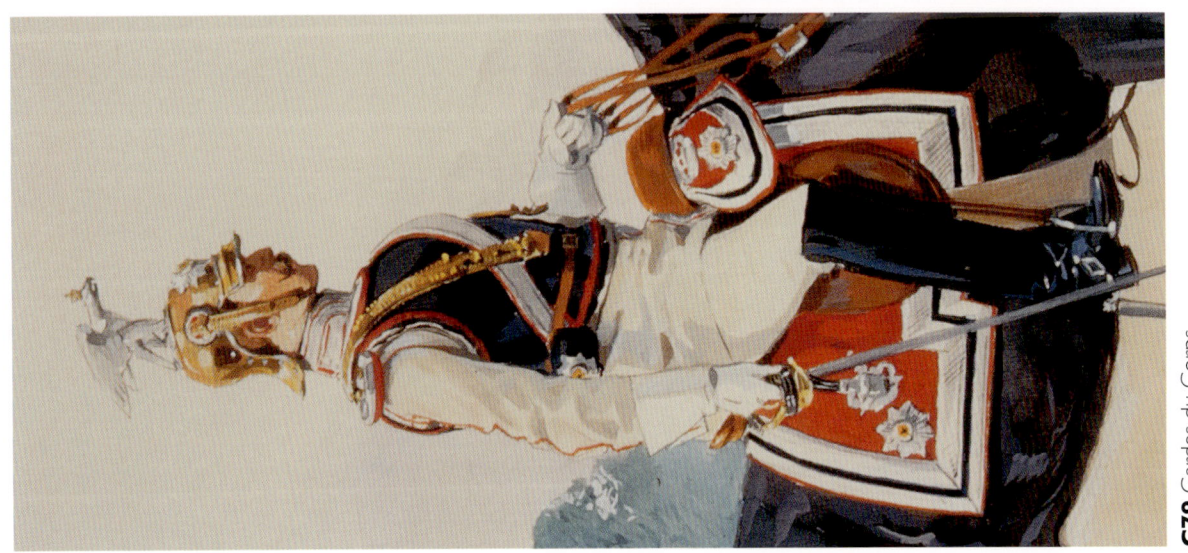

C79 Gardes du Corps

C78 1st Foot Guards

C83 Jäger zu Pferde trooper

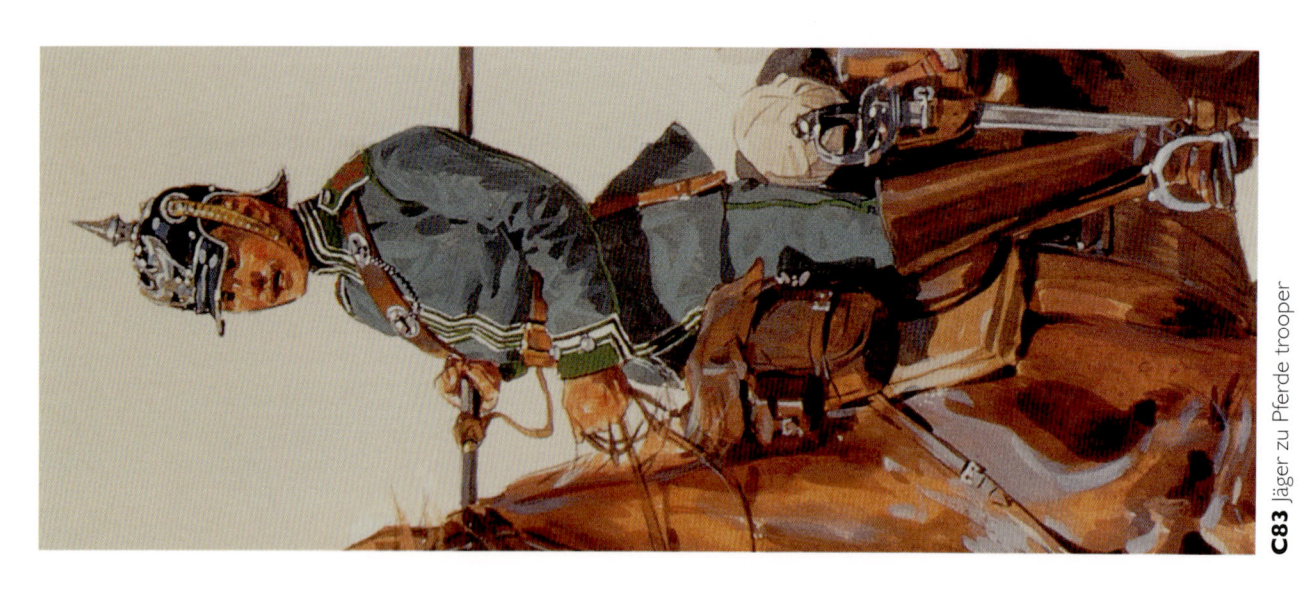

C82 19th Hussars (Saxon)

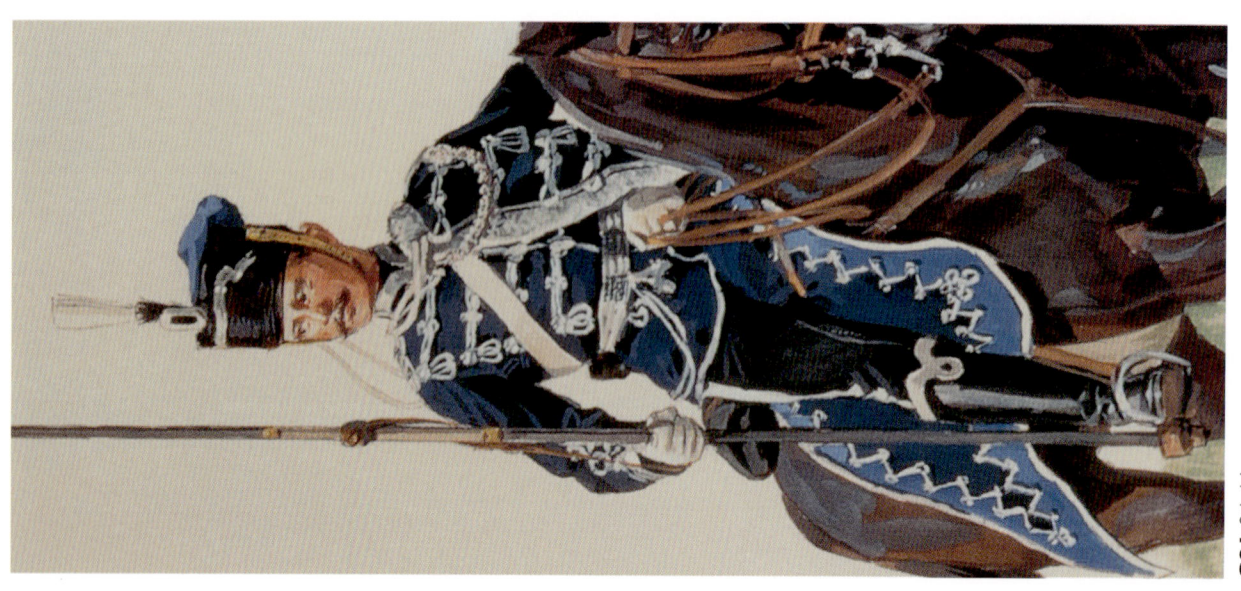

C81 8th Hussars

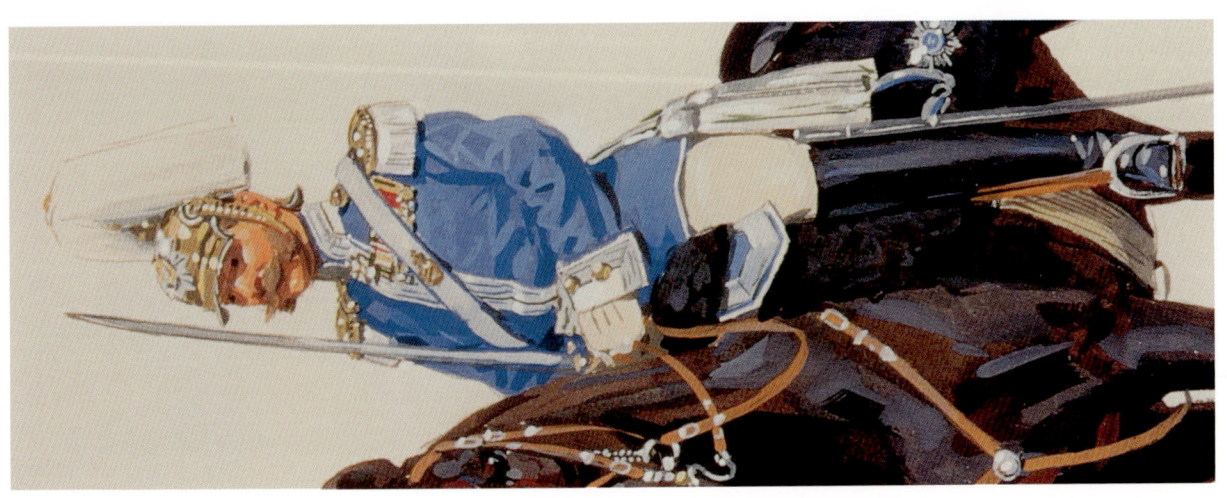

C84 Saxon 1st (Guard) Heavy Reiter

C85 Bavarian Schwere Reiter

C86 2nd Saxon Carabiniers

C89 Bavarian 11th Infantry

C88 11th Jägers (Mecklenburg)

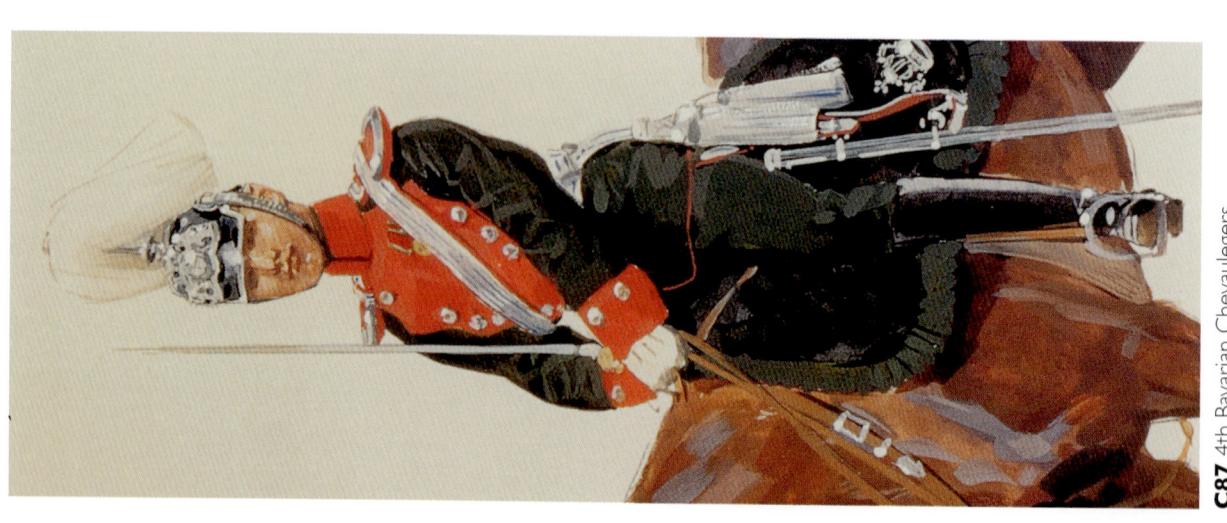

C87 4th Bavarian Chevaulegers

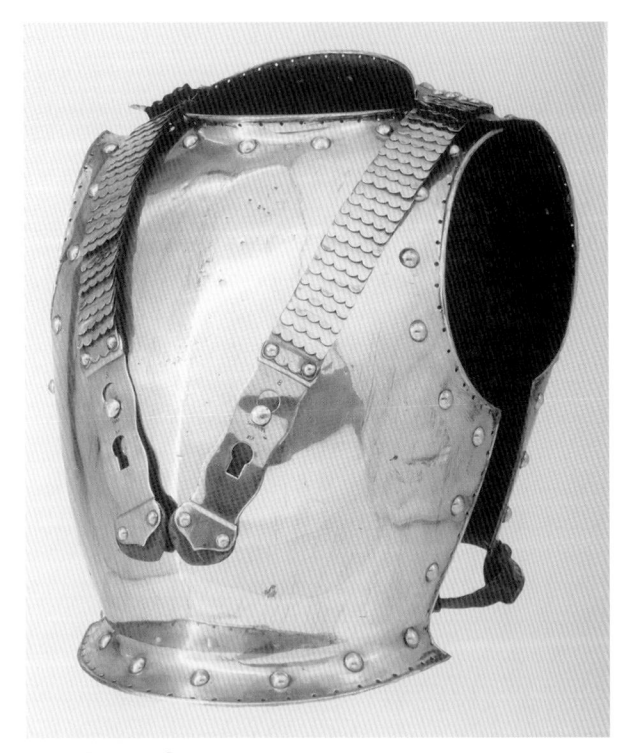

Cuirass

Both officers and other ranks of the guard cuirassier regiments wore cuirasses in full dress, but only when they were in mounted service (Images V:27, V:28, and V:29). For foot service, the cuirass was not worn except under special circumstances (see Palace Guard Dress, below). The cuirass was never worn outside of service. In regular dress, it was only worn when the helmet was also being worn.

The cuirass was made of brass. It was trimmed with cording the colour of the other ranks' full dress shoulder straps (Table V.5.a.1). The cording ran around the openings for the head and arms, down the side seams from the bottom of the armholes, and around the entire bottom edge of the cuirass. The lining of the shoulder straps and the belt was red leather.

V:27 Russian Cuirass

V:28 Subaltern in Full Dress Helmet with Double-Headed Eagle, Wearing Cuirass
Note how this in this studio photograph the officer has elected to have his pouch belt come below where the cuirass shoulder strap is fastened to the cuirass. He is wearing standard black riding boots that come to just below his knee.

V:29 Subaltern Officer in One of the Four Guard Cuirassier Regiments
Note how he has elected to have his pouch belt go above where the cuirass shoulder strap fastens to the cuirass. The officer's sash is worn beneath the cuirass. His black riding boots are patent leather.

Trumpets and drummers of the guard cuirassier regiments did not wear the cuirass.

Officer Epaulettes

Officers of the guard cuirassiers wore guard infantry model epaulettes in full dress. The lining and piping of the officers' epaulettes were the colour of the shoulder straps worn by the troops in full dress (Table V.5.a.1).

The 1st Squadron – and only the 1st Squadron – of both the Horse Guards and the Emperor's Cuirassiers bore the monogram H II for Nicholas II on the epaulette. The monogram was gold for the Horse Guards and silver for the Emperor's Cuirassiers. See §V-3-1 for details on epaulettes.

Other Ranks Shoulder Straps

Other ranks wore coloured shoulder straps in full dress. The colour of the shoulder strap varied by regiment, but all shoulder straps had white piping (Table V.5.a.1). In the 1st Squadron of the Horse Guard and of the Emperor's Cuirassiers, the shoulder straps bore the monogram H II for Nicholas II in smooth metal the colour of the button. See §V-3-1 for details on shoulder straps.

The other ranks had an additional set of shoulder straps that was worn with the walking-out tunic. These shoulder straps were black with piping in the colour of the full dress shoulder straps. Monograms were the same as for the full dress shoulder straps.

Gala Dress

Officers of the guard cuirassier regiments had three different types of uniform that were assigned for different ceremonies or other occasions of varying levels of formality: gala dress, ball full dress, and ball undress.

For gala dress, the helmet was worn with the eagle. Officers of the Emperor's and Empress's Cuirassiers wore the white full dress koller, and officers of the Chevalier Guards and the Horse Guards wore the gala dress red koller. Epaulettes were worn with the kollers. Gala trousers (charivari) were worn with shoes and ball spurs, and the outfit was completed with white gloves – regular, not gauntlet. A lath (type of sword) was worn on a belt over the tunic.

Full ball dress included the helmet with the grenade affixed to the top, the walking-out tunic (*vice-moundir*) with epaulettes, gala trousers (charivari), shoes, ball spurs, white gloves, and a sword.

Ball undress could either be the helmet and grenade with the walking-out tunic or sometimes even the undress jacket (*redingote*) worn with the cap. Long trousers were worn instead of breeches. All other accessories were the same as for full ball dress.

Walking-Out Tunic (*Vice-Moundir*)

Officers and other ranks of the guard cuirassier regiments wore different styles of walking-out tunic.

For the officers, the *vice-moundir* was double-breasted, with two rows of six buttons down the front. It was supposed to be made of dark royal green cloth according to regulation, but only the officers of the Horse Guard actually followed this rule; officers of the other three regiments of guard cuirassiers insisted on black cloth, which was the same colour as worn by the troops. The rounded collar and straight Swedish cuffs were the same colour as the tunic, with piping the colour of the other ranks' shoulder straps. The false rear pockets had the same colour of piping, and were cut straight with two buttons, one at the top (waist-level) and one at the bottom. There were no buttons on the cuff or on the sleeve above the cuff. The epaulette straps were the same as on the full dress tunic.

Other ranks wore a black single-breasted vice-moundir with nine buttons down the front. It had a rounded collar and Swedish cuffs, both black like the rest of the tunic with piping the colour of the full dress shoulder straps. The cuffs did not have any buttons, but on the outside seam of the sleeve above the cuffs were two buttons. The rear false pockets were straight, piped in the same colour as the collar and cuffs. They had one button at the top (waist-level) and one at the bottom. The black shoulder straps were worn with the vice-moundir.

Undress Jacket (*Redingote*)

The undress jacket, or *redingote*, was sometimes worn by officers in ball dress. It was dark green for the Horse Guard and black for the other regiments of guard cuirassiers. Like the officers' walking-out jacket, it was double-breasted with two rows of six buttons. The collar and cuffs were the colour of the rest of the jacket, and the piping of collar, cuffs, and pockets was the colour of the other ranks' full dress shoulder straps. The false rear pockets were straight, with one button at the top (waist-level) and another at the bottom.

The lining of the redingote was white.

Palace Guard Dress

Palace Guard duty was typically assigned to the Horse Guard and the Chevalier Guard. For palace duty, both officers and other ranks wore the helmet with the eagle. The white full dress koller and the *supravest* were worn with white suede breeches. Officers wore epaulettes, and other ranks wore their full dress shoulder straps. Officers also wore the pouch belt and pouch for palace duty; other ranks did not wear these items. White gauntlet-style gloves and black jackboots with spurs completed the outfit. The lath and revolver were carried for palace duty.

The Emperor's and Empress's Cuirassiers were not usually assigned palace duty. If they happened to be serving in one of the palaces, though, they wore the helmet with the eagle, the white full dress koller, the white suede breeches, and the jackboots with the cuirass, since they did not have the supravest. This was the one exception where the cuirass could be worn in foot service instead of mounted service.

Supravest

The Chevalier Guards and Horse Guards had special over-garments called *supravests*, which were worn only for palace duty. Both officers and other ranks wore supravests when on palace duty. They were made of cloth, but mimicked the shape of the brass cuirass which was worn in full dress. The supravest was supposed to be for the entirety of the two regiments, but in practice was usually only worn by the officers and men in the 1st and 4th Squadrons, who were usually the ones picked for palace duty because of their larger size.

The supravest was made of red cloth and had braid around the neck, the armholes, and the fitted waist. The braid was made of three stripes (Image V:30). The centre stripe was light blue for the Chevalier Guards, dark blue for the Horse Guards. The two outer stripes on the braid were orange for the other ranks and in the button colour for the officers, silver for the Chevalier

V:30 Front View of the Horse Guards Supravest

V:31 Subaltern of the Chevalier Guards Wearing Supravest
This was basically the uniform worn on palace guard duty. Also note the patent leather jackboots.

V:32 Side View of Chevalier Guard Officer
This shows the back of the supravest. Note the shape of the top of the jackboot.

V:33 Chevalier Guard Regiment, c. 1890s
In this photograph, an officer and trooper are both wearing supravests. Note the soft boots which later went out of style.

V:34 Subaltern of the Horse Guard Regiment Wearing a Supravest
He has placed the pouch belt in relationship to the double-headed eagle on the supravest. Also note the patent leather jackboots and the cords leading down to a holster and pistol.

Guards and gold for the Horse Guards. Below the braid (at waist-level) was a short flared skirt made of a series of rounded flaps of cloth, light blue for the Chevalier Guards and dark blue for the Horse Guards. The flaps were bordered with orange braid for the troops and gold or silver braid for the officers according to the button colour.

The front and the back of the supravest bore decorations.[66] For the Chevalier Guards, the decoration was a large silver St Andrew's guard star (Images V:31, V:32, and V:33). The diameter of the star from point to point was 22.23 cm (8.75 inches), and the interior diameter from angle to angle was 12.78 (5.03 inches). The centre of the star was enamelled. The decoration for the Horse Guards was a gold gilt metallic double-headed eagle (Image V:34). The decoration was 21.11 cm (8.31 inches) in both width and height.

RIDING BREECHES, TROUSERS, AND CHARIVARI

All ranks of guard cuirassiers usually wore standard breeches in full dress. Officers also had full-length trousers that could be worn with the walking-out tunic. Both the breeches and the officers' trousers were blue with narrow piping down the outside seam of each leg. Piping was the colour of the shoulder straps (Table V.5.a.1). Officers had an additional band in the same colour as the piping, 4.45 cm (1.75 inches) wide, which went around the top of the waist of the breeches and trousers, which was unusual.

The charivari worn by officers in gala and ball dress were blue with two wide bands in the colour of the shoulder strap (Table V.5.a.1) running down the outside of the leg. In between the two bands, on the blue outer seam, there was also piping in the shoulder strap colour.

For palace duty, the guard cuirassier regiments had a unique style of breeches that were made of white suede (deerskin) or elk skin.

The officers of the Chevalier Guards, probably the Horse Guards, and possibly the other Guard Cuirassier regiments had an unusual custom when they were called upon to perform palace guard duty in their palace guard dress inside the different palaces of the Czar.

Their white breeches were cut as tight as possible. The officers would not wear underpants. Then to fit into the tight breeches they would cover their lower body with soap and water to help squeeze into the smallest, tightest possible pair of white breeches. Once the breeches were on the body, water was thrown on them with the aim of making them shrink. This was done so that the breeches would not show creases.[67] Another way to achieve the tight breeches was to have two men 'shake' one into the dampened breeches powdered with soap sprinkled inside.[68] The end product was a garment that clung closely to the wearer, something like wearing wet Spandex.

It was said that the ladies of the court, unencumbered by a strict Victorian modesty, would admire the officers' manly builds as they walked by. Men who cut fine figures in this dress were great favourites with the court ladies. (Interview with Wrangel, c. July 1973.)

UNIFORM ACCESSORIES

Officers' Accessories
Officers of the guard cuirassiers wore the standard model pouch with a silver St Andrew's guard star decoration on the cover flap in full dress (*§V-3-1*). The Chevalier Guards had a special cuirassier-style braid which covered their pouch belt. The braid was silver to match the button colour, and was textured with five ridges that ran along it lengthwise. The officers of the other three regiments of guard cuirassiers had the standard smooth braid in their button colour on the pouch belt.

Officers also wore the standard officer's sash in full dress.(*§V-3-1*).

Other Ranks' Accessories
Other ranks of the guard cuirassiers wore a wide white patent leather belt in full dress. The belt had either a gold or silver buckle plate according to the button colour, and was decorated with the double-headed eagle. With the vice-moundir, the other ranks wore a narrow white leather belt with a regular buckle in the button colour. The straps on the belt which held the lath were white leather.

Other Accessories
Basic riding boots were worn by all ranks in full dress with the regular breeches (Image V:35). When charivari were worn by officers in full, gala, or ball dress, shoes were worn instead of boots. Shoes were also worn with officers' full-length trousers in walking-out dress. Jackboots were worn by all ranks for palace duty.

All ranks of the guard cuirassiers wore white gauntlet gloves in full dress and palace guard dress (Image V:35). Standard white gloves were worn by officers in gala dress, full ball dress, and ball undress. Standard brown gloves were worn by all ranks in walking-out dress. See §V-3-1 for more details on accessories.

V:35 Subaltern of the Four Guard Cuirassier Regiments
Note that he is wearing blue breeches. Also note the cord which goes around his neck and down to a pistol in a holster on his right side. The pistol and holster were items of full dress.

§V-5-b GUARD DRAGOONS AND HORSE GRENADIERS[69]

GUARD DRAGOONS

The Dragoon Regiment of the Imperial Guard was formed on 3 April 1814 as a regiment of horse chasseurs. Later that month, it entered the Young Guard as the Horse Chasseur Regiment of the Imperial Guard. In 1831, it became part of the Old Guard, and in 1833, it took its definitive name, Dragoon Regiment of the Imperial Guard. In 1909, Grand Duchess Maria Pavlovna was named honorary chief of the regiment.

HORSE GRENADIERS

The Horse Grenadiers were created on 12 December 1809, when the Lancer Regiment of Grand Duke Constantine was split in half. Originally, the regiment was simply named Dragoons of the Guard, and it entered the Old Guard in 1814. In 1831, its name was officially changed to the Horse Grenadier Regiment of the Imperial Guard, and with the title of grenadiers came its unique uniform.

Although the Horse Grenadiers did not officially bear the title of 'dragoons' they were considered, along with the Guard Dragoon Regiment, to make up part of the dragoon element of the Imperial Guard. The uniforms of both regiments were thus very similar in many respects, with the exception of the headdresses, which were completely unique to each regiment and are described in separate sections below.

UNIFORM

DRAGOON SHAKO

The Dragoon Regiment of the Imperial Guard wore a shako-style headdress in full dress (Image V:36).

For officers, the body of the shako was made of dark (royal) green cloth. For the other ranks, it was made of black waxed felt. The top and visor of the shako

V:36 Guard Dragoons
Note the different shapes of the eagles on the men's kivers. This photograph was apparently taken soon after they changed over to this type of dragoon uniform, and the officers and men wore different shaped double-headed eagles. Soon after this photo was made, officers and men wore the same shape eagle, the type worn by the officers with wings down. Also note the very different colours of the tunics worn by the officers and men.

were black patent leather, and the visor had a border of white metal 0.83 cm (0.33 inch) wide. There was also a band of black patent leather around the bottom edge of the shako, and a 'V' of the same material on either side, extending from the bottom edge – where the chinstrap attached – to the top edge of the headdress. The chinstrap was made of overlapping white metal scales. The scales alternated between having three scallops and two scallops. The chinstrap, more decorative than functional, was worn above the shako visor.

Shako Cording

Around the top edge of the shako there was a border of cording with a small loop at the back of the shako where the cap line could be attached. The cording was silver filigree for officers and regular white cording for other ranks.

The shako featured additional decorative cording comprising four individual strands of the same silver or white cording that was around the top edge of the shako. It started on the left side of the shako, where all four strands were attached near the top edge. The ends hung down almost to the bottom edge of the shako, where they were gathered into a flat tassel 3.11 cm (1.42 inches) long. From the point of attachment on the shako, the four strands of cording were divided so two strands could pass in front of the shako and two in back. The strands were braided together, however, giving the appearance of substantial thickness. This wider braided cording dipped down slightly at both the front and back – falling low enough on the front to avoid obstructing other headdress decoration – before coming back up to attach near the top edge on the right side of the shako, where all four strands of cording met again. The four strands then hung down 52.23 cm (20.56 inches) and ended in a series of three 3.89 cm (1.53 inch) tassels. The first tassel gathered all four cords together, and had a loop so it could be attached to the top button on the right front panel of the full dress tunic. At the bottom of the tassel, two cords came out and formed two flounders. There was another tassel at the bottom of each flounder.

NCOs had tassels and slides that were mixed white, black, and orange instead of plain white. Among the officers there was no further distinction for rank included in the cording except that the flounders of superior officers tended to be thicker than those of subalterns.

Decorations and Plume

The decoration on the front centre of the shako for both the officers and the other ranks of the guard dragoons was a silver double-headed eagle with the guard star of St Andrew on its breast. However, it was the 1814 model eagle, so its wings were extended to either side, but still pointed down rather than being completely raised and pointing upwards as was seen in later models of the eagle. Some pictures do exist, though, which show the officers wearing the regulation 1814 model eagle and the other ranks wearing the 1857 model eagle with upraised wings at the same time, so there may have been some initial experimentation before the 1814 model was definitively adopted (Image V:36).

Centred at the top edge of the front of the shako was a cockade. For the other ranks, it was the standard cockade but had the monogram H II (Nicholas II) in silver superimposed on it. Officers had a special cockade that was 4.72 cm (1.86 inches) high and 3.89 cm (1.53 inches) wide. In the centre of the cockade was another oval, 2.22 cm (0.88 inch) high and 1.67 cm (0.66 inch) wide. This oval had a silver monogram H II mounted on a background of St George's black-and-orange striped ribbon. The central oval was surrounded by four rows of sequins. The back of the cockade was green patent leather.

In full dress, a plume was mounted on the shako above the cockade. Other ranks wore a plain white horsehair plume. For officers, the plume was also white but had a base that was silver, braided with black and orange. The base was 2.5 cm (0.98 inch) high, and the plume itself was 23.89 cm (9.41 inches) high, and rounded at the upper end. Generals wore the hussar general's style of plume. See §V-5-d for details.

Cap Line

In addition to the above-described cording, the shakos worn by the Regiment of Guard Dragoons had a cap line for officers of silver filigree. Instead of being round like typical cording, it had a square cross-section. Other ranks had a plain white cap line.

Neither the officers or the other ranks had tassels on their cap lines.

The cap line always started with a large loop that went around the neck, fastening at the back of the tunic collar. If it was being worn while with the other ranks, it draped down the back to the level of the shoulder-blade before being brought back up to fasten to the cording loop on the back of the shako by means of a toggle on the end of the line. If the cap line was being worn outside the ranks or in foot service, after the neck loop it draped one-third of the way down the back before being brought back up, passing between the epaulette strap and the sleeve seam on the right shoulder, and falling down the front right side between the arm and the body of the tunic, finally attaching to the second button down on the right side of the plastron by passing the toggle through the buttonhole.

V:38 Horse Grenadiers NCO
Note the long-service stripes on the upper portion of his left arm. The large transverse crest on the helmet stands out prominently, and the bag hanging down can just be seen. Note also the old-style soft boots.

V:37 Made-up helmet of Horse Grenadier Regiment with Transverse Crest (this item shows why one should be very careful in viewing old uniform items)
The crest of the Guard Horse Grenadiers was noticeably larger than those worn by line cuirassiers and dragoons. Something has happened to this crest – it should be smooth. In addition., it seems too large. The bag which would hang down the back of the helmet and the shape of the braid that goes along the outside and centre of the bag seems correct. However, the badge on the front of the helmet is a line eagle and not the eagle and St Andrew star worn by the Guard Horse Grenadiers. The wrong front badge shows that this is a modern reproduction using some older elements.

V:39 The man on the left is an officer in the Horse Grenadiers. This gives a good view of the trim on the hanging bag. Note the newer-style boots and the location of the pouch. The man on the right is wearing a pre-1908 dragoon uniform.

Horse Grenadier Helmet

The Horse Grenadiers of the guard wore helmets in full dress. The shell and visor of the helmet were of black patent leather. The visor was bordered in copper. The chinstrap was copper as well, and outside the ranks the chinstrap was worn on the back of the helmet, resting on the neck-cover. There was a flaming grenade decoration on the helmet behind each chinstrap where it attached to the helmet. On the front of the helmet there was a gilt double-headed imperial eagle with the silver guard star of St Andrew on its breast. Above the eagle was a gilt distinction badge. The crest, which was transverse, was made of black horsehair. It was much higher than the transverse crest worn by line dragoons and cuirassiers (Image V:38). In full dress a long decorative triangular pennant was attached behind the crest. It was red, with trim running the length of the two long sides and down the centre as well (Image V:39). The trim was orange wool braid for other ranks and gold square-weave braid for officers. At the end of the pennant was a tassel, either orange or gold, to match the trim.

Tunic

The full dress tunic worn by both regiments was double-breasted, with two rows of seven buttons (for the 1908 Horse Grenadier Regiment, see Image V:40). For the officers, it was made of dark (royal) green cloth, while for the other ranks it was made of black cloth. The plastron for both regiments was red, as was the piping along the front edge of the tunic, which outlined the shape of the plastron on the right side before continuing down to the bottom hem of the tunic. The tunic skirt had scalloped false pockets which were piped in red and had three buttons, one on each point of the scalloping. The buttons were gold for the Horse Grenadiers, silver for the Dragoons.

The collar was red and cut on an angle for both regiments, piped in the colour of the tunic – green for officers, black for other ranks. The total height of the

V:40 Group Photo of Horse Grenadiers
Note how high the transverse crest is, and the difference in colour between the officer's tunic and the other rank's tunic.

collar varied from 4.45 cm (1.75 inches) to 5.56 cm (2.19 inches), and there were two simple litzen in the chapter shape on each side of the collar. For officers, the litzen was in the button colour, gold for the Horse Grenadiers and silver for the Dragoons. Other ranks of both regiments had orange litzen that were 1.39 cm (0.55 inch) wide with a red thread running through them. The collar litzen did not contain buttons.

The tunic had pointed (lancer-style) cuffs which were also red for both regiments. The cuffs did not have any piping. There was one litzen, the same colour and style as on the collar, on each cuff, but unlike the collar litzen the cuff litzen did have a button. Above the cuff on each sleeve, near the back arm seam, there were two buttons.

Epaulettes

Officers of both regiments wore cavalry model epaulettes in full dress. The epaulettes were gold for the Horse Grenadiers and silver for the Dragoons, with red piping and lining for both regiments.

Other ranks of both regiments wore metal trooper model epaulettes in full dress, gold metal for the Horse Grenadiers and white metal for the Dragoons. The epaulette lining was red in both cases. The Horse Grenadiers' epaulettes had a special red fringe that hung from the gold metal crescent. Theirs were the only trooper model epaulettes that had this feature.

For more details regarding models of epaulettes, see §V-3-1.

Shoulder Straps

Shoulder straps were worn in regular dress and walking-out dress. For both regiments, the shoulder straps were red. Horse Grenadiers had dark green piping on their shoulder straps, the Dragoons black.

For more details regarding shoulder straps, see §V-3-1.

Gala Dress

There were two levels of gala dress for the Guard Dragoon and Horse Grenadier officers.

Full ball dress was full winter parade dress for outside the ranks, meaning that charivari and shoes with ball spurs were worn instead of regular breeches and boots. The officer's sash, pouch, and pouch belt were not worn, and the cap line was worn affixed to the plastron rather than the shako. The sword belt was worn over the tunic.

Regular ball dress was regular winter dress for outside the ranks: the walking-out tunic was worn with charivari and shoes with ball spurs. However, epaulettes were worn instead of shoulder straps and white gloves were worn in place of brown.

Walking-Out Tunics

Two separate models of walking-out tunic were worn by the two regiments. Buttons were gold for the Guard Horse Grenadiers and silver for the Guard Dragoons.

Horse Grenadier Walking-Out Tunic

The Horse Grenadier Regiment of the Guard wore a vice-moundir, or undress jacket. The vice-moundir was double-breasted with two rows of seven gold-coloured buttons and cut to the shape of the plastron on the front, like the regular tunic. However, the collar was rounded at the corners rather than cut on an angle. The entire tunic, including the collar and pointed cuffs, was dark green, and there was red piping on the collar, cuffs, and front edge of the tunic. Above the cuff, near the back seam on each sleeve, were two buttons. The back skirt of the vice-moundir had scalloped pockets like the tunic which were piped in red and had three buttons, one at each point of the scalloping. The lining of the vice-moundir was white.

Dragoon Walking-Out Tunic

The Guard Dragoon Regiment wore a jacket called a *dragounka* instead of the vice-moundir (undress) jacket which was typical for walking-out dress. The dragounka was double-breasted with two rows of seven silver buttons, but was cut straight on the front rather than in the shape of a plastron. It was made of black cloth and had no piping. On the front panels of the jacket below the waist were pockets. The openings of the pockets were lined with black sheepskin. The sheepskin was bordered by 0.56 cm (0.23 inch) silver cording which encircled the entire pocket, with a loop at the top of the opening and a trefoil at the bottom of the opening.

Made of black sheepskin, the collar of the dragounka was rounded and worn folded down. A silver pelisse cord, or *mentichket*, like that worn by the hussars, was worn around the collar of the dragounka. It started on the right shoulder under the shoulder strap, draped slightly down in the front, and passed up the left side of the neck, around the back of the collar, and back down the right side of the neck, draping down slightly again as it crossed back over itself and went up to attach underneath the left shoulder strap.

The cuffs of the dragounka were pointed and made of black sheepskin. The cuffs were bordered in silver braid: 4.45 cm (1.75 inch) wide general's (zigzag) braid for generals, 2.78 cm (1.09 inch) wide hussar (zigzag) braid for superior officers, and 1.39 cm (0.55 inch) wide hussar braid for subalterns.

The lining of the dragounka was black.

Prior to being assigned the dragounka, the Guard Dragoons had worn a black vice-moundir similar to that worn by the Horse Grenadiers as their walking-out jacket.

Riding Breeches, Trousers, and Charivari

Officers and other ranks of both regiments typically wore standard breeches in full dress. Officers also had full-length trousers that were worn with the walking-out tunic, and with either the dragounka for the dragoons or the vice-moundir for the grenadiers. Both the breeches and the officers' trousers were blue with red piping down the outside seam of each leg.

The officers in both regiments also had dark green charivari that were sometimes worn in full dress with shoes rather than boots. The charivari had two wide red bands running down the outside of the leg. In between the two red bands, on the dark green outer seam, there was red piping. See §V-3-1 for more details.

Uniform Accessories

Officers' Accessories

Guard Dragoon and Horse Grenadier officers wore the standard model pouch and pouch belt in full dress. The pouch belt was in the button colour, silver for the dragoons and gold for the grenadiers. The pouch ornament was the silver guard star. Officers also wore the officer's sash in full dress. See §V-3-1 for further description.

Other Ranks' Accessories

Other ranks wore a striped girdle in full dress. The girdle was made of woven fabric with three horizontal stripes and piping at the top and bottom. The centre stripe was black, with a red stripe above and below it. The piping on the outside of the girdle was black. The buckle was covered in the same fabric as the belt.

Other Accessories

All ranks of both regiments wore standard knee-high riding boots and standard white wrist gloves in full dress. Standard brown wrist gloves were worn in walking-out dress. See §V-3-1 for more details on accessories.

§V-5-c GUARD LANCERS[70]

The guard was late in forming a lancer component. In 1803, a regiment named the Hussars of Odessa was formed from squadrons of hussars that dated back to 1651. Later in 1803, the Odessa Hussars' name was changed to Lancers of His Imperial Highness the Czarevich. In 1809, this regiment was divided into guard dragoons and guard lancers. It was made part of the Old Guard in 1814. Then, in 1849, it was named the Lancers of His Imperial Highness and Heir Czarevich. When the czarevich became Czar Alexander II in 1855, he gave his name to the regiment and it gained its 1914 title Lancers of His Majesty the Emperor.

The Lancers of Her Majesty budded from the Lancers of Hussars of Odessa in the 1803–4 period. Its existence closely tracked the regiment that would become the Lancers of His Majesty. It was not until 1894 that it received the name Lancers of the Guard of Her Majesty Empress Alexandra Feodorovna.

UNIFORM

Table V.5.c.1: Guard Lancers

Regiment	Plastron, Cuff, and Tunic Trim Colour	Button Colour	Collar Colour	Collar Shield Colour	Czapska[a] Stem Cloth Covering	Officer Litzen[b]	Trooper Litzen[b]	Monograms	Epaulette[c]	Distinction Banner[d]
Guard Lancers of the Emperor	Red[e]	Silver	Red	None	Yellow	Silver, guard-style	Orange, guard-style	H II – 1st Squadron only[f]	Silver	Descriptive
Guard Lancers of the Empress	Red[e]	Gold	Red	None	Red	Gold, guard-style	Orange, guard-style	None	Gold	Descriptive

Notes: [a] This is a Polish word that has several different spellings in English; czapska is the most common. Others are tschapska and chapka (see Marrion, *Lancers*; Thorburn, *French Army*; Mollo, *Uniforms*; Head, *Napoleonic Lancer*; Preben Kannik, *Military Uniforms*).
[b] Unless otherwise noted, all litzen were in the chapter shape.
[c] The epaulettes were made of metal for both officers and troops.
[d] See §V-2-2 for more details on banners.
[e] The top and front of the collar were piped in dark blue, the same colour as the tunic.
[f] Silver monogram of Czar Nicholas II.

Headdress

Lancer Helmets

The guard lancers had a slightly different helmet from that worn by the line: The two guard regiments' shell and visor were patent leather rather than the plain black leather worn by the line.

We do not have the measurements of the guard stem, but it is clearly shorter and thicker than that worn by the line. This made the guard czapska seem more squat and the mortarboard larger than that of the line. But the mortarboards of both the line and the guards were the same size (see also §V-7-b).[71]

Stem Cloth

In full dress, the stem was covered with a piece of removable cloth, the colour of which varied by regiment (Table V.5.c.1).

The guard lancers' stem cloth ended at the bottom of the stem and the cap line wrapped around it at the base, like that of the Prussian lancers.

Stem Cloth Trim

The stem cloth for the troops of the guard was edged at the top and the bottom with white or orange wool braid to match the buttons, and the ridges of the czapska stem were highlighted with orange and black cording.

For the officers of the guard, the top edge of the stem cloth was bordered with a 1.67 cm (0.66 inch) stripe of square-weave braid, while the bottom trim varied according to rank: a 1.39 cm (0.55 inch) stripe of square-weave braid for subaltern officers, a 2.78 cm (1.09 inch) stripe of square-weave braid for superior officers, or a 2.22 cm (0.88 inch) stripe of generals' (zigzag) braid for generals. All officers' rank braids were either gold or silver according to the button colour. The ridges of officers' czapska stems were highlighted with silver cording stitched with black and orange 0.56 cm (0.23 inch) wide.

Helmet Plate

The helmets worn by guard lancers had a guard star on top of a double-headed eagle on the front. The eagle was either gold or silver to match the colour of the buttons and epaulettes, while the guard star was always silver. Both guard regiments had a distinction banner above the eagle.

Cockade and Plume

A cockade was fixed to the front left edge of the mortarboard, along with a plume in full dress. Both officers and men wore a plume of white horsehair that fell to the side. Generals had plumes of black, orange, and white feathers. The plume rose up and then fell down, just like the tail of a spirited horse.

Cap Line

In full dress, the cap line started at the front right corner of the czapska mortarboard. From there, it had enough slack to fall about shoulder-blade level at the back before coming up to the neck. After wrapping around the neck, it passed between the collar and the epaulette strap on the left side of the tunic. It ended with the tasselled ends, which were sewn together and attached to the top button on the front left side of the tunic.

For the troops of the guard, the cap line was either yellow or white according to the button colour. NCOs also had slip-rings, flounders that were a mixture of black, orange, and white thread, and tassels of orange mixed with black.

Officers of the guard wore cap lines that were 0.56 cm (0.23 inch) thick. They were silver stitched with black and orange silk and had tassels which varied according to rank. The tassel fringe was thick for superior officers and thicker for generals, while the tassels worn by subalterns had a fine fringe.

Tunic[72]

The double-breasted tunic was dark blue for both regiments (Image V:41). There were two rows of seven buttons in front that ranged from 25.56 to 27.78 cm (10.06 to 10.94 inches) apart at the top buttons, 18.89 to 21.11 cm (7.44 to 8.31 inches) apart at the second buttons from the top, and 11.11 to 13.34 cm (4.38 to 5.25 inches) apart at the bottom buttons. The buttons were silver for lancers of the czar and gold for lancers of the czarina.

In full dress, both regiments buttoned on red plastrons, which added colour to a monochrome dark uniform.

The tunic piping was also red, the plastron (facing) colour. Unlike the Germans, whose lancer tunics had piping on both sides of the plastron, the front piping ran only along the right side of the plastron to the bottom of the tunic (Image V:42). Piping also ran around the bottom edge of the tunic, along the back seams of the sleeves, and along the two seams on the back of the tunic, extending down to the skirt.

V:41 Subaltern Officer of the Guard Lancers of Her Majesty
The lancer's helmet has a slightly different shape from that worn by the line lancers. Note the regimental badge worn on the left side of his tunic.

Collars

The guard collar was red. The guard and line lancer regiments wore different tunic collars. The guard lancers' collars were cut on the diagonal in the front, coming to a distinct point at the corners (Image V:41). The total height of the collar, including the trim, varied from 4.45 to 5.56 cm (1.75 to 2.19 inches). On each side of the collar were two litzen, gold or silver, depending on button colour, for the officers, and orange wool for the troopers. The troopers' guard litzen had a red central light. The officers' litzen was solid gold or silver colour, depending on the regiment.

Epaulettes

In full dress, all ranks of the guard lancers wore metal epaulettes. These were gold or silver colour, depending on the regiment's button colour. The metal epaulettes worn by officers were 'cavalry model' epaulettes, and other ranks wore the 'trooper model'. The lining for the epaulettes for both regiments was red. See *§V-3-1* for description.

Shoulder Straps

Guard lancers only wore shoulder straps in walking-out dress, on the *oulanka,* described below.

When they wore them, both regiments of guard lancers had red shoulder straps with dark blue piping. Only the 1st Squadron of the Emperor's Lancers had a silver metallic monogram H II for Nicholas II on the shoulder strap.

V:42 Two Officers of the 16th Lancers
One of the men has the plastron buttoned on and one does not. Note how the cap line lies across the chest on the man on the left and how the cap line is covered up when the plastron is buttoned on. Also note that both are wearing a holster and pistol on their right side and cords that lead to it. These are items of full dress.

Cuffs and Rear Skirts

The tunic had Polish-style pointed red cuffs (Image V:8(5)). The officers and the troops had single guard litzen behind the button on each cuff. Two other buttons were sewn off to the side above the cuff near the seam piping on the sleeve itself. For officers, the cuff litzen was gold or silver colour, depending on regimental button colour, and had no centre coloured line. For other ranks, the litzen was orange with a red centre line to match the cuff.

The rear skirts of the guard lancers had three buttons. Red piping connected the skirt false pocket buttons. The trim was in the typical lancer scallop pattern (Image V:43).

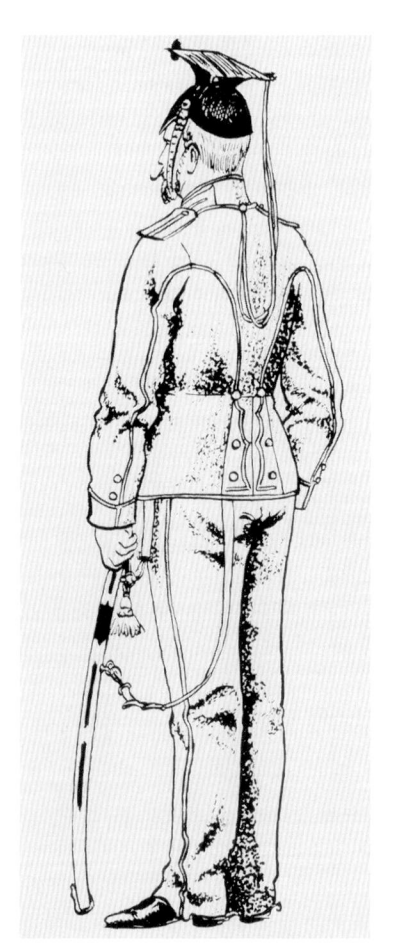

V:43 Back of a Lancer's Tunic, Showing Trim
Note where the cap line falls at the back.

Gala Dress

For the guard lancers, gala dress was the same as full winter dress but had the following modifications because it was worn by officers while they were not in the presence of their troops. The officer's girdle and pouch belt were not worn, and the sword belt was worn over the tunic. The cap line did not attach to the helmet. Instead, it began at the third button from the top on the right breast of the tunic. From there, it went up to the right shoulder and passed between the epaulette strap and epaulette button on the right side, then looped down about one-third of the length of the back before coming back up, going around the neck, passing between the epaulette and the collar on the left side, and attaching to the top left tunic button. It ended there, with the fringe showing.

Walking-Out Tunics

The guard walking-out coat was called the *oulanka*. It was a double-breasted lancer's tunic and cut a bit tighter at the waist, with two rows of seven buttons. The oulanka was dark blue with dark blue lining and had red piping in the same places as the normal lancer's tunic, with the exception of the two back seams. Instead of scalloped false pockets at the back, it had pockets with diagonal slashes on each skirt panel. The collar, which was red velvet, had rounded corners and was worn folded down. The cuffs, also of red velvet, were pointed and had rank stripes placed 0.28 cm (0.11 inch from the edge: a 2.22 cm (0.88 inch) wide general's (zigzag) braid for generals, a 2.78 cm (1.09 inch) wide hussar (zigzag) braid for superior officers, or a 1.39 cm (0.55 inch) wide hussar braid for subalterns. On each sleeve above the cuff there were two buttons. A pelisse cord, or mentichket, in gold or silver according to the button colour, was also worn with the oulanka. The cord was short and did not have a function. It started under the collar, made a small loop on the front, and then went back under the shoulder board to the back of the collar (see §V-5-d, Pelisse).

A pouch, pouch belt, and girdle were not worn with this order of dress.

Riding Breeches, Trousers, and Charivari

All ranks of the guard lancers wore standard breeches in full dress. The officers also had full-length trousers that were worn with the walking-out tunic, the oulanka. Both the breeches and the trousers were dark blue with narrow piping down the outside seam of each leg. Piping was red for both regiments.

The guard lancers also had dark blue charivari, sometimes worn by officers in full dress with shoes rather than boots. The charivari had two wide red bands running down the outside of the leg. On the dark blue band between the two red bands there was a line of narrow red piping. See §V-3-1 for details.

Uniform Accessories

Officers' Accessories

Guard lancer officers wore the standard model pouch and pouch belt in full dress. Guard officers wore the officer's girdle in full dress.

V:44 Trooper of the Guard Lancers of Her Majesty with his Plastron Buttoned on, c. 1890s
The helmet's double-headed eagle and guard star can be seen clearly in this photograph, as can the other ranks' lancer's girdle. He is wearing the old-style soft boots.

Other Ranks' Accessories

Other ranks of the guard wore a lancer trooper's girdle in full dress. The girdles were made of fabric that had three horizontal stripes and piping at the top and bottom. The buckle was covered in the same fabric, but it was turned to go up and down. On the girdle, the top and bottom stripes were red. The central stripe and the top and bottom piping were dark blue.

Other Accessories

All ranks of both the guard lancer regiment wore standard riding boots (Image V:44) and standard white gloves in full dress. Standard brown gloves were worn in walking-out dress. See §V-3-1 for more details on accessories.

§V-5-d GUARD HUSSARS[73]

The Hussars of His Majesty traced their origins back to a Life Squadron of hussars created by Catherine II, the Great, in 1775. In the early days, the Russians were not quite sure what to make of the hussars, as is shown by the fact that these hussars were joined in 1796 to Cossack units to become the Regiment of Hussar-Cossacks. Then, in 1798, the hussar element was broken out of the regiment to form the Life Guard Regiment of Hussars. They kept this form down to 1914. In 1855, they were given the title of Life Guard Hussars of His Majesty.

The Grodno Hussars were the other guard hussar regiment. Created in 1824 in Poland from Polish officers and men taken from the 1st, 2nd, and 3rd Hussar Divisions and the Lithuanian Lancers, the regiment was originally part of the Young Guard. In 1831, after taking part in the repression of the Polish revolt, it was promoted to the Old Guard. At this time the uniform colours were changed to those worn until 1914 because the old uniform was considered too Polish in its colours.[74]

UNIFORMS

Table V.5.d.1: Guard Hussars

Regiment	Button Colour	Busby Bag[a]	Attila	Pelisse and Lining	Monogram	Distinction Banner[b]
Emperor's Hussars	Gold	Red	Red	White Lining: red	H II[c]	Descriptive
Grodno Hussars	Silver	Raspberry	Dark green	Dark green Lining: raspberry	H II[c]	None

Notes: [a] For the guard hussars, the busby bag comes to a rather sharp point. The busby bag on the line hussars' bonnet comes to a rounded point.
[b] See §V-2-2, Distinction Banners, for banner type.
[c] Nicholas II.

In 1882, the line cavalry regiments were reorganised and underwent a uniform change. These changes did not affect the two guard hussar regiments. They wore hussar uniforms throughout this period.

The two guard hussar regiments, the Guard Hussar Regiment of His Majesty and the Grodno Hussar Regiment of the Guard, wore slightly different uniforms from those worn by the line hussar regiments after 1908. The guard regiments had started wearing their hussar uniforms in the mid-1800s and had not changed them when so much of the army became dragoons in 1881. Images V:45 and V:46 show the full uniforms of both regiments.

Headdress

Busby

Both guard hussar regiments wore a busby of dark brown, long-haired fur. For officers, it was made of beaver fur (Images V:47 and V:48). On the front of the busby was a silver St Andrew's guard star (Image V:49). Additionally, the Emperor's Hussars had a distinction banner made of gilded metal placed over the star (Image V:50). A cockade was placed near the upper edge of the front of the busby, above the guard star (and the distinction banner, for the Emperor's Hussars). The busby had a decorative chinstrap which was either gold or silver, according to the regiment's button colour (Table V.5.d.1).

V:45 Colonel of the Emperor's Hussars

V:46 Colonel of the Grodno Hussars

V:47 Grodno Hussars Officer Wearing an Overcoat
He is wearing his pouch belt over the overcoat, and this photograph gives a good view of the regiment's pouch belt. It also shows the pointed busby bag and the badge on the front of the busby.

V:48 Soldiers and NCOs of the Emperor's Hussars in Full Dress
Note how the fur busbies are over-sized and worn low on the head.

V:49 Young Officer of the Emperor's Hussars
The white pelisse he has over his back shows that he is from this regiment.

V:50 The Emperor's Hussars
The man on the left is wearing a pelisse. The man on the right gives an idea of how the pelisse looked when it was carried on the back.

Busby Bag

The guard hussars had decorative busby bags that were attached to the top of the busby with a hook-and-loop fixture and fell to the right side of the headdress. While line hussar busby bags were rounded, those of the guard hussars came to a distinct point (Image V:51).

The busby bag was made of red cloth for the Emperor's Hussars or raspberry cloth for the Grodno Hussars, and had trim that did not vary by rank for regimental officers.[75] The trim lined both sides of the pointed busby bag, and an additional piece of trim ran down the centre of the bag. The busby bag trim for troops was plain orange or yellow braid, according to the button colour. Officers of all ranks had trim made of gold or silver hussar (zigzag) braid, according to the button. Generals had the same trim as officers, but with additional soutache (a type of narrow braid) running along the inside edges of the hussar's braid and forming a series of loops.

V:51 Officer of the Grodno Hussars
Note the pointed busby bag's trim to the right and the breeches' decorations. Also note the way the pelisse is worn on the back and the way the hussar sash around the waist is tied.

Busby Plume

In full dress, a plume was attached to the front centre of the busby, above the cockade. Officers, NCOs, and the troops all wore white horsehair plumes. The plume was normally much taller than that worn by line hussars. The base of the plume varied by rank: white for the troops (Image V:53), white mixed with black and orange for NCOs, and silver for officers. Generals wore a special plume that was made of very fine white, orange, and black feathers. Instead of a regular plume base, generals had a small metallic tube which held the plume. The metal tube was decorated with a small imperial eagle and fine chains.

ATTILA[76]

The Emperor's Hussars wore a red *attila* (a short jacket) with red lining (Image V:48). The Grodno Hussars wore a dark green attila with raspberry lining.

Each side of the front panels of the attila had pockets with diagonal openings. The pocket openings were decorated with the cording, which formed a loop at the top end of the opening and crows' feet at the bottom.

OFFICERS' ATTILA

The officers' attila had five rows of gold or silver frogging on its front (Image V:49). The frogging was filigreed or woven of fine gold or silver threads according to the regiment's button colour. Each row consisted of two strands of this filigree braid. It went across the chest and ended with two falling loops of filigree braid. The top row of frogging was longer than that of the fifth row. Each row ended with a button, and below the button were two falling loops of filigree braid. The buttons were gold for the Emperor's Hussars and silver for the Grodno Hussars. They had a double-headed eagle on them. Halfway to the outside of the chest and the end of the frogging, there were two small loops in the frogging, one above the top strand of frogging and one below the bottom.

The front skirts of the attila had pockets on either side, as is shown by a photograph of a line attila (Image V:52). The pockets were trimmed in filigree braid and had a loop at the top and crows' feet (trefoil) at the bottom.

on the front of the attila. On each side of the rear skirt, going down from one of the toggles, were three columns of filigree braid. Each ended in a trefoil.

Collar

The collar was the same colour as the rest of the attila. For the guard regiments, it was cut on an angle at the front edges, whereas the line regiments had a rounded front edge. Collar trim varied according to rank.

Officers' Collar Trim

Officers' collars were outlined on all sides with the same gold or silver filigree braid that decorated the attila. The collars also had additional braid that varied according to rank, either gold or silver, depending on the button colour. Generals had 4.45 cm (1.75 inch) wide general's (zigzag) braid which covered the entire collar. Field officers had 2.78 cm (1.09 inch) wide hussar (zigzag) braid which lined only the top and front edges of the collar. Subalterns had 1.39 cm (0.55 inch) wide hussar's braid which lined all sides of the collar – top, bottom, and front. This braid also was applied to the cuffs.

This braid was lined with additional cording on its inside edges. For field officers, the size of the hussar's braid left a small panel of the attila's colour. The additional cording went around the outside of this panel and had two small loops dropping down from the top line of the cording on each side of the collar, a total of four on the collar. For the subalterns, this interior cording formed a single loop on the top edge on the inside edge of the collar and three loops on the bottom edge of each side of the collar for a total of eight loops: two on top, six on the bottom.

There was also a large trefoil at the back of all officers' collars.

Shoulder Cording

In place of epaulettes or shoulder boards the attila had cord braiding on the shoulders. This was worn by both officers and other ranks. It started at a button placed near the collar and extended to the end of the shoulder, where it formed a loop and then doubled back to the button. Badges of rank were beads worn on the cords. Additional rows of cords were added if

V:52 Line Hussar
Note the two rank beads on his shoulder and a spiral on his toggle buttons. The busby bag in this photograph looks pointed but in actuality is rounded. Note how the officer's sash is tied and the zigzag braid on the pouch belt.

The officers' attila was buttoned with a gold or silver toggle depending on the regiment's button colour. The toggle for officers had a spiral pattern.

The collar of the attila was outlined in filigree braid. This braid continued down the front of the attila, around the bottom of the attila skirt, to the rear skirt, where it outlined the rear vent.

The back of the attila had filigree braid along the rear seam line which accentuated the taper of the waist. This was common in all hussar uniforms of the period. There were two columns of this braid, one on either side of the attila.

At the top of each column of filigree braiding was a trefoil.

At waist-level, at the bottom of each column of seam braid, where the sash could rest on them, were two horizontal toggle buttons, the same as those worn the regiment had a monogram to be worn on their shoulder cords. See §V-7-c for details on the cords and badges of rank.

Cuffs

The cuffs were the same colour as the rest of the attila, and were outlined in filigreed cording which formed a Hungarian knot at its top. The cuffs came to a slight point, and trim varied according to rank.

Officers' Cuff Trim

Officers' cuff trim was made of a combination of the same gold or silver filigreed cording and gold or silver braid that was used on the collars. Generals had the 4.45 cm (1.75 inch) wide general's (zigzag) braid around the cuff. It formed an angle with somewhat rounded edges. The upper edge of the general's braid was lined with the filigreed cording, which was arranged so it formed a succession of round loops. Field officers had 2.78 cm (1.09 inch) wide hussar (zigzag) braid which went around the cuff and formed an angle.

Like generals, field officers had filigreed cording arranged in a series of loops along the upper edge of the braid. Subalterns had 1.39 cm (0.55 inch) wide hussar's braid which went around the cuff and formed a chevron (Image V:49). There was filigreed cording all around the cuff above the braid. Where the cording came to the point of the braid chevron, it formed a Hungarian knot.

Other Ranks' Attila

The attila had five rows of white or orange frogging across the front (Images V:53 and V:54). The frogging consisted of two strands of cords, ending on the outside of the chest with two falling loops. Above each set of loops was a white or yellow button, depending on the regiment. Halfway to the outside of the chest and the end of the frogging, there were two small loops in the frogging, one above the top strand of frogging and one below the bottom. The trim on the back of the other ranks' attila was the same as that on guard officers' uniforms, except it was in cord.

V:53 The seated other ranks is wearing the pelisse of a Grodno Hussar, and the standing officer is wearing the tunic of an Emperor's Hussar with a pelisse worn on his back.

V:54 Three NCOs of the Grodno Hussars
Note the guard star on the front of the busby and the medallion on the front of the hussar boots. Also note their service chevrons on their upper left arm and the way their hussar sashes are tied.

The attila was buttoned with a smooth toggle button that was white or yellow, depending on the regiment's button colour.

Other Ranks' Collar Trim

Other ranks' collars were the colour of the attila and cut at an angle like those of officers. The collars were outlined on all sides with the same white or orange cording that decorated the attila. On the front edge of each side of the collar, the cording formed two small inside loops. On the bottom edge of each side of the collar there were two additional inside loops of cording, for a total of four small loops on the bottom edge. As noted above, there was a trefoil at the back of the collar. NCOs wore *polouchtabski* braid on the top and front edges of the collar, immediately inside the cording. The NCO braid was either white or orange according to the button colour. Other ranks wore a plain braid that was orange for both regiments.[77] The braid had a central thread in the colour of the collar.

The collars of the other ranks were outlined in white or orange cording depending on the regiment's button colour.

Shoulder Cording

The shoulder cording in the guards followed the same pattern as line hussars. See §V-7-c, Line Hussars, for a full discussion.

Cuffs

The cuffs of the enlisted men were basically the same as the officers' cuffs. They were in the same colour as the attila.

Other ranks' cuffs were trimmed with cording that came to a slight point, white or orange according to button colour. On the outside of the cuff and sleeve, the cording formed a Hungarian knot above the point of the cuff trim. Below the cording and Hungarian knot was a band of orange braid that had a central thread in the colour of the attila (Image V:54). NCOs had an additional band of NCO braid marking their status.

Pouch Belt

The two regiments of guard hussars both wore a pouch belt in full dress, but the type of braid it was made of varied.

In place of the general pouch belt described in §V-3-1, the Emperor's Hussars wore a special braid unique to their regiment. It was gold with dark blue silk detailing, made up of five stripes. The central stripe was diagonal gold and blue silk stripes. The two stripes on either side of the central stripe were plain gold, and the two outer stripes were gold with dark blue silk 'teeth' – rows of triangles pointing outward. On the upper part of the pouch belt near the chest and shoulder, a gold award was attached (Image V:14). On the bottom part of the pouch belt was the monogram 'H II' for Nicholas II in gold on a backing of dark blue velvet, surrounded by a crown of leaves (Image V:13). Both of these badges were on the front of the pouch belt.

The Grodno Hussars' pouch belt was covered with the standard hussar braid in silver.

Pouch

Both regiments of guard hussars wore the standard model pouch with a silver St Andrew's guard star on the cover flap in full dress.

For more details on the pouch, see §V-3-1.

Waist Sash

The sash for all officers of the guard consisted of three thin silver cords mixed with black and orange darts. Each cord carried three silver slides (Image V:48). The style of the sash worn by Russian hussars was unusual: the three cords reached only halfway around the wearer's waist. Under each arm, the three cords were gathered and the balance of the sash consisted of two cords. The cord on the right terminated in a toggle button. The left-hand cords formed a fastening loop used to secure the sash. The two left-hand cords continued around to the wearer's right-hand side to be interwoven with the sash cords in front. The cords, after being interwoven with the sash in front, terminated in silver tassels. The size of the tassel cords was another indication of rank, those of senior officers being larger than those of junior officers.

For the other ranks in the guard regiments, the cords were orange wool for the Emperor's Hussars and white wool for the Grodno Hussars. The Emperor's Hussars had blue slides, while the Grodno Hussars had raspberry slides.

Side Arms

Like other Russian army officers, guard hussar officers and NCOs wore a revolver and a black leather holster when parading with their men. See §V-3-1 for details.

Riding Breeches, Trousers, and Charivari

The guard hussars of all ranks wore special riding breeches in full, ordinary, and walking-out dress. Special riding breeches were typically only worn by guard regiments in full and/or gala dress. See §V-3-1 for a more detailed description.

The special riding breeches were blue for the Emperor's Hussars and raspberry for the Grodno Hussars. For ordinary and walking-out dress, officers had hussar (zigzag) braid in the regiment's button colour along the outside seam. Other ranks had plain white or orange braid at the seam according to button colour, and had a central thread in the background colour of the breeches, either blue or raspberry.

The guard hussar regiments had special riding breeches for full dress and gala dress. These breeches were identical to the regular riding breeches, but had additional decoration. On the front of each leg, at the upper thigh, was a Hungarian knot made out of the same trim as on the side seams, for both the officers and the other ranks. Officers had additional soutache outlining the loops of the Hungarian knot.

Boots

Hussars of both the guard and the line wore special 'hussar-style' boots, very similar to the Hessian boots worn by British hussars. Boots were black leather, decorated in the front with a metal rosette in the regiment's button colour. The boots were cut with a pronounced 'V' in the front and a scooped-out area in the back. There was no trim on the top of the boots. The spurs for officers in all regiments were silvered metal. Other ranks wore white metal spurs.

Walking-Out Dress

The two regiments of guard hussars had a special walking-out tunic called the *venguerka*. This garment came in two styles, a winter model and a summer model. In addition to being worn as the walking-out tunic, the winter model of venguerka was worn in standard gala or ball dress.

The winter venguerka closely resembled the pelisse, but was always fully put on instead of left hanging from the shoulders as the pelisse was sometimes worn. For the Emperor's Hussars, it was dark blue with red lining, for the Grodno Hussars it was dark green with raspberry lining. The fur trim was black sheepskin. The cording trim differed slightly from that used on the attila and pelisse: instead of filigreed gold or silver, it was smooth gold or silver mixed with black and orange stitching. The stripes and cording on the sleeves had the same variations according to rank as the attila sleeves did.

The summer venguerka was much like the winter model, except that its lining was the same colour as the outside, and there was no fur trim. Officers and generals had the same collar trim as on the attila, but utilized the smooth cording described above for the winter venguerka.

Gala Dress

Guard hussars also had special gala or ball dress. There were two different levels of gala dress for the regiments of guard hussars. For full gala dress, they wore full winter dress with a few modifications: the revolver belt, cord, and revolver were not worn. The pelisse was worn instead of the attila, and the pouch, pouch belt, and waist belt were not worn. Regular gala dress was regular winter dress instead of full dress, again with several modifications: the venguerka was worn with special guard gala breeches and white gloves. The pouch, pouch belt, waist belt, revolver belt, revolver, and cord were not worn.

Pelisse

One other standard item of winter full dress remains to be considered: the pelisse (Image V:55). The pelisse was worn either as a jacket or hanging down the wearer's back. It was not worn covering one shoulder, as was done in the German and Austro-Hungarian armies.

or mentichket, was used to attach the pelisse to the attila and keep it in place. The pelisse cord was made of double cording, comprised of two halves starting on either side of the pelisse collar, where they were attached to the shoulder braid buttons by means of loops of fine cording. One half ended with a loop, and the other with a toggle button, so the pelisse cord could be fastened behind the collar of the attila after each half had passed under the attila shoulder braid on its respective side, gone across the chest, and passed under the attila shoulder braid on the other side.

Officers' Pelisse

The fur trim for the pelisses worn by the officers was made of dark brown beaver. On the cuffs, the fur trim formed a diamond shape. All other cuff and sleeve trim for officers was the same as on the attila.

The mentichket was made of thick filigreed silver or gold cording, according to the regiment's button colour, and had several slides. While the basic purpose of the pelisse cord remained the same, the squadrons of the Emperor's Hussars each had special ways of wearing the mentichket.

Other Ranks' Pelisse

Fur trim for the other ranks was black sheepskin. On the cuff the fur formed the same shape as the attila cuffs bordered by orange braid that had central thread in either red or dark green to match the regiment's colours. Above this braid was a Hungarian knot made of cording. On the front panels of the pelisse were diagonal pockets, the openings of which were lined with black sheepskin, which were in turn lined with cording that formed a loop at the top of the pocket and a trefoil at the bottom.

The pelisse cord was orange or white according to the regiment's button colour. NCOs had cords with mixed black and orange darts.

V:55 Officer Wearing a Pelisse
Note the shape of the cuff. The shape of the chest frogging indicates that this is a line regiment, and only the 3rd Hussars had a white pelisse.

The pelisse was white with red lining for the Emperor's Hussars and dark green with raspberry lining for the Grodno Hussars. The collar, front and lower edges, pockets, and cuffs were all trimmed with fur. The shoulder braid, trim (frogging), buttons, and toggles were the same as for the attila for both the officers and the other ranks. In full dress, the pelisse was worn hanging from the shoulders, attached to the attila somewhat like a cape. A pelisse cord,

§V-5-e GUARD COSSACKS[78]

The Cossack element of the Russian Imperial Guard comprised the Emperor's Cossacks, the Ataman Cossacks, and the Combined Cossack Regiment.

THE EMPEROR'S COSSACKS

The Emperor's Cossacks began as Catherine II's escort. Created on 20 April 1775 in Moscow, it was originally made up of only Don and Chuguev Cossacks. In 1796, it became known as the Regiment of Gatchina Cossacks, and later that year was combined with a regiment of Life Hussars and entered the Old Guard. At different points over the course of the nineteenth century, sotnias of Black Sea Cossacks and Crimean Tartars were added to the regiment so that eventually the Guard Cossacks had seven and then eight squadrons. Those squadrons eventually separated from the regiment, however, and in 1872 the six remaining squadrons took the definitive name of the Imperial Guard Cossack Regiment of His Majesty. Later, a part of the regiment would go to make up part of the Combined Cossack Regiment of the Imperial Guard.

With the emperor as its chief, the regiment was a very prestigious one, and during the twilight years of Imperial Russia, at least two grand dukes were listed among the regiment's ranks, in addition to the emperor himself.

The Ataman Cossacks

The Ataman Cossacks began from a concept that Catherine II had in 1775 for creating a Cossack regiment that would serve as a model for the other Cossack regiments. She decided that the new regiment would be placed directly under the command of the *ataman* (commander) of the Don Cossacks. On 20 April 1775 the new regiment was created according to her wishes: it was made up entirely of young Cossacks and was led by the Don Cossack ataman at the time, Alexei Ivanovich Ilovsky. The regiment became associated with the guard in 1829, when the Grand Duke Crown Prince Alexander Nikolaevich was named ataman of all the Cossack units. However, it did not officially enter the Young Guard until 1859. In 1874, half of the regiment was taken to create part of the Combined Cossack Guard Regiment. Finally, in 1878, it entered the Old Guard in recognition of its bravery during the second Turkish War.

The Combined Cossack Regiment

On 27 May 1906, the Combined Cossack Regiment was officially created. It represented all the different hosts of Steppes Cossacks, and thus was composed of a Ural sotnia, an Orenburg sotnia, a Siberian half-sotnia, a Semerechya platoon, an Astrakhan platoon, ½ Trans-Baikal Sotnia, an Amur platoon and a Ussuri platoon.

The 1st Sotnia, which was the Ural sotnia, came from the guard, and had a history which dated back much further than 1906 – all the way to 1798, when it had been formed as the Ural Life Sotnia under Paul I. It entered the Young Guard in 1830 as the Division of Ural Cossacks of the Guard. The division had been associated directly with the emperor as its commander since 1864 under Alexander II, so when Nicholas ascended the throne and became regimental chief in 1899, it became His Majesty's Sotnia of Ural Cossacks of the Imperial Guard. Even when the combined regiment was officially created with the addition of the other components in 1906, the Ural Sotnia, as its oldest and most distinguished component, kept the title 1st Ural Sotnia of His Majesty, of the Combined Guard Cossacks.

UNIFORM

Headdress

The guard Cossacks wore a busby as their headdress. It was made of black sheepskin, and flared very slightly outward at the top. The busby was 15.56 cm (6.13 inches) high. The busby bag, rather than coming to a point, was rounded (Image V:56), attached to the busby by means of a hook, and fell to the right side. It was not decorated with any braid, and varied in colour by regiment (Table V.5.e.1).

On the front of the busby was the silver guard star. Above the star, the Emperor's Cossacks and the Ataman Cossacks had distinction banners. On the left side at the top of the busby there was a cockade. In full dress, a white horsehair plume was worn attached at the cockade. This plume on the left gave the Cossacks a very different look. The plume base varied by rank: silver for officers, white mixed with black and orange for NCOs, and plain white for the

Table V.5.e.1: Guard Cossacks

Regiment	Tunic Colour	Busby Bag	Collar and Cuff Colour	Collar Trim	Cuff Trim[a]	Undress Jacket Collar Trim	Undress Shoulder Strap	Mono-grams	Distinction Banner
Emperor's Cossacks	Red	Red	Red	None	None	Red	Red	H II – 1st Sotnia only[b]	Yes[c]
Ataman Cossacks	Sky blue	Sky blue	Sky blue	None	None	Sky blue	Sky Blue	None	Yes[c]
Combined Regiment:									
1st Ural Sotnia	Raspberry	Raspberry	Raspberry	None	White	Raspberry	Raspberry	H II[b]	No
2nd Orenburg Sotnia	Sky blue	Sky blue	Sky blue	None	White	Sky blue	Sky blue	None	No
3rd Mixed Sotnia:									
½ Siberian Sotnia	Red	Red	Red	None	White	Red	Red	None	No
Semerechya Platoon	Raspberry	Raspberry	Raspberry	Dark blue	White	Dark blue	Raspberry	None	No
Astrakhan Platoon	Orange	Orange	Orange	None	White	Orange	Orange	None	No
4th Mixed Amur Sotnia:									
½ Trans-Baikal Sotnia	Orange	Orange	Orange	Raspberry	White	Raspberry	Orange	None	No
Amur Platoon	Orange	Orange	Orange	Sky blue	White	Sky blue	Orange	None	No
Ussuri Platoon	Orange	Orange	Orange	Red	White	Red	Orange	None	No

Notes: [a] For both the full dress tunic and the undress jacket.
[b] Nicholas II.
[c] See §V-2-2, Distinction Banners.

other ranks. Generals wore a special plume – the same as the plumes worn by hussar generals – made of fine white, orange, and black feathers, with its base a metal tube bearing a small imperial eagle with fine chain-work.

The busby was decorated with braided cording, silver for officers and orange for other ranks. The cording was in two strands and started at the left side of the busby, where both pieces attached to the plume base with the flounders and tassels hanging down. From there, they passed in front and back of the busby, dipping down slightly in a crescent shape, passing below the guard star on the front (Image V:56) before coming back up to attach beneath the busby bag. Both cords then fell down to the right shoulder, attaching to the epaulette or shoulder strap button before ending in flounders and tassels.

The black leather chinstrap, part of most headdresses, was sewn to the interior of the busby.

Tunic

The tunic worn by the guard Cossacks was in the Cossack cut, which meant it did not have any buttons and closed by means of hooks at the front (Image V:57). In the back, below the waist, the tunic skirt was pleated. The tunic had no pockets. It was in cloth of the regimental colour for the Emperor's Cossacks and

V:56 Subaltern of the Emperor's Cossacks
Note the special collar and cuff trim given to this regiment in 1914 and the distinction banner above the guard star.

V:58 Officer and Trooper of the Ataman Cossacks
Note how both the officer and trooper's cap lines rest on their right chest.

V:57 Ataman Cossacks, c. 1895
Note the shape of the fur headdress they are wearing and the small guard star and distinction banner on that headdress.

V:59 Emperor Nicholas II and his Son in the Post-1908 uniform of the Combined Cossack Regiment
Since this photograph is in black and white, we cannot see the colour of the tunic; therefore, we do not know which Cossack host's uniform they are wearing.

the Ataman Cossacks (Image V:58), and in the sotnia or even platoon colour for the parts of the Combined Regiment (Table V.5.e.1). The lining was in the same colour as the tunic.

The collar was cut on a slant in the front, with points rather than rounded corners. It was the same colour as the rest of the tunic, and sometimes had piping (Table V.5.e.1). There were two litzen on each side of the collar. For the officers, the litzen was plain silver, in the chapter shape. Other ranks had orange wool litzen, with a thread the colour of the tunic running through it. For groups in the Combined Regiment where the tunic was orange, red threads ran through their litzen, since orange thread would not have been visible in orange litzen. There were no buttons on the collar.

The cuffs were pointed (lancer style), and were the colour of the tunic. The Emperor's Cossacks and the Ataman Cossacks did not have any piping on their cuffs, but the Combined Regiment had white cuff piping in all sections (Image V:59). The litzen was the same as on the collar, but there was only one instead of two on each cuff. There were no buttons on the cuffs.

In 1914, officers of the Emperor's Cossacks were assigned special traditional embroidery. The embroidery took the place of the regular litzen on the collar and cuffs (Images V:56 and V:60).

Epaulettes

Both officers and other ranks of the guard Cossacks wore epaulettes in full dress. Officers wore cavalry model epaulettes, and other ranks wore trooper-style epaulettes. Epaulettes were silver and bore monograms where applicable (Table V.5.e.1). Epaulette lining – and piping, in the case of officers – was the colour of the undress shoulder straps. See §V-3-1 for more details on epaulettes.

Shoulder Straps

Shoulder straps were worn in regular and walking-out dress (for colours see Table V.5.e.1). If a sotnia had monograms on its epaulettes, it had the same monogram in metal mounted on the shoulder strap. For more details regarding shoulder straps, see §V-3-1.

V:60 Grand Duke Nicholas Wearing the Uniform of the Emperor's Cossacks
Note the shape of the buttonhole on the cuff. Also note how the headdress bag lies across the top of the headdress.

Walking-Out Tunic

The walking-out tunic for the guard Cossacks was the vice-moundir (undress jacket). It was the same cut and style as the regular tunic and was made of dark blue cloth for all regiments. The collar and cuffs were also dark blue, usually with piping (see Table V.5.e.1 for colours, regiments without piping). Both officers and other ranks had litzen which was the same as for the full dress tunic, including the embroidery for officers of the Emperor's Cossacks mentioned above.

Tchekman

The Guard Cossacks had an additional undress jacket called the *tchekman*. This was a version of native jacket which was quite long and comparable to the frock coats more popular in Europe. It took the place of the redingote, a type of undress jacket which many of the guard units had. For instance, the guard cuirassiers had a redingote which was sometimes worn in ball dress.

V:61 Don Cossack Wearing a Tchekman
Note the shape of his old-style fur headdress.

V:62 Officer
He is in what is believed to be a uniform of the Ataman Cossacks after 1908.

The tchekman was dark blue and went down to the knees (Image V:61). It had no piping on the front, but often had piping on the dark blue collar and cuffs. The cuff and collar piping were the same as for the vice-moundir (Table V.5.e.1).

Breeches, Trousers, and Charivari

Both officers and other ranks of the guard Cossacks wore blue breeches in full dress. The breeches did not have any piping. Officers had additional blue full-length trousers that were worn in walking-out dress with the undress jacket (vice-moundir).

The officers of the guard Cossacks also had blue charivari trousers that were sometimes worn in full dress with shoes rather than boots. The charivari had two wide bands the colour of the shoulder straps running down the outside of the leg (Table V.5.e.1). In between the two bands, on the outer seam, there was narrow piping, also in the colour of the shoulder strap (Image V:62). See *§V-3-1* for details.

Uniform Accessories

Officers' Accessories
Officers of the Emperor's Cossacks and the Combined Regiment wore the standard model pouch and pouch belt in full dress. The pouch ornament was the silver guard star, and the pouch belt was silver with piping in the colour of the shoulder straps. See *§V-3-1* for more description.

The officers of the Ataman Cossacks also wore the standard pouch with the guard star ornament but had a special type of braid which covered their pouch belt. The braid was composed of three silver stripes and two sky blue checked stripes arranged in an alternating pattern. On the top and bottom edge of the braid there was additional sky blue piping. They also had two badges on their pouch belt. On the upper portion of the belt, at the shoulder, there was a helmet, breast armour, and battle trophies (Image V:14). On the lower right front end of the belt was the monogram of Czar Nicholas II (Images V:13 and V:63). See also *§V-3-7*.

V:63 Young Subaltern of the Ataman Cossacks
Note the badge on the lower portion of his pouch belt (see §V-3-7-a) and the design of his pouch belt.

Officers also wore the officer's sash in full dress (Image V:63). See §V-3-1.

Other Ranks' Accessories
Other ranks of guard Cossacks wore a wide white cloth waist belt with the tunic in full dress. The buckle was covered in the same white fabric.

Additional Accessories
When the undress jacket was being worn, a narrow white leather belt was worn by both officers and other ranks in place of the usual full dress sash or belt.

All ranks of the guard Cossacks wore standard riding boots and standard white gloves in full dress. Standard brown gloves could be worn in walking-out dress. See §V-3-1 for more details on accessories.

§V-5-f EMPEROR'S GUARD ESCORT[79]

The Emperor's Escort section of the guard was made up of four sotnias, two from Kuban and two from Terek.

The history of the Kuban sotnias began on 18 May 1811, when the Black Sea Sotnia of the Imperial Guard was created as part of the guard Cossacks. In 1842 it was detached from the guard Cossacks and became a group of squadrons, or half-regiment. Over the course of the next fifty years, the squadrons were constantly being reorganised. Starting in 1861, they joined with the Caucasus Cossack Guard Squadron (the future Terek sotnias; see below) to become the 1st, 2nd, and 3rd Squadrons of Caucasus Cossacks, formally associated with the emperor's personal guard. Finally, in 1891 they officially changed from squadrons back to sotnias and took the names 1st and 2nd Kuban Sotnias of the Emperor's Escort.

The origins of the Terek sotnias dated from 12 October 1832, when a detachment of line Caucasus Cossacks was formed to serve as an escort for the emperor alongside the squadron of Caucasus Highlanders which had been formed in 1828. In 1861 it joined with the Black Sea group of squadrons (mentioned above) and formed the 1st, 2nd, and 3rd Squadrons of Caucasus Cossacks, and from that point on the histories of the sotnias were very similar. In 1891, when the squadrons returned to being sotnias, they were called the 3rd and 4th Terek Sotnias of the Emperor's Escort.

UNIFORM

Headdress
The full dress headdress for the Emperor's Escort was a black fur *papakha* with a red cloth top. The cloth top was decorated by rank. Officers had a large silver cylindrical piece in the centre of the cloth top. From the centre ornament, eight rays of silver braid with a gold stripe extended to the edge of the cloth top, and more of the same braid went around the border of the

cloth top. Other ranks did not have the decorative metal piece. They had plain orange braid sewn in the shape of a cross with more of the same braid around the border of the cloth top.

On the front of the papakha, a silver distinction banner was worn in full dress and when serving with other troops. At other times, the banner was not worn.

Tunic

The full dress tunic worn by the Emperor's Escort was a red cloth *cherkeska*, a long robe-like garment similar to that worn by the Caucasus Cossacks, who had similar origins. Officers had ten decorative cartridges on each side of the chest (Image V:64). The cartridges were made of birchwood carved into the proper shape with an oxidized silver metal tip attached. Each pair of cartridges had a silver chain connecting them to a silver metal rosette above the cartridges. Thus, on each side of the chest there was a row of five silver metal rosettes, each with a chain that went down to the five pairs of cartridges. The cartridges themselves were mounted on roughly shield-shaped patches on the chest indicating the placement of the interior breast pockets beneath. The cartridges, along with the rest of the shield-shaped patch, were covered with dark blue velvet. Other ranks had a similar decoration, except they had only eight cartridges instead of ten mounted on the shield-shaped exterior of the breast pocket (see Image V:65, where NCOs have nine). Other ranks had ordinary cartridges instead of the specially carved birchwood ones, and there were no metal chain and rosette decorations like those on the officer's model (Image V:65). For other ranks, the velvet covering of the cartridges and shield-shaped pocket exterior was dark blue for combatants and dark green for noncombatants.

The cherkeska included trim in a number of locations. The placement of the trim was the same for officers and other ranks, but officers had silver metallic trim with a gold stripe running through it, while other ranks had orange braid with blue thread along

V:64 Full Dress Uniforms of the Officers of the Emperor's Escort (Konvoy)
Note their Caucasian-type dress. The two men in the foreground are holding nagyka whips. Also note the soft boots worn by the officers in the front rows.

V:65 More Uniforms of the Emperor's Escort
The man on the far left is a bugler. Buglers always rode next to the czar, ready to relay his orders. The other three men are troopers wearing various levels of dress. The man in front and the man on the right are holding nagyka whips. This photograph gives an idea of how long the whip portion was and what the weight at the end of the whip looked like.

V:66 General Count Alexander Grabbe, Commander of the Emperor's Escort in Full Dress Uniform, 1917
Note his decorative short sword scabbard. During this period, officers were allowed to wear non-regulation swords if they were 'antique family heirlooms'. Note also his aiguillette worn on the right side as a member of the czar's personal staff. On his left breast, he has the Maltese Cross of a graduate of a the Page de Corps school. As a senior officer, his epaulettes have heavy thick fringe. Note also the trim down the front of his cherkeska and around the bottom and at the end of his sleeves and how it is different from the trim worn by the officers in Image V:64.

the sides. A double row of trim ran lengthwise across the velvet that covered the cartridges. An additional single row of trim was in a roughly triangular shape below the cartridges, coming to a point as it outlined the velvet patch under the cartridges (Image V:66).

Single rows of trim went around the V-shaped neck, down the front edges, along the bottom hem, and around the edges of the cherkeska's sleeves, as well as around the false pockets located at the back of the cherkeska immediately below waist-level. NCOs, unlike the rest of the other ranks, had the officer's style silver braid with a gold stripe on the cartridges and silver NCO's braid on the sleeves, but had the standard orange and blue other ranks' braid in all the other locations.

Bechmet

Like the Caucasus Cossacks, the Emperor's Escort wore a *bechmet*, or long shirt with standing collar, beneath the full dress cherkeska. The full dress bechmet was white with trim around the top and the bottom of the collar as well as down the front. The trim was silver with a gold stripe running through it for officers, and plain orange for the other ranks. NCOs had the regular orange other ranks' braid around the bottom of the collar and down the front of the bechmet, but had wider silver braid along the top and front edges of the collar. Because the cherkeska was collarless and had a V-shaped neckline, the bechmet collar and its decorative

V:67 Members of the Emperor's Escort in Less than Full Dress Uniforms
The officers on the far left and far right are holding nagyka whips.

trim were visible in full dress. In less than full dress other colours were worn, but the trim was the same (Image V:67).

Epaulettes

Epaulettes were worn only by the officers in full dress (Image V:67). They were cavalry-style epaulettes made of silver metal with red piping and lining. The epaulette crescent bore the monogram H II for Nicholas II in silver. See *§V-3-1* for details on epaulettes.

Shoulder Braids

Other ranks wore shoulder braids instead of epaulettes or shoulder straps in both full and ordinary dress. The shoulder braids were similar to those worn by the hussars, and were made of braided orange cording (Image V:65). Like the officers' epaulettes, they bore the monogram H II for Nicholas II in silver.

Shoulder Straps

Shoulder straps were worn by officers in ordinary and walking-out dress with the undress tunic. The braid covering the shoulder straps was silver, in the hussar (zigzag) style. The shoulder strap piping and the stripe running the length of the centre of the shoulder strap were both red. The shoulder strap bore the monogram H II for Nicholas II in silver.

Walking-Out Tunic

The tunic officers wore in walking-out and ordinary dress was a cherkeska like the full dress tunic, but was made of dark blue cloth. It had officer's trim in all the same places as the full dress tunic.

While the dark blue cherkeska was the regulation walking-out tunic, officers were permitted to wear brown, red-orange, grey, or black cherkeskas according to personal preference. With these alternative cherkeskas they could either wear the standard red undress bechmet with decorative trim or a plain black bechmet.

Walking-Out Bechmet

The bechmet officers wore in walking-out and ordinary dress beneath the blue undress cherkeska was red instead of white. However, in all other respects, including the trim, it was identical to the full dress model.

Cossack Charivari

Both officers and other ranks wore dark blue Cossack charivari in full dress. These were tucked into soft knee-high Circassian boots. The Cossack charivari had braid lining the outside seams of the legs. The braid was silver with a gold stripe running through it for officers and plain orange for other ranks. Officers wore the same full dress garments in walking-out and ordinary dress. Because of the length of the cherkeska, the Cossack charivari were not typically visible.

Other Items of Dress

Both officers and other ranks had a compass-holder in full dress, worn over the left shoulder and passed under the right arm. The compass attached to it was placed in the front right interior pocket, which was behind the decorative cartridges. The compass holder was covered with decorative gold braid with a gold tassel that hung down at the back of the tunic. For ordinary dress, other ranks had an additional model of compass-holder made of black silk ribbon material with a silver tassel at the back. Officers wore the gold-trimmed compass-holder in all uniforms, including undress and ordinary dress.

In full dress, both officers and other ranks wore a waist belt with decorative braid and a silver buckle. For officers the belt was covered with silver braid that had a gold stripe running through it. For other ranks the belt was red with orange braid running along the top and bottom edges. Officers wore the same silver and gold belt with all of their uniforms, but troops had an additional waist belt that was worn in ordinary dress. It was made of black patent leather and had silver ornaments which could be attached to it.

Officers and other ranks all wore standard black riding boots in full dress except for balls and Winter Palace guard duty, when officers wore soft Caucasus-style boots instead of the stiffer standard riding boots. In full dress, officers wore standard white wrist gloves. They did not wear any gloves in undress or ordinary dress, and other ranks never wore gloves. See §V-3-1 for a full description of accessories.

§V-6 GUARD INFANTRY

§V-6-a GUARD INFANTRY AND RIFLES[80]

Young boys, including young royals from ancient Egypt onwards, have liked to play with toy soldiers. Young Peter, not yet the Great, outdid them all. As a youth of eleven, while living at his mother's palace near the village of Preobrazhenskoye outside Moscow, he was allowed playmates from the children of Boyar families and court servants. These were formed into an army of his own. He dressed them in his uniforms, drilled them, marched them to and fro, and fought mock-battles with them. He did all this with the advice of a mercenary, General Patrick Gordon. He eventually outgrew Preobrazhenskoye and spread into the next village of Semenovskoye. These formed the basis for the two senior guard regiments, the Preobrazhensky and Semenovsky Regiments, whose seniority is dated from 1683.[81]

Preobrazhensky Regiment
Over the course of its history, the Preobrazhensky Regiment received many awards and distinctions. Because it had been created by Peter the Great, right from its inception the regiment had the czar as its regimental chief, and many members of the nobility such as grand dukes, could be found among its ranks.

Semenovsky Regiment
The Semenovsky Regiment had roughly the same origins as the Preobrazhensky, as part of Peter the Great's 'toy army' which was formed in 1683. It officially broke from the Preobrazhensky and became associated with the name Semenovsky a few years later, in 1687. Because of their common origins, though, the two regiments are often referred to as brother regiments.

In 1820, the regiment refused to obey the orders of its commander, a man known for his brutality, resulting in the regiment's dissolution and its troops' dispersal. The regiment was then reformed with all new men drawn from the grenadiers. Still, the Semenovsky, even in its new form, was not accorded the privileges of the Old Guard which it had previously held, and instead remained part of the Young Guard for the next three years. In late 1823, the regiment was finally restored to its former position in the Old Guard.

Izmailovsky Regiment
The Izmailovsky Regiment of the Imperial Guard dated from 22 September 1730, when Empress Anna Ioannovna created it from the Ukrainian land militia. It did not get its definitive name of Izmailovsky until 1801. The name came from Izmaylovo, a village located in the Moscow area on Romanov hereditary property.

Yegersky Regiment
The Yegersky (or Jaeger or Chasseur) Regiment of the Imperial Guard originated on 9 November 1796, when chasseurs from the Semenovsky and Izmailovsky Regiments, as well as chasseur companies from Gatchina (near St Petersburg), were formed into a guard chasseur battalion. It officially became a regiment in 1810.

Moscow Regiment
On 12 October 1817, the first two battalions of the Lithuanian Regiment (discussed below) were taken away and used to form the basis for the new Moscow Regiment. Thus, it dated its origins to 1811, when the Lithuanian Regiment was formed, instead of 1817.

The other ranks were pawns in the revolt of December 1825, a well known event in Russian history. They stood in the Senate Square all day chanting slogans they did not understand. At dusk, grapeshot drove them off. The regiment's officers were punished and the men sent to serve outside the guards.

Grenadier Regiment
Originally created on 30 March 1756 under the reign of Empress Elizabeth as the 1st Grenadier Regiment,

this regiment did not officially become part of the guard until 1813, when it was admitted into the Young Guard as a result of its meritorious actions. It entered the Old Guard on 6 December 1831.

Paul Regiment

The Paul Regiment considered 15 May 1790 to be its date of origin because that was the origin date of the regiment in Moscow that formed it. On 19 November 1796, parts of that regiment were taken to form the Grenadier Regiment of General Major Vadkovski. Only three days later, though, its name was changed to Paul, after the village Pavlovskaya. It entered the Old Guard in 1831.

The Paul Regiment of the Guard is one of the most famous and celebrated of all the regiments in the Russian army. Part of its fame comes from its unique grenadier's mitre which captured the public's imagination and was often depicted in art.

The regiment was the only one permitted to keep its grenadier mitre when mitres were removed from the rest of the regiments during the 1805 reforms. Some of these mitres had bullet holes in them from earlier fighting.

Finland Regiment

The Finland Regiment was created on 12 December 1806 as an imperial militia battalion made up of peasants from the imperial domains in Finland, Gatchina, Oranienbaum, Krasnoye Selo, and Strielna. It entered the guard in 1808, but did not officially become a regiment until 1811.

Lithuanian Regiment

The Lithuanian Regiment was formed on 7 November 1811 from two battalions taken from the Preobrazhensky Regiment and various elements from other units of the guard and the line. It was part of the Old Guard from its inception. When the first two battalions were taken from the regiment to form the basis for the new Moscow Regiment in 1817 (discussed above), the 3rd Battalion was replenished using Polish elements from other parts of the guard in an effort to keep the 'Lithuanian' tradition suggested by the regiment's name.

Kexholm Regiment

The Kexholm Regiment (see Image C62 (bottom right)) was created around 1709/1710 as the Grenadier Regiment of Prince Bariatinsky. Over the course of the next 200 years, it was reorganised and renamed no fewer than twenty times. It officially became the Life Guard Kexholm Regiment of the Emperor of Austria in 1894, in recognition of its honorary regimental chief. However, at the outset of World War I in 1914, the appellation was changed to simply Life Guard Kexholm Regiment. The Emperor of Austria could no longer be the regiment's honorary chief because Austria and Russia were on opposite sides of the war.

St Petersburg Regiment

The St Petersburg Regiment was created on 6 July 1790 as the Regiment of Grenadiers of St Petersburg. Originally, it was made of elements taken from the Tenga and Navaga Line Infantry Regiments. Because the regiment bore the name of its honorary chief in its title, the title changed many times throughout the years. In 1894, when Nicholas II ascended the throne, the regiment finally entered the Old Guard under the name Imperial Guard St Petersburg Regiment of King Frederick Wilhelm III of Prussia. When World War I broke out in 1914, it became simply the Imperial Guard Petrograd Regiment, because Petrograd was a more traditionally Russian name, and Frederick Wilhelm III as one of the enemy sovereigns could no longer be its honorary chief.

Volynsky Regiment

The Volynsky Regiment was created on 7 December 1817 from a battalion of the Finland Regiment and soldiers from other different regiments of the guard who shared a common Polish origin. Thus, its date of origin is placed at 1806, when the Finland Regiment was formed, instead of 1817. It was part of the Old Guard from its inception.

1st Rifle Regiment

The 1st Rifle Regiment of His Majesty was formed on 27 March 1856 under the name Battalion of Guard Rifles. It was originally made up of men taken from among the rifle companies of the 1st Division of the

Guard (Preobrazhensky, Semenovsky, Izmailovsky, and Yegersky Regiments). In 1910, the battalion became a regiment and took its definitive name.

2nd Rifle Regiment

Like the 1st Rifles, the 2nd Rifle Regiment was formed on 27 March 1856, but from men taken from the rifle companies of the 2nd Division of the Guard (Moscow, Grenadier, Paul, and Finland Regiments). It too began as a battalion and did not officially become a regiment until 1910, when it was given the official name of Imperial Guard 2nd Regiment of Rifles of Tsarskoye Selo.

3rd Rifle Regiment

The 3rd Rifles was a unique regiment. Created on 29 June 1799, it was originally made up of the garrison battalion of the guard and brought together all the guard soldiers who had become unfit for campaign service. At various points during its history, it was considered part of the guard's reserve infantry, but eventually came to be known simply as the 3rd Regiment of Guard Rifles of His Majesty.

Because of the nature of the regiment and the soldiers it was made up of, the 3rd Rifles did not participate in military campaigns.

4th Rifle Regiment

The 4th Rifle Regiment of the Imperial Family is known as Nicholas II's favourite regiment. Created during the Crimean War, on 25 October 1854, from peasants from the czar's land in the regions of Novgorod, Archangelgorod, and Vologda, this regiment immediately took the name Rifle Regiment of the Imperial Family and was equipped with a unique Russian-style uniform, described below. When the Crimean War was over, it became part of the Young Guard. Its numbers were then filled or completed with men from regular units: the Grenadier Corps, the 1st Reserve Division, the 1st and 2nd Second Reserve Divisions, and the Finnish battalions. In 1884, it was incorporated into the Old Guard, and in 1910 it took its definitive name, 4th Rifle Regiment of the Imperial Family. Unlike most regiments, it was made up of only two battalions.

Structure of the Russian Guard Troops

The guard infantry was made up of three infantry divisions of four regiments each, and one rifle brigade, which also had four regiments. The 1st Guard Infantry Division included the Preobrazhensky, Semenovsky, Izmailovsky, and Yegersky (sometimes written Jaeger or Chasseur) Regiments. The 2nd Division included the Moscow, Grenadier, Paul, and Finland Regiments, and the 3rd Division was made up of the Lithuanian, Kexholm, St Petersburg, and Volynsky Regiments. The Guard Rifle Brigade comprised the 1st, 2nd, 3rd, and 4th Rifles. The 4th Rifles had the distinction of being the regiment most closely associated with the Imperial Family, in addition to its unique history, so its uniform was considerably different from the rest of the guard infantry and rifle regiments. The 4th Rifles uniform was designed to resemble the traditional garb of Russian peasants, because the unit had been created by a mass conscription that had occurred during the war of 1854–5, during which peasants were recruited from land owned by the Czar.[82]

UNIFORM

Headdress

Guard Infantry Kiver

All regiments of guard infantry except the Paul Regiment and the 4th Rifle Regiment wore the guard infantry model kiver. This was a throwback to the model of headdress introduced in 1812 and at that time called a kiver.[83] For officers, the body of the kiver was covered with dark (royal) green cloth, and the top was made of black patent leather. For other ranks, the kiver was made of black felt, and the top was black waxed leather. The top was angled slightly, with the front slightly higher (14.45 cm or 5.69 inches) than the back (13.89 cm or 5.47 inches). The top and sides were

Table V.6.a.1: Guard Infantry

Regiment	Button Colour	Shako Officer Plume Colour[a]	Shako Top Band Colour	Shako Bottom Band Colour	Tunic Plastron	Tunic Collar	Tunic Cuff Horizontal	Tunic Cuff Vertical	Officer Epaulette	Trooper Shoulder Strap	Officer Litzen[b]	Trooper Litzen[c]	Monogram	Notes
Preobrazhensky	Gold	White	Red	Red	Red[d]	Red	Red[d]	Red[d]	Gold	Red	Special	Guard	H II[e,f]	A, E, G
Semenovsky	Gold	White	Red	Light blue[h]	Red[d]	Light blue	Red[d]	Red[d]	Gold	Red	Special	Guard	H II[e,f]	A, E, G
Izmailovsky	Gold	White	Red	White[h]	Red[d]	Same as tunic[g]	Red[d]	Red[d]	Gold	Red	Special	Guard	H II[e]	A, E, G
Yegersky	Gold	Black	Red	Same as tunic[g,h]	Light[d] green	Same as tunic[g,h]	Same as tunic[g,h]	Red[d]	Gold	Red	Special	Guard	H II[e]	A, E, G
Moscow	Gold	White	Red	Red	Red	Red	Red	Red	Gold	Red	Special	Guard	—	A
Grenadier	Gold	White	Red	Light blue[h]	Red	Light blue	Red	Red	Gold	Red	Special	Guard	H II[e]	A, E, G, I
Paul	Gold	Wore a mitre			Red	Same as tunic[g]	Red	Red	Gold	Red	Special	Guard	H II[e]	C, E, G
Finland	Gold	Black	Red	Same as tunic[g,h]	Same as tunic[g,h]	Same as tunic[g]	Same as tunic[g,h]	Red	Gold	Red	Special	Guard	---	A
Lithuanian	Silver	White	Yellow[g]	Yellow[j]	Yellow[j]	Yellow[j]	Yellow[j,j]	Yellow[j]	Silver	Red	Special	Guard	---	A
Kexholm	Silver	White	Yellow	Sky blue[k,n]	Yellow	Sky blue[k]	Yellow	Yellow	Silver	Red	Special	Guard	F I[f,l]	A, E, G, H
St Petersburg	Silver	White	Yellow	White[m,n]	Yellow	Same as tunic[g]	Yellow	Yellow	Silver	Red	Special	Guard	FW III[m]	A, E, G, H
Volynsky	Silver	Black	Yellow	Same as tunic[g,n]	Same as tunic[g,n]	Same as tunic[g]	Same as tunic[g,n]	Yellow	Silver	Red	Special	Guard	H II[e]	A, E, G
1st Rifles	Gold	Black	Raspberry	Same as tunic[g,o]	Raspberry	Same as tunic[g]	Same as tunic[g,o]	Raspberry	Gold	Raspberry	Special	Guard	H II[e]	B, E, G
2nd Rifles	Silver	Black	Raspberry	Same as tunic[g,o]	Raspberry	Same as tunic[g]	Same as tunic[g,o]	Raspberry	Silver	Raspberry	Special	Guard	—	A
3rd Rifles	Silver	Black	Raspberry	Raspberry	Raspberry	Raspberry	Raspberry	Raspberry	Silver	Raspberry	Special	Guard	H II[e]	B, E, G
4th Rifles	Gold	Wore a special bonnet			Wore a special jacket, no plastron or collar		Same as tunic[g,o]	—	Gold	Raspberry	Simple[p]	Simple[q]	H II[e]	D, F, G

Notes: ᵃ White plume for other ranks in all cases.

ᵇ Nearly all of the guard infantry regiments had unique embroidery in place of litzen, either gold or silver to match the colour of the buttons. Two on the collar; three on the cuffs.

ᶜ Two on the collar; three on the cuffs. Litzen were orange and in the chapter shape unless otherwise specified.

ᵈ White trim.

ᵉ Monogram of Nicholas II.

ᶠ Some of the men in the 3rd Company were also part of a Boat Crew. These men wore the monogram P. P. (for Peter the Great) combined with an anchor to denote their additional status. However, the naval uniforms of these units are beyond the scope of this work. See Zweguintzow, *Uniformes Russe*, pp. 42–4 and Plates A5, B7 and B73 for information on the uniforms of these troops.

ᵍ Czar's green for officers, black for troops. The tunics worn by the officers were easily distinguished from those worn by the other ranks.

ʰ Red trim.

ⁱ The yellow for the Lithuanian Regiment was known as 'canary' or 'lemon' yellow, meaning that it was lighter than the yellow worn by the other regiments in the division.

ʲ Trim in the colour of the tunic: czar's green for officers, black for troops.

ᵏ The Kexholm Guard Infantry Regiment's distinctive colour had previously been light blue; it changed to sky blue in 1912.

ˡ Monogram of the Emperor of Austria, see §V-3-5.

ᵐ Monogram of Frederick Wilhelm III, King of Prussia, see §V-3-5.

ⁿ Yellow trim.

ᵒ Raspberry trim.

ᵖ Two simple gold litzen on the cuffs only, in the chapter shape.

ᵠ Two simple orange wool litzen on the cuffs only, in the chapter shape.

A: Guard star on the shako with distinction banner above.
B: Guard star on the shako.
C: Guard star on the mitre with distinction banner above.
D: Cross (of the mass conscription) on the special bonnet.
E: Officers: metal monogram in button colour mounted on epaulette.
F: Officers: metal monogram in button colour mounted on epaulette of 1st Company only.
G: Troops: metal monogram in button colour mounted on shoulder straps of 1st Company only.
H: Troops: monogram painted in yellow on shoulder straps of all except the 1st Company.
I: After 1913, both officers and men again wore an aiguillette on their right shoulder.

V:68 Kiver of the Volynsky Regiment
The kiver was worn by enlisted men. Note the distinction banner above the guard star and placement of the guard star.

V:69 Guard Kiver for Other Ranks of the Volynsky Regiment
This partial side view gives an idea of the scooped-out nature of the top of the kiver and the cording and tassels on the side and back of the kiver. The cockade is missing.

slightly concave, so viewed from the front it appeared to flare slightly at the top. The visor was made of black patent leather for both officers and other ranks, and had a 0.83 cm (0.33 inch) metal border in the colour of the button. The chinstrap, which was typically worn decoratively above the visor, was also in the button colour and made of overlapping rows of three metal scales each (Images V:68 and V:69). See Table V.6.a.1 for regiment button colours.

Trim and Piping

The bottom edge of the kiver had a 2.22 cm (0.88 inch) wide cloth band that varied in colour by regiment. In some cases, the cloth band was trimmed on the top and bottom edges with 0.28 cm (0.11 inch) piping, the colour of which also varied, normally depending on which division the regiment belonged to. On either side of the kiver, the vertical seam could be trimmed with 0.28 cm (0.11 inch) piping as well. For the four regiments of the 1st Division of Guard Infantry, this side piping was white, while for the regiments of the 2nd Division – with the exception of the Paul Regiment, who did not wear the kiver – it was red, and for the regiments of the 3rd Division, yellow. The rifles did not have this piping. The top edge of the kiver had a border of coloured piping that varied by regiment. Immediately below the piping, actually touching it, was braid that varied by rank, as follows (see Table V.6.a.1 for colours).

Officers had braid that was either gold or silver according to the button colour. Subalterns had 1.67 cm (0.66 inch) wide square-weave braid. Superior officers had the same braid, but with an additional band of 0.56 cm (0.22 inch) wide superior officer's braid placed below it at a spacing of 0.56 cm (0.22 inch). Generals had 2.22 cm (0.88 inch) wide general's (zigzag) braid.

For the other ranks, the upper braid was either orange or white according to button colour, and varied by rank. Regular soldiers had a narrow 0.7 cm (0.27 inch) braid. NCOs had wider braid, 1.67 cm (0.66 inch). Adjutants and chief adjutants had both braids, with the wider braid on the top edge immediately adjacent to the kiver piping, with the narrow braid below it at a spacing of 0.56 cm (0.22 inch).

Kiver Decorations

Mounted on the front of the kiver was a silver guard star of St Andrew, 11.81 cm (4.65 inches) in diameter. Above the star, a cockade was mounted, sticking up slightly past the top edge of the kiver (see §V-3-1 for more information on cockades). If the regiment had received a distinction banner, it was mounted on the front of the kiver between the guard star and the cockade, usually overlapping with those other two decorations, sometimes concealing the lower half of the cockade (see Table V.6.a.1 for which guard regiments had distinction banners and §V-2-2 for information on what type).

On either side of the kiver, at the top of the side seam piping, there was a uniform button. From these two buttons hung a crescent of cording woven into wide flat braid that draped across the back of the kiver, with a loop on either end of the crescent which attached to the uniform button. A small flat woven flounder or tassel of cording, 2.78 cm (1.09 inches) long, hung down from the button on each side.

For the other ranks, the crescent and flounder or tassels were made of either white or orange cording, depending on the regiment's button colour (Table V.6.a.1). For officers, the flounders had black and orange threads in the centre, surrounded by gold or silver cording according to button colour, and varied by rank. Subalterns had matt-finish cording that was 0.21 cm (0.08 inch) in diameter, superior officers had matt-finish cannetille (spirally twisted thread) 0.28 cm (0.11 inch) in diameter, and generals had cannetille with a shiny finish, 0.42 cm (0.16 inch) in diameter. Similar cording and/or cannetille made up the woven crescent mentioned above. Generals, honorary *chefs*, and unit commanders had an additional crescent of decorative cording which passed around the front of the shako.

Pompoms

In full dress the other ranks always wore white pompoms on their kivers. For NCOs, the pompom was white, but infused with black and orange threads that were visible from the top.

Officers did not wear pompoms on their kivers in full dress, but did wear silver guard infantry model pompoms in regular dress. The pompoms were silver, surrounded by coated silk threads which varied by rank: subalterns had plain smooth thread, superior officers had matt-finish cannetille 0.28 cm (0.11 inch) in diameter, and generals had shiny-finish cannetille 0.42 cm (0.16 inch) in diameter. The top section of the pompom had two rows of sequins around the edge, with mixed black and orange threads visible in the centre. For the Preobrazhensky, Semenovsky, Izmailovsky, Yegersky (Chasseur), Grenadier, Volynsky, 1st Rifle and 3rd Rifle Regiments of the Imperial Guard, the upper section of the pompom included an imperial monogram on a St George's (black-and-orange striped) ribbon background. The monogram was made of silver metal for officers, white metal for other ranks.

Plumes

Officers and generals wore plumes on the kiver in full dress. Generals of the guard infantry regiments had plumes made of white, orange, and black feathers. The white feathers stood the highest, at 17.78 cm (7 inches) tall. The next layer was the orange feathers, which stood 8.33 cm (3.28 inches) high. The bottom layer of the plume was black feathers 5 cm (1.97 inches) high. Plumes were slightly shorter in the guard rifle regiments: feather heights for generals' plumes were 14.45 cm (5.69 inches), 6.67 cm (2.63 inches) and 3.89 cm (1.53 inches) for white, orange, and black feathers, respectively.

For other officers, the plume was made of horsehair, white in the Preobrazhensky, Semenovsky, Izmailovsky, Moscow, Grenadier, Lithuanian, Kexholm and St Petersburg Regiments, and black in the Yegersky, Finland, and Volynsky Regiments and the 1st, 2nd, and 3rd Rifle Regiments. The standard plume stood 15.56 cm (6.13 inches) high and was straight up and down. For the Rifle Regiments, though, it only stood 12.22 cm (4.81 inches) high and flared slightly towards the top.

GRENADIER'S MITRE

The Paul Regiment of the Imperial Guard wore a grenadier's mitre in place of the standard guard infantry kiver (see Image C61). The metal front plate of the mitre, which was gilt metal for officers or brass for other ranks, was engraved with the eighteenth-century style of the double-headed imperial eagle (Image V:70). This style of eagle had the wings fully extended with the wingtip feathers pointed upward. On the breast of the eagle was a silver guard star of St Andrew, with a distinction banner immediately above it (Image V:71). The headband of the mitre, which was of white cloth, was visible only from the sides and

V:70 Old-Style Mitre without a Guard Star of the Paul Regiment
It was used from 1825 to 1878, at which time they began putting the guard star on the front of it (Mollo, *Military Fashion*, p. 204).

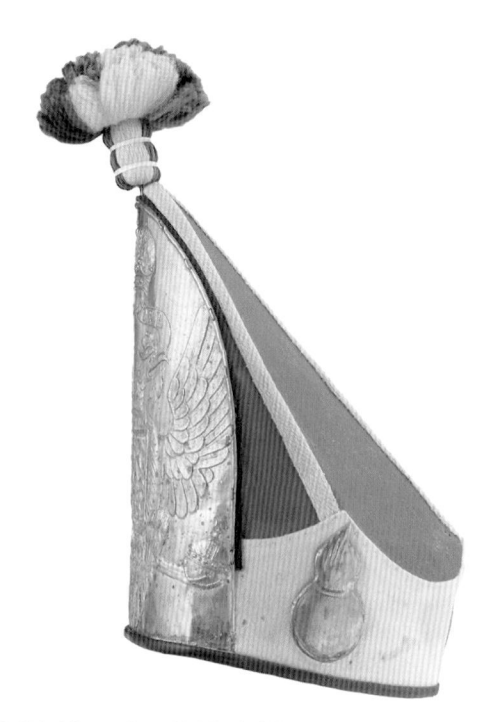

V:72 Side View of an Old-Style Mitre
This shows the cloth back of the mitre and its grenade decoration.

V:71 Officer of the Paul Regiment Wearing Mitre with a Guard Star and Distinction Banner
Note the collar and cuff litzen.

V:73 Private of the Paul Regiment Standing Guard Duty
This photograph provides a good side view of the other ranks' mitre.

back, as the metal mitre plate concealed it in the front. Above the headband, the backing and sides of the mitre were made of red cloth, with decorative braid on the seams. The braid was white for the other ranks, while for officers it was narrow silver page corps style (diagonally striped) braid. There were three decorative metal grenades on the white headband, one on either side where the chinstrap attached and one on the back (Images V:71 and V:72).

The chinstrap was made of overlapping rows of scalloped metal scales. The chinstrap and grenades were all of the same colour of metal as the mitre plate, gilt for officers or brass for other ranks. Below the chinstrap attachment and decorative grenade on the right side of the mitre was a large round cockade, 6.11 cm (2.41 inches) in diameter (see *§V-3-1* for more information on cockades). At the peak of the mitre, a pompom was worn in full dress, angled to jut out slightly in front of the headdress (Image V:73). Officers had a silver pompom, with sequins in the case of superior officers, while other ranks wore white pompoms.

It should be noted the 4th Battalion of the Paul Regiment wore a mitre, but it was not quite as tall and had a slightly different shape, similar to the one worn by the fusiliers from 1796 to 1800. The pompom was oriented vertically rather than tilted towards the front as it was in the other three regiments. However, the colours were all the same (Image V:74).

The Paul Regiment retained over 600 mitres from the 1807 Battle of Friedland.[84] The 1st Company wore those mitres (Image V:75), with the front plates of many of them bearing between one and four bullet holes. The name of the soldier to whom the mitre had originally belonged was hammered into the base of the plate. The mitres were a battle honour, given by Czar Alexander I after the Battle of Friedland as a visible mark of bravery and the Czar's grace.

4th Rifles Bonnet

The 4th Rifle Regiment wore a unique headdress comprising a wide fur headband and a cloth upper portion (Image V:76). The headband was made of black sheepskin, while the cloth upper portion was either black for the troops or dark (royal) green for the officers, the same colour as the tunic (discussed below). From the front, the cloth upper portion had

V:74 Mitres of the Paul Regiment with the Guard Star and Distinction Banner
Note the mitre of the 4th Battalion of the regiment on the right with its smaller front plate and cloth bag on the back. Note also how the plume on top is placed.

V:75 Mitres in the Regimental Museum
Note the bullet holes in the mitre plates. The regiment kept some mitres with bullet holes from the 1807 Battle of Friedland.

somewhat the appearance of a low, squat pentagon, with long lines sloping downwards from the centre peak of the cap to the outside edge, angling down and slightly inwards for a short distance to meet the headband. On the front of that portion, there was a cockade with the cross of the mass conscription superimposed over it (Image C62). The cross was brass for the troops, gilded for the officers.

Guard Infantry Tunic

The guard infantry model tunic worn by all of the regiments of guard infantry and rifles except the 4th Rifles, was double-breasted, with two rows of seven buttons on the front. The cloth of the tunic was dark royal green for the officers, black for the other ranks (Image C62, top). The front edge of the

V:76 Officers of the 4th Rifle Regiment in their Raspberry-Coloured Blouses
Note the shoulder boards worn on the blouse and the officer's belt. The blouse was often worn just like this. Note the unique headdress of this regiment and their baggy trousers.

Plastron

Uniquely, the Russian guard infantry in full dress wore plastrons as a part of their uniform. These were first introduced into the Russian army in 1817[85] and had a sporadic existence within the guard thereafter. The colour of the plastron varied according to regiment, and the plastron sometimes included piping as well (Table V.6.a.1, see Image V:77). The 4th regiment of each of the 1st, 2nd, and 3rd Guard Infantry Divisions (Yegersky, Finland, and Volynsky Regiments) had green plastrons to honour their previous designation as rifle regiments. The 3rd Division of Guard Infantry – with the exception of the aforementioned Volynsky Regiment, which had yellow trim – wore yellow plastrons, harking back to their Polish origins. In 1817, Grand Duke Constantine Pavolovitch was named Viceroy of the Kingdom of Poland, and a guard brigade (the Lithuanian and Volynsky Regiments) was formed for him. The Polish infantry traditionally had yellow as its distinctive colour. Later, the St Petersburg Regiment (at the time a grenadier regiment) and the Kexholm Regiment were added, and the brigade became a division. The St Petersburg and Kexholm Regiments were given yellow as their distinctive colour (see Image C62, bottom right). Eventually, these regiments were added to the guard. There was a tendency among the Russian guard to have their plastrons fly away at the top (Images V:78 and V:79). This was a non-regulation affectation.

tunic had piping in the shape of a plastron, white for the regiments of the 1st Division, red for the 2nd Division, yellow for the 3rd Division, and raspberry for the Rifle Regiments. The rear skirt of the tunic had false pockets, cut straight not scalloped, and had two buttons, one at waist-level at the top of the opening, and one at the bottom. The pockets were piped in red for the 1st and 2nd Divisions, yellow for the 3rd Division, and raspberry for the Rifles. For officers, the tunic also had coloured lining. The lining was red for the Preobrazhensky, Semenovsky, Izmailovsky, Moscow, Grenadier, and Paul Regiments. It was yellow for the Lithuanian, Kexholm, and St Petersburg Regiments, and dark green for the Yegersky, Finland, Volynsky, and Rifle Regiments.

Collar

The collar was cut on the diagonal at the front of the tunic. The height of the collar varied from 4.45 cm (1.75 inches) to 5.56 cm (2.19 inches), and it had 0.28 cm (0.11 inch) piping on the top and front edges. The collar and its piping varied in colour by regiment (see Table V.6.a.1). Each side of the collar included two litzen. For officers, the litzen were a special embroidery of lace, the design varying for most of the regiments of the guard infantry. Other ranks had double yellow-orange guard model litzen with red trim. Each litzen was 22.97 cm (9.04 inches) long, and they were arranged to fall the same distance from the top collar piping as from the bottom edge of the collar. The space showing between the two litzen was the colour of the collar for all except the Lithuanian Regiment, where the space between the two litzen was red instead of the canary yellow of the collar (Table V.6.a.1).

V:77 Subaltern of the Preobrazhensky Regiment
He has the Preobrazhensky gorget and the white piping of the 1st Guard Division on his plastron and cuffs. Note that the bottom button on the cuff is not buttoned.

V:78 Officer of the Volynsky Regiment
Note his flyaway plastron and the shape of his gorget. This regiment wore a plastron the same colour as the tunic.

V:79 Officer of a Regiment in the 1st Guard Division
Note the white piping on the flyaway plastron. White piping on the plastron was worn by all regiments of the 1st Guard Division.

Cuffs

The guard infantry tunic had Brandenburg-style cuffs, meaning a regular horizontal cuff with an additional tab of fabric oriented vertically, perpendicular to the regular cuff, that had officer's lace, litzen, and/or buttons when applicable. The total width of the horizontal cuff – including its 0.28 cm (0.11 inch) piping – was 5.56 cm (2.19 inches). The vertical cuff tab was 8.89 cm (3.5 inches) high and 5.56 cm (2.19 inches) wide. The horizontal and vertical cuffs and their piping varied in colour by regiment (Table V.6.a.1).

The vertical cuff tab had three sets of lace or litzen, each with a button. The lace or litzen was placed at equal intervals, one at the top, one in the middle, and one at the bottom of the tab. The litzen were 1.11 cm (0.44 inch) thick and extended horizontally, stopping 0.56 cm (0.22 inch) from either edge of the tab. The lace was again in the special embroidery for the officers and yellow-orange guard style for the other ranks, with the central space between the litzen of the other ranks in the colour of the cuff tab underneath instead of the collar colour. As was standard practice in the

Russian army, the bottom button on each officer's cuff was left undone (see §V-3-1 for the history of this custom). The other ranks buttoned all three cuff buttons (Image C62).

Guard Officer's Special Designs

The officer's lace mentioned above had special embroidered designs. Although most regiments had unique embroidery designs, several shared designs because they were related in some way. The Lithuanian Regiment had the same pattern as the Preobrazhensky because two of the battalions of the Preobrazhensky had been taken to form it. The Finland and Volynsky Regiments shared an embroidery pattern because the 1st Battalion of the Finland Regiment had been taken to form the basis of the Volynsky Regiment. The Semenovsky, Izmailovsky, Yegersky, Moscow, Grenadier, Paul, Kexholm, and St Petersburg Regiments each had a unique embroidery pattern. The 1st, 2nd, and 3rd Rifles also each had unique embroideries (see §V-3-3, Images V:8 and V:9).

4TH RIFLES TUNIC

The full dress tunic for the 4th Rifle Regiment was called a *polukaftan* or 'demi-caftan'. A caftan typically refers to a long robe-like garment and derives from a type of dress worn in some Asian, Middle Eastern, and African cultures (see Image C62, top). The demi-caftan worn by the 4th Rifles was not a traditional caftan: it was only slightly longer than the dress tunic worn by the other guard infantry and riles regiments and was fitted rather than flowing. It was collarless like a caftan, and closed in the front somewhat like a robe, with the left front panel extending across the front over much of the right front panel (Image C62). The left front panel buttoned to the right breast of the tunic on a diagonal by means of six loops of cording, each of which attached to one of the buttons that was on the right side of the chest. The buttons were gold, and the loops which attached to them were gold cording for officers, orange cording for other ranks. The tunic was made of dark royal green cloth for officers and black cloth for other ranks, and did not have any pockets. Officers' tunics had raspberry-coloured lining.

V:80 Czar Nicholas II in the Polukaftan (Demi-Caftan) of the 4th Rifle Regiment of the Imperial Family
This demi-caftan was worn over the raspberry blouse in full dress.

V:81 Full Uniform of the 4th Rifle Regiment
Note how the raspberry-coloured blouse buttons on the side of the neck and the demi-caftan buttons on the right side of the chest. Also note the length of the demi-caftan. The trim on the demi-caftan is raspberry.

Although the tunic did not have a traditional collar, it did have trim that ran around the neck and down the front panel edge to the bottom hem of the tunic. For officers the trim was gold hussar-style (zigzag) braid (Image V:80). Other ranks had 0.28 cm (0.11 inch) raspberry piping. Immediately inside the piping was 1.11 cm (0.44 inch) wide orange wool braid with a black thread running through it.

The tunic had straight-cut Swedish cuffs the colour of the tunic, with raspberry piping. There were two vertical litzen on each cuff. Each litzen had a button (Image V:81). Officers had simple gold litzen, while other ranks had orange wool litzen with a black central space.

Shirt

Because of the cut of the tunic and because it lacked a collar, the shirt worn underneath was visible and bears mentioning. The shirt was in what was called the 'Russian cut'. It was roughly the same length as the tunic, but did not button all the way down the front (Image V:82). Instead, it opened on the left side of the collar and partially down the left side of the chest so it could be pulled on over the head. Then the opening was buttoned up, with two gold buttons on the left side of the collar. The collar and buttons were visible above the V-shaped neckline formed by the demi-caftan tunic. The colour of the shirt was raspberry.

Epaulettes

Officers wore guard infantry model epaulettes in full dress, either all gold or all silver with piping the colour of the shoulder straps. For some regiments, the epaulette included a monogram (Table V.6.a.1). See §V-3-1 for epaulette details.

Shoulder Straps

Other ranks wore shoulder straps in full dress. The shoulder straps were either red or raspberry in colour and often included monograms (Table V.6.a.1).

Officers wore shoulder straps in walking-out dress. The shoulder straps were the same colour as for the other ranks, but the styles of the monograms differed somewhat. The officers of the Kexholm and St Petersburg Regiments had embroidered monograms, except

V:82 Nicholas II in the Blouse of the 4th Rifle Regiment Note how the blouse opened and where the buttons are located. The blouse had to be pulled over the head when being put on.

in the 1st Company of each regiment, where they were made of silver metal and mounted on the strap.

The monograms of the Preobrazhensky, Semenovsky, Izmailovsky, Yegersky, Grenadier, Paul, and Volynsky Regiments and the 1st, 3rd, and 4th Rifles Regiments were made of metal and mounted on the strap. In the Preobrazhensky, Semenovsky, and Kexholm Regiments, the commanders and adjuncts of the 3rd Companies wore the monogram P. P. with an anchor, made of metal and mounted on the strap. Officers of the 4th Rifles had gold hussar braid on the shoulder strap, in addition to the monogram specified in Table V.6.a.1.

Gorget

The gorgets were worn only by officers of the Preobrazhensky, Semenovsky, Izmailovsky, Moscow, Finland, Lithuanian, Kexholm, St Petersburg, and Volynsky Regiments. The Yegersky, Grenadier, Paul, and 1st–4th Rifles Regiments did not have gorgets. For those regiments which had them, the gorgets varied in model. This meant different shapes and designs.

Preobrazhensky and Semenovsky Model

The gorget worn by the Preobrazhensky and Semenovsky Regiments was the same because they were brother regiments with the same origins. Uniquely, the design varied by rank. Centred on the crescent for all ranks was a gold crown, detailed with red, white and blue enamel.

Below the crown was the cross of St Andrew. For subalterns, the cross was gold, in raised relief work, and was flanked by gold palm branches (Image V:16(2)). For superior officers and generals, the cross was blue enamel, with the figure of St Andrew in flesh-coloured enamel, and the letters S, A, P, and R, one in each extremity of the cross. There were no palm branches on the superior officer's gorget (Image V:16(1)).

The top of the crescent read '1683–1850–1883' in metal lettering for all ranks. Subalterns and captains had additional script on the bottom of the crescent below the palm branches which read '1700 No 19' in memory of the Battle of Narva in 1700. The casualties among senior officers at the Battle of Narva were so high that the regiment ended up being commanded by subalterns and captains. In the 1st Company of the Preobrazhensky Regiment only, all ranks had '1741' and 'Ho 25' in metal on either side of the cross, the date Empress Elizabeth Petrovna ascended the throne.

For all ranks, the back of the gorget was lined in red cloth. It was worn around the neck, suspended from sky blue ribbon. The metal colours of the gorget and its detailing described above varied according to rank and is outlined in Table V.6.a.2.

Izmailovsky Model

The gorget worn by officers of the Izmailovsky Regiment was the 1731 model; it was more bib-shaped than crescent-shaped (Image V:16(3)). It measured 16.11 cm (6.34 inches) vertically at its longest point and 14.17 cm (5.58 inches) horizontally at its widest point. The gorget itself was made of polished metal, silver for subalterns and gold for superior officers and generals. Around the outside of the entire gorget was a metal border, 0.56 cm (0.22 inch) wide, which was grooved, giving it the appearance of being a double border. The border was silver for subalterns, gold for superior officers and generals.

Table V.6.a.2: Preobrazhensky and Semenovsky Regiments' Special Gorgets

Rank	Gorget	Border	1683–1850–1883	1700 No 19[a]	1741 Ho 25[b]
Second lieutenant	Silver	Gold	Silver	Silver	Gold
Lieutenant	Silver	Gold	Gold	Silver	Gold
Second-in-command	Gold	Silver	Silver	Silver	Gold
Captain	Gold	Gold	Gold	Silver	Gold
Colonel	Gold	Gold	Silver	---	Gold
General	Gold	Gold	Gold	---	Gold

Notes: [a] Subalterns and captains only.
[b] 1st Company of the Preobrazhensky Regiment only.

The designs on the gorget were the same for all ranks of officers. In the centre of the gorget was the double-headed imperial eagle, with raised wings. The eagle's body, tail, neck and wings were painted with black enamel. The eagle's heads and legs, as well as the main part of the three crowns (one on each head and a larger one over them both), the sceptre, and the orb were in matt gold. The detailing on the crowns and the eagle's beaks and eyes were painted with red enamel. On the eagle's breast was a shield of white enamel, bordered in gold. The shield had the cross of St Andrew in blue enamel, with the figure of the saint painted on it in white. Below that shield was another smaller shield, on the eagle's tail. It had the monogram of Empress Anna Ivanovna on it in gold. Below the eagle was a series of decorations, including two flags (larger, to the left of the eagle), two standards (smaller, with fringed edging, on its right), two halbards, two cannons, and two drums. The back of the gorget was lined in red cloth and it was worn around the neck, suspended from a sky blue ribbon.

Moscow, Finland, Lithuanian, and Volynsky Model

Officers of the Moscow, Finland, Lithuanian, and Volynsky Regiments all wore the same model of gorget because these four regiments were closely related to each other: the first two battalions of the Lithuanian Regiment had been used to form the Moscow Regiment, while the first battalion of the Finland Regiment had been taken to form the

Volynsky Regiment. Moreover, the Lithuanian and Volynsky Regiments each retained Polish elements in honour of their heritage.

The gorget was the 1808 model, bib-shaped with both the length at the longest points and the width measuring 13.34 cm (5.25 inches). It had a grooved triple border, 0.56 cm (0.22 inch) wide (Image V:16(4)). Both the border and the gorget itself were made of polished gold or silver. In the centre was the imperial double-headed eagle in matt-finish metal. Its right head was raised slightly higher than its left, and it held a crown of laurels in its left foot while the right foot held a torch and a bolt of lightning. The eagle's breast had a shield bearing the emblem of Moscow. Below the eagle was a laurel branch on the right and an oak branch on the left, and below the branches were decorations: four flags, two quartermaster's flags, two tessaks (a type of sword), two trumpets, two rifles with bayonets, two cannon swabs, four cannons, two timpanis, two grenades, two piles of cannonballs, a drum, a helmet, and an oboe.

The back of the gorget was lined with red cloth, and the gorget was worn around the neck on a sky blue ribbon. The colours of metal used for the various parts of the gorget varied by rank, and are elucidated in Table V.6.a.3.

Table V.6.a.3: Standard Gorgets

Rank	Gorget	Eagle and Decorations	Border
Second lieutenant	Silver	Silver	Gold
Lieutenant	Silver	Gold	Silver
Second-in-command	Silver	Gold	Gold
Captain	Gold	Silver	Gold
Colonel, general	Gold	Gold	Gold

St Petersburg Model

The gorget worn by subalterns of the St Petersburg Regiment was silver, in a rounded bib shape (Image V:16(5)). The lower border of the gorget had a gold garland decoration. In the centre of the gorget was a blue enamelled cross of St Andrew on a plain silver oval shield, surrounded by a gold garland. Above the shield and garland was a gold crown with red enamel detailing.

The gorget worn by superior officers and generals was the same design as for subalterns, but all of the metal parts were gold. The cross of St Andrew stayed blue, and the crown maintained its red enamel detailing.

The gorget for all ranks had red cloth lining on the back. It was worn suspended from the neck by silver or gilt cording.

Kexholm Model

The Kexholm Regiment had a gorget that was in the 1698 model. It was more U-shaped than the other gorgets, and had corners and flat edges at the top instead of having completely smooth rounded edges.

The gorget was entirely of silver metal for subalterns, entirely of gold metal for superior officers and generals. In the centre of the gorget was the cross of St Andrew with a crown above it, both in blue enamel. The figure of the saint was on the cross, painted with nude-coloured enamel.

For all ranks the gorget had red cloth lining on the back. It was worn suspended from the neck by gold or silver cording.

V:83 Yegersky Regiment
Note the unique braid on his collar and cuff and the white piping on the plastron and cuffs. The white piping shows that this regiment was in the 1st Guard Division.

V:84 Senior Officer of the Artillery or Engineers of the Guard
This shows what a guard officer looked like when standing up and wearing his kiver. The collar and cuff lace was worn by technical troops.

V:86 Side View of a Subaltern in the Paul Regiment
This provides a good view of the trim of the bag worn behind the metal mitre. Note the lace on his collar.

V:85 Subaltern of the St Petersburg Regiment
Note braid on collar. Also note the large gorget worn by this regiment and the badge worn on his left chest just below the plastron.

V:87 Semenovsky Regiment
Note white trim on his flyaway plastron, showing this regiment was in the 1st Guard Division, and the special lace on his cuffs and collars. He is wearing the gorget worn by officers of the Semenovsky and Preobrazhensky Regiments. On his left chest, he has a regimental badge of the Semenovsky Regiment and a school badge of the Corps de Pages.

V:88 Guard Officer in Undress Blouse
The white trim on the cuffs and down the front means that his regiment is in the 1st Guard Division. He is wearing the gorget of the Izmailovsky Regiment.

V:90 Highly Decorated Russian Senior Officer
The lace on his collar was worn by the Preobrazhensky and the Lithuanian Regiments.

V:89 Subaltern of the Izmailovsky Regiment in Full Dress
Note the white trim on his plastron indicating 1st Guard Division. The lace on his collar and cuffs and his gorget were both worn by the Izmailovsky Regiment.

V:91 Subaltern of the Semenovsky Regiment
Note the white trim on his plastron and cuffs and the regimental badge on his left chest. He is wearing the gorget of a junior officer in spite of what seems to be his advanced age. Note the Semenovsky lace on his cuffs.

WALKING-OUT TUNIC

The walking-out tunic for all regiments of the guard infantry except the 4th Rifles was the redingote. It was made of czar's green cloth and double-breasted, with two rows of six buttons. The collar was rounded and was the same colour as the full dress tunic collar. If the full dress tunic collar had piping, then the redingote collar did as well, in the same colour (Table V.6.a.1). The redingote had pockets on the rear skirt like the tunic, with two buttons and the same piping. The cuffs were straight, not pointed, and were czar's green like the rest of the walking-out tunic. They were piped in white for the 1st Infantry Division and the 1st Rifles, red for the 2nd Infantry Division, yellow for the 3rd Infantry Division, and raspberry for the 2nd and 3rd Rifles.

The 4th Rifles did not have a walking-out tunic. For undress they could wear their normal tunic and shirt, or even just the raspberry-coloured shirt without the tunic with shoulder boards (V:82).

PANTALOONS AND TROUSERS

Both officers and other ranks wore pantaloons in full dress. These were the colour of the tunic, so officers' pantaloons were czar's green, the other ranks' black. Officers had additional full-length trousers, which were also czar's green.

Both the pantaloons and the full-length trousers had coloured piping running down the outside of each leg. The piping was red for the regiments of the 1st and 2nd Guard Infantry Divisions, yellow for the 3rd Guard Infantry Division, and raspberry for the four regiments of Guard Rifles.

UNIFORM ACCESSORIES

4th Rifles' Boots

The 4th Rifles wore fairly flexible black boots that came to the knee like other infantry boots. They differed in that the top had a 2.23 cm (0.88 inch) 'V' on each boot, coloured raspberry for the officers. Other ranks wore the same type of boot, but they had a braid band around the top of their boots that was narrower than the band worn by officers.

Officers' Accessories

Officers of the guard infantry and rifles wore the standard model officer's sash in full dress, with standard white wrist gloves worn for full dress and brown wrist gloves for regular or walking-out dress.

Officers had black shoes which could be worn in walking-out dress with the trousers.

Other Ranks' Accessories

Other ranks of the guard infantry regiments and the 1st, 2nd, and 3rd Rifles wore a leather belt over the tunic in full dress. The first three battalions of the Preobrazhensky, Semenovsky, Izmailovsky, Moscow, Grenadier, Paul, Lithuanian, Kexholm, and St Petersburg Regiments all had white leather belts. The 4th Battalions of each of these regiments – which had been formed from the rifle companies of those regiments – had black leather belts. All four battalions of the Yegersky, Finland, and Volynsky Regiments and the 1st, 2nd, and 3rd Rifle Regiments also had black leather belts. The belt plate was the colour of the button (see Table V.6.a.1) and had the double-headed eagle on it.

Other ranks of the 4th Rifle Regiment wore a belt that was made of raspberry-coloured cloth. The belt buckle was covered with the same raspberry cloth.

Unlike the officers, the other ranks were not assigned gloves for full dress.

Rifle Slings

The other ranks of the guard infantry and rifle regiments carried red leather rifle slings in full dress.[86] This distinguished them from the line soldiers, whose rifle slings were brown leather.

Other Accessories

All ranks of the guard infantry and the 1st, 2nd, and 3rd Rifle Regiments wore standard knee-high black leather boots in full dress. See §V-3-1 for more details on boots.

The Guard Grenadier Regiment had a unique accessory, the aiguillette. It was worn in both full and walking-out dress by both the officers and the other ranks of the regiment (Image V:92). The Grenadier Regiment was awarded this decoration by Catherine II in recognition of the victory at the Battle of Kagul against the Turks in 1770. Aiguillettes were later replaced by litzen under Alexander I, but were reintroduced with the uniform modifications of 1913. The aiguillette was worn on the right shoulder, gathered into several loops and passing under the epaulette or shoulder strap. For the officers, the aiguillette cording and the metal points on the end were both gold. Other ranks had yellow wool aiguillette cording with brass points. There was a silver monogram 'E II' for Catherine II on both the officer and other rank model of aiguillette. See §V-3-1 for more details on accessories.

Regimental Honours

The Paul Regiment was allowed to march with their rifles held in the 'attack' position.[87] For years, this was a unique honour in the Russian army. Then, in 1912, the 11th Grenadiers gained this honour thanks to some inner-palace, inner-family politics with the czar. Image V:93 shows the Paul Regiment marching in the attack position. They also hold their rifles in this position when standing at attention for review (Image V:94).

V:92 Young Subaltern in the Guard Grenadier Regiment
Note the aiguillette worn on his right shoulder, an honour unique to this regiment which was won before they were a guard regiment. Also note the distinctive lace on his collar and the way his plastron juts out at the top.

V:93 The Paul Regiment in their Summer Uniforms
They are marching with their rifles held at the attack position. For most of the nineteenth and early twentieth century, holding their rifles this way was an honour held only by the Paul Regiment. In 1912, the 11th Grenadiers were also given the honour of marching with their rifles at the attack position. Note the very long strides being taken by these marching men.

V:94 Troops of the Paul Regiment on Parade
Note how they are holding their rifles at the attack position, and also how their mitres look when worn by a mass of men.

§V-6-b COMBINED GUARD INFANTRY

On 1 March 1881, Emperor Alexander II was assassinated. As a result of this event, it was determined that a special guard detachment should be devoted to the protection of the Imperial Family. Thus, on 23 March 1881, a special guard company was created. It initially included men from the 1st and 2nd Guard Infantry divisions, the Guard Rifle battalions, and the Guard Reserve Infantry.

In time, additional guardsmen and infantry line men were added to this unit. Then, in 1907, the battalion was reconfigured as a regiment, with two battalions of four companies each. In this new form, the regiment included men representing all of the line infantry regiments. Thus, on any given day the emperor might encounter individuals from all parts of his army, a system which helped him to monitor troops' morale.[88]

Because of the unique nature of the regiment as a personal guard for the emperor, it was not deployed with the rest of the army for wars. Thus, the Combined Guard Regiment does not have the distinguished battle history shared by most other guard regiments. Additionally, the Combined Guard Regiment did not have a single standard uniform. Instead, all of the men in the regiment wore the uniform of their original regiment. This system, wherein a soldier's original regimental affiliation was maintained by his uniform, undoubtedly made it easier for the emperor to identify the individual parts of his army that were represented within the regiment.

§V-7 LINE CAVALRY

§V-7-a DRAGOONS[89]

§V-7-a-1 DRAGOONS TO 1907/1908

The dragoon arm goes right back to the beginnings of the Russian army under Peter the Great. In 1694, Peter assumed the rule of the Muscovite state from his mother. In 1698, a revolt of the Streltsy – the part-time troops that passed for a standing army – took place. The goal was to depose Peter and put his half-sister Sophia in his place. The revolt was put down while Peter was in Western Europe, but on his return he destroyed the Streltsy, and, in effect, the old army.

Peter had already raised a few Western-style regiments (See §V-6-a), and the city-state had a small number of regiments trained along Western lines and commanded by Western mercenary officers.[90]

Now these became the only soldiers in the Russian army. The czar could also call on the Cossacks, but they were an uncertain tool. Peter began raising an army of regiments trained in the Western style. At the end of Peter's rule, there were thirty-three dragoon regiments.[91]

Thereafter, dragoons were almost always a part of the Russian army. Alexander III chose to transform all the line cavalry into dragoons and give them quasi-peasant dress as uniforms.

Upon the accession in 1881 of Czar Alexander III, a new, plainer and cheaper style of uniform was adopted for the Russian army. For the cavalry, this meant a

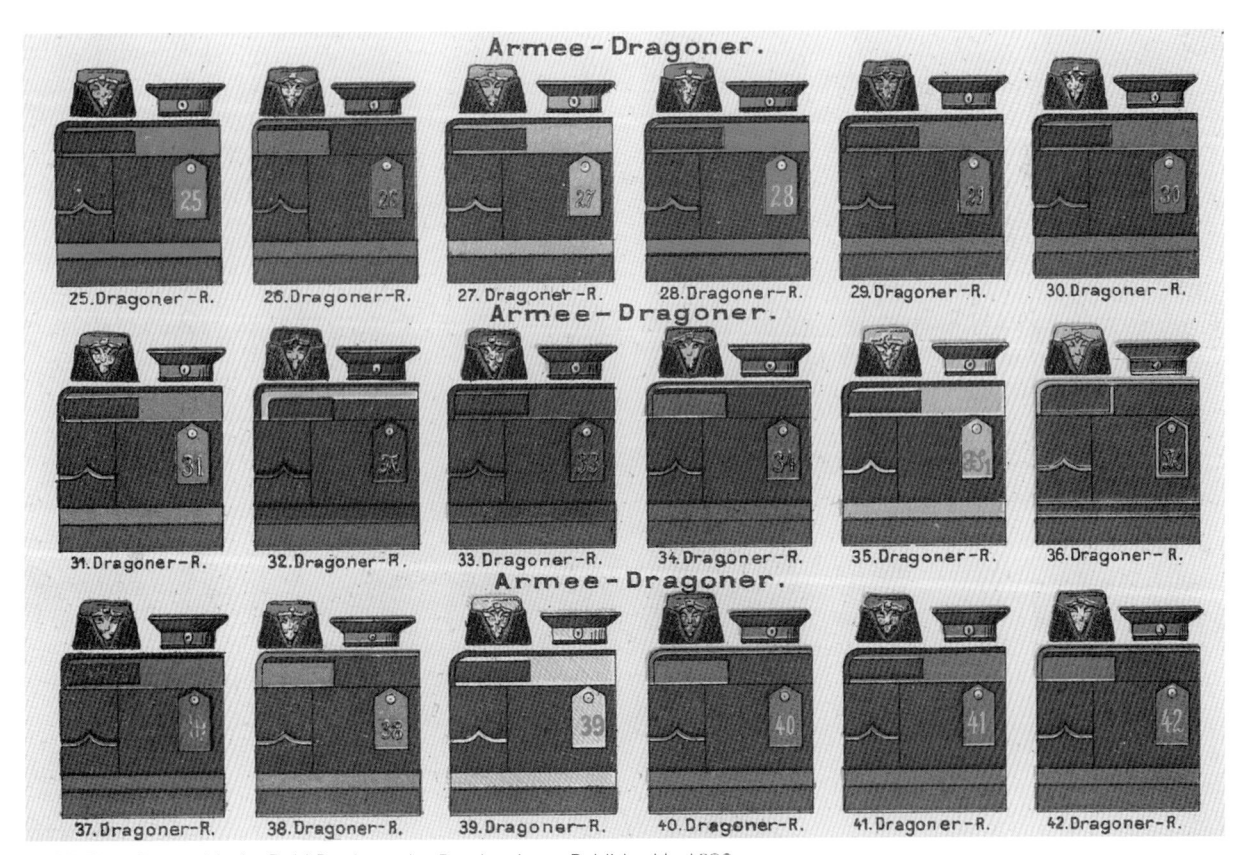

V:95 Plate from a Moritz Ruhl Book on the Russian Army Published in 1890
At this time, all cavalry in the Russian army were dragoons. This shows the similarity of all the uniforms worn by dragoon regiments during the period up to 1908.

V:96 Dragunka (Dragoon's Cap) for Enlisted Men of the 2nd Pskov Dragoons, 1881–1907
Note how it is cut away in front, leaving space for the double-headed eagle badge.

V:97 Dragoon Officer, Before 1908
Note his headdress and his tunic without buttons.

dark green[92] somewhat formless double-breasted tunic without buttons, fastened with hooks that did not show. The cuffs were the colour of the jacket, outlined with trim in the regimental colour. There were no buttons on the cuff; the only buttons were on the shoulder for the shoulder straps. The colour of the buttons varied by regiment (see Table V.7.a.1.1) NCOs wore trim in their button colour to show their rank. On the upper left arm, chevrons were worn to show years of service (Images C64 and V:95).

The headdress was a short fur truncated fez-like item, 7.62 or 10.16 cm (about 3 or 4 inches) high (Image V:96). The top was made of cloth. In the front, the fur had a pronounced notch in it to show the cloth top and its colour, which varied by regiment (Table V.7.a.1.1). In the notch the guard regiments wore a St Andrew's guard star. The line wore a double-headed eagle. Above these badges were worn distinction banners by those regiments entitled to one.

The breeches were grey-blue with piping that matched the tunic cuff piping. Long and fairly soft black boots that came to the knees were worn (Image V:97).

Post-1907 Dragoon Uniform

A series of reforms was undertaken to improve the morale of the Russian soldiers following their shocking defeat in the Russo-Japanese War. One of the morale-building steps was to bring back the old distinctions of lancers, hussars, and cuirassiers and their uniforms. While no one could bring themselves to reissue cuirasses, they did designate some dragoons as cuirassiers and did reintroduce a type of cuirassier uniform for this type of dragoon.

These changes opened the door for the regiments to press for old regimental distinctions on their uniforms. One example is the 2nd Pskov Dragoons, who, after 1910, had one of the most unusual helmet badges in the world, a miniature cuirass.[93] The regiment attempted to gain permission to wear cuirasses and then to wear forage caps in the colours worn by cuirassiers. They based this effort on a claim that during the Napoleonic War they had defeated a French cuirassier regiment, and as an honour they had been allowed to wear the regiment's cuirasses. They were denied both of these honours. Eventually, the czar's mother, Maria Feodorovna, became involved.

Table V.7.a.1.1 Russian Dragoon Regiments: Uniforms 1881–1908 [94]

Regiment	Metal	Tunic Collar[a]	Collar Shield	Colour of: Cloth Portion of Headdress; Shoulder Strap; Piping on Cuff and Pantaloons	Officers' Buttonholes
1st Moscow Life	Gold	Dark green P: red	Red	Red	Simple
2nd St Petersburg	Gold	Dark green P: brick red	Brick red	Brick red	Distinction
3rd Sumy	Gold	Dark green P: pink	Pink	Pink	Distinction
4th Pskov Life	Silver	Dark green P: pink	Pink	Pink	Simple
5th Kurland Life	Gold	Dark green P: orange	Orange	Orange	Simple
6th Pavlograd Life	Gold	Dark green P: turquoise	Turquoise	Turquoise	Simple
7th New Russia	Gold	Dark green P: light blue	Light blue	Light blue	Braid[b]
8th Smolensk	Gold	White P: dark green	Dark Green	White	Simple
9th Elizabetgrad	Gold	Dark green P: lilac	Lilac	Lilac	Braid*
10th Ekaterinoslav	Gold	Light green P: dark green	Dark green	Light green	Distinction
11th Kharkov	Silver	Orange P: dark green	Dark green	Orange	Braid[b]
12th Mariupol	Gold	Dark green P: brown	Brown	Brown	Braid[b]
13th Kargopol	Silver	White P: dark green	Dark Green	White	Braid[b]
14th Lithuanian	Silver	Dark green P: red	Red	Red	Braid[b]
15th Alexandria	Silver	Pink P: dark green	Dark Green	Pink	Braid[b]
16th Glukhov	Silver	Dark green P: white	White	White	Braid[b]
17th Volynsky	Silver	Dark green P: brick red	Brick red	Brick red	Braid[b]
18th Klyastitsi	Silver	Dark green P: lilac	Lilac	Lilac	Braid[b]
19th Kinburn	Gold	Dark green P: yellow	Yellow	Yellow	Braid[b]
20th Olviopol	Silver	Brown[c] P: dark green	Dark Green	Brown	Braid[b]
21st White Russian	Silver	Brick red P: brick red	Dark green	Brick red	Braid[b]

Regiment	Metal	Tunic Collar[a]	Collar Shield	Colour of: Cloth Portion of Headdress; Shoulder Strap; Piping on Cuff and Pantaloons	Officers' Buttonholes
22nd Astrakhan	Silver	Dark green P: yellow	Yellow	Yellow	Braid[b]
23rd Voznesensk	Silver	Dark green P: brown	Brown	Brown	Braid[b]
24th Lubny	Silver	Yellow P: dark green	Dark green	Yellow	Braid[b]
25th Kazan	Gold	Red P: red	Dark green	Red	Braid[b]
26th Bug	Gold	Brick red P: dark green	Dark green	Brick red	Distinction
27th Kiev	Gold	Pink P: dark green	Dark green	Pink	Braid[b]
28th Novgorod	Silver	Red P: dark green	Dark green	Red	Braid[b]
29th Odessa	Gold	Lilac P: dark green	Dark green	Lilac	Braid[b]
30th Ingermanland	Silver	Lilac P: dark green	Dark green	Lilac	Braid[b]
31st Riga	Gold	Light blue P: dark green	Dark green	Light blue	Braid[b]
32nd Chuguev	Gold	Dark green P: white	White	White	Simple
33rd Izyum	Gold	Brown P: dark green	Dark green	Brown	Distinction
34th Starodub	Silver	Light blue P: dark green	Dark green	Light blue	Braid[b]
35th Belgorod	Gold	Yellow P: dark green	Dark green	Yellow	Simple
36th Akhtyrka[d]	Gold	Brown P: yellow	Yellow	Yellow	Distinction
37th Military Order (St George)	Gold	Orange P: dark green	Black[e]	Orange	Simple
38th Vladimir	Silver	Dark green P: light blue	Light blue	Light blue	Braid[b]
39th Narva	Silver	Dark green P: orange	Orange	Orange	Braid[b]
40th Little Russian	Gold	Dark green P: light green	Light green	Light green	Braid[b]
41st Yamburg	Silver	Light green P: dark green	Dark green	Light green	Braid[b]
42nd Mitau	Silver	Dark green P: light green	Light green	Light green	Braid[b]
43rd Tver	Gold	Dark green P: raspberry	Raspberry	Raspberry	Distinction

Regiment	Metal	Tunic Collar[a]	Collar Shield	Colour of: Cloth Portion of Headdress; Shoulder Strap; Piping on Cuff and Pantaloons	Officers' Buttonholes
44th Nizhni-Novgorod	Gold	Raspberry P: dark green	Dark green	Raspberry	Distinction – double
45th Seversk	Silver	Dark green P: raspberry	Raspberry	Raspberry	Distinction – double
46th Pereyaslav	Silver	Raspberry P: dark green	Dark green	Raspberry	Simple
47th Tatar[f]	Silver	Dark green P: turquoise	Turquoise	Turquoise	Braid[b]
48th Ukrainian[f]	Silver	Turquoise P: dark green	Dark green	Turquoise	Braid[b]
49th Archangelgorod[g]	Gold	Turquoise P: dark green	Dark green	Turquoise	Braid[b]
50th Irkutsk[d,g]	Silver	Brown P: yellow	Yellow	Yellow	Braid[b]

Notes: [a] P = Piping.
[b] Between 1881 and 1908 there were three types of buttonholes on dragoon uniforms. Two were embroidered; there was regular embroidery for simple buttonholes and special embroidery for distinction buttonholes. The third type was made of braid instead of embroidery. Braid buttonholes were discontinued when uniforms were changed in 1908, and most regiments which had worn braid buttonholes prior to 1908 had simple litzen on their new uniforms.
[c] See §V-7-c, Line Hussars, Uniform Changes of 1908, Attila, for an explanation of why they wore brown.
[d] Had a brown tunic instead of standard dark green.
[e] Black velvet for officers only.
[f] Formed in 1891.
[g] Formed in 1895.

With her influence, the regiment was given the right to have an image of a cuirass on their helmets instead of the normal double-headed eagle.

The headpiece badge was a small cuirass breastplate with a guard star of St Andrew on it (Image V:98). The badge jutted out like a real breastplate, so only the edges were attached to the helmet. The central portion was hollow, coming out, at one point, ⅛ vershok (0.56 cm or 0.22 inch) from the helmet. There were two types of cuirass badges, one for officers and one for other ranks.

V:98 2nd Pskov Dragoons Regiment
Note special badge on the front of the helmet in the shape of a cuirass. Officers and other ranks had slightly different cuirass badges.

Officer's Helmet Cuirass of the Pskov Dragoons

The officer's cuirass was polished tombac with a ¼ vershok (1.11 cm, 0.44 inch) silvered trim on the neck and arm openings and along the bottom. The cuirass was very detailed: rivets, waist belt, chest straps and chain links. The polished silvered star was soldered in the centre of the breastplate. In the centre of the eight-rayed star was a silvered matt circle. In the centre of the circle was a silvered crowned 'M', for Empress Maria Feodorovna. The cuirass had a raised silver matt ridge down the centre, foreshortened to give a trompe l'oeil depiction of thickness.

The cuirass was very colourful. The waist belt was matt silver with a polished silver buckle. The chest straps were filled with pink enamel. Along the sides were enamel strips that gave the appearance of flat polished gilt chain links. The chest belt straps below the chain links had a pink enamel centre and polished matte edging. At the top of the chest straps were tiny matt gilt lion heads and at the bottom polished gilt end pieces with rivets and engraved palm branches.

The badge was fastened to the helmet by pins and screws.

Other Ranks' Helmet Cuirass of the Pskov Dragoons

The cuirass of the other ranks was made of stamped white metal (a copper, zinc, and nickel mixture). This badge also had a raised centre ridge and an eight-rayed star stamped on the centre of the cuirass. The star had the monogram 'M' with a crown and was bent along its vertical axis to conform to the ridge on the cuirass.

The badge showed the linked chains and end pieces of the chest straps, rivets, the waist belt, and the buckle. The surface of the plate was polished; the star and the chest strap except for its indentations, rivets, and waist belt buckle were painted in yellow lacquer. The waist belt was covered in a light brown enamel. The ends of the chest straps were painted with scarlet enamel. The cuirass also had foreshortening to give the illusion of thickness.

The badge was fastened to the helmet by means of leather or wooden pins and soldering.[95]

The new headpiece badge, announced in November 1910, prompted speculation by military historians over whether, and where, the French cuirasses were captured. The controversy went on until World War I, and it is still occasionally revisited with no clear answer.

The 13th Dragoons

The 13th Dragoons carried the unusual name 'Military Order Dragoon Regiment'. The Military Order was understood to refer to the St George Order or the St George Cross, which is the equivalent of the British Victoria Cross or the US Medal of Honor. Given this and with the knowledge that the regiment, then the 3rd Cuirassiers, had its name changed to the Military Order Regiment in the late 1770s, one naturally concludes that the regiment was awarded this order for a spectacular feat of arms. Reports of such a feat are not readily available in any English sources.

After research was conducted and cross-checked using English and Russian regimental histories and other available sources in Moscow, it was determined that what seems to have happened is that in the late 1770s the officers of the regiment were replaced. The new officers all held the Cross of St George. It is not clear whether this was done because of a whim of the ruler or to make the regiment a model training regiment. Because all the officers had a St George medal, the regiment's name was changed to the St George Order Regiment. It was simple chance that the 3rd Cuirassiers was chosen for this officer exchange.

§V-7-a-2 Dragoons after 1907/1908

Uniform[96]

Headdress

In 1914, three distinct types of headdresses were worn by different groupings of dragoon regiments. The 1st, 3rd, 5th, 7th, 11th, 15th, 19th and 20th Dragoons and the 2nd, 4th, 6th, 8th, 9th, 10th, 12th, 13th and 14th Dragoon Cuirassiers all wore the standard dragoon helmet, though with slight variations. The 16th, 17th, and 18th Dragoons, which were part of the Caucasus Corps, wore a fur bonnet in the so-called Asian style. Finally, the Premorsky Dragoons wore a tall cylindrical black fur headdress called a papakha.

Crested Dragoon Helmet

The standard dragoon helmet was made of black patent leather and had a black leather visor with a 0.83 cm (0.33 inch) border in the button colour (Images V:99–V:101). The chinstrap was made up of two rows of metal scales in the button colour. On the right side of the helmet, below where the chinstrap was fastened, was a large round cockade in the imperial colours (Image V:100). See §V-3-1 for cockade details.

The crest of the standard dragoon helmet was transverse, meaning it ran across the top of the helmet from side to side rather than from front to back. The crest was made of bearskin, black for the standard dragoons (Image V:102) and white for the dragoon cuirassiers (Image V:103). The crest was 8.89 cm (3.5 inches) thick in the middle and decreased in thickness towards the ends, so the thickness of the crest at either end ranged from 2.22 cm (0.88 inch) to 2.78 cm (1.09 inches). The maximum length of the hair making up the crest was 4.45 cm (1.75 inches).

Crested Helmet for Dragoon Cuirassiers

The helmet of the dragoon cuirassiers was exactly like that of the standard dragoons except the transverse crest was coloured white (Image V:103).

Helmet Badge and Distinction Badges

On the front of the helmet was the double-headed eagle, either gold or silver according to the button colour. If the regiment had a distinction badge, it was placed above the eagle (Tables V.7.a.2.1 and V.7.a.2.2 detail regiments entitled to these badges, and see Image V:101). Overall, 57 per cent of dragoon regiments had been awarded a distinction badge.

The table gives a breakdown of the three different types of dragoons:

Dragoon Type	Number of Regiments	Regiments with Distinction Banner	Percentage[a]
Standard dragoons	9	5	56%
Dragoon cuirassiers	9	4	44%
Caucasus dragoons	3	3	100%
Total	21[b]	12[b]	57%

Notes: [a] Percentage of each type with a distinction banner.
[b] Includes the Premorsky Dragoons.

Other Helmet Elements

Several dragoon regiments had special decorations added to their standard crested dragoon helmet. As described in §V-7-a-1, the 2nd Pskov Dragoons had miniature cuirasses decorated with the guard star of St. Andrew on the front of their helmets in place of the imperial eagle (Image V:98). The 13th Dragoons of the Military Order of St George replaced the eagle with the gilt star of St George, 8.20 cm (3.23 inches) in diameter (Image V:104). In the centre of the star was an orange circle bearing the monogram of St George, surrounded by a black band inscribed with the Military Order motto: 'For Service and Courage'. The 13th Dragoons also had an additional unique feature: flaming grenade decorations mounted on each side of the chinstrap.

Papakha

The papakha worn by the Premorsky Dragoons was a type of native headdress. It had a cylindrical body that narrowed slightly, somewhat like a fez, and was made of black fur. But instead of having a flat top like a fez, it had a domed cloth top that was the colour of the tunic cloth (czar's green for officers, black for troops), with trim around the perimeter and in the shape of a cross along the seams of the dome (Image V:105). The dome would collapse when worn so it could not be seen. On the front of the fur body of the papakha was a cockade, with a distinction banner mounted above it if one had been earned (Image V:105). (Five of the six squadrons of the Premorsky Dragoons had one. See §V-2-2.) See §V-3-1 for cockade details.

V:99 Enlisted Man's Helmet of the 20th Dragoons, After 1908
Note lack of a distinction banner.

V:101 Front View of a Line Dragoon Helmet of the 3rd, 5th, or 11th Dragoons, After 1908
Note the placement of the distinction banner.

V:100 Side View of a Line Dragoon Helmet of the 3rd, 5th, or 11th Dragoons, After 1908
Note distinction banner behind the crown on the front plate and the very large cockade.

V:102 Officer of the Line Dragoons with Distinction Banner

V:103 The Czar Nicholas II's Daughter, Maria, in the uniform of the 9th (Cuirassiers) Dragoons
Note the white colour of the transverse crest on her helmet and the Swedish cuffs. She is wearing cuirassier-style braid on her tunic. Also note that she is wearing a regimental badge on the left side of her tunic.

V:105 Premorsky Dragoons
This regiment was stationed in the extreme far east, and they were the only dragoon regiment to wear a papahka in full dress. This drawing shows the front, back, and top of the papahka, as well as the piping on the rear of the dragoon's tunic. Note the officers wore cap lines even though they did not fasten to the papahka.

V:104 Officer of the 13th St George Order (Cuirassier) Dragoons
Note the special star of the St George Order on the front of his helmet. As a cuirassier-style dragoon, he is wearing the transverse crest and the cuirassier trim down the front of his tunic and at the collar and cuffs.

V:106 Subaltern of the 17th or 18th Dragoons
This was a Caucasus unit. Note the distinction-style litzen on his collar and the monogram on his subaltern's epaulette. Also note the Caucasus-style cartridge holders on his tunic and the special bonnet.

Table V.7.a.2.1: Line Dragoons in 1914

Regiment	Button Colour	Tunic Collar	Tunic Collar Shield	Tunic Piping and Cuff Colour	Officer Epaulette Colour[a]	Troop Shoulder Straps[b]	Officer Litzen[c]	Trooper Litzen[c]	Monograms	Distinction Banner[d]	Other Notes
1st	Gold	Same as tunic[e]	Red	Red	Gold	Red	Gold simple	White simple[f]	P.P.-A III[g]	—	B, C, H
3rd	Gold	Same as tunic[e]	Raspberry	Raspberry	Gold	Raspberry	Gold simple	None	None	Simple	A, C, I
5th	Gold	Same as tunic[e]	White	White	Gold	White	Gold simple	None	None	Simple	A, C, I
7th	Silver	Same as tunic[e]	Yellow	Yellow	Silver	Yellow	Silver simple	None	None	—	B, C, I
11th	Gold	Light blue	Same as tunic[e]	Light blue[h]	Gold	Light blue	Gold simple	None	None	Descriptive	A, C, I
15th	Silver	Raspberry	Same as tunic[e]	Raspberry[h]	Silver	Raspberry	Silver simple	White simple[j]	A III[i]	Descriptive	A, C, H
16th	Gold	Same as tunic[e]	Raspberry	Raspberry	Gold	Raspberry	Gold distinction	None	A[k]	Descriptive	A, D, H
17th	Gold	Raspberry	Same as tunic[e]	Raspberry[h]	Gold[l]	Raspberry	Gold distinction[m]	St George[m]	N II[n]	Simple	A, D, E, H
18th	Silver	Same as tunic[e]	Raspberry	Raspberry	Silver	Raspberry	Silver distinction[m]	St George[m]	C IX[o]	Simple	A, D, E, H
19th	Silver	Same as tunic[e]	Red	Red	Silver	Red	Silver simple	None	None	—	B, C, I
20th	Silver	Yellow[p]	Same as tunic[e]	Yellow[h,p]	Silver	Yellow[p]	Silver simple	None	None	—	B, C, I
Premorsky	Gold	Same as tunic[e]	None	See notes	Gold	Yellow	Gold simple	None	None[q]	Descriptive	A, F, G

Notes: [a] Officer epaulettes were made of metal. The embossed monogram, when present, was probably in the contrasting metal colour (silver for gold epaulettes or gold for silver epaulettes) unless otherwise noted.
[b] Shoulder strap piping was in the tunic colour for all except the Premorsky Dragoons, who did not have piping on the shoulder straps.
[c] Unless otherwise noted, all litzen were in the chapter shape. Standard litzen for officers was one simple litzen on each side of the collar and on each cuff. For troops the standard uniform had no litzen.
[d] See §V-2-2 for more details on the banners.
[e] Czar's green for officers, black for troops. The tunics worn by the officers were easily distinguished from those worn by the other ranks.
[f] Single litzen at collar; no litzen at cuffs.
[g] Combined monogram of Peter the Great and Alexander III.
[h] The top and front of the collar was piped in the colour of the tunic rather than the colour of the rest of the piping and cuffs.
[i] Single litzen at both collar and cuffs.
[j] Monogram of Alexander III.
[k] Monogram of Crown Prince Grand Duke Alexis.
[l] Embossed monogram was in gold, the colour of the epaulette, rather than the inverse metal colour.
[m] Double litzen at collar; single litzen at cuffs.
[n] Monogram of Nicholas II.
[o] Monogram of the King of Denmark.
[p] Up to 1907, the regimental colour for the 20th Dragoon Regiment was light blue. In 1908, it changed to yellow.
[q] The Premorsky Dragoon Regiment did not technically have a monogram. However, since it did not have a regimental number either; 'Пpм,' an abbreviation of Premorsky, was on the other ranks' shoulder straps. This abbreviation followed the rules governing regimental numbers, and was therefore not included on the officers' epaulettes.

A: The headdress had a double-headed eagle with a distinction banner above it.
B: The helmet had a double-headed eagle.
C: Black transverse bearskin crest on the helmet.
D: Caucasus bonnet instead of regular crested dragoon helmet.
E: Six antique cartridges on either side of the chest of the tunic. Officers had a small medallion above each set of cartridges with fine chains running from the medallion to the cartridges (see Image V:106).
F: Instead of having tunic cuffs and tunic piping in facing colour like the rest of the line dragoon regiments, the Premorsky Dragoons had cuffs that were the same colour as their tunic, czar's green for the officers and black for the troops, with piping (standard dragoon cuffs did not have piping). All of the tunic piping, including the collar and cuff piping, was yellow.
G: Wore a fur cap, like that worn by the Siberian Rifles (see Image V:105).
H: Monogram included a crown.
I: In the absence of a monogram, the other ranks' shoulder strap had the regimental number as its marking.

Table V.7.a.2.2: Dragoons (Cuirassiers) in 1914

Regiment	Button Colour[a]	Tunic Collar	Tunic Collar Shield	Tunic Piping and Cuff Colour[b]	Officer Epaulette Colour[c]	Troop Shoulder Straps[d]	Officer Litzen[e]	Trooper Litzen[e]	Monograms	Distinction Banner[f]	Notes
2nd	Silver	White	Pink	Pink	Silver[g]	Pink	Silver simple	White plain[h]	M.Θ.[i]	–	C, E, F, G
4th	Silver	White	Orange	Orange	Silver	Orange	Silver distinction	None	None	Simple	A, E, H
6th	Silver	White	Light blue	Light blue	Silver	Light blue	Silver simple	White plain[j]	E II[k]	Simple	A, E, G
8th	Silver	White	Yellow	Yellow	Silver	Yellow	Silver simple double[l]	None	H. H.[m]	–	B, E, G
9th	Gold	White	Red	Red	Gold	Red	Gold simple	None	None	–	B, E, H
10th	Gold	White	Raspberry	Raspberry	Gold	Raspberry	Gold simple	None	W[n]	–	B, E, G
12th	Gold	White	Light blue	Light blue	Gold	Light blue	Gold simple	None	None	Descriptive	A, E, H
13th	Gold	White	Black	White	Gold	White	Gold simple	None	None	–	D, E, H
14th	Gold	White	Light green	Light green	Gold	Light green	Gold simple	None	None	Simple	B, E, H

Notes: [a] Cuirassier tunics did not have buttons down the front of the tunic, but they could have them on their cuffs. The term 'button colour' is used here only for convenience and consistency; it is used here as a term of art.
[b] Collar was piped in white.
[c] Officer epaulettes were made of metal. The embossed monogram, when present, was probably in the contrasting metal colour (silver for gold epaulettes or gold for silver epaulettes) unless otherwise noted.
[d] Shoulder strap piping was white for all except the 13th Dragoons, who had orange shoulder strap piping.
[e] Unless otherwise noted, all litzen were in the chapter shape. Standard litzen for officers was one simple litzen on each side of the collar and two simple litzen on each cuff. For troops the standard uniform had no litzen.
[f] See §V-2-2, Distinction Banners, for banner type.
[g] Embossed monogram was in silver; the colour of the epaulette, rather than the inverse metal colour.
[h] Single litzen at collar; double litzen at cuffs.
[i] Empress Maria Feodorovna.
[j] Single litzen at collar; no litzen at cuffs.
[k] Catherine II.
[l] Notation of 'double' refers to the collar litzen, which normally would have been single. The cuffs had double litzen as well, but that was standard.
[m] Grand Duke Nicholas Nikolaevich.
[n] King of Württemberg.

A: The helmet had a double-headed eagle with a distinction banner above it.
B: The helmet had a double-headed eagle.
C: The helmet of the 2nd Dragoons had an unusual badge on it. The badge consisted of a cuirass with a star or St Andrew on it.
D: The 13th Dragoons of the Order of St George had grenades instead of buttons on their collars. For the officers, the grenade was on the litzen. For the troops, who did not have litzen, the grenade was sewn directly to the collar. In both cases, the grenade was situated so that the flames pointed to the outside. They also had the star of St George on the front of their helmets.
E: White transverse bearskin crest on the helmet.
F: The 2nd Cuirassier Dragoons were one of only two regiments who maintained the crown design on their buttons instead of changing to the double-headed eagle when the buttons changed as part of the uniform modifications of 1907 (the other was the 13th Grenadiers).
G: Monogram included a crown.
H: In the absence of a monogram, the other ranks' shoulder strap had the regimental number as its marking.

The trim (perimeter and cross) on the upper cloth cap of the papakha varied by rank. Generals had 2.22 cm (0.88 inch) general's (zigzag) braid, while officers had gold braid in a tight square weave ('belt-style' braid). The other ranks had yellow piping.

Asian Bonnet

The Asian bonnet worn by the 16th, 17th, and 18th Dragoon Regiments of the Caucasus Cavalry Division was made up of two main parts: a black fur band 10 cm (3.94 inches) high, and a cloth domed top, 6.67 cm (2.63 inches) high (Image V:106). The cloth top had piping sewn in a cross on the seams and braid around the perimeter which varied according to rank. For the 16th Dragoons, the domed top was the colour of the tunic, with raspberry coloured piping. The 17th and 18th Dragoons had the inverse, with the domed top in raspberry and the piping in the colour of the tunic. On the front of the fur headband was an imperial eagle in the button colour, with a distinction banner and cockade mounted above (Image V:106). See §V-3-1 for cockade details.

Officers' Asian Bonnet

For officers, the black fur headband was made of karakul, a particular type of wool from the Central Asian karakul sheep. The cloth dome was topped with a metal half-sphere in the button colour which covered the place where the piping crossed. The piping was either raspberry or the colour of the tunic. The braid around the perimeter of the cloth dome varied according to rank and was either gold or silver according to the button colour. Subalterns had 1.67 cm (0.66 inch) wide square-weave 'basic' braid. Superior officers had the same braid as subalterns, but also had an additional 0.56 cm (0.22 inch) wide, diagonally striped braid (page's braid) placed at a spacing of 0.56 cm (0.22 inch) above the basic braid. Generals had 2.22 cm (0.88 inch) wide general's braid. The commander of the regiment and the honorary chief had trim like that of superior officers, but with additional 0.56 cm (0.22 inch) wide diagonally striped page's braid placed at a spacing of 0.28 cm (0.11 inch) on each side of the piping, meeting the perimeter braid at the bottom so it effectively formed triangles of braid in each quadrant of the cloth dome.

Other Ranks' Asian Bonnet

For the other ranks, the black fur headband was made of regular sheepskin. The cloth dome was topped with a standard uniform button at the place where the piping crossed. The piping was either raspberry or the colour of the tunic, as for officers, but the braid around the perimeter of the cloth dome was either white or orange according to button colour and, again, varied by rank. Regular soldiers had narrow 0.7 cm (0.27 inch) braid. NCOs had the same type of braid but wider, 1.67 cm (0.66 inch). Adjutants and chief adjutants had 0.7 cm (0.27 inch) braid, with a second piece of narrow 0.7 cm (0.27 inch) braid placed at a spacing of 0.56 cm (0.22 inch) above it.

Tunic

The line dragoons were made up of three groups. The 1st, 3rd, 5th, 7th, 11th, 15th, 19th, 20th, and Premorsky Dragoon regiments wore the standard dragoon tunic. The 2nd, 4th, 6th, 8th, 9th, 10th, 12th, 13th, and 14th Dragoon regiments wore a modified cuirassier's tunic because they had been cuirassier regiments until they were fused into the newly uniformed dragoons in 1860.[97] The 16th, 17th, and 18th Dragoon Regiments had a long history of service in the Caucasus. They all wore standard dragoon tunics, but the 17th and 18th were allowed unique Caucasus touches.

Standard Dragoon Tunic

The standard dragoon tunic was single-breasted and had a row of eight buttons down the front. Each of the rear skirts had scalloped trim with three buttons. The tunic was black for the troops, czar's green for the officers. Both the front edge of the tunic and the false rear pockets were edged with piping in the regimental colour, 0.28 cm (0.11 inch) wide (see Table V.7.a.2.1 for colours, and Images V:102, V:106, and V:107).

Buttons were either gold or silver according to the regiment (Table V.7.a.2.1).

The collar had rounded corners and was 5.56 cm (2.19 inches) high, although for NCOs it could be up to 6.67 cm (2.63 inches) high. The collar and its piping could be either the regimental colour or the tunic colour, but always contrasted with each other (Table V.7.a.2.1). All of the line dragoon regiments except the Premorsky Dragoons had coloured shields on their collars (Table V.7.a.2.1). The shields were 4.45 cm (1.75 inches) tall from top to bottom and ranged from 13.34 cm (5.25 inches) to 15.56 cm (6.13 inches) long. They were placed 0.56 cm (0.22 inch) from the front edges of the collar. If the uniform included collar litzen (Table V.7.a.2.1), the litzen was sewn to the collar shield, and stopped at a distance of 0.28 cm (0.11 inch) to 0.42 cm (0.16 inch) from the edges of the shield. If no collar shield was present, as in the case of the Premorsky Regiment, the litzen was sewn directly to the collar. The shield always included a button, which was either sewn to the far end of the litzen, if there was only one litzen, or between the far ends of the two litzen if there were two collar litzen. If the collar did not have a shield, there was just a lone button on the collar (Image V:107).

The cuffs were pointed. At the points, they were 8.89 cm (3.5 inches) high, while at the narrowest part they were 5 cm (1.97 inches) high. On the side of the cuff, 3.33 cm (1.31 inches) below the cuff trim point, a button was placed. If the uniform included cuff litzen (Table V.7.a.2.1), the litzen was sewn in this location as well, and the button was on it. The cuff litzen was 6.11 cm (2.41 inches) long, with its bottom edge 0.83 cm (0.33 inch) from the edge of the cuff.

The standard dragoon tunic for officers included one litzen on each side of the collar and one litzen on each cuff. The litzen were gold or silver depending on the regiment's button colour and were usually simple, in the chapter shape. In certain cases, though, the litzen could be for distinction rather than simple, and there were some regiments where the officers had two litzen on each side of the collar instead of one (Table V.7.a.2.1).

The standard dragoon tunic for troops did not have any litzen. However, if the regiment had been awarded litzen, the troops could have either single or double litzen at the collar and/or cuffs, either white or St George (orange and black).

The 17th and 18th Dragoons had long served in the Caucasus and had Asiatic touches on their tunics. These were permitted by Nicholas II, who had a fondness for the Caucasus troops. For both regiments, decorative antique cartridges were attached to the breast of the standard tunic on both the right and left sides (Images V:106, V:108, and V:109). Each decoration consisted of six cartridges placed side by side, so the total width was 7.22 cm (2.84 inches), with a total height of 10.56 cm (4.16 inches) from top to bottom. The cartridges were covered with cloth the same colour as the rest of the tunic, with a piece of raspberry-coloured cloth at the base of each cartridge.

Additionally, situated underneath each cartridge unit, was a small pocket the colour of the tunic with raspberry-coloured lining. For the troops, the cartridge units were edged with St George's braid, composed of three black stripes and two orange stripes, 1.39 cm (0.55 inch) wide. The top edge also had raspberry cording. For the officers, the braid around the cartridges was either gold or silver and included a raspberry-coloured thread. Officers' cartridges were represented by pieces of wood covered with a metal tip, either gilt or silvered, depending on button colour, with oxidised decorations. They were connected by means of fine chains to a Caucasus-style rosette situated above (Image V:106). For the troops the cartridges were 1.11 cm (0.44 inch) carbine cartridge casings.

V:107 Line Dragoons Second Lieutenant
Why this dragoon officer does not have litzen on his collar to go with his full dress epaulettes is a mystery. Note the unusually high collar. Prior to World War I, it was the style to wear as high a collar as one could get away with.

V:108 (Left) 17th Dragoons Staff Officer
V:109 (Right) 17th Dragoons Sergeant Major
Note how this man, even though he is a senior NCO, does not have any chains attached to the cartridges on his chest.

False Cap Line

Like the lancers, the 1st, 3rd, 5th, 7th, 11th, 15th, 16th, 17th, 18th, 19th, 20th, and Premorsky Dragoons wore a cap line in full dress. However, the dragoon cap line never actually attached to the helmet like the lancer cap line did – hence it is referred to here as a false cap line, and treated as a tunic decoration.

The false cap line began at the third button from the top on the front of the standard dragoon tunic. From there it ran up to the right shoulder and passed underneath the narrow part of the epaulette, near the epaulette button. It dipped down slightly on the back before going up to the collar and around the neck. After circling the neck it attached to the back of the collar and fell about one-third the length of the back before retracing its initial path over the right shoulder, passing again beneath the epaulette and reattaching to the third button.

For officers, the false cap line was made of smooth cording, either gold or silver according to the button colour. Other ranks wore either orange or white false cap lines, also according to button colour (Images V:102 and V:107).

Cuirassier Type Tunic

The dragoon regiments which had previously been cuirassier regiments regained the cuirassier-style tunic. For the troops, this tunic was black, and for the officers it was czar's green. On the rear skirts of the tunics were straight false pockets, piped in the colour of the shoulder straps (Table V.7.a.2.2). There were also two buttons in either white metal or brass according to the regiment's braid colour. The first was at the top of the false pocket, at waist-level, while the second was in the point of the false pocket formed by the piping.

The main distinguishing feature of the cuirassier tunic was that it had no buttons on the front (Images V:103 and V:104). Instead, it had 2.78 cm (1.09 inch) wide trim running around the top edge of the collar and down the front edges of the tunic on both sides to the bottom hem. The trim was composed of three stripes: a central stripe that ranged in width from 1.95 cm (0.77 inch) to 2.22 cm (0.88 inch), and two side stripes that ranged from 0.42 cm (0.16 inch) to 0.28 cm (0.11 inch) in width. For the troops, the central stripe was either yellow or white depending on the regiment's button colour, and the side stripes were the colour of the shoulder strap (Table V.7.a.2.2). The 13th Dragoons were the exception to this rule: they had a central stripe in black and orange, the colours of St George, with white side stripes.

For the officers, the trim was the same total width, but the central stripe was square-weave belt-style braid in either gold or silver depending on the regiment's button colour. The side stripes in the colour of the shoulder strap were 0.56 cm (0.22 inch) wide. Officers of the 13th Dragoons again had specialised trim, with the central stripe made up of three black stripes and two gold stripes, the colours of St George. The side stripes were white.

The standard cuirassier tunic for officers included one litzen on each side of the collar and two litzen on each cuff. The litzen were gold or silver depending on the regiment's button colour and were usually simple, in the chapter shape. There were exceptions. The litzen could be for distinction, rather than simple, and the officers could have two litzen on each side of the collar instead of one (Table V.7.a.2.2).

The standard cuirassier tunic for troops did not have any litzen. However, if the regiment had been awarded litzen, the troops could have single litzen at the collar and/or double litzen at the cuffs. The litzen was white with a central thread the colour of the shoulder straps in these cases (Table V.7.a.2.2).

The cuirassier tunic collar had rounded ends and was 5.56 cm (2.19 inches) high. It was white and had a shield the colour of the shoulder straps for all regiments except the 13th Dragoons, who had a black collar shield with white shoulder straps (Table V.7.a.2.2). The shield was 3.33 cm (1.31 inches) tall and 7.78 cm (3.06 inches) to 8.89 cm (3.5 inches) long. If the uniform included collar litzen, the litzen was sewn to the shield and was 0.28 cm (0.11 inch) to 0.42 cm (0.16 inch) shorter than the shield itself. The buttons were sewn to the litzen, or in the absence of litzen, to the collar shield itself, 0.56 cm (0.22 inch) from the far edge of the shield. The 13th Dragoons had gold grenades or litzen (sources differ) instead of buttons on the collar shield (see Image V:110).

The cuirassier tunic had Swedish cuffs. They were the colour of the shoulder straps and had the same trim as the collar and front edges of the cuirassier tunic (described above), placed 0.28 cm (0.11 inch) from the edge of the cuff. If the uniform included cuff litzen, there were two litzen on each cuff, 2.22 cm (0.88 inch) wide and 3.33 cm (1.31 inches) to 3.61 cm (1.42 inches) long. Both cuff litzen contained buttons. If the uniform did not include cuff litzen, then two buttons were sewn directly to the cuff.

The standard cuirassier tunic for officers included one litzen on each side of the collar and two litzen on each cuff. The litzen were gold or silver depending on the regiment's button colour and were usually simple, in the chapter shape. There were exceptions, though, where the litzen was for distinction rather than simple, and where the officers had two litzen on each side of the collar instead of one (Table V.7.a.2.2).

The standard cuirassier tunic for troops did not have any litzen. However, if the regiment had been awarded litzen, the troops could have single litzen at the collar and/or double litzen at the cuffs. The litzen was white with a central thread the colour of the shoulder straps in these cases (Table V.7.a.2.2).

The false cap line worn with the standard tunic by the regular line dragoons was not worn with the tunic of the dragoon cuirassiers.

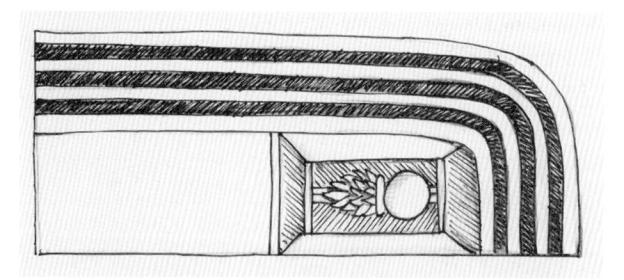

V:110 13th (Cuirassiers) Dragoons Collar
This was the special collar worn by the Military Order Regiment, and the stripes were orange and black.

Officer Epaulettes

In full dress, officers of the line and cuirassier dragoons wore metal 'cavalry model' epaulettes, either gold or silver according to button colour (see Tables V.7.a.2.1 and V.7.a.2.2 for button colour). The lining and piping of the epaulettes varied in colour by regiment, and were the colour of the shoulder straps that were worn by the troops (Tables V.7.a.2.1 and V.7.a.2.2) Officer epaulettes included repoussé monograms where applicable. If the regiment did not have a monogram, no marking – not even the regimental number – was worn on the epaulette. See §V-3-1 for description of epaulettes.

Shoulder Straps

Shoulder straps were worn by all other ranks in full dress. The shoulder straps varied in colour by regiment and bore the monogram of the regiment's honorary *chef* where applicable (Tables V.7.a.2.1 and V.7.a.2.2). Monograms were either yellow or red according to standard regulation (see §V-3-1 for more detail), with the exception of the 2nd Dragoons, who had a white monogram on their pink shoulder strap. In the absence of the monogram, the regimental number was on the shoulder strap.

Officers did not wear shoulder straps in full dress, but did wear them in walking-out dress.

Walking-Out Tunic

The walking-out tunic worn by the line and cuirassier dragoons was called the vice-moundir, a term which comes from the original Russian term for 'undress uniform'. There were two different styles of vice-moundir worn by the two groups of dragoons.

Standard Dragoon Vice-Moundir

The regular Dragoon regiments, including the 16th, 17th, and 18th Dragoons, who were part of the Caucasus Corps, all wore the standard dragoon vice-moundir for their walking-out tunic. It was made of dark green cloth and was single-breasted, with eight buttons down the front.[98] The piping on the front was the colour of the shoulder straps (Table V.7.a.2.1). The collar was rounded, with piping, and included collar shields if the regular tunic had them. The colours of the collar, its piping, and its shields (where applicable) were the same as on the regular tunic. However, the collar of the vice-moundir did not have litzen, and only included a button if the shield was present. The cuffs came to a point and were dark green with piping the colour of the shoulder strap.[99] On the sleeve above the cuff there were two buttons along the outer sleeve seam. The rear skirt false pockets were scalloped, also with piping the colour of the shoulder strap, and included three buttons. The lining of the standard dragoon vice-moundir was white.

Cuirassier Vice-Moundir

The regiments of dragoons which had previously been cuirassiers retained the cuirassier-style vice-moundir as their walking-out tunic. Like the standard dragoon vice-moundir, it was made of dark green cloth and was single-breasted with eight buttons on the front. Its piping was the colour of the shoulder straps (Table V.7.a.2.2), as was the collar, but with no dark green piping. The tunic had Swedish cuffs and a rear skirt with false pockets. Both were the colour of the rest of the tunic, with piping the colour of the shoulder straps. The false pockets, which were straight, had two buttons. The lining of the cuirassier vice-moundir, like that of the standard dragoon model, was white.

Because they had the distinction of being the Military Order of St George, the 13th Dragoons had several special features on their walking-out tunic. It was made entirely of black cloth instead of dark green, including the cuffs. Additionally, it had a black velvet collar with white piping.

RIDING BREECHES AND TROUSERS

All ranks of line and cuirassier dragoons wore standard breeches in full dress. Dragoon officers also had full-length trousers that could be worn with the walking-out tunic. Both the breeches and the officers' trousers were blue with narrow piping down the outside seam of each leg. Piping was in the colour of the shoulder straps (Tables V.7.a.2.1 and V.7.a.2.2).

An exception was the breeches and trousers of the 17th and 18th Dragoons, which had wide bands down the outside seams instead of narrow piping. The band was 4.45 cm (1.75 inches) wide in the colour of the shoulder straps. Additionally, troops on the general staff did not have piping on their breeches.

UNIFORM ACCESSORIES

Officers' Accessories

Dragoon officers wore the standard model pouch and pouch belt in full dress. The pouch ornament was usually the imperial eagle in the button colour. However, the 13th Dragoons had a special ornament, a gold star of St George like the one on their helmet. Additionally, from 1904 to 1906, the 2nd Dragoons had a special ornament, an 'M' in silver for the Empress Maria Feodorovna.

Officers also wore the officer's sash in full dress.

Other Ranks' Accessories

Other ranks of the line dragoons wore a brown leather belt in full dress. The belt had a buckle that was gold or silver, with a double-headed eagle, according to the button colour.

Other Accessories

All ranks of both the guard and the line wore standard riding boots and standard white gloves in full dress. Standard brown gloves were worn in walking-out dress. See §V-3-1 for more details on accessories.

§V-7-b LANCERS[100]

Little is known in the West about the line lancer regiments as so much history was lost during the Russian Revolution and the rest is in Russian-language books.

UNIFORM

The line lancers underwent the two major uniform changes of the Russian army between 1880 and 1914.

Uniform Changes in 1882
In 1882, almost all line cavalry regiments were made dragoons and given a simplified form of dress. This was worn until 1908. During this period, the classification of line lancers and their uniforms disappeared. See §V-7-a-1 for a description of the uniforms worn during this period.

Uniform Changes of 1908
Following the debacle of the Russo-Japanese War, the czar's government undertook a programme to reorganise the army and rebuild its morale. One step was the revival of the old classifications and dress for the regiments of line cavalry. This reversed the reform of 1882 where line cavalry regiments had become dragoons. This Indian summer for Russia saw the lancers reintroduced to the line cavalry and their traditional uniforms brought back. Some elements of this 'new' traditional uniform were modelled on the lancer uniforms worn by the period's German army.

Headdress

Helmets
The Russian lancer helmet, often called the czapska, was made of black leather (Image V:111). It was fairly shallow, 11.67 cm (4.59 inches) at its tallest point, and did not cover the ears. On the front of the helmet was a visor (brim), also of black leather, with a 0.83 cm (0.33 inch) metal border in the regimental button colour.

Attached to the top of the helmet was a stem. The square stem measured 4.72 cm by 4.72 cm (1.86 inches by 1.86 inches) and was approximately 5.56 cm (2.19 inches) high from the top of the helmet shell to the bottom edge of the mortarboard. The total height of the czapska, including shell and stem, ranged from 17.78 cm (7 inches) at the front to 15 cm (5.91 inches) at the back when the angle of the mortarboard was taken into account.

The stem led to a square mortarboard, 17.78 cm (7 inches) on each side. The mortarboard was set on the helmet so one of the corners pointed directly to the front of the helmet, as was the norm for Prussian lancers. Because the stem was attached off-centre, slightly towards the rear of the helmet, the entire helmet was angled so the overall height of the czapska was slightly taller in the front than in the rear: 17.78 cm (7 inches) in the front and 15 cm (5.91 inches) in the back for the line lancers.

The czapska stem had a square cross-section, aligning with the edges and corners of the mortarboard rather than the round cross-section favored by the

V:111 3rd Lancer's Helmet

Table V.7.b.1: Lancers, *c.* 1914

Regiment	Plastron, Cuff, and Tunic Trim Colour	Button Colour	Collar Colour[f]	Collar Shield Colour	Czapska[a] Stem Cloth Covering[f]	Officer Litzen[b]	Trooper Litzen[b]	Mono-grams	Epaulette[c]	Distinction Banner[d]
1st	Red	Gold	Dark blue[e] T: R	Red	Red T: D	Gold distinction	None	None	Gold	Simple
2nd	Light blue	Gold	Dark blue[e] T: B	Light blue	Light blue T: D	Gold simple	White simple	X ii[g]	Gold	Simple
3rd	White	Gold	Dark blue[e] T: W	White	White T: D	Gold simple	White simple	A III[h]	Gold	Simple
4th	Yellow	Gold	Dark blue[e] T: Y	Yellow	Yellow T: D	Gold simple	None	None	Gold	Simple
5th	Red	Silver	Dark blue[e] T: R	Red	Red T: D	Silver simple	None	V. E. III[i]	Silver	---
6th	Light blue	Silver	Dark blue[e] T: B	Light blue	Light blue T: D	Silver simple	None	None	Silver	---
7th	White	Silver	Dark blue[e] T: W	White	White T: D	Silver simple	None	A. XIII[j]	Silver	Simple
8th	Yellow	Silver	Dark blue[e] T: Y	Yellow	Yellow T: D	Silver simple	None	None	Silver	Simple
9th	Red	Gold	Red[e] T: D	Dark Blue	Red T: B	Gold distinction	None	None	Gold	Simple
10th	Light blue	Gold	Light blue[e] T: D	Dark blue	Light blue T: –	Gold simple	None	None	Gold	Simple
11th	White	Gold	White[e] T: D	Dark Blue	White T: –	Gold simple	White simple	M. Θ.[k]	Gold	---
12th	Yellow	Gold	Yellow[e] T: D	Dark Blue	Yellow T: –	Gold simple	None	F. J. I[l]	Gold	Descriptive
13th	Yellow	Silver	Yellow[e] T: D	None	Yellow T: –	Silver simple double	None	None	Silver	Descriptive
14th	Light blue	Silver	Light blue[e] T: D	None	Yellow T: D	Silver simple double	None	None	Silver	—
15th	Raspberry	Silver	Dark blue[e] T: R	Raspberry	Raspberry T: D	Silver simple	None	None	Silver	—
16th	Red	Silver	Red[e] T: D	None	White T: –	Silver simple	None	None	Silver	—

Regiment	Plastron, Cuff, and Tunic Trim Colour	Button Colour	Collar Colour[f]	Collar Shield Colour	Czapska[a] Stem Cloth Covering[f]	Officer Litzen[b]	Trooper Litzen[b]	Mono-grams	Epaulette[c]	Distinction Banner[d]
17th	Raspberry	Gold	Raspberry[e] T: D	None	Raspberry T: D	Gold simple	None	None	Gold	–

Notes: [a] This is a Polish word that has several different spellings in English; czapska is the most common. Others are tschapska and chapka (See Marrion, *Lancers*; Thorburn, *French Army*; Mollo, *Uniforms*; Head, *Napoleonic Lancer*; Preben Kannik, *Military Uniforms*).
[b] Unless otherwise noted, all litzen were in the chapter shape.
[c] The epaulettes were made of metal for both officers and troops.
[d] See §V-2-2 for more details on distinction banners.
[e] The top and front of the collar was piped in trim colour.
[f] Trim colours: R=Red, Y=Yellow, B=Light blue, W=White, D=Dark blue, T=Trim.
[g] Silver monogram of Czar Peter II.
[h] Silver monogram of Czar Alexander III.
[i] Gold monogram of King Victor Emmanuel III of Italy.
[j] Gold monogram of King Alfonso XIII of Spain.
[k] Silver monogram of Empress Maria Feodorovna.
[l] Silver monogram of Emperor Franz Joseph I of Austria.

Germans. The size of the stem swelled outwards from its base width of 6.67 cm (2.63 inches) from point to opposing point.

Stem Cloth

In full dress, the stem was covered with a piece of removable cloth, the colour of which varied by regiment (Table V.7.b.1). The cloth covering the stem in the Russian line lancers came down lower on the helmet shell than was common in the German or British lancers. The bottom of the cloth, often covered in braid, came down about two or three fingers below the base of the stem. The Prussian and British lancer stem cloth covering stopped at the bottom of the stem, whereas the Russian line lancer cloth came down to a point under each corner of the mortarboard (Image V:111).

Stem Cloth Trim

The stem cloth for the troops of the line was edged at the top with narrow braid in orange or white to match the buttons, while at the bottom the width of the braid varied by rank: 0.7 cm (0.27 inch) for regular troopers, 1.67 cm (0.66 inch) for NCOs, and 2.78 m (1.09 nches) for adjutants and chief adjutants. Adjutants and chief adjutants also had an additional narrow braid (0.7 cm or 0.27 inch) above the wider braid at a spacing of 0.56 cm (0.23 inch). On three of the four bottom corners of the stem cloth – all except the front corner – there was a button, and the ridges of the stem were highlighted with orange or white cording depending on the button colour.

For the officers of the line, the top edge of the stem cloth was bordered with a 1.67 cm (0.66 inch) stripe of square-weave belt-style braid, while the bottom trim again varied according to rank: both subaltern and superior officers had a 1.67 cm (0.66 inch) square-weave braid at the bottom edge of the cloth, but superior officers also had a narrow 0.56 cm (0.23 inch) special diagonally striped braid, in the style of the pages corps, placed above the wider braid at a spacing of 0.56 cm (0.23 inch).

Helmet Plate

The czapskas worn by regiments of line lancers had the double-headed imperial eagle affixed to the front. The eagle was either gold or silver to match the colour of the buttons and epaulettes. The distinction banner, where applicable, was located above the eagle (Image V:112, and Table V.7.b.1). Fifty-nine per cent of the line lancer regiments had distinction banners. See §V-2-2 for information on Distinction Banners and which regiments had earned them.

V:112 Close-Up of the Double-Headed Eagle and Distinction Banner on the Helmet of the 3rd Lancers
Note that the distinction banner is of the simple descriptive type.

V:113 Subaltern in a Line Lancer Regiment
He has his helmet at the regulation right tilt. Also note the unusual way his cap lines fall down across his right chest.

Cockade and Plume

Line lancers wore the same cockades and plumes as the guard lancers. See §V-5-c for details.

Cap Line

The cap lines of line lancers were affixed to the mortarboard and wrapped around the tunic in the same way as the guard lancers. Cap lines were either orange or white depending on the button colour. NCOs had slip-rings and flounders that were a mixture of black, orange, and white thread.

Line officers wore the same cap lines and fringe as officers of the guard lancers. See §V-5-c for details.

Tunic

The line lancers wore the same double-breasted dark blue tunic as the guard lancers. The pattern of the two rows of seven buttons was the same as the guard lancers. See §V-5-c for details.

The buttons were either gold or silver depending on the regiment's button colour (Table V.7.b.1). The buttons had a double-headed eagle design on them. Regiments with the emperor or empress as honorary chief had crowns rather than eagles until 1907, when they adopted the eagle-design button.

In full dress, the buttons held a plastron in the facing colour to the tunic, providing colour to the dark uniform (Table V.7.b.1).

Collars

The collars of the line lancers came in a wide range of colour and design (Table V.7.b.1). The line lancers' collars, instead of being cut on the diagonal like the guard lancers' collars, came to a right angle with a rounded corner (Image V:114). The collar could be either dark blue like the tunic or in the facing colour depending on the regiment (Table V.7.b.1). With the exceptions of the 13th, 14th, 16th, and 17th Regiments, line regiment collars had rectangular shields on either facing colour (Table V.7.b.1). Officers had single litzen behind the button on the cuffs, gold or silver according to the regiment's button colour. Enlisted men had a button on each cuff, but only some regiments had litzen (Table V.7.b.1). In those cases, the litzen was white with a coloured centre line the colour of the cuff. As in the guard, both officers and men had two additional buttons sewn above the cuff along the seam of each sleeve.

The rear skirts of the line lancer regiments had three buttons. Piping of the facing colour connected the skirt's false pocket buttons. The trim was in the typical lancer scallop pattern (Image V:43).

Epaulettes

In full dress, line lancers of all ranks wore metal epaulettes, gold or silver colour according to button colour. Officers wore cavalry model epaulettes. The lining and piping varied in colour by regiment and were the colour of the tunic plastron for all regiments except the 14th Lancers, who had yellow epaulette lining and piping even though their plastron was light blue (see Table V.7.b.1 for plastron colour). Other ranks of the line wore trooper model epaulettes, with lining in the colour of the tunic plastron, again with the exception of the 14th Lancers, mentioned above. See §V-3-1 for epaulette details.

Shoulder Straps

For their walking-out dress, the line lancers had shoulder straps that were the colour of the czapska stem cloth for each regiment (Table V.7.b.1), with dark blue piping. Shoulder straps bore a monogram or the regimental number according to the colours and standards described in §V-3-1. For officers, the monogram of the 11th Lancers only was made of metal in the colour of the button and was mounted on the shoulder strap. Monograms for officers of all other line lancer regiments were embroidered on the shoulder strap in metallic thread that was the opposite of the button colour.

V:114 *Czar Nicholas II's Daughter, Tatiana, in the Uniform of the 8th Line Lancers*
She is wearing her helmet at the regulation tilt down over the right eyebrow. As a senior officer in the regiment, the tassels at the end of her cap line are large. Also note the shape of the top part of her helmet, which is different from that found on guard helmets.

side in a colour contrasting with the colour of the collar (Table V.7.b.1). On each shield was a button. If the regiment had received litzen, these were on the shield, or, in the absence of a shield, directly on the collar itself. All officers had at least one simple litzen in either gold or silver. Officers could also have double litzen and in certain cases distinction litzen (Table V.7.b.1). In some regiments the troops also had single litzen which were white with a centre line the colour of the cloth underneath. All litzen were in the chapter shape.

Cuffs and Rear Skirts

For the line regiments, the Polish pointed cuffs, worn by officers and enlisted men, were in the regiment's

Walking-Out Tunic

The walking-out tunic worn by the line lancers was called the vice-moundir. Like the lancer's tunic, it was double-breasted, but it was cut a bit tighter at the waist. It had two rows of seven buttons on the front. The cloth, lining and piping were identical to those of the lancer's tunic. If the regiment's tunic had collar shields, then its walking-out tunic had identical collar shields, but, unlike the tunic, the walking-out coat never had litzen. The pointed Polish cuffs were dark blue like the coat itself and had piping the colour of the plastron. On each sleeve just above the cuff were two buttons near the seam. The rear skirt pockets, which were the colour of the plastron, were scalloped with three buttons. Shoulder boards were worn and they had a gold or silver scheme depending on the regiment's button colour.

The pouch, pouch belt, and girdle were not worn with the vice-moundir.

Riding Breeches and Trousers

All ranks wore standard riding breeches in full dress. Officers also wore trousers with their walking-out tunic, the vice-moundir. Both the breeches and the trousers were dark blue with narrow piping down the outside seam of each leg. Piping was the colour of the plastron (Table V.7.b.1).

Uniform Accessories

Pouch, Pouch Belt and Sash

Line lancer officers wore the standard model pouch and pouch belt in full dress. The pouch ornament for officers of the line lancers was the imperial eagle in the button colour.

Line officers wore the officer's sash in full dress (Images V:113 and V:114).

Other Ranks' Accessories – Trooper's Girdle

Other ranks of the line wore a lancer trooper's girdle in full dress. The girdles were made of fabric that had three horizontal stripes and piping at the top and bottom. The buckle was covered in the same fabric, but it was turned to go up and down.

On the girdle for troops of the line, the top and bottom stripes were the colour of the plastron (Table V.7.b.1). The central stripe and the top and bottom piping were dark blue.

Other Accessories

The boots and gloves worn by the line lancers were the same as those worn by guard lancers. See §V-3-1 and §V-5-c for details about accessories.

Officers and senior NCOs wore black leather holsters and Nagant revolvers in full dress when parading with their troops. They also wore regimental and school badges.

Regimental Badges

Line lancer officers wore regimental badges on full dress uniforms on the left side of the chest just below the plastron. Higher school badges were worn at the same level on the right. When an order of dress did not call for a plastron the badges were worn a little higher on the chest.

By 1914 most of the line lancer regiments had regimental badges. The badge of the 1st Lancers notes their claim to have captured two French eagles at the 1807 battle of Preussich-Eylau.[101] A unique achievement indeed, and one that outshines the Scots Greys and the 1st Royal Dragoons with their single captured eagles.[102] However, French records are available to researchers and they do not show two eagles being lost in this battle to a single Russian regiment.[103] A search was made of Russian sources in Moscow, including the regimental history. They noted the claim of two eagles captured by the 1st Lancers but did not say which French regiments the eagles were taken from. Without this detail, it is hard to believe this claim, given the information we now have.

The regimental badge of the 4th Lancers is a Warsaw Cross. It recalls with pride the regiment's capture of Tadeusz Kosïuszko of the Polich patriots, the leader of the Polish army in the 1794 fight against the Second Partition of Poland. Earlier, Kosïuszko had served the Americans in their revolutionary army and had designed their defences at the battle of Saratoga, the turning point of the revolution, and planned the defences at West Point.

The 4th Lancer's badge also noted their claim to being one of the oldest regiments in the Russian army, tracing their founding to 1651.[104]

§V-7-c HUSSARS[105]

There is a shortage of information in English on the history of the different Russian line regiments. Occasionally bits of information turn up. For example, we know that the Kiev and Ingermanland Regiments[106] attacked the 'thin red line' of the 93rd Highlanders (later Princess Louise's (Argyll and Sutherland Highlanders)) at Balaclava.[107]

These are, however, just slivers of light in a generally unknown area. The date the different hussar regiments were formed is given at §V-2-1. The hussars were some of the oldest regiments in the army because their date of origin related back to Cossack outposts or other guard stations when they were not yet operating regiments.

UNIFORM

Uniform Changes in 1882

In 1882, almost all line cavalry regiments were made dragoons and given a simplified form of dress. This was worn until 1908. During this period, the classification of line hussars and their uniforms disappeared. See §V-7-a-1 for a description of the uniforms worn during this period.

Uniform Changes of 1908

Following the Russo-Japanese War, the Russian government undertook a programme to reorganise the army and rebuild its morale. One step in this process was the revival of the old classifications and dress for the regiments of line cavalry. This reversed the reform of 1882 where line cavalry regiments had become dragoons. This produced some of the most colourful uniforms in Europe, and among the most dazzling of these was worn by the eighteen regiments of line hussars (see Shenk Plates at §V-3-6, Images C64–C74 and Table V.7.c.1).

When the classification of hussar was re-established, the traditional hussar uniform was revised, but reserved for winter ceremonial occasions. A more modern-style dress was worn in the summer when the troops were engaged in both manoeuvres and parades. The effect of modern war was recognised in a wholly utilitarian combat uniform.

Table V.7.c.1: Hussars

Regiment	Button Colour[a]	Busby Bag[b]	Attila	Pelisse and Lining	Monogram	Distinction Banner[c]	Notes
1st	Gold	Red	Light blue	(Light blue Lining: red)[d]	None	Simple	A
2nd	Gold	Turquoise	Dark green	Dark green Lining: turquoise	A III[e]	Simple	A
3rd	Gold	White	Light blue	White Lining: White	None	Simple	A
4th	Gold	Yellow	Dark blue	(Dark blue Lining: yellow)[d]	None	Descriptive	A
5th	Silver	Red	Black	(Black Lining: red)[d]	A. Θ.[f]	Descriptive	B
6th	Silver	Light blue	Dark blue	(Dark blue Lining: light blue)[d]	None	Simple	A
7th	Silver	White	Light blue	(Light blue Lining: white)[d]	A I[g]	Descriptive	A

Regiment	Button Colour[a]	Busby Bag[b]	Attila	Pelisse and Lining	Monogram	Distinction Banner[c]	Notes
8th	Silver	Yellow	Dark blue	(Dark blue Lining: yellow)[d]	None	Simple	A
9th	Gold	Red	Dark green	(Dark green Lining: red)[d]	None	Simple	A
10th	Gold	Light blue	Light blue	(Light blue Lining: light blue)[d]	None	None	A
11th	Gold	Red	Red	Dark blue Lining: red	None	Simple	A
12th	Gold	Yellow	Cinnamon brown	(Cinnamon brown Lining: yellow)[d]	None	Descriptive	A
13th	Silver	Yellow	Light blue	(Light blue Lining: yellow)[d]	W II[h]	Descriptive	A
14th	Silver	Yellow	Dark green	(Dark green Lining: yellow)[d]	None	None	A
15th	Silver	Light blue	Pink	(Black Lining: light blue)[d]	None	None	A, C
16th	Gold	Raspberry	Dark green	(Dark green Lining: raspberry)[d]	None	None	A
17th	Gold	White	Dark Green	(Dark Green Lining: White)[d]	None	Descriptive	A, D
18th	Silver	Light Blue	Dark Green	(Dark Green Lining: Light Blue)[d]	None	Simple	A

Notes: [a] Attilas and pelisses did not have buttons. Toggles were used in their place. The term 'button colour' is a term of art and is used here only for convenience and consistency.
[b] The busby bag on the line hussars' bonnet comes to a rounded point in contrast to the guard hussars' busby bag, which comes to a rather sharp point.
[c] See §V-2-2 for distinction banner type. Banners are sometimes referred to as scrolls.
[d] Parentheses denote that wearing of the pelisse in these regiments was only permitted for generals and the honorary regimental chief.
[e] Alexander III. In the 1st Squadron only, a gold metal monogram H II for Nicholas II was worn instead.
[f] In the 1st Squadron only, silver metal monogram of Empress Alexandra Feodorovna.
[g] Alexander I.
[h] Emperor Wilhelm II of Germany.

A: Double-headed eagle on the busby.
B: From 1908 to March 1914, a double-headed eagle. From March 1914 on, a large skull and crossbones badge on the busby.
C: By the normal rules this pelisse would be pink rather than black but the regimental chief was the czar's sister, Grand Duchess Xenia Alexandrovna. Having a pink pelisse on a pink attila, with its suggestion of flesh on flesh, was felt to be improper and too suggestive for such a lady. So black was substituted.
D: Only the 1st, 4th, and 5th Squadrons wore a distinction banner.

Winter Uniform

Headdress

Busby

In winter full dress, the attila was set off by a black lambswool busby topped with a white horsehair plume. On the front of the busby, for seventeen of the regiments, was an impressive imperial double-headed eagle in the regiment's button colour. Regiments that had earned the right to wear a distinction banner wore it above the eagle. Seventy-eight per cent of the hussar regiments had a banner. See §V-2-2 for information on distinction banners and which regiments earned them.

In March 1914, the 5th Alexandria Hussars were granted a skull and crossbones as their busby badge.[108] Since the change was granted late, and because of subsequent political events, there is a lack of good photographic evidence as to the exact size and shape

V:115 Group of the 5th Line Hussars
The man in the middle is wearing a busby with a small death's head badge.

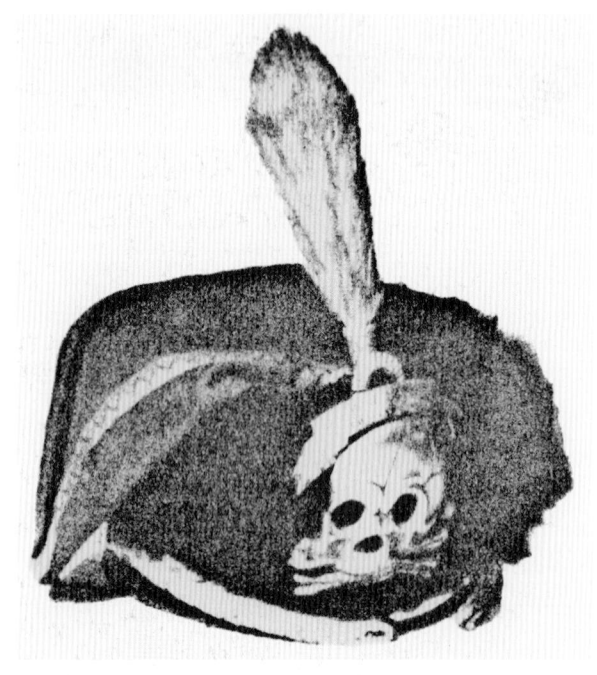

V:116 5th Hussar's Busby with Death's Head Badge
Since the death's head badge was only awarded in 1914, it is extremely difficult to locate photos of a busby with a badge on it, and consequently one must settle for poor-quality photos to illustrate the badge.

of the badge. A photograph of the small badge of the other ranks can be seen at the centre of Image V:115. For the much larger officer's busby, see Image V:116. Over the badge, the regiment carried a distinction scroll of the description variety.

All regiments had an oval cockade above the busby badge, which was often partially covered either by the crown of the double-headed eagle or by the distinction banner. Above the cockade was a white metal receptacle for the plume. For officers and under-officers, a black and orange swirl decoration was added. Troopers had a plain white receptacle. The busby was secured by a metal chinstrap in a double D pattern. It was often worn resting across the front of the busby and covering the lower part of the eagle badge. Its colour followed that of the regiment's button colour.

A cloth busby bag fell on the right side of the busby. For the line regiments it terminated in a rounded point (Image V:117). Its colour varied by regiment (Table V.7.c.1). The seams of the bag were trimmed with a welt or lace in the regiment's button colour. NCOs wore plain lace on the seams. In addition to this lace, senior NCOs, sergeants and warrant officers had

V:117 A Well-Decorated Line Hussar
The rounded point of his busby bag can easily be seen in this fine character study, as well as how his chest and collar frogging lie on the tunic.

a welt along the inside of the lace. Officers wore hussar lace along the seam. Senior officers had another welt along the inside of the lace. The welt carried by senior NCOs and senior officers was placed so the busby bag could be seen between the lace and the welt.

The back of the busby worn by other ranks was decorated with a strand of braid which hung loosely from buttons on either side of the busby. A short cord and tassel hung from each button, but on the right this was covered by the bag. This lace was white or orange, depending on the regiment's button colour. Officers had an elaborate chain-link-looking festoon in lieu of the other ranks' braid. A second festoon was worn on the front of the busby by regimental commanders and honorary commanders (Image V:118). Cap lines which attached to the body of the uniform were not worn by Russian hussars.

Attila

The most distinctive item of winter dress uniform was the attila. In the Russian army, there was not one standard colour for this item; rather, as in the case of German hussars, a wide variety of colours was worn. The most distinctive of the new uniforms was the 15th Ukrainian Hussars, who wore pink. The pink was an orange-rose shade, known as 'mermaid pink' in the regiment. Tradition attributes the pink worn by the regiment to Catherine the Great. She was a lusty woman with a habit of making her important advisors her lovers. With high officials playing these two roles, it was natural that official business would often be discussed in intimate surroundings. During one such conference, the question of a uniform colour for a new hussar regiment, the Ukrainian, was raised. Catherine, in a joking mood, slapped her uncovered thigh and said, 'Let this be their colour.' Since Catherine was an absolute monarch, this instruction was followed.

The colour of the 12th Akhtyrka Hussars was always brown but the final exact shade was not set until 1814. Prior to this conversion, they wore chestnut brown

V:118 Czar Nicholas II's Daughter, Olga, in the Uniform of the 3rd Hussars
Her uniform has the extra-wide braiding of a senior officer. As the *chef* of the regiment, she is entitled to wear a white pelisse with white lining.

uniforms. In 1814, the Russian army, having driven the French out of Russia and fought its way into France, was preparing for a victory parade in Paris. After a full two years of fighting, the brown uniforms of the 12th Akhtyrka Hussars were rather ragged. In a warehouse near Paris the commanding officer found a large supply of bolts of brown cloth that were to be used to make habits for the Franciscan order of monks. He ordered his regimental tailors to make new attilas out of this cloth. Later, Czar Alexander I noticed soldiers in his army wearing an unfamiliar shade of brown and asked for a report on this matter. Upon being informed what had happened, he told the regiment this would be their uniform colour forever. True to the Czar's orders, the regiment always wore that shade of Franciscan brown, even when converted to dragoons, when the rest of the Russian cavalry wore dark green tunics.[109]

Other regiments were dressed in light and dark blue, dark green, red, black, and brown (Table V.7.c.1).

The attila had five rows of braid. In line regiments, the braid on each side of the chest terminated in an elongated trefoil. In the middle of each row was a set of decorative loops. The button worn at the base of each trefoil carried the imperial double-headed eagle in 1914 (Image V:52).

The collar and cuffs were the same colour as the attila. The collar was trimmed at the top and bottom with braid (Image V:52). For senior officers, colonels and lieutenant colonels, a row of hussar (zigzag) lace in the regimental button colour was added at the top of the collar (Image V:118).

The shape of the braid on the cuff depended on the wearer's rank. For troopers and junior officers, major and below, the cuff took the shape shown in Image V:52. For senior officers the shape was modified and hussar lace added (Image V:118).

The attila had pockets on the front skirts. trimmed in braid and decorated with a loop at the top and a trefoil at the bottom (see Image V:52 of a line hussar officer at §V-5-d). The right front edge of the attila was also trimmed in braid. This braid continued around the bottom of the skirt and outlined the rear vent. As is traditional for hussars, the shape of the braid on the back accentuated the taper of the waist. Each skirt was decorated with three columns of braid which ended in trefoils. The back of the collar was decorated with a set of loops which were part of the trim at the base of the

V:119 | 12th Hussars
This shows the front and back of a line hussar's attila and the position the pouch was worn in.

collar. Trim went up the back on each side and ended in a trefoil (Image V:119).

The braid for other ranks was wool, and for officers it was cord or gimp chain. The normal form of officer's braid was cord, but the 1st Sumy, the 2nd Pavlograd, the 11th Izyum, and the 12th Akhtyrka Hussars wore gimp chain. The gimp chain was marked by a small bump midway between the first loop and the centre of the attila on either side of the chest.

The colour of the braid, gimp chain and the buttons was gold and silver, orange or white for other ranks, depending on the regiment's button colour (Table V.7.c.1). An exception to this was the 11th Izyum Hussars, whose braid was white for other ranks but the button colour was gold. Officers of this regiment had gold braid.

The cord worn by officers was decorated with darts of black and orange. When silver cord was worn, the black dart was inside the orange dart. For gold cord, this position was reversed.

The toggle button was in the regiment's button colour. Those worn by officers had a swirl pattern. The officers of the 1st Sumy, 2nd Pavlograd, 11th Izyum, and 12th Akhtyrka Hussars wore toggle buttons whose swirl pattern was closer together than that of the other line hussar regiments.[110] This close pattern was like that worn by the guard hussars. In addition to those worn on the chest, there were two horizontal toggle buttons on the back of the attila. These were worn on each column of braid and were placed so the sash rested on them.

For certain regiments, lace was introduced on the cuff and/or collar. Junior officers of the 2nd Pavlograd, the 5th Alexandria, and the 7th White Russian Hussars had hussar lace on the collar and cuffs just below the braid. On the collar, this was just below the braid at the top of the collar. It was about two-thirds as thick as the lace worn by senior officers. On the cuff, the lace was just below the bottom line of braid. Other ranks of these regiments had plain white lace on the collar. Only the 5th Alexandria Hussars troopers had extra white lace on the cuff (Image V:115).

NCOs with the rank of junior corporal and above wore plain lace on the collar just below the top row of braid and on the cuffs just below the bottom of the braid. In regiments entitled to extra lace on the collar and cuff, the rank lace seems to have been worn in addition to the extra lace. The rank lace was gold or silver, depending on the regiment's button colour.

SHOULDER CORDS

The shoulders were decorated with braid, cord or gimp chain for officers and wool for other ranks. Next to the collar the braid wrapped around a domed button, which bore the imperial eagle. The braid looped over itself at the point of the shoulder, and the outer edge of the loop extended just past the point of the shoulder. For regiments authorised to carry monograms, a knot inside the loop carried the monogram, making for a wider loop. The monogram was metal, its colour the reverse of the regiment's button colour. Men serving as one-year volunteers were designated by a braid of black, orange, and white stripes worn around the outside of the shoulder braid (Table V.7.c.1 shows which regiments wore monograms).

V:120 Line Hussar Officer
Note the beads of a senior officer on his shoulder cords and the badge of upper schooling on his right chest.

Officers' ranks were shown by beads, each with a star, strung on the shoulder braid. Second lieutenants wore two beads (Image V:52), lieutenants and lieutenant colonels wore three, captains four (Image V:120), and majors and colonels none (Image V:117). In the unlikely event of confusion over whether an individual was a lieutenant or lieutenant colonel, the shape of the braid on the cuff clarified it. Other ranks wore beads without stars on the shoulder braid to show their rank. Senior privates wore one bead, junior corporals two, senior corporals three. These were, again, white or orange according to the regiment's button colour. Sergeants had one bead of gold or silver, depending on the regiment's button colour. Warrant officers wore the cord of an officer as their shoulder braid with a sergeant's bead.

POUCH AND POUCH BELT

In the line hussars, the pouch belt and pouch were only worn by officers in full dress. The standard model pouch was worn and had a double-headed eagle emblem on the cover flap in the regiment's button colour. The pouch belt had gold or silver hussar lace according to the button colour (Image V:120). See §V-3-1 for more details on the pouch and pouch belt.

Waist Sash

The sash for all officers of the line hussars consisted of three thin silver cords mixed with black and orange darts. Each cord carried three silver slides (Image V:52). The style of the sash worn by Russian hussars was unusual: the three cords reached only halfway around the wearer's waist. Under each arm, the three cords were gathered and the balance of the sash consisted of two cords. The cord on the right terminated in a toggle button. The left-hand cords formed a fastening loop and continued around the wearer's right-hand side to be interwoven with the sash cords in front. The cords, after passing through the sash, terminated in silver tassels. The size of the tassel cords was another indication of rank, those of senior officers being larger than those of junior officers.

For other ranks of the line, the cords were of wool, orange or white depending on the regiment's button colour. The slides match the colour of the busby bag. For under-officers, orange and black darts were added to the tassel.

Side Arms

Officers wore side arms. Anachronistic with the historic and romantic hussar's outfit, a black leather holster and a Nagant revolver were a regulation item of full dress for line hussar officers and senior NCOs when parading with their men.

Sabretaches

Officers of the 2nd Pavlograd and 3rd Elizabetgrad Hussars, when wearing full dress and not parading with their men, were entitled to carry a sabretache. The Elizabetgrad Regiment's sabretache had a white cloth background. It carried a monogrammed OH for its honorary commander Olga Nicolaievna, the czar's daughter. The monogram, banner, crown, and the trim on the sabretache's cord and lace were gold. The sabretache of the Pavlograd Hussars had a turquoise cloth background and a gold trim. It carried a monogram of Alexander III topped by a crown.

Charivari Breeches

The Russian hussars' breeches were unique: both the guard and the line hussars of all ranks wore riding breeches in full, ordinary, and walking-out dress. Charivari breeches were typically only worn by guard regiments, in full and/or gala dress. See §V-3-1 for a detailed description.

Riding Breeches

The riding breeches worn with the attila were normally brick red, a flat dull red colour with no highlights. However, the 5th Alexandria Hussars wore black breeches,[111] and the 11th Izyum Hussars wore dark blue.[112] The outer seams were piped. For other ranks in most regiments the piping was a welt of orange or white wool, depending on the button colour. The Izyum Hussars had white wool. The troopers of the 2nd Pavlograd, 5th Alexandria and 7th White Russian Hussars wore a wider strip of braid with a stripe the colour of the riding breeches in the middle of the braid. The Pavlograd Hussars' braid was orange, and that of the Alexandria and White Russian Regiments was white. With certain exceptions, the braid on officers' breeches followed the patterns set by the attilas as to the colour of the cord or gimp chain. However, officers of the Pavlograd, Alexandria and White Russian Hussars had hussar lace, matching the regiment's button colour, on their breeches.

When in full dress but not parading with their men, officers were allowed to wear blue trousers. The trousers carried a thin strip of trim in the colour of the regimental busby bag. The trousers could also be worn in walking-out dress. Trousers were worn with ankle boots or shoes rather than the standard knee-high riding boots.

Boots

Hussars of both the guard and the line wore special 'hussar-style' boots of black leather, decorated in the front with a metal rosette in the regiment's button colour. The rosette for the 11th Izyum Hussars was copper. The boots were cut with a pronounced 'V' in the front and the back and no trim on the top of the boots. The spurs for officers in all regiments were silvered metal. Other ranks wore white metal spurs.

Walking-Out Dress

Winter walking-out dress for the line, with certain exceptions, was essentially the same as full dress. The pouch belt, sabretache, sash and revolver were not worn. Officers and senior NCOs replaced the busby with a peaked cap. The body of the cap was the colour of the attila and the band was the colour of the busby bag. The edge of the crown and the top and bottom of the band were piped in yellow or white welts depending on the regimental button colour. The 17th Chernigov Hussars were distinguished by a brick red cap and band, both trimmed in yellow. A cockade similar to that worn on the busby was worn on the front of the band. Other ranks wore a peakless cap of the same colours. They would wear it as far to the right side as possible, a tendency still evident in the modern Russian soldier. Indeed, some photos show the edge resting on the right ear, but since a chinstrap was not worn, this is doubtlessly a position that had been carefully composed to look as smart as possible when the wearer's picture was being taken.

Pelisse

Some line hussar officers, like their brother officers in the guards, wore a pelisse in winter full dress. It could be worn as a jacket or Russian-style, hanging down the wearer's back. It was not worn covering one shoulder as was done in the German and Austro-Hungarian armies.

The pelisse was worn by three line regiments in 1914. The 2nd Pavlograd Hussars wore a pelisse of dark green with turquoise lining. The pelisse of the 3rd Elizabetgrad Hussars was white with light blue lining and that of the 11th Izyum Hussars was dark blue with red lining. The braid was cord or chain filigree depending on what was worn on the attila. Other ranks wore wool braid which matched their button colour, with the exception of the 11th Izyum Hussars, whose other ranks had white braid on the pelisse. The shape of the chest and back braid was the same as the attila. There was shoulder braid with rank beads. The

V:121 5th Hussar in the Blouse worn by the Russian Army Note the school and regimental badge worn on the left pocket and the monogram on his shoulder strap.

collar, front, bottom, rear vent, and cuffs of the pelisse were trimmed with black fur. The pelisse of officers of the 2nd Pavlograd Hussars, like their attila, had gold hussar lace below the bottom of the cuff braid. The fur was below the lace. Because of this, in place of the diamond-shaped patch of fur below the cuff knot, their cuff fur took the shape of a pencil point. The cuff of other ranks was similar in design to the attila, with the portion of the cuff below the bottom of the braid being in fur.

The honorary commanders of the other regiments were also allowed to wear a pelisse. In such a case the colour was that of the attila, the lining that of the busby bag, and the braid in the regiment's button colour. If the regiment had gimp chain on the attila, this would also be on the pelisse. The one exception was the 15th Ukrainian Hussars, where the honorary colonel, the czar's sister Olga, wore a pelisse of black with light blue lining. It is suggested by Zweguintzow that this was done to save the honorary colonel from the embarrassment of wearing of one flesh-coloured garment on top of another.[113]

The commander of the 11th Izyum Hussars did not wear a pelisse. This tradition commemorated a day when Catherine the Great was reviewing the regiment. The weather unexpectedly turned chilly, and the commander gallantly gave the empress his pelisse.

Normally uniforms other than winter full dress are beyond the scope of this work. Image V:121 is included to show where officers wore their regimental and school badges. This style of blouse was worn by officers of all branches. The regimental and school badges can be seen on the left pocket. The shoulder straps, worn with the blouse, were secured near the collar by a button bearing the imperial eagle, the colour of which was the opposite of the regiment's button colour. In Image V:121 the shoulder strap carried the monogram of the honorary commander, Empress Alexandria.

UNIFORM ACCESSORIES

By 1914, the majority of hussar regiments had been allowed to adopt regimental badges. These were often, but not always, worn on the winter full dress uniform, and when worn were carried on the left-hand side of the chest. When worn on the hussar winter uniform, the badge was normally carried between the second and third row of braid; this can just be seen in Image V:52.

The badge was a much more important part of the summer dress uniform as the colour combinations of the attila, busby bag, and button colour were often not sufficient to distinguish between regiments. In summer uniform, the badges were worn on the pockets of the tunic or blouse. The 5th Alexandria Hussars had a second regimental badge to mark the fifth anniversary of Empress Alexandra being the honorary commander of the regiment (Image V:122). The 15th, 16th, and 18th Regiments did not have regimental badges. An officer could also wear the badge of his military college on the left-hand side of the chest, along with the badges of each school he had attended to receive advanced training in the military sciences, riding school, machine-gun school, translators' school, etc. On the right side of the chest the badges of the staff college were worn (Image V:120).

Regimental Customs

The 5th Alexandria Hussars had two unusual customs. Upon joining the regiment, a new officer took the name of an officer who had served (and been killed) in the regiment during the Napoleonic Wars. He was thereafter referred to by that name within the regiment while he served as a regimental officer. Because of this custom, the regiment was known as the 'immortals'.[114]

The other custom started just before World War I. Certain officers of the 5th Hussars, perhaps the young *beau sabreur* type, began wearing a gold earring while in uniform. It is unclear what initiated this custom. Perhaps it went with the pirate theme of the skull and crossbones badge on their busby, which the regiment received in 1914. What is certain is that the earring wearing caused a scandal.[115]

Age of Regiments

It can be noted from looking at the formation dates for hussar regiments in §V-2-1 that several of them date back to 1651. This makes them among the oldest regiments in the Russian army, and indeed in Europe. They were originally formed as Cossack outposts on the frontiers of the old Moscow state. They held on as cavalry units through the centuries with their cavalry type shifting as needs and military fashions changed.

V:122 Regimental Badge of the 5th Hussars

§V-8 STEPPES (OR PLAINS) COSSACKS

The Russian line Cossacks were composed of two different types of Cossacks: the Steppes (or Plains) Cossacks and the Caucasus (or Mountain) Cossacks. Although all were Cossacks, their uniforms differed in many ways, so they are treated separately in this work.

It is the Steppes Cossacks that most people have in mind when they think of Russian Cossacks. The Steppes Cossacks were divided into several different groups or hosts – Don Cossacks, Orenburg Cossacks, etc. – each with its own internal administration. These groups formed their own regiments.

UNIFORM

Headdress

The Steppes Cossacks' headdress was the papakha. There were two slightly different models of papakha assigned to the different Steppes Cossack Hosts. The Don, Orenburg, Astrakhan, Siberian, and Semirechye Cossacks wore a papakha with a cylindrical body that narrowed slightly, made of short-haired fur. In the 1890s, the way in which the sides of the papakha narrowed was fairly obvious, and the effect was somewhat like wearing an inverted flowerpot on the head (See Images V:56 and V:61). As the papakha continued to evolve between the 1890s and 1914, however, the sides became less and less slanted, so by 1914 it was almost completely cylindrical but still

V:123 Officer of the Astrakhan Cossacks, c. 1912
Note the wide band on the outside of his trousers and the shape of his papakha. Also note his long hair. Cossacks did not have to wear their hair short like the men in the regular Russian army. They also had the privilege of wearing facial hair if they wished to do so.

V:124 Ural Guard Cossacks Officer, 1890s
Note the thick fur of the papakha and the badge on the lower right side of his pouch belt. The cord falling from around his neck down to his right side leads to the regulation holster and pistol.

Table V.8.1: The Steppes Cossacks

Host	Button and Epaulette Colour	Tunic, Collar, and Cuff Colour	Collar & Cuff Trim Colour	Shoulder Straps	Pantaloon Stripe and Papakha Top	Monograms/Markings Epaulette	Monograms/Markings Shoulder Strap[a]
Don Cossack Host: 17 regiments and 6 separate sotnias	Silver	Dark blue	Red	Dark blue[b]	Red	A	B
Orenburg Cossack Host: 6 regiments, 1 demi-regiment and 2 separate sotnias	Silver	Dark green	Light blue	Light blue	Light blue	C	D
Astrakhan Cossack Host: 1 regiment	Silver	Dark blue	Yellow	Yellow	Yellow	E	F
Ural Cossack Host: 3 regiments	Silver	Dark blue	Raspberry	Raspberry	Raspberry	E	G
Siberian Cossack Host: 3 regiments	Silver	Dark green	Red	Red	Red	E	H
Semirechye Cossack Host: 1 regiment	Silver	Dark green	Raspberry	Raspberry	Raspberry	E	I
Trans-Baikal Cossack Host: 4 regiments	Silver	Dark green	Yellow	Yellow	Yellow	E	J
Amur Cossack Host: 1 regiment	Silver	Dark green	Yellow	Dark green[c]	Yellow	E	K
Ussuri Cossack Host: 1 regiment	Silver	Dark green	Yellow	Yellow	Yellow	E	L
Other Steppes Cossacks: Irkutsk Sotnia and Krasnoyarsk Sotnia	Silver	Dark green	Yellow	Yellow	Yellow	E	M

Notes: [a] The notes indicated in this column give the colour of the marking as it was embroidered on the shoulder straps of the other ranks. When officers wore shoulder straps, they had the same markings, but in the inverse button colour (gold metallic).
[b] Red trim.
[c] Yellow trim.

A: 2nd Don Cossack Regiment – silver monogram A (Crown Prince Grand Duke Alexis). Other regiments and sotnias – no monogram; epaulette bears same marking as shoulder strap in inverse button colour.
B: 1st Don Cossack Regiment – regimental number in red. 2nd Don Cossack Regiment – white monogram A (Crown Prince Grand Duke Alexis) with a crown above it. 3rd–17th Don Cossack Regiments – individual regimental numbers in red. 1st–6th Separate Don Cossack Sotnias – regimental number followed by letter Д. in red.
C: 1st Orenburg Cossack Regiment – silver monogram A (Crown Prince Grand Duke Alexis). Other regiments and sotnias – no monogram; epaulette bears same marking as shoulder strap in inverse button colour.
D: 1st Orenburg Cossack Regiment – white monogram A (Crown Prince Grand Duke Alexis) with a crown above it. 2nd, 5th, and 6th Orenburg Cossack Regiments – individual regimental numbers in yellow. 3rd Orenburg Cossack Regiment – regimental number in yellow followed by abbreviation У.-С. 4th Orenburg Cossack Regiment – regimental number in yellow followed by abbreviation И.-С. 1st and 2nd Separate Orenburg Sotnias – sotnia number in yellow. Separate Orenburg Cossack Demi-Regiment – yellow letter О.
E: No monogram – epaulette bears same marking as shoulder strap in inverse button colour.
F: 1st Astrakhan Cossack Regiment – regimental number in red.
G: 1st–3rd Ural Cossack Regiments – regimental number in yellow.
H: 1st–3rd Siberian Cossack Regiments – regimental number followed by abbreviation Сб. in yellow.
I: 1st Semirechye Cossack Regiment – regimental number followed by abbreviation См. in yellow.
J: Regimental numbers and abbreviations in red. Regiment numbers and abbreviations were as follows: 1st Nerchinsk – Нрч; 1st Verkhneudinsk – В.-Уд; 1st Chita – Чт; 1st Argun – Арг.
K: 1st Amur Cossack Regiment – regimental number in yellow.
L: Regiment of Ussuri Cossacks – abbreviation У. in red.
M: Irkutsk Sotnia – abbreviation Ир. in red. Krasnoyarsk Sotnia – abbreviation Крн. in red.

retained a hint of its former shape (Image V:123). Meanwhile, the Ural, Trans-Baikal, Amur and Ussuri Cossack Hosts, as well as the Irkutsk and Krasnoyarsk Cossack Sotnias, had a papakha that was completely cylindrical and did not taper at all at the top. It was thicker than the other model and made with long-haired fur (Images V:124, V:125, and V:126). Apart from these differences in shape, however, the papakhas were fundamentally the same, so the descriptions that follow apply to both styles.

In full dress and regular dress, the papakha had to be made of black fur. In daily dress for officers, however, papakhas made of sheepskin were worn. The colour did not particularly matter, so the sheepskin could be any colour except white, which was reserved for the Emperor's Escort in the guard. The colour of the cloth top of the papakha for daily dress was also left up to the wearer, provided it was not too conspicuous. The cloth tops of the black fur full dress papakhas were regulated and varied in colour by host (Table V.8.1).

V:125 (Above) Ural Guard Cossacks Other Rank, 1890s
Note the thick fur and the shape of the papahka.

V:126 (Below) Cossacks
Note the singers in the front of the unit and the fact that the lances do not have pennants. Cossacks carried lances without pennants. Also note the large size and thick fur of their papakhas.

The cloth top of the papakha was decorated according to rank. NCOs and adjutants had white braid sewn to the top of the papakha in the shape of a cross. Officers also had braid in the shape of a cross, and additional braid which went around the perimeter of the cloth papakha top. Officer's braid was metallic, in the colour of the button, and varied by rank as follows: for subalterns, the braid was 1.39 cm (0.55 inch) wide Caucasus-style braid, meaning it was a plain metallic braid with a thread the colour of the cloth beneath running through the centre. Superior officers had 2.78 cm (1.09 inches) wide hussar (zigzag) braid, and generals had 2.22 cm (0.88 inch) wide general's (zigzag) braid.

There was a cockade placed in the front middle of the papakha and, if applicable, a distinction banner. See §V-3-1 for details on cockades and §V-2-2 for list of regiments with distinction banners.

Steppes Cossacks when not in full dress often wore a cap with a wide top and a narrow visor. The Cossacks had two different widths of tops. One was the standard Russisn army shape, the other had a wider top (see Image V:127).

V:127 Cossack Band
Note relatively long hair on the man in front and the large topped hats often worn by Cossacks.

In March 1914, the 17th Don Cossack Regiment was given a silver skull and crossbones badge for the front of their papakha. The badge was the same design as that worn by the 5th Hussars (Images V:115 and V:116).[116] The regiment's distinction banner was placed above the skull, and the obligatory cockade was above the banner.

Earlier, in 1909, the 17th Don Cossacks were granted a special regimental flag in memory of General Yakov Baklanov. The flag was black and had a large white skull and crossbones on one side together with a statement in Cyrillic that translates as: 'I hope in the resurrection of death and eternal life. Amen.'[117] This was the flag Colonel Baklanov used as his personal banner while he was fighting in the Caucasus in command of the 17th Don Cossack Regiment. The Russians believed the flag caused a feeling of superstitious fear and inevitable defeat among the resisting mountain tribes.[118] The other side was black with '17Д' ('17D') in white.

Tunic

The full dress tunic worn by the Steppes Cossacks was in the distinctive Cossack cut: single-breasted, without any buttons, closing in the front by means of hooks instead (Image V:128). It was made of either dark blue or dark green cloth according to regiment (Table V.8.1) and did not have any piping on the front or any pockets. The lining of the tunic was the same colour as the rest of the tunic.

The standing collar of the Cossack tunic was rounded, and the same colour as the rest of the tunic. It was trimmed with 0.28 cm (0.11 inch) wide coloured piping (Table V.8.1). There was a single litzen on each side of the collar. The collar litzen was simple (chapter shape) and was 13.34 cm (5.25 inches) long and 2.22 cm (0.88 inch) wide. For officers, the litzen was in the button colour, while for other ranks it was white, with a central light (spiegel) that was the colour of the collar piping. There were no buttons in the collar litzen.

The cuffs were pointed, in the colour of the tunic with the same colour of piping as the collar. The cuffs had litzen of the same colour and style as the collar, one on each cuff. The cuff litzen did not contain buttons.

V:128 Line Cossack Officer
Note wide coloured band on his trousers in this view. Also note the wide white pouch belt. he buckle in front has slid down out of sight.

Epaulettes

Officers of the Steppes Cossacks wore epaulettes with the tunic in full dress. The epaulettes were cavalry-style, and were in the silver button colour for all regiments. The piping and lining were the colour of the collar trim (Table V.8.1). Officer epaulettes included repoussé monograms where applicable (Table V.8.1). If the regiment did not have a monogram, no marking, not even the regimental number, was worn on the epaulette. See §V-3-1 for more details regarding types of epaulettes.

Shoulder Straps

Shoulder straps could be worn by officers of the Steppes Cossacks in regular and walking-out dress. Other ranks wore shoulder straps with all uniforms. The colour of the strap and its trim (where applicable) varied by host. Shoulder straps usually bore either monograms, numbers, or other markings (Table V.8.1). See §V-3-1 for details on shoulder straps.

Tchekman

The officers had an additional undress jacket, the tchekman, which could be worn in walking-out dress. This was a form of native jacket which was quite long, and simlar to European frock coats. The tchekman was the same colour as the full dress tunic (Table V.8.1) and went down to the knees. It didn't have piping on the front. The rounded collar and straight cuffs were the same colour as the rest of the tchekman, piped in the same colours as the tunic. The tchekman did not have litzen.

Cossack Charivari

Both officers and other ranks of the Steppes Cossacks wore blue Cossack charivari in full dress. There were 4.45 cm (1.75 inch) wide Cossack-style bands in the host's colour (see Table V.8.1 for the colour of the outside band on the garments' legs). See §V-3-1 for more details on Cossack charivari and bands.

The tchekman was always worn with Cossack charivari that had simple piping rather than the distinctive Cossack-style band described above.

Uniform Accessories

Officers' Accessories

Officers of the Steppes Cossacks wore the patrontach-style pouch and standard model pouch belt in full dress. The pouch ornament was the silver double-headed eagle. The pouch belt was silver and buckled on the chest because it was being worn with the patrontach rather than the standard model lyadunka pouch.

Belts

Other ranks of the Steppes Cossacks wore a brown leather belt in full dress. Officers wore the officers' sash in full dress.

Boots and Gloves

All ranks of the Steppes Cossacks wore standard riding boots and standard white gloves in full dress. Standard brown gloves could be worn in regular and walking-out dress. See §V-3-1 for more details on accessories.

Nagyka Whip

The Cossacks did not wear spurs. Instead, they carried a short, thick whip called a *nagyka*. The whip had a thick leather handle, usually with a decorative tassel at the top. From the handle and tassel came a long braided cord, usually composed of three strips of leather tightly woven together. At the end of the cord was a leather-covered weighted tip made of lead or another metal. The primary use for the nagyka was urging a horse. It also proved to be an effective method of crowd control. When unruly mobs congregated in Russian cities, the Cossacks were often called in by the government authorities. Using whips on the crowds was seen as an effective, but still fairly humane and non-lethal method, so the Cossacks had no qualms about using the nagyka on the people. With its metal-weighted tip, however, the nagyka could still inflict quite a bit of damage – i.e. cut to the bone – and the crowds learned to disperse quickly when the Cossacks arrived. The men on the right of the front and back rows in Image V:65 are holding nagyka whips.

Horses

Traditionally, Cossacks supplied their own horses, equipment and some weapons. In exchange, they were given certain rights, such as the right not to cut their hair while in the army. The result was Cossacks often rode horses that were not as fit as those issued by the government (Images V:129 and V:130).

V:129 Cossack Band, 1890s
Note the shape of the papahkas.

V:130 Cossacks of the Far East
Note small horses and the men's facial hair.

§V-9 CAUCASUS (OR MOUNTAIN) COSSACKS

The so-called Caucasus (or Mountain) Cossacks originated from the time when certain Cossack hosts were sent to hold the line and encroach on land held by natives of the Caucasus. One of the groups the Cossacks came into contact with was the Circassians. There followed a long period of raid and counter-raid. During these long years, the Cossacks adopted the colourful dress of their native enemies, with its distinctive long coat and cartridges on the chest.

UNIFORM

Table V.9.1: Caucasus Cossacks

Host	Button and Epaulette Colour	Cherkeska Colour	Cherkeska Piping	Bechmet Colour	Bechmet Piping	Shoulder Straps	Papakha Top	Monogram Epaulettes	Monogram Shoulder Straps[a]
Kuban Cossack Horsemen: 11 regiments and 1 demi-regiment	Silver	Black	—	Red		Red	Red	A	B
Terek Cossack Host: 4 regiments	Silver	Black		Light blue	Red	Light blue	Light blue	—	C

Notes: [a] The notes in this column give the colour of the marking as it was embroidered on the shoulder straps of the other ranks. When officers wore shoulder straps, they had the same markings, but in the button colour (silver for Kuban Horsemen and Terek Cossacks).

A: 1st Kuban Regiment – silver monogram M (Grand Duke Michael Nikolaevich). 1st Zaporozhian Regiment – silver monogram E II (Catherine II). All other regiments and demi-regiment – no monograms.

B: 1st Kuban Regiment – yellow monogram M (Grand Duke Michael Nikolaevich) with a crown above it. 1st Zaporozhian Regiment – yellow monogram E II (Catherine II) with a crown above it. All other regiments and the demi-regiment had abbreviations of their regimental name in yellow as follows: 1st Yekaterinodar Regiment – E; 1st Uman Regiment – Ум; 1st Black Sea Regiment – Ч; 1st Poltava Regiment – Пл; 1st Laba Regiment – Л; 1st Caucasian Regiment – К; 1st Line Regiment – Лн; 1st Taman Regiment – Тм; 1st Khoper Regiment – Х; Kuban Cossack Demi-regiment – Кб.

C: All of the regiments originally had abbreviations of their regimental name in yellow as follows: 1st Kizlyar-Grenebskii Regiment – К.-Г.; 1st Mountain-Mozdok Regiment – Г.-М.; 1st Volga Regiment – Вг; 1st Sunsha-Vladikavkaz Regiment – С.-В. In 1915, the Mountain-Mozdok Regiment was given a white monogram Н II (Nicholas II) with a crown above it, and the Volga Regiment was given a white monogram A (Grand Duke Crown Prince Alexis) with a crown above it.

Headdress

Caucasus Cossacks in full dress wore the papakha. It was cylindrical in shape and covered in short-haired black fur, with a slightly rounded cloth top that varied in colour by regiment type (see Table V.9.1). There was a cockade on the front, with a distinction banner above it if the regiment had been awarded one (see §V-2-2 for details about distinction banners).

The cloth top of the papakha was decorated according to rank. Other ranks did not have any decoration. NCOs and adjutants had white braid sewn in a cross. Officers had braid sewn in a cross with additional braid around the border of the cloth top. Officer's braid was in the button colour (Table V.9.1) and varied according to rank. Generals had

2.22 cm (0.88 inch) wide general's (zigzag) braid, superior officers had 2.78 cm (1.09 inch) wide hussar (zigzag) braid, and subalterns had 1.39 cm (0.55 inch) wide Caucasus-style braid, which was plain metallic with either one or two stripes the colour of the cloth underneath which ran the length of it. The braid making up the cross had a single stripe in the cloth colour, while the braid that went around the edge had two stripes.

Officers had an additional papakha that could be worn in walking-out dress. It was not as tall as the full dress model, and the colour was not specified. The fur on the cylinder could be any colour besides white or anything else very bright, and the cloth top could be any colour, provided it was not flashy or garish.

Tunic

The model of tunic worn by the Caucasus Cossacks was the cherkeska, a long robe-like jacket which did not have any buttons or cuffs. Instead of a collar, it had a V-shaped neckline so that the collar of the bechmet (shirt, see below) was visible beneath it. The cherkeska was black, with ten decorative cartridges on either side of the chest, and it fell below the knee for the Kuban Horsemen and the Terek Cossacks (Image V:131).

The Kuban Plastuns were not typical mounted Cossack regiments, but foot Cossacks, organised into battalions like rifle regiments but divided into sotnias instead of companies. Their cherkeskas were slightly shorter than the others, falling at or slightly above knee-level. See §V-13 Cossack Infantry for information on Plastuns' uniforms.

Along the bottom edge of the sleeve, where a cuff normally would have been, there was trim which varied according to rank. Regular troopers had white braid with a stripe running through it which was the colour of the shoulder straps (Table V.9.1). NCOs and adjutants had embroidered braid in the button colour which went around the edge of the sleeve and around the rows of cartridges on either side of the chest. Subalterns and superior officers did not have any sleeve trim, but generals had 4.45 cm (1.75 inch) wide general's braid in the button colour.

Among the guard regiments, Caucasus Cossack dress was worn by the Emperor's Guard Escort. Only one regiment of the Caucasus Cossacks, the Sunsha-Vladikavkaz Regiment of the Terek Cossack Host, had litzen. It had two distinction-style litzen on each sleeve. The litzen did not have buttons. See §V-5-f for more images of this dress, for example Images V:64, V:65, and V:67.

V:131 Senior Officer of the Mountain Cossacks in a Cherkeska

Bechmet

A long, collared, shirt-like garment called a bechmet was worn underneath the cherkeska by Caucasus Cossacks. Because the cherkeska had a V-shaped neckline instead of a collar, the standing collar and top portion of the front of the bechmet was visible (Image V:132). In some cases, it added colour to the otherwise rather dark uniforms the Cossacks wore (Table V.9.1). For plastuns, there was raspberry-coloured piping which went around the upper edge of the collar and down the front edges of the bechmet. When there was additional braid, it was directly below or inside this piping.

The trim on the bechmet varied according to rank. On the top and front edges of the collar, regular troops typically had white braid with a stripe in the colour

V:132 Caucasus Cossack in a Cherkeska
This photograph gives a good view of the dagger carried by Caucasus Cossacks and how the shirt (bechmet) clearly shows behind the cherkeska. Note also the relatively large size of the papakha.

of the bechmet cloth running through it, while NCOs and adjutants had embroidered braid in the button colour. An exception was the 1st Sunsha-Vladikavkaz Regiment of the Terek Cossack Host, which had braid in the colours of St George – white, black and orange – for distinction.

Officers had plain Caucasus-style braid in the button colour with a stripe the colour of the shoulder strap (Table V.9.1) running through it. The braid went around all the collar (top, bottom, and front edges) and continued down the front edges of the bechmet. Officers of the 1st Sunsha-Vladikavkaz Regiment had a single distinction-style litzen on each side of the collar in addition to the trim. Generals had 4.45 cm (1.75 inch) wide general's braid, which effectively covered the entire collar.

Epaulettes

Officers of the Caucasus Cossacks wore epaulettes with the tunic in full dress.

The epaulettes were cavalry-style for the Terek Cossacks and the Kuban Horsemen. They were in the silver button colour, with piping and lining the colour of the shoulder straps (Table V.9.1). Officer epaulettes included repoussé monograms where applicable.

The epaulettes were in the line infantry model for the Kuban Plastuns. The body of the epaulette was raspberry-coloured, while the metal parts of the epaulette were gold. The epaulettes included gold metal monograms where applicable (Table V.9.1). See §V-3-1 for more details about epaulettes.

Shoulder Straps

Shoulder straps could be worn by officers of the Caucasus Cossacks in regular and walking-out dress. Other ranks wore shoulder straps with all uniforms. The strap colour varied by unit (Table V.9.1). Shoulder straps usually bore either monograms, numbers, or other markings. See §V-3-1 for more details on shoulder straps.

Walking-Out Tunic

Officers had a second cherkeska which could be worn for walking-out dress. The colour was left to the discretion of the wearer, with dark colours such as wine and dark blue being preferred. In winter, the V-shaped neckline of the walking-out tunic could be lined with black sheepskin for extra warmth. Shoulder straps were still worn with the walking-out cherkeska, even though they did not always match the cherkeska colour the officer had chosen.

The walking-out cherkeska was worn with a plain white or black bechmet rather than the full dress bechmet.

Cossack Charivari

Caucasus Cossacks of all ranks wore blue Cossack charivari in full dress. For the other ranks, the Cossack charivari were plain. For officers, there was piping in the colour of the shoulder strap (Table V.9.1) running down the seam on the outside of the legs. Officers had additional trousers in a colour of their choice which could be worn with the walking-out tunic.

Bashlyk

The *bashlyk* was a pointed cloth cap which had long flaps that came down on either side to cover the ears and wrap around the neck. It was sometimes worn in full dress over the normal papakha, ostensibly for additional protection against the Russian winter. According to regulation, the bashlyk worn by the Caucasus Cossacks was supposed to be grey. However, because it was, at times, being worn with the black full dress cherkeska, the men took advantage of an opportunity to add some colour to their attire. Thus, several regiments adopted their own more colourful bashlyks in place of grey: the Uman, Caucasian, Yekaterinodar and Line Regiments of the Kuban Cossacks adopted red, while the Poltava Regiment, one sotnia of the demi-regiment, and the Volga Regiment of the Terek Cossacks chose white, and another sotnia of the demi-regiment picked raspberry.

Uniform Accessories

Officers' Accessories

Officers of the Caucasus Cossacks had a braided compass-holder which was worn over the left shoulder and passed under the right arm. The compass attached to it was placed in the front right interior pocket behind the decorative cartridges. There were two models of compass-holder: in wartime, it was made of black silk and had a tassel in the button colour. In times of peace, the entire compass-holder was covered in braid the colour of the button, with a tassel in the button colour.

The belt worn by officers was made of black leather, like that of the other ranks. However, in full dress, the belt was trimmed above and below with braid in the button colour. Additionally, officers had optional silver ornaments which could be attached to the belt in full dress.

Officers wore standard white wrist gloves and black leather boots in full dress. See §V-3-1 for more details on accessories.

Other Ranks' Accessories

Other ranks wore a plain black leather belt in full dress. Like the officers, they wore standard black leather riding boots. However, other ranks did not wear gloves in full dress.

§V-10 THE NATIVE HORSE REGIMENTS

The Native Horse Regiments were part of the line cavalry, but were distinct from the categories of dragoons, lancers, hussars, or Cossacks. Each had unique uniform elements which reflected their heritage from particular regions of the multiethnic Russian Empire.

§V-10-a THE CRIMEAN CAVALRY

The Crimean Cavalry was also known as the Crimean or Tartar Horse Regiment. It was formed as a way of keeping a tradition of Crimean Tartar regiments which appear throughout the Russian army's history, dating back to the time of Catherine the Great. A platoon of Crimean Tartars of the Guard existed from 1827 to 1890.

UNIFORM

HEADDRESS

The Crimean Cavalry wore a black sheepskin busby in full dress. The busby bag, which came to a point, attached to the top of the headdress by means of a hook and fell to the right side. The bag was outlined on both sides with trim, and had additional trim which ran down the centre, dividing the triangular busby bag in half. For the officers, the trim was silver braid with a red stripe running through it. Other ranks had white braid.

On the front centre of the busby there was a silver imperial double-headed eagle. On the left side of the busby at the upper edge was a cockade, and in full dress a 20 cm (7.88 inch) tall white horsehair plume was attached near the cockade. The chinstrap was made of overlapping rows of metal scales, each row having two scales. See *§V-3-1* for more on cockades.

TUNIC

The tunic worn by the Crimean Cavalry was in a special Tartar-style cut (see Image C63, top). It was single-breasted and did not have buttons, closing instead with hooks. The tunic and its standing collar were made of black cloth, and it did not have pockets. Instead of cuffs, there was trim around the bottom of the sleeves. The same trim also went around the bottom hem of the tunic, on the top, bottom, and front of the collar, and down the front edges. For officers, the trim was silver braid with a red stripe running through it. For the other ranks, it was plain red braid. The tunic was much shorter than that worn by the other Native Horse or cavalry regiments, coming down only slightly below waist-level.

Officers had an additional full dress tunic that they wore outside the ranks. It was exactly the same cut as the regular full dress tunic with the same type of trim, but was made of red cloth instead of black.

EPAULETTES

Officers of the Crimean Cavalry wore cavalry model epaulettes in full dress. The epaulettes were in the silver button colour with red lining and piping. The crescent of the epaulette bore the silver monogram A. Ѳ. for Empress Alexandra Feodorovna. See *§V-3-1* for details of epaulettes.

SHOULDER STRAPS

Other ranks wore shoulder straps in all forms of dress including full dress. The shoulder straps were red and had the monogram A. Ѳ. (Empress Alexandra Feodorovna) in white with a crown above it.

Officers wore shoulder straps in ordinary and walking-out dress. Their shoulder straps were also red but had the monogram in gold metal. See §V-3-1 for more details on shoulder straps.

Redingote

Officers had an additional tunic called a redingote that could be worn in walking-out dress. The redingote was black cloth and double-breasted, with two rows of six buttons each on the front. It had a standing collar and straight-cut cuffs in black with red piping. The redingote also had straight, not scalloped, rear false pockets with red piping at the opening and two buttons, one at the top of the opening at waist-level and one at the bottom.

Cossack-Style Charivari and Trousers

Officers typically wore blue Cossack-style charivari in full dress. These had silver braid with a red stripe running along the outside seams of the legs. However, officers also had blue full-length trousers with simple red piping on the outside seam. The full-length trousers were worn in full dress outside the ranks, with the red full dress tunic instead of the normal black one. The full-ength trousers could also be worn in walking-out dress with the redingote.

Other ranks wore blue Cossack-style charivari with plain red piping on the outside seams of the legs in full dress.

Uniform Accessories

Officers wore the Cossack model of pouch (patrontach) and pouch belt in full dress. The pouch had silver braid around the edges of the cover flap and the silver double-headed eagle in the centre. The pouch belt was covered in silver braid with four red stripes running through it and red piping on either side. Other ranks did not wear the pouch or the pouch belt.

Officers wore the standard model officer's sash in full dress. Other ranks wore a brown leather belt.

All ranks typically wore standard black leather riding boots and white wrist gloves in full dress. However, when officers were in full dress outside the ranks, wearing the red tunic and blue full-length trousers, they wore shoes instead of boots. In standard and walking-out dress, brown wrist gloves were worn by all ranks. See §V-3-1 for more information on accessories.

§V-10-b THE DAGESTAN REGIMENT AND THE OSSETIAN DEMI-REGIMENT (CAUCASUS NATIVE HORSE)

These regiments were drawn from natives of the Caucasus. The Dagestan is a region that resisted the Russians for years, led by Shamyl. The Ossetians were friendlier with the Russians and gave the Russians the key pass across the Caucasus mountains.

UNIFORM

The two regiments wore very similar uniforms. Their uniforms, in turn, were nearly identical to those worn by the Caucasus Cossacks, which is only logical since those Cossacks copied their dress from the native people of the Caucasus.

Headdress

The headdress worn by both the Dagestan Regiment and the Ossetian Demi-Regiment was the papakha. It was identical to the model of papakha worn by the Caucasus Cossacks (see §V-9, Headdress).

Cherkeska

The regiments wore slightly different models of tunic in full dress (Table V.10.b.1).

The Ossetian Demi-Regiment wore a black cherkeska with ten cartridges on each side of the chest, much like the one worn by the Caucasus Cossacks. It

Table V.10.b.1: Uniform Colours of Native Horse Regiments

Regiment	Button	Cherkeska Colour	Cherkeska Piping	Bechmet Colour	Bechmet Piping	Shoulder Straps	Papakha Base
Dagestan Regiment	Silver	Light brown	White[a]	White	–	Red	White
Ossetian Demi-Regiment	Silver	Black	–	Light blue	–	Light blue	Light blue

Notes: [a] This was actually cording rather than piping, and was only worn by the troops.

had no piping around the neckline and no trim on the bottom edges of the sleeves, except in the case of generals, who had 4.45 cm (1.75 inch) general's (zigzag) trim on the sleeves.

The Dagestan Regiment also wore the cherkeska with ten cartridges on either side of the chest, but in light brown cloth. The troops had white cording around the V-shaped neckline and the bottoms of the sleeves. NCOs and adjutants had silver embroidered braid around the cartridges and the sleeves. Officers did not have the white cording trim, but did have trim on the cartridge holders for the decorative cartridges on the chest, on the small interior pockets which were located below the cartridges, and around the sleeves. Subalterns and superior officers had plain Caucasus-style silver braid with a red stripe running through it, while generals had 4.45 cm (1.75 inch) general's braid.

Bechmet

As was the case with Caucasus Cossacks, a long, collared, shirt-like garment called a bechmet was worn underneath the cherkeska. The V-shaped neckline on the cherkeska allowed the standing collar and top portion of the front of the bechmet to show (see Table V.10.b.1 for bechmet colours).

The trim on the bechmet varied according to rank. On the top and front edges of the collar, NCOs and adjutants had embroidered braid in the button colour. Officers had plain Caucasus-style braid in the button colour with a stripe the colour of the shoulder strap running through it (Table V.10.b.1). The braid went around the top, bottom, and front edges of the collar, continuing down the front edges of the bechmet. Generals had 4.45 cm (1.75 inch) wide general's braid, which effectively covered the entire collar.

Epaulettes

Officers of the regiments wore silver cavalry model epaulettes in full dress. The lining and piping of the epaulettes were the colour of the shoulder straps (see Table V.10.b.1). Neither regiment had monograms on the epaulettes; however, the epaulettes did have abbreviations representing the name of the regiment.

V:133 Drawing of a Man in the Daghestan Regiment
This type of local native dress was essentially copied by the Caucasus Cossacks. Dagestan was the area of the Caucasus that offered the stiffest resistance to the Russians' efforts to conquer the region.

For the Dagestan Regiment, it was Дг., while the Ossetian Demi-Regiment had the abbreviation Ос. The abbreviations were embossed on the epaulette crescent just like a monogram would have been, and were silver. See §V-3-1 for more details regarding epaulettes.

Shoulder Straps

Shoulder straps could be worn by officers of the Dagestan Regiment and the Ossetian Demi-Regiment in regular and walking-out dress. Other ranks of both regiments wore shoulder straps with all uniforms. The strap colour varied by regiment (Table V.10.b.1), and the shoulder straps bore the same abbreviations as on the officers' epaulettes. For officers the regimental abbreviation was in silver metal; for other ranks it was embroidered in yellow. See §V-3-1 for more details regarding shoulder straps.

Walking-Out Tunic

Officers had a second cherkeska which could be worn for walking-out dress. The colour was left up to the discretion of the wearer, with dark colours such as wine and dark blue being preferred. In winter, the V-shaped neckline of the walking-out tunic could be lined with black sheepskin for extra warmth. Shoulder straps were still worn with the walking-out cherkeska, even though they did not always match the cherkeska colour that the officer had chosen.

The walking-out cherkeska was worn with a plain white or black bechmet rather than the full dress bechmet.

Cossack-Style Charivari and Trousers

Both officers and other ranks wore blue Cossack-style charivari in full dress. For the other ranks, the Cossack-style charivari were plain. For officers, the garment was piped in the colour of the shoulder strap (see Table V.10.b.1). This ran down the seam on the outside of the legs. Officers had additional trousers in a colour of their choice which could be worn with the walking-out tunic.

Bashlyk

The bashlyk was a sort of pointed cloth cap which had long flaps that came down on either side to cover the ears and wrap around the neck. It was sometimes worn in full dress over the normal papakha, ostensibly for additional protection against the Russian winter. The bashlyk was red for the Dagestan Regiment, white for the Ossetian Demi-Regiment.

Accessories

Officers' Accessories

Officers' accessories were the same as those carried by officers of the Caucasus Cossacks. The Caucasus Native Horse officers had a braided compass-holder which was worn over the left shoulder and passed under the right arm. The compass which was attached to it was placed in the front right interior pocket, which was behind the decorative cartridges. There were two models of compass-holder: in wartime, it was made of black silk and had a tassel in the button colour. In peacetime, the entire compass-holder was covered in braid the colour of the button, and also had a tassel in the button colour.

The belt worn by officers was made of black leather, like that of the other ranks. However, in full dress, the belt was trimmed above and below with braid in the button colour. Additionally, officers had silver ornaments which could be attached to the belt in full dress, but which were optional.

Officers wore standard white wrist gloves (see §V-3-1). Officers and men wore boots made of thin black leather. The boots did not have soles or heels, only the plain leather.

Other Ranks' Accessories

Other ranks wore a plain black leather belt in full dress. Their boots were the same as those worn by the officers. However, other ranks did not wear gloves in full dress.

§V-10-c THE TURKMAN DEMI-REGIMENT

The Turkman (or Turkoman) Demi-Regiment was formed in the latter half of the nineteenth century after the Russian conquest of the areas then known as Turkestan. The Turkmen, as they were known by Europeans, were a Muslim ethnic group who led a nomadic existence throughout a large swath of western Central Asia, along the Persian and Afghan frontiers. They were best known for raiding overland caravans, taking plunder and slaves. The Russian conquest of the Turkmen began in the 1860s, but did not end until 1873, when the last outpost fell. Originally, the officers wore a uniform similar to that of the Ossetian Demi-Regiment (Images V:134 and C63, bottom), while the other ranks wore a uniform based on the local style of dress (Images C63, bottom, and Image V:135). By 1894, though, the officer's full dress parade uniform had become more like that of the other ranks, and the full dress uniform for outside the ranks had evolved to resemble a lancer's uniform. In 1911, officers were officially assigned the lancer-style uniform to be worn outside the ranks (Image V:136). Thus, by 1914, the regiment's uniforms had taken on a hybridised appearance that made them one of the more unique regiments in the Russian army.

V:134 Turkman Officer, Before 1911
Note how he is wearing a cherkeska.

V:135 Turkman Other Ranks Full Dress
This full dress uniform, called a khalat, is quite colourful, having carmine red, white, and yellow stripes.

V:136 Turkman Officer's Dark Green Lancer Tunic Worn When Not with the Ranks
The litzen was silver, and the piping was yellow. The buttons are silver.

UNIFORM

Headdress

Full Dress Papakha

Officers and other ranks both wore the papakha in full dress. Their papakha was very large, cylindrical, and made entirely of long-haired black sheepskin. Unlike other models of papakha, which had cloth tops, the model worn by the Turkmen had a fur top as well as sides. The top was decorated according to rank. Officers had plain silver braid with a yellow stripe sewn in a cross on the papakha top, while NCOs had a narrower plain silver braid, also sewn in a cross. Regular troops did not have papakha trim. On the front of the papakha, all ranks had an oval-shaped cockade (Image V:135). See §V-3-1 for cockade details.

Undress Papakha

The undress papakha was the same shape as the full dress model but could be made of black, brown, or white sheepskin. It did not have decorations on the top.

Officers' Czapska

Officers of the Turkmen Demi-Regiment wore a lancer's helmet in full dress and undress outside the ranks (Image V:136). The lancer's helmet was the model worn by the guard lancers, lower than the line lancers, but had a silver double-headed eagle on the front and no guard star. The lancer's helmet covering cloth was yellow and could be removed for undress outside the ranks. The chinstrap was silver, the button colour, made up of overlapping rows of two metal scales each. A black horsehair plume was worn on the lancer's helmet in full dress but removed for undress.

Tunic

Full Dress Khalat

The full dress tunic was a style of garment called a *khalat* and was based on the native Turkestan dress (see Image C63, bottom, and Image V:135). It was a robe-like garment that went almost to the feet, with long sleeves and a collar standing upright in the back but open in the front so the *kourtaktcha* (type of shirt) beneath it was visible (Image V:137). The khalat was made of striped cloth, common for the native dress. The stripes were alternating carmine red, 0.79 cm (0.31 inch) wide, and white edged with yellow, 0.48 cm (0.19 inch) wide.

The khalat trim went around the collar, down the front edges, around the bottom hem, and at the bottoms of the sleeves. For the other ranks, the trim was carmine red braid. Officers had braid varying according to rank. Superior officers and subalterns both had 2.22 cm (0.88 inch) wide silver braid, but superior officers had two yellow stripes in their braid while subalterns only had one. Generals had 2.22 cm (0.88 inch) wide general's (zigzag) braid. On the

V:137 Russian Officer in the Same Dress as Worn by the Turkmen
The shirt, called a kourtaktcha, worn under the coat, is clearly visible in this photograph. The kourtaktcha was yellow, and the officer's trim that went up the chest and around the top of the collar was silver braid with a yellow stripe.

sleeves above the braid, officers of all ranks had thin silver cording in an interlaced lozenge design (Images V:138 and V:139).

Undress Khalat
Officers had an additional khalat which could be worn in undress and service dress. It was identical to the full dress khalat, but did not have any of the braid or trim.

Officer's Tunic
In full dress and undress while outside the ranks, officers wore a lancer's tunic which was similar to the one worn by the guard lancers, with two rows of seven silver buttons on the front. It was made of dark green cloth and had yellow piping.[119] It did not have a plastron. The standing collar had front edges cut on the diagonal, not rounded, and the cuffs were pointed, in the lancer style. Both collar and cuffs were the same colour as the tunic, and both had yellow piping. There were two silver litzen on either side of the collar, and one silver litzen on each cuff. The cuff litzen had a button. The false pockets on the rear skirt were scalloped, with yellow piping and three buttons, one on each point of the scalloping.

Kourtaktcha

Full Dress Kourtaktcha
The kourtaktcha was a type of long shirt worn beneath the khalat, much like the bechmet worn under the cherkeska by the Caucasus Cossacks, the Dagestan Regiment, and the Ossetian Demi-Regiment. It was yellow, with trim around the neckline and front opening at the chest. For officers, the trim was plain Caucasus-style silver braid with a yellow stripe, while, for other ranks, it was carmine red braid.

Undress Kourtaktcha
Officers had a kourtaktcha which was worn with the undress khalat for undress and service uniforms. It was nearly identical to the full dress kourtaktcha, except without trim.

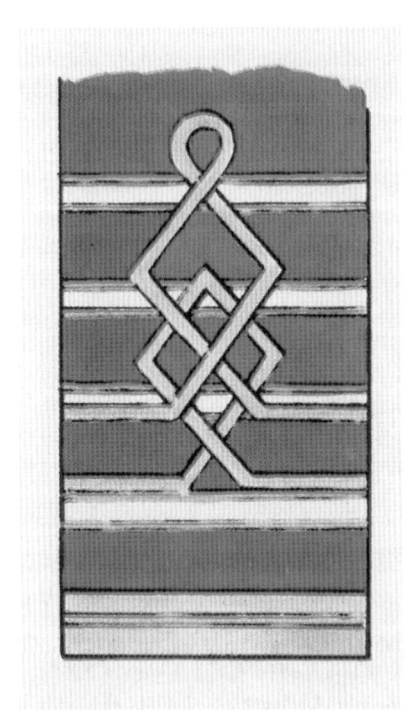

V:138 Officer's Lozenge Design on Sleeve
Rank is shown by braid below the lozenge. There is one yellow stripe on the bottom of the sleeve showing subaltern rank.

V:139 General's Sleeve
This has the lozenge design on the sleeve. Below that is the general's (zigzag) braid showing rank.

Epaulettes

Officers wore cavalry model epaulettes in full dress when appearing with the troops and away from the troops. The epaulettes were silver with yellow lining and piping. The regiment's abbreviation, Трк, was on the crescent of the epaulette in gold. See §V-3-1 for more details on epaulettes.

Shoulder Straps

Officers wore shoulder straps in undress both on and off ranks and in regular dress. Other ranks wore shoulder straps in all uniforms, including full dress. Shoulder straps were yellow and bore the same marking as officer epaulettes in red. See §V-3-1 for more details on shoulder straps.

Cavalry-Style Charivari and Trousers

In full dress, officers wore plain carmine red cavalry-style charivari without piping. Other ranks also wore cavalry-style charivari, but the colour was left to the wearer's discretion, and they did not have piping. For full dress outside the ranks and undress, officers had additional full-length trousers, blue with yellow piping. The full-length trousers were always worn with the lancer's tunic.

Accessories

In regular full dress, both officers and other ranks wore a belt that was a large piece of cloth folded and wound around the waist several times. The cloth was 1.07 m (about 3.50 feet) wide by 2.49 m (8.17 feet) long, and had to be of a darker colour, although the ends could be decorated with brightly coloured wool. For undress, the cloth was grey wool. The regiment also had leather belts that could be worn, black for the other ranks and red for the officers.

In full dress outside the ranks, when wearing the lancer-style uniform, officers wore a standard model officer's sash. Officers also wore the standard model pouch and pouch belt in full dress outside the ranks. The pouch belt was silver, without piping, and the pouch had a silver imperial eagle on the cover flap.

In both full dress and undress outside the ranks, officers wore standard brown gloves. Gloves were not worn by officers in regular full dress or by the other ranks. Boots were worn by both officers and other ranks in full dress. In full dress outside the ranks, officers wore shoes rather than boots with the lancer-style tunic and trousers. See §V-3-1 for more details.

§V-11 THE LINE INFANTRY AND GRENADIERS

These regiments were the largest branch and the heart of the Russian army. In 1914, there were 208 infantry regiments and sixteen grenadier regiments. In addition, there were large numbers of rifle troops stationed outside Europe, in Siberia and Turkistan, and in Finland, that were really just infantry. They are covered §V-12, Line Rifles. These huge numbers mesmerised both friends and foes and made Russia a desirable ally and a country one thought twice about crossing.

The grenadiers were considered a cut above the regular infantry and the the Caucasian Grenadiers, Regiments 13 through 16, a cut above the others. Their status was similar to that of the old British Indian army's Punjab Frontier Force and the Punjab Irregular Force. Like them, it was considered to be a *corps d'élite*.

The regimental number of the infantry and grenadiers does not have any real meaning. It was merely a product of what division the regiment was in. If the regiment moved to another division, its number changed. For many years, regiments did not have a regiment number on their uniform, only the division number they were in and a notation of which brigade they belonged to within that division.

The name of the regiment was the main part of its title, a tradition started by Peter the Great. In most cases, the name did not indicate where the regiment was raised, where it was recruited, or have any other logical relationship to the regiment. However, once given, the regiment, the city, town, or region would make some effort to build a relationship with each other. The applicable civil body might present samovars, silver, or certificates to the regiment. The regiment in turn could send delegations to attend important civil anniversaries or other events.

UNIFORM

Table V.11.1: Russian Line Infantry Regiments in a Division

	Cap Band[a]	Button Colour	Collar Colour[b]	Regimental Trim Colour	Shoulder Straps Colour	Officer's Litzen	Other Ranks Litzen	Notes
1st Regiment	Red T: —	Gold	Red T: —	Red	Red	Chapter shape	—	
2nd Regiment	Light blue T: red	Gold	Light blue T: red	Red	Red	Chapter shape	—	
3rd Regiment	White T: red	Gold	Tunic colour[c] T: red	Red	Light blue	Chapter shape	—	
4th Regiment	Tunic colour[c] T: red	Gold	Tunic colour[c] T: red	Red	Light blue	Chapter shape	—	

Notes: [a] T = trim.
[b] Between 1907 and 1912, the collar was the colour of the tunic and had a shield that went from the front of the collar to the shoulder strap. The shields were: 1st Regiment in the division, red; 2nd Regiment, light blue; 3rd, white; and the 4th did not have a coloured shield (see Zweguintzow, *Uniformes Russe*, p. 54).
[c] Tunic colour for other ranks was black. For officers, it was czar's green.

Table V.11.2: Russian Grenadiers – 1914

Regiment	Cap Band Colour[a]	Facing Colour,[b] Coat, Trousers	Collar Colour	Collar Trim	Button Colour	Officer Litzen	Troop Litzen	Shoulder Straps[a]	Mono-gram	Notes
1	Red T: –	Red	Red	–	Gold	Simple[c]	White simple[b,c]	Yellow T: red	H II and A II[e]	A, B
2	Light blue T: red	Red	Light blue	Red	Gold	Simple[c]		Yellow T: red	M[f]	A
3	White T: red	Red	Tunic colour	Red	Gold	Simple[c]		Yellow T: red	F W IV[g]	A
4	Tunic colour[b] T: red	Red	Tunic colour	Red	Gold	Simple[c]		Yellow T: red	H[h]	A
5	Red T: –	Red	Red	–	Gold	Simple[c]		Yellow T: Light Blue	A[i]	A
6	Light blue T: red	Red	Light blue	Red	Gold	Simple[c]		Yellow T: light blue	M[j]	A
7	White T: red	Red	Tunic colour	Red	Gold	Simple[c]		Yellow T: light blue	C[k]	A
8	Tunic colour[b] T: red	Red	Tunic colour	Red	Gold	Simple[c]		Yellow T: light blue	F M[l]	A
9	Red T: –	Red	Red	–	Gold	Simple[c]		Yellow T: white	H H[m]	A
10	Light blue T: red	Red	Light blue	Red	Gold	Simple[c]		Yellow T: white	M.P.[n]	A
11	White T: red	Red	Tunic colour	Red	Gold	Simple[c]		Yellow T: white	Δ Φ[o]	A
12	Tunic colour[b] T: red	Red	Tunic colour	Red	Gold	Simple[c]	White simple[c,d]	Yellow T: white	H II and A III[p]	A, B
13	Red T: –	Red	Red	–	Silver	Distinction	St George[c,d]	Yellow T: –	H II and M Θ[q]	A, B
14	Light blue T: red	Red	Light blue	Red	Silver	Distinction	St George[c,d]	Yellow T: –	A[r]	A, C
15	White T: Red	Red	Tunic colour	Red	Silver	Distinction	St George[c,d]	Yellow T: –	K[s]	A
16	Tunic colour[b] T: red	Red	Tunic colour	Red	Silver	Distinction	St George[c,d]	Yellow T: –	D[t]	A

Notes: [a] T = trim.
[b] Worn on caps, tunic, and outside of officer's trousers.
[c] Chapter-shape litzen.
[d] Worn on collar and cuffs.
[e] Czar Alexander II.
[f] Grand Duke Michael Alexandrovich.
[g] King Frederick William IV (Prussia).
[h] 'N' for Nesvijz.
[i] Grand Duke Héritier Alexis.
[j] Grand Duke Michel Nicolaiévitch.
[k] 'S' for Samoguitski.
[l] Grand Duke Frederick (Mecklenburg-Schwerin).
[m] Grand Duke Nicholas Nicolaevich.
[n] 'M.R.' for 'Malorossiiski' and Maréchal 'Rumyantzev'.
[o] 'D.F.' for Grand Duke Dmitri Pavlovitch and Phanagoria.
[p] Czar Alexander III.
[q] 'H II' for Nicholas II (first Company) and Czar Michael Fedorovich for rest of regiment.
[r] Alexis, Heir to the Throne.
[s] Grand Duke Constantine Constantinovitch.
[t] Grand Duke Dimitri Constantinovich.

A: The tunic is black for other ranks. It is a mid-green (czar's green) for officers.
B: 1st Company had monogram 'H II'.
C: 1st Company had monogram 'A'.

Headdress

Cap

The full dress headwear for the line infantry was a cap. Other ranks wore a cap without a brim (Image V:140); the officer's cap had a brim (Image V:88). The cap was czar's green for the officers and black for the other ranks, with red piping for infantry and grenadiers. In summer full dress, a khaki version of the cap was worn (Image V:88). The headband varied in colour according to regiment (Tables V.11.1 and V.11.2) On the front of the headband was a cockade. In full dress, the distinction banner was worn on the cap above the headband if the regiment had been awarded one. See §V-3-1 for details on headwear, and §V-2-2 for more on distinction banners.

Papakha

The papakha was worn by the officers and men of the regiments stationed in the military regions of Siberia – Omsk, Irkutsk, and Amur – and the 22nd Army Corps stationed in Finland. This, in theory, could apply to the infantry but there were no infantry regiments stationed in the two areas. The area's foot soldiers were all rifle battalions and regiments.[120] Other troops in these areas – cavalry, artillery, and support troops – would wear it. The papakha style was widely worn by the Cossacks (see §V-12, Line Rifles, for a description of the trim on the top of the papakha).

Image V:105 is a drawing of papakha which shows the top and the difference between the trim of an enlisted man and an officer. The drawing shows a soldier of the Premorsky Dragoons, a regiment which was stationed in Siberia and thus wore the papakha. Images V:123, V:124, and V:125 show papakhas worn by different Cossack troops. Image V:141 shows a papakha worn by Plastuns, the Cossack infantry.

Before the 1910 style was adopted, soldiers had worn the 1875 model, made of long-haired black fur and a top the colour of the tunic cloth, with the same trim.

Shako

In the line infantry, the shako was reserved for generals and honorary chiefs of the different regiments – as long as the regiment was not one of the ones where the papakha was worn. The shako was the same model worn by the guard infantry (§V-6-a). The top portion of the shako was covered with dark royal green cloth. On the front, grenadier regiments had metal plaques in the button colour. The plaques were decorated with the imperial double-headed eagle in honor of the mitres worn by grenadiers in the past. The rest of the non-grenadier regiments (regular line infantry, etc.) simply had the imperial double-headed eagle in the button colour mounted directly on the shako.

V:140 Enlisted Man, Taken 1905
In spite of this date, he seems to be wearing a post-1908 uniform. Very few pictures of enlisted infantry men or officers in full dress winter uniforms of the post-1902 era have made their way to the West. The cap band is the same colour as the cloth of the cap with red piping at the top and bottom of the cap band, because the 184th is the 4th regiment in his division (the 46th). The yellow regimental number on the shoulder strap has shown up dark. His tunic has two rows of six brass buttons. Note that the rows are closer together than the buttons on the guard plastrons. In fact, that the rows of buttons are so close raises the possibility the tunic is one that dates from Alexander II's reign (1855–81) (for a drawing showing this type of tunic, see Mollo, *Uniforms*, p. 136, nos. 101 and 103 and Plate 39). The collar of the tunic was also the same colour as the tunic and had red piping. The red piping on his cuffs can just be seen. More clearly visible is the red piping on the front of his double-breasted tunic and the double-headed eagle on his belt buckle.

The shako's headband was the same colour as the headband on the cap. Generals had a single thick braid of cording on the front of the headband, while honorary chiefs had two of the braids, one on the front and one on the back. There was no piping on the vertical side seams, but in the grenadier regiments there was a grenade in the button colour on either side of the shako. The metal chinstrap of the shako was in the button colour, made of overlapping rows of metal scales.

If the regiment had a distinction banner, it was worn on the front of the shako above the imperial double-headed eagle. In cases where the shako had a distinction banner, the gorget was not worn, because it was inscribed with the same award as the distinction banner. In full dress, a plume was worn on the front of the shako. It was made of white, orange, and black feathers and was the model worn by the guard infantry.

Tunic

The tunic worn by the line infantry was double-breasted, with two rows of six buttons down the front (Image V:140). It was made of czar's green cloth for officers and black cloth for the other ranks.[121] The front of the tunic had straight edges, rather than curved edges like the guard infantry and lancer tunics, because it did not have a plastron. There was piping along the front edge of the tunic – red for infantry and grenadiers. The rear skirt of the tunic had two false pockets, one on each side. The pockets had straight edges that were piped in the trim colour. Each pocket had two buttons, one at the top at waist-level and one at the bottom.

All of the piping of the 1st Neva Infantry and the 2nd Sofia Infantry – front edge of the tunic, collar, cuffs, pockets – was white regardless of what colour they would have normally had as the 1st and 2nd regiments of the division, respectively. This unique white piping dated from 1882 and commemorated the two regiments' previous history as marine infantry regiments. An exception was the piping on the cap, which was red.

Collar

The standing collar of the tunic was 4.45 cm (1.75 inches) in height. In 1914, for all regiments except the 1st regiment of each infantry and grenadier division, the collar had 0.28 cm (0.11 inch) red piping (Table V.11.1). The front edges of the collar were rounded, and there could be two litzen on either side of the collar. The litzen were the chapter style and were 1.39 cm (0.55 inch) wide, positioned equal distances from the piping at the top of the collar and the bottom edge of the collar. The litzen varied according to rank. All officers had litzen that were embroidered in the button colour and could either be plain (smooth) or for distinction (ridged). There were relatively few regiments where the officers had distinction litzen instead of the standard plain litzen; they were the 13th, 14th, 15th and 16th Grenadiers, the 17th Archangelgorod Infantry, the 34th Sevsk Infantry, the 80th Kabarda Infantry, the 84th Shirvan Infantry, and the 98th Yuriev Infantry.

Other ranks did not usually have litzen, but if the regiment had been awarded litzen it was either white with a stripe (central light) the colour of the collar underneath (regular) or in the colours of St George (orange, white, and black, for distinction). See §V-3-2, Table V.11.2, and Table V.11.3.

From 1907 to 1912, the grenadier and regular infantry and rifle regiments and battalions had coloured shields on the front of the collar (see C68a–C70a (top)). The shields were the height of the collar, and for the other ranks they extended from the front edge of the collar to the front edge of the shoulder strap, a length which could be from 7.78 cm (3.06 inches) to 10 cm (3.94 inches) long, depending on what size the tunic was. Officers had shields which extended to the back edge of the epaulette strap. The collars included litzen, but the litzen worn by the other ranks, when they had it, was necessarily shorter in length than that of the officers because of the smaller shield size. Within each infantry division, the shield of the 1st regiment was red, the 2nd light blue, the 3rd white, and the 4th did not have the shield.

Beginning in 1912, the collar shields were eliminated, and instead the entire collar became red for the 1st regiment of each infantry division (no piping), light blue with red piping for the 2nd, and the colour of the tunic (czar's green for officers, black for other ranks) with red piping for the 3rd and 4rth regiments of each division.

Cuffs

The cuffs were straight, not scalloped, and had 0.28 cm (0.11 inch) piping. For the 1st and 13th Grenadiers, the cuffs were red, while for all the other regiments they were the colour of the tunic[122] with piping that was white for the 1st and 2nd Infantry and red for all other regiments. The total height of the cuff, including the piping, was 5.56 cm (2.19 inches).

Beginning in 1912, the line grenadier regiments had Brandenburg-style cuffs, which had the standard circular cuff with a red perpendicular cuff tab that was 5.56 cm (2.19 inches) wide and 8.89 cm (3.5 inches) high. For officers, the tab had three litzen, each with a button. For other ranks, if the regiment had received litzen (Table V.11.3), there were three on the cuff tab, and the buttons were sewn to the litzen. If the other ranks did not have litzen, the buttons were sewn directly to the cuff tab, 0.56 cm (0.22 inch) from the back edge of the tab and spaced equally from each other. As in the guard, the bottom button was not buttoned into its buttonhole on the cuffs of officers' tunics.

The rest of the line infantry – all non-grenadier regiments – did not have cuff tabs. Instead they had plain Swedish-style cuffs, with two vertical litzen, plain or distinction as described above on each cuff for officers. If the other ranks had white simple or St George's litzen, they also had two vertical litzen on the cuff; otherwise their cuffs only had the standard piping. The litzen on the cuffs had buttons on them (Table V.11.3).

EPAULETTES

Officers of the line infantry and grenadiers wore line infantry model epaulettes in full dress. Epaulettes were gold or silver according to button colour, with a cloth centre that varied in colour by regiment and matched the colour of the trooper shoulder straps (see Tables V.11.1 and V.11.2). Epaulettes bore a marking in the button colour on the centre fabric. For grenadiers, the marking was the monogram of the regiment's honorary chief or other sign (Table V.11.2). For infantry, the marking was usually the regimental number. However, some regiments bore monograms instead, or had a monogram and a number (Table V.11.4). See §V-3-1 for a full description of epaulettes.

Table V.11.3: Other Ranks' Litzen

Regiment Name	Litzen Type	Litzen Location
2nd Sofia Infantry	White[a]	Collar
9th Ingria Infantry	White[a]	Collar
34th Sevsk Infantry	St George's	Collar and cuffs
48th Odessa Infantry	White[a]	Collar
65th Moscow Infantry	White[a]	Collar and cuffs
68th Borodino Life Infantry	White[a]	Collar
80th Kabarda Infantry	White[a]	Collar and cuffs
81st Apsheron Infantry	White[a]	Collar
84th Shirvan Infantry	White[a]	Collar and cuffs
145th Novocherkassk Infantry	White[a]	Collar

Notes: [a] This was a standard simple litzen which had a central stripe (central light) in the colour of the collar or cuff under it.

Shoulder Straps

Shoulder straps were worn by other ranks in full dress, and by officers in regular and walking-out dress. For all of the regiments of grenadiers, the shoulder straps were yellow, with piping (Table V.11.2). For the line infantry, the shoulder straps were red for the 1st and 2nd regiments of each infantry division, and light blue for the 3rd and 4th regiments. Shoulder straps for infantry did not have piping. For more details on shoulder straps, see §V-3-1.

The markings on the shoulder straps were the same as those on the epaulettes, but were not in the button colour (Table V.11.1). Infantry primarily had yellow shoulder strap markings (Table V.11.4).

GORGET

Officers of the line infantry and grenadiers whose regiments had earned a distinction insignia all wore the same model of crescent-shaped gorget in full dress (Image V:16(7)). The gorget was either completely gold or silver coloured, according to the regiment's button colour, and did not have any distinctions for the different ranks of officers. The imperial double-headed eagle was in the centre of the gorget. On the gorget was either a simple 'For Distinction' wording or more complex details of the date and battle where the honour had been won (see §V-2-2). The gorget

Table V.11.4: Line Infantry Monograms

Regiment Name	Monogram and Meaning	Notes
1st Neva Infantry	Г. I – King George I, Greece	A
2nd Sofia Infantry	A III – Emperor Alexander III	A
5th Kaluga Infantry	W I – Emperor Wilhelm I, Germany	A
6th Libau Infantry	F. L. – Prince Frederick Leopold, Prussia	A
9th Ingria Infantry	P. P. – Emperor Peter the Great	A
14th Olonets Infantry	П. I – King Peter I, Serbia	A
18th Vologda Infantry	C. C. – King Carol I, Rumania	A
39th Tomsk Infantry	L.V. – Archduke Ludwig Victor, Austria	A
48th Odessa Infantry	A I – Emperor Alexander I	A
51st Lithuanian Infantry	A – Crown Prince Grand Duke Alexis	B
54th Minsk Infantry	Ф – King Ferdinand I, Bulgaria	A
65th Moscow Infantry	H II – Emperor Nicholas II	B
67th Tarutino Infantry	F. A. – Grand Duke Frederick August of Oldenburg	A
68th Borodino Life Infantry	A III – Emperor Alexander III	A
80th Kabarda Infantry	H II – Emperor Nicholas II	C
81st Apsheron Infantry	E II – Empress Catherine II	A
84th Shirvan Infantry	H II – Emperor Nicholas II	B
85th Vyborg infantry	W II – Emperor Wilhelm II, Germany	A
89th White Sea Infantry	A – Grand Duke Crown Prince Alexis	B
145th Novocherkassk Infantry	A III – Emperor Alexander III	A
206th Salyany Infantry	A – Grand Duke Crown Prince Alexis	B

Notes:
A: Crown above monogram.
B: On the shoulder straps, the monogram of the 1st Company is gold instead of yellow. The monogram is yellow for the rest of the regiment.
C: Monogram is worn by only the 1st company of the regiment. On the shoulder straps, it is gold instead of yellow. All other companies of the regiment have the standard regimental number marking on the epaulettes and shoulder straps.

was lined at the back with felt, red for the grenadier and infantry regiments. The felt backing was cut slightly larger than the metal front piece, so it formed a 0.28 cm (0.11 inch) border around the gorget. The gorget hung from the epaulette in full dress or shoulder strap in ordinary dress buttons by means of gold or silver cording depending on the button colour.

The 11th Phanagoria Grenadier Regiment was the only line regiment with a unique gorget (Image V:16(6)). It was the same size and shape as the regular gorget and was made of polished gold metal, but had a gold border of matt-finish metal. The central imperial double-headed eagle was the design used during the reign of Catherine II and was also in matt-finish gold metal. Above the imperial eagle was a polished gold metal decoration made up of two medallions, one with the monogram of Catherin II (E II) and one with the monogram of Field Marshal Alexander Suvorov. It had white lining instead of red, and the lining did not form a border around the gorget as it did for the rest of the regiments. The gorget was worn around the neck suspended from orange and black cords attached to grenade decorations made of oxidised metal.

In units where the full dress headdress was the papakha instead of the cap, officers did not wear the gorget in full dress. Instead, they had a metallic distinction banner on the front of the papakha. This was also the case for generals who wore the papakha in place of the shako in full dress.

Redingote

Officers had a redingote, or undress jacket, in addition to the full dress tunic. The redingote was czar's green and double-breasted, with two rows of six buttons down the front. The standing collar had rounded corners at the front and was the same colour as on the full dress tunic, but without trim or embroidery.

Short Pantaloons and Trousers

Both officers and other ranks wore short pantaloons in full dress. These were the same colour as the full dress tunic, czar's green for officers and black for other ranks. Only officers had piping on the outside seams of the legs of these garments. The piping was red for all of the grenadier and infantry regiments except the 1st Neva and 2nd Sofia Infantry, which had white piping.

Officers had additional full-length trousers, also czar's green, with red piping (white for the 1st and 2nd regiments). The trousers could be worn in walking-out dress with the undress or the full dress tunic.

UNIFORM ACCESSORIES

Both officers and other ranks wore standard black leather boots in full dress, with the exception of the 81st Apsheron Infantry (see §V-3-1). Officers also had black shoes that could be worn in walking-out dress with the full-length trousers.

Officers wore white wrist gloves in full dress, and brown wrist gloves in ordinary and walking-out dress. Other ranks did not wear gloves.

Officers wore the standard officer's waist sash in full dress. Almost all other ranks wore a standard black leather belt. The exception was the grenadiers: in 1914 the first three battalions of a regiment wore white belts, the fourth wore a black belt. Earlier the other ranks of all four battalions had worn black belts.

A buckle in the button colour was worn. For in the line infantry, it had a double-headed eagle after 1904.[123] The grenadier regiments had a grenade on theirs.

For more details about accessories, see §V-3-1.

§V-12 LINE RIFLES

The Russian army contained a large number of rifle battalions and regiments. In 1914, the following types of rifles existed:

Types	Number of Regiments or Battalions
European	20
Caucasus	8
Siberian	44
Finnish	12
Turkestan	22

UNIFORM[124]

All rifle regiments wore essentially the same uniform. Except for trim, the shoulder straps, and, in some cases, the headwear, these were the same as the uniforms worn by the line infantry (see §V-11). The different types of rifles were identified by initials on their shoulder straps, and in some cases by their headdress.

Table V.12.1: Line Rifle Trim

Rifle Group	Headdress	Button Colour	Cap Headband	Cap Piping	Tunic Collar	Tunic Trim	Shoulder Straps	Piping on Officers' Breeches and Trousers
Rifle Group 1: European Caucasus Turkestan	Cap	Gold	Tunic colour[a] Trim: raspberry	Raspberry	Tunic colour[a] Trim: raspberry	Raspberry	Raspberry	Raspberry
Rifle Group 2: Finnish Siberian	Papakha	Gold	Khaki[b]	Raspberry for other ranks[c]	Tunic colour[a] Trim: raspberry	Raspberry	Raspberry	Raspberry

Notes: [a] Tunic for other ranks was dark green/black. For officers, it was a lighter shade of dark green (czar's green).
[b] After 1910. Before 1910, it was tunic colour.
[c] Raspberry for other ranks. NCOs and officers had special trim. See text.

Headdress

Cap
The full dress headwear for the rifles was a cap. It was the same cap as the line infantry and grenadiers'. It was mid green (czar's green) for the officers and dark green/black for the other ranks. Other ranks wore a cap without a brim (Image V:140); the officer's cap had a brim (Image V:88). The cap had raspberry piping. The headband was the colour of the cap, with raspberry piping. A cockade was worn on the front of the headband. If a regiment had been awarded a distinction banner it was worn over the cockade in full dress (see §V-2-1 for distinction banners).

In summer full dress, a khaki version of the cap was worn (Image V:88).

Papakha

The papakha was worn by the officers and men of the regiments stationed in the military regions of Siberia and the 22nd Army Corps stationed in Finland (see Rifle Group 2 in Table V.12.1). It was worn by all troops in these areas, which included cavalry, artillery, and support troops. When it came to foot soldiers, however, the rule applied mostly to rifles as few infantry units were stationed in these areas.

The papakha-style headdress was widely worn by the Cossacks (Images V:123, V:124, and V:125).

In 1914, the 1910 model of papakha was worn by the rifles. It was made of short grey fur and had a cockade on the front. If the regiment or battalion had a distinction banner, it was also on the front of the papakha. Sometimes it covered the lower part of the cockade.

The top of the model 1910 papakha was made of khaki cloth and had trim along the seams, forming a cross. Other ranks had 0.56 cm (0.22 inch) wide cording that was raspberry for rifles. NCOs had cording that was mixed white, orange, and black. Officers had trim in a cross shape like the other ranks, but also had additional trim going around the edge of the papakha top in a circle. For subalterns, it was plain Caucasus-style trim in the button colour with two stripes of raspberry running through it. Superior officers had narrow hussar (zig-zag) braid in the button colour, and generals had general's (zig-zag) braid in the button colour.

Before the 1910 style was adopted, soldiers had worn the 1875 model made of long-haired black fur and a top the colour of the tunic cloth but with the same trim.

Shako

As in the line infantry, the shako was reserved for generals and honorary chiefs of the different rifle regiments and battalions, unless the unit was one where the papakha was worn. The shako was the same model as that worn by the guard infantry (see §V-6-a). The top portion of the shako was covered with dark royal green cloth. On the front of the shako was a gold imperial double-headed eagle.

The shako's headband was the same colour as the headband on the cap, i.e. officer's caps were czar's green. Generals had a single thick braid of cording on the front of the headband, while honorary chiefs had two of the braids, one on the front and one on the back. There was no piping on the vertical side seams. The metal chinstrap of the shako was gold, made of overlapping rows of metal scales.

If the regiment or battalion had a distinction banner, it was worn on the front of the shako above the imperial double-headed eagle. In cases where the shako had such a distinction banner, the gorget was not worn. In full dress, a plume was worn on the front of the shako. It was made of white, orange, and black feathers and was the same as that worn by the guard rifles.

Tunic

The tunic worn by the rifles was the same as that worn by the line infantry. The piping was raspberry (see §V-11).

Collar

The standing collar of the tunic was also the same as that of the line infantry (see §V-11). Collar shields were not worn in the rifles. The gold litzen worn by the officers of most rifle units was the plain smooth type. Only one unit, the 1st Caucasus Rifles, wore a ridged distinction litzen (Images V:9(18)). Other ranks did not wear litzen unless it had been awarded to their regiment or battalion as a battle award (Table V.12.2).

Cuffs

The rifles had the same Swedish cuffs as the line infantry (see §V-11). Their cuffs had gold buttons and raspberry trim. Officers' cuffs had plain litzen behind their buttons, except for the 1st Caucasus Rifles, who had been awarded St George distinction litzen for collar and cuffs.

Other ranks did not wear litzen on their cuffs unless they were one of the five units that had been awarded litzen as a battle distinction (Table V.12.2).

Epaulettes

The rifles' gold epaulettes were identical to those of the line infantry except for minor rifle touches. The centre cloth for all rifle regiments was raspberry. On the raspberry cloth, the officers had their unit designation, usually a number and a Russian letter showing the rifle group (Table V.12.3). In a few cases a monogram was on the cloth as the unit's designation (Table V.12.4). These designations were in gold.

Some of the rifle battalions and regiments were given the right to carry monograms (see Table V.12.4).

Shoulder Straps

Raspberry shoulder straps were worn in full dress by other ranks and by officers in regular and walking-out dress. There was no trim on the straps.

The unit designation on the straps was yellow. These markings were the same as those on the epaulettes (see Tables V.12.3 and V.12.4 for exceptions).

Gorget

Rifle officers wore the same gorget as line infantry officers (see §V-11). The rifles' gorget was gold because of their gold button colour (Image V:16(7)).

Undress Jacket

Officers of rifle units wore the same redingote as that worn by line infantry officers. It had no trim or embroidery.

Breeches and Trousers

Riflemen and officers wore the same breeches and trousers as the line infantry in the same orders of dress. Only officers had piping on their breeches and trousers. The piping was raspberry. In service dress, soldiers in Turkestan often wore trousers of buffalo-skin dyed red. These were known by their Turkish name, *chambari*.[126]

Uniform Accessories

The boots, shoes, belt, belt buckle, double-headed eagle on the buckle, officer's waist sash, and gloves were all the same as those worn in the line infantry.

Table V.12.2: Other Ranks' Litzen

Regiment Name	Litzen Type	Litzen Location
16th European Rifles	White[a]	Collar
1st Caucasus Rifles	St George's	Collar and cuffs
1st Siberian Rifles	White[a]	Collar and cuffs
11th Siberian Rifles	White[a]	Collar and cuffs
21st Siberian Rifles	White[a]	Collar and cuffs

Notes: [a] This is a simple white chapter-shaped litzen with a central light in the colour of the collar and, if applicable, cuff under it (Zweguintzow, *Uniformes Russe*, p. 9 and Plate 73).

Table V.12.3: Rifle Group Letters[125]

Rifle Group	Russian Letters
Finnish	Ф
Caucasus	К[a]
Siberian	Сб[b]
Turkestan	Т

Notes: [a] Zweguintzow shows K_B. (see Zweguintzow, *Uniformes Russe*, Plate B19).
[b] Zweguintzow shows C_6 (see Zweguintzow, *Uniformes Russe*, Plate B19).

Table V.12.4: Rifle Monograms, 1914

Regiment Name	Monogram and Meaning	Notes
13th European Rifles	Н. Н. – Grand Duke Nicholas Nicholaevich	A
15th European Rifles	Н. I – King Nicholas I, Montenegro	A
16th European Rifles	A III – Emperor Alexander III	A
1st Caucasus Rifles	М. – Grand Duke Michael Nicholaevich	
1st Siberian Rifles	Н II – Emperor Nicholas II	B
11th Siberian Rifles	М. Ѳ. – Grand Duchess Maria Feodorovna	B
12th Siberian Rifles	A – Grand Duke Crown Prince Alexis	B
21st Siberian Rifles	A. Ѳ. – Grand Duchess Alexandra Feodorovna	B

Notes:
A: With regimental number below monogram.
B: On the shoulder straps, the monogram of the 1st Company is gold instead of yellow. The monogram is yellow for the rest of the regiment.

§V-13 COSSACK INFANTRY (KUBAN PLASTUN BATTALIONS)

The fighting in the Caucasus was often in mountainous broken terrain. This called for infantry, and the Cossacks responded by developing the plastuns. The word means creeper, slitherer, or crawler. The Plastun Battalions were usually manned by the poorer Cossacks who would have had trouble providing themselves with horses.

UNIFORM

The plastuns dressed exactly like the Kuban Cossacks (see §V-9), except for the trim differences noted in Table V.13.1 and a few other differences.

Cherkeska

The plastuns were not typical mounted Cossack regiments, but foot Cossacks, organised into battalions like rifle regiments but divided into sotnias instead of companies. Their dark cherkeskas were slightly shorter than the others, falling to or slightly above knee-level (Image V:141). Plastuns also had raspberry-coloured piping which went around the V-shaped neckline. This was different from the mounted troops, who did not have piping at the neckline. Compare the length of the cherkeskas in Image V:131 (a regular cherkeska) to Image V:141 (a plastun cherkeska). The cherkeskas had ten decorative cartridges on either side of the chest.

Bechmet

A long, collared, shirt-like black bechmet was worn underneath the cherkeska by Caucasus Cossacks. Because the cherkeska had a V-shaped neckline instead of a collar, the standing collar and top portion of the front of the bechmet was visible. In some cases, it added a splash of colour to the rather dark and understated uniforms the Cossacks wore. The plastuns' bechmet had raspberry-coloured piping which went around the upper edge of the collar and down the front edges of the bechmet. When there was additional braid, it was directly below or inside this piping.

The trim on the bechmet varied according to rank. On the top and front edges of the collar, regular troops typically had white braid with a stripe in the colour of the bechmet cloth running through it, while NCOs and adjutants had embroidered braid in the button colour. An exception was the 1st Sunsha-Vladikavkaz

Table V.13.1: Kuban Cossack Plastuns

Host	Button and Epaulette Colour	Cherkeska Colour	Cherkeska Piping	Bechmet Colour	Bechmet Piping	Shoulder Straps	Papakha Top	Monogram Epaulettes	Monogram Shoulder Strap[a]
Kuban Cossack Plastuns: 6 battalions	Gold	Black or other dark colour	Raspberry	Black	Raspberry	Raspberry	Raspberry	A	B

Notes: [a] The notes in this column give the colour of the marking as it was embroidered on the shoulder straps of the other ranks. When officers wore shoulder straps, they had the same markings, but in the gold button colour.

A: 1st Battalion – gold monogram M (Grand Duke Michael Nikolaevich). 2nd–6th Battalions – no monogram.

B: 1st Battalion – yellow monogram M (Grand Duke Michael Nikolaevich) with a crown above it. 2nd–6th Battalions – battalion number in yellow. Beginning in 1915, the 3rd Battalion had a yellow monogram A (Grand Duke Crown Prince Alexis) and the 6th Battalion had a yellow monogram H II (Nicholas II).

Regiment of the Terek Cossack Host, which had braid that was in the colours of St George (white, black, and orange) for distinction.

Officers had plain Caucasus-style braid in the button colour with a stripe the colour of the shoulder strap (Table V.13.1). running through it. The braid went around the collar's top, bottom, and front edges and continued down the front edges of the bechmet.

Epaulettes

Officers of the Caucasus Cossacks wore epaulettes with the cherkeska in full dress.

The epaulettes were in the line infantry model for the Kuban Plastuns. The body of the epaulette was raspberry-coloured, while the metal parts of the epaulette in gold. The epaulettes included gold metal monograms where applicable.

The shoulder straps, walking-out tunic, Cossack charivari, and bashlyk were all like those worn by the mounted regiments.

The officer accessories of compass-holder and belt were also the same as used by the mounted men. See §V-3-1 for details of accessories.

V:141 Kuban Plastun
Note the short black cherkeska worn by the plastuns (Kuban Cossack infantry) and the distinction banner worn by the 1st and 2nd Battalions only.

§V RUSSIAN EMPIRE: NOTES

1. Geary, *Labor Protest*, p. 122.
2. 'Russia,' *1911 Encyclopaedia Britannica*, pp. 908–9.
3. N. Riasanovsky, *History*, p. 471.
4. Ibid., p. 472.
5. Ibid., p. 471.
6. Kennedy, *Rise/Fall*, pp. 237–8.
7. Gatrell, *Rearmament*, p. 139.
8. Regimental names are from Conrad's *1914 Army*. Formation dates and regimental creation dates are from Zweguintzow, *Army*, pp. 24–6.
9. Correspondence with Conrad dated 16 September 2015.
10. Seaton, *Horsemen/Steppes*, p. 178.
11. Ibid., pp. 179–80.
12. Ibid., p. 180.
13. Information for the discussion on distinction banners is from Zweguintzow, *Army*, pp. 52–101, and Zweguintzow, *Uniformes Russe*, Plate B-65. At places these two sources do not agree with each other. I have elected to adopt the information in *Army* as it is the more detailed and thus more likely to be correct.
14. Drawings of most of the distinction banners can be found in Zweguintzow, *Uniformes Russe*.
15. Gorokhoff, *Garde Russe*, p. 17.
16. Given different years.
17. Tihon Kulikovsky, interview at his home outside Toronto, Canada, spring 1983.
18. Zweguintzow, *L'Armée Russe-7ᵉ*, pp. 904–5. These pages give the best list of squadron horse markings one is likely to find.
19. By Kayleigh Heubel and the author. In general, see Zweguintzow, *Uniformes Russe*.
20. Ibid., p. 3.
21. Ibid.
22. Zweguintzow, *Uniformes Russe*, p. 11.
23. Kovalevsky, Galitzine, and Stelletesky.
24. Gorokhoff, *Garde Russe*, p. 17.
25. Mollo, *Uniforms*, p. 131, no. 72 and Plate 27.
26. Andolenko, *Badges*, pp. 6–7. This book, while quite hard to find, provides extensive coverage of the hundreds of imperial Russian regimental badges.
27. Ibid., p. 7.
28. Conversation with V. Stelletesky, spring 1976.
29. See Zweguintzow, *Uniformes Russe*, Plates A1 through A18.
30. Mollo, *Swords*, p. 54.
31. They can be found in Zweguintzow, *Uniformes Russe*, p. 9.
32. Curtiss, *Russian/Nicholas I*, p. 233.
33. Ibid., p. 111; Shtern, *Jews/Army*, p. 55. The reserve force created was too small to be helpful in time of war. See Curtiss, *Russian/Nicholas I*, p. 111.
34. N. Riasanovsky, *History*, pp. 418–19. Over time the six-year obligation was reduced to three years for the infantry and four years for the cavalry. Golovin, *Russian Army/WWI*, p. 4.
35. Ross, 'NCOs/Continent – 1879,' pp. 244–5.
36. Ibid.
37. Ibid.
38. Intelligence, *Strength/Russia – 1882*, pp. 130 and 132. Candidates for combatant appointments also wore an extra-wide gold chevron.
39. The Russian term is *podpraporshtchik* in the infantry, *estandart junker* in the cavalry, and *podkhorundji* in the Cossacks. Ross, 'NCOs/Continent – 1879,' p. 129.
40. Intelligence, *Strength/Russia – 1882*, p. 132.
41. Gorokhoff, *Garde Russe*, p. 148.
42. This is the implication of an entry in a table on p. 22 of Zweguintzow's *Uniformes Russe*. While the entry is not clear when it comes to service chevrons, it also seems to say that the chevrons were in the regiment's button colour. This could explain why the account in the description immediately above did not cover the colour of the chevrons.
43. Zweguintzow, *L'Armée Russe-7ᵉ*, p. 794.
44. Ibid.
45. Ibid., p. 801.
46. Ibid., p. 802, no. 59.
47. Ibid., pp. 806–7.
48. Mayzel, 'General Staff,' p. 311.
49. Kuprin, *The Duel*, p. 42.
50. Ponomareff, *Political Loyalty*, p. 31.
51. The bulk of the uniform information for both parts of the general staff comes from Zweguintzow, *Uniformes Russe*, pp. 35–6, 43, 47, 48, 60, 61.
52. Ibid., p. 35, Plates A1, nos. 5 and 6; B53, no. 5.
53. Ibid., p. 35, Plate B1.
54. The officer's collar and cuffs in the photo could be a dark red, but that does not account for the velvet appearance.
55. http://www.warstar.info/glinka_russky_army_kostjum/illustrazii_glinka4.html and http://warstar.info/glinka_russky_army_kostjum/illustrazii_glinka3.html contain images of GS officers. They are from 1856 and 1907 respectively.
56. Zweguintzow, *Uniformes Russe*, pp. 43 and 48.
57. Ibid., p. 43.
58. Ibid.
59. Ibid., pp. 53–4.
60. Ibid., p. 53. None of the other sources mention GS distinctions for these officers.
61. By Kayleigh Heubel and the author; Zweguintzow, *Uniformes Russe*, pp. 64–5.
62. Gorokhoff, *Garde Russe*, pp. 171–2. See Riasanovsky, *History*, p. 263 for the founding tradition, and Ignatyev, *Subaltern/Russia*, p. 60 for the Kavalergardia.
63. Gorokhoff, *Garde Russe*, pp. 178–9.

64 Ibid., p. 187; Zweguintzow, *Chronology/Army*, p. 7.
65 Gorokhoff, *Garde Russe*, p. 193; Zweguintzow, *Chronology/Army*, pp. 7 and 16; Zweguintzow, *Army*, p. 55.
66 However, examples of chevalier supravests without back decorations are known.
67 Mansel, *Pillars*, p. 168.
68 Currie, *Scandinavian Story*, p. 99.
69 By Kayleigh Heubel and the author. Zweguintzow, *Uniformes Russe*, pp. 66–7.
70 This section was written by Kayleigh Heubel and the author. Uniform information mostly from Zweguintzow, *Uniformes Russe*.
71 Letter from Wladimir Zweguintzow to author, no date, Paris.
72 Zweguintzow, *Uniformes Russe*, pp. 68–9, 80–1, 86.
73 By Kayleigh Heubel and the author.
74 Mollo, *Uniforms*, p. 132, no. 75.
75 Zweguintzow, *Uniformes Russe*, p. 69.
76 Ibid., pp. 69–71. The sections on the guard hussar attila are by Kayleigh Heubel and the author.
77 Zweguintzow, *Uniformes Russe*, pp. 6, 21.
78 This section was written by Kayleigh Heubel and the author. In general see Zweguintzow, *L'Armée Russe-7ᵉ*.
79 Gorokhoff, *Garde Russe*, pp. 297–8. In general see Zweguintzow, *Uniformes Russe*, pp. 62–3.
80 By Kayleigh Heubel and the author. Generally see Zweguintzow, *Uniformes Russe*, pp. 40–9.
81 Mollo, *Uniforms*, p. 4.
82 Ibid., p. 143, no. 141 and Plate 53.
83 Ibid., p. 128, no. 55 and Plate 21.
84 Ibid.
85 Ibid., p. 130, no. 67 and Plate 25.
86 Zweguintzow, *Uniformes Russe*, p. 44.
87 Ibid.
88 Mollo, *Uniforms*, p. 139.
89 By Kayleigh Heubel and the author.
90 Mollo, *Uniforms*, p. 5; Riasanovsky, *History*, pp. 238, 243–4.
91 Mollo, *Uniforms*, pp. 7–8 and 118, no. 7.
92 Nicholson, 'Reminiscences', p. 31.
93 See Kilovskii, 'Trophy Cuirass', pp. 30–7. This can be found on the Conrad website (http://marksrussianmilitaryhistory.info/PskovCuir4-13.htm).
94 Zweguintzow, *L'Armée Russe-7ᵉ*, pp. 855–6.
95 Ibid., pages vary.
96 Zweguintzow, *Uniformes Russe*, pp. 77–80.
97 Ibid., p. 78.
98 Ibid., p. 79.
99 Ibid.
100 This section by Kayleigh Heubel and the author. Uniform information mostly from Zweguintzow, *Uniformes Russe* .
101 Andolenko, *Badges*, p. 118. Also known as Eylau.
102 The eagles captured were from the 45th and 105th Regiments respectively.
103 For example, see Letrun, *French Flags*.
104 Andolenko, *Badges*, p. 119.
105 This section by Kayleigh Heubel and the author.
106 In 1914, these regiments had the numbers 9 and 10. See §V-2-1. However, apparently in 1854 their numbers were 11 and 12. Mollo, *Uniforms*, p. 134, no. 91. Assuming the Mollo brothers are accurate, and I believe this is a fair assumption because the Mollo family owned and had access to a large collection of information on the Imperial Russian Army, this change of number between 1854 and 1914 is a good example of how Russian regimental numbers could change as regiments were moved between divisions.
107 Ibid.
108 Zweguintzow, *L'Armée Russe-7ᵉ*, p. 862.
109 Nicholson, 'Reminiscenes', p. 31; Alexis Wrangel interview, July 1973.
110 Zweguintzow, *Uniformes Russe*, Plate 90.
111 The right to wear black breeches was granted in 1909. Zweguintzow, *L'Armée Russe-7ᵉ*, p. 862.
112 The right to wear dark blue charivari breeches was granted in 1912. They were worn in both full and combat dress. Ibid., p. 863.
113 Interview W. Zweguintzow at his home in Paris, spring 1984.
114 Prince Nicholas Galitzine interview at his home in Washington, DC, July 1973; V. Stelletesky, interview at the Rodina Museum (Motherland Museum), Howell, NJ, August 1978.
115 Both Prince Galitzine and V. Stelletesky in interviews cited in the preceding endnote mention this peculiarity.
116 Zweguintzow, *L'Armée Russe-7ᵉ*, p. 867.
117 Ibid.
118 'Baklanov'.
119 Zweguintzow, *Uniformes Russe*, p. 95.
120 Zweguintzow, *Army*, pp. 1, 16, and 17; Conrad, *1914 Army*, pp. 9–10, 21–3, and 28.
121 Zweguintzow calls the other ranks' uniform black in his books. The drawings in Mollo, *Uniforms* show green/black uniforms for officers and other ranks from 1881 to 1913.
122 Zweguintzow, *Uniformes Russe*, p. 54.
123 Gorokhoff, *Garde Russe*, p. 17.
124 Zweguintzow, *Uniformes Russe*, pp. 53–5, tables, pp. 58–61.
125 *Handbook Russian Army*, pp. 236, 240–2.
126 Mollo, *Uniforms*, p. 137, entry 104.

§V RUSSIAN EMPIRE: BIBLIOGRAPHY

Interviews and Correspondences

Conrad — Mark Conrad, a long-time student of the Russian army and other armies of the great powers *c.* 1914. He maintains a very informative website on the Russian army (http://marksrussianmilitaryhistory.info).

Galitzine — Prince Nicholas Galitzine, veteran of the Ice March. His family traditionally served in the Horse Grenadier Regiment of the Imperial Guard.

Kovalevsky — Gabriel Dolenga-Kovalevsky, former lieutenant in the pre-World War I Russian Army. He served in the Imperial Guard Cuirassiers Regiment of His Majesty and rose to the rank of colonel during World War I.

Kulikovsky — Tihon Kulikovsky, son of Grand Duchess Olga, sister of Czar Nicholas II. His mother was the honorary commander of the 12th Alexandria Hussars in 1914.

Stelletesky — V. Stelletesky, former Lieutenant of 10th Odessa Lancers. He founded the Motherland Military Museum.

Wrangel — Alexis Wrangel, son of Baron Pyotr N. Wrangel, the last commanding general of the Southern White Armies in the Russian Civil War. Prior to World War I his father had been an officer in the Chevalier Guards.

Zweguintzow — W. Zweguintzow, son of a chevalier Russian guard officer. He made the Imperial Russian Army the subject of a lifetime's study, and he was considered the leading authority on the czar's army in the period 1870–1922.

Books and Articles

Andolenko, *Badges* — Serge Andolenko, *Badges of Imperial Russia*, translated and enlarged by Robert Werlich (Washington, DC: Quaker Press, 1972).

'Baklanov' — Wikipedia Contributors, 'Бакланов, Яков Петрович' (in English 'Yakov Petrovich Baklanov') Wikipedia, https://ru.wikipedia.org/wiki/Бакланов,_Яков_Петрович, accessed 27 July 2015.

Conrad, *1914 Army* — Mark Conrad, *Russian Army Order of Battle, 1914: A Compilation Showing the Organization of the Russian Army and its Units in 1914* (Privately printed, n.d.).

Currie, *Scandinavian Story* — Teresita Currie, *A Scandinavian Story: Two Families Allied in Art and Marriage* (Xlibris Corp, 2007).

Curtiss, *Russian/Nicholas I* — John Shelton Curtiss, *The Russian Army Under Nicholas I, 1825–1855* (Durham, NC: Duke University Press, 1965).

Gatrell, *Rearmament* — Peter Gatrell, *Government, Industry, and Rearmament in Russia, 1900–1914* (Cambridge: Cambridge University Press, 1994).

Geary, *Labor Protest* — Dick Geary, *European Labor Protest, 1848–1939* (New York: St Martin's Press, 1981).

Golovin, *Russian Army/WWI* — Nikolai Nikolaevich Golovin, *The Russian Army in World War I* (originally titled *The Russian Army in the World War*) (Hamden, CT: Archon Books, 1969) (originally published in 1931).

Gorokhoff, *Garde Russe* — Patrick de Gmeline and Gerard Gorokhoff, *La Garde Imperiale Russe 1896–1914* (Paris: Charles-Lavauzelle, 1986).

Handbook Russian Army — British General Staff, *1914 Handbook of the Russian Army*, 6th ed. (Nashville, TN: Battery Press, Inc., 1996).

Head, *Napoleonic Lancer* — Michael Head, *French Napoleonic Lancer Regiments* (London: Almark Publishing Co. Ltd, 1971).

Ignatyev, *Subaltern/Russia* — Aleksei Ignatyev, *A Subaltern in Old Russia* (New York: Hutchinson & Co., 1944).

Intelligence, *Strength/Russia – 1882* — Intelligence Branch of the Quarter-Master-General's Department, Horse Guards, War Office, *The Armed Strength of Russia* (London: His Majesty's Stationery Office, 1882).

Kannik, *Military Uniforms* — Preben Kannik, *Military Uniforms in Color* (New York: Macmillan Company, 1968).

Kennedy, *Rise/Fall*	Paul Kennedy, *The Rise and Fall of the Great Powers* (New York: Random House Inc., 1987).
Kilovskii, 'Trophy Cuirass'	Aleksandr Kilovskii, 'Trophy Cuirass of the Pskov Dragoon Regiment', *Tseikhgauz*, no. 13 (January 2001): pp. 30–7 (trans. Mark Conrad).
Kuprin, *The Duel*	Aleksandr Kuprin, *The Duel* (New York: Macmillan Co., 1916).
Letrun, *French Flags*	Ludovic Letrun, *French Infantry Flags* (Paris: Histoire et Collections, 2009)
Mannerheim, *Memoirs*	Carl Mannerheim, *The Memoirs of Marshal Mannerheim* (New York: E.P. Dutton & Co., 1954).
Mansel, *Pillars*	Philip Mansel, *Pillars of Monarchy: An Outline of the Political and Social History of Royal Guards, 1400–1984* (London: Quartet Books, 1984).
Marrion, *Lancers*	R.J. Marrion, *Lancers and Dragoons* (New Malden: Almark Publishing Co., 1975).
Mayzel, 'General Staff'	Matitiahu Mayzel, 'The Formation of the Russian General Staff, 1880–1917: A Social Study', *Cahiers du Monde Russe et Soviétique*, vol. 16, no. 3–4 (July–December 1975): pp. 297–321.
Mollo, *Military Fashion*	John Mollo, *Military Fashion* (New York: G.P. Putnam's Sons, 1972).
Mollo, *Swords*	E. Mollo, *Russian Military Swords*, (London: Historical Research Unit, 1969).
Mollo, *Uniforms*	Boris Mollo, *Uniforms of the Imperial Russian Army* (Poole: Blandford Press, 1979).
Nicholson, 'Reminiscences'	'Reminiscences of Imperial Russia Part III', an edited version of 'Among the Horses in Russia, by Captain M.H. Hayes, 1900', *Tradition Magazine*, ed. Lt-Col J.B.R. Nicholson, ret., no. 62 (n.d): pp. 28–31.
Ponomareff, *Political Loyalty*	Dmitry Ponomareff, *Political Loyalty and Social Composition of a Military Elite: The Russian Officer Corps, 1861–1903* (Santa Monica, CA: Rand Corporation, 1977).
Riasanovsky, *History*	Nicholas V. Riasanovsky, *A History of Russia* (New York: Oxford University Press, 1963).
Ross, 'NCOs/Continent – 1879'	John Ross, 'Non-Commissioned Officers in Continental Armies', *Journal of the Royal United Service Institution*, vol. 22 (London: W. Mitchell and Co., 1879): pp. 221–60.
'Russia', *1911 Encyclopaedia Britannica*	'Russia', *Encyclopaedia Britannica*, 11th ed., vol. 23 (Cambridge: Cambridge University Press, 1911).
Seaton, *Horsemen/Steppes*	Albert Seaton, *The Horsemen of the Steppes: The Story of the Cossacks* (London: Bodley Head, 1985).
Shtern, *Jews/Army*	Yohanan Petrovsky-Shtern, *Jews in the Russian Army, 1827–1917* (Cambridge: Cambridge University Press, 2009).
Thorburn, *French Army*	W.A. Thorburn, *French Army Regiments and Uniforms: From the Revolution to 1870* (London: Arms and Armour Press, 1969).
Zweguintzow, *Army*	W. (Vladimir) Zweguintzow, *Русская Армія 1914г* (*Russian Army 1914*) (Paris: privately published, 1959 (in Russian)).
Zweguintzow, *Chronology/Army*	W. (Vladimir) Zweguintzow, *Хронологія Русской Арміи, 1700–1917г* (*Chronology of the Russian Army, 1700–1917*) (Paris: privately published, 1961 (in Russian)).
Zweguintzow, *L'Armée Russe-7ᵉ*	W. (Vladimir) Zweguintzow, *L'Armée Russe, 7ᵉ Partie 1881–1917* (Paris: privately published, 1980 (in French)).
Zweguintzow, *Uniformes Russe*	W. (Vladimir) Zweguintzow, *Uniformes de l'Armée Russe, 1914* (Paris: privately published, 1968 (in French)).

§VI

GERMAN EMPIRE

§VI-1 COUNTRY BACKGROUND

For most of Germany's history, there were two types of Germans: Prussians and everyone else. Napoleon said the Prussians were hatched out of cannonballs. Most of the rest of Germany's populace were proudly known as 'A Nation of thinkers, of poets, and dreamers', as Wilhelm Rein (1847–1929) of the University of Jena put it.

Frederick II, father of King of Prussia Frederick William II (r. 1786–97), worried that one day the world would no longer think of Germany as a nation of 'Thinkers, and philosophers, poets, and artists, idealists and enthusiasts'.[1] About the same time, Voltaire said that England ruled the seas, France the land, and Germany the clouds.

The Prussians, on the other hand, were, as a general rule, seen as sedate and serious people who attended to business. The core of the state had been inherited from the Teutonic Order of warrior-monks, who had given it the germ of a very good bureaucracy. Under Frederick the Great, the Prussian state was organized for war, instituting a system to extract the maximum number of men for the army. This set-up was not unique to Prussia. The smaller state of Hesse-Cassel used the same practices during the same time period in order to produce as many regiments possible for its rulers to rent out as mercenaries.

Frederick's well-drilled soldiers punched above their weight during the wars of his period, but it is often forgotten that the men were religiously motivated. At the Battle of Leuthen in 1757, the soldiers who were marching to the flank – a move that won the battle – spontaneously began singing a hymn. Officers wanted to order them to stop, but Frederick is reputed to have said, 'Let them sing; with men such as these I am sure of victory'. After the Battle of Leuthen, a soldier standing beside Frederick the Great began singing, and the hymn was taken up by the whole army. The hymn is now known as the Leuthen Chorale. This spontaneous singing of hymns also happened during or after other battles.

In 1813, the Prussian army adopted the Russian army's custom of evening hymns. On the night after victory over the French was sealed on the field of Sedan, the camped Prussian soldiers did not cheer or celebrate their overwhelming success. Their response was to sing the hymn 'Nun danket alle Gott …'

Napoleon's overwhelming victories over Prussia at Jena showed that the Prussian soldier was not invincible, but they did set into motion a train of events that would have far-reaching effects. There were only two German states that firmly opposed Napoleon: Austria in the Catholic south and Prussia in the Protestant north. At the Congress of Vienna, Prussia was given large blocks of land in the Rhinelands of Germany to act as a counterweight against the day France again became aggressive. In the east, Prussia was given large territories taken from the state of Saxony, which had remained allied with France to the end. This allocation of territory strained relations between the two states until 1914, and soldiers from the two had to be kept apart on manoeuvres because they would tend to get into fistfights.

After the Napoleonic Wars were over, there was much soul-searching by the army, which led to military reforms. These events set the path for Prussia's in the nineteenth century. The Rhinelands turned out to be rich in iron and coal and inventive entrepreneurs and the area became a major centre for Prussia's industrial growth.

The reforms led to the creation of the General Staff, which organized the army and planned its campaigns. Prussia's rise to power as the centre of Germany was accomplished by the army in Bismarck's wars of 'blood and iron'.

The important role of the Prussian army in Prussia's rise to greatness gave the military tremendous prominence, but the rising industrial class that was making Prussia and Germany rich also had great prestige. It is debateable which group was more influential. Certainly some of the less predictable decisions made by Germany – such as building the fleet – were made in response to the desires of the industrialists to sell metal. With a little political bargaining, they had the influence to get their wishes passed into law. Nothing needs metal like warships.

§VI-2 THE ARMY

§VI-2-1   German Cavalry Regiments and Dates Formed – 1914
§VI-2-2   German Infantry Regiments and Dates Formed –1914
§VI-2-3   Physical Characteristics
§VI-2-4   Battle Souvenirs

§VI-2-1 GERMAN CAVALRY REGIMENTS AND DATES FORMED – 1914

Cuirassiers

Regiment	Year Formed
Garde du Corps Regiment	1740
Garde Cuirassier Regiment	1815
Life Cuirassier Regiment Great Elector (Silesian) No. 1	1674
Cuirassier Regiment Queen (Pomeranian) No. 2	1717
Cuirassier Regiment Count Wrangel (East Prussian) No. 3	1717
Cuirassier Regiment von Driesen (Westphalian) No. 4	1717
Cuirassier Regiment Duke Friedrich Eugen of Württemberg (West Prussian) No. 5	1717
Cuirassier Regiment Czar Nicholas I of Russia (Brandenburg) No. 6	1691
Cuirassier Regiment von Seydlitz (Magdeburg) No. 7	1815
Cuirassier Regiment Count Gessler (Rhine) No. 8	1815

Saxon Schwere Reiter (Heavy Cavalry)

Royal Saxon Guard Reiter Regiment (1st Heavy Regiment)	1680
Royal Saxon Carabinier Regiment (2nd Heavy Regiment)	1849

Dragoons

Regiment	Year Formed
1st Guards Dragoon Regiment Queen Victoria of Great Britain and Ireland	1815
2nd Guards Dragoon Regiment Empress Alexandra of Russia	1860
Dragoon Regiment Prince Albert of Prussia (Lithuanian) No. 1	1717
Dragoon Regiment (1st Brandenburg) No. 2	1689
Horse Grenadier Regiment Baron von Derfflinger (Newmark) No. 3	1704
Dragoon Regiment von Bredow (1st Silesian) No. 4	1815
Dragoon Regiment Baron von Manteuffel (Rhine) No. 5	1860
Dragoon Regiment (Magdeburg) No. 6	1860
Dragoon Regiment (Westphalian) No. 7	1860
Dragoon Regiment King Frederick III (2nd Silesian) No. 8	1860
Dragoon Regiment King Carol of Rumania (1st Hanoverian) No. 9	1805
Dragoon Regiment King Albert of Saxony (East Prussian) No. 10	1866
Dragoon Regiment von Wedel (Pomeranian) No. 11	1866
Dragoon Regiment von Arnim (2nd Brandenburg) No. 12	1866
Dragoon Regiment (Schleswig-Holstein) No. 13	1866
Dragoon Regiment (Kurmark) No. 14	1866
Dragoon Regiment (3rd Silesian) No. 15	1866
Dragoon Regiment (2nd Hanoverian) No. 16	1813
Dragoon Regiment (1st Grand Ducal Mecklenburg) No. 17	1819
Dragoon Regiment (2nd Grand Ducal Mecklenburg) No. 18	1867
Dragoon Regiment (Oldenburg) No. 19	1849
Life Dragoon Regiment (1st Baden) No. 20	1803
Dragoon Regiment (2nd Baden) No. 21	1850
Dragoon Regiment Prince Karl (3rd Baden) No. 22	1850
Life Dragoon Regiment (1st Grand Ducal Hessian) No. 23	1790

Regiment	Year Formed
Life Dragoon Regiment (2nd Grand Ducal Hessian) No. 24	1859
Dragoon Regiment Queen Olga (1st Württemberg) No. 25	1813
Dragoon Regiment King (2nd Württemberg) No. 26	1805

Prussian and Saxon Hussar Regiments

Regiment	Year Formed
Life Guard Hussar Regiment	1815
1st Life Hussar Regiment No. 1	1741
2nd Life Hussar Regiment Queen Victoria of Prussia No. 2	1741
Hussar Regiment von Zieten (Brandenburg) No. 3	1730
Hussar Regiment von Schill (1st Silesian) No. 4	1741
Hussar Regiment Prince Blücher of Wahlstatt (Pomeranian) No. 5	1758
Hussar Regiment Count Goetzen (2nd Silesian) No. 6	1808
Hussar Regiment King Wilhelm I (1st Rhine) No. 7	1815
Hussar Regiment Czar Nicholas II of Russia (1st Westphalian) No. 8	1815
Hussar Regiment (2nd Rhine) No. 9	1815
Hussar Regiment (Magdeburg) No. 10	1813
Hussar Regiment (2nd Westphalian) No. 11	1813
Hussar Regiment (Thuringian) No. 12	1791
Hussar Regiment King Humbert of Italy (1st Electorate of Hesse) No. 13	1813
Hussar Regiment Landgraf Friedrich II of Hesse-Homburg (2nd Electorate of Hesse) No. 14	1813
Hussar Regiment Queen Wilhelmina of the Netherlands (Hanoverian) No. 15	1803
Hussar Regiment Emperor Franz Joseph of Austria, King of Hungary (Schleswig-Holstein) No. 16	1866
Hussar Regiment (Brunswick) No. 17	1809
Hussar Regiment 'King Albert' (1st Royal Saxon) No. 18	1734
Hussar Regiment (2nd Royal Saxon) No. 19	1791
Hussar Regiment (3rd Royal Saxon) No. 20	1910

Lancers (Uhlans)

Regiment	Year Formed
1st Guard Lancer Regiment	1819
2nd Guard Lancer Regiment	1819
3rd Guard Lancer Regiment	1860
Lancer Regiment Czar Alexander III of Russia (West Prussian) No. 1	1745
Lancer Regiment von Katzler (Silesian) No. 2	1745
Lancer Regiment Czar Alexander II of Russia (1st Brandenburg) No. 3	1809
Lancer Regiment von Schmidt (1st Pomeranian) No. 4	1815
Lancer Regiment (Westphalian) No. 5	1815
Lancer Regiment (Thuringian) No. 6	1813
Lancer Regiment Grand Duke Friedrich of Baden (Rhine) No. 7	1734
Lancer Regiment Count zu Dohna (East Prussian) No. 8	1812
Lancer Regiment (2nd Pomeranian) No. 9	1860
Lancer Regiment Prince August of Württemberg (Posen) No. 10	1860
Lancer Regiment Count Haeseler (2nd Brandenburg) No. 11	1860
Lancer Regiment (Lithuanian) No. 12	1860
King's Lancer Regiment (1st Hanoverian) No. 13	1803
Lancer Regiment (2nd Hanoverian) No. 14	1805
Lancer Regiment (Schleswig-Holstein) No. 15	1866
Lancer Regiment Henning of Treffenfeld (Altmark) No. 16	1866
Lancer Regiment Emperor Franz Joseph of Austria, King of Hungary (1st Royal Saxon) No. 17	1867
Lancer Regiment (2nd Royal Saxon) No. 18	1867
Lancer Regiment King Karl (1st Württemberg) No. 19	1683
Lancer Regiment King Wilhelm I (2nd Württemberg) No. 20	1809
Lancer Regiment 'Kaiser Wilhelm II, King of Prussia' (3rd Royal Saxon) No. 21	1905

Jäger zu Pferde (Mounted Rifles)

Regiment	Year Formed
Royal Jäger zu Pferde Regiment No. 1	1901
Jäger zu Pferde Regiment Nos 2–3	1905
Jäger zu Pferde Regiment No. 4	1906
Jäger zu Pferde Regiment No. 5	1908
Jäger zu Pferde Regiment No. 6	1910
Jäger zu Pferde Regiment Nos 7–13	1913

Bavarian Schwere Reiter (Heavy Cavalry)

Regiment	Year Formed
1st Bavarian Schwere Reiter Regiment Prince Karl of Bavaria	1814
2nd Bavarian Schwere Reiter Regiment Archduke Franz Ferdinand of East Austria	1815

Bavarian Chevaulegers (Light Horse)

Regiment	Year Formed
1st Royal Bavarian Chevaulegers Regiment Czar Nicholas II of Russia	1682
2nd Royal Bavarian Chevaulegers Regiment Taxis	1682
3rd Royal Bavarian Chevaulegers Regiment Duke Karl Theodore	1724
4th Royal Bavarian Chevaulegers Regiment King	1744
5th Royal Bavarian Chevaulegers Regiment Grand Duke Friedrich of Austria	1776
6th Royal Bavarian Chevaulegers Regiment Prince Albrecht of Prussia	1803
7th Royal Bavarian Chevaulegers Regiment Prince Alfonse	1905
8th Royal Bavarian Chevaulegers Regiment	1909

Bavarian Lancer Regiments

Regiment	Year Formed
1st Royal Bavarian Lancer Regiment Kaiser Wilhelm II, King of Prussia	1863
2nd Royal Bavarian Lancer Regiment King	1863

§VI-2-2 GERMAN INFANTRY REGIMENTS AND DATES FORMED – 1914

Regiment	Year Formed
Foot Guards Regiment No. 1	1688
Foot Guards Regiment No. 2	1813
Foot Guards Regiment No. 3	1860
Foot Guards Regiment No. 4	1860
Foot Guards Regiment No. 5	1897
Guard Fusilier Regiment No. 1	1826
Guard Grenadier Regiment Czar Alexander No. 1	1814
Guard Grenadier Regiment Emperor Franz No. 2	1814
Guard Grenadier Regiment Queen Elizabeth No. 3	1860
Guard Grenadier Regiment Queen Augusta No. 4	1860
Guard Grenadier Regiment No. 5	1897
Grenadier Regiment Crown Prince (1st East Prussian) No. 1	1655
Grenadier Regiment King Frederick William IV (1st Pomeranian) No. 2	1679
Grenadier Regiment King Frederick William I (2nd East Prussian) No. 3	1685
Grenadier Regiment King Frederick the Great (3rd East Prussian) No. 4	1626
Grenadier Regiment King Frederick I (4th East Prussian) No. 5	1689
Grenadier Regiment Count Kleist von Mollendorf (1st West Prussian) No. 6	1772
Grenadier Regiment King Wilhelm I (2nd West Prussian) No. 7	1797
Life Grenadier Regiment King Frederick William III (1st Brandenburg) No. 8	1808
Kolberg Grenadier Regiment Count Gneisenau (2nd Pomeranian) No. 9	1808
Grenadier Regiment King Frederick William II (1st Silesian) No. 10	1808
Grenadier Regiment King Frederick III (2nd Silesian) No. 11	1808
Grenadier Regiment Prince Karl of Prussia (2nd Brandenburg) No. 12	1813
Infantry Regiment Herwarth von Bittenfeld (1st Westphalian) No. 13	1813
Infantry Regiment Count Schwerin (3rd Pomeranian) No. 14	1813
Infantry Regiment Prince Frederick of the Netherlands (2nd Westphalian) No. 15	1813
Infantry Regiment Baron von Sparr (3rd Westphalian) No. 16	1813
Infantry Regiment Count Barfuss (4th Westphalian) No. 17	1813
Infantry Regiment von Grolman (1st Posen) No. 18	1813
Infantry Regiment von Courbière (2nd Posen) No. 19	1813
Infantry Regiment Count Tauentzien von Wittenberg (3rd Brandenburg) No. 20	1813

Regiment	Year
Infantry Regiment von Borcke (4th Pomeranian) No. 21	1813
Infantry Regiment Keith (1st Upper Silesian) No. 22	1813
Infantry Regiment von Winterfeldt (2nd Upper Silesian) No. 23	1813
Infantry Regiment Grand Duke Frederick Franz II of Mecklenburg-Schwerin (4th Brandenburg) No. 24	1813
Infantry Regiment von Lützow (1st Rhine) No. 25	1813
Infantry Regiment Prince Leopold of Anhalt-Dessau (1st Magdeburg) No. 26	1813
Infantry Regiment Prince Louis Ferdinand of Prussia (2nd Magdeburg) No. 27	1815
Infantry Regiment von Goeben (2nd Rhine) No. 28	1813
Infantry Regiment von Horn (3rd Rhine) No. 29	1813
Infantry Regiment Count Werder (4th Rhine) No. 30	1812
Infantry Regiment Count Bose (1st Thuringian) No. 31	1812
Infantry Regiment (2nd Thuringian) No. 32	1815
Fusilier Regiment Count Roon (1st East Prussian) No. 33	1749
Fusilier Regiment Queen Viktoria of Sweden (1st Pomeranian) No. 34	1720
Fusilier Regiment Prince Heinrich of Prussia (1st Brandenburg) No. 35	1815
Fusilier Regiment General Field Marshal Count Blumenthal (1st Madgeburg) No. 36	1815
Fusilier Regiment von Steinmetz (1st West Prussian) No. 37	1818
Fusilier Regiment Field Marshal Count Moltke (1st Silesian) No. 38	1818
Fusilier Regiment (1st Lower Rhine) No. 39	1818
Fusilier Regiment Prince Karl-Anton von Hohenzollern (1st Hohenzollern) No. 40	1818
Infantry Regiment von Boyen (5th East Prussian) No. 41	1860
Infantry Regiment Prince Moritz of Anhalt-Dessau (5th Pomeranian) No. 42	1860
Infantry Regiment Duke Karl of Mecklenburg-Strelitz (6th East Prussian) No. 43	1860
Infantry Regiment Count Dönhoff (7th East Prussian) No. 44	1860
Infantry Regiment (8th East Prussian) No. 45	1860
Infantry Regiment Count Kirchbach (1st Lower Silesian) No. 46	1860
Infantry Regiment King Ludwig III of Bavaria (2nd Lower Silesian) No. 47	1860
Infantry Regiment von Stülpnagel (5th Brandenburg) No. 48	1860
Infantry Regiment (6th Pomeranian) No. 49	1860
Infantry Regiment (3rd Lower Silesian) No. 50	1860
Infantry Regiment (4th Lower Silesian) No. 51	1860
Infantry Regiment von Alvensleben (6th Brandenburg) No. 52	1860
Infantry Regiment (5th Westphalian) No. 53	1860
Infantry Regiment von der Goltz (7th Pomeranian) No. 54	1860
Infantry Regiment Count Bülow von Dennewitz (6th Westphalian) No. 55	1860
Infantry Regiment Vogel von Falkenstein (7th Westphalian) No. 56	1860
Infantry Regiment Duke Ferdinand of Brunswick (8th Westphalian) No. 57	1860
Infantry Regiment (3rd Posen) No. 58	1860
Infantry Regiment Baron Hiller von Gaertringen (4th Posen) No. 59	1860
Infantry Regiment Margrave Karl (7th Brandenburg) No. 60	1860
Infantry Regiment von der Marwitz (8th Pomeranian) No. 61	1860
Infantry Regiment (3rd Upper Silesian) No. 62	1860
Infantry Regiment (4th Upper Silesian) No. 63	1860
Infantry Regiment General Field Marshal Prince Frederick Karl of Prussia (8th Brandenburg) No. 64	1860
Infantry Regiment (5th Rhine) No. 65	1860
Infantry Regiment (3rd Magdeburg) No. 66	1860
Infantry Regiment (4th Magdeburg) No. 67	1860
Infantry Regiment (6th Rhine) No. 68	1860
Infantry Regiment (7th Rhine) No. 69	1860
Infantry Regiment (8th Rhine) No. 70	1860
Infantry Regiment (3rd Thuringian) No. 71	1860
Infantry Regiment (4th Thuringian) No. 72	1860
Fusilier Regiment Field Marshal Prince Albrecht of Prussia (1st Hanoverian) No. 73	1803
Infantry Regiment (1st Hanoverian) No. 74	1813
Infantry Regiment Bremen (1st Hanseatic) No. 75	1866
Infantry Regiment Hamburg (2nd Hanseatic) No. 76	1866
Infantry Regiment (2nd Hanoverian) No. 77	1813

Regiment	Year
Infantry Regiment Duke Frederick William of Brunswick (1st East Frisian) No. 78	1813
Infantry Regiment von Voigts-Rhetz (3rd Hanoverian) No. 79	1838
Fusilier Regiment von Gerdsdorf (Electorate of Hesse) No. 80	1813
Infantry Regiment Landgraf Friedrich I von Hessen-Cassel (1st Electorate of Hesse) No. 81	1813
Infantry Regiment (2nd Electorate of Hesse) No. 82	1813
Infantry Regiment von Wittich (3rd Electorate of Hesse) No. 83	1813
Infantry Regiment von Manstein (1st Schleswig) No. 84	1866
Infantry Regiment Duke of Holstein (1st Holstein) No. 85	1866
Fusilier Regiment Queen (1st Schleswig-Holstein) No. 86	1866
Infantry Regiment (1st Nassau) No. 87	1809
Infantry Regiment (2nd Nassau) No. 88	1808
Grenadier Regiment (1st Grand Ducal Mecklenburg) No. 89 (I and III Battalions from Mecklenburg-Schwerin; II Battalion from Mecklenburg-Strelitz)	1782
Fusilier Regiment Kaiser Wilhelm (1st Grand Ducal Mecklenburg) No. 90	1788
Infantry Regiment (Oldenburg) No. 91	1813
Infantry Regiment (Brunswick) No. 92	1809
Infantry Regiment (Anhalt) No. 93	1807
Infantry Regiment Grand Duke of Saxony (5th Thuringian) No. 94	1762
Infantry Regiment (6th Thuringian) No. 95	1807
Infantry Regiment (7th Thuringian) No. 96 (II Battalion from Reuss; III Battalion from Schwarzburg-Rudolstadt)	1702
Infantry Regiment (1st Upper Rhine) No. 97	1881
Infantry Regiment (Metz) No. 98	1881
Infantry Regiment (2nd Upper Rhine) No. 99	1881
Life Grenadier Regiment (1st Royal Saxon) No. 100	1670
Grenadier Regiment Kaiser Wilhelm, King of Prussia (2nd Royal Saxon) No. 101	1670
Infantry Regiment King Ludwig III of Bavaria (3rd Royal Saxon) No. 102	1709
Infantry Regiment (4th Royal Saxon) No. 103	1709
Infantry Regiment Crown Prince (5th Royal Saxon) No. 104	1701
Infantry Regiment King Wilhelm II of Württemberg (6th Royal Saxon) No. 105	1701
Infantry Regiment King Georg (7th Royal Saxon) No. 106	1708
Infantry Regiment Prince Johann Georg (8th Royal Saxon) No. 107	1708
Rifle (Fusilier) Regiment Prince Georg (Royal Saxon) No. 108	1809
Life Guard Grenadier Regiment (Baden) No. 109	1803
Grenadier Regiment Kaiser Wilhelm I (2nd Baden) No. 110	1852
Infantry Regiment Margrave Ludwig Wilhelm (3rd Baden) No. 111	1852
Infantry Regiment Prince Wilhelm (4th Baden) No. 112	1852
Infantry Regiment (5th Baden) No. 113	1861
Infantry Regiment Kaiser Frederick III (6th Baden) No. 114	1867
Life Guard Infantry Regiment (1st Grand Ducal Hessian) No. 115	1621
Infantry Regiment Kaiser Wilhelm (2nd Grand Ducal Hessian) No. 116	1813
Infantry Life Guard Regiment Grand Duchess (3rd Grand Ducal Hessian) No. 117	1697
Infantry Regiment Prince Carl (4th Grand Ducal Hessian) No. 118	1791
Grenadier Regiment Queen Olga (1st Württemberg) No. 119	1673
Infantry Regiment Kaiser Wilhelm, King of Prussia (2nd Württemberg) No. 120	1673
Infantry Regiment Old Württemberg (3rd Württemberg) No. 121	1716
Fusilier Regiment Emperor Franz Joseph of Austria (4th Württemberg) No. 122	1806
Grenadier Regiment King Karl (5th Württemberg) No. 123	1799
Infantry Regiment King Wilhelm I (6th Württemberg) No. 124	1673
Infantry Regiment Kaiser Frederick, King of Prussia (7th Württemberg) No. 125	1809
Infantry Regiment Grand Duke Friedrich of Baden (8th Württemberg) No. 126	1716
Infantry Regiment (9th Württemberg) No. 127	1897
Infantry Regiment (Danzig) No. 128	1881
Infantry Regiment (3rd West Prussian) No. 129	1881
Infantry Regiment (1st Lorrainian) No. 130	1881
Infantry Regiment (2nd Lorrainian) No. 131	1881

Regiment	Year
Infantry Regiment (1st Lower Alsatian) No. 132	1881
Infantry Regiment (9th Royal Saxon) No. 133	1881
Infantry Regiment (10th Royal Saxon) No. 134	1881
Infantry Regiment (3rd Lorrainian) No. 135	1887
Infantry Regiment (4th Lorrainian) No. 136	1887
Infantry Regiment (2nd Lower Alsatian) No. 137	1887
Infantry Regiment (3rd Lower Alsatian) No. 138	1887
Infantry Regiment (11th Royal Saxon) No. 139	1887
Infantry Regiment (4th West Prussian) No. 140	1890
Infantry Regiment (Kulm) No. 141	1890
Infantry Regiment (7th Baden) No. 142	1890
Infantry Regiment (4th Lower Alsatian) No. 143	1890
Infantry Regiment (5th Lorrainian) No. 144	1890
King's Infantry Regiment (6th Lorrainian) No. 145	1890
Infantry Regiment (1st Masurian) No. 146	1897
Infantry Regiment (2nd Masurian) No. 147	1897
Infantry Regiment (5th West Prussian) No. 148	1897
Infantry Regiment (6th West Prussian) No. 149	1897
Infantry Regiment (1st Ermland) No. 150	1897
Infantry Regiment (2nd Ermland) No. 151	1897
Teutonic Order Infantry Regiment (1st Alsatian) No. 152	1897
Infantry Regiment (8th Thuringian) No. 153 (I and II Battalions from Saxe-Altenburg)	1807
Infantry Regiment (5th Lower Silesian) No. 154	1897
Infantry Regiment (7th West Prussian) No. 155	1897
Infantry Regiment (3rd Silesian) No. 156	1897
Infantry Regiment (4th Silesian) No. 157	1897
Infantry Regiment (7th Lorrainian) No. 158	1897
Infantry Regiment (8th Lorrainian) No. 159	1897
Infantry Regiment (9th Rhine) No. 160	1897
Infantry Regiment (10th Rhine) No. 161	1897
Infantry Regiment Lübeck (3rd Hanseatic) No. 162	1897
Infantry Regiment (Schleswig-Holstein) No. 163	1897
Infantry Regiment (4th Hanoverian) No. 164	1813
Infantry Regiment (5th Hanoverian) No. 165	1813
Infantry Regiment (Hessen-Homburg) No. 166	1897
Infantry Regiment (1st Upper Alsatian) No. 167	1897
Infantry Regiment (5th Grand Ducal Hessian) No. 168	1897
Infantry Regiment (8th Baden) No. 169	1897
Infantry Regiment (9th Baden) No. 170	1897
Infantry Regiment (2nd Upper Alsatian) No. 171	1897
Infantry Regiment (3rd Upper Alsatian) No. 172	1897
Infantry Regiment (9th Lorrainian) No. 173	1897
Infantry Regiment (10th Lorrainian) No. 174	1897
Infantry Regiment (8th West Prussian) No. 175	1897
Infantry Regiment (9th West Prussian) No. 176	1897
Infantry Regiment (12th Royal Saxon) No. 177	1897
Infantry Regiment (13th Royal Saxon) No. 178	1897
Infantry Regiment (14th Royal Saxon) No. 179	1897
Infantry Regiment (10th Württemberg) No. 180	1897
Infantry Regiment (15th Royal Saxon) No. 181	1897
Infantry Regiment (16th Royal Saxon) No. 182	1912

Jäger and Schützen Battalions

Regiment	Year Formed
Guards Jäger Battalion	1744
Guards Schützen Battalion	1814
Jäger Battalion Count York von Wartenburg (East Prussian) No. 1	1744
Jäger Battalion Prince Bismarck (Pomeranian) No. 2	1744
Jäger Battalion (Brandenburg) No. 3	1815
Jäger Battalion (Magdeburg) No. 4	1815
Jäger Battalion von Neumann (1st Silesian) No. 5	1808
Jäger Battalion (2nd Silesian) No. 6	1808
Jäger Battalion (Westphalian) No. 7	1815
Jäger Battalion (Rhine) No. 8	1815
Jäger Battalion (Lauenburg) No. 9	1866
Jäger Battalion (Hanoverian) No. 10	1803
Jäger Battalion (Electorate of Hesse) No. 11	1813
Jäger Battalion (1st Royal Saxon) No. 12	1809
Jäger Battalion (2nd Royal Saxon) No. 13	1809
Jäger Battalion (Grand Ducal Mecklenburg-Schwerin) No. 14	1821

Bavarian Infantry Regiments

Regiment	Year Formed
Infantry Life Guard Regiment	1814
1st Infantry Regiment King	1778
2nd Infantry Regiment Crown Prince	1682
3rd Infantry Regiment Prince Karl of Bavaria	1698
4th Infantry Regiment King Wilhelm of Württemberg	1706

Regiment	Year
5th Infantry Regiment Grand Duke Ernst Ludwig of Hesse	1722
6th Infantry Regiment Kaiser Wilhelm, King of Prussia	1725
7th Infantry Regiment Prince Leopold	1732
8th Infantry Regiment Grand Duke Friedrich II of Baden	1753
9th Infantry Regiment Wrede	1803
10th Infantry Regiment King	1682
11th Infantry Regiment von der Tann	1805
12th Infantry Regiment Prince Arnulf	1814
13th Infantry Regiment Franz Joseph I, Emperor of Austria and Apostolic King of Hungary	1806
14th Infantry Regiment Hartmann	1814
15th Infantry Regiment King Friedrich August of Saxony	1722
16th Infantry Regiment Grand Duke Ferdinand of Tuscany	1878
17th Infantry Regiment Orff	1878
18th Infantry Regiment Prince Ludwig Ferdinand	1881
19th Infantry Regiment King Victor Emmanuel III of Italy	1890
20th Infantry Regiment Prince Franz	1897
21st Infantry Regiment Grand Duke Friedrich Franz IV of Mecklenburg-Schwerin	1897
22nd Infantry Regiment Prince Wilhelm von Hohenzollern	1897
23rd Infantry Regiment	1897

Bavarian Jäger Battalions

Regiment	Year Formed
1st Jäger Battalion King	1815
2nd Jäger Battalion	1825

§VI-2-3 PHYSICAL CHARACTERISTICS

§VI-2-3-1 GERMAN HORSE COLOURS

The Prussian army did not generally attempt to mount its cavalry regiments on certain colour horses. The exceptions to this were the 1st and 2nd Line Hussars, the Death's Head Hussars: the 1st Hussars rode white or grey horses, while the 2nd Hussars had black mounts.[2]

The other regiments did, however, have designated colours for their regimental trumpeters and drum horses, as shown in Table VI.2.3.1.1.

Table VI.2.3.1.1: German Horse Colours, 1913

Regiment	Trumpeters	Drum Horse
Gardes du Corps	Chestnuts	Chestnut
Guard Cuirassiers	Blacks	Black
1st Cuirassiers	Blacks	Black
2nd Cuirassiers	Blacks	Black
3rd Cuirassiers	Bays	Bay
4th Cuirassiers	Blacks	Black
5th Cuirassiers	Blacks	Black
6th Cuirassiers	Blacks	Black
7th Cuirassiers	Light browns	Light brown
8th Cuirassiers	Dark browns	Dark brown
1st Dragoon Guards	Chestnuts	Chestnut
2nd Dragoon Guards	Blacks	Black
1st Dragoons	Chestnuts	Skewbald
2nd Dragoons	Blacks	White
3rd Dragoons	Chestnuts	Chestnut
4th Dragoons	Blacks	None
5th Dragoons	Chestnuts, Browns & Blacks	None
6th Dragoons	Blacks	None
7th Dragoons	Chestnuts	None
8th Dragoons	Blacks	None
9th Dragoons	Reddish brown	Piebald
10th Dragoons	Blacks	None
11th Dragoons	Chestnuts	None
12th Dragoons	Chestnuts	None

Regiment	Trumpeters	Drum Horse	Regiment	Trumpeters	Drum Horse
13th Dragoons	Chestnuts, Browns & blacks	None	19th (Saxon) Hussars	Blacks	None
14th Dragoons	Blacks	None	20th (Saxon) Hussars	Chestnuts with white markings	None
15th Dragoons	Blacks	None	1st Guard Lancers	Brownish Blacks	None
16th Dragoons	Blacks	None	2nd Guard Lancers	Chestnuts	None
19th Dragoons	Blacks	None	3rd Guards Lancers	Chestnuts, browns & blacks	None
20th Dragoons	Chestnuts	Burnt bay	1st Lancers	Dark browns	None
21st Dragoons	Blacks	None	2nd Lancers	Chestnuts	None
22nd Dragoons	Mainly browns	None	3rd Lancers	Chestnuts	None
Life Guard Hussars	Whites	White	4th Lancers	Mainly browns	None
1st Hussars	Whites	Dapple grey	5th Lancers	Chestnuts	Chestnuts
2nd Hussars	Blacks	Piebald	6th Lancers	Chestnuts	None
3rd Hussars	Chestnuts with white markings	Chestnut	7th Lancers	Blacks	Black
4th Hussars	Piebalds	Piebald	8th Lancers	Blacks	None
5th Hussars	Blacks	None	9th Lancers	Light browns	None
6th Hussars	Chestnuts	None	10th Lancers	Browns	None
7th Hussars	Chestnuts	Chestnut	11th Lancers	Blacks	None
8th Hussars	Blacks	None	12th Lancers	Chestnuts	None
9th Hussars	Chestnuts	None	13th Lancers	Chestnuts	Chestnuts
10th Hussars	Chestnuts	None	14th Lancers	Chestnuts	None
11th Hussars	Chestnuts	None	15th Lancers	Browns	None
12th Hussars	Chestnuts	None	16th Lancers	Chestnuts	None
13th Hussars	Blacks	Skewbald	1st Jäger zu Pferde	Chestnuts	None
14th Hussars	Chestnuts	None	2nd Jäger zu Pferde	Browns	None
15th Hussars	Blacks	None	3rd Jäger zu Pferde	Chestnuts	None
16th Hussars	Chestnuts	Chestnut	4th Jäger zu Pferde	Chestnuts	None
17th Hussars	Blacks	Dapple grey	5th Jäger zu Pferde	Chestnuts	None
18th (Saxon) Hussars	Whites	None	6th Jäger zu Pferde	Chestnuts	None

Source: Hagger, Personal correspondence, 1980.
Notes: 7th–13th Jäger zu Pferde were formed in 1913; their horse colours are unknown.

A piebald horse is white with black patches; a.skewbald is white with brown patches.

§VI-2-3-2 SIZE OF HORSES AND MEN

The cuirassiers, lancers, and Jäger zu Pferde were considered heavy cavalry. Light cavalry was made up of hussars, dragoons, and Bavarian chevaulegers. Different types of horses and men went into these regiments. Light cavalry horses were bred at state studs in East and West Prussia. The horses were about 1.55 m (4.92 feet or 14 hands 3 inches) high and averaged 450 kg (992 lbs). The mounts for heavy cavalry came from northern farms in Hanover, Holstein, and Mecklenburg. Their height ranged between 1.65 and 1.75 m (5.41 and 5.74 feet, or 16 hands 1 inch and 17 hands 1 inch). They weighed between 600 and 700 kg (1,322.77 and 1,543.24 lb). If the state studs did not supply enough horses, the animals were bought on the open market.[3]

In the Prussian army, heavy cavalrymen were to be between 1.67 and 1.75 m (5.48 and 5.74 feet) tall. Light cavalrymen had a height range of 1.57 to 1.72 m (5.15 feet to 5.64 feet).[4]

§VI-2-4 BATTLE SOUVENIRS

The Prussian army was the polar opposite of the British army when it came to regiments carrying souvenirs of past battles and triumphs. British regiments have coloured hackles, bearskins, back badges, captured kettledrums, etc. to remind them and others of past successful battles. The Prussians were extremely parsimonious when it came to allowing such displays. Almost all of the helmet and cuff bands that recalled past campaigns and battles were awarded by the other states in the German federation (see §VI-3-6, §VI-3-7, and §VI-3-8).

However, the Prussians did allow one unusual souvenir of a successful battle to be displayed. At the Battle of Sadowa – also known as Königgrätz – in 1866, the 43rd Regiment captured a bass drum from the Austrian 77th Erzherzog Karl Salvator of Tuscany Regiment (in 1914, the 77th Philipp Herzog von Württemberg).[5] What made the capture unique was that the 43rd also captured a two-wheeled cart to carry the drum. The cart and drum were pulled in the Austrian army by a St Bernard dog, so the Prussian 43rd obtained their own St Bernard to pull the cart and drum. They took the cart and drum back to their home station at Königsberg.

The 43rd was given permission to use the dog, cart, and drum in parades, and the combination participated in many parades over the years up to 1914 and, because it was so unique, was always a hit with the viewing public.[6]

After World War I, in the reduced German army, the dog, cart, and drum were passed on to the 1st Infantry Regiment.[7]

§VI-3 UNIFORM INFORMATION

§VI-3-1   *Standard Uniform Items*
§VI-3-2   *Collar and Cuff Lace*
§VI-3-3   *Guard Eagle versus Grenadier Eagle*
§VI-3-4   *Helmet Badges*
§VI-3-5   *Minor States' Helmet Badges*
§VI-3-6   *Banners on Cavalry Helmets*
§VI-3-7   *Banners on Infantry Helmets*
§VI-3-8   *Background to Helmet Banners*
§VI-3-9   *Cavalry Regiment Plumes*
§VI-3-10 *Infantry Regiment Plumes, Litzen and Lace*
§VI-3-11 *Colour of Helmet Badges*
§VI-3-12 *Cockade and Helmet Front Badges*
§VI-3-13 *German Helmet and Uniform: Identifying Accessory Details – 1914*
§VI-3-14 *Prussian Plume and Litzen*
§VI-3-15 *Non-Prussian Plume and Litzen*
§VI-3-16 *States Wearing Only the Prussian Line Eagle and a State Cockade*
§VI-3-17 *Lance Pennant Colours*
§VI-3-18 *Cavalry Shoulder Strap and Epaulette Monograms*
§VI-3-19 *Infantry Shoulder Strap and Epaulette Monograms*
§VI-3-20 *Army Corps Distinguishing Colour Trim*
§VI-3-21 *Army Corps Shoulder Strap and Cuff Plate Piping Details*
§VI-3-22 *Regiments with Non-Standard Uniform*
§VI-3-23 *Prussian Army Epaulettes, Shoulder Cords and Weapons Proficiency Badges*

§VI-3-1 STANDARD UNIFORM ITEMS[8]

COCKADES

Cockades were used on all of the headdresses worn by the different branches of the German army. The cockades were circular and consisted of three concentric bands of colour, sometimes around an open centre. The size of the cockade and the individual widths of the coloured bands varied according to rank and were usually regulated very specifically.

Before 1897, the state cockades were the only ones used. Their colours often varied from state to state within the German Empire, even though the entire army was technically under Prussian control and direction. This was often a concession made by the Prussians to appease the contingents from the sovereign states, who did not want their unique identities subsumed by Prussian dominance.

On 22 March 1897, though, a cockade in the imperial colours was adopted for the entire German Empire. While cockades continued to vary in size and band-width depending on rank, the colours were consistent across the entire Empire: red, white, and black. The centre of the cockade – or the innermost band, in the case of cockades with empty centres – was red, and could be ridged but did not have to be. The centre band was white and smooth in texture. The outermost band was black, and always had a ridged texture and a scalloped edge. The Reich cockade (black, white, and red) was worn together with the state cockades (see *§VI-3-12* for their colours).

Litzen

Some but not all regiments had a special type of trim called *litzen* at the collar, cuffs, or both. The most common shape was rectangular with ends that flared out slightly. This was called the 'chapter' or 'chapel' shape – the names are used interchangeably. There was a coloured stripe that ran lengthwise through the centre of the rectangle, called a *spiegel*. Often, but not always, the spiegel was the colour of the cloth underneath the litzen. The litzen was made of braid that was in the button colour. For other ranks, it was normally made of white linen, but where yellow litzen were worn they were made of camel yarn. The litzen was silver or gold metallic for officers, although some exceptions existed. Litzen could also be made of either plain or patterned braid.

Collar litzen could be either single or double. The cuff litzen was placed one per button on the cuff. This meant there were two on the Saxon cuff and three on the Brandenburg cuff.

Infantry Trousers and Breeches

Other Ranks

Regular other ranks' trousers were wool, of a standard cut, typically made of mottled dark blue cloth with 2–3 mm (0.08 to 0.12 inch) coloured piping down the outside seam. The piping was usually red, as it was in the Prussian branch of the army, but it could be other colours in some of the contingent armies. Most of the army, including the contingents, wore this same style of trousers. An exception was the Bavarian force, who had light blue trousers the same colour as their coats, but still had red piping and a similar cut to the Prussian trousers. In the infantry, trousers were typically worn tucked inside the boots. The Saxon contingent army, though, preferred to wear the trousers over the boots.

White linen and occasionally twill trousers were also issued to the other ranks. They were only authorised to be worn during the summer months, from May to September. Because of their light colour, the white trousers were not the most practical choice for combat or manoeuvres, so they were eventually reserved almost exclusively for full dress and other special occasions. A second pair of sturdy grey trousers took their place for everyday wear during the summer months. Neither the white linen trousers nor the grey summer trousers had coloured piping.

Officers

Infantry officers were assigned the same mottled dark blue trousers as the other ranks. However, in practice they were often black and could be made of finer fabrics than those worn by the other ranks. The piping, usually red, on the outside seam could be no more than 1.5 mm (0.06 inch) in width. Officers' trousers had stirrups at the bottom which were supposed to keep them in place and prevent creasing.

In 1896, officers were also assigned breeches, which were quite similar to the riding breeches assigned to cavalrymen in that the bottom part of the leg was fairly tight so it could be worn inside the standard black boots. While all officers could have breeches, only mounted officers were permitted to have breeches that were reinforced with leather at the seat and on the inside of the legs. The breeches were the same colour as the full-length trousers and had the same piping on the outside seams.

Like the other ranks, officers had white linen summer trousers.

Infantry, jäger, and rifle officers also had gala trousers. From 1843 to 1896, the gala trousers were white cashmere. In 1896, dark blue-black gala trousers were assigned instead. The colour and style of the gala trousers was to be identical to the regular full-length trousers, right down to the stirrups sewn to the bottom of the trouser-legs. The only difference was that gala trousers had additional 3 cm (1.18 inch) red stripes sewn 0.5 cm (0.2 inch) from either side of the standard outside seam piping. Officers of the Bavarian infantry were not assigned gala trousers, so they wore the white linen trousers for court and gala dress instead.

Cavalry Netherwear

Riding Breeches

Riding breeches were the basic type of netherwear for both officers and other ranks of the cavalry. Starting in 1867, because of the heavy wear such breeches had to sustain, the hussars began wearing breeches that were reinforced on the seat and inner legs with leather for other ranks, or cloth or suede for officers, a practice which soon became standard in the rest of the cavalry. The typical riding breeches were made of dark blue mottled cloth: wool for other ranks, kersey for the officers. Unlike the infantry trousers, cavalry breeches did not have coloured piping down the outer seams. The hussars did, however, have their distinctive braid where the piping normally would have been. There were several variations on the standard model: mounted jägers, for instance, were assigned grey-green riding breeches – wool for other ranks, kersey for officers – which matched their tunics, instead of the standard dark blue, and cuirassiers wore white kersey breeches.

Saxon cavalrymen had cornflower blue breeches, and the other ranks of the Bavarian cavalry had light blue breeches and initially wore a slightly different cut of leather-reinforced breeches, but eventually adopted the Prussian style. Meanwhile, most Bavarian cavalry officers had light blue breeches which matched their tunics. The exception was the Bavarian Schwere Reiter, who wore the regulation blue-black trousers without piping instead of the light blue.

Trousers

All ranks of the cavalry also had long wool trousers. Trousers were only worn in walking-out dress by the other ranks, and in walking-out and mess dress by the officers. They were typically only issued to the cuirassiers and jägers, but men from the dragoons and lancers could wear them if they purchased them privately. Prussian hussars of all ranks were not permitted to wear the full-length trousers. The trousers were typically dark mottled blue with 2–3 mm (0.08–0.12 inch) red piping on the outside seams. As was the case with the breeches, though, jägers wore grey-green instead of dark blue, and Saxons had cornflower blue.

Bavarian full-length trousers, like the breeches, matched the tunic instead of always being the standard dark blue. Beginning in 1873, they had a single 5 cm (1.97 inch) stripe down the outside seam, in contrast to the narrow piping typically used. These trousers were discontinued for a time, but in 1884 they became standard for walking-out dress in both the Bavarian and Prussian branches of the cavalry. One interesting regulation concerning the full-length trousers was that they were never under any circumstance to be ironed with a crease down the front of the leg.

Like the infantry, all ranks of the Prussian and Saxon cavalry had white full-length linen trousers for summer full dress. The white trousers did not have any braid or piping on the side seams. The Württemberg and Bavarian contingent army cavalry did not have the white trousers.

Gala Trousers

Cavalry officers had special trousers that were typically worn in the gala uniform for events such as balls and weddings. An exception was the officers of the cuirassiers and the mounted jägers, who only wore the gala trousers to such events if they were planning on dancing. The gala trousers were of the same cut as the regular full-length trousers. For dragoons and lancers, there were coloured stripes down the outside of the leg. The stripes were two bands, 3 cm (1.18 inches) wide each, placed at a distance of 5 mm (0.20 inch) on either side of the outer seam piping. Cuirassiers, guard hussars, and horse jägers had unique models of gala trousers: cuirassier and jäger gala trousers were made of white satin, kersey, or cashmere, with braid on the outside seam matching the braid on their tunic. Guard hussars wore gala breeches with hussar braid down the outside seams and additional braid on the front of each leg in the shape of a Hungarian knot with loops of soutache, a type of flat narrow braid, around it.

Line hussars did not have separate gala trousers, and instead wore the regular full-length trousers, with the exception of the 18th and 19th Saxon Hussars, who did have gala trousers, and the 7th Hussars, who simply never stopped wearing the above-mentioned gala breeches when they were discontinued for the rest of the line hussar regiments in 1868. Saxon lancers also wore the regular full-length trousers in place of special gala trousers. The Bavarian officers wore white cashmere trousers for gala dress until 1873. When those were discontinued, they began wearing the regular full-length trousers for gala dress.

RANK BADGES FOR NCOs AND OTHER RANKS

Senior privates (*gefreite*) in both the infantry and the cavalry had a 2.5 cm (0.98 inch) wide button on either side of the tunic collar to denote their rank. The button bore the coat of arms of each contingent of the cavalry. In the infantry the button typically had the Prussian eagle on it, but several of the contingent armies bore their own markings. If the tunic collar included litzen, the button was in the outer corner of the litzen. These collar buttons were usually aligned with the button on the shoulder strap.

NCOs had special braid on their collar and cuffs to denote their rank. As of 1903, NCOs' braid in both the cavalry and the infantry was usually 2.1 cm (0.83 inch) wide for guard regiments, and 2 cm (0.79 inch) wide for non-guard regiments. However, depending on the branch of service in the cavalry, other widths were also assigned. The braid was in the button colour.

Sergeanten, as the highest rank of junior NCO, had buttons that were 2.9 cm (1.14 inches) in diameter on the collar of the tunic in both the cavalry and the infantry. The button had the markings of the Prussian army or of the contingent army the junior NCO belonged to. If the collar had litzen, the buttons were sewn to the centre stripe of the litzen.

Staff sergeants were called *vizefeldwebel* in the infantry and *vizewachtmeister* in the cavalry. They were considered senior NCOs and were permitted to wear an officer's cockade on their headdress. Otherwise, their rank badges were the same as for sergeanten (see above).

Master sergeants were *feldwebel* in the infantry and *wachtmeister* in the cavalry. They had all the same rank badges as staff sergeants (see above), but with additional NCO's braid that was 1.6 cm (0.63 inch) wide placed 7 mm (0.28 inch) above the regular cuff braid on the tunic.

Pouch and Pouch Belt

Both officers and other ranks of the cavalry wore a decorated pouch which held ammunition. It was worn on a bandolier-style belt that passed over the left shoulder and under the right arm.

Other ranks had a black leather rectangular pouch with a leather cover flap. The cover flap could have decorations on it. Cuirassiers and dragoons typically had a round brass ornament on the cover flap. The ornaments pictured an eagle with trophies. Lancer and hussar pouch cover flaps did not usually have decorations. Other ranks in the guard regiments and the light hussars were permitted to wear a silver guard star on the pouch cover flap. The pouch belt for other ranks was typically white. It was worn by other ranks of all types of cavalry of all the states after 1890.[9]

Officers' pouches were usually made of black patent leather and were slightly smaller than the other ranks' pouches. For officers of guard regiments, the pouch cover flap bore a silver guard star. For all the other regiments of the Prussian cavalry, a gold-plated monogram of Frederick William III was on the cover flap. The typical pouch belt had metal fittings in the button colour and was made of braid, also in the button colour.

Contingent armies sometimes had their own models of officer pouch and pouch belt. The Saxon contingent, for instance, had a pouch that was made of coloured cloth on the back and black leather on the front, with a gold-plated brass cover flap that had the Saxon coat of arms and trophies on it in silver. The pouch belts for all but one Saxon regiment were silver with coloured backing. Meanwhile, officers of the Bavarian contingent had a pouch covered in red morocco leather with a white metal lid with the Bavarian coat of arms. Their pouch belt was covered on the front with braid that had four wide silver stripes alternating with three narrow blue stripes, and the backing and piping were red.

Footwear

Footwear varied slightly between the cavalry and the infantry.

The officers and other ranks of the infantry had two types of footwear. The first was the regular infantry boots which, although much shorter than the cavalry-style riding boot, were supposed to be high enough to keep out the elements. Through trial and error, however, it was eventually determined that the boots were too short. Over the years the height of the boots was gradually increased so that by the late 1800s boots that went up to the kneecap were permitted for both officers and other ranks of the infantry. The soles of infantry boots had many metal studs on them, likely intended to keep the soles from wearing out too quickly.

The second type of footwear were leather shoes with laces, worn with full-length trousers. The shoes were gradually replaced by short laced boots. Once knee-high boots had been adopted as the standard footwear, the short laced boots worn with leather gaiters were sometimes worn as a more comfortable alternative to the knee-high boots.

The basic footwear in the cavalry was the black leather riding boot. For the dragoons and the lancers, the boots came up to the kneecap in the front and dipped slightly lower in the back. The cuirassiers, jägers, and Saxon Schwere Reiter wore a different model of boot that went over the knee but was made of soft leather that could be turned down when the men were on foot. Hussars had a unique model of boot with trim at the top (see §VI-6-d). The boots that were worn in parade dress could be patent leather instead of regular leather.

Black leather shoes and later black leather lace-up 'short boots' were assigned as the alternative footwear the cavalry wore with full-length trousers. If riding breeches were being worn, the riding boots described above were the logical choice.

Boots varied in height in the contingent armies, and changes in boot or shoe model were not always adopted at the same time as in the Prussian army. Both the riding boots and the short boots could be worn with spurs that either screwed or snapped on, in different shapes and sizes depending on the branch of service and the occasion. Bavarian cavalry footwear was unique in that all the spurs were attached buckle style, rather than snapping on or screwing in.

Lance

The general trend in the German cavalry around 1890 was to replace old wooden lances with newer metal models. The Prussians were assigned a cast-iron lance that was carried by all of the other ranks of the cavalry and was 3.2 m (10.5 feet) long. In the Württemberg and Bavarian contingents, steel lances were adopted, beginning in 1891 and 1890, respectively, but lances were only carried by the other ranks and NCOs of the lancers rather than the entire cavalry. Schwere Reiter of the Bavarian army carried wooden lances. The Saxon army did not switch to metal at all. The entire Saxon cavalry after 1899 was equipped with pinewood lances that were slightly shorter than the cast-iron/steel Prussian model, and they kept those pine lances right up to 1914.

Prussian Other Ranks' Belt

In the infantry, other ranks wore a leather belt with a rectangular 'box-type' buckle. The belt itself was made of either white chamois or black tanned leather. Beginning in 1887, the white leather model was only worn by guard and grenadier regiments, and all other infantry regiments wore the black model. The belt buckle was the same for all Prussian regiments. It was made of brass with a nickel-plated round shield design that had a crown in the centre with a laurel branch beneath it and the phrase 'Gott Mit Uns' ('God [is] with Us') above it. The buckle was 4.5 cm (1.77 inches) high by 6 cm (2.36 inches) wide, and the round shield centred on it was 4 cm (1.58 inches) in diameter. Other states had their own designs on their belt buckles.

In the Prussian cavalry, other ranks wore a leather belt that was 4.2 cm (1.65 inches) wide and about 4 mm (0.16 inch) thick. It had a brass buckle with two prongs, instead of a buckle plate like the infantry model. The belt was made of white leather for all of the cavalry except the mounted jägers, whose belt was brown. Hussars and lancers wore their belt underneath the tunic. Cuirassiers, dragoons, and mounted jägers wore the belt over the tunic.

Officer's Sash

Officers of the infantry and the cavalry wore a decorative sash that was generally made of silk or metal webbing, 4.3 cm (1.69 inches) wide. The sash was cinched around the waist, and had silver tassels on the ends that hung down 25–30 cm (9.84–11.81 inches). Stripes 0.5 cm (0.2 inch) wide in the contingent army's state colours ran through the belt and into the tassel, so that while the outer layer of the tassels was silver, the interior was in the stripe colour. Typically, there were only two coloured stripes in the belt, but the contingent army from Hesse had three stripes in its colours. The basic colour of the belt was silver for all except the Mecklinburg-Schwerin 17th and 18th Dragoon Regiments, which instead had yellow as the base colour of the belt but still had coloured stripes in the state colours. Hussars had a special sash (see §VI-6-d). After 1896, the tassels on the officer's sash were considered too unwieldy for regular wear, so the officer's sash was worn only for gala and parade dress.

There was also an adjutant's sash, which, at 6–7 cm (2.36–2.76 inches), was considerably wider than the regular officer's sash. The adjutant's sash was worn over the right shoulder, where it attached to the shoulder button, and was tied at the left hip. It was the same colour and had the same stripes as the officer's sash, but the coloured stripes were wider, 0.9 cm (0.35 inch). Typically, adjutants only wore the adjutant's sash and thus did not wear the regular waist sash. In the case of hussar adjutants, however, the adjutant's sash was worn under the hussar's waist sash.

Sword Knots

Sword knots would normally be beyond the scope of coverage of this work, but in the German army they carried so much information that they are covered here.

Each knot can be described as comprising a strap, a slide, a crown, and a fringe.

Squadron	Strap	Slide	Crown	Fringe
1st	Leather dyed red	Braided leather	White	White
2nd	Leather dyed red	Braided leather	Red	White
3rd	Leather dyed red	Braided leather	Yellow	White
4th	Leather dyed red	Braided leather	Light blue	White
5th	Leather dyed red	Braided leather	Green	White

The Gardes du Corps, until 1888, had ten companies with an entirely different colour scheme for crowns and fringe.[10]

NCOs' and Sergeants' Straps

The strap and slide were leather dyed red. The crown and fringe was wool mixed with the state colours – for example, black for Prussian regiments, light blue for Bavarian, etc.

NCOs' straps and slides were the same colour as those of the other ranks. However, the crown and the fringe were in the state's colours, e.g. black and white for Prussia.

Re-enlisted other ranks wore an additional special brown leather strap sword knot and slide with a crown in the squadron colour. The fringe was like the NCOs', in a mixture of the colours of the state.[11]

Officers

Officers' and senior NCOs' sword knot had a distinctive shape and were made in silver braid. The straps and slides in silver had four silk stripes in the state's colours, with black for Prussia. The silver fringe was closed and for Prussia had a black core at the bottom.

Fatherland Banner

The Prussian regiments had the so-called Fatherland banner across the line eagle after 1860. It read 'Mit Gott Für König and Vaterland' – 'With God for King and Fatherland'.

As other state forces came into the imperial army, some wore the Prussian eagle. For them, the word 'Fürst' – 'prince' or 'sovereign' – was used in place of 'Koenig' on the banner. Examples of this usage are found in the helmets of Infantry Regiments 92, 93, 95, 96 (2nd and 3rd Battalions only), and Regiment 153 (1st and 2nd Battalions only) after 1868.

§VI-3-2 COLLAR AND CUFF LACE[12]

The old and elite regiments of the German army wore special lace on their collars and cuffs. In most cases, this was granted between the turn of the twentieth century and 1914.

Images VI:1 and VI:2 show the lace designs worn on the collars and cuffs by the following: officer's chapter-style lace; men's chapter-style lace; old Prussian lace – troopers of Foot Guards Regiment No. 5 and Guard Grenadier Regiment No. 5; Prussian Guard Grenadiers; Prussian Guard Grenadiers, prior to 1837; Foot Guards Regiment No. 5 and Guard Grenadier Regiment No. 5; Guard Grenadiers (men's lace); Grenadier Regiment Crown Prince (1st East Prussian) No. 1; Grenadier Regiment King Frederick

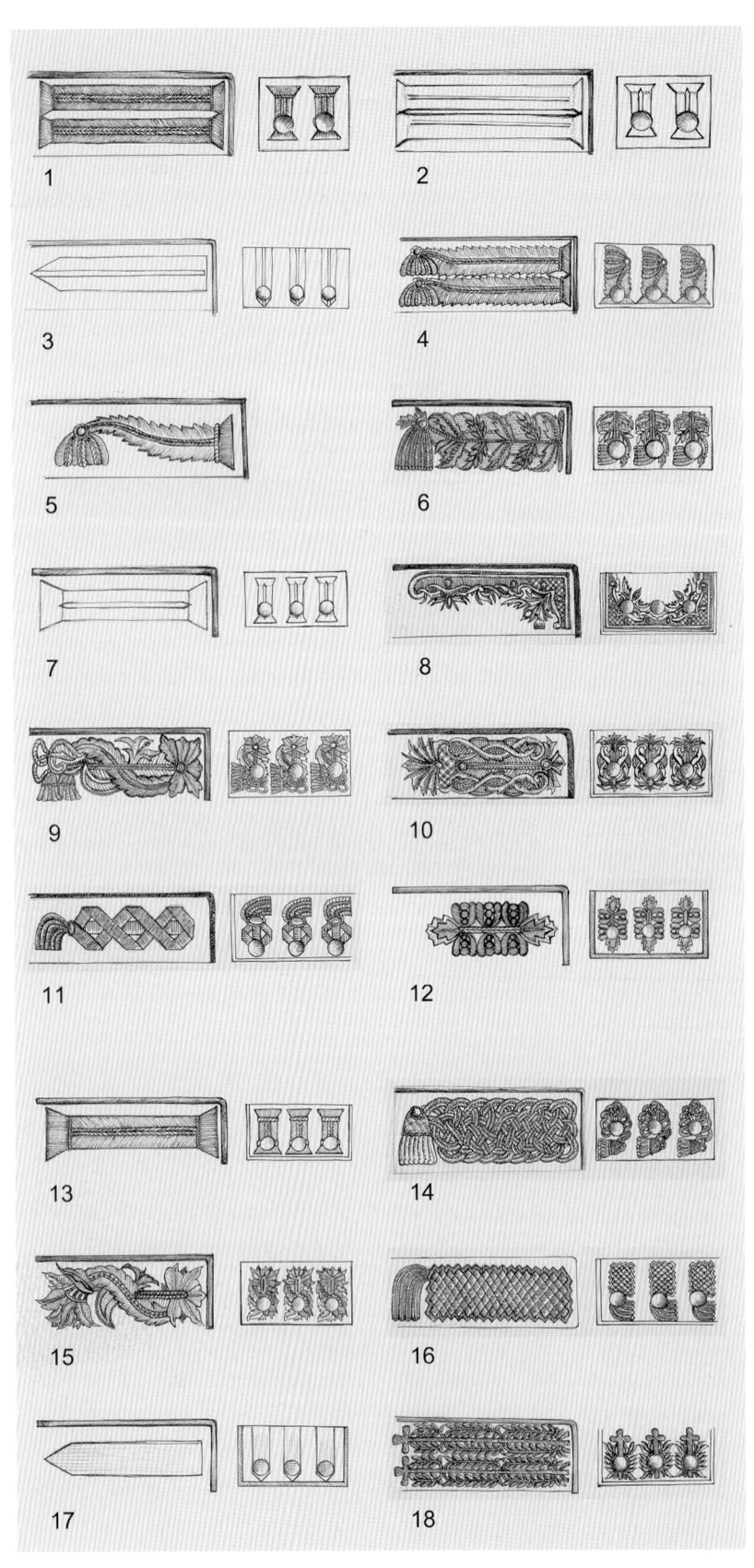

VI:1 Lace Designs on Collars and Cuffs[a]
1. Officers' chapter-style lace.
2. Men's chapter-style lace.
3. Old Prussian lace – troopers of Foot Guards Regiment No. 5 and Guard Grenadier Regiment No. 5.
4. Prussian Guard Grenadiers' lace.
5. Prussian Guard Grenadiers' lace, prior to 1837.
6. Foot Guards Regiment No. 5 and Guard Grenadier Regiment No. 5 officers' lace.
7. Guard Grenadiers – Men's lace.
8. Grenadier Regiment Crown Prince (1st East Prussian) No. 1 officers' lace.
9. Grenadier Regiment King Frederick William IV (1st Pomeranian) No. 2 officers' lace.
10. Grenadier Regiment King Frederick William I (2nd East Prussian) No. 3 officers' lace.
11. Grenadier Regiment King Frederick the Great (3rd East Prussian) No. 4 officers' lace.
12. Grenadier Regiment King Frederick I (4th East Prussian) No. 5 officers' lace.

Note: [a] Shirreffs, 'Lace and Emroidery', pp. 2–7.

VI:2 Lace Designs on Collars and Cuffs[a]
13. Grenadier Regiment Count Kleist von Mollendorf (1st West Prussian) No. 6 and Grenadier Regiment King Frederick III (2nd Silesian) No. 11 officers' lace.
14. Grenadier Regiment King Wilhelm I (2nd West Prussian) No. 7 officers' lace.
15. Life Grenadier Regiment King Frederick William III (1st Brandenburg) No. 8 officers' lace.
16. Fusilier Regiment von Gerdsdorf (Electorate of Hesse) No. 80 officers' lace.
17. Fusilier Regiment von Gerdsdorf (Electorate of Hesse) No. 80 – troopers' lace.
18. Grenadier Regiment (1st Grand Ducal Mecklenburg) No. 89, Ist and IIIrd Battalions' officers' lace.

Note: [a] Shirreffs, 'Lace and Emroidery', pp. 2–7.

William IV (1st Pomeranian) No. 2; Grenadier Regiment King Frederick William I (2nd East Prussian) No. 3; Grenadier Regiment King Frederick the Great (3rd East Prussian) No. 4; Grenadier Regiment King Frederick I (4th East Prussian) No. 5.

Image VI:1 show the lace designs worn on the collars and cuffs by the following regiments: Grenadier Regiment Count Kleist von Mollendorf (1st West Prussian) No. 6 and Grenadier Regiment King Frederick III (2nd Silesian) No. 11; Grenadier Regiment King Wilhelm I (2nd West Prussian) No. 7; Life Grenadier Regiment King Frederick Wiliam III (1st Brandenburg) No. 8; Fusilier Regiment von Gerdsdorf (Electorate of Hesse) No. 80; Fusilier Regiment von Gerdsdorf (Electorate of Hesse) No. 80 (troopers' lace); Grenadier Regiment (1st Grand Ducal Mecklenburg) No. 89, 1st and 2nd Battalions' lace.

§VI-3-3 GUARD EAGLE VERSUS GRENADIER EAGLE

When writing about pre-World War I German *pickelhauben*, or spiked helmets, some sources often refer to eagles with outstretched wings and no guard star as a 'guard eagle without a star'. Technically, in most cases, this is not correct. It is an eagle badge but very different one from the guard eagle. It is better referred to as a grenadier eagle.

It is easy to tell the two eagles apart (see Images VI:3 and VI:4). Notice how the crossguard of the sword and the tail feathers between the legs are different. The crossguard is curved and the tail feathers of the grenadier eagle (Image VI:4) are fuller than those of the guard eagle (Image VI:3). The wings are also slightly different, but that is harder to spot.

VI:3 Guard Pickelhaube with Guard Eagle and Guard Star
Note the shape of the sword guard and the tail feathers.

VI:4 Grenadier Eagle
Note how the tail feathers and the sword guard are different from those of the guard eagle. The sceptre and wing feathers are also different, but these are harder to spot.

§VI-3-4 HELMET BADGES

While the German uniforms were very similar, there was a wide variation in the badges worn on the helmets. These reflect the several different states that formed the German Confederation, special events in the history of the regiment wearing the helmet, and battle awards.

Images VI:5 through VI:15 show a sample of these helmet plates and shako badges. A very detailed study of this fascinating subject cannot be undertaken here as it would swallow up the book – there are multivolume works covering pickelhauben. However, some aspects of the helmets can be found at *§VI-3-5 through §VI-3-17*.

Note that helmet and badge coat of arms for Mecklenburg-Strelitz 89th Infantry Regiment (2nd Battalion) is the same as the coat of arms of Mecklenburg-Schwerin (VI:7) except the crown and wreath are missing.

VI:6 Standard Prussian Eagle
This was the most common helmet badge worn in the Prussian army.

VI:5 Grenadier Eagle of the 9th Grenadiers with Colberg Banner
Note the tail feathers and sword guard.

VI:7 Helmet Plate for Mecklenburg-Schwerin
This was worn by the 1st and 3rd Battalions of the 89th Infantry Regiment and the 90th Fusilier Regiment.

§VI-3 Uniform Information

VI:8 Oldenburg Infantry Regiment 91 Helmet Plate
This is the standard Prussian line eagle with the addition of a badge for Oldenburg (officer's helmet).

VI:9 Helmet Plate for Brunswick Infantry
This was worn by the 1st and 2nd Battalions of Regiment 92 up to 1912. The leather helmet is covered with grey-green cloth, which was done by troops going to put down the Boxer Rebellion. This is a standard Prussian line eagle with the addition of the Brunswick badge and honour scroll.

VI:10 Brunswick Infantry Regiment 92 Helmet Plate
Before 1912, only the 3rd Battalion wore a skull and crossbones helmet plate. After 1912, all three battalions wore it. For the regiment's 100th anniversary, all three battalions were temporarily allowed to wear the death's head badge, associated with the Napoleonic Black Horde. However, the other two battalions proved so unwilling to give up the death's head badge that it was extended to all three battalions. It was the custom to put black velvet behind the nose and eye sockets to produce an eerie effect.

VI:11 Officer's Helmet of Saxe-Weimar Infantry Regiment 94
Prussian eagle with Saxe-Weimar badge on it.

VI:12 Enlisted Man's Helmet
Thuringian (Saxon Duchies) Infantry Regiment 95.

VI:14 Enlisted Man's Helmet of the 3rd Battalion of Infantry Regiment 96 (Schwarzburg-Rudolstadt)

VI:13 Helmet of Infantry Regiment 96 (3rd Battalion, 7th Thuringian (Saxon Duchy)) (Schwarzburg-Rudolstadt)
Note the Fürst on the Fatherland banner and the Schwarzburg coat of arms on the eagle. This helmet was worn by only fourteen officers of the 3rd Battalion.

VI:15 Bavarian Infantry Helmet and Plate
This late model plate shows that much of the extra foliage decoration has been removed.

§VI-3-5 MINOR STATES' HELMET BADGES –1914

State and Regiment	Badges on Prussian Line Eagle	Fatherland Banner[a]
Anhalt 93	White eight-pointed star on Prussian line eagle with state coat of arms on it. The coat of arms was topped by a white crown.	Für Fürst*
Brunswick 92 (I & II Bn) prior to 1912	Star and badge of the Order of Heinrich the Lion on Prussian line eagle with a Peninsula banner under badge; star, badge, and Peninsula banner white for other ranks; badge enamelled for officers. All on Prussian line eagle.	Für Fürst*
Brunswick 92 (III Bn) prior to 1912	Wore white skull and crossbones in white on Prussian line eagle; white Peninsula banner under it.	Für Fürst*
Brunswick 92 after 1912	All three battalions had white Peninsula banner, and a white skull and crossbones on Prussian line eagle.	Für Fürst*
Mecklenburg-Schwerin 89 (I & III Bns)	Yellow sunburst, white coat of arms and laurel wreath. The coat of arms was topped by a white crown.	n/a
Mecklenburg-Schwerin 90	Yellow sunburst, white coat of arms and laurel wreath. The coat of arms was topped by a white crown.	n/a
Mecklenburg-Strelitz 89 (II Bn)	Yellow sunburst and white coat of arms. Coat of arms was the same as for Mecklenburg-Schwerin but no wreath and no crown.	n/a
Oldenburg 91	White eight-pointed star and state coat of arms on a Prussian line eagle. The coat of arms was topped by a white crown.	Für König**
Reuss (Elder and Junior lines) 96 (II Bn)	Eight-pointed star and state coat of arms enclosed by a laurel wreath, all in white, on a Prussian line eagle. The coat of arms was topped by a white crown.	Für Fürst*
Saxe-Altenburg 153 (I & II Bn) after 1897; prior to 1897, Regiment 96 (I Bn)	Saxon coat of arms (Saxon shield) enclosed by a laurel wreath, all in white, on a Prussian line eagle. The coat of arms was topped by a white crown.	Für Fürst*
Saxe-Coburg and Gotha 95 (I & III Bns)	Saxon coat of arms (Saxon shield) enclosed by a laurel wreath, all in white, on a Prussian line eagle. The coat of arms was topped by a white crown.	Für Fürst*
Saxe-Meiningen 95 (II Bn)	Saxon coat of arms (Saxon shield) enclosed by a laurel wreath, all in white, on a Prussian line eagle. The coat of arms was topped by a white crown.	Für Fürst*
Saxe-Weimar-Eisenach 94	Saxon coat of arms (Saxon shield) enclosed by a wreath of laurel and oak leaves, all in white, on a Prussian line eagle. The coat of arms was topped by a white crown.	Für Fürst*
Schwarzburg-Rudolstadt 96 (III Bn)	Eight-pointed star with state coat of arms enclosed by a laurel wreath, all in white, on a Prussian line eagle. The coat of arms was topped by a white crown.	Für Fürst*

Sources: Rankin, *Helmets*; Johansson, *Pickelhauben*; and Larcade, *Casques*, vol. 1.

Note: [a] *Für Fürst = For prince/ruler; **Für König = For king.

§VI-3-6 BANNERS ON CAVALRY HELMETS

Year Given	Regiment Name	Honour	Antecedent Unit	
			Unit in Action Commemorated	Name of Unit in 1866
1902	Cuirassier Regiment 1	Pro Gloria et Patria		1st Cuirassier[a,b]
1861	Cuirassier Regiment 2	Hohenfriedberg 4 June 1745		2nd Cuirassier[b]

Year Given	Regiment Name	Honour	Antecedent Unit	
			Unit in Action Commemorated	Name of Unit in 1866
1899	Dragoon Regiment 9	Peninsula, Waterloo, Göhrde	3rd Hussars KGL[c]	Duke of Cambridge Dragoons[d]
1899	Dragoon Regiment 16	Waterloo	Hussar Regt. Lüneburg	Crown Prince Dragoons[d]
1899	Hussar Regiment 15	Peninsula, El Bodon	1st Hussars KGL[c]	Garde Hussar Regt[d]
		Waterloo, Barossa	2nd Hussars KGL[e]	Köningen Hussar Regt[d]
1867 & 1873	Hussar Regiment 17	Sicily, Peninsula, Waterloo, Mars la Tour[f]	Brunswick-Oels Hussars	Brunswick Hussar Regt
1899	Lancer Regiment 13	Peninsula, Garzia Hernandez, Waterloo,	1st Light Dragoons KGL[c]	Gardes du Corps[d]
1899	Lancer Regiment 14	Peninsula, Garzia Hernandez, Waterloo	2nd Light Dragoons KGL[c]	Guard Curassier Regt[d]

Sources: Rankin, *Helmets*; Johansson, *Pickelhauben*; Williams, 'Battle Honours'; and Larcade, *Casques*, vol. 2.
Notes: [a] After 1902, special eagle of the era of Frederick the Great.
[b] Prussian army.
[c] On the British Establishment, KGL = King's German Legion.
[d] Hanover army.
[e] This regiment also had a Peninsula battle honour.
[f] From Franco-Prussian War.

§VI-3-7 BANNERS ON INFANTRY HELMETS

Year Given	Regiment Name	Honour	Antecedent Unit	
			Unit in Action Commemorated	Name of Unit in 1866
1889	1st Foot Guard (I Bn and staff) (III Bn)	Semper Talis Pro Gloria et Patria		1st Foot Guard 1st Foot Guard (on mitre only)
	Guard Jäger	1860[a]		Guard Jäger[b]
	Guard Schützen	1860[a]		Guard Schützen[b]
1888	Grenadier Regiment 1	1655		1st Grenadier[b,c]
1888	Grenadier Regiment 4	1626		1st Grenadier[b,d]
1897	Grenadier Regiment 7	22 Marz 1797[e]		7th Grenadier[b]
1849	Grenadier Regiment 9	Colberg 1807		9th Grenadier[b]
1865	Infantry Regiment 33[f] 5th & 6th Companies of II Bn	Für Auszeichnung des vormaligen Konigl. Schwedischen Leibregiments Königin[g]		Fusilier Regt. Graf Roon[b]
1843	Infantry Regiment 34[h]	Same inscription as 33rd Regiment, I & II Line Bns (inscription noting service as part of Swedish Life Guards)		Fusilier Regt. Queen Victoria of Sweden[b]
1899	Infantry Regiment 73	Peninsula, Waterloo	I & II Line Bns KGL[i] V & VIII Line Bns KGL[i]	Garde Regt[j]

§VI-3 Uniform Information

Year Given	Regiment Name	Honour	Antecedent Unit — Unit in Action Commemorated	Antecedent Unit — Name of Unit in 1866
	Infantry Regiment 73	Waterloo	VI & VII Line Bns. KGL[i] Field Bn Verden Lt Field Bn Grubenhagen Landwehr Bn Nienburg Landwehr Bn Quackenbrook Landwehr Bn Melle	7 Inf. Regt[j]
1901	Infantry Regiment 73	Gibraltar cuff band[k]		
1899	Infantry Regiment 74	Waterloo	Landwehr Bn Hildesheim Landwehr Bn Peine Landwehr Bn Saizgitter Landwehr Bn Celle Landwehr Bn Gifhorn Landwehr Bn Uelzen	3 Inf. Regt[j]
1899	Infantry Regiment 77	Waterloo	Field Bn Bremen Landwehr Bn Bremersvörde Field Bn Calenberg Landwehr Bn Verden Landwehr Bn Bremerlehe Landwehr Bn Hoya	5 Inf. Regt[j]
1899	Infantry Regiment 78	Waterloo	Lt Field Bn Osnabrück Duke of York Landwehr Bn Osnabrück Landwehr Bn Bentheim Landwehr Bn Diepholz	6 Inf.-Regt[j]
1899	Infantry Regiment 79	Gibraltar cuff band[k]		1 or Life Regt[j]
1899	Infantry Regiment 87	La Belle Alliance	Ducal Nassau 1. Inf.-Regt.	1 Inf. Regt[j]
1899	Infantry Regiment 88	Mesa de Ibor, Medellin, La Belle Alliance	Ducal Nassau 2. Inf.-Regt.	2 Inf.-Regt[j]
1867	Infantry Regiment 92	Peninsula	Brunswick-Oel Jäger Regt	Life Guard Bn, Line Regt[m]
1871	Infantry Regiment 115	1621		1st Grand Ducal Hessian
1897	Infantry Regiment 117[n]	1697, 1897		Grand Duchess's Infantry (3rd Grand Ducal Hessian)
1899	Infantry Regiment 164	Waterloo	Landwehr Bn Hanover Landwehr Bn Hameln Landwehr Bn Alfeld	2 Inf. Regt[j]
1899	Infantry Regiment 165	Waterloo	Lt Field Bn. Lüneburg Landwehr Bn. Lüneburg	4 Inf. Regt[j]
1899	Jäger Battalion 10	Peninsula, Venta del Pozo, Waterloo	I & II Lt Bns KGL[i] III & IV Line Bns KGL[i]	2nd Guard Jäger Bn[j]
	Jäger Battalion 10	Waterloo[o]	Landwehr Bn Münden Landwehr Bn Northeim Landwehr Bn Osterode	2. Lt. Bn[j]
1901	Jäger Battalion 10	Gibraltar cuff band[k]		

Sources: Rankin, *Helmets*; Johansson, *Pickelhauben*; Williams, 'Battle Honours'; and Larcade, *Casques*, vol. 1.

Notes: [a] On ribbon around star: 'Mit Gott Fur Koenig und Vaterland' motto added in 1860.

[b] Prussian army.

[c] A banner with the year '1619' had been awarded to the regiment for being the year of founding of the oldest regiment in the Prussian army. In 1888, this year was changed to 1626 as it was found the earlier date was wrong, and they were not actually the oldest regiment in the army. The banner could not

very well be taken away from them, so, a correct date was put on it, and everyone made the best of it.

[d] In the late 1880s, it was learned that this regiment was really the oldest in the Prussian army rather than the 1st Grenadiers. This was very embarrassing to the authorities. The 4th Grenadiers were quietly given a banner with the date of their founding, and everyone moved on.

[e] The day Kaiser Wilhelm I was born.

[f] Worn by officers and men of the 5th and 6th Companies of the 2nd Battalion.

[g] This translates as 'For distinction of the former Royal Swedish Life Guard Regiment Queen'.

[h] Worn by other ranks of I and II Battalions, and all officers wore banner.

[i] On the British establishment, KGL = King's German Legion.

[j] Hanover army.

[k] The Hanoverian regiments present at the siege of Gibraltar of 1779–83 were Infantry Regiments von Reden, de la Motte, and von Hardenberg, subsequently the 3rd, 5th, and 6th Regiments. These units ceased to exist in 1803 when the French disbanded the Hanover army. It is not clear how Kaiser Wilhelm II selected these Prussian regiments as successors to the Gibraltar regiments and thus entitled to be awarded a Gibraltar cuff band in 1901.

[l] Nassau army.

[m] The Life Guard Battalion was considered a successor to the Napoleonic Jäger Regiment and wore their skull and crossbones on their shako. The line regiment had two battalions that wore a star on their shako. After 1912, all wore a skull and crossbones and Peninsula banner.

[n] The 9th Company had an anchor with a crossed pickaxe and axe on it on top of an anchor, all on top of the helmet badge. The regiment's origins were as an engineer company.

[o] Only one Waterloo honour was worn on the helmet.

§VI-3-8 BACKGROUND TO HELMET BANNERS[13]

Battle	Description
Waterloo	Fought 18 June 1815.
Colberg 1807	Colberg was a Prussian port on the Pomeranian coast and was under siege by the French from April to July of 1807 when a treaty was signed between France and Prussia. It was the only Prussian fortress to successfully withstand a siege during the Napoleonic campaign against Prussia of 1806–7.
Peninsula	The Peninsula honour was for service in Spain, Portugal, and Southern France from 1808 to 1814.
Peninsula-Waterloo-Göhrde	Göhrde was fought on 16 September 1813 in northern Germany near a stream and a small village of the same name. A combined English–German–Prussian force under Lieutenant General Count Wallmodembaun and a French force under General Pecheux met in battle.
Hohenfriedburg	Fought 4 June 1745. In this major battle of the Second Silesian War, the Bayreuth Dragoons, in one charge against the Austrian infantry, numbering some twenty battalions, captured 2,500 prisoners and took sixty-six battle colours. The Cuirassier Regiment Queen (Pomeranian) No. 2 continued the traditions of the Bayreuth Dragoons after 1807.
Peninsula-Waterloo-Venta Del Pozo	Venta Del Pozo was a rearguard action in Spain, fought on 23 October 1812. In this action, the I and II Light Battalions, KGL, broke up heavy French cavalry charges by forming squares.
Peninsula-Waterloo-El Bodon-Barossa	El Bodon was an honour won by the 1st Hussars during the battle in Spain, fought 25 September 1811. The 2nd Hussars fought at the battle of Barossa on 5 May 1811.
Peninsula-Sicily-Waterloo-Mars la Tour	Mars la Tour was fought on 16 August 1870 during the Franco-Prussian War and was one of the few non-Napoleonic War honours in the German army.
La Belle Alliance	The name Le Belle Alliance is one proposed for the battle of Waterloo by Blücher, but rejected by Wellington as being 'too French'.
Mesa de Ibor-La Belle Alliance-Medellin	Mesa de Ibor (17 March 1809) and Medellin (28 March 1809) were fought in Spain when the Nassau Regiment was fighting Spanish forces on the side of the French.
Peninsula-Waterloo-Garzia Hernandez	At Garzia Hernandez, 23 July 1812, two heavy dragoon regiments broke three formed squares of French infantry in what was viewed as the greatest cavalry action against infantry in the entire Peninsular War.

§VI-3-9 CAVALRY REGIMENT PLUMES

Regiment	Plume Colour
1st Guards Dragoon	White
2nd Guards Dragoon	White
1st Dragoons	Black
2nd Dragoons	Black
3rd Dragoons	Black
4th Dragoons	Black
5th Dragoons	Black
6th Dragoons	Black
7th Dragoons	Black
8th Dragoons	Black
9th Dragoons	Black
10th Dragoons	Black
11th Dragoons	Black
12th Dragoons	Black

Regiment	Plume Colour
13th Dragoons	Black
14th Dragoons	Black
15th Dragoons	Black
16th Dragoons	Black
17th Dragoons	Black
18th Dragoons	Black
19th Dragoons	Black
20th Dragoons	White
21st Dragoons	White
22nd Dragoons	White
23rd Dragoons	Black
24th Dragoons	Black
25th Dragoons	White
26th Dragoons	Black

§VI-3-10 INFANTRY REGIMENT PLUMES, LITZEN AND LACE

Regiment	Plume Colour	Other Ranks Litzen	Litzen Colour	Officers' Special Lace[a]
1st Foot Guards (I & II Bns)	White	Double	White	Double[b]
(III Bn)	Black	Double	White	Double[b]
2nd Foot Guards (I & II Bns)	White	Double	White	Double[c]
(III Bn)	Black	Double	White	Double[c]
3rd Foot Guards (I & II Bns)	White	Double	White	Double[c]
(III Bn)	Black	Double	White	Double[c]
4th Foot Guards (I & II Bns)	White	Double	White	Double[c]
(III Bn)	Black	Double	White	Double[c]
5th Foot Guards (I & II Bns)	White	Old Prussian	White with red centre line	Special[d]
(III Bn)	Black	Old Prussian	White with red centre line	Special[d]
1st Guards Grenadier (I & II Bns)	White	Double	White	Special[e]
(III Bn)	Black	Double	White	Special[e]
2nd Guards Grenadier (I & II Bns)	White	Double	White	Special[e]
(III Bn)	Black	Double	White	Special[e]
3rd Guards Grenadier (I & II Bns)	White	Double	White	Special[e]
(III Bn)	Black	Double	White	Special[e]
4th Guards Grenadier (I & II Bns)	White	Double	White	Special[e]
(III Bn)	Black	Double	White	Special[e]
5th Guards Grenadier (I & II Bns)	White	Old Prussian	Yellow with red centre line	Special[d]
(III Bn)	Black	Old Prussian	Yellow with red centre line	Special[d]

German Empire

Regiment	Plume Colour	Other Ranks Litzen	Litzen Colour	Officers' Special Lace[a]
Guard Fusiliers	Black	Double	White	
Guards Jäger	Black	Double	Yellow with green centre lines	None
Guards Schützen	Black	Double	Yellow with black centre lines	None
1st Grenadier	Black	Single	White	Special
2nd Grenadier	Black	Single	White	Special
3rd Grenadier	Black	Single	White	Special
4th Grenadier	Black	Single	White	Special
5th Grenadier	Black	Single	White	Special
6th Grenadier	Black	Single	White	Special
7th Grenadier	Black	Single	Yellow with red centre fields	Special
8th Grenadier	Black	Single	White	Special
9th Grenadier	Black	None		
10th Grenadier	Black	None		
11th Grenadier	Black	Single	White	Special
12th Grenadier	Black	None		
25th Infantry	Black	None		
80th Fusilier	Black	Old Prussian	White without centre line	Special
86th Fusilier	Black	None		None[f]
89th Grenadier (I & III Bns)	Black	Double	White	Special
(II Bn)	White	Double	Yellow	None[f]
92nd Infantry	Black	None		
100th Grenadier	Black	Double	White	None
101st Grenadier	Black	Double	White	None
109th Grenadier (I & II Bns)	White	Double	White	None
(III Bn)	Black	Double	White	None
110th Grenadier (I & II Bns)	White	None		None
(III Bn)	Black	None		None
115th Infantry	Black	Double	White	None
116th Infantry	Black	None		
117th Infantry	Black	None		
119th Grenadier	White	Double	White	None[f]
120th Infantry	Black	None		
123rd Grenadier	Black	Double	White	None[f]
145th Infantry	Black	None		
1st Jäger	Black	None		
2nd Jäger	Black	None		
3rd Jäger	Black	None		
4th Jäger	Black	None		
5th Jäger	Black	None		
6th Jäger	Black	None		
7th Jäger	Black	None		
8th Jäger	Black	None		

Regiment	Plume Colour	Other Ranks Litzen	Litzen Colour	Officers' Special Lace[a]
9th Jäger	Black	None		
10th Jäger	Black	None		
11th Jäger	Black	None		
14th Mecklenburg Jäger	Black	Double	White with green centre lines	Special[g]

Notes: [a] The designs of special lace for different regiments are shown in Images VI:1 and VI:2.
[b] Silver.
[c] Gold.
[d] These wore the same lace.
[e] All wore the same design.
[f] Officers had normal litzen.
[g] Silver chapter litzen.

§VI-3-11 COLOUR OF HELMET BADGES

Regiment	Colour of Helmet Badge	Officers[a]	Regiment	Colour of Helmet Badge	Officers[a]
1st Foot Guard	White guard eagle with white star	Same	10th Grenadier	Yellow grenadier eagle	Same
2nd Foot Guard	Yellow guard eagle with white star	Same	11th Grenadier	Yellow grenadier eagle	Same
3rd Foot Guard	Yellow guard eagle with white star	Same	12th Grenadier	Yellow grenadier eagle	Same
4th Foot Guard	Yellow guard eagle with white star	Same	13th Infantry	Yellow Prussian line eagle	Same
5th Foot Guard	White guard eagle with white star	Same	14th Infantry	Yellow Prussian line eagle	Same
			15th Infantry	Yellow Prussian line eagle	Same
Guard Fusilier	White guard eagle with white star	Same	16th Infantry	Yellow Prussian line eagle	Same
			17th Infantry	Yellow Prussian line eagle	Same
1st Guard Grenadier	Yellow grenadier eagle with white star	Same	18th Infantry	Yellow Prussian line eagle	Same
2nd Guard Grenadier	Yellow grenadier eagle with white star	Same	19th Infantry	Yellow Prussian line eagle	Same
			20th Infantry	Yellow Prussian line eagle	Same
3rd Guard Grenadier	Yellow grenadier eagle with white star	Same	21st Infantry	Yellow Prussian line eagle	Same
			22nd Infantry	Yellow Prussian line eagle	Same
4th Guard Grenadier	Yellow grenadier eagle with white star	Same	23rd Infantry	Yellow Prussian line eagle	Same
			24th Infantry	Yellow Prussian line eagle	Same
5th Guard Grenadier	Yellow grenadier eagle with white star	Same	25th Infantry	Yellow Prussian line eagle	Same
1st Grenadier	Yellow grenadier eagle	Same	26th Infantry	Yellow Prussian line eagle	Same
2nd Grenadier	Yellow grenadier eagle	Same	27th Infantry	Yellow Prussian line eagle	Same
			28th Infantry	Yellow Prussian line eagle	Same
3rd Grenadier	Yellow grenadier eagle	Same	29th Infantry	Yellow Prussian line eagle	Same
4th Grenadier	Yellow grenadier eagle	Same	30th Infantry	Yellow Prussian line eagle	Same
5th Grenadier	Yellow grenadier eagle	Same	31st Infantry	Yellow Prussian line eagle	Same
6th Grenadier	Yellow grenadier eagle	Same	32nd Infantry	Yellow Prussian line eagle	Same
7th Grenadier	Yellow grenadier eagle	Same	33rd Fusilier	Yellow Prussian line eagle	Same
8th Grenadier	Yellow grenadier eagle	Same	34th Fusilier	Yellow Prussian line eagle	Same
9th Grenadier	Yellow grenadier eagle	Same			

Regiment	Colour of Helmet Badge	Officers[a]	Regiment	Colour of Helmet Badge	Officers[a]
35th Fusilier	Yellow Prussian line eagle	Same	74th Infantry	Yellow Prussian line eagle	Same
36th Fusilier	Yellow Prussian line eagle	Same	75th Infantry	Yellow Prussian line eagle	Same
37th Fusilier	Yellow Prussian line eagle	Same	76th Infantry	Yellow Prussian line eagle	Same
38th Fusilier	Yellow Prussian line eagle	Same	77th Infantry	Yellow Prussian line eagle	Same
39th Fusilier	Yellow Prussian line eagle	Same	78th Infantry	Yellow Prussian line eagle	Same
40th Fusilier	Yellow Prussian line eagle	Same	79th Infantry	Yellow Prussian line eagle	Same
41st Infantry	Yellow Prussian line eagle	Same	80th Fusilier	Yellow Prussian line eagle	Same
42nd Infantry	Yellow Prussian line eagle	Same	81st Infantry	Yellow Prussian line eagle	Same
43rd Infantry	Yellow Prussian line eagle	Same	82nd Infantry	Yellow Prussian line eagle	Same
44th Infantry	Yellow Prussian line eagle	Same	83rd Infantry	Yellow Prussian line eagle	Same
45th Infantry	Yellow Prussian line eagle	Same	84th Infantry	Yellow Prussian line eagle	Same
46th Infantry	Yellow Prussian line eagle	Same	85th Infantry	Yellow Prussian line eagle	Same
47th Infantry	Yellow Prussian line eagle	Same	86th Infantry	Yellow Prussian line eagle	Same
48th Infantry	Yellow Prussian line eagle	Same	87th Infantry	Yellow Prussian line eagle	Same
49th Infantry	Yellow Prussian line eagle	Same	88th Infantry	Yellow Prussian line eagle	Same
50th Infantry	Yellow Prussian line eagle	Same	89th Grenadier (I & III Bns)	Yellow sunburst with white Mecklenburg-Schwerin coat of arms enclosed by a white wreath[b, c]	Same
51st Infantry	Yellow Prussian line eagle	Same			
52nd Infantry	Yellow Prussian line eagle	Same			
53rd Infantry	Yellow Prussian line eagle	Same	89th Grenadier (II Bn)	Yellow sunburst with white Mecklenburg-Strelitz coat of arms[c] (no wreath)	Same
54th Infantry	Yellow Prussian line eagle	Same			
55th Infantry	Yellow Prussian line eagle	Same	90th Fusilier	Yellow sunburst with white Mecklenburg-Schwerin coat of arms enclosed by a white wreath[b, c]	Same
56th Infantry	Yellow Prussian line eagle	Same			
57th Infantry	Yellow Prussian line eagle	Same			
58th Infantry	Yellow Prussian line eagle	Same	91st Infantry	Yellow Prussian line eagle with white star and Oldenburg coat of arms[b, c]	Same
59th Infantry	Yellow Prussian line eagle	Same			
60th Infantry	Yellow Prussian line eagle	Same			
61st Infantry	Yellow Prussian line eagle	Same	92nd Infantry	Yellow Prussian line eagle with Peninsula banner and white death's head (after 1912)[c]	Same
62nd Infantry	Yellow Prussian line eagle	Same			
63rd Infantry	Yellow Prussian line eagle	Same	93rd Infantry	Yellow Prussian line eagle with white star and Anhalt coat of arms[b, c]	Same
64th Infantry	Yellow Prussian line eagle	Same			
65th Infantry	Yellow Prussian line eagle	Same	94th Infantry	Yellow Prussian line eagle with white star and Saxe-Weimar-Eisenach coat of arms (Saxon shield) enclosed by a white wreath[b, c]	Same
66th Infantry	Yellow Prussian line eagle	Same			
67th Infantry	Yellow Prussian line eagle	Same			
68th Infantry	Yellow Prussian line eagle	Same			
69th Infantry	Yellow Prussian line eagle	Same	95th Infantry	Yellow Prussian line eagle with white star and the Saxe-Coburg-Gotha and Saxe-Meiningen coats of arms (Saxon shield) enclosed by a white wreath[b, c]	Same
70th Infantry	Yellow Prussian line eagle	Same			
71st Infantry	Yellow Prussian line eagle	Same			
72nd Infantry	Yellow Prussian line eagle	Same			
73rd Infantry	Yellow Prussian line eagle	Same			

§VI-3 Uniform Information

Regiment	Colour of Helmet Badge	Officers[a]
96th Infantry (I Bn)	Prior to 1897 yellow Prussian line eagle with white Saxe-Altenburg coat of arms (Saxon shield) within a white wreath. After 1897 Bn was Prussian and wore a yellow Prussian line eagle Also see 153rd Infantry[b,c]	Same
96th Infantry (II Bn)	Yellow Prussian line eagle with white star and coat of arms of Reuss enclosed by a white wreath[b,c]	Same
96th Infantry (III Bn)	Yellow Prussian line eagle with white star and coat of arms of Schwarzburg-Rudolstadt enclosed by a white wreath[b,c]	Same
97th Infantry	Yellow Prussian line eagle	Same
98th Infantry	Yellow Prussian line eagle	Same
99th Infantry	Yellow Prussian line eagle	Same
100th Grenadier	White sunburst with yellow coat of arms enclosed by a yellow wreath	Same
101st Grenadier	Yellow sunburst with white Saxon coat of arms enclosed by a white wreath	Same
102nd Infantry	Yellow sunburst with white Saxon coat of arms enclosed by a white wreath	Same
103rd Infantry	Yellow sunburst with white Saxon coat of arms enclosed by a white wreath	Same
104th Infantry	Yellow sunburst with white Saxon coat of arms enclosed by a white wreath	Same
105th Infantry	Yellow sunburst with white Saxon coat of arms enclosed by a white wreath	Same
106th Infantry	Yellow sunburst with white Saxon coat of arms enclosed by a white wreath	Same
107th Infantry	Yellow sunburst with white Saxon coat of arms enclosed by a white wreath	Same
108th Rifle	Yellow sunburst with white Saxon coat of arms enclosed by a white wreath with white hunting horn	Same
109th Grenadier	White griffin with white star and order star	Same
110th Grenadier	Yellow griffin	Same
111th Infantry	Yellow griffin	Same
112th Infantry	Yellow griffin	Same
113th Infantry	Yellow griffin	Same
114th Infantry	Yellow griffin	Same
115th Infantry	White lion with white star	Same
116th Infantry	Yellow lion	Same
117th Infantry	Yellow lion[d]	Same
118th Infantry	Yellow lion	Same
119th Grenadier	White Württemberg coat of arms	Same
120th Infantry	Yellow Württemberg coat of arms	Same
121st Infantry	Yellow Württemberg coat of arms	Same
122nd Fusilier	Yellow Württemberg coat of arms	Same
123rd Grenadier	White Württemberg coat of arms	Same
124th Infantry	Yellow Württemberg coat of arms	Same
125th Infantry	Yellow Württemberg coat of arms	Same
126th Infantry	Yellow Württemberg coat of arms	Same
127th Infantry	Yellow Württemberg coat of arms	Same
128th Infantry	Yellow Prussian line eagle	Same
129th Infantry	Yellow Prussian line eagle	Same
130th Infantry	Yellow Prussian line eagle	Same
131st Infantry	Yellow Prussian line eagle	Same
132nd Infantry	Yellow Prussian line eagle	Same
133rd Infantry	Yellow sunburst with white Saxon coat of arms enclosed by a white wreath	Same
134th Infantry	Yellow sunburst with white Saxon coat of arms enclosed by a white wreath	Same
135th Infantry	Yellow Prussian line eagle	Same
136th Infantry	Yellow Prussian line eagle	Same
137th Infantry	Yellow Prussian line eagle	Same
138th Infantry	Yellow Prussian line eagle	Same
139th Infantry	Yellow sunburst with white Saxon coat of arms enclosed by a white wreath	Same

Regiment	Colour of Helmet Badge	Officers[a]
140th Infantry	Yellow Prussian line eagle	Same
141st Infantry	Yellow Prussian line eagle	Same
142nd Infantry	Yellow griffin	Same
143rd Infantry	Yellow Prussian line eagle	Same
144th Infantry	Yellow Prussian line eagle	Same
145th Infantry	Yellow grenadier eagle	Same
146th Infantry	Yellow Prussian line eagle	Same
147th Infantry	Yellow Prussian line eagle	Same
148th Infantry	Yellow Prussian line eagle	Same
149th Infantry	Yellow Prussian line eagle	Same
150th Infantry	Yellow Prussian line eagle	Same
151st Infantry	Yellow Prussian line eagle	Same
152nd Infantry	Yellow Prussian line eagle	Same
153rd Infantry	Yellow Prussian line eagle with white star and 'Saxe-Altenburg' coat of arms (Saxon shield) enclosed by a white wreath. Battalion I and II 1897–1914. Battalion III formed in 1913 was Prussian, and wore a yellow Prussian line eagle.[b, c]	Same
154th Infantry	Yellow Prussian line eagle	Same
155th Infantry	Yellow Prussian line eagle	Same
156th Infantry	Yellow Prussian line eagle	Same
157th Infantry	Yellow Prussian line eagle	Same
158th Infantry	Yellow Prussian line eagle	Same
159th Infantry	Yellow Prussian line eagle	Same
160th Infantry	Yellow Prussian line eagle	Same
161st Infantry	Yellow Prussian line eagle	Same
162nd Infantry	Yellow Prussian line eagle	Same
163rd Infantry	Yellow Prussian line eagle	Same
164th Infantry	Yellow Prussian line eagle	Same
165th Infantry	Yellow Prussian line eagle	Same
166th Infantry	Yellow Prussian line eagle	Same
167th Infantry	Yellow Prussian line eagle	Same
168th Infantry	Yellow lion	Same
169th Infantry	Yellow griffin	Same
170th Infantry	Yellow griffin	Same
171st Infantry	Yellow Prussian line eagle	Same
172nd Infantry	Yellow Prussian line eagle	Same
173rd Infantry	Yellow Prussian line eagle	Same
174th Infantry	Yellow Prussian line eagle	Same
175th Infantry	Yellow Prussian line eagle	Same
176th Infantry	Yellow Prussian line eagle	Same
177th Infantry	Yellow sunburst with white Saxon coat of arms enclosed by a white wreath	Same
178th Infantry	Yellow sunburst with white Saxon coat of arms enclosed by a white wreath	Same
179th Infantry	Yellow sunburst with white Saxon coat of arms enclosed by a white wreath	Same
180th Infantry	Yellow Württemberg coat of arms	Same
181st Infantry	Yellow sunburst with white Saxon coat of arms enclosed by a white wreath	Same
182nd Infantry	Yellow sunburst with white Saxon coat of arms enclosed by a white wreath	Same
Guard Jäger	White star of the Order of the Black Eagle	Same
Guard Schützen	White star of the Order of the Black Eagle	Same
1st Jäger	Yellow Prussian line eagle[d]	Same
2nd Jäger	Yellow Prussian line eagle[d]	Same
3rd Jäger	Yellow Prussian line eagle	Same
4th Jäger	Yellow Prussian line eagle	Same
5th Jäger	Yellow Prussian line eagle[e]	Same
6th Jäger	Yellow Prussian line eagle[e]	Same
7th Jäger	Yellow Prussian line eagle	Same
8th Jäger	Yellow Prussian line eagle	Same
9th Jäger	Yellow Prussian line eagle	Same
10th Jäger	Yellow Prussian line eagle	Same
11th Jäger	Yellow Prussian line eagle	Same
12th Jäger	White sunburst with yellow Saxon coat of arms enclosed by a yellow wreath and white hunting horn	Same

Regiment	Colour of Helmet Badge	Officers[a]
13th Jäger	White sunburst with yellow Saxon coat of arms enclosed by a yellow wreath and white hunting horn	Same
14th Jäger	Yellow sunburst with white Mecklenburg-Schwerin coat of arms enclosed by a white wreath	Same
1st Bavarian Infantry	White Bavarian coat of arms	Same
2nd Bavarian Infantry	Yellow Bavarian coat of arms	Same
3rd Bavarian Infantry	Yellow Bavarian coat of arms	Same
4th Bavarian Infantry	Yellow Bavarian coat of arms	Same
5th Bavarian Infantry	Yellow Bavarian coat of arms	Same
6th Bavarian Infantry	Yellow Bavarian coat of arms	Same
7th Bavarian Infantry	Yellow Bavarian coat of arms	Same
8th Bavarian Infantry	Yellow Bavarian coat of arms	Same
9th Bavarian Infantry	Yellow Bavarian coat of arms	Same
10th Bavarian Infantry	Yellow Bavarian coat of arms	Same
11th Bavarian Infantry	Yellow Bavarian coat of arms	Same
12th Bavarian Infantry	Yellow Bavarian coat of arms	Same
13th Bavarian Infantry	Yellow Bavarian coat of arms	Same
14th Bavarian Infantry	Yellow Bavarian coat of arms	Same
15th Bavarian Infantry	Yellow Bavarian coat of arms	Same
16th Bavarian Infantry	Yellow Bavarian coat of arms	Same
17th Bavarian Infantry	Yellow Bavarian coat of arms	Same
18th Bavarian Infantry	Yellow Bavarian coat of arms	Same
19th Bavarian Infantry	Yellow Bavarian coat of arms	Same
20th Bavarian Infantry	Yellow Bavarian coat of arms	Same
21st Bavarian Infantry	Yellow Bavarian coat of arms	Same
22nd Bavarian Infantry	Yellow Bavarian coat of arms	Same
23rd Bavarian Infantry	Yellow Bavarian coat of arms	Same
1st Bavarian Jäger	Yellow Bavarian coat of arms	Same
2nd Bavarian Jäger	Yellow Bavarian coat of arms	Same

Notes: [a] If a star was present in the other ranks' helmet badge, then the officers' was the same, with the exception that the star was enamelled.
[b] With crown.
[c] For details on the badges see §VI-3-5 Minor States Helmet Badges.
[d] 9th Company also had a white coat of arms.
[e] Had the monogram 'FWR' in an oval shield on the eagle's breast.

§VI-3-12 COCKADE AND HELMET FRONT BADGES

State[a]	Cockade[b]	Front Badge
Reich	Black, yellow, red	
Prussia	Black, white, black	Prussian eagle[c]
Anhalt	Green	Prussian eagle with badge
Baden	Yellow, red, yellow	Griffin
Bavaria	White, light blue, white	State coat of arms[c]

State[a]	Cockade[b]	Front Badge
Brunswick	Blue, yellow, blue	Prussian eagle with badges[d]
Bremen (75, I & II Bns)	White with red cross[e]	Prussian eagle
Hamburg (76)	White with red cross[f]	Prussian eagle
Lübeck (162, I & II Bns)	White with red cross[g]	Prussian eagle

State[a]	Cockade[b]	Front Badge	State[a]	Cockade[b]	Front Badge
Hesse	White, red, white, red	Lion[c]	Saxe-Meiningen and Saxe-Coburg-Gotha (95)	Green, white, green	Prussian eagle with badge
Lippe-Detmold (55, part of III Bn)	Yellow, red	Prussian eagle	Saxe-Weimar-Eisenach (94)	Green, yellow, black	Prussian eagle with badge
Mecklenburg-Schwerin (89, I & III Bns; 90)	Blue, yellow, and red	Sun and badge	Schaumburg-Lippe (55, part of III Bn)	White, red, blue[h,j]	Prussian eagle
Mecklenburg-Strelitz (89, II Bn)	Blue, yellow, and red	Sun and badge	Schwarzburg-Rudolstadt (96, III Bn)	Blue, white, blue	Prussian eagle with badge
Oldenburg (91)	Blue, red, blue	Prussian eagle with badge	Schwarzburg-Sonderhausen (71, I Bn)	White, light blue, white	Prussian eagle with badge
Reuss (96, II Bn)	Yellow, red, black	Prussian eagle with badge	Waldeck-Pyrmont (83, III Bn)	Yellow, red, black	Prussian eagle
Saxony	White, green, white	Star and badge	Württemberg	Black, red, black	State coat of arms
Saxe-Altenburg (153, I & II Bns; 7th Jäger)	Green, white, green[i]	Prussian eagle with badge			

Sources: For front badges see, generally, Bowman, *Pickelhaube*, vol. 1; Laine, *L'Armée Allemande*.

Notes: [a] Numbers in parentheses show the regiment and battalion in which the state's contingencies served.
[b] Colours listed from outside to inside.
[c] The helmet badge had different designs and variations.
[d] Badge for I and II Battalions, skull crossbones for III Battalion. After 1912, skull and crossbones for all.
[e] A Maltese cross to 1897, after that white, red, white.
[f] Up to 1897, a Maltese cross; after that, the cross of the Teutonic Order (the iron cross) (Bowman, *Pickelhaube*, vol. 1, p. 76).
[g] A Maltese cross. This was retained after 1897 (Bowman, *Pickelhaube*, vol. 1, p. 76).
[h] Up to 1897, after that a Prussian cockade, according to some sources; others show the state cockade being worn until 1914. Other sources list other colours.
[i] After 1987. Prior to that yellow, green, black.
[j] Likely not worn after 1897 as too few men.

§VI-3-13 GERMAN HELMET AND UNIFORM: IDENTIFYING ACCESSORY DETAILS – 1914

Regiment	State	Shoulder Strap	Cuff Type[a]	Cuff Plate Piping	Army Corps[b]	Helmet Banner	Plume	Mono-grams
1st Foot Guard (I & II Bns)	Prussia	White	Sw	None	Guard-C.	Yes	White[c]	No
1st Foot Guard (III Bn)	Prussia	White	Sw	None	Guard-C.	Yes	Black[d]	No
2nd Foot Guard (I & II Bns)	Prussia	Red	Sw	None	Guard-C.	No	White	No
2nd Foot Guard (III Bn)	Prussia	Red	Sw	None	Guard-C.	No	Black	No
3rd Foot Guard (I & II Bns)	Prussia	Yellow	Sw	None	Guard-C.	No	White	No
3rd Foot Guard (III Bn)	Prussia	Yellow	Sw	None	Guard-C.	No	Black	No
4th Foot Guard (I & II Bns)	Prussia	Light blue	Sw	None	Guard-C.	No	White	No
4th Foot Guard (III Bn)	Prussia	Light blue	Sw	None	Guard-C.	No	Black	No
5th Foot Guard (I & II Bns)	Prussia	White		None[e]	Guard-C.	No	White	No
5th Foot Guard (III Bn)	Prussia	White		None[e]	Guard-C.	No	Black	No

§VI-3 Uniform Information 683

Regiment	State	Shoulder Strap	Cuff Type[a]	Cuff Plate Piping	Army Corps[b]	Helmet Banner	Plume	Mono-grams
Guard Fusilier	Prussia	Yellow	Sw	None	Guard-C.	No	Black	No
1st Guard Grenadier (I & II Bns)	Prussia	White		None[e]	Guard-C.	No	White[f]	Yes
1st Guard Grenadier (III Bn)	Prussia	White		None[e]	Guard-C.	No	Black[g]	Yes
2nd Guard Grenadier (I & II Bns)	Prussia	Red		None[e]	Guard-C.	No	White	Yes
2nd Guard Grenadier (III Bn)	Prussia	Red		None[e]	Guard-C.	No	Black	Yes
3rd Guard Grenadier (I & II Bns)	Prussia	Yellow		None[e]	Guard-C.	No	White	Yes
3rd Guard Grenadier (III Bn)	Prussia	Yellow		None[e]	Guard-C.	No	Black	Yes
4th Guard Grenadier (I & II Bns)	Prussia	Light blue		None[e]	Guard-C.	No	White	Yes
4th Guard Grenadier (III Bn)	Prussia	Light blue		None[e]	Guard-C.	No	Black	Yes
5th Guard Grenadier (I & II Bns)	Prussia	White		None[e]	Guard-C.	No	White	No
5th Guard Grenadier (III Bn)	Prussia	White		None[e]	Guard-C.	No	Black	No
1st Grenadier	Prussia	White		White	I A.C.	Yes	Black	Yes
2nd Grenadier	Prussia	White		None	II A.C.	No	Black	Yes
3rd Grenadier	Prussia	White		White	I A.C.	No	Black	Yes
4th Grenadier	Prussia	White		White	I A.C.	Yes	Black	Yes
5th Grenadier	Prussia	Yellow		Light blue	XVII A.C.	No	Black	Yes
6th Grenadier	Prussia	Yellow		White	V A.C.	No	Black	No
7th Grenadier	Prussia	Yellow		White[e]	V A.C.	Yes	Black	Yes
8th Grenadier	Prussia	Red		White	III A.C.	No	Black	Yes
9th Grenadier	Prussia	White		None	II A.C.	Yes	Black	No
10th Grenadier	Prussia	Yellow		None	VI A.C.	No	Black	Yes
11th Grenadier	Prussia	Yellow		None	VI A.C.	No	Black	Yes
12th Grenadier	Prussia	Red		White	III A.C.	No	Black	No
13th Infantry	Prussia	Light blue		White	VII A.C.	No	No	No
14th Infantry	Prussia	White		None	II A.C.	No	No	No
15th Infantry	Prussia	Light blue		White	VII A.C.	No	No	No
16th Infantry	Prussia	Light blue		White	VII A.C.	No	No	No
17th Infantry	Prussia	Light green		White	XXI A.C.	No	No	No
18th Infantry	Prussia	Light blue		Light blue	XX A.C.	No	No	No
19th Infantry	Prussia	Yellow		White	V A.C.	No	No	No
20th Infantry	Prussia	Red		White	III A.C.	No	No	No
21st Infantry	Prussia	Yellow		Light blue	XVII A.C.	No	No	No
22nd Infantry	Prussia	Yellow		None	VI A.C.	No	No	No
23rd Infantry	Prussia	Yellow		None	VI A.C.	No	No	No
24th Infantry	Prussia	Red		White	III A.C.	No	No	No
25th Infantry	Prussia	Light blue		None	VIII A.C.	No	Black	No
26th Infantry	Prussia	Red		None	IV A.C.	No	No	No
27th Infantry	Prussia	Red		None	IV A.C.	No	No	No

German Empire

Regiment	State	Shoulder Strap	Cuff Type[a]	Cuff Plate Piping	Army Corps[b]	Helmet Banner	Plume	Mono-grams
28th Infantry	Prussia	Light blue		None	VIII A.C.	No	No	No
29th Infantry	Prussia	Light blue		None	VIII A.C.	No	No	No
30th Infantry	Prussia	Yellow		Yellow	XVI A.C.	No	No	No
31st Infantry	Prussia	White		Yellow	IX A.C.	No	No	No
32nd Infantry	Prussia	Red		Yellow	XI A.C.	No	No	No
33rd Fusilier	Prussia	White		White	I A.C.	Yes	No	No
34th Fusilier	Prussia	White		None	II A.C.	Yes	No	Yes
35th Fusilier	Prussia	Red		White	III A.C.	No	No	No
36th Fusilier	Prussia	Red		None	IV A.C.	No	No	No
37th Fusilier	Prussia	Yellow		White	V A.C.	No	No	No
38th Fusilier	Prussia	Yellow		None	VI A.C.	No	No	No
39th Fusilier	Prussia	Light blue		White	VII A.C.	No	No	No
40th Fusilier	Prussia	Light blue		None	XIV A.C.	No	No	No
41st Infantry	Prussia	White		White	I A.C.	No	No	No
42nd Infantry	Prussia	White		None	II A.C.	No	No	No
43rd Infantry	Prussia	White		White	I A.C.	No	No	No
44th Infantry	Prussia	White		White	I A.C.	No	No	No
45th Infantry	Prussia	White		White	I A.C.	No	No	No
46th Infantry	Prussia	Yellow		White	V A.C.	No	No	No
47th Infantry	Prussia	Yellow		White	V A.C.	No	No	Yes
48th Infantry	Prussia	Red		White	III A.C.	No	No	No
49th Infantry	Prussia	White		None	II A.C.	No	No	No
50th Infantry	Prussia	Yellow		White	V A.C.	No	No	No
51st Infantry	Prussia	Yellow		None	VI A.C.	No	No	No
52nd Infantry	Prussia	Red		White	III A.C.	No	No	No
53rd Infantry	Prussia	Light blue		White	VII A.C.	No	No	Yes
54th Infantry	Prussia	White		None	II A.C.	No	No	No
55th Infantry	Prussia	Light blue		White	VII A.C.	No	No	No
56th Infantry	Prussia	Light blue		White	VII A.C.	No	No	No
57th Infantry	Prussia	Light blue		White	VII A.C.	No	No	No
58th Infantry	Prussia	Yellow		White	V A.C.	No	No	No
59th Infantry	Prussia	Light blue		Light blue	XX A.C.	No	No	No
60th Infantry	Prussia	Light green		White	XXI A.C.	No	No	No
61st Infantry	Prussia	Yellow		Light blue	XVII A.C.	No	No	No
62nd Infantry	Prussia	Yellow		None	VI A.C.	No	No	No
63rd Infantry	Prussia	Yellow		None	VI A.C.	No	No	No
64th Infantry	Prussia	Red		White	III A.C.	No	No	No
65th Infantry	Prussia	Light blue		None	VIII A.C.	No	No	No
66th Infantry	Prussia	Red		None	IV A.C.	No	No	No
67th Infantry	Prussia	Yellow		Yellow	XVI A.C.	No	No	No
68th Infantry	Prussia	Light blue		None	VIII A.C.	No	No	No

§VI-3 Uniform Information

Regiment	State	Shoulder Strap	Cuff Type[a]	Cuff Plate Piping	Army Corps[b]	Helmet Banner	Plume	Mono-grams
69th Infantry	Prussia	Light blue		None	VIII A.C.	No	No	No
70th Infantry	Prussia	Light green		White	XXI A.C.	No	No	No
71st Infantry	Prussia	Red		Yellow	XI A.C.	No	No	No
72nd Infantry	Prussia	Red		None	IV A.C.	No	No	Yes
73rd Fusilier	Prussia	White		Light blue	X A.C.	Yes	No	No
74th Infantry	Prussia	White		Light blue	X A.C.	Yes	No	No
75th Infantry	Prussia	White		Yellow	IX A.C.	No	No	No
76th Infantry	Hamburg	White		Yellow	IX A.C.	No	No	No
77th Infantry	Prussia	White		Light blue	X A.C.	Yes	No	No
78th Infantry	Prussia	White		Light blue	X A.C.	Yes	No	No
79th Infantry	Prussia	White		Light blue	X A.C.	Yes	No	No
80th Fusilier	Prussia	Light blue		Yellow	XVIII A.C.	No	Black	Yes
81st Infantry	Prussia	Light blue		Yellow	XVIII A.C.	No	No	No
82nd Infantry	Prussia	Red		Yellow	XI A.C.	No	No	No
83rd Infantry	Prussia	Red		Yellow	XI A.C.	No	No	No
84th Infantry	Prussia	White		Yellow	IX A.C.	No	No	No
85th Infantry	Prussia	White		Yellow	IX A.C.	No	No	No
86th Fusilier	Prussia	White		Yellow	IX A.C.	No	Black	Yes
87th Infantry	Prussia	Light blue		Yellow	XVIII A.C.	Yes	No	No
88th Infantry	Prussia	Light blue		Yellow	XVIII A.C.	Yes	No	Yes
89th Grenadier (I & III Bns)	Mecklenburg-Schwerin	White		Red[e]	IX A.C.	No	Black	Yes
89th Grenadier (II Bn)	Mecklenburg-Strelitz	Red	F*	Red[e]	IX A.C.	No	White	Yes
90th Fusilier	Mecklenburg-Schwerin	White		Yellow	IX A.C.	No	No	Yes
91st Infantry	Oldenburg	White		Light blue	X A.C.	No	Black[h]	Yes
92nd Infantry	Braunschweig	White		Light blue	X A.C.	Yes	Black	Yes
93rd Infantry	Anhalt	Red		None	IV A.C.	No	No	Yes
94th Infantry	Saxony-Weimar	Red		Yellow	XI A.C.	No	No	Yes
95th Infantry	Saxony-Meiningen-Coburg-Gotha	Red		Yellow	XI A.C.	No	No	Yes
96th Infantry (I Bn)	Prussia	Red		Yellow	XI A.C.	No	No	No[j]
96th Infantry (II Bn)	Reuss	Red		Yellow	XI A.C.	No	No	No[j]
96th Infantry (III Bn)	Schwarzburg-Rudolstadt	Red		Yellow	XI A.C.	No	No	No[j]
97th Infantry	Prussia	Light green		White	XXI A.C.	No	No	No
98th Infantry	Prussia	Yellow		Yellow	XVI A.C.	No	No	No
99th Infantry	Prussia	Red		Light blue	XV A.C.	No	No	No

Regiment	State	Shoulder Strap	Cuff Type[a]	Cuff Plate Piping	Army Corps[b]	Helmet Banner	Plume	Mono-grams
100th Grenadier	Saxony	Prussian blue[i]	Sw	Dark blue	XII A.C.	No	Black	Yes
101st Grenadier	Saxony	Prussian blue[i]	Sw	Dark blue	XII A.C.	No	Black	Yes
102nd Infantry	Saxony	Prussian blue[i]	Sa	None	XII A.C.	No	No	No
103rd Infantry	Saxony	Prussian blue[i]	Sa	None	XII A.C.	No	No	No
104th Infantry	Saxony	Prussian blue[i]	Sa	None	XIX A.C.	No	No	Yes
105th Infantry	Saxony	Prussian blue[i]	Sa	None	XV A.C.	No	No	No
106th Infantry	Saxony	Prussian blue[i]	Sa	None	XIX A.C.	No	No	Yes
107th Infantry	Saxony	Prussian blue[i]	Sa	None	XIX A.C.	No	No	No
108th Rifle	Saxony	Very dark green[i,k,l]	Sa[m]	Red	XII A.C.	No	Black	No
109th Grenadier	Baden	White	Sw	None	XIV A.C.	Yes	White[n]	Yes
110th Grenadier	Baden	White		None	XIV A.C.	No	White[n]	Yes
111th Infantry	Baden	Red		None	XIV A.C.	No	No	Yes
112th Infantry	Baden	Light yellow		None	XIV A.C.	No	No	No
113th Infantry	Baden	Light blue		None	XIV A.C.	No	No	No
114th Infantry	Baden	Light green		None	XIV A.C.	No	No	Yes
115th Infantry	Hessen	Red		None	XVIII A.C.	Yes	Black	Yes
116th Infantry	Hessen	White		None[o]	XVIII A.C.	No	Black	Yes
117th Infantry	Hessen	Bright mid-blue		None[p]	XVIII A.C.	Yes	Black	Yes
118th Infantry	Hessen	Light yellow		None[q]	XVIII A.C.	No	No	No
119th Grenadier	Württemberg	Red	Sw	None	XIII A.C.	No	White	Yes
120th Infantry	Württemberg	Red		Light blue	XIII A.C.	No	Black	Yes
121st Infantry	Württemberg	Red		Light blue	XIII A.C.	No	No	No
122nd Fusilier	Württemberg	Red		Light blue	XIII A.C.	No	No	No
123rd Grenadier	Württemberg	Red	Sw	None	XIII A.C.	No	Black	Yes
124th Infantry	Württemberg	Red		Light blue	XIII A.C.	No	No	Yes
125th Infantry	Württemberg	Red		Light blue	XIII A.C.	No	No	Yes
126th Infantry	Württemberg	Red		Light blue	XV A.C.	No	No	No
127th Infantry	Württemberg	Red		Light blue	XIII A.C.	No	No	No
128th Infantry	Prussia	Yellow		Light blue	XVII A.C.	No	No	No
129th Infantry	Prussia	Yellow		Light blue	XVII A.C.	No	No	No
130th Infantry	Prussia	Yellow		Yellow	XVI A.C.	No	No	No
131st Infantry	Prussia	Light green		White	XXI A.C.	No	No	No

§VI-3 Uniform Information

Regiment	State	Shoulder Strap	Cuff Type[a]	Cuff Plate Piping	Army Corps[b]	Helmet Banner	Plume	Mono-grams
132nd Infantry	Prussia	Red		Light blue	XV A.C.	No	No	No
133rd Infantry	Saxony	Prussian blue[i]	Sa	None	XIX A.C.	No	No	No
134th Infantry	Saxony	Prussian blue[i]	Sa	None	XIX A.C.	No	No	No
135th Infantry	Prussia	Yellow		Yellow	XVI A.C.	No	No	No
136th Infantry	Prussia	Red		Light blue	XV A.C.	No	No	No
137th Infantry	Prussia	Light green		White	XXI A.C.	No	No	No
138th Infantry	Prussia	Light green		White	XXI A.C.	No	No	No
139th Infantry	Saxony	White	Sa	None	XIX A.C.	No	No	No
140th Infantry	Prussia	White		None	II A.C.	No	No	No
141st Infantry	Prussia	Yellow		Light blue	XVII A.C.	No	No	No
142nd Infantry	Baden	Light yellow		None	XIV A.C.	No	No	No
143rd Infantry	Prussia	Red		Light blue	XV A.C.	No	No	No
144th Infantry	Prussia	Yellow		Yellow	XVI A.C.	No	No	No
145th Infantry	Prussia	Light blue		Yellow	XVI A.C.	No	Black[f]	Yes
146th Infantry	Prussia	Light blue		Light blue[e]	XX A.C.	No	No	No
147th Infantry	Prussia	Light blue		Light blue	XX A.C.	No	No	No
148th Infantry	Prussia	Light blue		Light blue[e]	XX A.C.	No	No	No
149th Infantry	Prussia	White		None	II A.C.	No	No	No
150th Infantry	Prussia	Light blue		Light blue[g]	XX A.C.	No	No	No
151st Infantry	Prussia	Light blue		Light blue[g]	XX A.C.	No	No	No
152nd Infantry	Prussia	Light blue		Light blue[e]	XX A.C.	No	No	No
153rd Infantry	Saxony-Altenburg	Red		None	IV A.C.	No	No	Yes
154th Infantry	Prussia	Yellow		None[o]	V A.C.	No	No	No
155th Infantry	Prussia	Yellow		White	V A.C.	No	No	No
156th Infantry	Prussia	Yellow		None[o]	VI A.C.	No	No	No
157th Infantry	Prussia	Yellow		None	VI A.C.	No	No	No
158th Infantry	Prussia	Light blue		None[o]	VII A.C.	No	No	No
159th Infantry	Prussia	Light blue		White	VII A.C.	No	No	No
160th Infantry	Prussia	Light blue		None[o]	VIII A.C.	No	No	No
161st Infantry	Prussia	Light blue		None	VIII A.C.	No	No	No
162nd Infantry	Lübeck	White		Yellow[o]	IX A.C.	No	No	No
163rd Infantry	Prussia	White		Yellow	IX A.C.	No	No	No
164th Infantry	Prussia	White		Light blue[o]	X A.C.	Yes	No	No
165th Infantry	Prussia	Red		None	IV A.C.	Yes	No	No
166th Infantry	Prussia	Light green		None[o]	XXI A.C.	No	No	No
167th Infantry	Prussia	Red		Yellow	XI A.C.	No	No	No
168th Infantry	Hesse	Red		None	XVIII A.C.	No	No	No
169th Infantry	Baden	Red		None	XIV A.C.	No	No	No

German Empire

Regiment	State	Shoulder Strap	Cuff Type[a]	Cuff Plate Piping	Army Corps[b]	Helmet Banner	Plume	Mono-grams
170th Infantry	Baden	Light blue		None	XIV A.C.	No	No	No
171st Infantry	Prussia	Red		Light blue[o]	XV A.C.	No	No	No
172nd Infantry	Prussia	Red		Light blue	XV A.C.	No	No	No
173rd Infantry	Prussia	Yellow		Yellow[o]	XVI A.C.	No	No	No
174th Infantry	Prussia	Light green		White	XXI A.C.	No	No	No
175th Infantry	Prussia	Yellow		Light blue[o]	XVII A.C.	No[s]	No	No
176th Infantry	Prussia	Yellow		Light blue	XVII A.C.	No	No	No
177th Infantry	Saxony	Prussian blue[i]	Sa	None	XII A.C.	No	No	No
178th Infantry	Saxony	Prussian blue[i]	Sa	None	XII A.C.	No	No	No
179th Infantry	Saxony	Prussian blue[i]	Sa	None	XIX A.C.	No	No	No
180th Infantry	Württemberg	Red		Light blue	XIII A.C.	No	No	No
181st Infantry	Saxony	Prussian blue[i]	Sa	None	XIX A.C.	No	No	No
182nd Infantry	Saxony	Prussian blue[i]	Sa	None	XII A.C.	No	No	No
Guards Jäger	Prussia	Red	Sa	None	Guard-C.	Yes	Black	No
Guards Schützen	Prussia	Red	F	Red	Guard-C.	Yes	Black	No
1st Jäger	Prussia	Red	Sa	None	XX A.C.	No	Black	No
2nd Jäger	Prussia	Red	Sa	None	II A.C.	No	Black	No
3rd Jäger	Prussia	Red	Sa	None	III A.C.	No	Black	No
4th Jäger	Prussia	Red	Sa	None	IV A.C.	No	Black	No
5th Jäger	Prussia	Red	Sa	None	V A.C.	No	Black	No
6th Jäger	Prussia	Red	Sa	None	VI A.C.	No	Black	No
7th Jäger	Schaumburg-Lippisch	Red	Sa	None	VII A.C.	No	Black	No
8th Jäger	Prussia	Red	Sa	None	XV A.C.	No	Black	No
9th Jäger	Prussia	Red	Sa	None	IX A.C.	No	Black	No
10th Jäger	Prussia	Red	Sa	None	X A.C.	Yes	Black	No
11th Jäger	Prussia	Red	Sa	None	XI A.C.	No	Black	Yes
12th Jäger	Saxony	Dark green[i,k,l]	Sa	Red[m]	XII A.C.	No	Black	No
13th Jäger	Saxony	Dark green[i,k,l]	Sa	Red[m]	XII A.C.	No	Black	No
14th Jäger	Mecklenburg-Schwerin	Light green	Sw	Red[t]	XV A.C.	No	Black	No
Bavarian Life Guards	Bavaria	Red	Sw	White	I B.A.C.	No	No	Yes
1st Bavarian Infantry	Bavaria	Red		White	I B.A.C.	No	No	Yes
2nd Bavarian Infantry	Bavaria	Red		White	I B.A.C.	No	No	Yes
3rd Bavarian Infantry	Bavaria	Red		White	I B.A.C.	No	No	Yes
4th Bavarian Infantry	Bavaria	Red		None	II B.A.C.	No	No	No

Regiment	State	Shoulder Strap	Cuff Type[a]	Cuff Plate Piping	Army Corps[b]	Helmet Banner	Plume	Monograms
5th Bavarian Infantry	Bavaria	Red		None	II B.A.C.	No	No	No
6th Bavarian Infantry	Bavaria	Red		Yellow	III B.A.C.	No	No	Yes
7th Bavarian Infantry	Bavaria	Red		Yellow	III B.A.C.	No	No	No
8th Bavarian Infantry	Bavaria	Red		None	II B.A.C.	No	No	No
9th Bavarian Infantry	Bavaria	Red		None	II B.A.C.	No	No	No
10th Bavarian Infantry	Bavaria	Red		Yellow	III B.A.C.	No	No	Yes
11th Bavarian Infantry	Bavaria	Red		Yellow	III B.A.C.	No	No	No
12th Bavarian Infantry	Bavaria	Red		White	I B.A.C.	No	No	No
13th Bavarian Infantry	Bavaria	Red		Yellow	III B.A.C.	No	No	No
14th Bavarian Infantry	Bavaria	Red		Yellow	III B.A.C.	No	No	No
15th Bavarian Infantry	Bavaria	Red		White	I B.A.C.	No	No	No
16th Bavarian Infantry	Bavaria	Red		White	I B.A.C.	No	No	No
17th Bavarian Infantry	Bavaria	Red		None	II B.A.C.	No	No	No
18th Bavarian Infantry	Bavaria	Red		None	II B.A.C.	No	No	No
19th Bavarian Infantry	Bavaria	Red		Yellow	III B.A.C.	No	No	No
20th Bavarian Infantry	Bavaria	Red		White	I B.A.C.	No	No	No
21st Bavarian Infantry	Bavaria	Red		Yellow	III B.A.C.	No	No	No
22nd Bavarian Infantry	Bavaria	Red		None	II B.A.C.	No	No	No
23rd Bavarian Infantry	Bavaria	Red		None	II B.A.C.	No	No	No
1st Bavarian Jäger	Bavaria	Light green		None	I B.A.C.	No	No	No
2nd Bavarian Jäger	Bavaria	Light green		None	I B.A.C.	No	No	No

Sources: Friedag, *Heer & Flotte*; Nash, *German Infantry*; Laine, *L'Armée Allemande*; Knötel, *Deutsche Heer*; Herr, *German Infantry*, vols 1 and 2; Pietsch, *Preußischen Heeres*; Rankin, *Helmets*; Knötel, *Uniforms World*.

Notes: [a] Cuff type is Brandenburg if cuff type not given. Sw = Swedish cuff; Sa = Saxon cuff; F = French cuff; F* = French cuff for officers.
[b] Guard-C. = Guard Corps; A.C. = Army Corps; B.A.C. = Bavarian Army Corps.
[c] For full dress, wore a baroque-style silvered tin grenadier mitre.
[d] For full dress, wore a baroque-style silvered fusilier mitre, which was shorter than the grenadier mitre.
[e] Dark blue cuff plate.
[f] For full dress, I and II Battalions wore an old-style grenadier mitre, which had been worn by the 1st Foot Guards in the 1700s.
[g] For full dress, III Battalion wore an old-style fusilier mitre, which had been worn by the 1st Foot Guards in the 1700s. All three battalions also wore a helmet (pickelhaube) and plumes in less than full dress.
[h] Received in 1913.
[i] Square-topped shoulder strap trimmed in red.
[j] Wore regimental number rather than monograms because they were made up of so many contingents (Herr, *German Infantry*, Vol. 2, p. 589).
[k] Had a hunting horn in addition to the battalion number.
[l] Tunic and shoulder strap close to British rifle green (Kinna, *Jäger*, p. 2).
[m] Black cuff.
[n] III Battalion had a black plume.
[o] White cuff plate.
[p] Bright mid-blue cuff plate same as shoulder straps. This special shade of light aniline potassium blue was known as potassium blue in the regiment (Kinna, *Jäger*, p. 518).
[q] Yellow cuff plate.
[r] Helmet had a yellow grenadier eagle awarded on 16 June 1913, the twenty-fifth anniversary of Kaiser Wilhelm II's reign. The Kaiser was close to the regiment as it often provided a guard of honour at the Kaiser's holiday home, because it was stationed near it.
[s] Grenadier eagle rather than normal line eagle.
[t] Light green cuff.

§VI-3-14 PRUSSIAN PLUME AND LITZEN

Regiment	Plume	Litzen	
1st Foot Guard	White[a]	Double	
2nd Foot Guard	White[a]	Double	
3rd Foot Guard	White[a]	Double	
4th Foot Guard	White[a]	Double	
5th Foot Guard	White[a]	Old Prussian	
Guard Fusilier	Black	Double	
1st Guard Grenadier	White[a]	Double	
2nd Guard Grenadier	White[a]	Double	
3rd Guard Grenadier	White[a]	Double	
4th Guard Grenadier	White[a]	Double	
5th Guard Grenadier	White[a]	Old Prussian	
1st Grenadier	Black	Single[f]	Litzen awarded May 1900
2nd Grenadier	Black	Single[f]	Litzen awarded May 1897
3rd Grenadier	Black	Single[f]	Litzen awarded Sept. 1901
4th Grenadier	Black	Single[f]	Litzen awarded May 1911

Regiment	Plume	Litzen	
5th Grenadier	Black	Single[f]	Litzen awarded June 1913
6th Grenadier	Black	Single[f]	Litzen awarded Aug 1913
7th Grenadier	Black	Single[f]	Litzen awarded March 1897
8th Grenadier	Black	Single[f]	Litzen awarded June 1898
9th Grenadier	Black		
10th Grenadier	Black		
11th Grenadier	Black		Litzen awarded August 1913
12th Grenadier	Black		
25th Infantry	Black		Plume awarded June 1913
80th Fusilier	Black	Single[c]	Plume awarded June 1913
86th Fusilier	Black		Plume awarded Oct. 1895
145th Infantry	Black		Plume awarded Oct. 1895
Guard Jäger	Black	Double[d]	
Guard Schützen	Black	Double[e]	

Sources: Herr, *German Infantry*, vol. 1, pp. 353–5, 367–9, and 391. Most of the data on plumes are from Rankin, *Helmets*, pp. 28–9.
Notes: [a] III Battalion wore black plumes.
[b] Litzen were normally white with red centre lines; the 7th Grenadiers had yellow litzen with a red centre line.
[c] Litzen were normally white with red centre lines; the 80th Regiment had old Prussian litzen with no centre line from 1903.
[d] Litzen were normally white with red centre lines; the Guard Jäger had yellow with red centre lines.
[e] Litzen were normally white with red centre lines; the Guard Schützen had yellow with black centre lines to match their collar and cuffs.
[f] At the collar. Cuffs had three litzen.

§VI-3-15 NON-PRUSSIAN PLUME AND LITZEN

Regiment	Plume	Litzen	Guard
89th (I & III Bns)	Black	Double	Yes[a]
89th (II Bn)	White		Yes[a]
90th	None	Old Prussian	
91st	Black[b]		Yes[a]
92nd	Black		Yes[a]
100th	Black	Double	Yes

Regiment	Plume	Litzen	Guard
101st	Black	Double[c]	
109th	White[d]	Double	Yes
110th	White[d]		
115th	Black[e]	Double	Yes
116th	Black[f]		
117th	Black[g]		

Regiment	Plume	Litzen	Guard
119th	White	Double	
120th	Black[h]		
123rd	Black	Double	

Regiment	Plume	Litzen	Guard
14th Jäger	Black	Double[i]	
Bavarian Life Guards	None[j]	Double[k]	

Sources: Herr, *German Infantry*, vol. 2, pp. 442–699 (sections on helmets and tunics); Rankin, *Helmets*, pp. 28–9 for plumes.
Notes: [a] Only infantry regiment or unit of duchy.
[b] Plume awarded August 1913.
[c] White litzen awarded November 1872.
[d] III Battalion wore black plumes.
[e] Plume awarded end of 1871.
[f] Plume awarded June 1898.
[g] Plume awarded September 1883.
[h] Awarded August 1899.
[i] Litzen were normally white with red centre lines; 14th Jäger had a green centre line.
[j] Bavarian Infantry did not wear plumes.
[k] Worn after 1873.

§VI-3-16 STATES WEARING ONLY THE PRUSSIAN LINE EAGLE AND A STATE COCKADE

State[a]	Regiment
City of Bremen	75 (I & II Bns)[b]
City of Hamburg	76[c]
City of Lübeck	162 (I & II Bns)[d]
Lippe	55 (III Bn)
Schwarzburg	71 (I Bn)
Waldeck	83 (III Bn)
Schaumburg-Lippe	7 Jäger

Source: Herr, *German Infantry*, vol. 1, p. 18.
Notes: [a] These states often could not supply a full regiment or battalion and had to be filled out by Prussians. After 1897, the Prussians were ordered to wear the state cockade if serving in these battalions.
[b] After 1893. Prior to that, I Battalion only.
[c] After 1897. Prior to that, I and II Battalion only.
[d] After 1897. Prior to that, III Battalion of Infantry Regiment 76.

§VI-3-17 LANCE PENNANT COLOURS

Each German state had its own colours for the pennants carried on the lances of its cavalrymen. Corporals carried a different pennant, which was a solid colour with a heraldic device denoting the state.

Image C75 shows these colours. The state pennants shown are: Prussia; Bavaria; Saxony; Württemberg; Oldenburg; Mecklenburg-Schwerin; Baden; Hesse. Not shown is the pennant of 17th (Brunswick) Hussars, which had a light blue over yellow pennant for other ranks and a yellow pennant with a white horse and a crown on a red medallion for NCOs.

VI:16 Cavalry Shoulder Strap and Epaulette Monograms
See §VI-3-18 for details.
1. 1st Cuirassier.
2. 2nd Cuirassier.
3. 6th Cuirassier.
4. 8th Cuirassier.
5. Saxon Guard Reiter (shoulder cords and overcoats only).
6. 1st Guard Dragoons.
7. 2nd Guard Dragoons.
8. 3rd Horse Grenadiers.
9. 8th Dragoons.
10. 9th Dragoons.
11. 10th Dragoons.
12. 17th Dragoons.
13. 18th Dragoons.
14. 19th Dragoons.
15. 20th Dragoons.
16. 23rd Dragoons.

VI:17 Cavalry Shoulder Strap and Epaulette Monograms
See §VI-3-18 for details.
17. 24th Dragoons.
18. 25th Dragoons.
19. 26th Dragoons.
20. 1st Lancers.
21. 3rd Lancers.
22. 6th Lancers.
23. 13th Lancers.
24. 16th Lancers.
25. 17th Lancers.
26. 19th Lancers.
27. 20th Lancers.
28. 21st Lancers.
29. 2nd Hussars.
30. 7th Hussars.
31. 8th Hussars.
32. 13th Hussars.

VI:18 Cavalry Shoulder Strap and Epaulette Monograms
See §VI-3-18 for details.
33. 15th Hussars.
34. 16th Hussars.
35. 18th Hussars.
36. 19th Hussars.

§VI-3-18 CAVALRY SHOULDER STRAP AND EPAULETTE MONOGRAMS

See Images VI:16, VI:17 and VI:18.

Number in Images	Regimental Number/Name	Monogram	Namesake
Image VI:16			
1	1st Cuirassier	WR	King Wilhelm I
2	2nd Cuirassier	L	Queen Luise of Prussia
3	6th Cuirassier	H I	Czar Nicholas I of Russia
4	8th Cuirassier	GR V	King George V of England
5	Saxon Guard Reiter (shoulder cords and overcoats only)	FAR	Friedrich August III, King of Saxony
6	1st Guard Dragoons	VR	Queen Victoria of Great Britain and Ireland
7	2nd Guard Dragoons	A	Czarina Alexandra of Russia
8	3rd Horse Grenadiers	G mirrored V	King Gustav V of Sweden
9	8th Dragoons	FR III	Frederick III, briefly as German Kaiser, and King of Prussia
10	9th Dragoons	CR IX	King Carol of Rumania
11	10th Dragoons	AR	King Albert of Saxony
12	17th Dragoons	FF III	Grand Duke Friedrich Franz III of Mecklenburg-Schwerin
13	18th Dragoons	A	Queen Duchess Alexandra of Mecklenburg-Schwerin
14	19th Dragoons	A	Grand Duke August of Oldenburg
15	20th Dragoons	Crown	
16	23rd Dragoons	L	Grand Duke Ludwig of Hessen
Image VI:17			
17	24th Dragoons	N II	Czar Nicholas II of Russia
18	25th Dragoons	O	Queen Olga of Württemberg
19	26th Dragoons	W	King Wilhelm II of Württemberg
20	1st Lancers	A III	Czar Alexander III of Russia
21	3rd Lancers	A II	Czar Alexander II of Russia
22	6th Lancers	CR IX	King Christian IX of Denmark
23	13th Lancers	WR II	Kaiser Wilhelm II, King of Prussia
24	16th Lancers	GR	King Georg of Saxony
25	17th Lancers	FJ	Kaiser Franz Joseph of Austria, King of Hungary
26	19th Lancers	KR	King Karl of Württemberg
27	20th Lancers	W I	King Wilhelm I
28	21st Lancers	W	Kaiser Wilhelm II of Prussia
29	2nd Hussars	V	Queen Victoria of Prussia
30	7th Hussars	WR I	Kaiser Wilhelm I
31	8th Hussars	H II	Czar Nicholas II of Russia
32	13th Hussars	U	King Umberto of Italy
Image VI:18			
33	15th Hussars	W	Queen Wilhelmina of the Netherlands
34	16th Hussars	FJ	Emperor Franz Joseph I of Austria
35	18th Hussars	AR	King Albert of Saxony
36	19th Hussars	C	Queen Carola of Saxony

§VI-3-19 INFANTRY SHOULDER STRAP AND EPAULETTE MONOGRAMS

See Images VI:19, VI:20 and VI:21.

Number in Image	Regimental Number/Name	Monogram	Namesake
Image VI:19			
1	Guard Grenadier Regiment Czar Alexander No. 1	A I	Czar Alexander I of Russia
2	Guard Grenadier Regiment Emperor Franz No. 2	F I	Emperor Franz I of Austria
3	Guard Grenadier Regiment Queen Elizabeth No. 3	E	Queen Elizabeth
4	Guard Grenadier Regiment Queen Augusta No. 4	A	Queen Augusta
5	Grenadier Regiment Crown Prince (1st East Prussian) No. 1	FR III	Kaiser Frederick III
6	Grenadier Regiment King Frederick William IV (1st Pomeranian) No. 2	FWR IV	King Frederick William IV
7	Grenadier Regiment King Frederick William I (2nd East Prussian) No. 3	FWR I	King Frederick William I
8	Grenadier Regiment King Frederick the Great (3rd East Prussian) No. 4	FR II	King Frederick II
9	Grenadier Regiment King Frederick I (4th East Prussian) No. 5	FR I	King Frederick I
10	Grenadier Regiment King Wilhelm I (2nd West Prussian) No. 7	WR I	King Wilhelm I
11	Life Grenadier Regiment King Frederick William III (1st Brandenburg) No. 8	FWR III	King Frederick William III
12	Grenadier Regiment King Frederick William II (1st Silesian) No. 10	FWR II	King Frederick William II
13	Grenadier Regiment King Frederick III (2nd Silesian) No. 11	FR III	King Fredrick III
14	Fusilier Regiment Queen Viktoria of Sweden (1st Pomeranian) No. 34	V	Queen Viktoria of Sweden
15	Infantry Regiment King Ludwig III of Bavaria (2nd Lower Silesian) No. 47	L[b]	King Ludwig III of Bavaria
16	Infantry Regiment (5th Westphalian) No. 53	Crown	Kaiser Frederick III[c]
17	Infantry Regiment (4th Thuringian) No. 72	F	King Ferdinand of Bulgaria
18	Fusilier Regiment von Gerdsdorf (Electorate of Hesse) No. 80	VF	Empress and Queen Victoria as Empress Friedrich[d]
19	Fusilier Regiment Queen (1st Schleswig-Holstein) No. 86	AV	Queen Augusta Victoria
20	Infantry Regiment (2nd Nassau) No. 88	K	King Constantine of Greece
Image VI:20			
21	Grenadier Regiment (1st Grand Ducal Mecklenburg) No. 89 (I & III Bns)	FFGvM	Grand Duke Friedrich Franz II of Mecklenburg-Schwerin
22	Grenadier Regiment (1st Grand Ducal Mecklenburg) No. 89 (II Bn)	FW	Grand Duke Friedrich Wilhelm
23	Fusilier Regiment Kaiser Wilhelm (1st Grand Ducal Mecklenburg) No. 90	W	Kaiser Wilhelm II
24	Infantry Regiment (Oldenburg) No. 91	P	Duke Peter Friedrich Ludwig of Oldenburg
25	Infantry Regiment (Brunswick) No. 92	W	Duke Wilhelm
26	Infantry Regiment (Anhalt) No. 93	LF	Duke Leopold IV
27	Infantry Regiment Grand Duke of Saxony (5th Thuringian) No. 94	CA	Grand Duke Carl Alexander

VI:19 Infantry Shoulder Strap and Epaulette Monograms
See §VI-3-19 for details.

1. Guard Grenadier Regiment Czar Alexander No. 1.
2. Guard Grenadier Regiment Emperor Franz No. 2.
3. Guard Grenadier Regiment Queen Elizabeth No. 3.
4. Guard Grenadier Regiment Queen Augusta No. 4.
5. Grenadier Regiment Crown Prince (1st East Prussian) No. 1.
6. Grenadier Regiment King Frederick Wilhelm IV (1st Pomeranian) No. 2.
7. Grenadier Regiment King Frederick Wilhelm I (2nd East Prussian) No. 3.
8. Grenadier Regiment King Frederick the Great (3rd East Prussian) No. 4.
9. Grenadier Regiment King Frederick I (4th East Prussian) No. 5.
10. Grenadier Regiment King Wilhelm I (2nd West Prussian) No. 7.
11. Life Grenadier Regiment King Frederick Wilhelm III (1st Brandenburg) No. 8.
12. Grenadier Regiment King Frederick Wilhelm II (1st Silesian) No. 10.
13. Grenadier Regiment King Frederick III (2nd Silesian) No. 11.
14. Fusilier Regiment Queen Viktoria of Sweden (1st Pomeranian) No. 34.
15. Infantry Regiment King Ludwig III of Bavaria (2nd Lower Silesian) No. 47.
16. Infantry Regiment (5th Westphalian) No. 53.
17. Infantry Regiment (4th Thuringian) No. 72.
18. Fusilier Regiment von Gerdsdorf (Electorate of Hesse) No. 80.
19. Fusilier Regiment Queen (1st Schleswig-Holstein) No. 86.
20. Infantry Regiment (2nd Nassau) No. 88.

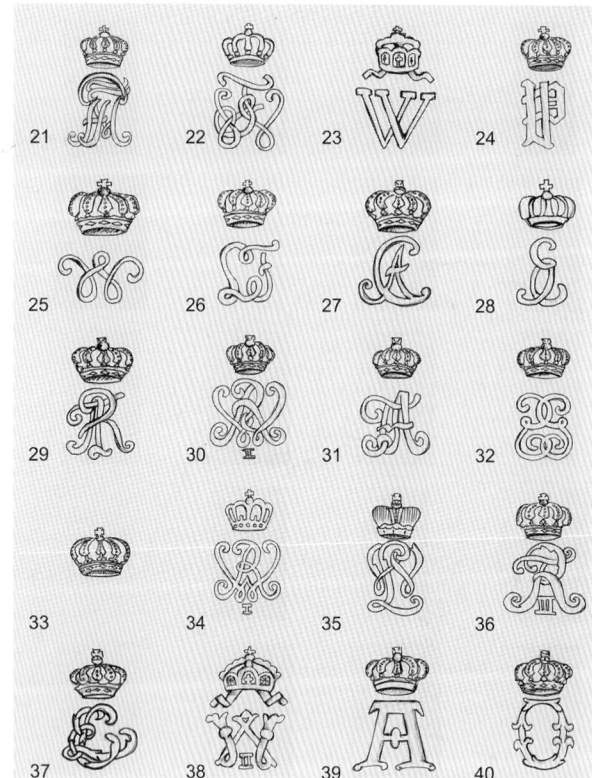

VI:20 Infantry Shoulder Strap and Epaulette Monograms
See §VI-3-19 for details.

21. Grenadier Regiment (1st Grand Ducal Mecklenburg) No. 89, 1st and 3rd Battalions.
22. Grenadier Regiment (1st Grand Ducal Mecklenburg) No. 89, 2nd Battalion.
23. Fusilier Regiment Kaiser Wilhelm (1st Grand Ducal Mecklenburg) No. 90.
24. Infantry Regiment (Oldenburg) No. 91.
25. Infantry Regiment (Brunswick) No. 92.
26. Infantry Regiment (Anhalt) No. 93.
27. Infantry Regiment Grand Duke of Saxony (5th Thuringian) No. 94.
28. Infantry Regiment (6th Thuringian) No. 95.
29. Life Grenadier Regiment (1st Royal Saxon) No. 100.
30. Grenadier Regiment Kaiser Wilhelm, King of Prussia (2nd Royal Saxon) No. 101.
31. Infantry Regiment Crown Prince (5th Royal Saxon) No. 104.
32. Infantry Regiment King Georg (7th Royal Saxon) No. 106.
33. Life Guard Grenadier Regiment (Baden) No. 109.
34. Grenadier Regiment Kaiser Wilhelm I (2nd Baden) No. 110.
35. Infantry Regiment Margrave Ludwig Wilhelm (3rd Baden) No. 111.
36. Infantry Regiment Kaiser Friedrich III (6th Baden) No. 114.
37. Life Guard Infantry Regiment (1st Grand Ducal Hessian) No. 115.
38. Infantry Regiment Kaiser Wilhelm (2nd Grand Ducal Hessian) No. 116.
39. Infantry Life Guard Regiment Grand Duchess (3rd Grand Ducal Hessian) No. 117.
40. Grenadier Regiment Queen Olga (1st Württemberg) No. 119.

Number in Image	Regimental Number/Name	Monogram	Namesake
28	Infantry Regiment (6th Thuringian) No. 95	EG	Duke Ernst II of Saxe-Coburg and Gotha and Georg II of Saxe-Meiningen
29	Life Grenadier Regiment (1st Royal Saxon) No. 100	FA	King Friedrich August III
30	Grenadier Regiment Kaiser Wilhelm, King of Prussia (2nd Royal Saxon) No. 101	WR I	Kaiser Wilhelm I
31	Infantry Regiment Crown Prince (5th Royal Saxon) No. 104	FA	Prince Friedrich August, as King Friedrich August III
32	Infantry Regiment King Georg (7th Royal Saxon) No. 106	Mirrored G	Prince and King Georg
33	Life Guard Grenadier Regiment (Baden) No. 109	Grand ducal crown	Reigning grand duke
34	Grenadier Regiment Kaiser Wilhelm I (2nd Baden) No. 110	WR I	King Wilhelm I
35	Infantry Regiment Margrave Ludwig Wilhelm (3rd Baden) No. 111	LW	Margrave Ludwig Wilhelm of Baden-Baden
36	Infantry Regiment Kaiser Frederick III (6th Baden) No. 114	FR III	Kaiser Frederick III
37	Life Guard Infantry Regiment (1st Grand Ducal Hessian) No. 115	EL	Grand Duke Ernst Ludwig of Hesse
38	Infantry Regiment Kaiser Wilhelm (2nd Grand Ducal Hessian) No. 116	W IIe	Kaiser Wilhelm II
39	Infantry Life Guard Regiment Grand Duchess (3rd Grand Ducal Hessian) No. 117	A	Grand Duchess Alice of Hesse
40	Grenadier Regiment Queen Olga (1st Württemberg) No. 119	O	Queen Olga of Württemberg
Image VI:21			
41	Infantry Regiment Kaiser Wilhelm, King of Prussia (2nd Württemberg) No. 120	WR	Kaiser Wilhelm I
42	Grenadier Regiment King Karl (5th Württemberg) No. 123	KR	King Karl of Württemberg
43	Infantry Regiment King Wilhelm I (6th Württemberg) No. 124	WI	King Wilhelm I of Württemberg
44	Infantry Regiment Kaiser Frederick, King of Prussia (7th Württemberg) No. 125	FR	Kaiser Frederick III
45	King's Infantry Regiment (6th Lorrainian) No. 145	WR II	King Wilhelm II
46	Infantry Regiment (8th Thuringian) No. 153 (I & II Bns from Saxe-Altenburg)	Mirrored E	Duke Ernst I
47	Infantry Life Guard Regiment	Crown	Represents the Kingdom of Bavaria
48	1st Infantry Regiment King	MJ	King Max I Joseph of Bavaria
49	2nd Infantry Regiment Crown Prince	ME	Elector Max Emanuel of Bavaria
50	3rd Infantry Regiment Prince Karl of Bavaria	IRPK 3	Prince Karl of Bavaria
51	6th Infantry Regiment Kaiser Wilhelm, King of Prussia	W	Kaiser Wilhelm I
52	10th Infantry Regiment King	L	King Ludwig III of Bavaria
53	Jäger Battalion (Electorate of Hesse) No. 11	M	Queen Marguerita of Italy
54	Rifle (Fusilier) Regiment Prince Georg (Royal Saxon) No. 108	Hunting horn and 108[a]	

Note: [a] Standard shoulder strap for Saxon rifle battalions and the 108th Infantry Regiment.
[b] Some sources show the monogram with the letters PR.
[c] From Bredow-Wedel, *Historische*, vol. 1, pp. 470–1.
[d] From Bredow-Wedel, *Historische*, vol. 1, p. 410.v
[e] Sources differ. Some say Wilhelm I, others say Wilhelm II.

VI:21 Infantry Shoulder Strap and Epaulette Monograms
See §VI-3-19 for details.
41. Infantry Regiment Kaiser Wilhelm, King of Prussia (2nd Württemberg) No. 120.
42. Grenadier Regiment King Karl (5th Württemberg) No. 123.
43. Infantry Regiment King Wilhelm I (6th Württemberg) No. 124.
44. Infantry Regiment Kaiser Friedrich, King of Prussia (7th Württemberg) No. 125.
45. King's Infantry Regiment (6th Lorrainian) No. 145.
46. Infantry Regiment (8th Thuringian) No. 153 (1st and 2nd Battalions from Saxe-Altenburg).
47. Infantry Life Guard Regiment.
48. 1st Infantry Regiment King.
49. 2nd Infantry Regiment Crown Prince.
50. 3rd Infantry Regiment Prince Karl of Bavaria.
51. 6th Infantry Regiment Kaiser Wilhelm, King of Prussia.
52. 10th Infantry Regiment King.
53. Jäger Battalion (Electorate of Hesse) No. 11.
54. Rifle (Fusilier) Regiment Prince Georg (Royal Saxon) No. 108.

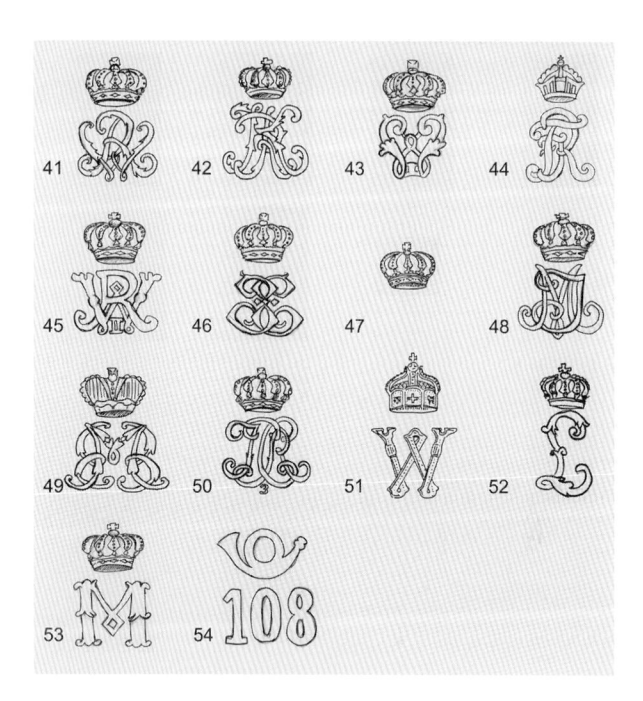

§VI-3-20 ARMY CORPS DISTINGUISHING COLOUR TRIM

Army Corps (location of headquarters)	When Added to Prussian Army	Cuff Plate Colour	Piping Colour	Shoulder Strap Colour
Guard (Berlin)		Varies[a]	None	Varies[b]
I (Königsberg (East Prussia))	Part of original army	Red	White	White
II (Stettin (Pomerania))	Part of original army	Red	None	White
III (Berlin (Brandenburg))	Part of original army	Red	White	Red
IV (Magdeburg (Prussian Saxony))	Part of original army	Red	None	Red
V (Posen (Lower Silesia)	Part of original army	Different colours[c,d] (7)	White	Yellow
VI (Bleslau (Silesia))	Part of original army	Different colours[e]	None	Yellow
VII (Münster (Westphalia))	Part of original army	Different colours[f]	White[g]	Light blue
VIII (Coblenz (Rhineland))	Part of original army	Different colours[h]	None	Light blue
IX (Altona (Schleswig-Holstein and Mecklenburg))	Added to army after Austro-Prussian War of 1866	Different colours[d,i] (89)	Yellow[j]	White[k]
X (Hanover (Hanoverian))	Added to army after Austro-Prussian War of 1866	Different colours[l]	Light blue	White
XI (Cassel (Thuringia and Nassau))	Added to army after Austro-Prussian War of 1866	Red	Yellow	Red
XII (1st Saxon) (Dresden)	Added to army after Austro-Prussian War of 1866	Red	None	Prussian blue with red piping (square top)

German Empire

Army Corps (location of headquarters)	When Added to Prussian Army	Cuff Plate Colour	Piping Colour	Shoulder Strap Colour
XIII (Württemberg (Stuttgart))	Added to army after Franco-Prussian War of 1870–1	Red[m]	Light blue	Red
XIV (Karlsruhe (Baden))	Added to army after Franco-Prussian War of 1870–1	Red[m]	None	Different colours[n]
XV (Strassburg)	Added to army after Franco-Prussian War of 1870–1	Different colours[o]	Light blue	Red
XVI (Metz)	Added to army after expansion of 1890	Different colours[p]	Yellow	Yellow[q]
XVII (Danzig (West Prussia))	Added to army after expansion of 1890	Different colours[r]	Light-blue	Yellow
XVIII (Frankfort-on-Main) (mostly Hessian)	Added to army after expansion of 1899	Red (Hesse regts different colours)[s]	Yellow (Hesse regts had none)	Light blue (Hesse regts had different colours)[t]
XIX (2nd Saxon) (Leipzig)	Added to army after expansion of 1899	Red	None	Prussian blue with red piping (square top)
XX (Allenstein)	Added to army after expansion of 1912	Different colours[u]	Light-blue	Light blue
XXI (Saarbrücken)	Added to army after expansion of 1912	Different colours[v]	White[w]	Light green
I Bavarian (Munich)	Added to army after Franco-Prussian War of 1870–1	Red[x]	White	Red
II Bavarian (Würzburg)	Added to army after Franco-Prussian War of 1870–1	Red	None	Red
III Bavarian (Nürnburg)	Added to army after expansion of 1890	Red	Yellow	Red

Notes: [a] Cuff plate colours were as follows: red (1st–5th Foot Guard, Guard Fusilier, and 5th Guard Grenadier); dark blue (1st–4th Guard Grenadier).
[b] Shoulder strap colours were as follows: white (1st and 5th Foot Guard, 1st and 5th Guard Grenadier); red (2nd Foot Guard and 2nd Guard Grenadier); yellow (3rd Foot Guard, 3rd Guard Grenadier, and Guard Fusilier); Light blue (4th Foot Guard and 4th Guard Grenadier).
[c] Cuff plate colours were as follows: red (6, 19, 37, 46, 47, 50, 58, 155, and 157); white (154).
[d] The cuff plates on the Brandenburg cuffs were blue for the 7th and 89th Grenadiers.
[e] Cuff plate colours were as follows: red (10, 11, 22, 23, 38, 51, 62, 63, and 157); white (156).
[f] Cuff plate colours were as follows: red (13, 15, 16, 39, 53, 55, 56, 57, and 159); white (158).
[g] The 158th Regiment had no piping.
[h] Cuff plate colours were as follows: red (25, 28, 29, 65, 68, 69, and 161); white (160).
[i] Cuff plate colours were as follows: red (31, 75, 76, 84, 85, 86, 90, and 163); white (162).
[j] The 89th Regiment had red piping.
[k] The 89th Regiment, II Battalion had red shoulder straps.
[l] Cuff plate colours were as follows: red (73, 74, 77, 78, 79, 91, and 92); white (164).
[m] If a Brandenburg cuff was worn by a line regiment, it was red.
[n] Shoulder strap colours were as follows for Baden regiments: white (109 and 110); red (111 and 169); light yellow (112 and 142); light blue (113 and 170); light green (114).
[o] Cuff plate colours are as follows: red (99, 105, 126, 132, 136, 143, and 172); white (171).
[p] Cuff plate colours were as follows: red (30, 67, 98, 130, 135, 144, and 145); white (173).
[q] The 145th Regiment had blue shoulder straps.
[r] Cuff plate colours were as follows: red (5, 21, 61, 128, 129, 141, and 176); white (175).
[s] Cuff plate colours were as follows for Hesse regiments: red (115 and 168); white (116); blue (117); yellow (118).
[t] Shoulder strap colours were as follows for Hesse regiments: red (115 and 168); white (116); bright mid-blue (117); light yellow (118).
[u] Cuff plate colours were as follows: red (18, 59, and 147); white (146, 148, and 152); yellow (150); light blue (151).
[v] Cuff plate colours were as follows: red (17, 60, 70, 97, 131, 137, 138, and 174); white (166).
[w] The 166th Regiment had no piping.
[x] If Brandenburg cuff was worn, it was red.

§VI-3-21 ARMY CORPS SHOULDER STRAP AND CUFF PLATE PIPING DETAILS

Table VI.3.21.1: Shoulder Strap Colours

Colour	Corps
White	I, II, IX, X
Red	III, XI, XIII, XV
	Bavarian I, II, III
Yellow	IV, V, VI, XVI, XVII

Colour	Corps
Light blue	VII, VIII, XVIII, XX
Light green	XXI
Varied	Guard, XIV
Dark blue, trim red	XII, XIX (both Saxon)

Source: See Herr, *German Infantry*, vol. 1, p. 52.

Table VI.3.21.2: Shoulder Strap Colours and Cuff Plate Trim

Army Corps	Shoulder Strap Colour	Cuff Plate Trim[a]
Guard	Varies[b]	None
I	White	White
II	White	None
III	Red	White
IV	Red	None
V	Yellow	White
VI	Yellow	None
VII	Light blue	White
VIII	Light blue	None
IX	White	Yellow
X	White	Light blue
XI	Red	Yellow
XII (Saxon)	Dark blue with red piping	None

Army Corps	Shoulder Strap Colour	Cuff Plate Trim[a]
XIII (Württemberg)	Red	Light blue
XIV (Baden)	Varies[c]	None
XV	Red	Light blue
XVI	Yellow	Yellow
XVII	Yellow	Light Blue
XVIII	Light blue (other than Hesse regts)	Yellow[d]
XIX	Dark blue with red piping	None[d]
XX	Light blue	Light blue
XXI	Light green	White
Bavarian I	Red	White
Bavarian II	Red	None
Bavarian III		

Source: See Herr, *German Infantry*, vol. 1, p. 52.
Notes: [a] When Brandenburg cuffs worn
[b] See Table VI.3.21.3, Guards.
[c] See Table VI.3.21.4, Baden Corps.
[d] Other than Hesse regiments (see Table VI.3.21.5, Hesse Regiments).

Table VI.3.21.3: Guard Regiment Shoulder Strap Colours and Cuff Plate Trim

Guard Regiment	Shoulder Strap Colour	Cuff Plate Trim
1st Foot Guard	White	Swedish cuffs, n/a
2nd Foot Guard	Red	Swedish cuffs, n/a
3rd Foot Guard	Yellow	Swedish cuffs, n/a
4th Foot Guard	Light blue	Swedish cuffs, n/a
5th Foot Guard	White	None
Guard Fusilier	Yellow	Swedish cuffs, n/a

Guard Regiment	Shoulder Strap Colour	Cuff Plate Trim
1st Guard Grenadier	White	None
2nd Guard Grenadier	Red	None
3rd Guard Grenadier	Yellow	None
4th Guard Grenadier	Light blue	None
5th Guard Grenadier	White	None

Source: Herr, *German Infantry*, vol. 1, pp. 309–10, 337.

Table VI.3.21.4: Baden Corps Shoulder Strap Colour

Regiment Number	Shoulder Strap Colour
109	White
110	White
111	Red
112	Light yellow
113	Light blue
114	Light green
142	Light yellow
169	Red
170	Light blue

Source: Herr, German Infantry, vol. 2, p. 456.
Note: The Baden Corps did not have cuff plate piping; it had Swedish cuffs.

Table VI.3.21.5: Hesse Regiments Shoulder Strap, Cuff Plate and Trim Colours

Regiment Number	Shoulder Strap Colour	Plate Colour	Cuff Plate Trim Colour
115	Red	Red	None
116	White	White	None
117	Bright mid-blue[a]	Potassium blue	None
118	Light yellow	Light yellow	None
168	Red	Red	None

Source: Herr, German Infantry, vol. 2, p. 512.
Note: [a] Called Potassium blue in the regiment (Herr, German Infantry, vol. 2, p. 518).

§VI-3-22 REGIMENTS WITH NON-STANDARD UNIFORM[14]

Table VI.3.22.1: Regiments without Yellow Button

Regiment	Button Colour
1st Foot Guards	White
5th Foot Guards	White
Guard Fusilier	White
89th[a]	White
90th (Mecklenburg-Strelitz)	White
100th (Saxon)	White
109th (Baden)	White

Regiment	Button Colour
115th (Hesse)	White
116th (Hesse)	White
117th (Hesse)	White
118th (Hesse)	White
168th (Hesse)	White
Bavarian Life Guards	White with a crown

Note: [a] I and III Battalions.

Table VI.3.22.2: Regiments with Cuff Plate Colour Other than Red

Regiment	Cuff Plate Colour
7th Grenadier	Dark blue[a]
89th	Dark blue
116th (Hesse)	White
117th (Hesse)	Bright mid-blue[b]
118th (Hesse)	Yellow
146th (Prussian)	White
148th (Prussian)	White
150th (Prussian)	Yellow
151st (Prussian)	Yellow
152nd (Prussian)	White

Regiment	Cuff Plate Colour
154th (Prussian)	White
156th (Prussian)	White
158th (Prussian)	White
162nd (Prussian)	White
164th (Prussian)	White
166th (Prussian)	White
171st (Prussian)	White
173rd (Prussian)	White
175th (Prussian)	White

Notes: [a] To mark the 100th anniversary of Wilhelm I's birth, on 22 March 1897, the regiment was granted blue cuff plates like those worn by the Guard Grenadiers (Herr, *German Infantry*, vol. 1, p. 380).

[b] This special shade of light aniline potassium blue was known as potassium blue in the regiments (Herr, *German Infantry*, vol. 2, pp. 512 and 518).

Other deviations from the standard were the Prussian 145th Line Regiment, who had a grenadier eagle on their helmets instead of the Prussian line eagle. The officers and NCOs of the 108th (Saxon) Regiment had black velvet collars and cuffs.[15]

Table VI.3.22.3: Regiments with White Eagle, Device, or Coat of Arms

Regiment	Type of White Badge for Other Ranks	Regiment	Type of White Badge for Other Ranks
1st Foot Guards	Star with the Order of the Black Eagle on it	119th (Württemberg)	State coat of arms: lion, stag, shield, and crown
5th Foot Guards	Eagle with the Order of the Black Eagle on it	123rd (Württemberg)	State coat of arms: lion, stag, shield, and crown
Guard Fusilier	Eagle with the Order of the Black Eagle on it	Bavarian Life Guard	State coat of arms: two lions, shield, and crown[b]
100th (Saxon)	White star with yellow Saxon coat of arms[a]	Guard Jäger	Star of the Order of the Black Eagle
109th (Baden)	Griffin with the star and cross of the Order for Loyalty	Guard Schützen	Star of the Order of the Black Eagle
115th (Hesse)	Hessian Lion, extra laurel and oak wreaths, and the star of the Order of Ludwig	Jäger 12 (Saxon)	Star with yellow Saxon coat of arms surrounded by a white French (curved) hunting horn
		Jäger 13 (Saxon)	Star with yellow Saxon coat of arms surrounded by a white French (curved) hunting horn

[a] Line regiments had a yellow star and a white coat of arms.

[b] The badge was made smaller in 1914 (Herr, *German Infantry*, vol. 2, p. 686).

§VI-3-23 PRUSSIAN ARMY EPAULETTES, SHOULDER CORDS AND WEAPONS PROFICIENCY BADGES

Officers' Epaulettes

Image VI:22 shows epaulettes for Prussian army officers. The numbers on it show the following ranks: superior general (the best approximation – no English equivalent exists); field marshal; brigadier; major general; general; major; lieutenant colonel; colonel; second lieutenant; lieutenant; captain.

Officers' Shoulder Cords

Image VI:23 shows shoulder cords for Prussian army officers: major general; lieutenant general; general; superior general (the best approximation – no English equivalent); major; lieutenant colonel; colonel; second lieutenant; lieutenant; captain.

Weapons Proficiency Badges

Specialist badges were awarded for the achievement certain skill levels in fighting with the lance and sword. These badges were worn on the upper arm of the koller and *waffenrock* (see *§VI-6-a*, Walking-Out Tunic (Waffenrock)). Image VI:24 shows the twelve classes of badge.

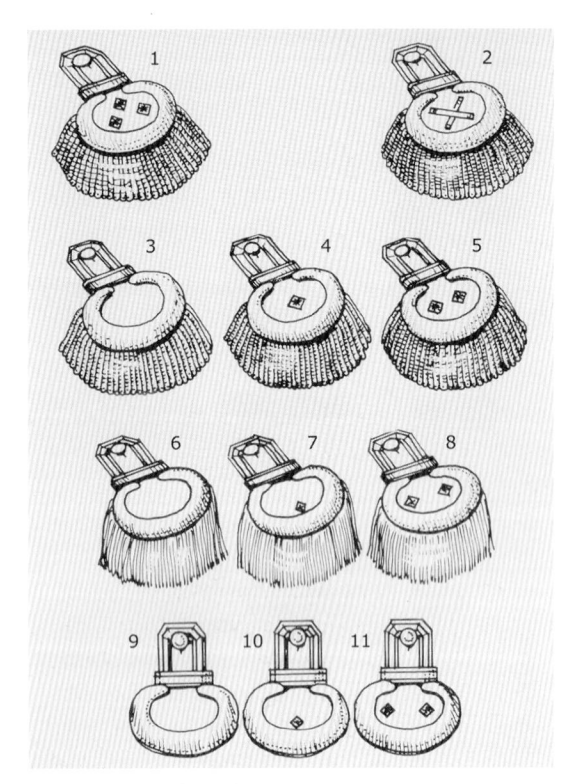

VI:22 Prussian Officers' Epaulettes
1. No English equivalent of this rank; the best translation is superior general.
2. Field marshal.
3. Brigadier.
4. Major general.
5. General.
6. Major.
7. Lieutenant colonel.
8. Colonel.
9. Second lieutenant.
10. Lieutenant.
11. Captain.

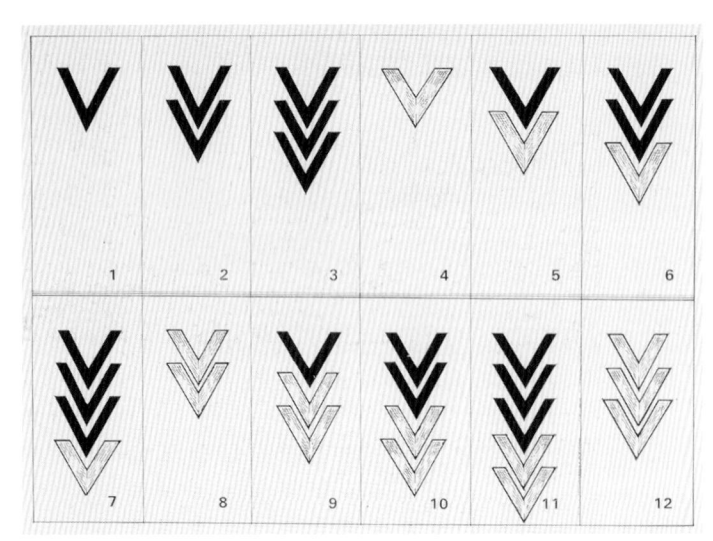

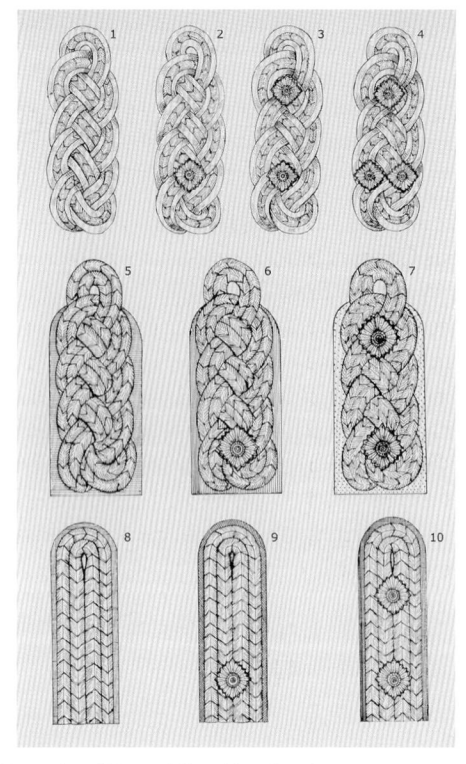

VI:23 Prussian Officers' Shoulder Cords
1. Major general.
2. Lieutenant general.
3. General.
4. No English equivalent of this rank; the best translation is superior general.
5. Major.
6. Lieutenant colonel.
7. Colonel.
8. Second lieutenant.
9. Lieutenant.
10. Captain.

VI:24 Prussian Army Weapons Proficiency Badges
1. 1st Class – one woollen chevron in the facing colour.
2. 2nd Class – two woolen chevrons in the facing colour.
3. 3rd Class – three woollen chevrons in the facing colour.
4. 4th Class – one gold or silver lace chevron.
5. 5th Class – one gold or silver lace chevron and one woollen.
6. 6th Class – one gold or silver lace chevron and two woollen.
7. 7th Class – one gold or silver lace chevron and three woollen.
8. 8th Class – two gold or silver lace chevrons.
9. 9th Class – two gold or silver lace chevrons and one woollen.
10. 10th Class – two gold or silver lace chevrons and two woollen.
11. 11th Class – two gold or silver lace chevrons and three woollen.
12. 12th Class – three gold or silver lace chevrons.

§VI-4 GENERAL STAFF

After regimental service, the next major step for an ambitious German officer was to attempt to gain entry into the War Academy. If he did well there he might be chosen for the General Staff and join the men whom Bismarck termed the 'demigods'.[16] Recruits had to pass a series of very difficult exams and a probation period in order to join.[17] Each year, only about 1 or 2 per cent of the officers who began the long process made it on to the General Staff.[18] The competition was greater among the infantry, who were more career-minded than the aristocratic cavalry.[19]

Uniform

HELMET
Standard black leather helmet with a square front brim. The metal items on the helmet – spike, trim, etc. – were silver.

The badge was a silver guard eagle with a guard star on it for Prussian officers. Officers from other contingents wore their state badges on their helmets.[20] A white buffalo-hair plume was worn for parades by all staff officers, including Bavarian general staff officers.[21] It is not known what type of plume a general staff officer wore if he was a general: buffalo hair or a general's feather plumes.

TUNIC
The single-breasted tunic was Prussian blue and cut like those of guard officers. The tunic had eight buttons down the front. The buttons were a plain dome shape and without a design on them. They were silver-coloured, but could be either silver-plated or white copper. They are referred to here by their colour, 'silver'. The front edges of the tunic and rear skirt were piped in the general staff's distinctive carmine (wine colour). The rear skirt piping was in the Brandenburg shape and had three silver buttons.

Collar
The squared collar was carmine and had a form of embroidery known as Kolben. Image VI:25 shows Kolben on the collar of a uniform worn by Alfred Graf von Schlieffen.

Cuffs
Each of the carmine Swedish cuffs had two silver buttons. Each button had Kolben litzen behind it (Image VI:25).

EPAULETTES AND SHOULDER CORDS
For epaulettes, the ground colour was carmine, and the crescents were silver-plated. The normal rules on the size of the fringe and badges of rank applied.

VI:25 Alfred Graf von Schlieffen in a General Staff Uniform
The trim at his collar and cuffs is a special trim. He is wearing the Kolben embroidery. For general staff officers, the Kolben was silver. War Ministry officers also wore Kolben in gold embroidery.

The backing on the shoulder cords was carmine, and the cord was silver with black threads for Prussian officers. Officers from other states had threads in their state's colour. The normal rules on badges on rank applied.

TROUSERS AND RIDING BREECHES
The trousers and riding breeches were black. They had two 4 cm (1.57 inch) stripes of carmine cloth placed on either side of a band of carmine piping that ran along the garment's side seam. This is quite different from the 1.5 mm (0.06 inch) wide piping worn on these items by infantry officers. They are the most noteworthy mark of a general staff officer. This was the same width of stripe as worn on these garments by Prussian generals and members of the Prussian and Bavarian War Ministries.[22]

The stripes were probably fastened to the clothing the same way that wide stripes were put on infantry gala trousers.[23] The general staff trousers and breeches stripes would be laid out as follows: piping 1.5 mm (0.06 inch) wide on the side seam of the garment; on the right and left of the side seam carmine stripes of cloth 4 cm (1.57 inches) wide were added. The inside edges of the stripes were placed 0.5 cm (0.2 inch) from the side seam, i.e. no attention was paid to the piping when placing the carmine stripes.[24] This created a very narrow band of 0.38 cm (0.15 inch) of black between the central carmine piping and the carmine stripes on each side.

ADJUTANT'S SASH
While not part of the dress uniform, it is worth noting that Prussian regulations stated members of the general staff, when on duty, were to wear a Prussian adjutant's sash. This was worn over the tunic or frock coat and in place of the Prussian officer's sash.

§VI-5 PRUSSIAN GUARD INFANTRY

The regiments of Prussian guard infantry, surprisingly, were not old units when compared with the British foot guards or the Russian guard infantry. True, the 1st Foot Guards claimed a founding date of 1688, but three guard regiments only dated back to the Napoleonic War era. Four were founded in 1860 and two in 1897. The first two guard grenadier regiments, while having a formation date of 1814, had to wait until 1820 to become guard regiments.[25] Furthermore, with the exception of the 1st Foot Guards, the guard regiments had seen very little combat.

The Prussian guards were often accused by the many enemies of the Prussians and Germans as being arrogant. But they probably were no worse in this area than fortune's other winners: students at Oxbridge or the Ivy Leagues, star athletes, rock stars, or subalterns in other countries' elite guard regiments, etc.

The Guard was divided into five types of troops, each with slightly different uniforms: foot guards or *Zu Fuss* (five regiments); guard fusiliers (one regiment); guard grenadiers (five regiments); guard jägers (one battalion); and guard rifles or guard *Schützen* (one battalion).

Table VI.5.1: Prussian Guard Uniforms

Regiment	Button Colour	Facing Colour	Helmet Eagle	Guard Star	Cuff Type[a]	Cuff Colour	Vertical Plate	Shoulder Strap Colour	Plume I & II Bns	Plume III Bn	Litzen[b]	Notes
1st Foot	White	Red	White	White	Sw	Red	—	White	White	Black	Chapter Silver	A, B, D, F
2nd Foot	Yellow	Red	Yellow	White	Sw	Red	—	Red	White	Black	Chapter Silver	D, F
3rd Foot	Yellow	Red	Yellow	White	Sw	Red	—	Yellow	White	Black	Chapter Silver	D, F
4th Foot	Yellow	Red	Yellow	White	Sw	Red	—	Light Blue	White	Black	Chapter Silver	D, F
5th Foot	White	Red	White	White	B	Red	Dark blue	White	White	Black	Special	E, F
Fusiliers	White	Red	White	White	Sw	Red	—	Yellow	Black	Black	Chapter Silver	D, F
1st Grenadiers	Yellow	Red	Yellow	White	B	Red	Dark blue	White	White	Black	Special	C, D, F
2nd Grenadiers	Yellow	Red	Yellow	White	B	Red	Dark blue	Red	White	Black	Special	D, F
3rd Grenadiers	Yellow	Red	Yellow	White	B	Red	Dark blue	Yellow	White	Black	Special	D, F
4th Grenadiers	Yellow	Red	Yellow	White	B	Red	Dark blue	Light Blue	White	Black	Special	D, F
5th Grenadiers	Yellow	Red	Yellow	White	B	Red	Dark blue	White	White	Black	Special	E, F

Notes: ᵃ Sw = Swedish-style cuff; B = Brandenburg-style cuff.
ᵇ See §VI-3-2 for shape of special braid and litzen.

A: Mitre given by Prussian King Frederick William III in 1824. New baroque mitre given in 1894 by Kaiser Wilhelm II (Herr, *German Infantry*, vol. 1, p. 274).
B: 'Semper Talis' banner worn by I Battalion. This started with the 3rd and 4th Companies of the battalion, who were deemed to be descendants of the Giant Guards and later expanded to the entire battalion.
C: Wore 1st Foot Guards' old mitres, given to them in 1896.
D: Other ranks wore chapter-shaped litzen.
E: Old Prussian braid (litzen) for other ranks.
F: Had a rear skirt with three buttons and a scallop design piped in red on each skirt

§VI-5-a FOOT GUARDS

Uniform

The distinguishing marks of the first four foot guard regiments were their Swedish cuffs and the chapter litzen on the collars and cuffs of the officers and men (Images VI:26 and VI:27 (officers), VI:28 and VI:29 (other ranks)). The 5th Regiment was formed late, in 1897, and broke the pattern by having Brandenburg cuffs and special lace on the collars and cuffs of officers. The other ranks of the 5th Foot Guards wore old Prussian lace (Image VI:30). By an old custom, the princes of Prussia became lieutenants in the 1st Foot Guards on their tenth birthday (Image VI:31). One proud young prince wrote back to his mother how pleased he was that he kept up in the parade following his appointment as lieutenant, in spite of his short legs.

The 1st Foot Guards, in addition to their normal spiked helmets, also had mitres. Over the years they wore two styles. The first style is often said to have been a gift to the regiment from the Russian czar following the Napoleonic Wars. However, it seems that the mitres were awarded to the 2nd Battalion of the regiment by Frederick William III in 1824. These were given for no other reason than to honour the old army.[26] In the same year, the 1st Battalion also received the mitres. Then in 1843 the 3rd (Fusilier) Battalion was given a modified, shorter mitre.[27]

In 1889, the 3rd and 4th Companies were given a 'Semper Talis' banner for their mitres because of a tenuous tie, through prisoners of war returned after the Battle of Jena, to the old Giant Guards (or Giant Grenadiers) of King Frederick William I and a banner he had awarded the 1st Battalion in 1713. The right to wear the banner was expanded to all of the 1st Battalion in 1889.

The design of the mitre was very plain. For other ranks it consisted of a brass sheet stamped with a guard star and a centre-piece of the Order of the Black Eagle. The star was surmounted by a stamped crown. (Image VI:32 shows this mitre after it was turned over to the 1st Guard Grenadiers.) All three battalions had an upright cloth 'fringe' made of white wool with a black centre. There was a cloth bag in the rear of the brass plate. For the first two battalions it was red with three white tape trim lines on it. One was in the middle; the others were off to the side, but not all the way to the edge of the red cloth bag. Around the bottom of the cloth bag, going all the way around the back, was a border of white cloth about 10.16 cm (4 inches) high. In the middle of the back of the mitre and behind the point where each of the chin straps fastened to the mitre was a brass flaming grenade. Behind each grenade the white cloth border rose slightly up to a point. (Image VI:33 is a side view of a Russian mitre of the same period. It shows how the back band forms the slight point and the placement of the trim tape. The Prussians, however, used a grenade of a different shape from that of the Russians.)

The mitre for the 3rd or Fusilier Battalion was basically the same as that worn by the first two Prussian battalions. (Image VI:34) The front plate was not as tall but it had the same design. The 'fringe' was white with a black centre, but it was not as tall. The bag trim and border in the back was red and white. However, it had small Prussian eagles in place of the flaming grenades. Furthermore, the eagles on the side were a little above or even off to the side of where the chin scales fastened to the mitre rather than being right behind it.

Officers' mitres had a few differences (Image VI:35). They wore a fringe of silver wire, called a *puschel*, at the top of the mitre. It had an intertwined core of black. They had a large gilded brass front plate

VI:26 Crown Prince Wilhelm, c. 1895 in the Uniform of the 1st Foot Guard Regiment
Note the shape of the litzen at the collar and cuffs and the absence of spiegel.

VI:28 1st Foot Guard Regiment Other Ranks' Tunic
Note the shape of the litzen at the collar and cuffs. Also note the spiegel on the litzen for enlisted men.

VI:27 Young Officer of the 1st Foot Guard Regiment, c. 1900
Note his silver mitre and adjutant's sash worn over his right shoulder.

VI:29 Enlisted Man of the 4th Foot Guards
The white belt and white plume on his helmet show he served in the 1st or 2nd Battalion of the regiment.

VI:30 Other Ranks of the 5th Foot Guard Regiment
Note old Prussian lace worn by other ranks in this regiment on collar and cuffs.

VI:32 1st and 2nd Battalion of the Kaiser Alexander Guard Grenadiers Enlisted Men's Mitre
The decorations are just stamped in the middle. Note the holes left after the 'Semper Talis' banner was removed from this mitre after it was passed on to the 1st Guard Grenadier Regiment.

VI:31 1st Foot Guards
The princes of Prussia became officers of this regiment at the age of ten. Note the side view of the officer's mitre.

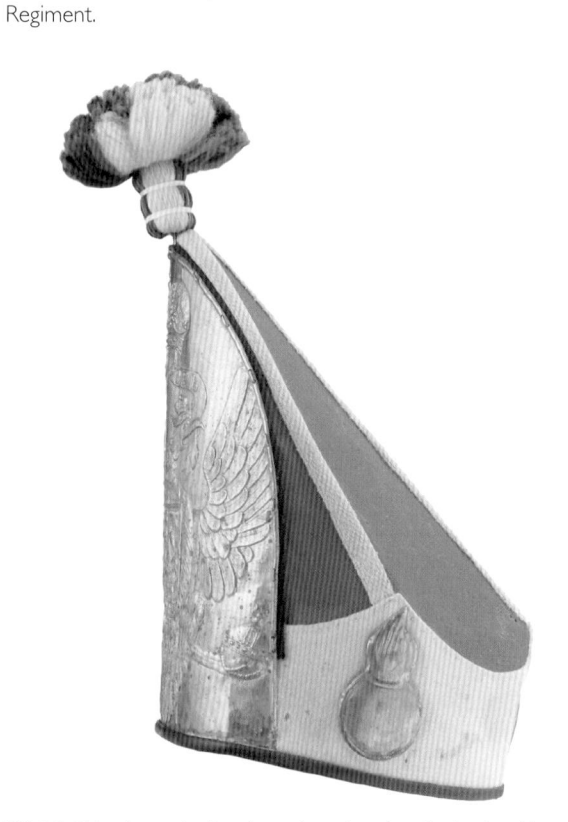

VI:33 Side view of a Russian mitre showing the back white cloth trim of the Russian mitre and the positioning of the cloth decoration at the top. This shows the great similarity between Russian and Prussian mitres.

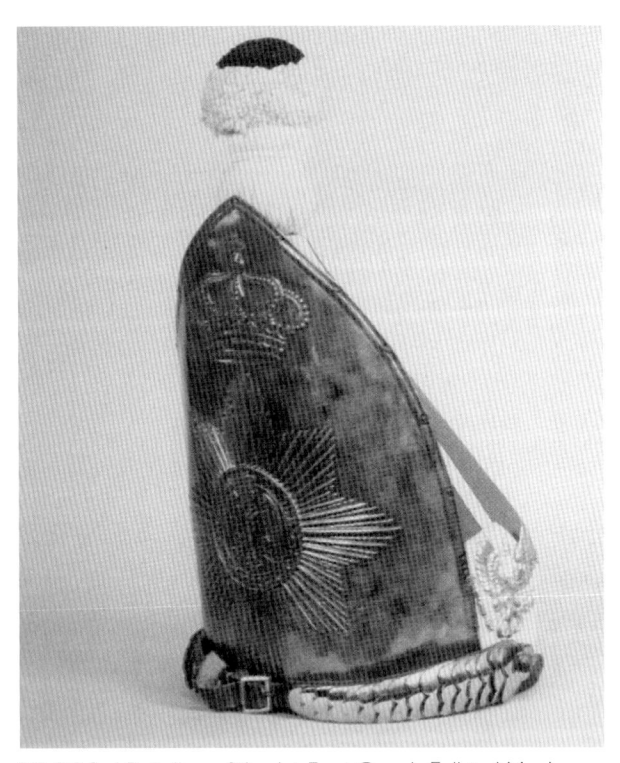

VI:34 3rd Battalion of the 1st Foot Guards Enlisted Men's Mitre (1849–97)
Note eagle decoration on the white cloth band that goes around the rear.

VI:36 Foot Guards' Mitre
This is the second style mitre worn by this regiment.

VI:35 Officer's Parade Mitre
Note the fringe of silver wire, called a puschel, at the top of the mitre.

VI:37 Other Ranks' M1884 Mitre of the 1st Foot Guards
Note the 'Semper Talis' motto above the eagle.

carrying a star of the Order of the Black Eagle in frosted silver with an enamelled eagle of the order in the centre. Above the star was a silver, frosted, pierced crown.[28] See Image VI:31 for the contrast between officers' and other ranks' mitres, and note the summer white trousers. Officers wore silver lace on the cloth bags in place of the white tape of other ranks.

NEW SILVER MITRES

In 1894, Kaiser Wilhelm II awarded new mitres to the 1st Battalion of the 1st Foot Guards. He paid for these mitres out of his personal funds. The Prussian War Ministry then paid for new mitres for the 2nd and 3rd Battalions.[29]

The new silver mitres were a very different style, being modelled more or less on the mitre worn by Infantry Regiment 35 (1764–1806) in the time of Frederick the Great (1712–86). This produced a baroque-style mitre (Image VI:37). The 'Semper Talis' phrase was now stamped on the mitre plates of the 2nd Battalion, as well as being carried by the 1st Battalion. The mitre plate of the Fusilier Battalion was given a stamped banner, 'Pro Gloria et Patria' ('For

VI:39 Side View of the 3rd (Fusilier) Battalion of the Foot Guards' Mitre
Note the shape of the band at the back of the mitre.

VI:38 Mitre for the 1st Foot Guards, 3rd Battalion
Note banner above the eagle. Also note the officer's puschel at the top of the mitre.

VI:40 Back View of the Mitre of the 1st Foot Guards, 3rd (Fusilier) Battalion
Note the design of the metal back band on this mitre and the shape and design of the officer's braid on the cloth bag in the back of the mitre.

Glory and Fatherland'; see Images VI:36 and VI:38). This had been on the grenadier mitres of Frederican Infantry Regiment 35.[30]

The front plate was silvered tin for other ranks. It had a cloth back whose colour varied by battalion. In place of the white back-cloth borders of the old M1824 mitre, the new mitres had a baroque silvered tin border around the back of the mitre at the bottom of the cloth bag (Image VI:40). The border was decorated with grenades, flags, and scrolls (Image VI:39).[31] The cloth bag for the other ranks of the 1st and 2nd Battalions was red with white tape trim (Image VI:37). The Fusilier Battalion had a yellow wool body with white tape cloth braid. The front plate of the Fusilier 3rd Battalion was shorter than those of the first two battalions.

The new mitre for the other ranks was topped by a white woollen fringe with a red centre for the 1st and 2nd Battalions. In the Fusilier 3rd Battalion, the centre was yellow.

Officer's Mitre

The front and back border of the M1894 mitre for officers was stamped silver.[32] The cloth bags were the same colour as those worn by the other ranks, but their white trim was replaced by strips of silver lace (Images VI:40 and VI:41).

At the top of the officer's mitre was a field badge in place of the other ranks' fringe (Images VI:38 and VI:41). To make it, cannetille (a type of filigree) threads were wrapped around a pear-shaped piece of wood. This required skilled workmanship and made this item very expensive.

Helmet and Uniform

The helmets had the guard eagle with a guard star with the Order of the Black Eagle on it (Image VI:26). When the black polished leather helmet was worn with a plume, the plume colour carried by all five regiments was the same. The 1st and 2nd Battalions had white plumes and the 3rd (fusilier) Battalion black.

The tunic, except for the Swedish cuffs, was a standard Prussian model. It was single-breasted and dark blue with eight yellow dome buttons without any designs down the front (Images VI:27 and VI:28). The collar and cuffs were red. The front was piped in red.

VI:41 Officer's Mitre of the 1st Foot Guards, 1st and 2nd Battalions after 1894

There were false pockets on each of the two rear skirts and each had three buttons, with one placed at the waist. The others were connected by red piping in a scalloped pattern. The piping was just like that found on British infantry skirts. In fact, the British trim was sometimes called Prussian trim. Trousers were blue-black with red piping along the outside seams.

Officers wore chapter litzen. For the 1st Foot Guards they were silver. The 2nd through 4th Foot Guards wore gold-coloured litzen. The other ranks' chapter litzen for these regiments followed these colours but were made of less valuable material. The officers wore an officer's sash. Other ranks wore belts (Image VI:29), white for the 1st and 2nd Battalions and black for the 3rd Battalion.

The 5th Foot Guard Regiment had a Brandenburg cuff. Its cuff plate was dark blue. The officers had elaborate lace on their collars and cuffs (§VI-3-2, Image VI:1(6)). Other ranks had white old Prussian lace on theirs (Image VI:30).

Image C78 shows the entire uniform and its colours.

§VI-5-b GUARD FUSILIER REGIMENT

Uniform

The guard fusiliers' uniform was very similar to that of the foot guards. They wore a pickelhaube with guard eagle and star (Table VI.5.1). They wore the basic Prussian uniform with red collars and cuffs. Their tunic had a Swedish cuff (Image VI:42). The regiment wore chapter litzen. Because of its status as a fusilier regiment, all three battalions wore black belts; in most Prussian regiments the first two battalions wore white belts and the third was deemed a fusilier battalion and normally wore a black belt. All three battalions wore a black plume. The trousers were the standard blue-black with scarlet piping.

§VI-5-c GUARD GRENADIERS

Uniform

The uniform of these regiments followed the Prussian standard of dark blue uniform with yellow button colour, facing colour red, Brandenburg cuffs and blue-black trousers (Images VI:43 and VI:44).

All the regiments wore a pickelhaube with a yellow guard eagle and a white guard star after 1889.[33] The helmet plates, after 1889, were the same as those of the 2nd through 5th Foot Guards for both officers and men.

In 1896 the old M1824 mitres, which had been replaced by the silver mitres and were no longer being used by the 1st Foot Guards, were passed on to the 1st Guard Grenadier Regiment (Image VI:45). Before the mitres could be worn, the 'Semper Talis' banners that had been added to the mitres for the 1st Foot Guards

VI:42 Guard Fusilier Regiment Other Ranks
Note his black belt and the black plume on his helmet. He is wearing a marksman award on his right chest.

VI:43 1st Guard Grenadier's Tunic and Frock Coat
Note guard grenadier braid on the cuff of the tunic.

VI:44 3rd Guard Grenadier Regiment Other Ranks' Tunic Officers in the grenadiers wore special guard grenadier lace, but other ranks wore simple chapter litzen on the collar and cuffs.

VI:46 3rd Guard Grenadier Regiment Note the white belt and white plume showing he is a member of the 1st or 2nd Battalion of the regiment.

VI:45 1st Guard Grenadier Regiment Other Ranks This is obviously after they were given their mitres.

VI:47 4th Guard Grenadier Regiment Note the way the helmet plume falls and covers the helmet badge. Also note the length of the plume. This fierce man has elected to have his photo taken with his mother.

VI:48 Guard Grenadier Other Rank
He is wearing the black belt and black plume of the 3rd Battalion of a guard grenadier regiment.

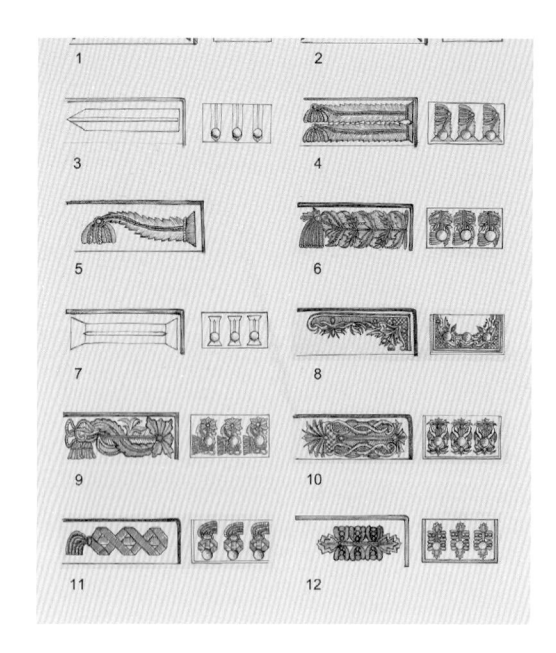

VI:49 Other Ranks of the 5th Guard Grenadiers
Note old Prussian lace on collar and cuffs and on his overcoat. The belt buckle shows up particularly well in this photograph, and the crown on the circular badge in the middle of the brass buckle can be clearly seen.

had to be removed. Since these had been on a separate strip of metal which was fastened to the mitre via a bolt, their removal left a hole in the mitre. This did not matter to the thrifty Prussians, and the 1st Guard Grenadiers wore the mitres, holes and all, on parade. See Image VI:32 for an example of a passed-on mitre with the hole.

The upright plates of the Brandenburg cuff were dark blue, a unique feature worn almost exclusively by guard regiments (Images VI:43 and VI:44). The officers of the 1st through 4th Guard Grenadier Regiments had the same type of special lace embroidery on their collars and cuffs. Prior to 1837, the 1st and 2nd Regiments had worn the gold lace pattern shown in *§VI-3-2*, Image VI:1(5) on their collars only. After that they wore the pattern shown in *§VI-3-2*, Image VI:1(4).

When the 3rd and 4th Guard Grenadier Regiments were raised in 1860 they took the same pattern lace that was being worn on the collars of the 1st and 2nd Regiments. This pattern can now fairly be called guard grenadier lace. In 1874, the guard grenadier lace was extended to be worn on the cuffs also. The other ranks of these regiments wore chapter litzen (Images VI:46 and VI:47). Image VI:48 shows a soldier of a 3rd Battalion wearing a black plume and a black belt.

When the 5th Guard Grenadiers were raised in 1897, they and the 5th Guard Foot Regiment were given the same pattern lace (*§VI-3-2*, Image VI:1(6)). The other ranks wore old Prussian lace (*§VI-3-2*, Image VI:1(3)) that was the same design as the 5th Foot Guards (Image VI:49), but in yellow.

§VI-5-d GUARD JÄGER AND RIFLES

Uniform

These units, one battalion each, are covered below, where the line jägers are described. See *§VI-10*, Jägers and Rifles.

§VI-6 PRUSSIAN CAVALRY

§VI-6-a PRUSSIAN CUIRASSIERS

The cuirassiers were the senior cavalry army of the Prussian army. They included many regiments credited with being among the oldest in the Prussian army.

Since they wore armour, one might think that the origins of the cuirassiers lay in medieval knights. However, the truth is more prosaic. If one digs into the genealogy of the cuirassier regiments, their origins, in almost all cases, lay in a dragoon regiment. The only exception to this is the 6th Cuirassiers, who were formed in 1691, before dragoons were really created. Their 'founding' regiment was a gendarme squadron. Gendarmes at the time were lightly armoured cavalry.

Table VI.6.a.1: Dates Cuirassier Regiments First Organised

Old Regiment Title	New Regiment Title	Date Formed
Gardes du Corps	Gardes du Corps	1740
Guard Cuirassiers	Guard Cuirassiers	1815
Cuirassier Regt (Silesian No. 1)	1st Cuirassiers	1674
Dragoon Regt (Queen's)	2nd Cuirassiers	Into Cuir: 1819[a]
Cuirassiers Regt (East Prussian No. 2)	3rd Cuirassiers	1717;[b,c] 1808[a]
Dragoon Regt No. 2	4th Cuirassiers	1717, 1819[a]
Dragoon Regt No. 4	5th Cuirassiers	1717, 1819[a,b]
Cuirassier Regt (Brandenburg No. 3)	6th Cuirassiers	1691
Cuirassier Regt No. 4	7th Cuirassiers	1815
Dragoon Regt No. 8	8th Cuirassiers	1819[a]

Sources: Fosten, *Cuirassiers, etc.*, p. 8; Bredow-Wedel, *Historische*, vols 1 and 2.
Notes: [a] Converted into cuirassiers in this year.
[b] Traces origins to old 'Porcelain Regiment' (see below).
[c] After the downsizing of 1808, it was combined with elements of other regiments and formed into the 2nd Cuirassiers, which in turn became the 3rd Cuirassiers in 1819 (Bredow-Wedel, *Historische*, vol. 1, pp. 257–8).

The cuirassier regiments have an unusually interesting background. The Life Cuirassiers Great Elector (Silesian) No. 1 was formed in 1674 as a regiment of bodyguard dragoons from two regiments: the 'Dragoons of the Court' and the 'Dragoons of the Kitchen'. The latter's duty was to escort convoys bringing seafood to the kitchens of Great Elector Frederick William I of Prussia. The regiment was converted into cuirassiers in 1718. In 1866, it was given the largely honorary title of Bodyguard Regiment and entitled to add 'Life' in front of its regimental title.[34]

The 2nd Cuirassier Regiment was said to trace its ancestry to the Bayreuth (also spelled Baireuth) Dragoons of Frederick the Great.[35] The dragoons had performed well on many battlefields during Frederick's wars, but their day of glory came at the Battle of Hohenfriedberg in 1745 against the Austrians. In an attack on several lines of Austrian infantry numbering some twenty battalions, they captured sixty-six standards and at least 2,500 prisoners. The Hohenfriedberg March, one of the best-known German marches, was written in their honour, allegedly by Frederick the Great himself. Frederick gave them the nickname 'The Caesars of Hohenfriedberg'.[36]

In 1806, they were given the title Queen's Dragoons. When this regiment was converted to cuirassiers in 1819, all these traditions went with it.

The 3rd Cuirassiers had a unique background. Europe had long coveted porcelain. For centuries, the secret of making porcelain was known only in China. So, by the time a piece got to Europe, it was incredibly expensive. A porcelain cup is shown in Montegna's 1490 painting *Adoration of the Magi* as one of the treasures offered to the Christ child.[37]

Porcelain became easier to obtain after the Portuguese and then the Dutch reached China, but it was still fabulously expensive. In the sixteenth and seventeenth centuries, there was a craze for porcelain in Europe. Among the most avid collectors was Augustus I, 'Augustus the Strong', Elector of Saxony and King of Poland. He spent so much that his advisors feared he would bankrupt the kingdom.

Augustus coveted porcelain held by the Prussian King Frederick William I. Sources disagree whether the desired items were a tea/coffee set studded with amber[38] or a collection of 151 mixed items of porcelain made up of monumental vases and many other smaller items. To pay for the porcelain, on 19 April 1717 a regiment of 600 men was sent from Augustus' army to the Prussians.[39] (The dragoon vases are still in Dresden.[40]) The Prussians formed a dragoon regiment with the men, which was given the nickname the 'Porcelain Regiment'. In 1806, the regiment was the 6th Dragoons. In 1807, it was divided into two parts: a 2nd Cuirassier Regiment that in 1819 became the 3rd Cuirassiers, and a 2nd Dragoon Regiment that in 1819 became the 4th Cuirassiers (see Table VI.6.a.1). They had the same founding date, 1717 – that of the old Porcelain Regiment – since they were both split off from that regiment.

The 5th Regiment of Cuirassiers also had a founding date of 1717 because it traced its origins back to the Porcelain Regiment. Its ancestor was split off from that regiment in 1727 and, after further splits, in 1806 it was the 8th Dragoons. In 1808, it changed to the 4th Dragoons, and in 1819, as noted in Table VI.6.a.1, it became the 5th Cuirassiers.

The cuirassier regiments seemed to draw the largest number of nobles prior to World War I and, in fact, were a noble enclave within an aristocratic force.

Table VI.6.a.2: Cuirassiers' Uniform Details

Regiment	Koller Trim Colour	Button Colour	Helmet Colour	Monogram	Cuirass Colour[a]	Notes
Gardes du Corps	Poppy red	White[b]	Yellow[c]		Brass or Black[d]	A, B, C, D
Guard Cuirassiers	Cornflower blue	White	Yellow[e]		Yellow[d]	A, B, C
1st Cuirassiers	Black[f]	Yellow[c]	White[g]	Yes[h]	White[g]	E, F
2nd Cuirassiers	Crimson	White	White[g]	Yes[i]	Yellow[j,k]	G, H
3rd Cuirassiers	Light blue	White	White[g]		White[g]	I
4th Cuirassiers	Poppy red	White	White[g]		White[g]	
5th Cuirassiers	Rose red/pink	Yellow	White[g]		White[g]	
6th Cuirassiers	Russian blue	Yellow	Yellow[e]	Yes[l]	Yellow[j,k]	
7th Cuirassiers	Lemon yellow	White	White[g]		White[g]	
8th Cuirassiers	Light green	Yellow	White[g]	Yes[m]	White[g]	

Notes: [a] Cuirasses are steel (white) unless otherwise noted.
[b] In the guards, the buttons were made of nickel silver, in the other 'white' regiments of nickel.
[c] Buttons made of tombac, an alloy of copper and zinc. The name comes from the Malaysian word *tembaga* ('Tombac', *Webster's Unabridged Dictionary*, p. 1993).
[d] Steel cuirass plated with brass. The Gardes du Corps also had a black cuirass, which was worn for the spring parade and other special events (Herr, *German Cavalry*, p. 268).
[e] Helmet made of tombac.
[f] Officers of the 1st Regiment had facings of black velvet.
[g] Made of steel.
[h] 'WR' monogram under crown for King Wilhelm I.
[i] 'L' under crown for Queen Luise of Prussia (granted 1888).
[j] Steel cuirass plated with tombac for officers. Those of NCOs plated with brass.
[k] NCOs wore a brass-plated cuirass.
[l] Cyrillic 'N' (i.e. an 'H') and 'I' or 'I' under crown. Other ranks had Arabic '1' and officers a Roman 'I' (granted 1826) (Herr, *German Cavalry*, p. 241).
[m] 'GR' monogram and 'V' under crown for George V of Britain (granted 1911).

A: Guard eagle.
B: Guard star.
C: Litzen (white).
D: Gorget, given 1912.
E: Helmet plate of eagle flying to the left. Eagle design is from regimental flags used by Frederick the Great. Banner with motto 'Pro Gloria et Patria', which was also from the flags (Herr, *German Cavalry*, p. 231). Given in 1902.
F: Gorget, given 1896.
G: 'Hohenfriedburg 1775' banner, given 1889.
H: Gorget, given 1895.
I: Special koller trim braid, given 1901.

Uniform

Helmet

The spiked helmet worn by Prussian cuirassiers was distinctive in its shape. It had been introduced in 1842 and maintained its basic design, with minor changes, down to 1914. As with most Prussian helmets, it tended to become lower and lighter as the years passed.

The helmet worn by the guard had an imposing eagle on it (Images VI:51 and VI:52). Along with the rest of the uniform, it could create an impressive picture (Image VI:50). One unusual feature of these helmets was that they did not cover the ears.

In 1889, the helmets of the other ranks were given a rounded front visor. Officers' front visors were more square and tended to jut out at the bottom at a ninety-degree angle (Images VI:53, VI:54, and VI:52).

In general, the helmets of the other ranks, in addition to having a different front visor, were not as tall and did not have as massive a 'tail' as those of the officers (Image VI:51).

The helmets were polished steel except for the Gardes du Corps, the Guard Cuirassiers, and the 6th Cuirassiers. Theirs were made of tombac. The steel helmets had brass mountings, and the tombac helmets' mountings were German silver. The spike on steel helmets was brass. The tombac helmets had a column and collar of steel, but the spike was tombac.[41] For parades and ceremonial duties, the Gardes du Corps and the Guard Cuirassiers wore, in lieu of the spike, an impressive crowned eagle with outstretched wings. The eagle of the other ranks was made of German silver, the officers' eagle silver. The crown was gilded.[42]

Koller

Cuirassiers wore a special type of tunic called a koller. The colour for both officers and other ranks was often said to be yellow-white but, judging from photographs and physical examinations, the colours tends to be almost pure white for both.

The koller had Swedish cuffs and a standing collar. Both had cuirassier braid. The two guard regiments wore litzen. On the cuffs, there were the customary two buttons, each with chapter litzen running vertically. On the collar, they had a single chapter litzen that

VI:50 Kaiser Wilhelm in the Full Dress of the Gardes du Corps (Cuirassier) Regiment

ran on each side of the collar from where the collar closed in front to halfway around the collar. The litzen was placed below the collar's cuirassier braid (Image VI:55). Line officers did not have litzen (Image VI:56).

A notable feature of the koller was that it did not have buttons. It was closed by sixteen hooks and eyes for other ranks. For officers, the number was supposed

VI:51 M1894 Enlisted Man's Helmet of Guard Cuirassiers or the Gardes du Corps
Note how the rear tail is shorter than that found on an officer's helmet.

VI:53 Prussian Line Cuirassier Officer's Helmet
This was worn by the 3rd, 4th, 5th, 7th, and 8th Prussian Line Cuirassier Regiments. It had a nickel-plated steel skull with gilded tombac mountings. The eagle has frosted gilding and the rear brim is lined with black velvet.

VI:52 M1889 Helmet for Officers of the Gardes du Corps or Cuirassier Guard
Note the fine detail of the eagle worn on the top of the helmet in full dress.

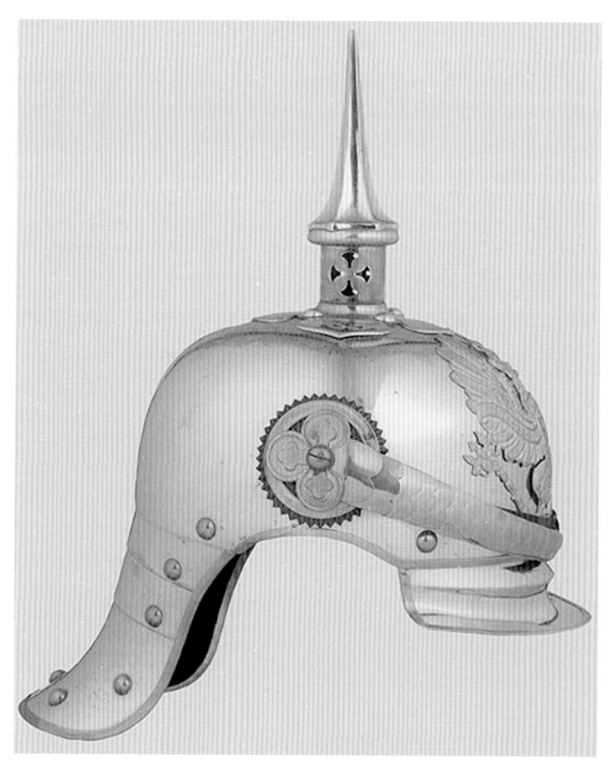

VI:54 Side View of the Cuirassier Helmet
Note how the front brim juts straight out, and the back portion of the helmet had an exaggerated lobster-tail shape.

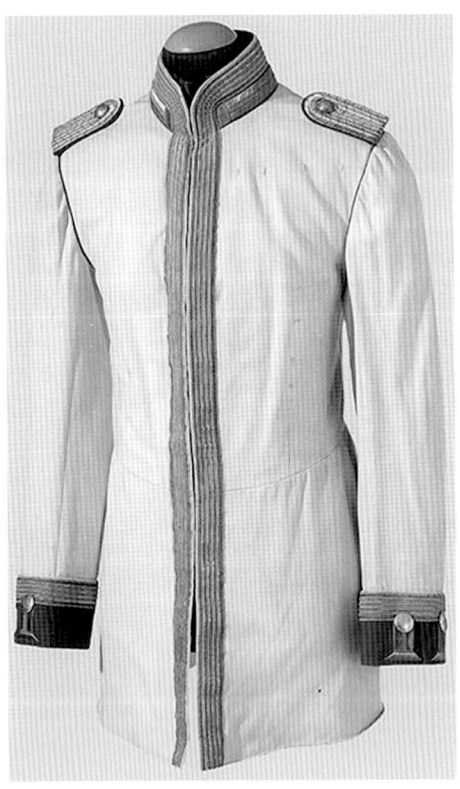

VI:55 Cuirassier Officer's Koller
This is for a guard regiment. Note how the shoulder straps are worn on this officer's koller.

VI:57 2nd Cuirassiers Other Ranks
Note the other rank cuirassier braid on collar, down the front, and at the cuffs, and the regiment's gorget for an NCO.

VI:56 2nd Cuirassier Regiment Officer's Koller
Note the epaulettes.

VI:58 Other Ranks Cuirassier

to be twenty-two, but the actual number varied as the kollers were privately purchased.[43]

The braid was very different for officers and other ranks. See Image VI:57 for an other ranks' koller. However, for both, it was to be 3.6 cm (1.42 inches) wide with trim of the regiment's facing colour of 2 mm (0.08 inch) on each side.[44]

For other ranks, the braid consisted of three stripes. The two outside stripes were in the regiment's facing colour, and the inside stripe was white (referred to herein as 'men's cuirassier braid') (Image VI:58). On the collar, the men had a top line of white trim over the braid, and this continued down the front of the koller, creating a line of white trim where the koller closed. The cuffs had narrow lines of white trim above and below the braid.

The 3rd Regiment had special braid. In place of the centre white stripe, they wore a light-blue stripe on each edge with light blue lozenges in the middle (Image VI:59).[45]

The shoulder straps, armhole seams, back arm seams, and seams on the back of the koller were also piped in the facing colour. The rear skirt had three buttons and a scalloped pattern trim (Image VI:60) in the facing colour.

Sergeants wore sergeant's braid in place of the central band of white on the men's cuirassier braid (Image VI:61).

The officers' cuirassier braid looked very different. In place of the other ranks' central white band, the officers wore gold or silver braid, depending on the regiment's button colour. This braid, the same as the men's cuirassier braid, was 3.6 cm (1.42 inches) wide. On either side, it had trim in the regiment's facing colour 2 mm (0.08 inch) wide.

The officers' cuirassier braid consisted of strips of raised braid alternating with strips of flat braid. This has been described as a corduroy pattern (Image VI:62). Image VI:63 is a closeup of this type of braid used in Russia. It is almost exactly the same as German officers' cuirassier braid.

In the 1st Cuirassiers, the officers' collar patches and cuffs were black velvet.[46]

Epaulettes and Shoulder Straps

In full dress, officers wore epaulettes, and for other duties, shoulder cords. The epaulette consisted of

VI:59 3rd Cuirassiers' Collar and Cuff Braid

a shoulder board of white, the colour of the koller, edged with silver and black striped lace. The large metal crescent was the button colour. It was held to the koller by a small strip of cloth and a button near the collar. Rank was shown by a combination of the thickness of the epaulette's fringe, or lack of fringe and the number of stars on the epaulette (see §VI-3-23, Officers' Epaulettes).

Generals and field marshals had thick silver fringe. The fringe was always mixed with 'darts' in the colour of the state raising the regiment, and this custom was followed by the cuirassiers. A field marshal carried crossed batons. The other generals carried up to three stars as their rank grew higher. Field officers had what might be called regular fringe, thinner than the fringe of generals. They carried from no stars up to two as their rank grew from major to colonel. Officer ranks from captain on down did not have fringe. Their stars grew from one for a lieutenant to two for a captain (see §VI-3-23, Officers' Epaulettes, and Image VI:22).

For less than full dress, officers wore shoulder cords on a cuirassier tunic (see below). The cords grew thicker as the man's rank grew higher, and the system of stars followed the pattern used on epaulettes (see §VI-3-23 and Image VI:23).[47]

Cuirass

Surprisingly, the Prussian cuirassiers had an on-again, off-again relationship with their body armour, the breast plate and back plate that gave them their name. They had worn armour under Frederick the Great, but towards the end of the reign of King Frederick William II (1744–97), it was done away with in an effort to make them more mobile.[48] Then, in 1814, Prussian cavalry in France began wearing captured French cuirasses.[49] When the new permanent cuirassier regiments were formed in 1808–19, they followed the practice of wearing armour. The cuirasses were worn in battle in the

§VI-6 Prussian Cavalry   721

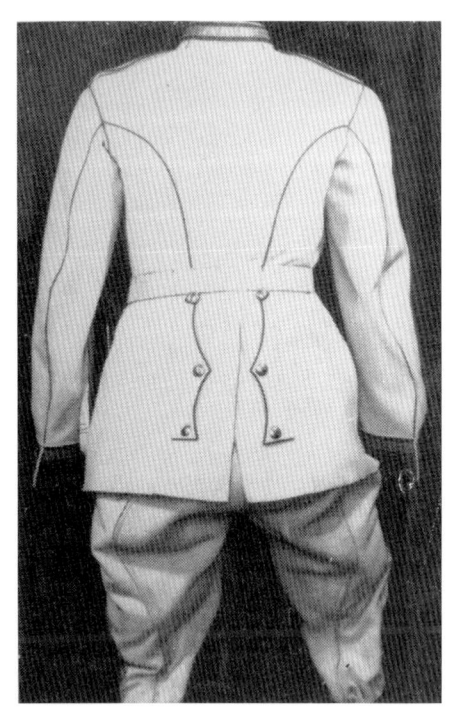

VI:60 Rear View of a Koller and Breeches
Note the trim on the back of the koller and the reinforcing on the inside of the breeches.

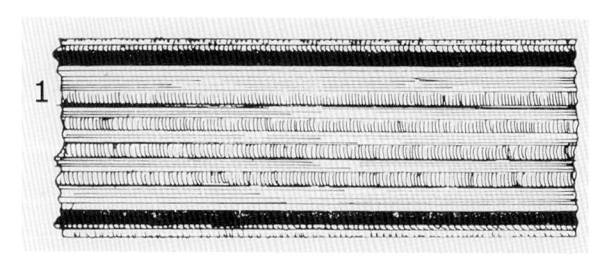

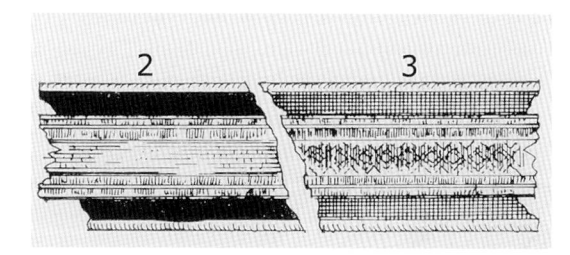

VI:62 Examples of Different Types of Lace
1. The corduroy lace worn by Prussian cuirassier officers on their kollers.
2. Line lace.
3. Guard lace.

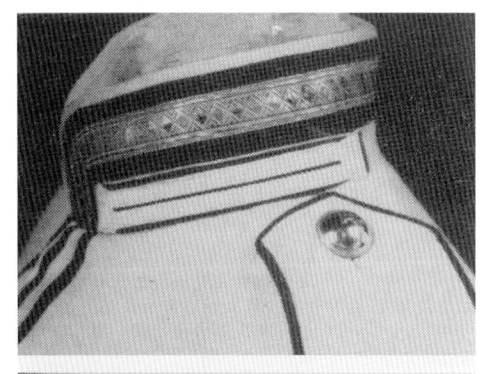

VI:61 Detailed View of the Collar and Cuffs of an NCO's Pattern of Koller Worn by Guard Regiments
Note guard pattern NCO lace and the litzen worn by guard cuirassiers.

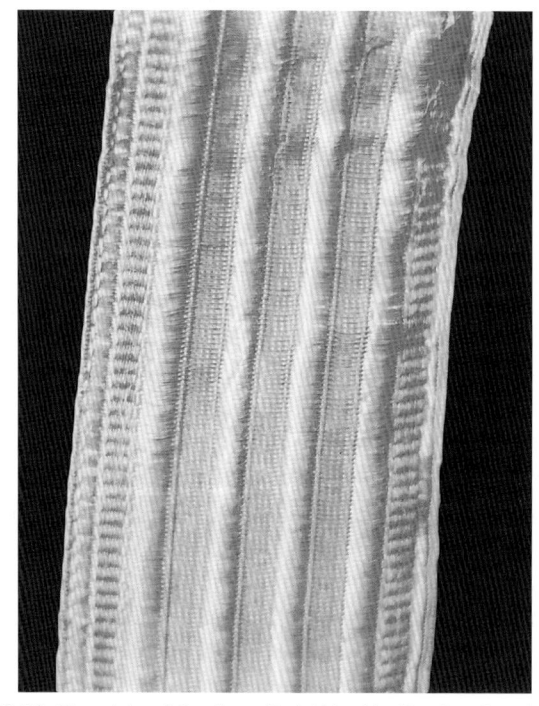

VI:63 Close-Up of Corduroy Braid Used by Russian Guard Cuirassier Officers
This is close to the shape of the corduroy braid used by German cuirassier officers. It lacks the outer bands of facing colour.

wars with Denmark, Austria, and France, as well as at important peacetime events.

Orders came in 1888 that the armour would henceforth only be worn as parade dress. After that, it was rarely worn except for the two guard regiments and the 1st and 2nd Regiments, which were considered extremely aristocratic and elite. In the other regiments, it was not unusual to have officers who did not own a cuirass or officers who only put them on to have their photograph taken.[50]

From 1880 to 1914, several different patterns of cuirasses were worn: a steel cuirass, worn by most regiments; a steel cuirass plated with tombac worn by all ranks of the Gardes du Corps; the special black cuirass of the Gardes du Corps (see below); and a steel cuirass plated with tombac for officers and NCOs of Regiments 2 and 6.[51]

It goes without saying that the officers' cuirasses were more elegant, better fitting, and of a higher quality than those of the other ranks.

The steel cuirass weighed about 7.7 kg (16.98 pounds.) It had a twill lining to protect the koller from wear. There was lining at the neck, arm, and waist openings, which sometimes extended outside the cuirass.[52]

The strap and scales holding the two plates of armour together came down noticeably farther in front on the officers' cuirass than on the other ranks' (including NCOs') cuirasses (Images VI:64, VI:65, and VI:66). And, of course, the officers' straps were much more elaborate. The officers' models differed between themselves and from the other ranks in details of rivets, the moulding of the cuirass, the scales holding the two parts of the armour together, etc., which are beyond the scope of this work.

The Gardes du Corps had special cuirasses in addition to their brass-coated steel cuirasses. In 1814, as part of the *bonhomie* following the defeat of Napoleon, the Allies took several steps to show their goodwill towards each other. One such step was by Czar Alexander I, who gave the Gardes du Corps Russian black iron cuirasses, which were quite heavy. They were worn on special occasions, such as the spring parade, on mounting guard in the palace, weddings, etc.

Even with limited use, by the end of the nineteenth century the Russian cuirasses were starting to wear out. In 1897, Kaiser Wilhelm II gave the regiment new steel cuirasses that were lacquered black. These had straps with brass (golden) scales going over the shoulders, to hold the cuirass on, and red trim. The combination made a striking and attractive uniform item (Images VI:67 and C79).

Two of the line cuirassier regiments were awarded gorgets: the 2nd in 1895 and the 1st in 1896. The gorgets appeared on the cuirasses. In the 2nd Regiment, the entire shield-shaped gorget was screwed onto the cuirass (Image VI:66). These were attached to the centre of the upper chest a little below the neck opening. There were different models of gorgets for other ranks, NCOs, and officers.[53]

The 1st Regiment wore only the central portion of their gorget on their cuirass. These were attached in the same place as the 2nd Regiment's (Image VI:68). There were different models for other ranks, NCOs, and officers.

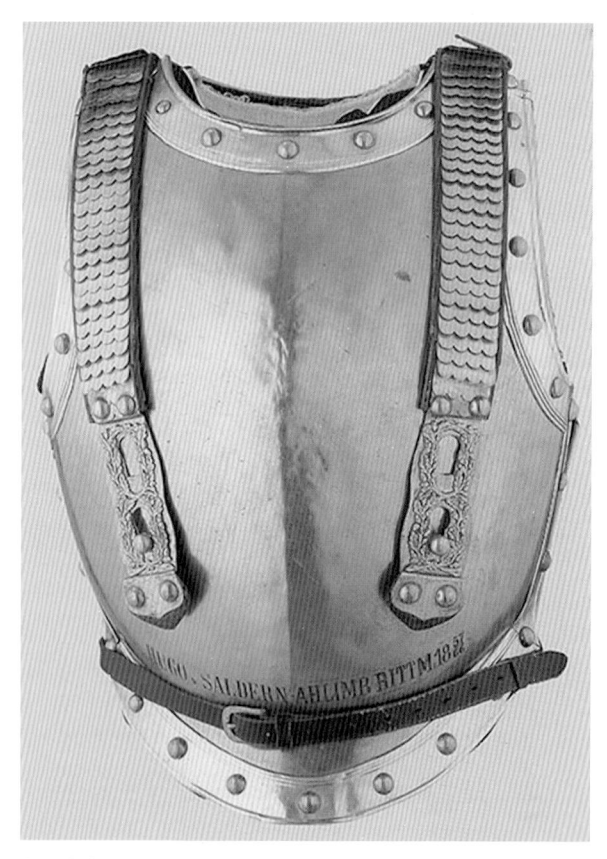

VI:64 Gardes du Corps or Cuirassier Guard Regiment Officer's Cuirass
It was customary for the officers to have their names and joining dates put on their cuirasses when they retired. These could be hung in either the officer's home or the regimental mess.

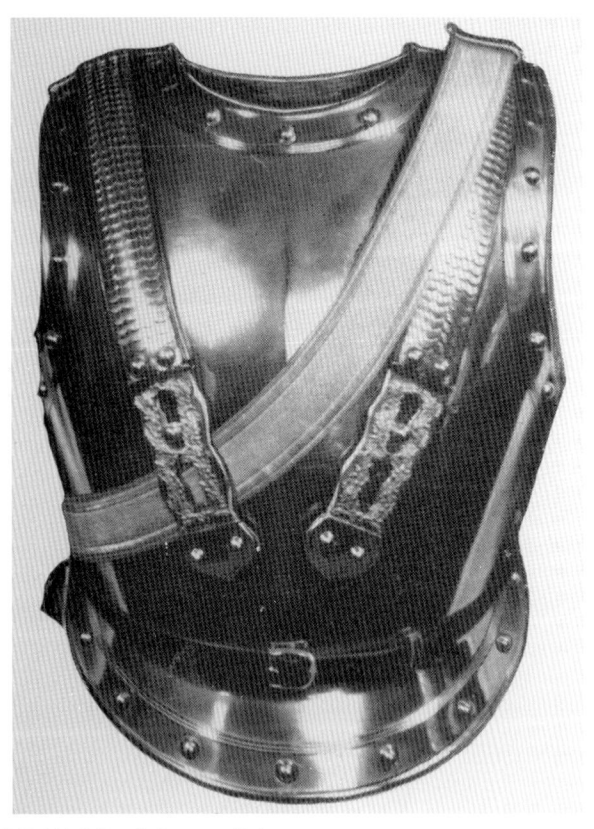

VI:65 Officer's Pattern Cuirass

VI:67 Kaiser Wilhelm II Wearing the Lacquered Black Cuirass of the Gardes du Corps
Note how he is wearing short white gloves and a separate gauntlet-shape cuff to go with the short gloves. Apparently, even emperors need to economise.

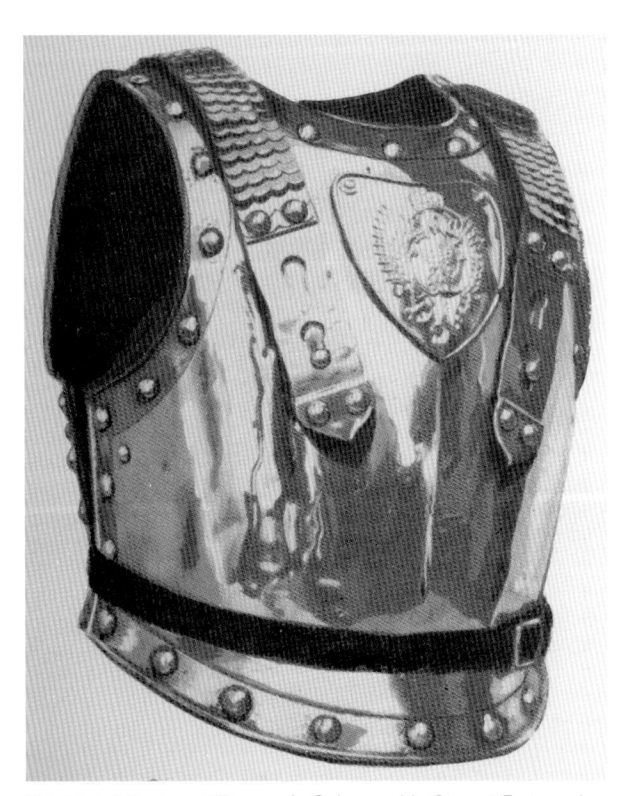

VI:66 1st Regiment Trooper's Cuirass with Gorget Fastened to the Cuirass

VI:68 2nd Regiment Trooper's Cuirass with Part of the Regimental Gorget Attached to the Cuirass

In 1912, the Gardes du Corps was awarded a gorget. The central portion of the gorget was attached to both the regular guard cuirass and the black cuirass. They were attached at the same location set out in the discussion of the 2nd Cuirassiers. The Gardes du Corps' gorget came in three types: the other ranks', NCO's and officer's models. An idea of what these looked like can be gained by looking at the discussion of Gardes du Corps gorgets below and Images VI:75 and VI:80. The central part of the gorget was worn on the cuirass.

Gala Tunic

For court functions and balls, both Guard Cuirassier regiments wore a special poppy red single-breasted tunic. The tunic was introduced in 1856 for the Gardes du Corps and in 1862 for Guard Cuirassiers. They hark back to gala tunics worn at the time of Frederick the Great.[54]

The tunics for the two regiments were almost identical. Neither had officers' cuirassier braid. Both had square-cut collars and Swedish cuffs. The Gardes du Corps wore dark blue trim (Image C76), and the Guard Cuirassiers wore cornflower blue, a fairly dark shade of blue (Image C77).

The collars hooked closed in front. The tunics had eight plain, silver, domed buttons in front. The back skirts had three buttons on each side, and a simple pointed trim. The collars had double litzen, and each button on the cuffs had framing litzen. The litzen was the chapter style.

Standard full dress epaulettes were worn with the gala tunic. The Gardes du Corps wore their gorget with this order of dress after it was awarded to them (Image C76). The tunics were lined with white silk.

The only difference between the red tunics of the two regiments, besides their facing colours, was the trim on their tunics. The Gardes du Corps had thin dark blue trim. The Guard Cuirassiers had thin white trim. The thin trim ran around the top of the collar, down the front of the collar and the front of the tunic, around the top of each cuff, and between each set of buttons on the rear skirt of the gala tunic. In the Gardes du Corps, the trim was not visible, because the trim was the same colour as the collar and cuffs. The helmet with an eagle and white gala breeches (see below) completed this striking uniform.[55]

Gala Palace Guard Dress

The gala palace guard duty order of dress consisted of five elements: the supravest; pouch belt, also called a bandolier; pouch; sword belt; and sabretache. It was worn by specially selected members of the Life Company of the Gardes du Corps when performing ceremonial duties at grand events at the Royal Court. A similar supravest had been worn by the regiment in the reign of Frederick the Great.

Supravest

The supravest was worn over the koller. It was a short-skirted crimson cloth vest that had the basic shape of a cuirass. However, the supravest had a short pleated skirt below the waist. It fastened under the left arm and at the left shoulder with hooks. The supravest for troopers was trimmed by a simple form of men's cuirassier braid that ran around all the outside edges of the vest, including the left side where it was hooked together and the shoulders, where each side had two white lines.

The officer's supravest, until 1900, was made of poppy red cloth and had 3.2 cm (1.26 inch) wide silver braid around the edge as well as red stripes. This, in effect, was the officer's braid on the koller, only a little smaller.

After 1900, the officer's supravest was made of red velvet and had new silver braid in a unique pattern (Images VI:69 and VI:70).

In the middle of the front and back of the troopers' supravest, there was a white embroidered star of the Order of the Black Eagle. It had a red centre circle bearing a black Prussian eagle. The eagle's crown, beak, talons, and sword were yellow, as were the thunderbolts around it. Around the red circle was a white circular band bordered in black. The band contained the words 'SUUM CUIQUE' in yellow embroidery and two sprays of green laurel below the lettering. The laurel had red berries.

The officer's star had the same design, but with silver wire in place of the white embroidery, and gold wire in place of the yellow on the badge. Coloured silk was used to provide the coloured elements.[56]

VI:69 Gardes du Corps Gala Supravest
On the left is an other ranks' supravest. On the right is an officer's supravest.

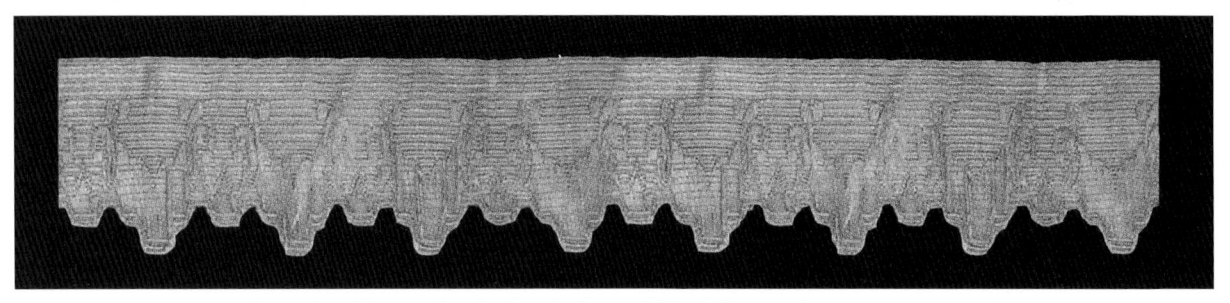

VI:70 The Lace which is Part of the Trim on the Gardes du Corps Officer's Sabretache

Pouch Belt

A special bandolier was worn in this order of dress. A normal bandolier and pouch box had been worn until 1883, when the Kaiser ordered special models to be used. For other ranks, the old belt was white lacquered leather with crimson worsted braid on either side, positioned to leave a small line of white leather on the outside of the braid. It had silver mountings.

The belt of officers was the same up to 1900. After 1900, for officers, it was made of red velvet and had silver patterned braid. No photograph of this pattern can be found, but see Image VI:69.

Pouch

Until 1883, a normal cuirassier pouch was worn, at which point a white leather box replaced it. The lid was white lacquered leather with cuirassier trim. In the centre was the guard star.

In 1883, officers began wearing a poppy red pouch with a lid of the same colour. The lid was trimmed with a row of officers' cuirassier braid. It also had a guard star, but in better quality materials. After 1900, the cover of the pouch lid was made of red velvet, and the red trim on the officer's pouch was changed to embroidered silver braid in the same pattern used on the officer's supravest (see Images VI:69 and VI:70).

Sword Belt

The sword and the sabretache were both carried on the same belt and type of carrying strap. The belt had the same basic braid as the bandolier. The belt was worn out of sight, under the tunic. The belt, carrying straps and sling straps were all white and decorated with a red braid 1.3 cm (0.5 inch) wide. This left a white edge on both sides[57] that was 3 mm (0.12 inch) wide.[58]

Sabretache

Sabretaches as a general rule are not covered in this work. However, an exception is made here since the sabretache was such an integral part of the court ceremonial dress.

For other ranks, the sabretache was red leather with a red cloth flap cover. The cover was trimmed with two rows of men's cuirassier braid (Image VI:71). In the centre was the crowned monogram 'FR' for Frederick the Great. The crown had red and green 'stones' in its brow band.

The officer's sabretache was first issued to officers in 1883. It had the same basic design as the other ranks' sabretache: a crowned 'FR' monogram in the centre with braid around the edges. The pouch was red leather. Up until 1900, the cover was the same as that used by the other ranks. In 1900, the cover was changed to red velvet and the trim to the type of silver braid used on the officer's supravest.[59]

BOOTS AND BREECHES

In court ceremonial dress, two other items completed the dress: white chamois breeches and black jackboots. The boots reached 8 cm (3.15 inches) above the knees in front and were cut out in the back.[60]

WALKING-OUT TUNIC (WAFFENROCK)

While the koller looked very elegant, its white surface could be easily stained. For this reason, cuirassier officers and men are most often seen in their walking-out tunic, the single-breasted, dark blue *waffenrock*, which was a cross between the koller and the red gala tunics of the guard regiments.

It had a high standing collar and Swedish cuffs that were, with a few exceptions – like the 6th and the 8th – in the regiment's facing colour. It is believed these regiments changed the piping colour on their walking-out tunics for aesthetic reasons.[61] See Table VI.6.a.3 below for a full listing of waffenrock facing details.

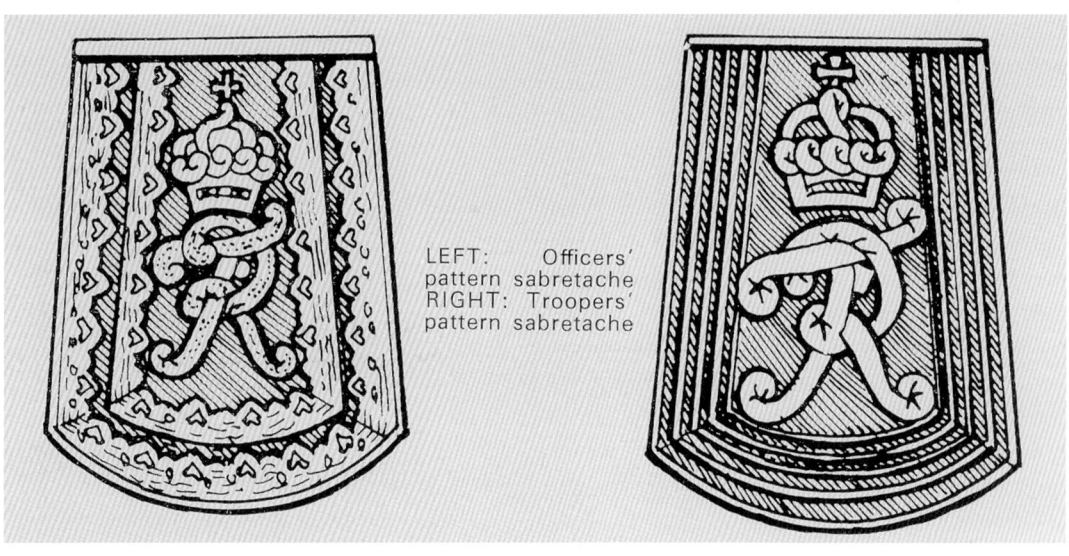

LEFT: Officers' pattern sabretache
RIGHT: Troopers' pattern sabretache

VI:71 Gala Sabretache of the Gardes du Corps

Table VI.6.a.3: Walking-Out Tunic (Waffenrock) Details

Regiment	Collar and Cuffs	Buttons	Piping	NCO & Trooper Monogram Shoulder Strap Colour
Gardes du Corps	Red with white or silver litzen	White	Red	–
Guard Cuirassiers	Cornflower blue[a] with white or silver litzen	White	Red	–
1st Regt (black velvet facings)	Black	Yellow	White[b]	Yellow
2nd Regt	Crimson[c]	White	Red	Red
3rd Regt[d]	Light blue	White	Light blue	–
4th Reg.	Poppy red[e]	White	Red	–
5th Regt	Rose red/pink[f]	Yellow	Rose/pink	–
6th Regt	Poppy red[g]	Yellow	Poppy red	Yellow
7th Regt	Lemon yellow	White	Yellow	–
8th Regt	Light green[h]	Yellow	White[b]	Yellow

Source: Fosten, *Cuirassier, etc.*, p. 67.
Notes: [a] The cornflower blue could appear fairly dark on the uniform.
[b] White piping was worn to show better against the dark waffenrock.
[c] The shade of crimson worn by 2nd's officers was lighter than worn by other ranks.
[d] After 1901, the regiment wore braid from the era of Frederick the Great..
[e] The 4th's officers wore vermillion red rather than poppy red.
[f] The rose red/pink of the 5th's officers was a softer richer pink.
[g] The 6th's officers wore poppy red to have it show better against the dark waffenrock.
[h] The officers of the 8th wore a rich sea green.

Because in the past the better cloth of officers' uniforms took the dyes of the period differently from those of the other ranks, the shade of the officers' uniforms were slightly different, even when they were supposed to be the same colour. In time, these differences became traditional features of the regimental uniforms.

In the 4th Regiment, the officers' trim was vermillion rather than poppy red. The rose red/ pink of the officers of the 5th was a softer rich pink. The Russian blue of the officers of the 6th had a dark ultramarine blue. In the 8th, the officers wore a rich sea green. The facings of the officers of the 2nd were a lighter shade of crimson than that worn by the other ranks.[62]

The collar and Swedish cuffs were trimmed in cuirassier braid. The other ranks' tunic had eight flat buttons down the front (Image VI:72). The eight buttons of officers were domed. There were three on each rear skirt flap (Image VI:73). The rear skirts were the same as those on the red tunics.

The collar and cuffs of the men and the officers were in the regiment's facing colour. The collars and cuffs of the other ranks had a patch in the facing colour,[63] and the patch was so large it left only a small portion of the back of the collar uncovered.

VI:72 NCO's Walking-Out Tunic for 6th Cuirassier Regiment

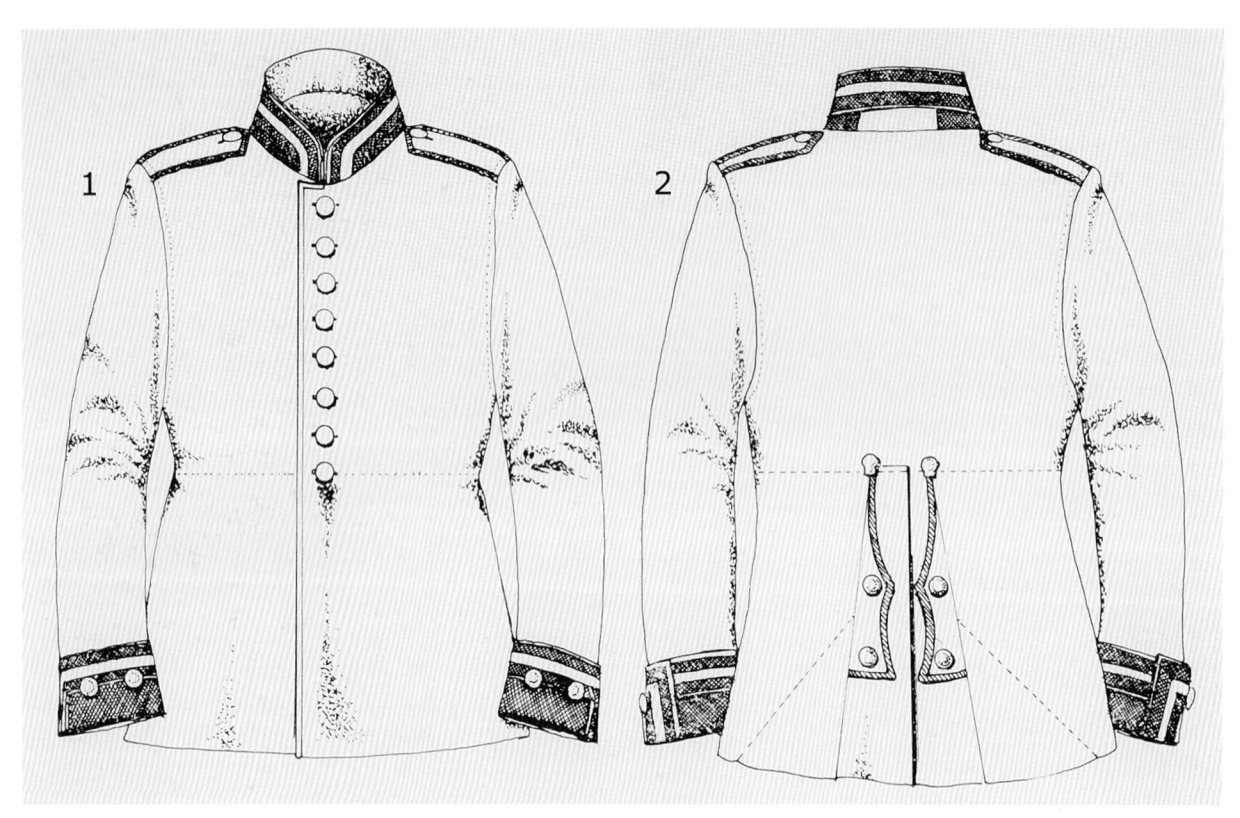

VI:73 Waffenrock (Undress or Walking-Out Tunic)

The other ranks' shoulder straps were the same colour as on the koller.

The collars and cuffs of the officers carried the same corduroy braid that the koller had at its collar and cuff.

Officers could wear either epaulettes or shoulder cords on their walking-out tunics (see above for a description of both items). Since this tunic was less formal, shoulder cords were normally worn.

Pouch Belt

Other ranks wore a thick white leather pouch belt over their left shoulder. Officers wore a cloth belt of the regiment's facing colour with officers' cuirassier braid in a corduroy pattern over the left shoulder. The braid was placed so only a thin edging of the facing colour showed along the outside of the belt pouch.

Pouch and Pouch Lid Devices[64]

The cartouche pouch for officers and other ranks was made of black polished leather. The officers had cloth pouch belts in their regiment's facing colour covered by braid, which was in the regiment's button colour. The belt was edged on both sides with cord in the regiment's facing colour. The belt was cut so the pouch was worn on the right side at waist level, about where the two edges of the cuirass joined together, or in the middle of the back at the belt line.

The pouch lid had different decorations as detailed below.

Guard

The other ranks of the Gardes du Corps had a silver-plated guard star on the lid. The lid had two rows of silver trim around the outside edge. The officer's star was silver and the outside trim was a silver baroque pattern inside a silver edge. The troopers of the Guard Cuirassiers had a brass-plated guard star on their pouch. The star of the officers was silver with enamelling.

Line Troopers

The 1st Regiment's pouch device was an oval brass plate with the old Brandenburg eagle from the time of Frederick the Great, which was awarded in 1902.

The 2nd Regiment had a circular centre ornament with the Prussian line eagle hovering over trophies of cannon, drums, and flags. On the eagle's breast was the monogram 'FWR'. On both bottom corners of the pouch lid was a large brass flaming grenade.

The 3rd to 8th Regiments had pouch lids with a circular plate that was just like that worn by the 2nd Regiment, except the eagle did not have a monogram on its chest (Image VI:74).

Line Officers

The pouch of the officer was smaller than that worn by the other ranks, and this, of course, made the pouch lid smaller. It was generally made of black patent leather.[65]

Line officers did not wear a circular plate. Rather, the devices found inside the plates of the other ranks' plates were put on officers' pouch lids without a surrounding plate.

The officers of the 1st Regiment wore the old Brandenburg eagle with a baroque wreath of palms around it. Under the wreath was a banner with the dates '1674' and '1902'. The whole was topped by a crown.

The 2nd Regiment had the cut-out line eagle with trophies and monogram. Cut-out flaming grenades were at the corners.

The pouch lid of officers of the 3rd to 8th Regiments had a cut-out 'FWR' monogram with a crown over it. For line officers, all lid devices were gilt (Image VI:74).[66]

Officer's and Adjutant's Sashes

For full dress, a sash was worn around the waist, tied on the left hip by a slide with tassels descending 10 cm (3.94 inches) above knee level. The sash had two stripes in the Prussian colours, silver with black lines, with netted knots above the tassels.[67] For details on the sash, see §VI-3-1. Adjutants wore the normal adjutant's sash over their right shoulder (see §VI-3-1).

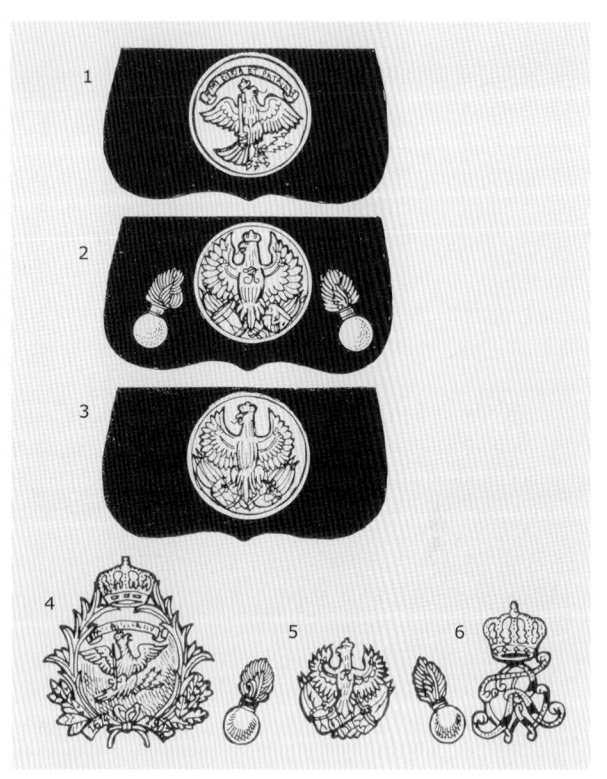

VI:74 Pouch Lid Ornamentations
1. 1st Cuirassier Regiment Other Ranks.
2. 2nd Cuirassier Regiment Other Ranks.
3. 3rd–8th Cuirassier Regiments Other Ranks.
4. Officer's pouch belt, pouch lid decoration for 1st Cuirassier Regiment.
5. Officer's pouch belt, pouch lid decoration for officer of the 2nd Cuirassier Regiment.
6. Pouch lid decoration for officers of the 3rd–8th Cuirassier Regiments.

Sword Belt

A 4.2 mm (0.17 inch) white leather sword belt was worn over the koller and the waffenrock by other ranks. It was 4.2 cm (1.65 inches) wide. It had an open square brass buckle with two prongs for all regiments, except the 6th, the Gardes du Corps, and Guard Cuirassiers, whose buckles were tombac.

Officers wore white leather sword belts faced with button-colour lace and edged with piping in the regiment's facing cloth.

The belt was normally worn under the uniform. The only time the belt was worn over the uniform was when dancing at a court ball and the broadsword was being carried. Adjutants would wear a special, slightly wider, belt over their uniforms with parade and gala uniforms.[68]

Lance
The other ranks of the cuirassiers carried a lance from 1888. They were the first non-lancer units in the German army to be armed with the lance.

Riding Breeches
The riding breeches of the other ranks were white kersey with a reinforcement of white chamois leather. This was the general cavalry model. For walking out, long blue-black trousers were worn during the winter months. They had a red stripe down the outside of each leg. Exceptions to this general rule were the 2nd Regiment, which had crimson stripes, and the 5th, which had rose red piping. During hot weather, white linen trousers were worn.

Officers wore the same breeches and long trousers, although officers' trousers tended to have a tighter cut.

For gala dress, line officers wore trousers of white satin, kerseymere, or kersey. They had trim along the side of the same braid found on the officers' koller.[69]

Footwear
In 1867, the Brandenburg boot was introduced. This was black leather and reached to about mid-thigh. However, the leather above the knee was soft and could be turned down if the wearer wished.

In the 1886–8 period, black boots were introduced that came above the knee in front and had a scooped out section behind the knee. The front section came about 4 cm (1.57 inches) above the knee in front and was scooped out enough in the back of the knee to allow the knee to bend easily.

The two guard regiments wore a special version of jackboot, which was slightly higher in front.[70]

Gauntlet Gloves
The gauntlet gloves were worn for parades and other events when the koller and riding breeches were worn.

The gauntlet gloves were made of white washed leather, and the stitched-on stiff pointed cuff was made of 2.5 mm (0.1 inch) thick white chamois leather. The cuff was at least 14 cm (5.51 inches) long with flaring wings. The wing portion was much wider than the arm and thus stood well away from the rest of the glove.

Many officers, in lieu of the gauntlet glove called for in formal full dress, wore a regular short white glove and added a separate large cuff with the required flaring wings (see, for example, Image VI:67).

Standard Gloves
For gala and social events, short white gloves made of suede, kid leather, wool or cotton were to be worn by officers. The short white glove was worn with the guard's red gala tunic.[71]

Gorget
The 2nd Cuirassiers was given gorgets in 1895 on the anniversary of the Battle of Hohenfriedberg (Images VI:75 and VI:76). The trooper's gorget and its chain were highly polished brass with a German silver ornament in the centre. The ornament consisted of a cartouche bearing the line eagle surrounded by flags and cannon barrels with a baroque plate under it with the date 1745, the year of the battle. The ornament was surmounted by a crown. The NCO's gorget was nickelled and its central ornament (and rim?) were all brass (see Image VI:57). The ornament was the same as above. The officer pattern had the same ornament, but it was a silver/gilt gorget with a gilded rim, the central ornament silvered and gilded, the cartouche red enamelled, the eagle black and gold, the oak leaves green and gold, and the flags silver. The shield and chain used to hold the gorget around the neck were lined with crimson cloth.

The following year, in 1896, the 1st Regiment was also awarded a gorget (Images VI:77, VI:78, also Image VI:75). The ornament for other ranks and officers was much the same. It was a circular centre bearing an old Prussian eagle, flying from the earth to the sun with a motto scroll around it and crown above it. Inside the scroll was a shell-shaped baroque cartouche and below it a 'W II' monogram, and on either side '1674' and '1896'. On either side of the central circle were trophies of armour surrounded by four flags, pikes, and cannons.

The troopers' gorget was in German silver, and the central ornaments were brass. The NCO's gorget was also German silver, but the centre was in silvered metal, with a black enamelled eagle. The officer pattern was plated silver but had a gilded central trophy and a gilt

VI:77 1st Life Cuirassiers Officer's Gorget

VI:75 Gorget Patterns
Top: Gorget pattern for 1st Life Cuirassier Regiment.
Bottom: Gorget pattern for 2nd Cuirassier Regiment.

VI:76 Cuirassier Regiment No. 2 Officer in Waffenrock with Epaulettes and Gorget

VI:78 Cuirassier Regiment No. 1 Officer in Walking Out Tunic (Waffenrock) with Gorget
Note that he is wearing epaulettes with the waffenrock.

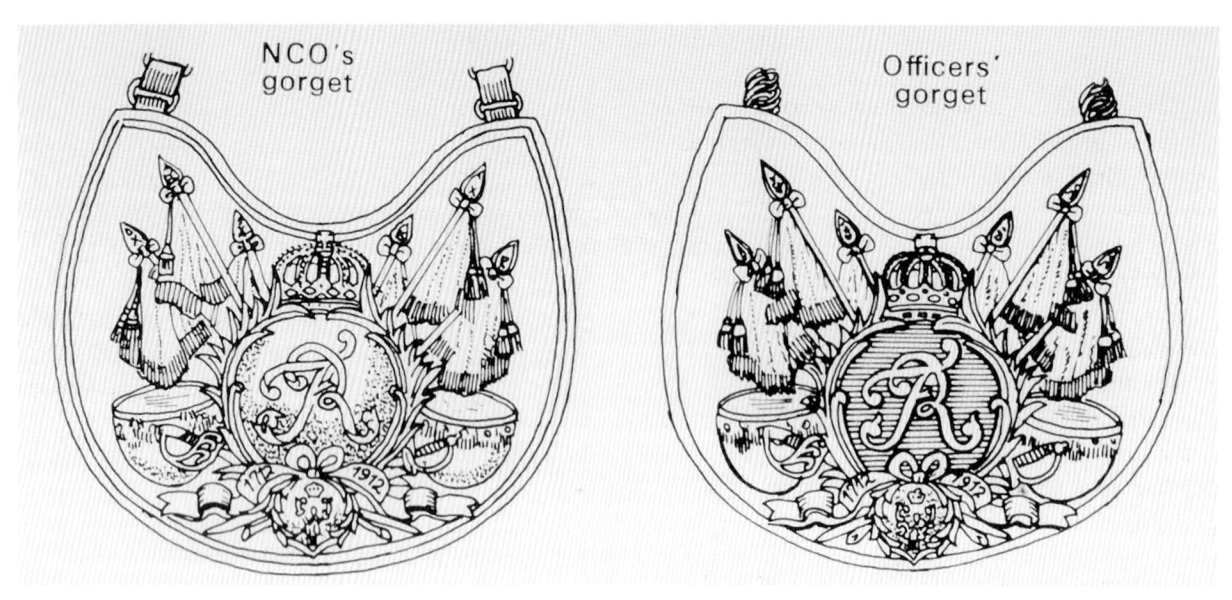

VI:79 Gardes du Corps NCO's and Officer's Gorgets

rim. For officers, the central cartouche was silver, the eagle black and gold, the sun gold, the scroll red and gold with the motto 'Non soli cedit', the earth green, and the sky light blue. Gorgets of the officers of the 1st Regiment were lined with black velvet.

The Gardes du Corps received a large and very elegant brass gorget in 1912 on the 200th anniversary of the birth of Frederick the Great (Images VI:79 and VI:80). The central design on the gorget was an oval with baroque palm leaves around it. The oval had a 'FR' monogram. This was surrounded by flags and kettledrums with crossed swords at the foot. At the bottom was another oval with the initial 'W' with a crown over it and 'II' below it. Just above the bottom oval was a ribbon with '1712' on the left and '1912' on the right. The oval was topped by a large crown.

For other ranks, the central design seems to have been white metal. The central oval for NCOs was gilded. For officers, the metal parts were silver. The oval was enamelled red with the monogram in gilt. The border trim was also silver.

The flat link chain holding the gorget was brass. For officers, it was backed with red cloth.[72]

The gorget was worn with both the full dress and undress tunics.[73] When the cuirass was worn, a type of gorget was worn on the breast of the cuirass. For the Gardes du Corps and the 1st Regiment, this was the central part of the gorget and for the 2nd a small version of the entire gorget.

VI:80 Gardes du Corps Regiment Other Ranks' Gorget

§VI-6-b DRAGOONS

As was the case for dragoons in other armies, German dragoons began their life as infantry mounted on horses, which enabled them to reach the scene of the battle faster. For this reason, their uniforms have always been similar to those of the infantry. In fact, in their early days, the dragoons carried drums.[74]

However, as time passed, they became another arm of the cavalry and lost their mounted infantry role. As cavalry, their role grew in importance, and by the time of the death of Frederick the Great in 1786, there were twelve dragoon regiments in the army. In addition, another two were added before 1806.[75] This was probably to utilise the additional manpower gained from the partitions of Poland.

After Napoleon shattered the Prussian army in 1806, it was reduced from 200,000 men to 40,000. After 1806, six reorganised dragoon regiments were formed, mostly from the odds and ends of the old dragoons. In 1815, the 1st Guard Dragoons were formed. Shortly thereafter, another two dragoon regiments were created, bringing the dragoon total to one guard regiment and eight line regiments.

In 1819, four of the line dragoon regiments were converted to cuirassiers, leaving four line dragoon regiments: the old 3rd Lithuanian, 5th Brandenburg, 6th New Mark, and 7th Rhine. These were renumbered the 1st Lithuanian, 2nd Brandenburg, 3rd New Mark, and 4th Rhine Line Dragoons, and they kept these numbers until 1914. The first three also kept their names until 1914; however, the 4th's Rhine name was changed in the course of time to the 1st Silesian, and this was its subtitle in 1914.

Uniform

Table VI.6.b.1: Dragoons, 1914

Regiment	Tunic Colour	Facings	Button Colour	Litzen	Tunic Variations	Monogram[a]	Plume Colour	Colour of Helmet Plates[b]	Other
1 Guard	Cornflower blue	Red	Yellow	Yellow		VR[c]	White	Tombac & silver[d]	
2 Guard	Cornflower blue	Red	White	White		A[e]	White	Tombac & silver[d]	
1	Cornflower blue	Red	Yellow	–		–	Black	Brass[f]	
2	Cornflower blue	Black	Yellow	–	Note A	GV[g]	Black	Brass[h]	F, G, H
3	Cornflower blue	Pink	White	–		–	Black	Silver[f]	I
4	Cornflower blue	Pale yellow	White	–		–	Black	Silver[i]	
5	Cornflower blue	Red	White	–		–	Black	Silver[i]	
6	Cornflower blue	Black	White	–	Note A	–	Black	Silver[i]	H
7	Cornflower blue	Pink	Yellow	–		–	Black	Brass[i]	
8	Cornflower blue	Yellow	Yellow	–		FRIII[j]	Black	Brass[i]	
9	Cornflower blue	White	Yellow	–		C[k]	Black	Brass[i]	
10	Cornflower blue	White	White	–		AR[m]	Black	Silver[i]	
11	Cornflower blue	Crimson	Yellow	–	Note A	–	Black	Brass[i]	H, J
12	Cornflower blue	Crimson	White	–	Note A	–	Black	Silver[i]	H, J
13	Cornflower blue	Red	Yellow	–	Note B	–	Black	Brass[i]	
14	Cornflower blue	Black	Yellow	–	Notes A, B	–	Black	Brass[i]	H
15	Cornflower blue	Rose red	White	–	Note B	–	Black	Silver[i]	

German Empire

Regiment	Tunic Colour	Facings	Button Colour	Litzen	Tunic Variations	Mono-gram[a]	Plume Colour	Colour of Helmet Plates[b]	Other
16	Cornflower blue	Yellow	White	–	Note C	–	Black	Silver[n]	
17 (Mecklenburg)	Cornflower blue	Red	Yellow	Yellow		FF III[o]	Black	Brass sun & silver coat of arms[p]	
18 (Mecklenburg)	Cornflower blue	Black	White	White	Note L	A[q]	Black	Brass sun & silver coat of arms[p]	
19 (Oldenburg)	Cornflower blue	Black	White	–	Notes A, D	A[r]	Black	Silver & brass star[s]	H
20 (1st Baden)	Cornflower blue	Poppy red	White	–		Crown[t]	White	Silver[u]	
21 (2nd Baden)	Cornflower blue	Light yellow	White	–		–	White	Silver[u]	
22 (3rd Baden)	Cornflower blue	Black	White	–	Notes A, E	–	White	Silver[u]	H
23 (1st Hesse)	Dark green	Red	White	White		L[v]	Black	Silver[w]	K
24 (2nd Hesse)	Dark green	White	White	–		H II[x]	Black	Silver[w]	K
25 (1st Württemberg)	Cornflower blue	White	Yellow	White		O[y]	White	Silver[z]	
26 (2nd Württemberg)	Cornflower blue	Lemon yellow	White	–		W[aa]	Black	Silver[bb]	

Notes: [a] To view drawings of monograms, see §VI-3-18.
[b] For helmet plates, see §VI-3-4 and for special helmet banners, see §VI-3-6.
[c] Queen Victoria of Great Britain (1st Guard).
[d] Guard eagle.
[e] Czarina Alexandra of Russia (2nd Guard).
[f] Guard eagle without star.
[g] King Gustav V of Sweden (3rd).
[h] Dragoon eagle with, from 1913, a shield with the Prussian sceptre.
[i] Dragoon eagle.
[j] Frederick III of Prussia (8th).
[k] King Carol of Rumania (9th).
[l] Dragoon eagle with 'Peninsula-Waterloo-Göhrde' banner.
[m] King Albert of Saxony (10th).
[n] Dragoon eagle with 'Waterloo' banner.
[o] Grand Duke Friedrich Franz III of Mecklenburg-Schwerin (17th).
[p] Dragoon eagle with sunburst and Mecklenburg arms in centre.
[q] Grand Duchess Alexandra of Mecklenburg-Schwerin (18th).
[r] Grand Duke August of Oldenburg (19th).
[s] Dragoon eagle with a star and Oldenburg Arms in centre.
[t] Crown awarded 1869 (20th).
[u] Baden coat of arms (griffin).
[v] Grand Duke Ludwig of Hesse (23rd).
[w] Hessian lion.
[x] Czar Nicholas II of Russia (the 'H' is a Cyrillic 'N') (24th).
[y] Queen Olga of Württemberg (25th).
[z] Württemberg coat of arms.
[aa] King Wilhelm of Württemberg (26th).
[bb] Württemberg coat of arms with star of the Order of the Crown of Württemberg on it.

A: Velvet collars and cuffs (Herr, *German Cavalry*, p. 347).
B: White piping on collar and cuffs (Herr, *German Cavalry*, p. 349).
C: White piping on all edges of the uniform.
D: White shoulder straps (ibid.).
E: Poppy red piping around collar, shoulder straps, pocket flaps, and on the front (ibid.).
F: Awarded a shield with the old Brandenburg sceptre in June 1913.
G: The 2nd Dragoons wore a 2.5 cm (0.98 inch) yelllow Prussian eagle, a small version of the helmet plate, on their *mutze*, an undress cap worn for walking out. This was not part of their full dress uniform, but is mentioned because of its interest. It is said that this badge was earned during the Wars of Liberation (1813–15). The men of the regiment were riding bareback to water their horses. They wore soft caps not helmets. Suddenly, they were attacked by French cavalry. They were able to repel the attack in spite of their clear disadvantages (Herr, *German Cavalry*, p. 344).
H: The facing colours were in velvet. The others wore woollen cloth (Herr, *German Cavalry*, p. 347).
I: Awarded a guard eagle (with outstretched wings) without star in March 1897 (Herr, *German Cavalry*, p. 325).
J: The crimson was so dark as to be almost purple/violet (Herr, *German Cavalry*, p. 347).
K: Hessian helmets had round front visors (Herr, *German Cavalry*, p. 326).
L: After 1894 black velvet (ibid., p. 348).

Helmet

The helmet worn by dragoons was very similar to that of the infantry, except the front brim was cut square. A variation from this was the two Hessian dragoon regiments, the 23rd and 24th, which had rounded front visors like the infantry. The helmet was made of boiled black leather that was then polished to a high shine. The front brim had a strip of metal trim.

All regiments wore plumes in full dress. Up to 1896 both officers and men wore horsehair plumes. After 1896 officers wore buffalo hair plumes. See Table VI.6.b.1 for information on what helmet plate was worn on the front and its colour.

The badges the regiments wore on their helmets as members of the different states are shown in the images of helmet plates at §VI-3-4. In 1913, the 2nd Dragoons were given an oval with a Prussian sceptre. The oval was topped by a crown (Image VI:81).

VI:81 2nd Dragoon Helmet with Medallion and Crown on Eagle Awarded in 1913
The medallion has the sceptre of the electors of Brandenburg. Note the cross on the eagle's chest denoting a reserve officer.

Tunic[76]

The standard tunic for dragoons was cornflower blue with a standing collar and Swedish cuffs. Cornflower blue is a mid-blue (see Image C80). After 1900, officers tended to wear a very pale shade – perhaps down to a pale sky blue – of the colour. This made them stand out from the troopers.[77] The exceptions to this were the two Hessian dragoon regiments, which retained their old dark green tunic when Hesse joined the confederation.

The tunic was single-breasted with eight domed buttons down the front (Image VI:82). There were two buttons at the back at waist level to hold up the waist belt. The back skirt of the tunic was slit and each side had two vertical scalloped pocket flaps with two buttons (three when the waist button is counted) on each side.

The other ranks of all regiments wore a pointed shoulder strap. The collar front was normally rounded. Some regiments had litzen on their collars. For these regiments, both Guard Dragoons and the 23rd (Hessian), the collars were higher and cut square. Other regiments with litzen on the collars, the 17th, 18th (both Mecklenburg with guard litzen), and 25th (Württemberg with normal litzen), kept rounded collars until 1896 and 1892. The 17th and 18th changed to a square cut in 1896.[78] The 25th wore square collars after 1892.[79]

VI:82 Prussian Dragoons Other Ranks
Note the square-cut brim of the helmet worn by almost all dragoons, the open-faced buckle on his waist belt and the shape of his helmet badge. This shape of eagle was worn by the majority of the dragoon regiments.

The collar, Swedish cuff, and shoulder strap were all in the regiment's facing colour. See Table VI.6.b.1 for colours.

The buttons were plain domed without any devices. See Table VI.6.b.1 for the colours assigned to each regiment.

The other ranks' collar was plain unless it had litzen or NCO lace (compare Image VI:82 with Image VI:83). The collar was to be 6 cm (2.36 inches) high according to regulations,[80] but many officers wore it higher as that was fashionable.

The Swedish cuffs had two buttons. Some carried litzen (Table VI.6.b.1). NCOs wore their lace on it as well as the collar. Regulations state the cuff was to be 4.75 cm (1.87 inches) high.[81]

The pointed shoulder strap colours are listed in Table VI.6.b,1, as are what regiments had monograms to carry on them. After 1889 regiments that did not bear a monogram carried a number. For other ranks, the monogram or number was yellow unless the shoulder strap was yellow or white. In those cases, the monogram or number was red. An exception was the 23rd, which had a red shoulder strap and a white monogram for other ranks.[82]

Officers wore epaulettes. The epaulettes followed the normal rules as to whether or not there was fringe and how thick the fringe was. The crescent was in the button colour. The area inside the crescent and shoulder pad was either silver metal webbing or, in the cases of the 2nd, 6th, 11th, 12th, 14th, 19th, and 22nd Regiments, velvet.

Riding Breeches and Trousers[83]

Riding Breeches

For other ranks, the riding breeches were a blue-black mixture, tending towards black, for all regiments. Officers' breeches were dark blue for all regiments. For all ranks, they were without piping.

Trousers

Trousers were worn for walking out and undress during the winter months from November to April. They were a very dark blue-black. Trousers were not standard issue for other ranks, but could be bought. Most regiments had trousers with poppy red piping 1.5 mm (0.06 inch) wide down the outside seam on each leg. Exceptions were: the 3rd, 7th, and 15th with pink piping; the 11th and 12th with crimson piping; and the 24th with white piping. During the summer months, trousers of white linen without piping were worn by all ranks of most regiments. However, the Württemberg regiments (Nos 25 and 26) did not wear the white trousers, except for minor exceptions.[84]

Officers also wore the white linen trousers to levees and balls.

Gala Trousers

Gala trousers were worn by officers for state events and balls and their own weddings. For most regiments, they were cornflower blue with two 4 cm (1.57 inch) broad stripes down the outside of each leg. Between the two broad stripes was a band of narrow 1.5 mm (0.06 inch) wide piping. The stripes were 0.5 mm (0.02 inch) from the piping. The stripes and piping were in the regiment's facing colour. These were velvet for the 2nd, 6th, 11th, 12th, 14th, 19th, and the 22nd Regiments. After 1894, the 18th also had stripes and piping of velvet. The 22nd was a bit of an exception in that its central piping was red, while the two outer velvet stripes were black piped in red on the outer sides.

VI:83 Dragoon NCO's Walking-Out Tunic

The major exception to this system was the two Hessian dragoon regiments, the 23rd and the 24th. They had black jersey gala trousers. The 23rd had red stripes and piping and the 24th white.

Pouch Belt[85]

Most of the other ranks wore a plain white leather belt (Image VI:82). The 23rd and 24th Hessian dragoon other ranks had a black pouch belt.

The officer's pouch belt in most regiments was cloth of the regiment's tunic colour covered in braid in the regiment's button colour. An edge of cloth 2 mm (0.08 inch) wide showed on each side of the braid. The braid was to be 4.6 cm (1.81 inches) wide. The exceptions to this were the two Hessian regiments, the 23rd and 24th. Their belt was red Moroccan leather. The belt was overlaid with lace of the button colour, silver, and had trim on the edges as was done with the balance of the dragoons, i.e. the red leather showed. A further difference was that the braid of these regiments had two red stripes along the length of the belt, which divided the braid into three parts.

The two Hessian regiments, the 23rd and 24th, had a special undress pouch belt which was worn when the dress pouch belt was not required. It was black Moroccan leather with a row of silver domed studs down the centre (Images VI:84 and VI:85).

The pouch belts of some non-Prussian regiments, 17th and 18th Mecklenburg, the 23rd and 24th Hessian, and the 25th Württemberg, were embellished by decorations. The 17th, 18th, 23rd, and 24th had a lion's head near the front top of the pouch belt. The head anchored two small link chains which connected to an oval plate which held two small signal pipes or whistles. The embellishments of all four regiments were silver or silver-plated.[86] See Image VI:86 for the decorations for the 17th and 18th Dragoons, Image VI:87 for those of the 23rd and 24th, and Image VI:88 for the 25th's. The drawings also show how the 23rd and 24th's pouch belt differed from the 17th and 18th's by having their two red stripes in the silver lace.

The 25th Württemberg had a different set of decorations. They had, on the upper part of the belt, a silver-plated oval plate. Resting on the plate was a gilt crowned shield, which held a 'WII' monogram. From this shield fell two small linked silver-plated chains. The chains went to another silver-plated oval plate

VI:84 Dragoon Regiment 24 (Hessian), Undress Pouch Belt

VI:85 Dragoon Regiment 24 (Hessian) Lieutenant
He is wearing a frock coat and service pouch belt with studs on it.

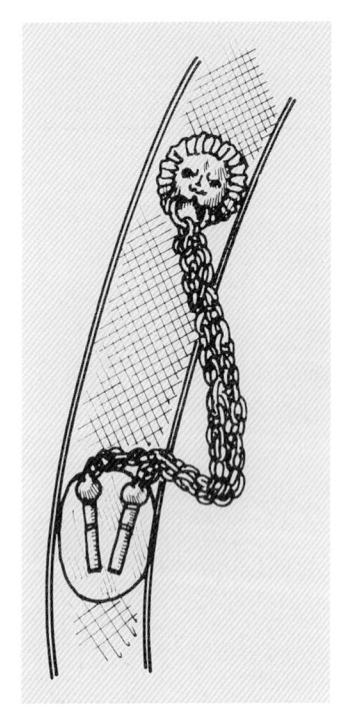

VI:86 Dragoon Regiment 17 and 18, Pouch Belt and Decoration

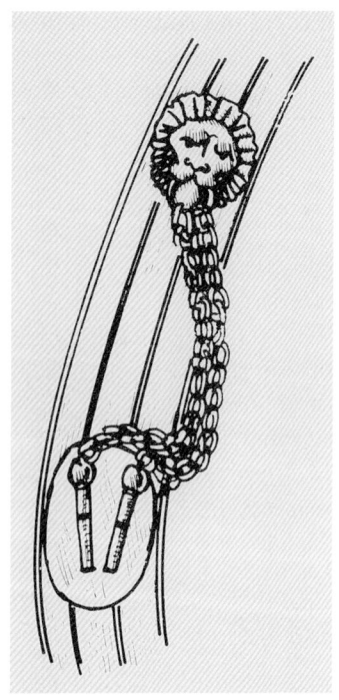

VI:87 Dragoon Regiments 23 and 24, Pouch Belt and Decoration

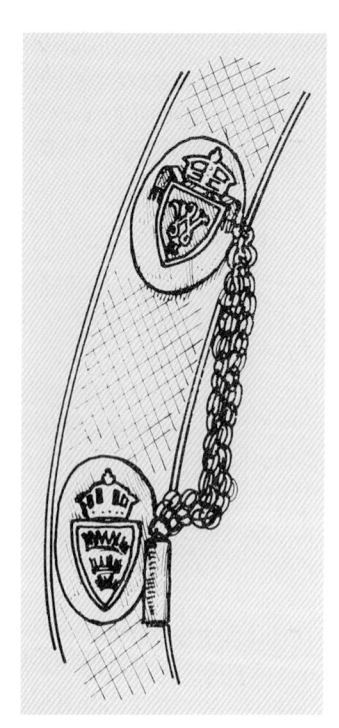

VI:88 Dragoon Regiment 25, Pouch Belt Decoration

with another crowned shield in gilt. The lower shield held the coat of arms of Württemberg. The chains went to small tube on the side of the lower shield. The tube held a small silver signal pipe or whistle (Image VI:88).

Other ranks of the 25th also had these embellishments on their white leather pouch belts. For them, the upper plate was German silver with a brass 'WII' and crown, and the lower plate had the same metals used in it. The chains, tube, and whistle were German silver.[87]

Pouch

The decorations on the covers of the dragoon pouch varied widely. Here as much as anywhere an old adage, 'German dress regulations consists of one paragraph and five pages of exceptions' applies. In addition, coverage of this subject is patchy and the sources do not agree. Table VI.6.b.2 and its detail is an attempt to provide a synthesis of the available information:

The Prussian guard regiments had pouch ornaments consisting of the star of the Order of the Black Eagle (guard star). The 1st Guard Regiment had brass badges (gilt for officers), and the 2nd Guard Regiment had white metal (silver for the officers).

See Image VI:89 for examples of some of the pouch badges.

Belt

The other ranks of the dragoon regiments, except for the 23rd and 24th Hessian, wore the standard cavalry belt (see §VI-3-1). The Hessians wore a black belt with a rectangular buckle. The buckle had the crown of the grand duke.

Officers wore their sabre belt under their tunic.

Boots

The black leather riding boots reached to just below the knees in front. They were cut about 6 cm (2.36 inches) lower in back. A smaller and lighter boot was worn with trousers.

Table VI.6.b.2: Line Pouch Ornaments – 1914

Regiment	Other Ranks	Officers	Regiment	Other Ranks	Officers
1	A	B	14	A	B
2	A	B	15	A	B
3	C	C	16	A	B
4	A	B	17 (Meck)	D	E
5	A	B	18 (Meck)	D	E
6	A	B	19 (Olden)	A	F
7	A	B	20 (Baden)	G	B
8	A	B	21 (Baden)	G	B
9	A	B	22 (Baden)	G	B
10	A	B	23 (Hesse)	H	I
11	A	B	24 (Hesse)	H	I
12	A	B	25 (Württ)	J	K
13	A	B	26 (Württ)	L	M

Sources: Marrion, *Lancers, etc.*, p. 34; Herr, *German Cavalry*, pp. 67–72 and 368–73; Knötel, *Deutsche Heer*, vol. 2, plates 77–84a; Laine, *L'Armée Allemande*, pp. 121–35.

Notes:
A: A brass circular plate with the Prussian eagle impressed in the centre upon a trophy of arms, drums, and flags. The rim of the plate was raised.
B: A gilded FWR monogram with a crown above.
C: Officers had a gilt guard star with gilt flaming grenades set at angles in each corner. The star and grenades were brass for other ranks.
D: A Mecklenburg coat of arms and star in brass.
E: A silver-plated pouch, the lid edged with gilt and a gilt Mecklenburg star with a silver Mecklenburg coat of arms in the centre.
F: A gilded Gothic FWR monogram with a crown above.
G: Other ranks had circular white metal plates impressed with the Baden griffin clutching a shield in its front paws, all on a trophy of arms.
H: NCOs and troopers wore a pouch ornament consisting of a brass L with a crown above it.
I: Officers wore an L with a crown over it in silver, surrounded by a gilded half-open oak and laurel wreath and with the edge of the pouch decorated with a gilt trim.
J: The NCOs and troopers had plain pouches.
K: Officers had a gilded Gothic KR and crown ornament. This stood for Karl Rex (Karl, King of Württemberg), and it was worn even after his death in 1891.
L: For NCOs and troopers, the star of the Order of the Crown of Württemberg in white metal after 1905. Prior to that, they had plain pouches.
M: Officers wore the star of the Order of the Crown of Württemberg in silver with an enamelled centre after 1905. Prior to that, they wore the badge type K.

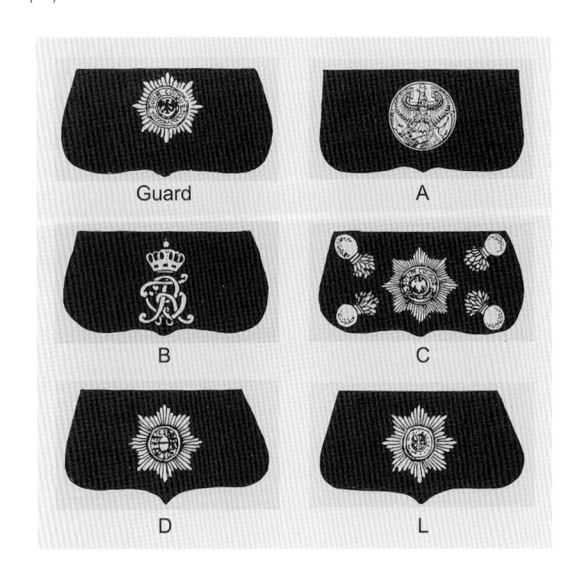

VI:89 Pouch Belt Ornaments Worn by Certain Dragoon Regiments
Guard: Ornament worn by guard dragoon regiments. It is a star of the Order of the Black Eagle.
A. Brass plate worn by other ranks of Prussian dragoon regiments.
B. Monogram 'FWR' and crown worn by Prussian officers and Baden officers.
C. Star with flaming grenades worn by the 3rd Horse Grenadier (Dragoon) Regiment.
D. Star with Mecklenburg coat of arms on top of it.
L. Star of the Order of the Crown (Württemberg).

§VI-6-c LANCERS (UHLANS)

The lancers were considered somewhat exotic by the early staid Prussians, thus becoming a bit of a collection of oddments of regiments and units. This is, in part, shown by their coming last on the cavalry list for many years.

An ideal example of the unique quality of the lancers is what became the 6th Lancers in 1815. They had formerly been one of the most famous of the Free Corps of the wars of German Liberation, Free Corps Lutzow.[88] The Lutzow Free Corps was composed of infantry and cavalry. They acted as guerillas and spies behind French lines in the campaigns of 1813–14. It had a reputation of being composed of students, artists, poets, intellects, and adventurers. They were known for their daring attacks and crazy frivolity out of battle. In addition to being the basis of the 6th Lancers, the Free Corps also formed the 25th Prussian Line Infantry.[89]

It is said their dress was the basis for the German black, red, and gold national colours. They did not have uniforms, so they dyed their civilian clothes black to have a uniform colour. In their dress, they wore gold-coloured buttons. On their black clothes, the rank was noted by red trim. This combination of colours became associated with the republican movement in Germany and in time translated into the flag.

The 7th Regiment (Rhine) was created in 1815 from the cavalry of Free Corps Hellwig, a Saxon lancer regiment of the Prince Clemens and squadrons of cavalry commanded by Major Von Shill in Hamburg.

The 8th was formed in 1815 from the men of the Russian-German Legion, which had been created in 1812 as a home for German deserters and prisoners of war who wanted to fight the French. In time, the legion grew to a strength of two hussar regiments. Command of the regiment passed to the Prussians in 1814. In 1815, personnel from the two hussar regiments of the legion were used to form the 8th Lancers (2nd Rhineland). The subtitle of the regiment was changed to East Prussia in 1860, a title they kept until 1914.

The 9th Lancers were formed in 1860 from squadrons of the 4th and 8th Cuirassiers and the 5th, 7th, and 8th Lancer Regiments. The 10th Lancers were formed in the same year, from squadrons of the 1st and 5th Cuirassiers and the 1st and 2nd Lancers.

The 11th Lancers were also formed in 1860 from squadrons of the 6th and 7th Cuirassiers, as well as squadrons of the 3rd, 5th, and 6th Lancers. The 12th Lancers were formed that year too, from the 2nd and 3rd Cuirassiers, as well as the 4th and 8th Lancer Regiments.

After the Austro-Prussian War, Prussia seized states or parts of states that it had defeated, often because the land was needed for a clear path to Prussia's Rhineland, and sometimes merely because they had opposed Prussia. Most notably, the land was taken from the kingdom of Hanover, the electorate of Hesse-Cassel, the duchy of Nassau, and the Free City of Frankfurt am Main. This led to more regiments being formed.

The 13th Lancer Regiment (1st Hanoverian) was created by squadrons from three guard lancer regiments and a squadron from the Gardes du Corps. The 14th Lancer Regiment (2nd Hanoverian) was formed from squadrons of the 4th, 8th, 9th, and 12th Prussian Lancers. Later, in 1899, Kaiser Wilhelm invented, completely from his imagination, a historical link for the regiment with the Hanoverian Guard Cuirassiers.

The 16th Lancer Regiment, with its subtitle Altmark referring back to old Prussia, is a less obvious creation of the 1866 expansion. It was made by drawing squadrons from the 2nd, 5th, 6th, and 7th Prussian Lancers. In the Franco-Prussian War, the 16th took part in Von Bredow's famous death ride at the Battle of Mars-le-Tour.

After the Austro-Prussian War, Saxony was brought into the North German confederacy and assigned to supply two lancer regiments. It did this by creating two new ones. The 17th Saxon Lancers were created in 1867 from the Saxon Guard Reiter Regiment and the 1st and 3rd Reiter Regiments. The 18th Saxon Lancers were created in 1867 from the 1st, 2nd, and 3rd Reiter Regiments.

In 1905, a third Saxon lancer regiment was formed, the 21st (Royal Saxon) Lancers. It seems to have been created by budding off personnel from the other two Saxon lancer regiments.

After the Franco-Prussian War, the kingdom of Württemberg became part of the German Empire. It created two line lancer regiments, the 19th and

20th, as part of the general army reorganisation that took place at that time. The 19th (1st Württemberg) Lancers were budded off from the 1st Württemberg Reiter Regiment in 1871. As such, they kept this Reiter regiment's history and formation date of 1683. The 20th (2nd Württemberg) Lancers were budded off from the 3rd Württemberg Reiter Regiment in 1871. This allowed them to keep the 3rd Reiter Regiment formation date of 1809 and history.

Uniform

Table VI.6.c.1: Cavalry Lancer Uniform

Regiment	Facing Colour	Button	Czapska Mortarboard Cover	Plastron	Collar and Cuff Colour	Collar Piping Colour[a]	Litzen on Collar and Cuff[b]	Epaulette Field	Monograms on Shoulders	Notes
1st Guard	White, piped red	White	White	White, piped red	Red	none	Two rows of litzen in white	White	None	A, B, C
2nd Guard	Red	Yellow	Red	Red	Red	none	Two rows of litzen in yellow	Red	None	A, B, C
3rd Guard	Golden yellow	White	Golden Yellow	Yellow	Golden yellow	none	Two rows of litzen in white	Yellow	None	A, B, C
1st	Red	Yellow	White	Red	Poppy red	Blue	None	White	'A III' surmounted by a crown	D
2nd	Red	Yellow	Red	Red	Poppy red	Blue	None	Red	None	D
3rd	Red	Yellow	Yellow	Red	Poppy red	Blue	None	Yellow	'A II' surmounted by a crown	D
4th	Red	Yellow	Light blue	Red	Poppy red	Blue	None	Light blue	None	
5th	Red	White	White	Red	Poppy red	Blue	None	White	None	
6th	Red	White	Red	Red	Poppy red	Blue	None	Red	'CR IX' surmounted by a crown	
7th	Red	White	Yellow	Red	Poppy red	Blue	None	Yellow	None	E
8th	Red	White	Light blue	Red	Poppy red	Blue	None	Light blue	None	
9th	White	Yellow	White	White	White	Blue	None	White	None	
10th	Crimson	Yellow	Crimson	Crimson	Crimson	Blue	None	Crimson	None	
11th	Yellow	Yellow	Yellow	Yellow	Lemon yellow	Blue	None	Yellow	None	

Regiment	Facing Colour	Button	Czapska Mortarboard Cover	Plastron	Collar and Cuff Colour	Collar Piping Colour[a]	Litzen on Collar and Cuff[b]	Epaulette Field	Monograms on Shoulders	Notes
12th	Light blue, piped white	Yellow	Light blue	Light blue piped white	Light blue Collar: white piping Cuffs: white piping around the top	White	None	Light blue	None	F
13th	White	White	White	White	White	Blue	None	White	'WR II' surmounted by a crown	G
14th	Crimson	White	Crimson	Crimson	Crimson	Blue	None	Crimson	None	H
15th	Yellow	White	Yellow	Yellow	Lemon yellow	Blue	None	Yellow	None	
16th	Light blue, piped white	White	Light blue	Light blue piped white	Light blue Collar: white piping Cuffs: white piping around the top	White	None	Light blue	'GR' surmounted by a crown	F
17th (Saxon)	Crimson	Yellow	White	Crimson piped white	Crimson collar: white piping around the bottom Cuff: white piping around the top	Light blue	Two rows of guard litzen in yellow	Light blue[c]	Crown	F, I
18th (Saxon)	Crimson	Yellow	Crimson	Crimson piped white	Crimson collar: white piping around the bottom Cuff: white piping around the top	Light blue	Two rows of litzen in white	Light blue[c]	None	F, I

Regiment	Facing Colour	Button	Czapska Mortar-board Cover	Plastron	Collar and Cuff Colour	Collar Piping Colour[a]	Litzen on Collar and Cuff[b]	Epaulette Field	Monograms on Shoulders	Notes
19th (Württemberg)	Red	White	Red	Red	Red	Blue	Two rows of litzen in white	Red	'KR' surmounted by a crown	J
20th (Württemberg)	Yellow	Yellow	Yellow	Yellow	Lemon yellow	Blue	None	Yellow	'KR' surmounted by a crown	J
21st (Saxon)	Crimson	White	Light blue	Crimson piped white	Crimson collar: white piping around the bottom Cuff: white piping around the top	Light blue	Two rows of litzen in white	Light blue[c]	Crown	F, I
1st Bavarians	Crimson	Yellow	Crimson	Crimson	Crimson	Steel green[d]	None	Crimson	None	K, L
2nd Bavarians	Crimson	White	Crimson	Crimson	Crimson	Steel green[d]	None	Crimson	None	L

Source: Marrion, *Lancers, etc.*, pp. 76–7 and 87–92.
Notes: [a] Cuffs did not have piping except as shown below.
[b] NCOs only had one bar of litzen on their collar because of the NCO lace. The cuff in all cases had one bar of litzen when the collar had litzen. The litzen was in the chapter shape unless otherwise noted.
[c] All-metal epaulettes.
[d] This colour (*stahlgrun*) was a dark green with an olive green overtone

A: Guard eagle and silver star.
B: Guard lace.
C: Eagle in button colour.
D: Monogram 'FWR' on helmet eagle on an oval shield.
E: In 1913 given a guard eagle without a star.
F: White piping on top of cuffs.
G: Guard eagle with guard star and 'Peninsula-Waterloo-Garzia Hernandez' banner on helmet.
H: Same banner as worn by 13th Lancers on helmet.
I: Yellow star with white Saxon coat of arms on helmet.
J: White Württemberg coat of arms on helmet.
K: Helmet badge in button colour.
L: Yellow Bavarian coat of arms on helmet.

Headdress[90]

The German lancers wore a helmet of a special shape called a *czapska*.[91] The helmet body was fairly small and did not come down anywhere close to the ears. It was made of highly polished black lacquered leather for both officers and troopers. Coming out of the top was a narrow round stem, which, at its top, had a flat crown, often called a mortarboard because of its shape. Near the top of the stem, it swelled out to reach the edges of the mortarboard (Image VI:90).

On the front of the czapska, the guard regiments had a guard star on a guard eagle. The eagle matched the button collar, and the star was always silver (Image VI:91).

The eagles of the Prussian line lancers were somewhat complicated as there were several different styles worn. The first general rule to note is that the eagle colour followed the button colour.

VI:90 Standard Prussian Lancer Helmet (Czapska)
The helmet and the badge on the front were the norm for most of the Prussian lancer regiments and were supposed to be just like the badge worn by line infantry regiments. Note where cap lines are attached on the right side of the mortarboard.

VI:91 Czapska of the 3rd Guard Lancer Regiment
Note the guard star and guard eagle. This helmet belonged to an NCO. Note the black and white colouring on the slides and tassels. Note also the black and white horsehair plume denoting NCO status.

VI:92 3rd Line Lancers Officer's Czapska
Note the shape of the officer's tassel at the end of the cap line and the black and white darts.

VI:93 13th Prussian Lancers Czapska
Note the honour scroll denoting service in the Napoleonic Wars. Note also the eagle on this helmet – the guard eagle with guard star worn by this regiment, which was the only regiment in the German army to have a guard eagle and a Napoleonic banner. The Kaiser was the colonel-in-chief of the regiment. The device for securing the cap line shows quite clearly in this photograph.

§VI-6 Prussian Cavalry   745

VI:94 7th Lancers Other Ranks' Helmet
Note the guard eagle without a star. This helmet's white metal badge was worn after June 1913.

VI:96 Lancer Regiment 20 (Württemberg) Officer's Czapska

VI:95 Saxon Regiment 17. NCO's Czapska
Note eight-pointed star with the Saxon coat of arms surrounded by a laurel wreath and topped by a crown.

VI:97 1st Bavarian Lancer Regiment's Helmet

The 1st to 3rd Lancers had a standard cavalry eagle with upturned wings. But these eagles had an oval plaque on the breast with the monogram 'FWR' on it (Image VI:92). The 13th Lancers had a guard eagle with a star and the battle honours 'Peninsula-Waterloo-Garzia Hernandez' (Image VI:93). The 14th Regiment had a standard eagle with the same battle honours as the 13th.

Regulations stated that the standard eagle, which was worn by the rest of the Prussian lancer regiments, was to be the same as that worn on the infantry pickelhaube (Image VI:90). Its size was to be 9.5 cm (3.7 inches) high and 14 cm (5.5 inches) wide. In actuality, however, lancer units often wore larger badges.[92] The badge was an eagle with upturned wings. On its breast the eagle carried the block letters 'FR'. A Fatherland banner was above the letters.

In 1913 the 7th Lancers were granted a guard eagle without a guard star (Image VI:94).[93] Unusually for a regiment wearing this type of device, their 'guard eagle' was actually a guard eagle with a squared crosspiece on the sword, an eagle on the sceptre, and the guard eagle tail feather pattern.

The 17th, 18th, and 21st Regiments had the Saxon star with the Saxon coat of arms on their helmets (Image VI:95). In the 17th and 18th Regiments, the star was yellow, and the coat of arms was white. In the 21st, the star was white, and the coat of arms was yellow.

The helmets of the 19th and 20th Regiments carried the Württemberg coat of arms in white on the front (Image VI:96).

The Bavarian 1st and 2nd Lancer Regiments had the arms of Bavaria in yellow. In 1914, the laurels were removed from the coat of arms.[94] This created a cleaner look (Image VI:97).

The 3rd Lancers had a wide band of gold braid around the helmet at the base of the helmet stem.

Prussian Mortarboard
The regulation size of the mortarboard was 14.5 cm by 14.5 cm (5.71 inches by 5.71 inches). However, this could vary slightly depending on the body size of the wearer. A mortarboard the author measured was 14.61 cm by 14.61 cm (5.75 inches by 5.75 inches). The stem of the sample measured had a diameter of about 5.08 cm (2 inches). Below the stem the parade facings on the underside of the mortarboards of the officers of the 3rd Lancers had gold braid. This was a gift from Czar Alexander of Russia in 1862. The braid was 3.8 cm (1.5 inches) wide.[95]

With only two exceptions, the chin scales for all regiments were brass regardless of their regiment's button colour.[96] The exceptions were the 21st (Saxon) and the 2nd Bavarian Lancers. Both had white metal or silver-coloured chin scales.[97]

The top of the mortarboard was black leather. For full dress, the bottom of the mortarboard and sides of the stem were covered with a cloth whose colour varied by regiment (see Table VI.6.c.1 for colour). For officers, the edges of the cloth were trimmed with button-colour braid. The other ranks had white braid. The top of the mortarboard was left uncovered.

On the centre of the left side of the mortarboard was a large oval metal state cockade. For Prussia, it was black and white (Image VI:90); Saxony, green and white; Württemberg, red and black; and Bavaria, light blue and white. For officers, the white part was silver cord (Image VI:93).

VI:98 One-Year Volunteer Wearing His Lancer's Helmet
Note the regulation tilt of the helmet to the right.

VI:99 Prussian Lancer Other Ranks
Note how he has moved the cap lines to hang to the side rather than down to the back for this photograph. Also note the other ranks' girdle around his waist.

VI:100 Saxon Lancer Other Ranks
This man does not have his cap lines fastened to his helmet. Note how the cap lines are worn when not attached to the helmet.

A horsehair plume was worn, coming out from behind the cockade. Buffalo hair plumes were introduced in 1895 and after that date officers' plumes could be made of either. It looked exactly like a horse's tail in that it rose up and then drooped down (Image VI:97). The plumes of generals were made of egret feathers. The horsehair plume was white for troopers in all states. In Prussia, it was black and white for NCOs and officers (Image VI:91). The NCOs and officers in Bavarian regiments wore light blue and white; Saxons, green and white; and Württembergers, a mixture of black, white, and red.

Because of the weight of the cockade and the plume on the left side of the helmet, the regulations provided that the helmet be worn cocked to the right to offset the weight. The front visor (peak) was to be worn at all times 3 cm (1.18 inches) over the right eyebrow and 5 cm (1.97 inches) above the left eyebrow.[98] However, another respected source states that regulations called for the front visor to cover the right eyebrow (Image VI:98).[99] Whatever the exact rule, the way it was worn gave the lancers a jaunty look.

Two cap lines were fastened to a hook on the back right of the mortarboard, wrapped around the stem and fell to about the upper middle of the back. Then they looped up and came up to the collar in the back, where they separated with one strand going around each side of the collar. They were then caught up and hung just below the epaulette on the wearer's left side tunic breast (Image VI:99).

With the Saxons, when mounted, the cap line went from the helmet to the right epaulette. From there, it looped across the right breast to the collar in front. At the collar, the two cap lines separated, ran around the collar, and joined in back. There, they joined together, fell down the back and then up to the left shoulder epaulette, where the tassel showed in front, high on the left chest near the epaulette (Image VI:100).

When the soldier was not mounted, the cap line was not hooked to the czapska. Instead, the cap lines were anchored to the right epaulette. From there, they looped across the chest below the first loop and hooked to the left epaulette near the tassels.

The cap lines were white linen cord for troopers. Officers wore silk cords with darts in the state's colours. The guard regiments had flounders above their tassels. Guard NCOs had officers' cap lines, but only their tassels, flounders, and slides had the state's colours. Line NCOs had troopers' cap lines, but the fringe and tassels were in the state colours.

VI:101 Lancer's Tunic (Ulanka) with Plastron
The bar on the right sleeve is for attending the Dresden riding school. Note NCO lace on collar and cuffs.

VI:102 Two German Soldiers
The man on the right is wearing a lancer's tunic without a lancer's girdle. On his left upper arm the badge shows he was a trained machine-gun specialist.

Ulanka[100]

The Prussian lancers and the Württemberg contingent wore a dark blue double-breasted tunic called an *ulanka*. The uniform of the 19th and 20th Württemberg Lancers followed those of the Prussian lancers almost exactly, but they, of course, had the Württemberg coat of arms, cockades, plume colours, cap line, darts, etc. The Saxons wore cornflower blue (more a mid-blue) and the Bavarians steel green.

The ulanka had two sets of seven buttons running down the front, one on either side of the chest. For other ranks, they were nickel (white) or tombac (yellow), depending on the regiment's button colour (Table VI.6.c.1) Like all lancer tunics, the buttons were wider apart near the top of the chest and closer together as they moved down to the waist (Images VI:101 and VI:102). In full dress, a detached plastron was worn (see Table VI.6.c.1 for the colour of the plastron). The red piping on the 1st Guard Lancers' plastron recalled that they had, until 1860, worn a red plastron.[101] In 1895, white piping replaced light blue on the collars and cuffs of the 12th and 16th Prussian Regiments, who were authorised to wear white piping on their plastrons. The plastrons of the 17th and 18th Saxon Lancers had white piping from 1867 (Image VI:108).[102]

With the exception of the 12th, 16th, 17th, 18th, and 21st Regiments, the lancers' tunic had trim and their collars and cuffs in the regiments' facing colour. The exception regiments had white trim. The trim outlined where the plastron would be, and from the plastron continued down on both sides of the ulanka until it reached the bottom of the tunic's skirt. The bottom of the skirt was piped in this colour all the way around, as were the seams on the back of the sleeves.

The back seam of the ulanka was also piped in this colour. This trim started at the arm hole and went down to the two buttons used to hold up the lancer's girdle. From there it went straight down to the trim along the bottom of the skirt.

As noted above, the 12th, 16th, 17th, 18th, and 21st Regiments were exceptions. They did not have trim on their arm and back seam in their facing colour and their collars and cuffs were not in that colour. The 12th and 16th Lancers were Prussian regiments. Their arm and back seam trim was white. The collar for both regiments was light blue with white piping around the top. On the cuffs they both had white piping around the top of their light blue cuffs. This gave them a very different look from the normal Prussian lancer regiments, which had dark blue trim. This dated back to army orders of 1889.[103] The 17th, 18th, and 21st were Saxon lancers, and they traditionally had white trim at the bottom of their crimson collar and at the top of the cuffs (Table VI.6.c.1).[104]

In photographs, the lancers' dress could appear rather dark (Images VI:103 and VI:104). But in person, with their plastrons, they could be quite colourful (Images VI:105 and VI:106).

On the back skirts of the tunic, outside the lines that continued down from the back seams, were two false pockets. There were three buttons on either skirt, the top one at waist level and the others below that in a scallop pattern. These were connected by trim in the facing colours with the exceptions noted above. The trim was scalloped. An example of a tunic of a second

VI:103 Thuringian (Saxon Duchies) Lancer Regiment 6

VI:104 One-Year Volunteer 3rd Guard Lancers
Note plume and white pouch belt.

VI:105 3rd Guard Lancers Bandmaster
He wore a red plume. Note his musician's wing and the fringe hanging from the wings.

VI:106 20th Württemberg Lancers
Note the Württemberg coat of arms and czapska. This regiment wore a yellow plastron, yellow trim, and lemon yellow collar and cuffs.

lieutenant in the Württemberg lancers from the early twentieth century shows a collar 8 cm (3.1 inches) high, 2 cm (0.8 inch) higher than the regulation 6 cm (2.4 inch) height, confirming young officers' love of high collars.[105]

The tunic collar was squared in front for the Prussian guard regiments and the 17th, 18th, 19th, and 21st Regiments, none of which was a Prussian regiment (Table VI.6.c.1). The others had a slightly round front. The colour of the collars was the same as the plastrons and had the same piping (Table VI.6.c.1). The litzen of the troopers' collar of the 1st and 3rd Guards was linen and that of the 2nd Guards was made of camel hair. The 1st and 2nd Guard Lancers' litzen had a central light (spiegel) of red. The 3rd Guards' spiegel was yellow. The officers' litzen were either gold or silver embroidered litzen and did not have the spiegel of the other ranks. The collar was 4.75 cm (1.9 inches) high, a bit higher than the 4 cm (1.6 inch) infantry collar.[106] Officers, especially the younger ones, wore it higher when they could get away with it. The Saxon tunic generally followed the Prussian design as to the buttons in front and in back. The rear skirt had a scalloped false pocket and three buttons.

The cuffs, the so-called Polish cuff, were pointed with one button. In the Prussian army, the tip of the point was 11 cm (4.3 inches) from the bottom of the cuff. The Saxon pointed cuffs were a bit different in that they were larger than the Prussian cuffs: 14 cm (5.5 inches) to the point of the cuff.[107] The three Saxon lancers, the 17th, 18th, and 21st, had litzen on their collars and cuffs. The Prussian cuffs were the same colour as the collar and the plastron. Their piping was normally either dark blue or the colour of the cuff so it did not stand out. The exceptions were the 12th, 16th, 17th, 18th, and 21st Lancers, who had white piping even though their cuffs were another colour (Table VI.6.c.1).

The Bavarian 1st and 2nd Lancers' tunics showed several differences from the Prussian model. First, the tunic was steel green, a dark green with an olive green overtone. The trim was also slightly different. On the front, the trim along the outside of the plastron went to the bottom of the tunic skirt on the right side only.

Rank among the troopers was shown by a combination of braid and buttons:

Lance corporal	Small heraldic button on each side of collar near shoulder strap.
Corporal	Lace, gold or silver according to button colour, on cuffs and collars.
Sergeant	Corporal's lace plus a large heraldic button on either side of the collar.
Regimental sergeant major	Sergeant's lace and collar button with 1.6 cm (0.6 inch) wide gold or silver lace encircling each sleeve 7 mm (0.03 inch) above each cuff.

The heraldic button had an eagle for Prussian regiments, the Saxon coat of arms for Saxon regiments, the Bavarian rampant lion for Bavarian regiments, etc.

The NCOs' braid, according to regulations, was 2 cm (0.78 inch) wide for the line regiments and 2.1 cm (0.82 inch) for the guards. In addition, senior sergeants wore an extra line of braid 1.6 cm (0.6 inch) wide above the cuff. However, the rule stipulating size was not always followed. Being revered beings, they often wore wider braid.[108]

VI:107 NCO of the 2nd Guard Lancers
Note NCO braid on collar and cuffs.

In the guards, the braid was placed 3 mm (0.1 inch) from the top of the collar and cuffs. This allowed a thin strip of the cuff collar and the cuff piping to show above the braid (Image VI:107). In the line, it was placed 2 mm (0.08 inch) from the top.

Epaulettes

The Saxon regiments wore an all-metal epaulette, which is detailed below. The Prussian epaulette consisted of three parts: a cloth strap that extended to the collar, a metal crescent, and – for certain officers – a fringe. Within the crescent was an area of cloth often called the field. The field was connected to the collar by a strap of cloth. The strap was edged on each side with a strip of metal scaling that matched the crescent colour.¹⁰⁹ The strap and the field were the same colour as the plastron. The crescent was brass for the other ranks and gilt for officers, except for the 1st and 3rd Guards, and the 13th, 15th, and 20th Line Regiments, which had white metal (silver for officers). The 21st Regiment had epaulettes wholly of white metal.¹¹⁰ The regimental number or monogram was in yellow metal and was placed in the crescent field.

Field officers and generals wore bullion fringe off their crescents. The fringe of generals was thicker than that of the field officers.

A unique feature of the Saxon lancers was that their officers and ranks wore all-metal epaulettes. These consisted of a crescent, a metal field, and metal scales where the strap would extend to the collar. The other ranks of the 17th Regiment had an Austrian crown repoussé into its field after 1891, and the 21st had an imperial German crown repoussé in the field after 1905.

The metal epaulettes of officers had raised lines in the field and on the crescent. This precluded placing monograms or crowns in the field.¹¹¹ Rank was shown by stars in a contrasting colour from that of the epaulette. The stars were placed in the crescent field.

VI:108 Colonel Hans von Mangoldt of Saxon Lancer Regiment 17
Note waist sash worn by lancer officers.

Girdle¹¹²

The lancers' girdle was leather, 5.5 cm (2.2 inches) wide and was worn around the waist and over the tunic. The leather was covered with cloth divided into three equal strips. The two outer strips were the regiment's facing colour. The middle strip was dark blue. Most of the regiments had a dark blue strip on the top and bottom 3 mm (0.1 inch) wide. The 12th and 16th Regiments were exceptions with white piping on the top and the bottom. The 6 cm (2.4 inch) high buckle was concealed behind a band of cloth with the same design as the girdle cloth. The buckle was worn in the front centre of the waist.¹¹³ The cloth on the buckle was placed so the stripes were vertical (Image VI:99).

The Bavarian lancers did not wear a girdle. Rather, they wore a white waist belt with a brass open buckle.

Officers wore the standard waist sash.

Riding Breeches

The Prussian and Württemberg regiments wore the standard dark blue-black riding breeches. Other ranks had double twill reinforcements on the insides of the legs after 1875.¹¹⁴ Regulations did not provide for reinforcements on officers' breeches.¹¹⁵ The breeches of these states did not have any trim. The Saxon breeches were light blue with trim in the regiment's facing colour. The Bavarians' breeches were steel green and did not have piping.¹¹⁶

Trousers¹¹⁷

Other ranks could wear woollen trousers in walking-out dress only. In the lancers, they had to be privately purchased by the individual, but had to conform to certain rules. They were dark blue and had piping, usually red, along the side seam of each leg. The 10th and 14th Regiments had crimson piping.¹¹⁸ It is not clear if the 12th and 16th Regiments had white piping. The piping was 2–3 mm (0.07–0.1 inch) wide. The trousers were to be worn without a crease.¹¹⁹ In Prussia and Saxony only, the men wore white linen trousers in the summer months between May and October. The white trousers did not have piping.

In Saxony, the trousers were cornflower-blue with crimson piping on the side seams. The Bavarian regiments wore steel green with piping in the regiment's facing colour.

Officers' woollen trousers followed the same pattern. Their side piping had to have 1.5 mm (0.06 inch) visible.[120] White linen trousers were worn by the Prussian and Saxon lancer officers only during the summer months.

Gala Trousers[121]

Prussian officers wore gala trousers for court balls and their own weddings. These trousers were dark blue and cut like the walking-out woollen trousers. The basic design of the side stripes on the gala trousers was piping along the seam, a space of 0.5 mm (0.02 inch) for the trouser colour to show, and a stripe 3 cm (1.2 inches) wide on either side of the piping. The piping and stripes were normally the facing colour, but there were exceptions. The 1st Guard Lancers had red piping and red side stripes. The 12th and 16th Lancers had white piping and light blue side stripes.

Saxon lancers did not have gala trousers. Bavarian lancers did not have them after 1873. Officers in these states wore standard wool trousers to court and special events.

Pouch Belt

Other lancer ranks in all states wore a white leather pouch belt that was 4 cm (1.6 inches) wide after 1890. Prussian lancer officers wore pouch belts of standard lace of white or yellow, depending on the button colour. The cloth backing was dark blue. The exception was the 1st Guard Lancers, who had a poppy red belt backing that showed on either edge of the lace.

Saxon lancers wore the standard Saxon pouch belt with a crimson leather backing that showed on both edges of the silver lace belt. The belt also carried on its front a gilt Saxon shield and surmounted crown surrounded with wreaths. The pouch belt for officers of the Bavarian lancers was the standard Bavarian pouch belt. It was made of red leather covered with silver lace. The lace had three lines of light blue silk spaced equally along the silver lace (see §VI-3-1 for more details).

Pouch

The pouch of other ranks after 1890 was black leather without decorations on the lid for the lancer regiments of all the states. There were a few exceptions. The guard lancer regiments carried the guard star of the Order of the Black Eagle in nickel silver on their black leather pouch lids. After 1891, the pouch lid carried by other ranks in the 13th Lancers had a crowned 'WRII' on its lid. The front of the pouch was made of polished brass.[122] Herr in *German Cavalry* on p. 69 states that NCOs of most Prussian line lancers carried a brass circular plate on their black leather pouch lids. The plate had a Prussian eagle impressed in the centre upon a trophy of arms, drums and flags. The rim of the plate was raised. Laine in *L'Armée Allemande* (pp. 155–6) shows these plates on the troopers' pouches of only regiments Nos. 1–3. NCOs in Saxon regiments (Nos. 17, 18 and 21) had a cut-out round Saxon shield surmounted by a crown and surrounded by a wreath on their black leather pouch lid.

The pouch of Prussian officers was smaller than that of other ranks and was generally made of black patent leather. The three guard lancer regiments had a guard star on their lid with the centre picked out with wonderful workmanship. Most of the line lancer officers' pouch lids had the standard monogram 'FWR' under a crown. The 13th Regiment all had a 'WRII' monogram rather than the 'FWR' monogram.

The officers of the Württemberg Lancers (Nos. 19 and 20) carried the monogram of King Karl I (or Charles I) under a crown. This was carried after his death in 1891 until 1914.

The bottom and front of the Saxon officers' pouch was covered by black leather. The back was crimson cloth. The lid was made of gold-plated brass. It carried on it a Saxon shield under a crown surrounded by flags. At the bottom of the shield was a sprig of leaves, a sheaf of grain, and two cannon barrels. The outside border of the lid was decorated with a trim of 'Saxon trefoils' (stylised clover leaves on a stem). Outside that, on the very edge, there was a border of very tall thin lozenges alternating with small elongated dots. The shield, crown, and trophies were silver. The balance of the lid, including the border trim, was gold-plated.

The Bavarian officers' pouch lid was a slightly different size. It measured 12.4 cm (4.9 inches) across, 2.2 cm (0.9 inch) in depth, and 7.2 cm (2.9 inches) in height. The body was made of red leather and had a silver-plated lid. The lid had the Bavarian coat of arms on it, also in silver. The Bavarian coat of arms filled the entire lid.

§VI-6-d HUSSARS

The guard hussars were formed in 1815 from elements of the guard light cavalry and the Eastern Prussian national cavalry. In 1888, they were named the Life Guard Hussar Regiment.

The 1st Hussars, the Death's Head Hussars, traced their creation back to 1741 (see section on Busby Badges below for the history of their unusual uniform). They went by several different names and numbers in the early years as their colonels changed. In 1808, they were designated Life Hussars No. 4. In 1812, elements marched with the French Grand Army into Russia. After a period of chaos during the Wars of Liberation, they were designated the 1st Hussars (1st Life Hussars) in 1816. In 1860, this changed to 1st Life Hussar Regiment (1st Regiment). Normally the term 'life' with a regimental title denotes guard status but, in the case of this regiment and the 2nd Hussars, it was an honorary distinction without much practical meaning, although it did make some difference to their uniforms.

The 2nd Hussars were budded off from the 1st Hussars in 1808. As such, they carried the same founding date and regimental history as the 1st Hussars. They also carried the same death's head badge. They were given a similar title to the 1st Hussars in 1816, only it stated 2nd. In 1860, they were also named the 2nd Life Hussars Regiment (2nd Regiment).

The hussars were, as in most armies that had them, the most colourful and one of the most expensive branches of service in the German army. In the German army they alone (like the Russian hussars after 1905) retained different coloured uniforms for different regiments throughout the nineteenth century. This bright plumage and their profusion of gold and silver braid made for a striking uniform sure to call attention to the wearer and to set romantic feminine hearts aflutter. Nor was this image damaged by the fact that the officers had to be wealthy to be able to afford all this splendour and to serve in the cavalry in general.

The first Prussian hussars were said to have been formed in 1721 in response to hussar and other light cavalry units formed by the Austrians and Russians to carry out raids behind enemy armies. Both of those armies had populations that naturally produced light cavalrymen. The Prussians did not; the concept and dress of light cavalry was alien to the Prussian soldier. General von Pape wrote in 1887 that his great-grandfather was ordered by Frederick William I to bring order to the riff-raff that had been collected for Prussia's first hussar regiment. He put on the hussar's 'harlequin get-up', took a look at himself in the mirror, and fell dead from a stroke.[123]

Uniform

BUSBY

The other ranks' busby was made of sealskin, dyed black, stretched over a cane frame. It became lower and lower after its introduction in 1850, and by 1914 was 13.5 cm (5.31 inches) high.[124]

Officers' busbies were dark brown otter skin until 1912, when the material was changed to 'grey' opossum skin (Images VI:109, VI:110 and VI:111, also Image VI:122 below). While officially grey, the opossum skin looked brown. Some of the officers of the Brunswick Hussar Regiment No. 17 wore a bearskin busby as a regimental distinction. The officer's busby could be as high as 15 cm (5.91 inches) but no higher.[125] However, some officers, if they could get away with it, wore taller busbies.

VI:109 1st or 2nd Prussian Life Hussar's Possum Fur Busby After 1912

Table VI.6.d.1: German Hussars – 1914

Regiment	Attila	Braid	Monogram	Busby Badge	Pelisse	Busby Bag
Life Guards	Bright red	Yellow		Guard star	Yes	Red
1st Hussars	Black	White		Death's head and crossbones	Yes	Red
2nd Hussars	Black	White	Officers and other ranks[a]	Death's head and crossbones	Yes	White
3rd Hussars	Bright red	White		King and Fatherland scroll	Yes	Red
4th Hussars	Brown	Yellow		King and Fatherland scroll		Yellow
5th Hussars	Dark red	White		King and Fatherland scroll	Up to 1870[c]	Dark red
6th Hussars	Dark green	Yellow		King and Fatherland scroll		Red
7th Hussars	Russian blue	Yellow	Officers only[d]	Monogram[b,p]		Red
8th Hussars	Dark blue	White	Officers and other ranks[f]	King and Fatherland scroll	Yes	Light blue[g]
9th Hussars	Cornflower blue	Yellow		King and Fatherland scroll and honours		Cornflower blue
10th Hussars	Dark green	Yellow		King and Fatherland scroll		Pompadour red[h]
11th Hussars	Dark green	White		King and Fatherland scroll		Red
12th Hussars	Cornflower blue	White		King and Fatherland scroll	Yes	White
13th Hussars	Cornflower blue	White	Officers and other ranks[j]	King and Fatherland scroll	Yes	Red
14th Hussars	Dark blue	White		King and Fatherland scroll		Red
15th Hussars	Dark blue	White	Officers and other ranks[k]	King and Fatherland scroll plus, after 1899, laurel leaves with four battle honours	Yes	Yellow
16th Hussars	Cornflower blue	White	Officers only[l]	King and Fatherland scroll	Yes	Yellow
17th (Brunswick) Hussars	Black	Yellow		Special skull and crossbones scroll with Napoleonic battle honours[i]		Red
18th (Saxon) Hussars	Light blue	Yellow	Officers only[m]	Saxon star with Saxon coat of arms on it		Red
19th (Saxon) Hussars	Light blue	White	Officers only[n]	Saxon star with Saxon coat of arms on it		Purple red (crimson)
20th (Saxon) Hussars	Field grey	Field grey	Officers and other ranks[o]	Saxon star with Saxon coat of arms on it		Light blue

Notes: [a] 'V' for Queen Victoria of Prussia.
[b] Monogram of King Wilhelm I.
[c] Wore a pelisse up to 1870 (Sanders, *Hussars*, Vol. 1, p. 167).
[d] 'WRI' for King William of Prussia.
[e] King and Fatherland scroll.
[f] 'HII' for Czar Nicholas II of Russia.
[g] For officers: turquoise blue.
[h] Deep pink.
[i] Also had Mars la Tour on their scroll.
[j] 'U' for King Umberto of Italy.
[k] 'W' (Gothic) for Queen Wilhelmina of Holland.
[l] 'FJI' for Emperor Franz Joseph of Austria.
[m] 'AR' for King Albert of Saxony.
[n] 'C' for Queen Carola of Saxony. Worn only by officers who had served in the regiment prior to her death on 15 December 1907.
[o] '20'.
[p] Small King and Fatherland scroll below monogram.

VI:110 1st or 2nd Life Hussars Officer After 1912
Note officer-style sash around his waist.

VI:111 Ordinary Line Officer's Grey Opossum Busby Adopted in 1912
As can be seen, it was rather bulkier than the pre-1912 pattern busby.

The busby bag fell to the left (see Table VI.6.d.1 for the colours). The bag did not have any trim on it. It should be noted that the different regiments would often use different shades of the same colours for their bags. For example, the Guard, 1st, 3rd, 6th, 7th, 11th, 13th, 14th, 17th, and 18th Regiments' red was one shade. The 5th's was a darker red. The 10th wore a dark pink bag called Pompadour red, because the shade was the favourite of Madame Pompadour, mistress of France's King Louis XV. The 19th (Saxon) Hussars had a purple-red (crimson) shade of red called *Karmesinrot* in German.[126] The blue bags had different shades, as noted in Table VI.6.d.1.

The plumes for the Prussian other ranks was made of white horsehair and from 1865 to 1903 fell to the right (see Image VI:113 below). After 1903, it was upright and was not to be higher than 18 cm (7.09 inches) above the sheath.[127] The Brunswick (17th) and Saxon (18th, 19th, and 20th) Hussars always wore upright plumes. Saxons wore white plumes, which they would sometimes fan out. Brunswickers wore white over light blue plumes until 1886, when they received white plumes.[128]

After 1903, NCOs on parade were to wear black horsehair around the lower third of the white plume. The exceptions to this included: the 17th, where the black covered the lower half of the plume, and the Saxon Hussars (18th, 19th, and 20th), where green horsehair was substituted for black around the lower third. Any NCO could substitute buffalo hair for horsehair in his plume at his own expense.[129]

Officers also wore white plumes. There were two types of officers' plumes: heron feathers and vulture feathers, which had replaced the cockerel feathers worn earlier. The following regiments wore heron feathers: Life Guard, 1st, 2nd, 3rd, 7th, 17th, 18th, and 19th. The others wore vulture feathers. The regulation height of the two types was different. The overall height of the Prussian heron plume could not exceed 35 cm (13.78 inches). The plume had a base of black ostrich feathers, not higher than 9 cm (3.54 inches) (see Image VI:122). The vulture feathers could not exceed 23 cm (9.06 inches). The black base could be no higher than 7.5 cm (2.95 inches). Brunswick (17th) and Saxon (18th and 19th) Hussars wore heron plumes. The Saxons wore the bottom base only after 1903.[130] Again, some officers would try to wear taller plumes.

The government provided the other ranks' busbies, but officers had to supply their own, like other uniform items. The cost would vary, but an average busby cost about 50 marks (£2.41 or $11.71) just before World War I.[131] (This equates to a current value of £235 or $277.) The cap and cord cost about 6 marks (5 shillings 10 pence or $1.41) (current cost about £28 or $33). For the guard everything was more expensive. Their tassels alone cost 12.5 marks (12 shillings or $2.93) (current cost about £59 or $69).[132] Vulture plumes cost about 8 to 10 marks (7 shillings 7 pence to 9 shillings 7 pence or $1.87 to $2.34) (current cost about £38 to £47 or $44 to $55) and heron plumes 36 to 43 marks (£1.73 to £2.07 or $8.43 to $10.07) (current cost about £169 to £202 or $199 to $238).[133]

The busby had a cap line whose purpose was to keep the busby from being lost if it fell off during rapid cavalry movement such as a charge or combat. The lines for line regiments attached to the back and top of the busby.

The cap lines fell from the busby to about the shoulder blades and then split and ran around the uniform at neck level. They fastened under the first olive on the front of the attila. The hussars' cap lines simply ended at the same olive of the attila. No part of the cap line hung across the chest, as was the case with British hussars. In the Guard Hussars, the other ranks' cap line was fastened to the right side of the busby. It had two flat elaborate woven knots, often called flounders, and three tassels affixed to the right-hand side of the busby.[134]

For non-NCO other ranks, unless noted, the cap line was white. The cap line of the 17th Hussars was lemon yellow.

On dismounted service, the cap line was tied up in an elaborate loose knot on the right side of the busby (Image VI:112).

Prussian NCOs had the white olive and slides of the cap lines marked by black zigzag pattern. In the Life Guards, the sergeant major's cap line, flounder, and tassels were a mixture of black and silver.[135]

The cap lines of officers were made of silver bullion. Prussian regiments had interwoven black thread; the Saxons, the 18th, 19th, and 20th, had green added. The Brunswick Regiment, the 17th, had light blue added to the silver.

Busby Badges

The most striking busby badge, and perhaps the most striking headdress badge worn in any army, was the large skull and crossbones worn by the 1st and 2nd Hussars (Images VI:113, VI:114 and VI:115). Its origins are said to come from the 1740 funeral trappings of Prussian King Frederick William I, which were, of course, black and had a large right-facing

VI:112 Examples of How and Where the Cap Lines of the Busby Were Folded Up When Not in Use

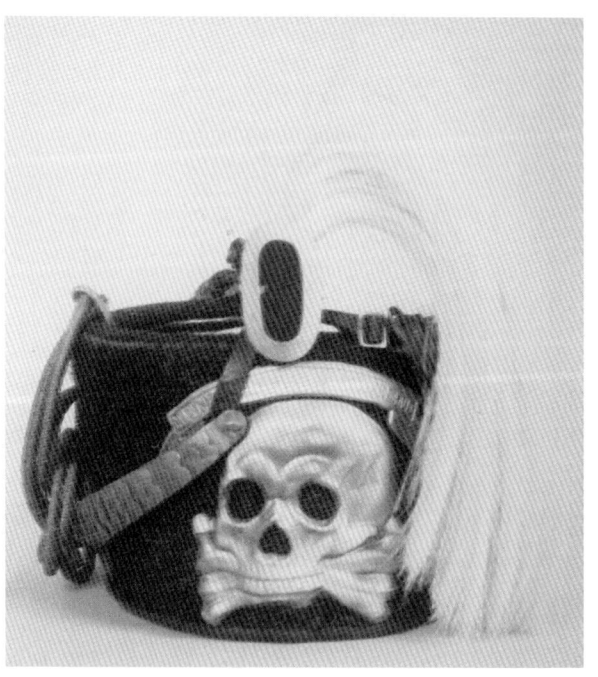

VI:113 Busby of a Prussian Enlisted Man of Life Hussar Regiment 2
Note the old-style drooping plume.

jawless death's head with bones lying behind the skull, embroidered in silver bullion. In his memory, when a new hussar regiment, the 5th Hussars, was formed in 1741, it took black as the colour of its uniform and wore the skull and crossbones on its headdress.[136] In time, the 5th Hussars became the 1st and 2nd Hussars. The death's head motif was popular with the elite stormtroops that were formed towards the end of World War I and with the Freikorps (free corps) that formed spontaneously after the end of the war.[137]

Given this background, it was perhaps inevitable that the new SS would adopt the death's head (*Totenkopf*) in 1923. At first they used a badge exactly like that worn by the hussars; they even ordered devices from firms that used pre-war dyes to manufacture their products. However, in 1934, the new German Panzer Corps began using the old Prussian Totenkopf badge as their distinctive badge, so the SS had to make a change. The Prussian Totenkopf had both upper and lower rows of teeth, but did not have a lower jaw. After 1934, the SS death's head kept the teeth and added a jaw bone for a skull that seemed to be grinning. This was the badge they wore throughout World War II, a subtle difference from the Prussian Totenkopf.

VI:114 Bandmaster of the 1st Life Hussar Regiment
He is wearing the 1908 pattern uniform. It appears from the wearer's decorations that this photo was taken after 1918.

VI:115 Kaiser Wilhelm in Uniform as 1st Life Hussar Regiment's Colonel-in-Chief
He wears the old-style death's head hussar busby.

VI:116 17th Brunswick Hussars Enlisted Man's Busby and Helmet Plate
Notice the shape of the death's head badge. This was called the apothecary's death's head, because it was shaped like the sign used by apothecaries to warn of deadly drugs. Also note the scroll above the skull carrying Napoleonic and Mars La Tour battle honours.

VI:117 17th Brunswick Hussars Other Ranks
Note his Brunswick-style death's head and battle honour banner on his busby. Also note his enlisted man's hussar sash around his waist.

VI:118 Close Up of the 17th Brunswick Hussar's Busby Decorations

The 17th (Brunswick) Hussars also had a skull and crossbones on their busby. However, it was a different design from that worn by the 1st and 2nd Hussars (Images VI:116 and VI:117). They were called the Apothecary Death's Head Regiment, because their Totenkopf resembled the poison symbol used by druggists on their medicine.[138] The busby also had a banner which read 'Peninsula, Sicilien, Waterloo, Mars la Tour' (Image VI:118).

Both of these badges were borne by the regiment thanks to a bit of sleight of hand. In 1807, Napoleon took over the Duchy of Brunswick, and its ruler, Duke Friedrich Wilhelm, was dispossessed. In an effort to regain his birthright, he formed a military corps known as the Black Brunswickers in Britain and the Black Horde in German. The unit consisted of both infantry and hussars. Austria supplied much of the equipment.[139] In addition, it is said that the duke borrowed against his duchy of Oels in Prussian Silesia, which he still controlled.

To show his intensity of purpose, the duke dressed his troops in black and gave them a skull and crossbones badge. It was this dress that gave them the name the Black Horde, and him the name the Black Duke. At first the Horde fought alongside Austria, but when Austria made peace with the French in 1809, the duke decided to fight his way to the coast and sail on British ships to England.

They duly reached the German coast on 6 August and sailed for England in stages. After refitting, they landed in Lisbon on 8 October 1810. Both the infantry and the cavalry took full part in the fighting in the Peninsula. The hussars served on the eastern side of Spain and helped in the invasion of Sicily. They remained in British service until mid-1815.[140]

When Napoleon was defeated in 1814, the Black Duke returned to his duchy and raised a hussar regiment of completely new men.[141] This regiment had absolutely no connection to the hussars of the Black Horde as the horde were still serving with the British. It was this new regiment that fought at Waterloo.

The mystique of the Black Horde was very strong. In 1867, the new regiment was granted the right to carry the 'Sicily and Peninsula' battle honours won by the hussars of the Black Horde. The newly formed hussar regiment was also given a 'Waterloo' honour to which they were entitled. Then, in 1873, the 'Mars la Tour' honour was added for the battle in the

VI:119 Other Ranks' Guard Hussar Busby
Note the shape of the guard star and the three tassels and the flounder just above the tassel.

Franco-Prussian War. Not satisfied with that, in 1883, the regiment was given the death's head badge worn by all units of the Black Horde.[142] Once again there was no regimental connection, as the British army would view it, to justify the awarding of this badge.

The badge of the Guard Hussars, as might be expected, was the guard star with the Order of the Black Eagle on it. For officers, the circular centre was enamelled. The star was not to be any larger than 9.2 cm (3.62 inches) in diameter (Image VI:119).[143]

Most of the regiments had a Fatherland banner on their busby (Image VI:120).

VI:121 7th Hussars NCO's Busby
Note the two colours in the plume and the monogram 'WRI' on the front, which are the initials of King Wilhelm I of Prussia. The fact that the monogram has the roman numeral "I" on it shows that this monogram was made after Wilhelm II ascended to the throne. Note also the very small and discreet Fatherland banner below the monogram.

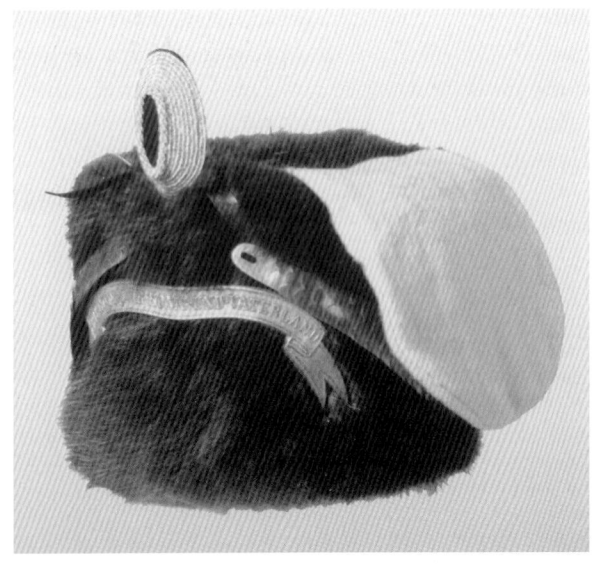

VI:120 Hussar Busby with God and Fatherland Banner

VI:122 M1912 Hussar Officer's Busby for Regiment 7
In 1912, grey opossum fur was adopted for hussar officers' busbies. The vulture plumes on this busby are replacements.

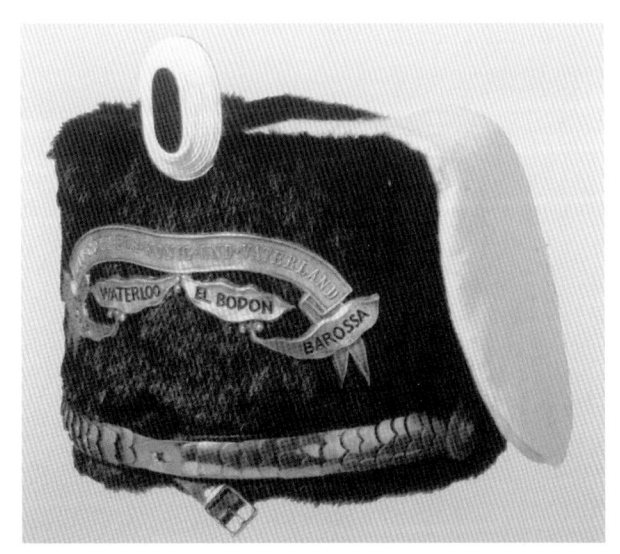

VI:123 Busby of Hussar Regiment 15
This has Peninsula, Waterloo, El Bodon, and Barossa banners added to the Fatherland banner.

The 7th Hussars had an unusual busby badge. It consisted of the crowned monogram of King Wilhelm I. The monogram was awarded to the regiment in 1861. The Roman numeral 'I' was added to the monogram when Kaiser Wilhelm II came to the throne in 1888. The monogram was 9 cm (3.54 inches) high and 9 cm (3.54 inches) wide. Below the monogram was a small, discreet Fatherland banner (Images VI:121 and VI:122).

The 15th Hussars had the Fatherland banner with honours won by the King's German Legion in Spain. These were 'Peninsula', 'El Bodon', 'Waterloo', and 'Barossa' and were awarded by Kaiser Wilhelm II in 1899 (Image VI:123). Since they came to the Prussian army by way of disbanded Hanoverian regiments, there was no connection to the Spanish honours under the stricter British army standards.

ATTILA

The twenty hussar regiments wore a variety of coloured attilas. This was one of the things that made them so fascinating (see Table VI.6.d.1 for the colours and Images C81 and C82). Not only did the regiments wear different colours, but there was a wide range of shades within those colours. In early days, because officers' uniforms were made of better cloth, they took and held the dyes of the era better. This meant the shade of the officers' uniforms in most armies was different from the other ranks', and in time, these differences became traditional features of the different regiments' uniforms.

The cornflower blue of the 9th, 12th, 13th, and 16th was a rather deep sky blue but the officers had a much lighter shade. It is said that they could be distinguished from other ranks at a distance of more than half a mile. The officers' tunics of the 9th, 12th, 13th, and 16th Regiments were of a much lighter blue than those of other ranks, perhaps as light as the blue worn by the Prussian dragoons.[144] The light blue of the Saxon regiments was much lighter than their Prussian counterparts. The officers of the 7th Regiment wore a lighter shade of Russian blue. In the 4th, although the other ranks wore a tobacco brown colour, the officers had a red-brown shade. The officers of the 5th had a tunic of an appreciably different hue, more pink than dark red. It was similar to the carmine shade of the Prussian General Staff.[145]

The dark blue mentioned in Table VI.6.d.1 'was a much brighter colour than the dark blue worn in the British army. Russian blue was a soft medium dark blue distinctly different from the dark blue clad regiments. The red of the Life-Guard Regiment and of the 3rd was a very brilliant colour'.[146]

There is confusion among the sources about the shade of dark green attila worn by officers of the 6th, 10th, and 11th Hussars when compared to those of the other ranks. Table VI.6.d.2 shows the colours stated in the books by D.H. Hagger and Ulrich Herr and Jens Nguyen, and the colours I found in examining photographs of NCOs' and officers' attilas in Paul Sanders' book.[147] It should be noted that photos at times do not properly show the true colours of an item because of lighting factors when the photo was made and on ink limitations when a book is printed.

Table VI.6.d.2: How Officers' Colours Varied from Other Ranks' Dark Green Attilas

Regiment	Sanders' Interpretation	Herr's Interpretation	Hagger's Interpretation
6th	Darker	Darker	Lighter
10th	Darker	Lighter	Lighter
11th	Darker	Darker	Lighter

Sources: Sanders, *Hussars*, Vol. 1, p. 187; Vol. 2, pp. 68, 71, and 83; Herr, *German Cavalry*, p. 42; Hagger, *Hussars, etc.*, p. 21.

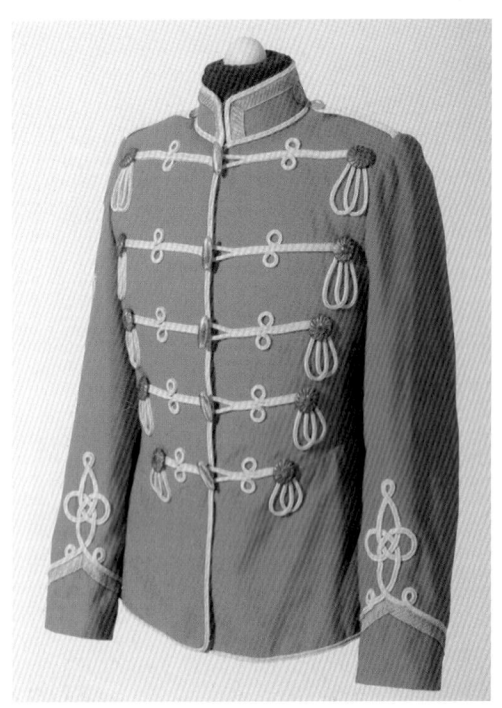

The attila had five rows of white or yellow braid, sometimes called frogging, down the front, with one exception (Table VI.6.d.1). The braid for other ranks consisted of two strands of flat wool cords. It ended on the outside of the chest with two falling loops of cord. Halfway to the end of the side of the chest, there were two small loops in the braid, one above the line of braid and one below it (Images VI:124 and VI:125).

The officers' attila followed the same general pattern as the men's. However, their attila frogging was gold or silver chain-stitch cord or flat cord. If cord was used, it could either be pure silver or gold thread or a cheaper substitute (Image VI:126).

The attila was buttoned with a toggle button the colour of the braid. For other ranks prior to 1888, the toggle had a swirled pattern, but by 1914 this had changed to a smooth pattern. The end of the row of frogging and the top of the loops was covered by a metal rosette button the colour of the braid with one exception.[148] The button had a swirled pattern on it.

The exception mentioned above was the 20th Hussars. They were formed in 1910 and given field grey dress as their dress uniform. Their frogging was field grey. They did not have rosettes, but instead

VI:124 3rd Hussars Attila
This is a tunic for a gefreite (lance corporal), shown by the braid on his collar and cuff, as well as the size of the button on his collar.

VI:125 Hussar Regiment 12 or 13 Sergeant's Attila
Note how the sergeant's braid on the collar and cuffs is a bit thicker and the button on the collar than that worn by a gefreite.

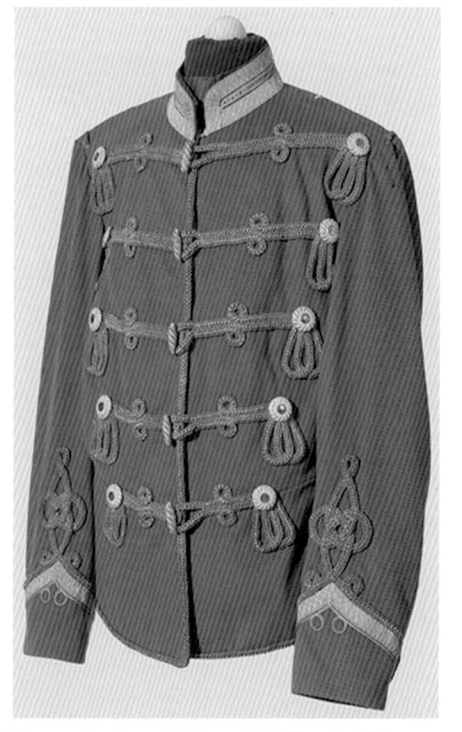

VI:126 Hussar Regiment 12 or 13 Officer's Attila
Note the gimp chain frogging on his attila. The trim pattern shows he is either a captain or subaltern.

§VI-6 Prussian Cavalry

VI:127 Front and Rear Views of the Tunic of a One-Year Volunteer Lance-Corporal of the King's Hussar Regiment 7
The tunic is privately tailored from good-quality cloth and with a heavily padded chest.

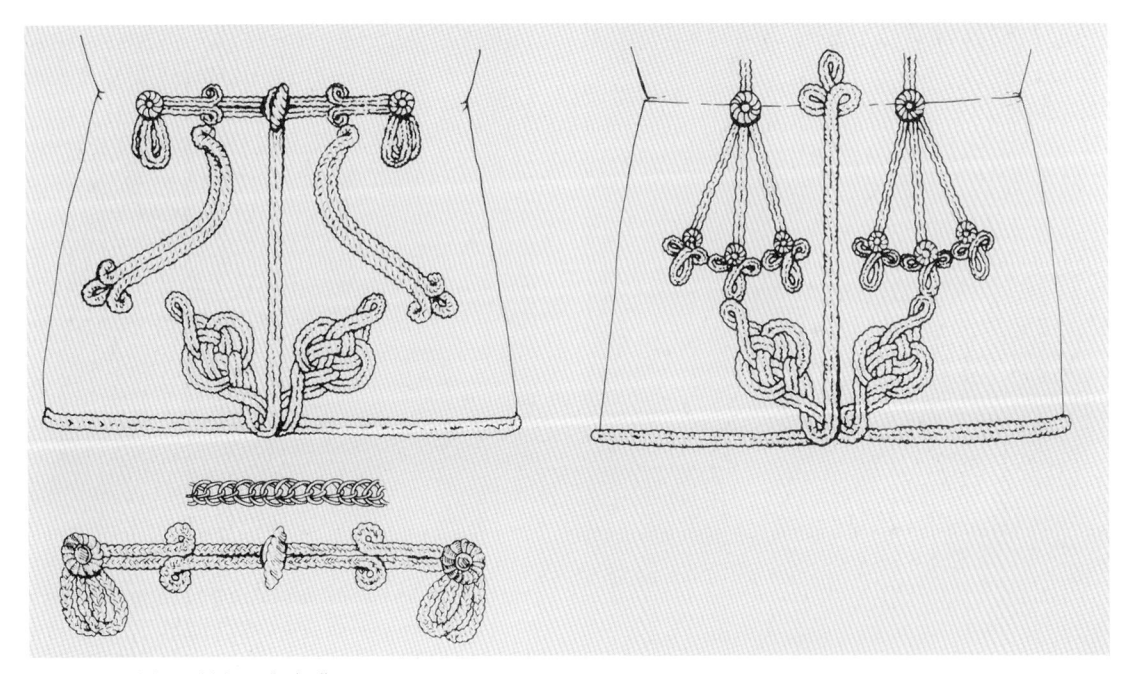

VI:128 Details of Guard Hussar's Attila
On the left is the front of the attila. On the right is the back of the attila. Note that the Guard's attila has extra buttons at each of the six crow's feet on the skirt. Also note the extra knots at the corners of the front and back of the attila. Below the attilas are drawings of the gimp chain used in the frogging and the way the frogging loops on the tunic.

had only loops of braid. Their toggles were black. However, their shoulder straps were a mix of white and cornflower blue cords and bore the regiment's number, 20, in brass (see below).[149]

The cuffs, which were the same colour as the attila, were trimmed in the same cord braid used on the chest and had a Hungarian knot. The slit at the back of the cuff was sewn up and traced with cord braid after 1895.

The front opening of the attila was trimmed with cord braid. This braid continued around the bottom of the attila and up the left rear skirt. There it ended in an elongated trefoil (crow's foot) shape (Image VI:127). The front and rear edges of the attila of officers in the Guard Hussars had Hungarian knots on them (Image VI:128).

Curved pockets which ended in a trefoil were a feature of many, if not all, of the officers' front skirts (Image VI:129). Prior to June 1899, officers in the 17th Hussar Regiment had worn straight pockets on their attilas. They then changed to curved pockets. Also in 1899, Saxon hussars were ordered to wear diagonal pockets on their attilas.[150]

The officers of the Guard Hussars and the 17th Hussars had a spiral button at waist level on either side of the skirt at the back. In addition, they had one above each of the columns and one next to each of the three crows' feet on each of the two rear skirts (Image VI:128). The buttons were gold or gold substitute for these regiments because their frogging colour was yellow.

The officers' toggles on the front of the attila had a swirl pattern. Some regiments had special regimental distinctions. Officers of the 17th Hussars had small slides on either side of the five rows of braid on the front of the attila. The slides were between the toggle or toggle loops and the small loops in the cord braid halfway to the spiral buttons (Image VI:130).

From an unknown early date the sergeant majors of the 2nd Hussars were allowed to wear silver braid along the outside of their attilas just to the inside of the metal buttons at the end of each row of frogging. In 1897, this privilege was extended to sergeant majors of the 1st Hussars. Then in 1908, the trumpet majors of both regiments gained the right to wear this braid.[151]

The officers in the 5th Hussars wore a silver fringe on the attila, connecting the braid looping on each side of the wearer's chest (Image VI:131). The fringe on the 5th Hussars' uniforms was as had been worn by the regiment in 1808, and given to them in 1843 for their dolman. When the hussars changed to attilas in 1853, this grant was no longer valid, but in 1861 this distinction was granted for wear on the regiment's attilas.

It has proved difficult to find the origins of the wearing of the fringe back beyond 1808. The 5th Regiment traced its origins to a hussar battalion raised in 1758 by a von Belling. However, the 5th was a regiment reformed in 1808 from bits and pieces of several different regiments. The von Belling Hussars do not seem to have worn fringe on their uniform. But wearing fringe was not unknown among Frederick the Great's Hussars. For example, the 6th Hussars of von Werner had it on their uniform in 1785. It is possible that one of the other regiments brought the concept of wearing fringe to the 5th in 1808 when the regiment was reformed. Certainly in a time of military despair

VI:129 Hussar Regiment 7 (King Wilhelm I)

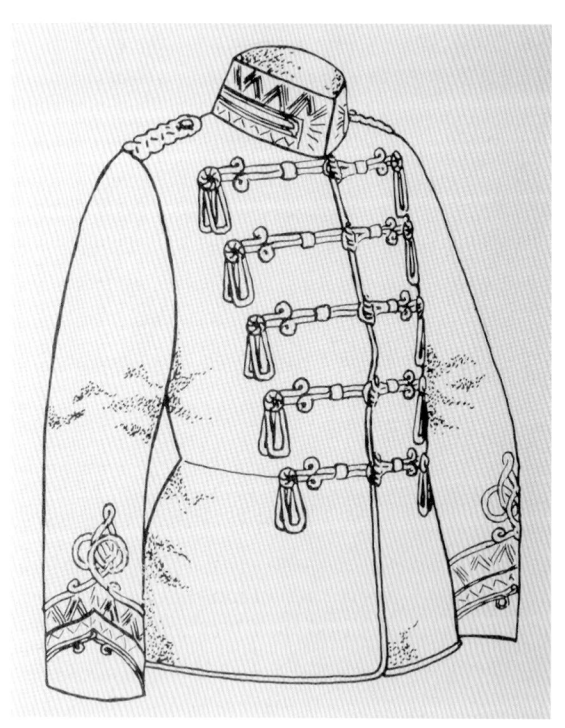

VI:130 17th Brunswick Hussars Officer's Tunic
Note the extra slide on each set of frogging on the front of the attila.

soldiers would likely be looking back to the traditions of Frederick the Great's soldiers for inspiration.

The back of the two seams of the attila was traced with cord braid. This braid formed an elongated trefoil shape at the level of the shoulder blade and then came down to waist level, where there was a toggle on each rear skirt for line regiments.

Each rear skirt of the line regiments had three lines of cord braid ending in crows' feet below the waist on each skirt.

The collar for other ranks was the same colour as the attila. It was trimmed on the top and bottom and had a trefoil on the back of the collar. The Guard Hussar Regiment, as a regimental distinction, wore yellow braid on their collars and cuffs. On the collar, it was worn under the top level of collar trim, and on the cuff, under the cuff trim. This 'guard braid' had a thin red line through the centre of it. If NCO braid was worn, the guard braid was worn below the rank braid with a thin space between them to show the red attila colour.

Other ranks of German hussars did not wear shoulder straps. Rather, they wore yellow or white cords to match the frogging colour. If the regiment

VI:131 Prince Albert Victor of Britain in the Uniform of the 5th Pomeranian Hussars
This shows the fringe worn on either side of the chest. Note also the officer's sash around his waist.

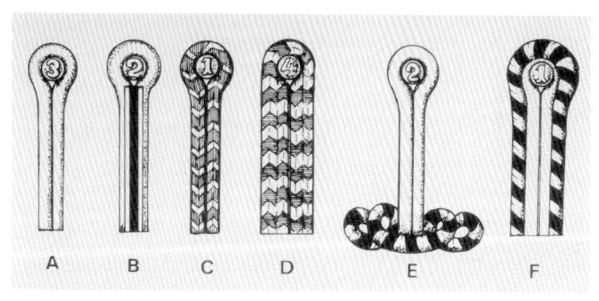

VI:132 Different Designs of the Hussars' Shoulder Cords
Note that the cords go around a button that has the squadron number.
A. Ordinary pattern.
B. Graduate of cavalry telegrapher school.
C. Graduate of military riding school at Hanover (one-year course).
D. Graduate of military riding school at Hanover (two-year course).
E. Re-enlisted men.
F. One-year volunteers.

did not have a monogram, there were normally four to six cords on each shoulder. These were held down by a button in the frogging colour (Image VI:132). Regiments with a monogram had upwards of fourteen cords in order to be able to hold the monogram (Table VI.6.d.1).

It is interesting to see the cost of German attilas and compare them to what British officers were paying for their uniforms (see §II, British Empire). In 1871, a young officer noted in a letter home that his 7th Hussars attila cost 70 thalers (currently £1,633 or $1,989).[152] The 7th Hussars' chief was the Prussian king, so it was an aristocratic regiment. The officer's family must have been well-placed for him to find a commission in the regiment, yet he was concerned about the cost.

Officers' Attila

The collars were trimmed top and bottom with officer's braid. They also had braid which showed rank (Image VI:133). The Guard Regiment had different

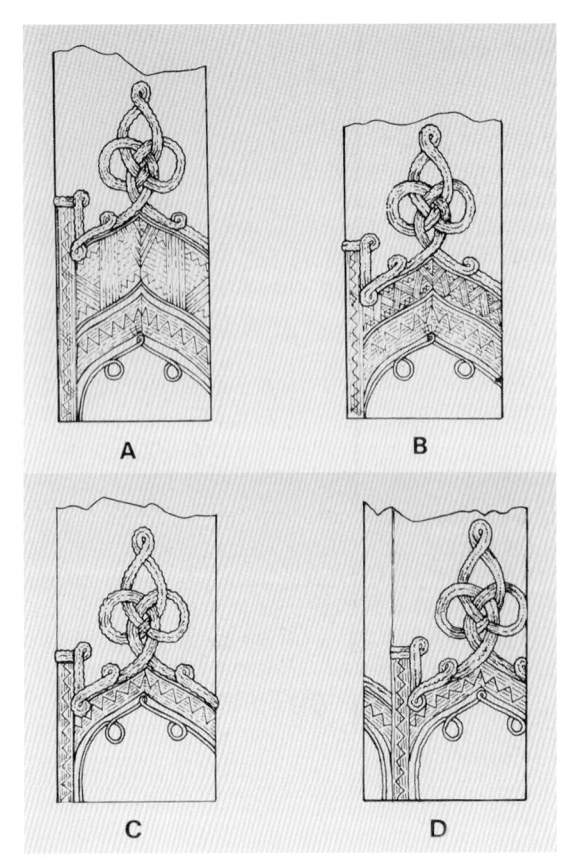

VI:134 Details on Cuff Lace for Hussar Officers
A. Generals.
B. Field officers.
C & D. Captains and subaltern officers.

rank braid. At the back of the collar, the bottom braid made a loop which could, depending on the person's rank, fill most of the collar space.

The officers' cuffs also had rank braid on them (Image VI:134). The collar and cuff rank braid were in addition to the badges of rank worn on the shoulder cords.

Interim Attila

While it is not an item of full dress, a word should be said about the 'interim attila'. These were simplified versions of the attila for everyday use whose purpose was to reduce the wear and tear on the expensive attila. Since they were the same colour as the attila and had roughly the same frogging, they are easy to confuse with the proper attila. This, in turn, can lead to confusion about other elements of the uniforms. The easiest way to tell a proper attila and an interim attila

VI:133 Details of Collar Lace for Hussar Officers
A. Generals.
B. Field officers.
C. Captains and subaltern officers.
D. Captains and subaltern officers of the Life Guard Hussar Regiment.

VI:135 Undress Attila
Notice the difference in the cuff braid between this tunic and the full dress attila.

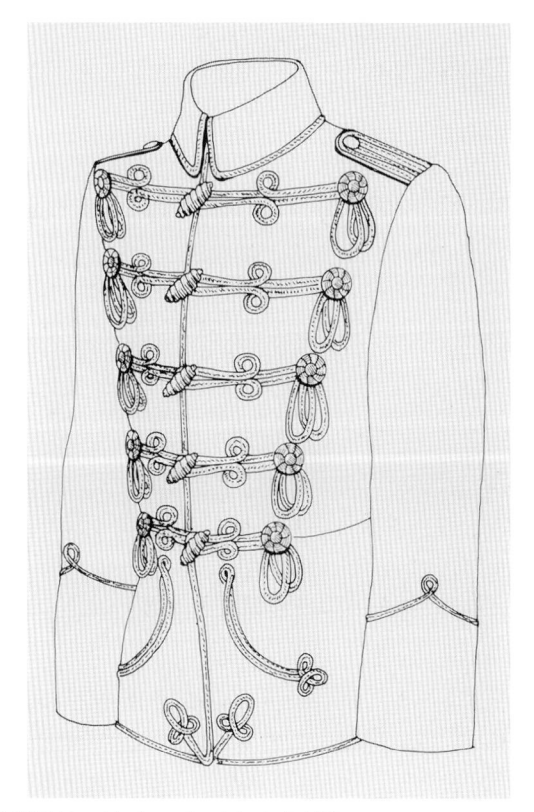

VI:136 Line Undress (or Interim) Attila

apart is to look at the sleeves. An interim attila has one row of cord braid with a single loop placed halfway up the forearm. The proper attila has Hungarian knots and rank braid (Images VI:135 and VI:136).

Hussar Sash

Around their waist, most of the hussar regiments, except for the 20th, wore a hussar sash. The sash for other ranks, except for the 17th Hussars, normally consisted of many strands of white wool collected into groups in front by three sets of long, hollow tubes. The wool strands continued around to the wearer's back, where they were collected into two strands by tubes. The sash was buttoned by a toggle going through a loop made of the strand coming from the other end of the sash. Extra strands extended beyond the cord and looped around to the front of the sash, where they were woven through the sash. These extra cords ended in a small tube, and for other ranks, two stylised acorns (Image VI:137). The long and short tubes and the acorns all had zigzags in the state's colours, black for the Guard Hussars and 1st to 16th Prussian Hussar Regiments, and green for the 18th and 19th Saxon Hussars.

The 17th Brunswick Hussars wore blue wool for their sash and their hollow tube slides. Toggles and acorns were white without zigzags.[153]

The 20th Hussars, raised in 1910, were given the field grey uniform which was to be introduced in 1911. Since the sash was not worn in the field, they were issued a brown belt instead of a sash. The belt had a silver-coloured buckle. On the buckle was a

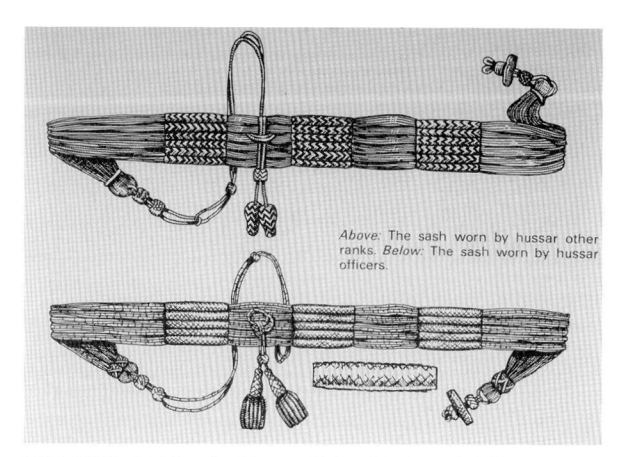

VI:137 Sash Worn by Hussar Other Ranks and Officers

Above: The sash worn by hussar other ranks. *Below:* The sash worn by hussar officers.

round brass shield, which probably had the Saxon crown and the 'Mindful of Providence' motto.

The officer's sash was similar to that of the other ranks but made of more costly materials and had a larger, closed bullion tassel. The sash cords were silver thread mixed with black, light blue, or green silk, depending on whether the officer came from Prussia, Brunswick, or Saxony. The hollow tube slides and tassels were also silver. The sash knot where the cord from the back was tucked into the sash in front was more complicated (Image VI:137).[154]

The officer's sash cost between 29 and 98 marks (£1.40 to £4.73 or $6.81 to $23.09) in the 1910–14 period.[155] That converts to a current price range of approximately £137 to £465 or $160 to $541.

Pouch Belt

The other ranks of the Prussian and Saxon hussars wore a pouch belt of white leather. The pouch belt of the 17th Brunswick Hussars was black leather.

Prussian officers wore a belt of silver lace with a trim of tunic colour. The 17th Hussar officers wore a red leather belt with gold trim based on British models.

Officers of the Saxon 18th Hussars had a gold lace belt, and the 19th had a silver lace belt. These regiments had the Saxon coat of arms on their belts in a colour that was the reverse of the belt colour. The 20th Saxon Hussars, in keeping with their simple field dress uniform, wore a plain brown leather belt.

Pouch

The pouch for all other ranks was black leather. The Guard Hussars had the star of the Order of the Black Eagle in brass on theirs. The 1st and 2nd Hussars had the same design on theirs in brass. The other ranks in an average Prussian hussar regiment had a pouch with no devices on it. The black pouch of the other ranks of the 3rd–7th Hussars had a brass circular plate with the same devices as those carried on the pouches of the 1st, 2nd, and 3rd line lancers (see §VI-6-c Lancers pouch section above). The 17th had a brass star with the monogram 'W' on it. The NCOs only of the 18th and 19th Saxon Hussars had the Saxon coat of arms in brass. This was cut out so the black leather of the pouch showed through. The troopers of the Saxon 20th Hussars carried a plain brown pouch.

Prussian officers had the gilded monogram 'FWR' with a crown over it. The 17th Hussars, following British practice, had a pouch of red Moroccan leather with sides and a flap of silver. The flap had the Brunswick coat of arms in gold on it and a flower border trimmed in silver. This was in a style close to the pouch design worn by the British 18th Hussars (see §II-7-c, British Hussars). The Saxon 18th and 19th Hussars had the sides and flap in gilt. The flap had the arms of Saxony with a stand of flags behind the arms and a crown over the arm in silver. The edge of the flap had a clover leaf trim. Officers of the Saxon 20th wore a plain brown pouch in keeping with their field dress uniform.[156]

Riding Breeches

Other ranks in Prussian and Brunswick regiments wore blue-black riding breeches. The breeches had braid on the outside seam the same colour as the chest braid on the attila (Table VI.6.d.1). The outside braid

VI:138 Side View of an Officer of the 5th Hussars
This shows the width of the lace braid on an officer's breeches.

continued across the upper back of the breeches' seat to form a circle in the middle of the seat.

Saxon hussars in the 18th and 19th Regiments wore cornflower blue breeches that matched their attilas (Image C82). Their braid matched the chest braid of their attilas, yellow for the 18th and white for the 19th. The Saxon 20th had field grey braid on their riding breeches.

All other ranks' breeches had leather reinforcement on the inner side of the leg and the seat.

The officers' riding breeches followed the same pattern. Their braid was fairly wide (Image VI:138) and was either silver or gold, depending on the regiment's chest braid.

Trousers

From May through October, other ranks could wear long white linen trousers. These trousers were without trim. The Saxon 18th and 19th Regiments had trousers of attila colour to wear in garrison. The trim matched that of the riding breeches. For the 20th Hussars, the trousers were attila colour, but the trim was red.

Boots

The hussar boot, which was black, was distinctive in that it had a 1.4 cm (0.55 inch) band of leather trim around the top of the boot the colour of the chest braid. The top of the boot was cut to form a 'V' notch in the front centre. Just below the notch cut-away, the coloured trim formed a pronounced loop (Image VI:139).

The officers' boots followed the same pattern, but their silver or gold braid around the top of the boot was 2 cm (0.79 inch) wide.[157] For officers, a rosette replaced the other ranks' loop. Officers normally went to the expense of buying patent leather boots.

Patent leather boots could be worn by other ranks for walking out if they wished to go to the expense of purchasing them privately.

Monograms

Certain regiments had been honoured by having members of the nobility named honorary commanders, or otherwise had ties to the regiment. When this happened, the noble's monogram was

VI:139 A Group of Hussar Other Ranks Enjoying Their Beer
Note their cloth caps (*mützes*) with Reich cockade on the top and the state cockade below. Note also the leather-reinforced breeches and the trim at the top of their boots.

given to the regiment to be worn on its shoulder strap or, in the hussars, its shoulder cords. In the hussars, the other ranks' shoulder cords had to be wider in order to contain the monogram.

There were two classes of monograms: those that could be worn only by officers and those that could by worn by officers and other ranks:

Officers and Other Ranks

2nd Regiment	Queen Victoria of Prussia, 'V'
8th Regiment	Czar Nicholas II of Russia, 'HII'
13th Regiment	King Umberto of Italy, 'U'
15th Regiment	Queen Wilhelmina of Holland, 'W' (Gothic)

Officers Only

7th Regiment	King William I of Prussia, 'WRI'
16th Regiment	Emperor Franz Joseph of Austria, 'FJI'
18th Regiment	King Albert of Saxony, 'AR'
19th Regiment	Worn only by officers who had served in the regiment prior to the death of the Dowager Queen Carola of Saxony in December 1907, 'C'.[158] Monogram 'FR' worn by officers who had served before the death of Kaiser Frederick III in 1888.[159]

For the designs of the monograms, see §VI-3-18.

PELISSE

In addition to the attila, certain regiments wore a pelisse. The pelisse, like the rest of hussar dress, originated from Hungary. It was worn hanging from the wearer's back in Russia, and off the shoulder in Germany. It is said to have had its origins in Hungarian troopers not having time to get fully dressed as they responded to enemy raids. They would hurriedly dress and throw their top jacket over their shoulder as they rode out to face the foe.

Originally, the pelisse was a standard part of all hussars' dress. But then a fashion of simplifying their dress took hold, and the pelisse was done away with almost everywhere. However, in some countries, a simplified pelisse was reintroduced as a reward to a regiment for an outstanding performance in combat or as a gift from the regiment's patron. In Prussia and Germany, the funds for almost all regimental pelisses came from regimental patrons. The only exception was the Guard Hussars, who received theirs at the government's expense.

Table VI.6.d.3 shows the regiments that carried a pelisse in 1914, the year they received it, and the source of the funds for the pelisses:[160]

Table VI.6.d.3: Hussar Regiments Carrying a Pelisse

Regiment	Date Pelisse Received	Pelisse Funded by
Life Guards	1865	Government issue
1st Regiment	1895	Gift of Kaiser Wilhelm II
2nd Regiment	1896	Gift of the Dowager Empress Frederick of Prussia
3rd Regiment	1873	Gift of Prince Friedrich Karl of Prussia
8th Regiment	1896	Gift of Czar Nicholas II of Russia
12th Regiment	1881	Gift of Grand Duke Vladimir of Russia
13th Regiment	1913	Gift of King Victor Emmanuel III of Italy
15th Regiment	1876	Gift of Grand Duke Friedrich Franz II of Mecklenburg-Schwerin
16th Regiment	1888	Gift of Emperor Franz Joseph of Austria

Between May and October, the summer months, the pelisse was worn only for parades or by officers in gala dress. During these months, it was worn hanging from the left shoulder. During the other months, in theory, it could be worn closed as a jacket in full and walking-out dress by both other ranks and officers. But, in reality, only officers wore it this way.[161]

The sash was never worn over a closed pelisse.

There is some doubt as to whether or not the entire 13th Hussars ever wore their pelisses. The gift was made on the regiment's centenary, August 1913. The first chance to wear it would have been January 1914 at

VI:140 Front and Rear Views of the Hussar Officers' Pelisse
This was worn by officers of all hussar regiments except the Guard and the 3rd and 15th Regiments.

the Kaiser's birthday parade, but it was so cold that only greatcoats were worn. The next big parade was during the autumn, but by that time, World War I had started.

The pelisse was the same basic shape as the attila. It was, however, a little longer. It had five rows of braid on the chest, which had the same design as the attila braid. The toggles and the buttons were the same as the attila (Image VI:140).

The pelisse, unlike the attila, had fur trim down the front, around the bottom, at the collar, and at the cuffs. In most regiments, the curved pockets on either front side of the officers' pelisses were trimmed in fur. Other ranks did not have visible pockets in their pelisses, and thus there was no fur trim there.[162] The bottom edge of both front corners of the pelisse had a Hungarian knot (Image VI:141). In addition, on officers' pelisses, there was a Hungarian knot just

VI:141 Fur Cuff Trim Worn on the Pelisse of the 1st, 2nd, 8th, 12th, 13th, and 16th Hussars
It is probably not the 1st or 2nd as the pelisse does not seem to be black. On the other hand, the pelisse seems too dark to be cornflower blue (a light blue), which rules out the 12th, 13th, and 16th. This leaves the 8th as the most likely candidate. Note also the trim and boss at the top of his boots.

below the centre of the collar in the back (Image VI:140). The Guard Hussars had extra buttons on the rear skirt of their pelisses in the same pattern as on the rear of their attilas. Other ranks of the Guard, 1st, and 2nd Hussars had a button rather than a toggle at waist level on either side of the rear skirt of the pelisse. It is unclear whether line officers' pelisses had the toggles or buttons on the back waist. Most, other than the Guard, 1st, and 2nd Hussars, had toggles, but the sample is too small to make a firm statement.

The pelisse colours and cuff shapes are shown in Table VI.6.d.4.

Table VI.6.d.4: German Pelisse Colours and Trim

Regiment	Pelisse Colour	Fur Trim Officers	Fur Trim Other Ranks	Pelisse Lining	Cuff Type
Life Guard	Dark blue	Pale grey	Black	White	Other ranks: Brandenburg with guard braid Sergeant major: modified Brandenburg with heavy rank braid Officers: pointed cuff with braid with a single loop of cord braid above it
1st	Black	Pale grey	Pale grey	White	Pointed
2nd	Black	Pale grey	Pale grey	White	Pointed
3rd	Dark blue	Pale grey	Pale grey	White	Brandenburg
8th	Dark blue	Pale grey	White	Light blue	Pointed
12th	Cornflower blue	Pale grey	White	White	Pointed
13th	Cornflower blue	Pale grey	Pale grey	White	Pointed
15th	Dark blue	Pale grey	Black	Yellow	Brandenburg
16th	Cornflower blue	Pale grey	White	Yellow	Pointed

Source: Hagger, *Hussars, etc.*, p. 25.

See Image VI:142 for the shape of the pelisse cuff. Examples of cuff shapes and braid can be seen at Images VI:143 through VI:146.

The fur for officers' pelisses was supposed to be made from the wool of newborn lambs of a breed of sheep found primarily in the Crimean. However, some officers trimmed their pelisses in the plain sheep's wool used by other ranks.[163] Others used an imitation fur.[164]

The pelisse's coloured lining was silk for officers and wool for other ranks. The pelisse followed the same pattern as the attila when it came to extra buttons on the back.

The Guard Hussars' pelisse for other ranks was trimmed in guard braid with the red line in it between the fur trim and the cord braid. The cuff for the regiment's sergeant-majors is set out in Table VI.6.d.4 above.

VI:142 Pelisse Cuffs
A. Officers of the Life Guard Hussars.
B. Officers of all regiments except the Guard, 3rd and 15th Regiments.
C. Officers of the 3rd and 15th Regiments.
D. Sergeant Major of the Life Guard Hussar Regiment.

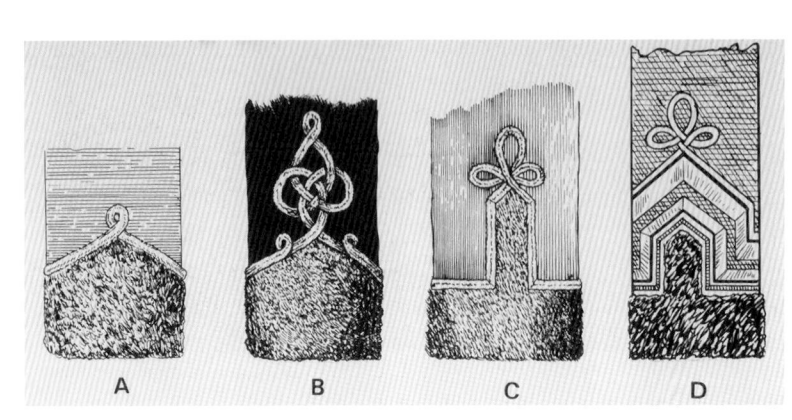

VI:143 Pelisse and Attila of an Other Ranks in the Hussar Life Guards Regiment

VI:145 Guards Hussar Officer Wearing Pelisse

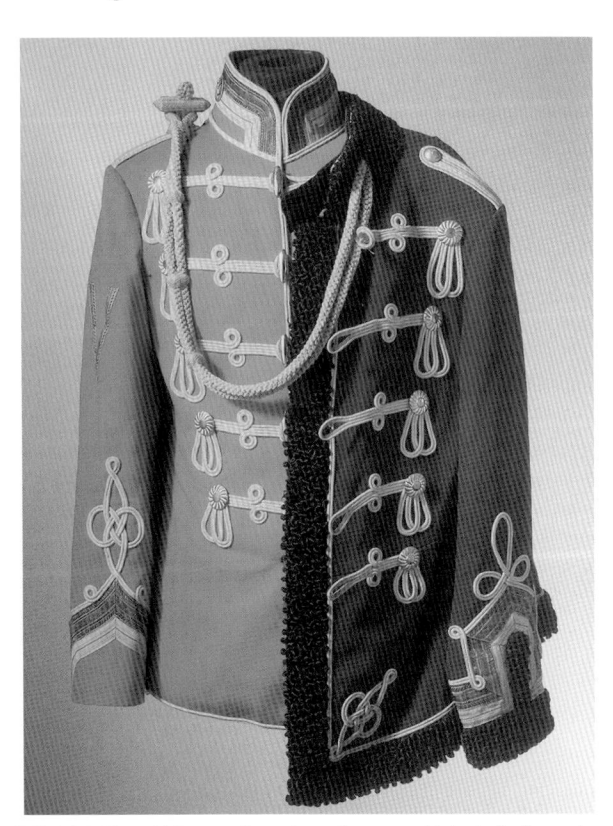

VI:144 Guard Hussars Squadron Sergeant Major's Attila and Pelisse
Note the shape of the fur cuff on the pelisse.

VI:146 Colonel of 3rd Hussars
Note shape of pelisse cuff. This cuff shape was worn only by the 3rd and 15th Hussars.

VI:147 Czar Nicholas II of Russia as Colonel-in-Chief of the 1st Westphalian Hussar Regiment No. 8
He is wearing gala breeches worn only by colonels-in-chief. Note the non-standard fur trim on his pelisse.

VI:148 Edward VII of the United Kingdom in Pelisse of the 5th Pomeranian Hussar Regiment
He was entitled to wear this as he was the honorary chief of the regiment. Note that the fringe worn on the attila was also on the pelisse (see Image VI:131). It was rumoured that Kaiser Wilhelm II, who did not particularly like Edward, made him chief of a hussar regiment because that would force Edward to wear the tight-fitting clothes of a hussar, and thus show off his pudgy physique. Edward had been gaining weight for years, and by 1902, the year of his coronation, both his chest and his waist measured 121.92 cm (48 inches). Edward's social set called him Tum-Tum and Jumbo behind his back. Edward seems to have outsmarted Wilhelm in this photo by wearing the pelisse to camouflage his size. Note also the officer's sash and how it is tied in front.

The officers' pelisses did not have rank lace on the cuffs or collar. However, the shoulder cords were the same as those worn on the attila.

The pelisse had two long cords 60 cm (23.62 inches) long. These were made of chain-braided cord for officers and wool for other ranks. These were used to hold the pelisse on when it was worn off the shoulder (Image VI:147). When the pelisse was worn as a jacket, these thick cords were draped down in front to about mid-chest level and fastened at the back just below the neckline. The cords were in the form of two sets of two cords, one set falling either side of the central line of fur on the front of the pelisse (Image VI:145). Chiefs (*chefs*) of hussar regiments and men supernumerary to the regiment (*à la suite*) could wear a pelisse in the regiment's colours. The pelisse for the 5th Hussars had a fringe (Image VI:148).

Gala Dress

Gala dress was a colourful order of dress worn for royal weddings, receptions, and court balls. It was limited to officers and not worn by other ranks. In theory, the only regiment whose officers were allowed to wear gala dress was the Guard Hussars. However, it does appear that the officers of the 7th Hussars also wore it, in violation of regulations, up to 1914. A possible reason they were able to ignore the rules was that their chief from 1857 to 1888 was Wilhelm I, the king of Prussia and first German Kaiser.

In addition to regimental officers, gala dress was worn by *chefs* and men *à la suite*. Senior military men and royalty both liked to be appointed *à la suite* to hussar regiments so they could wear their colourful uniforms. Being allowed to wear their gala dress was a bonus.

Gala dress had been worn by all hussar regiments up to 1868, but after that date only the officers listed above were entitled to wear it.[165]

Gala dress consisted of the regiment's pelisse if it had one. Only the officers of regiments listed in Table VI.6.d.3 had an official pelisse. Officers of regiments that did not have an official pelisse wore a pelisse the colour of their attila in gala dress. These special gala dress pelisses had brown sable for fur and a white silk lining (Image VI:148). A broad band of lace, either gold or silver depending on the regiment's braid colour, was placed on the sleeve of the pelisse between the fur cuff and the Hungarian knot.[166] The 5th Hussars had once had a dark blue pelisse, but it was changed to the attila colour in 1899.

Gala Breeches

The most eye-catching element of the gala dress was the colourful riding breeches with the mass of braid on each thigh. The braid took the form of an elaborate Hungarian knot with a border of eyelets around it (Images VI:149, VI:150 and VI:151). The loop at the back of the breeches also had small eyelets around it. However, the Saxon hussars did not have a border of eyelets on their breeches.[167] Table VI.6.d.5 lists the colour of the regiments' gala breeches and braid.

Horse Colours

As was the case in the British army, a few regiments limited themselves to horses of certain colours. In the case of the Prussian hussars, there were only two, the 1st Hussars, who rode white or grey horses, and the 2nd Hussars, whose mounts were black.[168]

By tradition, the Prussian army limited themselves to certain horse colours for their trumpeters and drum horses. These did not change over the years, as was often the case in the British army. (Image VI:152 and §VI-2-3-1.)

VI:149 Hussars Zieten Regiment No. 3 Gala Uniform Worn by Arthur, Duke of Connaught and Strathearn, colonel-in-chief of the regiment.

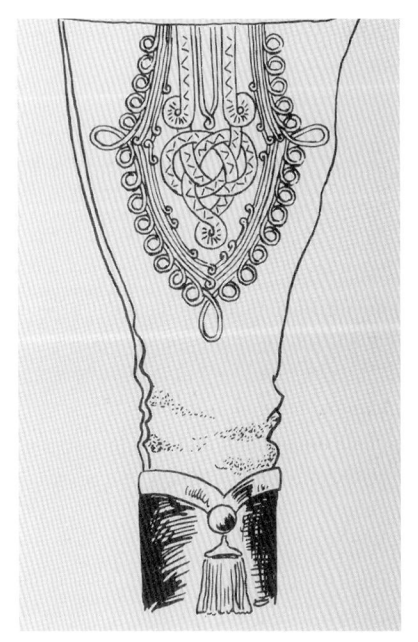

VI:150 Pattern of Lace Worn on Gala Uniform Breeches of Hussar Chefs and a Few Others

Table VI.6.d.5: Colour of Gala Breeches and Braid

Regiment	Colour of Breeches	Braid
Life Guards	Dark blue	Gold
1st Hussars	Black	Silver
2nd Hussars	Black	Silver
3rd Hussars	Dark blue	Silver
4th Hussars	Cornflower blue	Gold
5th Hussars	Black	Silver
6th Hussars	Poppy red	Gold
7th Hussars	Poppy red	Gold
8th Hussars	Dark blue	Silver
9th Hussars	Cornflower blue	Gold
10th Hussars	Deep pink	Gold
11th Hussars	Poppy red	Silver
12th Hussars	Cornflower blue	Silver
13th Hussars	Cornflower blue	Silver
14th Hussars	Dark blue	Silver
15th Hussars	Dark blue	Silver
16th Hussars	Cornflower blue	Silver
17th Hussars	–	–
18th (Saxon) Hussars	Light blue	Gold[a]
19th (Saxon) Hussars	Light blue	Silver[a]
20th (Saxon) Hussars	–	–

Sources: Hagger, *Hussars, etc.*, p. 28; and Herr, *German Cavalry*, p. 468.
Note: [a] Did not have the border of eyelets.

VI:151 Lieutenant General in the Gala Uniform of the 10th Hussars
Note the tassel hanging loose from the top of his boots. This was a part of the hussars' gala uniform.

VI:152 Death's Head Hussars on Parade
Judging by the horse colours and lance pennant, this is probably the 1st Hussars Regiment. Note how long the German lances were.

VI:153 Group of Other Ranks of the 1st Hussars
Note lance pennants with skull and crossbones on them and the trim on the top of their boots.

Lance Pennants

Until 1892, all Hussar regiments carried the same Prussian army lace pennants. (*§VI-3-17*) Then in 1892, the 1st (Death's Head) Hussars were granted a black pennant with a white skull and bones. The 2nd Regiment was given a white pennant with a black skull and bones in 1894.[169] These were carried by all non-officers. This was a unique distinction in the German army (Images VI:152 and VI:153).

§VI-6-e MOUNTED RIFLES (JÄGER ZU PFERDE)[170]

The origin of the Mounted Rifles lies in small detachments formed in the 1890s to carry dispatches. They looked somewhat similar to the uniforms the Jäger zu Pferde would ultimately wear, but some wore hussar dress.

In 1901, there were eight Jäger zu Pferde squadrons, each numbered to correspond with the army corps in which it served, except the XIth Corps, which had two squadrons, the 10th and the 11th.

In 1905, the squadrons were consolidated into three regiments, 1–3. Between 1905 and 1910, three additional regiments were raised. Then, in 1913, the last of the 'old-style' regiments, No. 7, was raised. In October 1913, six 'new-style' Jäger zu Pferde regiments were raised. These regiments, 8–13, wore different helmets and had different button colours.

Uniform

Table VI.6.e.1: Jäger zu Pferde

Regiment	Facing Colour	Type of Coat	Type of Helmet	Date Formed	Breeches and Trousers After 1911	Colour of Button and Helmet Trim	Collar and Cuff	Notes
1	White	Tunic	Cuirassier	1901	Grey-green	White	Light green	A, B, C, D
2	Red	Tunic	Cuirassier	1905	Grey-green	White	Light green	A, B, C, D
3	Lemon yellow	Tunic	Cuirassier	1905	Grey-green	White	Light green	A, B, C, D
4	Light blue	Tunic	Cuirassier	1906	Grey-green	White	Light green	A, B, C, D
5	Black	Tunic	Cuirassier	1908	Grey-green	White	Light green	A, B, C, D
6	Dark blue	Tunic	Cuirassier	1910	Grey-green	White	Light green	A, B, C, D
7	Pink	Tunic	Cuirassier	1913	Grey-green	White	Facing colour	B
8	White	Tunic	Dragoon	1913	Grey-green	Yellow	Facing colour	E, F
9	Red	Tunic	Dragoon	1913	Grey-green	Yellow	Facing colour	E, F
10	Lemon yellow	Tunic	Dragoon	1913	Grey-green	Yellow	Facing colour	E, F
11	Light blue	Tunic	Dragoon	1913	Grey-green	Yellow	Facing colour	E, F
12	Black	Tunic	Dragoon	1913	Grey-green	Yellow	Facing colour	E, F
13	Dark blue	Tunic	Dragoon	1913	Grey-green	Yellow	Facing colour	E, F

Notes:
A: Koller discontinued in 1910 (Herr, *German Cavalry*, p. 612).
B: These regiments wore a cuirassier-style helmet carried over from when they were squadrons.
C: Cuirassier eagle worn on the helmet until 1905, when it was replaced by a dragoon eagle.
D: Light green trim on riding breeches up to 1911.
E: Army orders in 1913 provided for blackened cuirassier helmets for other ranks. But, until they could be issued, the troopers wore dragoon helmets.
F: Officers bought their own cuirassier-style helmets.

Helmet

A blackened cuirassier pattern helmet was worn (see Image C83). From the force's formation until 1905, it had a cuirassier eagle. After that, it had a dragoon-style eagle. The badge and fittings were nickelled silver for other ranks, silver for officers. When Regiments 8–13 were formed in 1913, the idea was that they would wear the same type of blackened helmet.[171] There was no time to produce and issue all NCOs and other ranks cuirassier-style helmets, so instead they were given leather dragoon helmets with dragoon eagles on them. These regiments' button colours were gold or yellow.

Officers of the new regiments, Nos 8–13, who purchased their own uniforms, bought the proper blackened cuirassier-style helmet with the gold dragoon eagle on it. The officers also sometimes wore helmets that were not blackened, but rather had a high polish.[172]

Koller

The koller was worn by the original regiments, Nos 1–6, from their formation until 1910, when kollers were discontinued. They were, except for very minor differences and colour, like those of Prussian cuirassiers described above (for a description, see §VI-6-a).

The koller colour was grey-green with a green stand-up collar and Swedish cuffs. Its piping was green/light green. The Swedish cuffs had cuirassier braid in the same pattern as that worn by cuirassiers. The rear skirts had three buttons on each skirt, one at the waist, and were connected by piping in a scalloped shape. The piping was green.

When the koller was done away with in 1910, the Mounted Rifles began wearing their walking-out tunic as their full dress uniform. The tunic was grey-green and had eight dome buttons with a crown for all ranks. It had a stand-up collar and Swedish cuffs. The rear skirt was the same as that of the koller.

The stand-up collar had the same cuirassier braid as was found on the kollers. The Swedish cuffs also had the same 3.3 cm (1.3 inch) cuirassier braid as the koller. The model of tunic worn, M1910, which replaced the koller,[173] had buttonless side pockets on the front skirts. It also had green piping down the front and around the hem.[174]

Pouch Belt

The pouch belt of officers of Regiments 1–6 of the Mounted Rifles was brown patent leather with a brass Prussian eagle on an oval shield at the top of the belt and, on the lower end, a crowned monogram 'WII' on an oval shield in brass. The two plates were nickel silver. A small nickel silver chain ran from the top plate to the bottom plate. The chain held a whistle which went into a sheath on the bottom plate.

The pouch belt of other ranks for these regiments had the same decorations, with the ornaments being in white metal.

For Regiments 8–13, the pouch belt had gold-plated fittings overlaid with gold-plated decorations. The whistle and chain and its sheath were also gold-plated.[175] Other ranks of Regiments 7–13 did not have a pouch belt.

Pouch

The trooper's pouch for Regiments 1–6 was tanned brown leather, made darker in 1908. On the lid was a brass French hunting horn. Other ranks of Regiments 7–13 did not carry a pouch.

In 1905, Kaiser Wilhelm named himself colonel-in-chief of Jäger zu Pferde Regiment No. 1. This meant that Wilhelm II's monogram was placed over the hunting horn on the pouch lid, and both had an imperial crown above it. It also meant the Kaiser's monogram was on the shoulder straps and epaulettes of Regiment No. 1.

Breeches and Trousers

The colour of the breeches and trousers underwent a number of changes as the nature of these units moved from squadron to regiment size.

	Squadrons	1905 Regiments	Notes
Men's breeches	White	Grey-green Trim: green	A
Men's trousers	Grey-green Trim: green	Grey-green Trim: green	
Officers' breeches	White	Grey-green Trim: green	A
Officers' trousers	Black Trim: red	Grey-green Trim: green or Black Trim: red	B
Officers' gala	White Trim: gold cuirassier braid	White Trim: same braid as worn on the koller	

Notes:
A: Green piping trim dropped in 1911.
B: Black trousers discontinued in 1907.

Boots

The Mounted Rifles other ranks wore brown turn-down boots that came above the knee. The shade of brown was darkened in 1908.

When Regiments 7–13 were formed in 1913, they were ordered to wear the black boots of dragoons and lancers.[176] However, Regiment No. 7, as a semi-old regiment, continued to wear their brown boots.[177]

§VI-7 BAVARIAN CAVALRY

§VI-7-a BAVARIAN HEAVY CAVALRY (SCHWERE REITER)

The two heavy cavalry regiments early on were cuirassiers. The 1st was formed in 1814, and its title changed until 1822, when it was named the Garde Reiter Regiment. Then, in 1875, when its function changed (see below), it added the subtitle '1st Heavy Regiment'. However, officially the subtitles were not to be used. Another Bavarian cavalry regiment was formed in 1849 as the 3rd Reiter Regiment, which acted as a cuirassier force. In 1875, its function also changed, and it was renamed the Carabinier Regiment (2nd Heavy Regiment).[178]

In 1876, the Bavarian Cuirassiers were ordered to give up their cuirass. It took a little time, but they also exchanged their steel helmet and heavy boots for lighter items.[179]

Uniform

Table VI.7.a.1: Bavarian Heavy Reiter

Regiment	Tunic	Facings	Button Colour	Monograms	Helmet[a]	Plume
1st	Light blue	Poppy red	Silver (white)	None	Prussian dragoon-style	White horsehair[b]
2nd	Light blue	Poppy red	Brass (yellow)	None	Prussian dragoon-style	White horsehair[b]

Notes: [a] Prussian helmet adopted in 1886. The helmet had the Bavarian coat of arms on the front in the regiment's button colour.

[b] Officers' plumes were usually made of buffalo hair (Herr, *German Cavalry*, p. 309).

Helmet

The Bavarian helmet, as worn by cuirassiers and heavy reiters prior to 1886, had an outline that was like a shallow Prussian helmet, but instead of a spike, it had a crest, often with a 'caterpillar' on it. The caterpillar of other ranks was made of black horsehair, and those of NCOs and officers black bearskin.

In 1879, as a halfway step towards converting to conform with the Prussian model, a 7 cm (2.76 inch) spike replaced the crest and caterpillar. A white plume replaced the spike for parades and other full dress occasions. The plume was to fall to reach the top of the front visor.

In 1886, the final step to conformity was taken, and the Prussian black polished leather, square-visored dragoon helmet was adopted. The white plume continued to be worn for parades and other formal events. Presumably, the length of the plume remained the same. The plume was horsehair for the other ranks and officers, but most officers elected to go to the expense of buying buffalo hair plumes.

The badges on the front of the helmets prior to the adoption of the Prussian helmet had been the initials of the rulers of Bavaria. When the Prussian dragoon-style helmet was adopted, the Bavarian coat of arms was worn on the front of the helmet. For other ranks in the 1st Regiment, the device was German silver, and it was brass for the 2nd. Officers' devices were silvered for the 1st Regiment and gilded for the 2nd (Image VI:154). Note that the lions in the crest had two tails. The motto below the device was 'In Treue Fest' ('Steadfast in Fidelity'). The centre oval shield on officers' badges was enamelled so the pale blue, black, red, and white stood out. The Reich cockade was worn on the right of the helmet, and the light blue and white Bavarian on the right.[180]

Tunic

The heavy reiters wore a single-breasted tunic of Bavarian light blue, which is really more of a

VI:154 Three Variants of the Bavarian Helmet Plate
Top and middle: Coat of arms in reduced size and simplified by removing branches and leaves. These pictures are variants of this change ordered for officers in 1914 and made for enlisted men in 1896.
Bottom: Traditional style with branches and leaves between the lions' legs.

mid-blue, with a standing collar and Swedish cuffs. It was identical to the Prussian dragoon tunic. The collar and cuff were poppy red (see Image C85).

After 1904, the collar could be up to 6 cm (2.36 inches) high for officers. This was always an important limit as officers tried to make their collars as high as possible in order to be fashionable. This height was a concession to the young blades, as earlier the height had been 4.5 cm (1.77 inches) in 1900 and 3.5 to 4.5 cm (1.38 to 1.77 inches) before that. From 1886, the top and front of the collar had 3 mm (0.12 inch) wide piping.

There were eight buttons down the front of the tunic after 1873. The buttons were white for the 1st Regiment and were at first made of tin. After 1887, they were nickel. After 1887, the 2nd's buttons were tombac, having earlier been brass. The buttons were

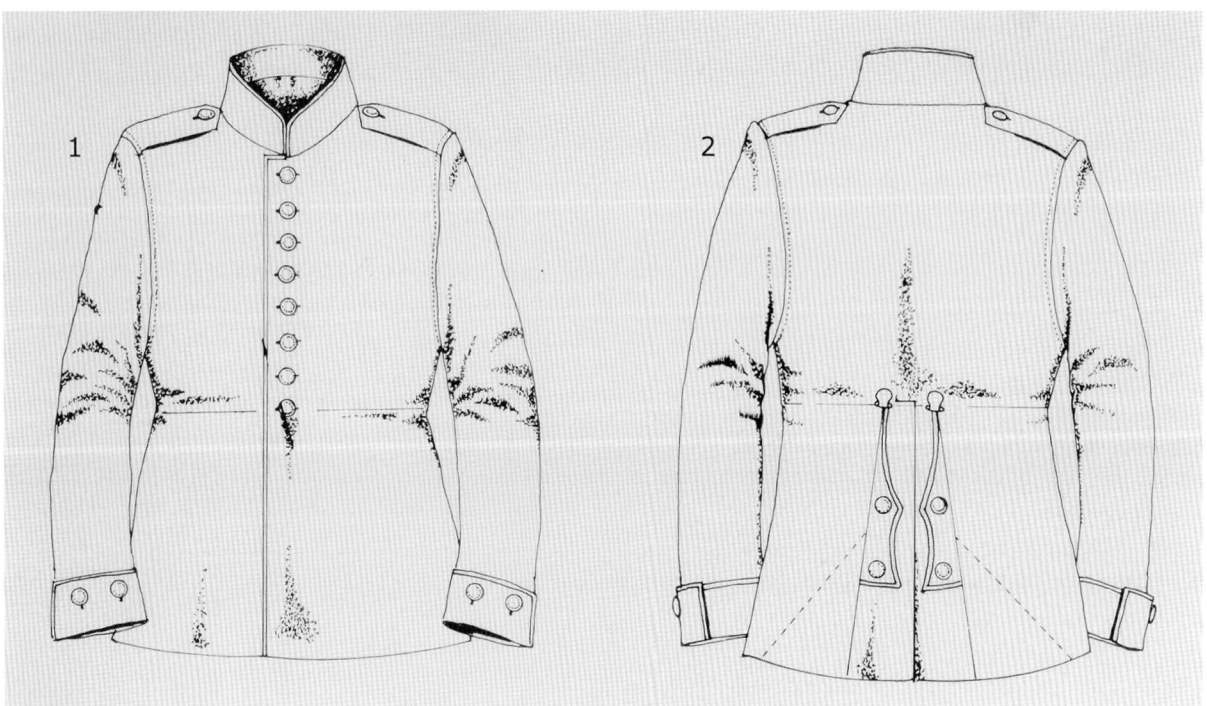

VI:155 Bavarian Heavy Cavalry Full Dress Tunic
1. Front view.
2. Back views. Note scallop pattern trim.

domed without any design on them. The button colour was the only difference between the uniforms of the two regiments.

The tunic was piped down the front edge in poppy red. The piping seems to have been 3 mm (0.12 inch) wide. The rear skirt was divided in two and each side had three buttons connected by red piping in a scallop pattern (Image VI:155). The distance between the buttons after 1904 was 25 cm (9.84 inches). Earlier it had been 22 to 24 cm (8.66 to 9.45 inches).

The Swedish cuff had two buttons and no trim or piping. After 1904, the cuffs were 8 cm (3.15 inches) deep; previously they had been 7 cm (2.76 inches).[181]

Shoulder Straps and Epaulettes

Other ranks wore 6.5 cm (2.56 inch) wide red shoulder straps. The straps did not have a monogram or regimental number.

The officers' epaulettes followed the Prussian model in regard to number of rank stars and fringe. The epaulettes had a red ground inside the crescent and on the flat surface on the shoulder. The fringe and crescents were in the regiment's button colour.[182]

Pouch Belt

The troopers and NCOs had a white leather pouch belt. In 1903, its width was 4 cm (1.57 inches). The Bavarians had adopted the Prussian bandolier in 1890.

The officer's belt was red, faced with silver lace placed so the red showed only as outside trim on both sides of the belt. The silver lace belt had three light blue lines of silk.

Pouch

The other ranks' pouch was black leather without decoration. The pouch for officers was somewhat unusual in that it was squarer than the normal pouch. It measured 12.4 cm (4.88 inches) across, 2.2 cm

VI:156 Bavarian Officer's Pouch
It has the state coat of arms and laurel sprays beneath. Bavarian pouches were made more square.

(0.87 inch) in depth, and 7.2 cm (2.83 inches) in height. It was made of red Moroccan leather and had a silver-plated lid. The lid carried the Bavarian coat of arms in high relief and was the same for all Bavarian regiments (Image VI:156).[183]

Breeches and Trousers

The riding breeches for other ranks were Bavarian light blue until 1878. After that, they wore dark blue-black breeches without piping.

Officers' breeches at first were also light blue without trim from 1870. But, in 1879, these changed to a dark blue-black without trim.

Other ranks and officers wore trousers of Bavarian light blue with a 5 cm (1.97 inch) red stripe on the outside seam for walking out and other formal dismounted events.[184]

Footwear

From 1873 to 1878, long soft over-the-knee boots in the Prussian style were worn in full dress. After 1879, normal black riding boots were worn.[185]

§VI-7-b BAVARIAN LANCERS

The 1st Bavarian Lancers were formed on 21 December 1863 from squadrons of the 3rd and 4th Chevaulegers. The same year the 2nd Bavarian Lancers were formed from the 1st and 5th Chevaulegers. Both regiments led a peaceful life except for the Franco-Prussian War, in which they fought as part of the Bavarian army.

Uniform

Table VI.7.b.1: Bavarian Lancers

Regiment	Plume	Helmet Cloth Colour	Button Colour	Coat Colour	Facing Colour	Collar and Cuff Colour	Plastron Colour
1st	White	Crimson	Yellow	Steel green[a]	Crimson	Crimson	Crimson
2nd	White	Crimson	White	Steel green[a]	Crimson	Crimson	Crimson

Note: [a] The steel green had an olive green tint to it.

Helmet

The helmet worn by the Bavarian lancers upon their creation looked to Austria for its form. It was not until 1886 that the Bavarian lancer helmet assumed the shape of the Prussian helmet. Thereafter, except for the helmet plate, it followed the Prussian model closely.

Tunic

The Bavarian tunic was like its Prussian counterpart, but in *stahlgrun*, a steel green colour (a dark green with an olive green overtone). The piping was in the facing colour: crimson for both regiments. The Bavarian lancers had an outlining of the plastron as was normal, but this piping did not continue down the hem on the left side on the Bavarian lancer's tunic the way it did for other German tunics.[186]

Belt

Bavarian lancers wore a white belt with a plain brass buckle rather than the lancers' girdle worn by other German lancers.

Pouch Belt

The troopers' pouch belts were plain white leather.

Officers' belts were red leather covered by silver lace with three light blue silk lines.

Pouch

Troopers had plain black leather pouches and lids.

The pouches of the officers were red Moroccan leather, and the lid was covered with a silver plate holding the Bavarian coat of arms.

Breeches and Trousers

The riding breeches were steel green for all ranks.

Steel green trousers could be worn inside the garrison after 1875 if privately purchased; therefore details on them are not given in the regulations.[187]

§VI-7-c BAVARIAN LIGHT HORSE (CHEVAULEGERS)

The Bavarian Chevaulegers were the equivalent of dragoons in other armies. The 1st Chevaulegers were formed as a cuirassier regiment in 1682 from three existing and three new reiter (horse) companies. Thereafter, it was changed to a reiter regiment in 1785, back to a cuirassier in 1790, and to dragoons in 1804, before becoming the 1st Chevaulegers in 1811.

The 2nd Regiment was also formed in 1682 and underwent several changes in designation: in 1682, they were cuirassiers; in 1785, reiters; in 1790, dragoons; and in 1811, chevaulegers. In 1835, they were given the name Taxis. This was an important name in Austria and Southern Germany. The Taxis family had grown rich and powerful through their monopoly on mail-carrying throughout the Holy Roman Empire.

The 3rd Regiment was formed in 1724 out of elements of the Guard Carabiniers, the Horse

Grenadiers, and a dragoon regiment. In 1799, they became the 3rd Chevaulegers. Thereafter, they underwent a number of changes, until 1811, when they permanently became the 3rd Regiment.

The 4th was formed in 1744 as a heavy reiter regiment from squadrons of the Life Carabiniers and other reiter and cuirassier regiments. In 1799, it became the 4th Chevaulegers. It underwent a number of changes before settling on that number in 1811. In 1835, it was given the distinction 'King'.

The 5th was formed in 1776 as a dragoon regiment from life dragoon, reiter, and newly raised squadrons.

In 1788, its designation was changed to Chevauleger, and it underwent the inevitable number of changes until 1811, when it permanently became the 5th.

The 6th Chevaulegers trace their origins to an 1803 merging of the dragoons and hussars units of the bishop of Wurtzburg and the dragoons of the bishop of Bamberg. These were formed into a dragoon regiment that underwent several changes down to 1811. In 1811, they were made the 6th Chevaulegers.

The 7th Chevaulegers were created in 1905 and the 8th in 1909 as the manpower of Bavaria grew.

Uniform

Table VI.7.c.1: Bavarian Chevaulegers

Regiment	Facing Colour	Button Colour	Plastron Colour	Shoulder Strap, Collar, Cuffs, Tunic Trim	Walking-Out Trouser Stripes
1st	Crimson	Yellow	Crimson	Crimson	Crimson
2nd	Crimson	White	Crimson	Crimson	Crimson
3rd	Pink (peach)	Yellow	Pink (peach)	Pink (peach)	Pink (peach)
4th	Scarlet	White	Scarlet	Scarlet	Scarlet
5th	Scarlet	Yellow	Scarlet	Scarlet	Scarlet
6th	Pink (peach)	White	Pink (peach)	Pink (peach)	Pink (peach)
7th	White	Yellow	White	White	White
8th	White	White	White	White	White

Source: Marrion, *Lancers etc.*, pp. 102–5.

Note: All regiments wore white horsehair plume for ceremonial events. Their black leather helmets had square front visors.

Helmet

A spiked helmet was introduced in 1886. They were black leather with square front visors. All regiments wore white horsehair plumes for ceremonial events.[188] All metal fittings and the Bavarian coat of arms on the front of the helmet were in the button colour.[189]

Tunic

The chevaulegers wore a tunic of *stahlgrun*, steel green (see Image C87). This was a fairly dark green with olive green tones. The chevaulegers' coat resembled a modified lancer's tunic in its cut and trim (Image VI:157). Like lancers' coats, they had two rows of seven buttons down the front of the tunic in the same pattern. The rear skirts had a scalloped design on each side of the central vent flap. It had the same three buttons on each rear skirt and piping in the regimental colour between the buttons. The rear vent flap was also in the regimental colour.

For parades and ceremonial events, a plastron was worn (see Table VI.7.c.1 for the colour.

A major difference from the standard German lancer tunic was that the front of the chevauleger tunic was trimmed in piping only along the right side of where a plastron would be worn (Image VI:158). This trim continued down to the bottom of the tunic and around its bottom. The sleeves and back seams were not trimmed, which is different from the lancer tunic.

VI:157 Bavarian Chevauleger Tunic
The views show the front and back. Except for the cuffs, this tunic is very similar to that worn by the lancers.

The pointed shoulder straps, stand-up collar, and Swedish cuffs with two buttons were in the regiment's facing colour (Table VI.7.c.1). NCOs had button colour braid on the collar and cuffs. The edges of the collar were piped in steel green for all ranks.

Breeches and Trousers
Breeches were steel green without trim for all ranks.

The walking-out trousers were steel green with a wide facing-colour stripe down the outside of each leg.

Pouch Belt and Pouch
The pouch belt was a plain white leather belt with an open brass bucket. All ranks had a plain black pouch.

Boots
They wore the standard Bavarian riding boots which came up to the knee, and ankle boots with the trousers.

VI:158 A Bavarian Chevauleger
In full dress, he would wear a plastron. Note the open-faced belt buckle.

§VI-8 SAXON CAVALRY

§VI-8-a SAXON HEAVY CAVALRY (SCHWERE REITER)

In 1842, the Saxon cavalry consisted of three reiter regiments: the guard and two others. The guard dated from 1680, the 1st Regiment to 1734, and the 2nd to 1791.

In 1849, a fourth regiment was formed, the 3rd, and the helmet was changed (see below).

In 1876, the 1st and 2nd Regiments were converted into the 18th and 19th Saxon Hussars respectively (*§VI-6-d*). The Guard Reiter Regiment became heavy cavalry, as did the 3rd Regiment. The 3rd Regiment took the title 2nd Heavy (Carabinier) Regiment.[190]

Uniform

Table VI.8.a.1: Saxon Heavy Cavalry Uniform Colours

Regiment	Koller Colour	Koller Trim Colour	Button Colour	Helmet Colour	Plume Colour	Monogram	Notes
Guard Reiter	Saxon cornflower blue	White	Tombac (yellow)	Tombac	White	'FAR' with crown over it	A, B, C
2nd Heavy (Carabinier)	Saxon cornflower blue	Black[a]	Tombac (yellow)	Tombac	White	None	A

Notes: [a] Black velvet for officers and, after 1 January 1892, for senior NCOs.

A: Brass shoulder scales instead of shoulder straps worn by all ranks. Officers' scales were gilded.

B: Had a crown on their shoulder scales.

C: A crouching lion was worn on the top of the helmet after 1907.

HELMET[191]

Following the Napoleonic Wars, in 1821 the Saxon cavalry adopted a helmet that looked very much like the 'Roman helmet' worn by the British cavalry of the same period. In 1849, the crest on the helmet was changed to a crest with an outline that looked much like the crest worn by Austrian dragoons in 1914. Then, in 1867, the crest was changed again to add a wool 'caterpillar' to the top.

In 1876, the Kingdom of Saxony was forced into a military convention with Prussia. As part of the convention, the military dress of the Saxons was brought into general conformity with the Prussians.

The Saxon heavy cavalry regiments (Table VI.8.a.1) received a helmet that was almost identical to the Prussian cuirassier helmet. The helmet was tombac for both regiments, with nickel silver fittings. The helmet underwent slight modifications until 1914. In 1904, the spike was set at 11 cm (4.33 inches) high.

For officers, it was 11 to 12.5 cm (4.33 to 4.92 inches) high.

As a result of the changes introduced by the Prussians, both regiments wore white horsehair plumes on parades. The official length of the plumes varied somewhat over the years. The 1904 Regulations stated it should come exactly to the middle of the visor.[192]

The helmet plate was a Saxon star in German silver with a Saxon coat of arms and laurel leaf wreath around it in tombac. Over the star and wreath was a crown in tombac. For officers, the star was silvered and the arms, wreath, and crown gilded.

After 1897, the Reich cockade was worn on the right and the Saxon on the left of the helmet.

In 1907, the Guard Reiter Regiment was awarded a crouching lion to be worn on the top of their helmets, the way the Prussian cuirassiers wore an eagle. The award was given on the 100th anniversary of the

VI:159 M1889/1907 Helmet for Royal Saxon Guard Reiter Regiment Enlisted Men
It has a tombac skull and silver-plated eight-pointed star with coat of arms under a crown. It has the initials 'FAR' within the oval ring on the shield the lion is holding.

VI:160 Side View of a Helmet for an Officer of the Royal Saxon Guard Reiter Regiment (1st Heavy Regiment)

VI:161 Royal Saxon Guard Reiter Regiment (1st Heavy Regiment) Officer's Helmet
This photograph offers a full view of the lion worn on the helmet.

day the regiment was promoted to the guards and renamed the Life Cuirassier Guards. This is surely one of the most unique and memorable uniform items worn by any antebellum army. The lion of Meissen was an emblem of the old margrave of Meissen, who was said to be an ancestor of the king of Saxony.

The lion, made of German silver, supported with its right paw an upright German silver shield with a cartouche. The cartouche had a tombac corded border and in the centre the monogram 'FAR' under a crown, both in tombac (Images VI:159 to VI:161).

Officers had silvered ornaments, and the tombac trim was gilded.

Koller

The koller worn by the Saxon heavy cavalry was very similar in cut to the Prussian koller (see Image C84). However, it was in Saxon cornflower blue, a shade that was a bit darker than the cornflower blue worn by Prussian dragoons. The collars and Swedish cuffs were in the facing colour and were piped in

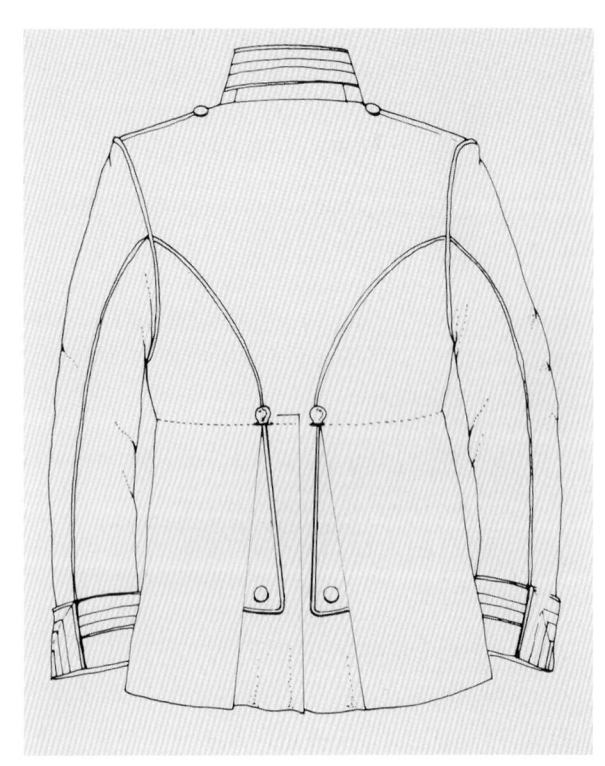

VI:162 Back of a Saxon Koller
It has trim along the seams of the back and the back of the sleeves. Note also the shape of the piping on the rear skirts.

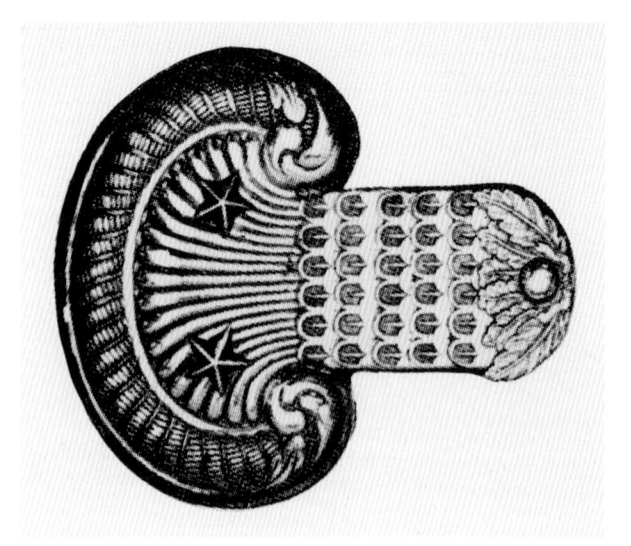

VI:163 Saxon Heavy Cavalry Metal Epaulette

cornflower blue. The koller had piping around the armholes, down the back seams, along the back seams of the sleeves, and on the rear skirts. The piping for both regiments was white. The rear skirts had 'Saxon trim', which consisted of two buttons on either side of the rear slit and straight white trim running between them (Image VI:162).

The koller for other ranks had cuirassier braid with cornflower blue stripes on the outside for the Guard Reiter Regiment and black wool for troopers and junior NCOs of the Carabiniers after 1892 (see Image C86).

Officers wore silver officers' corduroy-style cuirassier braid.[193] The Guard Reiter officers had trim of light blue silk, and the Carabiniers had black velvet.

NCOs wore plain gold braid, but after 1904, the Guard Reiter NCOs wore patterned braid. After 1892, black velvet collars and cuffs could be worn by senior NCOs and officer candidates (ensigns).

A unique feature of the Saxon heavy cavalry was their brass epaulettes with brass crescents on a cornflower blue backing. The other ranks of the Guard Reiter Regiment had a crown within the crescent.

The flat part of the epaulettes of the other ranks was decorated with D-shaped flat plates.

Officers' brass epaulettes were gilded and were without any regimental distinctions. They had five-pointed Saxon stars to show rank, rather than the many-rayed four-pointed Prussian star (Image VI:163). Field officers wore silver fringe on their gilded brass epaulettes.[194]

Special Cuffs

The Swedish cuff was slit at the back and, on most uniforms, the front of the cuff stood out from the sleeve. The regulations provided that the 'fly-away cuff' was to be no more than 1.5 cm (0.59 inch) away from the sleeve. This unusual type of cuff was seen on both regiments and was a long-standing uniform feature (Image VI:164).[195]

BREECHES AND TROUSERS

At first both regiments wore cornflower blue riding breeches with white piping. Then, in 1896, the regiments changed over to white riding breeches.

The Saxon reiter regiments wore cornflower blue trousers with white piping on the outer seams almost from the beginning.

Officers wore gala trousers of cornflower blue with 4 cm (1.57 inch) wide stripes on either side of the trousers' white piping. The stripes were in the regiment's colour and in woollen cloth for the Guards and in velvet for the Carabiniers. These were worn at balls, and after 1897 at the soldiers' own weddings.[196]

From 1875, the Guard Reiter Regiment wore white riding breeches for formal palace wear.

POUCH BELT

The pouch belt for other ranks was thick white leather.

The pouch belt for officers in the Guard Reiter Regiment was cornflower blue, and it was black velvet for the Carabiniers. Both had silver lace along the belts' outside edges.

On the belt, at mid-chest, was a gilt ornament. It was a shield-shaped Saxon coat of arms surrounded by a laurel sprays, and the whole was surmounted by a crown (Image VI:165).

POUCH

Troopers carried a black pouch without decorations.[197] Saxon NCOs had a black leather pouch and pouch lid. On the lid, they had a brass Saxon coat of arms surrounded by a wreath of laurel and surmounted by a crown.

The bottom and front of the officers' pouch was covered in black leather. The back was covered in cloth of the regiment's facing colour. The pouch lid was covered with a gold-plated brass plate.

The outside border had an elaborate border design of stylised clover leaves (Image VI:166). On the face of the lid was an ornament in the form of the Saxon coat of arms surrounded by flag trophies and cannons, and surmounted by a crown.[198]

VI:164 Wilhelm Ernst, Grand Duke of Saxe-Weimar in the Uniform of the Saxon Carabinier Regiment
Note how the cuffs stood well out and away from the sleeve.

VI:165 Saxon Officer's Pouch Belt and Badge Worn on Pouch Belt

VI:166 Saxon Cavalry Pouch Lid
Note stylised clover leaves around the edge.

VI:167 Officers and NCOs of the Saxon Guard Reiter Regiment
They are in kollers and wearing the parade lion on the helmet. This photograph was taken after 1904, when a waist belt with a brass buckle was issued to other ranks. The man on the left is an officer, as can be seen by his officer's belt.

Belt and Officer's Sash

An unusual feature of the Saxon heavy cavalry was that for years the other ranks did not wear a waist belt. It was not until 1904 that one was issued to them. The new belt was 4.5 cm (1.77 inches) wide and made of white chamois leather. It had a rectangular brass buckle with a round shield on it, which held a crown and the Saxon motto 'Providentiae Memor' ('Mindful of Providence').

Reiter officers did not wear a sash until 1896.[199] The two stripes on the white sash were green. Saxon generals wore three stripes on their sashes.[200]

Adjutant's Sash

Until an officer's waist sash was adopted, the only sash worn by Saxon officers was the adjutant's sash. This was 5.5 cm (2.16 inches) wide, until 1897 when it changed to 6 cm (2.36 inches) to match the Prussian model.[201]

Boots

As of 1875, the Saxon Reiters wore black turn-down boots that came 2.54 cm (1 inch) over the knees. These were worn with every type of dress, except walking-out. In drill order, short boots could be worn.[202]

For views of the entire uniform, see Images VI:168 and VI:169; also see Image VI:167.

VI:168 Saxon Guard Reiter Parade Dress (Other Ranks)

VI:169 Saxon 1st Guard Reiter Officer
Note Saxon coat of arms badge on his pouch belt, and cuirassier braid on his koller.

§VI-9 LINE INFANTRY

PRUSSIA AND STATE CONTINGENT

The Prussian army was the creation of Frederick William, the Great Elector (r. 1640–88). He created a standing force and instituted its special relationship with the Junkers (the landed nobility of Prussia).[203] From these beginnings, it grew into a large well-organised and drilled force, 83,000 men, under King Frederick William I (r. 1713–40). He was able to maintain this by following a policy of rigid economy.[204] It was the fourth largest army in Europe, although Prussia was tenth in territory and thirteenth in population.[205] This was the army that his son, Frederick the Great, used to fight his many wars. The army atrophied after Frederick's death, and was destroyed at Jena, Auerstädt, and their aftermath.

A new army and military system was created, beginning in 1807, by a small band of men. The best-known are Stein, Scharnhorst, Gneisenau, Boyen, and Grolman.[206] The Prussian infantry that became famous was the product of these men.

VI:170 Russian Infantry Helmet Introduced in the 1840s and Worn During the Crimean War.
This helmet was very similar to the early Prussian pickelhaube. Note the flame on top of the helmet rather than the spike found on Prussian helmets.

Uniform

The uniform of the Prussian infantry during the nineteenth century was always simple and straightforward, in keeping with the frugal traditions of the Prussian state.

HEADDRESS

Until 1842, the line infantry wore shakos of different shapes and styles. Then, in 1842, the pickelhaube was introduced. There are different stories about where the shape came from. Probably the most believable is that a model of a similar shape was seen in Russia by the Prussian king. A glance at the helmet the Russians introduced just after the Prussians brought in their pickelhaube shows the similarity between the two helmets (Image VI:170). Prussia was able to introduce its model first because it was a smaller country and had a more efficient bureaucracy. The helmet introduced by Prussia in 1842 is shown in Images VI:171, VI:172 and VI:173. The close similarity to the Russian helmet (Image VI:170)

VI:171 M1842 Prussian Helmet
Many believed that this was copied from a Russian model of helmet. Note the guard eagle and guard star on the front and the massive high dome and front and rear brims.

VI:172 Front View of the M1842 Prussian Helmet
Note its high dome and wide front brim. The helmet plate is often described as the grenadier eagle. The initials on the oval shield are 'FWR'.

VI:173 M1842 Helmet with a Prussian Eagle on the Front
At this time the Fatherland banner had not yet been placed on the eagle.

can easily be seen. The photographs of the Prussian helmet also show the early helmet plates used in the Prussian army: guard eagle and guard star (Image VI:171), grenadier eagle (Image VI:172), and line eagle (Image VI:173).

The spiked helmet issued in 1842 was rather tall and heavy, and over the years, via several modifications, it became shorter and lighter. From the beginning, the helmet carried the line version of the Prussian eagle with upturned wings, though the shape changed somewhat over time.[207] In 1860, the Fatherland banner was added to the eagle.[208]

§VI-9-a PRUSSIAN LINE GRENADIERS

In 1860, the old regiments, numbers 1 through 12, were given the name grenadier regiments, but they were still treated and numbered as line regiments.

Helmet

The grenadier regiments wore a special eagle on the helmet. At first, it was a line eagle with an oval shield on the eagle's breast. On the shield was the monogram 'FWR' for Frederick William Rex. Later, under Kaiser Wilhelm II, these eagles were replaced, over a span of several years, by the type of grenadier eagle with outstretched wings formerly worn by the guard grenadier regiments (Image VI:4). It had the letters 'FR' ('Friedrich Rex') on its breast. This device dated back to at least the eighteenth century. The 1st, 4th, 7th, and 9th Grenadier Regiments had banners of one type or another on their eagles (*§VI-3-7* and *§VI-3-8*). Whatever the shape of the eagle, it was yellow, following the button colour.

Originally only the 8th Regiment among the line infantry had worn plumes (black) on their headdress. But, in 1860, when the grenadier title was granted to the first twelve regiments of the line, these regiments were all also granted the right to wear black plumes on their helmets.

Tunics

The grenadiers wore the standard Prussian dark blue single-breasted tunic with yellow buttons and red trim (Image VI:174). There were eight buttons down the front and three on each rear skirt, connected by red trim in a scallop shape. The trim was in the same shape as that used in British infantry uniforms, and the British trim was often called 'Prussian trim'. The stand-up collar was red, as were both parts of the Brandenburg cuffs. The cuffs held three buttons. Grenadiers and line infantry officers wore the lower cuff button unbuttoned until 1896. An exception to this was the 7th Grenadiers, who, after 1897, had the vertical portion of their Brandenburg cuffs in blue, like some guard regiments (§VI-3-13). This was done to mark the 100th anniversary of the birth of Wilhelm I, the namesake of the regiment.

Between 1897 and 1913, Kaiser Wilhelm II awarded special collar and cuff trim to most of the line grenadier regiments (§VI-3-2) This trim was based on uniform trim worn during the era of Frederick the Great.

The Prussian army did not grant special coloured shoulder straps to each regiment. Rather, they assigned cuff trim and shoulder strap colours to different army corps. As a regiment moved between army corps, their

VI:174 This photograph presents a nice identification puzzle. At first glance, the soldier is a typical Prussian infantryman, but the plume belies this. Most Prussian line infantry regiments did not have plumes. The helmet can be seen clearly enough to show that there is nothing on the eagle's chest to indicate that this is a regiment from a contingent state. This could be the uniform of the 86th Line Infantry. They were the only line regiment that had this combination of a Prussian eagle, black plume (after 1895), no litzen, and, after 1867, a white shoulder strap. It could also be the 3rd (Fusilier Battalion) of certain grenadier regiments. The 3rd Battalions of all the grenadier regiments wore black belts, unlike the first two battalions who wore white belts. In 1860, the line grenadier regiments were given black plumes. Until it was replaced, regiment by regiment, during the period 1897 to 1913, all grenadier regiments wore an eagle that had upturned wings and an oval shield with the monogram 'FWR' on its chest. Other than the shield and monogram, the eagle was just like the standard Prussian line eagle. (This eagle was still worn by some Prussian jäger regiments in 1914. An example of it can be seen in §VI-10, Jägers, at Image VI:197.) The 3rd Battalions of the grenadier regiments that meet the conditions of a black belt, no litzen, black plume, white shoulder straps, and Prussian line-style eagle were the 2nd, 3rd, and 4th Grenadiers during a range of years. The range would all start in 1860 with the regiments receiving their black plumes. For the 2nd, these years were up to 1897, when it received the new-style grenadier eagle with outstretched wings (and litzen), For the 3rd, the years were up to 1901, when it received the new-style grenadier eagle (and litzen). The 4th Grenadiers received a banner with '1626' on it to wear on the eagle in 1888. The helmet shows that the banner is not present. Thus the 4th's possible years are 1860 to 1888.

Note also the Kaiser's marksmanship badge on the man's upper right sleeve. This was awarded to the personnel of the best shooting company in each army corps. This award was established in 1895. If the photograph is of a soldier in the 2nd Grenadiers, this further narrows the period of the time in which the photograph could have been taken, to between 1895 and 1897.

cuff trim and shoulder straps colours would change. Table VI.3.13 shows these colours as of 1914 and to which army corps they regiments were assigned.

In addition, the line grenadiers were notable by the high percentage of regiments that had monograms on their shoulder straps and epaulettes. See §VI-3-19 to see the grenadier regiments with monograms and the monograms themselves.

Trousers and Breeches

The line grenadiers wore the standard trousers and breeches (§VI-3-1).

§VI-9-b PRUSSIAN LINE INFANTRY

The heart and soul of the Imperial German army was the steady and self-sacrificing Prussian infantry. After annexing Hanover, Hesse-Cassel, and territory of other states, Prussia made up of approximately 60 per cent of imperial Germany. The line infantry, not counting line grenadiers, had a strength of 121 regiments. When guard and line grenadier regiments were added to the line infantry regiments, Prussia could field 217 infantry regiments. These made up 60 per cent of the total line infantry regiments.[209]

The original Prussian line regiments occupied regimental numbers 13 to 72. Numbers 73 to 88 were from Hanover, Nassau, Hesse-Cassel, the city states, such as Hamburg and Bremen, and other smaller territories absorbed by Prussia in 1866.

At this point, contingent states joined the army list, and the Prussian regiments' number ranges are broken. They were: 97 (part) to 99; 128 to 132; 136 to 138; 140 to 145; 147 to 167, 153 (part); and 171 to 176. The breaks in the numbers were caused by several factors. Numbers 97 through 99 were left unfilled in 1867 when integrating the Saxon army with the Prussian army so as to allow the Saxon regiment numbers to reflect their Saxon army regimental numbers. The Saxon line numbers began at 101. A Saxon guard regiment was number 100. Similar steps were taken in the British Indian army to preserve old regiment numbers. The numbers 97 to 99 were only filled in 1881.

Another factor that caused the number range to be broken was population movements within Prussia and Germany. As Prussia and Germany became industrialised, there was, generally speaking, an internal migration from the rural agricultural Prussian east to Berlin and west to the urban industrial Rhineland. The growth of industry also pulled in people from other states to these and other industrial areas.

In addition, a tremendous population growth occurred between 1871 and 1914. The population grew from 41 million in 1871 to 68 million in 1913. The growth was uneven and not across all corps areas.

This growth and movement meant that new regiments could be formed over the years and that new army corps had to be formed. That, in turn, often meant that regiments needed to be moved from their old corps. Some regiments – for example, the 14th and 17th Regiments – had their cuff piping and shoulder

VI:175 One-Year Volunteer of Infantry Regiment 116 Kaiser Wilhelm (2nd Grand Duke Grossherz Hesse)
Note the white cuff plate.

strap colour changed several times as they moved between corps. It also meant the old colour system stopped being sufficient, and new colours, such as white cuff plates, were introduced (§VI-3-20 and Image VI:175).

By 1914, the number of line infantry regiments, Prussian and the other states', had grown to 182, with another twenty-four in the Bavarian army. See Tables VI.3.13 and VI.3.21 for lists of regimental shoulder strap and cuff plate piping colours.

Helmet

The line infantry regiments wore the same black lacquered leather helmet as was worn by the line grenadiers. On the front, they wore the Prussian line eagle with an 'FR' on its chest (§VI-3-4, Image VI:6).

Because of general Prussian conservatism, there were very few variations from the standard line eagle. The 5th and 6th Companies of the 2nd Battalion of the 33rd Regiment and 1st and 2nd Battalions of the 34th Regiment wore a banner showing their tie with the Swedish Life Guard Regiment before another bit of Pomerania, ruled by Sweden, was taken over in 1815.

The 145th King's Infantry Regiment was awarded a 'guard eagle' in 1913. It is unclear whether this eagle was a true guard eagle or a grenadier-style eagle.[210] It is said that this award was because one of Kaiser Wilhelm II's vacation homes was located near where the 145th was stationed. For this reason, the 145th often provided guard details for the Kaiser and his family, and the Kaiser became familiar with the officers. In 1893, three years after the regiment was formed, Wilhelm named the regiment after himself, and it became the 145th King's Regiment. Consequently, on the twenty-fifth anniversary of his reign, Wilhelm awarded a special eagle to the regiment. They had earlier, in 1895, been given the right to wear a black plume.

Also in 1913, the 25th Regiment was granted the right to wear a black plume on their helmet. The regiment was a descendant of the most famous free corps in the Wars of Liberation, the Lützow Free Corps.[211]

Regiments numbers 73 to 88 were Prussian line regiments. Wilhelm II, towards the turn of the twentieth century, started recognising the history of the states that supplied men to the regiments. Some of the regiments were issued helmet banners and uniform decorations based on what were very tenuous connections to the old regiments and the honours they had won.

Regiments 89 through 96 were drawn from regiments that had entered the Prussian army list in 1866 as part of the North German Confederation. As such, they were recognised by combinations of helmet badges and cockades. Some of the places of origin, such as the cities of Bremen, Hamburg, and Lübeck, the Duchy of Lippe-Detmold, and the principalities of Schaumburg-Lippe, and Waldeck-Pyrmond, had their participation in the army noted only by cockades on the regiments' helmets. See §VI-3-12 for a list of cockade colours.

Other larger states were recognised by being allowed to place their state's coat of arms on the Prussian line eagle and to use a Fürst banner in place of the Fatherland banner. Oldenburg was an exception to the Fürst banner rule, which is interesting because – if one goes back to the time of Peter III – one finds that he was a German and grandson of Peter the Great of Russia and came from a junior branch of the ruling family of Oldenburg. This caused Oldenburg and Russia to have close relations down the years. That the Oldenburg regiment was given the Fatherland banner may have been the relatively new Hohenzollerns snubbing the Romanovs. On the other hand, the state's regiment was granted an eight-pointed white star and a badge for the eagle in 1870 and a black plume in 1913. In addition, the helmet of reserve officers had a Fürst banner.[212]

See §VI-3-5 for regiments in the range 89 to 96 who had their coat of arms on their helmet. A sample of these helmet plates can be seen at §VI-3-4, Images VI:7 to VI:14.

Mecklenburg-Schwerin was able to obtain a very good bargain from the Prussians in terms of uniform details and the number of military units it was able to carry into the contingent state army. Its ruler at the time was a nephew of Prussian King Wilhelm II and had been a Prussian general since 1842. The state had a history of good relations with Prussia. This goes far in explaining why the two Mecklenburg states were not forced to adopt the Prussian eagle for their helmets in 1867.

As contingent states joined the army, they were often more free in granting helmet banners. Brunswick is an example. Another source of the uniform variation is the fact that many of the regiments pulled into the Prussian army list acted as guard regiments in their grand duchies, duchies, and principalities, and as such wore litzen.

See §VI-3-5 for a list of helmet badges, §VI-3-10 for the infantry regiments that wore plumes, §VI-3-11 for the colours of the helmet badges, §VI-3-12 for the colours of the state's cockades, §VI-3-13 for the regiments' cuff piping and shoulder strap colours and whether or not they wore monograms, §VI-3-19 for infantry monograms; and §VI-3-15 for a list of regiments in this range that wore litzen, what type, and whether or not they were considered guard units.

§VI-9-c HESSE LINE INFANTRY

Confusingly, in the 1700s and early 1800s there were at least two Hessian states, Hesse-Cassel and Hesse-Darmstadt.

HESSE-CASSEL[213]

Hesse-Cassel made a specialty of renting out mercenary regiments during the eighteenth century. It was the state's main source of income. Britain was a major customer, and at times kept Hesse-Cassel on retainer in order to have ready access to its fighting men. Britain made extensive use of Hesse-Cassel's regiments in the American Revolutionary War, and the Americans hated and feared the 'Hessians', which became a general term for all British German mercenaries.

During the Austro-Prussian War Hesse-Cassel sided with Austria. After the war, Prussia annexed the state because the main route to its Rhine provinces ran across the state. The territory formed four Prussian regiments, 80 through 83. There was nothing on the regiments' helmet or uniform to reflect the area's 'Hessian' history; only regimental titles recalled Hesse-Cassel.

HESSE-DARMSTADT

Hesse-Darmstadt also sided with Austria against Prussia in 1866. The state lost territory but remained in existence, perhaps because the sister of the ruler of Hesse-Darmstadt, Louis Ludwig III, was the wife of the czar of Russia.

Uniform

HELMET[214]
The basic helmet plate for Hesse-Darmstadt (hereinafter 'Hessian') regiments was a left-facing crowned lion holding a sword. The lion was surrounded on the left and right by a wreath – oak leaves on the left, laurel on the right. For most regiments the plates and fittings were brass. There were some variations from the basic pattern.

In 1871 Regiment 115 was given a brass banner to be worn above the lion with '1621' to commemorate the year of the regiment's establishment. In 1897 the helmet plate and fittings were changed to silver. The wreaths were made double and a star of the Hessian Order of Ludwig was added. The star had the motto 'Gott Ehre Vaterland' ('God, Honour, Fatherland'). The centre of the officers' star was enamelled.

In 1897 Regiment 117 was awarded two banners. One on the left, over the oak leaves, had '1697' in black. The other banner, on the right, over the laurel leaves, had '1897' in black. These commemorate the 200th anniversary of the regiment. In 1871 the 9th Company

VI:176 Standard Hessian Helmet

VI:178 Helmet of Hessian Infantry Regiment 117
Note the banner with the dates 1697–1897 on the wreath. These dates commemorate the 200th anniversary of the regiment. The helmet banner was issued in 1889.

VI:177 Helmet of Hessian Regiment 115
Note the double set of leaves, the banner at the top of the badge, and the star of the Order of Ludwig.

of the regiment had a white metal anchor between the legs of the lion. On the anchor were placed a crossed pickaxe and axe. These recalled that the regiment was reformed based on an engineering company in 1871.

Black plumes were worn on parades by Regiments 115 (after 1871), 116 (after 1898) and 117 (after 1883).[215] The other regiments, i.e. 118 and 168 (after being formed in 1897) did not have plumes. All regiments except for No. 115 had yellow brass lion plates on the helmets and brass fittings.

Tunic[216]

The tunics of the Hesse regiments followed the Prussian colour and style with few exceptions. The Hesse regiments, like the Prussians, wore Brandenburg cuffs. An exception was that the vertical flap of the cuff for each of the first four regiments was a different colour: 115 – red; 116 – white; 117 – potassium blue; and 118 – yellow. Regiment 168 when formed in 1897 was given a red flap.

VI:179 Prussian Infantry Regiment in Full Dress
This photograph gives a good idea of what an average Prussian infantry regiment looked like in full dress. The thrifty Prussians used their somewhat shop-worn old full dress as a number two dress to get more use out of it.

Until 1897 shoulder straps were straight at the top near the collar. After that they were pointed like the rest of the army (except the Saxons).

The Life Guard Infantry Regiment 115 had litzen on their collars and cuffs. Until 1884 these were rectangular in shape. After that they took the chapter shape.

Hesse regiments, like the rest of the Prussian army, left the bottom button on the vertical flap of their Brandenburg cuff unbuttoned. In 1896, when the order came to button all bottom buttons, the officers of the Hesse Life Guard Regiment 115 kept them unbuttoned. They did so at least until 1914.[217] A possible reason for this might have been family ties: the custom of leaving the bottom button unbuttoned came from Russia and in 1896 the Empress of Russia, Alexandra, was a daughter of Ludwig IV, the ruler of Hesse until 1892, and sister of the ruler in 1896.

Trousers and Belts

Other ranks' and officers' trousers and breeches conformed to the Prussian practice.

The other ranks of all regiments wore black belts. The buckle was rectangular and had a ducal coronet (crown) on it. For all regiments except No. 115, the buckle was brass. The buckle for Regiment 115 was nickel silver after 1897.

Officers

Officers wore a white cloth belt that had three rows of red vertical dashes. The buckle was round. In its centre was the ruler's monogram under a ducal coronet.

§VI-9-d SAXON LINE INFANTRY

The Saxon army had fought on the side of Austria in the Austro-Prussian War of 1866. In fact, they formed the Austrian army's left flank at the showdown Battle of Sadowa, also called the Battle of Königgratz. But, soon after the war, Saxony, with what grace it could muster, joined the military convention of 1867, which brought so many states under the control of the Prussian army.

When the Saxon army came onto the Prussian army list, the Saxons had eight infantry regiments, one of which, the 1st, served as a guard unit, as well as a special rifle regiment. They received the numbers 100 through 108, with the rifle regiment taking number 108.

In the following years, new regiments were added as follows:

- 1881　133 (9th Saxon) and 134 (10th Saxon)
- 1887　139 (11th Saxon)
- 1897　177 through 181 (12th through 15th Saxon)
- 1912　182 (16th Saxon) and a third battalion for each of the 177–181 Regiments (12th through 15th Saxon)

They also kept their old numbers, and the prefix 'Royal Saxon' was carried by all regiments. They are not often shown on lists and tables in this work in the interest of space. The Saxon army formed the XII and XIX Army Corps in 1914.

Uniform

All uniform descriptions below will be those of the Saxon troops after the state came under the sway of Prussia in 1867.

HELMET

The Saxons wore the Prussian helmet with a star and a crowned Saxon coat of arms within an oak and laurel wreath on it (*§VI-3-4*, Images VI:180 and VI:181, and Table VI.3.11). The starburst for the 100th (Life Guard) Grenadier Regiment was silver with a brass (gilt for officers) crown and coat of arms. The line regiments had the colours reversed, brass (gilt for officers) starburst and silver coat of arms.

VI:180 Saxon Infantry Officer's Helmet
The Saxon numbering range started at 100.

VI:181 Other Ranks' Saxon Infantry Helmet
Notice the wreath is not cut out. Also note the Saxon cockade on the left of the helmet and the very different spike worn by the other ranks.

Regiment 108 wore the uniform of a jäger regiment and is covered in the section on jägers.

Regiments 100 and 101 had black plumes (*§VI-3-10*).

TUNIC

The Saxons wore a Prussian dark blue tunic that had a slightly different cut from the regular Prussian tunic. It was about 8 cm (3.15 inches) shorter than the Prussian tunic, and unlike the Prussian, only half-covered the seat.[218] The collar and Saxon cuffs were red and piped in dark blue. Both sides of the front of the tunic had red piping. The red piping continued around the bottom of the tunic on both sides and went up the opening slit at the back of the tunic. The back of the tunic had two buttons on each side of the rear skirt. One was at the waist and the other below it. The two were connected by a straight line of trim that went just under the bottom button. The button and trim combination on the left rear skirt was well away from the point and to the right of where the left skirt met the right skirt.

There were eight buttons down the front, one falling under the belt, in white for the 100th, brass for all others.

The Regiments 100 and 101 (Saxon Grenadier) carried litzen on the collar and Saxon cuffs. It was white (silver for officers) for No. 100 (Image VI:182), and white for the other ranks of Regiment 101 and gold for officers.[219] The litzen was in the chapter shape for both regiments. The two regiments with litzen had square collars; on the other regiments, it was rounded.

The Saxon army was also marked by its use of a different type of shoulder strap. It was rectangular in shape and piped on top and the two sides by red piping (Image VI:183). The bottom of the strap had a narrow red woollen cord that was used in rolling up the shoulder strap.[220] The shoulder strap was the colour of the tunic, dark blue, with yellow numbers or

VI:182 Officer of Saxon Life Grenadier Regiment 100
Note eight-pointed star and Saxon coat of arms on his helmet and the chapter litzen worn by this regiment.

VI:183 Saxon 5th Infantry Regiment 104 (Prince Friedrich August)
Note the helmet plate and shape of the shoulder strap.

VI:184 Saxon NCO
Note the extra lace worn above the cuff by the regimental sergeant major.

VI:185 One-Year Volunteer, Saxon Infantry Regiment 104 or 181

monograms, with white for Regiment 100 after 1893.[221] Four regiments had monograms during the period 1880–1914 (see §VI-3-13 for a list of the regiments and §VI-3-19 and Image VI:20 for illustrations of the monograms).

Trousers and Breeches

The Saxons wore the same dark blue-black trousers and breeches as the Prussian army (Image VI:184).

Belt and Buckle

The black belt was the same as that used in the Prussian army. Most carried a brass buckle with a round shield of nickelled silver (Image VI:185). However, there were some variations in the belt buckles used by the Saxons. Regiment 100 had a silver buckle with a tombac shield.[222] The shield for most regiments consisted of a crown with the motto 'Providentiae Memor' ('Mindful of Providence') around it. After 1896, Regiment 108's buckle had the monogram of its *chef*, Crown Prince and then King Georg. After 1896 Regiment 107 also carried the monogram 'JG' of its *chef*, Prince Johann Georg.[223]

Sash

The officer's sash was the same as that worn in Prussia, except it had two green stripes rather than Prussia's two black ones. In 1872 regulations provided for an adjutant's sash that was 5.5 cm (2.1 inches) wide. It was silver with two broken green lines. It ended in long green and silver tassels. By 1904 its size was the same as in Prussia, 6 to 7 cm (2.3 to 2.75 inches) wide.[224]

Shoes

The Saxons wore the same boots and shoes as the Prussians. As a side note, the Saxons never tucked their trousers into their boots, as was the Prussian practice.[225]

§VI-9-e BADEN LINE INFANTRY

The state of Baden followed a course of balance between the Prussians and the Austrians. It sided with Austria in the 1866 war and did not join the North German Confederation or become part of the military convention in 1867. But, after the war, the state cooperated with Prussia and became subject to Prussian regulations. In addition, a Prussian general took command of the Baden division.

Bismarck had tied Baden, along with the other south German states, to treaties committing them to fight France in the event of war. Following the Franco-Prussian War, the Baden army became a component part of the Prussian army as Regiments 109 through 114. It, like the Saxons, kept its regimental names and numbers in addition to its number in the new Imperial army.

In 1890, Regiment 142 (7th Baden) was formed. This was followed in 1897 by Regiments 169 (8th Baden) and 170 (9th Baden).[226] The regiments no longer had the name 'Grand Duchy' in their names; they were just referred to as Baden, much like a Prussian province designation. Baden supplied the regiments for the XIV Corps, but no special notation was made of the fact that it was a Baden corps, as one Prussian regiment, the 40th in 1914, was needed to make it a full corps. This was unlike what was done for the larger Saxon and the slightly larger Württemberg army in the XIII Corps, who could supply full corps.

Uniform

The Baden uniform had tracked that of Prussia since the 1850s; there were few changes that needed to be made to the uniform when the Prussians took over.

Helmet

The Baden regiments' helmet was similar to that worn by the Prussians, and it changed as the Prussian helmet changed. The plate on the front was a brass Baden griffin (gold-plated for officers) with a banner reading 'Mit Gott F. Fuerst U. Vaterland' under it (§VI-3-4, Image VI:186). In 1885, the 109th Life Guard Grenadiers were given a nickel-silver griffin with a nickel-silver star. For officers, the griffin was silver-plated, and the star had coloured enamelling (§VI-3-4, Image VI:187).[227]

The 1st and 2nd Battalions of Regiments 109 and 110 wore white horsehair plumes for parades and other full dress events. Officers would wear plumes of buffalo hair. The 3rd Battalions of those regiments wore black plumes.

Tunic

The tunic worn by the Baden regiments closely followed the Prussian model in all respects, and therefore only identifying differences will be noted here.

VI:186 Baden Infantry Officer's Parade Helmet

VI:187 Officer's Helmet of Infantry Regiment 109 (Baden Life Grenadiers)
This consists of the standard Baden griffin with the addition of the star and cross of the Order of Loyalty.

As in Prussia, all regiments wore red collars and cuffs. The Life Guard Grenadier 109th Regiment had Swedish cuffs (Image VI:188); all the other regiments had Brandenburg cuffs (Image VI:189). The uniform of the 109th Life Guards was quite similar to that of the Prussian 1st Foot Guards. It also had a square collar, white chapter litzen (silver for officers), and after 1885, white buttons. NCOs wore white braid.

The Baden shoulder strap colours did not follow the normal pattern, having an extra light blue colour added to the range. In addition, the colours ranged widely. The best way to follow their colours is to see §VI-3-13.

Four regiments had monograms or crowns on their shoulder straps in 1914. See §VI-3-13, §VI-3-19, and Image VI:20 for a list of the regiments and to see the monograms.

Trousers, Breeches, and Footwear

The Baden regiments wore the standard Prussian items.

VI:188 Baden Life Guard Regiment 109
Note the crown on his shoulder strap and the litzen worn by this regiment. Also note the shape of the belt buckle.

VI:189 6th Baden Infantry Regiment 114 (Kaiser Friedrich III)
Note griffin plate on his helmet.

Sash

The officer's and adjutant's sashes of certain contingents were the same size and colour as those of Prussia, but had a red thread added down the middle. In this way they showed the imperial colours. These sashes were worn by: Baden, Oldenburg, Anhalt, Reuss, Saxe-Altenburg and Gotha, Saxe-Meiningen, Saxe-Weimar and Schwarzburg-Rudolstadt.[228]

Belts

The regiments wore a Prussian black belt with a Prussian buckle.[229]

§VI-9-f WÜRTTEMBERG LINE INFANTRY

After fighting on the side of Austria in 1866, Württemberg drew closer to Prussia and took part in the Franco-Prussian War on its side. After the war, the Wüttermberg regiments entered the Prussian army lists as numbers 119 through 126, and they also carried the designation 1st to 8th Württemberg Regiments. In 1897, Regiments 127 and 180 were formed (9th and 10th Württemberg Regiments) as part of a wholesale expansion of the German army. These regiments formed the XIII (Württemberg) Army Corps.

Uniform

Helmet

A Prussian helmet was adopted in 1871. Other ranks wore the standard black leather helmet with a rounded front visor. However, the officers were an exception in that they had a square front visor. The helmet plate was the Württemberg coat of arms (*§VI-3-4*, Image VI:190). It was brass (gold-plated for officers) for all regiments, with two exceptions up to 1896. After that, it was tombac.[230] The exceptions were Grenadier Regiments 119 and 123, which had nickel-silver (silver-plated for officers) coats of arms as their helmet plates.

After 1871, Regiment 119 wore white plumes, and 123 wore black plumes. Regiment 120 was granted black plumes in 1899.[231]

Tunic

In 1871, Württemberg regiments wore a dark blue double-breasted tunic, and the army continued to wear these until 1892. Early on it adopted the Prussian red collar and cuffs on the double-breasted tunics to

VI:190 Standard Württemberg Helmet Plate Showing Wurttemberg Coat of Arms
The Württemberg range of regimental numbers was 119 to 127, and 180.

blend with Prussia. In 1892, the Prussian tunic was introduced, but the old double-breasted models continued to be worn until they were worn out. In reality, this took a long time.

The dark blue double-breasted tunic had two rows of six buttons down the front. The right edge of the front was piped in red. The tunic had a red stand-up collar piped in dark blue. The regiments had red Brandenburg cuffs, with two exceptions. The two exceptions, the 199th and 123rd Grenadiers, wore red Swedish cuffs. Both of these regiments had white linen (silver for officers) litzen on their collars and cuffs. The litzen were in the chapter shape. These two regiments, because of the litzen, had square tunic collars. All the others had rounded collars.

The buttons were made of tombac for all regiments.

Because the regiments were in the XIII Corps, they wore red shoulder straps and had light blue trim on their Brandenburg cuff plates.

The rear skirts had three buttons on each side, with one at the waist. The buttons were connected by red piping in a scalloped shape.

The Prussian tunic was introduced in 1892. As in Prussia, it was single-breasted with eight buttons down the front, and the front was trimmed with red piping. All the other details of the double-breasted tunic as to colour and shape of collar and cuffs, litzen, back trim, etc. were carried over from the Prussian tunic.

By 1914, five regiments had monograms on their shoulder straps and epaulettes.

See §VI-3-13 and §VI-3-19 and Images VI:20 and VI:21 for a list of regiments that carried monograms and to see the monograms.

Trousers and Breeches

With the exception of white linen trousers, the regulations that applied in Prussia also applied in Württemberg.[232] Württemberg soldiers did not wear white trousers, but officers, and presumably NCOs and men, sent to the Prussian army wore white trousers to conform to Prussian practice while there.

Belt and Buckle

A black belt that conformed to the Prussian style was worn. The belt buckle was brass, tombac, or aluminium bronze. On it was a round white metal shield with the state's coat of arms in the centre. Around the coat of arms was the motto 'Furchtlos und Trew' ('Fearless and True').[233]

§VI-9-g BAVARIAN LINE INFANTRY[234]

Bavaria in the south-west of Germany was one of the largest states in Germany and a Catholic counterweight to Prussia. An old saying goes that the Bavarians had the charm of the Prussians and the efficiency of the Austrians (who were famous for their fecklessness). In 1914, Rupprecht, the Crown Prince of Bavaria, was the leading Stuart heir to the thrones of England and Scotland. Every year on the anniversary of the death of Charles I, white roses filled the Bavarian royal palace.[235]

After opposing Prussia in 1866, Bavaria entered into a treaty that brought its army under the command of the Prussians in the event of a future war. That conflict, the Franco-Prussian War, soon came. After the war, Bavaria joined the Imperial Confederation, but its army remained self-contained and outside Prussian command in peacetime. However, their uniforms were made to conform in many ways to the Prussian model, although they retained their own uniform colour.

When the Bavarians joined the Imperial Confederation, they had sixteen regiments to field, one guard and fifteen line.

After that the army was expanded as follows:

1878   two regiments, Nos 16 and 17
1881   one regiment, No. 18
1890   one regiment, No. 19
1897   four regiments, Nos 20 to 23

By 1914, Bavaria supplied three separate army corps to the German army.

Uniform

Helmet

The Bavarians fought the French in their own Tarleton-style leather helmet. On the top, it had a black crest, called a caterpillar, which was bearskin for officers.

In 1886, a Prussian-style black leather pickelhaube was adopted. It is said that it had a square front visor, and the spike was slightly different.[236] The officers continued to wear a square visor up to 1914, but in 1896 other ranks changed over to rounded front visors as

VI:191 Bavarian Infantry Regiment 16 (Grossh' Ferdinand von Toscana)
Note the tunic and trousers are the same colour. Also note the Bavarian coat of arms on his helmet.

VI:192 Bavarian Infantry Regiment 15 (King Albert von Sachsen)
This photograph clearly shows that the tunic and trousers are the same colour. Note piping around the cuff plate.

part of a general modification taking place in Prussian helmets.[237] See *§VI-3-4*, Image VI:15, and also Images VI:191 and VI:193. Also see Image VI:192, which shows the old other ranks square-fronted helmet. The front plate was now the Bavarian coat of arms rather than the traditional king's monogram (*§VI-3-4*, Image VI:15). The coat of arms was nickel-silver for other ranks of the Life Guard Regiment (silver-plated for officers). For all other regiments, it was tombac (gold-plated for officers). In February 1914, the officers' coat of arms was modified by being reduced in size and doing away with some of the foliage between the lions and the central oval shield. This new model helmet is rare because officers, who paid for their own helmets, were allowed time to switch over to the new style. There is photographic evidence that other ranks also received the new, smaller, and simpler coat of arms.

In 1914, chin scales were generally abolished for other ranks, and officers were granted convex chin scales.[238]

No Bavarian regiment wore a plume.

Tunic

The Bavarians stood out because they wore a 'light blue' (really a mid-blue) tunic. Historically, the Bavarians had their own uniform design, and it took time to bring them into conformity with the Prussian style, which was provided for in the 1870 treaty between Prussia and Bavaria.[239] The Bavarians adopted Brandenburg cuffs, new collars, a different number of buttons, new insignia, different collar colours, and a new style of shoulder straps.

Image C89 shows how the Bavarian tunic, as

VI:193 NCO of Bavarian 11th Infantry
Note location of NCO braid on cuffs and collar.

VI:194 Officer of the Bavarian Life Guards
Note the shape and design of the officer's litzen on his collar and cuffs.

modified, closely followed the Prussian style except for its colour. The single-breasted tunic had, with one exception, eight brass buttons down the front. In 1887, the buttons were changed to tombac. The exception was the Life Guard Regiment, which had eight tin buttons until 1887 and nickel-silver ones after that. All of their buttons, as a mark of special distinction, were decorated with a crown, which was the badge carried on the shoulder strap.

The front of the tunic was piped in red. The cuffs were piped in white for all ranks. On the rear skirt there were buttons and piping on each side of the central vent. Each rear skirt had three buttons. One button was at waist level; the other two buttons were connected by red piping in a scalloped shape, as was used in the Prussian infantry.

The stand-up collar and cuffs were red. The collar after 1886 had piping the colour of the tunic. The collar for the line regiments was slightly rounded in front. The collar for the Life Guards was square since they had litzen on their collars. With one exception, the infantry wore Brandenburg cuffs with three yellow buttons. The Brandenburg cuffs were red and the cuff plate was piped to show what corps the regiment belonged to. They were: I Corps, white; II Corps, none; and III Corps (after being formed in 1900), yellow (Image VI:191). The exception was the Life Guard Regiment, which had red Swedish cuffs with two white buttons. The cuffs were piped in white for all ranks (Image VI:194).

The Life Guard Regiment had white litzen on the collar and cuffs. There were two on the cuffs and two on the collars. The officers' litzen were silver and did not have a spiegel.

All regiments wore a red shoulder strap regardless of what corps they belonged to. The shoulder strap came to a point near the collar just like the Prussian shoulder straps. The regimental badges, insignias, and monograms were all yellow.

The Life Guards had a crown on their shoulder straps, and in 1914, five line regiments carried monograms. Monograms in the Bavarian army started being granted only at the end of the nineteenth century and were used very sparingly.[240] The last, that of King Ludwig III of Bavaria, was granted in November 1913.[241] See *§VI-3-13* for a list of regiments that had monograms and *§VI-3-19* and Image VI:21 for the monograms.

Badges of rank for NCOs and officers followed the Prussian system, with only minor variations. Up to 1873, Bavarian officers had worn gorgets, but those were dropped in that year.[242]

TROUSERS AND BREECHES

Trousers
After 1873 the Bavarian army wore trousers of the same cut as those of the Prussian army. However, the Bavarians' trousers were the same shade of blue as their tunics, officially light blue, but really more of a mid-blue (Images VI:191 and VI:193). The trousers had 2 mm (0.08 inch) wide red piping along each outside seam.

In the summer months, both officers and men wore only white trousers.[243]

Breeches
Mounted officers were authorised to wear breeches reinforced with leather insets. These breeches were the same colour as the tunic and had the same piping on the outside seams as the trousers.

Gala Trousers
There were no official gala trousers, so Bavarian officers wore their white summer trousers to events that called for gala trousers.

BELT AND BUCKLES

The Bavarians wore a black leather belt 4.86 cm (1.91 inches) wide.

Until about 1887, they wore a brass double-pronged buckle that was only slightly wider than the belt. After that, a Prussian-style brass box-type buckle was introduced and the belt became 5 cm (1.97 inches) wide. A nickel-silver round shield was in the centre of the buckle. The shield had the same motif as the Prussian shield, a crown in the centre with a motto around it. The Bavarians motto was 'In Treue Fest' ('Steadfastly Loyal').

In 1896, the width of the black belt dropped from 5 cm to 4.5 cm (1.97 to 1.77 inches).

FOOTWEAR

The Bavarian infantry after 1873 wore the same half-boots with iron nails in the soles as were worn by the Prussians. They also wore the same shoes with laces, knee-high boots, and riding boots as the Prussians.

OFFICER'S AND ADJUTANT'S SASH

After 1873, an officer's sash was worn around the waist. It was silver with two lines made up of checked stripes (or dashes) of light blue in it. The tassels were a mix of silver and light blue.

An adjutant's sash of the same colours, but with the wider width used in the Prussian army, was worn over the right shoulder and fell across the chest to the left hip.

§VI-10 JÄGERS AND SCHÜTZEN (RIFLES)[244]

The first green-coated jäger units were said to have been formed by what became the Electorate of Hesse-Cassel in 1631. They were attached to and subordinate to regular infantry regiments and fought on the side of Gustav Adolphus in the Thirty Years' War.[245] Other German states soon raised their own Jäger units, Bavaria in 1645 and Brandenburg in 1674, as well as several smaller states, such as Hanover, Ansbach-Bayreuth, and Brunswick. Originally, there was a difference between Jägers and Schützen. Jägers were drawn from professional foresters and specialised in difficult terrain. They often acted on their own well in advance of the main body of the army. Schützen were expert marksmen and also had high levels of fieldcraft.

Frederick the Great formed a permanent Jäger establishment for Prussia in 1744 with men exclusively drawn from a forestry background.[246] The Jäger and Schützen troops were part of the light battalions of the line infantry regiments. They did well during Frederick's wars and gained a very good reputation.

Jäger units were among the German troops Britain sent to America to help put down the revolt. Their combination of excellent marksmanship and good fieldcraft gave the Americans a healthy respect and fear of them. Some say their fieldcraft was better than that of the frontiersmen. Certainly their discipline was better.

The debacle of Jena caused the Prussian army to be reorganised in 1808. The Guard and the 1st and 2nd Jägers were formed as separate battalions. These acquired an outstanding reputation during the Wars of Liberation (1813–15).

Frederick I and his heirs ruled Brandenburg and Neuchatel in a personal union. In 1814, Neuchatel formed a guard battalion for the king. Then the king lost the principality of Neuchatel, which is located on the eastern side of Switzerland, in a bloodless revolution. Switzerland took it over, and today Neuchatel is still a canton of that country. The Guard Schützen was originally staffed by men from Neuchatel, but after 1848, Prussians supplied the personnel.

The 3rd and 4th Battalions were formed as a fighting unit in 1815 from the Russian German Legion (made up of men who were deserters from the French army and prisoners of war in Russia), part of the Saxon Jäger Corps, and a Saxon volunteer unit that had formed in 1813 to fight the French. They were known as the 2nd Jäger Battalion until 1821, when they split into the 3rd and 4th Jäger Battalions, but they kept the same commander until 1831.[247]

The 5th and 6th Jäger Battalions were created in 1808 as a Silesian Rifle Battalion made up of light infantry companies from Silesia that had formed during the 1806–7 war. They did not become Jägers until 1845.[248]

The 7th Jägers were formed in 1815 as the 2nd Schützen (Rhine) Battalion from existing volunteer jägers and men from former Berg Jägers and Saxon and Nassau light infantry. They became the 7th Jägers in 1845. In 1867, Schaumberg-Lippe came into the German Confederation, and the Schaumberg-Lippe contingent became part of the 7th Jägers.[249]

The 8th Jägers had the same origins as the 7th Jägers. In 1845, they became the 8th Jägers after splitting off from the 2nd Schützen.[250]

The 9th Jägers were formed in 1866, taking men from the 1st Companies of all the other Jäger battalions and the Guard Schützen Battalion.[251]

In 1866, Prussia annexed Hanover. The 10th Jägers were formed by taking men from Guard Jägers, Guard Schützen, and the 1st, 2nd, 5th, and 6th Jäger Battalions. They also had some Hessian troops. In addition, the Prussians also kept two officers and 138 men from the former Hanoverian Jäger Battalion.[252] They had no relationship to the Gibraltar regiments (see *§VI-3-7*) as the Hanoverian army had been disbanded in 1803 when the French overran the country.

The victory in the Franco-Prussian War and the formation of an empire-wide army brought the Saxon, Mecklenburg-Schwerin, and Bavarian Jäger battalions into the united army. The Saxons came under the control of the Prussian army and were given numbers 12 and 13. The Mecklenburgen battalion took number 14. The Bavarian Jägers remained a part of a separate Bavarian army.

Uniform

Table VI.10.1: Jägers and Schützen

Battalion	Tunic Colour	Button Colour	Helmet Badge	Collar & Cuffs	Cuff Type	Piping Colour	Notes
Guard							
Jägers	Dark green	Yellow	Guard star	Red	Swedish	Red	1, 2, 4
Schützen	Dark green	Yellow	Guard star	Red	French	Red	1, 2, 3, 4
Line							
1st Jägers	Dark green	Yellow	A	Red	Swedish	Red	---
2nd Jägers	Dark green	Yellow	A	Red	Swedish	Red	---
3rd Jägers	Dark green	Yellow	B	Red	Swedish	Red	---
4th Jägers	Dark green	Yellow	B	Red	Swedish	Red	---
5th Jägers	Dark green	Yellow	A	Red	Swedish	Red	---
6th Jägers	Dark green	Yellow	A	Red	Swedish	Red	---
7th Jägers	Dark green	Yellow	B	Red	Swedish	Red	5
8th Jägers	Dark green	Yellow	B	Red	Swedish	Red	---
9th Jägers	Dark green	Yellow	B	Red	Swedish	Red	---
10th Jägers	Dark green	Yellow	B	Red	Swedish	Red	6, 7
11th Jägers	Dark green	Yellow	B	Red	Swedish	Red	8
Contingent Troops							
12th Saxon Jägers	Rifle green	White	C	Black	Saxon	Red	9, 10
13th Saxon Jägers	Rifle green	White	C	Black	Saxon	Red	9, 10
108th Saxon Rifles	Rifle green	Yellow	D	Black	Saxon	Red	9, 10
14th Mecklenburg-Schwerin Jägers	Dark green	White	E	Light green	Swedish	Red	4, 11
Bavarian Army							
1st Jägers	Light blue	Yellow	F	Light green	Swedish	Light Blue	
2nd Jägers	Light blue	Yellow	F	Light green	Swedish	Light Blue	

Notes:
A: Prussian eagle with 'FWR' on its chest.
B: Standard Prussian eagle.
C: Saxon badge. White star and hunting horn with gold Saxon coat of arms. Worn on special Saxon shako which had the shape of a tall kepi.
D: Same as C but with colours of star, hunting horn, and coat of arms reversed.
E: Twelve-rayed tombac yellow sun with white (silvered for officers) crowned Mecklenburg-Schwerin coat of arms within a laurel wreath.
F: Bavarian coat of arms in yellow metal.

1: Officer's shako made of felt with a cloth covering. Only top and visor were leather (Herr, *German Infantry*, vol. 2, p. 754).
2: Officer's plumes made of buffalo hair (Herr, *German Infantry*, vol. 2, p. 754).
3: Officers had velvet collars and cuffs.
4: Officers and men wore chapter litzen.
5: The battalion wore a Schaumburg-Lippe cockade.
6: Had the banner 'Peninsula-Waterloo-Venta Del Pozo' on their shako plate for a supposed tie with the King's German Legion that fought in Spain with the British (§VI-3-7).
7: Wore a Gibraltar band on right arm for the supposed tie to the Hanoverian units that served there during siege of 1779–83. The Hanoverian army was disbanded in 1803; so, no direct tie existed (§VI-3-7) (Williamson, *Cuffbands*, p. 16). Awarded to the battalion in 1901.
8: The 11th Battalion had the monogram of Queen Marguerita of Italy.
9: Other ranks wore a hunting horn over the battalion number on their dark green square-topped shoulder straps. Shoulder straps had red trim on all four sides.
10: Bottom of collar trimmed red where it met the body of the tunic. Front and top of collars trimmed dark green. Cuffs trimmed in red.
11: The 14th Jägers wore the very distinctive quartered cockade of Mecklenburg which was carmine/dark blue, superimposed with a yellow cross, both enclosed within a yellow woollen oval (Kinna, *Jäger*, p. 23).

Helmet

Jägers had worn the pickelhaube when it was introduced in 1842. In 1854, it was switched for a leather shako whose shape was similar to the one worn in 1914, but it was taller and had a wider top so it did not have the 'bump' in the back. After that, over the years, the shako became shorter, lighter, and the top smaller. Along the way, it developed the characteristic bump or swelling at the back of the shako. This was one of the more successful headdresses developed in the nineteenth century. German police were wearing it as late as the 1970s.

In 1860, a line eagle with the Fatherland banner was put on the front of the shako for line battalions (Image VI:196); Guard battalions had the guard star (Image VI:195). Battalions 1, 2, 5, and 6, which were old battalions, had worn the monogram 'FWR' on their shako. They now wore the line eagle with this monogram on the eagle's chest (Image VI:197). In 1899, Battalion 10 was given a banner reading 'Peninsula, Waterloo, Venta Del Pozo' to note a supposed tie with the King's German Legion, who fought in Spain under Wellington (Image VI:199).

The Saxon jäger shako was covered with black velveteen with, around the crown, a black velvet band upon which staff officers displayed three, and company officers two, rings of silver embroidery. For Schützen Regiment 108 the embroidery was golden.[253]

It should be noted that all ranks wore a black plume (horsehair for other ranks; buffalo hair for officers) that fell in front of the shako and covered the shako plates (Images VI:204 and VI:205).

Tunic

The tunic worn by the Prussian Jägers and Schützen was identical to the tunics of the Prussian line infantry as to cut and length. The colour of the Prussian Jäger and Schützen tunic was dark green. It was single-breasted and fastened down the front with eight yellow buttons. Each rear skirt had a pocket with three buttons, one being at waist level. The buttons were connected by piping in a scallop shape.

All Jägers had red collars and red Swedish cuffs. The Guard Schützen had black collars. Their tunics had French cuffs which consisted of black turn-down cuffs with a dark green horizontal bar with three buttons and the arched piping that marked a French cuff (Images I:1(4), VI:205, and VI:206).

The tunic for Jägers had 2 mm (0.08 inch) wide piping down the front, on the front, and top of the collar (Image VI:207), on the top of the cuffs, and in a scallop pattern between the buttons on the rear skirts. The Guard Schützen Regiment had red piping the same size in the same places. The horizontal cuff bar had piping on the top and bottom, on the forward edge, and halfway up the bar in the back where the vertical piping runs into the vertical bar.

The Guard Jägers and Schützen had chapter litzen on their collars and cuffs. There were two on the collar and a litzen for each button on the cuff (Images VI:208 and VI:209). The guard had square-cut collars and the Prussian line battalions (Nos 1–11) had half-rounded front collars (Images VI:210 and VI:211).

Jäger Battalion 10 was given a 'Gibraltar' cuff band in 1901 (Images VI:204, VI:207, and VI:212). This was based on a fictitious link between the imperial regiments recruited in Hanover and the old Hanoverian army that fought under the Hanoverian kings of Britain. The letters on the 2.8 cm (1.1 inch) wide bright blue cloth band were stitched in yellow wool for other ranks.[254] Officers had gold silk or wire on theirs. The band was worn on the right sleeve 4 cm (1.57 inches) above the Swedish cuff.[255]

All Prussian battalions wore red pointed shoulder straps. The Guard battalions did not wear any devices on theirs. The line battalions had their number, except for Battalion 11, which carried the monogram of Queen Marguerita of Italy after 1897. The number or monogram was yellow.

All Jäger battalions wore black belts.

Guards Officers

The officers' tunic was a lighter shade of green than that worn by the other ranks. The stand-up collar was higher and stiffer than the men's. While the square-fronted collar was to be no higher than 6 cm (2.36 inches), this height limit was often violated in the name of fashion. The Guard Schützen collars and cuffs were black velvet.

The front and upper edges of the Jäger officers' collar was piped in dark green. The Schützen had red piping along these spaces.

VI:195 Prussian Officer's Guard Shako with Prussian Guard Star

VI:196 Prussian Line Shako
This shako plate was worn by Battalions 3, 4, 7, 8, 9, and 11. Note the 'FR' initials on the eagle's chest.

VI:197 Prussian Line Shako Helmet
Note the intertwined 'FWR' on the oval shield on the eagle's chest. This shako plate was worn by Jäger Battalions 1, 2, 5, and 6.

VI:198 Side view of Standard Jäger Shako Note the bump at the back of the shako.

VI:199 Shako of the Jäger Battalion 10 (Hanoverian)
The banners on the helmet reflect battle honours won fighting against the French during the Napoleonic Wars.

VI:200 Shako of the Mecklenburg-Schwerin Jäger Battalion 14

VI:201 Shako of Saxon Jägers (Early Model)

VI:202 Shako of Saxon Schützen Regiment 108 (Other Ranks)
Note the bugle horn.

VI:203 1st and 2nd Bavarian Jäger Regiments Shako (Officer's Model)

VI:204 10th (Hanoverian) Jäger Battalion
This battalion was granted the right to wear a Gibraltar cuff by Kaiser Wilhelm II because of a supposed relationship to a Hanoverian regiment that took part in the Siege of Gibraltar.

VI:206 Soldiers of the Guard Schützen Battalion
Note the litzen on collar and cuffs.

VI:205 NCO of the Guard Rifles Wearing White Summer Trousers
Note the marksmanship badge on right upper sleeve, guard star, and NCO braid. Note also this regiment has French cuffs.

VI:207 Close-Up of an Enlisted Man of the 10th (Hanoverian) Jäger Battalion
Note the shoulder straps and the Gibraltar banner.

VI:208 Duke Henry of Mecklenburg-Schwerin (later Prince Henry of the Netherlands)
He is wearing the uniform of the Prussian Guard Jäger Battalion

VI:210 Tunic of the 6th Jäger Battalion
Notice the marksmanship cord coming from the right shoulder to the fifth button of the tunic. This is an error. It was supposed to go to the second button of the tunic. There are ten separate grades of marksmanship cords.

VI:209 One-Year Volunteer of the Prussian Guard Schützen Battalion
Note the guard star on shako, French cuffs and NCO braid on collar and cuffs. Also note the Kaiser's badge for marksmanship on his right sleeve. This award was given to the company within an army corps which had the highest standard of marksmanship. NCOs retained this badge for the duration of service with the company.

VI:211 Prussian Jäger One-Year Volunteer (Officer Candidate)
Note the black and white cord around his shoulder straps denoting status. He has pulled the shako plume apart to show the shako badge which otherwise would be covered by the plume.

Line Officers

The line officers had tunics of the same lighter shade of green as guard officers. They had collars of the same height, but theirs were rounded. In all other respects, their tunics were like those of the guards. Officers with the Gibraltar band of Battalion 10 had the Gibraltar name in gold embroidered block letters.

Saxons

The Saxons provided Battalions 12 and 13. Although they were brought into the Imperial system, and given numbers in the imperial numbering system, they were still able to keep Saxon touches.

Shako

The Saxons wore a shako with a unique shape found only in the Saxon Jägers and the 108th (Saxon) Rifles. The 108th, while technically a line regiment, will be covered here because its dress was so similar to that of Jägers.

The Saxon shako was shaped like a kepi with a black straight peak.

Other Ranks

The shako was covered in black cloth for other ranks (Images VI:201 and VI:202). The front badge was an eight-pointed star of German silver. On the star was a crowned Saxon coat of arms within a laurel leaf wreath, all in tombac. After August 1909, under the coat of arms was a hunting horn which was also of German silver. The 108th Regiment had the same front badge, but the colours were reversed; i.e. tombac star and hunting horn, and German silver crowned Saxon coat of arms and wreath.

The other ranks of all of these units wore a black horsehair plume that rose from the top front of the shako and swept to the left side of the shako, where it was fastened to the shako by a bow and retained by a small black leather buckled strap. By custom, the 12th Battalion had a rising plume, the 13th a drooping plume, and the 108th a horizontal plume (Image VI:214).[258] Behind the point where the plume was fastened to the shako of the 108th Regiment, and probably for the two Jäger battalions, was a small metal device that could allow the end of the plume to

VI:212 10th Hanoverian Jäger with Regimental Standard
He is wearing the gorget of a standard bearer. Note the Gibraltar sleeve band on his right lower arm and the Peninsula-Waterloo banner on the shako plate, which can just be made out.

The domed buttons, in the same numbers and places as the other ranks, were gilt for both guard battalions. They wore epaulettes or shoulder cords to show rank.

The cuffs were larger than those worn by men. The Swedish cuff of the Guard Jägers was 8 cm (3.15 inches) high. The Guard Schützen rectangular plate was 14 cm (5.51 inches) high and 7 cm (2.76 inches) wide, including piping.[256]

The collar chapter litzen had double twisted cord in place of their spiegel (central lights). The same twisted cord also replaced the spiegel in the litzen on the cuffs.[257]

§VI-10 Jägers and Schützen (Rifles)

VI:213 108th Saxon Rifle Regiment
Soldier has used a small flip of the kepi to make the plume stand away from the kepi.

VI:214 Officer of the 108th (Saxon) Rifles
Note how the plume is pulled back to the side of his shako, and the two rows of lace around the top of his kepi.

be flipped out at a ninety-degree angle to the shako. I have never heard of a reason for this device and certainly the plume was never worn this way except in photos, where the riflemen seem to have liked to flip out the plume for the occasion (Image VI:213). Around the top of the shako there were one or two braid rings to show rank. The colour of the rings followed the unit's button colour.

Officers

Officers wore the same shako as the other ranks, but there were some differences. Officers' shakos were covered in black velveteen, and their plumes were buffalo hair. On the front badge, in place of tombac, the badge elements were gilt, and in place of German silver, the devices were silver-plated. The top of the officers' shako had a black velvet band which held bands of braid showing rank: field officers had three and company officers two. The bottom band had a pronounced downward 'V' at the middle back of the shako. The colour of the braid followed the unit's button colour.

Tunic

Other Ranks

The Saxon tunic had several special characteristics. Its colour was a darker green than those of the Prussians, and came close to being the shade of dark green used by British rifle regiments. The Saxon tunic was about 8 cm (3.15 inches) shorter in the seat than the Prussian tunic and covered only half the wearer's behind.[259] The black collar had a half-round shape and had no piping. However, along the bottom of the collar, where it met the tunic, there was red piping (Image VI:213).

VI:215 *Saxon Jäger Battalion 15*
Note square top on the shoulder strap. This battalion was disbanded on 1 April 1900. The men were used to form Saxon Infantry Regiment 181. The uniform is rife green with black cuffs and red trim. Note the hunting horn on the shoulder strap. This was worn on the shoulder straps of all Saxon jäger battalions and the 108th Saxon Rifle Regiment.

The cuffs were Saxon-style in shape and piped red (Image VI:215). The dark green shoulder straps were also uniquely Saxon in that they were square on top and piped on the top (near the collar) and on the two sides in red. The bottom side also had narrow red 1 mm (0.04 inch) piping. The shoulder straps had the number of the unit under a hunting horn (Image VI:215). Both were red.

The domed buttons of the Saxon Jägers were white and those of the 108th Rifles yellow.

The rear pocket flaps were straight with two buttons and not scalloped with three buttons. The tunic trim was red.

Officers

The Saxon officers' tunics showed a few differences from those of the other ranks. The most noticeable difference was that officers' collars were piped on the front and top edges in red as well as having red piping along the bottom of the collar.

Their collars were rounded in front and of black velvet. The Saxon cuffs were black velvet with red piping. The officers of Jäger battalions had silver buttons, and those of the 108th Regiment had gilt buttons.

Mecklenburg-Schwerin

Thanks to shrewd bargaining (helped no doubt by the fact that the grand duke at the time, Frederick Franz II, was a nephew of Prussian King Wilhelm II and a general in the Prussian army), the state of Mecklenburg-Schwerin was able to preserve its light infantry unit and incorporate it into the imperial army when other states saw their units disbanded. They even won the right to continue to wear their blue tunics for a while; They did not begin wearing the Prussian jäger green tunics until 1890, and even then they kept some Mecklenburg touches (see Image C88).

SHAKO

On the standard Prussian shako, the 14th (Mecklenburg-Schwerin) Jägers had a front plate that consisted of a truncated twelve-rayed tombac sun. On the sun was a German silver crowned shield with the Mecklenburg coat of arms within a German silver laurel leaf wreath (Image VI:200).

The cockade was very distinctive. It was quartered, with the first and third quarters being dark blue and the second and fourth quarters carmine (purplish-red to crimson). Superimposed on the quarterings and marking their edges was a yellow cross. The quarterings and cross were enclosed within a yellow woollen oval (Image VI:216). Black horsehair plumes were worn by the other ranks.

Officers

The sun on the officers' front plate was gilt and the coat of arms and wreath were silver or silver-plated. The plumes were black buffalo hair. The cockade consisted of an outer border of silver cords and an inner oval of a velvet field quartered dark blue and carmine by a gold cross, and the whole outlined by a gold cord.[260]

§VI-10 Jägers and Schützen (Rifles)

VI:216 14th Mecklenburg-Schwerin Jäger Battalion. Note NCO braid and button on the collar. Also note the Mecklenburg-Schwerin shako and the very distinctive four-quartered cockade.

Tunic

Other Ranks
The tunic was basically the Prussian jäger tunic with a square-fronted collar. The collar and cuffs were light green. The collar was piped on all three sides in red, and the Swedish cuffs had red piping. The tunic had white chapter litzen on the collar (two) and cuffs (two on each cuff). The spiegel was light green. White domed metal buttons were worn.

The men wore light green pointed shoulder straps piped red with a red number. Rear skirts had three buttons and scalloped red piping on each side.

Officers
The officers had a particularly light shade of grass green collar and cuffs.[261] Silver chapter litzen were on the collar (two) and cuffs (two on each cuff).

Bavaria

Shako
The Bavarians after 1895 wore a shako that conformed to the Prussian model. Prior to that, they had worn several other types of helmets. Between 1868 and 1886, they wore a Tarleton helmet with a side plume, and then between 1886 and 1895, they wore a spiked helmet of the Prussian model.

On the front, the other ranks' shako had the Bavarian coat of arms, a shield with two crowned lion supporters mounted on a scroll with the motto '*In Treue Fest*' ('Steadfastly Loyal'). The coat of arms was in tombac. The cockade was white and light blue. The Bavarians did not wear plumes.

Officers
Officers wore the same helmet, but their coat of arms was gilted. Their cockade had an outer section of twisted silver metallic cord (Image VI:203).

Tunics

Other Ranks
The Bavarian single-breasted tunic conformed to the Prussian model but was light blue (really a mid-blue). It had light green collar and cuffs. The domed buttons were yellow metal and without any devices. The tunic had light green piping down the front of the tunic. The rear skirts had three buttons and scalloped light green piping connecting the buttons.

The pointed shoulder straps were light green and carried the battalion number in yellow.

The half-round collar was piped around the front and along the upper edge in light blue. The Swedish cuffs were also piped in light blue along the outside edges.

Officers
The tunic was the same as for other ranks, but the buttons were gilted.

Trousers and Breeches

Trousers
All states except Bavaria wore dark blue/black trousers. There was 2–3 mm (0.08–0.12 inch) wide piping down the outside of each leg. The trousers were worn form October 1 to April 30 with black laced ankle boots. For summer months, May 1 to September 30, white linen trousers without piping could be worn.

Breeches
These were the same colour and had the same piping as the trousers. However, the bottoms of the legs were tapered to fit inside the marching boot (Image VI:212).

Officers
Officers' trousers were the same colour but had a somewhat different cut. They were cut narrower than those of the other ranks and had stirrups that went under the shoe to cause a tight, smooth fit. The waist was cut high to hide any big stomachs. The piping on each leg was to be no larger than 1.5 mm (0.059 inch) wide. Officers often had their trousers made of satin or kersey.[262]

Bavarians
The trousers of the Bavarians were the same colour as their tunics: light blue. They had light green piping. They wore white trousers in the summer. Mounted officers wore breeches of light blue with light green piping. They had the same cuts as the Prussian trousers and breeches. White trousers were often worn on parade.[263]

§VI-11 OVERSEAS TROOPS

The early German colonies were acquired by entrepreneurs and adventurers. In spite of public support for the concept of acquiring colonies, Bismarck saw no value in having German colonies and turned down opportunities to acquire them.

Trading companies from Hamburg established trading posts on the coast of Cameroon in 1868. Other companies followed. Once the German government became involved in 1884, the Germans pushed inland and acquired more territory. In 1911, as a *quid pro quo* for France having a free hand in Morocco, French territory in Central Africa was ceded to the Cameroons. This almost doubled the size of the German Cameroons (France took the ceded land back after World War I).

One of the first Germans to act to acquire land in Africa was Adolf Luderitz. Starting in 1881, he began buying land around the only good harbour on the south-west African coast that had not already been claimed by one country or another. This expanded to absorb the area known in 1914 as German South-West Africa. In 1884, Bismarck agreed to take over the territory that Luderitz had been acquiring.

The other early mover came out of public agitation for acquiring colonies. Dr Karl Peters bought land in East Africa from tribes, paying almost nothing. In 1885, the German government accepted a protectorate over the area. After a revolution by the coastal Arabs in 1888, known as the Abushiri Rebellion, the government took direct control of the area.

Footholds were established on the coast of Togo by German adventurers at gunpoint in February and July 1884.

The hope of government and Bismarck in agreeing to assume control over these territories was that they could be given to a well-financed private company which would manage them. That never happened: the new colonies were money pits and had problems with the local people. No private companies wanted to get involved.

In 1884, Germany's protectorate over all these areas was formalised by the Berlin Conference held in 1884–5 to divide up Africa. Later that year, Germany obtained the first of its Pacific holdings by obtaining land in New Guinea. More Pacific land would follow in 1885–8.

In 1897, two German missionaries in China were murdered. Germany used this as a reason to seize the port of Tsingtao and the land around it.

In 1896, a standard uniform for all the African colonies was introduced. Before describing the new uniform, it may be well to take a brief look at the uniforms worn in the different colonies prior to that date.

§VI-11-a GERMAN EAST AFRICA UP TO 1896

The German East African Company had conducted business in the area and had a force of armed men to protect its property. In 1888, a revolt broke out among the coastal populations, likely upset that the new order was interfering with their slave trading. Troops had to be raised to deal with the uprising. The result was the so-called Wissmann Troops or Reich Commissioner's Troops, named after Hermann von Wissmann, who had been appointed commissioner for East Africa. He raised a mixed force of Swahili-speaking coastal Africans, *askaris*, taken over from the local trading company, Sudanese, and Zulus from Portuguese East Africa. They served under German officers and NCOs who had volunteered for African service. To do so, they had to leave the army.

The ranks were the normal German ones, but a rank called 'effendi' emerged. Effendi is an honorific used in Egypt and the Sudan, but as used in the German colonial army it denoted a senior NCO or junior officer rank (see Table VI.11.g.2). The men who first filled the rank had been native Sudanese officers in the six companies of Sudanese supplied by Khedive Tawfiq in 1889 to the Wissmann Troop.[264]

The uniforms[265] were a mix, and who wore what depended on what group the soldier belonged to.

Sudanese

These troops wore the Egyptian red fez and black tassel or the cloth wrapping that had gone around the fez and formed a turban in the Sudanese regiments. Later, the turbans were grey or tan and were wrapped around the red fez. This, in time, developed into the *tarbusch*, which was standard wear.

The tunic or shirt was light tan (khaki) with five yellow buttons down the front. It had a khaki turn-down collar and khaki shoulder straps. It was similar to that worn in the Egyptian army.

The men wore khaki knickerbockers and dark blue puttees. Native officers could wear long trousers while in the garrison.

The belt was natural colour (brown) and had a square buckle carrying an imperial crown.

Brown lace-up ankle boots were worn.

Zulus

The Zulus had a very different uniform at first, one with a naval flavour. They had a red fez, and the tassel colour varied by company – black for the 1st and white for the 2nd.

The tunic was a light blue jumper with a wide navy, boat-neck collar and half sleeves. It fastened with four black buttons.

The trousers came down to the calves. White puttees were sometimes worn, but at other times, no puttees were worn. They did not wear shoes.

This uniform was unsatisfactory, and in 1889 the Zulu companies changed over to the uniform worn by the Sudanese with a red fez. They still went without shoes.

Swahili

At first, they wore the same naval-oriented uniform as worn by the Zulus, only in all-white. This proved unsatisfactory so they also changed over to a Sudanese-style uniform with a red fez and no shoes.

Officers

The officers' full-dress uniform was based on the naval uniform with the addition of a white pith helmet. The force had a strong naval flavour. Their warrant officers were first known as pursers and later as deck officers.

The dark blue tunic had a fold-down collar the same colour as the tunic, with six gold buttons (white buttons for deck officers). It was without trim on the collar and down the front. Rank was shown by braid on the lower sleeves. At first, this was in black, silver, and red braid. Later, the braid was changed to gold with the executive curl in the top braid, as found among deck officers in the British navy.

The trousers were in the same dark blue as the tunic and had no piping. Shoes were black. A naval officer's sash was worn around the waist.

In the field, the officers, after a few false starts, came to wear khaki tunics and trousers cut in the same way as the blue full dress. Brown boots that came up to the knee were worn.

Schutztruppe, 1891–6[266]

A law passed in 1891 changed the status of the German East Africa (GEA) troops, and this brought uniform changes. The troops were placed under the Admiralty while the Colonial Office controlled how they were stationed.

The different Sudanese, Zulu, and Swahili companies were mixed together. During this period, the Sudanese and Zulu personnel started to be phased out. The number of Sudanese available for the German East Africa force had been greatly reduced in the early 1890s; the British in Egypt were having trouble obtaining enough Sudanese to man their own Sudanese regiments.[267]

The new order did not bring any changes for the African other ranks. They continued to wear the Sudanese-style uniform of red fez with a black tassel, light khaki tunic or shirt and knickerbockers, blue puttees, and brown boots if footwear was used.

The officers' full dress did see some changes.

The pith helmet was replaced by a black leather pickelhaube with a square front visor (Image VI:217). It had the Reich cockade on it. The front plate had an imperial eagle in red brass for NCOs and gilt for officers.

The dark blue tunic was modelled on the naval infantry and had eight red brass buttons (gold-plated for officers) down the front. It had a fold-down collar of dark blue, which allowed the white shirt collar to show behind it. The trim colour was white. The lower edges of the collar were trimmed white, as was the

VI:217 Black leather pickelhaube for German East African Officers, c. 1891–6
The eagle is an imperial eagle made of brass. Note that the front visor is square cut.

VI:218 Tropical Helmet for Officers and NCOs of German East Africa, c. 1891–6
Again a brass imperial eagle was on the front. The spike is removable.

front edge of the tunic. On the sleeves, white trim outlined the shape of a Brandenburg cuff, but both the horizontal and vertical sections of the cuff were the same colour as the tunic. The shoulder cords were like those worn in the navy.

A gold-plated imperial crown was at the ends of the rounded turn-down tunic collar for both officers and NCOs.

All officers wore aiguillettes in full dress with gold cords. These went from a button at the end of the man's left shoulder cords, hung across the chest, and ended at the third button on the front of the tunic.

The officers continued to wear the naval officer's sash and adjutant's sash in the imperial colours – silver with black and red darts forming two lines in it.

The NCOs wore chevrons in place of the shoulder cords and did not wear sashes or aiguillettes. They wore a brown belt and brass buckle. The buckle had the imperial crown on it.

Both officers and NCOs wore trousers of dark blue with white piping on the side seams.

Tropical Uniform

There was also a tropical uniform. The headdress consisted of a high-domed white pith helmet with an imperial eagle on the front (Image VI:218). The helmet also had a removable spike. All metal was in brass (gilt for officers).

The tunic was much like the blue uniform, only in white. It had six buttons in front rather than eight, and pockets on both chests and both front skirts. The Brandenburg cuffs were the same white as the tunic, but were outlined in blue, as were the shoulder straps. Other than these two elements, the tunic was without piping.

White trousers without piping were worn.

In 1896, a standard uniform for all German colonial troops was created. This and its effect on German East Africa troops will be covered below.

§VI-11-b GERMAN SOUTH-WEST AFRICA[268]

1889–91

At first there was a small force, some forty-five to fifty men, just large enough to provide a guard for the commissioner. The headdress was a grey slouch felt hat of the type that became standard wear for the Germans in Africa (Image VI:219). The turned-up right side was held in place by the Reich cockade. The hats of other ranks were smaller than those of officers until 1894.[269] Officers' hats were distinguished by trimmings of cornflower blue silk rep.[270]

All ranks wore a light grey corduroy tunic with six buttons made of horn on the front. There was a pocket on the left chest and on each front skirt. The stand-up collar had no trim and neither did the cuffs. There were no shoulder straps.

VI:219 Felt Hat First Worn in German South-West Africa. It was later adopted for all German colonies. The white band on this hat shows that it was worn by an officer or NCO in German East Africa.

1891–4[271]

In 1891–4, the uniform was smartened by adding trim and piping to it and modifying the headdress.

The other ranks' hat became the same size as those of the officers. All hats were given light blue trim around the edge of the brim and a band of the same colour around the crown. A white high-domed pith helmet with a spike and eagle on the front was worn for parades. Its fittings were like those worn in East Africa. It had the standard colonial eagle with upturned wings, a crown, and a large spike with a large cruciform base (Image VI:218). A version with a khaki cloth cover could be worn on other occasions. These helmets were in service for only a few years in German South-West Africa (GSWA). A kepi-style cap was also issued. It too had a short life.

The corduroy tunic continued to have a stand-up collar until 1894, when it was changed to a turn-down style. The collar, whether stand-up or turn-down, and new lancer pointed cuffs were cornflower blue (a mid-blue). The tunic was light grey and had patch pockets on each side of the chest. It had six white buttons (silver-plated for officers) down the front. The buttons had an imperial crown on them.

There was one white litzen (silver for officers) in the chapter shape on either side of the collar and on each cuff. The cuffs also had a button on each litzen. The other ranks' litzen had a red central light (spiegel) while the officers' silver litzen had none.

All ranks wore an aiguillette on their left chest made of white (troopers) or silver (officers) cords.

The trousers and breeches were grey corduroy. The trousers had cornflower blue piping, but the breeches were without piping.

Long brown riding boots were worn. Brown ankle boots were also issued. The men were also equipped with large bowie knives, named after their inventor, Jim Bowie, an American frontiersman who died at the Alamo.

Lances, when carried, had a pennant with three stripes – from the top down, black, white, and red.[272]

§VI-11-c CAMEROON

A military force was not created in the Cameroons until 1893, and it was very small. It was first formed by employing slaves from Dahomey, but it was not a success. Next, soldiers from the Sudan via German East Africa were tried in 1895, but, the West African climate was as deadly to them as it was to Europeans.

The Sudanese were slowly replaced by men from the British colonies of Sierra Leone and Niger. It was not until about 1900 that the Germans began recruiting from the local tribes.

The size of the force in the Cameroons grew from one company in 1894 to six in 1905. Then, between 1905 and 1914, another six companies were added, bringing the 1914 total to twelve.

The force had three to five German NCOs and one or two officers assigned to each company.

When the Sudanese came from German East Africa, they brought their Sudanese style of dress with them, and this was the uniform of the early troops in the Cameroons. Then the soldiers came under the universal uniform provisions of 1896.

§VI-11-d TOGO

The colony of Togo never raised a military force as such. Rather, this small colony relied on armed police to keep order.

§VI-11-e TSINGTAO (JIAOZHOU)

Tsingtao in China was a port for the German East Asia Fleet, and there was a small area of land behind it leased for ninety-nine years, which made up the Tsingtao territory. Since the port was important to the navy, the area was under the control of the Admiralty and garrisoned by the III Marine Battalion. It will be discussed below.

§VI-11-f SOUTH PACIFIC COLONIES

While today it is largely forgotten, Germany, prior to 1914, had fairly large colonial holdings in the South Pacific. These had come about, for the most part, by businesses following missionaries, and government following the businessmen. The German rule in this far-flung region did not call for a military force, and there were no soldiers stationed in the area.

§VI-11-g COMMON UNIFORMS OF 1896

There were three colonies with non-naval military forces: German East Africa (GEA), German South-West Africa (GSWA), and Cameroon. In 1896, a common uniform was ordered for the soldiers in all these colonies. This new uniform was modelled on the uniform worn in GSWA and had facing colours introduced for each colony. The uniforms for native soldiers were modelled on those worn in GEA.

Table VI.11.g.1 shows the colony facing colours as of 1914.

HAT FOR EUROPEANS

Officers and men wore the hat that had been worn in GSWA made of grey felt with a crown that was 15 cm (5.91 inches) high. The crown always had a dent or indentation in it, normally running from front to back

Table VI.11.g.1: Identifying Colours of German Colonies in 1914

East Africa	White
South-West Africa	Cornflower blue
Cameroon	Poppy red
Togo	Yellow
New Guinea and other South Pacific islands	Green
Samoa	Pink

Source: Knötel, *Deutsche Heer*, vol. 1, p. 359.

(Image VI:219). The brim was 12 cm (4.72 inches) wide, turned up on the right and pinned to the crown by the Reich cockade.

The hat had a 3.5 cm (1.38 inch) high band of coloured rep with a bow on the left. The brim was trimmed with a 1 cm (0.39 inch) wide band that was the same colour as the hat band. The hat band and edge trim was wool for enlisted men and silk for officers.

The colours on the hats were different for the different protectorates/colonies (see Table VI.11.g.1).

TUNIC FOR EUROPEANS
Originally, the GSWA's corduroy uniform was adopted as the standard uniform for colonial troops; after a year, in 1897, it was changed to light grey cloth. The corduroy uniform, however, lived on in GSWA.[273] The single-breasted cloth tunic had eight white metal (silver-plated for officers) buttons down the front (Image VI:220). The buttons had the imperial crown on them. The turn-down collar was the colour of the colony and had a single white wool litzen (silver for officers) (Images VI:220 and VI:221). The Swedish cuffs were the in the colony's colour and had two white or silver-plated buttons and two white (silver for officers) litzen. The litzen were in the chapter shape. Those of the other ranks had a red central light (spiegel), but those of the officers did not have a spiegel.

Other ranks had shoulder straps made of four white cords, much like the cords worn by the Prussian hussars. The white cords had black and red darts on them to make the imperial colours. Subalterns wore the same style shoulder cords as worn by junior officers in the home army (see §VI-3-23, Officers'

VI:220 Captain (Hauptmann) von Raven, a German Colonial Officer serving in German Cameroon
The trim on the outside of the hat's brim, collar, and cuffs for officer and NCOs in Cameroon was poppy red. Almost all German personnel in the colonies wore aiguillettes on their left side. This photograph provides an excellent view of how the aiguillette cords were interlaced.

Shoulder Cords), only in a silver colour. They had red and black darts. Majors and above wore standard German army shoulder cords for officers of that rank, but in silver cord with red and black darts. There was a pad under the cords in the colony's colour.

In full dress, all ranks wore aiguillettes. The cords of other ranks' aiguillettes were made of white wool with white, black, and red darts, while the officers' consisted of silver cords (Image VI:220). These went from a button at the end of the man's left shoulder cords, hung across the chest, and ended at the third button on the front of the tunic. The aiguillette consisted of two sets of two cords, one tied to the other, and a thick woven length of cord braid (Image VI:220).

VI:221 Paul von Lettow Vorbeck Prior to World War I in the Uniform of German South-West Africa
In German South-West Africa, the facing colour was cornflower blue, and this can be seen on the cap band, the trim of the brim, the collar, and the cuffs.

The front edge of the tunic was piped in the colony's facing colour. The collar of the white shirt worn under the tunic showed behind the fold-down collar. In 1914, the colour of the tunic was changed from light grey to field grey.

Each rear skirt of the tunic had three buttons, one at waist level, which were connected by scalloped shape piping in the colony's colour.

NCOs wore rank lace that was the type worn by other ranks of guard units on their collars and cuffs. They also had collar buttons.[274]

Trousers and Breeches

All ranks wore light grey trousers with piping of the colony's colour along the outside seam. The cut and quality of the other ranks' and officers' trousers differed.

All mounted ranks could also wear light grey breeches. The breeches had piping in the colony's colours along the outside seam. The breeches of officers and other ranks had minor differences.

Officers also had gala trousers after 1899. They were light grey with a 3 cm (1.18 inch) wide stripe in the colony's colour over the outside seams.[275]

Belt and Buckle

The belt for other ranks was of natural leather, which was a shade of brown. The buckle was brass and rectangular. On it was a white metal round shield with an imperial crown in the centre. Around the crown was the motto 'Gott Mit Uns' ('God [is] with Us') and a wreath of laurels. NCOs also had a black leather belt.

The officers' belt consisted of a silver cloth belt over leather with two black stripes. Between the two black stripes was a very thin red stripe. The belt buckle was round and silver-plated. In the centre was an imperial crown. All the way around the crown was a laurel wreath.

Footwear

Light brown knee-high boots were normally worn by all German ranks. With trousers and gala trousers, black ankle boots were worn.

Tropical Uniform

The piping and trim on these uniforms did not reflect the colony's colour but rather was cornflower blue for everyone. The uniform would vary by the colony, with GSWA being the exception. In 1896, regulations for a tropical uniform for wear in the colonies were also issued. These provided for both khaki and more formal white dress. The standard undress tropical uniform, worn in GEA and Cameroon, was a pith helmet or khaki-brimmed cloth cap with khaki tunic and trousers. They also wore a high-domed pith helmet that would be covered in either khaki or white cloth. In GSWA, they retained their old light grey corduroy uniforms, tunics, trousers, and breeches.

The white uniform was for full dress. It will be covered first and in detail.

VI:222 *Askaris Being Inspected*
The German officers and NCOs are wearing white tropical uniforms. Note a few of the officers, or more likely NCOs, have on black belts with their tropical whites.

PITH HELMET

A new pith helmet was issued in 1896. It was made of pressed cork and covered with white cloth for full dress. These helmets no longer had spikes or front eagle badges.[276] Period photos tend to show that for parades and reviews, the felt hat with the turned-up brim was normally worn, but not always (Image VI:222).

WHITE TUNIC

In GEA and Cameroon, a white single-breasted tunic with six silver-coloured buttons down the front was worn as tropical full dress. In GSWA, soldiers continued to wear their corduroy uniforms until 1913, when they adopted the white tropical tunic.

The white tunic had large pockets with an external pocket flap and a silver button on each side of the chest and on each front skirt. The turn-down collars had cornflower blue piping, as did the cuffs. The front edge of the tunic had the same cornflower blue piping, but the rear skirts were without piping. Photographs of men in the formal white uniform do not show any trim. So, either the trim was not worn, or it was very thin.

TROUSERS

White trousers were worn in tropical full dress, and these had cornflower blue piping along the outside seams. Again, this trim does not show in period photographs.

BELT AND BELT BUCKLE

German NCOs wore black belts with a standard belt buckle. Officers wore their standard officer's belt.

FOOTWEAR

Lace-up shoes of white, brown, or black could be worn. According to photographs, white shoes were normally worn.

Khaki Uniform

A tan khaki uniform worn by both officers and other ranks for field and garrison wear was also issued. It was just like the white uniform; only the colour differed. It was a tan khaki single-breasted tunic that had six white metal buttons down the front. The buttons had the imperial crown. The turn-down collar and front edge of the tunic were piped in the cornflower blue which was worn in all the colonies. The cuffs were tan khaki and outlined by a straight cornflower blue line. There was no piping on the rear skirt or the shoulder strap.

Each side of the chest had large pockets with an external top flap and button. Each lower front skirt had the same type of pocket. Their belt was brown, and their belt buckle was the standard brass with a white metal shield bearing an imperial crown, 'Gott Mit Uns' motto, and a laurel wreath. The shoulder cords were different for officers and other ranks (see above).

Helmet

A pith helmet in the same shape as the white helmet was worn in this order of dress. The only difference was that the cork body was covered by a tan khaki cloth rather than a white one.

Image VI:223 shows the uniform worn by Kaiser Wilhelm II when he visited Palestine in 1898. On that trip, his headdress and tunic were essentially that worn by colonial officers, except for trim details. The helmet has the shape of the GEA or GSWA helmets of 1891, and is close to the 1896 universal colonial helmet. The image shows how the helmet sat on the wearer's head. The eagle in front is a guard eagle – neither it nor the helmet spike would be found on a colonial helmet (spikes were made for colonial helmets, but photographs do not show them being worn). The tunic is basically a colonial tunic. Note how the shirt collar under the tunic shows under the tunic's turn-down collar. The aiguillette is not the colonial aiguillette, which was worn on the other shoulder. Rather, it is the aiguillette of a Prussian general.

Tunic/Shirt

A light brown single-breasted tunic/shirt was issued to German other ranks and NCOs. The only other ranks to wear them were in GSWA. The tunic had six white metal buttons down the front. The fold-down collar and Swedish cuffs were both tan. The buttons had an imperial crown on them. Both the collar and cuffs were trimmed in cornflower blue for all colonies, and neither had buttons nor anything else on them anywhere but down the front. The rear skirts were without buttons or trim. The tunic/shirt had shoulder cords of the hussar pattern with black and red darts on them.

The chest on either side had large external pockets with an outside pleat. At the top was a flap which was closed with a tunic button. Each front skirt had large external pockets which also had a flap and closed with a tunic button. Officers wore the same tunic/shirt with silver-plated buttons and officer's shoulder cords buttoned on.

The new light brown tunic/shirts were destined to outlive Germany's colonial empire. In the early 1920s, a young up-and-comer in a new party, the National Socialist German Workers' Party, was having success in recruiting new members to the party's fighting unit and wanted to put them all in uniforms. Through a friend, he was able to cheaply acquire shirts that had been readied for shipment to Africa before World War I.[277] The new party grew and became better known as the Nazis. The shirts gave his unit its popular name, the 'Brownshirts', and they became the brawling arm of the Nazis.

VI:223 Kaiser Wilhelm II
He wore this uniform when he went to Palestine, Turkey, and other eastern location in 1898. The helmet plate and aiguillette are completely different from those worn in Africa. However, the helmet and the tunic are similar to those worn in Africa and give an idea of how these clothing items looked when worn.

Trousers and Breeches

Trousers in this order of dress were tan with cornflower blue piping for all the colonies.

Tan breeches could also be worn by mounted officers. These had cornflower blue piping, regardless of the colony.

German South-West Africa

GSWA did not adopt the white tropical uniform until 1913. Before then, its troops, all Germans, continued to wear the old corduroy uniforms or tan khaki uniforms. Since the corduroy faded with many washes, old salts took pride in having a very pale brown corduroy uniform, just as old salts in the French Foreign Legion took pride in having a very pale kepi cover.

GERMAN EAST AFRICA NATIVE TROOPS

Effendi

The native troops in GEA were all known as askaris by the 1900s, a term that had originally applied to only the coastal Swahili troops. Their uniforms owed much to the Egyptian army influence that the Sudanese mercenaries had brought to the early GEA troops.

In GEA, rank among the askaris was denoted using Turkish titles as shown in Table VI.11.g.2.

Table VI.11.g.2: Ranks Used for Native Soldiers in German East Africa and a Comparison of Titles Used in Egypt

Askari (Turkish) Title	Egyptian Title	German Title	English Title
Ombascha	None	Gefreite	Lance corporal
Schausch	Ombashi	Unteroffizier	Corporal
Bet-schausch	Shawish	Sergeant	Sergeant
Sol	Bash shawish	Feldwebel	Sergeant major
	Solkologasi		Warrant officer[a]
Effendi	No equivalent	No equivalent	No equivalent

Sources: Askari titles from Windrow, *Osprey*, p. 287; Knötel, *Deutsche Heer*, vol. 1, p. 365. Egyptian titles from Lamothe, *Slaves/Sudanese*, p. xv.

Notes: Note how in GEA the Egyptian army titles have been mutated and applied to a rank one lower in the table of ranks.
[a] In spite of the name, this is an NCO and not an officer.

Effendi was a Turkish honorific and not a military title in Egypt. It was used in Egypt to show respect for status. Second lieutenants and some higher ranks were addressed as effendi. In GEA, effendi was an ambiguous rank. It was considered a very senior NCO rank, but it could also be viewed as a very junior officer rank. By 1914, there were only two men with the rank of effendi in GEA.[278] The practice of using Turkish ranks was said to exist because in the founding days there had been a strong presence of Sudanese men who had served in the Egyptian army, which was technically under Turkish rule and used Turkish titles and words of command.

Uniform

There was very little difference between the full dress and the field dress worn by the African troops. In both orders of dress, they wore basically the same khaki tunic/shirts and knickerbockers. Only in the headdress and the puttees in some colonies might differences be found. The differences will be noted below.

Headdress

The red fez had been relegated to undress wear. For full dress, a tarbusch was worn. The tarbusch was a

VI:224 German East African Askaris Band
This image provides a good look at German East African askari uniforms as actually worn.

modified fez where a woven cane structure in the shape of a tall, thick fez was made, with a brown khaki cover pinned over it. The GEA tarbusch always had a neck flap of brown khaki attached to it (Image VI:224). It also usually had a white metal German eagle or battalion number pinned to the front.

Tunic

A tan to brown khaki single-breasted shirt/tunic was worn by askaris. It was shorter than the tunics worn by Germans, coming down only to crotch level. It had five domed nickel buttons down the front (Images VI:224 and VI:225). The buttons had no decorations. There were khaki shoulder straps and turn-down collars. The other ranks' tunic had no trim and did not have pockets (Images VI:224 and VI:225).

Effendi[279]

Askaris who held the rank of effendi wore the tunic of a German NCO, but the only piping they had

VI:225 German East African Askari Uniforms

(cornflower blue) was on the cuff. The effendis' tunics had a large pocket on each chest and each front skirt. Each pocket had an external flap at the top and was closed with a nickel button. They wore three Egypt (five-pointed) stars on their khaki shoulder straps. As noted above, there were only two men holding the rank of effendi in 1914.

Knickerbockers and Trousers
Khaki knickerbockers without trim were worn. In full dress, dark blue-grey puttees were worn. Khaki puttees were worn most of the time. Effendis could wear khaki trousers while in garrison.[280]

Belt and Belt Buckle
The soldiers wore a brown belt with a rectangular brass belt buckle. The buckle had no devices on it.

Footwear
The askaris wore brown leather lace-up ankle boots.

CAMEROON NATIVE SOLDIERS

Uniform
The native soldiers in the Cameroons wore the same basic uniform as their counterparts in GEA. However, there were some key differences.

Shirt/Tunic
Their single-breasted khaki tunic had five, or often four, plain brass buttons. Their turn-down collars had red trim along the outside edge and had one red litzen-type bar in the middle. This tunic, too, was shorter than the tunic worn by Germans. The khaki cuffs were outlined with red piping that came to a point. It had plain khaki shoulder straps. They wore the same khaki knickerbockers as the GEA askaris. Khaki puttees were normally worn, but dark blue puttees could be worn. The belt and belt buckle were the same as those worn in the GEA. The men wore brown lace-up ankle boots or went barefoot.[281]

Sergeant Majors[282]
Sergeant majors showed their rank by wearing the German grey domed felt hat with red trim and piping. It had the right brim turned up.

They also wore the khaki colonial uniform worn by German soldiers, but their shoulder straps were khaki cloth rather than cord. In addition, their rank chevrons were red rather than being the white metal chevrons of German NCOs.

Other Ranks' Headdress
Other rank African native soldiers wore a low red felt fez, the so-called rolled fez. Image VI:226 gives an idea of its size – note the eagle badge worn on the front. In the field, a khaki cover and back cloth was worn. For full dress, a blue-black tassel, which tended to fall to the left, was worn.

VI:226 This photograph is to show the size of the low red felt fez, the so-called rolled fez. The actual fez cannot be seen because a camouflage covering with neck flap is over it. Note the badge worn on the front of the fez. This was worn on the red fez also.

MARINES IN TSINGTAO (KIAUTSCHOU)

In 1897, two German missionaries were murdered in the far south-west portion of Shandong Province, China. Shandong is the province that contains the port of Tsingtao, which the Germans had had their eyes on for several years as a base for the East Asia Fleet and an entry to the Chinese markets. The murders were used as a reason by the Germans to obtain a ninety-nine-year lease over Tsingtao and a security zone around it (today Qingdao, Jiaozhou) in Shantung (now Shandong) Province. This area was under the jurisdiction of the Admiralty since it was technically not a colony but a naval base on a long leasehold. The well-known Chinese beer Tsingtao originated in the city while it was under German rule.

The marines had been formed in 1848, and in 1889 a second battalion was added. In 1895, the marines no longer served on ships, and they were designated policing duties in German colonies. They had helped suppress a mutiny among native troops in the Cameroons in 1894. The two home battalions, 1st and 2nd, sent out a composite battalion to serve in the Boxer Rebellion. Troops were also sent to GSWA to fight in the Herero Rebellion of 1904.

In 1897, the 3rd Marine Battalion was formed to provide a military presence in Jiaozhou and the rest of China. In 1914, the 3rd Battalion was stationed at Tsingtao and had detachments at Peking (one company, two artillery sections, and a platoon of mounted marines) and Tientsin.[283] To the normal companies at Tsingtao was added an extra one. The 5th Company of the Battalion at Tsingtao was mounted and had the derisive nickname 'Kauliang Hussars'.[284]

The other ranks were all volunteers and came from all parts of Germany. The officers were seconded from the army. The marines had developed a very good reputation and several young officers, such as Erich Ludendorff and Paul von Lettow-Vorbeck, who went on to fame, served in the marines.

Uniform[285]

The uniform of the marines was a blend of naval and army elements.

Shako

A shako for marines was adopted in 1862. In 1872, a front badge of an imperial eagle on an anchor was added (Image VI:227). Then, in 1882, the shako took

VI:227 Marine Infantry Officer's Shako
The badge on the shako is an Imperial eagle over an anchor.

VI:228 German Sea Battalion (Marines) Shako (Officer's Model)

the form of a line jäger shako, black leather (black cloth for officers) with a falling black horsehair plume in front (red for the band). Their cockade was in the national colours: red, white, and black. Other ranks had black leather chinstraps and officers' chinstraps were made of brass.

Tunic

The tunic was dark blue, but it was lighter blue than the Prussian army infantry tunic. It was single-breasted with eight yellow buttons that were domed and without decorations. The front edge of the tunic was piped in white. Each rear skirt had three buttons, one at waist level, and they were connected with white piping in a Prussian scalloped pattern.

The stand-up collar was white after 1875. Yellow litzen (gold for officers) were added to the collar in 1888. The litzen were in the chapter shape, and the other ranks had two on their collars, while officers had one large stylised chapter litzen (Image VI:229). If an enlisted man wore NCO lace at the collar, only one litzen bar was worn. The other ranks' collar litzen did not have a central light (spiegel), but the officers' litzen had a very thin blue spiegel.

The cuffs were in the Brandenburg shape with the horizontal portion white and the vertical plate the colour of the tunic. On the officers' cuffs, two sides of the vertical plate were outlined with white trim (Image VI:229). The cuffs of the other ranks did not have trim.

There were three yellow litzen on the other ranks' cuffs. The litzen was in the chapter shape and had a blue spiegel. The three chapter-shaped litzen of officers were gold and had a very thin blue spiegel. The two yellow crossed lightning bolts on the lower left sleeve of the other ranks' tunic in Image VI:230 are the insignia of a telegrapher.

Other ranks wore white cloth shoulder straps. The strap had an imperial crown and under it crossed anchors. Below the crossed anchors was the battalion number expressed in Roman numerals, III for the 3rd Battalion. All of these were in yellow cloth or sometimes yellow silk. As was standard, there was a button, yellow, at the pointed collar end of the shoulder strap.

VI:229 Marine Officer's Tunic
Note how the upper portion of the blue vertical cuff plate is trimmed in white. Note also the shape of the litzen on the collar and how the cuff litzen has the slightest trace of a blue central light.

VI:230 Marine Other Ranks Tunic
Note the Brandenburg cuffs with blue vertical plate. The crossed lightning bolts on the lower left sleeve are the insignia of a telegrapher. The chapter litzen on the collar cuff were yellow, and those on the cuff had a blue central light.

Officers wore epaulettes in full dress. These had a white field and a gilt metal crescent. The fringe was silver (see §VI-3-23, Officers' Epaulettes for who was entitled to wear fringe and how thick shaped it was for the different ranks). The outside of the white shoulder board was trimmed with silver lace that had the imperial colours, black and red.

The officers' epaulettes bore crossed anchors, sometimes without battalion numbers (Image VI:231), but there are descriptions and photographs of officers' epaulettes with crowns.[286] Other ranks' shoulder straps bore crowns, crossed anchors, and the battalion number.[287] The epaulettes rested on a base of white cloth.

Trousers and Breeches

Trousers of the same darkish blue as the tunic were worn. These had white piping down the outside seams. White trousers without piping could be worn in the summer. Mounted troops wore breeches of the same colour without white piping.[288]

Gala Trousers

Officers had gala trousers for balls and state occasions. These were the normal trousers with the addition of a broad band of gold lace on the outside seams.[289]

Belt and Belt Buckle

The belt for other ranks was black leather. The belt buckle was the same as worn by the colonial troops. It was a brass rectangle with a white metal oval shield. In the centre of the shield was an imperial crown. Around the top outside edge was the motto 'Gott Mit Uns' ('God [is] with us'). Around the bottom in an arc was a wreath of laurel leaves. The officers wore a naval officer's belt, which consisted of silver-coloured cloth over leather that had three lines of rectangles woven into it. The two outer lines of rectangles were black and the inner line was red. Their gilt buckle was a circle which had a wreath of laurel leaves around the outside. In the centre was an anchor with an imperial crown above the top portion of the anchor and the letter 'W' on top of the anchor.[290]

VI:231 German Marines Officer's Epaulette
Note the silver braid around the shoulder board with its lines of black and gold, the imperial colours. The device on this epaulette is a simple crossed anchors. Many if not most officers' epaulettes had in addition to the crossed anchors crowns and a Roman numeral showing what battalion they were assigned to.

CHINESE MARINES[291]

In 1899, the German naval authorities, impressed with the military potential of the local population, raised a company of Chinese men to serve alongside the 3rd Marine Battalion. The three officers and ten NCOs came from the 3rd Marines. There were even visions of fielding enough Chinese recruits to be able to send them to Africa. However, the unit did not work out and the company had a short life, suffering a high desertion rate. Military service was not an honoured profession in China; there is an old Chinese saying: 'Good iron is not made [into] nails, good men are not made [into] soldiers'. Men who volunteered to serve in the British and German armies were under strong social pressure from their families and neighbours to change their minds. The unit was considered unreliable during the Boxer Rebellion and was disbanded in 1901.

Uniform

Any description of the Chinese Marines' uniform must be viewed as tentative because of a shortage of source material. For example, it is not clear that they had a dress uniform, much less what it looked like.

Headdress

No fewer than four different types of headdress existed: 1) a large grey-green or blue cloth cap with a large brim. It had ear flaps that could be folded up and tied on top, which seems to be how it was normally worn, except during periods of extreme cold (Image VI:232). 2) A black Kilmarnock hat with a black touri on the top. 3) A straw coolie-style straw hat (see Image IV:77 in §IV-9-c, Tonkinese and Annamite Tirailleurs, for its shape). From the top streamers or tassels of black, red, and white, the imperial colours, were worn. And 4) A loose turban of blue cloth.

The men wore a pigtail, *de rigueur* for all Chinese men in Imperial China. Sometimes, they tucked it into their belts at the back.

Shirt/Tunic

Summer Uniform

In the summer, a short tan khaki shirt/tunic was worn. It came down to crotch level. In the front, it had five toggle buttons. Some photographs show six buttons. Going out to either side of the toggle were lines of tan khaki or yellow. See Image VI:232 for an idea of how the front of the shirt/tunic looked. It had a low standing collar, but no shoulder straps or pockets. There was no trim.

Winter Uniform

The winter uniform was basically the same as the summer uniform only in a grey-green colour. The lines coming from the toggles were yellow, so they showed up very clearly. The cuffs had yellow trim. The trim formed a loop on the outside of the sleeve. The uniform shown in Image VI:232 did not have the yellow trim.

Trousers

Long khaki trousers were worn (grey-green in winter). They had no trim. The trousers seemed to have been cut close to the calf below the knee to accept puttees.

Belt and Belt Buckle

A brown or black belt was worn. The belt buckle was the standard buckle worn by enlisted men in the German marines.

VI:232 Front and Back View of Chinese Marine Uniform
This is one version of the different uniforms that this unit seems to have worn in its short life. Note the long pigtail going down the soldier's back and tucked into his belt.

PUTTEES
Puttees were not always worn, but they do seem to be present during more formal events. The puttees were dark blue/green.

FOOTWEAR
The Chinese marines wore either brown ankle boots or Chinese shoes with white socks.

ETHNIC COMPOSITION OF COLONIAL TROOPS

GERMAN EAST AFRICA
In 1914, about 27 per cent of the GEA native troops were from tribes who lived outside the colony.[292] These were mostly Sudanese and men who were ex-King's African Rifles soldiers released as their battalions were disbanded. The balance of the askaris came from local tribes, mostly the Ngoni, Manyema, and especially the Sukuma.[293]

GERMAN SOUTH-WEST AFRICA
The soldiers were all Germans.

CAMEROON
The soldiers in the Cameroon came from the local tribes: mostly the Yaounde, Wute, and Bule.[294]

SIZE OF COLONIAL FORCES[295]

German East Africa	14 companies[296]
German South-West Africa	9 companies: 6 companies mounted on horses (1st, 2nd, 3rd, 6th, 8th, 9th); 1 camel-mounted and machine-gun company (7th), and 2 machine-gun companies (4th, 5th)
Cameroon	12 companies
3rd Marines[297]	
Tsingtao (now Qingdao)	5 companies (one mounted)[298]
Tientsin (now Tainjin)[299]	2 companies and 1 machine-gun platoon[300]
Peking (now Beijing)	1 company, 1 machine-gun platoon, and 1 mounted platoon[301]

§VI GERMAN EMPIRE: NOTES

1. Excerpt from Frederick II's diary, Hay, *Europe Rules*, p. 93.
2. Hagger, Personal correspondence, 1980.
3. Herr, *German Cavalry*, p. 17.
4. Ibid., p. 16.
5. Lucas, *Fighting Troops*, p. 76.
6. Behrend, 'Paukenhunde', p. 17.
7. Kennedy, *German Campaign*, p. 10.
8. This section written by Kayleigh Heubel and the author.
9. Herr, *German Cavalry*, p. 67.
10. Herr, *German Cavalry*, p. 116.
11. Fosten, *Cuirassiers, etc.*, pp. 103–4; Herr, *German Cavalry*, pp. 116–19.
12. Herr, *German Infantry*, vol. 1, pp. 367–9, 424–7; vol. 2, pp. 538–44; Laine, *L'Armée Allemande*, pp. 25–39, 56 and 59.
13. Johansson, *Pickelhauben*, pp. 8–12.
14. Herr, *German Infantry*, vols 1 and 2; Laine, *L'Armée Allemande*; Spemann, *Deutsche Heer*.
15. Herr, *German Infantry*, vol. 2, p. 612.
16. Sater, *Grand Illusion*, p. 12.
17. Samuels, *Command/Control*, p. 20.
18. These percentages were computed using figures from ibid., p. 25; Buchholz, *War/Dawning*, p. 114.
19. Kitchen, *German Officer*, p. 6.
20. Knötel, *Deutsche Heer*, vol. 2, plate 7.
21. Ibid.
22. Herr, *German Generals*, pp. 90–1, 337–8, and 346.
23. These were 3 cm (1.18 inches) wide. Herr, *German Infantry*, vol. 1, p. 75.
24. Ibid.
25. Bredow-Wedel, *Historische*, vol. 1, pp. 182 and 187.
26. Herr, *German Infantry*, vol. 1, p. 276.
27. Ibid., p. 274.
28. Johansson, *Pickelhauben*, p. 30.
29. Herr, *Germany Infantry*, vol. 1, pp. 274–5.
30. Ibid., p. 275.
31. Johansson, *Pickelhauben*, pp. 27–8.
32. Herr, *German Infantry*, vol. 1, p. 292.
33. Ibid., pp. 328–9.
34. Larcade, *Casques*, vol. 2, pp. 7–8.
35. This is another rare case where the regiment was not reduced and amalgamated with several other regiments. Bredow-Wedel, *Historische*, vol. 1, p. 298.
36. Larcade, *Casques*, vol. 2, p. 8.
37. Degenhardt, 'Cracking Mysteries/China', p. 136.
38. Larcade, *Casques*, vol. 2, p. 8.
39. Ibid.
40. Gleeson, *Arcanum*, p. 127. It was Augustus's lust for porcelain that led to the Europeans discovering how to make porcelain. Augustus had hired an alchemist, Johann Bottger, to produce gold for him. When the alchemist was unable to deliver, Augustus ordered him to produce porcelain and had him locked up in a castle in Meissen in 1705, and in 1708, he created porcelain. After that, Augustus's money problems vis-à-vis porcelain were largely over. The whole fascinating story is told in Janet Gleeson's *The Arcanum*. But, while the Saxons could now make porcelain, they could not match the technical skills of the Chinese. That is why Augustus traded the soldiers for the vases in 1717. He wanted to obtain underglaze-blue-coloured items that could only be made in the Far East.
41. Fosten, *Cuirassiers, etc.*, pp. 51–2.
42. Ibid., pp. 31–2, 52–3.
43. Ibid., p. 61.
44. Herr, *German Cavalry*, p. 241.
45. Fosten, *Cuirassiers, etc.*, p. 61.
46. Ibid., p. 63.
47. For epaulettes and rank markings on epaulettes and cords, see ibid., pp. 10–14.
48. Herr, *German Cavalry*, p. 222.
49. Ibid.
50. Ibid., p. 268.
51. Ibid.
52. Ibid.
53. Ibid., p. 277.
54. Ibid., p. 256.
55. See generally Fosten, *Cuirassiers, etc.*, pp. 33, 36, and 43; Herr, *German Cavalry*, pp. 256–8.
56. For general coverage, see Fosten, *Cuirassiers, etc.*, pp. 33 and 49; Herr, *German Cavalry*, pp. 278–80.
57. Fosten, *Cuirassiers*, pp. 33 and 49; Herr, *German Cavalry*, p. 278.
58. See ibid., p. 7 for width of strap.
59. In general, see Fosten, *Cuirassiers, etc.*, pp. 49–50; Herr, *German Cavalry*, pp. 278 and 280.
60. Fosten, *Cuirassiers, etc.*, p. 43; Herr, *German Cavalry*, pp. 261 and 263.
61. Herr, *German Cavalry*, pp. 254–5.
62. Fosten, *Cuirassiers, etc.*, p. 63.
63. Ibid., p. 64.
64. Ibid., pp. 92–3; Herr, *German Cavalry*, pp. 71 and 267.
65. Herr, *German Cavalry*, p. 70.
66. Fosten, *Cuirassiers, etc.*, pp. 92–4; Herr, *German Cavalry*, pp. 68–70, 267.
67. Fosten, *Cuirassiers, etc.*, p. 94; Herr, *German Cavalry*, pp. 76–7.
68. Fosten, *Cuirassiers, etc.*, pp. 102–3; Herr, *German Cavalry*, pp. 74–5, 266.
69. Fosten, *Cuirassiers, etc.*, pp. 88–9; Herr, *German Cavalry*, pp. 261 and 263.
70. For netherwear and footwear, see Fosten, *Cuirassiers, etc.*, pp. 88–9; Herr, *German Cavalry*, pp. 261–5.
71. Herr, *German Cavalry*, pp. 48 and 258.
72. Fosten, *Cuirassiers, etc.*, p. 43.
73. Ibid., pp. 90–2; Herr, *German Cavalry*, pp. 276–7.
74. Marrion, *Lancers, etc.*, p. 7.
75. Ibid.
76. In general, see Marrion, *Lancers, etc.*, pp. 21–3.
77. Herr, *German Cavalry*, p. 347.
78. Ibid., p. 348.
79. Ibid., p. 350.
80. Ibid., pp. 352, 359.

81 Ibid. p. 359. They may have the collar and cuff numbers reversed. See ibid., p. 352.
82 Ibid., p. 350.
83 Marrion, *Lancers, etc.*, p. 28; Herr, *German Cavalry*, pp. 35–40, 366.
84 Herr, *German Cavalry*, p. 37.
85 Marrion, *Lancers, etc.*, pp. 32–3; Herr, *German Cavalry*, pp. 70–3.
86 Marrion, *Lancers, etc.*, pp. 32–3; Herr, *German Cavalry*, pp. 369, 372.
87 Marrion, *Lancers, etc.*, p. 33. Laine, *L'Armée Allemande*, p. 135 shows them as yellow brass.
88 Larcade, *Casques*, vol. 2, p. 30; Bredow-Wedel, *Historische*, vol. 2, p. 755.
89 Ogden, *Famous*, pp. 167–70; Bredow-Wedel, *Historische*, vol. 2, p. 639.
90 Marrion, *Lancers, etc.*, pp. 84–6.
91 This is a Polish word that has several different spellings in English; 'czapska' is the most common. Others are 'tschapska' and 'chapka' (see Marrion, *Lancers, etc.*; Thorburn, *French Army*; Mollo, *Uniforms*; Head, *Napoleonic Lancer*; and Kannik, *Military Uniforms*).
92 Herr, *German Cavalry*, p. 536.
93 Ibid., p. 538.
94 Ibid., p. 508.
95 Ibid., p. 535.
96 Marrion, *Lancers, etc.*, p. 84.
97 Laine, *L'Armée Allemande*, p. 166 (21st Saxon); Herr, *German Cavalry*, p. 552 (2nd Bavarian).
98 Marrion, *Lancers, etc.*, p. 85.
99 Herr, *German Cavalry*, p. 512.
100 Marrion, *Lancers, etc.*, pp. 67–73, 87–95; Herr, *German Cavalry*, pp. 554–73.
101 Herr, *German Cavalry*, pp. 556 and 564.
102 Ibid., p. 556; Marrion, *Lancers, etc.*, p. 88.
103 Herr, *German Cavalry*, pp. 554 and 556.
104 Ibid., p. 556.
105 Ibid., p. 570.
106 Ibid., p. 557.
107 Ibid., p. 571.
108 Ibid., p. 558.
109 Marrion, *Lancers, etc.*, p. 89; Herr, *German Cavalry*, p. 577.
110 Ibid.
111 Herr, *German Cavalry*, p. 577; Laine, *L'Armée Allemande*, pp. 165–7.
112 Herr, *German Cavalry*, p. 586; Marrion, *Lancers, etc.*, p. 92.
113 Herr, *German Cavalry*, p. 586; Marrion, *Lancers, etc.*, p. 92.
114 Herr, *German Cavalry*, p. 38.
115 Ibid.
116 Ibid., pp. 38, 40.
117 Ibid., pp. 584–5.
118 Marrion, *Lancers, etc.*, p. 82.
119 Herr, *German Cavalry*, p. 35.
120 Ibid., p. 37.
121 Marrion, *Lancers, etc.*, p. 92; Herr, *German Cavalry*, p. 41.
122 Knötel, *Deutsche Heer*, vol. 2, plates 99–106, 110, 111, 113 and 114. Herr, *German Cavalry*, p. 588.
123 Demeter, *Officer-Corps*, p. 5.
124 Herr, *German Cavalry*, p. 393.
125 Hagger, *Hussars, etc.*, p. 15 (Brunswick regiment); and Herr, *German Cavalry*, p. 394 (busby height).
126 Sanders, *Hussars*, vol. 1, p. 11.
127 Herr, *German Cavalry*, pp. 393–4.
128 Ibid., p. 394.
129 Ibid.
130 Ibid., pp. 395 and 412; Hagger, *Hussars, etc.*, p. 16.
131 Herr, *German Cavalry*, p. 405.
132 Ibid., p. 409.
133 Ibid., p. 412.
134 Hagger, *Hussars, etc.*, p. 15.
135 Ibid.
136 Lumsden, *Black Order*, p. 142.
137 Ibid., pp. 142–3 and Jones, *Hitler's Heralds*, pp. 7–8.
138 Larcade, *Casques*, vol. 2, p. 107.
139 Pivka, *Black Brunswickers*, p. 7.
140 Ibid., p. 17.
141 Ibid.
142 Larcade, *Casques*, vol. 2, pp. 106–7.
143 Ibid., p. 66.
144 Hagger, *Hussars, etc.*, p. 21; Herr, *German Cavalry*, p. 424.
145 Hagger, *Hussars, etc.*, p. 21.
146 Ibid., pp. 21–2.
147 See generally Sanders, *Hussars*.
148 Herr, *German Cavalry*, p. 422.
149 Ibid., pp. 423 and 424.
150 Ibid., p. 424.
151 Ibid., pp. 424 and 434; Hagger, *Hussars, etc.*, p. 21.
152 von Bülow, *Memoirs*, p. 250. The current value was calculated using 1 thaler = 3 marks. Multiple sources cite this figure, often tied to 1873, but an 1871 figure was unavailable.
153 Herr, *German Cavalry*, p. 481.
154 Hagger, *Hussars, etc.*, pp. 53–4.
155 Herr, *German Cavalry*, p. 482.
156 Hagger, *Hussars, etc.*, pp. 54–5; Herr, *German Cavalry*, pp. 68–9 and 484.
157 Herr, *German Cavalry*, p. 461.
158 Hagger, *Hussars, etc.*, pp. 22 and 24.
159 Herr, *German Cavalry*, 424.
160 Hagger, *Hussars, etc.*, p. 22.
161 Ibid., p. 24.
162 Herr, *German Cavalry*, p. 452.
163 Ibid, p. 449.
164 Ibid., p. 455.
165 Hagger, *Hussars, etc.*, p. 27.
166 Ibid.
167 Herr, *German Cavalry*, p. 468.
168 Hagger, Personal correspondence, 1980.
169 Somers, *German Uniforms*, vol. 3, pp. 1203–4.
170 Herr, *German Cavalry*, pp. 594–9 and 605–26; Hagger, *Hussars, etc.*, pp. 78–92.
171 Herr, *German Cavalry*, p. 606.
172 Ibid., p. 609.
173 Ibid., p. 616.
174 Ibid.
175 Ibid., p. 625.
176 Ibid., p. 622.
177 Ibid.
178 Bredow-Wedel, *Historische*, vol. 3, pp. 1412 and 1414.
179 Larcade, *Casques*, vol. 2, pp. 95–7.
180 Larcade, *Casques*, vol. 2, pp. 95–9; Fosten, *Cuirassiers, etc.*, pp. 113–15; Herr, *German Cavalry*, pp. 308–15.
181 Herr, *German Cavalry*, pp. 316–18; Fosten, *Cuirassiers, etc.*, p. 115.
182 Fosten, *Cuirassiers, etc.*, p. 115; Herr, *German Cavalry*, p. 318.

183 Fosten, *Cuirassiers, etc.*, p. 117; Herr, *German Cavalry*, pp. 67, 72, and 73.
184 Herr, *German Cavalry*, pp. 38, 40, and 320; Fosten, *Cuirassiers, etc.*, p. 117.
185 Herr, *German Cavalry*, p. 320.
186 Marrion, *Lancers, etc.*, p. 88.
187 Herr, *German Cavalry*, p. 584.
188 See Herr, *German Cavalry*, p. 377; Larcade, *Casques*, vol. 2, p. 104.
189 Marrion, *Lancers, etc.*, pp. 103–4,
190 Larcade, *Casques*, vol. 2, p. 119.
191 In general see Fosten, *Cuirassiers, etc.*, pp. 123–5; Larcade, *Casques*, vol. 2, pp. 118–20; Herr, *German Cavalry*, pp. 290–7.
192 Herr, *German Cavalry*, p. 290.
193 Ibid., p. 298.
194 Ibid., pp. 301 and 303; Fosten, *Cuirassiers, etc.*, pp. 122 and 126.
195 Herr, *German Cavalry*, pp. 298 and 300.
196 Ibid., p. 304; Fosten, *Cuirassiers, etc.*, pp. 127–8.
197 Herr, *German Cavalry*, p. 67.
198 Ibid., pp. 67, 69, and 71; Fosten, *Cuirassiers, etc.*, p. 128.
199 Herr, *German Cavalry*, p. 76.
200 Ibid., pp. 74, 76, and 305; Fosten, *Cuirassiers, etc.*, p. 128.
201 Herr, *German Cavalry*, p. 76.
202 Ibid., p. 304.
203 Craig, *Politics/Army*, pp. 2–6.
204 Ibid., p. 8.
205 Ibid.
206 Ibid., p. 37.
207 See Larcade, *Casques*, vol. 1, pp. 7–15.
208 Johansson, *Pickelhauben*, p. 16.
209 Herr, *German Infantry*, vol. 1, p. 388.
210 See ibid., pp. 391 and 428 versus Larcade, *Casques*, vol. 1, p. 41. Herr may be using the term 'guard eagle' to refer to the old guard grenadier eagles.
211 Ogden, *Famous*, p. 170.
212 Herr, *German Infantry*, vol. 2, p. 560.
213 Showalter, 'Hessians'.
214 Herr, *German Infantry*, vol. 2, pp. 501–9; Larcade, *Casques*, vol. 1, p. 75–9; Johansson, *Pickelhauben*, pp. 49–51.
215 Herr, *German Infantry*, vol. 2, p. 501. Laine, *L'Armée Allemande*, p. 72 does not show a plume for the 116th. But Knotel, *Deutsch Heer*, vol. 2, plate 39 does.
216 Herr, *German Infantry*, vol. 2, p. 512–20; Laine, *L'Armée Allemande*, pp 72–3 and 89.
217 Herr, *German Infantry*, p. 512.
218 Kinna, *Jäger*, p. 2.
219 Herr, *German Infantry*, vol. 2, p. 613.
220 Ibid., p. 617.
221 Ibid., p. 615.
222 Ibid., p. 636.
223 Ibid., pp. 636–7.
224 Ibid., p. 638.
225 Ibid., p. 640.
226 Ibid., p. 443.
227 Ibid., p. 444.
228 Ibid., p. 461.
229 Ibid., p. 461.
230 Ibid., p. 650.
231 Ibid.
232 Ibid., p. 672.
233 Ibid.
234 Ibid., pp. 678–701, 710–11, and 726–7.
235 Tuchman, *Guns of August*, p. 208.
236 Herr, *German Infantry*, vol. 2, p. 680.
237 Ibid., pp. 688–9.
238 Ibid., p. 680.
239 Ibid., p. 692.
240 Ibid., p. 701.
241 Ibid., p. 692.
242 Ibid., p. 693.
243 Ibid., p. 710.
244 In general, see Kinna, *Jäger*, pp. 1–2, 5–6, 22–31, and 40–1; Herr, *German Infantry*, vol. 2, pp. 740–70, 776, 783–4, 787–93, and 797–815.
245 Kinna, *Jäger*, p. v.
246 Ibid.
247 Bredow-Wedel, *Historische*, vol. 1, p. 335, and vol. 2, p. 669.
248 Ibid., vol. 1, pp. 403 and 436.
249 Ibid., vol. 1, pp. 474–5.
250 Ibid., vol. 2, p. 648.
251 Ibid., vol. 1, p. 541.
252 Ibid., vol. 2, p. 670.
253 Kinna, *Jäger*, p. 41.
254 Herr, *German Infantry*, vol. 2, p. 766.
255 Williamson, *Cuffbands*, p. 20.
256 Kinna, *Jäger*, p. 26.
257 Ibid.
258 Ibid., p. 23.
259 Ibid., p. 2.
260 Ibid., p. 41.
261 Ibid., p. 27.
262 Herr, *German Infantry*, vol. 1, p. 74.
263 Kinna, *Jäger*, p. 30.
264 Lamothe, *Slaves/Sudanese*, p. 47. See British Author's Note for full citation.
265 See generally, Kraus, *Colonial Troops*, pp. 250–3.
266 Ibid., pp. 254–60.
267 Lamothe, *Slaves/Sudanese*, pp. 28–9.
268 'German South West Africa – Francois-Truppe Uniforms, 1899–91', at www.germancolonialuniforms.co.uk.
269 Kraus, *Colonial Troops*, p. 266.
270 Ibid.
271 Knötel, *Uniforms World*, p. 459; Kraus, *Colonial Troops*, pp. 266–7, 269.
272 Knötel, *Deutsche Heer*, vol. 3, plate 175c.
273 Kraus, *Colonial Troops*, p. 276.
274 Ibid., p. 294.
275 Ibid., p. 309.
276 Knötel, *Deutsche Heer*, vol. 1, p. 366; vol. 3, plate 175; Kraus, *Colonial Troops*, pp. 354–8.
277 Tolstoy, *Long Knives*, pp. 30–1. There is some disagreement about who was behind the buying of the brown shirts. This author says Ernst Röhm.
278 'Effendi: Askari Officers of the German East African Schutztruppe and Polizeitruppe', at www.germancolonialuniforms.co.uk.
279 Knötel, *Deutsche Heer*, vol. 1, p. 367; vol. 3, plate 173; Kraus, *Colonial Troops*, p. 428.
280 Kraus, *Colonial Troops*, p. 428.
281 See Funcken, *La Guerre 1914*, p. 107.
282 Knötel, *Deutsche Heer*, vol. 1, p. 371; vol. 3, plate 175.
283 Marrion, 'German Marine', p. 358.
284 Ibid., p. 356.

285 Knötel, *Deutsche Heer*, vol. 1, pp. 344–54 and vol. 3, plate 175b; Marrion, 'German Marine', pp. 356–60.
286 Marrion, 'German Marine,' p. 359.
287 Ibid., p. 357, illustration L.
288 Ibid., p. 360.
289 Ibid., p. 359.
290 Knötel, *Deutsche Heer*, vol. 3, plate 168.
291 'Tsingtao Chinese Company: Chinese Soldiers in German Service 1899–1901', at www.germancolonialuniforms.co.uk; Marrion, 'German Marine', p. 358.
292 Kraus, *Colonial Troops*, p. 136.
293 Sibley, *Tanganyikan Guerilla*, p. 18.
294 Kraus, *Colonial Troops*, p. 162.
295 Friedag, *Heer & Flotte*, pp. 330–1.
296 Ibid., p 331 states 12: most authorities say 14.
297 Ibid., p. 288.
298 The mounted company always had the next higher number, viz., the 5th in 1914. In World War I in 1914, it took the Japanese 18th Division, the 2nd South Wales Borderers, and the 36th Sikhs nearly two months to capture Tsingtao.
299 Tientsin (Tianjin) was the port city for Peking (Beijing).
300 Kraus, *Colonial Troops*, p. 175.
301 Ibid.

§VI GERMAN EMPIRE: BIBLIOGRAPHY

Correspondance
Hagger, Personal correspondence   D.H. Hagger, Personal correspondence, winter and spring 1980.

Books and Articles

Behrend, 'Paukenhunde' — Hermann Heinrich Behrend, 'Die Paukenhunde von Königsberg: Die vierbeinigen Militämusiker waren die Lieblinge der ganzen Stadt – Trophäe von Königsgrätz', *Das Ostpreußenblatt*, vol. 21, no. 36 (5 September 1970): p. 17.

Bowman, *Pickelhaube*, vol. 1 — J.A. Bowman, *The Pickelhaube, Volume 1: Line Infantry* (Lancaster: Imperial Publications, 1889).

Bredow-Wedel, *Historische* — Claus von Bredow and Ernst von Wedel, *Historische Rang- und Stammliste des deutschen Heeres*, vols 1–3 (Krefeld: Verlag Heere d. Vergangenheit Olmes, 1974).

British Staff, *Handbook 1914* — British War Office, *Handbook of the German Army (Home and Colonial), 1912 (Amended to August 1914)*, 4th edn (London: Imperial War Museum, 2002).

Buchholz, *War/Dawning* — Frank Buchholz, Joe Robinson and Janet Robinson, *The Great War Dawning* (Vienna: Verlag Militaria, 2013).

Carsten, *Junkers* — F.L. Carsten, *A History of Prussian Junkers* (London: Scolar Press, 1989).

Craig, *Politics/Army* — Gordon Craig, *The Politics of the Prussian Army, 1640–1945* (New York: Oxford University Press, 1964).

de Quasada, *Colonial Troops* — Alejandro de Quasada and Chris Dale, *Imperial German Colonial and Overseas Troops, 1885–1918* (New York: Osprey Publishing, 2014).

Degenhardt, 'Cracking Mysteries/China' — Jane Hwang Degenhardt, 'Cracking the Mysteries of "China": China(ware) in the Early Modern Imagination', *Studies in Philology*, vol. 110, no. 1 (Winter 2013): pp. 132–67.

Demeter, *Officer-Corps* — Karl Demeter, *The German Officer-Corps in Society and State 1650–1945* (London: Weidenfeld and Nicolson, 1962) (originally published in German).

Fosten, *Cuirassiers, etc.* — D.S.V. Fosten, *Cuirassiers and Heavy Cavalry* (London: Almark Publishing Co. Ltd, 1972).

Friedag, *Heer & Flotte* — B. Friedag, *Führer Durch Heer und Flotte; Elfter Jahrgang 1914* (Krefeld: Verlag Heere der Vergangenheit J Olmes, 1974).

Funcken, *La Guerre 1914* — Liliane Funcken and Fred Funcken, *L'Uniforme et les Armes de Soldats de la Guerre, 1914–1918, I: Infanterie, etc.* (Tournai: Casterman, 1970).

Gleeson, *Arcanum* — Janet Gleeson, *The Arcanum: The Extraordinary True Story* (New York: Warner Books, Inc., 1999).

Hagger, *Hussars, etc.* — D.H. Hagger, D.S.V. Fosten, and R.J. Marrion, *Hussars and Mounted Rifles: Uniforms of the Imperial German Cavalry, 1900–1914* (New Malden, Surrey: Almark Publishing Co. Ltd., 1974).

Hay, *Europe Rules* — Jeff Hay (ed.), *Europe Rules the World*, vol. 7 (San Diego, CA: Greenhaven Press, Inc., 2002).

Head, *Napoleonic Lancer* — Michael Head, *French Napoleonic Lancer Regiments* (London: Almark Publishing, 1971).

Herr, *German Cavalry* — Ulrich Herr and Jens Nguyen, *The German Cavalry from 1871 to 1914: Uniforms and Equipment* (Vienna: Verlag Militaria, 2006).

Herr, *German Generals* — Ulrich Herr and Jens Nguyen, *The German Generals as well as the War Ministries and General Staffs from 1871 to 1914* (Vienna: Verlag Militaria, 2012).

Herr, *German Infantry* — Ulrich Herr and Jens Nguyen, *The German Infantry from 1871 to 1914*, vols 1 and 2 (Vienna, Austria: Verlag Militaria, 2008).

Johansson, *Pickelhauben* — Eric J. Johansson, *Pickelhauben (Spiked Helmets), the Glittering Age: German Headdress from the Seventeenth to the Twentieth Century 1650–1918* (Independence, MO: H.S.M. Publications, 1982).

Jones, *Hitler's Heralds*	Nigel H. Jones, *Hitler's Heralds: The Story of the Freikorps 1918–1923* (New York: Dorset Press, 1992).
Kannik, *Military Uniforms*	Preben Kannik, *Military Uniforms of the World in Color*, ed. William Carman (New York: Macmillan, 1968).
Kennedy, *German Campaign*	Robert M. Kennedy, *The German Campaign in Poland (1939)* (Washington, D.C.: Department of the Army, 1956).
Kinna, *Jäger*	H. Kinna and D.A. Moss, *Jäger and Schützen Dress and Distinctions, 1910–1914* (Watford: Argus Books Ltd, 1977).
Kitchen, *German Officer*	Martin Kitchen, *The German Officer Corps 1890–1914* (Oxford: Clarendon Press, 1968).
Knötel, *Deutsche Heer*	Herbert Knötel, Paul Pietsch, and Baron Collas, *Uniformenkunde Das Deutsche Heer: Friedensuniformen bei Ausbruch des Weltkrieges*, vols 1–3 (Stuttgart: Spemann, 1982).
Knötel, *Uniforms World*	Richard Knötel, Herbert Knötel, and Herbert Sieg, *Uniforms of the World, 1700–1937*, trans. Robert Ball (New York: Charles Scribner's Son, 1980).
Kraus, *Colonial Troops*	Jurgen Kraus and Thomas Muller, *The German Colonial Troops from 1889 to 1918* (Vienna: Verlag Militaria, 2009).
Laine, *L'Armée Allemande*	Didier Laine, *L'Armée Allemande en 1914* (Paris: Chromos Services, 1984).
Lamothe, *Slaves/Sudanese*	Ronald Lamothe, *Slaves of Fortune: Sudanese Soldiers and the River War, 1896–1898* (Woodbridge: James Currey, 2011).
Larcade, *Casques*, vol. 1	Jean-Louis Larcade, *Casques à Pointe et Coiffures Prestigieuses de l'Armée Allemande: 1842–1918, Tome 1: Troupes à Pied* (Paris: J. Grancher, 1983–5).
Larcade, *Casques*, vol. 2	Jean-Louis Larcade, *Casques à Pointe et Coiffures Prestigieuses de l'Armée Allemande: 1842–1918, Tome 2: Troupes à Cheval* (Paris: J. Grancher, 1983–5).
Lucas, *Fighting Troops*	James Lucas, *Fighting Troops of the Austro-Hungarian Army, 1868–1914* (Tunbridge Wells: Spellmount Ltd, 1987).
Lumsden, *Black Order*	Robin Lumsden, *Himmler's Black Order: A History of the SS, 1923–45* (Thrupp: Sutton Publishing Ltd, 1997).
Marrion, 'German Marine'	Bob Marrion, 'German Marine Infantry Uniform Detail in Full Colour', *Military Modelling*, vol. 18, no. 6 (June, 1988): pp. 356–60.
Marrion, *Lancers, etc.*	R.J. Marrion, *Lancers and Dragoons* (New Malden: Almark Publishing Co. Ltd, 1975).
Meria, *Die Uniformierung*	Klaus-Peter Meria, *Die Uniformierung* (Berlin: Brandenburgisches Verlagshaus, 2001).
Mollo, *Uniforms*	Boris Mollo, *Uniforms of the Imperial Russian Army* (Poole: Blandford Press, 1979).
Nash, *German Infantry*	David Nash, *German Infantry 1914–1918* (London: Almark Publishing Co. Ltd, 1971).
Ogden, *Famous*	H.A. Ogden (H.A. Hitchcock, collaborator), *Young People's Book of Famous Regiments* (New York: McBride Co., Inc., 1957).
Pietsch, *Preußischen Heeres*	Paul Pietsch, *Die Formations und Uniformierungsgeschichte des Preußischen Heeres 1808 bis 1914* (Hamburg: Helmul Verlag Gerhard Schulz, 1963).
Pivka, *Black Brunswickers*	Otto von Pivka, *The Black Brunswickers* (Reading: Osprey Publishing Ltd, 1973).
Rankin, *Helmets*	Colonel Robert H. Rankin, *Helmets and Headdress of the Imperial German Army, 1870–1918* (New Milford, CT: N. Flayderman & Co., 1965).
Samuels, *Command/Control*	Martin Samuels, *Command or Control?* (Portland, OR: Frank Cass, 1995).
Sanders, *Hussars*	Paul Sanders, *Uniforms and Accoutrements of the Imperial German Hussars, 1880–1919*, vols 1 and 2 (Atglen, PA: Schiffer Military History, 2004).
Sater, *Grand Illusion*	William Sater and Holger Herwig, *The Grand Illusion: The Prussianization of the Chilean Army* (Lincoln, NE: University of Nebraska Press, 1999).
Shirreffs, 'Lace and Embroidery'	William Shirreffs, 'Lace and Embroidery Patterns in the Prussian Infantry, 1814–1914', *Tradition*, no. 69 (n.d.): pp. 2–7.
Showalter, 'Hessians'	Dennis Showalter, 'Hessians the Best Armies Money Can Buy', *Military History*, vol. 24, no. 7 (October 2007): pp. 36–43.
Sibley, *Tanganyikan Guerilla*	J.R. Sibley, *Tanganyikan Guerilla: East African Campaign, 1914–18* (New York: Ballantine Books, Inc., 1971).
Somers, *German Uniforms*, vol. 3	Johan Somers, *Imperial German Field Uniforms and Equipment, 1907–1918*, vol. 3 (Atglen, PA: Schiffer Military History, 2007).
Spemann, *Deutsche Heer*	W. Spemann, *Uniformenkunde Das Deutsche Heer: Friedensuniformen bei Ausbruch des Weltkrieges*, vol. 2 (Stuttgart: W. Spemann, 1982).
Thorburn, *French Army*	W.A. Thorburn, *French Army Regiments and Uniforms: From the Revolution to 1870* (London: Arms and Armour Press, 1969).

Tolstoy, *Long Knives*	Nikolai Tolstoy, *Night of the Long Knives* (New York: Ballantine Books, Inc., 1972).
Tuchman, *Guns of August*	Barbara W. Tuchman, *The Guns of August* (New York: Bonanza Books, 1982).
von Bülow, *Memoirs*	Prince Bernhard von Bülow, *Memoirs of Prince von Bülow, Volume IV: Early Years and Diplomatic Service, 1849–1897*, trans. Geoffrey Dunlap and F.A. Voigt (Boston, MA: Little, Brown Co., 1932).
Webster's Unabridged Dictionary	*Webster's Unabridged Dictionary*, 2nd edn (New York: Random House, 2001).
Williams, 'Battle Honours'	J. Robert Williams, 'Battle Honours Shared by British and German Regiments, as Reflected by Devices Worn by Units of the Imperial German Army in 1914', *Bulletin of the Military Historical Society*, vol. 23, no. 92 (May 1973): pp. 97–103.
Williamson, *Cuffbands*	Gordon Williamson and Thomas McGuirl, *German Military Cuffbands, 1784–Present* (San Jose, CA: R. James Bender Publishing, 1998).
Windrow, *Osprey*	Martin Windrow (ed.), *Osprey Men-At-Arms: A Celebration* (Oxford: Osprey Ltd., 2008).
www.germancolonialuniforms.co.uk	C. Dale, 'German Colonial Uniforms', www.germancolonialuniforms.co.uk, accessed 13 June 2017.

§VII

AMERICAN EMPIRE

§VII-1 COUNTRY BACKGROUND

The United States grew from tiny toeholds planted along the Atlantic coast in the late sixteenth and early seventeenth century. The early ones failed, but eventually some were successful through finding ways to make a living. Almost at once they came into conflict with the native peoples who already lived there, and this was the beginning of an almost 300-year process of settlers encroaching on Native American land, the Native Americans reacting, with a 'war' between the white man and the American Indian being the result.

The availability of free or very cheap land drew in migrants from the Old World, whose numbers caused the encroachment on the American Indian lands. The estimated population of the American colonies and country grew as follows:

Table VII.1.1: American Colonial Population[1]

Year	1620	1790	1830	1860	1880	1910
Population (in millions)	0.0023	3.9290	12.866 0	31.4433	50.1892	92.2285

Much of this growth, and many of the so-called Indian Wars, took place behind the protective shield and within the trading system of the British Empire. It was not until the middle of World War II that the United States had been independent of British rule for longer than it had been a British colony.

The first British colonies were not the only colonies from European countries. The Spanish had reached America first and had settlements in what today are the southern states of Florida and Georgia. The Dutch and Swedes also had colonies. In the north, in Canada, France controlled large swathes of land. It was thinly settled, but, for that reason, France had very good relations with the First Nations. Early on, the British removed the Dutch and the Swedes, but not before the Swedes taught the American settlers how to make log cabins. The Spanish colony declined, along with Spanish power. France was ejected as a result of the Seven Years' War, called the French and Indian War in America.

To win the war, Britain incurred large debts that had to be serviced and paid back. Another result of the war was that the interests of Britain and the American settlers diverged. The British, trying to balance the interests of the colonists and the Native Americans, barred the forward movement of settlements into the west. This upset all classes of colonists – the poor who wanted the land and the upper classes who had been speculating in western land. The British also clamped down on smuggling in order to collect the customs duties. This, of course, was not liked by communities such as Boston, whose economy received a large amount of money from smuggling. Other taxes were imposed, which the Americans – who had been fairly lightly taxed up to this point – resented. The British government also made some unpopular decisions.

The outcome of all of this was the American Revolution, a gruelling long war in which the American settlers outlasted the British will to keep fighting and the colonies declared their independence as the United States of America. However, the Americans were greatly aided by other European countries, one after another, entering the war on the American side.

When the peace treaty was signed in 1783, the Americans were amazed by British generosity. The new country obtained all the territory between Canada and Florida – which was held by Spain – and between the Atlantic and the Mississippi River. They did not receive Louisiana or the city of New Orleans.

During the Napoleonic Wars, New Orleans and the Louisiana Territory passed into the hands of the French. Cut off from it by the Royal Navy, Napoleon sold it to the Americans in what is the second most important expansion step in American history. It brought what would later become almost thirteen new states into the Union, and also the port of New Orleans, which gave the country a route to ship its western products overseas. The land from the treaty that ended the American Revolution was the most important territorial gain because of the raw material wealth in it, and it set up future expansion.

Then, between 1810 and 1819, the United States took advantage of Spain's weakness to acquire Florida, partly through naked seizure and partly through a treaty.

Post-1815 Economic Developments

At the end of the Revolution, the United States was in economic and political shambles. The states negotiated a better union and signed the United States Constitution in 1787, which solved many of the political and economic problems. Gold was discovered in North Carolina in 1799, which added a valuable source of wealth to the country.

The country's manufacturing base began in 1790 with theft of intellectual property from Britain. Britain had developed machinery that could increase tenfold the amount of cotton thread a worker could spin in a day. In 1793 Eli Whitney, a Yale Yankee living in the South, invented the cotton gin, which could clean the seeds from the cotton at a rate of fifty pounds a day.[2] This changed everything. Whitney is also generally credited with developing the concept of American mass production in around 1800, whereby products such as muskets and, later, cars and planes were produced with interchangeable parts.[3] Cotton cloth output grew 15.4 per cent per year from 1815 to 1833 and 5.1 per cent from 1834 to 1860.[4] During this period, the amount of income generated by cotton manufacturers in America was greater than that generated by the iron industry.[5] In addition to supplying the cotton for the Northern mills, the Southern cotton also accounted for more than half the dollar value of American exports. It was worth nearly ten times the exports of its nearest competition, wheat and flour from the North.[6] Growing cotton made many rich, and the South probably the richest region of the country.

There were two problems. First, it needed a large, cheap labour force, and that meant slaves. In the years between 1800 and 1860, more and more people in America and Britain turned against the evils of slavery. Second, and perhaps equally pressing, was that many in the North wanted higher and higher tariffs to protect Northern industries. The South, which had become an agricultural-producing economy, had to buy most of the manufactured items it needed. Most came from overseas. If tariffs were higher, overseas goods would be more expensive, and Northern manufacturers, with less competition, could raise their prices. The political system could not resolve these conflicts, and tensions between the two parts of the country grew more and more strained.

Adding to the political stress were the long-term trends. Increasing numbers of migrants were coming into the North, where there were factory and other jobs, or they passed on to the West, where they could set up farms they would work themselves. The areas where cotton could be grown were nearly all settled, so new states that came into the Union would not be ones sympathetic to the slaveholders' point of view.

Finally the American Civil War began. The war was won by the North, which had an overwhelming advantage in manpower and industrial capacity. The American Civil War is the bloodiest war the country has ever had. The casualties – two-thirds from disease – were higher than American losses in World War I, World War II, and the Korean War combined. In addition, these losses were suffered by a much smaller population. The two sides were completely unevenly matched. The North had more than three times as many white men. It had 110,000 manufacturing establishments to the South's 18,000.[7]

The central fact of American economic, political, and social history between 1865 and 1950 is that the North won the Civil War. The South lost almost all of its overseas markets and ownership of almost all its assets. The infrastructure of the South was destroyed, and in effect it became a very poor colony of the North. Through control of the railways that were built with Northern capital after the Civil War, the rest of the country was also more or less a Northern economic colony until many decades later.

FOREIGN WARS

Between the end of what the Americans call the War of 1812 with Britain and the US entry into World War I, the Americans were engaged in only two foreign wars in addition to their Civil War, the wars with Mexico and Spain, and their constant very low-level skirmishes with Native Americans on the western frontier.

In 1846–8, the United States fought a war with Mexico. Americans in Texas, which was a part of Mexico, had revolted in 1836, and they won their independence. The last stand at the Alamo took place during this revolt. The Americans/Texans formed a Republic of Texas which lasted until 29 December 1845, when it joined the Union as a state. Texas brought its border disputes with Mexico with it when it joined the Union. The Americans had tried to buy the disputed areas and other Mexican land, but Mexico was in no mood to sell anything. The war with Mexico began in one of the disputed areas.

Today, especially in historical accounts written during period of the Vietnam War, the war with Mexico is viewed as big America bullying a smaller country. But the countries were more closely matched then, and most European military experts thought Mexico, with its larger army professionally trained by Europeans, would win every battle. In addition, the Americans would be fighting at the end of very long supply lines.

The Americans won the war by succeeding in some very hard-fought battles and taking reckless military risks. In some battles, they were all but beaten, but saved by hard fighting by one American unit or another. The American volunteer soldiers often outfought the Mexican peon soldiers, who had been drafted against their will and poorly supplied and mistreated once in the army. In addition, the American army leadership managed to keep political jockeying for future political office from interfering with their military decisions better than the Mexican generals. There were cases where, during a battle, one Mexican commander did not send aid to another commander who was a possible future political rival.

In the 1848 peace treaty following the war, the US acquired a large area of land, most of six western states that Mexico nominally owned. The US government paid $15 million to Mexico and assumed a little over $3 million in debts that the Mexican government owed American citizens. This was about the same amount that had been paid for the Louisiana Purchase, and less than half what the US had offered to buy Mexican land prior to the war. Much of this territory Mexico had inherited from Spain, whose claim to it went back, more or less, to when the Pope had divided the world between Spain and Portugal. Neither Spain nor Mexico had done much to settle this land, and Mexico owned it because in the past people in the chancelleries of Europe had drawn lines establishing borders on a blank map without knowing anything about the land.

There were settled areas which America took over. Mexico had planted a string of missions in California that reached up to just beyond San Francisco, and a few people had established large ranches. There were also some seaports. The Americans in California revolted, declaring a California Republic in April 1846, after the Mexican War had begun. It is not clear whether or not they had news of the outbreak of war at the time of their revolt. The US acquired the area of what is now California in the peace treaty. This was land Mexico might not have been able to hold onto anyway.

There were also long-standing settlements in southern New Mexico and Arizona which the US took over. All of this made a large territorial expansion for the United States. In 1853, the US purchased additional land along the Rio Grande from Mexico – Mexico chose to sell its land that time.

The United States came close to going to war with Mexico when Mexico had broken out in a confusing, multi-sided civil war. In January 1916, one of the leaders of a faction in that war, Poncho Villa, feeling the US had been working against him, carried out a raid on a US town. This led to an American punitive expedition into Mexico to try to track him down.[8]

NATIONAL GUARD-MEXICAN BORDER

Things went from bad to worse, and in the summer of 1916, a large percentage of the regular army was on the Mexican border. All of the National Guard was also mobilised and sent there.[9] The National Guard had the potential to form ten infantry divisions and six separate brigades which could be formed into two more infantry divisions.[10]

This was the last listing of the old militia numbers and state titles which went back to colonial days. Shortly thereafter, the militias lost their state ties and names and went to a less personal system. A local touch was lost, although the old system could be confusing: by this time, it was possible to have forty-nine different 1st infantry regiments.

As relations with Germany soured, the Americans reduced their conflicts with the Mexicans and returned the National Guard soldiers to their homes. Then, on 26 April 1917, the US declared war on Germany.

§VII-2 THE ARMY

§VII-2-1   The Army and its Background
§VII-2-2   Officers' Promotions
§VII-2-3   'Indian Campaigns' Considered 'Wars'

§VII-2-1 THE ARMY AND ITS BACKGROUND

The traditional American viewpoint of the military was that of the British motherland, modified by the experiences in fighting to win independence from Britain. The US inherited a strong distrust of standing armies. The American Revolution had been won, in large part, because the British, at the end of a very long supply chain, had not been able to stamp out the small American forces. The Americans held on long enough for other major European countries to join in the fight against Britain. Finally, for Britain, the game was not worth the effort.

Once independence was won, the pattern that would be followed for the rest of the century was established. The central government had a small army and each state maintained a militia in such a state of readiness as it saw best. When a war, such as the Mexican–American War, the Civil War, or the Spanish–American War, occurred, most of the fighting men were supplied by the state troops.

This system worked for the United States because, for a century, it faced no enemies on its borders other than the Mexicans, who were beaten in a war in the 1840s – a war most European military experts had thought the Mexicans would win. The Canadians, a British colony, were intent on settling their wild frontiers, and while there were many sharp disagreements about where the border between Canada and the US should be drawn as both moved west, these were always settled peacefully and fairly logically.

All of this meant the American army could be quite small between 1815 and 1898, except during the American Civil War, when it grew to a great size. The duty of the army during this period was mostly to protect the settlers from the Native Americans as the settlers encroached on the American Indians' land. The high point of this 'Indian-Fighting Army' came between 1865 and 1898, the end of the Civil War and the beginning of the Spanish–American War.

During this period, the army was stationed in small groups throughout the west. There were 111 western posts in 1880.[11] With the help of Native American scouts, they launched expeditions to try to track down Native American bands and camps. The foe was much more mobile than the US troops, who were completely tied to their supply lines. Even the forage for the cavalry horses and supply animals had, at times, to be shipped in as they often could not live by grazing on the native plains grass.[12] One American soldier likened the situation to that of a large dog on a chain: 'within the length of the chain irresistible, beyond it powerless.'[13]

Life in the frontier army was hard for officers, troops, and families. The posts were almost always in remote areas; obtaining creature comforts was very hard. They suffered from climate extremes. The soldiers on the ever-changing frontier often had to build their own posts. In the south-west these were often made of adobe, claylike dirt blocks, locally cut logs, or logs split into boards. One post for the Dakotas built in the winter was made of mud. The floors were normally dirt, as were the roofs. Almost none of them had outer walls.[14]

The author of *Black Infantry in the West* goes into some detail describing the poor living conditions at frontier posts and particularly those suffered by the 24th and 25th (Black) Infantry Regiments.[15] This could lead the unwary to believe that the army's black soldiers suffered substandard housing. This is not the case. Almost all frontier posts were crude because they had originally been built by soldiers who did not have special construction training, using whatever materials were on hand. After the were built, there was almost no effort made to maintain the posts. The army command took the view that the posts were temporary establishments, which is why they made little effort to build sound quarters or to repair them when they deteriorated. The author of *Black Infantry in the West* makes the point that the black infantry regiments served for many years in such western posts, but most of the white regiments were also stationed on the frontier between 1865 and 1895.[16]

On top of that, the political class saw little reason to spend money on the army. One House member in 1869 spoke for almost all political classes in peacetime: 'If we continue to make these appropriations of the people's money to keep up this great army, our constituents will run every one of us into the Potomac.'[17] Another congressman in 1876 suggested doing away with the army and vesting its peacetime functions in the Interior Department.[18] When the South was able to send representatives to Congress after the Civil War, they had long memories of what their region had suffered from the national army during the Civil War and the occupation of the South that had followed it. They resisted giving money to the army. On two occasions, in 1877 and 1879, the fiscal year ended without money being approved for the army. In 1877, funds were not allocated until three months into the next year, and in 1879, it took two months. During these periods, the officers and men went without pay.[19]

During the Indian Wars, the American Indians almost never made mounted attacks on forts or attacked wagon trains by riding around them in circles. In fact, most forts did not have outside walls.[20] These were devices adopted by the touring Wild West shows put on by showmen, such as Buffalo Bill Cody and others, for audiences in the eastern United States and Europe. These devices were necessary to fit the action within the limited confines of a show tent or an exhibition hall, and so that all members of the audience could see the action and actors. This, in turn, was picked up by the film industry.

The Indian Wars were dirty wars waged against a relatively small number of people. There were fewer than 100,000 hostile American Indians facing the United States in 1866 at the start of the final struggle for the American West.[21] This number includes women and children; the number of fighting men was much smaller. Some of the most well-known fighting tribes were very small: the Cheyenne, 3,500 in 1780; the Pawnee, 4,686 in 1856; the Comanche, 7,000 in 1690; and the Dakota Sioux (all bands), 25,000 in 1780.[22] Needless to say, these numbers are all rough estimates and include all ages and sexes. At first it may seem that the number of people in a tribe in 1690 or 1780 is useless when considering fighting numbers in the period 1866–90 but it must be remembered that in the days before modern medicine and antibiotics populations grew very slowly and often fell. In addition, the tribes were engaged in constant warfare with each other and this led to many deaths. They also stole women from each other; both of these factors would act to curtail a tribe's numbers. For these reasons the stated population numbers ninety or even a hundred years before the period of the Indian Wars do give a good rough idea of the tribes' sizes during the period 1866–90.[23]

Since the frontier army's American Indian opponents were not numerous and the fighting was basically a low-intensity guerrilla war, the army's losses in fighting them were relatively low, surprisingly so for a period of warfare that forms what is probably the US's main founding story. Between 1865 and 1898, the army had only 1,056 officers and soldiers killed in battle with the American Indians. There were another ninety-three American Indian scouts and police and 118 civilians killed who were working with the army.[24]

Because the army lacked mobility, it brought the American Indians to battle where it could, in their villages with their families. This was often most successful in winter.[25] There were, of course, women and children in the attacked villages. Some army officers tried to kill them, but most tried hard to not harm them.[26] Whatever happened, the attacks were very traumatic and surrender often followed.

The American frontier is said to have closed in 1890, and the army began the process of closing its small bases. They were down to sixty-two by 1891 from 111 in 1880.[27]

Then, in 1898, came war with Spain. The war started after a period of tension with Spain when sections of the American people were aggressively unhappy with Spain's policy in its colony of Cuba and wanted US intervention in Cuba to help the rebels. The event that triggered the war was the blowing up of a US battleship in a Cuban harbour. It was well timed and in accordance with the bellicose parties' desire for war with Spain; it was so disastrous for Spain that suspicions have always existed that a mine was used to set off the explosion.

For the war, the state militias, now called the National Guard, were called out. When it was over, America occupied Cuba, Puerto Rico, the Philippines, and several other Pacific islands. The American politicians in power convinced themselves that the state of the world required the United States to maintain control of most of this territory. After an occupation of several years, US forces were withdrawn from Cuba. It would have looked too unseemly to take over the island America had gone to war to free.

To occupy what could now be called the American Empire, additional soldiers were needed and the army was expanded from tiny to small. The Indian-Fighting Army had been around 28,000 officers and men,[28] with the fighting being done by twenty-five infantry regiments (including two black regiments) and ten cavalry regiments (including two black regiments). After the outbreak of the Spanish–American War, the calls upon the army to fight beyond the continental United States in the Spanish–American War, in the Philippines, and in the Boxer Rebellion in China made the US Congress see that a larger army was needed. The authorised size of the army increased to 97,000,[29] the size of the army of an average Balkan country of the period.

This was accomplished when Congress passed a law in 1902 adding five additional cavalry and five additional infantry regiments to the army.[30] Most of these were organised in 1902.[31] These additions brought the army up to fifteen cavalry regiments, numbered 1 to 15, and thirty infantry regiments, numbered 1 to 30. The number of black regiments was not changed or increased – they remained the 24th and 25th Infantry and the 9th and 10th Cavalry.

PHILIPPINE SCOUTS

There had been an independence movement in the Philippines when the Americans arrived there. When it became clear that the Americans intended to take over rule of the islands from the Spanish, the movement turned to fight the Americans. Another outcome of this action was that Rudyard Kipling wrote the poem which opens, 'Take up the White Man's burden'.[32] This viewpoint would not last much longer.

The resistance movement turned into a guerrilla war centred mostly among the Tagalog ethnic group who lived around Manila on the main island, Luzon. This fighting absorbed large numbers of American troops. As part of this effort, early on the Americans raised scouts from among the Macabebes, an ethnic group that had traditionally served the Spanish as soldiers. This experiment was a great success. In 1901, Congress authorised the formation of the Philippine Scouts, who would be a part of the US army. In time, the Scouts were formed into fifty companies of one hundred men each. The majority of the men were from the tried and proven Macabebe group. The next largest group was the Ilocanos, who, like the Macabebes, were traditional foes of the Tagalogs. The new Scouts also contained men from the Bicol region, the Cagayan area, the Visayan Islands,[33] and even Tagalogs. The Ilocanos lived on the north-west coast of Luzon. The Bicol region was in southern Luzon, the Cagayan was on the northern tip of Luzon, and the Visayan Islands were the central islands of the Philippine archipelago.[34]

The United States then undertook a task the Spanish had never really attempted: making their rule a reality on the rest of the thousands of islands that made up the Philippines. This involved many long and hard campaigns in tropical conditions and the raising of more Scouts.

By 1910, the Scouts had almost achieved their final form. There were twelve battalions of Scouts, each with four companies. The companies and battalions came from different parts of the Philippines and were often stationed away from their homeland to reduce the likelihood of the soldiers supporting civilian leaders in a revolt. The units were usually recruited from one geographic area and named after that area.

To give an idea of the intensity of the fighting in the Philippines, consider the following: the Medal of Honor was awarded to thirty soldiers during the Spanish–American War, to four during the Boxer Rebellion, and to seventy men during the Philippine Insurrection.[35]

Table VII.2.1.1 shows the ethnic composition of the different companies and where they were stationed. Their location reflects the fact that there was still fighting against the Moros taking place.

Table VII.2.1.1: Philippine Scout Battalions, Organisation in 1910[36]

Battalion	Companies	Ethnic Group	Station
1st	1st, 2nd, 3rd, 6th	Macabebes[a]	Mindanao
2nd	12th, 13th, 14th, 18th	Ilocanos[b]	Luzon
3rd	29th, 30th, 31st, 34th	Tagalogs[c]	Mindanao
4th	37th, 43rd, 48th, 49th	Visayans[d]	Mindanao
5th	15th, 16th, 21st, 24th	Ilocanos[b]	Mindanao
6th	17th, 20th, 22nd, 23rd	Ilocanos[b]	Samar
7th	7th, 9th, 10th, 11th	Macabebes[a]	Corregidor
8th	35th, 38th, 39th, 41st	Visayans[d]	Leyte
9th	25th, 26th, 27th, 28th	Cagayans[e]	Luzon
10th	36th, 40th, 44th, 50th	Visayans[d]	Luzon
11th	42nd, 45th, 46th, 47th	Visayans[d]	Samar
12th	4th, 5th, 8th, 33rd	Macabebes[a]	Palawan
Unattached	19th	Ilocanos[b]	Luzon
Unattached	32nd	Bicols[f]	Luzon
Unattached	51st	Moros[g]	Mindanao
Unattached	52nd	Moros[g]	Mindanao

Notes: [a] The Macabebes took their name from the town of Macabebe in Pampanga Province. The province is located in central Luzon, just above the waist of the island. The town is located in the southern part of the province. Central Luzon was home to the Kapampangan people, one of the larger ethnic groups in the Philippines. Pampanga contained only a portion of them.
[b] A language/ethnic group that lived primarily on the north-western coast of Luzon near the tip of the island.
[c] Tagalogs were the major language/ethnic group on Luzon and the second largest in the Philippines. In addition to living in much of Luzon, they lived in Manila. They were the group that first resisted the coming of the Americans. They lived in southern and central Luzon and the islands of the Luzon island group.
[d] An ethnic group whose members shared a cultural and linguistic affinity. They lived on a group of islands within the Visayan Sea, one of the three major island groups in the Philippines. The language group was the largest in the Philippines.
[e] A language/ethnic group that lived primarily on the northern tip of Luzon.
[f] A language/ethnic group that lived on the south-west peninsula of Luzon.
[g] Moros were Muslims who lived on the island of Mindanao, Sulu, and smaller islands to the southeast. The Mindanao island group, with the Luzon and Visaya groups, is one of the three main island groups in the Philippines. The term Moro covers several different ethnic groups. The Moros had made a spirited resistance to the Spanish when they ruled the Philippines. In 1910, they were doing the same with the Americans, but some had elected to serve in the American armed forces.

The organisation meant that the battalions had a limited ethnic makeup. But apart from the Macabebes the Americans tended to ignore ethnicity. After early problems, they were, however, careful not to mix ethnic groups within a company.

The company numbers are somewhat misleading because the army changed the numbers between 1901 and 1914 and then again after 1914. They could also change the companies in a battalion, as long as the battalion kept the same ethnic group.

Porto Rico Regiment

The other major area absorbed after the war was the island of Puerto Rico. There, the Americans moved in with no trouble and formed a Puerto Rican regiment. The Porto Rico Regiment of Infantry (as it was spelled at the time), formed to garrison the island, had a Puerto Rican rank and file. The lieutenant colonel and majors were regular army men. The captains, for the most part, were men up from the ranks of the regular army, but a few were directly appointed to the regiment, and some had been National Guard officers.

All the lieutenants were native Puerto Ricans, or at least people with Spanish names.

§VII-2-2 OFFICERS' PROMOTIONS

Prior to 1890, the speed of an officer's promotion generally depended on his regiment. Eligibility for promotion in the infantry and cavalry depended on an officer's seniority in his regiment. This could cause classmates from the West Point military academy to have very uneven rates of promotion. If one regiment had heavy casualties from battle or disease, or high numbers of its senior officers retired, resigned, or were promoted, the junior officers gained fast promotions.

In 1890, promotion below the grade of brigadier general was changed to be within each branch of the army rather than within each regiment.[37] A seniority list was kept for the infantry and another for the cavalry. Others were kept for different branches, corps, and departments of the army. This did away with the vagaries of regimental experience and allowed for smoother transfer between regiments. The same rule also provided promotion exams for officers below the rank of major.[38]

§VII-2-3 'INDIAN CAMPAIGNS' THAT WERE CONSIDERED 'WARS'

The following campaigns against Native Americans ('Indian campaigns') were defined as wars:[39]

- Campaigns in southern Oregon and Idaho and northern parts of California and Nevada, 1865–8.
- Campaign against the Cheyennes, Arapahoes, Kiowas, and Comanches, in Kansas, Colorado, and Indian Territory, 1867, 1868, and 1869.
- Modoc War, 1872 and 1873.
- Campaign against the Apaches of Arizona, 1873.
- Campaign against the Kiowas, Comanches, and Cheyennes, in Kansas, Colorado, Texas, Indian Territory, and New Mexico, 1874 and 1875.
- Campaigns against the Northern Cheyennes and Sioux, 1876 and 1877.
- Nez Perce War, 1877.
- Bannock War, 1878.
- Campaign against the Northern Cheyennes, 1878 and 1879.
- Campaign against the Ute in Colorado and Utah, September 1879 to November 1880.
- Campaign against the Apaches in Arizona, 1885 and 1886.
- Campaign against the Sioux in South Dakota, November 1890 to January 1891.

Service stripes were awarded to the enlisted men that participated in the above wars.

§VII-3 UNIFORM INFORMATION

§VII-3-1   *Service and War Service Stripes*
§VII-3-2   *Different Shades of Cavalry Yellow*
§VII-3-3   *Montana Peak Hat*

§VII-3-1 SERVICE AND WAR SERVICE STRIPES

The first United States service stripes were issued in 1782 during the Revolutionary War. A white stripe to be worn on the upper arm was granted for four years of unblemished service. Later, this was changed to three years of service with a second stripe for six years. The colour of the stripe was changed to the colour of the man's corps.[40] The use of service awards ended when the Revolutionary War was over.[41]

Service stripes were reintroduced in 1832 in the form of an inverted 'V' above the elbow of the coat sleeve. One was granted for five years' service with additional stripes being added for each additional five years of service. War service was marked by red trim on each side of the stripe that marked the war service.[42]

In 1851, service stripes were moved to the lower arm. They were to be worn diagonally, and were 1.27 cm (½ inch) wide and in branch colour.[43]

The diagonal service stripes, or half-chevron, as they were known,[44] were worn on the lower sleeve of both arms. The lowest stripe was 1.27 cm (½ inch) above the front corner of the cuff facing. Additional stripes were placed 6.4 mm (¼ inch) above earlier stripes.[45] In the infantry, it was made of blue cloth and in the cavalry of yellow cloth.

In 1866, Congress set cavalry enlistments at five years and infantry enlistments at three years. In 1869, by an act of Congress, five-year enlistments were set for all branches.[46] Then, in 1894, standard army enlistment was reduced from five years to three.[47]

The service stripes were different for men who had served in wartime. Prior to 1873, war service was noted by a red stripe 1.91 cm (¾ inch) wide with an overlay of the branch colour 1.27 cm (½ inch) wide.[48]

In 1873, the adjutant general ordered that wartime service, in the future, would be shown by a diagonal stripe of the colour of the branch the soldier was in when the man rendered the war service.[49] Since it was common for men to move between branches, soldiers could have several different coloured service stripes on their coats.

VII:1 Post Ordnance Sergeant in M1885 Dress Uniform with Pseudo-Brandenburg Cuffs
The cuffs and collars are crimson trimmed in white. Note the five service stripes, which indicate at least fifteen years' service, and one wound stripe. The star and chevrons show his rank of post ordnance sergeant.

Between 1884 and 1902, service stripes consisted of gold lace with backing in the branch colour. The lace stripe was 1.27 cm (½ inch) wide and sewn on a 1.91 cm (¾ inch) cloth of the branch colour to show war service. Otherwise, it was sewn on blue cloth. For infantry, the branch colour was white. For cavalry, between 1884 and 1887, the backing colour was medium yellow.[50]

The subject of American service stripes and which ones were to be worn when is very complex. Staff members of the quartermaster general and the inspector general wrote several studies in the 1880s to explain how the system worked.[51] These works show that even the staff officers were not always sure of what was to be worn in all cases.[52]

After 1902, wartime service was noted by a diagonal stripe of white edged with the branch colour. Three or five years of service was shown by a stripe in the branch colour.[53] A gold wound stripe could also be worn along with the service and war service stripes.[54]

The 1912 Dress Regulations state that all enlisted men who had served for a period of three years, *continuously or otherwise*, wore a service stripe of their arm of service. For each additional three years of service, *continuously or otherwise*, an additional service stripe should be worn (emphasis added).[55]

The regulations go on to state that if the soldier had moved between service arms, the stripe would be the colour of arm, corps, or department where the major portion of the three-year period was served. The stripes were worn diagonally on both sleeves of the lower portion of each coat. The stripes extended from coat seam to seam. The lowest stripe was about 8.89 cm (3½ inches) from the bottom of the sleeve. Additional stripes were added above the first stripe in the order in which they were earned. There was 6.4 mm (¼ inch) space between each stripe.[56] The stripes were 1.27 cm (½ inch) wide.[57] During the period 1886 to 1912, minor changes were made to the width of the service stripes. These, because they were minor, have not been covered. Between 1902 and 1910, the infantry branch stripes were light blue. Then, between 1910 and 1917, they were white. The cavalry colour for this period was yellow.[58]

Campaign medals began to be issued in 1905.[59] Their introduction led, in time, to the end of war service stripes in 1910.[60]

War Service

The following was considered war service:

Served in War of the Rebellion (Civil War).
Served in the designated Indian Wars (See *§VII-2-3*).
Served in the Regular or Volunteer Army of the United States between 21 April 1898 and 11 April 1899 (Spanish–American War).
Served in the Philippine Islands between 11 April 1898 and 4 July 1902.
Served with the China Relief Expedition (i.e. in China against the Boxers), 1900–1.

§VII-3-2 DIFFERENT SHADES OF CAVALRY YELLOW

Up to 1887, the shade of yellow used by cavalry facings was a lemon yellow. After that date, the facings changed to a deeper yellow colour.[61]

§VII-3-3 MONTANA PEAK HAT

Sources disagree on when the distinctive 'Montana' peak hat was introduced for wear with the service uniform. This style of hat is still being worn in the United States by certain police forces and is known as the 'Smokey the Bear' hat, because it is worn by federal forest rangers and featured in a series of very successful ads starring a bear mascot urging the public to be careful not to start forest fires.

One source states the hat was 'officially' introduced in 1905.[62] Another source dates the hat to the 1912 Regulations, which provide for a service hat to be peaked with four indentations, calling it the Model 1911 service hat.[63]

In the British army, it was widely worn in Southern Africa, where it went by the name 'wide awake hat'. In World War I New Zealand soldiers also wore this style of hat, known as a 'lemon-squeezer' hat. The Montana peak hat was the headdress Baden-Powell chose for the first boy scouts.

§VII-4 GENERAL STAFF

A general staff, in the European sense, was late in coming to the United States, and when it did come, entry into it took a different form from that found in Europe.

In 1901, a law was passed creating an Army War College and a tiered system of schooling for officers. Officers would move from instruction in the regiment to a General Service and Staff College at Fort Leavenworth, Kansas, for the best officers of all branches. Then, the best officers could attend the Army War College in Washington, DC.[64] Graduates expected to receive a senior command or, after it was created, a senior staff appointment.[65]

Because of resistance by army bureaucrats and their congressional allies, a General Staff Act was not passed until 1903. When it was passed, forty-two officers were assigned to the general staff.[66] These forty-two officers entered a situation that was rather nebulous. During the pre-World War I period, the duties of the staff were still being worked out, as was the relationship between the general staff and the Army War College.[67]

Early on, the War College was used to train staff officers. Only after a reservoir of trained staff officers had been created did the War College turn to preparing the general career officer for a senior career.[68]

The American general staff was modelled on the Prussian general staff and had two components: the 'War Department General Staff', stationed in Washington, DC, and the 'General Staff Serving with the Troops'.[69] The War Department General Staff had three departments. Simplified, these were: First Department – mobilisation, combat developments for the infantry, cavalry, and field artillery, and the officer education system; Second Department – military information; and Third Department – campaign and contingency planning, joint operations with the navy, and combat developments for the coastal artillery and technical services.[70]

While a system of education was in place, its impact should not be overemphasised. In 1916, less than 10 per cent of the officer corps had attended either the Staff or War Colleges.[71] In addition, less than half of the 202 officers picked for the general staff in the pre-World War I era had any military postgraduate education.[72] Some claim the War College did not really train a person for staff work, because staff duties were not thoroughly understood.[73]

The general staff officers would learn their roles through on-the-job training, first in the mobilisation of the army on the Mexican border in 1916 and then during World War I in France.[74]

Uniform

Staff officers did not have a special uniform. They wore the normal uniform of their rank and branch of service with the addition of aiguillettes (Image VII:2).

VII:2 General Staff Officers, c. 1902–7
Their status as staff officers during the period 1902–7 is shown by large gold aiguillettes worn on the right shoulder. The two officers on the right, who are below the rank of general, wear general staff insignia, a silver star with the United States coat of arms on it, in the open space below their Hungarian knots on their sleeves. The figure on the right of the group is a general. During this period, generals did not wear staff officers' insignia.

As can be seen, the aiguillettes made quite a show. Ogden shows them as golden and hanging from the right shoulder during the period 1902–7.[75] However, the 1912 United States Dress Regulations state that the aiguillettes were to be worn on the left shoulder by all staff officers, except the chief of staff and a few other exceptions that do not concern us here.[76]

Staff officers below the rank of general were also identified by general staff insignia worn on the full dress uniform. That uniform consisted of a frock coat with rank shown by the number of gold Hungarian knots on the sleeves. In the space that the scroll trim leaves at the bottom of the sleeves, officers wore the insignia of their branch of service. At this spot the insignia of the general staff was worn (Image VII:2).

The general staff insignia consisted of a general's silver star with the eagle and shield of the United States coat of arms (Image VII:3) superimposed on it.[77]

Prior to 1911, the only mark of general staff duty for generals was the general staff aiguillette. After 1911, they wore the general staff insignia on their epaulettes. Only staff officers who were generals wore an insignia of assignment to the general staff on their epaulettes.[78] The insignia was worn together with rank stars.

In keeping with America's small army, the general staff in 1903 also provided that forty-two officers would be assigned to the General Staff Corps.[79] By 1916, this had grown to fifty-five officers, with not more than half in Washington, DC.[80] In 1917, it rose to eighty-eight general staff officers, plus the chief of staff and four generals assistant chief of staff.[81] When the United States entered World War I, these low numbers must have been recognised as inadequate for the much larger army the United States would field. The limitation on the number of staff officers was suspended.[82]

VII:3 United States Coat of Arms

§VII-5 CAVALRY AND INFANTRY

As perhaps befits a republic with Puritan roots, the uniforms of the United States army have always been rather plain and utilitarian. Fancy dress was left to the National Guard units, who often personally paid for their uniform upgrades.

In 1872, new uniforms were issued for the post-Civil War army. This, with minor modifications, would be the dress uniform for the Indian-Fighting Army.

§VII-5-a CAVALRY

HELMET

A helmet that some say was inspired by the Prussian *pickelhaube* was issued to the cavalry in 1872. There was a general issue of a slightly modified version of the helmet in 1881, and the infantry received the helmet at that time.[83] The cavalry branch helmet had yellow plumes that fell from a spike. On the front was an American eagle with a shield on its breast. Under the shield, and large enough to show around it, were the crossed sabres of cavalry, showing that the men served in the cavalry branch. The regiment number was shown on the shield (Images VII:4 and VII:5).

The helmet of the other ranks had yellow woven cords that hooked on the left side and looped deeply

VII:4 Cavalry Officer in the Pre-1902 Uniform
Note the spiked helmet with plume worn by mounted personnel. This officer had unhooked his cap lines from his helmet and attached them to his tunic.

VII:5 Two Infantrymen in a Pre-1902 Uniform after 1884
Note the white trim on the collar, shoulder straps, front of the tunic, and cuffs. Also note the pseudo-Brandenburg shape of the cuffs.

down to the brim in the front and the back. It was deep enough to show the helmet badge in front. High on the left side of the helmet, where the woven cords began, a short cord with a tassel hung down. The tassel stopped at the side edge of the helmet. The helmet also had two other cords attached to the left side of the helmet at the same place as the woven helmet cords. These two cords came down to the left shoulder, where they became part of the tunic decoration. They will be covered under tunics below.

The officer's helmet was the same, except the cords were in gold.

Tunic

Officers

Officers wore a long double-breasted dress coat that showed French influences. It fell to mid-thigh and generally had nine buttons in two rows on the front of it. The number of buttons would vary over the years and by rank (Images VII:4 and VII:6). The coat had gold shoulder knots. The rear skirt had two buttons on either side of the rear skirt divide. Each had a straight line of trim from the top (waist) button to the bottom, which was about two-thirds of the way down the rear skirt.

During several periods, including 1902–14, the army used gold scroll Hungarian knot sleeve trim to show rank. The knots came halfway to the elbow. The Confederate troops had used this type of braid during America's Civil War. They are said to have picked up the idea from the Crimean War. Northern Zouave units also used this type of arm trim. The braid showed rank (see Table VII.5.a.1):

When a colonel moved up to general, the scroll braid was replaced by oak leaves around the cuffs and stars to show the grade of general.

The scroll sleeve trim left a space at the bottom of the sleeves. Within this space was put the insignia of the officer's branch of service. The cuff itself was of the Swedish shape without buttons. It had gold lace around its bottom edge where the Hungarian knots began.

During another period, the cuffs for field officers had three buttons and three braid stripes behind them. Each stripe was gold and consisted of two vertical stripes going from the cuff edge to the button on either side of the button. This left a space of tunic

VII:6 Infantry Subaltern Officer in a Pre-1902 Uniform
He wears a helmet but, not being mounted, does not wear a plume. Note the white collar, the length of his coat, and the double row of buttons on his coat.

Table VII.5.a.1 Sleeve Braid and Ranks

Rank	Sleeve Braid
Second lieutenant	None
First lieutenant	One strand
Captain	Two strands
Major	Three stands
Lieutenant colonel	Four strands
Colonel	Five strands

between them. The two stripes of braid came together in a point just past the button. Company officers had two such gold braid stripes and buttons. In addition to the buttons connected by the braid, the officer's coat had three gold buttons on the cuff.[84]

The helmet had gold wire cap lines that fell from the left side of the helmet, forming a major part of the tunic's decoration. In 1886 orders stated that they were to fall to the left shoulder, where they were closed by a slide. One cap line then went around the back of the collar and the other around the front. They met under the right shoulder strap where a slide closed them again. They then separated and went around the right arm and were pulled together by a slide at the armpit. The two gold lines then looped across the chest to the second button down from the top in the left column of the buttons on the chest. From that button, the cap lines, each with a flounder and tassels, hung down on the left side of the chest.

The reality was a bit different. A large number of photographs show that the slides on the right side of the collar have loosened, and the cords have slipped loose to make large loops on the chest before going to the end of the right shoulder strap. There, the two cap lines, each with a flounder and tassels, hung down to about mid-chest level (Image VII:4).

When on foot and not wearing a helmet, the cord that would have been fastened to the helmet was brought to the front of the coat and hooked to the top button on the right-hand column of buttons (Image VII:4).

Other Ranks

The other ranks of the cavalry arm were issued a new model full dress tunic in 1872. It was dark blue and had eight buttons. The facings were yellow and showed on the collar, cuffs, rear skirts, and front piping. However, the type of collar facing would change over the years between 1872 and 1900. Some years, the entire collar would be yellow, while other years, it would be dark blue with a yellow shield. The regiment's number was always shown on the collar in dark blue.

The yellow cuffs had three buttons. These were shown on a vertical bar with a scalloping between

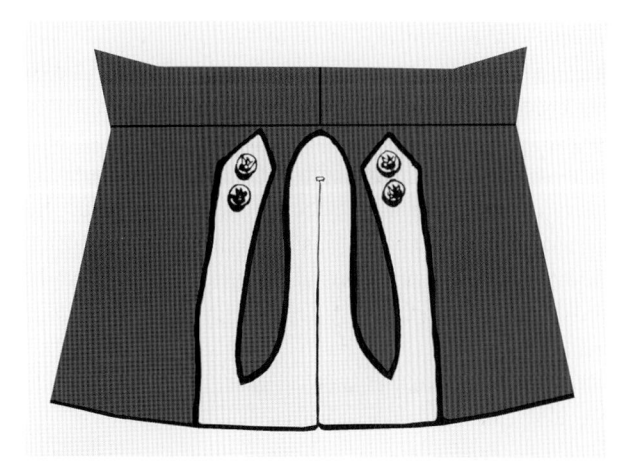

VII:7 Rear Trim Skirt Worn by Cavalry Troopers after 1887
The portion that is lighter in this drawing was yellow, and the dark portion was blue.

the middle button and the two outside buttons. The scalloping faced to the outside. From 1884 to 1887, the trim on the rear skirt had three buttons and was coloured in a scalloped pattern. The scalloping faced the inside. After 1887, the rear skirts had an unusual yellow trim that is better seen than described (see Image VII:7).

The cord cap lines of the other ranks went from helmet to body in the same way as the cap lines of officers. But, in the case of the other ranks, the cord cap lines looped across the chest to the left shoulder strap button near the collar.[85] From there the two cords, each with a flounder and tassels, hung down to about mid-chest level.

Trousers

The trousers were a mid-blue shade that was much lighter than the dark blue of the tunic or coat worn by the other ranks or officers. For this reason, they were often called light blue. Once the wearer rose above the rank of private, the trousers had yellow stripes of different widths that, in a rough way, showed his rank.

§VII-5-b INFANTRY

The uniform of the infantry was, except for a few details as to trim colour, plumes, and badges, exactly the same as that worn by the cavalry. The description below will therefore only note the differences between the infantry and the cavalry, which was described above.

Helmet

The infantry branch did not receive a helmet until the reissue of the modified helmet in 1881. After that, the infantry had the same general helmet and badge in front as the cavalry. It carried the crossed rifles of the infantry behind the shield, and the regimental number on it. Other ranks, NCOs, and officers below the rank of field officer had a simple spike on their helmet (Image VII:6). Infantry field officers, because they were mounted, had a plume on their helmet.[86]

Tunic

The tunic was the same as that worn by the cavalry. The trim and helmet cords were in the colour of the infantry branch, which changed during the period. In 1884, it was changed to white.[87] Before that, it had been light blue.

Other ranks had on their cuffs a horizontal bar with three buttons and scalloping between the buttons (Images VII:5 and VII:1). The bar was in the colour of the branch of service. The tunic had a low collar, which was also in the colour of the branch of service.

Long service stripes were worn on the lower arms, and a man with enough service could build up an impressive number of stripes, as is shown in Image VII:1. Prior to 1894, it took five years of service to obtain a service stripe. After that, they were awarded for three years of service (see §VII-3-1, Service and War Service Stripes).

Image VII:1 shows a black soldier who had served in the ordnance division. It is a common mistake to believe that black men only served in the 9th and 10th Cavalry and 24th and 25th Infantry; a few were allowed to serve in other branches. Once in the army, the black soldiers tended to stay for a long time as conditions were better than those they faced as civilians. The army recognised this. Officers often said that for white soldiers the army was a refuge, while for black soldiers it was a career.

Trousers

The trousers were the same as those worn by the cavalry but had stripes of different widths to show ranks above private. The trim colour was light blue or white, depending on the regulations in force that year.

§VII-5-c NEW DRESS UNIFORMS

Infantry and Cavalry

The year 1902 saw the introduction of new dress uniforms. Perhaps it was because of the end of the Spanish–American War or a reaction to the turn of the century. Numerous other countries also introduced new uniforms during this time period.

Headdress

The most noticeable change was the replacement of the helmet by a brimmed cloth cap. The cap was 8.89 cm (3½ inches) high and 22.23 cm (8¾ inches) tall across the top. The side consisted of two sections. The upper cloth crown section was 3.81 cm (1½ inches) tall and stiffened with hair cloth and wire around the crown. The second section was a band 4.45 cm (1¾ inches) wide, which had a stripe of silk in the branch's facing colour 1.91 cm (¾ inch) wide. This coloured stripe was flanked on the top and bottom by gold lace 1.27 cm (½ inch) wide. On the front was a brim (visor) of black patent leather that drooped at an angle of forty-five degrees. The brim was 1.59 cm (⅝ inches) at its deepest point, with gold oak leaves embroidered on its upper surface for field officers (Image VII:8).[88]

The United States coat of arms, an eagle with a shield, was on the front of the cap in gold so that it lay across both the cap band and the upper part of the cap (Image VII:9).

The enlisted men wore a cloth cap of the same dimensions and colour. The cap band had a stripe of cloth in the colour of the branch of service, yellow for cavalry, light blue for infantry. In full dress, a 1.91 cm (¾ inch) stripe of dark blue cloth (the colour of the cap) was placed over the middle of the coloured cloth.[89] For dress wear, a step down from full dress, the blue band was removed.[90] In place of the officer's eagle, the enlisted men wore a yellow metal insignia

VII:8 Field and Company Officers of the Infantry in Full Dress
They are wearing post-1902 uniforms with the early model cap. The trim of these uniforms was a mix of white and the old infantry colour of light blue. The stripes on the trousers and breeches are white, one of two new infantry branch colours. The two figures on foot are a lieutenant (on the left) and a colonel (on the right). Notice how the number of buttons on their tunics varies by rank, as do the Hungarian knots on their sleeves.

VII:9 Charles Young, the Last Nineteenth-Century Black Graduate of West Point, 1916
He is wearing the uniform adopted in 1902, and his hat shows the slight modifications made a few years after 1902. Just above his cuff, the crossed sabres and the '9' show he is or was an officer in the 9th Cavalry, whose enlisted men were all black. He is wearing a medal presented to him by the National Association for the Advancement of Colored People. The two strands in his Hungarian knot indicate the rank of captain.

that showed their branch of service, regiment, and troop (cavalry) or company (infantry). For cavalry, this consisted of crossed sabres, the number of the regiment in the upper angle, and the letter of the troop in the lower angle. Infantry had the same concept, only they had crossed rifles and showed company letters. The insignia was placed on the upper part of the cap above the cap band.

In 1912, the cap was changed slightly. The regimental officer's cap band was now silk in the branch colour with two bands of gold lace about 1.27 cm (½ inch) thick, one on the top and one on the bottom.[91] The crown size was increased. It was now to be 26.67 cm (10½ inches) from front to rear and 24.13 cm (9½ inches) from side to side.[92]

Only the front of the cap had stiffening, which caused the rear of the cap to fall in. This meant the cap had a very different silhouette from that of the 1902 model, which had a flat top in silhouette.

Tunic

Officers

Officers continued to wear the double-breasted frock coat that fell to mid-thigh. It had two rows of gold buttons (Image VII:8). The number of buttons varied by rank (see Table VII.5.c.1). This continued as the custom, with variation, found in the Indian-Fighting Army.

The coats of all officers between the ranks of lieutenant and colonel had nine buttons after 1913.[93]

The most noticeable change in the uniform was the loss of the cap lines.

The stand-up collar was trimmed on the top, bottom, and front with gold braid. The middle was the colour of the wearer's branch of service. The two rear skirts had two gold buttons, one at the waist and one lower down set at a slight right angle. Braid, if any, did not stand out except in the case of engineers.

Table VII.5.c.1: Buttons on Officers' Frock Coat, 1902–12[94]

Rank	Number of Buttons	Spacing
General	12	Buttons by fours[a]
Lieutenant general	10	Buttons at the upper end and lower end by threes (middle group had four)[a]
Major general	9	Buttons by threes[a]
Brigadier general	8	Buttons by pairs[a]
Colonel, lieutenant colonel and major	9	Buttons at equal intervals
Captain, first and second lieutenant	7	Buttons at equal intervals

Note: [a] Generals' uniforms differed from those of other officers in that they had oak leaves on their cuffs, collar, and cap, and one or more stars on their cuffs.

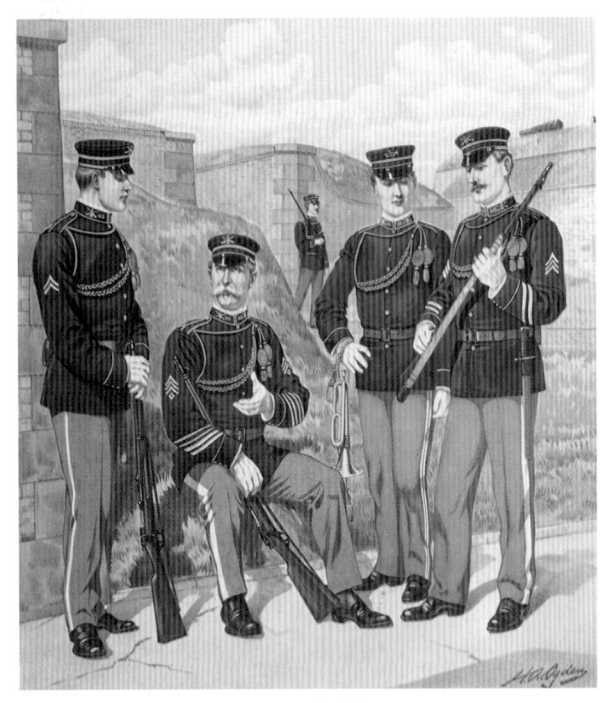

VII:10 Other Ranks Infantry in Full Dress
The man on the left is a corporal. He has a narrow white stripe on his blue trousers. The rest of his trim, including the chest cords, is light blue. His shoulder straps and cuffs are tunic colour with light blue trim. The cap band is light blue with a tunic colour band over it, as was worn in full dress. The sitting sergeant's sleeves have two blue stripes, showing two periods of peacetime army service of three to five years and two white stripes trimmed light blue for two bouts of wartime service. The sergeant on the right has a gold wound stripe and a blue service stripe above it.

In 1912, more changes were made to the full dress coat. The individual's strands of the braid in the Hungarian knots grew from 3.2 mm (⅛ inch) to 6.4 mm (¼ inch) wide.[95] This made for a larger Hungarian knot on the sleeve (Image VII:8).

Other Ranks

The 1902 enlisted men's uniform, while retaining the dark blue tunic, changed many of the trim details. It now had six buttons down the front. The collar was higher and dark blue with branch colour trim on the top, front, and bottom (Image VII:10).

The enlisted men's stand-up collar was dark blue. Up to 1905, both sides of the collar had the United States coat of arms and an insignia showing the branch of service: crossed sabres for cavalry and crossed rifles for infantry. In 1905, the letters 'U.S.' replaced the coat of arms.

The cuffs were in a Swedish shape but had three buttons. They were trimmed around the top in the branch colour. The shoulder straps were now the colour of the tunic and had trim in the branch colour at the two side edges, but not at the end.

By far the most noticeable change in the enlisted men's uniform was that they now wore the helmet cords across their chest, even though they did not have a helmet. The mohair cords followed the same general path set out above, with one exception (Image VII:11).

The cords, which were in the wearer's branch colour, started at the top of the left shoulder strap near the collar. From there they went around the front and back of the collar, but no longer went tightly around the collar. (Perhaps the authorities had taken notice that the slides and the cap lines around the collar tended to come loose.) Rather, they went down between the first and second button across the chest and fastened to the end of the right shoulder strap. From there, they followed the same path set out above, across the chest to the left shoulder strap and falling down the chest in the same way.

Trousers

The trousers were light blue with stripes on the outside seam that varied in width depending on the man's rank. The stripes were white for infantry and

VII:11 US Private of Infantry Posing for a Photograph to Send Home to his Family
Note the collar and cuffs are the same colour as the tunic and only have trim in infantry white. He is wearing the early model cloth cap. His chest cord, flounder, and tassels are all white. On the back of this photograph, he assured his folks back home that everything was going fine.

yellow for cavalry. Cavalry enlisted men did not have full dress breeches.[96]

Enlisted Men
The trouser stripes were as follows:

Rank	Stripe[97]
Private	None
Corporal	1.27 cm (½ inch)
Sergeant	3.18 cm (1¼ inches)
Musician	two 1.27 cm (½ inch) stripes

VII:12 American Cavalryman
Note the crossed-sabre badge on his hat and collar. At the top of where the sabres cross is a '1', designating his regiment. Across his chest, he wears cords that end in a flat flounder and acorns. He is wearing both a side arm and a sword. The hat style shows this photo was made close to 1900.

Officers
Officers wore trousers and breeches that were a bit darker, closer to a mid-blue. They had a 3.81 cm (1½ inch) wide stripe on the outside seam. The stripe was yellow for cavalry and white for infantry.[98]

SABRE BELT
The waist belt for enlisted men was brown leather, about 3.81 cm (1½ inches) wide with an open-faced belt buckle.[99]

Field officers had a dress belt with one broad stripe of gold lace on a black-enamelled leather belt.[100]

Company-grade officers had a belt with four stripes of gold wire lace and three stripes of silk in the colour of their arm of service (light blue or yellow).

VII:13 Officers and Enlisted Men of the Cavalry in Full Dress, pre-1905
The mounted sergeant in the foreground has two types of service stripe on his lower left sleeve. The upper diagonal stripe is yellow and represents a peacetime three-year tour of service. The stripe below it is white edged in cavalry yellow to signify wartime service. The belts and shoes are russet brown (black boots for officers). The other ranks wear leather strap-on russet gaiters above the shoes.

The officers' belt buckle was a gilt rectangle with the US coat of arms on it in silver.[101]

Footwear

Enlisted men wore black shoes with trousers. When wearing breeches for mounted duties, cavalry other ranks wore russet brown shoes with russet brown leather gaiters held in place by straps (Image VII:13).

Officers could wear either brown or black shoes. When cavalry officers wore boots, they were black.

§VII-5-d PHILIPPINE SCOUTS

As covered in §VII-2-1, the Philippine Scouts consisted of a rank and file made up of local ethnic groups. Their officers were American army officers.

Uniform

The Philippine Scouts did not have a separate uniform. With one exception (see below), all scouts wore the standard-issue uniforms of the rest of the US army. The scouts did not wear the full dress uniform worn by the rest of the army. Rather they wore service dress on occasions that called for dress uniforms. Dress uniforms were not worn in the Tropics.[102] The only thing to mark a scout was his insignia. He would have a 'P' in place of the regimental number on the crossed rifles or sabres worn in the regular army.[103]

The 1912 Regulations state the scouts were to wear the olive-drab cotton uniform with Philippine Scouts insignias.[104] However, other sources state that they wore cotton khaki service dress.[105] There were two types of service dress – woollen and cotton. Cotton was worn in warm weather.[106]

Headdress

Officer's Peaked Service Cap
A peaked cotton khaki service cap was worn by officers with khaki service dress. A size 7 cap had a diameter across the top of 20.95 cm (8¼ inches) and a depth of 8.89 cm (3½ inches). The top was to be 3.18 mm (⅛ inch) larger or smaller for every size above or below size 7[107].

Officer's Service Hat
Officers could also wear a service hat that consisted of a crown and wide brim. Prior to *c.* 1911 the service hat had a crease that ran from back to front (see Image VII:14 – man on the left). After 1911 or so they wore Montana peak service hats (see Image VII:14 – man on the right).

The officers' service hats had a double cord that was made of gold bullion for general officers and of intermixed gold bullion and black silk for all other officers.[108] Until about 1906 crossed rifles or sabres

VII:14 Philippine Scouts in the Field
The six men on the right are wearing Montana peak hats with cords. The cords can best be seen on the man on the far right. The cords are the branch of service colour. The Scouts wore blue for infantry. The man on the far left is still wearing his hat with the old-style crease running along the crown. The men are wearing shirts and puttees rather than the old-style canvas leggings.

with the company letters were worn on the front of service hats.[109]

Other Ranks

Beginning in about 1911, the headdress of the other ranks changed over to the Montana peak hat (service hat) (Image VII:14 and see §VII-3-3). The hat was worn with double cords 4.76 mm (³⁄₁₆ inch) in diameter. The cords were blue for infantry and yellow for cavalry.[110] They went around the crown of the hat and rested on the brim.

The 1912 Regulations stated that the peaked service cap was not authorised for other ranks in the Philippines. The service hat was to be worn in the field; and the (sun) helmet at other times.[111] The supply of sun helmets ran out about 1906.[112]

TUNIC

Service Coat

In 1902, the regulations prescribed a new service coat for officers. It had four outside bellows pockets. Two were above the waist and two below. It had falling collars that were 2.54–3.81 cm (1–1½ inches) long, depending on the height of the officer. The shoulder strap was of the same material as the coat. Branch insignia were worn on the collar and rank badges on the shoulder straps.[113] The coat had seven bronze buttons down the front. In 1907 a strip of 1.27 cm (½ inch) brown braid was added to each sleeve, 7.62 cm (3 inches) from the bottom of the sleeve.[114] The braid at the bottom of the sleeve was to be black for officers of the general staff.[115] In 1912 the coat was made tighter and smarter. The collar became a standing collar. Branch insignia was moved to the collar.

Shirt

Native other ranks did not wear a tunic. Up to 1904 a dark blue flannel shirt was worn.[116] After that, other ranks wore a Model 1904 olive-drab shirt (see Image VII:14). The shirt had three buttons on the front and was open only to the middle of the chest. This meant it had to be pulled on over the head. It had a pocket on each side of the chest that closed with a button. The sleeves had a slit that opened almost to the elbow. Each cuff was closed with a button. The shirt had

VII:15 Moro (Muslim) Philippine Scouts, 1910
Particularly noteworthy is their Tuban headgear shaped to allow Muslim Moros to touch their foreheads to the ground during their five daily prayers. Also note the bolo bayonet and the two styles of canvas leggings.

VII:16 These men are believed to be Philippine Scouts, but could be Philippine (military) police. Note the bolos they are carrying.
Also of interest is the sun helmet (pith helmet) worn by these men. This is an item that was generally discontinued in the main army but continued to be worn in the Philippines because of its hot climate.

small falling collars.[117] This model of shirt was worn by officers and men until 1916. In 1916 the chest pockets officially received pocket flaps.[118]

Service Trousers and Breeches

Officers and Other Ranks
Service trousers were made of khaki-coloured material and had no stripe, welt, or cord.[119] The same was true of service breeches. They were cut loose above the knee and were to fit closely below it (Image VII:14).[120]

Infantry wore khaki trousers and breeches. Cavalry wore khaki breeches. Both had small strips of cloth and a buckle in the back just below the waist.[121] This allowed the garments to be tightened for a better fit.

Tuban Headdress
One uniform item that was unique to the scouts was the tuban headdress. The term tuban means turban in the language spoken by the Moros. The tuban was worn only by the Muslim Moros in the Moro units of the scouts – the 51st and 52nd Companies in 1910. It was shaped to allow the Moros to touch their foreheads to the ground during their daily prayers. The Moros lived on the island of Mindanao and in the Jolo Archipelago in the Philippines.

Belt

The belt was a dark russet colour. It closed with an open-faced buckle.[122] The belt was about 3.81 cm (1½ inches) wide.[123]

Leggings

Canvas leggings were worn by scouts cavalry until about 1907. After that they wore russet-coloured leather leggings.[124] Infantry wore puttees (Image VII:14).

Shoes

There were two types of shoes – marching and garrison. Both were made of russet leather. The differences between them were how far up the leg the shoe came and the cut.[125]

Bolos

The Philippine Scouts carried a special and unique knife, the bolo, which is somewhat analogous to the Gurkhas' kukri. The bolo was adapted from knives used for agricultural purposes. The scouts underwent regular drills on how to use the bolos in combat, just as they had drills in bayonet fighting. Bolos were issued to American army cavalry machine-gun troops to help them clear fields of fire.[126]

§VII-5-e PORTO RICO (PROVISIONAL) REGIMENT OF INFANTRY

This regiment served only in Puerto Rico. As noted in §VII-2-1, the other ranks were Puerto Ricans, as were the lieutenants. The officers above the rank of lieutenant were American army officers. The regiment wore the same uniform as the regular infantry except the letters 'P.R.' in Gothic lettering replaced the regiment number.[127]

AMERICAN EMPIRE: NOTES

1. *Historical Statistics*, p. 1168; *Census 1990*, p. 2.
2. Robertson, *History/Economy*, p. 115.
3. *World Book – M*, p. 211. Not everyone agrees; see Robertson, *History/Economy*, p. 211.
4. Lee, *Economic/History*, p. 85.
5. Robertson, *History/Economy*, p. 117.
6. Ibid., pp. 116–17.
7. Kennedy, *Rise/Fall*, p. 180.
8. See Clendenen, *Blood/Border*, pp. 196–267.
9. Ibid., pp. 287–91.
10. National Archives, Box 8750, September 30, 1916, 1916, *Report of the Quartermaster General*, exhibit 13, pp. 433–4; 108 regiments of infantry and seven additional battalions and three regiments of cavalry, thirteen squadrons and twenty-two troops of cavalry were called on 9 May and 18 June 1916. 1917, *Report of the Chief of Staff* (printed in 1918), p. 190.
11. Utley, *Frontier Regulars*, p. 47.
12. Ibid., p. 48.
13. Ibid.
14. Nevin, *The Soldiers*, pp. 28–9, 47.
15. Fowler, *Black Infantry*, pp. 22–3.
16. Fletcher, *Black Soldier*, p. 22; Coffman, *Old Army*, p. 254.
17. Utley, *Frontier Regulars*, p. 59.
18. Ibid., p. 60.
19. Coffman, *Old Army*, p. 246.
20. Nevin, *The Soldiers*, p. 47.
21. Utley, *Frontier Regulars*, p. 5.
22. Lowie, *Indians/Plains*, pp. 10–11.
23. Losses from European disease would not have been a major factor during this period. The native people would have suffered their population crashes before 1690 during their first contact with Europeans.
24. Johnson, *No Greater Calling*, yearly totals as corrected and p. 392 for American Indian Police. This wonderful book is a labour of love of a type so useful to researchers. The figures are from a mammoth and detailed work listing every army versus American Indian firefight that took place in the American West c. 1865–98 and the army dead and wounded in the battle. It has its problems. Appendix A, by showing only named deaths, does not provide a complete count of the number of deaths during the period 1865–98. There has been some carping that this or that number is incorrect. But that can happen when a 400-page book of detailed information is produced.
25. Utley, *Frontier Regulars*, p. 50.
26. Ibid., p. 51.
27. Ibid., p. 47.
28. Coffman, *Regulars*, p. 3.
29. Ibid., p. 140.
30. Steffen, *Horse Soldier*, vol. 3, p. 93.
31. Ibid.
32. Kipling, *Kipling's Verse*, pp. 321–3.
33. Flake, *Loyal Macabebes*, p. 74.
34. Ibid.
35. Pakula, *Ogden Uniforms*, notes to Plate XVIII, fig. 4.
36. 'Heritage of Valor,' p. 6. See Flake, *Loyal Macabebes*, p. 74 for the location of the ethnic groups. But see Franklin, *History/Philippine Scouts*, pp. 1–6, which shows different companies in these battalions in 1910 and in other years between 1901 and 1914.
37. Ganou, *History/Army*, p. 365.
38. Ibid.
39. *House Reports*, vol. 3, Report no. 1084, p. 6, citing Adjt. Gen. F.C. Ainsworth, in a letter to the Committee on Pensions of the House, in the 62nd Congress, under the date of 13 January 1912.
40. Emerson, *Chevrons*, pp. 51 and 54.
41. Ibid., p. 55.
42. Ibid.
43. Ibid.
44. McChristian, *Army/West*, p. 66.
45. Ibid., pp. 66–7.
46. Ganou, *History/Army*, pp. 307 and 324.
47. Dawson, *Late/Army*, pp. 219–20.
48. McChristian, *Army/West*, p. 19.
49. Ibid., p. 67.
50. Emerson, *Chevrons*, pp. 76–7, 82.
51. Ibid., p. 75.
52. Ibid., opinion cited.
53. Pakula, *Ogden Uniforms*, Plate VI and text for figs 3 and 6, Plate XI and text for figs 2 and 5; Steffen, *Horse Soldier*, vol. 3, p. 119, which sets out the 1902 Regulations on this subject.
54. Pakula, *Ogden Uniforms*, Plate XI and its text, fig. 5.
55. *U.S. Regulations, 1912*, ¶84(g), not paginated.
56. Ibid.
57. Steffen, *Horse Soldier*, vol. 3, p. 140.
58. Emerson, *Chevrons*, pp. 137–8, tables 5-4 and 5-5.
59. Ibid., p. 136.
60. Ibid.
61. Steffen, *Horse Soldier*, vol. 3, p. 5.
62. Katcher, *Army 1890*, p. 24.
63. Steffen, *Horse Soldier*, vol. 3, pp. 148, 171, and 153, citing 1912 *Regulations and Specifications for the Uniform of the United States Army*.
64. Stiehm, *War College*, p. 28.
65. Ibid.
66. Ball, *Responsible*, p. 76.
67. Nenninger, *Leavenworth Schools*, pp. 54–5; Pappas, *Prudens Futuri*, p. 1.
68. Pappas, *Prudens Futuri*, pp. 1–2; Ball, *Responsible*, p. 82. Of the 256 army graduates during the period 1904 to 1917, 57 per cent became generals and 20 per cent major unit chief of staffs by 11 November 1918. Steihm, *War College*, p. 30; Ball, *Responsible*, pp. 137–8.
69. Ball, *Responsible*, pp. 81–2.
70. Ibid., p. 82.
71. Coffman, *Regulars*, p. 185.
72. Ibid.
73. Ibid.
74. Clendenen, *Blood/Border*, p. 289; Nenninger, *Leavenworth Schools*, pp. 139–40.

75 Pakula, *Ogden Uniforms*, Plate IV.
76 *US Regulations, 1912*, ¶ 55.
77 Emerson, *US Insignia*, p. 309.
78 Ibid., p. 14, caption for fig. 2-24.
79 Ball, *Responsible*, p. 76.
80 Emerson, *US Insignia*, p. 309.
81 Ibid.
82 Ibid.
83 Utley, *Frontier Regulars*, p. 74; Howell, *US Headgear*, p. 62.
84 Langellier, *Bluecoats*, p. 35.
85 Howell, *US Headgear*, p. 71.
86 Ibid., p. 70; Langellier, *Bluecoats*, p. 78.
87 Ibid., p. 74.
88 Langellier, *Hats Off*, p. 126.
89 Ibid. pp. 126–7.
90 Ibid., p. 130.
91 Ibid., p. 149–50.
92 Ibid., p. 150.
93 Ibid., p. 153.
94 Steffen, *Horse Soldier*, vol. 3, p. 97.
95 Ibid., p. 153.
96 Ibid., p. 111.
97 Ibid., p. 113.
98 Ibid., pp. 100 and 103.
99 Ibid., pp. 119 and 111, fig. 302 (men on left and right).
100 Ibid., p. 105.
101 Ibid.
102 Ibid., p. 172
103 Ibid., p. 132 (drawing 320).
104 *US Regulations, 1912*, ¶33, not paginated.
105 Steffen, *Horse Soldier*, vol. 3, p. 132.
106 Ibid.
107 Ibid., pp. 103 and 104.
108 Ibid., p. 104.
109 Ibid., p. 140.
110 Ibid., p. 115.
111 Ibid., p. 172.
112 Ibid., p. 134.
113 Ibid., p. 100.
114 Ibid., p. 141.
115 Ibid., p. 152.
116 Ibid., p. 143.
117 Ibid., p. 124 (drawing 314).
118 Ibid., p. 180 (fig. 339 and text).
119 Ibid., p. 103.
120 Ibid.
121 Ibid., p. 150 (drawing 325).
122 Ibid., p. 121 (drawing 309).
123 Ibid., p. 119.
124 Ibid., p. 140.
125 Ibid., pp. 115 and 122 (drawing 311).
126 Ibid., pp. 177, 247, and 248 (drawing 347(A)).
127 Ibid., p. 135.

AMERICAN EMPIRE: BIBLIOGRAPHY

Ball, *Responsible*	Harry Ball, *Of Responsible Command: A History of the U.S. Army War College* (Carlisle Barracks, PA: Alumni Association of the United States Army War College, 1983).
Census 1990	United States Bureau of the Census, *1990 Census of Population and Housing: Population and Housing Unit Counts, United States* (Washington, DC : US Dept of Commerce, Economics and Statistics Administration, Bureau of the Census, 1993).
Clendenen, *Blood/Border*	Clarence Clendenen, *Blood on the Border: The United States Army and the Mexican Irregulars* (New York: Macmillan, 1969).
Coffman, *Old Army*	Edward Coffman, *The Old Army: A Portrait of the American Army in Peacetime, 1784–1898* (Oxford: Oxford University Press, 1986).
Coffman, *Regulars*	Edward Coffman, *The Regulars: The American Army, 1898–1941* (Cambridge, MA: Belknap Press, 2004).
Dawson, *Late/Army*	Joseph G. Dawson, *The Late 19th Century U.S. Army, 1865–1898* (New York: Greenwood Press, 1990).
Emerson, *Chevrons*	William Emerson, *Chevrons* (Washington, DC: Smithsonian Institution Press, 1983).
Emerson, *US Insignia*	William Emerson, *Encyclopedia of United States Army Insignia and Uniforms* (Norman, OK: University of Oklahoma Press, 1996).
Flake, *Loyal Macabebes*	Dennis Edward Flake, *Loyal Macabebes: How the Americans Used the Macabebe Scouts in the Annexation of the Philippines* (Angeles City, Philippines: Juan D. Nepomuceno Center for Kapampangan Studies, Holy Angel University, 2009).
Fletcher, *Black Soldier*	Marvin Fletcher, *The Black Soldier and the Officer in the United States Army: 1891–1917* (Columbia, MO: Curators of the University of Missouri, 1974).
Fowler, *Black Infantry*	Arlen Fowler, *The Black Infantry in the West, 1869–1891* (Westport, CT: Greenwood Publishing Co., 1971).
Franklin, *History/Philippine Scouts*	Charles Franklin, *History of the Philippine Scouts 1899–1934*, Washington DC: Historical Section Army War College, 1935).
Ganou, *History/Army*	William Addleman Ganou, *The History of the United States Army* (Ashton, MD: Eric Lundberg, 1964).
'Heritage of Valor'	'Heritage of Valor: A History of the Philippine Scouts, 100th Anniversary,' revised version (Sam Houston, TX: Preservation Fort Sam Houston, 2001 (originally published by the Fort Sam Houston Museum)).
Historical Statistics	United States. Bureau of Census, *Historical Statistics of the United States: Colonial Times to 1970, Part 2* (Washington, DC: US Dept of Commerce, Bureau of the Census, 1975).
House Reports, vol. 3	*House Reports (Public)*, vol. 3, 63rd Congress: 2nd Session, 1 December 1913–24 October 1914 (Washington, DC: Government Printing Office, 1914).
Howell, *US Headgear*	Edgar Howell, *United States Army Headgear, 1855–1902* (Washington, DC: Smithsonian Institution Press, 1975).
Johnson, *No Greater Calling*	Eric Johnson, *No Greater Calling: A Chronological Record of Sacrifice and Heroism during the Western Indian Wars, 1865–1898* (Atglen, PA: Schiffer Publishing Ltd, 2012).
Katcher, *Army 1890*	Philip Katcher, *The US Army, 1890–1920* (London: Osprey Publishing Ltd, 1978).
Kennedy, *Rise/Fall*	Paul Kennedy, *The Rise and Fall of the Great Powers* (New York: Random House Inc., 1987).
Kipling, *Kipling's Verse*	Rudyard Kipling, *Rudyard Kipling's Verse*, definitive edition (Garden City, NY: Doubleday and Co., Inc., 1940).
Langellier, *Bluecoats*	John Langellier, *Bluecoats: The US Army in the West, 1848–1897* (London: Greenhill Books, 1995).
Langellier, *Hats Off*	John Langellier, *Hats Off: Headdress of the U.S. Army, 1872–1912* (Atglen, PA: Schiffer Publishing Ltd, 1999).
Lee, *Economic/History*	Susan Lee and Peter Passell, *A New Economic View of American History* (New York: W.W. Norton & Co., 1979).
Lowie, *Indian/Plains*	Robert Lowie, *Indians of the Plains* (Lincoln, NE: University of Nebraska Press, 1954).
McChristian, *Army/West*	Douglas McChristian, *The U.S. Army in the West, 1870–1880* (Norman, OK: University of Oklahoma Press, 1995).

National Archives, Box 8750, September 30, 1916	Box 8750-2378529, September 30, 1916, National Archives of the United States.
Nenninger, *Leavenworth Schools*	Timothy Nenninger, *The Leavenworth Schools and the Old Army* (Westport, CT: Greenwood Press, 1978).
Nevin, *The Soldiers*	David Nevin, *The Soldiers* (Alexandria, VA: Time-Life Books, 1973).
Pakula, *Ogden Uniforms*	Marvin Pakula, *Uniforms of the United States Army*, with paintings by Henry Ogden (New York: Thomas Yoseloff, 1960).
Pappas, *Prudens Futuri*	George Pappas, *Prudens Futuri, U.S. Army War College, 1901–1967* (Carlisle Barracks, PA: Alumni Association of the United States Army War College, 1967).
Robertson, *History/Economy*	Ross Robertson, *History of the American Economy*, 3rd edn (New York: Harcourt, Brace, Jovanovich, Inc., 1973).
Steffen, *Horse Soldier*, vol. 3	Randy Steffen, *The Horse Soldier, 1776–1943*, vol. 3 (Norman, OK: University of Oklahoma Press, 1978).
Stiehm, *War College*	Judith Stiehm, *The U.S. Army War College* (Philadelphia, PA: Temple University Press, 2002).
US Regulations, 1912	*U.S. Regulations (Uniform) 1912*, compiled and edited by Jacques Jacobsen, Jr. (Staten Island, NY: Manor Publishing, 1975).
Utley, *Frontier Regulars*	Robert Utley, *Frontier Regulars: The United States Army and the Indian 1866–1891* (Lincoln: NE: University of Nebraska Press, 1973).
World Book – M	'Mass Production', *The World Book Encyclopedia, M*, vol. 13 (Chicago: World Book Inc., 1983).

§VIII CODA

The old uniforms remained, recalling past glories, but times were changing.

VIII:1 Planes and Plumes just before World War I

CREDITS

ILLUSTRATION CREDITS

A.C. Lovett, drawings in Major G.F. MacMunn, DSO, *The Armies of India* (London: Adam and Charles Black, 1911)
III:79, III:85, III:92, III:115

Carl Becker from Anne S.K. Brown Military Collection, Brown University Library
VI:106, VI:169, VI:205, VI:214

Claude Robert
IV:2

Courtney Branch
II:39, II:44, II:46, II:48–51, II:132, III:35–36, VI:1–2, VI:16–21, VI:59

Don Fosten
C76–77, VI:137, VI:166

Doug Hagger
V:136, V:138–139, VI:24, VI:69, VI:86–88, VI:165

Don Fosten and Doug Hagger
II:126, II:131, V:43, VI:22–23, VI:62, VI:71, VI:73–75, VI:79, VI:89, VI:101, VI:128, VI:130, VI:132–134, VI:136, VI:140, VI:142, VI:150, VI:155, VI:157, VI:162

Francais Calume
IV:62

Henry Ogden
VII:2

Herbert Knötel from Anne S.K. Brown Military Collection, Brown University Library
V:42, V:50, V:77, V:105, V:108–109, V:119

R.J. Marrion
C75, II:37, II:194, V:58, VI:66, VI:68, VI:85, VI:105, VI:168

Wladimir Zweguintzow
V:110

PHOTO CREDITS

Anne S.K. Brown Military Collection, Brown University Library
C1–10, C18–23, C61–74, C78–89, II:2, II:35, II:102, II:116, II:133, II:150, II:154, III:29–30, V:23, V:45, V:95, V:133, VI:138, VI:193–194

Author
C11–17, C26–42, I:1, II:3–34, II:36, II:70, II:123, II:173–178, II:181, III:31, III:45–46, III:57, III:112, III:118, V:1–2, V:4–7, V:11–15, V:18–19, V:25, V:33, V:62, V:110, VI:31, VI:45, VI:179, VII:3, VII:7–8, VII:10, VII:13

Bibliothèque nationale de France
V:26, V:31–32, V:44, V:47, V:53–54, V:57, V:61, V:64–65, V:94, V:97, V:124–125

Cedric Demory
IV:3, IV:13–14, IV:16, IV:18–20, IV:34–35, IV:37–42, IV:45, IV:47, IV:52, IV:63, IV:67–73

Chris Dale
VI:232

Columbia University
V:10

David Linaker
II:25(2, 9, 16)

Doug Hagger
III:52, VI:135

Durham University Library
II:188–190

Eric Johansson
VI:9–12, VI:14, VI:32, VI:34–35, VI:91–95, VI:97, VI:113, VI:116, VI:121, VI:170–173, VI:176, VI:186–187, VI:197, VI:202–203, VI:217–219, VI:226, VI:228

Fort Sam Houston Museum
VII:15–16

FR ANOM. Aix-en-Provence (FR ANOM 65Fi B92)—All Rights Reserved
IV:78

Gary Gerber
VI:30, VI:48–49, VI:58, VI:82, VI:99–100, VI:102, VI:117, VI:139, VI:141, VI:153, VI:188, VI:204, VI:206–207, VI:209, VI:211–213, VI:216

Gary Schultze
II:172

General Sir John Chapple
II:193, II:195

George Eastman House
IV:77, V:36

Getty Images
V:59–60, V:67, V:93, V:103, V:114, VI:50, VI:67

Gordon Dine
II:25(1, 3, 4, 5, 6, 8, 11, 12, 13, 14, 15), II:72

Grabbe Family Collection
V:66

Gurkha Museum
III:117

Hermann Historica
V:20–22, V:27, V:30, V:37, V:68–70, V:72, V:81, V:96, V:99–101, V:111–112, VI:5–8, VI:13, VI:15, VI:28, VI:33, VI:36–41, VI:43–44, VI:51–57, VI:64, VI:72, VI:77, VI:80–81, VI:83, VI:90, VI:96, VI:109, VI:118–120, VI:122–126, VI:143–144, VI:159–161, VI:177–178, VI:180–181, VI:190, VI:195–196, VI:198–201, VI:210, VI:215, VI:227, VI:229–231

Imperial War Museums
III:17–24, III:90, VIII:1

Jerome Discours
IV:5, IV:7, IV:24–25, IV:29–30, IV:46, IV:55, IV:64

Mark Conrad
VII:11

Mary Evans Photo Service, London
II:155, II:191–192, VI:27

Musée de l'Armée
C43–60, IV:1, IV:4, IV:6, IV:8–12, IV:15, IV:17, IV:21–23, IV:26–28, IV:31–33, IV:44, IV:48–51, IV:53, IV:57–61, IV:65–66, IV:74–75

Mohamed Ali Foundation and Durham University Library
II:182–187

Motherland or Rodina Museum
V:17, V:24, V:28–29, V:34, V:41, V:52, V:55–56, V:63, V:71, V:73–76, V:78–79, V:82–92, V:98, V:102, V:104, V:106–107, V:115, V:117–118, V:120–122, V:127–128, V:132, V:137

National Army Museum, London
C25, II:127, II:165–166, II:168–169, III:6–7, III:25, III:32, III:40, III:50, III:55, III:59–60, III:63–65, III:67–69, III:72–74, III:81, III:84, III:89, III:91, III:94, III:99, III:103, III:106, III:110–111

© National Museums Scotland
II:149, II:156, II:158

Ohio Historical Society
II:162, VII:9

Oxfordshire and Buckinghamshire Light Infantry Chronicle (1907 reproduced in Oct., 2017 *Stand To!* No. 110, p. 12)
Insert 1

Credits

Philip Warner
III:62

Private Collection
C24, II:38, II:40–43, II:45, II:47, II:52–59, II:62–64, II:66–69, II:71, II:73–77, II:79, II:80–86, II:89–90, II:93, II:95–99, II:101, II:103–105, II:109–114, II:117, II:121–122, II:124–125, II:128–130, II:140, II:142, II:144, II:147, II:152–153, II:157, II:159–161, II:179–180, II:190, III:1–5, III:8–16, III:26–27, III:33–34, III:37–39, III:41–44, III:47–49, III:51, III:53–54, III:56, III:58, III:61, III:66, III:70–71, III:75–77, III:80, III:82–83, III:86–88, III:93, III:95–98, III:102, III:104–105, III:107–108, III:113–114, IV:36, IV:43, IV:54, IV:56, IV:76, V:8–9, V:16, V:35, V:38–40, V:46, V:48–49, V:51, V:80, V:113, V:116, V:123, V:126, V:129–131, V:134–135, V:140–141, VI:3–4, VI:25–26, VI:47, VI:63, VI:65, VI:70, VI:78, VI:84, VI:108, VI:110–112, VI:114–115, VI:127, VI:145, VI:148, VI:152, VI:154, VI:156, VI:158, VI:167, VI:184, VI:222–225, VII:1, VII:4–6, VII:12

Public Domain
V:3

R.G. Harris
III:101, III:109, III:116, VI:164

R.J. Marrion
II:78, II:87–88, II:91–92, II:94, II:100, II:106–107, II:119, II:136–139, II:141, II:143, II:145–146, II:148, II:151, II:163–164, II:167, II:170–171, III:78, III:100, VI:29, VI:42, VI:46, VI:60–61, VI:76, VI:98, VI:103–104, VI:107, VI:129, VI:146–147, VI:149, VI:151, VI:163, VI:174–175, VI:182–183, VI:185, VI:189, VI:191–192, VI:208, VI:220–221

Ray Westlake
II:1, II:108, II:115, II:118, II:120, II:135

Royal Collection Trust/© Her Majesty Queen Elizabeth II 2014
II:60–61, II:134, VI:131

Sean Weir
III:28

Smithsonian Institution
IV:79

US National Archives and Records Administration, Still Picture Branch, College Park, MD
VII:14

W. Lambert
II:25(7, 10)

INDEX

The index is grouped by Empire: British, India, French, Russian, German, American.
Page numbers in **bold** refer to black and white illustrations and photographs. References in **bold** preceded by '**C**' refer to colour plates.

BRITISH EMPIRE

Aden, 11, 12
aiguillette, 95, 98, **100**, 100–01, **101, 102**
Alamanza, Battle of, 142
Alexandria, Battle of, 12
　see also Egypt
Argentina, 5
aristocracy, 5–6
Australia, 5
Austrian knot, 4
axe, farrier's, **104**

back flash, Royal Welch Fusiliers, 15–16, **16**
badges, 40–93, **60–65, 114**
　1904 Regulations, 42–59
　1911 Regulations, 66–93
　cavalry arm, 41, 118–19, **131, 132,** 135
　collar, 135, **135,** 143, 145
　Lancer NCO arm, 125–26
　rank, 139
　scout, 140, **140**
　special, 142
　Chinese Regiment, **188**
　Gloucestershire Regiment, 12, 63, 142, **143**
　　back badge, xiii, 12
　Hong Kong Regiment, 187, **187**
　Northumberland Fusiliers, 14
　see also helmet plates; shoulder, titles
band uniform, 112
battle honours, cavalry, 119
bearskins

2nd Dragoons (Royal Scots Greys), 13, 113, **114**
5th (Royal Irish) Lancers, 13
Grenadier Guards, 13, 106, **107**
see also headdress
belt, 111, 118, 141, 150, 154, 187
　buckle, 42–46
　cartouche, 102
　pouch, 118, 126, 128, 132–33, 150
　shoulder, 102
Bermuda, 11, 12
Black Brunswick Hussars, 148
black lines on lace and shoulder cords, 15, 20, **21**
blouse, Hong Kong Regiment, 185–86
Boer War, 14
bonnet
　Highland regiments, 150–51
　Lowland regiments, 162–63
boots, 118, 127, 134–35, 142
　Hessian, 134
　jackboots, 102, **103**
Boston Massacre, 142
Bourbon flags, 15th (The King's) Hussars, 17
breeches, riding, 3, 102, 109–10, 126–27
　see also pantaloons
British Empire, background, 5–6
Brodrick cap, **108**
buckle, belt *see* belt, buckle
buff cloth, South Staffordshire Regiment, 15

Burma, 11, 12
busby, 14, 127
　Rifle, 146–47
　Royal Scots Fusiliers, 163
　see also headdress
buttons
　1904 Regulations, 42–59
　1911 Regulations, 66–93
　Chinese Regiment, 189
　Duke of Edinburgh's (Wiltshire Regiment), 15
　dents in, xiii, 15
　Foot Guards tunics, 109

Canada, 5, 15
cap *see* headdress
Carrickfergus Castle, 15
cartouche belt, 102
cavalry
　arm badges *see* badges, cavalry arm
　names and dates formed, 7
　regiments
　　1st (King's) Dragoon Guards, 41, 112, **115**
　　1st Life Guards, **97–101, 103, 104, C11**
　　1st (Royal) Dragoons, 41, 112
　　2nd Dragoon Guards (Queen's Bays), 41, 112, **114, 116**
　　2nd Dragoons (Royal Scots Greys), 41, 112, **114**
　　　bearskins, 13
　　2nd Life Guards, **98**
　　3rd (King's Own) Hussars, **131**

cavalry, regiments (*continued*)
   3rd (Prince of Wales's) Dragoon Guards, 41, 112, **117, C18**
   4th (Queen's Own) Hussars, **131, 134**
   4th (Royal Irish) Dragoon Guards, 41, 112, **117**
   5th (Princess Charlotte of Wales's) Dragoon Guards, 112, **115**
   5th (Royal Irish) Lancers, 120, **C15**
    bearskins, 13
   6th Dragoon Guards (Carabiniers), 112, **116, C13**
   6th (Inniskilling) Dragoons, 41, 112, **C14**
   7th (Princess Royal's) Dragoon Guards, 41, 112
   7th (Queen's Own) Hussars, **131**
   9th (Queen's Royal) Lancers, 41, 120–21, **122, 123, 125**
   10th (Prince of Wales's Own Royal) Hussars, **130**
   11th (Prince Albert's Own) Hussars, 41, **114, 129, 130**
   12th (Prince of Wales's Royal) Lancers, 120
   13th Hussars, **130, 133**
   14th (King's) Hussars, 41, **129, 135**
   15th (The King's) Hussars, 41, **129, 132**
   16th (The Queen's) Lancers, 120, **120, C16**
   17th (Duke of Cambridge's Own) Lancers, 41, 120, **124, 126**
   18th (Queen Mary's Own) Hussars, 41, **133**
   19th (Queen Alexandra's Own Royal) Hussars, 41, **C17**
   20th Hussars, **134**
   21st (Empress of India's) Lancers, 41, 120, **125**
   Royal Horse Guards, 42, **99, 103**
   (*see also* Dress Regulations; uniform composites)
Central African Regiment, 173
chain, chin *see* strap, chin
Chillianwallah, Battle of, 12–13
China, 12

Chinese Regiment, 188, **188**
Churchill, Winston, **131**
coat colours, 4
Connaught, Prince Arthur, Duke of, **131, 160**
cord, shoulder, 15, 20, **21**, 94, 98, 100
  see also strap, shoulder
cords, gold (field officer), 184
Corunna, 15
country background, 5–6
crown types, 105, 111, 137
cuff types, 3, 139, 186
cuirass, 102–4, **103**
Culloden, Battle of, 14–15
Cumberland, Duke of, 14–15
cummerbund, 171, 186

death duties, 6
Depression, Great, 5–6
Dettingen, Battle of, 142
Disraeli, Benjamin, 5–6
doublet, Scottish regiments, 152, 161, 164
Dragoon guards, 112–19
  see also under cavalry, regiments
Dragoons, 112–19
  see also under cavalry, regiments
Dress Regulations
  1900 *see* uniform composites
  1904, 42–59
    (*see also* uniform composites)
  1911, 40, 66–93

East African Rifles, 173
Egypt, 11, 12
  see also Alexandria, Battle of
Egyptian Army, **180, 181,** 180–84, **182–84**
  cavalry, 183, **183**
Emsdorff, Battle of, 17
England, land area, 1
'enlisted men', 3

facings, collar, 116, 141, **141**
farriers, 104, **104**
fez, 183
  King's African Rifles, 173
  West African Regiment, 171
Fitzgeorge, Captain George, **134**
flap, slash, tunic, 95
flashes, garter, 154
Foot Guards, 106–11

  see also under infantry, regiments
footwear *see* boots
France, British battalions in, 1914, 12
free trade, 5
frock, Chinese Regiment, 188, **188**
Frowd Walker, R. S. (Malay State Guides), 179

gaiters, **158,** 181, 187
  West India Regiment, **168,** 169
Garter, Order of the, 137
general staff, 94, **94,** 95
gentry, landed, 5–6
Gibraltar, 12
girdle, Lancer, 126
gloves, 104, 126
gorget patch, 95
grain production, 5
Great Depression, 5–6
Guard cavalry *see* Household cavalry

Haig, Colonel Sir Douglas, **122**
Hamilton, Colonel Henry, **129**
Hanover army, 13
hat, cocked, 94, **94**
headdress
  Brodrick cap, **108**
  Chinese Regiment, 188, 189
  Dragoons and Dragoon Guards, 113–14
  Foot Guards, 106–8
  Fusilier, 143–45, **144**
  General Staff, 94, **94**
  Highland Light Infantry, 159–61
  Highland regiments, 150–51
  Hong Kong Regiment, 185, 187
  Household Cavalry, 96–97
  Hussar, 127
  Kilmarnock bonnet, 162, **162**
  Lancer, 120–24
  Rifles, 145–47
  West African Regiment, 171
  West India Regiment, **167,** 168
  see also bearskins; busby; helmet
height, men's, 104, 113
helmet, 172
  Albert Pattern, 96–97
  badge, Gloucestershire Regiment (28th and 61st Foot), 12–13
  colonial (Egyptian pattern), 173
  colonial (Wolseley), 21, **34,** 170, 172, 178

Dragoons and Dragoon Guards, 113–14
Lancer *see* headdress, Lancer
Line Foot, 136–38
helmet plates, **60–65,** 96
    1904 Regulations, 48–59
    1911 Regulations, 66–93
    see also badges
Hompesch, Ferdinand de, 150
    see also infantry, regiments, King's Royal Rifle Corps (60th Foot)
Hong Kong, 12
Hong Kong Regiment, 185–87
horses, 104–5
Household Cavalry, 96–105
    see also under cavalry, regiments
Hungarian knot, 4, 148
Hussars, 127–35
    see also under cavalry, regiments
Hussars, Black Brunswick, 148

Imperial crown (on helmet plate), 137
India, 11, 12
infantry
    distribution in 1914, 11–12
    names and dates formed, 7–11
    regiments, 13, 14–15
        Black Watch (Royal Highlanders) (42nd and 73rd Foot), 151, **153, 157, 158, C3**
        Cameronians (Scottish Rifles) (26th and 90th Foot), 136, 145, **164,** 164–65, **165, C10**
        Cheshire Regiment (22nd Foot), 142, **C21**
        Coldstream Guards, **107, 109, 110**
        Connaught Rangers (88th and 94th Foot), 20, **137**
        Duke of Cambridge's Own (Middlesex Regiment) (57th and 77th Foot), **140**
        Duke of Cornwall's Light Infantry (32nd and 46th Foot), **140**
        Duke of Edinburgh's (Wiltshire Regiment) (62nd and 99th Foot), 15

Duke of Wellington's (West Riding Regiment) (33rd and 76th Foot), 141
Durham Light Infantry (68th and 106th Foot), **139**
East Surrey Regiment (31st and 70th Foot), 20
East Yorkshire Regiment (15th Foot), 20
Essex Regiment (44th and 56th Foot), 137
Gloucestershire Regiment (28th and 61st Foot), 142, **143**
    helmet badges, 12–13, **143**
Gordon Highlanders (75th and 92nd Foot), 20, 151, **156, 157, C6**
Green Howards, 19
Grenadier Guards, 106, **106–10**
    bearskins, 13
Hampshire Regiment (37th and 67th Foot)
    Minden Rose, 13
Hertfordshire Regiment
    see infantry, regiments, Bedfordshire Regiment
Highland Light Infantry (71st and 74th Foot), 159–61, **160, 161, C4**
Irish Guards, **110**
King's Own Scottish Borderers (25th Foot), 162, **162, C7**
    Minden Rose, 13
King's Own (Yorkshire Light Infantry) (51st and 105th Foot)
    Minden Rose, 13, **14**
King's Royal Rifle Corps (60th Foot), 145, 147, **148, 149**
Lancashire Fusiliers (20th Foot), **144**
    Minden Rose, 13
Leicestershire Regiment (17th Foot), 20
Lincolnshire Regiment (10th Foot), **138**
Loyal North Lancashire Regiment (47th and 81st Foot), 20
Manchester Regiment (63rd and 96th Foot), **C19**

Norfolk Regiment (9th Foot), 20, 142
Northumberland Fusiliers (5th Foot), 145
    plumes, 13–14
    regimental badge, 14
Oxfordshire and Buckinghamshire Light Infantry (43rd and 52nd Foot), 143
Prince Albert's (Somerset Light Infantry) (13th Foot), 142
sashes, 14–15
Princess Louise's (Argyll and Sutherland Highlanders) (91st and 93rd Foot), 151, **158, C2**
Princess Victoria's (Royal Irish Fusiliers) (87th and 89th Foot), 14
Queen's Own Cameron Highlanders (79th Foot), 151, **155, C1**
Rifle Brigade (The Prince Consort's Own), 115–16, 145, **147–49, C23**
Royal American Regiment, 147 (*see also* King's Royal Rifle Corps (60th Foot))
Royal Fusiliers (City of London Regiment) (7th Foot), 16, **144**
Royal Inniskilling Fusiliers (27th and 108th Foot), **144**
Royal Irish Rifles (83rd and 86th Foot), 145, **149**
Royal Scots Fusiliers (21st Foot), 163, **163, 164, C8**
Royal Scots (Lothian Regiment) (1st Foot), 137, 162, **162, C9, C22**
Royal Sussex Regiment (35th and 107th Foot), 142
Royal Welsh Fusiliers (23rd Foot), **C20**
    back flash, 15–16, 141
    Minden Rose, 13
Scots Guards, **108**
Seaforth Highlanders (Ross-Shire Buffs, The Duke of Albany's) (72nd and 78th Foot), 151, **155, 156, C5**

infantry, regiments (*continued*)
    Sherwood Foresters (Nottinghamshire and Derbyshire Regiment) (45th and 95th Foot), 137
    South Staffordshire Regiment (38th and 80th Foot) buff cloth, 15
    Suffolk Regiment (12th Foot) Minden Rose, 13
    Welsh Regiment (41st and 69th Foot), 20
    West India Regiment, 65
    Worcestershire Regiment (29th and 36th Foot), 142
        pouch star, 16–17
    York and Lancaster Regiment (65th and 84th Foot), 20
    (*see also* uniform composites)
'Inverness' skirt *see* doublet, Scottish regiments

jacket
    West African Regiment, 172
    West India Regiment, 168, **168**
'jam pot' cuffs, 139

Kent, Duke of, 16
Kilmarnock bonnet, 162–63
kilt, 153
King's African Rifles, 173, **174**, 175, **175**
King's crown (on helmet plate), 137
knickerbockers, **167**, 169, 171, 181, 186
    see also pantaloons
kulla, 185

lace, 15, 95, 121, 132
lance, 127
Lancers, 120–27
    see also under cavalry, regiments
land area, 1
land ownership, 5–6
landed gentry, 6
Lansdowne, Baron, 5–6
levee dress, 154, **157**, 184
Line Foot infantry, 136–42
    see also under infantry, regiments

Malay, 12
    State Guides, 179, **179**

Malta, 11, 12
Maltese Cross, 150
manufacturing, 5
marching pace, 143
Massacre, Boston, 142
Mauritius, 11, 12
Meeanee, Battle of, 142
Meinerzhagen, Richard (KAR), **175**
Minden
    Battle of, 13, 14
    Regiments and Roses, 13
Moore, Sir John, 15

Napoleon, 13
navy, 5
New Zealand, 5
Nicholas II, Czar, **114**
Nova Scotia, 15

Other ranks *see* 'enlisted men'

pace, marching, 143
pantaloons, 3, 95, 102, 118, 127, 133
    see also breeches, riding; knickerbockers
pennant, 127
Peterborough, Earl of, 15
Peters, Major Cecil, **134**
pickers, 118
    see also belt, shoulder
Pierce's Foot *see* infantry, regiments, Prince Albert's (Somerset Light Infantry) (13th Foot)
plaid, shoulder, 154
plastron, 124, **124**, 125
plumes, 106, **106**, 112, 121, 142, 147
    crimping, 113, **120**, 123
    Fusiliers, 145
    Guard cavalry, 97, 104
    Royal Northumberland Fusiliers (5th Foot), 13–14
pouch belt *see* belt, pouch
pouch star, Worcestershire Regiment (29th and 36th Foot), 16–17
Prince, German Crown, **129**
puggaree badge, 60, 62, 64
Pulteney's Foot *see* infantry, regiments, Prince Albert's (Somerset Light Infantry) (13th Foot)
puttees, 171

Quebec, 15
Queen's crown (on helmet plate), 137

Ramillies, Battle of, 13
rank badges *see* badges, rank
ranks
    comparison across countries, 2
    infantry and cavalry, 2
    Household cavalry, 105
Regulations, Dress *see* Dress Regulations
Rolica, Battle of, 142
roses of Minden regiments, 13, 14

sabretache, **129, 130, 134**
Salisbury, Marquess of, 5–6
sash, **109**, 110, 139, 141, **142**
    Prince Albert's (Somerset Light Infantry) (13th Foot), 14–15
    Scottish regiments plaid, 154
scabbard and stripe, Royal Fusiliers (City of London Regiment) (7th Foot), 16
scales, chin, 97
Sengalese *see* Egyptian Army
sgian dubh, 154
shabraque, 17
shako, 138
    Cameronians (Scottish Rifles), 164
    Highland Light Infantry, 159–61
    Royal Irish Fusiliers, 14
    Royal Northumberland Fusiliers, 14
    see also headdress
shirt
    West African Regiment, 171
    West India Regiment, 169, **169**
shoulder
    belt, 102
    cord *see* cord, shoulder
    shoulder plaid, 154
    strap *see* strap, shoulder
    titles, 18, 19, 111
    (*see also* individual regiments)
Sikh army, 12–13
Singapore, 12
sling, rifle, 150
South Africa, 11, 12
Spain, 15
special uniform items, 12–17
sporran, 152–53
spurs, 150

St Edward's crown (on helmet plate), 137
strap, chin, 106
strap, shoulder, 99–101, 111, 140, **140**, 141, 186
  see also cord, shoulder
stripe, long service, **99**
Sudan, 11, 12
Sudanese see Egyptian Army
Swithinbank, Lieutenant Harold, **129**

tartan, 153, 161
Thurot, François, 15
trade, 5
trews, 153, 161, 165
trousers, 95, 102, 109–10, 118, 133, 141, 150
  West African Regiment, 172
  West India Regiment, 170
  see also breeches, riding; kilt; knickerbockers; pantaloons; trews
tunic
  Dragoons and Dragoon Guards, 114–17
  Egyptian Army, 181, 184
  Foot Guards, 108–9
  Fusiliers, 145
  general staff, 95
  Highland regiments doublet, 152, 161
  Hong Kong Regiment, 185–87
  Household cavalry, 97–100
  Hussars, 127, 132
  Lancers, 124–25
  Line Foot, 138–41
  Rifles, **147**, 147–50
  West African Regiment jacket, 172
  West India Regiment jacket, 168, **168**

Uganda Rifles, 173
uniform composites, 21–22
  Colonial helmets (prior to 1904), **34**
  Colonial (Wolseley) helmet (1904 Regulations), **34**
  Dragoons (1900 Regulations), **26**
  Dragoons (1904 Regulations), **27**
  Foot Guards (1900 Regulations), **24**
  Foot Guards (1904 Regulations), **25**
  Highland Scots (1900 Regulations), **36**
  Highland Scots (1904 Regulations), **37**
  Household Cavalry (1900 Regulations), **22**
  Household Cavalry (1904 Regulations), **23**
  Hussars (1900 Regulations), **28**
  Hussars (1904 Regulations), **29**
  Lancers (1900 Regulations), **30**
  Lancers (1904 Regulations), **31**
  Line infantry and fusiliers (1900 Regulations), **32**
  Line infantry and fusiliers (1904 Regulations), **33**
  Rifles (1900 Regulations), **35**
  Rifles (1904 Regulations), **35**
  Scottish Rifles (1900 Regulations), **38**
  Scottish Rifles (1904 Regulations), **39**
  see also individual regiments

La Vigie, battle of, 13

Waterloo, Battle of, 13, 108
West African Frontier Force, 176–78, **177**
West African Regiment, **171**, 171–72
West India Regiment, 137, **166**, 166–70, **167–70**
West Indies, 13, 15, 142, 145
Wilhelmstahl, Battle of, 13–14
wings, bandsman's, **139**, **156**
Wolfe, James, 15
Wolseley helmet see helmet, colonial (Wolseley)

Zouave uniform, 166

INDIA

Aden, 199
aiguillette, 253
alkalak, **254**, 289, 300
Arcot, Nawab of, 298
Army, Indian, history of, 204
'Army in India', British, 206
Atkinson, Lieutenant Frederick, **255**
Auchinlek, Second Lieutenant Claude, **350**

badges, 228
  see also turban, badges
Baluchs, 207, 217
bands, **358**, **361**
Bangalore Brigade, 27th, 226
Bengal
  army, 204, 205–7 (see also Mutiny, Indian (1857))
  cavalry, 208–10, **292**, **295**, **296** (see also under cavalry, regiments)
  Dress Regulations, 290
  infantry, 315, 349
  Irregular Cavalry, 288–98 (see also under cavalry, regiments)
  knot, **293**
Bombay
  army, 205–8
  cavalry, 300–304
  infantry, 316, 366–67, 369–73
  Irregular Cavalry, 301 (see also under cavalry, regiments)
Brahmins, 207
Burma regiments, 365
  see also Madras, infantry

Campbell-Harris, Lieutenant, **293**
Canartic, 208
caps, forage, 228–29
castes, 206–7
cavalry
  class composition, 208–10
  dates raised, 208–10
  ratings after inspection, 220–21
  regiments (see also cavalry, uniform)
    1st Duke of York's Own Lancers (Skinner's Horse), 289, 290, **294**, **296**, 299, **C27**
    2nd Lancers (Gardner's Horse), 289, 290, 299
    3rd Skinner's Horse, 289, **C27**
    4th Cavalry, 289, **C26**
    5th Cavalry, 289, **C26**

cavalry, regiments (*continued*)
   6th King Edward's Own Cavalry, 289, **C28**
   7th Hariana Lancers, 217, 289, **293**
   8th Cavalry, 289, **C28**
   9th Hodson's Horse, **255, 294**
   11th King Edward's Own Lancers (Probyn's Horse), **283, 296, C26**
   12th Cavalry, 198, 229, **294, 296**
   13th Duke of Connaught's Lancers (Watson's Horse), **293, 297**
   14th Murray's Jat Lancers, 217, **C29**
   15th Lancers (Cureton's Multanis), 217, **254**
   16th Cavalry, **294, C26**
   17th Cavalry, **297, 298, C26**
   19th Lancers (Fane's Horse), **C30**
   20th Deccan Horse, 310, 311, **C32**
   23rd Cavalry (Frontier Force), **C26**
   25th Cavalry (Frontier Force), **309**
   26th King George's Own Light Cavalry, 298, 299, **C26**
   27th Light Cavalry, 298, 299, **C31**
   28th Light Cavalry, 298, 299, **C31**
   29th Lancers (Deccan Horse), 310, **313, C32**
   30th Lancers (Gordon's Horse), 310, **C32**
   31st Duke of Connaught's Own Lancers, **304**
   32nd Lancers, **298, C33**
   33rd Queen Victoria's Own Light Cavalry, **C33**
   34th Prince Albert Victor's Own Poona Horse, 219, **304, C33**
   35th Scinde Horse, 219
   37th Lancers (Baluch Horse), 304, **305**
   38th King George's Own Central India Horse, **C34**
  Aden Troop, 210, 266, 281, 287
  Bhopal, 218
  Body guard, 287
  Bombay cavalry, 208
  Central India Horse, 208
  Guides, Queen's Own Corps of, 207, 215, 305–7, **307**
  uniform, 208–10 (*see also* cavalry, regiments)
   British officers, 257–66, 268–69
   Indian officers, 270–82
   other ranks, 284–87
Central India Horse, 312–14
Christians, 207
Churchill, Winston, 198
class make up, 216, 217
colleges, staff, 253
country background, 197–203
cummerbund, 300

Dawson, Captain H. L., **255**
Dehra Dun, 219
Dogras, 207
Downing, Captain, 219
Dress Regulations, Bengal, 290
dress terms, 256, **256**

East India Company, 198, 204, 288, 298, 315
Elphinstone, Lieutenant Colonel A. P., **367**
Erinpura, 219
Expeditionary Force, Indian, 225–26

forage cap, 228–29
Forster, Henry, 219
Frontier Force, 204, 205, 207, 208, 209, 305
  cavalry, 305–09
  infantry, 374–79
   Punjab, 374–75
   Sikh, 375–78
   Guides, 379
  see also under cavalry, regiments; infantry, regiments

General staff, 253
glossary, Indian words and terms, 200–03
Gordon, Lieutenant Colonel J. C. F., **292**
Guides, Queen's Own Corps of
  see under cavalry, regiments; infantry, regiments

Gurkhas, 207, 208, 380–86
  1st King George's Own Gurkha Rifles (Malaun Regiment), 219
  2nd King George's Own Gurkha Rifles (Sirmoor Rifles), 219, **381**
  5th Gurkha Rifles (Frontier Force), **351, 386**
  6th Gurkha Rifles, **C42**
  ratings after inspection, 225
  see also infantry, regiments
Gwalior, 218

headdress
  Bengal infantry, 351
  Bombay cavalry, 300, 301, 302
  Central India Horse, 313, 314
  Hyderabad Contingent, 310
  Madras cavalry, 299, 300
  Madras infantry, 365
  see also helmet; turban
helmet
  lancer, 301
  Wolseley, 253
history of Indian Army, 204
honours, battle, 219–20
horses, 198
Hyderabad Contingent, 207, 208
  cavalry, 309–12, **313**
  infantry, 366

Imperial Service Brigade, 226
Indian Mutiny (1857), 198, 204, 288, 289
infantry
  class composition, 210–15
  dates raised, 210–15
  ratings after inspection, 222–25
  regiments (*see also* Gurkhas)
   1st Brahmins, 217, **352, 356, 358**
   2nd Queen Victoria's Own Rajput Light Infantry, 217
   3rd Brahmins, 217
   4th Prince Albert Victor's Rajputs, 217
   5th Light Infantry, **C35**
   6th Jat Light Infantry, 217, **C35**
   7th Duke of Connaught's Own Rajputs, **352**
   9th Bhopal Infantry, 218, **350**

Index (India)

10th Jats, 217
11th Rajputs, 217, **351**
12th Pioneers (Kelat-i-Ghilzie Regiment), 219, **355**
13th Rajputs (Shekhawati Regiment), 217, 219, **353**
14th King George's Own Ferozepore Sikhs, 217, 218
15th Ludhiana Sikhs, 217, 218, **356, C24**
16th Rajputs (Lucknow Regiment), 220
17th Infantry (Loyal Regiment), 220, **355, 358**
18th Infantry, **362**
19th Punjabis, **355, 357**
20th Duke of Cambridge's Own Infantry (Brownlow's Punjabis), **350**
22nd Punjabis, **361**
23rd Sikh Pioneers, 217
30th Punjabis, **357**
32nd Sikh Pioneers, 217, **357**
33rd Punjabis, **359, C37**
34th Sikh Pioneers, 217, **353**
35th Sikhs, 217, **C36**
36th Sikhs, 217, **354**
37th Dogras, 217
38th Dogras, 217, **359**
39th Garhwal Rifles, **352, C38**
40th Pathans, 205, **360**
42nd Deoli, 208, 219, **362, C25**
43rd Erinpura, 208, 219, **363**
44th Merwara Infantry, **363**
45th Rattray's Sikhs, 217, 219, **354, 358, 361, C39**
47th Sikhs, 217
51st Sikhs (Frontier Force), 217
52nd Sikhs (Frontier Force), 217, **376**
53rd Sikhs (Frontier Force), 217, **377**
54th Sikhs (Frontier Force), 217
57th Wilde's Rifles (Frontier Force), **378**
58th Vaughan's Rifles (Frontier Force), **377**
61st King George's Own Pioneers, **364**
62nd Punjabis, **350**
83rd Walajabad Light Infantry, 218

101st Grenadiers, **367, C40**
102nd King Edward's Own Grenadiers, **C40**
103rd Mahratta Light Infantry, 217
105th Mahratta Light Infantry, **369**
106th Hazara Pioneers, 217, **367**
107th Pioneers, **368**
110th Mahratta Light Infantry, 217
114th Mahrattas, 217
116th Mahrattas, 217
119th Infantry (Mooltan Regiment), 220
120th Rajputana Infantry, **369**
124th Duchess of Connaught's Own Baluchistan Infantry, 217, **218**
126th Baluchistan Infantry, 217, **371**
127th Queen Mary's Own Baluch Light Infantry, 217, 371–72, **C41**
128th Pioneers, **368**
129th Duke of Connaught's Own Baluchis, 217, 371–72
130th King George's Own Baluchis (Jacob's Rifles), 217, 371–72
Guides, Queen's Own Corps of, 207, 305–7, **307, 378**, 379
uniform, 210–15 (*see also* Gurkhas; infantry, regiments)
British officers, 317–24
Indian officers, 326–37
other ranks, 339–47
Irregular cavalry
Bengal, *see* Bengal, Irregular Cavalry
Bombay *see* Bombay, cavalry

jacket
Bombay cavalry, 300, 301
Zouave, 356, **356**
Jats, 207
John Company *see* East India Company

Khan, Hulagu, 217
Kilmarnock cap, 351, **351, 381**
King's Commissioned Officer (KCO), 204–5
King's Indian Orderly Officer, 230, **230–44**
Kitchener, Earl, 253
Kuch Levy, 301
kurta, 257–66, 270–82, **283, 292, 293**
see also tunic

lances, 228–29
Lucknow, Siege of, 220

Madras
army, 205–8
cavalry, 298–300
infantry, 315, 364–65
Malwa Contingent, 218, **361**
Marathas, 207
Meena Battalion *see* infantry, regiments, 42nd Deoli
Merats, 219
Mers, 207, 219
Meywa Bhil Corps, **363**
Mollo, Colonel E., **381**
Mutiny, Indian (1857), 198, 204, 288, 289

names, regimental, 216–19
Napier, General Sir Charles, 219
'native officer' *see* Viceroy Commissioned Officer
Nepal, 380
number, regimental, 216

Orderly Officer, King's Indian *see* King's Indian Orderly Officer
Oudh Irregular Horse, 289

pantaloons, 253, 300, 310
de Pass, Frank Alexander, VC, **304**
Peale Commission, 204–6
see also Mutiny, Indian (1857)
pennant colours, lance, 228–29
'Piffers' *see* Frontier Force
pioneers, 216–17
see also under infantry, regiments
Plassey, Battle of, 197
plastron, **255**, 256
Bengal cavalry, 292
Priestley, Lieutenant Colonel C. E. N., **C25**

Punjab
  cavalry, 307–9
  Frontier Force (*see* Frontier Force)
  infantry, 374–75

quoit, 202, **354**

Rajputana, 219
Rajputs, 207
ranks, 220
  comparison across countries, 2
  Indian infantry and cavalry, 2, 220
  ratings after inspection
    cavalry, 220–21
    Gurkhas, 225
    infantry, 222–25
Rebellion, Indian (1857), 198
recruitment, 217, 226–27
religious sensitivity, 205
replacement, casualty, 226–27
Rifle Brigade (British army), 208

seniority, regimental, 216
Sepoy Mutiny *see* Mutiny, Indian (1857)

shako, 301
Shekhawati Local Force, 219
  see also infantry, regiments, 13th Rajputs (Shekhawati Regiment)
Shujah, Shah, 219–20
Sikh
  infantry, 375–78
  War, First, 218
sikhs, 217
silladar system, 254
  see also cavalry, regiments
Sirmoor, 219
Skinner, James and Robert, 289
spending, military, 198, 199
staff colleges, 253
Suez Canal, 226

Tamils, 207
Truncheon, Queen's, 385, **385**
  see also Gurkhas
tunic
  Bengal cavalry, 289
  Bengal infantry, **350**
  Bombay cavalry, 302

British officers, cavalry, 268–69
cavalry, 254, **255**, 256
Central India Horse, 313
Gurkha, 381, 382, 383–84
Hyderabad Contingent, 310
Madras light cavalry, 299
staff officer, 253 (*see also under* British Empire, tunic)
Zouave, 208
see also kurta
turban
  badges, unofficial infantry, 348–49, **354**
  colours, 245–49
  'humbug', **C24**
  shapes, 249, **250–52**
  see also headdress

Untouchables, 207

Viceroy Commissioned Officer (VCO), 200, 302, 312, 314

Waler (horse), 198
Welby Commission, 198

FRENCH EMPIRE

d'Afrique, Armée, 422, 437–56
Algeria, 440–41, 447, 448, 452
alpenstock, 435
amalgamations, 399–400
André, General Louis, 407
armband colours, General Staff, 409
artillery, colonial, 457

du Barail, General, 418
Barb (Barbary horse), 440
beret, 432–34
  Alpins, 432, **433**, **434**
  Alipine infantry, 436, **436**
bigors, 457
blouse, 464
Blue Devils *see* infantry, Chasseurs Alpins
breeches, **415**, 417, 422, 440
Brunck, Colonel, **426**
burnous *see* headdress, Spahi

cavalry, 411–23
  regiments, names, numbers and dates formed, 395–96

4th (Saxe) Hussars, 399
15th (Royal Allemand) Cavalry, 399
Chasseurs d'Afrique, 437–40, **438**, **439**, **440**, **C52**
Cuirassiers, 411–15, **412**, **413**, **C46**, **C47**
Dragoons, 415–18, **416**, **C50**
history, 399–400
Light Cavalry, 418–22, 418–23
  Chasseurs à Cheval, **419**, **422**, 423, **C49**
  Hussars, **419**, **421**, 422–23, **C48**
Moroccan Spahis, 445
Spahis, 440–45, **441**, **442**, **445**, **C59**, **C60**
Charlemagne, 393
chechia, **438**, 438–39, 447, **448**, 452
coat
  Colonial Line Infantry, 459–60
  colours, 404–5
Conseil Superieur de la Guerre, 407
country background, 393–94

crest, cuirassier, **410**
Crimea, 437
Crusade, First, 393
cuirass, 413–14, **414**
cummerbund, 444, 451, 454, 455, 462

dolman *see* tunic, Light Cavalry
Dreyfus Affair, 394, 407
Dutch fleet, xiv

epaulette colours, 404–5

Faidherbe, Louis, 461
Fashoda, 466
Ferron, General, 407
Ferry, Jules, 461
Foreign Legion *see* infantry, Foreign Legion
Franco-Prussian war, 407, 437

gaiters, 451
General Staff, 407–10, **410**
gloves, 415
guenhour *see* headdress, Spahi

Index (French Empire)

haik *see* headdress, Spahi
Hartmannswillerkopf (HWK), 435
headdress
   Chasseurs à Cheval helmet, 420
   Chasseurs Alpin beret, 432
   Chasseurs d'Afrique, 437–39
   Colonial Line Infantry, 458–59
   Cuirassier helmet, 411–12, **412**
   Dragoon helmet, 415–16, **416**
   General Staff, 408
   Hussar helmet, **420**
   Indochinese Tirailleurs, 463–64
   kepi *see* kepi
   Senegalese Tirailleurs, 461
   shako
      Chasseurs à Cheval, 418, **418**, 419, **419**, 423, **C49**
      Chasseurs d'Afrique, 437, 438, **438**
      Hussars, 418, **419**, C48
   Spahi, 441–43, 444–45
   Tirailleurs Algériens, 452
   Tirailleurs Marocains, 455–56
   Zouave, 447
   see also kepi; shako
helmet *see under* headdress

infantry, 424–36, 455
   regiments, names, numbers and dates formed 396–98
   African Light Infantry, **446,** 446–47
   Alpine Infantry, 435–36, **436**
   Chasseurs à Pied, 431, **431, C45**
   Chasseurs Alpins, 432–35, **433, 434**
   Colonial Line Infantry, 457–60, **458, 459, 460**
   Foreign Legion, 429–30
   history, 398–99
   Indochinese Tirailleurs, 460–65, **461, 462, 465**
   Line Infantry, 424–29, **425, 426**
   Madagascan Tirailleurs, 465
   Senegalese Spahis, 463
   Tirailleurs Algériens, 452–55, **453, 454, C56, C57, C58**
   Tirailleurs Marocains, **455,** 455–56
   Zouave, 447–51, **448, 449, C53, C55**
insignia, General Staff, **409**

Isly, Battle of, 441

jacket
   ras de cul, 439, 447
   Senegalese Tirailleurs, **462**
   Spahi, **443,** 443–44
   Tirailleurs Algériens, 452
   Zouave, 447–50, **450**
   see also tunic
jambières, 451
Les Joyeux *see* infantry, African Light Infantry
jumper, Chasseurs Alpin, 432

kepi, 408, **C43**
   African Light Infantry, 446
   Chasseurs à Cheval, 419
   Chasseurs à Pied, 431
   colours, 404–5
   Foreign Legion, 429
   Hussars, 419
   Light Cavalry, 419
   Line infantry, **424,** 424–27, **425**
   Spahi, **443**
   see also headdress
knickerbockers, 455, 464

lances, 401, 417–18
loin cloth, 464

Marey-Monge, Colonel, 440
Mexico, 437
Moroccan Crisis, 407
mountain troops *see* infantry, Alpine infantry; infantry, Chasseurs Alpins
mutiny, 441

Napoleon, 399
North African Army *see* d'Afrique, Armée

pantaloons, 444, 451, **451,** 454
pennants, 401
Phoney War, 393
plume colours for staff, 408
puttees, 435, 462

ranks
   comparison across countries, 2
   infantry and cavalry, 2
   markings, officer, 406, 428

ras de cul, 447
Regiments Etranger *see* infantry, Foreign Legion
Revolution, French, 398, 399
Rocroi, Battle of, 394
Roi, Regiment du, 398

Saharan units, **465,** 466–68
The Sahel, 461
salacco, 463–64
sandals, 462
sash, Foreign Legion, 430
Senegal, 460–62
shako
   Chasseurs d'Afrique, 437–38, **439**
   Light Cavalry, **418**
   see also headdress
shama, Zouave, 447–50, 452
shoulder piece, **417**
spats, 429

themaggs, 444
Thirty Years War, 394
Tit attack and Battle, 467
tombo, 452–53, **C54**
Triple Alliance, 432
Tuareg, 467
Tuat, 466
tunic
   African Light Infantry, 446, 447
   Chasseurs à Pied, 431
   Chasseurs d'Afrique, 439–40
   Curassiers, 412–13
   Dragoons, 416–17
   Foreign Legion, 429–30, **430**
   General Staff, 408–9
   Light Cavalry, 420–22, 423
   Line infantry, **427,** 427–28, **C44**
   Zouave, 450–51
   see also jacket; jumper, Chasseurs Alpin
Tunisia, 440
Turcos *see* infantry, Tirailleurs Algériens

uniform, pre-1900, 401, **402–3**

Valmy, Battle of, xiv

Zouaves *see* infantry, Zouave

RUSSIAN EMPIRE

2nd Pskov Dragoons, xiv
77th Tenga Infantry, xiv
81st Apsheronsk Infantry, xiii

aiguillette, 519
Alexander II, Czar, 582
Alexander III, Czar, 583
Asian bonnet, 595
attila, 547–50, 609–11

badges
    pouch belt, 513–14, **514**
    regimental, 496–97, **514**, 515, 605, **614**
Balaclava (Crimea), 606
bands, **619, 620**
banners, distinction *see* distinction banners
bashlyk, 624, 628
bechmet, 560–561, 622–23, 627, 643–44
belt, pouch, 496
blouse *see* shirt
bonnet, 571
boots, Hussar, 612
breeches, 497, 599
    General Staff, 519
    Guard cavalry, 532–33, 539, 543, 551, 557
    Hussar, 612
    Lancer, 605
    line Rifles, 642
busby, 625
    Guard Hussar, 545, 547
    Hussar, 606–09
buttons, 495–96

Caucasus Native Horse, 626–28, **627, C73a**
    see also Cossacks, Caucasus
cavalry, line
    combat dress, **C71b**
    Crimean (Tartar) Horse Regiment, **C71b**
    Dragoons, 499, **583**, 583–99, **584, 591, 596, C64a, C70b, C71a, C71b**
    Hussars, 500, 606–14, **609, C73a, C73b, C74**
    Lancers, 500, **542**, 600–05, **603, 604, C72a, C72b, C73a**

regiments
    5th Alexandria Hussars, 614
    11th Izyum Hussars, 610
    12th Akhtyrka Hussars, 609–611, **610**
    13th Dragoons, 588
    17th Dragoons, **597**
    names and dates formed, 481–84
    Premorsky Dragoons, 589, **591**
    Pskov Dragoons, 587–88, **588**
    see also Caucasus Native Horse; Crimean Cavalry; Imperial Guard, cavalry; Turkman Demi-Regiment
cavalry school uniform, **C74**
changes, uniform, 1880-1914, 517
characteristics, physical
    horses, 490, 491, 492
    Guard men, 491
charivari, 497
    Caucasus Cossack, 623
    Caucasus Native Horse, 628
    Cossack, 619
    Crimean Cavalry, 626
    Guard Cossack, 557, 562
    Guard Cuirassier, 532
    Guard Hussar, 551
    Guard Lancer, 543
    Horse Grenadier, 539
    Hussar, 612
    Turkman Demi-Regiment, 632
cherkeska, 559–60, 622, 626–27, 643
chevrons, service, 515
cockades, 493–494
collar, Dragoon, 598
colours
    horse, 491, 492
    uniform, 493
Cossacks
    band, **618, 620**
    Caucasus, 621–24 (*see also* Caucasus Native Horse)
    infantry, 643–44, **644**
    names and dates formed, 483
    Mountain (*see* Cossacks, Caucasus)
    Plains (*see* Cossacks, Steppes)
    Steppes, **615**, 615–20, **617, 619**
    see also Imperial Guard, cavalry, Cossacks

country background, 475
Crimean Cavalry, 625–28
cuffs, 527
cuirass, 529, **529**
customs, 514, 614

Daghestan Regiment *see* Caucasus Native Horse
decorations (medals), 498
distinction banners, 484–90, 589
dragunka, **584**

embroidery, 521
epaulettes, 494–95
    Caucasus Cossack, 623
    Caucasus Native Horse, 627–28
    Cossack infantry (Plastuns), 644
    Crimean Cavalry, 625
    Dragoon, 598
    Emperor's Guard Escort, 561
    General Staff, 519
    Guard Cuirassier, 530
    Guard Dragoon, 538
    Guard Horse Grenadier, 538
    Guard infantry, 575
    Guard Lancer, 542
    Lancer, 604
    line infantry, 637
    line Rifles, 642
    Steppes Cossack, 619
    Turkman Demi-Regiment, 632
    see also shoulder straps

Feodorovna, Maria, 584, 587
footwear, 497
Friedland, Battle of, 571

gala uniform, **528,** 530, 538, 543, 551
    General's, **C74**
General Staff, 518–523, **519,** 522
gloves, 498
Gordon, General Patrick, 563
gorget, 515–16, **516,** 575–79, **578, 579,** 637–38, 642
Grabbe, General Count Alexander, **560**

headdress, **508**
    Caucasus Cossack, 621–22
    Caucasus Native Horse, 626

Crimean Cavalry, 625
Dragoon, 589, **590**
Dragoons, 595
Emperor's Guard Escort, 558–59
General Staff, 518, 520
Guard Cossacks, 553–54
Guard Cuirassiers, 525–26, **526**
Guard Lancers, 540–41, **541**
Hussar, 606–09
Lancers, 600–03
line infantry, 635–36
Line Rifle regiments, 640–41
Steppes Cossack, 615–18
Turkman Demi-Regiment, 630
see also Asian bonnet; *bashlyk*;
    bonnet; busby; *dragunka*;
    helmet; kiver; mitre; shako
helmet
    Dragoon, 584, 587, **587**, 589, **590**
    Guard Lancers, 540–41
    Horse Grenadiers, **536**, 537
    Lancers, **600**, 600–03, **603**
    see also headdress
Highlanders, 93rd (British), at
    Balaclava, 606
horses, 620
    colours, 490–91, 492

Imperial Guard
    cavalry, 499, **506**, **C65b, C66a,
        C66b, C67a, C67b**
    Cossacks, 552–58, **555**
    Cuirassiers, 524–33, **526, 527,
        529, 533**
    Dragoons, **534**, 534–39
    Emperor's Guard Escort,
        558–62, **559, 560**
    Horse Grenadiers, 534–39, **536,
        537**
    Hussars, 544–52, **545, 546, 547,
        549**
    Lancers, 539–44
    infantry, 563–82, **C64b, C65a, C67b**
        Combined Guard Infantry, 582
        Guard Rifles, 565, 571, **572,
            C65a, C67b**
        regiments, 563–65, **573, 577,
            578, 579, 581**
    names and dates formed, 477
    regiments
        Cheval Guards (*see* Horse
            Guards)

Chevalier Guard Regiment, 524,
    526, 531, 532
Cuirassiers of the Emperor, 524
Cuirassiers of the Empress, 524
Horse Guards, 524, **532**
infantry, line, 633–39
    regiments, names and dates
        formed, 478–81
    Grenadiers, 634, 638, **C68a, C68b**
    regular regiments, **C69a, C69b**
    Rifle regiments, 640–42, **C70a**
    see also Cossacks, infantry;
        Imperial Guard, infantry

jacket, 530–531, 642
    see also *attila*; koller; tunic

Kavalergardia see Imperial Guard,
    regiments, Chevalier Guard
    Regiment
khalat, 630–31
kiver, 518, 565–569, **568**
    see also headdress
koller, **526**, 527, 528, **528**
    see also tunic
kourtaktcha, 631

lace, collar and cuff, 505–06
lance
    pennant, 498–500
    pole, 500–01
lancer other rank girdle
    guard, 544
    line, 605
line infantry *see* infantry, line
line Rifle regiments *see under*
    infantry, line
litzen, 494, 501–06, 528, 541–42,
    596, 601–02
lyadunka, 496

marching step, 492
mitre, Grenadier's, 569–71, **570, 571**
monograms, general, 507–09, **508**
    Caucus Cossacks, 621, 623
    Cossack Infantry, 643
    Crimean Cavalry, 625, 626
    Guard Cossacks, 554, 556
    Guard Cuirassier, 530
    Guard Infantry, 566–67, 575
    Guard Lancers, 540
    Guard Rifles, 575

Line Dragoons, 592–94, 598
Line Hussars, 611
Line Lancers, 601–02, 604
Line Rifles, 642
Steppes Cossacks, 616, 619
nagyka whip, 620, **560, 561**
Nicholas, Grand Duke, **556**
Nicholas II, Czar, **555, 574**
    daughters, **591, 604, 609**

Ossetian Demi-Regiment see
    Caucasus Native Horse

'painting with the toe' marching, 492
Palace Guard dress, 531
pantaloons, 497, 580, 638–39
papakha, 589, 615–18, 621–22, 626,
    630, 635, 640–41
patrontach, 496
Paul I, Czar, 524
pelisse, **546**, 551–52, **552**, 613
Peter the Great, 524, 563, 583
Plastuns *see* Cossacks, infantry
plates, Shenk, 509, **C64–C74**
plume, 535
polouchtabski braid, 550
pouch belt badges, 513, **514**

ranks
    comparison across countries, 2
    infantry, cavalry and Cossacks, 3
redingote, 530–31, 626, 638
regimental badges, **514**, 515, 605,
    614, **614**
revolutions, 475
revolver, Nagant, 498, 612
rifle attack position, 581, **581, 582**
Russo-Japanese War, 475

sabretache, 612
sash, hussar waist, 550–51, 612
sash, officer, 497
service chevrons, 515
shako
    Guard Dragoon, 534–36
    line infantry, 635–36
    line Rifles, 641
shashka, 498
Shenk, V. K., 509
Shenk plates, **C64–C74**, 509–13
shirt, 575, 613
    see also *kourtaktcha*

Index (German Empire)

shoulder straps, 495
  Caucasus Cossack, 623
  Caucasus Native Horse, 628
  Dragoon, 598
  Emperor's Guard Escort, 561
  Guard Cossack, 556
  Guard Cuirassier, 530
  Guard Dragoon, 538
  Guard Horse Grenadier, 538
  Guard infantry, 575
  Guard Lancer, 542
  Hussar (cords), 611
  infantry, line, 637
  Lancer, 604
  Rifles, line, 642
  Steppes Cossack, 619
  Turkman Demi-Regiment, 632
  see also epaulettes
side arms, 498
spiegel, 494, 618, 661, 707, 750, 809, 816, 819, 824, 826, 834
spurs, 498
St Andrew guard star, 496, 533
St George's star, 496
straps
  rifle, 517
  shoulder (*see* shoulder straps)
Streltsy revolt, 583
supravest, **531,** 531–32

tchekman, 556–57, 619
trousers, 497, 532, 539, 543, 557, 580
tunic, 619
  Caucasus Cossack, 622
  Crimean Cavalry, 625
  Dragoons, line, 595–98
  Emperor's Guard Escort, 559–60
  General Staff, 518–19, 520
  Guard Cossacks, 554–56
  Guard infantry, 571–73, 574
  Guard Lancers, 541–42, **542**
  Guard Rifles, 571–73
  Horse Grenadiers, 537–38
  infantry, line, 636–37
  Rifles, line, 641
  Steppes Cossack, 618
  Turkman Demi-Regiment, 630–31
  see also attila; cherkeska; jacket; khalat; koller; pelisse; tchekman; walking-out tunic
Turkman Demi-Regiment, **629,** 629–32, **630, 631, C73a**

venguerka, 551
vice-moundir, 530, 599

walking-out tunic
  Caucasus Cossack, 623
  Caucasus Native Horse, 628
  Dragoon, 598–99
  Emperor's Guard Escort, 561–62
  Guard Cossack, 556
  Guard Cuirassier, 530
  Guard Dragoon, 538–39
  Guard Horse Grenadier, 538
  Guard Hussar, 551
  Guard infantry, 580
  Guard Lancer, 543
  Hussar, 613
  Lancer, 604–05
  see also tunic
whip, *nagyka,* **560, 561,** 620

GERMAN EMPIRE

Abushiri Rebellion, 821
Academy, War, 703
accessory details, identifying, 682–89
Adolphus, Gustav, 810
aiguillettes, 826
Albert Victor, Prince (of Britain), **765**
Army Corps, 697–701
askari, 821, **828,** 830, **831,** 831–32, 837
attila, **765, 767, 773**
  Prussian Hussar, 761–67, **762, 763**
  see also pelisse, Prussian Guard Hussar
Augustus I, King, of Poland, 715–16
Austro-Prussian War, 740

background, country, 649–50
badge
  busby, 757–61 (*see also* busby)
  Death's Head, 757–60
  helmet, **667–70,** 667–71, 677–82 (*see also* cockade; helmet)
  Bavarian cavalry, 780, **781**
  Prussian line infantry, **792, 793**
rank, 662–63
weapons proficiency, 701–2
bands, **831**
banner
  1626, xiv, 653, 672, 673
  Fatherland, 665, 710–11
  Fürst, 796
  helmet, 671–74, 797–98
  Hohenfriedburg 4 June 1745, xiv, 674, 716
  'Semper Talis' (1st Foot Guards), 706, 710, 712
  'Pro Gloria et Patria', 1st Foor Guards, 3rd Btn, 672, 710
Bavarian cavalry
  Chevaulegers (Light Horse), 783–85, **785, C87**
  Lancers, 782–83
  Schwere Reiter (Heavy Cavalry), 780–82, **C85, C86**
Bayreuth Dragoons, xiv, 674, 715
belt
  Bavarian Lancer, 783
  Bavarian Line Infantry, 809
  Chinese marine, 836
  colonial troops, 827
  German East African troops, 832
  Hesse Line Infantry, 799
  pouch, 725–26, 728, 737–38, **737–38,** 753, 768, 779
  Bavarian Chevaulegers, 785
  Bavarian Lancer, 783
  Bavarian Schwere Reiter, 782
  Saxon Schwere Reiter, 789, **789**
  Prussian Dragoons, 738
sword, 726, 729
tropical uniform, 828
Tsingtao marines, 835
Berlin Conference, 821
von Bismark, Otto, 821
Black Eagle, Order of the, 706, 710, 711, 738
Boxer Rebellion, 833, 836
  see also Tsingtao marines
braid, 720, **721**
breeches
  Bavarian Chevaulegers, 785

Bavarian Lancer, 783
Bavarian Line Infantry, 809
Bavarian Schwere Reiter, 782
General Staff, 704
khaki uniform, 829–30
Mounted Rifles (Zäger zu Pferde), 779
Prussian Cuirassiers, 730
Prussian Dragoons, 736
Prussian Hussars, 768–69, **775**
Prussian Lancers, 752
Saxon Schwere Reiter, 788–89
Britain, 470, 739, 799, 810, 812
busby, Prussian Hussar, 754–61
see also czapska; helmet; shako

Cameroon, 824–25, 832, 833
see also South-West Africa, German
cannetille, 711
'caterpillar', 780
cavalry
2nd Cuirassier battle honour, xiv, 715
regiments, names and dates formed, 651–53
Bavarian (*see* Bavarian cavalry)
Prussian (*see* Prussian cavalry)
Saxon (*see* Saxon Schwere Reiter (Heavy Cavalry))
cockade, 660, 681–82, 796, 834
State, 691
see also badge, helmet; helmet
collar, General Staff, 703
colonial troops, 821–37
ethnic composition, 837
see also Cameroon; East Africa, German; South-West Africa, German; Tsingtao marines
colours, German national, 740
Connaught and Strathearn, Arthur, Duke of, **775**
country background, 649–50
Court, Dragoons of the *see* Prussian cavalry, Cuirassiers
crown, helmet *see* czapska
cuirass, Prussian Cuirassier, 720–24, **722, 723**
czapska, 743–48, **744, 745, 746**
see also busby; helmet; shako

dog, drum, 659
dolman, 764

eagle, helmet, 667–71
East Africa, German, 821–23, 825–32, **831**
Edward VII, King (of United Kingdom), **774**
effendi (rank), 821, 830
epaulette
Bavarian Schwere Reiter, 782
General Staff, 703–04
monogram, 692–97
Prussian Army, 701–02
Prussian Cuirassier, 720
Prussian Lancer, 751–52
Saxon Schwere Reiter, **788**
Tsingtao marines, 835, **835**
Württemberg Line Infantry, 805–6
see also gala uniform; pelisse, Prussian Guard Hussar; walking-out tunic

fez, 822, 830–31
Cameroon native soldier, 832, **832**
footwear, 663–64
Franco-Prussian War, 740–41
Frederick II (The Great), King, 710
Frederick William I, King, 757, 792
Frederick William II, King, 649
Frederick William III, King, 706

gala uniform
Bavarian Line Infantry, 809
Prussian Dragoons, 736–37
Prussian (Guard), Cuirassier, 724–26, **725, 726**
Prussian Hussars, 774–75, **775, 776**
Prussian Lancers, 753
Tsingtao marines, 835
see also trousers; tunic
Gardes du Corps *see* Prussian cavalry, Cuirassiers
General Staff, 703–04
facing colour, 704
special braid, 703
wide stripes, trousers and breeches, 704
Giant Grenadiers (Giant Guards), 706
Gibraltar regiments, 810

Gibraltar arm band, xiv, 673, 674, 811, 812, **814**, 816
girdle, 752
gloves, Prussian Cuirassiers, 730
gorget, Prussian Cuirassiers, 722, 724, 730–32, **731, 732**

headdress
Chinese marine, 836
German colonies, common, 825–26, **826**
German South-West African troops, 824, **824**
see also busby; czapska; helmet; shako
helmet, **667–70**, 667–91
Baden Line Infantry, 803, **803, 804**
badge (*see* badge, helmet)
Bavarian Chevaulegers, 784
Bavarian Lancer, 783
Bavarian Line Infantry, 806–07
Bavarian Schwere Reiter, 780
Foot Guard, 711
General Staff, 703
German East African troops, 822–23, **823**
Guard Cuirassier, 718
Hesse Line Infantry, 797–98, **798**
Jägers and Schützen, 811–12
khaki uniform, 829
Line Cuirassier, 718
Line infantry, **792**, 792–93, **793**
Mounted Rifles (Zäger zu Pferde), 778
Prussian Cuirassier, 717
Prussian Dragoons, 735, **735**
Prussian Line Grenadier, 793
Prussian Line Infantry, 796–97
Russian, **792**
Saxon Line Infantry, **800**, 800–801
Saxon Schwere Reiter, 786–87, **787**
tropical uniform, 828
Württemberg Line Infantry, 805, **805**
see also busby; czapska; shako
Henry, Duke of Mecklenburg-Schwerin, **815**
Herero Rebellion, 833
see also Tsingtao marines
Hesse, 735
Hohenfriedberg, Battle of, xiv, 715, 730

Hohenfriedberg March, 715
horses, 658–59
   colours, 775, **776**
hymns, 649

infantry
   regiments, names and dates formed, 653–57
   Line (*see* Line infantry)
   Prussian Guard (*see* Prussian Guard infantry)

Jägers and Schützen, 810–20, **813, 814, 815, 816**
   Bavarian battalions, 819–20
   Mecklenburg-Schwerin battalion, **815**, 818–19, **819, C88**
   Saxon battalions, 816–18
   see also Line Infantry; Prussian cavalry; Prussian Guard infantry
Jena, Battle of, 706, 810
Jiaozhou *see* Tsingtao marines

khaki uniform, 828–30
Kiautschou *see* Tsingtao marines
King's African Rifles, 837
Kitchen, Dragoons of the *see* Prussian cavalry, Cuirassiers
knots, sword, 665
Kolben embroidery, 703, **703**
koller
   Mounted Rifles (Zäger zu Pferde), 778–79
   Prussian Cuirassiers, 717, 719, 720, **721**
   Saxon Schwere Reiter, 787–88, **788**
Königgrätz, Battle of, 659, 800

lace, collar and cuff, 666–67, **721, 766**
   Foot Guards, 714
   infantry regiments, 675–77
lance, 664
   pennant, 691, 777, **777, C75**
   Prussian Cuirassiers, 730
Legion, King's German, 812
von Lettow-Vorbeck, Paul, **827**, 833
   see also Tsingtao marines
Leuthen, Battle of, 649
Liberation, Wars of, 810

Life Cuirassiers Great Elector (Silesian) No. 1 *see* Prussian cavalry, Cuirassiers
Line infantry, 792–809
   Baden Line Infantry, 803–05, **804**
   Bavarian Line Infantry, 806–09, **807, 808, C89**
   Hesse Line Infantry, 797–99
   Prussian Line Grenadiers, 793–95, **794**
   Prussian Line Infantry, **795**, 795–97, **799**
   Saxon Line Infantry, 800–03, **801, 802**
   Württemberg Line Infantry, 805–06
litzen, 661, 663, 675
   Baden, 804, **804**
   Bavaria, 808, **808**, 809
   Cavalry
      Cuirassiers, 717, **721**, 724, 727
      Dragoons, 733, 734, 735, 736
      Lancers, 741–43, 750, 751
   Colonial, 824, 826, 832
   General Infantry, 675–77, 690–91
      General Staff, 703
      Guard Infantry, 705–06, **707**, 711, 712, **713**, 714, 716
   Jägers, 811, 812, **814**, 816, 819
   Line Grenadiers, 794
   Line Infantry, 797, 799
   Marine, 834, **834**
   Saxon, 801, **801**
   Württemberg, 806
Louis Ludwig III, 797
Ludendorff, Erich, 833
   see also Tsingtao marines
Luderitz, Adolph, 821
Ludwig III, King, of Bavaria, 809
Lützow Free Corps, 740, 796
   see also Prussian cavalry, Lancers

von Mangoldt, Colonel Hans, **752**
marines
   Chinese, 835–37 (*see also* Tsingtao marines)
   Tsingtao (*see* Tsingtao marines)
Meissen, lion of, 787, **787**
mitre, 706–11, **708, 709, 710, 711, 712**

monograms, all states, cavalry and infantry, 692–97, **692, 695, 697**, 769–70
   Cavalry
      Cuirassiers, 716
      Dragoons, 733, 734, 736
      Lancers, 741, 742, 743, 752
      Hussars, 755, 765, 766
      Mounted Rifles, 779
      Saxon Schwere Reiter, 786
   Infantry
      Bavarian, 806, 809
      Jägers, 811, 812
      Prussian grenadiers, 795
      Saxon, 695, 696, 802
mortarboard *see* czapska

netherwear
   cavalry, 661–62
   infantry, 661
Neuchatel, 810
Nicholas II, Czar (of Russia), **774**

pelisse, Prussian Guard Hussar, 770–74, **771, 772, 773, 774**
   see also attila
pennant, lance *see* lance, pennant
Peters, Dr Karl, 821
pickelhaube see helmet
plate, helmet *see* badge, helmet
plume, 690
   Baden Line Infantry, 803
   Bavarian Chevaulegers, 784
   Bavarian Schwere Reiter, 780
   cavalry regiments, 675
   Hesse Line Infantry, 798
   infantry regiments, 690–91
   Jägers and Schützen, 812
   Prussian Dragoons, **735**
   Prussian Hussars, 756
   Prussian Lancers, 747
   Prussian Line Grenadier, 793, **794**
   Prussian Line Infantry, 796
   Württemberg Line Infantry, 805
   see also cockade
Porcelain Regiment, 716
   see also Prussian cavalry, Cuirassiers
pouch, 663
   Bavarian Chevauleger, 785
   Bavarian Lancer, 783
   Bavarian Schwere Reiter, 782, **782**

Mounted Rifles (Zäger zu Pferde), 779
Prussian Cuirassiers, 725, 728–29, **729,** 739, **739**
Prussian Dragoons, 738
Prussian Hussars, 768
Saxon Schwere Reiter, 789, **789**
pouch belt *see* belt, pouch
Prussian cavalry, 665
    Cuirassiers, 665, 715–32, 719, **C76, C77, C79**
    Dragoons, 733–39, **735, 737, C80**
    Gardes du Corps (*see* Prussian cavalry, Cuirassiers)
    Hussars, 754–77, **756, 757, 764, 768, 769, 776, C81, C82**
    Lancers, 740–53, **746, 747, 749, 750, 751, 752**
    Mounted Rifles (Zäger zu Pferde), 777–79, **C83**
    see also cavalry; Saxon Schwere Reiter (Heavy Cavalry)
Prussian Guard infantry, 705
    Foot Guards, 706–11, **707, 708, C78**
    Grenadiers, **712,** 712–13, **713, 714**
    Jäger, 714, 812, **815**
    Rifles (*Schützen*) Battalion, 714, 812, **814**
    see also infantry
Prussian Line Eagle, 691
puschel, 706

Queen's Dragoons *see* Prussian cavalry, Cuirassiers

ranks, 662–63, 720
    comparison across countries, 2
    German East Africa, 830
    infantry and cavalry, 2
von Raven, Captain, **826**
Reich Commissioner's Troops, 821
Rein, Wilhelm, 649
Rifle regiments *see* Jägers and Schützen
Royal Swdish Bodyguards, xiv, 672, 674
Rupprecht, Crown Prince of Bavaria, 806
Russian-German Legion, 740

Sadowa, Battle of, 659, 800

sash, 664–65
    adjutant's, 704, 726, **726,** 729, 790
    Baden Line Infantry, 805
    Bavarian Line Infantry, 809
    Prussian Hussar, **767,** 767–68
    Saxon Line Infantry, 802
    Saxon Schwere Reiter, 790
    Saxon Schwere Reiter (Heavy Cavalry), 786–91, **789, 790, 791, C84**
    see also Prussian cavalry, Hussars
von Schlieffen, Alfred Graf, 703
Schützen *see* Jägers and Schützen
shako
    Jägers and Schützen, 812, **813**
    Bavarian battalions, 819
    Mecklenburg-Schwerin battalion, 818
    Saxon battalions, 816–17, **817**
    Tsingtao marines, **833,** 833–34
shoulder
    cord
        General Staff, 703–04
        Prussian Army, 701–02
        Prussian Hussars, **765**
    Spiegel, 661, **707,** 750, 809, 816, 819, 824, 826, 834
    strap
        Army Corps, 699–700
        Baden Line Infantry, 804
        Bavarian Line Infantry, 809
        Bavarian Schwere Reiter, 782
        colonial troops (European), 826
        monogram, 692–97
        Prussian Cuirassier, 720
        Saxon Line Infantry, 801
        Tsingtao marine, 834
        South Pacific Colonies, 825
South-West Africa, German, 821, 824, **827**
souvenirs, battle, 659
stahlgrün (steel green), 783, 784
Sudanese troops, 822
    see also East Africa, German
supravest, 724, **725**
Swahili troops, 822
    see also East Africa, German

tarbusch, 822, 831
Taxis *see* Bavarian cavalry, Chevaulegers (Light Horse)
Togo, 821, 825

    see also South-West Africa, German
tombac, 787, 806
totenkopf see badge, Death's Head
tropical uniform, 827–28, **828,** 830
trousers
    Bavarian Line Infantry, 809
    Chinese marine, 836
    colonial troops, 827
    General Staff, 704
    German East African troops, 832
    Jägers and Schützen, 820
    Prussian Dragoons, 736
    Prussian Hussars, 769
    Prussian Lancers, 752–53
    Prussian Line Infantry, 799
    tropical uniform, 828
    Tsingtao marines, 835
    see also gala uniform
Tsingtao marines, 825, 833
    see also marines, Chinese
tunic
    Baden Line Infantry, 803–04
    Bavarian Chevauleger, 784–85, **785**
    Bavarian Lancer, 783
    Bavarian Line Infantry, 807–09
    Bavarian Schwere Reiter, 780–82, **781**
    Cameroon native soldier, 832
    Chinese marine, 836
    colonial troops (European), 826–27
    General Staff, 703
    German East African troops, 823, 831–32
    Jägers and Schützen, 812, 816
    Bavarian battalions, 819
    Mecklenburg-Schwerin battalion, 819
    Saxon battalions, 817–18, **818**
    khaki uniform, 829
    Mounted Rifle (Zäger zu Pferde) (*see koller*)
    Prussian Curassier (*see koller*)
    Prussian Dragoon, 735–36
    Prussian Hussar (*see attila*)
    Prussian Lancer (*see ulanka*)
    Prussian Line Grenadier, 794–95
    Saxon Line Infantry, 801–02
    tropical uniform, 828
    Tsingtao marines, 834–35

Index (American Empire)

tunic (*continued*)
   see also gala uniform; walking-out tunic

uhlans *see* Prussian cavalry, Lancers
ulanka, **748,** 748–51
uniform, non-standard, 700–01

waffenrock see walking-out tunic

aiguillette, **857,** 857–58

background
   Army, 849–52
   country, 845–48
badge, helmet, 859–60
belt, 866, 869
bolo (knife), **868,** 869
Boxer Rebellion, 851
braid, sleeve, 860
buttons, frock coat, 864

Canada, 845, 846, 849
cap *see* headdress, new dress uniform
cavalry, 859–61, **863, 865, 866**
Civil War, American, 846–47, 849
coat, frock *see* tunic
Coat of Arms, United States, 858, **858,** 862
Cody, Buffalo Bill, 850
cotton, 846
country background, 845–48
Cuba, 851

dress uniform, new, 862–66

facings, cavalry yellow, 855
Fire (House) Zouaves, xiv
footwear, 866, 869

General Staff, **857,** 857–58
Guard, National *see* National Guard

half-chevron *see* stripes, service
hat, Montana peak, 856, 867
   see also headdress
headdress
   new dress uniform, 862–63

walking-out tunic, 726–28, **727, 728**
   Prussian Cuirassiers, **731**
   Prussian Dragoons, **736**
   see also tunic
weapons proficiency badge, Prussian Army, 701–02
Wilhelm, Crown Prince, **707**
Wilhelm Ernst, Grand Duke of Saxe-Weimar, **789**

AMERICAN EMPIRE

Philippine Scouts, 868
   Scouts, Philippine, 866–67
   see also hat, Montana peak; helmet
helmet
   cavalry, 859–60
   infantry, 862
   see also headdress
Honor, Medal of, 851

Indian wars, 845, 849–50, 853
infantry, **860,** 861–66, **863, 864, 865**
   see also Porto Rico (Provisional) Regiment of Infantry

Kipling, Rudyard, 851
knot, Hungarian, 858, 860

leggings, 869
'light blue' *see* trousers
lines, cap, 861
Louisiana Purchase, 847

Macabebe group, 851
   see also Scouts, Philippine
medals, campaign, 855
Mexico, American war with, 847
Moros 851, 868, **868**
   see also Scouts, Philippine

National Guard, 848, 851

The Philippines, 851–52
   see also Scouts, Philippine
plume, 859, 862
population, American colonial, 845
Porto Rico (Provisional) Regiment of Infantry, 852, 869
   see also Puerto Rico
promotion, officers', 853

Wilhelm I, King, **764**
Wilhelm II, Kaiser, 710, **717, 723,** 779, **829**
von Wissmann, Hermann, 821

Zulus, 822
   see also East Africa, German

Puerto Rico, 851
puttees, 869

ranks, 860
   comparison across countries, 2
   infabntry and cavalry, 2
Revolution, American, 846, 849

Scouts, Philippine, 851–52, 866–69, **867, 868**
service, war, 855
Seven Years' War, 845
shirt *see* tunic, Philippine Scouts
slavery, 846
Spanish-American War, 850–51
Spanish colonisation, 845
stripes, service, 854–55

Tiger Zouaves, xiv
trousers
   cavalry, 861
   infantry, 862
   new dress uniform, 864–65
   Philippine Scouts, 868
tuban headdress *see* headdress, Philippine Scouts
tunic
   cavalry, 860–61, **861**
   infantry, 862
   new dress uniform, 863–64
   Philippine Scouts, 867–68

Villa, Poncho, 847

War College, Army, 857
Whitney, Eli, 846

Young, Charles, **863**